New York Family History Research Guide and Gazetteer

New York Genealogical and Biographical Society

The map on the cover is a detail from *The Tourist's Map of the State of New York* . . . made by William Williams (Utica, NY: William Williams, 1831) and engraved by Galch, Stiles & Co., New York, 1831. Courtesy of the Lionel Pincus and Princess Firyal Map Division, the New York Public Library, Astor, Lenox and Tilden Foundations.

Published by the New York Genealogical and Biographical Society
36 West 44th Street, New York, NY 10036
NewYorkFamilyHistory.org

Library of Congress Control Number: 2014955433

Library of Congress Cataloging-in-Publication Data

New York family history research guide and gazetteer / prepared by The New York Genealogical and Biographical Society ; managing editors, Naomi Joshi, Michael J. Leclerc, Cathy Michelsen, Susan R. Miller, McKelden Smith, Catherine Ziegler.
    pages cm
 Includes bibliographical references and index.
 ISBN 978-0-692-31998-7 (softcover : alk. paper) 1. New York (State)--Genealogy--Handbooks, manuals, etc. 2. New York (State)--Genealogy--Archival resources. 3. New York (State)--Genealogy--Library resources. I. Joshi, Naomi, editor. II. New York Genealogical and Biographical Society.
 F118.N46 2014
 929.1072'0747--dc23
                        2014046318

New York Family History Research Guide and Gazetteer

prepared by the
New York Genealogical and Biographical Society

Managing Editors

Naomi Joshi
Michael J. Leclerc
Cathy Michelsen
Susan R. Miller
Catherine Ziegler
McKelden Smith

Project Staff

Naomi Joshi
Project Director and Editor, Gazetteers

Colleen Bennett, *Book Design*
Elizabeth Bennett, *Production Consultant*
Amber Gartung, *Map Designs*
Nancy Soriano, *Copy Editor*
Claire Aquilano, *Design Assistant*
Curtis Tow, *Design Concept*

Review Committee

Harry Macy Jr., FASG, FGBS
Consulting Editor

Ruth A. Carr
Laura Murphy DeGrazia, CG, FGBS
James D. Folts, PhD
Karen Mauer Green, CG, FGBS
Henry B. Hoff, CG, FASG, FGBS
Terry Koch-Bostic
Michael J. Leclerc
Anita A. Lustenberger, CG, FGBS
Suzanne McVetty, CG, FGBS
Jane E. Wilcox

Contributing Authors

Stanton Biddle, PhD
Victoria Boutilier
Ruth A. Carr
Mary Collins, CG
Laura Congleton
James D. Folts, PhD
Wayne Kempton
David Kleiman †

Kate Myslinski Kleiman
Terry Koch-Bostic
Michael J. Leclerc
Karen E. Livsey
Harry Macy Jr., FASG, FGBS
Rhoda Miller, EdD, CG
John T. Spellman
Paula Stuart-Warren, CG, FUGA

Contributors and Advisors

Moriah Amit
Brian G. Andersson
Maurita Baldock
Lynn Bassanese
Charles Fourquet Batiz
Michael Benowitz
Richard R. Berg
Mary Bertschmann
F. Warren Bittner, CG
Dag Blanck, PhD
Philip Blocklyn
Brian Carpenter
Tanya Chebotarev
Robert Clark
Kenneth R. Cobb
Brigitte H. Conkling
Pamela Cooley
Katherine Cordes
John Daggan
Catherine Daly
June DeLalio
Joseph Ditta
Dorothy Dougherty
Donald Eckerle
Charles Egleston
Elaine Engst
Stefani Evans, CG
Paul Friedman
Margaret Frost
Russell L. Gasero
Charles A. Gehring, PhD
Leonora A. Gidlund†

Aaron Goodwin
Johanna Gorelick, PhD
Eric G. Grundset
Barbara Gunvaldsen
Richard Haberstroh, PhD, AG
Janine E. Hakim
Michael J. Hall
Richard H. Harms, PhD
Leslie Harris, PhD
Victoria Hofmo
Cara Janowsky
Melissa A. Johnson
Henry Z Jones, FASG, FGBS
Arthur C. M. Kelly
Nancy Kelly
Marcia Kirk
Matthew Knutzen
Joan Koster-Morales
Carl Laurino
Joseph Lieby
Maira Liriano
Lauren A. Maehrlein
Nancy Maliwesky
Jackson McPeters
Stephen Michie
Gary Mokotoff
Christopher P. Moore
Kevin Newburg, PhD
Patricia Nixon
Denise Oliansky
Janet Lynne Peterson
Carla L. Peterson, PhD

Molly Poremski
Constance Potter
Timothy B. Powell, PhD
Laura G. Prescott
Shawn Purcell
Laura Redish
Michael Robison
Robert Roeckle
Mary Frances Ronan
Eric J. Roth
Judy Russell, CG, CGL
Marie Scalisi, CG
Kerry Sclafani
Craig Roberts Scott, CG, FUGA
Jill Seaholm
Marian L. Smith
Karen Staulters
Anthony Stevens
Edward R. Stewart
Francis J. Sypher, Jr., PhD
Loretto D. Szucs
D. Joshua Taylor
Mary M. Tedesco
Kathleen Tesluk
Karim Tiro, PhD
Lindsay Turley
Janny Venema, PhD
Eric Wakin, PhD
Guy R. Warner
Jessica Watson
Meldon J. Wolfgang, FGBS†

County Guides: Contributors and Advisors
Public Historians, Genealogists, Archivists, and Research Librarians

Patricia Bryce, Albany County
Ellen Gamache, Albany County
Jill Hughes, Albany County
Susan E. Leath, Albany County
Antony Opalka, Albany County
Don Rittner, Albany County
Craig Braack, Allegany County
Patricia Hilliker Forsberg, Allegany County
Richard Langdon, Allegany County
Rondus Miller, Allegany County
Mark Voorheis, Allegany County
Elizabeth Nico, Bronx County
Lloyd Ultan, PhD, Bronx County (Borough of the Bronx)
Richard Blythe, Broome County
Gerald R. Smith, Broome County
Sharon Fellows, Cattaraugus County

Maggie Fredrickson, Cattaraugus County
Jessica Armstrong, Cayuga County
Linda Frank, PhD, Cayuga County
Robert Kolsters, Cayuga County
Jean Lanning, Cayuga County
Cheryl Longyear, Cayuga County
Michelle Henry, Chautauqua County
Rachel Dworkin, Chemung County
J. Kelsey Jones, Chemung County
J. Arthur Kieffer, Chemung County
Mary Ellen P. Kunst, Chemung County
Earl Robinson, MD, Chemung County
Bruce Whitmarsh, Chemung County
Patricia E. Evans, Chenango County
Ronald & Carol Allen, Clinton County
Anastasia L. Pratt, PhD Clinton County

† deceased

Robert Tegart, Clinton County
Mary Howell, Columbia County
Diane Shewchuk, Columbia County
Alex Aloi, Cortland County
Jeremy Boylan, Cortland County
Jeff Guido, Cortland County
Anita Wright, Cortland County
Anthony Liberatore, Delaware County
Gabrielle Pierce, Delaware County
Wayne W. Wright, Delaware County
Joyce C. Ghee, Dutchess County
Eileen Mylod Hayden, Dutchess County
Linda Koehler, Dutchess County
Valerie LaRobardier, Dutchess County
Lynn K. Lucas, Dutchess County
Elizabeth C. Strauss, Dutchess County
Melissa N. Brown, Erie County
Douglas Kohler, Erie County
Cynthia Van Ness, Erie County
Margaret Gibbs, Essex County
Terry DeCarr, Franklin County
Carol P. Poole, Franklin County
Peter Betz, Fulton County
Susan L. Conklin, Genesee County
David C. Dorpfeld, Greene County
Patricia Morrow, Greene County
Wayne W. Wright, Greene County
Bill Zullo, Hamilton County
James M. Greiner, Herkimer County
Susan R. Perkins, Herkimer County
James Ranger, Jefferson County
John B. Manbeck, Kings County (Borough of Brooklyn)
Ron Schweiger, Kings County (Borough of Brooklyn)
Jerry E. Perrin, Lewis County
Amie Alden, Livingston County
Rhea Jean Walker, Livingston County
Virginia Keith, Madison County
Matthew Urtz, Madison County
Kathy Kanauer, Monroe County
Bill Poray, Monroe County
Carolyn Vacca, PhD, Monroe County
Kelly Yacobucci Farquhar, Montgomery County
Thomas Saltzman, Nassau County
Edward J. Smits, Nassau County
Sharon Wilkins, New York County (Borough of Manhattan)
Craig Bacon, Niagara County
Ronald Cary, Niagara County
Catherine L. Emerson, Niagara County
Brian Howard, Oneida County
Phyllis Ricco, Oneida County
Elizabeth Batlle, Onondaga County

Sandy Beglinger, Onondaga County
Dennis Connors, Onondaga County
Dorianne Gutierrez, Onondaga County
Dorothy Heller, Onondaga County
Mike Hoppe, Onondaga County
John G. Horner, Onondaga County
Ruth Hotaling, Onondaga County
Bonnie Kisselstein, Onondaga County
Kimberly Kleinhans, Onondaga County
Thomas B. Mafrici, Onondaga County
Susan Millet, Onondaga County
Peg Nolan, Onondaga County
Pamela Priest, Onondaga County
Margaret M. Riker, Onondaga County
Barbara S. Rivette, Onondaga County
Holly Sammons, Onondaga County
Jane Tracy, Onondaga County
Laurie Winship, Onondaga County
Hans-J. Finke, PhD, Ontario County
Preston Pierce, PhD, Ontario County
Rosemary Switzer, Ontario County
Cornelia W. Bush, Orange County
Mary Cardenas, Orange County
Suzanne Isaksen, Orange County
Norma Schadt, Orange County
Marilyn Terry, Orange County
C.W. Lattin, Orleans County
Delia Robinson, Orleans County
Justin White, Oswego County
Wayne W. Wright, Otsego County
Denis Castelli, Putnam County
Sallie Sypher, Putnam County
Jack Eichenbaum, PhD, Queens County (Borough of Queens)
Charles Filkins, Rensselaer County
Don Rittner, Rensselaer County
Kathryn T. Sheehan, Rensselaer County
Sarah Clark, Richmond County (Borough of Staten Island)
Thomas W. Matteo, PhD, Richmond County (Borough of Staten Island)
Barnett Shepherd, Richmond County (Borough of Staten Island)
Steven Cobb, Rockland County
Craig H. Long, Rockland County
Joanne Potanovic, Rockland County
Lauren Roberts, Saratoga County
Don Rittner, Schenectady County
Daniel J. Beams, Schoharie County
Wayne W. Wright, Schoharie County
Marion M. Boyce, Schuyler County

Carol Fagnon, Schuyler County
Andrew Tompkins, Schuyler County
Walter Gable, Seneca County
Gail H. Snyder, Seneca County
Twila O'Dell, Steuben County
Nancy Boeye, St. Lawrence County
Patricia Davis, St. Lawrence County
Dennis E. Eickhoff, St. Lawrence County
Pamela Ouimet, St. Lawrence County
Trent A. Trulock, St. Lawrence County
Norman Young, St. Lawrence County
Bradley Harris, Suffolk County
Toni Raptis, Suffolk County
Edward H. L. Smith III, FGBS, Suffolk County
John Conway, Sullivan County
Frank V Schwarz, Sullivan County
Louise Smith, Sullivan County
Emma M. Sedore, Tioga County
Alan Chaffee, Tompkins County
Carol Kammen, Tompkins County

Anne M. Gordon, Ulster County
Linda Queipo, Ulster County
John D. Austin, FASG, Warren County
Marilyn Van Dyke, PhD, Warren County
Ann McCann, Warren County
Loretta Bates, Washington County
William Cormier, Washington County
Donna Crandall, Washington County
Carol Greenough, Washington County
Peter Evans, Wayne County
June Hamell, Wayne County
Sandy Hopkins, Wayne County
Barbara Meeks, Wayne County
Sally J. Millick, Wayne County
Jackie Graziano, Westchester County
Daniel Kelly, Westchester County
Maureen Koehl, Westchester County
Patrick Raftery, Westchester County
Doris A. Bannister, Wyoming County
Jeanne Mest, Wyoming County
Frances Dumas, Yates County

Research Associates

Joshua Blair
Hallie J. Borstel
Madeline Bourque Kearin
Wendy L. Oborne
William B. Roka
Anna Romagnoli

Research Assistants

Marguerite Adams
Ben Atkinson
Trisha Battoo
Brendan Birth
Ivory Butler
Noelle Butler
Sarah Cassone
Amirah Cisse
Annabel Coleman
Anna Gibertini
Rachel Glasberg
Todd Hirsch
Laura Hoffman
Elisabeth Hyde
Shayra Kamal
Jeremy Karson
Evans Forbes Kelley
David Kurkovskiy

Jason Lalljee
Joy Lee
Timothy Levin
Ted Levin
Michael LoSasso
Jaime Lowen
James Macksoud
Harriet Mayer
Michael Pascual
Emily Powell
Christine Rai
Jenna Ray
Kelsey Riddle
Gretchen Schumacher
Donovan Soleyn
Kim Tambascia
Tamara Whitehouse

Table of Contents

Part One
Each chapter includes a selected bibliography and suggestions for further reading, as well as descriptions of selected repositories and online resources.

Part Two

Three years ago the New York Genealogical and Biographical Society set out to produce a definitive guidebook to the genealogical research resources of New York State, including an updated gazetteer. This was no small undertaking, even for an organization that has contributed substantially to the scholarship in the field for 145 years.

While much has been written on numerous subjects relevant to New York research, no one volume has embraced the full range of resources of importance to family historians. And the most recent scholarly gazetteer of the state was prepared over a century ago. The production of the *New York Family History Research Guide and Gazetteer* has been a monumental effort, and I have so many people to thank.

We are extraordinarily indebted to Harry Macy Jr., who it is fair to say is *the* undisputed authority on New York families and genealogy. As consulting editor for the project, he has read and commented extensively on every chapter in Part One of this book, and on key sections of Part Two, and added his own critical insights to the chapter text and bibliographies. Mr. Macy's standards for thoroughness and fine-tuned detail, as well as big-picture observation, immeasurably benefited the book, and provided inspiration to the project staff.

I am grateful to the review committee, a blue-ribbon panel of New York experts, for editing the first draft of the manuscript, and steering us in the right direction as we approached the finish line. All members of the review committee rolled up their sleeves and made valuable contributions to many of the chapters and county guides.

Naomi Joshi brought her wide-ranging talents and dedication to high standards for this challenging enterprise. She enlisted the support of New York's enthusiastic genealogical community, which resulted in expert contributions from more than 200 historians, archivists, librarians, genealogists, volunteers, and interns. It was truly a crowd-sourced project.

I would like to especially thank the professionals at of the NYG&B for truly heroic work on the book, particularly Cathy Michelsen, Sue Miller, McKelden Smith, and Catherine Ziegler. Without their intensive focus on the project, this book would have taken *at least* another year to produce.

I thank all of our friends from the professional genealogical community who not only reviewed chapters, but undertook supplementary research and provided encouragement along the way. These individuals unselfishly shared their knowledge and are recognized in the acknowledgment pages of this book.

I thank the generous friends and trustees of the NYG&B who contributed financially to help underwrite the costs of this complex project from research to publication. These special friends are listed on the opposite page.

People often say that research in New York State is a difficult task. We hope that, in ways large and small, this book will make your work more productive. And we encourage you to publish your own research in print or online so that others will benefit from your discoveries. Perhaps this book will help you solve a problem, compile a genealogy, or transcribe a previously unknown manuscript that could become the basis for an article in the *New York Genealogical and Biographical Record*.

And so we didn't publish this book for our coffee tables. We published this book for all of us who endeavor to discover and tell the stories of our New York families. Many of our immigrant ancestors arrived on these shores through the great gateway port of New York City. Some migrated to New York from other cities and states, or came across the national borders. Some of our ancestors traveled here forcibly, as slaves, and some were in New York before the first Europeans arrived.

That is why our organization's purpose is to help people of all backgrounds explore and document their family histories. This work is life enriching—particularly when we find our own places in the continuum of American history, connect with family members past and present, and build community.

We welcome your suggestions to improve this book. After all, at the end of the day, we are all one extended family.

Jeanne Sloane
Chairman, Board of Trustees
New York Genealogical and Biographical Society

For more than 150 years New York was the most populous state in the Union, so it is not surprising that a huge number of people living today have New York roots. Many discover their connection to the Empire State only through genealogy, while others know they are New Yorkers from an early age, and I was in the latter category. Born on Long Island, I began searching my roots as a teenager, eventually became a professional genealogist doing work for clients, and in 1986 joined the staff of the New York Genealogical and Biographical Society (NYG&B), where for 20 years I edited the Society's journal, the *NYG&B Record*. New York's genealogical resources stretch back to the 1600s, and in the course of my career I have used a wide variety of them and have untangled endless genealogical mysteries. I have also experienced firsthand the dramatic changes that have occurred in the field of genealogy in recent decades.

I was fortunate when I started my research because many sources I needed were in print or on microfilm, and I could access them in several good libraries. Numerous original records were also available in those libraries and other local repositories. I ran into some roadblocks but was able to fill in a great deal of my ancestral chart rather quickly, confirming that I was a 13th generation New Yorker. Thus I was surprised to hear other genealogists complain that New York genealogy was so difficult to research, a complaint one still hears today. In fact New York has wonderful resources for the genealogist, but they may differ from sources found in other states, and one has to learn what they are and how to use them effectively.

One thing that sets New York apart from many other states is its long and unusually complex history. Before becoming a state it was an English colony, and before that it was part of the Dutch colony of New Netherland. From the beginning there have also been complicated multiple levels of local government. The state's major regions—Long Island, New York City, the Hudson Valley, the North Country, and central and western New York—have distinct histories that can affect research. New York City alone has more people than forty states, and extensive records covering nearly 400 years.

Researchers with more than a little New York ancestry are apt to find a great amount of diversity in their family tree. This diversity, in terms of race, ethnicity, and religion, began to grow in the early 1600s. In the nineteenth and early twentieth centuries the port of New York received the vast majority of free immigrants to the United States, many of whom remained in the state, and from the seventeenth century onward there was migration into New York from New England, other colonies or states, and Canada.

An amazing number of records have survived from the colonial period to the present. They have been published, microfilmed, or preserved in government offices, archives, and libraries, and are now becoming increasingly accessible online. In addition to government records at all levels, there are records of numerous religious denominations, as well as records created by private enterprises and individuals. More than a few of these records are in languages other than English.

Over the years genealogy in New York State has been supported by local, regional, and statewide societies. The oldest and most prominent of these is the NYG&B, founded in New York City in 1869 at a time when interest in American genealogy was rapidly growing. Many families had been here for 200 years or more, but details of their family histories had been largely forgotten. The effort to recapture those histories was spearheaded by individuals who had the time and money to do the research and publish their findings. The result was a flood of genealogies, local histories, and transcripts or abstracts of records that we still use today. Several of those individuals were early members of the NYG&B.

In 1870 the NYG&B began publishing its quarterly, the *NYG&B Record*, now in its 145th year, the second-oldest continuously published genealogical journal in the English language. In its thousands of pages are genealogies of New York families and transcripts and abstracts of New York records, the largest collection of reliable New York family history under one title. The *Record* participated in the development of scholarly genealogy, and today it is one of the few peer-reviewed American scholarly journals in the field, a magnet attracting the best and brightest researchers and writers. Anyone who fails to include the *Record* in their research, especially when working on New York families before 1900, risks missing unique and crucial information, and thus repeating old errors or creating new ones. Even when a family is not found in the *Record*, reviewing its articles will help in understanding how scholarly genealogy should be written, and how New York sources can be used.

Of course the NYG&B is more than the *Record*. The Society accumulated one of the largest genealogical collections in the country, now housed at the New York Public Library. The Society's staff and many of its volunteers are New York experts, who conduct a wide range of educational programs, as well as contribute to publishing aids for New York research in addition to the *Record*. Over the past forty years or so the number of genealogical researchers has skyrocketed. More and more nineteenth and twentieth century records have been made available, making genealogy a subject of interest to all Americans, not just those with colonial roots. The Internet has given everyone access to sources that were once available only in a few cities. As genealogy has evolved in this new world, so has the NYG&B. Its publications and many other resources are now available to members on the Society's ever-growing website, *NewYorkFamilyHistory.org*.

To cope with New York's extensive and often complicated records in today's genealogical world, a comprehensive, accurate, and up-to-date, statewide research guide has long been needed. Continuing its long history of publishing New York research aids, the NYG&B now introduces the *New York Family History Research Guide and Gazetteer*. Since no one person can be an expert in every aspect of New York genealogy, the knowledge of many experienced researchers has been drawn on to create the chapters that follow. The resulting work is designed to help everyone, from those attempting New York genealogy for the first time to experienced researchers who may have hit a brick wall. It is a book that should be in every New York genealogist's personal library, always on hand for ready reference.

Harry Macy Jr., FASG, FGBS
Consulting Editor
New York, New York
December 2014

This book is a guide to the genealogical research resources for New York State—the first of its kind ever written—and is meant to serve everyone from beginners to professionals. Its purpose is to open doors that will lead, with the application of effort, to genealogical discovery.

Part One

Part One describes the key genealogically-pertinent records that have been kept for New York and provides guidance on how to locate both original and derivative records, as well as record substitutes and authored works.

New York's complex history—as a colony, ruled variously by the Dutch and the English, and as one of the most populous and earliest states—produced idiosyncrasies in its record keeping. Part One begins with a chapter on New York's colonial period, which is followed by chapters that describe major record groups and other research resources; identify resources with special relevance to the ethnic and religious groups that have had a significant presence in New York; catalog repositories and resources that provide national and statewide coverage; and identify the fundamental, easily accessible New York research references in current use.

Though this is a reference book, researchers are encouraged to read all of Part One. That's because the record groups and resources are interconnected, often in surprising and unexpected ways, and knowledge of the whole may well lead to breakthroughs that a cherry-picking approach will miss.

Part Two

Guides to New York's 62 counties—including the five boroughs of New York City, each of which is its own county—comprise Part Two. Each County Guide has three components: a cover page with an original map and key details about the county; a gazetteer of place names, past and present; and a list of research resources specific to each county.

Getting the most from the County Guides requires reading the introduction to Part Two, which defines geographic terms and explains how the state is organized governmentally, how public records particular to the county are distributed, and how to understand the gazetteer.

Additions and Corrections

The amount of detail in this book is vast. Despite input from dozens of informed people in every county and area of specialty, omissions and errors are inevitable. Readers are invited to submit additions and corrections to NYGuide@nygbs.org with the sincere thanks of the editors.

Frequently Used Abbreviations in This Book	
CNYGS	Central New York Genealogical Society
DAR	National Society Daughters of the American Revolution
FHL	Family History Library
HDI	Historical Documents Inventory
LOC	Library of Congress
MUNI	Municipal Archives of New York City
NARA	National Archives and Records Administration, Washington, DC
NARA-NYC	National Archives at New York City
NEHGS	New England Historic Genealogical Society
NYG&B	New York Genealogical and Biographical Society
N-YHS	New-York Historical Society
NYPL	New York Public Library
NYSA	New York State Archives
NYSHA	New York State Historical Association
NYSL	New York State Library
WPA	Works Progress Administration/Work Projects Administration

This timeline shows the major highlights of New York history that are especially relevant to people studying New York families and that are, for the most part, *particular to New York State*. The chart's purpose is to provide the general historical framework that shapes any researcher's exploration of the people of New York and the records they left behind. An emphasis is placed on events that affect record keeping. The population statistics from the federal censuses are from the website of the United States Census Bureau; the statistics from the state censuses are from the official state reports.

1609	Henry Hudson explored area around New York Harbor and Hudson Valley region representing the Dutch East India Company; Samuel de Champlain explored what is now northeastern New York representing France
1614	New Netherland Company formed in Amsterdam; Fort Nassau built near present-day Albany; colony of New Netherland established in area between Delaware and Connecticut rivers.
1621	Dutch West India Company chartered
1624	First European colonists—most of them Walloons—arrived in New Netherland; West India Company established Fort Orange at site of present-day Albany
1626	First African slaves brought to the colony; beginning of settlement on Manhattan Island surrounding Fort Amsterdam; Manhattan acquired from American Indians
1628	First church (Dutch Reformed) organized in Manhattan
1629	First large land grant by the Dutch; Patroonship of Rensselaerswyck established; later became Van Rensselaer Manor
1640	First English settlements on eastern Long Island
1650	By the Treaty of Hartford, the English and Dutch divided Long Island just west of Oyster Bay
1653	New Amsterdam chartered as a city
1654	Twenty-three Sephardic Jews from Brazil arrived in New Amsterdam
1657	The Flushing Remonstrance, perhaps the earliest demand for religious freedom by American colonists, drafted in response to persecution of Quakers by the Director-General of New Netherland
1664	British captured New Netherland renaming it New York (formalized with Treaty of Breda in 1667); English towns on Long Island added to new colony
1664	New Jersey, part of New Netherland, became a separate colony
1665	"Duke's Laws" adopted, reorganizing local government and introducing English legal system including probate records; City of New York created by charter
1660s–1700s	Early manors and early eastern patents granted
1673–1674	Brief recapture of New York by the Dutch; Treaty of Westminster established English control
1682	First Jewish congregation formed (Shearith Israel, in New York City)
1683	Election of first General Assembly, which drafted Charter of Liberties and Privileges, reorganizing government and recognizing basic rights including religious liberty for most (but not Catholics); Assembly divided the colony into 12 counties: Albany, Cornwall, Dukes, Dutchess, Kings, New York, Orange, Queens, Richmond, Suffolk, Ulster, and Westchester; Dukes (Martha's Vineyard and Nantucket) and Cornwall (part of present-day Maine) later ceded to Massachusetts

1685	French king revoked Edict of Nantes, stimulating exodus of Huguenots from France
1691	Colonial court structure significantly revised
1693	1693 Ministry Act passed, leading to recognition of Church of England as the established church in four counties: New York, Richmond, Westchester, and Queens
1698	First census of New York colony: total "White" population: 15,897; total "Negro" population: 2,170
1709–1710	First group of Palatine Germans settled in the Hudson Valley
1723	Stone Arabia Patent: one of the earliest large land grants given directly to settlers (Palatine Germans)
1725	The *New-York Gazette*, New York's first newspaper, began publication, followed in 1733 by the *New-York Weekly Journal*
1730s–1760s	First Great Awakening, an evangelical religious movement, influenced the shape of Protestant churches, particularly Congregational, Presbyterian, Dutch Reformed, and Baptist denominations, and, towards the end of the period, the Methodist denomination just then becoming established in New York
1731	Present-day boundary of New York and Connecticut established; Connecticut recognized Rye as a New York town and New York ceded any claim to Connecticut towns of Greenwich and Stamford; the disputed two-mile wide "Oblong" tract along the border with Connecticut and Massachusetts ceded to New York
1753	A colonial act required all mortgages be recorded with city or county clerks
1756–1763	French and Indian War: French lands in northern and western New York fell to the British; royal proclamation in 1763 prohibited European settlement west of Appalachians
1769	Present border with New Jersey was settled; line surveyed and marked in 1774
1773	Boundary dispute with Massachusetts partially settled
1775–1783	The American Revolution: New York City, Long Island, and southern Westchester continuously occupied by the British 1776–1783; at war's end, thousands of New York Loyalists emigrated to Canada, Britain, and elsewhere
1777	New York State's first constitution adopted
1779–1785	Loyalist land confiscations
1784	Legislature lifted ban on Catholic worship, which had been in effect since the Dutch period except for Dongan Administration in the 1680s; first Catholic church founded in New York City
1785–1790	New York City served as capital of the United States; George Washington inaugurated as the President in New York City in 1789
1786	First city directory printed in New York City
1787	State legislature created office of Surrogate in each county to have jurisdiction over estates and keep related records, subject to state Court of Probates created in 1778
1788	Reorganization Act recognized most county boundaries, created a new county, recognized towns, and created new towns
1788	Fort Schuyler Treaty established first American Indian reservations in New York
1790	New York surrendered all claims to land in Vermont
1790s–1840s	Second Great Awakening, a national religious movement led by Baptists and Methodists, expanded churches and church membership; the "Burned Over District" in western New York particularly influenced by the movement
1790	First federal census reported a New York population of 340,120

1797	Albany became capital of New York State, replacing New York City
1799	New York's Gradual Emancipation Act passed
1800	Federal census reported a New York population of 589,051, a 73% increase since 1790
1804	The New-York Historical Society formed
1806	Catskill Turnpike completed, connecting Catskill (Hudson County) with Bath (Steuben County) about 200 miles due west and later extended to both Erie and Buffalo
1810	Federal census reported a New York population of 959,049, a 63% increase since 1800
1811	Commissioners' Plan of 1811 laid out Manhattan street grid
1812–1815	War of 1812: more than 75,000 New Yorkers served; significant action occurred on the border between New York and Canada
1817	Erie Canal construction began, creating new towns and settlements
1817	New York Stock and Exchange Board (later renamed New York Stock Exchange), tracing its origins to 1792, formally organized with a constitution and bylaws
1818	New York State Library founded
1820	Federal census reported a New York population of 1,372,812, a 43% increase since 1810
1820	Steerage Act of 1819 required passenger lists for arriving ships to be filed with U.S. Customs
1825	Erie Canal opened between Albany and Buffalo, linking New York City to the Great Lakes
1825	The first New York state decennial census taken; reported a population of 1,616,458 (state census repeated regularly, with last state census taken in 1925)
1827	Slavery ended in New York State with exceptions for non- and part-time residents
1829	New York State mandated petitions for probate or administration to identify all heirs-at-law and probate and administrative files to be kept permanently
1830	Church of Jesus Christ of Latter-day Saints organized in Fayette, Seneca County
1830	State statute mandated that county clerks record all deeds
1830	Federal census reported a New York population of 1,918,608, a 40% increase since 1820
1831–1851	New York's first successful, regularly scheduled railroad connected Albany and Schenectady (Mohawk and Hudson Railroad); railroads connected Albany with Buffalo by 1841; New York City and Albany connected by railroads by 1851; Long Island Rail Road Company chartered in 1834
1835	The New York Herald began publication; became the nation's largest circulating paper
1835	New York State conducted a statewide census; reported population to be 2,174,517
1839–1845	Anti-Rent Wars led to end of manorial system
1840	Federal census reported a New York population of 2,428,921, a 27% increase since 1830
1842	Webster-Ashburton Treaty confirmed border with Canada
1845	General property taxation standardized and collected on a regular basis throughout New York State (state property taxes abolished in 1928)
1845	New York State conducted a statewide census; reported a population of 2,604,495

1845–1852	The Great Famine in Ireland drove millions to immigrate to New York and elsewhere
1847	Major reorganization of the state court system
1848	Revolutionary movements and crop failures in Europe led to surge in political refugees from the continent to New York and elsewhere
1849	Gold discovered in California set off the Gold Rush, prompting migration out of New York and other states
1850	Federal census reported a New York population of 3,097,394, a 28% increase since 1840
1851	The *New York Daily Times* began publication and became the *New York Times* in 1857
1854	First of the "orphan trains" departed from New York City, mainly to the Midwest and West
1855	Massachusetts and New York finally settled long-standing border dispute
1855	Castle Garden opened as a state-run immigrant processing center in New York City; eight million immigrants processed there until its operations ceased in 1890
1855	New York State conducted a statewide census, the first state census with all names recorded; reported a population of 3,466,118
1860	Federal census reported a New York population of 3,880,735, a 25% increase since 1850
1861–1865	The American Civil War: about one-sixth of the Union service members were New Yorkers
1862	The federal Homestead Acts (starting 1862) encouraged outward migration by offering land at little or no cost on federal land in western states
1863	Draft riots in New York City, which turned into violent race riots, put down by federal troops and state militia
1865	New York State conducted a statewide census; reported a population of 3,831,751
1869–1870	New York Genealogical and Biographical Society founded in 1869; publication of the *New York Genealogical and Biographical Record* began in 1870
1870	Federal census reported a New York population of 4,382,759, a 13% increase since 1860
1875	New York State conducted a statewide census; reported a population of 4,698,958
1878	First commercial telephone exchange in New York opened in Albany; first telephone directory published in New York City
1880	Federal census reported a New York population of 5,082,871, a 16% increase since 1870
1880–1881	Collection of vital records expanded from the cities to the entire state; but nearly 35 years before full compliance achieved
1881	Assassination of Russia's Czar Alexander II, for which Jews were scapegoated and suffered reprisals, resulted in very large Jewish immigration to New York
1882	Chinese Exclusion Act passed by the U.S. Congress prohibiting Chinese immigration; not lifted until 1943
1886	Statue of Liberty dedicated
1890	Federal census reported a New York population of 6,003,174, an 18% increase since 1880
1890	Castle Garden closed in April, ceasing operations as a New York State immigration station; succeeded by Federal Barge Office (April 1890–December 1891)
1891	The Immigration Act of 1891: Federal government began taking over immigration management from the states

1892	Ellis Island opened as an immigration station; burned in 1897; reopened in 1900; processed 12 million immigrants until closure in 1924 but remained a detention facility until 1954.
1892	New York State conducted a statewide census (no state census in 1885 or 1895); reported a population of 6,513,343
1894–1895	U.S. immigration ports of entry established along the Canadian border in 1894; record-keeping began on immigration from Canada into New York began in 1895
1898	The modern City of New York is formed creating the five boroughs of the Bronx, Brooklyn, Queens, Staten Island (then called Richmond), and Manhattan
1898	Spanish-American War: the United States acquired Puerto Rico, setting the stage for future migration to the United States
1900	Federal census reported a New York population of 7,268,894, a 21% increase since 1890
1905	New York State conducted a statewide census; reported a population of 8,067,308
1907	Ellis Island's peak year: over one million immigrants processed
1910	Federal census reported a New York population of 9,113,614, a 25% increase since 1900
1916–1930	The first wave of the "Great Migration" of African Americans from the southern states to New York City and elsewhere
1911	Fire in the Capitol in Albany destroyed or damaged large part of the New York State Library (including many of the State's archives which at that time were part of the Library)
1914	The last county formed in New York State: Bronx County
1915	New York State conducted a statewide census; reported a population of 9,687,744
1917	The United States entered World War I
1917	American citizenship extended to residents of Puerto Rico
1917	New York State granted women the right to vote in state elections
1918	The influenza pandemic killed thousands
1920s	Harlem emerged as a center of African American life and spurred the "Harlem Renaissance" cultural movement
1920	Federal census reported a New York population of 10,385,227, a 14% increase since 1910
1920	19th Amendment gave women the right to vote in national elections
1924	Act passed by the U. S. Congress sharply limited immigration and effectively closed Ellis Island as an immigration center; it remained open as a detention center
1925	New York State conducted its last statewide census; reported a population of 11,162,151
1929	The New York Stock Market Crash marked the beginning of the Great Depression
1930	Federal census reported a New York population of 12,588,066, a 21% increase since 1920
1940	Federal census reported a New York population of 13,479,142, a 7% increase since 1930
1939–1945	World War II; the U.S. entered the War in 1941

Part One

Guide to Record Groups and Research Resources

African American	English	Jewish
American Indian	French and French-Speaking	Polish
Austro-Hungarian (and related, but distinct ethnicities)	German	Russian (and related, but distinct ethnicities)
	Hispanic	
Chinese	Irish	Scandinavian
Dutch	Italian	Scots and Scots-Irish

Baptist	Episcopal	Presbyterian
Catholic	Jewish	Quaker (Society of Friends
Congregational (also Independent)	Lutheran	Reformed (Dutch, Huguenot,
Eastern Rite Catholic and Eastern	Methodist	German, Christian)
Orthodox	Mormon (Latter-day Saint)	

Historical Overview

New York was a colony for more than 150 years before it became a state, first as part of Dutch New Netherland and then as English New York. During those years, numerous records were created that are of value to genealogists. Most of them fall into the same categories as later records, and are clearly the ancestors of today's records, but some are different enough to warrant special consideration.

Genealogists who find they have roots in the Dutch colony are often confused by its name. It was New Netherland, without an "s" at the end, and not New Amsterdam, which was actually the name of its capital city located on the southern tip of Manhattan Island.

Dutch traders frequented what became colonial New York before actual settlement began. Juan Rodriguez, a free man of African and Hispanic descent who was born on the island of Hispaniola, was aboard one of those vessels in 1613, and he remained for at least a year in the harbor area where he helped set up a trading post.

From a genealogical standpoint, however, colonial New York begins in 1624 when the first European settlers arrived on the Dutch ships *Eendracht* and *Nieuw Nederland*. The latter ship bore the name of the colony created by the West India Company, which extended from the Connecticut River to the Delaware, far beyond the present boundaries of New York. New Netherland quickly became a "melting pot" of people from all over Europe, as well as Africans, both slave and free. They included Christians of many denominations and a few Jews and Muslims living in settlements surrounded by the native peoples that had been in the region for millennia.

At the same time that New Netherland was being settled, English settlers founded towns on Long Island from Oyster Bay eastward. Most of those towns were affiliated with the Connecticut or

New Haven colonies, and research before 1664 must include the published records of those colonies in addition to town records. English people also settled within the boundaries of New Netherland under Dutch rule.

In 1664 the English seized New Netherland, and King Charles II gave the former Dutch colony to his brother, the Duke of York. The new colony (later province) of New York was created from both the Dutch and English parts of Long Island plus Staten and Manhattan Islands, extending up the Hudson River to north of Albany, and along the Mohawk River to Schenectady. The Duke almost immediately made his friends Berkeley and Carteret proprietors of the territory between the Hudson and Delaware rivers, which became the separate colony of New Jersey. From that point forward, New Jersey and New York have their own records, despite the fact that they sometimes shared a governor.

In 1673 during the Third Anglo-Dutch War, the Dutch recaptured New York, restoring the name New Netherland. Under the treaty ending the war in 1674, each side agreed to give up any captured lands, and English rule was restored. New York remained an English colony (or province) until the American Revolution.

In 1688–1689 New York was briefly part of the Dominion of New England under a governor seated at Boston. Several New York wills were proved and recorded in Boston during this period, but most records were not affected. The Dominion was dissolved after the "Glorious Revolution" of 1688 in England, when the Catholic King James II (the former Duke of York) was ousted in favor of the Protestant William and Mary (James's daughter Mary and her husband, Prince William of Orange, a grandson of Charles I).

In New York, Jacob Leisler assumed the office of lieutenant governor, pending the arrival of a new governor from London.

There followed a period of unrest known as the Leisler Rebellion, in which the colony's population was deeply divided between pro- and anti-Leisler factions. Some of this division reflected growing Dutch concern over Anglicization. While some of the leading Dutch merchants and clergy opposed Leisler, the Dutch rank and file were among his most avid supporters.

When the new governor eventually arrived, Leisler was arrested and executed for treason, but his conviction was reversed several years later. From the many records of this period, it is often possible to determine which side a particular family favored in this conflict. The Leisler Papers Project at New York University, under the direction of David William Voorhees, has done much to correct earlier historians' negative treatment of Leisler and to clarify the importance of this period of New York history.

During the eighteenth century, Dutch was still the language of much of the population, but its use slowly declined in favor of English. Immigration from the Netherlands virtually ceased after 1675, but immigrants continued to arrive from France, Germany, Scotland, Ireland, and England, and more African slaves were brought into the colony. At this time there was also the beginning of a migration out of New England into the Hudson Valley. By the time of the American Revolution, New York had an estimated population of 200,000. Studies of surnames in the 1790 census indicate that people of English descent had become a bare majority of New York's people, making it and New Jersey the least English of the thirteen colonies.

The Revolution revealed another deep division among New Yorkers, between supporters of independence and those who remained loyal to the English king. Others remained neutral, including the colony's numerous Quakers. As the British Army prepared to leave late in 1783, many Loyalists also departed, most of them going to Nova Scotia (which then included New Brunswick) and Ontario (many of those from the Mohawk River Valley). Other Loyalists remained in the new state, resigning themselves to the new order.

Records of the Colonial Governments

Though New Netherland was settled in 1624, its records, both civil and religious, do not begin until 1638–1639. Some of that gap is filled by documents in the notarial archives of Amsterdam and the few surviving records of the West India Company. A collection of very early documents was discovered in the early twentieth century and published in 1924 as *Documents Relating to New Netherland 1624–1626*, edited by Arnold J. F. van Laer. For information about the known documents from the Dutch period, see the *Guide to Dutch Manuscripts Relating to New Netherland*, best accessed from the New Netherland Institute website, *newnetherlandinstitute.org*; updated 2010–2012, the *Guide* identifies and locates Dutch manuscripts in numerous repositories. See also Charles T. Gehring's "A Survey of Documents Relating to New Netherland."

A large number of colonial New York records survive from 1638 forward, but the originals tend to be in fragile condition; access is generally limited to microfilm or digital copies, printed transcriptions, extracts, or abstracts. The earliest records are difficult to read, as they are written in old handwriting that can be hard to decipher, and many are in seventeenth-century Dutch. There is an ongoing project to transcribe and translate them as described below. Many colonial government records were destroyed or damaged in a fire at the New York State Library (NYSL) in 1911, though some lost in that fire had fortunately been published prior to that date. For more information on the fire and documents destroyed or remaining, see Harry Macy Jr.'s "The 1911 State Library Fire and Its Effect on New York Genealogy."

Records were kept by every level of government on both sides of the Atlantic. These records detail interactions between colonists, their governments, and one another. The extensive records of the governments of New Netherland and English New York accumulated in the colonial capital, New York City (the former New Amsterdam). These colony-level records were inherited by New York State in 1783, and were moved to Albany when it became the state capital in 1797. Early in the nineteenth century, concern was expressed for the preservation of these records, and Francis Adriaen vander Kemp was hired to begin translating records that were written in Dutch, but most of his work was lost in the 1911 fire. The state also sent John Romeyn Brodhead to The Hague, London, and Paris to copy records in the Dutch, British, and French archives that related to New York.

In 1850 New York State hired Edmund Bailey O'Callaghan to translate and edit the documents found by Brodhead, and the result was volumes 1–11 of *Documents Relative to the Colonial History of the State of New York*. Dr. O'Callaghan also undertook the preservation of the state's own colonial records, reorganizing them into a series of volumes that are now in the New York State Archives (NYSA) and commonly referred to as the New York Colonial Manuscripts. O'Callaghan's *Calendar of Historical Manuscripts in the Office of the Secretary of State, Albany, New York*, giving brief descriptions of the contents of every page of every volume, was published in 1865–1866 in two parts, Dutch (1630–1664) and English (1664–1776, including the Dutch records for 1673–1674). These calendars are a gateway to the various published versions of the Colonial Manuscripts described below.

Portions of the colonial manuscripts were published in O'Callaghan's four-volume *Documentary History of the State of New York*, in volumes 12–14 of the *Documents Relative* series (retitled *Documents Relating to the Colonial History of the State of New York*) edited by Berthold Fernow, and in various later volumes translated and edited by Arnold J. F. van Laer. As a result of the 1911 fire, many of these records survive only because of the work done by these men.

In 1974 the Holland Society of New York, which collects and preserves information concerning early Dutch communities in New York and New Jersey, sponsored publication of the first four volumes of the New York Colonial Manuscripts, under the new title *New York Historical Manuscripts: Dutch*, translated earlier by Van Laer. This was the beginning of a series, since renamed *New Netherland Documents*, undertaken by the New Netherland Project (NNP), now called the New Netherland Institute (NNI), which will eventually provide new translations of all the Dutch documents in the NYSA. See also chapter 14, Peoples of New York, the section on the Dutch, including the NNP/NNI. The website of the NNI (*newnetherlandinstitute. org*) offers a very extensive bibliography of sources for the Dutch period in the colonial era and extensive text introducing volumes of translated Dutch documents.

The Holland Society of New York has also supported publication of the series *New York Historical Manuscripts: English* (now called *New York Historical Manuscripts*), covering the records of the English colonial government beginning in 1664. Peter R. Christoph and the late Florence A. Christoph transcribed and edited the volumes published to date, covering the records of the English colonial government from 1664 through 1691. Peter R. Christoph has edited most of the volumes, some with his wife Florence A. Christoph as co-editor. In both the Dutch and English series, when all or part of an original record was lost due to the 1911 fire, it has sometimes been possible to fill the gap with a copy of a record from a pre-1911 publication.

These records were those of the top level of government in the colony. It is important to stress that when doing New York colonial research, the records of all levels of government must be consulted. Extensive records survive from the counties, towns, and cities that existed in the colonial era. These include land records, probate and other court records, town meeting records, and city council records, all of which continued to be kept after the Revolution with relatively few changes. The original records are still in the custody of the county or local governments, or have been transferred to archives. Many of these records have been published in full or as abstracts, and have also been microfilmed and are now being digitized. For example, the New York City Municipal Archives (MUNI) has launched an initiative to make images of its New Amersterdam records 1647–1674 accessible online at *www.archives.nyc*. For further detail, see references to the colonial period in the chapters that follow.

Records from Nongovernmental Sources

In addition to government records, colonial churches and other institutions left behind a tremendous number of record books, and individuals, too, left records of their lives. The major landowners, called patroons in the Dutch period and lords of manors under the English, left many nongovernmental records. See chapter 7, Land Records, for information on those records.

Religious Records

Religious records are among the most important resources for colonial New York genealogy, as the principal substitute for the lack of civil vital records. In New Netherland, only the Dutch Reformed Church was permitted to hold public worship. Individuals of other religions were limited to privately worshipping in their own homes. Even if they had been Lutheran, Mennonite, or Roman Catholic in the old country, they were required by New Netherland law to be married in the Dutch Reformed Church; they may also have had their children baptized in the Dutch Reformed Church as well. The English Puritans, who founded several towns within New Netherland, were exempted from this restriction, as they were viewed as fellow Calvinists. When the first Jews arrived in New Amsterdam in 1654, an attempt to prevent them from staying in the colony was thwarted by the directors of the West India Company, and the Jewish community became well established during the remainder of the colonial era.

In English New York, the Dutch Reformed Church remained strong, and the ban on other public worship was lifted except for Roman Catholics. New churches were created by the Lutherans and Huguenots, and later by the German Reformed, Moravians, and others. Most of the Puritan congregations eventually became Presbyterian, while other English in the colony turned to the Church of England (Anglican), Baptists, or Quakers. The seven volume *Ecclesiastical Records, State of New York* includes numerous documents concerning the Dutch, English, and other churches in the colony, their interaction with their mother churches in Europe, and with the colonial authorities. For additional information see the relevant sections of chapter 14, Peoples of New York, and chapter 15, Religious Records.

When the first Quakers arrived in 1657, Director-General Pieter Stuyvesant tried to banish them from the colony. The inhabitants of Flushing sent him a Remonstrance, now considered to be one of the most important documents in the struggle for religious freedom in the thirteen colonies. The text of the Remonstrance, written in English, reminded him of "The law of love, peace, and liberty in the states [of the Netherlands] extending to Jews, Turks, and Egyptians, as they are considered the sonnes of Adam, which is the glory of the outward state of Holland," and they defiantly told him that anyone "whether Presbyterian, Independent, Baptist or Quaker" who should "come in love unto us, we cannot in good conscience lay violent hands upon them, but give them free egresse and regresse unto our Town, and houses." And they pointed out their position was in accordance with the patent and charter given to Flushing "in the name of the States General [the Dutch parliament]." It took five years for the West India Company to overrule Stuyvesant, but in the end the remonstrants prevailed. Quakers subsequently became a major denomination in New York's diverse religious landscape.

Genealogists doing research in the English colonies are familiar with the September 1752 calendar change, when the "new style" calendar now in use was introduced by skipping ahead eleven days, so that what would have been 3 September 1752 became 14 September. This adjustment was necessary to synchronize the calendar with the earth's annual orbit around the sun. The new calendar also called for the year to start on January 1 instead of March 25, doing away with "double-dating" the year between those dates. The new calendar had actually been promulgated in 1582 by Pope Gregory, and thus is called the Gregorian calendar. The old calendar it replaced was known as the Julian calendar because it dated back to the time of Julius Caesar. In 1582 most non-Roman Catholic churches and countries refused to adopt the new calendar, but they eventually accepted it, as England did in 1752.

The province of Holland adopted the Gregorian calendar in 1583, and New Netherland followed the laws and customs of that province, so New Netherland records are dated "new style" at the same time that the neighboring English colonies were using the old calendar. Once New Netherland became New York, official documents were dated according to the old calendar, but at least some Dutch church and family records continue to reflect certain aspects of "new style" dating. For example, even if they were using an "old style" (Julian) calendar, they still treated January 1 as the first day of the new year and avoided double-dating.

It is best genealogical practice to copy a date exactly as written, and not try to convert an old style date to new style. However, if the date in an English document is between January 1 and March 25 and the year is not double-dated, records preceding or following it need to be studied to determine the correct year. For example, in a series of chronological records, if one is dated February 15, 1688, and a few records later the date is April 1, 1689, the February date was most likely 1688/9.

Family Bible records or cemetery inscriptions created after 1752 may adjust pre-1752 birth and marriage dates from old style to new, but this is not always evident and, again, it is wise practice just to copy the dates as written.

New York's numerous Quakers followed their faith's practice of numbering months and days instead of using their "pagan" names. For example, Sunday, June 20, is First Day, 20th of 6th month. If a record shows a date written in the Quaker style, it is best genealogical practice to copy it as written, perhaps inserting the name of the month in parentheses after the month number. Researchers need to keep in mind that under the old calendar before 1752, March was the first month, and February the twelfth. If numbered months are converted to their names and don't take this into consideration, dates will be two months off.

Personal Papers and Accounts

Not to be overlooked are the personal papers and related materials of colonial New Yorkers held in special collections at libraries, archives, and other repositories both in New York, like the Rensselaerwyck Manor Records, 1630–1899, held at the NYSL and outside New York State. These collections contain correspondence, account books, copies of land patents, and many other records produced by individuals or businesses during the colonial era.

The *National Union Catalog of Manuscripts Collections* can be very helpful in this search. It is an online database available at *www.loc.gov/coll/nucmc* (originally published in book form) containing catalog records for archival and manuscript collections in repositories throughout the United States. While not all families left extensive personal papers, locating even one ancestor can make the effort of the search worthwhile.

Also in this category are family records of births, marriages, and deaths, usually kept in Bibles, which, like religious records, can fill the gap caused by the lack of civil vital records. The Bible Records of New York State, collected by the Genealogical Records

Committee of the Daughters of the American Revolution, make up the largest such collection and include records from many colonial era Bibles. (See chapter 16, National and Statewide Repositories & Resources for the DAR listing). Colonial Bible records have also been published in periodicals, including the *NYG&B Record*, while others are unpublished and can be found in library manuscript collections.

Names

Genealogists working in the colonial era quickly learn that personal names were not spelled consistently, often even within the same document. This was especially true in New York State, where recorders were often unfamiliar with the language spoken by the persons whose names they were recording, and those individuals were often unable to spell their names, even in their own language. When families first became English-speaking, or when they were illiterate for one or more generations, the family surname might appear spelled in records in ways that could be unrecognizable to their forebears.

Dutch naming custom is a subject by itself. See chapter 14, Peoples of New York, for the section on the Dutch.

Online Reference
New Netherland Institute

www.newnetherlandinstitute.org/research/online-publications
The New Netherland Institute has translated from Dutch over 7,000 pages of records, and the website provides digital copies of many of the sources cited within this chapter. The introductions to the *New York Historical Manuscripts: Dutch/New Netherland Documents* series provide an overview of the documents and various translations (*www.newnetherlandinstitute. org/files/1814/0574/3519/New_Netherland_Documents_ Introductions.pdf*).

Selected Bibliography and Further Reading

Colonial Laws of New York from the Year 1664 to the Revolution . . . . 5 vols. Albany: J. B. Lyon, State Printer, 1894.

Gehring, Charles. "A Survey of Documents Relating to New Netherland" in Joyce D. Goodfriend, ed., *Revisiting New Netherland, Perspectives on Early Dutch America* (Leiden and Boston: Brill, 2005). This essay describes known colonial and local documents from the Dutch period.

Hastings, Hugh, ed. *Ecclesiastical Records, State of New York.* 7 vols. Albany: J. B. Lyon, State Printer, 1901–1916.

Hoadly, Charles J., ed. *Records of the Colony and Plantation of New Haven from 1638–1649.* 2 vols. Hartford: Case, Lockwood and Co., 1858. For pre-1664 references to Southold, Long Island.

———. *Records of the Colony or Jurisdiction of New Haven, from May, 1653, to the Union [1664]. Together with New Haven Code of 1656.* 2 vols. Hartford: State Printers, 1857–1858.

Klein, Milton M., ed. *The Empire State, A History of New York.* Ithaca and London: Cornell University Press with the New York Historical Association, 2001. Specifically Part 1, "Before the English," by Oliver C. Rink, and Part 2, "The English Province," by Ronald W. Howard, plus the Selected Readings for Parts 1 and 2.

Macy, Harry, Jr. "The 1911 State Library Fire and Its Effect on New York Genealogy." *NYG&B Newsletter* (now *New York Researcher*), Spring 1999. Updated 2011 and published as a Research Aid on *NewYorkFamilyHistory.org*.

———. "The Calendar and Colonial New York." Published as a Research Aid, 2011, on *NewYorkFamilyHistory.org*.

New York Historical Manuscripts: Dutch. Baltimore: Genealogical Publishing Co. (GPC), 1974-1983; and Syracuse: Syracuse University Press (SUP), for the Holland Society and New Netherland Project/Institute. Called *New Netherland Documents* since 1987. See relevant county guides for volumes covering local records.

Gehring, Charles T., trans. and ed. *Council Minutes, 1652–1654* (GPC, 1983) and *1655–1656* (SUP, 1995); *Land Papers, 1630–1664* (GPC, 1980); *Laws and Writs of Appeal, 1647–1663* (SUP, 1991); *Correspondence, 1647–1653* (SUP, 2000) and *1654–1658* (SUP, 2003).

Van Laer, Arnold Johan Ferdinand, trans. and ed. *Register of Provincial Secretary.* 3 vols. 1638–1660; *Council Minutes, 1638–1649.* Edited and added indexes by Kenneth Scott and Kenn Stryker-Rodda (GPC, 1974).

New York Historical Manuscripts: English. Baltimore: Genealogical Publishing Co. (GPC) and Syracuse: Syracuse University Press (SUP), for the Holland Society, 1980–2002. Called New York Historical Manuscripts since 1989. Peter R. Christoph and Florence A. Christoph, eds., *Books of General Entries of the Colony of New York, 1664–1673* [and] *1674–1688* (GPC, 1982); *Records of the Court of Assizes for the Colony of New York, 1665–1682* (GPC, 1983); *Andros Papers,* vol. 1, 1674–1676; vol. 2, 1677–1678; vol. 3, 1679–1680 (SUP, 1989–1991). Peter R. Christoph, ed., *Administrative Papers of Governors Richard Nicolls and Francis Lovelace, 1664–1673* (GPC, 1982). *The Dongan Papers, 1683–1688,* Parts I and II (SUP, 1993, 1996). *The Leisler Papers, 1689–1691* (SUP, 2002). See relevant county guides for volumes covering local records.

New York State and Corwin, Edward T. *Ecclesiastical Records, State of New York.* Albany: J. B. Lyon, State Printer, 1901–1916. 7 vols.

O'Callaghan, Edmund B., trans. *Calendar of Historical Manuscripts in the Office of the Secretary of State, Albany, NY.* 2 vols. Albany: Weed, Parsons, 1865–1866. Part 1: Dutch Manuscripts, 1638–1664; Part 2: English Manuscripts, 1664–1776.

———, trans. and ed. *Documentary History of the State of New York.* 4 vols. Albany: State of New York 1849–1851 (octavo edition) and 1850–1851 (quarto edition with different pagination). [*Ancestry.com* has octavo edition]

———. *Laws and Ordinances of New Netherland 1638–1674.* Albany: Weed, Parsons, 1868.

O'Callaghan, Edmund B. and Berthold Fernow, eds. *Documents Relative to the Colonial History of the State of New York.* 15 vols. Albany: Weed, Parsons & Co., 1856–1887. Vol. 1–11 are documents collected by John Romeyn Brodhead. Title of vols. 12–15 is *Documents Relating* . . . .

Rensselaerwyck Manor Records, 1630–1899. Manuscript collection held at the New York State Library in Manuscripts and Special Collections.

Trumbull, J. Hammond, ed. *The Public Records of the Colony of Connecticut.* 3 vols. Hartford: State Printers, 1850–1859. For references to Long Island towns before 1664.

Van Laer, Arnold Johan Ferdinand, trans. and ed. *Documents Relating to New Netherland 1624–1626.* San Marino, CA: Henry E. Huntington Library and Art Gallery, 1924.

Vital Records

Table 1: Overall Summary: New York Vital Records	
Topic	**Key Information**
Vital Records in Colonial New York	Vital records are few and far between. Researchers turn to other types of records for information on births, marriages, and deaths. See sections in this chapter on Early Records and Substitutes for Vital Records. See chapter 1, Colonial Era.
Accessibility of Modern Vital Records	• Birth certificates, available if the birth occurred 75 years or more ago, and if the person is deceased. • Death certificates, available if the death occurred 50 or more years ago. • Marriage certificates, available if the marriage occurred 50 or more years ago, and when both parties are deceased. • Divorce certificates, available only to the persons who were divorced, or by court order. • Divorce records, sealed for 100 years. • Adoption records, permanently sealed.
Vital Records of New York State	Generally speaking, few vital records were kept by New York State until the 1840s and 1850s when sporadic record keeping began in various places. Some cities kept their own vital records beginning in the 1860s, and some continued to do so until 1908 for marriages, and 1914 for births and deaths. Statewide systematic record keeping did not begin until 1881, and did not hit full stride until 1913 For New York State vital records since 1881, most original records are at the New York State Department of Health in Albany, but some original records remain in the localities that generated them. Indexes are not published in any form, but are available on microfiche in ten locations in New York State. An exception is a limited range of death records (beginning in 1957) that are indexed online. Records must be purchased from the Department of Health before they can be seen. Some county marriage records have been digitized by *FamilySearch.org*.
Vital Records of New York City	Vital records for New York State and New York City are kept separately. Essentially, researchers must think of New York City as a separate state. The modern city of New York, comprised of the boroughs of the Bronx, Brooklyn, Manhattan, Queens, and Staten Island, was formed in 1898. Birth, marriage, and death records from 1898 to various dates in the twentieth century are at the Municipal Archives of New York City (MUNI) in Manhattan; indexes to these records have been published and microfilmed; many records at MUNI are indexed online. Most of the records available at MUNI have been microfilmed by the Family History Library (FHL), and copies of the film are in several locations. Later records are at the New York City Department of Health or the office of the City Clerk Marriage Bureau. These have not been filmed by the FHL. Pre-1898 original vital records for the cities of New York and Brooklyn, and originals or ledger copies of those for other municipalities that once existed in present-day New York City are for the most part at MUNI, and most have been microfilmed by the FHL with copies of the films at the NYPL; some original early records are only in Albany. References exist which identify the extant records, indexes, and their locations at a level of detail not provided in this chapter.

Introduction

Vital records provide official documentation of births, marriages, and deaths in a community. They generally include the date and place of the event and the name of the person or people involved. Sometimes they list addresses, occupations, causes of death, and places of interment, as well as other data that can help connect two generations, such as the names of the parents.

Researchers working in some states may find complete, well-kept, well-preserved vital records reaching back well into the eighteenth century or even earlier. Alas, this is not the case in New York. The subject of vital records in New York State is complicated. For a quick summary of vital records availability in New York, see table 1. Among the reasons for the subject's complexity are:

- New York State did not keep vital records completely and systematically until 1913, when new legislation went into effect.
- New York State and New York City maintain separate vital records. In fact, New York is the only state accommodating two unconnected vital records systems. There are, however, important exceptions noted throughout the chapter.
- Some other cities of New York State independently kept their own vital records as late as 1914.
- Published information about vital records, even on government websites, is often out of date, usually oversimplified, or sometimes just incorrect.

This chapter is organized as follows:

- History of Vital Records-Keeping in New York
- New York State: Accessing the Vital Records
- Vital Records of New York City
- New York City: Accessing the Vital Records

- Vital Records Resources in the Five Boroughs of New York City
- Other Records: Divorce and Adoption
- Substitutes for Vital Records (New York State and City)
- Selected Bibliography and Further Reading

History of Vital Record Keeping in New York

Finding vital records created in New York State after about 1913 is relatively straightforward, and the probability of success is high. Because the location of vital records in New York State is not necessarily intuitive, the chances of finding vital records for earlier years are significantly improved by a general understanding of the history of vital records in New York State and the history of the formation of the modern City of New York.

Early Records

There are few government-kept vital records for New York from the seventeenth and eighteenth centuries. The Dutch considered the keeping of such records to be a church function. After the English took over in 1664, a new law required the minister or clerk of every parish to "well and truly and plainly record all births marriages and burials," with a fine of five shillings imposed for noncompliance. See "New York's Vital Records Law of 1665" in the *NYG&B Record*, explaining why the law failed to motivate the systematic collection and preservation of vital records by the civil authorities. Some early government-kept records exist, but only for a few English towns (see below). Records were mainly preserved by churches, Quaker meetings, and the colony's lone synagogue; and those that have survived have been published.

The English also introduced marriage licenses, which permitted a couple to marry without the time required for, and formalities of, reading the banns in church, although the couple had to be married by a Protestant minister. *Names of Persons for Whom Marriage Licenses Were Issued by the Secretary of the Province of New York, Previous to 1784,* published by the State in 1860, lists couples who obtained licenses and the dates the licenses were issued (not their marriage dates). *Ancestry.com* has digitized this volume. Couples gave their licenses to the ministers who married them, and a few of those licenses survive, especially in historical society collections.

Bonds posted by these couples were retained by the government and were the principal, but not the only, source for the 1860 book. At that time there were 40 volumes of bonds in the Secretary of State's office, but most of them were destroyed or damaged in the 1911 New York State Library (NYSL) fire; those bonds that have survived are in the New York State Archives (NYSA) and were abstracted in Kenneth Scott's *New York Marriage Bonds 1753–1783.* A 1968 reprint of the 1860 book, titled *New York Marriages Previous to 1784,* identifies additional marriage licenses from other sources, and also abstracts a collection of licenses now at the New-York Historical Society (N-YHS). Harry Macy Jr.'s "Seven Queens County Marriage Licenses" abstracts a small Oyster Bay collection and includes the full text of one license. After British rule ended in 1783, marriage licenses were not issued again until the early-nineteenth century.

Civil marriages were also recognized in colonial New York. A few marriages performed by justices of the peace have been published in periodicals. For example, see "Record of Marriages by Roswell Hopkins, One of His Majesty's Justices of the Peace in the County of Dutchess."

Some town records from the colonial era contain vital records, most of which have been published in journals like the *NYG&B Record* and in books. (Those books out of copyright are easily found in online archives, such as *Archive.org* and *Hathitrust.org.*) These have appeared in the *NYG&B Record*:

- Lucy D. Ackerley's "Southold [Suffolk County], N.Y. Town Records, Vital Statistics from Libers D. and E. in the Town Clerk's Office [1661–1763]" published in four installments
- George D. A. Combes' "Early Vital Records of Hempstead, Long Island, N.Y., from the Minutes of the Meetings of the Town Justices and Vestry, Beginning 1704 and Continuing to 1784"
- Orville B. Ackerly's "Genealogical Data Found in the Printed Records of the Town of Huntington, Long Island [1665–1773]"
- Teunis G. Bergen's "Marriage Records, Gravesend, L.I. [1664–1702]"

A handful of divorces were granted by both the Dutch and English governments, but divorces were not granted during the colonial era after 1675. (See the section on divorce records below.)

Genealogists have dug deeply into all kinds of records to find vital records substitutes for these early years. For example:

- Terri O'Neill's "Birth and Death Records in New York Conveyances, 1687–1704: Early New York City Jewish Families"
- Francis J. Sypher, Jr.: "New York City Coroner's Reports, 1680–1684" in the *NYG&B Record* and *Minutes of Coroners Proceedings City and County of New York, John Burnet, Coroner 1748–1758.* Early town records may also contain records of coroners' inquests.
- "Some Deaths in New York City 1753–1756" lists names found in the daybook of coffin maker Joshua Delaplaine, now at the N-YHS

Early Vital Records Collection

Little happened in New York State between the American Revolution and the 1840s to make the keeping of vital records more methodical. The New York City Board of Health, however, began recording burials in ledgers beginning in 1801; from 1812 forward, these burial records are essentially complete, and beginning in 1843 they list all deaths in the city, regardless of place of burial.

Irregular birth and marriage records of New York City begin as early as the 1820s, but record keeping was inconsistent. The records that survive are at New York City Municipal Archives (MUNI) and on microfilm at the Family History Library (FHL) and the New York Public Library (NYPL). Where municipal vital records are lacking during this period, researchers will need to rely on other types of records. A large percentage of the early New York City burial and death registers show burials in cemeteries associated with a house of worship, a clue to religious records that might mention the family. For more suggestions, see the section on substitute records near the end of this chapter.

While most marriages recorded by New York City were religious, civil marriages also continued to be permitted in the state, and some have been published or made available to researchers. These include, for example, Ray Sawyer's typescript "Marriages Performed by the Various Mayors and Aldermen of the City of New York, as well as Justices of the Peace, etc., 1830–1854;" other examples were published in the *NYG&B Record*:

- Catherine F. Leigh's "Amenia [Dutchess County] Marriage Records [by Justice Jabez Flint, 1797–1814]"
- George D. A. Combes' "Marriages Performed by Justice William Mott of the Town of Hempstead, Long Island, 1793–1827"
- Charles Farrell's "Marriages by a Justice of the Peace in Morrisania [Westchester County] 1867–1873"
- "Marriages by Justice Ammon Blair, Orleans County, 1840–1850"

The National Medical Convention, meeting in Philadelphia in May 1847, made a vigorous call "to recommend and urge upon" state governments to require the recording of births, marriages, and deaths. And not "just for proofs of lineage, rights of dower, or bequests of property," but instead "for reasons more profound and far reaching, more important to the glory and welfare of man." Keeping such records would advance "the physical, moral, and civil condition of the human family." (The full *Minutes of the National Medical Convention*, the source of these quotations, is online at *books.google.com*.)

New York responded to this appeal, and the legislature mandated the keeping of vital records throughout New York State that same year. "An Act Providing for the Registry of Births, Marriages, and Deaths" (Law 1847, Chapter 152) was passed directing each of the state's many thousands of school districts to record those events and provide duplicate reports to town clerks or appropriate officials in cities, including New York City. It also required abstracts to be sent to the Secretary of State. This law is important, because for most municipalities in New York State it marks the date of the earliest extant vital records created systematically by the civil administration.

The 1847 law required physicians and professional midwives to record births, physicians to record deaths, clergymen to record funerals, and sextons to record deaths and burials. There was widespread objection to the law in many counties of New York State, because it was cumbersome and complicated to execute. Few school districts complied with the law after 1849, and it was for the most part ignored by the early 1850s. It was officially repealed in 1885 (L. 1885, C. 270).

The surviving records created during this period are in the custody of local governments, and in some instances, local historical societies. Some of these records have been transcribed and published in genealogical journals such as *Tree Talks* and by organizations like the National Society Daughters of the American Revolution (DAR). Some have been microfilmed and indexed. For example, records created as a result of the 1847 law for Suffolk County towns are held by the county clerk; these are also available on FHL microfilm as "Suffolk County Return of County Clerk's Records of Births, Marriages, and Deaths." They were published in the *Suffolk County Historical Society Register*, all issues from Vol. 17 (1991–1992) through Vol. 21 (1996). See the County Guides for more of the 1847 law records that have been published.

An act amending the 1847 law was passed in 1853 as it applied to New York City. The 1853 law affirmed the requirement to record births, marriages, and deaths, with fines for noncompliance.

A helpful inventory of vital records collected in New York State during this period and afterwards is the three-volume work produced by the Historic Records Survey of the Work Projects Administration (WPA), *Guide to Public Vital Statistics Records in New York State (including New York City)*. The inventories in each volume are by county and then by municipality, and are current as of 1942, the date of publication. Despite the subtitles of each volume (1. Births; 2. Marriages; and 3. Deaths) each volume contains references to all three record types. Not surprisingly, some records were missed in the survey. See Roger Joslyn's article, "Town of Ramapo Births in 1847" for an example of vital records missing from the WPA inventory. Other points to note about these three volumes:

- The inventory of records in Vol. 1 describes material from 1847 forward, except for some earlier nineteenth-century records in the boroughs of New York City; some very early records in Southampton, Suffolk County; and some records from the early-nineteenth century in a very few municipalities in some upstate counties.
- The inventory of records in Vol. 2 notes only a handful of records predating 1847. Some earlier New York City records and some from Southampton are mentioned.
- The inventory of records in Vol. 3 does not contain references to records created before 1847 except a few from New York County dating to 1837.

"An Act to Provide for the Registration of Deaths in the Several Towns and Wards of the State" was passed in 1864 (L. 1864, C. 380) requiring the recording of deaths and the deposit of copies of those records with the town or city clerk and with the Secretary of State in Albany; that law was repealed (L. 1865, C. 723) the following year. Few records were produced as a result of this short-lived law.

In 1866, the state legislature created New York City's Metropolitan Board of Health (L. 1866, C. 74) and charged it with collecting data on births, marriages, and deaths. For family historians, the most important event of 1866 was the introduction of birth, marriage, and death certificates in New York City and Brooklyn (though Brooklyn was already issuing *death* certificates from 1862).

The law was amended in 1870 (L. 1870, C. 137) to include a "Register of Records" to "record every birth, marriage, and death," among other changes. These laws did produce results.

About that time, some cities (other than New York City and Brooklyn), clearly growing impatient with the poor state of vital record keeping in New York, started maintaining vital records on their own. Albany began keeping its own vital records in 1870 by its revised charter, Yonkers began in 1875 by city ordinance, and Buffalo began in 1878, also by local ordinance. All three cities continued to keep vital records of their own until 1914, when they joined the state system. Long Island City, incorporated in 1870, kept vital records continuously beginning in 1871. Other cities attempting to keep their own records were Rochester, Syracuse, and Utica. Some records were made in Amsterdam, Binghamton, Elmira, Newburgh, and Poughkeepsie. See the city clerk's office listings in the County Guides for the specifics. See table 2 to identify the location of records.

Richmond County also briefly attempted to collect birth, marriage, and death records beginning in 1872. "An Act to Establish a Board of Health and of Vital Statistics in the County of Richmond, and to Define Its Powers and Duties" (L. 1872, C. 160) was repealed just two years later (L. 1874, C. 586).

Some towns recorded vital records in town minutes in the nineteenth century, including upstate towns, for example: Granville (Washington County); Ellery, Westfield, and Carroll (Chautauqua County); Royalton (Niagara County); and Canandaigua and Victor (Ontario County). These examples are cited in John Austin's "Genealogical Research in New York State–An Informal Finding List of Published Materials with Supplementary Notes," but there are undoubtedly others.

Modern System of Vital Records

Most reviews of vital records of New York give 1880 and 1881 as the official beginning of modern record-keeping in New York State. These dates, however, as a practical matter, are less important than one might assume, because start-up was uneven, and compliance over the next 30 years or more was far from perfect.

In 1880 New York State created a Board of Health and a Bureau of Vital Statistics. "An Act to Secure the Registration of Births of Children of Residents of the City of New York . . ." (L. 1880, C. 259) required the recording of births in New York City by the bureau of vital statistics of the health department. Another law that year (L. 1880, C. 512) required clerks in every town and village everywhere in New York State to record births, marriages, and deaths. It also required permits for burials; this law did not apply to cities.

In 1881 another law was passed (L. 1881, C. 431) which placed responsibility for the recording of births, marriages, and deaths in the hands of local boards of health in villages, towns, and cities. This law did not apply to Brooklyn, New York City, Yonkers, and Buffalo, presumably because systems of vital record keeping were already in place in those cities.

Death certificates issued in New York State and New York City, as a result of these two laws, included a place to name the parents, which makes those that were completed particularly valuable. An exception was the City of Brooklyn, which did not add this feature to death certificates until 1898, when it became part of the modern City of New York.

In 1885 "An Act for the Preservation of the Public Health and the Registration of Vital Statistics" (L. 1885, C. 270) was passed that continued the requirement for local boards of health in cities, villages, and towns to register births, marriages, and deaths, and issue permits for burials and transit of bodies, but exempted New York City, Buffalo, Albany, Yonkers, and Brooklyn from the law. This law was the first to require sending original certificates to the State Board of Health in Albany, and it provided for violations to be treated as misdemeanors, and for the offenders to be subject to prosecution. Amendments were made to this law in 1888 (L. 1888, C. 309).

"An Act Relating to the Domestic Relations . . ." (L. 1896, C. 272) was passed in 1896 that required marriage certificates to be recorded by clerks in cities and towns, where they would be retained. In 1907 that act was amended (L. 1907, C. 742) and required marriage licenses to be issued by the city, town, or village clerk where the bride resided (or if the bride or both parties were nonresidents, the place of marriage); the amendment spelled out at length the details of the requirement for record-keeping. The local clerks were then to file these documents with the county clerk, who would then send copies to Albany. This arrangement lasted until 1936, when a follow-up law (L. 1935, C. 535) required the municipal clerks themselves to forward the certificates to Albany, as they were already doing with birth and death records.

Despite attempts to build incentives for officials to conform to these laws, observance was irregular. The state statutes reflect the system's weaknesses. For example, a law passed in 1901 (L. 1901, C. 29) clearly expressed the frustration of state officials in obtaining local cooperation, and it toughened the consequences of noncompliance.

In 1913, however, "An Act to Amend the Public Health Law, in Relation to Vital Statistics" was passed (L. 1913, C. 619) applying to cities, villages, and towns and provided for serious fines and imprisonment for officials found in noncompliance. For uncooperative localities, the law provided for the state to take over the vital records registration process and the records themselves. Further, it spelled out in unprecedented detail the procedures for collecting vital records and listed the precise information that vital records must contain. A Division of Vital Statistics was created inside the New York State Department of Health. Thus, the modern system for vital records management in New York State was born. Some authorities believe that practically all events since 1913 have been recorded. Others believe that recording all events did not truly begin until a year or two later.

New York State: Accessing the Vital Records
Practical Information

The New York State Department of Health's Bureau of Vital Records is the agency that maintains vital records for New York State today. (For information on accessing official vital records of New York City, see the separate section below.) Their data collections began in 1880 and 1881 and became progressively more complete until 1913 or shortly thereafter, as noted above, when they were reliably complete.

Access to vital records is restricted by law. There are always exceptions to the rules, which are detailed online, but generally:

- Birth certificates are available for births 75 years or more ago, if the person is deceased
- Death certificates are available for deaths occurring 50 or more years ago

Table 2: Vital Records Held by Selected Cities from 1852 to the present

(Former City of Brooklyn and New York City excluded from this table.)

City	Available Records	Location / URL
Albany	Births and Deaths: 1870–present	City of Albany, City Clerk / *AlbanyNY.org*
	Births and Deaths: 1914–present	New York State Department of Health / *www.health.ny.gov/vital_records*
	Marriages: 1870–1946	Albany County Hall of Records (City of Albany only) / *albanycounty.com*
	Marriages: 1908–present	New York State Department of Health / *www.health.ny.gov/vital_records*
Buffalo	Births: 1878–present Deaths: 1852–present Marriages: 1877–present	Buffalo, City Clerk / *ci.buffalo.ny.us*
	Births, Marriages, and Deaths: 1914–present	New York State Department of Health / *www.health.ny.gov/vital_records*
Rochester	Marriages: 1908–present	Rochester, City Clerk (see also Rochester Municipal Archives & Records Center at *cityofrochester.gov*)
	Births and Deaths: starting 1880 with scattered earlier records	Monroe County Vital Records Office / *www2.monroecounty.gov*
	Births and Marriages: 1881–present Deaths: June 1880–present	New York State Department of Health / *www.health.ny.gov/vital_records*
Syracuse	Births and Deaths: 1873–present	Onondaga County Health Dept., Syracuse / *ongov.net*
	Marriages: 1908–present	Syracuse City Clerk / *Syracuse.ny.us*
	Births and Marriages: 1881–present Deaths: June 1880–present	New York State Department of Health / *www.health.ny.gov/vital_records*
Utica	Births and Deaths: 1876–present Marriages: 1874–present	Utica City Clerk / *cityofutica.com*
	Births and Marriages: 1881–present Deaths: June 1880–present	New York State Department of Health / *www.health.ny.gov/vital_records*
Yonkers	Births, Marriages, and Deaths: 1875–present	Yonkers City Clerk / *cityofyonkers.com*
	Births, Marriages, and Deaths: 1914–present	New York State Department of Health / *www.health.ny.gov/vital_records*

- Marriage certificates are available for marriages taking place 50 or more years ago, when both parties are deceased
- Divorce certificates, created beginning in 1963, are available only to the persons who were divorced, or by court order

Very detailed information on procedures for obtaining birth, marriage, and death certificates from the New York State Department of Health is on the Department of Health's website at *www.health.ny.gov/vital_records*. This site is frequently updated to reflect changing and variable details about obtaining certified vital records and vital records requested for genealogical purposes. These two types of requests vary by how they are obtained, fees, methods of acceptable payment, eligibility, and time required to fulfill orders. (Note that the New York State Department of Health is located in Albany, but the location to request vital records in person—where turnaround time can be shorter—is in the village of Menands, just north of Albany.) While applicants for genealogical records by mail may wait many months for fulfillment, the good news is that the Department of Health recognizes the need for records by genealogists and accommodates them on its website. Note that researchers at the NYSL may also conveniently drop off applications for vital records at the library.

Record Keeping Exceptions for Some New York Cities

As described in the previous section, some cities began keeping vital records before they were required to do so by the legislation passed in 1880 and 1881. Some cities did not fully participate in the move to consolidate vital record keeping at the state level but continued to keep their own records exclusively at the municipal level. Table 2 outlines the disposition of vital records for selected cities. Vital records issued between 1881 and 1913 in Albany, Buffalo, and Yonkers, as well as marriage records for Albany and Buffalo through 1908, are kept locally, and not with the New York State Department of Health. Directions for obtaining records from these three cities is on the Health Department website: *health.ny.gov/vital_records/genealogy.htm*.

Other Sources of Official New York State Vital Records

While the New York State Department of Health is the central repository for New York State vital records, it is not the exclusive source. Records of births, marriages, and deaths are also filed with the municipality where the events occurred.

Sometimes the originals went to Albany, and copies were kept locally, as is the case today. However, some statutes required the originals to be retained locally, with copies to the New York State Department of Health in Albany. There is no apparent pattern for the way local clerks complied or did not comply with this aspect of the law.

The town or city Clerk's offices provide directions on obtaining vital records held at the local level especially for cities (other than New York City). Some cities and counties have consolidated their vital records-keeping, but not always for all records; and some municipal and county clerks have genealogical webpages that reflect increasing volumes of requests by family historians. County and municipal websites have up-to-date information and special accommodations made for historians and genealogists. The design and content of these websites change frequently. Researchers should note that four counties in New York State (Chemung, Monroe, Onondaga, and Tompkins) are "consolidated districts" where vital records are kept at the county level.

Some New York State material is available online at *FamilySearch.org*. "New York, County Marriages, 1908–1935" includes records and licenses for many, but not all, New York counties; this dataset excludes New York City. *FamilySearch.org* offers some additional vital material (titled "New York Deaths and Burials: 1795–1952"; "New York Births and Christenings 1640–1962"; "New York Marriages 1686–1980") drawn from a variety of civil, religious, and other sources, and researchers will want to make an effort to identify and examine those original sources.

Indexes to Official Vital Records of New York State

Indexes to vital records beginning 1880–1881 exist, but have not been published (with one exception for a death index noted below). However, researchers may consult these indexes on microfiche available at one of ten locations in New York State. (See table 3.) Contact information for these locations is on the NYSL website: *www.nysl.nysed.gov/genealogy/vitrec.htm*.

Table 3: Locations of New York State Vital Records Microfiche Indexes

Repository	City	County
New York State Archives	Albany	Albany
Broome County Public Library	Binghamton	Broome
Steele Memorial Library	Elmira	Chemung
Buffalo & Erie County Public Library	Buffalo	Erie
Roswell P. Flower Memorial Library	Watertown	Jefferson
Rochester Public Library	Rochester	Monroe
National Archives at NYC	New York City	New York (Manhattan)
Onondaga County Public Library	Syracuse	Onondaga
Patchogue-Medford Library	Patchogue	Suffolk
Crandall Public Library	Glens Falls	Warren

Births that took place 75 or more years ago and deaths and marriages that took place 50 or more years ago are included. The indexes created by the state cover all of New York State except New York City, but:

- Include records of Kings County towns before they were annexed to the City of Brooklyn, and of municipalities of Queens, Richmond, and Westchester (now Bronx) counties before they were annexed to New York City;
- Exclude birth and death records for the cities of Albany, Buffalo, and Yonkers prior to 1914, and marriage records for those three cities prior to 1908.

The value of the microfiche New York State vital records index is that it confirms that a record exists, and it provides barebones information including name, location, date, and the certificate number. With this information, researchers must then take the next step to see the actual record by purchasing a certified or uncertified copy from the New York State Department of Health, by finding a copy of it locally, or by viewing it on the FHL microfilm if available.

The microfiche index is not online. However, an index of some New York State death records is online at the website of the New York State Department of Health: *https://health.data.ny.gov/Health/Genealogical-Research-Death-Index-Beginning-1957/vafa-pf2s*. (This index is also online at *FamilySearch.org*, but that version may not be current.) The index covers records beginning in 1957 and continues to the fifty-year cut off for death records. (For example, the 1970 records will be added to the index in 2020.) The index includes name, date and place of death, age at death, and certificate number.

Vital Records of New York City

As noted above, inventories of records for New York State were made by the WPA and published in 1942; these inventories include New York City. However, for inventories of New York City records, there are more recent and more comprehensive reviews:

- Harry Macy Jr.'s detailed research guide, "New York City Vital Records," updated in 2013 as a Research Aid at *NewYorkFamilyHistory.org*;
- Estelle M. Guzik's *Genealogical Resources in New York*. Her book, which focuses on New York City, is out of print but is easily obtainable. (The most recent edition is the second, published in 2003.) While some of the logistical information is out of date, detailed descriptions of holdings of the Municipal Archives, for example, may be current for years to come.

Harry Macy Jr's and Estelle Guzik's publications have the most comprehensive inventories of early records generated by cities, towns, and villages before they were absorbed by other municipalities and went out of existence, and before they became part of New York City; detail of this kind is much more extensive in these sources than appears in this chapter. Harry Macy Jr.'s article provides numbers for relevant FHL microfilm, call numbers for film at the NYPL, and comprehensive lists of sources in periodicals. Both publications provide excellent reviews of the indexes available for vital records in New York City, a subject as complicated as the records themselves.

For a short, up-to-date summary of New York City vital records, see Laura Murphy DeGrazia's *New York City, Long Island, and Westchester County* volume in the National Genealogical Society's Research in the States series.

What is New York City?

New York City has existed since the British took over New Amsterdam in 1664 and renamed the place New York. It consisted only of Manhattan Island (and smaller islands) until the late-nineteenth century, when parts of Westchester County were annexed to it. Those sections were called the "Annexed District."

Across the East River from New York City was the Village and later Town of Brooklyn, in Kings County. Brooklyn became an independent city in 1834 and expanded over time until 1896, when it took over the last bit of Kings County, and the city and county boundaries became contiguous. The City of Brooklyn began keeping its own vital records in ledgers from the 1840s; it started generating death certificates in 1862 and birth and marriage certificates in 1866. In fact, Brooklyn was the second city in New York State (after New York City) to keep vital records.

Table 4: Summary of New York City Vital Records Location and Accessibility

Record Type	Repository	Accessibility
Birth: Earliest dates (beginning in 1847) through 1909	MUNI	Unrestricted Note: See section on New York State for areas of New York City that have some early vital records in Albany.
Birth: 1910–present	NYCDH	Depends on the applicant's relationship to the person named in the certificate, the date of the birth, and whether the person named in the certificate is living or deceased. Birth certificates created 75 or more years ago are generally available.
New York City Department of Health Marriage Certificates: Earliest dates (1860s) through 1937	MUNI	Unrestricted Note that the New York City Department of Health did not issue marriage certificates after 1937.
Marriage Certificates: 1930–present	NYCMB	Available if the record was created 50 or more years ago. Access to more recent records is detailed at *www.cityclerk.nyc.gov/html/marriage/records.shtml*.
City Clerk marriage affidavits, licenses, and certificates (1908–1929)	MUNI	Unrestricted The index to marriages runs to 1951 even though records after 1929 are not available at MUNI on microfilm only.
Death: Earliest dates (from 1795) through 1948	MUNI	Unrestricted
Death: 1949–present	NYCDH	Depends on whether the applicant is related to the deceased, whether the cause of death information is required, and when the death occurred.

Table 5: Summary of New York City Vital Records Held at MUNI by Borough

Borough	Birth	Marriage	Death	Notes on Early Records
The Bronx	1898–1909	1898–1937	1898–1948	For places annexed from Westchester County in 1874 and 1875, see Westchester County for records made before annexation. For these places from annexation to 1898, see Manhattan.
Brooklyn	1866–1909	1866–1937	1847–1853 1857–1948	Includes what records exist for the City of Brooklyn since its founding; extant vital records from the municipalities annexed by the City of Brooklyn to 1896 are at MUNI. The earliest are from 1847.
Manhattan	1847–1848 1853–1909	1847–1848 1853–1937	1795 1802–1804 1808 1812–1948	Except for deaths, the earliest records are sparse. See also notes on early records of the Bronx in this table, above.
Queens	1898–1909	1898–1937	1898–1948	Also includes records from towns and villages of Queens created 1847–1849 and 1881–1897, and from Long Island City 1871–1897.
Richmond/ Staten Island	1898–1909	1898–1937	1898–1948	Includes records created before 1898 by towns and villages on Staten Island dating from 1847–1859 and 1881–1897.

Long Island City was created in 1870 from part of the Town of Newtown (including the Village of Astoria), in Queens County. As a city, it, too, began collecting its own vital records.

It was not until 1898 that the modern New York City was created, incorporating:

- What existed at that time as New York City and County (Manhattan and the Annexed District, renamed the Bronx in 1898)
- The western part of Queens County including Long Island City
- The City of Brooklyn (contiguous with Kings County)
- Richmond County (also known as Staten Island)

These places were reconstituted as the five boroughs of New York City: the Bronx, Brooklyn, Manhattan, Queens, and Richmond (later Staten Island). See Harry Macy Jr.'s Research Aid, "Before the Five-Borough City," in which he provides maps and a clear, detailed account of the pre-1898 municipalities in what is now New York City. (Estelle Guzik's book includes this article as Appendix H.)

With few exceptions, all extant vital records (originals or transcripts) created before 1898 in the areas that comprise today's New York City (New York County/Manhattan and the Bronx; the City of Brooklyn; Long Island City; and the former towns or villages of Kings, Queens, Richmond, and Westchester counties before they were annexed to New York or Brooklyn) are at MUNI. The vital records for the five boroughs of New York City from 1898 to the present are at MUNI and other centralized repositories located in Manhattan. (See below.)

Original birth, marriage, and death certificates for Queens and Richmond counties (1880–1897); eastern Bronx (1880–1895), when it was part of Westchester County; and the towns of Kings County (from 1880 until annexed to Brooklyn 1882–1896) are, for the most part, at the New York State Department of Health in Albany. Before the certificates were sent to Albany, the local clerks transcribed their content in ledgers, which are at MUNI. Most of those transcripts are available on microfilm created by the FHL; copies of most of that microfilm are at the NYPL. Surviving records for all these counties from the 1847 vital records law are also at MUNI and on microfilm at the FHL and the NYPL.

New York City: Accessing the Vital Records

Researchers looking for birth, marriage, and death records need to be familiar with the New York City Municipal Archives (MUNI), the New York City Department of Health and Mental Hygiene (NYCDH), and the Office of the City Clerk, New York City Marriage Bureau (NYCMB). See table 4. Vital records are located in all three of these repositories. What records are available and their accessibility is variable.

Many records held at MUNI, and corresponding indexes for the MUNI records, are on microfilm at the FHL and can be identified by the online catalog at *FamilySearch.org*. Copies of most, but not all, of this film are at the NYPL. (Other repositories such as the Center for Jewish History and the Family History Center at Lincoln Center, both located in Manhattan and which contain growing but incomplete film libraries, could also be consulted for film sourced from the FHL.)

MUNI's website (*www.nyc.gov/html/records/html/archives/archives.shtml*) has helpful information for genealogists, such as a description of many of their collections (not limited to vital records), as well as instructions for genealogists on

Table 6: Summary of New York City Marriage Records Held at MUNI

Borough	Health Department Certificates	City Clerk Affidavits, Licenses, and Certificates*	Other Marriage Records at MUNI
Bronx	1898–1937	1914–1929 (for records 1908–1913, see Manhattan)	County Clerk: Marriage license religious ceritificates 1914–1929
Brooklyn	1866–1897** 1898–1937	1908–1929	Delayed marriages: 1875–1934; Special marriages: 1898–1937 (Delayed and special marriages mean the same thing)
Manhattan	1866–1937	1908–1929	City Clerk: Certificates or marriage contracts 1902–1908 Delayed marriages: 1873–1916 Mayor's Office Marriage Registry 1875–1897 Marriages: "Registry by Judge Erlich" 1886–1895
Queens	1898–1937	1908–1929	Queens County Clerk summary volumes, 1908–1916; transcripts, 1917–1920. Indexes for 1908–1917 with gaps and for 1938 (in Queens, not MUNI).
Richmond/ Staten Island	1898–1937	1908–1929	

*The *index* to these records at MUNI goes to 1951.
**City of Brooklyn 1866–1897

obtaining copies of certificates. The websites of the NYCDH and the NYCMB (see table 4) have instructions for obtaining certificates, but they are not relevant to genealogical research, so they must be interpreted.

Table 5 differentiates records held by MUNI for each of New York City's five boroughs. See also the section below, Vital Records Resources in the Five Boroughs of New York City.

A Note About Marriage Records in New York City

Marriage records from what is now the five-borough city are found in city, town, and village records before 1898. Certificates in New York County and the City of Brooklyn begin in 1866. One might expect marriage records to begin in full force in 1898, when the five boroughs were created. The facts are somewhat more complicated, as outlined in table 6.

The New York City Department of Health issued marriage certificates beginning in 1866 in New York City (Manhattan); the City of Brooklyn also issued certificates beginning that year. The New York City Department of Health issued marriage certificates in all five boroughs beginning in 1898, continuing until 1937, when marriages were no longer reported to that department.

Meanwhile, the City Clerks in all five boroughs generated marriage records beginning in 1908, as required by New York State law. Records included the affidavits for license to marry completed by the bride and groom, the license itself signed by the City Clerk, and the City Clerk's marriage certificate. One

reason that the marriage records are incomplete before the state law of 1908 is that marriages were reported to the City by the persons performing them, and many of them failed to do so. Some researchers claim that most Catholic marriages in Manhattan were not recorded in city records before the 1908 law was passed.

For the years 1908 to 1937, New York City kept two sets of marriage records. Most, but not all, couples reported their marriages to both the City Clerk and the New York City Department of Health, and there are enough differences between these two certificates to justify obtaining both of them. For a detailed description of these documents and their value to genealogists, see Leslie Corn's article, "City Clerk's Marriage Licenses, New York City, 1908–1937: One of 20th Century Genealogy's Best Primary Sources," online as a Research Aid at *NewYorkFamilyHistory.org*. Leslie Corn shows how the City Clerk's records provide more genealogically relevant information than those issued by the New York City Department of Health; she also gives examples for using these records to best advantage.

Indexes to New York City Vital Records

There is no one index that covers all of New York City's vital records. Instead there are separate indexes for births, deaths, marriage certificates, and marriage licenses. Which index to consult depends on the date of the record and the county or borough where the event took place.

Table 7: Original Card Indexes to New York City Vital Records at MUNI

Record	Present-Day Borough	Pre-1898 Municipality	Dates Covered
Birth	Manhattan	New York City	1857–1897
	Brooklyn	City of Brooklyn	1866–1897
		Town of Flatbush	1847–1851; 1881–1895
	Queens	Long Island City	1871–1898
		Town of Jamaica	1881–1897
		Village of Jamaica	1889–1898
		Village of Flushing	1889–1897
		Town of Flushing	1881–1897
		Village of Whitestone	1889–1897
		Village of Rockaway	1897–1898
		Village of Far Rockaway	1889–1897
		Village of College Point	1889–1898
		Village of Richmond Hill	1895–1897
		Town of Newtown	1847–1849; 1881–1898
	Staten Island (Richmond until 1975)	All towns	1847–1852; 1859–1860; 1869; 1875; 1879; 1880–1897
Marriage (Groom)	Manhattan	New York City	1866–1910
	Brooklyn	All available municipalities	1866–1907
	Queens	All available municipalities	1881–1898
	Staten Island	The borough	1898–1932
		All towns	1882–1897
Marriage (Bride)	Manhattan	New York City	1866–1934
	Brooklyn	All available municipalities	1866–1910; 1931–1937
	Bronx		1898–1937
	Queens		1905–1937
	Staten Island		1898–1937
		All available municipalities	1882–1897
Death	Manhattan	New York City	1868–1890
	Brooklyn	City of Brooklyn	1848–1897 (gaps)
		Town of Flatbush	1847–1851; 1880–1896
		Towns of Flatlands, Gravesend, New Lots, New Utrecht	1881–1899
	Queens	Long Island City	1871–1897
		Town of Jamaica	1881–1897
		Village of Jamaica	1890–1897
		Village of Flushing	1889–1897
		Town of Flushing	1881–1897
		Village of Whitestone	1889–1897
		Village of Richmond Hill	1895–1897
		Village of Rockaway	1897–1898
		Village of Far Rockaway	1889–1897
		Village of College Point	1889–1897
		Town of Newtown	1881–1897
	Staten Island	All available municipalities	1847–1897 (gaps)

Table by Ken Cobb, Assistant Commissioner, New York City Municipal Archives

The Main Printed and Microfilmed Indexes

Indexes to births, marriages, and deaths in New York City are available in annual printed volumes published by the city's Department of Health (and before 1898 also by the Brooklyn Board of Health). These volumes begin in 1888 for what is now Manhattan and annexed portions of the Bronx, and in the 1890s for Brooklyn. Beginning in 1898 there are annual indexes for all five boroughs. Marriage indexes ceased in 1937 when the Department of Health ceased issuing marriage records, but indexes of births and deaths continued to be published until 1982. MUNI has microfilm of these volumes covering the records they possess. The FHL has all the volumes on microfilm through 1965, and the NYPL has all of the volumes either on paper, microfilm, or microfiche through 1982. There are also published soundex volumes.

There are card indexes to many of the earlier records not covered by the printed volumes, available on microfilm at MUNI. (See table 7 for a detailed list of vital records covered by the card indexes.) Most of the filmed indexes are at the FHL and the NYPL. The FHL microfilm numbers can be determined most easily through Steve Morse's One-Step website (*stevemorse.org*); they may also be found in the *FamilySearch.org* catalog. The NYPL has a finding aid for its patrons, and FHL and NYPL microfilm numbers are also indicated in Harry Macy Jr.'s "New York City Vital Records." See also the lists of both records and finding aids in Estelle Guzik's *Genealogical Resources in New York*, chapters on MUNI and the NYPL.

The online indexes created by the German and Italian genealogical groups (described below) include many, but not all, of the card indexes.

The indexes cover both certificates and some ledgers (also called libers), but for the most part the pre-1866 ledgers, such as those for New York City deaths or burials, are not indexed. Entries in ledgers are chronological but are grouped by the first letter of the surname, which helps limit the extent of a search.

There are also soundex indexes to births, created by the Department of Health, for Manhattan, Bronx, and Brooklyn, 1881–1919, and Queens and Staten Island, 1897–1919. MUNI has these soundex indexes through 1909, but the FHL and the NYPL have them on microfilm through 1919. The soundex was also used for the published indexes for all boroughs, covering the years 1943 to 1945.

FamilySearch.org has three finding aids: "Register of New York City Birth Records," "Register of New York City Marriage Records," and "Register of New York City Death Records," listing indexes filmed by the FHL, along with film numbers. Researchers can locate these finding aids in the FamilySearch catalog and then click to download the documents, which are lengthy. Alternatively, as noted above, the Steve Morse One-Step website may also be used to located film numbers.

Main Online Index to New York City Vital Records

Online indexes to the vital records held at MUNI have been created, are continually updated and corrected, and are offered free of charge by the German Genealogy Group (*germangenealogygroup.com*) and the Italian Genealogical Group (*italiangen.org*). Hundreds of volunteers created these indexes. (An edition of these indexes is now on *Ancestry.com*, but as the *Ancestry.com* database is updated only periodically, it most likely will not have the most current additions and corrections.) The indexes give researchers information needed to order copies of the actual records from MUNI, which charges fees to provide them. Researchers are advised to check the German and Italian websites for progress in completing the indexes. See table 8.

Table 8: Online Indexes to Vital Records Held by MUNI

Table covers MUNI certificates indexed by the German Genealogy Group (GGG) and the Italian Genealogical Group (IGG) as of July 2014. Check websites for updates and indexes for towns prior to 1898.

Record	Present-Day Borough	Dates Covered
Birth	Bronx	1898–1909, includes some Dec. 1897 births
	Brooklyn	1880–1909
	Manhattan	1878–1909, includes part of the Bronx until 1897; all of the Bronx from 1898 to 1909
	Queens	1898–1909
	Staten Island	1898–1909, includes some Dec. 1897 births
Marriage	Bronx	1898–1937
	Brooklyn	1871–1937: Brides; 1866–1937: Grooms
	Manhattan	1866–1937: Brides; 1866–1937: Grooms
	Queens	1905–1937: Brides and Grooms
	Staten Island	1898–1937: Brides and Grooms
Death	Bronx	1898–1948
	Brooklyn	1862–1948
	Manhattan	1867–1948
	Queens	1898–1948
	Staten Island	1898–1948

Geographical Indexes to Births at MUNI

Table 9 summarizes available indexes to births arranged by street address. The geographical indexes are not included in the online indexes listed in table 8.

In sum, there are four sources for indexes to New York City Vital Records: MUNI itself, the NYPL, the FHL, and the internet. Indexes at MUNI and the NYPL require site visits. Film may be rented from the FHL and viewed at local Family History Centers.

Vital Records Resources in the Five Boroughs of New York City

The sections on the five boroughs below describe vital records at various repositories, particularly at MUNI; note that most of the records at MUNI are also on FHL microfilm, with copies at the NYPL and possibly at other repositories that have also acquired copies. Also note that when a family is found in village records, the earlier records of the parent town should be checked.

Borough of the Bronx (Bronx County)

Researchers seeking early vital records for the Borough of the Bronx must be aware that the Bronx was once part of Westchester County until various dates in the late-nineteenth century.

In 1874 New York City (at the time, contiguous with New York County) annexed part of Westchester County west of the Bronx River; the annexed land included the towns of Morrisania, West Farms, and Kingsbridge. Vital records for this "annexed district" created from 1874 until 1898 are included with those of New York City and are at MUNI. The Westchester County Archives holds some earlier records from the 1847 law for Morrisania, West Farms, and Yonkers (predecessor of Kingsbridge). MUNI has 1872–1874 births from the Town of Morrisania which have not been filmed or published.

In 1895, New York City/County annexed another part of Westchester County, this time east of the Bronx River. The annexed land consisted of the Town of Westchester; the southern part of the Town of Pelham including City Island; and the southern part of the Town of Eastchester including the villages of Wakefield and South Mount Vernon. MUNI holds the ledgers from the Town of Westchester under the 1847 and 1880 laws (with a few marriages from the 1870s) and the villages of Wakefield and South Mount Vernon from 1890 to 1895 (plus 1878–1881 marriages); the certificates issued under the 1880 law and listed in these ledgers are in Albany. Pre-1895 records for other annexed parts of Eastchester and for Pelham are retained by those towns, which are still in Westchester County; their certificates under the 1880 law are in Albany. From 1895 until 1898 vital records for this "annexed district" are included with those of New York City and are at MUNI.

See Harry Macy Jr.'s article, "Vital Records of New York City" for a detailed list of records available for each town and village at

Table 9: Geographical Indexes to Births at MUNI	
Borough	**Dates Covered**
Bronx	1898–1910; see Manhattan for earlier years; there is also a hospital index for 1942–1944
Brooklyn	1898–1910
Manhattan	1880–1914; there is also a hospital index for 1880–1909
Queens	1898–1917
Staten Island	1898–1909

MUNI. He notes that the records of South Mount Vernon are incorrectly cataloged by the FHL as City of Mount Vernon, Westchester County.

The Borough of the Bronx was created in 1898, and Bronx vital records begin with that year; certificates are at MUNI for the same years as the other boroughs. (See table 5.) Bronx County was not created until 1914, but this event has little practical bearing on vital records. Needless to say, however, no records collected by a county clerk would have been collected for Bronx County before this date. Those would have been either New York City (Manhattan), New York County, or Westchester County records, depending on the date.

Borough of Brooklyn (Kings County)

Brooklyn was once one of several towns in Kings County. It became a city in 1834 and grew to encompass all of Kings County by 1896 through the annexation of the towns of Bushwick, Flatbush, Flatlands, Gravesend, New Lots, and New Utrecht, and the City of Williamsburg. All of these jurisdictions theoretically complied with the 1847 state vital records law, but only Town of Flatbush records (birth, marriage, and death) and City of Brooklyn death records survive.

The City of Brooklyn continued to register deaths (in ledgers) from 1847, and in 1866 started issuing birth, marriage, and death certificates and keeping records of stillbirths. Ledgers, however, continued to be kept for at least ten more years. Certificates and ledgers created for the City of Brooklyn are at MUNI. Brooklyn also began records of "delayed registration" marriages in 1875, which are also at MUNI.

The towns of Kings County came under the state vital records system in 1880, until they were annexed by Brooklyn. Certificates created by municipalities in Kings County before annexation to Brooklyn are in Albany; the ledgers are at MUNI for all the towns existing in 1880, namely Flatbush, Flatlands, Gravesend, New Utrecht, and New Lots.

From 1898 vital records for the Borough of Brooklyn have been part of the consolidated New York City system and are at MUNI. This includes "delayed marriages" (1898–1934) and "special marriages" (1898–1937) which are essentially the same thing, despite the fact that they have different names.

Borough of Manhattan (New York County)

The island of Manhattan has been called that from the earliest days of settlement, but the name was not often used until it came into official use in 1898. Researchers should note that some indexes categorize records created before 1898 as "Manhattan," when New York County or New York City would be more correct.

All vital records or copies of records pertaining to areas now part of the Borough of Manhattan may be found at MUNI or other consolidated repositories in the borough.

Records were kept in ledgers until 1866, when New York City began issuing certificates. However, even after the introduction of certificates, ledgers continued to be kept for another 20 or more years. Both sets of documents are at MUNI.

For other marriage records, see Ray Sawyer, "Marriages Performed by the Various Mayors and Aldermen of the City of New York, as well as Justices of the Peace, etc., 1830–1854," abstracted from various sources including "Marriages Performed by the Mayors of New York 1830–1850," two manuscript volumes at the County Clerk's Office (New York County) Division of Old Records in Manhattan.

Borough of Queens (Queens County)

Before 1898, Queens County included the towns of Flushing (including the villages of Flushing, College Point, and Whitestone); Jamaica (including the villages of Jamaica and Richmond Hill); Newtown; Long Island City which was created in 1870 from part of Newtown (including the Village of Astoria); and the Rockaway Peninsula section of Hempstead (including the villages of Far Rockaway and Rockaway Beach). All these municipalities ceased to exist when the Borough of Queens was created in 1898. The rest of the town of Hempstead and the towns of North Hempstead and Oyster Bay were also in Queens County, but were not included in the 1898 borough. In 1899 they formed the new county of Nassau.

The towns of Flushing, Jamaica, and Newtown recorded births, marriages, and deaths from 1847 to 1849. Long Island City began keeping its own vital records in 1871; and the entire county came under the state vital records system in 1880. Certificates created by Long Island City and the towns after 1880 and before 1898 were sent to Albany. Beginning in 1889, the villages took over this responsibility from their towns and also sent their certificates to Albany until 1898. Registers (ledgers) were kept in the various municipalities in Queens and are now at MUNI.

Since 1898, vital records for all parts of the Borough of Queens have been part of the consolidated New York City system.

See Harry Macy Jr.'s "Vital Records of New York City" for a detailed list of records from 1847 to 1897 kept by Long Island City and all the towns and villages named above except Astoria, which never created any vital records. He cautions researchers to beware of errors in descriptions of these records. He also notes that any 1847–1897 vital records of the Rockaway Peninsula other than those of the villages of Far Rockaway and Rockaway Beach are at Hempstead or Albany, not at MUNI.

Borough of Staten Island (Richmond County)

Richmond County, also known as Staten Island, before 1898 consisted of the towns of Castleton, Northfield, Southfield, Westfield, and Middletown, the last formed from Castleton and Southfield in 1860. Castleton included the Village of New Brighton which eventually covered the entire town. Northfield included the Village of Port Richmond, and Westfield included the Village of Tottenville, while the Village of Edgewater was divided between Middletown and Southfield. All these municipalities ceased to exist when Richmond County became the Borough of Richmond in 1898. The borough was renamed the Borough of Staten Island in 1975. The county name remains Richmond.

The former municipalities kept vital records for several years under the 1847 state law; these records are at MUNI. All towns and villages came under the state vital records system in 1880, though most of the villages did not take over registration from their towns until later. Vital records created between 1880 and 1897 are in Albany; ledgers including this information are at MUNI. See Harry Macy Jr.'s "Vital Records of New York City" for a detailed account of the records information available from each locality on Staten Island prior to 1898.

Since 1898 vital records for the Borough of Richmond/Staten Island have been part of the consolidated New York City system.

Other Records: Divorce and Adoption

Divorce Records (New York City and New York State)

A very small number of divorces, annulments, or legal separations were granted in New Netherland and the English colony of New York between 1655 and 1675, after which no marriages were legally dissolved in New York for over 100 years. For detail on these early matrimonial actions, see Matteo Spalletta's article, "Divorce in Colonial New York."

From 1787 to 1847, the state gave the Chancery Court the right to grant divorces for adultery, as well as legal separations and annulments. Records of these actions are found in the court's records both at the NYSA in Albany and the New York County Clerk's archives in Manhattan. Table 10 indicates how those records are divided beginning in 1823. For case files in Manhattan to 1840, see Charles Farrell's "Index to Matrimonial

Table 10: Location of Chancery Court Divorce Records (1823–1847) of New York City and State		
Dates	**Counties**	**Location**
1823–May 22, 1836	New York, Kings, Queens, Richmond, Suffolk	New York County Clerk, Division of Old Records
May 23, 1836–1847	New York, Kings, Richmond	
May 23, 1836–1847	Suffolk, Queens	New York State Archives
1823–1847	All others	

Actions 1787–1840, New York County Clerk's Office." This article includes an introduction by Harry Macy Jr. which demonstrates the genealogical value of the records; the index list is itself valuable, as it gives the names and dates for the separations, annulments, and divorces.

From 1847 divorce actions took place in the Supreme Court located in each county. (See chapter 5, Court Records, for an explanation of the function of the Supreme Court in New York State; the Supreme Court is not New York State's highest court, despite the name.) Until 1967 adultery remained the only grounds for divorce by the Supreme Court; divorce on other grounds required a special act of the legislature and was rare. Large numbers of New Yorkers went to other states or countries to have their marriages dissolved; see, for example, Henry Hoff's "New Yorkers in Some Connecticut Divorces [1719–1922]." Other couples separated without any legal process.

Divorce files in New York are sealed for 100 years, but the indexes for all years to those files are open to the public. The records are in the custody of the county clerks, who are also clerks of the Supreme Court in their counties. (There are exceptions; for example, divorce records from Richmond County from 1861 to 1933 are now at MUNI.) The index for New York County 1787–1910 (including other southern counties from 1787 to 1847) is available from the FHL, with a copy at the NYPL. (Charles Farrell's index noted above covers part of this.) The NYSA has a limited, unpublished manuscript index to Chancery Court records for the remainder of the state.

Divorce certificates have been issued in New York State since 1963; certificates for divorces in New York State and New York City are filed with the New York State Department of Health in Albany. Without a court order, the parties to the divorce are the only persons who may obtain certificate copies.

Sometimes divorce papers are filed with other records, and researchers may stumble on them serendipitously. For example,

copies of divorce papers may be filed with a second marriage license or in estate records.

Adoption Records

Adoption records in New York State are permanently sealed. Research in this field is specialized and not addressed in this book.

Substitutes for Vital Records (New York State and City)

If vital records are not available for a place or time period, there are many other records that can be used to identify some of the same information. For these kinds of records in seventeenth- and eighteenth-century New York, see the Early Records section near the beginning of this chapter and chapter 1, Colonial Era.

The general genealogical literature includes many books and articles about finding birth, marriage, and death information in all kinds of records, including religious, court, cemetery, census, Bible, immigration and naturalization, institutional, military, and probate records. Even city directories have some vital records value. And, of course, the Social Security Death Index, available online at *FamilySearch.org*, *Ancestry.com*, and other locations, is essential for more recent deaths. These general sources, discussed elsewhere, are not covered in this chapter. But note that most chapters in Part One of this book reference records which contain vital records-type information, especially deaths.

Newspaper and Serial Records

Mentions of marriages and deaths (and occasionally births) are recorded in newspapers everywhere; data for New York State publications abound. A lengthy list of sources of data on births, marriages, and deaths found in newspapers is in Estelle Guzik's book, *Genealogical Resources in New York*. Various sections of her book include abstracts and indexes to New York City newspapers, lists of holdings of papers (including ethnic papers) at the NYPL, the Bronx Historical Society, the Brooklyn Public Library, the Queens Library, the Staten Island Historical Society, and the Staten Island Museum.

The most frequently consulted books on this subject were prepared by Fred Bowman. Despite the title, his *Directory to Collections of New York State Vital Records, 1726–1989, with Rare Gazetteer* is essentially a guide to this kind of information in newspapers; his series of books and articles (for example, *10,000 Vital Records of Eastern New York, 1777–1834*), published in the 1980s and 1990s, covers newspaper references to marriages and deaths in most parts of New York State. For a list of these books, see chapter 12, Newspapers; the bibliography for this chapter does not include them. See also Marian Henry's guide to the series of books by Fred Bowman.

Other sources of vital records from various newspapers and publications include, but are not by any means limited to, the following list. See also the bibliographies in the County Guides.

- Typescripts by Ray Sawyer and Gertrude Barber noted in the catalogs of the NYPL, the New England Historic Genealogical Society (NEHGS), and other New York repositories; Gertrude Barber's extracts of deaths and marriages from the *Brooklyn Eagle* and the *New York Evening Post* are on *Ancestry.com*. (A lengthy bibliography of works by Sawyer and Barber is in the last installment of Roger Joslyn's six-part article "Gertrude Barber, Minnie Cowen, and Ray Sawyer, The Sisters Who Indexed New York.")
- Articles by Carolyn G. Stifel in the *NYG&B Record* about vital events noticed in early New York City magazines
- Various books and articles by Kenneth Scott noted in the bibliography below
- Joseph Gavit's index to deaths and marriages in upstate New York newspapers and the companion work by Kenneth Scott
- William Millet Beauchamp's book about marriages reported in newspapers of central New York State
- Henry Hoff's research aids on marriage and death notices in New York City and Long Island newspapers

Church Records

Information about births, baptismal records, marriages, and deaths collected by churches abound. The subject indexes to the *NYG&B Record*, online and freely available, provide leads to many church records. Kinship Books (*kinshipny.com*) has published many volumes of "vital records" for churches in New York State. The volumes of vital records from churches in New York City and New York State, published in 1942 by the WPA in the Historical Records Survey series, also provide excellent leads to church records. See also chapter 15, Religious Records, and the bibliographies in the County Guides for selected church record references.

Census Records

Researchers will find mortality schedules covering deaths occurring in the year preceding the taking of the census in some New York state censuses. See chapter 3, Census Records, for what has survived in the state censuses. The schedules for 1865 and 1875 list both marriages and deaths. *Tree Talks* has published many of these schedules. The mortality schedules in the federal census exist for all counties (1850–1880).

Coroners' Inquest Records

Coroners' records exist from the eighteenth century. See the Early Records section of this chapter for publications by Francis Sypher on the earlier coroners' records. See Kenneth Scott's article, "Early New York City Coroner's Reports [1795–1820 with gaps] in the *NYG&B Record* and his books *Coroners' Reports in New York City, 1823–1842* and *1843–1849* for later records. New York City coroners' records 1898–1917 are

in ledger books at MUNI. Coroners' records from the City of Brooklyn (1897–1916) and Richmond County (1851–1897) are also at MUNI. Some coroners' records were filmed by the FHL; most, but not all, of this film is also at the NYPL. MUNI also has investigation files from the Chief Medical Examiner's Office (1918–1939); access to these records has restrictions.

Records of the Poor and Indigent

The New York City Alms House kept death records of a kind. Though not strictly speaking vital records, these records include deaths and causes of death for inmates who died there. Those records, and the Alms House admissions and censuses, include ages and birthplaces of inmates. They are now at MUNI (1759–1916), and some have been filmed by the FHL, but they have not been indexed. Death records for those who died in the almshouse are duplicated in the city death records. See also information about Hart Island, the New York City Potters Field since 1869, in chapter 9, Cemetery Records. This cemetery contains nearly a million graves which are partially indexed online. Extant records from 1883 to 1961 are at MUNI and have been microfilmed. See also chapter 10, Business, Institutional, and Organizational Records, for other references to almshouses.

Epidemics

The earliest official record of New York City deaths is a list of persons who died in the yellow fever epidemic in 1795. See lists of published records in Rosalie Bailey's guide, and for similar lists from 1799 and 1800, see Harry Macy Jr.'s "New York City Vital Records," which updates Bailey's guide. See also B-Ann Moorhouse's Research Aid, "Little Publicized New York City Sources: Minutes of the Committee on Health 1798." These minutes, which are on microfilm at MUNI, record names and addresses of the sick and more information on those who died. The names of people (many with addresses) who died from cholera in Albany in 1832 have been transcribed by Carolyn Stifel in "Cholera Records, July and August 1832, Albany" from an original manuscript by Samuel Pruyn. This list pre-dates any City of Albany death records.

Probate Documents

Wills and Letters of Administration before 1830 sometimes include the names and relationships of next-of-kin, as well as the date and place of death and burial for the decedent. After 1830, including the next-of-kin data was required. See chapter 6, Probate Records.

Bodies in Transit

New York City was among those local governments that required bodies to be registered when arriving in, or traveling through, its jurisdiction. This registration was an attempt to stem the spread of disease. MUNI has ten volumes of these records covering 1859–1894, with some years missing. They have information both on those who were to be buried in New York City or New York State and those passing through for burial elsewhere. Biographical information can include name, age, place of birth, date and place of death, cause of death, and place of interment. Microfilm of these records is available at MUNI, the NYPL, and the FHL. See B-Ann Moorhouse's Research Aid, "Little Publicized New York City Sources: Bodies in Transit." The ledgers have not been indexed, but are arranged by year and are alphabetized within the year.

In another article with a similar title by B-Ann Moorhouse, "Little Publicized New York City Sources: The Landon Papers and Military Records," she notes a microfilm reel at MUNI entitled "U.S. Soldiers in Cuba and Puerto Rico: Deaths 1898–1900"; these are essentially bodies-in-transit records that contain names, addresses, dates and places of birth and death, places of interment, and other genealogically important data.

Private Records

Lists covering all births, marriages and deaths in a community were occasionally kept by private individuals; many of these are found in historical society collections. Probably the largest and best known of these was kept by several generations of the Salmon family of Southold, Suffolk County, with entries dated from 1696 to 1811. See William A. Robbins' "The Salmon Records." Bible records may also be classified as "private records"; see chapter 16, National and Statewide Repositories and Resources, for a description of Bible records collected by the DAR, and the NYG&B eLibrary at *New York Family History.org* for the American Bible Society collection and other Bible records. Of course, Bible records are found in many other places.

Selected Bibliography and Further Reading

Ackerley, Lucy D. "Southold [Suffolk County], N.Y. Town Records, Vital Statistics from Libers D. and E. in the Town Clerk's Office [1661–1763]." *NYG&B Record*, vol. 38 (1907) no. 3: 164–170; no. 4: 246–250; vol. 39 (1908) no. 1: 58–64, no. 2: 129–136. [NYG&B eLibrary]

Ackerly, Orville B. "Genealogical Data Found in the Printed Records of the Town of Huntington, Long Island [1665–1773]." *NYG&B Record,* vol. 50 (1919) no. 1: 72–76, no. 2: 127–133. [NYG&B eLibrary]

Austin, John. "Genealogical Research in New York State—An Informal Finding List of Published Materials with Supplementary Notes." Typescript, [Albany]: 1983. NYPL, New York.

Bailey, Rosalie Fellows. *Guide to Genealogical and Biographical Sources for New York City (Manhattan), 1783–1898.* New York: The Author, 1954. [*books.FamilySearch.org*] Reprinted with new introduction by Harry Macy, Jr. Baltimore: Clearfield Co., 1998. The original material for this book was published in the *New England Historical and Genealogical Register* (1952–1954). The 1998 edition contains an introduction by Harry Macy Jr. He notes that some of the information in the book, such as record locations and access, is out of date, but Bailey's descriptions of record content and many of her bibliographical references are not available elsewhere.

Beauchamp, William M. *Early Marriages from Newspapers Published in Central New York.* Finksburg, MD: Pipe Creek Publications, 1992. Originally compiled in the nineteenth century. With an appendix: "Manlius, NY, Obituaries and Marriages in the Early Nineteenth Century," supplied by H. C. Durston.

Bergen, Teunis G. "Marriage Records, Gravesend, L.I. [1664–1702]," *NYG&B Record*, vol. 4, no. 4 (1873): 199–200. [NYG&B eLibrary]

Blatt, Warren. "New York City Birth, Marriage and Death Records." *Newsletter of the Jewish Genealogical Society of Greater Boston*, Summer 1993; also published in *Resources for Jewish Genealogy in the Boston Area*. Boston: JGSGB, 1996; and *DOROT*, Jewish Genealogical Society (NY), 8 (Fall 1995): 6. See also *Ancestry*, 16 (Sept/Oct 1998): 32–33. [*jgsny.org*]

Bowman, Fred Q. For all titles by this author covering vital records in newspapers, see chapter 12, Newspapers.

Combes, George D. A. "Early Vital Records of Hempstead, Long Island, N.Y., from the Minutes of the Meetings of the Town Justices and Vestry, Beginning 1704 and Continuing to 1784," *NYG&B Record*, vol. 54, no. 1 (1923): 42–43. [NYG&B eLibrary]

———. "Marriages Performed by Justice William Mott of the Town of Hempstead, Long Island, 1793–1827." *NYG&B Record*, vol. 55, no. 2 (1924): 175–176. [NYG&B eLibrary]

Corn, Leslie. "City Clerk's Marriage Licenses, New York City, 1908–1937: One of 20th-Century Genealogy's Best Primary Sources." *NYG&B Newsletter* (now *New York Researcher*), Spring 1999. Updated 2003 and published as a Research Aid on *NewYorkFamilyHistory.org*.

———. "New York City Research Guide, Part One: Vital Records, Property Records, and Estate Records." Published as an article at *AmericanAncestors.org*.

DeGrazia, Laura Murphy. *Research in New York City, Long Island, and Westchester County.* Arlington, VA: National Genealogical Society, 2013.

FamilySearch.org. "New York Vital Records." A detailed wiki on vital records and vital records substitutes for New York. *https://familysearch.org/learn/wiki/en/New_York_Vital_Records*

Farrell, Charles. "Index to Matrimonial Actions 1787–1840, New York County Clerk's Office." *NYG&B Record*, vol. 129, no. 2 (1998): 81–88, with introduction by the editor, Harry Macy Jr. [NYG&B eLibrary]

———. "Marriages by a Justice of the Peace in Morrisania [Westchester County] 1867–1873." *NYG&B Record*, vol. 129, no. 3 (1998): 189–190. [NYG&B eLibrary]

Gavit, Joseph. "American Deaths and Marriages, 1784–1829: Taken from Upstate New York Newspapers." [Albany]: n.d. Card Index to 40,000 marriages and deaths; microfilms at the NYSL and NYPL. See also the companion work by Kenneth Scott listed below.

Guzik, Estelle M., ed. *Genealogical Resources in New York.* New York: Jewish Genealogical Society, 2003.

Henry, Marian S. "Early Vital Records of New York State: The Work of Fred Q. Bowman." Published in *New York Essays, Resources for the Genealogist in New York State Outside New York City.* Boston: New England Historic Genealogical Society, 2007.

Historical Records Survey. *Guide to Public Vital Statistics Records in New York State (Including New York City).* Albany: Historical Records Survey, 1942. Vol. 1. Birth Records; vol. 2. Marriage Records; vol. 3. Death Records. [Vols. 1 and 3 in NYG&B eLibrary; vol. 1 also at *Hathitrust.org* and *FamilySearch.org.*]

———. *Guide to Vital Statistics Records of Churches in New York State (exclusive of New York City).* Albany: Work Projects Administration, 1942. Two volumes, arranged by county. [NYG&B eLibrary]

———. *Guide to Vital Statistics Records of Churches in the City of New York.* Albany: Work Projects Administration, 1942. Five volumes (for each of the boroughs). [Brooklyn and Queens in the NYG&B eLibrary]

Hoff, Henry B. "Marriage and Death Notices in Long Island Newspapers." *NYG&B Newsletter* (now *New York Researcher*), Summer 1991. Updated December 2000 and published as a Research Aid on *NewYorkFamilyHistory.org.*

———. "Marriage and Death Notices in New York City Newspapers." *NYG&B Newsletter* (now *New York Researcher*), Spring 1991. Updated December 2000 and published as a Research Aid on *NewYorkFamilyHistory.org.* Lists all published or manuscript indexes and abstracts up to 1991.

———. "New Yorkers in Some Connecticut Divorces [1719–1922]." *NYG&B Newsletter* (now *New York Researcher*), Spring/Summer 2001; Fall 2001. Published as a Research Aid on *NewYorkFamilyHistory.org.*

Joslyn, Roger D. "List of the Cowen Sisters' Works," in his "Gertrude Barber, Minnie Cowen, and Ray Sawyer, The Sisters Who Indexed New York." *NYG&B Record,* vol. 143, no. 3 (2012): 226–234. This is the final installment of a six-part article. [NYG&B eLibrary]

———. "New York Vital Records." In *Red Book: American State, County, and Town Sources.* Edited by Alice Eicholz, 3rd edition. Provo, UT: Ancestry, 2004. See also similar article by the same author at *http://www.ancestry.com/wiki/index.php?title=New_York_Vital_Records*

———. "Town of Ramapo Births in 1847." *NYG&B Record,* vol. 132, no. 3 (2001): 168–169 [NYG&B eLibrary]

Kieval, Shelia. "New York Vital Records." *JewishGen.org,* January 1997. [*jewishgen.org/infofiles/ny-vital.html*]

Leigh, Catherine F. "Amenia Marriage Records [by Justice Jabez Flint, 1797–1814]." *NYG&B Record,* vol. 101 (1970) no. 4: 199–200; vol. 105 (1974) no. 3: 149. [NYG&B eLibrary]

Macy, Harry, Jr. "Before the Five-Borough City." *NYG&B Newsletter* (now *New York Researcher*), Winter 1998. Updated June 2011 and published as a Research Aid on *NewYorkFamilyHistory.org.*

———. "New York City Vital Records." *NYG&B Newsletter* (now *New York Researcher*), Summer 1998 and 1999. Completely revised January 2013 and published as a Research Aid on *NewYorkFamilyHistory.org.*

———. "Seven Queens County Marriage Licenses 1762–1768." *NYG&B Record,* vol. 119, no. 4 (1988): 226–227. [NYG&B eLibrary]

"Marriages by Justice Ammon Blair, Orleans County, 1840–1850." *NYG&B Record,* vol. 140, no. 4 (2009): 285–286. [NYG&B eLibrary]

Moorhouse, B-Ann. "Little Publicized New York City Sources: Minutes of the Committee on Health 1798." Originally published in *NYG&B Newsletter* (now *New York Researcher*), Spring 1993. Published as a Research Aid at *NewYorkFamilyHistory.org.*

———. "Little Publicized New York City Sources: Bodies in Transit." *NYG&B Newsletter* (now *New York Researcher*), Summer 1992. Published as a Research Aid at *NewYorkFamilyHistory.org.*

———. "Little Publicized New York City Sources: The Landon Papers and Military Records" *NYG&B Newsletter* (now *New York Researcher*), Fall 1994. Published as a Research Aid on *NewYorkFamilyHistory.org.*

New York Marriages Previous to 1784. A Reprint of the Original Edition of 1860 with Additions and Corrections. Baltimore: Genealogical Publishing Co., 1968. Includes facsimile of the first edition *Names of Persons for Whom Marriage Licenses Were Issued by the Secretary of the Province of New York, Previous to 1784.* Albany: Weed, Parsons, 1860, with extensive new material.

New York State Archives: "Guide to Birth, Marriage, and Death Records." *www.archives.nysed.gov/a/research/res_topics_gen_vitalstats.shtml.* This provides a general overview of vital records of New York State, prepared by the NYSA.

New York State Library. "New York State Vital Records (except New York City)." *www.nysl.nysed.gov/genealogy/vitrec.htm.* This is a general guide to New York State vital records.

"New York's Vital Records Law of 1665," *NYG&B Record*, vol. 132, no. 3 (2001): 170. [NYG&B eLibrary]

O'Neill, Terri B. "Birth and Death Records in New York Conveyances, 1687–1704: Early New York City Jewish Families." *NYG&B Record*, vol. 140, no. 4 (2009): 272–283, 275–277. [NYG&B eLibrary]

"Record of Marriages by Roswell Hopkins, One of His Majesty's Justices of the Peace in the County of Dutchess, State of New York [1763–1797]." *NYG&B Record*, vol. 39, no. 2 (1908): 126–129. [NYG&B eLibrary]

Remington, Gordon L. "Divorce Records, New York Style." *APG Quarterly*, vol. 12 (Sept. 1997): 90–91.

Robbins, William A. "The Salmon Records." *NYG&B Record*, vol. 47 (1916) no. 4: 344–360; vol. 48 (1917) no. 1: 20–32, 79, no. 2: 164–179, no. 3: 275–290, no. 4: 341–351; vol. 49 (1918) no. 1: 64–75, no. 2: 154–165, no. 3: 265–279. [NYG&B eLibrary]

Robison, Jeannie Floyd-Jones. *Genealogical Records; Manuscript Entries of Births, Deaths, and Marriages Taken from Family Bibles, 1581–1917*. New York: The National Society of Colonial Dames of the State of New York, 1917. Reprint: Baltimore: Genealogical Publishing Co., 1972.

Sawyer, Ray C., comp. and ed. "Marriages Performed by the Various Mayors and Aldermen of the City of New York, as well as Justices of the Peace, etc., 1830–1854." Typescript, 1935. NYPL. Also found at the FHL and *Ancestry.com*.

Scott, Kenneth. *Coroners' Reports in New York City, 1823–1842*. New York: New York Genealogical and Biographical Society, 1989. [NYG&B eLibrary]

— — —. *Coroners' Reports in New York City, 1843–1849*. New York: New York Genealogical and Biographical Society, 1991. [NYG&B eLibrary]

— — —. "Early New York City Coroner's Reports [1795–1820 with gaps]." *NYG&B Record*, vol. 119 (1988) no. 1: 76–79, no. 2: 145–150, no. 3: 217–219; vol. 120 (1989) no. 1: 18–20, no. 2: 88–92. [NYG&B eLibrary]

— — —. *Genealogical Data from Colonial New York Newspapers: A Consolidation of Articles from the New York Genealogical and Biographical Record*. Baltimore: Genealogical Publishing Co., 1977.

— — —. *Genealogical Data from the New York Post-Boy*. Washington: National Genealogical Society, 1970.

— — —. *Joseph Gavit's American Deaths and Marriages, 1784–1829: Index to Non-Principals in Microfilm Copies of Abstracts in the New York State Library, Albany, New York*. New Orleans: Polyanthos, 1976.

— — —. *New York Marriage Bonds, 1753–1783*. New York: Saint Nicholas Society of the City of New York, 1972.

Scott, Kenneth, and Kristin Lunde Gibbons, eds. *The New York Magazine, Marriages and Deaths, 1790–1797*. New Orleans: Polyanthos, 1975.

"Some Deaths in New York City 1753–1756." *New-York Historical Society Quarterly*, vol. 21 (1937): 127–130.

Spalletta, Matteo. "Divorce in Colonial New York." *The New-York Historical Society Quarterly*, 39 (October 1955): 422–440.

Stifel, Carolyn G. "Cholera Records, July and August 1832, Albany." *NYG&B Record*, vol. 138, no. 2 (2007): 133–137, 220–224. [NYG&B eLibrary]

— — —, comp. "Deaths from the *Ladies Miscellany or the Weekly Visitor*." See the bibliography in chapter 12, Newspapers, for a detailed entry for these transcripts.

Sypher, Francis J., Jr. *Minutes of Coroners Proceedings City and County of New York, John Burnet, Coroner 1748–1758*. New York: New York Genealogical and Biographical Society, 2004. [NYG&B eLibrary]

— — —. "New York City Coroner's Reports, 1680–1684," *NYG&B Record*, vol. 136, no. 4, (2005): 261–271. [NYG&B eLibrary]

Worden, Jean D. *Revised Master Index to the New York State Daughters of the American Revolution Genealogical Records Volumes*. Books 1 and 2, prepared by the General Peter Gansevoort Chapter. Albany and Zephyrhills, FL: Jean D. Worden, 1998.

Introduction

Most researchers are familiar with the federal decennial census mandated by the United States Constitution. The federal census has been conducted every ten years since 1790, and the existing census records are available to researchers through 1940. Federal census records are easily accessed online and on microfilm, and are usually among the first original sources to be consulted by genealogists.

The literature is replete with books and articles on making the most of the federal census in genealogical research. This chapter does not address the federal census in general, but begins with information specific to the federal census in New York State.

The second part of the chapter deals with the New York state census. William Dollarhide's book *New York State Censuses and Substitutes*, which is in print and ebook formats and easily obtainable, is a good source of information on this subject and more detailed than this chapter can be. It contains maps, county-by-county information, sample pages, and extensive bibliographic references. As it was published in 2005, aspects of it are out-of-date, particularly regarding the availability of online records and, of course, descriptions of the 1940 census, which was released in 2012. See also David P. Davenport's "The State Censuses of New York 1825–1925."

New York has some unusual census resources which are not well known, including some early censuses, and these are covered in the last section of this chapter.

Federal Census for New York State

The federal censuses from 1790 to 1840 include names for the heads of households and the number of people in each household in various demographic categories. Beginning in 1850 the federal censuses began adding a wide range of data, including the names of every individual in each household,

ages, birth locations, addresses, marital status, employment, and numerous other diagnostics.

These records are indexed on paper and electronically and are available at repositories across the country, on microfilm in many locations, and online through *Ancestry.com*, *FamilySearch.org*, *findmypast.com*, *Archive.org*, *HeritageQuest*, and probably others. Those sites that have incomplete images or incomplete indexes will likely get them in due course.

Except for the 1890 census (see below), most of the federal census records for New York have survived. William Dollarhide's book provides a table of the federal census records on microfilm from 1790 to 1930. (As noted, it was published before the release of the 1940 census.) The table serves as an overview of existing federal censuses of New York State by county and year.

In 1870 New York City was one of three cities that was granted a recount, so there are two 1870 censuses, one conducted in June and the other, known as the second enumeration, in December. Both censuses are available at *Ancestry.com*. The second enumeration recorded street addresses. Researchers will benefit by looking for their subjects in both censuses. If the indexes are flawed, a person found in one enumeration can be searched in the other enumeration using the ward and district numbers.

The 1890 federal census population schedules were almost entirely destroyed after they had been damaged in a fire in Washington, DC. The surviving fragments for New York State include parts of the town of Brookhaven (Suffolk County) and the town of Eastchester (Westchester County). The 1890 Union Veterans and Widows federal census records for New York also survived the fire and are available on *FamilySearch.org* and *Ancestry.com*. Researchers have the 1890 "Police Census" as a substitute for New York City, which included New York County (then comprised of the island of Manhattan and parts of the

Bronx), as well as the 1892 New York state census, both of which are discussed in this chapter. See the section on American Indians in chapter 14, Peoples of New York, for information about 1890 federal census data from Indian reservations.

Some county clerks maintained their own county copies of the federal census, which may differ from the copies sent to Washington, DC. More information about these county copies and their availability may be found in *New York State Census Records, 1790–1925* by Marilyn Douglas and Melinda Yates. This lengthy document is online at the website of the New York State Library (NYSL).

Federal Census Special Schedules

The federal census special schedule for 1820 (manufactures), and those for 1850 to 1880, can be a source of useful information but are frequently ignored by researchers. The 1820 special schedule is housed at the National Archives and Records Administration (NARA) in Washington, DC, and is on microfilm at the Family History Library (FHL) and the New York Public Library (NYPL). Those from 1850 to 1880 are at the New York State Archives (NYSA) in Albany, on film at the FHL and the NYPL, and also on *Ancestry.com*.

Agricultural schedules detail the property, employees, livestock, and crops of each farm, providing useful detail far beyond the simple label "farmer" assigned in the population schedules.

Industrial schedules provide information on small businesses (including self-employed men), such as employees, wages, materials, and products.

Mortality schedules list deaths, and causes of death, during the preceding year; this is especially significant where there are unreliable death records.

The Social Statistics schedules for the 1850, 1860, and 1870 federal censuses provide summaries for individual towns, including their libraries and churches, schools and students, property and taxes, criminals and paupers, and newspapers, but do not provide information about individuals.

The Supplemental schedules for the Defective, Dependent, and Delinquent Classes (DDD), which were only provided in the 1880 census, enumerate the inhabitants of institutions, poorhouses, and prisons; people considered insane or "idiots"; the deaf and the blind; the indigent; and homeless children. The DDD schedules are described in "The 'Forgotten' Census of 1880" by Ruth L. Hatten.

For more information on the special schedules, including which schedules exist for which years and locations, see Harry Macy Jr.'s Research Aid "Special Federal Census Schedules for New York State" online at *NewYorkFamilyHistory.org*.

The New York State Census

New York State periodically undertook its own censuses, as did many other states. (For an overview of all state censuses, see Ann S. Lainhart's *State Census Records*.) As noted, William Dollarhide's book provides the most detailed description of this resource.

The second New York State Constitution (1821) required that a census be taken in 1825 and every ten years after that. In 1825 the New York State Legislature passed an act (Law 1925, Chapter C) "to provide for taking future enumerations of the inhabitants of this state and for procuring useful statistical tables," specifying in detail what information was to be collected and reported, and by whom. The act required marshals in every city, town, and ward "to take a true and accurate enumeration of the inhabitants" and forward the results to the county clerk. The clerk in each county was required to prepare abstracts for the secretary of state. Consistent with the federal census, only the head of household was to be named; other household members in various demographic categories were simply to be counted.

The constitution and the act of 1825 initiated a series of New York state censuses that were indeed taken every ten years in the middle of each decade. This occurred through 1875. Because of various political and bureaucratic issues, there was no 1885 census. Instead, the state took a census in 1892, skipped the 1895 census, and then resumed the pattern, conducting state censuses in 1905, 1915, and 1925. In 1931, the New York State Constitution was amended to abolish the state census, so the 1925 state census was the last. The management issues that resulted in the state conducting a census in 1892 was a fortunate occurrence for genealogists, because that state census is a valuable substitute for the destroyed 1890 federal census.

Theoretically, the benefit for genealogists researching in New York State is that from 1820 through 1930, there was a census taken every five years (except for the irregularities noted above, and the loss of the 1890 federal census). As a practical matter, however, this is only true for a few counties in New York State, because the census records for 1825, 1835, and 1845 are mostly lost. "Lost counties" during those years include Albany, Dutchess, Kings, New York, Queens, Rensselaer, Saratoga, and Ulster, to name a few of the more populous counties. See table 1.

Like the federal census, the state census was conducted by county. During the nineteenth century, many new counties were created to keep pace with the burgeoning population. Researchers may find a person remaining in the same locality listed in the censuses of different counties in successive years. For example, the Town of Catharine will be found in Tioga County on the 1825 census, in Chemung County on the 1845 census, and in Schuyler County on the 1855 census. Occasionally a newly formed county will be included in the census of its parent; for example, Hamilton County was formed in 1821 but was listed with Montgomery County in the 1825 census. Part Two of this book provides guidance on where to look for census records for various places and dates.

The information included varies by year. The 1855 New York state census was the first to record the names of every individual in the household; previously only the head of household was named, along with the number of other household members by age and sex. Of particular importance in the 1855 census is that the relationship of the family members to the head of household was given. This question was not asked in the federal census until 1880. The 1855 census also provides the length of time that people had lived in their towns or cities and the state or country of birth for each; if the enumerated person was born in New York State, then the county of birth was noted. This information could prove particularly helpful to researchers tracking the movement of families within the state.

The type and amount of data collected in the state censuses varied widely. From 1825 until 1875 the census became increasingly rich in data. The 1865 census, taken just after the Civil War ended, was the most elaborate in New York State; the 1875 census was nearly as rich. After that, the data collected became continuously less detailed. See table 2 for a summary of questions asked on New York state censuses, and the NYSL website for the instructions given to the enumerators for taking the New York state census (*http://www.nysl.nysed.gov/scandocs/nyscensus.htm*).

The New York state censuses from 1855 to 1875 also feature special schedules, similar to the special schedules in the federal census. The special schedules for the state censuses are found with the population schedules.

Original New York State Census Records

Two sets of census schedules were prepared in every county for all New York state censuses from 1825 to 1925. One copy was kept by the county clerk, and the second copy was sent to the state census office in Albany. The devastating 1911 State Capitol fire destroyed the entire collection held by the state government of the New York state census records created between 1825 and 1905. Fortunately many county clerks had retained most of their censuses from the 1855 census until the fire, so the surviving "originals" for these years will usually be found with the county clerk. The censuses for Clinton, New York, Putnam, Queens, Seneca, Suffolk, and Westchester counties are the conspicuous exceptions, as most of their nineteenth-century census records are entirely lost.

Although the fire destroyed the state-owned copies of the state census, the NYSL has assembled microfilm copies of the county-owned versions for the years that burned, for on site use in Albany. An inventory of the NYSL's microfilm holdings in chart form is online at *http://www.nysl.nysed.gov/genealogy/nyscens.htm*.

For the New York state censuses conducted in 1915 and 1925, there is a complete set at the NYSA, and most county clerks also have their "originals" for these two census years. The phrase "duplicate originals" is frequently used for one set or another, as in most cases it is not clear which set of forms was completed first. Table 1 provides an overview of all available state censuses. For more detailed information, including the availability of indexes and transcriptions, consult the individual County Guides in Part Two of this book.

New York State Census and American Indians

The New York state census includes data gathered on Indian reservations using the same forms designed for the counties. In 1845 census takers complained of the difficulty of procuring information from American Indians. The instructions for the 1855 census state that "Special marshals will be appointed for taking the census of the Indians residing in the Allegany, Cattaraugus, Oneida, Onondaga, St. Regis, Tonawanda, and Tuscarora settlements." The town Marshals for the census were given instructions on how to list Indians who were not living on reservations. See the American Indian section in chapter 14, Peoples of New York.

Records on Microfilm

Nearly all existing records are available on microfilm at the NYSL, the NYSA, the NYPL, and the FHL. Public libraries with local history or genealogy sections frequently have microfilm copies for their respective counties, and occasionally for neighboring counties as well. For lists of all the repositories holding New York state censuses, both manuscripts and on microfilm by year and county, see William Dollarhide's book, and the online article by Marilyn Douglas and Melinda Yates.

Both the NYSL and county clerk sets of New York state censuses for 1915 and 1925 have been microfilmed for a number of upstate counties. Eventually all of these records will be digitized and indexed. Since all censuses contain human errors, having two sets to compare can be very useful. The FHL catalog differentiates between the two by describing the NYSL's version as "Secretary of State," and the county version as "County Clerk."

Online Availability

FamilySearch.org currently has the most extensive collection of New York state censuses online; they have digitized most of their microfilmed records and are in the process of indexing and adding the rest to their online collection.

Ancestry.com and *FamilySearch.org* are working in partnership with the NYSA to digitize New York state census material (and other records besides the census), and these efforts are ongoing. Researchers can check the catalogs for updates. New York State residents who do not have an *Ancestry.com* subscription can access the New York State material (census and otherwise) online without charge by creating an account; see the *Ancestry.com* entry in chapter 16 for details; access to *FamilySearch.org* is always free.

Table 1: New York State Census: Preserved and Lost Records

Virtually all existing census records from 1855 to 1925 are online at *FamilySearch.org*; *Ancestry.com* and other sites also have selected New York State census records online.

The dates of establishment are provided for those counties formed after 1825; see the County Guides for information on the whereabouts of census records for these areas before formation of the current county.

Key:
* See details in the indicated County Guide
Blue shading: records exist
White (no shade): records lost (or never existed)

County	1825	1835	1845	1855	1865	1875	1892	1905	1915	1925
Albany				▓	▓	▓	▓	▓	▓	▓
Allegany			*	▓	*	▓	▓	▓	▓	▓
Bronx (est. 1914)										
Broome	*			▓	▓	▓	▓	▓	▓	▓
Cattaraugus		*		▓	▓	▓	▓	▓	▓	▓
Cayuga				▓	▓	▓	▓	▓	▓	▓
Chautauqua	▓			▓	▓	▓	▓	▓	▓	▓
Chemung (est. 1836)				▓	▓	▓	▓	▓	▓	▓
Chenango				▓	▓	▓		▓	▓	▓
Clinton				*	▓	▓	▓	▓	▓	▓
Columbia			*	▓	▓	▓		▓	▓	▓
Cortland	▓		*	▓	▓	▓	▓	▓	▓	▓
Delaware			*	▓	*	▓	▓	▓	▓	▓
Dutchess				▓	▓	▓			▓	▓
Erie				▓	▓	▓	▓	▓	▓	▓
Essex				▓	▓	▓	▓	▓	▓	▓
Franklin				▓	▓	▓		▓	▓	▓
Fulton (est. 1838)			▓	▓	▓	▓	▓	▓	▓	▓
Genesee				▓	▓	▓	▓	▓	▓	▓
Greene				▓	▓	▓	▓	▓	▓	▓
Hamilton	*			▓	▓	▓	▓	▓	▓	▓
Herkimer	*			▓	▓	▓	▓	▓	▓	▓
Jefferson				▓	▓	▓		▓	▓	▓
Kings			*	▓	▓	▓		▓	▓	▓
Lewis	▓	▓		▓	▓	▓		▓	▓	▓
Livingston				▓	▓	▓		▓	▓	▓
Madison				▓	▓	▓	▓	▓	▓	▓
Monroe				▓	▓	▓	▓	▓	▓	▓

County	1825	1835	1845	1855	1865	1875	1892	1905	1915	1925
Montgomery	*	*	*							
Nassau (est. 1899)										
New York				*						
Niagara										
Oneida	*									
Onondaga										
Ontario			*							
Orange										
Orleans										
Oswego										
Otsego	*		*							
Putnam	*		*							
Queens										
Rensselaer										
Richmond										
Rockland										
Saratoga			*							
Schenectady			*							
Schoharie										
Schuyler (est. 1854)										
Seneca										
St. Lawrence		*	*		*		*			
Steuben										
Suffolk	*		*				*			
Sullivan							*			
Tioga			*							
Tompkins										
Ulster										
Warren										
Washington										
Wayne				*						
Westchester			*							
Wyoming (est. 1841)							*			
Yates			*							

New York City 1855 Census for Ward 17

Most of New York City's Ward 17 for the 1855 New York state census is available only in the New York Genealogical and Biographical Society's (NYG&B) eLibrary. As this Lower East Side ward was a temporary home for many new immigrants, this census was frequently the only record of their stay in New York City. The fact that all subsequent nineteenth-century New York County state census records have been lost makes the county's 1855 census all the more valuable.

Statistical Schedules

The statistical schedules for all New York state censuses, as well as the instructions for census takers and several preliminary reports, have been digitized by the NYSL and are available at *www.nysl.nysed.gov/scandocs/nyscensus.htm*. Statistical schedules enumerate the populations and economy of counties, cities, and towns. But since statistical schedules do not include names of individuals, they have limited genealogical value.

Table 2: New York State Census: Selected Questions Asked 1855–1925							
Questions on Population Schedule I*	1855	1865	1875	1892	1905	1915; 1925	Notes
Address				✓	✓	✓	
Material of which dwelling is built	✓	✓	✓				
Value	✓	✓	✓				
Name of everyone in household	✓	✓	✓	✓	✓	✓	1865, including name of anyone absent in army or navy
Age, sex, and color	✓	✓	✓	✓	✓	✓	1875, specified Indian
Relation to head of family	✓	✓	✓		✓	✓	
Place of birth	✓	✓	✓	✓	✓	✓	1855, 1865, and 1875 asked for county
Marital status	✓	✓	✓				
Number of times married		✓					
Colored not taxed	✓	✓					
Occupation	✓	✓	✓	✓	✓	✓	
Deaf, dumb, blind, insane, or idiotic	✓	✓	✓				
Parent of how many children		✓					
Native and naturalized voters	✓	✓	✓				
Years resident in this city or town	✓						
Number of years in United States					✓	✓	
Citizen or alien	✓	✓	✓	✓	✓	✓	
If naturalized, when and where						✓	
Owners of land	✓	✓	✓				
Usual place of employment		✓	✓				1875, asked for former home of men in military service
Infants under one year						✓	
Literacy	✓	✓	✓				
Inmates of institutions					✓	✓	
Servicemen (now or formerly)		✓					
*Questions pertaining to special schedules are not included in this table.							

Transcriptions and Indexes

Volunteers across the state and beyond continue to independently transcribe and index a variety of New York census records. It is always worth checking local genealogical societies, historical societies, and libraries for handwritten, typed, and printed works. An increasing number of transcriptions and indexes are available online. *NYGenWeb.net* is a good source of information gathered at the local level. As with any large-scale transcription project, human errors are inevitable, but researchers will find a wide range of detailed secondary source material. *Censusfinder. com* aims to identify and provide links to all available census records online. This website, which allows a search by state and county, can be a good starting point for locating and accessing online census records of many kinds.

Indexes and Finding Aids

Unlike the federal census, the New York state census is not comprehensively indexed in print; these indexes exist only for individual counties or towns and for certain years. An extensive list of published indexes, formerly held by the NYG&B and now housed at the NYPL, can be found under "Research Aids" on the NYG&B member webpages. The New York state censuses are partially indexed on *FamilySearch.org* and *Ancestry.com*, and it will only be a matter of a short time before they are fully indexed online.

Transcripts, abstracts, extracts, and other reports detailing the New York state census have been published and may be useful to those who are unable to locate their families through an index; researchers who use these resources may have to search by town. Dollarhide's book includes a town-by-town list of these resources.

For those sections not yet indexed, researchers looking in cities can be more efficient by first finding the family's address (found in local and city directories) and the Assembly District (AD) and Election District (ED) to which that address belongs; these can be found using AD/ED maps for the relevant year. Note that the AD/ED can change between census years. For New York City addresses, AD/ED for the years 1890 to 1925 can be identified by searching the Steve Morse One-Step website *www.stevenmorse.org/nyc/nyc.php*. Note that the acronym ED means "election district" for New York State records, while it means "enumeration district" for federal records. Identifying the AD/ED is rarely necessary for towns in rural areas.

Other Census Resources in New York State
Colonial Censuses

During the period of English rule (1664–1783), periodic censuses of the colony or province of New York were conducted, listing every inhabitant or, alternatively, just heads of households with statistics on the rest of the family. Any surviving original records of these censuses were destroyed in the 1911 State

Table 3: Transcriptions of Colonial Censuses

Year	County (and Towns if census not available for entire county)
1686	Suffolk (Southold)
1697	Albany
1698	Kings, Queens (Flushing, Hempstead, Newtown), Suffolk (Southold, Southampton), Westchester (Eastchester, Fordham, Mamaroneck, Morrisania, New Rochelle, Westchester)
1702	Orange
1703	New York (New York City)
ca. 1707	Richmond
1712	Orange
1714	Dutchess
1731	Kings
1771	Queens (Newtown), Suffolk (Shelter Island), Westchester (New Rochelle)
1776	Suffolk (all towns except Huntington)
1781	Queens (part of Oyster Bay)

Capitol fire; table 3 lists those that had previously been transcribed. Transcripts of these census records have been published as indicated in the County Guides or in Henry Hoff's "Pre-1750 Lists." See also *Early New York State Census Records, 1663–1772* by Carol Meyers.

Censuses of Electors

New York State conducted a census of electors (voters) in 1790. In addition to numerical data, this census recorded the head of household's name. The census data was to be returned to the Secretary of State of New York. Unfortunately the returns are lost, possibly destroyed in the 1911 Capitol fire. Only sections of Albany County and the Town of Huntington (Suffolk County) have been recovered. See Charles Street's *Huntington Town Records Including Babylon, Long Island, NY, 1653–1914*.

Approximately 4,000 names survive for Albany County, which is about half the number of names listed in the federal census of 1790. Interestingly, hundreds of the names differ from those in the federal census; details can be found in *New York State Census of Albany County Towns in 1790* by Kenneth Scott.

Statewide "electoral" censuses were conducted at irregular intervals between 1795 and 1821. These provided information on population and the number of eligible voters, but included few names. As a consequence they generally have little genealogical value.

In addition to federal and state censuses, counties, cities, towns, and even villages have sometimes conducted censuses. Dollarhide's book provides an extensive list of these censuses and lists, including those for poorhouses, almshouses, prisons, and similar institutions.

Settlers Census

The Holland Land Company in western New York State (see chapter 7, Land Records) conducted several small "censuses" between 1802 and 1806. In order to review progress being made on its land, the company recorded the names of resident lot owners, the number of men, women, and children living on the lot, and details of cattle, horses, crops, and the number of acres improved. These surveys covered settlers in Chenango and Madison counties.

One drawback for genealogists is that even though many of the lots had more than one owner, only an aggregate number was entered for men, women, and children. This prevents researchers from knowing which people were related or how many children belonged to a particular family. Most of the original records are in the Netherlands, but microfilmed records are available at the Library of Congress, the FHL, the NYPL, the NYSL, the Olin Library of Cornell University, and the Reed Library, SUNY Fredonia.

New York City Censuses

In addition to the New York state census, New York City officials conducted various censuses between 1795 and 1829 for the purpose of identifying potential jurors or to reapportion its state legislative districts. Surviving records are scarce, but can be extremely useful, as they provide the names of many adult women, very few of whom appear in the population schedules; they are available on microfilm at the New York City Municipal Archives (MUNI) and at the NYPL. (The original documents are at MUNI.) See table 4 for the questions on these censuses. See Roger Joslyn's "New York City Censuses for 1816, 1819, and 1821" for details on which jury census schedules survive for which specific wards of the City.

New York City "Police Census" of 1890

The New York City authorities felt the 1890 federal census was incomplete. Lower numbers meant the city would not get appropriate representation in Congress or receive correct levels of state and federal aid. (Note that in 1890 New York City included only present-day Manhattan and the western Bronx.) A second census, carried out later the same year by city police officers, produced a 13 percent increase over the population figures shown in the 1890 federal census. Of the 1,008 census books, 894 still exist. Some of the surviving records can be accessed online through *Ancestry.com*.

Table 4. Information Collected on the New York City Jury and Electoral Censuses

1816 and 1819 Jury Censuses	1821 Electoral Census
• Name, street address, age, occupation • Freeholder of $150; personal estate of $150 • Reason for exemption • Number of inhabitants broken down by sex, race (including free blacks), citizenship status (e.g., alien), slaves; tenants renting • Freeholders of £100 and up; Freeholders of £20 and under £100 • Number of jurors in the household; total in household; remarks	• Name of family head • Street address • Number of eligible voters (male)

The original surviving records are at MUNI. All are on microfilm there and at the NYPL and the FHL. Researchers using microfilm need to know the address of the family in order to locate it on the microfilm records. Addresses can be found in local and city directories. See Howard Jensen's *Aid to Finding Addresses in the 1890 New York City Police Census*. His book converts a street address to the book number and then converts the book number to the FHL film and AD/ED numbers. The AD/ED can also be identified by searching the Steve Morse One-Step website at *www.stevenmorse.org/nyc/nyc.php*. In addition, both MUNI and the NYPL have finding aids that cross reference the census book numbers to AD/ED numbers.

Almshouses and Poorhouses

The NYSA has census records of inmates in almshouses and poorhouses, from 1826 until 1921, with the bulk dating from 1875 to 1921 (series A1978). Information is available on the inmates themselves, their families, and their economic history. These records are also on *Ancestry.com*. See also chapter 10, Business, Institutional, and Organizational Records.

Military-related Information on Censuses

Since 1825, the New York state census has been collecting information relevant to military service. The 1825, 1835, and 1845 censuses counted men subject to military duty; in later years questions were asked about current or former service.

In the 1840 federal census, Revolutionary War veterans and widows receiving pensions were enumerated and published in *A Census of Pensioners for Revolutionary or Military Services* . . . . The listings for New York are divided into Northern and Southern districts, then by county, and then by town.

The veterans' schedules, listing Union veterans or their widows from the Civil War, taken with the 1890 federal census, survive and are online at *Ancestry.com*. The census recorded names, ranks, regiment (army) or vessel (navy), dates of enlistment and discharge, disability if any, length of service, and address.

Census Substitutes

When a census record is irretrievably lost, damaged, or incomplete, the researcher may seek other types of records that provide the information that would have been preserved in the census.

For census substitutes in the colonial period, see Henry Hoff's "Pre-1750 Lists" for a wide variety of records including assessment rolls or tax lists, lists of freemen and freeholders, and oaths of allegiance to the crown.

Tax lists can often be used as substitutes for the census. Information about New York tax lists, as well as a compilation of tax lists published in periodicals, can be found in Roger Joslyn's article "New York State Censuses and Tax Lists." See also chapter 13, Tax Records.

Other substitute records include voter registrations, religious records, military lists, local directories, and indexes of land, naturalization, and vital records. Dollarhide's book identifies substitute records for each county. These types of records are covered in other chapters in this book.

Selected Bibliography and Further Reading

A Census of Pensioners for Revolutionary or Military Services: With Their Names, Ages, and Places of Residence, As Returned by the Marshals of the Several Judicial Districts, Under the Act for Taking the Sixth Census [1840]. Washington: United States Census Office, 1841.

Davenport, David P. "The State Censuses of New York 1825–1925." *Genealogical Journal* (now *Crossroads*), vol. 14 no. 4 (1985–1986): 172–195.

Dilts, Bryan L. *1890 New York Census Index of Civil War Veterans and Their Widows*. Salt Lake City: Index Publishing, 1984.

Dollarhide, William. *New York State Censuses and Substitutes*. Baltimore: Genealogical Publishing Co., 2005.

Douglas, Marilyn, and Melinda Yates. *New York State Census Records, 1790–1925 Biography Bulletin 88*. Albany: State Education Department, 1981. [Link at *www.nysl.nysed.gov/scandocs/nyscensus.htm*]

Eichholz, Alice, and James M. Rose, comps. *Free Black Heads of Households in the New York State Federal Census 1790–1830*. Gale Genealogy and Local History Series, vol. 14. Detroit: Gale Research Co., 1981.

Hatten, Ruth L. "The 'Forgotten' Census of 1880: Defective, Dependent, and Delinquent Classes." *National Genealogical Society Quarterly*, vol. 80 no. 1 (March 1992): 57–70.

Hoff, Henry B. "Pre-1750 New York Lists." *NYG&B Newsletter* (now *New York Researcher*), Fall 1992. Published as a Research Aid on *NewYorkFamilyHistory.org*.

Inskeep, Carolee R. *The Children's Aid Society of New York: An Index to the Federal, State and Local Census Records of Its Lodging Houses, 1855–1925*. Baltimore: Clearfield Publishing Co., 1996.

— — —. *The New York Foundling Hospital: An Index to Its Federal, State and Local Census Records, 1870–1925*. Baltimore: Clearfield Publishing Co., 1995.

Jensen, Howard M. *Aid to Finding Addresses in the 1890 New York City Police Census*. Bowie, MD: Heritage Books, 2003.

Joslyn, Roger D. "New York City Censuses for 1816, 1819, and 1821." *NYG&B Newsletter* (now *New York Researcher*), Winter 1992. Published as a Research Aid on *NewYorkFamilyHistory.org*.

— — —. "New York State Censuses and Tax Lists." *NYG&B Newsletter* (now *New York Researcher*), Spring 1998. Published as a Research Aid on *NewYorkFamilyHistory.org*.

Lainhart, Ann S. *State Census Records*. Baltimore: Genealogical Publishing Co., 1992.

LeBarron, Laura. "Contents of the New York State Census." *NYG&B Newsletter* (now *New York Researcher*), Summer 1997. Published as a Research Aid on *NewYorkFamilyHistory.org*.

— — —. "Finding Aids at the NYG&B Library for New York State Censuses." *NYG&B Newsletter* (now *New York Researcher*), Spring 1997 and Summer 1997. Published as a Research Aid on *NewYorkFamilyHistory.org*.

Macy, Harry, Jr. "The 1820 U.S. Census of Manufactures." *NYG&B Newsletter* (now *New York Researcher*), Summer 1999. [NYG&B eLibrary]

— — —. "New York 1890 Census Substitutes." Published as a Research Aid on *NewYorkFamilyHistory.org* and checked for accuracy by the author in 2011.

— — —. "Special Federal Census Schedules for New York State." *NYG&B Newsletter* (now *New York Researcher*), Spring 1993. Updated 2011 by the author and published as a Research Aid on *NewYorkFamilyHistory.org*.

Meyers, Carol. *Early New York State Census Records, 1663–1772*. Gardena, CA: RAM Publishers, 1965.

O'Callaghan, Edmund Bailey. *Documentary History of the State of New York*. 4 vols. Albany: State of New York 1849–1851 (octavo edition) and 1850–1851 (quarto edition with different pagination). Portions reprinted in *Lists of Inhabitants of Colonial New York Excerpted from the Documentary History of the State of New York*. Baltimore: Genealogical Publishing Co., 1979. See table 3 in this chapter and County Guides for details.

Scott, Kenneth. *New York State Census of Albany County Towns in 1790*. Baltimore: Genealogical Publishing Co., 2003.

Street, Charles R. *Census of Huntington, 1790: Huntington Town Records Including Babylon, Long Island, NY, 1653–1914*. Vol. 3: 147–158. Huntington, NY: The Town, 1887–1889.

Online References

FamilySearch: New York State Census Wiki. See two URLs: *www.familysearch.org/learn/wiki/en/New_York_Census* *www.familysearch.org/learn/wiki/en/New_York_Census_ State_Censuses*. Identifies and provides locations (including online) for all extant New York state census records and indexes, organized by year and county.

New York State Library: New York State Census Records Available at the Library. *www.nysl.nysed.gov/genealogy/nyscens.htm*

Silinonte, Joseph M. *Street Index to the 1892 New York State Census, City of Brooklyn*. Brooklyn: J. M. Silinonte, 2001.

Stephen Morse: Obtaining AD/ED for the 1890–1925 New York State Census in One-Step. *www.stevenmorse.org/nyc/nyc.php*

Stephen Morse: New York State Census in One Step—Frequently Asked Questions. *www.stevenmorse.org/nyc/faq.htm*

Immigration, Migration, and Naturalization

Chapter 4

Introduction

New York's growth and development—from the earliest European settlements to modern times—has been greatly influenced by immigration from many countries and by migration. To clarify the terminology used, immigration records document the arrival in the United States (and, more specifically in this chapter, New York) of individuals from a foreign country; naturalization records document the process by which an alien residing in New York State obtained United States citizenship; migration refers to the movement of people from one region of the United States to another, including movements within New York colony and state.

It is useful to know that the port of New York was, and remains, the only official seaport of entry into the state; not until 1895 were locations along the northern land border with Canada designated as official ports for immigration purposes.

The content, provenance, and availability of immigration and naturalization records vary for different time periods. This chapter provides a historical overview, followed by specific information on where records can be found. Chapter 14, Peoples of New York, contains detailed information about research resources related to the immigration and migration of major ethnic populations in New York, including American Indians.

Pre-European Period

Prior to the arrival of European explorers, the territory that would become New York State had been home to American Indians for thousands of years. Best known are the "Five Nations" that united to form the Iroquois (Haudenosaunee) Confederacy: the Cayuga, Mohawk, Oneida, Onondaga, and Seneca, who were joined in the early-eighteenth century by the Tuscarora. Several Algonquian tribes also occupied territory now in New York State.

1609–1664: New Netherland

Immigration

Beginning in 1609 with Henry Hudson's voyage, Dutch ships visited New Netherland to trade with the native inhabitants. It was not until 1624 that the Dutch West India Company (WIC) began sending permanent settlers to the colony. This flow of immigrants continued until the English seized New Netherland in 1664. New Netherland returned to Dutch control briefly in 1673–1674, but there is little evidence of immigration during that period.

New Netherland's "Dutch" population was actually an extremely diverse mixture of European nationalities; probably no more than half of the population was native to the Dutch Republic. The Dutch colony also attracted numerous English settlers (and some Scots, Irish, and Welsh), most of whom went first to New England and then migrated to New Netherland. On Long Island, the settlements from Oyster Bay eastward were part of New England during this period. Beginning in 1626, the WIC began to import enslaved Africans, mainly from the Caribbean.

Migration

Within what is now New York State, the Dutch first settled at Fort Orange (which became Beverwijck and then Albany) and on Manhattan Island (which became New Amsterdam). From there they spread to Staten Island, western Long Island, the Esopus area (Wildwijck, now Kingston), and into the great patroonship of Rensselaerswijck surrounding Fort Orange. Some of the English chose to live in these Dutch settlements, but most of them preferred to form their own towns in New Netherland, either on western Long Island or in what would later become Westchester County.

Naturalization

Settlers sailing from Amsterdam and those arriving in the colony from elsewhere were required to take an oath of allegiance to the States General (Dutch parliament) and to the WIC.

1664–1783: The English and Revolutionary Periods

In September 1664 the English seized New Netherland and created the colony (later province) of New York, which included the former New England towns on eastern Long Island.

Immigration

There was very little immigration from the Netherlands after 1664, but nearly all of the "Dutch" settlers remained in the colony. Until the American Revolution there was a small but steady stream of immigration from Europe, mainly from Great Britain, Ireland, and the German states. Additionally, the small Jewish community in New York City experienced steady growth.

Occasionally there was a larger influx such as the Huguenots (in New York City, New Rochelle, New Paltz, and Staten Island) beginning in the 1680s and continuing into the early-eighteenth century; the German Palatines (in the Hudson, Schoharie, and Mohawk valleys) beginning in 1709; and the Scots who settled the Argyle Patent (in present-day Washington County) beginning in the 1730s. Peter Wilson Coldham's lists of the thousands of indentured servants, convicts, and other bonded emigrants whom the British government transported to the American colonies show that almost none was sent to New York. However, the colony's slave population grew considerably.

Migration

As rapid population growth quickly reduced the supply of vacant farmland in those areas settled first, many families had to seek land elsewhere. The Dutch from Kings County and New York City migrated east into Queens County, west to Staten Island and New Jersey, and north into the lower Hudson Valley. Those in and around Albany and Kingston spread out on both sides of the Hudson River and up the Mohawk and Schoharie valleys, along with Palatine immigrants, but were prevented from expanding further westward by treaties with the Iroquois.

English families on Long Island migrated north into Westchester, Dutchess, and Orange counties, and west to Staten Island and New Jersey. The eighteenth century saw the beginning of a steadily increasing migration of New Englanders into the Hudson Valley and areas north of Albany, concentrated at first where the Dutch had not settled. During this period there was some migration into New York City from surrounding areas, as well as from abroad.

The American Revolution largely halted immigration from Europe, but brought new waves of migration. Many New Yorkers remained loyal to the Crown, and the southern counties remained in British hands until the war ended in 1783. Some Loyalist refugees fled to those counties, while some supporters of independence fled from them. For a particularly large but temporary migration from eastern Long Island to Connecticut, see Frederic Mather's *Refugees of 1776 from Long Island to Connecticut*. When the British military evacuated New York in November 1783, large numbers of Loyalists left with them; most went to Nova Scotia and New Brunswick while others went to Upper Canada (Ontario), Quebec, and England. See, for example, Gavin K. Watt's *Loyalist Refugees: Non-Military Refugees in Quebec 1776–1784*.

Approximately 3,000 black Loyalists left New York with certificates of freedom from the British, who also arranged their transport to Nova Scotia. They were all listed in the "Book of Negroes"; a transcript and scanned images are online at *blackloyalist.info*. Many colonial New York families of all backgrounds have branches in Canada today.

Naturalization

In 1664 the English required the inhabitants of New Netherland to take an oath of allegiance to the king that made them British subjects; similar oaths were repeated at later dates. Immigrants entering the colony after 1664 had to be naturalized to enjoy the same rights as British subjects, including the right to own land. Naturalization was expensive, but a more affordable process known as denization also allowed for land ownership. Both of these procedures required action in London. However, in 1740 Parliament allowed the colonial government to naturalize aliens, provided that they had resided in the colony for seven years and had taken Protestant communion in the previous month. Quakers and Jews were exempted from the latter requirement.

During the Revolution oaths of allegiance—often made under duress—were demanded by both sides. Residents of the American-occupied counties became citizens under the state constitution of 1777; this was extended to the entire state at the end of 1783.

1783–1825: Early Statehood Period

After the Revolution the federal and state governments concluded treaties with the Iroquois nations that opened up central and western New York to settlement, except for small Native American reservations. The period leading up to the completion of the Erie Canal in 1825 thus saw significant changes in where people lived and who became landowners. By 1825 the population had exploded to five times what it had been in 1790. This was primarily due to high birth rates, but also to immigration from Europe and migration into New York from New England and other states.

Immigration

Although there are few passenger lists before federal records began in 1820, other evidence indicates that the number of immigrants from Europe remained relatively low during most of this period, with the largest numbers coming from Great Britain, Ireland, and the German states. Many immigrants who arrived between 1817 and 1825 helped build the Erie Canal.

Migration

The breakup of the colonial manors of the Hudson Valley and the "acquisition" of what is now northern, central, and western New York from the American Indians made huge amounts of land available for settlement. The new settlers included those born in New York, many migrants from New England, and some from New Jersey and Pennsylvania. Large numbers of American Indians left New York for Canada or the West. Beginning in 1786 those who remained were settled on reservations. See chapter 14, Peoples of New York, American Indian, for more information.

Land was offered to veterans of the American Revolutionary War. This "Military Tract" comprised 1.8 million acres through the center of the state. Some veterans moved to the proffered land, but many sold their tracts instead. See chapter 7, Land Records, for additional details. This period also saw dramatic growth in the state's cities. There were large migrations to New York City from Long Island, the lower Hudson Valley, New Jersey, and New England, as well as from Europe.

Naturalization

In 1790 Congress passed the first federal naturalization act, which delegated the responsibility of naturalization to any court (town, city, county, state, or federal) with a clerk and seal. This act made an alien eligible for naturalization after only two years of residence. That requirement was raised to five years in 1795, and then to 14 years in 1798, before returning to five years in 1802.

1825–1866: The National Period

In addition to the immigrants who came to America between 1817 and 1825 to help build the Erie Canal, large numbers of people relocated to work not only on the main canal but also on its subsequent extensions and tributaries. New settlements were built along the canal to house the workers and later to serve the flow of migrants. The Erie Canal was the first of many transportation revolutions to have an enormous impact on immigration and migration. Railroads also transformed land travel. The ease of moving people and goods led to new settlements and fueled an economic boom throughout the state.

Immigration

Throughout this period there was a substantial growth in New York's population largely due to an influx of immigrants, predominantly Irish and German peoples, including German Jews (see tables in the introduction to chapter 14, Peoples of New York). This influx reached a peak during the Great Famine (1845–1852) in Ireland and the crop failures and 1848 revolutions in the German states. The third largest group of immigrants came from Great Britain. At New York and other United States ports of entry, the cost involved in processing all these new arrivals, especially those who arrived in need of medical attention after a grueling voyage, led to spirited political debate.

New York State responded by establishing a Board of Emigration Commissioners and by opening a state "immigration station" at Castle Garden, in what is now lower Manhattan, in 1855.

Table 1: Selected Naturalization Records: Originals and Online Locations

Repository	Originator of Record— Declarations and Petitons	Time Frame	Index	Online
County Courts	County Courts	Varies by county 1790–1956	County Courts & image within record set	*FamilySearch.org* (some records for 45 counties)
NARA-NYC	NY Federal Courts and U.S. Military	1792-1960	NARA-NYC	*Ancestry.com, Fold3.com*
NARA-NYC	NYC Courts—Local, State, Federal	1792–1906	NARA-NYC GGG* & IGG*	*Ancestry.com, Fold3.com*
County Court	County Court—Clinton County	1840–1906		*FamilySearch.org*
NARA-NYC		1851–1906	GGG & IGG	*Ancestry.com, Fold3.com*
County Court	County Court—Essex County	1799–1956		*FamilySearch.org*
NARA-NYC		1840–1906	GGG & IGG	*Ancestry.com Fold3.com*

Other local, town, county, state, and federal court records are not currently online, see County Guides for more information

*German Genealogy Group (*germangenealogygroup.com*) or Italian Genealogical Group (*italiangen.org*). Jewish Genealogical Society (*jgsny.org*) for 1907–1924 Kings County index.

The Castle Garden website, *castlegarden.org*, has a name index, 1820–1913. The state agency managed immigrants "in distress," established a labor exchange, and arranged transportation west. To fund this activity, New York levied a "head tax" on each person who landed at the port; this created a steady income stream for the state.

Travel by ship—first sailing ships, then steamships—to the United States was not without danger. A surprising number of ships were wrecked, or sank, en route to New York and other ports, often with loss of life. Frank A. Biebel's recent book, *The Shipwrecked Passenger Book: Sailing Westbound From Europe for the Americas, 1817–1875*, lists many of these ships and their passengers and crew. Many of these names do not appear on other lists.

Some immigrants returned to Europe, either to visit or remain; if they returned they would show up again in later United States passenger lists. Between 1858 and 1870 the British government kept records of passengers arriving from North America at British or Irish ports, in an attempt to detect Fenians (Irish nationalists) or their supporters. James Maher's *Returning Home* gives the names of the more than 42,000 passengers in these records, roughly one-third each Irish, English, and Scottish, with a few "Americans."

Migration

More than one million New Yorkers left the state as part of the westward expansion movement. New Englanders continued to enter the state, though many of them just passed through on their way west. This period also saw continued migration from rural areas into the cities. The Civil War affected the movement of those who fought and those who moved to avoid fighting. The Underground Railroad moved thousands of fugitive slaves from the South on their way to freedom in northern states and Canada.

Naturalization

Since the American Revolution, when patriot soldiers were made citizens, army veterans have had special access to naturalization. In 1862 a law was passed allowing honorably discharged Army veterans of any war to petition for naturalization after living in the United States for one year; they were not required to file a declaration of intention. In 1894 this privilege was extended to honorably discharged five-year veterans of the Navy or Marine Corps.

1866–1924: Post-Civil War and Peak Immigration Period

The Industrial Revolution, and particularly advances in transportation, continued to bring significant increases to New York's population. This period saw the introduction of steamships that transported more immigrants more rapidly, facilitating the "Great Wave" of American immigration from about 1881 to 1924.

Immigration

The variety of business opportunities and the greater ease of travel led to an increasing number of immigrants entering the port of New York. Germans (including many German Jews) and Irish continued to be the largest immigrant groups, followed by the British and Scandinavians. Beginning at the turn of the twentieth century, immigration greatly increased by people from southern and eastern Europe, particularly Italians and the varied populations of the Austro-Hungarian and Russian Empires—including large numbers of Polish and Jewish immigrants. More than 20 million immigrants arrived in New York State in these four decades.

The rapid growth in the numbers of immigrants drew the attention of the federal government and led to the creation of the U.S. Immigration Service in 1891. In that year Congress took the regulation of immigration away from the individual states. Ellis Island opened in 1892 as a federal immigration station. It replaced the state-run Castle Garden, where immigrations had been processed from 1855 to April 1890, and its successor office, the federal government's temporary Barge Office (April 1890–1891).

In 1897 a major fire destroyed the Castle Garden immigration station and its records. For this reason researchers rely on U.S. Customs lists (ship's manifests) from 1819 to 1897, and U.S. Immigration lists for the years after 1897.

The huge influx of immigrants in the years prior to World War I significantly changed the composition of the population in many parts of the country and led to agitation to restrict the flow. During the war (1914–1918) few people could leave Europe, but when the conflict ended, large-scale immigration resumed. This motivated Congress to enact a restrictive quota system in 1921and to tighten it in 1924. The period between World War I and World War II saw an increase in people arriving from the West Indies, Cuba, Mexico, and other countries in the Americas, as well as migration from Puerto Rico.

Entering New York from Canada

Before 1895 many unrecorded immigrants entered America from Canada. Canada collected detailed information on its own immigrants but significantly less on those who were booked to travel on to America. These records can be found in the Library and Archives of Canada.

In 1894 the United States designated several immigration ports of entry along the northern border; immigration records for those ports date from 1895. Federal immigration inspectors were then stationed at Canadian ports of entry to collect complete United States passenger manifests for United States-bound passengers. Because the transatlantic crossing to Canada cost much less and entry through Ellis Island could be slow, many European passengers traveled to New York via Canada. From 1895 to 1954 all records were maintained in St. Albans, Vermont (a records center, not a port of entry).

Naturalization

The great wave of immigration in the late-nineteenth century led to a substantial increase in the number of people who sought to become citizens. This created a breeding ground for fraud and widespread corruption, which came to the attention of the federal government. Major legislation passed in 1906 created the federal Naturalization Service to standardize fees, forms, and procedures; the Bureau of Immigration became the Bureau of Immigration and Naturalization.

Before this date, the naturalization process was not standardized and could occur in any court. Courts collected different information and had different requirements, often according to the whim of the presiding judge, so documents sometimes contain minimal information.

After 1906 nonfederal courts could still process naturalizations, but they were required to record the information in a manner regulated by the federal government. This information included the names of family members, birth dates and places, marriage dates and places, names of ships and ports of arrival, previous residences, occupations, children's names, birthplaces, current residences, as well as names, occupations, and residences of witnesses.

All naturalization records from this period were required to be prepared in duplicate; the naturalization court retained the original, and the duplicate copy was sent to the Bureau of Immigration and Naturalization in Washington, DC, where it was added to the certificate or C-file. C-files contain copies of records granting naturalized United States citizenship by courts from 1906 to 1956. The Certificates of Citizenship to people who derived or resumed United States citizenship may also be in these files. Some, but not all, C-file documents are duplicated in the records of naturalization courts.

Gradually the new Naturalization Service worked to encourage all courts to relinquish their power to the federal courts. This was unpopular with the county and town courts as it deprived them of a source of income. New York was particularly reluctant to relinquish this power and continued to process naturalizations until the mid-1920s and to file declarations of intention until the 1950s. The federal naturalization process consists of a certificate of arrival verifying entry into the United States, a declaration of intention (commonly known as first papers), and the petition. The law does not require the certificate of arrival to be kept; the clerk of the court can decide whether to keep it.

There have been many adjustments to United States nationality law over the years, particularly as it relates to derivative citizenship for family members and changes in regulations regarding women. Before 1906 wives and children received derivative citizenship through their husbands but were rarely named on naturalization papers. Adult women were seldom naturalized individually until the law of September 22, 1922 (the Married Women's Act, also known as the Cable Act) required all women to file separately; see Marian Smith's article " 'Any Woman Who is Now or May Hereafter be Married . . .' Women and Naturalization, ca. 1802–1940." If persons arrived in the United States as minors, they were not always required to file declarations of intention when applying for citizenship.

Under the 1906 act, a woman who was a United States citizen lost her citizenship when she married an alien, and could regain it only by terminating her marriage. Right after women gained the right to vote, the 1922 Cable Act revoked this provision and created a procedure for women to regain their citizenship.

An act of May 9, 1918, allowed aliens serving in the United States armed forces during "the present war" (World War I) to file a petition for naturalization without requiring a declaration of intention or five years of residence. The National Archives and Records Administration (NARA) provides the statistic that over 192,000 aliens were naturalized under this act, between May 9, 1918, and June 30, 1919.

1924–Present

Immigration

The Immigration Act of 1924 created a permanent quota system that cut the 1921 annual quota from 358,000 to 164,000, reducing the immigration limit to two percent of each foreign group (whether born in their mother country or in the United States) living in the United States in 1890. The new law cut the quota by 29 percent for northern and western European countries and by 87 percent for southern and eastern Europe. It also barred entry to those designated ineligible for citizenship under existing laws, which effectively ended the immigration of all Asians. There had been very little Asian immigration to New York, and the largest group, the Chinese, had been barred from immigrating since 1882. See also the section on the Chinese in chapter 14, Peoples of New York. The quota system did not apply to countries in the western hemisphere. In the 1930s, for the first time in United States history, the number of people leaving the country was greater than the number of people entering it.

When the Immigration Act of 1924 was passed, all immigrants had to obtain visas from an American consul in their countries of origin. No longer needed as an immigration processing center, Ellis Island was used predominantly as a detainee station from 1924 to 1954; it is now the American Family Immigration History Center. The exhibitions tell the story of Ellis Island and feature a number of original records.

The Alien Act of 1940 required alien (noncitizen) registration, which generated records (A-files and AR-2 files) that are useful to family historians. Aliens living in the United States registered at their local post office; new immigrants over the age of 14 years registered upon arrival in the United States. Registration consisted of a two-page form and fingerprints. See table 2 for the differences between A-Files and AR-2 files.

Table 2: Differences Between AR-2 Files and A-Files

	AR-2 Files	A-Files
Time Period	Aug. 1, 1940–Mar. 31, 1944	Apr. 1, 1944–May 1, 1951
Format	Originals microfilmed then destroyed	Original records exist for any active case of an immigrant not yet naturalized
Location	U.S. Citizenship and Immigration Service (USCIS) maintains this microfilm containing nearly 6 million AR-2 forms	USCIS, Washington, DC (more than 70 million records)
A-number	These immigrants have an A-number below 8 million (A8000000), but unless their case was reopened after 1944 (e.g., for a naturalization application) they will have no A-file	These immigrants have an A-number above 8 million
Naturalization	When an alien is naturalized all records are moved to a C-File and the A-File ceases to exist	
Contents	Visas, photographs, applications, affidavits, correspondence, etc.	
Access	Available to all researchers through the USCIS Genealogy Program: *www.uscis.gov/genealogy*; fees apply	Records must be requested via the USCIS Freedom of Information and Privacy Act program

The War Brides Act of 1945 and its subsequent amendments allowed more than 100,000 non-Asian spouses and natural and adopted children of United States military personnel to enter the country between 1945 and 1948.

The 1924 quota system regulating immigration from many countries remained in force until 1965. The shortage in the labor force that it created was filled by migration from other parts of the country and by immigration to New York from the Caribbean, especially the British West Indies, which was not restricted by quotas. In the 1930s the relatively large German quota was used by many refugees escaping from the Nazis, and after the war other refugee groups were admitted by special legislation.

In 1965 Congress passed a new act that abolished the old quota system and gave immigrants from all countries equal access. The number of immigrants to be admitted from any one country in a given year was limited, but for most countries was generous compared to the old system. This law brought large numbers of new immigrants to New York from all over the world, but especially from Latin America, Asia, and Eastern Europe.

Migration

American cities continued to grow as a result of immigration and migration from rural areas of New York and other states. This growth continued until after World War II, when a large exodus from the cities to the suburbs began. The urban population loss from that exodus was offset by new waves of migration from other parts of the country. African Americans from the south who had been coming to New York in large numbers for many years continued to migrate after World War II, mostly to the cities. Puerto Ricans, who were made United States citizens in 1917, began migrating, particularly to New York City, especially during and after World War II.

Later in the twentieth century there was a noticeable migration out of New York to other states, especially to the so-called Sun Belt, but this decrease in population was offset by new immigration under the 1965 act. New York City and its suburbs remain a major destination for migrants, notably young people, as well as immigrants.

Immigration Records
1609–1664: New Netherland

Immigration records do not exist for many of those who arrived in the Dutch colony in this period, but see Harry Macy Jr.'s "Researching the People of New Netherland and Their Descendants . . ." for sources that identify passengers coming from Amsterdam, their ships, and dates. Resources include *Passengers to New Netherland 1654 to 1664; Noord Amerika Chronologie 1598–1750*; Pim Nieuwenhuis' article in *New Netherland Connections; Van Rensselaer Bowier Manuscripts: . . .*; and the Van Rensselaer Manor papers at the New York State Library (NYSL). A list of ships that sailed to the colony is available at *olivetreegenealogy.com*. It is sometimes possible to match a ship with an approximate date of arrival.

For immigration data on English settlers other than those who came by way of Amsterdam, researchers should consult research guides for New England, Virginia, or other English colonies. A good place to start is Robert Anderson's *Great Migration* series, which currently covers all New England settlers through 1635. Some of these settlers (or their descendants) ended up in either New Netherland or the English towns of eastern Long Island. See chapter 1, Colonial Era.

1664–1819: The English Colonial, Revolutionary and Early Statehood Periods

There are few immigration records for the period 1664–1819, a significant exception being those pertaining to the Palatines as shown in *The Palatine Families of New York* and other books by Henry Z Jones, Jr. Also see Carl Boyer's *Ship Passenger Lists: New York and New Jersey 1600–1825*.

1820–1891: U.S. Customs Records for Passenger Arrivals

During this period there was a significant increase in the number of available records generated. In 1819 Congress passed the Steerage Act that, beginning in 1820, required the captains of vessels arriving from foreign ports to file passenger lists with the United States Customs Collector. This led to limits on the number of people per ship, which greatly improved conditions for voyagers.

These lists are often referred to as the ship's manifest, ship list, ship passenger list, or passenger manifest. The passenger information recorded included name, age, sex, occupation, country of origin, and country of intended settlement; it might also say "died on board," and could provide information on the cause of death. Though customs records can be incomplete, the number of questions would grow in future years making these lists increasingly useful to genealogists.

As the United States Customs collector was a federal agent, the original United States Customs records are now held by NARA in Record Group 36 in two microfilm publications: M237, Passenger Lists of Vessels Arriving at New York, New York, 1820–1897 and M261, Index to Passenger Lists of Vessels Arriving at New York, New York, 1820–1846.

Most of this microfilm has been digitized and is available online from *Ancestry.com*. Indexes are available on *FamilySearch.org* and *Castlegarden.org*, although not all were created with the same level of accuracy or completeness. (Castle Garden's is known to be incomplete.)

1892–1924: Ellis Island and Other Federal Immigration Records

The manifest prepared at the port of departure was taken off each ship when it arrived at Ellis Island. The list is usually divided into cabin passengers (first and second class) and steerage (sometimes listed as third class). Ellis Island staff processed the manifests for all passengers (and crew); they also generated the additional "List of Detained Aliens" record and/or "Record of Aliens Held for Special Inquiry" lists. These records were often placed at the back of the ship's manifest at the end of the day. As a result, a passenger's name can appear more than once; researchers are advised to check the records placed at the end of the manifest, as these records can include additional information. Sometimes the records will provide a cross reference to other listings for the same person, e.g., 12/15, which means "page 12, line 15." Marian Smith's article "Manifest

Table 3: Selected Immigration Records (1820–1950s) and Indexes: Original Records and Online Locations

Type of Record	Location	Date Range	Repository/Website[1]

Passenger Arrivals
   U.S. Customs Lists 1820–1897
   U.S. Immigration Service post-1897
	New York	1820–1957
		indexes 1820–1846 and 1897–1948
		1820–1957
			NARA originals, *Ancestry.com*

Passenger Arrivals	Castle Garden, New York	1820–1890 Indexes 1855–1890	*Ancestry.com, castlegarden.org*
Passenger Arrivals	Barge Office	1890–1891	*Ancestry.com*
Passenger Arrivals	Ellis Island, New York[2]	1892–1954	*ellisisland.org*[2], *Ancestry.com*
Passenger Arrivals	Canada	1865–1957 1865–1935	Library and Archives of Canada *Ancestry.com*
Border Crossings	U.S.–Canada	1895–1954	NARA originals, *Ancestry.com*
Crew Lists	New York	1820–1957	NARA originals, *Ancestry.com*

1. Other websites also have online records or indexes, e.g., *FamilySearch.org*
2. Records include all passengers and classes arriving at the Port of New York (not only those processed at Ellis Island). For example, some manifests list passengers going on to Canada—their records might show who they are going to live with in Canada.

Markings: A Guide to Interpreting Passenger List Annotations," is a helpful aid for passenger lists with annotations.

Cabin passengers (first and second class) had the luxury of being "processed" on board ship instead of on Ellis Island. They were still asked the same questions and received a medical examination. Their information will be found in the Ellis Island records along with the steerage passengers. If they failed the medical exam, they would have been detained at Ellis Island and will appear on the detained passenger lists. For example, in 1905 there are records for 800,000 steerage passengers who passed through Ellis Island, but only 3,000 of 100,000 cabin passengers had to pass through Ellis Island for additional medical checks.

After 1906 the number of ship passengers who were American citizens increased. Passengers who were American citizens may be listed separately or listed with their passenger class (first, second, steerage, etc.). Some websites include those passengers, and some do not. Sometimes these lists were cross referenced, and sometimes not.

Some passengers may not be found because they traveled under assumed names or because their names were illegible and indexed incorrectly. Stowaways may not have appeared on the embarkation lists, but were usually found during the voyage. They will be identified as stowaways in Ellis Island records—sometimes listed with the crew members if they were made to "work their passage."

The Ellis Island records and the post-1895 Canadian border crossings are found in NARA record group 85, Records of the Immigration and Naturalization Service 1891–1857, Pacific and Atlantic Ports, 1895–1954 (M1464, 640 microfilm rolls), and are also available on *Ancestry.com*.

The website of the Ellis Island Foundation (*libertyellisfoundation.org*) has indexes and digitized images to most records from 1892 to 1957. The commemorative certificate offered by this website is compiled from transcriptions.

Not all federal immigration and naturalization records are digitized; see tables 1 and 3 for those records that are online as of the date of this publication.

Naturalization Records
1609–1782: New Netherland, English Colonial, and Revolutionary Periods
For naturalizations and related procedures, the first place to check is Kenneth Scott and Kenn Stryker-Rodda's *Denizations, Naturalizations, and Oaths of Allegiance in Colonial New York*, with its excellent introduction and several lists of names. Omitted from this book are naturalizations and denizations conferred in London, for which researchers can consult *Publications of the Huguenot Society of London* (*Quarto Series*), volumes 18, 24, and 27. Joel Munsell's *The*

Annals of Albany contains some oaths of allegiance. See also chapter 1, Colonial Era.

1782–1790: Early Statehood Period
Legislative sessions between 1782 and 1789 contain a few acts of naturalization. The original publications of the session laws are now rare books found only in a few large law libraries, but they have been reproduced on microfilm. The session laws between 1777 and 1801 were republished as *Laws of the State of New York* in five volumes. These volumes have been indexed and are available on microfilm at the New York State Archives (NYSA); the index and most volumes are online at *HathiTrust.org*.

1790–1933
Beginning in 1790 naturalization records may be found in court records at all levels of government. The counties of New York State are the primary repositories of these early records, as well as many records created after the 1906 legislation. See the County Guides for information on county holdings. Researchers will find some naturalization records and indexes online. A digitized card index is available on *FamilySearch.org* for some counties as early as 1790, but for most counties in the indexes start later, at various dates (e.g., 1820, 1847, 1859, or 1906). The court specified on the index may be searched for the original naturalization record.

The records for most naturalizations that took place in New York federal courts are held by NARA at New York City (NARA-NYC). Their holdings also include images of the dexigraphs (photostatic copies) from local, county, and state courts that were located in New York City. Researchers are advised to contact NARA-NYC prior to visiting to determine whether the record or microfilm required is available on site, or needs to be ordered from offsite storage.

Digitization partnerships have made most of these NARA naturalization records available to *Ancestry.com* and *Fold3.com* subscribers; over time, many of the records may become freely available on NARA's website. The Ancestry database names for these records are "New York, Naturalization Petitions 1794–1906" and "New York, Index to Petitions for Naturalization filed in Federal, State, and Local Courts located in New York City, 1792–1989." Record sets on *Fold3.com* often have names which closely match NARA titles.

For genealogists, naturalization records for 1906 and later are significantly more useful, as the information reported includes the applicant's and spouse's names and residences; occupations; the date and court where the applicant's declaration of intention was filed; applicant's and spouse's birth dates and places; marriage date and place; children's names, birthplaces, and current residences; name of ship and port of arrival; last foreign residence; and names, occupations, and residences of witnesses. All post-1906 naturalization records are filed by number.

1933–Present

In 1933 the Bureau of Immigration and the Bureau of Naturalization became the Immigration and Naturalization Service (INS). Seventy years later, in 2003, the INS function was divided, and the U. S. Citizenship and Immigration Service (USCIS) became the agency primarily concerned with immigration records and processes. The USCIS is now part of the Department of Homeland Security.

The INS/USCIS processes arrival records of all immigrants after July 1, 1924. For New York and New Jersey, most records for both immigration and naturalization will be found at NARA in New York City. The NARA Microfilm Reading Room in Washington, DC, holds a complete set of microfilmed Customs and INS arrival records. Additional correspondence and supporting materials can frequently be found in the USCIS Research Library. See table 3 for details on collections, locations, and access.

The USCIS Genealogy Program (*uscis.gov/genealogy*) has an index search program if the file number is not known or the researcher wishes to ensure all available files in the USCIS collection will be identified. Records available under this program include naturalization, alien and visa files, alien registration forms, and registry files. See listing below for dates of holdings.

Both the USCIS website and the NARA website (*www.archives. gov/research*) provide reliable information on the history of immigration and naturalization and the different types of records. The NARA website has searchable catalogs, so researchers can find details on existing records by series, title, or file group. NARA's Access to Archival Databases (AAD) allows searches for individual names. The AAD includes "Record Data Files" from documents in NARA's collections, as well as records that were created digitally; they do not include scanned images.

Selected Repositories

See the listings for NARA, NARA-NYC, and websites significant to research in chapter 16, National and Statewide Repositories & Resources.

United States Citizenship and Immigration Services (USCIS), Washington, DC

USCIS Genealogy Program • PO Box 805925
Chicago, IL 60680-4120 • (866) 259-2349 (for voice mail messages)
Email: Genealogy.uscis@dhs.gov • *uscis.gov/genealogy*
Contact information for local offices is on the website.

The USCIS has indexes of immigration and naturalization records and will perform searches (for a fee) that provide a list of file numbers for an individual. It holds Naturalization Certificate Files (C-files, 1906–1956; most on microfilm, some in paper form), Alien Registration Forms (AR-2 files, 1940–1944 on microfilm), Visa files (1924–1944 in paper form), Registry Files (1929–1944 in paper form) and Alien Files

(A-files, numbers below 8 million, documents dated prior to May 1, 1951 on microfilm; A-files numbered above eight million are subject to the Freedom of Information Act).

Center for Migration Studies

27 Carmine Street • New York, NY 10014 • (212) 337-3080
Office: 209 Flagg Place • Staten Island, NY 10304-1122
Email: archives@cmsny.org • *cmsny.org/archives*

The Center's collections include case histories of immigrants who received assistance from agencies on Ellis Island; papers of selected individual immigrants who achieved notable success; records of the National Catholic Welfare Conference, Bureau of Immigration; and photographs that document the immigrant experience with a focus on Italian Americans from the nineteenth to twenty-first centuries.

Ellis Island:
American Family Immigration History Center

The Statue of Liberty-Ellis Island Foundation, Inc.
17 Battery Place, #210 • PO Box ELLIS
New York, NY 10004-3507 • Email: historycenter@ellisisland.org
(212) 561-4588 • *LibertyEllisFoundation.org*

Twelve million immigrants passed through Ellis Island between 1892 and 1924. The digitized records of passenger arrivals can be accessed via the website. Visitors to Ellis Island can also access more than 22 million digitized records in the American Family Immigration History Center.

Immigrant Ships Transcribers Guild

The website (*Immigrantships.net*) provides free access to thousands of transcribed passenger manifests for New York ship arrivals from 1623 to 1956. Data is transcribed by volunteers from original documents, newspapers, and non-copyrighted publications.

Shipindex.org

The website includes listings of the ships on which immigrants arrived and information regarding those ships. It also includes a resource list with links. The site offers some free access; more recent content requires a subscription.

Selected Bibliography and Further Reading

See chapter 14, Peoples of New York, for additional resources that pertain to specific ethnic groups.

Immigration

Biebel, Frank A. *The Shipwrecked Passenger Book: Sailing Westbound from Europe for the Americas, 1817–1875*. Compact Disc. New York: The Author, 2013. [*books. FamilySearch.org and NYG&B eLibrary*]

Boyer, Carl. *Ship Passenger Lists, New York and New Jersey (1600–1825)*. Newhall, CA: C. Boyer, 1978.

Coldham, Peter W. *Emigrants from England to the American Colonies, 1773–1776*. Baltimore: Genealogical Publishing Co., 1998.

Colletta, John P. *They Came In Ships: A Guide to Finding Your Immigrant Ancestor's Arrival Record*. Salt Lake City: Ancestry, 2002.

Davis, Damani. "Ancestors from the West Indies: A Historical and Genealogical Overview of Afro-Caribbean Immigration, 1900–1930s." *Prologue*, vol. 45, no. 3 (Fall-Winter 2013): 66–72. While this article focuses on African American immigration, the sources cited can be used for all immigrant groups.

Filby, P. William. *Passenger and Immigration Lists Bibliography 1538–1900: Being a Guide to Published Lists of Arrivals in the United States and Canada*. 2nd edition. Detroit: Gale Research Co., 1988.

Filby, P. William, and Dorothy M. Lower. *Passenger and Immigration Lists Index: A Guide to Published Arrival Records of more than 1,775,000 Passengers Who Came to the New World between the Sixteenth and the Early Twentieth Centuries 1896–90 cumulated supplements*. Detroit: Gale Research Co., 1990.

Hoff, Henry B. *English Origins of American Colonists: From the New York Genealogical and Biographical Record*. Baltimore: Genealogical Publishing Co., 1991.

Jones, Henry Z, Jr. *The Palatine Families of New York*. 2 vols. Rockland, ME: Picton Press, 2001.

Macy, Harry, Jr. "Researching the People of New Netherland and Their Descendants: How to Identify and Make Best Use of the Available Sources." Program syllabus from Finding Your New Netherland Roots. New York: NYG&B Society, 2009. Published as a Research Aid on *NewYorkFamilyHistory.org*.

Maher, James P. *Returning Home. Transatlantic Migration from North America to Britain & Ireland, 1858–1870*. Dublin, Ireland: Eneclann, 2004.

Morton Allan Directory of European Passenger Steamship Arrivals for the Years 1890 to 1930 at the Port of New York and for the Years 1904 to 1926 at the Ports of New York, Philadelphia, Boston, and Baltimore. Baltimore: Genealogical Publishing Co., 2001. First published 1931 by Morton Allan.

New York State Library, Nicolaas de Roever, Arnold Johan Ferdinand van Laer, Kiliaen van Rensselaer. *Van Rensselaer Bowier Manuscripts: Being the Letters of Kiliaen van Rensselaer, 1630–1643, and . . . .* Albany: University of the State of New York, 1908. Includes appendix Settlers of Rensselaerswyck.

Nieuwenhuis, Pim. "Abstracts from Notarial Documents in the Amsterdam Archives." *New Netherland Connections*, vol. 4 (1999) no. 3: 65–70, no. 4: 90–93; vol. 5 (2000) no. 1: 23–28, no. 2: 50–56, no. 3: 78–81.

Noord Amerika Chronologie 1598–1750. Amsterdam, Netherlands: Gemeentearchief Amsterdam. Microfilm of 5000 cards containing abstracts from Amsterdam notarial records with places of origin for immigrants to New Netherland 1598–1750 many of them indicating places of origin for immigrants to New Netherland. [microfilm at NYPL, NYSL]

O'Callaghan, Edmund B. "Early Highland [Scots] Immigration to New York." *The Historical Magazine and Notes and Queries Concerning the Antiquities, History and Biography of America*, vol. V, no. 10. (October 1861): 301–304.

"Passengers to New Netherland 1654 to 1664." Year Book of the Holland Society of New York for 1902. New York: Knickerbocker Press, 1902.

Smith, Marian L. "By Way of Canada: U.S. Records of Immigration Across the U.S.-Canadian Border, 1895–1954 (St. Albans Lists)." *Prologue*, vol. 32, no. 3 (Fall 2000): 192–199. [*archives.gov*]

———. "A Guide to Interpreting Passenger List Annotations." Digitally published by JewishGen, 2002. *www.jewishgen.org/InfoFiles/Manifests*.

Tepper, Michael. *Immigrants to the Middle Colonies: a Consolidation of Ship Passenger Lists and Associated Data from the New York Genealogical and Biographical Record*. Baltimore: Genealogical Publishing Co., 1978.

Van Laer, Arnold Johan Ferdinand, ed. *Settlers of Rensselaerswyck, 1630–1658*. Reprinted Baltimore: Genealogical Publishing Co., 1965. Appendix to *Van Rensselaer Bowier Manuscripts* (see above). Transcription of *Settlers of Rensselaerswyck* text available online on Rensselaer County Genweb.

Migration

Anderson, Robert Charles. *The Great Migration Begins: Immigrants to New England, 1620–1633*. 3 vols. Boston: New England Historic Genealogical Society, 1995.

———. *The Great Migration: Immigrants to New England, 1634–1635*. 7 vols. Boston: New England Historic Genealogical Society, 2011.

Mather, Frederic G. *The Refugees of 1776 from Long Island to Connecticut*. Albany: J. B. Lyon, 1913.

Watt, Gavin K. *Loyalist Refugees: Non-Military Refugees in Quebec 1776–1784*. Milton, Ontario: Global Heritage Press, 2014.

Naturalization

Austin, John D. *Naturalization Records of New York State*. Syracuse: New York State Council of Genealogical Organizations, 2001.

Bockstruck, Lloyd DeWitt. *Denizations and Naturalizations in the British Colonies in America, 1607–1775*. Baltimore: Genealogical Publishing Co., 2005.

Corn, Leslie. "New York State Supreme Court Naturalization Records in the New York County Clerk's Office." *NYG&B Newsletter* (now *New York Researcher*), Fall 1999 and Winter 2000. Published as a Research Aid on *NewYorkFamilyHistory.org*. Part 1 1907–1924 and Part 2 Colonial Period through 1906.

Hoff, Henry B. "Published New York City Naturalizations." *NYG&B Newsletter* (now *New York Researcher*), Spring 1993. Published as a Research Aid on *NewYorkFamilyHistory.org*.

Munsell, Joel. *The Annals of Albany*. 10 vols. Albany: J. Munsell, 1849–1859. Available on microfiche.

Newman, John J. *American Naturalization Records, 1790–1990: What They Are and How to Use Them*. Bountiful, UT: Heritage Quest, 1998.

New York (State). *Laws of the State of New York (1887)*. Albany: Weed, Parsons, 1887.

———. *Laws of the State of New York: Passed at the Sessions of the Legislature Held in the Years 1777–1801*. 5 vols. Albany: Weed, Parsons, 1886–1887.

New York State Archives. "Naturalization and Related Records." Information Leaflet no. 6. www.archives.nysed.gov/a/research/res_topics_gen_naturalization.shtml.

———. "Pathfinder Chronology of Naturalization in New York State." www.archives.nysed.gov/a/research/res_tools_nysa_path_nat.shtml.

O'Neill, Terri Bradshaw. "Naturalizations in the New York Secretary of State Deeds, 1689–1717." *NYG&B Record*, vol. 139, no. 3 (2008): 186–196. [NYG&B eLibrary]

Penrose, Maryly B. "New York Naturalizations, 1789." *NYG&B Record*, vol. 112, no. 1 (January 1981): 16–17. [NYG&B eLibrary]

Publications of the Huguenot Society of London (Quarto Series), vols. 18, 24, and 27. London: Huguenot Society Publishing, 1911, 1921, 1923. Vol. 18, edited by William A. Shaw, *Letters of Denization & Acts of Naturalization (for Aliens) in England & Ireland, 1603–1700*. Vol. 24, edited by M. S. Giuseppi, *Naturalizations of Foreign Protestants in the American and West Indian Colonies (under Stat. 13 Geo II)*. Vol. 27, edited by William A. Shaw, *Letters of Denization & Acts of Naturalization in England & Ireland, 1701–1800*. [Vol. 24 on *Ancestry.com*]

Schaefer, Christina K. *Guide to Naturalization Records of the United States*. Baltimore: Genealogical Publishing Co., 1997.

Scott, Kenneth, and Kenn Stryker-Rodda. *Denizations, Naturalizations, and Oaths of Allegiance in Colonial New York*. Baltimore: Genealogical Publishing Co., 1975. Alphabetical listing of persons naturalized found in documents in England and in New York. [*Ancestry.com*]

Scott, Kenneth. *Early New York Naturalizations: Abstracts of Naturalizations Records from Federal, State, and Local Courts, 1792–1840*. Baltimore: Genealogical Publishing Co., 1999. [*Ancestry.com*]

———. *Naturalizations in the Marine Court New York City, 1827–1835*. New York: New York Genealogical and Biographical Society, 1990. [NYG&B eLibrary]

———. *Naturalizations in the Marine Court New York City, 1834–1840*. New York: New York Genealogical and Biographical Society, 1991. [NYG&B eLibrary]

Scott, Kenneth, and Rosanne Conway, comp. *New York Alien Residents, 1825–1848*. Baltimore: Genealogical Publishing Co., 1978.

Smith, Marian L. " 'Any Woman Who is Now or May Hereafter be Married . . .' Women and Naturalization, ca. 1802–1940." *Prologue*, vol. 30, no. 2 (Summer 1998): 146–153. [*Archives.gov*]

———. "Manifest Markings: A Guide to Interpreting Passenger List Annotations." Digitally published by JewishGen, Manifest Markings Home; last revised, September 29, 2002.

Szucs, Loretto Dennis. *They Became Americans: Finding Naturalization Records and Ethnic Origins*. Salt Lake City: Ancestry, 1998.

Wolfe, Richard J. "The Colonial Naturalization Act of 1740 with a List of Persons Naturalized in New York Colony, 1740–1769." *NYG&B Record*, vol. 94, no. 3 (1963): 132–147. [NYG&B eLibrary]

Court Records

Table 1: The New York State Unified Court System at a Glance

The New York State court system and its history are complex. This chart provides an outline of the present day New York judicial system in a simplified format and provides historical notes of interest to family historians.

Category	Court	Location	Jurisdiction	Historical Notes
Highest Court	Court of Appeals	Albany	Appeals of criminal and civil cases and matters handled by special courts.	Created in 1847 to replace the Court for the Correction of Errors, established in 1777.
Principal Trial and Appellate Court	Supreme Court (called Supreme Court of Judicature before 1847)	Organized in 13 districts with trial terms in all 62 counties; Appellate Division organized in four regional departments	Essentially unlimited jurisdiction; handles civil cases, matrimonial proceedings including divorce, separation and annulment, and felony cases in NYC. Appellate Division (with subsidiary Appellate Terms downstate) is the state's main appellate court though not its highest court.	Established in 1691 and reorganized in 1847 and 1896. Once called "Supreme Court of Judicature." Absorbed equity jurisdiction of the Court of Chancery when it was abolished in 1847. In 1896, statewide Courts of Oyer and Terminer (criminal), Circuit Courts (civil), NYC Superior Court, NYC Court of Common Pleas, City Court of Brooklyn, Superior Court of Buffalo merged into the Supreme Court.
Local Trial Courts	County Court (called Court of Common Pleas before 1847)	All counties except the five counties/boroughs of NYC	Felony cases and smaller stakes civil cases; some guardianship cases.	County Court formerly called Court of Common Pleas which had civil jurisdiction. Formed in 1691, replacing Court of Sessions, a county court established in 1684. Court of Common Pleas was reorganized and renamed in 1847. County Courts abolished in NYC outer boroughs in 1962. Court of General Sessions handled criminal cases before 1896, in Manhattan until 1962.
	Criminal Court Civil Court	New York City	Misdemeanor and violation cases; smaller stakes civil cases.	Established 1962. Succeeded NYC Municipal Court (civil) and Magistrates' Courts (criminal).
	City Courts	Cities except New York City		Established under each city charter.
	Justice Courts	In almost 1,300 towns and villages		Established in towns in the colonial period; formerly called justices of the peace (in towns) and police justices (in villages).
	District Courts	Serve Nassau County and the five western towns of Suffolk County		Established in stages starting in 1939.
Special Courts	Surrogate's Court	All counties	Probate of wills and supervision of decedent estates; some guardianship and adoption cases.	Established in 1787. Replaced the colonial Prerogative Court established in 1692 (headed by the Governor who had possessed probate jurisdiction since 1686) and its successor, the State Court of Probates (abolished 1823). Appeals lay to Court of Probates (1777–1822), Court of Chancery (1823–1847) or to Supreme Court Appellate Division (1847–present).
	Family Court	All counties	Matters involving minors; domestic disputes; adoption; guardianship. Note marital issues not in this jurisdiction.	Established 1962. Succeeded early-twentieth century Children's Court and NYC Domestic Relations Court.
	Court of Claims	Statewide jurisdiction	Claims against New York State and state institutions.	Originally established in 1883; made permanent in 1915.

Introduction

This chapter offers guidance on the resources available for researching the most genealogically pertinent court records in New York State, and explains how to locate the surviving records. Court records commonly used by genealogists can include records of civil litigation, criminal prosecutions, mortgage foreclosures, naturalizations, legal name changes, divorces, wills and estates, and bankruptcies. Information about some of these court records is found elsewhere in this book. For example:

- Chapter 6, Probate Records, covers wills and estates records created by Surrogate's Courts and predecessor courts, and guardianships
- Chapter 4, Immigration, Migration, and Naturalization, covers naturalizations and citizenship information found in court records
- Chapter 2, Vital Records, covers divorce and bastardy records

Court records are important for thorough genealogical research, but are a greater challenge than more accessible and user-friendly records such as the census. Research in court records requires time and patience. Christine Rose's *Courthouse Research for Family Historians* gives a general introduction to using court records in the United States.

Court records are created by local, state, and federal courts. The New York State courts operate on multiple levels—statewide, regional, county, district, city, town, and village. Federal courts handle cases arising under federal law, and they have a much smaller caseload than the state courts. Court records can include index books, court minutes, docket books, judgment and order books, and the actual files created in civil and criminal cases. They often provide summary documentation of a case, including the claims put forth by plaintiffs and defendants and the results of a trial, if any. If a case was appealed, the record may contain transcripts of the testimony of parties and witnesses, as well as other documents.

New York State has an unusually complicated legal system that developed when it was still a British colony, but it was restructured in 1823, 1847, 1896, and 1962. Some courts founded during and after the colonial era no longer exist today. New York State also has some uncommon legal nomenclature. For example, the New York Supreme Court is not the highest court in the state; it is primarily a trial court. The highest court in New York State is the Court of Appeals. The Historical Society of the New York Courts website is an excellent source of information on the legal history of New York (*www.nycourts.gov/history*).

Some courts have scanned recent records and made them available on their websites. A number of naturalization records are available online, but generally few court records are online or even microfilmed with the exception of probate and estate records. Court records that have been preserved can be difficult to find and use, even for legal professionals. Knowledge of legal procedures and terms as well as historical New York State court organization is ideal for in-depth research. The fourth edition of *Black's Law Dictionary* is recommended for genealogists, because it offers comprehensive definitions of archaic terms that are not included in later editions.

Before delving into court records researchers may find it helpful to have some information about the case, particularly the names and residences of the plaintiff and defendant (or petitioner if a nonadversarial case) and the type of case. Dockets and indexes are usually organized by range of dates and plaintiff's or party's name. The clues that point a researcher to court records will vary depending on the type of case. For example, a marriage certificate or a census record might include a notation that a person has been divorced, or a newspaper article may report in graphic detail on a scandalous trial civil suit, or make note of an arrest or conviction. Newspapers also print "Legal Notices" regarding bankruptcies and other legal proceedings. Newspaper articles are frequently the only surviving record of arrests and convictions for petty crimes, because few lower court records (except in New York City) survive. New York State's courts destroy noncurrent records according to a retention schedule (found on *www.nycourts.gov*) that requires permanent retention of all surviving records before certain dates, but only designated records thereafter.

Colonial Era Courts

In New Netherland the Director-General (Governor) and Council, sitting in New Amsterdam, acted as a court for the entire colony. Lower courts (of *schout* and *schepenen*) were eventually created in the various Dutch settlements. Jaap Jacobs' book *The Colony of New Netherland* gives a good description of the Dutch courts. Translations of the council minutes and records of the court at Beverwijck or Fort Orange (later Albany) have been published by the New Netherland Project (*www.nnp.org*). Arnold J. F. van Laer translated the *Minutes of the Court of Rensselaerswyck 1648–1652*. Berthold Fernow's seven-volume work, *The Records of New Amsterdam from 1653 to 1674 Anno Domini*, translates the records of New Amsterdam's city court. Proceedings of town courts during the Dutch period may be found in the records of the respective towns. English towns on eastern Long Island had courts resembling those in New England.

After assuming control of the colony in 1664, the English created a Court of Assizes in New York City (the capital of the colony), records of which have been published as part of the series *New York Historical Manuscripts: English*. Under that court were regional Courts of Session for Albany–Schenectady–Rensselaerswyck; Kingston–Hurley–Marbletown; the East, North, and West Ridings of Yorkshire (which encompassed present-day Long Island, Staten Island, and Westchester); and the Mayor's Court of New York City. A Court of Oyer and Terminer was held from time to time in the same areas to hear more serious cases. Records of some of these courts have survived and been published. Under these courts, in the lower part of the colony, were town courts whose proceedings may form part of the town records.

In 1683 New York was divided into twelve counties, and Courts of General Sessions of the Peace were established in each county. The Court of Assizes was abolished in 1684, and its jurisdiction assumed by the Court of Chancery, which had been established the previous year. In 1686 the governor of the colony was given the authority to approve probate of wills and grant letters of administration. In 1692 this jurisdiction was formalized into the Prerogative Court; local courts and "surrogates" performed administrative functions. See chapter 6, Probate Records.

The court structure was thoroughly revised in 1691 when the following changes were made:

- The Supreme Court of Judicature was established and assumed common-law and first-level appellate jurisdiction, which had been vested in the Court of Chancery since 1683.
- The Court of Chancery continued (with brief suspensions) as the colony's court of equity.
- Courts of Common Pleas were established in each county and had jurisdiction over civil suits similar to that of the Supreme Court of Judicature; the Courts of General Sessions of the Peace continued to have jurisdiction in criminal matters.

In New York City and County, the Mayor's Court was continued and functioned as a court of common pleas. The Court of Oyer and Terminer was also continued for felonies, with jurisdiction similar to the Court of General Sessions, but also included offenses punishable by death or life imprisonment. In counties with towns, the justices of the peace conducted town courts. All of these trial courts were continued after the Revolutionary War under the first state constitution of 1777, except the Prerogative Court, which was replaced by a Court of Probates. See also chapter 6, Probate Records. James Folts summarizes the history of the Supreme Court and other early courts in *"Duely & Constantly Kept": A History of the New York Supreme Court, 1691–1847 and an Inventory of Its Records (Albany, Utica, and Geneva Offices), 1797–1847*; see especially Appendix C, "Inferior Courts of Law."

New York State Courts and Court Structure

The judicial system in New York has been called the "New York State Unified Court System" since 1962 (see table 2). Its formal head is the Chief Judge of the Court of Appeals, New York's highest court. The Chief Administrative Judge is responsible for court operations statewide. The best place to start looking for information about New York State courts as they exist today is the New York State Unified Court System's comprehensive website (*www.nycourts.gov/courts*) which has:

- Records retention and disposition schedules that contain summary descriptions of records for civil, criminal, and appellate courts, as well as the specialized courts: Surrogate's Court, Family Court, and Court of Claims.
- Addresses and contact information for the courts operating on the state, county, city, district, town, and village levels, and for the county clerk's offices which hold those records of the Supreme Court and County Court that are not retained by the court clerks.
- Addresses and contact information for each county's public-access law library.
- Summary online data on civil cases in the Supreme Court, New York City Civil Court, Nassau and Suffolk District Courts, and city courts statewide as early as 1983 accessible

via the *eCourts* database at *http://iapps.courts.state.ny.us/webcivil/ecourtsMain*.

The *New York Law Journal* (*newyorklawjournal.com*) has been publishing legal news since 1888. Official reports of legally significant court decisions (case law) have been published since 1804; the reports are published commercially in the *New York Supplement*. There are also databases of case decisions for New York State published by Westlaw and Lexis; these subscription-only services are available at some public libraries. Sources of reported court decisions available at the New York State Library (NYSL) are listed at *www.nysl.nysed.gov/leghist/leghis12.htm*. For a comprehensive list, see the NYSL's list of law resources at *www.nysl.nysed.gov/collections/lawresources.htm* or a public-access law library. Many published reports on early New York cases are readily available online through resources such as *books.google.com*, *HathiTrust.org*, and *Archive.org*.

Children's Court (1921–1962); Family Court (1962–Present)

Special provisions for minors appearing before the courts were enacted in the nineteenth century, and children's courts were established in New York City and large cities upstate soon after 1900. In 1921 a Children's Court was authorized for each county; in New York City the court became part of the new Domestic Relations Court in 1933. Both courts were succeeded by the Family Court in 1962. Family Court handles cases involving juvenile delinquency; child and spousal support; child custody, abuse, and neglect; foster care; and adoptions. Case records of the Family Court and predecessor courts are legally restricted and are disclosed only by court order. Even indexes to adoption are closed.

County Court (1847–Present)

County Courts were established in 1847 for each of the counties outside New York County. They assumed the jurisdiction of the Courts of Common Pleas and Courts of General Sessions. County Courts are the main criminal courts outside New York City. These courts may also handle civil business but seldom do so; they also hear appeals from local justices' courts.

In New York County the Court of Common Pleas continued until 1895 when (along with the Superior Court) it was merged into the Supreme Court. Although Kings, Queens, and Richmond counties joined with New York County to become New York City in 1898, they continued to have their own County Courts until 1962. The present-day Bronx was part of the Westchester County Court system until 1874. From 1874 to 1914 the western Bronx was part of New York County, and from 1895 to 1914 the eastern Bronx was also part of New York County. In 1914, Bronx County was formed; the Bronx County Court was in session from 1914 to 1962.

The Family History Library (FHL) has some microfilm copies of historical County Court records. Researchers should check the catalog's listing for the county of interest. Most County Court records are in the custody of the county clerks.

Court of Chancery (1683–1847)

The Court of Chancery was established in 1683 and with a few gaps operated until 1847. Its equity jurisdiction included commercial cases, e.g., disputes over profits, payments, contracts, insurance policies, and fraud; it also assisted the common-law courts with writs of subpoena, injunction, etc. The court appointed and supervised guardians for the property of widows, minors, and other legally incompetent persons (such as "lunatics" and "drunkards"). The court also handled mortgage foreclosures and some real property partition cases. The governor of New York served as Chancellor during the colonial period; a separate Chancellor headed the court from 1778 to 1847. Under the second New York State constitution, eight circuits were established in 1823, each with its own Vice-Chancellor. The Court of Chancery became the court of appeal for these circuits, as well as for the Surrogate's Courts, though the Chancellor continued to decide some cases. The Chancery Court received jurisdiction over matrimonial cases (divorces and annulments) in 1787. The Court of Chancery was abolished in 1847, and its equity jurisdiction was transferred to the Supreme Court.

The Court of Chancery had its own court clerks. The major repositories of surviving Chancery Court records are the New York State Archives (NYSA) for the Chancellor and the upstate New York circuits (2nd through 8th) and the New York County Clerk's Division of Old Records for downstate New York (1st circuit). The FHL has microfilm copies of Chancery minutes and orders dating from 1701 through 1847; see the online catalog for more details. A copy of the FHL microfilm is available at the New York Public Library (NYPL). Also see Kenneth Scott's *Records of the Chancery Court, Province and State of New York, Guardianships, 1691–1815*.

Court of Common Pleas/Mayor's Court (1686–1895 in New York City and Albany County, 1691–1847 Elsewhere)

The Court of Common Pleas, established in the city/county of New York and Albany in 1686 and in each county in 1691, had common-law jurisdiction similar to that of the Supreme Court of Judicature. The Court of Common Pleas was superseded in 1847 by the County Court. An exception was in New York County (New York City) where the court was known as the Mayor's Court until 1821, when it was renamed the Court of Common Pleas. It was abolished in 1895 and its jurisdiction assumed by the Supreme Court, New York County, Civil Term. There were also Mayor's or Recorder's Courts in Albany and other cities, but their respective counties still had Courts of Common Pleas and, later, County Courts.

The Court of Common Pleas had civil jurisdiction almost identical to that of the Supreme Court, and usually handled lawsuits involving smaller sums. The court had administrative responsibilities such as issuing tavern licenses and military duty exemptions, authorizing name changes and naturalizations, and handling cases that in the present day would be heard in Family Court, such as child support. The court also heard appeals from determinations of justices of the peace.

Name changes are of particular interest to genealogists. John Austin's "Early Changes of Name in New York" explains the history of name changing in the state, by both the courts and the legislature, and lists many, but not all, persons whose names were legally changed between 1812 and 1901.

The NYG&B's manuscript collection of legal papers filed in New York City's Mayor's Court dating from 1775 to 1835 is now at the NYPL. See Megan Von Behren's "New York City and New York State Legal Documents from the 18th and 19th Centuries" for more information about this collection. For other counties, researchers can check the FHL's catalog for available microfilm.

Court for the Correction of Errors (1778–1847); New York State Court of Appeals (1847–Present)

Between 1778 and 1847 the Court for the Correction of Errors heard appeals from the Supreme Court of Judicature and the Court of Chancery that in turn heard first-level appeals from various lower courts. Records of the Court for the Correction of Errors are in the NYSA.

In 1847 the Court for the Correction of Errors was replaced by the New York State Court of Appeals. Located in Albany, it is the highest court in New York State and is presided over by a Chief Judge and six Associate Judges. It hears appeals from the Supreme Court Appellate Division (called Supreme Court General Term from 1847 to 1895). Appeals almost always concern significant issues of law, and the court hears fewer than 200 cases per year. The Court of Appeals transfers the clerk's set of records and briefs to the NYSA (series J2002, Cases and Briefs on Appeal). Law libraries and the NYSL hold duplicate sets of the records and briefs. The period 1847–1989 generated 15,761 volumes. Reports of cases decided in the Court of Appeals of the State of New York have been published in *New York Reports* (series 1, 1847–1955; series 2, 1956–2003; series 3 (2004–present).

Court of General Sessions of the Peace/Court of Quarter Sessions (1665–1847; New York County 1665–1962)

The Court of General Sessions of the Peace was also called the Court of Quarter Sessions when it was held quarterly. It was established in 1665 as the Court of Sessions in various parts of the colony, and it was continued as a county court in 1691 after the twelve original counties were created. The Court of General Sessions was the principal county criminal court, having jurisdiction in most felony cases (mainly those that were considered "vice crimes" such as theft, assault and battery, and bastardy). It was abolished in 1847 and succeeded by the

County Court everywhere in New York State, except New York County (Manhattan), where it continued to be held until 1962. Surviving records for the Court of General Sessions are maintained by the county clerk's office.

In the 1980s the National Genealogical Society published four volumes of genealogical extractions from Quarter/General Sessions in *New York City Court Records*, edited by Kenneth Scott, and covering the period 1684 to 1801. The New York City Municipal Archives (MUNI) and the New York County Clerk's Division of Old Records hold records of the New York County (Manhattan) Court of General Sessions. The minutes for 1683–1921 have been microfilmed.

Court of Oyer and Terminer and General Gaol Delivery (1683–1895)

The Court of Oyer and Terminer and General Gaol Delivery was established in 1683. This county-level court, which dealt with felony offenses (including cases in which the penalty was death or life imprisonment), was abolished in 1895. Supreme Court justices, rather than county judges, comprised its bench. The court's records are maintained by the county clerk's offices. The FHL has microfilmed Court of Oyer and Terminer records from several New York counties.

Justices of the Peace/Town Justice's Courts, City Courts outside New York City, Village Courts, and District Courts (1665–Present)

Courts with limited civil and criminal jurisdiction have functioned under various names since the colonial era. A 1665 law authorized justices of the peace to try debt cases involving amounts less than 40 shillings, and this authority was renewed several times, e.g., in 1827 and 1847. After 1732 justices of the peace also were empowered to adjudicate misdemeanors when a defendant could not post bail. Cities and villages have courts of limited jurisdiction, similar to that of town justices. (Nassau County, since 1939, and western Suffolk County, since 1964, also have District Courts.) By law, most records of the town, village, district, and city courts can be destroyed 25 years from the date of the initiation of proceedings, although minute and docket books are retained. Record retention schedules may be found at *www.nycourts.gov/Admin/recordsmanagement/sch_court_records.shtml*. Outside of New York City (see below) very few records of local courts have survived. They usually take the form of brief entries in docket books kept by a justice of the peace or police justice. The town clerk assumes custody of the records of retired town justices, but some of these dockets are found in libraries and historical societies.

New York City Court of Special Sessions (1732–1962); Police Court (1798–1895); Magistrates' Courts (1895–1962); New York City Criminal Court (1962–Present)

A 1732 law authorized New York City magistrates to hold expedited "special sessions" of the Court of General Sessions to arraign suspects and try (without a jury) persons charged with misdemeanors, such as petit (petty) larceny, prostitution, vagrancy, certain forms of assault, and other criminal offenses below the felony level. The Court of Special Sessions lasted until 1962. After 1798 appointed justices held a "police court." That court and the successor Magistrates' Courts, established 1896, adjudicated minor offenses and conducted preliminary hearings. Minor offenses could include disorderly conduct, trespassing, and loitering as well as nonmoving traffic offenses. Judgments were handed down with no jury trial available. In 1962 the New York City Criminal Court succeeded the earlier courts.

MUNI has extensive, and practically complete, records of the Police Court and Magistrates' Courts for the period 1799–1950 for New York County (Manhattan), and for Brooklyn (Kings County), Queens County, and the Bronx (Bronx County beginning in 1914) after they became boroughs of New York City. These records prior to 1931 have been microfilmed. MUNI also has Richmond County court records, labeled Staten Island Court, from 1848 to the 1930s (see the inventory in the NYG&B eLibrary).

New York City Justices' Courts (1787–1819); Marine Court (1819–1883); City Court (1883–1962); Assistant Justices' Courts (1807–1852); District Courts (1852–1897); Municipal Court (1898–1962); New York City Civil Court (1962–Present)

New York City civil courts possessing limited or intermediate jurisdiction have existed under various names. Few if any of their records survive. The only civil court record series at MUNI is a docket of naturalizations in the Marine Court, 1819–1846 (see the Naturalization bibliography in chapter 4, Immigration, Migration, and Naturalization, for NYG&B publications of these records). The New York City Civil Court continues as the city's civil court for small lawsuits, small claims, and housing disputes. Most civil court records are destroyed 25 years after the date of the initiation of proceedings. Records maintained permanently by civil court clerks include judgment and minute books and records of name changes.

Supreme Court of Judicature/Supreme Court (1691–Present)

The Supreme Court of Judicature, established by the New York Colonial Assembly in 1691, was a trial court that sat in New York City and periodically in the other counties. Its jurisdiction included common-law actions and proceedings concerning debts, contracts, and real property disputes such as tenant evictions. After the state capital was moved to Albany in 1797, records of this court were filed with clerks' offices in Albany and New York City, and additional offices were opened in Utica in 1807 and Geneva in 1829. The court was reorganized and renamed the Supreme Court in 1847.

See the New York County Clerk's Division of Old Records and NYSA (below) for surviving records of the Supreme Court of Judicature. The Supreme Court of Judicature records before

1847 that are held by NYSA are listed in James Folts' *Duely and Constantly Kept . . . .* The NYG&B manuscript collection of legal papers filed in the Supreme Court of Judicature dating from 1775 to 1835 is now at the NYPL. See Megan Von Behren's "New York City and New York State Legal Documents from the 18th and 19th Centuries" for more information about this collection. The FHL has microfilmed some Supreme Court indexes and records, especially *lis pendens* (notices of pending suits) for various counties.

From 1847 to the present, the Supreme Court has been New York State's principal trial court of general jurisdiction. The court is now organized in 13 districts with elected justices. In New York City it is divided into Civil and Criminal Terms and subdivided into Parts (branches or individual courtrooms); in other counties it may have specialized Terms. The Supreme Court handles major civil cases, real property disputes, and other types of actions and special proceedings in all counties, as well as criminal (felony) cases in New York City. The county courts handle criminal cases in counties outside the five boroughs.

Divorce, separation, and annulment in New York State are handled by the Supreme Court of the county in which the parties reside and are referred to as "matrimonial actions" in legal parlance. The researcher is advised to check both counties of residence if the parties live in different counties. See also chapter 2, Vital Records.

County clerks are responsible for keeping dockets and an index of Supreme Court cases, as well as the case files themselves, unless the court clerk maintains the records. Formerly, judgments, orders, and minutes were entered into books; now such documents are filed. Indexes to matrimonial actions are usually kept separately from the indexes to other Supreme Court cases. Although access to indexes to divorce decrees is not restricted, there is a statewide 100-year privacy restriction in place for papers on file (see chapter 2, Vital Records). In New York City, Supreme Court Civil Term and Criminal Term records are maintained separately by the respective court clerks.

Between 1847 and 1895 the Supreme Court General Term was the state's principal appellate court. Since 1896 the Supreme Court Appellate Division, organized in four departments (with courtrooms and clerk's offices in New York, Brooklyn, Albany, and Rochester), hears appeals from trial courts, including the Surrogate's Courts. The state's appellate court of last resort is the Court of Appeals (called Court for the Correction of Errors 1778–1847), which was discussed earlier in this chapter.

Relatively few civil and criminal cases are appealed. If that happened, the "record on appeal" provided to the New York Supreme Court General Term (1847–1895) or Appellate Division (1896–present) may be of interest to genealogists because it would contain detailed information about the facts of a case. A record on appeal includes copies of trial court documents such as transcripts of testimony and documentary exhibits. The record and the accompanying legal briefs of appellant and respondent are prepared in multiple copies. The largest collection of New York Supreme Court records and briefs is in the NYSL. Another large collection in New York City is being digitized by Google Books. A record on appeal can be located by supplying a law librarian with the citation to the published case report in the *Appellate Division Reports* or predecessor reporter. Reports of cases decided in the Appellate Division are published in *Appellate Division Reports* (series 1, 1847–1955; series 2, 1956–2003; series 3, 2004–present).

Federal Courts in New York State (1789–Present)

The United States District Court for the District of New York was one of the original 13 courts established in 1789. In 1814 New York was divided into Northern and Southern districts; the Eastern District was created in 1865 and the Western District in 1900. See *www.nywd.uscourts.gov*.

The United States Court of Appeals for the Second Circuit (*www. ca2.uscourts.gov*), an appellate court, is also located in New York City. It handles appeals from the U.S. District Courts, and its decisions can be appealed to the United States Supreme Court.

While genealogists often refer to federal court records for naturalizations, the records are also useful for researching civil and criminal cases lying within federal jurisdiction. Such cases include treason and smuggling, personal and corporate bankruptcies, tax evasion, bootlegging, equity, and *habeas corpus* cases.

The National Archives at New York City (NARA-NYC) acts as custodian for the records created before the 1970s by all federal courts located in New York State. A comprehensive guide to, and inventory of, NARA's federal court records collection and a pathfinder for obtaining more recent federal court records, are available at *www.archives.gov/nyc/public/courts.html*.

Major Repositories of Court Records of New York State

Larger courts may have a records room run by the clerk of the court. The clerk's office is usually located in the courthouse, although older records may need to be retrieved from an offsite storage location. This is discussed in further detail below.

Statewide

- **National Archives and Records Administration at New York City** (NARA-NYC) in Manhattan holds records of federal courts (trial and appellate) in New York State. *archives.gov/nyc*
- **New York State Archives** (NYSA) in Albany holds over 6,000 cubic feet of records of the Supreme Court of Judicature 1797–1847; Supreme Court, Appellate Division 1896–1983 (incomplete holdings); Court of Chancery 1704–1847, including the 2nd through 8th Circuits (located upstate) 1823–1847; Court of Probates 1665–1823; Court for the Correction of Errors 1777–1847; and Court of Appeals starting in 1847. *www.archives.nysed.gov/a/research/res_topics_gen_guide_court.shtml*
- **New York State Library** (NYSL) Law Collection in Albany has records on appeal from the New York State Court of Appeals starting in 1847; Supreme Court, General Term ca. 1850–1895; and New York State Supreme Court, Appellate Division, starting in 1896. *www.nysl.nysed.gov/collections/law.htm*
- **Family History Library** (FHL) possesses substantial microfilm collections of various nineteenth-century court records and indexes from Broome, Cattaraugus, Cayuga, Chemung, Chenango, Cortland, Delaware, Dutchess, Herkimer, Jefferson, Livingston, Madison, New York, Onondaga, Ontario, Orange, Otsego, Richmond, Saratoga, St. Lawrence, Ulster, Warren, Wayne, and Yates counties, and a smattering of other records, particularly *lis pendens* in Supreme Court and county court, from New York's other counties. Some of the FHL court records microfilm collection (donated by the New York Genealogical and Biographical Society) is at the NYPL. For the FHL catalog, see *FamilySearch.org*.

See also the New York County Clerk, Division of Old Records below. For records before 1797 when the capital of New York

Table 2: Federal Court Districts of New York State	
U.S. District Courts of New York	**Counties Currently in District**
Southern District (formed in 1814)	Bronx, Dutchess, New York (Manhattan), Orange, Putnam, Rockland, Sullivan, and Westchester
Northern District (formed in 1814)	Albany, Broome, Cayuga, Chenango, Clinton, Columbia, Cortland, Delaware, Essex, Franklin, Fulton, Greene, Hamilton, Herkimer, Jefferson, Lewis, Madison, Montgomery, Oneida, Onondaga, Oswego, Otsego, Rensselaer, Saratoga, Schenectady, Schoharie, St. Lawrence, Tioga, Tompkins, Ulster, Warren, and Washington
Eastern District (formed from Southern in 1865)	Kings (Brooklyn), Nassau, Queens, Richmond (Staten Island), and Suffolk
Western District (formed from Northern in 1900)	Allegany, Cattaraugus, Chautauqua, Chemung, Erie, Genesee, Livingston, Monroe, Niagara, Ontario, Orleans, Schuyler, Seneca, Steuben, Wayne, Wyoming, and Yates

moved to Albany, see the New York County Clerk's listing below. Small but unique collections of court records can often be found scattered among local historical societies and archives such as the Brooklyn Historical Society (*brooklynhistory.org*). It is always worth checking local institutions for "missing" records.

New York City

- **New York County Clerk, Division of Old Records** in Manhattan has records of the Supreme Court of Judicature 1691–1847 (scope is colony and statewide before 1797), including records of the court clerk's office in New York City 1797–1847 (files from downstate counties), and the Supreme Court in New York County (Manhattan) 1847–present. Also many records of the Court of Chancery ca. 1700–1847, including First Circuit (downstate counties) 1823–1847; Mayor's Court and Court of Common Pleas of the City and County of New York 1674–1895; and the Superior Court of New York City 1828–1895. *www.nycourts.gov/courts/1jd/supctmanh/county_clerk_records.shtml*

- **New York City Department of Records/Municipal Archives** (MUNI) in Manhattan has an extensive collection of court records pertaining to New York. Major series include records of felony prosecutions by the New York County District Attorney in the Court of General Sessions/Supreme Court 1664–1970s and felony prosecutions in the Kings County Court 1896–1940. MUNI also houses records of violations and misdemeanors in record series for Manhattan 1799–1950; Brooklyn 1881–1950; Queens, and the Bronx 1898–1950. Civil court records include case files from the Kings County (Brooklyn) Clerk's Office and Richmond County (Staten Island) Clerk's Office—not indexed. A list of felony indictments for trials in the New York County Court of General Sessions 1879–1892 are on the website, arranged by name of defendant. *www.nyc.gov/html/records/html/archives/collections.shtml*

John Jay College of Criminal Justice

524 West 59th Street • New York, NY 10019
guides.lib.jjay.cuny.edu/SpecialCollections

The special collections in the Sealy Library include trial transcripts and the "Crime in New York Images Archive 1850–1950." The images include the photo archive of Lewis Lawes, who was warden of Sing Sing Prison (1920–1941). Some of this material is online.

Selected Bibliography and Further Reading

Austin, John. "Beyond the Surrogate: Other New York Court Records." *Tree Talks*, vol. 35 (Spring 1995): 3–12.

———. "Early Changes of Name in New York." *NYG&B Record*, vol. 127 (1996) no. 3: 137–142, no. 4: 222–225; vol. 128 (1997) no. 1: 44–48, no. 2: 97–100. [NYG&B eLibrary]

———. *Family History Resources: Court Records (New York State as an Example)*. Salt Lake City: Church of Jesus Christ of Latter-day Saints, 1980.

Bailey, Rosalie Fellows. *Guide to Genealogical and Biographical Sources for New York City (Manhattan), 1783–1898*. New York: R. F. Bailey, 1954. [*FamilySearch.org*] Reprint with new introduction by Harry Macy Jr., Baltimore: Clearfield Co., 1998.

Bentley, Elizabeth Petty. *County Courthouse Book*. 3rd edition. Baltimore: Genealogical Publishing Co., 2009.

Bergan, Francis. *The History of the New York Court of Appeals, 1847–1932*. New York: Columbia University Press, 1985.

Black, Henry Campbell. *Black's Law Dictionary*. 4th edition. St. Paul, MN: West Publishing, 1951.

Chester, Alden, and E. Melvin Williams. *Courts and Lawyers of New York: A History, 1609–1925*. 3 vols. New York and Chicago: American Historical Society, 1925.

Fernow, Berthold, trans. and ed. *The Records of New Amsterdam from 1653 to 1674 Anno Domini*. 7 vols. New York: Published under the authority of the city by Knickerbocker Press, 1897. Records of the City Court. [*FamilySearch.org*]

Folts, James D., and Jeffrey A. Kroessler. "Courts." In *Encyclopedia of New York City, 2nd Edition*, edited by Kenneth T. Jackson, 321–326. New Haven: Yale University Press, 2010.

Folts, James D. "Courts, State." In *Encyclopedia of New York State*, edited by Peter Eisenstadt, 411–416. Syracuse: Syracuse University Press, 2005.

———. *"Duely & Constantly Kept": A History of the New York Supreme Court, 1691–1847 and an Inventory of Its Records (Albany, Utica, and Geneva Offices), 1797–1847*. Albany: New York State Court of Appeals, New York State Archives and Records Administration, 1991, 1–183. *http://www.courts.state.ny.us/history/legal-history-new-york/documents/History_Supreme-Court-Duely-Constantly-Kept.pdf*

Gardinier, Timothy P. "Courts, Federal." In *Encyclopedia of New York State*, edited by Peter Eisenstadt, 410–411. Syracuse: Syracuse University Press, 2005.

Guide to Federal, County, and Municipal Archives in the City of New York. New York: Department of Records and Information Services, Municipal Archives, 1989.

Guzik, Estelle M., ed. *Genealogical Resources in New York*. New York: Jewish Genealogical Society, 2003.

Hamlin, Paul M., and Charles E. Baker, eds. *Supreme Court of Judicature of the Province of New York, 1691–1704*. 3 vols. New York: New-York Historical Society, 1959.

Jacobs, Jaap. *The Colony of New Netherland*. Ithaca: Cornell University Press, 2009.

Joslyn, Roger D. "New York." In *Red Book: American State, County & Town Sources*, edited by Alice Eichholz, 480. 3rd edition. Provo, UT: Ancestry, 2004. [*www.ancestry.com/wiki*]

Manz, William H. *Gibson's New York Legal Research Guide*. 3rd edition. Buffalo: William S. Hein, 2004.

Morris, Richard B. *Select Cases of the Mayor's Court of New York City, 1674–1784*. Washington, DC, 1935.

New York Historical Manuscripts: Dutch, and *New Netherland Documents* (see chapter 1, Colonial Era, bibliography), particularly the Council Minutes volumes and also *Laws & Writs of Appeal 1647–1663*.

New York Historical Manuscripts: English. (See chapter 1, Colonial Era, bibliography.) Many of the volumes in this series contain some court records, but particularly *Records of the Court of Assizes for the Colony of New York 1665–1682*, and *Minutes of the Mayors Court of New York, 1674–1675*, 1983.

New York Law Journal. New York: New York Law Publishing Co., 1888–present.

New York Reports [1st]. Court of Appeals. Reports of Cases Argued and Determined in the Court of Appeals of the State of New York. New York and Albany: Banks & Brothers, Law Publishers, 1888–. Volumes 1–309 in 158 books reporting decisions 1847–1955, various publishers.

New York Reports [2nd]. Court of Appeals. Reports of Cases Argued and Determined in the Court of Appeals of the State of New York. Albany: Williams Press/Rochester: Lawyers Cooperative Publishing. Volumes 1–100 reporting decisions 1856–2003, various publishers.

New York Reports [3rd]. Court of Appeals. Reports of Cases Decided in the Court of Appeals of the State of New York. St. Paul, MN: Thomson/West, 2004.

New York State, and Esek Cowen. *A General Digested Index to the Nine Volumes of Cowen's Reports of Cases Argued and Determined in the Supreme Court and in the Court for the Trial of Impeachments and the Correction of Errors of the State of New York/by the Author of Those Reports*. Albany: W. and A. Gould: 1831.

New York State, and Supreme Court. *Reports of Cases Argued and Determined in the Supreme Court of Judicature: And in the Court for the Trial of Impeachments and the Correction of Errors of the State of New York [1828–1841]/by John L. Wendell*. Albany: Gould, Banks: 1829–1842. Microform. [NYPL Science, Industry and Business Library]

New York State Archives. "Records Relating to Criminal Trials, Appeals, and Pardons." Information Leaflet No. 9, Guides to Historical Records. 1999. *http://www.archives.nysed.gov/a/research/res_topics_legal_trials.pdf*.

Remington, Gordon L. "Divorce Records, New York Style." *APG Quarterly*, vol. 12 (1997): 90–91.

Rose, Christine. *Courthouse Research for Family Historians*. San Jose, CA: CR Publications, 2004.

Sankey, Michael. *The Sourcebook of Federal Courts, U.S. District and Bankruptcy: The Definitive Guide to Searching for Case Information at the Local Level within the Federal Court System*. Tempe, AZ: BRB Publications, 1993.

Scott, Kenneth, ed. *New York City Court Records, 1684–1760: Genealogical Data from the Court of Quarter Sessions*. Special Publication No. 50. Washington, DC: National Genealogical Society, 1982.

———. *New York City Court Records, 1760–1797: Genealogical Data from the Court of Quarter Sessions*. Special Publication No. 52. Washington, DC: National Genealogical Society, 1983.

———. *New York City Court Records, 1797–1801: Genealogical Data from the Court of General Sessions*. Special Publication No. 56. Arlington, VA: National Genealogical Society, 1988.

———. *New York City Court Records, 1801–1804: Genealogical Data from the Court of General Sessions*. Arlington, VA: National Genealogical Society, 1988.

———. *Petitions for Name Changes in New York City, 1848–1899*. Washington, DC: National Genealogical Society, 1984.

———. *Records of the Chancery Court, Province and State of New York, Guardianships, 1691–1815*. New York: Holland Society, 1971.

Sickels, H. E. *Reports of Cases Decided in the Court of Appeals of the State of New York, Vol. C*. Albany: Weed, Parsons, 1886.

The Sourcebook of County Court Records: A National Guide to Civil, Criminal, and Probate Records at the County and Municipal Levels within the State Court Systems. 4th edition. Tempe, AZ: BRB Publications, 1998.

Surrency, Erwin C. *History of the Federal Courts*. 2nd edition. Dobbs Ferry, NY: Oceana Publications, 2002.

Von Behren, Megan. "New York City and New York State Legal Documents from the 18th and 19th Centuries." *NYG&B Newsletter* (now *New York Researcher*), Spring-Summer 2001. Published as a Research Aid on *NewYorkFamilyHistory.org*.

Probate Records
Chapter 6

Introduction

Probate and other estate settlement records—including petitions, wills, letters of administration, inventories, accountings, and other documents—are important sources for research. Though research in these kinds of records in New York has its special challenges, pursuing a subject's estate records is well worth the effort. In addition to information about a decedent's estate, these records can contain vast amounts of data, including names, addresses, and relationships of family members (often minors and family members not mentioned in actual wills); information identifying undertakers, cemeteries, and grave markers; miscellaneous documents such as death certificates; and inventories of personal possessions and household furnishings that may contain revealing information about a subject's lifestyle, occupation, values, and other personal characteristics. Historians have written extensively about New York's nearly 400 years of probate and estate records. Consequently many records are relatively easy to find. Probate and estate records are generally well preserved because they have legal value.

This overview outlines the fundamentals of New York State probate and estate records and the major pathways to the genealogical information they contain. The courts having jurisdiction in estate matters changed in 1787, so this chapter addresses the pre-1787 and post-1787 periods separately.

The essential first step in researching probate material is to determine the subject's date of death. If the subject died *before* 1787, the researcher should consult published guides to probate records to pinpoint the place where the record, or an accessible copy or abstract of the record, can best be located. If the subject died *after* 1787, the most likely repository of the records is the Surrogate's Court in the county where the decedent resided at the time of death. Guides to probate records, such as Gordon Remington's book described in the next paragraph, note the exceptions to this practice, which can be complicated. Guides

can also indicate where microfilm copies can be accessed, and in some cases, where the records exist online.

Gordon L. Remington's book, *New York State Probate Records: A Genealogist's Guide to Testate and Intestate Records*, contains a detailed description of records in pre- and post-1787 New York as well as a county-by-county guide to printed, microfilmed, and online records. (The *second* edition is recommended.) Remington provides an excellent guide to microfilmed records in the Family History Library (FHL). As availability of the records changes (especially online records), the county guides section of Remington's book may not be completely up-to-date.

Information Leaflet #3, Probate Records in the New York State Archives, on the New York State Archive's (NYSA) website (*www.archives.nysed.gov*) contains a detailed guide to probate holdings at the NYSA and the New York State Library (NYSL) with catalog references or links. The leaflet is particularly helpful for locating the original records (and accessible microfilm copies) prior to 1787, and it helps navigate the unusual complexities of the division and relocation of record sets. Also on the NYSA website is the Probate Record Pathfinder, a research tool that provides descriptions of archival collections with links to Excelsior, the online catalog of the NYSA and the NYSL.

Records Before 1787
New Netherland

In Dutch New Netherland, which existed from the earliest years of European settlement until the English took control in 1664, wills were recorded *while the testator was alive*, so that upon death, the terms of the will were carried out without further legal ado. Dutch women were permitted to make wills. They usually did this by creating joint wills with their husbands. Settlers in New Netherland, including some of the English settlers, conformed to the Dutch system regardless of their respective nationalities.

Wills and related legal documents were drawn up and recorded by a notary or other official such as the secretary of the colony. The *Calendar of Historical Manuscripts in the Office of the Secretary of State, Albany, NY* for the Dutch period (edited by Edmund B. O'Callaghan) identifies some records relating to estates; the full texts are available in the *New York Historical Manuscripts* and the *New Netherland Documents* series. Records of two New Amsterdam notaries, Walewyn Van der Veen (1662–1664) and Salomon Lachaire (1661–1662), survive. Van der Veen's records are published in Berthold Fernow's *Minutes of the Orphanmasters . . . (Volume 2)*; Lachaire's are published separately as noted in the bibliography.

The orphanmasters of the *weeskamer* or orphan chamber protected the property of minors when one or both parents died. The records of the New Amsterdam chamber have been published: 1655–1663 translated and edited by Fernow, and 1663–1668 by O'Callaghan. Beverwijck (Albany) did not have an orphan chamber but did have two orphanmasters who reported to the Fort Orange Court, as explained in Janny Venema's *Beverwijck*. All of the records of this period were written in Dutch, but these published versions are in English. Also see chapter 1, Colonial Era, and chapter 14, Peoples of New York, Dutch.

Colony (later Province) of New York

The English took over New Netherland in 1664. This did not mean that Dutch probate practices (and the use of the Dutch language in wills) ended abruptly and were suddenly replaced by the English system. For the Dutch community, there was a transition period of about 20 or more years. This can be seen in local records of the various Dutch settlements, which begin before 1664 but continue to contain notarial or other estate records almost to the end of the century.

English law differed from the Dutch; the English system required wills to be recorded *after* the testator's death, when they were proved (authenticated) in court. This system is used in present-day New York. From 1664 until 1686 wills were proved at the Court of Assizes in New York City (the colonial capital) or in Courts of Sessions located in various regions of the colony. Some of these Courts of Sessions kept their own records, but most wills were sent to the centralized repository in New York City for probate and entered into "libers" of the "Court of Record." This was the beginning of the largest collection of colonial New York wills and administrations. Between 1686 and 1692, in cases in which the royal governor granted probate or letters of administration, the grant was made under the governor's own seal, not by a separate prerogative court.

Briefly (1688–1689) New York was part of the Dominion of New England under a governor seated in Boston. Several New York wills were proved and recorded in Boston during this period. See "New York Probates Recorded in Massachusetts, 1688–1689, During the Dominion of New England" by Henry B. Hoff.

In 1692 the court structure was changed by the Act of 1692 (chapter 27). From then until the Revolutionary War ended in 1783, the majority of estates were processed through the Prerogative Court in New York City, nominally overseen by the Governor but usually by "surrogates." This court had exclusive authority over wills and administrations in the counties of New York, Kings, Richmond, Westchester, and (until 1752) Orange. After 1692 Queens and counties farther away from New York City were permitted to prove wills and issue letters of administration for estates valued under £50, usually through their Courts of Common Pleas, and the records of these smaller estates are found in the respective county records. Estates valued at £50 or more continued to be sent to the Prerogative Court in New York City. Records of all Orange County estates after 1752 are found in New York City, even though the county had the power to prove wills and issue letters of administration after that date.

During the American Revolution, the authority of the Prerogative Court in the counties not controlled by the British was assumed by the new Court of Probates that met in Poughkeepsie. When the Revolution ended in 1783, the Court of Probates moved to New York City and assumed authority over the entire state.

Researchers interested in pre-1787 probate records of New York should start with the published abstracts. The New-York Historical Society (N-YHS) has published *Abstracts of Wills on File in the Surrogate's Office, City of New York 1665–1801*, edited by William S. Pelletreau in 17 volumes covering all counties 1665–1787 and New York County 1781–1800. (Note that corrections to volumes 1–11 appear in volumes 16 and 17.) Many libraries have these volumes; full-text digital versions of all 17 volumes are in the Family History Books collection at *FamilySearch.org*. Because the wills and administrations in these volumes were recorded in New York City and were held by the New York County Surrogate's Court at the time they were abstracted, they are sometimes referred to as New York County or New York City wills, but in fact the decedents lived in every county. Arthur Kelly's two-volume name index to these abstracts is very helpful.

Another set of province-wide abstracts, though incomplete, was compiled by Fernow from records that he found in Albany, many of them moved from New York City when Albany became the state capital. Almost all of those records are now at the NYSA. For these abstracts, see Fernow's *Calendar of Wills on File and Recorded in the Offices of the Clerk of the Court of Appeals*. Abstracts of wills and administrations recorded by the county clerks also may be consulted.

After consulting the abstracts to determine which wills need to be examined further, researchers can then consult the full text of the wills. For the Prerogative Court, hundreds of the original wills survive and more legible conformed copies (exact copies that include all original notations) of all the wills are found in the will books, or libers. A second set of the libers was made in the late-nineteenth century, but, as with all copies, this set may contain transcription errors. The original wills and original libers from 1665 to 1787 are at the NYSA in Albany, while the New York County Surrogate's Court holds the second set of libers. The NYSA also has the records of the State Court of Probates (1778–1823). The county clerks retain custody of the original records of their courts, including the recorded wills for small estates.

The wills in the will books or libers are indexed in Sawyer's "Index of Wills for New York County (New York City), from 1662–1850," also known as "Index of New York State Wills 1662–1850," which covers all counties until 1787, but only New York County from 1787 to 1850.

Indexes to the original wills from 1658 to 1829 were made in the 1960s by Scott, Bloch, and Hershkowitz and published in the *National Genealogical Society Quarterly*. These indexes must be consulted to obtain the will number before using the FHL microfilm of the original wills, which are from all counties until 1787, and only New York County from 1787 to 1829.

The provincial probate and estate records of the English colonial period have been microfilmed by the FHL. Copies of the microfilms are also available at the New York Public Library (NYPL) in Manhattan, the NYSA, the Queens Library (Queens County), and the Daughters of the American Revolution (DAR) Library in Washington, DC. Copies or abstracts of some of the county records of the period are also available at these libraries. Also see *FamilySearch.org* for records that are now online.

For New Yorkers who died intestate, letters of administration could be issued and recorded in the provincial or county will libers. Beginning in 1743 a separate set of libers was created for those letters of administration issued by the Prerogative Court; they are included in Barber's "Index of the Letters of Administration" which also covers later administrations of New York County. Numerous letters of administration, bonds, and related documents are held at the NYSA. Harry Macy Jr.'s article "New York Probate Records Before 1787" provides additional background on these and all the other provincial and county records and explains how they can be accessed in print, microfilm, or online.

Hundreds of inventories of estates prior to 1787 survive in separate collections at the NYSA, the New York County Surrogate's Court, and the N-YHS, or were recorded with their respective wills or administrations in provincial or county books. Those at NYSA are abstracted in Kenneth Scott and James Owre's *Genealogical Data from Inventories*, and those at N-YHS and the New York County Surrogate's Court are indexed in Scott's "Inventories of New York Estates." Inventories generally do not include real property, but often contain very detailed descriptions of the decedent's personal property. No other estate papers survive for those who died intestate. Also see chapter 1, Colonial Era, and chapter 14, Peoples of New York, Dutch.

Records After 1787
Surrogate's Courts

In 1787 the state Court of Probates, successor to the colonial Prerogative Court, was largely replaced by a system of Surrogate's Courts in each county. This system continues to the present day. Proving wills, issuing letters of administration, and supervising the administration of estates is almost entirely carried out by these courts. Legislation subsequent to 1787 expanded the powers of the Surrogate's Courts to include, for example, the appointment of guardians (1802) and maintenance of adoption records (1873, but today handled primarily in Family Court).

During the first half of the nineteenth century, the Surrogate's Courts maintained separate books for the "admeasurement of dower." These records indicate how property was divided to satisfy a widow's one-third "dower" right.

In 1829 the state introduced two new requirements of great importance to the genealogist. First, petitions for probate or administration had to identify all heirs-at-law, whether named in a will or not. Second, all documents pertaining to the settlement of an estate, which the courts had hitherto often discarded, now had to be kept on file permanently. As a result all counties have estate files dating from 1830, although how these files are organized, what they are called, how complete they are, and how they are indexed can vary from one county to another.

Beginning in 1830 the Surrogates' records also include files of Letters Testamentary; a few counties may have preserved these records from earlier dates. These letters are given to executors of wills, to confirm their appointment and authorize them to perform actions necessary to settle the estate. They correspond to the Letters of Administration issued in cases where there is no will, but unlike Letters of Administration they are of minimal value to the genealogist. Access to estate records varies widely from county to county, and availability of print and online indexes and records changes over time. Abstracts of some records in most counties have been published; see *WorldCat.org* for publications and nationwide library locations. Periodical indexes should also be checked as many abstracts have been published in genealogical journals. Communicating with court staff can be hit or miss, and record recovery can often be astoundingly expensive and time-consuming. Of course, researchers can visit Surrogate's Courts in person or employ local researchers to visit the courts on their behalf.

Microfilm of Surrogate's Court records is available from the FHL for all counties except Bronx (formed 1914), Nassau (formed 1898), Sullivan (burned 1909), and Suffolk. Cutoff dates for the microfilms vary from county to county, as do the types of records filmed. Many of the existing microfilms are also available at the NYPL. The NYSA holds the original will books (libers) of New York County 1787–1876, as well as microfilm copies, while the County Surrogate holds the second set of those books described earlier.

Table 1: Simplified Summary of Probate Jurisdiction in New York		
Time Period	**Court**	**Jurisdiction/Historical Notes**
Dutch Colonial Rule: 1624–1664		
1624–1664	None	There was no official probate court in New Netherland. During the Dutch colonial period, wills were recorded by a government official when the testator was living. The Orphanmasters Court dealt with estates inherited by minors.
English Colonial/Provincial Rule: 1664–1778/1783		
1664–1692	Court of Assizes (New York City) and Courts of Sessions (regional)	Probate was not suddenly changed; Dutch system transitioned over time to the English system.
1692–1778/1783	Prerogative Court established in New York City in 1692	Abolished in 1778 when New York State declared its independence but remained active in British New York until 1783. Smaller estates were handled locally by the Courts of Common Pleas. A few New York estates were settled in English courts.
Post-Revolutionary New York		
1778–1823	State Court of Probates created in 1778; it replaced the English colonial Prerogative Court	State Court of Probates had jurisdiction over independent New York until 1783 when it then covered all of New York State. Proved wills in special cases only after 1787. Abolished 1823.
Modern New York		
1787–present	County Surrogate's Courts created in 1787	A Surrogate's Court (a state court) was established in each county; Court of Probates kept jurisdiction over estates in multiple counties until abolished in 1823. While they were in existence, Court of Chancery (1777–1847) and Supreme Court of Judicature (1801–1829) shared jurisdiction with the Surrogate's Court in some situations. Appeals submitted to Court of Chancery (1823–1847) or Supreme Court (1847–present).

FamilySearch continues to digitize microfilm of Surrogate's Court records. Almost all counties have at least some records and indexes online at *FamilySearch.org*, under the general title New York Probate Records, sorted by county and then record group. With several exceptions, these digital records are those of the county Surrogate's Courts, beginning in 1787 and continuing to the early-twentieth century. Under New York and Albany counties are posted the colonial Prerogative Court records for the entire province, and under Albany and Dutchess counties are posted pre-1787 probate records kept by their county clerks. Some of the online records are searchable by name; otherwise the records must be browsed. However, for most counties the court indexes have also been posted, or there are manuscript indexes embedded in the record books themselves.

William Eardeley abstracted estate proceedings, 1787-1835, in 51 New York counties and indexed all of the names that appear in the abstracts. His manuscript is held by the Brooklyn Historical Society, which also microfilmed it. It has been digitized by the New England Historic Genealogical Society and is accessible at *AmericanAncestors.org* in the collection "Abstracts of Wills, Administrations and Guardianships in NY State, 1787-1835."

This collection also contains DeWitt Van Buren's abstracts of Kings County wills, 1787-1843, which Eardeley did not cover.

Online indexes are available for some county Surrogate's Courts. Researchers should check the website of the relevant court, as well as the websites listed below. Although Surrogate's Courts are microfilming and digitizing records, those digital records are not necessarily available online.

Other Courts

Although the Surrogate's Courts in the counties largely replaced the State Court of Probates in 1787, the State Court of Probates maintained jurisdiction in special cases: for example, New Yorkers who died out of state, residents of other states who died in New York, and New Yorkers with real property in multiple counties. This court was abolished in 1823 and its jurisdiction was turned over to the Surrogate's Courts; records (1778–1823) are at the NYSA.

The Court of Chancery (in Albany and New York City) proved some wills and appointed guardians; appeals from the Surrogate's Courts were made to the Court of Chancery. It was abolished in 1847. Since then appeals from the Surrogate's Courts have been made to the Supreme Court. Records from Albany (1704–1847) are at the NYSA.

The County Court of Common Pleas could, until 1829, prove wills that involved real estate. The Mayor's Court in New York City and the old Supreme Court had similar powers. Except for the Court of Common Pleas for New York County, all of these courts were abolished as of 1847, and their relevant records were turned over to the Surrogate's Courts, with some exceptions. For example, the books of recorded wills of the Supreme Court of Judicature (pre-1847) are at the NYSA, and some wills from the Supreme Court of New York City and New York County Court of Common Pleas are at the New York County Clerk's Division of Old Records. See abstracts by Ray Sawyer.

Guardianship Records

Guardianship records can be rich sources of genealogical information, because they can connect individuals with their parents and other family members and can reveal information about estates and important life events, including children's ages.

Protection of the assets of minors during the Dutch colonial period is mentioned above, in the section on New Netherland. During the English colonial period and into the early-nineteenth century, guardianships were the responsibility of the Court of Chancery. Kenneth Scott abstracted the Chancery guardianship records from 1691 to 1815, found at the NYSA and New York County Clerk's Division of Old Records. Some guardianships are also found in county Court of Common Pleas records until 1802 when power to appoint guardians was transferred to the county Surrogate's Courts; at the latter researchers will find letters of guardianship, bonds, and files. Details for locating records, including microfilm for the FHL (including film numbers) and copies of microfilm at the NYPL, are in Harry Macy Jr.'s two finding aids covering pre- and post-1787 probate records published at *NewYorkFamilyHistory.org*.

Roger Williams provides a detailed review of guardianship records covering the mid-nineteenth century to the mid-twentieth century in his article "Guardianship Records of New York State" published in *Tree Talks*. Essentially, he sends researchers to the Surrogate's Courts in the counties of New York. Many of these records have been filmed and indexed as described elsewhere in this chapter. Guardianship records for some counties have also been abstracted in issues of *Tree Talks*.

Selected Online Resources

Since online records change frequently, the county and non-governmental websites should be checked for additions. As described above, *FamilySearch.org* has millions of probate records spanning four centuries, organized by county and type of record. Since 1870, the *NYG&B Record* has published transcribed abstracts of probate records for several counties; these can be accessed online at *NewYorkFamilyHistory.org*.

AmericanAncestors.org offers the 14-volume index to Albany County Deeds 1630–1894 (which indexes some wills) and William Eardeley's *Abstracts of Wills, Administrations and Guardianships in NY State, 1787–1835*. Some publications of the New Netherland Project can be accessed at *www.newnetherlandinstitute.org/research/online-publications*. Also see chapter 1, Colonial Era, and the section on the Dutch in chapter 14, Peoples of New York. *Sampubco.com* is a private company offering probate material from most New York counties. Indexes are free; obtaining the records themselves (which are not online) requires payment.

Selected Bibliography and Further Reading

Barber, Gertrude Audrey. "Index of the Letters of Administration Filed in New York County from 1743–1875." Typescript. New York, 1950–1951. Prior to 1787, it covers all counties. [*Ancestry.com*]

Bloch, Julius M., Kenneth Scott, and Leo Hershkowitz. "[Index to Original] Wills of Colonial New York, 1736–1775." *National Genealogical Society Quarterly*, vol. 54 (1966): 98–124. The second of three articles; see Scott for the other two.

Christoph, Peter R., Florence A. Christoph, and Kenneth Scott, eds. *New York Historical Manuscripts: English*. Baltimore: Genealogical Publishing Co. 1980–1983, and Syracuse: Syracuse University Press, for the Holland Society, 1980–2002. Government records from 1665–1691.

Eardeley, William A. D. "New York State Abstracts of Wills." Covers 1787-1835, 51 New York counties;includes name index. Manuscript, 1929-1933. Brooklyn Historical Society, New York. Microfilmed by the Society, 1997. [*AmericanAncestors.org*]

Fernow, Berthold, trans. and ed. *Calendar of Wills on File and Recorded in the Offices of the Clerk of the Court of Appeals of the County Clerk at Albany, and of the Secretary of State, 1626–1836*. New York: Knickerbocker Press, 1896. Reprinted in 1967 by Genealogical Publishing Co., Baltimore. Most of the wills abstracted by Fernow are on *FamilySearch.org* under Albany County.

———. *The Minutes of the Orphanmasters of New Amsterdam, 1655 to 1663*. 2 vols. New York: F. P. Harper, 1902–1907. Vol. 2 includes Walewyn Van der Veen's notarial records 1662–1664. See O'Callaghan below for later Orphanmasters records. [NYG&B eLibrary]

Hoff, Henry B. "New York Probates Recorded in Massachusetts, 1688–1689, During the Dominion of New England." *NYG&B Record*, vol. 139, no. 4 (2008): 266–268. [NYG&B eLibrary]

Johnson, Herbert A. "The Prerogative Court of New York, 1686–1776." *American Journal of Legal History*, vol. 17 (1973): 95–144.

Kelly, Arthur C. M. *Index, Names of Principals: Abstracts of Wills on File in the Surrogate's Office, City of New York*. 2 vols. (Vol. 1. 1665–1776; vol. 2. 1777–1800). Rhinebeck, NY:

Palatine Transcripts, 1981. Indexes the abstracts by Pelletreau, see below; pre-1787 abstracts are from all counties.

Macy, Harry, Jr. "Library Resources for Research in New York Probate Records Since 1787." *NYG&B Newsletter* (now *New York Researcher*) Spring 1992. Updated by Harry Macy Jr., 2011 and published as a Research Aid on *NewYorkFamilyHistory.org*.

———. "New York Probate Records Before 1787." *NYG&B Newsletter* (now *New York Researcher*), Spring 1991. Updated by Harry Macy Jr., 2011 and published as a Research Aid on *NewYorkFamilyHistory.org*.

Narrett, David E. *Inheritance and Family Life in Colonial New York City*. Ithaca, NY: Cornell University Press, 1992.

New Netherland Institute. "New York Historical Manuscripts: Dutch/New Netherland Documents Series Introductions." *www.newnetherlandinstitute.org/research/online-publications* See also the bibliography in chapter 1, Colonial Era.

O'Callaghan, Edmund Bailey, trans. *Calendar of Historical Manuscripts in the Office of the Secretary of State, Albany, NY.* 2 vols. (Part 1: Dutch Manuscripts, 1638–1664; Part 2: English Manuscripts, 1664–1776). Albany: Weed, Parsons, 1865–1866. Reprint Ridgewood, NJ: Gregg Press, 1968. Indexes the documents translated or transcribed in the *New York Historical Manuscripts* series.

———. *The Minutes of the Orphanmasters of New Amsterdam, 1663 to 1668.* Kenn Stryker-Rodda and Kenneth Scott eds. Baltimore: Genealogical Publishing Co., 1976. Continues Fernow's translation noted above.

O'Callaghan, Edmund Bailey, Kenneth Scott, and Kenn Stryker-Rodda, eds. *New York Historical Manuscripts: Dutch: The Register of Salomon Lachaire, Notary Public of New Amsterdam, 1661–1662.* Baltimore: Genealogical Publishing Co., 1978.

Pearson, Jonathan, and Arnold J. F. van Laer, trans. and eds. *Early Records of the City and County of Albany, and Colony of Rensselaerswyck.* 4 vols. Albany: 1869–1919. Vol. 3 contains Notarial Papers 1660–1696, and vol. 4, Wills 1681–1765.

Pelletreau, William S., ed. *Abstracts of Wills on File in the Surrogate's Office, City of New York, 1665–1801.* 17 vols. New York: New-York Historical Society, 1892–1908. Pre-1787 wills and administrations are from all counties. Note that vols. 16–17 contain corrections to vols. 1–11.

Remington, Gordon L. *New York State Probate Records: A Genealogist's Guide to Testate and Intestate Records.* 2nd edition. Boston: New England Historic Genealogical Society, 2011.

Sawyer, Ray Cowen. "Abstract of Wills Probated in the Common Pleas Court (also known as Mayor's Court) 1817–1892, Supreme Court of Judicature 1821[sic, 1787]– . . . 1870, All of New York County, New York City." Typescript, New York, 1948. DAR Library, Washington, D.C.

———. "Index of Wills for New York County (New York City), from 1662–1850." 3 vols. Typescript, New York, 1931. Wills before 1787 are from all counties. [*Ancestry.com*]

Scott, Kenneth. "Appointment of Guardians, Mayor's Court, New York City, 1696–1737." *National Genealogical Society Quarterly*, vol. 56 (March 1968): 51–54.

———. *Genealogical Data from Administration Papers in the New York State Court of Appeals in Albany.* Middletown, NY: Trumbull Publishing Company, 1972.

———. *Genealogical Data from Further New York Administration Bonds 1791–1798.* Collections of the NYG&B Society. Vol. 11, 1971. [NYG&B eLibrary]

———. *Genealogical Data from New York Administration Bonds 1753–1799 and Hitherto Unpublished Letters of Administration.* Collections of the NYG&B Society. Vol. 10, 1969. [NYG&B eLibrary]

———. "[Index to] Early Original New York Wills [1658–1738]." *National Genealogical Society Quarterly*, vol. 51 (June 1963): 90–99ff. See Bloch, above, for the next index.

———. "Inventories of New York Estates." *National Genealogical Society Quarterly,* vol. 53 (June 1965): 133–143. Indexes inventories (from all counties) at the New York County Surrogate's Court and The New-York Historical Society.

———. *Records of the Chancery Court, Province and State of New York: Guardianships, 1691–1815.* New York: Holland Society of New York, 1971.

Scott, Kenneth, and James A. Owre. *Genealogical Data from Inventories of New York Estates 1666–1825.* New York: New York Genealogical and Biographical Society, 1970. Inventories from all counties, now in the New York State Archives. [NYG&B eLibrary]

Scott, Kenneth, and Leo Hershkowitz. "Index of Original [New York] Wills (1776–1829)." *National Genealogical Society Quarterly*, vol. 55 (June 1967): 119–145.

Skeele, Perle M., comp. *New York State Wills, 1791–1842.* Yonkers, NY: 1929.

Van Laer, Arnold Johan Ferdinand. *New York Historical Manuscripts, Dutch: Register of the Provincial Secretary.* 3 vols. Baltimore: Genealogical Publishing Co., 1974. [Digital version edited by Charles T. Gehring from Van Laer manuscript, vol. 1 (1638–1642) and vol. 2 (1642–1647)]. Contains some wills and estate inventories. [*nnp.org*]

Van, Buren D. W. *Abstracts of Wills of Kings County Recorded at Brooklyn, N.Y.* Salem, MA: Higginson

Venema, Janny. *Beverwijck, A Dutch Village on the American Frontier, 1652–1664.* Albany: SUNY Press, 2003.

Williams, Roger. "Guardianship Records in New York State." *Tree Talks*, vol. 53, no. 2 (2013): 67–72.

Introduction

In all land research, establishing who had jurisdiction at the time in question is critical to success. Because New York State was settled over the course of several centuries and under several different regimes, patterns of land ownership and record-keeping practices varied widely, depending on the time period and geographic area in question. The historical overview below provides readers with context for land-related research in New York.

Following the historical overview, this chapter provides information on how and where to find records of land transactions. The record types that are the basis of land research are deeds (conveyances), mortgages, patents, grants (including bounty land grants), leases, land company papers, surveys, maps, atlases, and gazetteers, as well as court records involving disputes, land confiscations, and estates. Note that some deeds were not recorded; see the New York State section in Records of Land Transactions later in this chapter for more details on unrecorded deeds.

Table 1 at the end of this chapter summarizes genealogically significant land-related events.

Historical Overview

New Netherland

The West India Company, chartered in 1621, administered the colony of New Netherland. It acquired land from the native inhabitants, which it then granted or leased to settlers, mostly as small farms or as city or village lots. Directors of the company were allowed to obtain larger tracts directly from the native peoples, with the idea that these "patroons" would rent portions to tenants whom they brought over from the old country. Only a handful of these patroonships (i.e., privately owned colonies) were created, and all but the largest, Rensselaerswijck, failed within a few years. The owners of the other patroonships sold their land back to the company.

New York under the English

Patents were grants of land given to individuals or groups by the Crown or governor and publicly documented; when given to a group, the individuals were known as "proprietors." In 1639 Lion Gardiner was issued a royal patent for Gardiner's Island at the east end of Long Island. The English founded settlements on eastern Long Island outside Dutch jurisdiction as early as 1640. When England seized New Netherland in 1664 and created New York, eastern Long Island was included in the new colony. Almost all of the inhabitants were small landowners, as was the case in the other territories the English acquired in 1664, including the Dutch and English villages of western Long Island, Staten Island, the area that became southeastern Westchester, Beverwijck (Albany), and Wiltwijck (Kingston), as well as the city of New Amsterdam (renamed New York).

The English honored the land grants that had been made by the Dutch and continued to grant patents for the colony's unsettled land to individuals or groups, some of whom chose to live on their patents, while others sold or leased their land. Twenty of these patents were designated as manors, starting with the Van Rensselaer Manor, which had been the patroonship of Rensselaerswijck. Most of the manors were small, but the Van Rensselaer, Van Cortlandt, Philipse, and Livingston families controlled extensive manors, which attracted large numbers of tenants.

New York's eastern border included a narrow strip of land (now referred to as the Oblong) that was also claimed by Connecticut, but was ultimately ceded to New York in 1731. The relatively small lots in the Oblong were owned by individuals, in contrast to the large manors or patents to the west. For strategies on how to find records, see Anita Lustenberger's "When Connecticut Became New York: Researching in the Oblong Before 1800."

The land farther north, which is now part of Vermont, was disputed between New York and New Hampshire. Researchers are advised to consult the records of Vermont and New Hampshire, in addition to New York's, for information on residents of this area.

In 1664 New Jersey was established as an autonomous colony separating itself from New York, though until 1739 the two colonies often shared a governor. While land disputes between New York and New Jersey continued until nearly the end of the twentieth century (e.g., Liberty and Ellis Islands), they rarely have a bearing on genealogical research.

New France

Until the end of the French and Indian War in 1763, France controlled the land to the north of New Netherland and New York, including Lake Champlain and Lake George, and there was no defined boundary between those colonies and New France. Although the French made grants of land in northern New York, the settlements struggled through years of hostilities in the area, but most of the land was regranted by the English once the area was clearly under their control.

Indian Lands and the Proclamation Line

The Royal Proclamation of 1763 was issued by King George III to manage Britain's new empire and to establish better relations with American Indians. It regulated settlement, land purchases, and trade, and forbade acquisition of Indian lands west of the Allegheny watershed. Many smaller grants of land were made by the colonial governors throughout the lands east of the 1763 proclamation line. The line ran the length of the Appalachian Mountains, assigning all land with rivers that flowed into the Atlantic to the colonies and land that drained into the Mississippi to the native Indian population. The proclamation was contentious, because there were pre-existing settlements and unresolved land claims beyond the line. After the Revolutionary War, with the help of the new federal government, these multiple overlapping claims were reconciled, borders were established, and American Indian rights were extinguished through new "treaties" with the Indian nations. The first American Indian reservations in New York were established in 1788 in present-day Onondaga and Madison counties, and most of the other reservations were formed in 1797. See the section on American Indians in chapter 14, Peoples of New York.

The Revolutionary War and the Military Tracts (New and Old)

After the Revolutionary War, settlement began to increase in the north as a result of large land grants made both to individuals and to groups of men. In the central area of the state was the Military Tract, 1.8 million acres allocated as bounty land for Revolutionary War soldiers by the New York State legislature in 1783. The land was intended both as a reward and to position loyal soldiers along the frontier. In fact by the time all the claims had been settled, most of the soldiers had sold their land, and the frontier had shifted. Initially the Military Tract was located in fertile land in present-day Cayuga, Cortland, Onondaga, and Seneca counties, as well as parts of Oswego, Schuyler, Tompkins, and Wayne; however, much of this land was legally owned by Indian nations.

In 1786 alternative land was found in Clinton, Essex, and Franklin counties, but it was much less arable. Owing to vigorous objections (mostly from land speculators who had already purchased the rights from war veterans), this land was rejected and became known as the Old Military Tract. In 1788 the original Military Tract land was acquired through treaties with the Onondaga and Cayuga tribes; and finally, in 1791 it was awarded to veterans and became known as the New Military Tract. *The Balloting Book*, compiled by Michael Connelly, contains a list of soldiers whose names were drawn in the balloting procedure through which the land was assigned. A name index for this book has been published, and the names are also easily accessed in Lloyd Bockstruck's index, *Revolutionary War Bounty Land Grants: Awarded by State Governments*. See the bibliography at the end of this chapter for more resources regarding the Military Tract.

Because of the involvement of speculators in the Military Tracts, many large land transactions differed from the Hudson River manor system. Purchases were made by those who intended selling for profit rather than retaining and leasing the land.

Expansion into Western New York

The 1786 Treaty of Hartford established that New York would cede land west of the 1763 proclamation line to Massachusetts with the proviso that, though Massachusetts could sell the land, New York would retain jurisdiction, meaning the land would be, and would remain, part of New York State. This land was known as the Massachusetts Reserve.

In 1788 Oliver Phelps and Nathaniel Gorham contracted to purchase six million acres from Massachusetts; however, changes in their finances allowed them to retain only about one-third of the land, and they began the process of selling land and creating amenities to entice settlers. The western section of the Massachusetts Reserve was sold to Revolutionary War financier Robert Morris in 1791. Morris also had financial problems and sold parts of his land in smaller pieces to other land speculators. He eventually sold the western 3.3 million acres to Dutch banking houses, which in 1794 established the stockholding company known as the Holland Land Company. The Dutch bankers held other land in New York State in the area of Madison and Chenango counties which were already settled. They also had land and other investments in other states, particularly in Pennsylvania.

New York— A State Land State

New York is a "state land state," which means that the colony, and later the state, controlled the granting of land. States created after the establishment of the United States government are "public land states," wherein the federal government was the grantor of the lands. Characteristic of state land states are the seemingly haphazard boundaries of each parcel of land. In New York the earliest farms and lots were laid out following the customs of the Netherlands and England, with boundaries set by metes and bounds (a descriptive method using physical features and distances), and this practice was continued in all of the eastern counties.

As settlement continued to the west and large tracts were split into small farms for the individual settlers, the land was surveyed into rectangular townships by township and range lines. A system of lotting was established within each surveyed township in which smaller plots of land were surveyed and sold; they often contained fewer acres than did a full lot. The smaller parcels were often surveyed and described in reference to the straight lines of the township and range lines. On paper these rectangular surveys may appear similar to the system used in the public land states, but they do not contain the same acreage and designations.

For an understanding of land surveys, established grants and tracts, as well as individual purchases during the early stages of land distribution, Joseph Bien's *Atlas of the State of New York*, published in 1895, is a good resource. In this atlas the county maps name the larger tracts, and show the surveyed lot lines and some of the lot numbers.

Records of Land Transactions

One of the best sources for information on the early land grants is French's 1860 gazetteer. This book has a chapter on land with tables of early manors, patents, and tracts, as well as a listing of most New York grants with dates, patentees' names, the location by county, and, frequently, the acreage. A reference to land in a named grant can help the researcher find the county in which it was located. In addition, there is a chapter on each county that includes more information on land distribution specific to that county. The names of early settlers are often provided in footnotes.

The major land records—patents, deeds, and land grant applications—of both the colonial and state governments can be found in the New York State Archives (NYSA) in Albany. In 1830 a state statute mandated that county clerks record all deeds. In spite of this law, many deeds were not recorded, but may appear in a chain of title in a deed recorded decades later. After the formation of a county, deeds and mortgages were held by the county clerk's office, although deeds might be found elsewhere as well—in town records, for example. *FamilySearch.org* has digitized land and property records from the seventeenth century into the twentieth, mostly from county courthouses. Many more land records of the colonial and state periods are available on microfilm from the Family History Library (FHL).

New Netherland

For a good overview of land ownership see Jaap Jacobs's *The Colony of New Netherland*. Records of grants by the West India Company are found in Charles T. Gehring's Land Papers volume of *New York Historical Manuscripts: Dutch*, which includes deeds given by the natives to the patroons, as well as grants of small tracts to various individuals. Subsequent sales between settlers are found in Van Laer's *Register of the Provincial Secretary* and in the local records of the various communities. Janny Venema's book on Beverwijck analyzes land ownership. For ownership of lots in New Amsterdam and farms on the rest of Manhattan Island, see *The Iconography of Manhattan Island, 1498–1909*, a six-volume work by I. N. P. Stokes.

New York under the English

The towns of eastern Long Island, which were not part of New Netherland, hold numerous land records from 1640 to 1664. For the colony (later province) of New York, created in 1664, there are land records at three levels of government, namely colony and province, county, and town.

Colony and province of New York land records include:

- Land patents, covering grants by the governor or the Crown; originals at the NYSA, microfilm copies at the FHL and the New York Public Library (NYPL), indexed by grantee and location.
- The *Calendar of N. Y. Colonial Manuscripts: Indorsed Land Papers in the Office of the Secretary of State of New York. 1643–1803*; originals at the NYSA relating to applications for patents and other grants.
- Deeds kept by the Provincial Secretary; originals at the NYSA with useful separate volumes of abstracts, indexed by grantor and grantee; microfilm copies at the FHL and (for the colonial period) at the NYPL.

Counties were first created in 1683, and each county began to keep a book containing various types of records, primarily deeds. These initial books became Liber A (i.e., Book A) of a series of volumes usually called *Deeds* or *Conveyances*. Under a 1753 law, counties were required to record mortgages and maintain a separate set of books for that purpose. All of the deed books and many of the mortgage books, with indexes, are available on FHL microfilm, with copies at the NYPL, and many of the deed books are digitized and available on *FamilySearch.org*. Some of the records have been published, usually in abstract form.

Towns that existed during the colonial period have records that contain numerous deeds, and many of these records have been published or microfilmed. Even after the formation of the counties, large numbers of deeds continued to be recorded at the town level.

New York State

When New York became a state, most of the colonial land records series were continued with little change, except for dropping references to the old political order. Thus, provincial land patents continued as state patents, and provincial secretary's deeds became deeds of the secretary of state, and are found at the NYSA and on microfilm as described above for the colony and province of New York. The counties continued their series of deed and mortgage books, but deeds are rarely found in town books after the Revolutionary War.

On March 7, 1788, the Reorganization Act was passed by the New York State legislature. The act recognized the boundaries of thirteen of the existing counties, and Clinton County was created from Washington County. There was also an unsuccessful attempt to regain the counties of Cumberland and Gloucester, which had been lost to Vermont in 1777. The act recognized existing towns and precincts throughout the state as towns, and some new towns were formed.

Several counties were established by law as of a certain date, but did not have their own governments until sufficient levels of population were attained. For example, Cattaraugus County was established by law in 1808, but was not "organized" until 1817. Between 1808 and 1817, it was attached to Niagara County, where deeds were recorded and other business transacted, including the 1810 federal census.

County deed and mortgage books are in the custody of the county clerks, except in New York City (see below). The FHL has microfilms of the records, in most cases extending to the end of the nineteenth century, and of the indexes up until the middle of the twentieth century; most of these have been digitized and are available on *FamilySearch.org*. The NYPL has copies of the microfilms for many of the counties, but with earlier cutoff dates for the deeds and mortgages. The grantor/grantee indexes for New York County and Albany County have been published to 1856 and 1894, respectively.

An 1830 statute mandated that all deeds be recorded by the county clerks, and in the newer counties of central and western New York, recording was required as early as the 1790s; despite these laws there are deeds that do not appear in the county books. Some counties (Suffolk, for example) have volumes of unrecorded deeds that were given to the county clerk, but never formally recorded. Such deeds may also be found in the collections of libraries, archives, historical societies, and town historians.

In New York State, political jurisdiction exists at the village, town, and city levels, as well as at the county level. A village remains part of a town even though it has its own government, but a city is separate from a town. In New York State the term "township" is not used as a unit of local government. A township only refers to a division of land created by a survey. See the introduction to the County Guides (Part 2) for a fuller explanation.

New York City

In four of the five boroughs of New York City, the Bronx, Brooklyn, Manhattan, and Queens, the Office of the City Register (*www.nyc.gov/html/dof/html/property/property_rec_property.shtml*) holds land records. Records for Staten Island are held by the Richmond County Clerk. In addition to the Office of the Register and the Richmond County Clerk's office, the Milstein Division of the NYPL has copies of the FHL films for New York County from 1654 to 1850, and for Kings, Queens, and Richmond counties from 1683 to 1850. The NYPL also has films of the mortgages for New York and Richmond counties from 1754 to 1800. At the FHL are additional films of these records extending into the twentieth century, including the grantor/grantee indexes to deeds (with separate indexes for New York County corporate grantors and grantees). The collection at the NYPL includes index films for each of these counties extending into the twentieth century, except the New York County grantee index ends at 1890. The FHL also has films of deeds relating to property in Bronx County, extracted from the records of its parent counties, Westchester and New York. Digital copies of all FHL films except Queens (and the Westchester extracts for Bronx) can be found on *FamilySearch.org*.

New York Manor and Early Patent Records

The manors kept records relating to their lands. Henry B. Hoff, in his article "Manors in New York," identifies the manors that existed within the present boundaries of New York State (six in the Hudson Valley, seven on Long Island and adjacent islands, three in southeastern Westchester County, two in what is now Bronx County, two on Staten Island, and one north of Albany). In each case he indicates which records survive and lists published works relating to each manor. Since the article was published, the New York State Library (NYSL) has created an online finding aid to its collection of Van Rensselaer Manor papers at *www.nysl.nysed.gov/msscfa/sc7079.htm*. The Livingston papers, formerly at the Morgan Library, have been moved to the New-York Historical Society, and some additional Livingston papers are held by Princeton University. See also Sung Bok Kim's *Landlord and Tenant in Colonial New York: Manorial Society, 1664–1775*.

Much has been written about early patents, notably Frank Doherty's exhaustive, multi-volume series, *Settlers of the Beekman Patent, Dutchess County, New York: An Historical and Genealogical Study of All the 18th Century Settlers in the Patent*. Researchers may find various records, including leases, rent books and rolls, account books, rent receipts, manor mill account books, store ledgers, and tax records mentioned as sources in the footnotes of Mr. Doherty's books. Jane E. Wilcox's "Exploring Research Resources for Hudson Valley Tenant Farmers" in the *New York Researcher* provides an in-depth look at these types of records, and her syllabus "Looking for Your New York Tenant Farmer:

Little-Used Resources" for the National Genealogical Society Conference (2014) lists locations for these records.

Later Land Leases

In many sections of the state, owners of large parcels of land did not always sell their land, but occasionally leased lots to individuals. For example, George Clarke, in what is now Otsego County, leased land to hundreds of tenants over decades. He kept records of the leases, transfers of leases, maps showing lots and tenants, and surveyor's field books describing each lot and its occupiers. Most of these records are held at Cornell University Library, Division of Rare Books and Manuscripts. If a researcher is looking for persons known to have lived in an area where landowners mostly leased land, they may be listed in the landowner's records.

Records of Assessors

Assessors' offices (county, city, town, or village) may hold property cards that record the history of the property, including the names of owners. Although current retention schedules require these to be kept permanently, losses may have occurred owing to fire, flood, and disposition before the retention schedule was in place. Assessors' offices may also have access to tax records, but more often the tax records are kept at the county level. Some tax records have been transferred to historical societies or town historians, or have been published. Sheriff's sales for unpaid taxes are usually recorded under the names of the sheriffs, so land transfers may be stored in the records under their names. It is helpful to know who the sheriff was at the time a transfer was made. Local historical societies are good places to access these names and dates, and many New York county sheriff websites list the names of past sheriffs. See also chapter 13, Tax Records.

Land Company Records

Land companies bought tracts of land hoping to make profits by dividing them into smaller lots to sell to settlers. Most found they had to invest in the land by conducting surveys and creating amenities, such as roads, before they could attract settlers. Many of the land companies and proprietors of the large tracts kept their own records of land transactions that occurred before the land was actually paid for and the deed recorded in the county courthouse. Some settlers did not complete their purchases, but moved on in search of better or cheaper land farther west. Others never received a deed that could be recorded. Official records for these transactions can be difficult to locate or may not exist.

Because the land company records belonged to the company, many have disappeared or have been scattered as they passed from generation to generation. One of the largest land company archives is that of the Holland Land Company (from 1794 to the 1840s). These records are now in the custody of the Stadsarchief Amsterdam (Municipal Archives of Amsterdam)

in the Netherlands. They have been arranged, described, and recorded on 202 rolls of microfilm. The microfilm is available at the NYPL, NYSL, Library of Congress, FHL, and at Reed Library SUNY College, Fredonia, New York, where it is available on interlibrary loan (*www.fredonia.edu/library*). The finding aid created by the Municipal Archives of Amsterdam (in English) is available on the first roll of microfilm or on the website of Reed Library, which also has a link to the hundreds of maps from this collection. Documents can also be found at the Division of Rare Books and Manuscript Collections, Cornell University Library (Holland Land Company Records 1802–1863, collection number 383). Karen Livsey's two-volume work, *Western New York Land Transactions, 1804–1835*, serves as an entry point for finding transactions involving individuals and the company, for identifying where the land was located, and for other information, such as correspondence and accounts.

Reed Library's Holland Land Company Manuscript Preservation Project has continued to locate related collections and has obtained microfilm copies of many of these records. One important collection is the Joseph Ellicott Papers, which include Ellicott's correspondence and copy books from the years 1800 to 1826, when he was the resident agent for the land company. After he was dismissed, he took these papers with him. The New York State courts upheld his right to keep the documents, and his family later donated them to the Buffalo and Erie County Historical Society. Other records from the family papers of people who worked for the Holland Land Company have been located, adding to the information about the company.

The NYSL has an excellent collection of land records, including the Phelps and Gorham papers from 1776 to 1892. Searching the NYSL/NYSA catalog at *www.nysl.nysed.gov* will lead to other papers relating to land company tracts.

The Historical Document Inventory (HDI) is particularly helpful in locating land company records, because these records may have remained with the families concerned and been deposited at different times at various repositories. A search for the words or phrase of the named tract, the proprietors, or the location may bring up related papers. The NYSL online catalog allows searching within the HDI. See the New York State Library entry in chapter 16, National and Statewide Repositories & Resources.

Loyalist Land Confiscations (1779–1785)

During and after the American Revolution, lands owned by Loyalists were confiscated in many areas of New York State, with major actions taking place in Dutchess, Putnam (then part of Dutchess), and Westchester counties. Names involved in the confiscations include Robinson, Morris, and Philipse. See William Ruddock's *Confiscated Properties of Philipse Highland Patent, Putnam County, New York, 1780–1785* for Putnam

County sales, Harry P. Yoshpe's *The Disposition of Loyalist Estates in the Southern District of the State of New York*, Theresa Hall Bristol's "Abstracts of Sales by the Commissioners of Forfeitures in the Southern District," and Anita Lustenberger's "Tenants of Commissioners of Sequestration in Westchester County 1778–1783." The Westchester County Archives has a purchaser name index on its website.

Mortgage Records

Many homeowners borrowed money to purchase land. If a mortgage was taken out, the mortgage record will indicate the name of the purchaser, the address of the property, information on finance and assets, and in some cases the names of other family members, if they were involved in providing money or guarantees. These records are most often found in the office of the county clerk.

Reservoir-Related Records

When large dams were constructed, the reservoirs behind them flooded land that often had been farmland, towns, or forests. Dams were constructed in many areas of New York for water supply, flood control, and hydroelectric power. As New York City's need for water increased, land was confiscated by eminent domain starting in the 1840s and continuing to the 1950s. While the bulk of these reservoirs were in Putnam, Saratoga, Sullivan, Ulster, and Westchester counties, other places were affected—for example, towns in Cattaraugus County by the Kinzua Dam constructed in Pennsylvania. Surveys were created that will generally be found in county records or archives. Land sales can be found in county grantor/grantee books. Lawsuits were filed in county courts, and some were appealed in state courts; documentation may be found in the records of both courts. Local, state and federal jurisdictions may all contain records that are relevant to land taken by eminent domain for reservoir use.

Surrogate's Court Records

Land can be transferred by will as well as by deed; in many cases a title search (see below) will include a copy of the will. If a deed cannot be found, the next step is to look for a will in the records held by the Surrogate's Courts. Sometimes when land is transferred by will, the transaction is not recorded until generations later, when the land is finally sold outside the family rather than inherited or sold within the family. As these land transfers may not have been recorded at the time they were made, it may be necessary to look through many subsequent years of the grantor/grantee indexes to find deeds. The real property of someone dying intestate may be found in the last partition books, usually found in the county's Surrogate's office. See also chapter 6, Probate Records, for information about Surrogate's Court records.

Title Searches and Maps

Finding a title (a document of ownership) for a property may answer many questions about land transfers. A "full title" search usually goes back 50 to 70 years; a "mineral title" search usually goes back as far as the original grant deed to the first subsurface ownership. "Title and Abstract" companies located in the county may have copies of older title searches, but these are expensive to acquire. An abstract of title lists all legal actions that have been executed on a property. Individual counties also hold maps showing subdivisions of lands within their jurisdiction. These are subdivisions of larger plots of land and not necessarily maps of recent housing subdivisions constructed in the suburbs. Because some deeds refer only to a lot number on a particular map and do not have the actual description of the parcel, these maps may be useful in identifying the location of a property.

Transportation-Related Records

The nineteenth-century system of canals and railroads in New York led to the creation of many records of land ownership. Surveys of the routes provided numerous details on adjacent landowners; disputes over boundaries and compensation were recorded and preserved; and railroad and canal companies purchased bordering land. Some of these records may be found at the county level in deeds, court records, and tax records. The NYSA holds all the records of the Canal Commissioners, the governing body overseeing most New York canals, including the Erie Canal.

Railroad companies kept their own records, which are now held in different locations. For example, the Delaware and Hudson Railroad records that were originally kept in their Albany offices are now held by the NYSL Manuscripts and Special Collections; and some records of the Delaware, Lackawanna, and Western Railroad can be found at the Special Collections Research Center of Syracuse University and the Cortland Historical Society. Researchers should consult the HDI to locate other New York-based repositories.

Selected Bibliography and Further Reading

Bailey, Rosalie Fellows. *Guide to Genealogical and Biographical Sources for New York City (Manhattan), 1783–1898*. New York: R. F. Bailey, 1954. [*Books.FamilySearch.org*] Reprint with new introduction by Harry Macy Jr. Baltimore: Clearfield Co., 1998. Excellent description of New York City land records.

Bien, Joseph R. *Atlas of the State of New York*. New York: Julius Bien & Co., 1895.

Bockstruck, Lloyd deWitt. *Revolutionary War Bounty Land Grants: Awarded by State Governments*. Baltimore: Genealogical Publishing Co., 1996.

Bowman, Fred Q. *Landholders of Northeastern New York 1739-1802*. Baltimore: Genealogical Publishing Co., 1983.

Bristol, Theresa Hall. "Abstracts of Sales by the Commissioners of Forfeitures in the Southern District of New York State." *NYG&B Record*, vol. 59 (1928) no. 2: 108–120, no. 3: 247–255, no. 4: 328–332; vol. 60 (1929) no. 1: 64–67, no. 2: 164–171. [NYG&B eLibrary]

Calendar of N.Y. Colonial Manuscripts: Indorsed Land Papers in the Office of the Secretary of State of New York; 1643–1803. Albany: Weed, Parsons, 1864.

Connelly, Michael, and New York State Secretary's Office. *The Balloting Book and Other Documents Relating to Military Bounty Lands in the State of New-York.* Albany: Packard & Van Benthuysen, 1825. Reprinted Ovid, NY: W. E. Morrison, 1983. Reprinted by the New York State Council of Genealogical Organizations. [NYSL digital collection, *tcpl.org*]

Doherty, Frank J. *Settlers of the Beekman Patent, Dutchess County, New York: An Historical and Genealogical Study of All the 18th Century Settlers in the Patent.* 11 vols. Pleasant Valley, NY and Orlando, FL: F. J. Doherty, 1990–2013. Additional volumes are planned. [*beekmansettlers.com*]

Evans, Paul Demund. "The Holland Land Company." PhD diss., Publications of the Buffalo Historical Society, vol. 28. Buffalo: Buffalo Historical Society, 1924. Reprint Fairfield, NJ: Augustus M. Kelley, 1979.

Fernow, Berthold, and Edmund B. O'Callaghan, eds. *Documents Relative to the Colonial History of the State of New York.* 15 vols. Albany: Weed, Parsons, 1856–1887. Vol. 1-11 are documents collected by John Romeyn Brodhead. Titles of vols. 12–15 is *Documents Relating . . . .*

Ferris, Mary Frances. *Index. The Balloting Book and Other Documents Relating to Military Bounty Lands in the State of New-York, Albany 1825.* Syracuse: Onondaga Historical Association, 1954.

French, John H. *Gazetteer of the State of New York.* Syracuse: Pearsall Smith, 1860. Reprint, Baltimore: Genealogical Publishing Company, 1998. The 1998 edition contains a supplementary index to place names. (See also *All-Name Index to the 1860 Gazetteer of New York State.* Interlaken, NY: Heart of the Lakes Publishing, 1993.)

Gehring, Charles T., trans. and ed. *New York Historical Manuscripts, Dutch: Volumes GG, HH, and II: Land Papers, 1630–1664.* Baltimore: Genealogical Publishing Co., 1980.

Guide to Historical Resources in [name] County, New York Repositories series. 62 vols. Ithaca, NY: New York. Historical Resources Center, Olin Library, Cornell University, 1978–1993. The resource descriptions within all volumes are online and searchable through Excelsior, the NYSL catalog, and *Worldcat.org*.

Hatcher, Patricia. *Locating Your Roots: Discover Your Ancestors Using Land Records.* Cincinnati: Betterway Books, 2003.

Henry, Marian S. "Bounty Lands in the Military Tract in Post-Revolutionary War New York State." *New York Essays: Resources for the Genealogist in New York State Outside New York City*, p. 125–137. Boston: New England Historic Genealogical Society, 2007.

Hoff, Henry B. "Manors in New York." *NYG&B Newsletter* (now *New York Researcher*), Fall 1999 and Winter 2000. Published as a Research Aid on *NewYorkFamilyHistory.org*.

Jacobs, Jaap. *The Colony of New Netherland.* Ithaca, NY: Cornell University Press, 2009.

Kim, Sung Bok. *Landlord and Tenant in Colonial New York: Manorial Society, 1664–1775.* Chapel Hill, NC: University of North Carolina Press, 1978.

Livsey, Karen E. *Western New York Land Transactions, 1804–1835: Extracted from the Archives of the Holland Land Company.* 2 vols. Baltimore: Genealogical Publishing Co., 1991.

Lustenberger, Anita A. "Tenants of the Commissioners of Sequestration in Westchester County 1778–1783." *NYG&B Record*, vol. 123 (1992) no. 4: 203–206; vol. 124 (1993) no. 1: 30–33. [NYG&B eLibrary]

———. "When Connecticut Became New York: Researching in the Oblong Before 1800." *Connecticut Ancestry*, vol. 47, no. 2 (September 2004): 169–178.

Pearson, Jonathan, and Arnold Johan Ferdinand van Laer, trans. and eds. *Early Records of the City and County of Albany, and Colony of Rensselaerswyck.* 4 vols. Albany: 1869–1919. Vols. 1–2 contain deeds 1656–1704 and vol. 4 contains mortgages 1658–1660.

Rose, Christine. *Courthouse Research for Family Historians: Your Guide to Genealogical Treasures.* San Jose, CA: CR Publications, 2004. Includes a chapter on the various types of deed indexes.

———. *Military Bounty Land 1776–1855.* San Jose, CA: CR Publications, 2011.

Ruddock, William T. *Confiscated Properties of Philipse Highland Patent, Putnam County, New York, 1780–1785.* Westminster, MD: Heritage Books, 2012.

Stokes, Isaac Newton Phelps. *The Iconography of Manhattan Island, 1498–1909.* 6 vols. New York: Robert H. Dodd, 1915–1928. Reprinted, New York: Arno Press, 1967. Early title history of original New Amsterdam lots, and farms on rest of Manhattan, as well as inventory of New York County land records.

Van Laer, Arnold Johan Ferdinand, trans. and ed. *New York Historical Manuscripts, Dutch: Register of the Provincial Secretary.* 3 vols. Digital version edited by Charles T. Gehring from Van Laer manuscript, vol. 1 (1638–1642) and vol. 2 (1642–1647). [*nnp.org*]

Venema, Janny. *Beverwijck: A Dutch Village on the American Frontier, 1652–1664*. Albany: SUNY Press, 2003.

Wilcox, Jane E. "Looking for Your New York Tenant Farmer: Little-Used Resources." Syllabus for the National Genealogical Society 2014 Family History Conference. [*Amazon.com*]

— — —. "Exploring Research Resources for Hudson Valley Tenant Farmers." *New York Researcher*, vol. 25, no. 2 (Summer 2014): 28–31. [NYG&B eLibrary]

Yoshpe, Harry P. *The Disposition of Loyalist Estates in the Southern District of the State of New York*. New York: Columbia University Press, 1939.

Maps

Introduction

Maps should not be overlooked as a resource for family history research.

Maps can lead researchers to records by pinpointing potential sources of undocumented information (for example, private cemeteries); they can also identify families and people, as names were often recorded on local maps.

While typically maps show roads, streets, and natural features, they can also help provide socio-economic context for other data. Insurance maps, for example, can show the precise dimensions of houses and other structures, and identify nearby churches, schools, and other institutions that could have records. The Sanborn Insurance Company and its predecessors produced thousands of highly detailed maps, many of which are archived in libraries; the New York Public Library has a particularly strong collection.

New York's map resources are exceptionally rich because parts of New York State were settled in the seventeenth century, and because large parts of the state became heavily populated and industrialized.

A good overview of New York maps is found in Jo Margaret Mano's "Annotated Bibliography of Selected New York State Maps: 1893–1900." It describes dozens of important maps. Her essay on nineteenth-century mapmaking, focusing on New York maps, and the bibliography are at *www.nysl.nysed.gov/msscfa/mapsbibl.htm*.

David H. Burr's *An Atlas of the State of New York* (1829) and Joseph R. Bien's *Atlas of the State of New York* (1895) are good starting points for New York cartography. Both of these are widely available online. Another useful source to consult is Albert Hazen Wright's *A Check List of New York State County Maps Published 1779–1945*.

David Y. Allen's lengthy, searchable, online bibliography, "The Mapping of New York State: A Study in the History of Cartography," is an essential resource. This document contains a very extensive bibliography about maps, and New York maps, far more ample than this one. A number of entries come with links to articles and maps. His bibliography provides sources of information about canals, turnpikes, and other topics relating to migration and travel through New York. He covers all aspects of maps, including, for example, natural history, natural resources, and geology.

The individual County Guides in this book pinpoint maps and atlases specific to each county, primarily from the nineteenth and early-twentieth centuries. Local historical societies and libraries sometimes have excellent local maps that have not been catalogued.

To learn about county boundary changes for New York (and all 50 states) see the astonishing *Atlas of Historical County Boundaries* published online at *http://publications.newberry.org/ahcbp* by the Newberry Library in Chicago. This interactive site shows graphically the boundary status of counties for New York from the late-seventeenth century to 2000, and provides detailed timelines on boundary changes for each county. Data may be downloaded in several formats. This project was preceded by the publication of Kathryn Ford Thorne's book, *Atlas of Historical County Boundaries: New York.*

For researchers interested in the Revolutionary War period, Eric G. Grundset's *New York in the American Revolution*, published by the DAR in 2013, has a bibliography of books about maps. Some titles focus on New York and others are more general.

Selected Repositories and Resources

See also chapter 16, National and Statewide Repositories & Resources, for full listings for the NYPL, the NYSA, the N-YHS, and the Library of Congress.

The Library of Congress (LOC)

The LOC has thousands of New York maps in its collection, and provides detailed cataloging data at *www.loc.gov/topics/maps.php*; an estimated ten percent of the New York material is online with images of various resolutions. The earliest maps feature New Netherland; the majority of online maps are from the nineteenth century. The collection includes the rare and staggeringly beautiful *Novi Belgii Novæque Angliæ* (New Netherland and New England), published in Amsterdam in 1685; it also contains overall maps of New York State as well as maps of counties, cities, towns, and villages from the eighteenth through twentieth centuries. The collection includes Sanborn insurance maps. Some topics within the map division that include New York maps are separately described on the LOC website, such as Railroad Maps (1828–1900); the Rochambeau Map Collection (1715–1795); and Panoramic Maps (1860–2000).

The New York Public Library: The Lionel Pincus and Princess Firyal Map Division

The division has maps of New York City, the metropolitan region, and New York State. Thousands of maps in their very large and growing collection are online. (In early 2014 the number of digitized maps passed the 20,000 mark.) The Map Division's website at *nypl.org/mapdivision* offers very detailed and continually expanding descriptions of it holdings of maps (digitized and not), atlases, and books about maps. The holdings are not limited to New York maps, but are global in scope. The Map Division's architecturally magnificent reading room offers books about maps on open shelves.

New York State Archives (NYSA)

The NYSA contains a collection of more than 80,000 maps, including maps of places in New York State and neighboring states, military maps, insurance maps, land patents and surveys, and New York county atlases. The maps date from the seventeenth century. A catalog of maps made in 1859 by David Mix is still the definitive index to early maps at the NYSA. The maps section of the NYSA's website offers a very detailed history of map-making in New York and a descriptive bibliography of selected maps. See *www.nysl.nysed.gov/msscfa/mapsbibl.htm*; the digital archive of the NYSA offers several thousand maps at *www.archives.nysed.gov/a/digital/images/browse.*

New-York Historical Society (N-YHS)

The Patricia D. Klingenstein Library at the N-YHS holds about 10,000 maps, a collection which is divided into printed maps and manuscript maps. Dating from the seventeenth century, the collection covers New York City and New York State and is national in scope. Maps made by Robert Erskine and Simeon DeWitt, the mapmakers for George Washington, are highlights of the manuscript map collection. A short description and links to searching the collection is at *http://dlib.nyu.edu/nyhs/maps.*

David Rumsey Historical Map Collection

David Rumsey's map collection at *davidrumsey.com*, covering places in North and South America, is an excellent source for New York maps. Though it is a commercial site, access is free. Of the approximately 150,000 items in his collection, about one-third are digitized.

American Geographical Society Library

The AGS library is at the University of Wisconsin-Milwaukee; until 1978 it was the library of the American Geographical Society of New York. The collection, described at *http://uwm.edu/libraries/agsl*, is huge and global in scope. It contains some New York material, and some New York maps have been digitized. Much of the collection may be searched through the University's online catalog, but the collection is in the early stages of reorganization.

Selected Bibliography and Further Reading

See the county guides in Part Two of this book for additional titles.

Allen, David Yehling. *Long Island Maps and Their Makers: Five Centuries of Cartographic History*. Mattituck, NY: Amereon House, 1997.

———. "Bibliography." The Mapping of New York State: A Study in the History of Cartography. Updated May 8, 2013. *www.dyasites.com/maps/nysbook/Bibliography.htm*. This document contains a very extensive bibliography about maps, and New York maps.

Ballon, Hilary, ed., *The Greatest Grid: The Master Plan of Manhattan, 1811–2011*. New York: Museum of the City of New York and Columbia University Press, 2012.

Bien, Joseph R. *Atlas of the State of New York*. New York, 1895. [NYPL Digital Gallery]

Burr, David H. *An Atlas of the State of New York*. New York, 1829. [NYPL Digital Gallery]

Carroll, Francis M. *A Good and Wise Measure: The Search for the Canadian-American Boundary, 1783–1842*. Toronto: University of Toronto Press, 2001.

Cohen, Paul E., and Robert T. Augustyn. *Manhattan in Maps, 1527–1995*. New York: Rizzoli, 1997.

Cumming, William P. *British Maps of Colonial America*. Chicago: University of Chicago Press, 1974.

Gronim, Sara Stidstone. "Geography and Persuasion: Maps in British Colonial New York," *The William and Mary Quarterly*, vol. 58, no. 2 (2001): 373–402.

Grundset, Eric. *New York in the American Revolution*. Washington: National Society Daughters of the American Revolution, 2012. See chapter 3 for an annotated bibliography of maps.

Homberger, Eric. *The Historical Atlas of New York City: A Visual Celebration of 400 Years of New York City's History*. New York: Henry Holt, 2005.

Mano, Jo Margaret. "Annotated Bibliography of Selected New York State Maps: 1793–1900." New York State Library. Updated January 29, 2014. *www.nysl.nysed.gov/msscfa/mapsbibl.htm#Annotated*

Mix, David E. E. *Catalogue of Maps and Surveys, in the Offices of the Secretary of State, State Engineer and Surveyor, and Comptroller, and the New York State Library*. Albany, 1859.

Munger, William Peres, ed. *Historical Atlas of New York State*. Phoenix, NY: F. E. Richard, 1941.

Rayback, Robert J., and Jeanne Meador Schwartz. *Richard's Atlas of New York State*. Phoenix, NY: F. E. Richards, 1968.

Schwarz, Philip J. *The Jarring Interests: New York's Boundary Makers, 1664–1776*. Albany: State University of New York Press, 1979.

Thorne, Kathryn Ford. *Atlas of Historical County Boundaries: New York*. New York: Simon and Schuster, 1993.

Wright, Albert Hazen. *A Check List of New York State County Maps Published 1779–1945*. Ithaca, NY: The Author, 1965.

———. *The New York Town Maps in Library of Congress and Cornell Archives*. Ithaca: The Author, 1965.

Wright, Albert Hazen, and Willard Waldo Ellis. *New York Historical Source Studies. Part I: Supervisor's Proceedings of Various Counties of New York. Part II: Checklist of the County Atlases of New York*. Ithaca, NY: The Author, 1943.

Table 1: Major Land Transactions: Grants, Patents, and Manors

Name (Year)	Counties Included	Acreage	Notes
Beekman Patent (1697)	Dutchess	ca. 100,000	Henry Beekman Sr.; boundaries redrawn 1703, divided among heirs and leased
Beekmantown Patent (1769)	Clinton	30,000	William H. Beekman; 1787 most of the land was leased as 100-acre farmsteads
Bentley Manor (1687)	Richmond	3,165	Granted to Christopher Billop, a captain in the Royal Navy, as "the Lordship and Mannor of Bentley"
Boston Ten Towns (1787)	Broome, Cortland, Tioga, Tompkins	230,400	First known as the Chenango Purchase; rights to sell land given to MA in 1786 Treaty of Hartford; purchased and mainly settled by families from Lenox and Stockbridge, MA
Burnetsfield Patent (1725)	Herkimer	ca. 9,400	Gov. William Burnet acquired land from Mohawk Indians in 1722; patented 1725; over 90, predominantly Palatine, individuals granted 100 acre parcels
Canadian & Nova Scotia Refugee Tract (1784)	Clinton	ca. 131,500	Law passed allocating land near Lake Champlain for patriot military personnel from Canada; 227 lots distributed 1786
Cassiltown(e) Manor (1687)	Richmond	ca. 25,000	Granted to John Palmer, Admiralty judge and supreme court Chief Justice, as "the Lordship and Mannor of Cassiltown"

Table 1: Major Land Transactions: Grants, Patents, and Manors

Name (Year)	Counties Included	Acreage	Notes
Chenango Twenty Townships (1789–1794)	Chenango, Madison, Oneida	ca. 500,000	Officially called Governor's Twenty Towns or Clinton's Purchase; surveyed 1789, purchases began 1791
Chesecock Patent (1707)	Orange, Rockland	40,000–75,000	Dr. John Bridges fronted the purchase; boundaries ill-defined, estimates on acreage vary greatly, and land involved in NY/NJ boundary disputes
Cortlandt Manor (1697)	Westchester	86,000	Stephanus van Cortlandt (NYC mayor 1677–1678, 1686–1688); first acquired Indian land in 1677; the manor connected land parcels and was granted as "the Lordship and Mannour of Cortlandt"
Cosby's Manor (1734)	Herkimer, Oneida	22,000–42,000	Original patentees conveyed land, before February 19, 1735, to William Cosby, Gov. of NY and NJ 1732–1736; estimates on acreage vary as Cosby bought two tracts in the same year
Eaton Manor (1686)	Suffolk	1,500	Granted to Richard and Alexander Bryan, CT merchants, as "the Lordship and Mannour of Eaton"
Fishers Island Manor (1668)	Suffolk	4,000	Granted to John Winthrop, Jr., Gov. of CT, as "an Intire Enfranchised Towneship Mannor & Place of itself"
Fordham Manor (1671)	Westchester	3,900	John (Jan) Archer mortgaged land to Cornelius van Steenwyck (NYC mayor 1668–1671, 1682–1684) as mortgage not paid, Steenwyck's widow inherited land; she left it to New York Reformed Dutch Church in 1695
Fox Hall Manor (1672)	Ulster	330	Granted to Thomas Chambers with local autonomy in 1672, rights extended to "Lordship and Mannor of Foxhall" in 1686
Gardiner's Island Manor (1665)	Suffolk	ca. 3,000	1639/40 King Charles I gave Lion Gardiner "the right to possess the land forever"; 1665 his son David was granted local autonomy, and 1686 rights were extended to "Lordshipp and Mannor of Gardiner's Island"
Great Nine Partners Patent (1697)	Dutchess	ca. 150,000	Caleb Heathcote, Augustine Graham, and seven speculators from NYC; also called Lower Nine Partners; divided and sold 1734
Hardenbergh Patent (1708)	Delaware, Greene, Sullivan, Ulster	1.5 million	Johannes Hardenburgh and others acquired land 1707, patent granted 1708; American Indians forced to relinquish ancestral lands to new settlers after the Revolution
Highland/Philipse Patent (1697)	Incorp. in Dutchess Co., later Putnam Co.	ca. 200,000	Adolphus Philipse; most of the land now in Putnam Co.; his nephew Frederick Philipse II inherited this patent, as well as Philipsburgh Manor
Holland Land Company Purchase (1792–1796)	Allegany, Cattaraugus, Chautauqua, Erie, Genesee, Niagara, Orleans, Wyoming	3.6 million	Dutch investors began purchasing land in 1792; they formed the Holland Land Company in 1796; early purchases included current Cazenovia and land along the upper Black River (the Oldenbarneveld Settlement); largest purchase (ca. 3 million acres) in western NY from Robert Morris; land sales began 1801 after American Indian land titles were resolved
Holland Patent (1769)	Oneida	ca. 20,000	Henry Fox (Lord Holland); sold most land before 1797; majority of early settlers were Welsh

Table 1: Major Land Transactions: Grants, Patents, and Manors

Name (Year)	Counties Included	Acreage	Notes
Kakiat(e) Patent (1696)	Rockland	100,000–185,000	Daniel Honan and Michael Hawdon; both sold their land by 1716; estimates of acreage vary greatly; land was claimed by other patents and involved in NY/NJ boundary disputes
Kayaderosseras Patent (1708)	Fulton, Montgomery, Saratoga, Schenectady, Warren	ca. 400,000	Authorized 1701 to Manning Hermanse and others; series of revisions 1703–1708; land finally divided and surveyed in 1771 after years of disputes with Mohawks over fraudulent deed
Kingsborough Patent (1753)	Fulton	20,000	Sir William Johnson and Arent Stevens; Johnson settled English, Scots, and Irish immigrants as tenants and laid out the market town of Johnstown
Kipsburgh Manor-Rhinebeck Patent (1697)	Dutchess	ca. 20,000	Gerrit Aertson, Hendrick Kip, and Henry Beekman Sr.; boundaries changed June 8, 1703
Little Nine Partners (1706)	Dutchess	18,000-60,000	Sampson Broughton and others; boundaries ill-defined—18,000 acre patent mapped as approx. 60,000; also called Upper Nine Partners; comprises most of Town of Northeast
Livingston Manor (1686)	Columbia	ca. 160,000	Robert Livingston, Secretary of Indian Affairs and Speaker of the General Assembly, granted "the Lordshipp and Mannor of Livingston"; leased land in ca. 84-acre plots to tenant farmers; in 1728 son Philip inherited the manor and most of the land; by 1766 he had 266 tenants
Macomb Purchase (1792)	Franklin, Herkimer, Jefferson, Lewis, Oswego, St. Lawrence	ca. 3.6 million	After 1791 NYS law authorized public land sales, Alexander Macomb made large land purchase in northern NY along the St. Lawrence River; land was later divided into smaller tracts and sold to speculators
Massachusetts Reserve (1786)	Allegany, Cattaraugus, Chautauqua, Erie, Genesee, Livingston, Monroe, Niagara, Ontario, Orleans, Schuyler, Steuben, Wayne, Wyoming, Yates	ca. 6 million	1786 Treaty of Hartford: MA gained the right to buy and resell land from the Indian Nations but NYS retained political jurisdiction—see Phelps and Gorham Purchase, Morris Reserve, and Holland Land Company Purchase
Military Tract—New (1782–1791)	Cayuga, Cortland, Onondaga, Oswego, Schuyler, Seneca, Tompkins, Wayne	ca. 1.5 million	Bounty land for Revolutionary War soldiers; Indian land claims delayed allocation, finally distributed in 1791
Military Tract—Old (1786)	Clinton, Essex, Franklin	ca. 640,000	Bounty land assigned in northern NY for Revolutionary War veterans because of the delay in allocating land in the "New Military Tract"; this land was rejected by veterans in favor of the former—more arable—land, and sold by the NYS land commissioners with the usual conditions of patents
Minisink Patent (1704)	Orange, Sullivan	200,000–300,000	Matthew Ling and others; land involved in protracted NY/NJ boundary dispute; estimates on acreage vary greatly; 1769 ruling in NY's favor established Hudson to Delaware boundary with NJ

Table 1: Major Land Transactions: Grants, Patents, and Manors

Name (Year)	Counties Included	Acreage	Notes
Morris Reserve (1791)	Allegany, Genesee, Livingston, Monroe, Orleans, Wyoming	750,000–800,000	Robert Morris bought 1.2 million acres of the Massachusetts Reserve from Phelps and Gorham in 1790 and swiftly sold to English investors; he bought another 4 million acres from MA and swiftly sold over 3 million to purchasers who became the Holland Land Company
Morrisania Manor (1697)	Westchester	1,920	Lewis Morris, Chief Justice of the Province of New York and Gov. of NJ, acquired 500 acres in 1660s; granted "the Mannour or Lordship of Morrisania" in 1697
Oblong Tract (1731)	Dutchess, Putnam, Westchester	50,000	Result of 1683 boundary treaty between NY and CT; patented and then sold to Equivalent Land Co. of 22 colonists; divided and sold lots in 1732; discrepancies over boundary lines caused disputes between tenants and other patents, e.g., Highland and Beekman Patents
Pelham Manor (1666)	Westchester	9,166	Land acquired from Indians in 1654 by Dr. Thomas Pell of CT; settled with 15 families and given royal grant in 1666 after English takeover of New Netherland; his nephew John Bell inherited 1669 and received a renewed patent with manorial privileges in 1687
Penet's Square (1788)	Jefferson	6,400	Ten square miles to Pierre Penet, part of land surrendered by Oneida Indians in Treaty of Fort Schuyler; land ownership later uncertain; John LaFarge established clear title in 1830
Phelps and Gorham Purchase (1788)	Allegany, Livingston, Monroe, Ontario, Schuyler, Steuben, Wayne, Yates	2.6 million	Phelps and Gorham (P&G) contracted to purchase land rights to all the Massachusetts Reserve (6 million acres); by 1790 the MA pound tripled in value so P&G could only afford the rights to 2.6 million acres and returned the rest; later in 1790 they sold 1.2 million acres to Robert Morris
Philipsburgh Manor (1693)	Westchester	ca. 90,000	Frederick Philipse; his son Adolphus owned Highland Patent, his grandson Frederick inherited both; as they were loyalists, manor confiscated by government and sold at public auction in 1779
Plum Island Manor (1675)	Suffolk	820	Granted to Samuel Wyllys with local autonomy, "an entire and enfranchized mannor and place of itself"
Queens Village Manor (1685)	Queens, Suffolk	2,900	Granted to Henry Lloyd, "henceforth be called the Lordship and Mannor of Queens Village"; on Lloyd's Neck which was ceded by Queens Co. to Suffolk Co. in 1886
Rensselaerwyck (1629)	Albany, Columbia, Rensselaer	ca. 1 million	Kiliaen van Rensselaer granted a patroonship by Dutch West India Co.; began purchasing land in 1630; 1664 given title of Rensselaerswick Manor by English
Rombout Patent (1685) also Rumbout	Dutchess	ca. 80,000	Francis Rombouts (NYC mayor 1779–1780) and Gulian Verplanck; awarded land tracts to encourage settlement
Royal Grant / Kingsland Grant (1765)	Herkimer	ca. 93,000	Sir William Johnson petitioned for 40,000 acres and received approx. 93,000; inherited by son John in 1774; John fled to Canada in 1776, after the Revolution the land holdings were forfeited and confiscated by NYS
Sacandaga Patent (1741)	Fulton, Hamilton	28,000	Lendert Gransevoort and others, Royal Patent; later taken over by Sir William Johnson

Table 1: Major Land Transactions: Grants, Patents, and Manors

Name (Year)	Counties Included	Acreage	Notes
Saratoga Patent (1684)	Rensselaer, Saratoga, Washington	ca. 150,000	Pieter Schuyler and others; acquired from Mohawk Indians in 1683, patent confirmed 1684, new patent confirmed Oct. 1708
Scarsdale Manor (1701/02)	Westchester	11,500	Caleb Heathcote, NYC mayor 1711–1713, also a Great Nine Partners patentee; Scarsdale was the last NY manor granted
Scriba Patent (1794)	Oswego	ca. 500,000	Originally called "Roosevelt Purchase," land bought by George Scriba in 1792; patented 1794
Shelter Island Manor (1666)	Suffolk	8,000	Nathaniel and Constant Sylvester acquired the island in 1651; in 1666 they received a patent with the right of local autonomy
St. Lawrence Ten Towns (1787)	St Lawrence	64,000	Established by NYS Land Commissioners from part of Macomb Purchase; each "town" was 10 square miles; only present-day Canton, De Kalb, Lisbon, and Potsdam retain original boundaries
St. Georges Manor (1693)	Suffolk	64,000	Col. William "Tangier" Smith; land added 1697; British used "Fort St. George" during the Revolution
Stone Arabia Patent (1723)	Montgomery	12,700	Issued to 27 patentees to promote settlement; majority were German Palatines
Totten & Crossfield Purchase (1771–1787)	Essex, Hamilton, Herkimer, Warren	ca. 1,150,000	Acquired from the Mohawks; 50 townships were planned for the area but only 24 were surveyed by the beginning of the Revolution
Vermont Sufferers Tract (1786)	Chenango	ca. 41,000	Land granted by NY to compensate 135 men whose land claims in Cumberland Co. were invalidated when NY ceded their land to VT after the Revolution
Watkins and Flint Purchase (1794)	Chemung, Schuyler, Tioga, Tompkins	ca. 300,000	Purchased 1791 by NYC investors, John Watkins and Royal Flint; patented 1794; Robert C. Johnson purchased approx. 100,000 acres in 1795
Waywayanda Patent (1703)	Orange	ca. 150,000	Acquired from Munsee Indians by 12 NYC residents; boundaries ill-defined—60,000 acre patent mapped as approx. 150,000; divided 1706 by the 12 residents

Introduction

Military records may lead to accounts of life in the military, as well as dates, places, and ranks. While this chapter often refers to men, it is important to remember that women served as well, especially in more recent conflicts. Societies formed by those in military conflicts or their descendants are an important resource and will be discussed below. Major repositories for military records are listed near the end of the chapter.

Record Types and Definitions

Compiled Military Service Records

Compiled military service records consist of record abstracts, usually from records about many men, such as muster rolls and pay rolls. These records generally provide information on the name, rank, military unit, and dates of service. In addition, there may be information on the date and place of enlistment and mustering in (a gathering of the troops), physical description of the soldier, residence, pay amounts and dates, wounds, capture, death, imprisonment, hospital stay, hospital release, oath of allegiance, desertion, promotion, battles, heroic action, reenlistment, leave of absence (or furlough), mustering out, and discharge.

New York State compiled military service records exist for the War of 1812, Civil War, Spanish-American War, Mexican Border Conflict (also known as the Mexican Punitive Campaign), and World War I. Federal compiled military service records exist for the American Revolutionary War, but due to fire, federal records are less complete after 1912. A check for both state and federal records is part of a thorough genealogical search.

Bounty Land Records (1755–1855)

The Province of New York granted lands for service in the Seven Years' War (1754–1763), known as the French and Indian War in the North American colonies. Federal records are applications and awards of land in return for military service in the Revolutionary War, the War of 1812, and the Mexican War. They usually contain a name, age, rank, and military unit, as well as dates and places of enlistment, service, wartime experience, and birth. State records of land grants are discussed below. The last bounty land act was passed in 1855. See also chapter 7, Land Records and Maps.

Military Claims

Claims of military participants for military back pay or equipment, and of civilians for supplies or service, usually list the name of the claimant, details of the claim, date of the claim, witnesses to the claim, and the amount awarded if the claim was accepted. The only New York State records that fit this category are War of 1812 veterans' claims, now in the New York State Archives (NYSA).

Military Unit Histories

If researchers know the unit in which a person served, they can try to find a unit history. Unit histories usually trace the events of the unit throughout a war, often referring to officers, enlisted men, battles, campaigns, and deaths, as well as dates and places of organization, mustering in, reorganization, mustering out, and other events. They may even contain information on reunions held by unit members after the conflict ended. Most of these publications are about Civil War regiments and World Wars I and II units; unit histories are rare for other conflicts.

Manuscript collections at libraries and archives throughout New York State contain original letters and diaries by officers and soldiers who served in New York units. These collections should be consulted, not only by surname, but also by unit for an ancestor. Often these personal writings describe the experiences of the author and the people with whom they served, allowing researches to indirectly find information about an ancestor.

Military Pension Records

These federal records usually contain significant genealogical information, because the veterans or surviving spouses were required to supply documentation (e.g., marriage certificate, testimony of witnesses) to support their claims. In some cases records may contain descriptions of battles in order to document the person's capture or death. Names and places of residence of witnesses may be found in affidavits. Researchers of New York veterans and widows of those who served in the military from 1775 to 1916 may search for pension files at the National Archives (NARA) in the General Index to Pension Files, 1861–1934 (microfilm T288, 544 rolls). Some Civil War widow's pension files have been imaged by NARA's digitization partners, *Ancestry.com* and *Fold3.com* (an *Ancestry.com* subsidiary). See NARA's repository listing below.

Censuses

Certain federal and state censuses asked questions that provide information on active soldiers and veterans. Many of the schedules have been published separately, and some may be found online. See chapter 3, Census Records, for details.

Historical Overview and Selected Resources
Colonial Wars (1639–1763)

During the Dutch period wars include Kieft's War, the First and Second Esopus Wars, and the Anglo-Dutch Wars; during the English period they include King Philip's War, King William's War, Queen Anne's War, The War of Jenkin's Ear, King George's War, and the French and Indian War (Seven Years' War).

The Dutch settlements surrounding Manhattan experienced frequent conflicts with their American Indian neighbors beginning in 1639, especially during Kieft's War (1640–1645). Similar troubles led to the First and Second Esopus Wars (1659 and 1663) in the region around Wiltwijck (Kingston). New Netherland went to war in 1655 to seize New Sweden at the mouth of the Delaware River, and was constantly on guard against the English, especially during the Anglo-Dutch wars of 1652–1654, 1664–1667, and 1672–1674, which led to the end of the Dutch colony in 1664 and its brief revival in 1673–1674.

To protect New Netherland, the West India Company employed several hundred professional soldiers recruited from various European countries, a few of whom remained in the colony and left descendants. They were augmented by local Burgher Guards, which the male European settlers were required to join (see Militia and National Guard, below, and also the Dutch section in chapter 14, Peoples of New York).

During the English period, men from New York participated in all of the colonial wars listed above. King Philip's War was a conflict in New England, though New York did receive many Indian refugees who settled at Schaghticoke in the upper Hudson River Valley. The 1911 Capitol fire destroyed most original muster rolls in the New York State Library (NYSL), but fortunately the rolls had already been published with a name index in *Muster Rolls of New York Provincial Troops, 1755–1764* and the 1896–1897 *Annual Report of the State Historian*. The NYSA has land grant records for veterans of the Seven Years' War in Military Patents, 1764–1797 (series A0447) and Applications for Land Grants (series A0272).

Revolutionary War and Frontier Conflicts (1775–1811)

All of New York was of strategic importance during the Revolutionary War. For the Patriots there were four types of military service:

- Continental Army: nine New York regiments (infantry, artillery, cavalry) served under General Washington
- New York State Militia
- New York Provincial Company of Artillery created by New York Provincial Congress in 1776
- Levies drafted from the militia and citizenry of New York to serve under Continental command either inside or outside of the state

Francis J. Sypher's book *New York State Society of the Cincinnati, Histories of New York Regiments of the Continental Army* contains detailed descriptions of all of the units listed above. More than 17,700 New York men served in the Continental Army; almost 4,000 were militiamen.

NARA has resources helpful for finding a Revolutionary War soldier from any state. These include the index and records of the Compiled Service Records of Revolutionary War Soldiers, Army Staff (series M881) for which images are available on *Fold3.com* (indexes available on *FamilySearch.org*), as well as the index and records of the Compiled Service Records of Naval Personnel during the Revolutionary War (series M880, microfilm available from the Family History Library).

The NYSA holds the extant Revolutionary War records of state government, including bounty land grants and applications for land grants. Records containing military service data include the following, and some of them are name-indexed on the NYSA's website:

- Military Patents (series A0447), land grants to Continental officers and soldiers (including drafted men, or "Levies") or their assignees
- Applications for Land Grants (series A0272), see abstracts in *Calendar of N.Y. Colonial Manuscripts Indorsed Land Papers, 1643–1803*
- Revolutionary War Accounts and Claims (series A0200), names abstracted in James A. Roberts, *New York in the Revolution as Colony and State*
- Audited Accounts (A0870, summarizing data in series A0200)
- Certificates Submitted by Disabled Revolutionary War Veterans (series A0174), covers 1779–1789 only.

Berthold Fernow's *New York in the Revolution* (Vol. 15 of *Documents Relating to the Colonial History of the State of New*

York) contains records from the NYSA. It overlaps with Roberts' *New York in the Revolution as Colony and State*, but each has unique material all burned in the Capitol fire of 1911.

Also see the New-York Historical Society's (N-YHS) *Muster and Pay Rolls of the War of the Revolution*. These rolls are in the N-YHS collections.

Note also that there are other Revolutionary muster rolls that were preserved in private collections and are found in published local histories.

Information on the burial of Revolutionary War soldiers can be found in Patricia Law Hatcher's *Abstract of Graves of Revolutionary Patriots*, digitized and searchable at *Ancestry.com*. This set is based on the National Society Daughters of the American Revolution's (DAR) listings of located and marked graves of soldiers and Patriots published in its annual report from the early-twentieth century to 1977. Subsequent markings, locations, and corrections are maintained by the DAR's Office of the Historian General (see chapter 16, National and Statewide Repositories & Resources).

The DAR's contribution to the Revolutionary War literature is extensive, and researchers can consult its website (*dar.org/library*) for resources. Eric Grundset's recent book on New York in the Revolutionary War is completely comprehensive. Names of many Revolutionary War soldiers buried in New York State may be found in the DAR's "Graves of Revolutionary Soldiers in New York." Local New York State chapters of the DAR have compiled information about New York Revolutionary soldiers that can be found by searching the DAR Library online catalog. The online DAR Genealogical Research System (*www.dar.org*) allows researchers to search for an ancestor by name and see whether the ancestor's lineage and Revolutionary War service has already been proven.

The National Society Sons of the American Revolution (SAR) was organized in 1889 as a fraternal and civic society. Membership is given to descendants of supporters of American independence, including soldiers and members of the Continental Congress. The *Register of the Empire State Sons of the American Revolution* provides information about the patriot ancestors of the SAR members and is online at *HathiTrust.org*. Membership applications (1899–1970) are available on *Ancestry.com*. The SAR Patriot and Grave Index is searchable online at *patriot.sar.org* and was created from previous SAR publications. See the section on lineage societies in chapter 16, National and Statewide Repositories & Resources.

A group of Continental Army officers established the Society of the Cincinnati in 1783. See Francis J. Sypher's book *New York State Society of the Cincinnati: Biographies of Original Members & Other Continental Officers*. The Society of the Cincinnati maintains its own archives, including minutes, proceedings, and correspondence. A finding aid is available on the Society's website (*societyofthecincinnati.org*). Some of the proceedings have been microfilmed by the Family History Library (FHL). For more detail about the Society of the Cincinnati, see chapter 16, National and Statewide Repositories & Resources.

The Daughters of the Cincinnati is a membership organization formed in 1894 by female descendants of Continental Army officers. The Ancestor Card File, A–Z; Card Index of Eligible Members, A–Z; and Application Packets, Membership List, and Roster of Ancestors are available on microfilm from the FHL.

Loyalists

New York City, Long Island, Staten Island, Westchester County, and certain upstate areas had concentrations of colonists who remained loyal to Great Britain. After the war many Loyalists left the new United States and petitioned the Crown for compensation for lost property. Both the NYSL and the New York Public Library (NYPL) have some original documents relating to Loyalists, and the NYSL has a bibliography for Loyalist records on its website. Both the NYPL and the NYSL hold "American Loyalist Claims" reproducing 146 volumes of Britain Public Record Office material (series A.O., 12, 30 microfilm reels). The NYPL also holds the second series, American Loyalist Claims (series A.O. 13, Series II, 145 reels). Researchers should check both the NYPL Milstein and Manuscript divisions for Loyalist records.

Also see numerous articles in the *NYG&B Record* about Loyalists in New York. Recently Gavin K. Watt, a prolific historian who has written extensively on the subject of Loyalists, published a report, *Loyalist Refugees: Non-Military Refugees in Quebec 1776–1784*, listing over 2,000 loyalists who went to Canada, most of whom were from New York.

Post-Revolutionary Wars to 1858 (1783–1858)

This period includes the War of 1812, Indian Wars, the Patriot War (Canadian), and the Mexican War.

NARA has microfilm indexes to records for the War of 1812, the Indian Wars and Disturbances 1815–1858 (microfilm M0629), and the Mexican War 1846–1848 (microfilm M0616). These records include pension and bounty land warrant applications, and compiled service records.

NARA's War of 1812 pension files, which have never been microfilmed, are being slowly digitized (in alphabetical order) and placed on *Fold3.com*. "Genealogical Records of the War of 1812" by Stuart L. Butler is useful for NARA holdings relating to the war. Copies of indexes are available through other repositories such as the FHL and the NYPL. The Mexican War Pension Index, 1887–1926, is online at *FamilySearch.org*.

The Patriot War—a conflict between some Canadians seeking independence and the English in late 1837 and early 1838—took place in what is now Quebec; a battle took place on Canadian soil near Niagara Falls, and Canadians and some American partisans retreated to the city of Buffalo. New York militia organized briefly in early 1838 to protect against incursion by these groups; service records are at NARA (series M0630) and on microfilm at the FHL.

The NYSA holds militia payroll transcriptions for the War of 1812 (series B0810 and B0811) that provide name, rank, organization, and the amount of pay for men who came under federal command during the war. The NYSA also has militia veterans' certificates of claim for reimbursement (series A0020 and A3352). These are microfilmed and are indexed in New York Adjutant General's Office's *Index of Awards on Claims of the Soldiers of the War of 1812*. The book *New York Military Equipment Claims, War of 1812* is available on *Ancestry.com* to those New Yorkers who have created a free New York account (see the NYSA entry in chapter 16 for details). The NYSA also holds claims by veterans of the one New York volunteer regiment that served in the Mexican War (series A1254).

Military Minutes of the Council of Appointment of the State of New York, 1783–1821, vol. 4, contains names of all militia officers commissioned by New York State governors from 1783 to 1821.

Civil War (1861–1865)

Union Army records include enlistment papers, draft files, muster rolls, prisoner-of-war papers, death reports, and more. Listings in *Civil War Muster Roll Abstracts of New York State Volunteers . . .* often contain the place of enlistment and soldier's description. These are available on *Ancestry.com* (at no charge with a free New York-records Ancestry account).

Although the vast majority of Union soldiers were volunteers, single men (age 20–45) and married men (20–35) were subject to conscription beginning in 1863. It was possible to avoid conscription by payment of a $300 fee or the hiring of a substitute.

There are three types of draft records at NARA:

- Consolidated lists (ARC Identifier 4213514)—these draft records usually include the man's name, place of residence, age as of July 1, 1863, occupation, marital status, state, territory, or country of birth, and the military organization of which he was a member. These records are filed by state and then by congressional district [*Ancestry.com*].
- Descriptive rolls—many entries are not completed, but these records might include a personal description, exact place of birth, and whether a person was accepted or rejected for service. These records are filed by state and then by congressional district.
- Case files on aliens who were drafted—these records concern aliens who were drafted and released from 1861 to 1864. The files are in alphabetical order by surname, and may include name, district, country of citizenship, age, length of time in the United States, and a physical description. See *research.archives.gov/description/865200*.

The Index to Compiled Service Records of Volunteer Union Soldiers Who Served in Organizations from the State of New York (microfilm M551, 157 rolls) and the General Index to Pension Files, 1861–1934 (microfilm T288, 544 rolls) are NARA microfilm sets that are available through the FHL, the NYPL, and online at *Ancestry.com* and *FamilySearch.org*. Some pension files held by NARA are currently being digitized by *Fold3.com* (widow's pensions as mentioned above).

The 1865 New York State census had questions regarding military service, specifically employment in military or naval service of the United States, on June 1, 1865, or earlier.

The NYSA holds extensive records of New York men who served in the Civil War, partially duplicating those held by NARA. An 1863 law required compilation of a record for every New Yorker who had volunteered for service. This resulted in registers of men who were currently or formerly in service, or who died in service as of 1865 (series A0389). An 1865 law required the clerk of each town and city to compile a record of soldiers and sailors who comprised that community's quota of troops (series 13774). Both sets of registers are arranged geographically by county, then by town or city, and are on microfilm. The town and city registers have been digitized and indexed by *Ancestry.com*. (Registers for some communities, including New York City, are missing, but lists of soldiers from those communities are included in series A0389.)

In 1876 New York started compiling abstracts of muster rolls of volunteer regiments, sharpshooters, and U.S. Colored Troops (series 13775). When completed circa 1900, the abstracts totaled 1,231 volumes containing 550,000 records. They are indexed in the "New York State Civil War Soldier" database on the NYSA website. Microfilmed images have been digitized by *Ancestry.com*. Core information in the abstracts, arranged by regiment, was printed in the annual reports of the New York Adjutant General, 1893–1905. Other Civil War abstracts for members of the Navy, Marines, and the New York National Guard are being digitized by *Ancestry.com*.

Researchers can consult Harold Holzer's *The Union Preserved: A Guide to Civil War Records in the New York State Archives* and Kenneth Munden and Henry Beer's *The Union: A Guide to Federal Archives Relating to the Civil War*.

The Civil War Soldiers and Sailors database on the website of the National Park Service (*nps.gov*) is searchable by name and state, and provides summary histories of the veteran's unit, including military engagements.

Histories of units can add color to an ancestor's story. However, NARA cautions the researcher not to assume that an individual participated in every battle fought by his unit. See NARA's Civil War records page for a detailed explanation at *www.archives.gov/research/military/civil-war/resources.html*. The New York State Military Museum's Unit History Project provides summary historical information for New York units in the Civil War. These include the artillery regiments and battalions. "Civil War Unit Histories: Regimental Histories and Personal Narratives," an extensive microfiche set of full-text sources, is available at the NYSL and the NYPL. It includes the New York State Adjutant-General's reports about Civil War regiments and many volumes from the NYPL.

The Hamilton College Library has an online collection of Civil War letters (cwl.dhinitiative.org) mostly from regiments from upstate counties, especially Oneida County where Hamilton College is located.

Grand Army of the Republic

The Grand Army of the Republic (GAR), founded in 1866, was an organization of Union Army veterans. GAR Records, Department of New York, 1865–1949 (including post rosters) are held at the NYSA (series B1706). They have not been microfilmed, digitized, or indexed, and are fragile. A finding aid is available on the NYSA website. Information on GAR posts and the men who held them can be found on Morrisville State College Library's website in the "New York State and the Civil War" page (library.morrisville.edu/localhistory.aspx). A few GAR rosters and encampment records are available through the FHL.

United States Sanitary Commission

The NYPL's Manuscripts and Archives Division holds the archive of the United States Sanitary Commission (USSC), a civilian organization that provided assistance to Union soldiers and sailors (and, in some circumstances, family members) during and after the war; it existed from 1861 until 1879. The archive is huge, at over 900 linear feet. It includes correspondence with soldiers, claim files, local agent records, diaries, scrapbooks, and other documents rich in genealogically relevant data in 20 series. The NYPL website has a detailed description of the collection. Not cataloged until 2013, it is largely unexplored by researchers. Some parts of the archive have been microfilmed; some images have been digitized. A finding aid of over 1,000 pages includes an index of about 40,000 names from claim files. The finding aid is online at nypl.org in sections; the largest section (the one with the listing of names) is at http://archives .nypl.org/uploads/collection/pdf_finding_aid/mss18809.pdf. Due to the fragility and scope of the collection, in-person research is usually necessary. Other repositories hold local agency or branch collections or other records of the USSC or related aid organizations.

Spanish-American War (1898)

NARA's "General Index to Compiled Service Records of Volunteer Soldiers Who Served during the War with Spain" is available through the FHL and the NYPL, and online at Ancestry.com and FamilySearch.org.

Spanish-American War veterans are included in NARA's General Index to Pension Files, 1861–1934 (microfilm T288) which is available through the FHL, the NYPL, and online at Ancestry.com and FamilySearch.org. The pension file documents are held by NARA, and are being digitized by Fold3.com.

The NYSA's Abstracts of Spanish-American War, Philippine-American War, and China Relief Expedition ("Boxer Rebellion") Military and Naval Service Records (series B0809) provide summary data in card form on New York men who served in the U.S. Army, Navy, and Marine Corps. Abstracts of Muster Rolls for National Guard and Naval Militia Units Mustered into Federal Service (series B0801) is described and indexed in New York in the Spanish-American War.

Theodore Roosevelt's First U.S. Volunteer Cavalry Regiment, otherwise known as the "Rough Riders," fought in Cuba. Books by Edward Marshall and Virgil Jones contain detailed lists of men who served in this unit.

Some Spanish-American War records are at the New York City Municipal Archives (MUNI). See B-Ann Moorhouse's "Little Publicized New York City Sources: The Landon Papers and Military Records." There are two reels of microfilm, "U.S. Soldiers in Cuba and Puerto Rico: Deaths 1898–1900" and "United Spanish-American War Veterans," recording deceased veterans.

World War I (1914–1918, United States entry 1917)

NARA holds U.S. World War I Draft Registrations Cards for 24 million men (approximately 25 percent of the total population); both aliens and United States citizens were required to register. The World War I draft consisted of three separate registrations:

- The First Registration in June 1917 was for men ages 21–31.
- The Second Registration in June 1918 was for men who had turned 21 after the first registration—and men not previously registered and not already in the military. A supplemental registration in August 1918 was for men who had turned 21 after June 5, 1918. A question about the registrant's father's birth place was asked.
- The Third Registration in September 1918 was for men age 18–21 and 31–45; this asked questions regarding citizenship and naturalization.

These records are available on Ancestry.com and FamilySearch.org (the index on FamilySearch.org was mostly complete at the time this book was published). The NYPL and NARA at New York City have microfilm copies of the New York City registrations.

After the United States entered World War I in 1917, New York State took a "Military Census" of men eligible for military duty. No census returns are now held in any state office or at the NYSA. The Manhattan census, however, is at the New York County Clerk's Division of Old Records and Brooklyn's at the Kings County Clerk's Office. Copies of the census may exist for other localities. Researchers should contact county clerk's offices for information.

For a summary of World War I holdings at NARA, see Mitchell Yockelson's "They Answered the Call, Military Service in the United States Army during World War I, 1917–1919."

The National Personnel Records Center (NPRC) holds most surviving twentieth-century service records for United States military personnel including those who served in WWI. See the entry for the NPRC later in this chapter.

The NYSA holds summary data on New York men who served in the U.S. Army, Navy, and Marine Corps, and on women who were Army or Navy nurses, in Abstracts of World War I Military Service (series B0808). More than 800,000 summary cards were prepared from federal personnel records later destroyed by fire in 1973. In addition, miscellaneous service information can be found in World War I Veterans' Service Data (series A0412), also available in "New York, World War I Veterans' Service Data, 1913–1919" on *Ancestry.com*.

Information on National Guard members mustered into federal service during World War I is found at the NYSA in Abstracts of National Guard Service in World War I (series 13721). Some of these are available in the NYSA Digital Collections on its website. See *A Spirit of Sacrifice: New York's Response to the Great War; A Guide to Records Relating to World War I Held in the New York State Archives*, a version of which is on the NYSA website.

A list of New Yorkers who died in World War I can be found in Brigadier General Kincaid's *Roll of Honor: Citizens of the State of New York Who Died While in the Service of the United States during the World War*.

World War II (1939–1945, U.S. entry 1941)

The National Personnel Records Center (NPRC) in St. Louis, Missouri maintains World War II Selective Service Records. The Selective Service System conducted six draft registrations during World War II. All males ages 21–36 were required to register on October 16, 1940, under the 1940 Selective Training and Service Act. This draft and the two subsequent drafts are not available due to privacy laws.

The fourth draft, often referred to as the "old man's registration," was conducted in 1942 and registered men who were not already in the military. It lists men born between April 28, 1877 and February 16, 1897—men 45 to 64 years old at the time of registration. Information available on the draft cards includes name, age, birth date, birthplace, residence, employer information, name and address of a person who would always know the registrant's whereabouts, and physical description of registrant. Records of the fourth draft are available on *FamilySearch.org, Ancestry.com,* and *Fold3.com*.

World War II Army enlistment records, 1938–1946, for the 8.3 million men and women who enlisted in the U.S. Army during

World War II, are available at NARA. These records are also available on *Ancestry.com*.

The NYSA has no World War II records, except microfilmed summary service cards for National Guard personnel who were inducted into the U.S. Army starting in 1940 (series B2001).

A bibliography of World War II unit histories, *Unit Histories of World War II, United States Army, Air Force, Marines, Navy,* was published in collaboration with Charles E. Dornbusch.

Post-World War II, including Korean War and Vietnam Era

The NPRC maintains Selective Service Records for this time period for all men born before 1960 (except men born between March 29, 1957 and December 31, 1959, when the program was suspended).

Veterans or surviving next of kin can request copies of service records from NARA for post-World War II veterans.

"Korean War Casualties" is a searchable database on *Fold3.com* covering casualties sustained by American soldiers between February 13, 1950 and December 31, 1953. Records usually give name, place of residence, birth year, service information, and casualty information. Records of soldiers who died while prisoners of war or while missing in action are included.

"Vietnam War, Casualties Returned Alive, 1962–1979" on *Ancestry.com* contains information from NARA's "Combat Area Casualties Returned Alive" file (subset of NARA record group 330). Files typically include personal information (name, age, marital status, and race), service information (branch of service, occupation, and date of tour), and information on the casualty.

Militia and National Guard

The first militia in New York, called the Burgher Guard, was organized in New Amsterdam in May 1640 to assist professional soldiers of the Dutch West India Company. Similar guards were organized later at other settlements. Both Dutch and British colonial rulers made militia service compulsory, British law requiring all men ages 16 to 60 to serve. Many muster rolls from the colonial period will be found in the 1896/97 *Annual Report of the State Historian* and O'Callaghan's *Documentary History of the State of New York*.

In 1792 a federal law required all free white men between the ages of 18 and 45 to enroll in their state's militia. Compulsory militia service was abolished in 1846, though the service obligation had to be commuted by a monetary payment until 1870.

Units of the state militia began to be called the National Guard in 1862. The militia units in New York were reorganized in response to the National Militia Act of 1903 and became the New York National Guard, a statewide organization, about 1906. In 1947 the New York National Guard was divided into the Air National Guard and the Army National Guard. Members of the militia and National Guard are not full-time soldiers; they are part of a reserve force and almost always hold civilian jobs.

The NYSA holds registers of the New York Militia and National Guard commissioned officers (1800–1909) and muster rolls of the National Guard (1878–1954; previous muster rolls were destroyed in the capitol fire of 1911). These are not indexed, microfilmed, or digitized. Information on National Guard members mustered into federal service during World War I can be found at the NYSA in Abstracts of National Guard Service in World War I (series 13721). Images for the "Harlem Hell Fighters" are available on the Digital Collections section of the NYSA website. This African American unit has been written about extensively, most recently by Jeffrey Sammons and John H. Morrow, Jr.

Ancestry.com has digitized some original records held by the New York State Military Museum, located in Saratoga Springs. The enlistment records can be found in "New York, 74th Infantry National Guard Enlistment Cards, 1889–1917" and "New York, U.S. National Guard Enlistment Cards, 1923–1947." These often contain the name, age, place and date of birth, physical characteristics, occupation, residence, and service information of the enlisted. Service cards for officers of the state militia and National Guard have also been digitized as "New York, Military Service Cards, 1816–1979." These almost always list name, rank, and unit, and may contain further personal information. The "New York, National Guard Monthly Roster, 1940–1945" includes both rosters and muster rolls. Rosters give name, unit, and rank; muster rolls give name, rank, age, date of enlistment, and enlistment term. In addition, the New York State Military Museum holds service cards for New York members of the National Guard called into service in the fall of 1940.

Towns may have militia or other military records not found in the state archives. For example, John Hammond's *Civil War Records: Town of Oyster Bay* includes a lengthy roll of the 15th Regiment New York State Militia, giving the local residence and age of each man, most of whom did not enter federal service; also included are town rolls relating to the Civil War draft and recruitment.

The early sections of *Military Minutes of the Council of Appointment* should also be consulted for more early militia-related records.

Repositories and Resources

Full listings for most of the repositories or resources in this section may be found in chapter 16, National and Statewide Repositories & Resources. Those not included in chapter 16 list addresses and phone numbers.

National
National Archives and Records Administration (NARA)
archives.gov

NARA has pre-World War I-compiled military service records, pension application files, pension ledgers, pension payment vouchers, bounty land files, and draft records including:

- Volunteer military service 1775–1902
- U.S. Army enlisted personnel 1789–October 31, 1912, and officers 1789–June 30, 1917
- U.S. Navy enlisted personnel 1798–1885, and officers 1798–1902
- U.S. Marine Corps enlisted personnel 1789–1904, some officers 1789–1895
- U.S. Coast Guard predecessor agencies 1791–1919 (Revenue Cutter Service, Life-Saving Service, and Lighthouse Service)
- Veterans' pension files and claims 1775–1916 (except for Confederates)
- Bounty land files 1775–1855
- Enlistment registers 1789–1914 (Adjutant General's Office)

There are compiled military service records for volunteers only; the rest are muster rolls, pay rolls, and other original records.

Some records can only be accessed in person at NARA in Washington, DC, in particular pension files (except those digitized by *Fold3.com*). However, microfilm copies of many military service-related indexes can be found in NARA branches, the FHL, the NYPL, and the NYSL. Some material is also online at *FamilySearch.org*, *Fold3.com*, and *Ancestry.com*. For copies of veterans' records from World War I to the present, NARA provides an online request form (*archives.gov/veterans*).

The National Personnel Records Center (NPRC)
One Archives Drive • St. Louis, MO 63138 • (314) 801-0800
E-mail: MPR.center@nara.gov • *archives.gov/st-louis*

This unit of NARA has military records for the twentieth century. Archival records (for veterans discharged more than 62 years ago) are open to the public, and federal records (veterans discharged less than 62 years ago) are restricted to the veteran or next of kin if the veteran is deceased.

A fire in 1973 destroyed 80 percent of the records for U.S. Army officers and enlisted men (including Army Air Force) discharged from 1912 to 1959. Seventy-five percent of Air Force records from 1947 to 1963 (surnames Hubbard through Z) were destroyed. In the years following the fire, the NPRC has collected numerous records (referred to as auxiliary records) that are being used to reconstruct basic service information. U.S. Navy and Marine Corps records sustained no losses due to this fire.

New York State

The New York State Archives (NYSA)

archives.nysed.gov

The NYSA holds records documenting individuals who served in the armed forces of colonial New York or New York State during conflicts prior to World War II, including collections such as registers of New York State Militia commissioned officers (1800–1909), and muster rolls of New York National Guard (1878–1954). Many records from colonial wars and the American Revolutionary War were damaged or destroyed by the 1911 Capitol fire in Albany.

NYSA has a web page, "Military Records | New York State Archives," with links for five research guides to military records (*www.archives.nysed.gov/a/research/res_topics_military. shtml*). For a listing of records that have been abstracted and/ or indexed in publications, see *New York State Archives Information Leaflet #4* on the NYSA website. The NYSA does not hold federal government records.

The New York State Library (NYSL)

nysl.nysed.gov

Collections of the NYSL include Military History and Genealogy; researchers are advised to check both areas on the NYSL website. Two guides available on the NYSL's website are "New York State Military Records before the Civil War" and "New York State Military Records Civil War and Following." The NYSL holds a large collection of Civil War regimental histories (print and microfilm), as well as an extensive collection of works compiled by New York State chapters of the DAR. The NYSL holds an unpublished 15-volume transcription, "Graves of Revolutionary Soldiers in New York" (1922–1955).

The New York Public Library (NYPL)

www.nypl.org

The NYPL holds a notable collection of regimental histories and naval cruise books, especially for the Civil War, World War I, and World War II. The NPRC refers veterans whose records were lost in the 1973 fire to the NYPL Milstein Division unit histories collections. In addition to unit histories, some muster rolls or compiled lists, research guides, and manuscripts contain New York military information.

New York State Military Museum and Veterans Research Center

6 Lake Avenue • Saratoga Springs, NY 12866 • (518) 581-5100 (518) 581-5121 for information on how to submit research questions • *dmna.ny.gov/historic/mil-hist.htm*

The museum, owned by the State of New York, focuses on New York's military and veterans. It contains a large collection of artifacts of all kinds representing all conflicts from the American Revolution to the present, and maintains a library and archives. The library contains books about military and New York State history, thousands of photographs, unit history files, letters, and ephemera. Many of the photographs are now on *Fold3.com*.

The New York State Military Museum Unit History Project provides summary historical information for New York units in the Civil War. These include the artillery regiments and battalions. There is a collection of newspaper clippings filed by New York unit, and service records of the New York National Guard from the 1880s to the mid-1960s. Also located here are the archives of the New York State Veteran Oral History Program and the Veteran Questionnaire Program. An advanced search function provides an opportunity to explore the collection in some detail.

County, City, and Town Clerks

Town or city clerks may hold military registers and enrollment books for volunteer New York militia service, and/or for money commutation of service, for the mid-nineteenth century. County clerks may also hold veterans' discharges (beginning with World War I). In 1920 a law was passed allowing veterans to file an honorable discharge. Filing was and still is optional; however privacy restrictions apply to most discharge records.

Hamilton College

Burke Library • 198 College Hill Road • Clinton, NY 13323 (315) 859-4471 • Email: askarch@hamilton.edu *hamilton.edu/library/collections/specialcollections*

The special collections are strong in New York State and local history, the Adirondacks, and regimental histories of the Civil War. For example, they hold the enlistment forms for the New York State 117th Volunteer Regiment; this collection has been transcribed, digitized, and put online. The library also holds special collections of books printed in Albany and Utica, among other resources.

Research Aids and Online Resources

Cyndi's List (*cydnislist.com*) has extensive links to military sites, many of which will provide background and leads for researchers to find sources of original records.

FamilySearch.org contains many nationwide indexes to military service records, as well as some transcriptions. The site includes links to *Fold3.com* where subscribers of *Fold3.com* can access original images. It has an online guide New York Military Records in the wiki: *https://familysearch.org/learn/wiki/en/ New_York_Military_Records*.

Fold3.com is a subscription site that specializes in information about military records and collections. This site is a NARA digitization partner. An extensive number of military records and indexes are available, both as original documents and transcriptions. Examples include service cards, army enlistment records, pension files, and draft registration cards. Some content is available on *Ancestry.com*, its parent company.

The *Guide to Genealogical Research in the National Archives of the United States* contains chapters on records of the regular army, service records of volunteers, naval and marine service records, pension records, bounty land warrant records, and other records relating to military service.

"Online Military Indexes & Records" is a directory of links to online military indexes and records (Revolutionary War through Vietnam), including rosters, databases of soldiers, and listings of military and war casualties (*militaryindexes.com*).

U.S. Army Heritage and Education Center in Carlisle, PA, provides research assistance in addition to an extensive catalog and some online holdings (*www.carlisle.army.mil/ahec/index.cfm*).

Selected Bibliography and Further Reading

Note that following the first ("general") section, this bibliography is arranged chronologically by war.

General

Horowitz, Lois. *A Bibliography of Military Name Lists from Pre-1675 to 1900: A Guide to Genealogical Sources.* Metuchen, NJ: Scarecrow Press, 1990. Compiled sources of veterans' names from 400 publications that collected data from cemeteries, rosters, newspapers, reunions, etc.

Plante, Trevor K. "An Overview of Records at the National Archives Relating to Military Service." *Prologue*, vol. 34, no. 3 (2002): 231. Author is an archivist who specializes in military records prior to World War II.

United States and National Archives and Records Service. *Guide to Genealogical Research in the National Archives of the United States.* 3rd edition. Washington, DC: National Archives and Records Service, 2001.

Colonial Wars

Calendar of N. Y. Colonial Manuscripts: Indorsed Land Papers in the Office of the Secretary of State of New York 1643–1803. Albany: Weed, Parsons, 1864.

Meyers, Carol M. *Early Military Records of New York, 1689–1738.* Saugus, CA: Ram Publishers, 1967. Her records are drawn from O'Callaghan's *Documentary History*; see below.

Muster Rolls of New York Provincial Troops, 1755–1764. New York: New-York Historical Society, 1892. The records in this book are also in the *Annual Report of the State Historian*, below, but both transcriptions should be checked as the transcribers sometimes read a name differently; original records were destroyed in the 1911 Capitol fire.

New York State. *Annual Report of the State Historian of the State of New York, 1896–97.* Albany and New York: Wynkoop Hallenbeck Crawford, 1897–1898. Contains New York colonial muster rolls, 1664–1775; the index is in the 1897 volume.

O'Callaghan, Edmund Bailey, trans. and ed. *Documentary History of the State of New York.* 4 vols. Albany: State of New York 1849–1851 (octavo ed.) and 1850–1851 (quarto ed. with different pagination).

American Revolutionary War

Bielinski, Stefan, ed. *A Guide to the Revolutionary War Manuscripts in the New York State Library.* Albany: New York State American Bicentennial Commission, 1976. Includes state government records transferred to the NYSA in 1978.

Bockstruck, Lloyd DeWitt. *Revolutionary Bounty Land Grants Awarded by State Governments.* Baltimore: Genealogical Publishing Co., 1996.

Chopra, Ruma. *Unnatural Rebellion: Loyalists in New York City during the Revolution.* Charlottesville: University of Virginia Press, 2011.

Fernow, Berthold, ed. *New York in the Revolution.* Vol. 15 of *Documents Relating to the Colonial History of the State of New York.* Albany: Weed, Parsons, 1887.

Flick, Alexander C. *Loyalism in New York during the American Revolution.* New York: Columbia University Press, 1901.

"Graves of Revolutionary Soldiers in New York." 1922–1955. Typescript. 15 vols. Compiled by the Daughters of the American Revolution. N.p.

Grundset, Eric G. *New York in the American Revolution: A Source Guide for Genealogists and Historians.* Washington, DC: National Society Daughters of the American Revolution, 2012. Indispensable for studying Revolutionary War soldiers in New York.

Hatcher, Patricia Law. *Abstract of Graves of Revolutionary Patriots.* 4 vols. Dallas: Pioneer Heritage Press, 1987–1988.

Jasanoff, Maya. *Liberty's Exiles: American Loyalists in the Revolutionary World.* New York: Alfred A. Knopf, 2011. Several prominent Loyalists in New York at the time of the Revolution (John Murray, governor of NY in 1770; Mohawk Indian, Joseph Brandt; Beverly Robinson and wife Susanna Philipse) are part of the in-depth characters the author uses to help the reader understand movements into and out of New York and other British held cities and the eventual migration destinations of many Loyalists as they flee the colonies.

Johnson, James M., Christopher Pryslopski, and Andrew Villani. *Key to the Northern Country: The Hudson Valley in the American Revolution.* Albany: State University of New York Press, 2013.

Kelby, William. *Orderly Book of Three Battalions of Loyalists in New York City*. 3 vols. New York: Printed for the New-York Historical Society, 1917.

New-York Historical Society. *Muster and Pay Rolls of the War of the Revolution, 1775–1783: Reprinted from the Collections of the New York Historical Society for the Years 1914 and 1915*. Baltimore: Genealogical Publishing Co., 1996.

O'Callaghan, Edmund Bailey, comp. *Calendar of Historical Manuscripts Relating to the War of the Revolution in the Office of the Secretary of State, Albany, NY*. 2 vols. Albany: Weed, Parsons, 1868.

Palmer, Gregory. *Biographical Sketches of Loyalists of the American Revolution*. Westport, CT: Meckler Publishing, 1984. Includes numerous New York Loyalists and is probably the best starting point for researching individual Loyalists.

Papas, Phillip. *That Ever Loyal Island: Staten Island and the American Revolution*. New York: New York University Press, 2007.

Pierce, Grace M. "The Military Tract of New York State." *NYG&B Record*, vol. 40, no. 1 (1909): 15–22. [NYG&B eLibrary]

Ranlet, Philip. *The New York Loyalists*. Knoxville: University of Tennessee Press, 1986.

Roberts, James A. *New York in the Revolution as Colony and State*. 2 vols. Albany: Weed-Parsons, 1897. 2nd edition. Albany: Press of Brandow Print. Co., 1898. Provides brief histories and registers of New York military units.

Scott, Kenneth. *Rivington's New York Newspaper, Excerpts from a Loyalist Press, 1773-1783*. New York: New-York Historical Society, 1973.

Sypher, Francis J., Jr. *New York State Society of the Cincinnati: Biographies of Original Members & Other Continental Officers*. Fishkill, NY: New York State Society of the Cincinnati, 2004.

———. *New York State Society of the Cincinnati, Histories of New York Regiments of the Continental Army*. Fishkill, NY: New York State Society of the Cincinnati, 2008.

Venables, Robert W. *The Hudson Valley in the American Revolution*. Albany: New York State American Revolution Bicentennial Commission, 1975. This is a revision of the original published by the New York State Historic Trust in 1968.

Watt, Gavin K. *Loyalist Refugees: Non-Military Refugees in Quebec 1776-1784*. Milton, Ontario: Global Heritage Press, 2014. This author has written other works on this topic. See *www.gavinwatt.ca*.

Yoshpe, Harry B. *Disposition of Loyalist Estates in the Southern District of the State of New York*. New York: Columbia University Press, 1939.

Post-Revolutionary Wars to 1858

Butler, Stuart L. "Genealogical Records of the War of 1812." *Prologue*, vol. 23, no. 4 (1991): 420–425.

Everest, Ellan Seymour. *The War of 1812 in the Champlain Valley*. Syracuse: Syracuse University Press, 1981.

Guernsey, R. S. *New York City and Vicinity during the War of 1812-15, Being a Military, Civic and Financial Local History of That Period*. 2 vols. New York: C. L. Woodward, 1889, 1895.

Hastings, Hugh. ed. *Military Minutes of the Council of Appointment of the State of New York, 1783–1821*. 4 vols. Albany: J. B. Lyon, 1901–02. Vol. 4 contains the name index to all four volumes.

Malcomson, Robert. "When Our Country Calls: The New York State Militia in the War of 1812." Typescript, 2007, Manuscripts and Special Collections, New York State Library, Albany.

New York State Adjutant General's Office. *Index of Awards on Claims of the Soldiers of the War of 1812*. Albany: Weed, Parsons, 1860. Reprint, Baltimore: Genealogical Publishing Co., 1969. The reprint includes an errata list compiled by the NYSL.

Phifer, Mike. *Lifeline: The War of 1812 Along the Upper St. Lawrence River*. Westminster, MD: Heritage Books, 2008.

Slosek, Anthony M. *Oswego and the War of 1812*. Oswego, NY: Heritage Foundation of Oswego, 1989.

Civil War

Annual Report of the State Historian of the State of New York 1896–98. 2 vols. Albany: New York State, 1897–1898.

Breshears, Guy, and William Wheeler. *Loyal till Death: A Diary of the 13th New York Artillery*. Bowie, MD: Heritage Books, 2003.

Dornbusch, Charles E., comp. *The Communities of New York and the Civil War: The Recruiting Areas of the New York Civil War Regiments*. New York: New York Public Library, 1962. Lists for each county, town, and city and the regiments in which those listed served.

———, comp. *Military Bibliography of the Civil War*. 4 vols. New York: New York Public Library, 1961–1987. A comprehensive bibliography of Civil War regimental histories and personal narratives that includes a section on New York State units.

Gillespie, Richard T., and Andrew H. Gale. *Civil War Letters and Diary of Andrew H. Gale of the 137th Regiment, New York State Volunteers*. Westminster, MD: Heritage Books, 2005.

Hammond, John E. *Civil War Records: Town of Oyster Bay*. Oyster Bay: The Town, 2011. [oysterbaytown.com]

Holzer, Harold, ed. *The Union Preserved: A Guide to Civil War Records in the New York State Archives*. New York: Fordham University Press and New York State Archives Partnership Trust, 1999.

Munden, Kenneth W., and Henry Putney Beers. *The Union: A Guide to Federal Archives Relating to the Civil War*. Washington, DC: National Archives and Records Administration, 1986; first published 1962.

New York Adjutant General. "Civil War Muster Roll Abstracts of New York State Volunteers, United States Sharpshooters, and United States Colored Troops [ca. 1861–1900]." New York State Archives (series 13775, microfilm, 1,185 rolls).

———. *A Record of Commissioned Officers, Non-Commissioned Officers and Privates . . . in Suppressing the Rebellion*. 8 vols. Albany: Comstock and Cassidy, 1864–1868. Muster-in rolls arranged by regiment and company, but not including all regiments.

———. *Register of New York Regiments in the War of the Rebellion*. 43 vols. Albany: New York State, 1894–1906. Compiled from the muster roll abstracts now in the New York State Archives.

Phisterer, Frederick, comp. *New York in the War of the Rebellion, 1861 to 1865*. 6 vols. 3rd edition. Albany: New York State, 1912. Includes histories of each military unit from New York, lists of commissioned officers with brief service histories, and roll of honor (fatalities).

Saunders, Lisa, Charles McDowell, and Nancy McDowell. *Ever True: Civil War Letters of Seward's New York 9th Heavy Artillery of Wayne and Cayuga Counties between a Soldier, His Wife and His Canadian Family*. Bowie, MD: Heritage Books, 2004.

Wilt, Richard A. *New York Soldiers in the Civil War, A Roster of Military Officers and Soldiers Who Served in New York Regiments in the Civil War as Listed in the Annual Reports of the Adjutant General of the State of New York*. Vol. 1, A–K; vol. 2, L–Z. Bowie, MD: Heritage Books, 1999, 2007. The rosters were printed without an index. These volumes are alphabetized and indexed by both name and regiment.

Post-Civil War

Dornbusch, Charles E. United States, Department of the Army, Office of Military History and the New York Public Library. *Unit Histories of World War II, United States Army, Air Force, Marines, Navy*. Washington, DC: Department of the Army, 1950.

Jones, Virgil C. *Roosevelt's Rough Riders*. Garden City, NY: Doubleday, 1971.

Karpiak, Christine. *A Spirit of Sacrifice: New York's Response to the Great War; A Guide to Records Relating to World War I Held in the New York State Archives*. Albany: State Archives, 1993.

Kincaid, Brigadier General J. Leslie, comp. *Roll of Honor. Citizens of the State of New York Who Died While in the Service of the United States during the World War*. Albany: Adjutant General, 1922.

Marshall, Edward. *The Story of the Rough Riders*. New York: G. W. Dillingham Co., 1899.

Moorhouse, B-Ann. "Little Publicized New York City Sources: The Landon Papers and Military Records." *NYG&B Newsletter* (now *New York Researcher*), Fall 1994. Published July 2011 as a Research Aid on *NewYorkFamilyHistory.org*.

New York Adjutant General. *New York in the Spanish-American War*. 4 vols. Albany: J. B. Lyon, 1900. Reprinted as *Index to the New York Spanish-American War Veterans 1898*. 2 vols. edited by Richard H. Saldana. Bountiful, UT: A.I.S.I. Publishers, 1987.

Sammons, Jeffrey T., and John H. Morrow, Jr. *Harlem's Rattlers and the Great War: The Undaunted 369th Regiment and the African American Quest for Equality*. Lawrence, KS: University Press of Kansas, 2014.

Yockelson, Mitchell. "They Answered the Call, Military Service in the United States Army during World War I, 1917–1919." *Prologue*, vol. 30, no. 3 (1998): 228–238.

Historical Overview

During the colonial era, both Dutch and English settlements usually included a community cemetery from the outset. Families living far from a town's center often conducted burials on their farms and sometimes shared that family ground with neighbors, creating a neighborhood cemetery. As houses of worship were built, almost all congregations created an adjoining cemetery.

When older burial grounds filled up, new ones had to be created. In the mid-nineteenth century this led to the creation of "garden" or "rural" cemeteries all over New York State, beginning with Green-Wood (Brooklyn) in 1838; other notable examples include Albany Rural Cemetery, Forest Lawn (Buffalo), Poughkeepsie Rural, and Woodlawn (then Westchester County, now the Bronx). Although these are nonsectarian cemeteries, at first they were used almost exclusively by Protestant families. Catholic dioceses and Jewish congregations created burial grounds for their dead in this garden style as well.

As cities grew and real estate pressures mounted, some of the older cemeteries became full and then closed, and the bodies were removed to new cemeteries farther from city centers. This also occurred with some family burial grounds in rural areas. In other cases cemeteries were closed, but the bodies were not moved; the monuments were buried and the grounds put to other uses. This was the fate of Manhattan's African Burial Ground, rediscovered in 1991 when old buildings covering the site were razed. Still other burial grounds were converted to parks.

Under state law towns and cities have title to abandoned cemeteries and are responsible for their maintenance and protection, though in some cases the large number of such cemeteries has made it impractical for the municipalities to fully exercise that responsibility.

All not-for-profit cemeteries and crematories in New York (about 1,800) are governed by the Department of State, Division of Cemeteries (*dos.ny.gov/cmty*). Approximately 4,000 religious, municipal, private, national, and family cemeteries do not fall under this jurisdiction.

Locating New York Cemeteries

In 1910 a list of all cemeteries in New York State was published as *The Fairchild Cemetery Manual: A Reliable Guide to the Cemeteries of Greater New York and Vicinity*. It provides descriptions of those in New York City and elsewhere within a 50-mile radius. It also lists cemeteries in nearby states.

Between 1995 and 1997 a project of the Association of Municipal Historians of New York State identified no fewer than 8,000 cemeteries in the state. Lists of these cemeteries were published in 1999 in three volumes: *New York State Cemeteries Name/Location Inventory, 1995–1997: Compiled by the Association of Municipal Historians of New York State*. These volumes list the name of deceased, location, date of first and last burial, religious or family affiliation, size, status (either active, inactive, or deserted) and contact information for the cemeteries.

Two additional cemetery finding aids are "A Snapshot of Cemetery Resources in New York State" in the *New York Researcher* and Marian Henry's "New York State Cemeteries: A Finding Aid" available on *AmericanAncestors.org*.

The NYG&B website has an online guide for cemetery research in New York State, including a listing with links to some major cemeteries. The largest in the state is Calvary Cemetery of the Catholic Archdiocese of New York, located in Queens, with over three million burials. Unfortunately, this cemetery has no name index to burials, but Rosemary Ardolina has compiled two volumes of its gravestone inscriptions.

Identifying a Cemetery

Death records indicate place of burial or cremation, and sometimes the date as well. When there is no government death record, other sources may identify the place of burial. These include family records, church and synagogue records, newspaper death notices, estate files (which may contain bills for the funeral or gravestone), and records of funeral homes or monument makers. If none of these sources is fruitful, local histories or city directories may include lists of cemeteries from which a likely burial place can be detected.

Gravestones

Before 1730 there was no professional stone carver in New York. Gravestones, usually of red sandstone or slate, had to be carved as far away as Boston and brought to New York by boat. Only the well-to-do could afford such monuments, so most of the earliest graves were marked, if at all, with stones crudely cut with an individual's initials and perhaps a date. Even after a carver set up business in New York City, most graves continued to be marked with these simple stones. Many have disappeared, often just by sinking into the ground. See Emily Wasserman's *Gravestone Designs* and Richard Welch's *Memento Mori: The Gravestones of Early Long Island, 1680–1810*.

In the nineteenth century gravestones began to be made with a less expensive, soft, white marble, replacing the older types of markers. Unfortunately, this marble has proved extremely vulnerable to erosion so that inscriptions are now often illegible. That is not a problem with the granite monuments that became popular late in the nineteenth century.

An 1823 New York City ordinance prohibited burials south of Canal, Sullivan, and Grand Streets, and an 1851 ordinance extended the ban to 86th Street, except for private vaults and cemeteries. After 1851 no new cemeteries could be established in New York County. Most cemeteries south of 86th Street were closed, and the bodies were removed to new cemeteries in the surrounding counties.

Until 1852 Quakers prohibited the use of grave markers, and the apparently unused sections of their oldest cemeteries actually contain the remains of those who died before the ban was lifted.

Gravestone Transcriptions

Beginning in the nineteenth century, volunteers all over New York State began copying the inscriptions from gravestones, especially in small family or community cemeteries. For some counties, such as Dutchess, Genesee, Orange, Putnam, Ulster, and Washington, nearly all of the older inscriptions have been published, either in book form or in periodicals such as the *NYG&B Record*. Many historical and genealogical societies continue to transcribe and publish headstones as part of their activities. For example, *Tree Talks*, a quarterly publication of the Central New York Genealogical Society, has included many cemetery abstracts.

Many more transcriptions are available as manuscripts or typescripts with limited distribution. See the County Guides in Part Two of this book to locate many typed or handwritten manuscripts in local libraries, historical societies, and genealogical societies, as well as with county and town historians. The Genealogical Records Committee (GRC) of the Daughters of the American Revolution (DAR) of New York State has been transcribing gravestones in cemeteries throughout New York State for almost a hundred years. The hundreds of volumes in their *Cemetery, Church and Town Records* series cover the entire population, not just DAR members or their descendants. The DAR's GRC catalog can be searched at *http://services.dar.org/public/dar_research/search*. The full series of New York transcriptions can be found at the DAR Library in Washington, DC, the New York State Library (NYSL), and the New York Public Library (NYPL). See also Jean Worden's *Revised Master Index to the New York State Daughters of the American Revolution Genealogical Records Volumes*.

Another large collection was assembled by Gertrude A. Barber and her sisters, Ray Sawyer and Minnie Cowen, who transcribed thousands of gravestones from Allegany, Cattaraugus, Chautauqua, Columbia, Erie, Orange, Otsego, Rockland, Schoharie, Sullivan, and Wyoming counties. Their publications are listed in the individual County Guides. Hundreds of published or manuscript Long Island cemetery transcriptions are identified in Herbert Seversmith and Kenn Stryker-Rodda's *Long Island Genealogical Source Material*. Library catalogs may reveal more recent transcriptions.

Unfortunately, some cemeteries disappeared before there was an interest in copying gravestones. Others have been transcribed more than once, in which case it is wise to seek out the oldest transcription, which may have been made before some stones disappeared or became difficult to read. By using the many transcriptions now available online, researchers can search for digitized versions of the original manuscripts, typescripts, or published versions. Since errors are inevitable when extensive transcripts are retyped, it is important to use the one that was made directly from the monuments if it is not possible to view the monuments themselves.

Burial Records

The larger cemeteries, where most burials of the past 150 years have taken place, maintain a record of burials, usually called the List of Interments. These should always be checked in addition to the gravestone inscriptions, since headstones often do not list all who are buried in a grave or plot. Many graves have never had a monument, but the burials will still be recorded in the cemetery's books. Families often bought large plots, and the names of those buried together in the plot, often bearing several surnames, can be extremely useful in reconstructing a family.

Most active cemeteries will perform a genealogical search upon request, and some charge a fee for this service, but the fee for a full list of a plot can be worth the expense. Researchers will sometimes need a date of interment because some cemetery records are filed by interment date, not an alphabetical index; Calvary Cemetery in Queens County is one of those with records filed by interment date. However, the interment dates of one or two people may reveal that they were buried in a family plot, and a full list of interments in that plot can then be obtained. An increasing number of cemeteries have online databases of the names of the interred, usually indicating the burial plot numbers.

If a church cemetery no longer exists, its records may have been retained by the church or transferred to another church. Sometimes a cemetery's interment records have been transferred to a local historical society or other organization, or that organization has obtained a copy of the records.

Cremation

Cremation was rare in New York before the twentieth century, and was (and still may be) prohibited by some religions. There was only one crematory a century ago in New York City, Fresh Pond Crematory in Middle Village (Queens County). Cremation is a much more common practice today. A death certificate may indicate that a body has been cremated, but usually will not indicate what was done with the cremated remains. If the cemetery used by the family is known, its records will disclose whether the remains were buried there or possibly to whom they were given. There may be a marker similar to one placed over a traditional grave. The German Genealogy Group (*germangenealogygroup.com*) and the Italian Genealogical Group (*italiangen.org*) each have a database containing more than 215,000 Fresh Pond Crematory records.

Potter's Fields

Parts of many cemeteries were set aside for burial of the indigent or unidentified, but the great number of such burials in cities required the creation of a separate "potter's field" for that purpose. In New York City, such public parks as Bryant Park, Madison Square Park, and Washington Square Park were once potter's fields.

Since 1869 New York City's potter's field has been on Hart Island on Long Island Sound, where almost one million people are buried on 101 acres, making it the largest tax-funded cemetery in the world. Its online database contains more than 65,000 names, from 1980 to 2011 (*www.nyc.gov/html/doc/html/hart_island/hart_island.shtml*). Efforts are underway to increase the online listings.

Institutional Cemeteries

People who died while confined to a prison or other state institution may have been buried on that institution's grounds. The New York State Archives (NYSA) may have records of such interments.

Military Cemeteries

More than three million United States service members, from the Revolutionary War to the present, are buried in cemeteries maintained by the Veterans Administration (*cem.va.gov*), though the first of these cemeteries was not created until 1862. There are seven in New York State:

- Albany Rural Cemetery Soldiers' Lot (Albany County)
- Bath National Cemetery (Bath, Steuben County)
- Calverton National Cemetery (Calverton, Suffolk County)
- Cypress Hills National Cemetery (Brooklyn, Kings County)
- Gerald B. H. Solomon Saratoga National Cemetery (Schuylerville, Saratoga County)
- Long Island National Cemetery (Farmingdale, Suffolk County)
- Woodlawn National Cemetery (Elmira, Chemung County)

West Point Cemetery in Orange County is the nation's oldest military post cemetery (*usma.edu*).

Many veterans are buried in private cemeteries. Union veterans of the Civil War may have been provided with marble gravestones by the United States government as a result of legislation passed in 1879. *Ancestry.com* has a searchable database of more than 166,000 of these gravestones. Some private cemeteries have special soldiers sections or monuments memorializing local veterans of various wars.

Selected Online Resources and Indexes

The online catalog of the NYSL is a good place to search by place name or keyword for cemetery records that are local and are often found within other collections. The following websites are databases of user-submitted information. Some include photographs of headstones or lists of those interred in a specific cemetery. These databases are often incomplete, but can be helpful because they are searchable by name as well as by cemetery. Keep in mind that the absence of a record in any online collection is not evidence that the person being searched is not buried there, even if spouses or other close family members are listed on the site.

Some cemeteries have their own online databases such as: Graceland Cemetery (*graceland-cemetery.com*) in Albany County, Holy Sepulchre (*holysepulchre.org*) in Monroe County, Cedar Grove Cemetery (*thecedargrovecemetery.com*) in Queens County, and Vale Cemetery (*valecemetery.org*) in Schenectady County. Famous residents are likely to be found on cemetery websites, including Albany Rural Cemetery (*albanyruralcemetery.org*), which lists prominent officials and important historical families such as the Van Rensselaers, even listing servants in the various households. Green-Wood Cemetery (Brooklyn) offers an online index and an efficient genealogical research service (*green-wood.com*).

For information about cemetery research specific to particular ethnic or religious groups, see chapter 14, Peoples of New York and chapter 15, Religious Records.

Billiongraves

Billiongraves.com allows users to search for a cemetery by state or county, specific name, birth year, and death year. An entry usually includes birth and death dates, the name of the contributor, and a photograph of the headstone.

FindAGrave

FindAGrave.com is a free nationwide website and lists more than 100 million grave records. Searches can be made by county, cemetery, or name of the deceased. A typical entry includes the name of the deceased, birth year, and death year; the cemetery name, location, and contact information; the date the record was added, the name of the person who added the record, and the unique FindAGrave memorial number. Many entries have maps with GPS coordinates and include photographs. Also note that FindAGrave includes records from sources other than the cemetery itself, a practice which can introduce errors.

Interment

The Interment website (*interment.net*) can be browsed by cemetery by first selecting a state and county. Name, location, and contact information are given for each cemetery, as well as the contact information for members who provided the transcriptions for that particular cemetery. Each entry gives birth date, death date, and age at time of death. Lists are organized alphabetically.

New England Historic Genealogical Society (NEHGS)

The NEHGS (*AmericanAncestors.org*) has a very large cemetery transcription database available to members or at libraries with institutional subscriptions.

New York City Cemetery Project

This project website (*nycemetery.wordpress.com*) offers links to cemeteries, as well as articles and blogs about recent developments—such as the rescue of the Brinckerhoff Cemetery in Fresh Meadows, Queens County.

New York Genealogical and Biographical Society (NYG&B)

The website *NewYorkFamilyHistory.org* offers NYG&B members numerous resources for cemetery research that are described in its online "Guide to Cemetery Research." Of particular interest are the Cemetery Transcriptions Collection in the NYG&B eLibrary that includes transcriptions from more than 300 cemeteries in 24 New York counties, a "List of Cemetery Transcriptions" in the *NYG&B Record*, Catherine Ellard's *A Selected Bibliography for New York State Cemetery Research*, which is organized by county, and "A Selection of Major Cemeteries in New York State," which describes their genealogical services and online features.

New York Gravestones

NewYorkGravestones.org only contains records with photographs, so some cemeteries have very few records. Entries usually include the name, birth date, and death date. Family relationships are given if known. The website can be browsed by cemetery or searched by name.

New York Tombstone Transcription Project

The New York Tombstone Transcription Project (*www.usgwtombstones.org/newyork/newyork.html*) is a volunteer-run initiative to gather transcriptions of headstones across New York State and make them available online. Transcriptions are organized by county, then cemetery. Some transcriptions are recent, while others have been copied from older books.

Northern New York Genealogy

Northern New York Genealogy (*nnygenealogy.com*) maintains a searchable database for cemeteries of Jefferson, Lewis, and Oswego counties.

Obituary Central

Obitcentral.com offers both obituary and cemetery searches. Searches can be made by keyword, which may include the name of the deceased, year of death, or county. A typical entry consists of a text-only transcription. The site also includes links to other cemetery and obituary websites.

Selected Bibliography and Further Reading

See the individual County Guides for cemetery transcriptions and abstracts for specific counties and regions.

Ardolina, Rosemary M. *Old Calvary Cemetery: New Yorkers Carved in Stone.* Bowie, MD: Heritage Books, 1996. The cemetery is in Queens.

———. *Second Calvary Cemetery: New Yorkers Carved in Stone.* Floral Park, NY: Delia Publications, 2000.

Bailey, Rosalie Fellows. *Guide to Genealogical and Biographical Sources for New York City (Manhattan), 1783–1898.* New York: The Author, 1954. [*books.FamilySearch.org*] Reprinted with new introduction by Harry Macy Jr. Baltimore: Clearfield Co., 1998.

Ellard, Catherine M., comp. *A Selected Bibliography for New York State Cemetery Research.* Digitally published by the NYG&B Society, 2006. [*NewYorkFamilyHistory.org*]

The Fairchild Cemetery Manual: A Reliable Guide to the Cemeteries of Greater New York and Vicinity. Brooklyn, NY: Fairchild Sons, 1910. Lists of cemeteries in Greater New York City, New York State, New Jersey, Connecticut, and Massachusetts.

Henry, Marian S. "New York State Cemeteries: A Finding Aid." *www.americanancestors.org/new-york-state-cemeteries-a-finding-aid.*

Inskeep, Carolee R. *The Graveyard Shift: A Family Historian's Guide to New York City Cemeteries*. Orem, UT: Ancestry Publishing, 2000.

Joslyn, Roger D. "Gertrude Barber, Minnie Cowen, and Ray Sawyer: The Sisters Who Indexed New York. List of the Cowen Sisters' Work." *NYG&B Record*, vol. 143, no. 3 (2012): 226–234. The final installment of this six-part article provides an extensive list, organized by county, of the New York cemeteries that the sisters transcribed. [NYG&B eLibrary]

New York State Cemeteries Name/Location Inventory, 1995–1997: Compiled by the Association of Municipal Historians of New York State. 3 vols. Bowie, MD: Heritage Books, 1999. A finding aid for this book by Marian Henry is listed above.

New York State Cemetery Records: Compiled by Missionaries and Members of the Eastern States Mission and Typed by the Genealogical Society of Utah. 23 vols. Salt Lake City: Genealogical Society of Utah, 1940–1969. [Microfilm of typescript, 8 reels, FHL]

"A Snapshot of Cemetery Resources in New York State." *New York Researcher*, Fall 2013. Published as a Research Aid on *NewYorkFamilyHistory.org*.

Seversmith, Herbert F., and Kenn Stryker-Rodda. *Long Island Genealogical Source Material: A Bibliography*. Arlington, VA: National Genealogical Society, 1987.

Wasserman, Emily. *Gravestone Designs: Rubbings & Photographs from Early New York and New Jersey*. New York: Dover Publications, 1972.

Welch, Richard. *Memento Mori: The Gravestones of Early Long Island, 1680–1810*. Syosset, NY: Friends for Long Island Heritage, 1983.

Worden, Jean D. *Revised Master Index to the New York State Daughters of the American Revolution Genealogical Records Volumes, Books 1 and 2*, prepared by the General Peter Gansevoort Chapter. Albany and Zephyrhills, FL: Jean D. Worden, 1998.

Table 1: Selected New York City Cemeteries Prior to 1900

County	Cemetery	Incorporated or earliest burial dates	Website
Bronx	New York City Cemetery (Hart Island Potters Field)	1869	www.nyc.gov/html/doc/html/hart_island/hart_island.shtml
Bronx	Woodlawn Cemetery	1863	thewoodlawncemetery.org
Bronx	Old St. Raymonds/St. Raymonds Cemetery	1842	www.straymondparish.org/cemetery.html
Kings	Green-Wood Cemetery	1838	green-wood.org
Kings (on Queens border)	Cypress Hills National Cemetery	1862/1870	www.cem.va.gov/cems/nchp/cypresshills.asp
Kings (on Queens border)	Cypress Hills Cemetery	1848	cypresshillscemetery.org
Kings	Holy Cross Cemetery	1849	www.ccbklyn.org/our-cemeteries/holy-cross-cemetery
Kings	Washington Cemetery	1857	No website; (718) 377-8690
Kings (on Queens border)	The Evergreens Cemetery	1849	theevergreenscemetery.com
New York	For New York Cemeteries, see cemetery tables in Rosalie Fellows Bailey, *Guide to Genealogical and Biographical Sources for New York City*		
Queens	Calvary Cemetery	1848	calvarycemeteryqueens.com
Queens	[Lutheran] All Faiths Cemetery	1857	allfaithscemetery.org
Queens	Cedar Grove Cemetery	1893	thecedargrovecemetery.com
Queens	Fresh Pond Crematory	1884	freshpondcrematory.com
Queens	Mount Zion	1893	mountzioncemetery.com
Richmond	Silver Lake	filled by 1909	www.hebrewfreeburial.org/cemeteries.html
Richmond	Moravian	1740 (1867–present records)	moraviancemetery.com

Business, Institutional, and Organizational Records

Chapter 10

Introduction

The records of businesses, institutions, and organizations are a potentially rich, but often neglected, resource for genealogists. Such records might include archives or publications of companies and small businesses and their employees, charitable institutions, professional organizations, educational institutions, or fraternal and benevolent organizations. For an overview of their value to genealogical research, see Ann Carter Fleming's "Overlooked Resources: Business, Organizational, and Institutional Records," Laura Szucs Pfeiffer's *Hidden Sources: Family History in Unlikely Places*, and Kay Haviland Freilich and Ann Carter Fleming's "Business, Institution, and Organization Records."

Ancestors who fell upon hard times due to illness or economic privations may have been dependent upon governmental or private charitable institutions at some point in their lives. The State Board of Charities was established in 1867 to bring some coordination to charitable activities throughout New York State. The Board issued comprehensive annual reports from 1867 through 1928 that included directories of public and private charities under its oversight. (The annual reports were continued subsequently by the State Board of Social Welfare and the State Department of Social Services). Many of these publications are online at *Archive.org* or *HathiTrust.org*, and there is some variation in the titles. Published in 1874, the *Directory to the Charities of New York* was the first attempt to list all the charities in New York City; it was followed by the *New York Charities Directory* (later called the *Directory of Social and Health Agencies*), published annually or biannually from 1883 to 1982. These directories can be exceptionally useful resources to identify hospitals, asylums for children and adults, missions, reformatories, benevolent societies, and other places functioning at a particular time, as well as their staff and board members.

Almost all modern records of this type are legally restricted; see comments on restrictions in the sections that follow. For information regarding access to records about individuals that are held by state and local government agencies in New York, one may consult the Committee on Open Government website at *www.dos.ny.gov/coog/index.html*.

The Historical Documents Inventory (HDI) conducted between 1978 and 1993 by the New York Historical Resources Center at Cornell University resulted in the publication of the series *Guides to Historical Resources in Repositories* for each county of New York State. These books can help identify and locate the archives of businesses, institutions, and organizations. The New York State Library (NYSL) provides instructions on where to obtain HDI volumes at *www.nysl.nysed.gov/hdi.htm*. Titles in the series will be found in the individual county bibliographies in Part Two of this book; many have been digitized and are available at *books.FamilySearch.org*. The collections that are documented in the HDI guides are recorded in the NYSL online catalog, which will identify which repository holds the item.

An introduction to some of the major categories of business, institutional, and organizational records follows.

Almshouses or Poorhouses
Early Records

The deacons of the early Dutch Reformed churches were responsible for the poor in their congregations, as shown by records that survive for the Albany and Flatbush churches. The first colonial Assembly passed an act providing that commissioners in every county, city, town, and precinct should provide for the maintenance of their poor; this eventually led to creation of Overseers of the Poor, elected annually by town meetings. Some of the Overseers' records have been published. See, for example, Rufus B. Langhans' records of the Overseers of the Poor of the Town of Huntington; these have been published in several volumes and cover records beginning in 1729.

In the four counties where the Anglican church was established under the Ministry Act of 1693, the maintenance of the poor was turned over to church wardens who were also elected, and, despite their title, did not represent a religious denomination. Kenneth Scott's "Church Wardens and the Poor in New York City 1693–1747" has an informative introduction followed by abstracts of data in the church wardens' records for New York County.

In later years county almshouses or poorhouses housed destitute individuals and families—often on a temporary basis—including orphans, the sick, unwed mothers, victims of domestic abuse, the disabled, the mentally ill, and those who could not lead financially independent lives. In 1824 New York State legislated the establishment of an institution for the poor in every county. A listing of New York State poorhouses by county is available at Linda Crannell's Poorhouse Story website, *poorhousestory.com*. County and city governments continue to operate residential facilities for the aged and infirm.

Almshouse or poorhouse records usually list the occupant's name, along with age, sex, race, birthplace, date of admission, and date of discharge or death. Even early nineteenth-century records give age and birthplace of each inmate. Beginning in 1875 the state mandated a complete census of inmates, which recorded the occupant's health and personal habits, marital status, parent's names and birthplaces, and level of education. Older records of residents are disclosable under New York law. However, modern records regarding social services recipients are legally restricted.

Almshouse or poorhouse records may be held by the institution's present-day equivalent or by the city or county archives; some records are held in local or regional historical societies. The Family History Library (FHL) has microfilmed some of these records; dates range from 1759 to 1948.

Repositories for Records

The New York City Municipal Archives (MUNI) collection, Almshouse Records, 1758–1953, includes records of the municipal almshouses, workhouses, and hospitals. Most of the records are in the form of ledger books listing names of occupants. Single and widowed women without family support are heavily represented in these records, and some books only list children. Some of these records are also available on microfilm through the FHL. See also, for example, Charles Farrell's *NYG&B Record* article for the names of children in the New York City Almshouse 1807–1810 abstracted from records at MUNI; and see Roger D. Joslyn's "Indentures of the Poor Children of Orange County, 1829–1847, 1871, 1884, 1885," also in the *NYG&B Record*.

The New York State Archives (NYSA) has a record series of "census" forms for almshouse or poorhouse inmates for 1826–1921 (series A1978), available on microfilm. Most of the records are from 1875 to 1921. They contain information on an inmate's family, as well as his or her personal and economic history. The collection is arranged alphabetically by county, then by institution name, then chronologically by census year. It may be accessed for free through the New York portal of *Ancestry.com*, which requires a New York State zip code to register for a free account. *Ancestry.com's* free New York records may be accessed from the NYSA website at *www.archives.nysed.gov*.

Potter's Fields

Many poorhouses had cemeteries on the grounds. Northern New York Genealogy includes the Poorhouse Cemetery in Watertown, New York in its online records; see burials at *nnygenealogy.com*. Some burial grounds for the indigent or unclaimed, also known as potter's fields, stood alone. New York City established City Cemetery as a potter's field on Hart Island in 1869; it now has over one million burials. The New York City Department of Correction has a database of burial records from 1980 to 2011 at *www.nyc.gov/html/doc/html/hart_island/hart_island.shtml*. Records from 1883 to the 1950s are on microfilm at MUNI.

Orphanage Records (1653–Present)

Orphanages have existed in New York since 1653, and have been operated by civil authorities, religious groups, and private benefactors. (See also chapter 1, Colonial Era, and chapter 15, Religious Records.) Orphanages served a varied population of minors, not only those who had lost one or both parents, but also those children who had emotional, mental, or physical disabilities, or whose parents could not care for them. Records vary in content and can be difficult to locate.

By 1850 New York had 27 public and private orphanages. Records usually include each child's name, age or birthdate, birthplace, and dates of admission and discharge. Files may also include information on parents, nearest kin, and whether the child was indentured as an apprentice after discharge. Researchers looking at orphanage records could potentially discover the trade the orphaned individuals took up after they left the institution; informal records also contain notes about the individuals. If the orphanage is still in operation, records may be kept at the institution. The NYSA holds the records of the Thomas Indian School, which was located on the Cattaraugus Indian Reservation and closed in 1957. See also the American Indian section in chapter 14. The Children's Aid Society, which is based in New York City, can also be helpful in identifying orphanages; its website includes information about historical events and records related to orphans at *www.childrensaidsociety.org/about/history*.

The records of closed orphanages could be with county clerks, historical societies, or agencies (local, religious, etc.) that operate successor institutions. Many orphanages were associated with religious institutions. (See also chapter 15, Religious Records.) Census records are another valuable resource when looking into finding information about orphans. Records of institutions such as orphanages are generally found on the last pages of an enumeration district.

Many children were orphaned as a result of the Civil War, leading to an increase in the number and size of orphanages. The high rate of maternal deaths was another factor, as working class men might not have the support system to care for minor children. The Foundling Hospital was created in New York City in 1869 by Catholic nuns concerned about the number of children orphaned by the Civil War. Archival records of the New York Foundling Hospital (1869–2009) and the nonsectarian Children's Aid Society (1853–1947) were donated to the New-York Historical Society (N-YHS). A finding aid for these records is at *http://dlib.nyu.edu/findingaids/html/nyhs/foundling*. Some of these records have restricted access and require advance permission to view them. The censuses of the Foundling Hospital (1870–1925), as well as records for both the New York and the Brooklyn Hebrew Orphan Asylum, may be accessed on *Ancestry.com*.

The N-YHS also maintains the records of the Colored Orphan Asylum (1836–1972, bulk 1850–1936), that relocated within Manhattan before moving to Riverdale (now in the Bronx) at the end of the nineteenth century, and the Leake & Watts Children's Home (1831–1949) which was in New York City until it moved to Yonkers in 1890. See William Seraile's book *Angels of Mercy...* .

Between 1853 and 1929 an estimated 200,000 New York City orphans were sent to foster homes in the Midwest and the West on "orphan trains" sponsored by the Children's Aid Society and the New York Foundling Hospital. The National Orphan Train Complex Museum in Concordia, Kansas, preserves stories and artifacts of participants in the Orphan Train Movement between 1854 and 1929. It maintains an online registry, *Orphantrain depot.com*, and does research for a fee. There is a large volume of literature on the orphan trains, with several dozen links provided on the subject on Cyndi's List, *cyndislist.com*.

Details of child inmates can also be found in Reformatory records. Some records are held by the NYSA. See Corrections and Prison Records later in this chapter for more information.

School Records

School records include official records of students (administrative records, class rosters, report cards, class photos, class lists, and yearbooks.) Student records of institutions receiving federal aid are restricted for 100 years by the 1974 Family Educational Rights and Privacy Act (FERPA), except for "directory" information

such as lists of graduates. For information regarding access to student records, consult the Committee on Open Government website at *www.dos.ny.gov/coog/index.html*.

Prior to the passage of the New York State Common School Act of 1812, there was no law mandating any form of public education for children. The 1812 Act required every town and city to organize school districts to provide public education for children ages five to fifteen. After 1867 public schools were free (and poorer families began to send their children to school), and in 1894, a guarantee of free primary and secondary education was added to the New York State Constitution. Some communities did set up schools prior to the 1812 Act. Early forms of New York school records began in the mid-1700s, and although rare, those that survive can provide important biographical information. Possible resources are local historical societies.

The clerk of the public school district was responsible for maintaining records of schools in that district, as well as predecessor school districts. County clerks and town clerks were required to file annual reports of local school officials between 1814 and 1912, though the reports do not list students prior to 1856. Local historical societies or other repositories may also hold these records, but the survival rate of school district annual reports is low. Annual reports of school districts to the State Education Department are in the NYSA. They start in 1904, but never include names of students. The New York State Historical Association (NYSHA) has older records of some school districts, especially in central New York. School censuses exist and can be surprisingly useful. For example, the Town of Huntington (Suffolk County) published its *School Trustee Annual Census Reports 1827–1863*.

Records of private, parochial, and boarding schools can be extensive; they may be found at the school or its successor or in the archives of a historical society or the religious organization that operated the school. Records of parochial schools operated by the Roman Catholic Church are generally found at the local parish; some records, particularly for closed schools, may be located in the diocese. See also chapter 15, Religious Records.

Many private schools have published histories. The Collegiate School, which still exists on the Upper West Side of Manhattan, traces its origin to the Dutch Reformed Church school started in Manhattan in 1628, the oldest school in New York. Henry Webb Dunshee's history of the school written in 1883 includes a list of the students beginning in 1790. Another example is the Albany Academy, which predated public schools in Albany. The NYSL's Manuscripts and Special Collections Department has a five-volume typescript prepared by Henry Hun in 1934, "Survey of the Activity of the Albany Academy; the Ancestry and Achievements of Its Students . . . ."

College and university records, such as enrollment, matriculation, and graduation information, are better preserved than primary and secondary school records. Many colleges and universities have archives containing alumni records. The Family Educational Rights and Privacy Act (FERPA) restricts access to records of post-secondary students for 100 years, except for "directory" information. Almost all colleges and universities have published alumni directories, which often give business and home addresses, class, degrees attained, occupations, maiden names, and other relevant data.

Albums resembling modern school yearbooks started being produced in the mid-1800s. College yearbooks began to be published in the late nineteenth century and can be found online or in the collections of local libraries. *Mocavo.com*, for example, has a large collection of high school and college yearbooks. *Ancestry.com* has a collection of 35,000 U.S. school yearbooks from 1884 to 2009.

MUNI holds the records of the New York City Board of Education from 1842 to 2001, and records of the Board of Education of the City of Brooklyn from 1853 to 1897. They document policy making and administration, but do not include student records. The collection includes 50,000 images of schools, classrooms, lectures, and events, ca. 1918–1970. A finding aid is available at *www.nyc.gov/html/records*; search "board of education."

Business and Employee Records

Business records may include personnel files, union records, insurance forms, customer records, legal documents, annual reports, tax information, photographs, directories, in-house publications, official company histories, and biographical sketches, depending on the type and size of business. Early indenture or apprentice records may also exist. Abstracts of 35 volumes of New York apprenticeship registers held by the N-YHS can be found in Kenneth Scott's *Nineteenth Century Apprenticeships in New York City*.

Pre-1900 business records were usually kept in bound ledgers. (See also the entry on the Emigrant Savings Bank records in the Irish section of chapter 14, Peoples of New York.) Post-1900 business records take the form of bound books, flat files, and other formats. The Cornell University Library Division of Rare Books and Manuscripts collects and preserves the records of many defunct New York businesses. Those records that do survive are usually financial and legal in nature. College and university libraries in the locality where a business was based may be another source. *WorldCat.org* can be searched to locate archival collections in libraries, including those identified by the Historic Document Inventory. See also chapter 16. Railroad employee records may be kept at either museums or historical societies and are sometimes available online. For an example, see the Erie Railroad Internet Employee Archive at *http://freepages.genealogy.rootsweb.ancestry.com/~sponholz/erie.html*.

The NYSA holds an extensive collection of New York State Canal System records which are described in Elizabeth Golding's online finding aid listed in the bibliography. The records include payrolls for state employees who maintained the canal system, 1827–1880 (series A0013), but the records are not indexed, microfilmed, or digitized, and are very difficult to search. Reports made by contractors working on the canal include lists of employers. The NYSA also holds state civil service employee history cards for the period ca. 1894–1954 (series 15029); they are name-accessible. Some canal images and maps may be viewed at *http://iarchives.nysed.gov/PubImageWeb/listCollections.jsp?id=68615*.

In New York City, the *Civil List* was published annually as a supplement to *The City Record*, 1883–1967. The *Civil List* recorded the names of all employees (police, fire, teachers, utility workers, etc.) of the City of New York, their home addresses, annual salaries, and dates of entrance into the civil service. The listings are broken down by department and further subdivided by functional unit such as precinct, within the police department. Those employees who were separated from their positions—including by death—were also published in *The City Record*. Copies of *The City Record* can be viewed on microfilm at MUNI and the New York Public Library (NYPL). Many pre-1923 volumes are available online at *HathiTrust.org*.

Union records can also be extensive. Records of the International Ladies Garment Workers Union (ILGWU) are now at the Kheel Center, NYS School of Industrial and Labor Relations, Cornell University. This library holds many other union records. An extensive collection of labor union records are at the Tamiment Library and Robert F. Wagner Labor Archives at New York University. Records of the New York Typographical Union No. 6 (1829–1988) may be found at the NYPL.

If unknown, the name of an ancestor's employer at the time of issuance of a Social Security card (1937–onward) can be obtained for a fee by requesting a copy of the original Social Security application form at *https://secure.ssa.gov/apps9/eFOIA-FEWeb/internet/main.jsp*.

City directories and county gazetteers can identify companies in business at specific times and locations. Business directories classified companies by subject or type of business, in the manner of telephone directory yellow pages; they could be statewide or local or cover one or more counties. Copartnership business directories can identify the business name and address, as well as the names of its partners, officers, directors, and agents—and sometimes the amount of its capitalization. See chapter 11, City Directories, for information on how to identify and where to access business directories.

Retrospective volumes of trade or professional directories such as the *Martindale-Hubbell Directory* (1868–1980) of lawyers or *American Medical Directory* (1906–1990), and biographical compilations (*Who's Who in . . ., Notable Men . . ., Old Merchants of . . .*), available in large research libraries, can identify business and professional men and women. County histories and "mug books," published in the nineteenth century, are other good sources for biographical information about the business community. County and town historians can be another important resource.

Major businesses often had their own corporate archives and libraries. However, many of these have been eliminated since the 1990s, and their collections dispersed or deposited elsewhere. Company archives, histories, annual reports, and periodicals might be located in library collections by searching *WorldCat.org*. Some businesses in the New York metropolitan area have records at the NYPL and N-YHS. Examples at NYPL include: Phelps, Dodge and Company records, 1818–1883 (import/export, mining, railroad); Macmillan Company Records, 1889–1960 (publishing); the records of merchant Samuel Ferguson (1769–1816); and the Account Books Collection, 1760–1936 (400 volumes maintained by businesses and individuals primarily in New York). Noteworthy collections at the N-YHS include mercantile records of the Beekman, Hendricks, and Leverich families; Ogden Day and Company (import/export); Brown Brothers Harriman (banking); and John Jacob Astor's American Fur Company. Numerous other libraries and historical societies in New York State have merchant account books; some have been published as articles in the *NYG&B Record* and other periodicals.

Fraternal and Benevolent Organizations

The role played by fraternal and benevolent organizations in the life of a community was especially important from the nineteenth century through the mid-twentieth century. Members of such organizations banded together on the basis of ethnicity, language, religion, town/region of origin, trade, or military service. Not only did these organizations provide members with a community of familiarity or interest, they often offered a form of insurance or mutual aid in the event of illness or death, credit unions, and scholarship funds, all of which was particularly meaningful in the days before social security or other government welfare programs. Ethnic-based organizations frequently provided services to help immigrants assimilate. The names of fraternal and benevolent organizations can generally be found in city and community directories; ethnic mutual aid societies are frequently listed in charity directories and the annual reports of the State Board of Charities.

Burial societies were important for many of the immigrant groups. Among Jews, the Landsmanshaftn (hometown associations) formed by immigrants from Central and Eastern Europe provided mutual aid and burial societies for members. For Roman Catholics, the Knights of Columbus was founded in 1882 as a way to assist widows and orphans and continues to provide insurance services today. The Turnverein of the Germans and Sokol of Czechs and Slovaks were athletic clubs

with historic political roots. For other examples of ethnic or religious fraternal organizations see chapter 14, Peoples of New York, and chapter 15, Religious Records.

Some fraternal organizations were "secret societies" with rituals known only to members in good standing. Perhaps the best known of these is the Freemasons, which started as a trade-based organization in Europe in the fourteenth century. Since colonial times, many prominent Americans have been members of the Masons, and masonic lodges are a feature on the American landscape in small towns and big cities. The Chancellor Robert R. Livingston Masonic Library at the Grand Lodge in Manhattan will do family membership searches for a fee (*www.nymasoniclibrary.org/genealogical-research*). Typical search results include the name of a member's lodge; his occupation when he joined; his age at the time of joining; the dates of his Masonic degrees; and a date of death if he remained a member in good standing throughout his life. At times, results will include information relating to offices held within a lodge, or other information relating to lodge activities.

Fraternal organizations records can include membership records and applications. Some organizations published newspapers or newsletters for members which featured reports of member activities, including life and death events. General interest newspapers often covered the public activities of fraternal organizations, such as dances, picnics, athletic competitions, dinners, and awards, and included the names of members participating. In obituary or death notices and on tombstones, a researcher may encounter the initials or insignia of a fraternal organization to which the decedent belonged. An extensive list of fraternal organizations and secret societies can be found online at the website of AAA Historical Americana-World Exonumia at *www.exonumia.com/art/society.htm*. Details about the history and purpose of fraternal organizations can be found in *The International Encyclopedia of Secret Societies and Fraternal Orders* by Alan Axelrod.

After the Civil War a number of veterans organizations were founded, the best known being the Grand Army of the Republic (GAR) for Union veterans. There were 600 GAR posts in New York. The NYSA holds series B1796, the New York State Historian GAR Records. Members met in "annual encampments," and these meetings are documented in publications and "rosters" that enumerate the names of participants. Many of these publications are in the holdings of the NYPL and the NYSL. The Sons of Union Veterans of the Civil War is sponsoring a project to identify repositories of records of the GAR, searchable by state, at *garrecords.org*.

Another veterans group, founded by former officers, is the Military Order of the Loyal Legion of the United States (MOLLUS). The New York Commandery of MOLLUS was formed in 1865 shortly after the assassination of President Lincoln. MOLLUS still exists as a patriotic and hereditary organization. The MOLLUS archives are on long-term loan to the library of the Civil War Heritage Center at the Union League of Philadelphia; an online catalog is at *ulheritagecenter.org*. Publications of MOLLUS are available at the NYPL. Some GAR and MOLLUS publications are online at *HathiTrust.org*.

While membership in many fraternal organizations was restricted to men, women often participated actively in female auxiliaries. However, reform-minded temperance organizations were the bastion of women. These groups provided comradeship and support for like-minded women, and produced newspapers and other publications. The Women's Christian Temperance Union (WCTU) was founded in 1873–1874 after protest marches on saloons in many towns in Ohio and New York. The women of Fredonia, New York are credited with being the first to march, and the organizational meeting establishing the WCTU took place in Chautauqua, New York. Temperance groups became a political outlet for women in a period when they were lacking voting rights and other legal protections. Records of various chapters of the WCTU in New York can be found in the Historic Document Inventory catalog. The records of the New York-based Friends Temperance Union (1876–1905) are held by Swarthmore College in Pennsylvania; a finding aid is online at *www.swarthmore.edu/library/friends/ead/4094tuny.xml*.

The *Brooklyn Eagle Almanac* is an outstanding resource for identifying fraternal and benevolent organizations in New York City and Long Island. See Harry Macy Jr.'s "The Brooklyn Eagle Almanac" in the *New York Researcher*.

Corrections and Prison Records

The first state prison, Newgate, opened in New York City in 1797. Auburn prison, built in Cayuga County in 1825, was considered a "model" prison embracing new thinking in prison design. Sing Sing Prison (Westchester County) opened in 1826 to replace Newgate Prison.

Other nineteenth- and early-twentieth-century correctional facilities included Clinton Prison, opened in 1845; Elmira Reformatory, 1876; Eastern Reformatory, 1892; Great Meadow Prison, 1911; Attica Prison, 1931; and Wallkill Prison, 1932. The Auburn Asylum for Insane Convicts, which opened in 1858, was succeeded by the Mattawan State Hospital, 1893, and Dannemora State Hospital, 1900. The Mount Pleasant Female Prison was opened at Sing Sing in 1839 and received inmates previously held at Bellevue Hospital's prison ward and Auburn Prison. When Mount Pleasant closed in 1877, the women were moved to county penitentiaries until a new women's prison opened at Auburn in 1893, succeeded by Bedford Hills Prison in 1933.

Sing Sing was the site of all executions in New York between 1892 and 1963, the last year an execution was performed in New York. Extensive, though incomplete, inmate records of most of these facilities are at the NYSA and *Ancestry.com* (see below).

Early records were written in registers or record books; after about 1900, case files gradually replaced registers. Prison records may include admission and discharge registers; biographical and descriptive registers; case files, including medical files; and registers of persons executed.

Prison records often contain extensive information about the prisoner's personal history and family background. Records for current inmates are maintained at the prison. Summary information on convicts in state prisons back to the 1970s is available in the "Inmate Lookup" database on the website of the New York State Department of Corrections and Community Supervision at *doccs.ny.gov*.

Records of state prison inmates in the NYSA are generally not indexed and are arranged by inmate identification number assigned at the time of admission. In order to search for records, or request that NYSA staff undertake a search, the inmate's full name, place of incarceration, and admission date or identification number must be known. Records can also be searched using date of conviction, as the date of admission usually took place shortly thereafter. Conviction dates can often be found in newspaper accounts, or in court records held by the county clerk. Because of the huge volume of modern prison records, the NYSA is preserving a two percent random sample of case files of inmates released after 1956. (The remaining records are destroyed.) While privacy laws make obtaining prison records difficult, contacting the prison's records department can be helpful in finding and accessing records.

Prison records from the NYSA are being added to *Ancestry.com*. Recent additions include:

- Discharges of Convicts by Commutation of Sentences, 1883–1913. Series A0604.
- Executive orders restoring citizenship rights, 1869–1931. Series B0046.
- Governor's Registers of commitments to prisons, 1842–1908. Series A0603. Records online are from Newgate, New York City, 1797–1810; Sing Sing Prison, Westchester County, 1855–1939; Clinton Prison, Clinton County, 1857–1882, 1926–1939; Auburn Prison, Cayuga County, 1853–1882; New York Penitentiary (Blackwell's Island, now Roosevelt Island), New York City; Kings County Penitentiary; Albany County Penitentiary; Onondaga County Penitentiary, Syracuse; Monroe County Penitentiary, Rochester, and others.
- Prisoners Received at Newgate State Prison, 1797–1810.

The first juvenile reformatory in the United States, the New York House of Refuge, opened in New York City in 1825. Though privately managed by the Society for the Reformation of Juvenile Delinquents of the City of New York, it received state funding. The institution closed in 1935. Administrative, operational, and inmate records are held at the NYSA and cover the Society and institution's lifespan; a detailed list of the collection is on their website. The NYSA also holds records of the Western House of

Refuge in Rochester, opened in 1849, later relocated and called the State Agricultural and Industrial School; the NYSA also holds the Western House of Refuge for Women, 1893, later called the Albion State Training School. Records include admission and discharge records, work records, and apprenticeship records. Although in the earliest years only boys were admitted, female sections were eventually added.

See the bibliography for the NYSA's online "Guide to Records of the Department of Correctional Services," which describes its extensive prison-related holdings. While basic information regarding adult inmates can be disclosed to researchers, access to other information is restricted under state or federal laws. When researchers use the NYSA records, the NYSA staff will determine access to inmate records on a case by case basis.

An index of prisoners incarcerated in federal facilities since 1982 is available online at *www.bop.gov/iloc2/LocateInmate.jsp*. The Federal Bureau of Prisons is in the process of transferring its pre-1982 inmate records to the National Archives (NARA).

Very few older county jail records have survived. Notably excepted are admission registers for the Albany County jail and penitentiary, which span the years 1829–1976, and are available at the Albany County Hall of Records.

In 1880 the U.S. Census included a supplementary schedule of Defective, Dependent, and Delinquent Classes. It captured the individual's name, race, gender, age, former residence, and, for prisoners, details regarding their imprisonment. Schedules for New York can be seen at the NYSL and are accessible for free at the *Ancestry.com*'s New York portal. See also chapter 3, Census Records.

Medical Records
Hospital Records

Hospital and physicians' medical records can be a useful source of genealogical information. However, in addition to state privacy laws, access to health records is also controlled by the Health Insurance Portability and Accountability Act (HIPAA). Changes to HIPAA's "Privacy Rule" effective September 2013 allow access to "protected" records 50 years after the death of a patient, but New York State law continues to restrict access to personal health information indefinitely. Generally, medical records are available only to the patient or other authorized individual or organization, including the administrator of the patient's estate.

Hospital archives policies and practices differ. When a hospital closes, records may transfer to the successor hospital. Early hospital registers usually list the name, age, place of birth, admission date, health condition, and date of discharge. Hospitals also kept death records, which usually included the name of the deceased, as well as the date and cause of death. This section provides basic information on some of the oldest hospitals in the state.

MUNI maintains records from the hospitals located on Blackwell's Island in New York City from 1758 to 1953. These records are contained in the "Almshouse" collection. (See the preceding section on Almshouses or Poorhouses in this chapter.)

The Archives of the New York Weill Cornell Medical Center, New York City, is the repository for the official records of many medical institutions in New York City including New York Hospital (1794–1796, 1801–1932); New York Infant Asylum (1871–1901, 1904–1909, with gaps); and Bloomingdale Asylum/Bloomingdale Hospital (1808–1932). The earliest records are dated 1771, and researchers can access patient records prior to 1932. The archives are open for research by appointment. Hours and details of the collections may be found on their website, *http://weill.cornell.edu/archives*.

The Lillian & Clarence de la Chapelle Medical Archives (*http://hslguides.med.nyu.edu/medicalarchives*) of the NYU Health Sciences Libraries house the historical records of the New York University Medical Center and the New York University School of Medicine, as well as records of institutions that have merged with the School or Medical Center such as the Bellevue Hospital Medical College. While the Archives collects personal papers and administrative records relating to faculty, alumni, and the NYU Langone Medical Center and School of Medicine, they do not collect student records and patient records. However, a collection of original Bellevue Hospital case books dating between 1860 to 1932 document various diseases, including infectious diseases, diseases of the circulatory system, chronic diseases, and injuries of the body. Microfilm copies are available to researchers.

The Mount Sinai Archives include records from the Mount Sinai Hospital (1852–present), and the Mount Sinai Hospital School of Nursing (1881–1971). The hospital began as the "Jews' Hospital in the City of New York" in the mid-1800s providing medical care for the Jewish immigrant community in New York City. In its first year of operation, the majority of patients were foreign-born. During the Civil War it cared for Union soldiers. In 1866 the hospital formally abandoned its sectarian charter and was renamed The Mount Sinai Hospital. The website provides details of the collection and research services at *http://library.mssm.edu/services/archives*.

The Albany Hospital was the first general hospital in the state outside of New York City. It was incorporated in 1849 and opened two years later to meet the needs of the poor, who could not afford private physicians, and to improve medical training by creating a teaching hospital. The Albany Medical College Archives include hospital records from 1844 to 1990. A description of the collection is at *www.amc.edu/Academic/Alumni/archives/Archives.cfm*.

Records of closed Catholic hospitals are often held by the diocese where the hospital was located. See chapter 15, Religious Records.

Psychiatric Institution Records

Records of psychiatric institutions often come in the form of handwritten casebooks. These large, bound volumes designate a page for every new patient, in order of admittance. Notes on the patient were made, and a second later page was used (and cross-referenced) if necessary. Most of these notes are observations of the patient's condition and behavior. The NYSA maintains the patient records of several state hospitals, now called psychiatric centers, the oldest of which (Utica) opened in 1843. Patient records of other facilities (many of which have closed) are maintained by the New York State Office of Mental Health. All information in those records is permanently restricted under federal and/or state law and is not disclosed for genealogical purposes.

When a patient died, the institution would file a death certificate with the New York State Department of Health, as required by a law passed in 1880. Staff from the institution frequently provided information for the death certificate. Some institutions maintained their own cemeteries, but the cemetery records are considered medical in nature and are legally restricted.

However, genealogical data can be gleaned from court records of commitments. In New York these cases were handled by the Courts of Common Pleas and successor courts. These court records may be in the County Clerk's offices. Typically, the court record of commitment to a mental hospital provides details of symptoms and name of the illness; examinations which led to the individual being ruled insane; the destination where the person would be sent; the names of concerned family members, usually a spouse or parent; guardianships for minor children; and the name of the examining physician. See also, chapter 5, Court Records.

The 1880 federal census contained a supplemental schedule, called the Defective, Dependent, and Delinquent Schedule. See the preceding section on Corrections/Prison Records in this chapter for details.

Selected Bibliography and Further Reading

Andress, Richard. "Guide to Records of the Department of Correctional Services." New York State Archives, Guides to Historical Records. 1992. [www.archives.nysed.gov/a/research/res_topics_legal_corrections.pdf]

Arons, Ron. Wanted! U.S. Criminal Records: Sources and Research Methodology. Oakland, CA: Criminal Research Press, 2009.

Axelrod, Alan. The International Encyclopedia of Secret Societies and Fraternal Orders. New York: Facts on File, 1997.

Bureau of Charities, New York City. Directory to the Charities of New York. New York, 1874.

Charity Organization Society of Buffalo. Annual Report. Buffalo, 1879–1928/29. Microfilmed by the NYPL.

Charity Organization Society of the City of New York. The New York Charities Directory. New York, 1883–1933/34. Also known as Classified and Descriptive Directory to the Charitable and Beneficent Societies and Institutions of the City of New York (1883–1887); Directory of Social Agencies of the City of New York (1927/28–1950/51); Directory of Social and Health Agencies of New York City (1952/53–1981/82).

Dunshee, Henry W. History of the School of the Reformed Protestant Dutch Church in the City of New York from 1633 [sic] to the Present Time. Revised edition, New York: Aldine Press, 1883.

Farrell, Charles. "Children of the New York City Almshouse 1807–1810." NYG&B Record, vol. 130 (1999) no. 1: 36–42, no. 2: 120–123, no. 3: 180–182, no. 4: 296–300; vol. 131 (2000) no. 1: 59–62. [NYG&B eLibrary]

Fleming, Ann Carter. "Overlooked Resources: Business, Organizational, and Institutional Records." OnBoard: Newsletter of the Board for Certification of Genealogists, vol. 13 (September 2007): 22–23. [www.bcgcertification.org/skillbuilders]

Freilich, Kay Haviland, and Ann Carter Fleming. "Business, Institution, and Organization Records." In The Source: A Guidebook to American Genealogy, edited by Loretto Dennis Szucs and Sandra Hargreaves Luebking. 3rd edition. Provo, UT: Ancestry, 2006. Digitally published 2010 at Ancestry.com.

Golding, Elisabeth A. "The Mighty Chain: A Guide to Canal Records in the New York State Archives." New York State Archives, Guides to Historical Records. 1992. [http://www.archives.nysed.gov/a/research/res_topics_trans_canal.pdf]

Hun, Henry. "Survey of the Activity of the Albany Academy: The Ancestry and Achievements of Its Students, Its Undeveloped Material and Its Finished Products." Typescript. New York State Library Department of Manuscripts and Special Collections, Albany, 1934.

Joslyn, Roger D. "Indentures of the Poor Children of Orange County, 1829–1847, 1871, 1884, 1885." NYG&B Record, vol. 137 (2006) no. 4: 294–303; vol. 138 (2007) no. 2: 144–150, no. 3: 227–231, no. 4: 312. [NYG&B eLibrary]

———. "New York." In Red Book: American State, County and Town Sources, edited by Alice Eicholz. 3rd edition. Provo, UT: Ancestry, 2004. Digitally published 2010 at Ancestry.com.

Langhans, Rufus B., and John J. O'Neil. Town of Huntington, Records of the Overseers of the Poor: Part 1, 1752-1804; Part 2, 1805-1861. Huntington, NY: The Town, 1986.

———. Town of Huntington, Records of the Overseers of the Poor: Addendum, 1729-1843. Huntington, NY: The Town, 1982.

Macy, Harry, Jr. "The Brooklyn Eagle Almanac." *New York Researcher*, Winter 2005. Updated September 2014 and published as a Research Aid on *NewYorkFamilyHistory.org*.

New York Historical Resources Center. *Guide to Historical Resources in . . . County New York, Repositories*. Ithaca, NY: Cornell University, 1980–1993. Titles in this series, which resulted from the Historical Documents Inventory, will be found in the individual county bibliographies in Part Two of this book. Many titles accessible at *books.FamilySearch.org*.

New York (State), Board of State Commissioners of Public Charities. *Annual Report of the Board of State Commissioners of Public Charities of the State of New York*. 6 vols. Albany: The Argus Co., 1868–1873.

New York (State). State Board of Charities. *Annual Report of the State Board of Charities of the State of New York*. 56 vols. Albany: Weed, Parsons and Co., 1874–1928.

New York (State). State Board of Charities. *Directory of the Charitable, Eleemosynary, Correctional and Reformatory Institutions of the State of New York*. Albany: J. B. Lyon, 1892.

New York (State) Legislature. Joint Legislative Committee Investigating Seditious Activities. "Citizenship Training in the State of New York." In *Revolutionary Radicalism, Its History, Purpose and Tactics with an Exposition and Discussion of the Steps Being Taken and Required to Curb It . . . Filed April 24, 1920, in the Senate of the State of New York*. Part II, "Constructive Movements and Measures in America," vols. 3 and 4. Albany: J. B. Lyon, 1920. This exhaustive report provides a wealth of information on the many organizations—private and public, ethnic- and religious-based, serving immigrants in New York State. [*books.Google.com*]

Pfeiffer, Laura Szucs. *Hidden Sources: Family History in Unlikely Places*. Orem, UT: Ancestry, 2000.

Richmond, Rev. John F. *New York and Its Institutions 1609–1872. A Library of Information, Pertaining to the Great Metropolis, Past and Present*. New York: E. B. Treat, 1872. Reprinted 2010 by Nabu Press.

Scott, Kenneth. "The Churchwardens and the Poor in New York City 1693–1747." *NYG&B Record*, vol. 99 (1968) no. 3: 157–164; vol. 100 (1969) no. 1: 18–26, no. 3: 141–147; vol. 101 (1970) no. 1: 33–40, no. 3: 164–173; vol. 102 (1971) no. 1: 50–56, no. 3: 150–156. [NYG&B eLibrary]

———. *Nineteenth Century Apprenticeships in New York City*. Special publication of the National Genealogical Society no. 55. Arlington, VA: National Genealogical Society, 1986.

Seraile, William. *Angels of Mercy: White Women and New York's Colored Orphan Asylum*. New York: Fordham University Press, 2011.

Stuhler, Linda S. "A Brief History of Government Charity in New York (1603–1900)." The Social Welfare History Project. [*www.socialwelfarehistory.com/organizations/brief-history-state-charity-new-york-1603-1900*]

Town of Huntington School Trustee Annual Census Reports, 1827–1863, Volumes 1–2. Huntington, NY: The Town, 1982.

City Directories and Other Directories

Chapter 11

Overview

The city directory, forerunner to the telephone book, can be a valuable tool for locating an ancestor, understanding historical context, and revealing information that may lead to other records. A methodical search over several years can provide information about a person's address history, job history, and business and family relationships, as well as name variations.

The first known directory in colonial America was compiled in 1665, one year after New York came under British control. It provided a simple listing of householders in New York City arranged by street. A more substantial directory of the city was printed in 1786 by David Franks and included a map, an almanac, and separate lists of prominent citizens and professionals. Franks published a second directory in 1787, and other publishers produced New York City directories every year from 1789 until the early-twentieth century.

Initially, the primary role of the city directory was as a tool for businesses; directories provided a catalog of potential customers and an outlet for printed advertising. Frequently printed by newspapers at the start, a field of directory publishers soon emerged. Often, multiple publishers might produce competing directories in a single city. Each publisher determined the criteria for inclusion in its directory, so the information contained might vary among directories. Canvassers were sent out to record the heads of households, with an emphasis on property owners and primary tenants, and men who were employed; widows were generally listed. Directories grew to be more inclusive and eventually listed all employed men and their wives, working women, and adult children; some directories listed people who worked in a city, even if they resided elsewhere.

City directories, or residential directories, began to be widely published in the late-eighteenth century, in cities and towns. They were typically organized alphabetically by the head of household, and provided a home address, occupation, and sometimes a business address. They might also include street listings and maps, ward boundaries, and listings of government offices, banks, cemeteries, religious institutions, schools, hospitals, and fraternal organizations. Reverse directories organized by street address were produced occasionally in the nineteenth century and became more common in the 1920s. Elite directories, also called social registers, blue books, or family directories, listing the names and addresses of prominent families in a community, sometimes included a reverse directory.

In rural communities, a rural or farm directory might provide information on a farmer's acreage and crops and the farm's map coordinates, in addition to the standard information of a city directory. For an example, see the 1917 *American Agriculturalist Farm Directory and Reference Book, Monroe and Livingston Counties, New York.*

City directories were generally published annually after May 1, which was for many years the traditional moving day and the annual start date for leases in New York City and elsewhere. In the twentieth century the publication of city directories became more sporadic with gaps between years. The city directory was eventually supplanted by the telephone directory, as the telephone became prevalent in many households. In New York City, the last city directory published was for the years 1933–1934; in some communities city directories continued to be published far later. The first telephone directory for New York City was published in 1878.

Business directories can identify companies that were in business at a specific time and place. They were typically organized by subject or type of business, in the manner of telephone directory yellow pages, and could be statewide or local, or cover one or more counties. A copartnership business directory can identify the business name and address, as well as the names of its partners, officers, directors, and agents— and sometimes the amount of its capitalization. Membership directories of professional or trade associations remain popular. See chapter 10, Business, Institutional, and Organizational Records, for information about directories of charities.

Specialized directories that might have an ethnic focus or a fraternal affiliation were sometimes produced. Examples include the *Rochester Italian Directory, 1931* and the *Rochester City Directory of Negro Business and Progress 1939–1940*, which provides a history of "Negro Progress in Rochester 1816–1839" and includes narrative sections on census data, property owners, and occupations, in addition to a listing of individuals and businesses. Both titles may be accessed through the Monroe County Library System website (see below). Published in 1894, the *Knights of Pythias Directory and Buffalo Street Directory and Guide* gives the names, addresses, and occupations of all lodge members in Buffalo and Erie County; the book is accessible at *Archive.org*.

Dorothea Spear has produced a *Bibliography of American Directories Through 1860*. However, there is no single, comprehensive bibliography that identifies every directory that has been published for every community of New York State. Most local and county libraries and historical societies maintain collections of directories relevant to their communities. Some provide lists of their holdings or finding aids online, sometimes with links to digitized directories. See the individual County Guides in Part Two of this book for listings of county repositories and resources. Many directories published before 1923 have been digitized and are available for free on the internet, Archive (*Archive.org*), Google Books (*books.google.com*), and the HathiTrust (*HathiTrust.org*).

Repositories and Online Resources

Below is a list of repositories and online resources that have significant collections of New York directories. See also chapter 16, National and Statewide Repositories & Resources.

Ancestry

Ancestry.com

This subscription website offers online access to numerous directories throughout New York State. At the date of publication, a total of 128 city directories and 131 business and professional directories were offered.

Brooklyn Genealogy Information Page

stevemorse.org

A large selection of digitized directories for Brooklyn and other parts of New York City and Long Island, 1796–1955, may be accessed at *http://bklyn-genealogy-info.stevemors e.org/ Directory*.

BuffaloResearch.com: Genealogy and Local History in Buffalo, NY

buffaloresearch.com

The website of librarian and historian Cynthia Van Ness has a very comprehensive catalog of links and provider information for city directories available for the City of Buffalo, Erie County, and western New York State, as well as research tips.

City Directories of the United States

uscitydirectories.com

This website is a work in progress. For the selected county in New York State, it provides a list of available years at some repositories, with a corresponding call number, and direct links to some online material.

Distant Cousin

distantcousin.com/Directories/NY

This free website offers a growing selection of online New York State city directories, and currently numbers 27.

Fold3

fold3.com

This subscription website offers online access to a selection of city directories for New York City (132), Brooklyn (48), Buffalo (63), and Rochester (27).

Library of Congress

loc.gov

The Microform Reading Room at the Library of Congress holds mid-nineteenth to mid-twentieth century directories for about 150 places in New York State. A full listing is accessible at *www.loc.gov/rr/microform/uscity/ny.html*. The research guide "Telephone and City Directories in the Library of Congress: Current Directories" is at *http://loc.gov/rr/genealogy/bib_guid/ telephon.html*.

Mocavo

Mocavo.com

Mocavo's growing collection of city directories numbers more than 100,000 at the date of publication and includes 6,000 directories for New York State. The collection may be searched by name and key word for free, and individual directories may be browsed. More sophisticated search options are available to paid subscribers.

Monroe County Library System

www3.libraryweb.org

The Monroe County Library System website provides remote access to its extensive digital directory collections for the city of Rochester and other cities, villages, farms, and businesses in or near the counties of Monroe, Genesee, Livingston, Ontario, Orleans, and Wayne. [*www3.libraryweb.org/lh.aspx?id=1128*]

New York Heritage Digital Collections

nyheritage.org

The New York Heritage website provides free access to selected digital collections of more than 200 partner organizations. Currently, the collection of directories includes more than 50 city and family directories for Buffalo (Erie County), more than 30 directories for Jamestown (Chautauqua County) and Olean (Cattaraugus County), and more than 20 directories for Oswego City.

New York Public Library

nypl.org

The New York Public Library maintains a collection of historical city directories on microfilm for the entire state that is accessible in the Milstein Division of U.S. History, Local History & Genealogy. It also has an extensive collection of telephone directories in print or on microfilm, and a large collection of social registers. They can be found in the online catalog, *catalog.nypl.org*, by keyword, searching locality name and the term "directories." (To search for a business directory, add the keyword "commerce"; to search for a social directory, add the keyword "elite.") Telephone directories for 1940 for the five boroughs of New York City may be accessed at *directme.nypl.org*. See the bibliography for Philip Sutton's article about city directories, which is on the NYPL website. Holdings for telephone directories (including reverse/address directories and yellow pages) for New York City, Nassau, Suffolk, and Westchester counties are listed on the NYPL's microforms web page at *www.nypl.org/locations/schwarzman/microforms*.

New York State Library

www.nysl.nysed.gov

A list of the city directories and telephone directories available on microfilm at the New York State Library may be accessed at *www.nysl.nysed.gov/genealogy/citydir.htm*. The list is arranged alphabetically by location.

Old Telephone Books

oldtelephonebooks.com

The free website provides access to a large collection of online telephone books for New York State.

Online Historical Directories

https://sites.google.com/site/onlinedirectorysite/Home/usa/ny

Miriam Robbins's free website provides links to an extensive and growing selection of online city directories for New York State.

Selected Bibliography and Further Reading

American Agriculturalist Farm Directory and Reference Book, Monroe and Livingston Counties, New York: A Rural Directory and Reference Book Including a Road Map of Monroe and Livingston Counties. New York: Orange Judd Company, 1917.

Bailey, Rosalie Fellows. *Guide to Genealogical and Biographical Sources for New York City (Manhattan), 1783–1898.* New York: The Author, 1954. [books.FamilySearch.org] Reprinted with new introduction by Harry Macy Jr. Baltimore: Clearfield Co., 1998.

Coles, Howard W., comp. *City Directory of Negro Business and Progress 1939–1940.* Rochester: Howard W. Coles, 1939. A digital version may be accessed on the website of the Monroe County Public Library at *http://www.libraryweb.org/~digitized/miscdir/City_Directory_of_Negro_Business_and_Progress_1939-1940.pdf*.

Franks, David C. *The New York Directory for 1786.* Preface by Noah Webster. 1786. Reprint, New York: Winthrop Press, 1905.

Kuebler, Albert J., and Fred Kraebel. *Knights of Pythias Directory and Buffalo Street Directory and Guide.* Buffalo: Kraft & Stern, 1894.

Meyerink, Kory L. *Effective Use of City Directories.* ProGenealogists. [www.progenealogists.com/citydirectories.htm]

Remington, Gordon L. "Directories." In *The Source: A Guidebook to American Genealogy* 3rd edition. Edited by Loretta Dennis Szucs and Sandra Hargreaves Luebking. Provo, UT: Ancestry, 2006. [Ancestry.com]

Rochester Italian Directory, 1931. Rochester: North Printing Company, 1931. A digital version may be accessed on the website of the Monroe County Public Library at *http://www.libraryweb.org/~digitized/miscdir/Italian_directory_1931.pdf*.

Spear, Dorothea N. *Bibliography of American Directories through 1860.* Worcester, MA: American Antiquarian Society, 1961.

Sutton, Phillip. "Direct Me NYC 1786: A History of City Directories in the United States and New York City." Digitally published by the New York Public Library, 2012. [nypl.org]

Wilson, James Grant, ed. "A Directory for the City of New York in 1665." In *The Memorial History of the City of New-York: From Its First Settlement to the Year 1892.* New York: New York History Co., 1892.

Newspapers

Introduction

Information found in newspapers can provide historical context and add details that bring names, dates, and places to life. In addition to birth, marriage, and death notices, newspapers include biographical material (occasionally with surprising detail), descriptions of social functions, school announcements, missing relatives, and even scandals, gossip, and crime that most families work hard to suppress.

Researchers will be most effective if they locate more than one account of an event, searching both the locale where the event occurred and where the person was born, lived, and died. While some newspapers may be online and text-searchable, others are available on microfilm or on paper.

Newspapers are not usually original sources. Sometimes the reporter was an eyewitness, but other times articles are compilations of information from sources such as interviews and reports of events from individuals not involved with the event. Many obituaries, especially in recent years, are written by family members often with very strong biases.

Historical Overview

The first newspaper published in the Province of New York was William Bradford's *New York Gazette*, established in New York City in 1725. By the time of the American Revolution, there were 22 newspapers in New York, all but one of them published in New York City.

Early newspapers consisted mainly of shipping news, stories reprinted from London papers, advertisements, official government notices, and essays that had appeared in British literary publications. But they did contain some genealogical information. For published or manuscript indexes and abstracts from early newspapers, see Henry Hoff's "Marriage and Death Notices in New York City Newspapers." After the American Revolution a lively press emerged with links to the main political factions of the day. By 1825 most of the larger New York State municipalities had newspapers. Innovations in printing and transportation led to dramatic circulation increases in the 1830s.

The "penny press," targeted towards a working class audience, proliferated and transformed newspaper publishing. The first successful penny paper was the *Sun* (1833) in New York City, and it was quickly imitated. By 1840 New York State had more than 200 newspapers, by 1855 it had more than 600, and by 1860 every city had one or more daily papers. Some newspapers developed around themes or segments of the population, for example, religious belief, immigrant groups, temperance, abolitionist support, the suffrage movement, agriculture, an industry, or political beliefs or parties. As New York City became the nation's economic hub, it also became a publishing center.

As immigrant populations grew, specialized foreign-language titles appeared. New York newspapers have been published in many languages, including Arabic, Chinese, Czech, Dutch, Finnish, French, German, Hebrew, Italian, Japanese, Norwegian, Polish, Russian, Spanish, Swedish, and Yiddish.

The growth and spread of newspapers across New York State (and the rest of the United States) can be seen graphically thanks to the Stanford University Data Visualization Project "Mapping Journalism's Voyage West" (*www.stanford.edu/group/ruralwest/cgi-bin/drupal/visualizations/us_newspapers*). This page also lists the newspapers and their dates of publication (sourced from the Library of Congress Chronicling America pages at *chroniclingamerica.loc.gov*).

Comprehensive histories of New York State or of individual counties include sections on newspapers. A short history of newspaper publishing in New York is on the website of the New York State Library (NYSL) at *www.nysl.nysed.gov/nysnp/history.htm*.

Lists of New York Newspapers

A key to effective newspaper research is identifying the local papers that would most likely have reported on the person, family, or community being researched. Researchers can find many resources for titles.

- The NYSL website page, New York State Newspapers in Print and on Microfilm, provides a database for newspapers in libraries and other repositories around the state (*www.nysl.nysed.gov/nysnp*). The listing provides links to the repositories. Researchers can limit their search to a county or city (town or place-name). This database was created as a result of New York's participation in the United States Newspaper Program (USNP) cited below.

- The Chronicling America website, *chroniclingamerica.loc.gov*, hosted by the Library of Congress (LOC), has a database, US Newspaper Directory, 1690–Present, that allows the user to search for newspapers published in the United States by title, locality, time period, or ethnicity, and provides information on locating a print or microfilm version of the paper itself. More than 12,000 New York newspaper titles are listed; however, not every newspaper is included. The Newspaper Directory is derived from the library catalog records created during the USNP, 1980–2007. This program funded state projects to locate, describe, and selectively preserve historic newspaper collections. (Note that only ten of those listed are available digitally on this site.)

- *Rowell's American Newspaper Directory* (1869–1877), *Ayer's American Newspaper Annual* (1880–1909), and *Ayer's American Newspaper Annual & Directory* (1910–1920) are available in the Digital Reference Collection of the Library of Congress Newspaper and Current Periodical Reading Room website at *www.loc.gov/rr/news*. These annual directories are organized by state, then locality, and list all titles published in that locality in that year.

- French's *Gazetteer of the State of New York: Embracing . . .* has listings of newspapers in each county and town up until 1860. Researchers can identify potentially relevant newspapers.

- The New York Public Library (NYPL) has a research page entitled Newspapers (*nypl.org/node/5623*), which, while not specific to genealogy, is a resource for finding not only the extensive NYPL holdings, but links to other newspaper sites as well. A 13-page list of New York newspapers includes NYPL call numbers and dates of the holdings.

- The University of Pennsylvania's Historical Newspapers Online is a national database and is organized by state. Many New York links are provided on this site at *http://guides.library.upenn.edu/historicalnewspapersonline*.

- Wikipedia's List of Online Newspaper Archives is a guide to accessible newspaper titles, with links. The list is organized by country and state at *http://en.wikipedia.org/wiki/Wikipedia:List_of_online_newspaper_archives*.

- Miriam J. Robbins has compiled a list of New York newspapers with links at *https://sites.google.com/site/onlinenewspapersite/Home/usa/ny*. This long list provides links to newspapers at principal sites such as Old Fulton New York Postcards and the Library of Congress, as well as smaller sites.

- The Center for Research Libraries (CRL), an international consortium of university, college, and research libraries, located in Chicago, has a notable newspaper collection on microfilm. Its online catalog at *crl.edu* provides clues to some unusual New York newspaper titles. CRL microfilm collections may be borrowed by member libraries through interlibrary loan. Colgate University, NYPL, and SUNY Binghamton are among the New York libraries that are members.

- The website of the New York Genealogical and Biographical Society has a useful finding aid, Guide to New York Newspapers That Are Online. This guide contains links to many local, state, and national online newspaper archives on *NewYorkFamilyHistory.org*.

Online Newspaper Resources

The array of New York newspapers online is extensive and continually growing. New York newspapers resources include *Ancestry.com*, ProQuest Historical Newspapers (*proquest.com*), *Genealogybank.com*, *NewspaperArchive.com*, Google News, Early American Newspapers (*Readex.com*), *WorldVitalRecords.com*, Nineteenth Century Newspapers (*gdc.gale.com*), and the website of the LOC (*loc.gov*). Most of these sites update and increase their holdings frequently and improve their search functions. Many require subscriptions to access; ProQuest and *Readex.com* may be accessed through local libraries which maintain subscriptions. (Note that not all sites offering online newspapers have New York titles.)

Links for well-known newspapers, such as the *Brooklyn Eagle*, will be found quickly, although not all websites cover the same publication dates. More specialized data or titles can be identified using sites like those listed below. The quality of the images and search engines varies from website to website. Many public libraries hold subscriptions to newspaper databases, and some libraries give their users remote access.

Old Fulton New York Postcards (*FultonHistory.com*) is a newspaper website of staggering size and utility. It offers millions of pages of newspapers from small towns to large cities in New York State, and some from other states. This site, by far the largest collection of New York newspapers online, has a full-text search engine. An index of newspaper titles and coverage dates, organized by county, may be accessed from the FAQ page. Access is free.

A number of important, large-circulation New York newspapers of record can be searched from their own websites and, in some cases, from other sites like ProQuest. Most of these proprietary websites require payment or a subscription for access to part or all of their collections. Among them are the *New York Times*, fully searchable from its start in 1851, and the *Wall Street Journal*, searchable from 1889. The *Brooklyn Daily Eagle* (1841–1955) is on the website of the Brooklyn Public Library at no charge (*http://newsstand.bklynpubliclibrary.org*) and other sites, some free, and others possibly requiring a subscription.

Other large city papers have their own newspaper archives, but their online archives tend to begin at relatively recent dates. These include the *Albany Times Union,* the *Buffalo News, Poughkeepsie Journal, New York Daily News, Rochester Democrat and Chronicle, Newsday* (Long Island), and the *Journal News* (Westchester County and Rockland County). All of these titles can be quickly located through any search engine.

Other resources for online newspapers are local libraries and historical societies. Examples include the *Andover Advertiser,* serving Allegany and Steuben counties, available at the Andover Free Library website (*AndoverFreeLibrary.org*); Nassau County Libraries Historic Newspaper Collections on *LongIslandMemories.org* includes issues of *Bethpage Tribune, Farmingdale Observer, Daily Review of Nassau County, Freeport News, South Side Messenger, Queens County Review, Nassau County Review, Nassau Post,* and the *Leader*; the Suffolk County Historical Newspaper Archive (*SuffolkCountyHistoricalSociety.org/library*) includes the *Corrector* (Sag Harbor), the *Long Island Traveler* (Cutchogue), the *Long Islander* (Huntington), the *Mid-Island Mail* (Medford Station), the *Patchogue Advance,* the *Port Jefferson Echo,* the *Sag Harbor Express,* the *South Side Signal* (Babylon), and the *Suffolk County News* (Sayville).

Among other websites for New York titles are:

- NYS Historic Newspapers. The site (*nyshistoricnewspapers.org*) has 178 town, county, and city digitized newspapers. This free site can be searched by county or city (or town) and publishes a complete list of titles and issues in the database. It includes newspapers digitized by the Guilderland Public Library in Albany County (*historicnewspapers.guilpl.org*), and the Northern New York Library Network (*news.nnyln.net*); the links for those sites direct the researcher directly to NYS Historic Newspapers.

- Hudson River Valley Heritage. The website (*news.hrvh.org*) includes four papers: *Rockland County Journal, Rockland County Messenger, Rockland County Times,* and the *Kingston Daily Freeman.*

- The database Historical Newspapers of the Rochester, New York Area (*rrlcnewspapers.org*) includes *Fairport Herald, Fairport Herald Mail, Fairport-Parrington Herald-Mail, and Monroe County Mail.* The site provides a list of issues.

- Paper of Record's website (*PaperofRecord.com*) has a subscription database that is international in scope and contains three New York papers: *Mackenzie's Gazette* (New York City), *New York Examiner* (New York City), and *Volunteer* (Rochester). A subscription is not required to view the list of papers on this website.

- *Freedom's Journal* (1827–1829) was published in New York City and is said to be the first African American owned and operated newspaper in the United States. It contains an extensive amount of information of genealogical interest. This newspaper is online at the Wisconsin Historical Society website (*WisconsinHistory.org*). All issues are available.

- *The Friend of Man* (1836–1842). This important antislavery and reform-movement paper, published in central New York, is online at Cornell University (*http://fom.library.cornell.edu*).

- *The Cornell Daily Sun* (1880–1989). Digitizing this college newspaper (*http://cdsun.library.cornell.edu*) is an ongoing project of the Cornell University Library. A large number of issues have been digitized and are searchable.

- The University at Buffalo's library provides links to various digitized newspaper sites at *http://libweb1.lib.buffalo.edu/guide/guide.asp?id=374.*

- The Vassar College paper is fully digitized and online from 1872 to the present (*specialcollections.vassar.edu*).

- New York Heritage Digital Collections. The website (*nyheritage.org*) provides free access to a selection of New York State newspapers from 19 counties with links to many of the websites listed above.

- The American Newspapers Online site offered by Cornell University (*http://guides.library.cornell.edu/content.php?pid=8983&sid=65905*) aggregates many of the websites listed above.

The websites listed above may duplicate information about online resources and links.

Obituaries may be archived online in various locations and provide New York data. Some sites with newspaper obituaries include *ObitCentral.com, ObituaryDatabase.com,* and *AncestorHunt.com.*

Print and Microfilm Newspaper Resources

The rise of digital newspaper resources creates the badly mistaken impression that New York newspapers can now be fully searched online. Print and microfilm resources remain essential and are vast in New York, as many newspapers are not published online.

The NYSL, the NYPL, and the New-York Historical Society hold original and microfilm copies of New York newspapers. Local libraries and historical societies frequently have archives of their community's newspapers in their holdings, and many offer locally produced indexes of their hometown newspapers that are searchable by name.

The holdings of New York State newspapers in print and microfilm are listed at the NYSL website (*nysl.nysed.gov/nine/index.html*). This page also gives access to lists of newspapers in other locations in New York State.

General or obituary indexes to many newspapers may be found as card files, in book form, or online and searchable. Local libraries will often check their local paper for a death notice or obituary when the date of death is provided. The County Guides in this book provide information on many of these resources. An example of a general index is a 1,742-volume manuscript index to the *New York Herald* (1835–1918) held by the NYPL. One online example is the Life Records database hosted by Monroe County Library System (*www3.libraryweb.org/lh.aspx?id=948*) that consists of birth, death, and marriage indexes to Rochester newspapers.

Henry Hoff's article "Marriage and Death Notices in Long Island Newspapers" catalogs a list of resources for genealogical information extracted from newspapers. In particular, he notes typescripts, manuscripts, and index-card resources located at the Brooklyn Historical Society, the NYPL, the Queens Library, and the East Hampton Library. Hoff's article "Marriage and Death Notices in New York City Newspapers" identifies similar information for City papers from the eighteenth to the twentieth centuries.

Newspapers maintained "morgues" of past articles filed by subject for the use of their reporters and editors. Many newspaper morgues have been transferred to libraries and archives. The LOC Newspaper and Current Periodical Reading Room website provides information about the location of newspapers morgues at *http://www.loc.gov/rr/news/oltitles.html*.

Gertrude A. Barber (1891–1974), a prolific transcriber of New York records, published a number of books of marriages, deaths, and other records from New York newspapers, including the *New York Evening Post*, the *Brooklyn Eagle*, *Cooperstown Federalist*, the *Delaware County Gazette*, the *Otsego Herald and Western Advertiser*, the *Republican Watchman* (Suffolk County), and the *Orange County Patriot*, among others. Larger genealogical libraries in New York State will have these volumes. Titles of works like these by Mrs. Barber and others, which are too numerous to list here, can be identified on *WorldCat.org*, as well as in the NYSL and the NYPL catalogs. The last installment of Roger Joslyn's multipart article in the *NYG&B Record*, "Gertrude Barber, Minnie Cowen, and Ray Sawyer: The Sisters Who Indexed New York. List of the Cowen Sisters' Work," provides a detailed listing.

Books like Mrs. Barber's are still being published and can be very useful to researchers. James Maher's multivolume index to marriages and deaths in the *New York Herald* is particularly useful. For genealogical data from New York City ethnic newspapers, see two books by Laura Murphy DeGrazia and Diane Fitzpatrick Haberstroh, *Voices of the Irish Immigrant*

and *Irish Relatives and Friends*; Frank Biebel's book, *Index to Marriage and Death Notices in the New-Yorker Staats-Zeitung, 1836–1870*; and Thomas Reimer's *Index to Deaths found in the New Yorker Volks-Zeitung, 1878–1920*.

Fred Bowman's series of books about "vital records" all report data sourced from newspapers.

Selected Bibliography and Further Reading

See the County Guides for additional listings of newspaper abstracts.

Benedict, Shelia. "Using Newspapers Effectively," *OnBoard*, vol. 9 (September 2003): 20–22. Digitally published by the Board for Certification of Genealogists—Skillbuilding: Using Newspapers Effectively. [*www.bcgcertification.org/skillbuilders/skbld039.html*]

Biebel, Frank A. *Index to Marriage and Death Notices in the New-Yorker Staats-Zeitung, 1836–1870*. New York: New York Genealogical and Biographical Society, 2000. Extracts data from a major German-language paper. [NYG&B eLibrary]

Bowman, Fred Q. *8000 More Vital Records of Eastern New York State, 1804–1850*. Rhinebeck, NY: Kinship, 1991. Index available from Berkshire Family History Association.

———. *10,000 Vital Records of Central New York, 1813–1850*. Baltimore: Genealogical Publishing Co., 1986.

———. *10,000 Vital Records of Eastern New York, 1777–1834*. Baltimore: Genealogical Publishing Co., 1987. Index available from Berkshire Family History Association.

———. *10,000 Vital Records of Western New York, 1809–1850*. Baltimore: Genealogical Publishing Co., 1985. Index available from Berkshire Family History Association.

———. *Directory to Collections of New York Vital Records, 1726–1989, with Rare Gazetteer*. Bowie, MD: Heritage Books, 1995.

Bowman, Fred Q., and Thomas J. Lynch. "1100 Vital Records of Northeastern New York 1835–1850." *NYG&B Record*, vol. 118 (1987), no. 3: 135–142, no. 4: 203–209; vol. 119 (1988), no. 1: 35–43, no. 2: 91–98, no. 3: 166–170. [NYG&B eLibrary]

———. *7000 Hudson-Mohawk Valley (NY) Vital Records, 1808–1850*. Baltimore: Genealogical Publishing Co., 1997. Index available from Berkshire Family History Association.

DeGrazia, Laura Murphy, and Diane Fitzpatrick Haberstroh. *Irish Relatives and Friends from "Information Wanted" Ads in the Irish-American, 1850–1871*. Baltimore: Genealogical Publishing Co., 2010.

———. *Voices of the Irish Immigrant: Information Wanted Ads in the Truth Teller, New York City, 1825–1844*. New York: The New York Genealogical and Biographical Society, 2005. Reports data from *Truth Teller*, the New York City's first Catholic newspaper. [NYG&B eLibrary]

French, J. H. *Gazetteer of the State of New York: Embracing a Comprehensive View of the Geography, Geology, and General History of the State, and a Complete History and Description of Every County, City, Town, Village, and Locality. With Full Tables of Statistics.* Syracuse: R. Pearsall Smith, 1860.

Gavit, Joseph. *American Deaths and Marriages, 1784–1829; Microfilm of Abstracts in the New York State Library.* Albany: New York State Library, 197-?. Microfilm. 40,000 marriage and death notices, mainly New York State.

Hoff, Henry B. "Marriage and Death Notices in Long Island Newspapers." *NYG&B Newsletter* (now *New York Researcher*), Summer 1991. Updated December 2000 and published as a Research Aid on *NewYorkFamilyHistory.org*.

— — —. "Marriage and Death Notices in New York City Newspapers." *NYG&B Newsletter* (now *New York Researcher*), Spring 1991. Updated December 2000 and published as a Research Aid on *NewYorkFamilyHistory.org*. Lists all published or manuscript indexes and abstracts up to 1991.

Joslyn, Roger D. "Gertrude Barber, Minnie Cowen, and Ray Sawyer: The Sisters Who Indexed New York. List of the Cowen Sisters' Work." *NYG&B Record*, vol. 143, no. 3 (July 2012): 226–234. [NYG&B eLibrary]

Maher, James P. *Index to Marriages and Deaths in the New York Herald 1835–1876.* 4 vols. Vols. 1–2 Baltimore: Genealogical Publishing Co. and Clearfield Co., 1987–1991. Vols. 3–4 Alexandria, VA: The Author, 2000–2006. Vol. 4 includes *U.S. Deaths in the Phoenix 1859–1861.*

— — —. *Index to Marriages and Deaths in the New York World 1860–1865.* Alexandria, VA: The Author, 2006.

Reimer, Thomas. *Index to the Deaths Found in the New Yorker Volks-Zeitung, 1878–1920.* Bowie, MD: Heritage Books, 2000.

Stifel, Carolyn G. "Deaths from the *Lady's Magazine and Musical Repository/The Lady's Monitor/The Weekly Visitor or Ladies' Miscellany*, New York, 1801–1810." *NYG&B Record*, vol. 133 (2002) no. 4: 279–285; vol. 134 (2003) no. 1: 61–66, no. 2: 136–147, no. 3: 198–206, no. 4: 271–278; vol. 135 (2004) no. 1: 56–67, no. 2: 136–145, no. 3: 212–219, no. 4: 303–307; vol. 136 (2005) no. 1: 30–32, no. 2: 110–118, no. 3: 215–221, no. 4: 296–302. Additions/Corrections: vol. 134, no. 4: 305–306; vol. 137, no. 4:309 (by Marguerite Adams). [NYG&B eLibrary]

— — —. "Marriages from *The Lady's Magazine and Musical Repository/The Ladies' Monitor/The Weekly Visitor or Ladies' Miscellany*, New York City, 1801–1805." *NYG&B Record*, vol. 139 (2008) no. 4: 275–280; vol. 140 (2009) no. 1: 55–62, no. 2: 127–130, no. 3: 230–238; Additions/Corrections: no. 4: 318. Hansen, James L. "Marriages from *The Weekly Visitor or Ladies' Miscellany*, New York City, 1803–1804." *NYG&B Record*, vol. 140 (2009) no. 4: 293–307; vol. 141 (2010) no. 1: 72–77, fills a gap in Carolyn G. Stifel's abstracts. [NYG&B eLibrary]

Stryker-Rodda, Harriet M. "Marriages of New Yorkers and Marriages in New York Reported in Morristown, New Jersey, *Genius of Liberty.*" *NYG&B Record*, vol. 114, no. 1 (1983): 16–18. [NYG&B eLibrary]

Periodicals: Journals, Magazines, and Newsletters

Introduction

Periodicals can be overlooked, but are a rich source of genealogically pertinent information about New York families, communities, resources, and historical context. Often, transcriptions of unpublished records are printed in periodicals in installments over a period of many years.

Scholarly Journals

Scholarly journals in the field of genealogy adhere to rigorous standards for research, documentation, and writing.

The *New York Genealogical and Biographical Record* has been published quarterly by the New York Genealogical and Biographical Society (NYG&B) since 1870. The full run of the *NYG&B Record* forms the largest single collection of published material on families that lived in New York and includes compiled genealogies; transcriptions and abstracts of original records and other source material from throughout New York State; articles that solve genealogical problems; and reviews of new scholarship. A search engine, which covers more than 1,000,000 names, and indexes (to subjects, places, titles, and authors) assists readers in mining the rich body of information in the *NYG&B Record*. Every issue has been digitized and is accessible to NYG&B members at *NewYorkFamilyHistory.org*. Issues published prior to 1923 are available at *findmypast.org*. The ProQuest American Periodicals database includes the full-text *NYG&B Record* from 1870 to 1910. *AmericanAncestors.org* offers out-of-copyright issues; selected out-of-copyright issues are available elsewhere online.

The NYG&B's *New York Researcher* (formerly the *NYG&B Newsletter*) is a quarterly review that provides instructive articles on genealogical research techniques and resources. All issues have been digitized and are accessible to members at *NewYorkFamilyHistory.org*. More than 100 articles of particular utility are organized in a collection of Research Aids on the website, many of which have been updated since their original publication.

The oldest journal in the field is the *New England Historical and Genealogical Register*, which has been published quarterly since 1847. Though its focus is on New England, it sometimes covers New York subjects, especially in its annual supplement, the *American Ancestors Journal*. All issues of the *Register* have been digitized and are accessible to members of the New England Historic Genealogical Society (NEHGS) at *AmericanAncestors.org*. The *Register* for 1847 to 1911 is at *Ancestry.com*; ProQuest American Periodicals has the *Register* for 1847 to1905.

Other scholarly journals that occasionally publish articles about New York subjects include the *National Genealogical Society Quarterly* (the NGSQ), *The American Genealogist* (TAG), and *The Genealogist*, published by the American Society of Genealogists.

Other New York-Focused Periodicals

Tree Talks has been published quarterly by the Central New York Genealogical Society since 1961 and is an exceptional resource for New York research. Its focus is to publish abstracts of source material, such as cemetery, census, church, tax, town, and vital records; guides to genealogical research; and publication reviews. It has published abstracted records of 49 New York counties and has consolidated these records into individual County Packets. Information about *Tree Talks* is at *www.rootsweb.ancestry.com/~nycnygs/publications.htm*.

The *Western New York Genealogical Society Journal* has been published quarterly since 1974. Its focus is on unpublished records relating to the eight counties of western New York, as well as Bible records, book reviews, articles for the beginning and advanced genealogist, and news in the field. An index is on the website of the Western New York Genealogical Society at *wnygs.org*.

The Northeastern New York Genealogical Society has published *Patents,* a bimonthly newsletter, since 1981. Its focus is on cemetery records, early vital records from various towns, family Bibles, newspaper articles, and family trees relating to Warren County and its neighboring counties. [*www.rootsweb.ancestry.com/~nywarren/community/nnygs.htm*]

Between 1984 and 1998 Arthur C. M. Kelly published four quarterlies of local record transcriptions from several New York counties that are referred to as the "Valley Quarterlies": the *Capital*, the *Columbia*, the *Mohawk*, and the *Saratoga*; an annual yearbook was produced for each title from 1999–2001. See the bibliography for a directory and every-name index.

Outside New York

New York topics are frequently covered by periodicals published outside the state whose focus is not exclusively on New York. Since 1990 the *New York Researcher* has published a column which points out relevant articles published outside New York State that might be otherwise overlooked; an index to the articles covered in these columns is at *NewYorkFamilyHistory.org*. The NEHGS has published a similar column annually since 2010 in *American Ancestors* magazine.

The NEHGS website offers access to a selection of periodicals produced by other genealogical societies and individuals, including the full run of *New Netherlands Connections,* which was edited and published quarterly by Dorothy Koenig between 1996 and 2010. The Society's quarterly magazine, *American Ancestors*, regularly addresses New York topics through its "Focus on New York" column.

Indexes to Periodicals

The following indexes can help identify articles published in periodicals that are relevant to genealogical research.

America: History & Life

www.ebscohost.com/academic/america-history-and-life

Historical Abstracts

www.ebscohost.com/academic/historical-abstracts

Together, these two bibliographic resources produced by EBSCO provide selective indexing for more than 4,000 journals from as far back as 1954 that cover history and culture of the United States and Canada. They are available through subscribing libraries and schools.

JSTOR

jstor.org

This site is a digital archive of full-text articles from more than 2,000 academic journals. Searching the JSTOR index and accessing articles published before 1923 is free. Full access to all articles on JSTOR is available through subscribing libraries and schools, which sometimes offer their patrons remote access. Many colleges offer free remote access to alumni; a list of such colleges is online. JStor's Register & Read program offers free read-online access to more than 1,500 journals to anyone who registers for a free account.

Periodical Source Index (PERSI)

search.findmypast.com/search/periodical-source-index

The Periodical Source Index contains over 2.5 million entries from thousands of periodicals that focus on genealogy and history. PERSI was originally developed by the staff of the Allen County Public Library Genealogy Research Center. A new partnership with *findmypast.com* will link thousands of individual genealogical periodicals and resources to the index, providing direct access to the original content.

Readers' Guide to Periodical Literature Retrospective 1890–1992

www.ebscohost.com/academic/readers-guide-retrospective

Readers' Guide to Periodical Literature

www.ebscohost.com/academic/readers-guide-to-periodical-literature

The Readers' Guide to Periodical Literature was for many years the primary, and sometimes the only, search tool for articles in periodicals. EBSCO offers two database indexes, one current and one retrospective, to subscribing libraries. The retrospective index provides coverage of major historical events which can be useful for researching historical context.

Selected Periodicals for New York Research

Below is a selection of principal periodical titles in current publication that covers multiple counties and subjects relevant to New York research. See the individual County Guides in Part Two for periodical titles that are relevant to county and local research. See chapter 14, Peoples of New York, for periodical titles that are relevant to ethnic research.

American Ancestors (formerly *New England Ancestors*, 2000–2009). Boston: New England Historic Genealogical Society, 2000–present. [*AmericanAncestors.org*]

American Ancestors Journal (annual supplement to the *Register*). New England Historic Genealogical Society, 2009–present. [*AmericanAncestors.org*]

The American Genealogist. Demorest, GA: David L. Greene, 1932–present. Previously titled *The New Haven Genealogical Magazine*, 1923–1931. [*americangenealogist.com*]

Connecticut Ancestry. Stamford, CT: Connecticut Ancestry Society, Inc., 1967–present. Focus on southwestern Connecticut and adjacent Westchester, Putnam and Dutchess counties. [*connecticutancestry.org*]

de Halve Maen. New York: Holland Society of New York, 1922–present. [*hollandsociety.com*]

Genealogical Magazine of New Jersey. Genealogical Society of New Jersey, 1925–present.

Hudson River Valley Review: A Journal of Regional Studies. Poughkeepsie, NY: Hudson River Valley Institute at Marist College, 2002–present. [*hudsonrivervalley.org*]

National Genealogical Society Quarterly. Arlington, VA: National Genealogical Society, 1912–present. [*ngsgenealogy.org*]

The Genealogist. American Society of Genealogists, 1980–present. [*fasg.org*]

Lifelines—Official Journal of the Northern New York American-Canadian Genealogical Society. Plattsburgh, NY: Northern New York American-Canadian Genealogical Society, 1984–present. [*nnyacgs.com*]

New England Historical and Genealogical Register. Boston: New England Historic Genealogical Society, 1847–present. [*AmericanAncestors.org*]

New York Genealogical and Biographical Record. New York: New York Genealogical and Biographical Society, 1870–present. [NYG&B eLibrary]

New York Archives. Albany: Archive Partnership Trust, 2003–present. [*www.archives.nysed.gov/apt/magazine/index.shtml*]

New York History. Cooperstown, NY: New York State Historical Association, 1921–present. [*nysha.org*]

New York Researcher (formerly *NYG&B Newsletter*, 1990–2003). New York: New York Genealogical and Biographical Society, 1990–present. [NYG&B eLibrary]

The Patents. Queensbury, NY: Northeastern New York Genealogical Society, 1981–present. [*www.rootsweb.ancestry.com/~nywarren/community/nnygs.htm*]

Prologue Magazine. Washington, DC: National Archives, 1969—present.

Tree Talks. Syracuse: Central New York Genealogical Society, 1961–present. [*www.rootsweb.ancestry.com/~nycnygs/publications.htm*]

Western New York Genealogical Society Journal. Hamburg, NY: Western New York Genealogical Society, 1974–present. [*wnygs.org*]

Selected Bibliography and Further Reading

Austin, John. "Genealogical Research in New York State. An Informal Finding List of Published Materials With Supplementary Notes. Compiled for Genealogical Conference of New York, Inc." [Glens Falls, NY:] 1983. Typescript. NYPL.

Burrows, Edwin G, and Mike Wallace. *Gotham: A History of New York City to 1898*. New York: Oxford University Press, 1999.

Carr, Ruth A. "Other Places Your Ancestors Might Be Hiding: Non-Genealogy Databases and Internet Resources to Explore." *New York Researcher*, Spring 2012. Also published as a Research Aid at *NewYorkFamilyHistory.org*.

Eisenstadt, Peter, ed. *Encyclopedia of New York*. Syracuse: Syracuse University Press, 2005.

Hinckley, Kathleen W. "Finding Ancestors in Periodicals." *Genealogy.com*. *Ancestry.com*, 2011. [*www.genealogy.com/34_kathy_print.html*]

Hoff, Henry B. "New York Families and Sources in some Genealogical Journals." *NYG&B Newsletter* (now *New York Researcher*), Winter 1995. Updated March 2001 and published as a Research Aid at *NewYorkFamilyHistory.org*. Titles include *Genealogical Magazine of New Jersey, Connecticut Ancestry, Genealogical Journal, The Genealogist, Huguenot Historian,* and *Somerset County Genealogical Quarterly*.

— — —. "New York Families in the *American Genealogist*." *NYG&B Newsletter* (now *New York Researcher)*, Summer 1994. Updated March 2001 and published as a Research Aid at *NewYorkFamilyHistory.org*.

— — —. "New York Families and Sources in the *National Genealogical Society Quarterly*." *NYG&B Newsletter* (now *New York Researcher*), Summer 1995. Updated March 2001 and published as a Research Aid at *NewYorkFamilyHistory.org*.

— — —. "New York Families and Sources in the *New England Historical and Genealogical Register*." *NYG&B Newsletter* (now *New York Researcher*), Summer 1995. Updated March 2001 and published as a Research Aid at *NewYorkFamilyHistory.org*.

— — —. "*New Netherland Connections* and Researching New York Dutch Families." *American Ancestors*, Winter 2012: 52–54.

— — —. "Using *de Halve Maen*." *NYG&B Newsletter* (now *New York Researcher*), Fall 1991. Digitally published 2011 as a Research Aid at *NewYorkFamilyHistory.org*.

— — —. "Using *Tree Talks*." *NYG&B Newsletter* (now *New York Researcher*), Winter 2001. Digitally published 2011 as a Research Aid at *NewYorkFamilyHistory.org*.

Hoff, Henry B., and Harry Macy Jr. "Guide to the Contents of *New Netherland Connections*." Digitally published 2011 as a Research Aid at *NewYorkFamilyHistory.org*.

Hoff, Henry B. and Harry Macy, Jr., eds. "New York State Genealogical and Historical Periodicals," *NYG&B Newsletter* (now *New York Researcher*), Summer 1991. Digitally published 2014 as a Research Aid at *NewYorkFamilyHistory.org*.

Jackson, Kenneth T. *The Encyclopedia of New York City*. 2nd edition. New Haven, CT: Yale University Press, 2011.

Joslyn, Roger D. "New York Periodicals, Newspapers, and Manuscript Collections." In *Red Book: American State, County, and Town Sources*. 3rd edition, edited by Alice Eichholz. Provo, UT: *Ancestry.com*, 2004.

Kelly, Arthur C. M. *Valley Quarterlies*. Directory of articles (vols.1–15) and every-name index of the *Capital*, the *Columbia*, the *Mohawk*, and the *Saratoga*. Rhinebeck, NY: Kinship, CD-ROM, 2000.

Klein, Milton M. *The Empire State: A History of New York*. 2001. Reprint, Ithaca: Cornell University Press, 2005.

New York Genealogical and Biographical Society. "Guide to Articles of New York Interest in Other Publications." Digitally published 2011 as a Research Aid at *NewYorkFamilyHistory.org*. Includes a list of titles published 1990–2011 in non-New York periodicals, which was compiled from columns in the *New York Researcher*.

Tax Records

Chapter 13

Introduction

Tax records can be used as a substitute for census records. They provide details of property and wealth, place of residence, and the number and names of taxable persons. Researchers can also extrapolate other information such as deaths (when a man's name disappears or is replaced by the name of his widow); birth order or age (when a person was added to the tax roll or became a head of household); changing residences (when someone was no longer listed); and occupations (expressed or implied by the paying of a license fee, for example).

Tax records are created more frequently than censuses, allowing a researcher to find records between the years the censuses were taken. They may record information in a more accurate or precise manner. For example, more effort will have been taken to differentiate between two people with the same name to ensure each is assessed the appropriate amount of tax. Taxes include:

- Real property taxes levied on a person's land (quitrents, paid by landowners to the government, are sometimes included in this category; quitrents were abolished in the early-nineteenth century)
- Personal property taxes (including slaves)
- Income taxes levied on the amount of money earned by an individual (passage of the 16th Amendment to the Constitution in 1909, ratified 1913, made this a permanent tax)
- Indirect taxes, such as excise taxes on alcohol or tobacco

Access to records depends on the type of tax. Federal tax records are available to researchers up to 1894, when Congress prohibited government officials from disclosing any details of an individual or corporate tax return. The only years in the twentieth century when both individuals and corporations had to make their tax payments public (though they were not required to share the entire return) were 1923 and 1924.

New York State individual and corporate income tax returns are likewise confidential. All real property tax records are open to the public.

Colonial Era

Tax records of interest to the genealogist from the Dutch colonial period are sparse. The Dutch West India Company obtained most of its nonbusiness revenue from indirect taxes (e.g., excise taxes) rather than property taxes.

After the British takeover of New Netherland in 1664, property taxes started to be collected throughout the New York colony. Property tax laws became better defined with the establishment of the Colonial Assembly in 1683. Assembly Acts of 1683, 1691, and 1703 established the local property system. Town and city officials assessed (assigned values to) real and personal property and levied and collected taxes annually. Provincial taxes on property were levied intermittently, usually during wartime. Landowners passed the costs of the quitrents they paid to the government on to their tenant farmers.

Records that exist include the taxpayer's names and the value of their real estate, house, and livestock. Gaps may appear in records during times of civil unrest along the frontier when the assessment and collection of property tax was suspended.

Those seventeenth- and eighteenth-century tax lists that survive are readily available for research. Henry Hoff's article "Pre-1750 New York Lists" inventories tax lists, rate lists, and assessments made before 1750 in the counties of Dutchess, Kings, New York, Queens, Suffolk, Ulster, and Westchester; it also pinpoints the location of published versions of these lists and where microfilm records exist. Some of the sources noted by Henry Hoff have since become available online at *Archive. org* and other online collections.

A 1709 tax list of Albany County discovered after Henry Hoff's article was published was transcribed by Ruth Piwonka for the *NYG&B Record*. Harry Macy's article "New York City Assessment Rolls 1699–1734" adds important details regarding a collection briefly listed by Hoff. John R. Sprague transcribed a 1746–1747 Hempstead tax list for the *NYG&B Record*. The New York State Archives holds the records "Accounts of quit rents and commutations, ca. 1728–1779," compiled by the Treasurer's Office of the Colony of New York.

Many of the property taxes levied in New York County after 1693 were specifically to pay for the Anglican minister's salary and poor relief managed by the churchwardens. There were similar taxes in the other three counties where the Anglican church was established (Queens, Richmond, and Westchester); Hoff does not show any surviving tax lists for those counties after 1693, but there are 1708/09 lists in the published Jamaica town records, and others may exist.

The article on New York Taxation on the FamilySearch wiki (*https://FamilySearch.org/learn/wiki/en/New_York_Taxation*) identifies many New York State tax records from the colonial era and provides the Family History Library (FHL) film numbers.

Dutchess County has the most complete set of colonial tax lists, covering 1718–1779 (with one short gap), forming a continuous list of adult males during that period. The County Guides in Part Two of this book may also be consulted for references to colonial tax records. Florence Christoph identified Albany County tax lists from 1760 to 1768 in her book *Upstate New York in the 1760s*. Henry Hoff transcribed 1761 and 1781 tax lists of Flatbush, Kings County, for the *NYG&B Record*, and "Tax List, Town of Hurley, 1783" was also published in the *NYG&B Record*.

Revolution and Post Revolution

For tax records of the Revolutionary period, see chapter 8 in Eric Grundset's *New York in the American Revolution*. Roger Joslyn's article "New York State Censuses and Tax Lists" is an essential Research Aid for those looking for tax lists from the early post-Revolutionary period to the mid-nineteenth century.

Special Provincial and State Taxes

Special taxes for provincial or state purposes were authorized by statutes of 1772, 1778, 1779, 1780, 1786, 1787, and 1788. The New York State Archives (NYSA) and the Manuscripts and Special Collections Department of the New York State Library (NYSL) have some of the surviving lists resulting from these statutes, mostly for the Hudson Valley counties. See New York State Archives, Treasurer's Office, Series A1201, Assessment Rolls, 1779–1814; A3210, Tax Assessment Lists, 1779–1788; A3206, Tax Assessment List for Van Rensselaer District, ca. 1750. These records contain lists for scattered Hudson Valley and Mohawk Valley towns and districts. The NYSA catalog entries for Series A1201 and A3210 are extremely detailed, providing

both collection descriptions and historical background for these records. See also the Lansing Papers at the NYSL that include assessment rolls and other material for most of New York State north of New York City from 1779 to 1802.

The Brooklyn Historical Society's Henry Onderdonk Papers contain his transcripts of tax lists (otherwise lost) for all Queens County towns for various years in the 1780s and 1790s, apparently based on the statutes noted above.

1798 Federal Direct Tax

In 1798 the Federal Direct Tax was levied on dwelling houses, other real property, and slaves. Original records connected with this tax are a gold mine of information, but unfortunately the original records of this tax for New York, except for some scattered fragments, are lost. Judith Green Watson's article in *Prologue* provides an incomplete list of information from New York (and other states) connected with this tax and where it can be found:

- New Windsor, Orange County (NYSA)
- Newburgh, Orange County (Historical Society of Newburgh Bay and the Highlands)
- Wallkill, Deer Park, and Minisink, Orange County (Historical Society of Middletown and Wallkill Precinct)
- Kingston, Marbleton, and Hurley, Ulster County (N-YHS)

Some transcribed information from Clinton County taxpayers was published in the *Republican* newspaper between 1892 and 1899, and that material (partly illegible) is on microfilm at the NYSL and the Plattsburg Public Library. Transcribed data for the towns of Plattsburgh, Champlain, and Peru, edited by David Kendall Martin, FASG, was published in the *NYG&B Record*.

Other records in New York State for this tax exist for New Paltz (Ulster County, available at the library in New Paltz) and for parts of Orange County (see C. R. Carey, "Town of Deer Park 1798 Assessment Records"). Ulster County lists for Hurley, Marbleton, and Kingston were published by Kenneth Scott ("Ulster County, New York, 1798 Tax List," *National Genealogical Society Quarterly*) drawing on material at the N-YHS. Edward H. L. Smith's article "1798 Property Valuations for Western Suffolk County," in the *NYG&B Record*, identified a likely transcript of the 1798 valuations for Brookhaven, Huntington, Islip, and Smithtown. His article includes an abstracted list of the owners and occupants of houses in Smithtown, and gives the value of the houses, land and the number of acres owned.

Occasionally, tax lists appear in nineteenth-century county histories. For example, a list of taxpayers in the Town of Patterson (Putnam County) in 1798 appears in William S. Pelletreau's *History of Putnam County, New York*.

Property Taxes

The colonial system of property taxes was continued with little change until 1799, when the state legislature reorganized the system of assessing and taxing real and personal property. The 1799 tax rolls used the assessments made for the 1798 direct tax. Each county was required to file a copy of the county's tax rolls and a list of unpaid taxes with the state comptroller's office. Other than New York County, only a few counties still have their real property tax assessment rolls prior to 1850. Researchers can contact the county treasurer, chief fiscal officer, town receivers of taxes, or county and/or town historian for information about them. Note that the county clerk's office is not the legal custodian of tax assessment records.

Real property tax records for New York City (Manhattan) are at the New York City Municipal Archives in the collection "Assessed Valuation of Real Estate, 1789–1989." They record the owner, or occupant, of the property, a description of the property (dimensions of the lot and building), and its assessed valuation. Tax Assessment holdings, by borough:

- Manhattan: 1789–1978/79
- Brooklyn: 1866–1974/75
- Queens: 1899–1987/88
- Bronx: 1897–1961/62
- Richmond: 1899–1978/79

Pre-1900 volumes at the Municipal Archives are on microfilm. Films for "New York City Assessment Rolls, 1790–1821" are available at the FHL and the New York Public Library (NYPL).

Although property holders continued to be taxed annually, few other lists prior to 1830 survive. Property assessment rolls (lists) were compiled annually by local assessors. The lists included the name of the taxpayer, value of real and personal estate, and the warrant or order of a local officer to levy and collect the tax. Property tax payers (with some exceptions, such as women who owned property) were enfranchised voters in New York until 1823, when the property qualification to vote was abolished. Beginning in 1805 tax assessment rolls were filed with the county treasurer and with town or city officials. The exception was Westchester County, where warrant tax rolls were retained only at the town level.

Estate Taxes

The NYSA holds the New York State Comptroller's Office records of "Tax Assessment Rolls of Real and Personal Estates" (1799–1803 for all counties, excluding New York County; 1804 for some counties). The records have been microfilmed (series B0950); the entry in the online catalog at *nysl.nysed.gov* provides a detailed description and includes a link to a finding aid. This material is on *Ancestry.com*.

Local governments generally have not preserved their old tax rolls, because the warrant copy of the tax roll held by the county is the official record. However, copies of older tax and assessment rolls may sometimes be found with city, town, or village clerks or county or town historians. Tax lists may also be found in other collections such as private libraries and historical societies.

The statewide Historical Documents Inventory resulted in the multi-volume series *Guide to Historical Records,* for each county in New York this invaluable aid to locating such records is described at *www.nysl.nysed.gov/hdi.htm*. See chapter 17, Reference Shelf, for a fuller description. Otherwise, since the location of local tax records varies widely among the counties and also among the towns within the counties, and tend to be distributed among multiple locations within each jurisdiction, researchers will have to undertake separate searches for each location and for each local tax record desired.

Federal Taxes

To raise funds during the Civil War, Congress passed the Revenue Act of 1861 (repealed ten years later) that imposed taxes on personal income and certain valuable property, such as carriages, silverware, and watches. The records at the National Archives (NARA), "Assessment Lists of the Federal Bureau of Internal Revenue, 1862–1866," have been digitized and are available at *Ancestry.com* and *FamilySearch.org*.

Lists of taxpayers, their incomes, and tax liabilities were frequently printed in newspapers. In 1865 the American News Company published a comprehensive list of New York City taxpayers in the volume *The Income Record: A List Giving the Taxable Income for the Year 1863, of Every Resident of New York.*

Federal assessment lists, and some other information regarding the collection of federal revenue in some places in New York State, from the post-Civil War years to the early-twentieth century, are in the records of the Internal Revenue Service held by NARA as Record Group 58. The set of "Records of New York Collection Districts" includes:

- Assessment lists, 1st–32nd Districts, 1867–1873
- Assessment lists, 2nd and 3rd Districts (Manhattan), 1911–1917
- Assessment lists, 14th District (Albany), 1914–1917
- Assessment lists, 21st District (Syracuse), 1883–1917
- Register of employees, 2nd District (Brooklyn), 1885–1919
- Records of the 28th, 30th, and 31st Districts (Buffalo), consisting of assessment lists, 1912–1917, and a register of employees, 1875–1919

In 1894 Congress enacted a flat rate federal income tax, which was ruled unconstitutional the following year by the United States Supreme Court. The passage of the Sixteenth Amendment to the United States Constitution, ratified in 1913, provided for a federal income tax on individuals and corporations. Records of individual tax returns are closed, except for selected data from 1923 and 1924 that was made available. For those years, the Internal Revenue authorities were required to make public reports of names, addresses, and tax payment of taxpayers; many newspapers printed these lists, including the *New York Times*, the *New York Herald*, the *Buffalo Morning Express*, and the *Syracuse Post Standard*. See Daniel Marcin's article,

"The Revenue Act of 1924," which lists the top taxpayers in the United States, many of whom were New Yorkers.

New York State Taxes

By the 1880s New York State property tax revenues no longer reflected the rapid economic growth in New York. Neither were they sufficient to support the infrastructure and services needed for a larger population. Simultaneously, other sources of state revenue (such as canal tolls) were being eliminated. This increased the pressure on the state to identify new tax revenue sources. Taxes on corporations were instituted in 1880, and an estate tax on wealthy individuals was imposed beginning in 1885. The state property tax ended in 1928.

Records of New York State taxation of estates (including wills, property appraisals, personal property inventories, and documents relating to the management of the estate) for the years 1885 to 1990 can be found at the NYSA as "Estate Tax Files" in series 19802. They are arranged alphabetically and pertain largely to wealthy individuals. The NYSL catalog description for this series is very detailed.

New York became the seventh state in the United States to institute a state income tax in 1919. These records are closed.

Selected Bibliography and Further Reading

See the County Guides in Part Two of this book for additional published tax lists for individual counties.

Carey, C. R. "Town of Deer Park 1798 Assessment Records." *Orange County Historical Society Publication*, no. 8 (1978–1979): 13–25.

Christoph, Florence A. *Upstate New York in the 1760s: Tax Lists and Selected Militia Rolls of Old Albany County 1760–1768.* Camden, ME: Picton Press, 1992. "Old" Albany County comprised an area much larger than the present-day county.

Clark, Jonathan. "Taxation and Suffrage in Revolutionary New York." *Hudson Valley Regional Review*, vol. 1: no. 1 (1984): 23–33.

Dollarhide, William. *New York State Census and Substitutes.* Baltimore: Genealogical Publishing Co., 2006. This book contains a wealth of information on tax lists, arranged by county.

Grundset, Eric G. *New York in the American Revolution.* Washington: National Society Daughters of the American Revolution, 2012. See chapter 8, "New York Finances and Taxation during the Revolutionary Era."

Hedlund, F. F. "Development of Assessment of Property and Collection of Taxes in Rural New York." *Cornell University Agricultural Experiment Station Bulletin.* Vol. 681 (1937).

Hoff, Henry B. "1761 Assessment List of Flatbush, Kings County" and "The 1781 Tax List of Flatbush, Kings County." *NYG&B Record*, vol. 137 (2006), no. 3: 188–190; no. 4: 291–293. [NYG&B eLibrary]

———. "Pre-1750 New York Lists." *NYG&B Newsletter* (now *New York Researcher*), Fall 1992. Also a Research Aid on *NewYorkFamilyHistory.org*.

The Income Record: A List Giving the Taxable Income for the Year 1863, of Every Resident of New York. New York: American News Company, 1865.

Joslyn, Roger D. "New York State Censuses and Tax Lists." *NYG&B Newsletter* (now *New York Researcher*), Spring 1998. Also a Research Aid on *NewYorkFamilyHistory.org*. This list covers both pre- and post-Revolutionary War New York State tax records in some detail.

———. "New York State Tax Records 1799–1804: A Newly Available Resource for Genealogists." *NYGB Newsletter*, Spring 1990. Also a Research Aid on *NewYorkFamilyHistory.org*.

Lansing, Gerrit Y. Papers, 1783–1843. New York State Library Manuscripts and Special Collections. This large collection includes tax assessment rolls and other material (some abstracted) for most of New York State north of New York City from 1779 to 1802, including present-day Albany, Cayuga, Columbia, Greene, Kings, Montgomery, Orange, Oswego, Rensselaer, Saratoga, Schenectady, Washington, and Westchester counties. An unpublished partial guide to the collection is available in the repository.

Macy, Harry, Jr. "New York City Assessment Rolls 1699–1734." *NYG&B Newsletter* (now *New York Researcher)*, Fall 1996. Updated June 2011 and published as a Research Aid on *NewYorkFamilyHistory.org*.

———. "New York City Assessment Rolls [1790–1821]," *NYG&B Newsletter* (now *New York Researcher*), vol. 4, no.1 (1993): 6. Describes contents of FHL films 481, 394–396. [NYG&B eLibrary]

Marcin, Daniel. "The Revenue Act of 1924: Publicity, Tax Cuts, Response." March 15, 2014. Marcin's paper, published online, provides various analyses of high-income taxpayer income derived from newspaper accounts tied to census records. When the article was written, the author was a PhD candidate in economics at the University of Michigan. [*www-personal. umich.edu/~dmarcin/JMP.pdf*]

Martin, David Kendall. "A 1798 United States Assessment List for Northern New York State." *NYG&B Record*, vol. 113 (1982) no. 2: 93–102; no. 3: 152–160; no. 4: 231–238. [NYG&B eLibrary]

New York Historical Resources Center. *Guide to Historical Records in . . . County New York, Repositories.* Ithaca, NY: Cornell University, 1980–1993. For a description of the Historical Documents Inventory (HDI), see chapter 17, Reference Shelf. Many titles at *books.FamilySearch.org*

New York State. Department of Taxation and Finance. *The New York State and Local Tax System*. Numerous editions of this publication were issued from the 1940s into the 1970s. These are described in the catalog of the NYSL.

O'Callaghan, Edmund Bailey. *Lists of Inhabitants of Colonial New York: Excerpted from the Documentary History of the State of New-York*. Indexed by Rosanne Conway. Baltimore: Genealogical Publishing Co., 1979. Does not include 1675 Kings County tax assessment rolls in vol. 4 of the Documentary History.

O'Callaghan, Edmund Bailey. *The Documentary History of the State of New-York, 1797–1880*. 4 vols. New York State Secretary's Office. Albany: Weed, Parsons, 1850–1851. (Note that the 1850–1851 publication dates are for the quarto edition; the dates for the octavo edition are 1849–1851.)

O'Callaghan, Edmund Bailey, and Berthold Fernow, eds. *Documents Relative to the Colonial History of the State of New York*. 15 vols. Albany: Weed, Parsons, 1856–1887. The only tax lists in these 15 volumes are in vols. 2 (New York City [then New Orange] 1674), 13 (Westchester town 1683 and 1675, Eastchester 1675), and 14 (Newtown and East Hampton 1678). See Henry Hoff's article "Pre-1750 New York Lists" above.

Pelletreau, William S. *History of Putnam County, New York*. Philadelphia: W. W. Preston, 1886.

Peterson, Nancy S. "Early Dutchess County Tax Lists, 1717–1779," *New York Researcher*, vol. 15 (Spring/Summer 2004). Published as a Research Aid on *NewYorkFamilyHistory.org*.

Piwonka, Ruth. "Tax Lyste van d Stadt en County van Albany 1708/9 (Tax List of the City and County of Albany)." *NYG&B Record*, vol. 139, no. 1 (2008): 55–62. [NYG&B eLibrary]

Schwab, John Christopher. "History of the New York State Property Tax." *Publications of the American Economic Association*, vol. 5, no. 5 (September 1890): 360–466.

Scott, Kenneth. "Ulster County, New York, 1798 Tax List." *National Genealogical Society Quarterly*, vol. 73 no. 1 (1985): 117–123. This publication is online at *ngsgenealogy.org*.

Smith, Edward H. L. "1798 Property Valuations for Western Suffolk County." *NYG&B Record*, vol. 127, no. 1 (1996): 12–16. [NYG&B eLibrary]

Sprague, John R. "Hempstead Tax List 1746–1747." *NYG&B Record*, vol. 128, no. 4 (1997): 219–222. [NYG&B eLibrary]

"Tax List, Town of Hurley, 1783." *NYG&B Record*, vol. 116, no. 1 (1985): 1–3. [NYG&B eLibrary]

Watson, Judith Green. "A Discovery: 1798 Federal Direct Tax Records for Connecticut." *Prologue Magazine*, vol. 39, no. 1 (Spring 2007): 6–15. This article contains information about the survival of the 1798 tax records and early tax records in general. [*archives.gov*]

Introduction

Many people who have made their home in New York, whether permanently or temporarily, have clustered together with others who share the same country of origin, language, religion, or cultural traditions. Consequently, specialized genealogical resources often exist that can facilitate research of individuals within a specific ethnic community. Needless to say, it is not possible to explore the full range of peoples who lived in and moved through New York in a book of this size. This chapter provides information relevant to sixteen ethnic groups that have been represented in large numbers in New York, and played an important role in its development:

- African American
- American Indian
- Austro-Hungarian (including many distinct ethnic groups of the former empire)
- Chinese
- Dutch
- English
- French and French-speaking
- German
- Hispanic
- Irish
- Italian
- Jewish
- Polish
- Russian (including many distinct ethnic groups of the former empire and the former Soviet Union)
- Scandinavian
- Scots and Scots-Irish

For each population, a historical overview is provided, along with a description of records, repositories, organizations, websites, a selected bibliography, and other resources that are especially pertinent. The complexities of history, migration, and settlement, as well as the availability of unique resources relevant to New York populations, determined the extent of each profile.

The information presented here is meant to be used in tandem with the records and resources described elsewhere in Part One of this book and in the County Guides that follow in Part Two. Cross references are given to other sections of the book that relate to, or expound on, a topic.

A Note about Indexes

Both online and printed indexes to various record and document collections have become widely available, and can greatly facilitate research. However, the reliability of indexes varies greatly, particularly when transcribers are not fluent in the language or handwriting style of the subject group, or when the criteria used in creating the index is not evident. Indexes can be nonetheless valuable to the researcher as a means to locate original records or in the absence of surviving records. For this reason, this chapter identifies many published indexes and online resources that are valuable, if not infallible.

Population Figures

The primary source of historical population figures for ethnic groups is the U.S. Census. In its section on Immigration, the *Encyclopedia of New York State* provides two tables on foreign-born New York residents based on data extrapolated from federal censuses 1860–2000. These tables are reprinted here with the permission of Syracuse University Press.

Early state and county gazetteers often provided information about the ethnicity of settlers, as did local histories. Selected titles may be found in the bibliographies in Part Two, in both the introduction and the individual County Guides.

Table 1: New York State's Foreign-born Population by Selected Place of Birth

Origin	1860	1870	1880	1890	1900	1910	1920
Africa	69	92	156	29	9 473	900	1,528
Asia[a]	206	105	81	358	1,744	420	744
Austria	—	3,928	6,530	33,135	78,491	245,004	151,172
Belgium	860	984	1,288	1,342	1,787	3,484	5,300
Canada[b]	55,273	79,042	84,182	93,193	117,535	124,580	114,614
Central America[c]	55	49	65	237	1,048	2,803	8,645
China	77	177	1,015	3,135	6,880	4,482	4,559
Cuba[d]	—	1,824	2,227	4,065	2,195	17,483	—
Denmark	1196	1,701	3,145	6,238	8,746	12,544	14,222
France	21,826	22,302	20,321	20,443	20,008	23,472	32,252
Germany	256,252	316,902	355,913	498,602	480,026	436,911	295,651
England	106,011	110,071	116,362	144,060	135,685	146,870	135,541
Ireland	498,072	528,806	499,445	483,375	425,553	367,889	284,747
Scotland	27,641	27,282	28,066	35,332	33,862	39,437	37,656
Wales	7,908	7,857	7,223	8,108	7,304	7,464	6,763
Greece	35	60	94	413	1,573	10,097	26,117
Holland	5,354	6,426	8,399	8,366	9,414	—	—
Hungary	—	709	4,440	15,598	37,168	96,843	78,374
India	—	102	310	349	403	361	624
Italy	1,862	3,592	15,113	64,141	182,248	472,201	545,173
Japan	—	9	32	209	392	1,163	2,393
Mexico	116	127	237	330	353	555	2,999
Norway	539	975	2,185	8,602	12,601	25,013	27,573
Pacific Islands[e]	11	6	96	112	113	220	320
Poland[f]	2,296	4,061	11,999	22,718	70,255	—	247,519
Portugal	353	237	295	284	362	660	1,481
Russia	1,013	1,473	5,438	58,466	165,610	558,256	529,243
South America[c]	312	442	754	921	1,130	—	—
Spain	809	818	1,216	1,603	1,614	3,766	12,722
Sweden	1,678	5,522	11,164	28,430	42,708	53,705	53,025
Switzerland	6,166	7,916	10,721	11,557	13,678	16,315	15,053
Turkey[g]	39	71	180	427	1,915	14,482	5,250
West Indies[d]	1,957	1,303	1,734	—	4,241	—	38,288

Source: US Census.
[a] Does not include China, Japan, and India, which are listed separately. [b] Includes French and English Canada and Newfoundland. [c] The data for Central American in 1910 and 1920 include South America. [d] The data for Cuba in 1890 and 1910 include other West Indies, except Puerto Rico after 1890; since 1900 persons born in Puerto Rico have been counted as native-born. [e] Does not include the Philippine Islands and other US possessions. [f] For the census of 1910 the Polish population is reported under Austria, Germany, and Russia. [g] From 1910 Turkey is divided into Turkey in Asia and Turkey in Europe. The data for Turkey in Asia and Turkey in Europe for 1910 are, respectively: 5,004 and 9,478; for 1920: 3,200 and 2,050. Compiled by Jacqueline Villarrubia-Mendoza.

Table 1: Villarrubia-Mendoza, Jacqueline, comp. "New York State's Foreign-Born Population by Selected Place of Birth 1860-1920." In *Encyclopedia of New York State*, p. 765. Syracuse: Syracuse University Press, 2005. Reprinted with permission from Syracuse University Press.

Table 2: New York State's Foreign-born Population by Selected Place of Birth

	1930	1940[a]	1950	1960	1970	1980	1990	2000
Total Population	12,588,066	13,479,142	14,830,192	16,783,604	18,236,882	17,558,072	17,990,455	18,976,457
Foreign-Born Population	3,262,278	2,916,645	2,578,973	2,289,314	2,109,776	2,388,938	2,851,861	3,868,133
Foreign-Born (%)	25.9	21.6	17.4	13.6	11.6	13.6	15.9	20.4
Birthplace								
Europe	2,961,265	2,644,647	2,277,832	1,933,562	1,438,531	1,108,392	842,395	879,307
Austria	142,298	172,347	149,955	107,101	65,606	38,779	19,275	11,299
Czechoslovakia	56,176	41,798	44,111	42,021	32,363	24,041	17,660	13,246
Denmark	17,407	14,304	11,627	9,462	6,366	3,681	2,778	—
England[b]	146,772	117,370	100,280	86,343	67,860	52,105	68,434	62,237
Finland	17,444	15,101	12,897	9,765	6,605	3,541	2,141	—
France	32,273	26,373	28,185	27,639	23,681	20,852	18,411	20,310
Germany	349,196	316,844	270,661	250,173	183,754	134,991	92,322	69,327
Greece	33,387	34,800	36,757	36,579	44,478	54,738	44,316	42,335
Hungary	70,631	75,254	65,276	60,382	43,506	31,732	22,337	17,401
Ireland	251,704	205,323	182,581	131,764	93,818	66,639	53,949	41,934
Northern Ireland	41,521	30,432	4,171	18,749	10,651	3,418	—	—
Italy	629,322	584,075	503,175	440,063	352,711	283,990	190,305	147,729
Netherlands	14,909	13,842	13,393	13,132	11,421	8,462	7,379	6,545
Norway	44,882	37,169	33,073	27,125	17,371	10,540	5,924	—
Poland	350,383	281,080	254,065	234,742	168,370	113,262	88,230	93,187
Romania	51,014	43,950	32,270	29,040	25,485	21,827	22,369	25,059
Russia[c]	481,307	436,028	354,197	245,068	147,993	112,725	98,576	94,595
Scotland	67,623	57,639	48,304	41,396	29,184	19,861	—	—
Sweden	61,233	48,317	36,747	23,516	13,534	7,741	4,646	4,305
Wales	7,037	4,752	4,725	3,383	2,200	1,495	—	—
Caribbean	64,466	14,986	73,305	100,997	246,099	463,759	682,991	1,004,344
Cuba	—	6,632	14,531	30,632	72,224	56,895	52,064	36,642
Dominican Republic	—	—	3,265	9,643	52,700	131,313	241,941	408,086
Haiti	—	—	445	3,180	21,466	55,363	87,215	125,475
Jamaica	—	—	6,081	12,441	44,916	107,130	146,829	226,470
Central and South America	20,145	14,322	24,252	41,540	110,892	250,474	448,353	726,079
Guatemala	—		415	692	1,793	7,049	17,883	33,208
Honduras	—	—	410	1,748	4,934	—	20,955	43,314
Panama	—	—	970	6,070	10,810	—	28,257	26,202
Colombia	—	—	1,775	5,477	25,502	48,486	82,767	111,727
Ecuador	—	—	980	3,019	17,105	42,426	68,954	139,226
Guyana	—	—	—	—	—	33,398	81,386	142,154
Peru	—	—	890	1,565	4,572	12,966	26,647	43,753
Asia	47,610	39,840	59,179	77,022	133,114	290,456	556,662	916,597
China[d]	7,512	—	14,752	22,251	42,425	68,839	155,352	301,735
India	920	—	1,475	2,013	8,537	33,434	66,851	117,238
Korea	—	—	346	822	3,965	27,104	71,975	97,933
Philippines	—	—	4,132	5,037	10,264	27,493	50,245	72,408
Turkey[e]	16,673	20,507	19,520	15,105	13,397	12,332	11,569	16,228
Canada	155,526	129,810	120,011	111,280	85,176	73,142	56,795	54,876
Mexico	5,218	3,567	4,290	4,496	4,806	10,676	43,505	161,189
All others	8,048	6,358	20,104	20,417	91,158	192,039	221,160	125,741

Source: US Census.

[a]In 1940 the foreign-born populations for specified countries includes only Whites; this was also true for most regions and countries in 1950. [b]Includes Scotland, Wales, and Northern Ireland in 1990 and 2000. [c]For the years 1940–1990 includes the non-Baltic Republics of the USSR. [d]Includes Hong Kong in 2000. [e]1930 and 1940 include Asian population only; from 1950 includes European population as well. Compiled by Timothy Calabrese.

Table 2: Calabrese, Timothy, comp. "New York State's Foreign-Born Population by Place of Birth 1930-2000." In *Encyclopedia of New York State*, p. 768. Syracuse: Syracuse University Press, 2005. Reprinted with permission from Syracuse University Press.

An Unlikely Resource

The exhaustive 1920 report of New York State's Joint Legislative Committee Investigating Seditious Activities includes a wealth of information on immigrants and ethnic groups in New York State and the many organizations—private and public, ethnic- and religious-based—serving them. New York City receives detailed coverage, and there are descriptions of ethnic mutual aid societies, community centers, schools, churches, missions, clubs, and civic and cultural organizations. Information provided on 47 other cities and towns illustrates the geographic distribution of ethnic groups across New York State (see volume 3, pp. 2569–2622). This exceptional resource is accessible in four separate volumes at *Archive.org* but might easily be overlooked because of its off-putting title, *Revolutionary Radicalism, Its History, Purpose and Tactics with an Exposition and Discussion of the Steps Being Taken and Required to Curb It . . . Filed April 24, 1920, in the Senate of the State of New York.* Especially relevant is the section "Citizenship Training in the State of New York." See below for a complete citation.

Selected Bibliography and Further Reading

The resources below provide broad coverage of ethnic groups in New York State. See also chapter 17, Reference Shelf, for additional general references. Bibliographies specific to each ethnic group appear at the end of each section in this chapter.

Bentley, Elizabeth P. *The Genealogist's Address Book: State and Local Resources: with Special Resources Including Ethnic and Religious Organizations.* Baltimore: Genealogical Publishing Co., 2009.

Burrows, Edwin G, and Mike Wallace. *Gotham: A History of New York City to 1898.* New York: Oxford University Press, 1999.

Eisenstadt, Peter R., and Laura-Eve Moss. *The Encyclopedia of New York State.* Syracuse: Syracuse University Press, 2005.

Gibson, Campbell, and Emily Lennon. "Region and Country or Area of Birth of the Foreign-Born Population, with Geographic Detail Shown in Decennial Census Publications of 1930 or Earlier: 1850 to 1930 and 1960 to 1990." U.S. Census Bureau, Population Division. Last Revised: October 31, 2011. *www.census.gov/population/www/documentation/twps0029/tab04.html*

Harvard University Library Open Collections Program. "Immigration to the United States, 1789–1930." *http://ocp.hul.harvard.edu/immigration*

Jackson, Kenneth T. *The Encyclopedia of New York City.* New Haven, CT: Yale University Press, 2011.

Library of Congress. "Immigrant Arrivals: A Guide to Published Sources." *www.loc.gov/rr/genealogy/bib_guid/immigrant/*

Nwosu, Chiamaka, Jeanne Batalova, and Gregory Auclair. "Frequently Requested Statistics on Immigration." Migration Policy Institute. April 28, 2014. *www.migrationpolicy.org/article/frequently-requested-statistics-immigrants-and-immigration-united-states*

New York State Legislature. Joint Legislative Committee Investigating Seditious Activities. "Citizenship Training in the State of New York." In *Revolutionary Radicalism, Its History, Purpose and Tactics with an Exposition and Discussion of the Steps Being Taken and Required to Curb It . . . Filed April 24, 1920, in the Senate of the State of New York.* Part II, "Constructive Movements and Measures in America," vols. 3 and 4. Albany: J. B. Lyon, 1920.

Powell, John. *Encyclopedia of North American Immigration.* New York: Facts On File, 2005.

Errors and Omissions

Readers who find errors or omissions in any section in this book are encouraged to inform the editors by sending an email to *NYGuide@nygbs.org.* By submitting additions and corrections, all researchers consulting future editions of this book will benefit.

African American

Historical Overview

Colonial Era

There has been an African presence in what is now New York City since the earliest days of European engagement. In fact, the first nonindigenous permanent settler in the area is said to have been Juan Rodriguez, a free man of African and Hispanic descent who was born on the island of Hispaniola. He served on the Dutch ship *Jonge Tobias*, which arrived on what is now Manhattan Island in 1613, and remained to set up a trading post. (See also the section on Hispanic people in this chapter.)

Around 1626 enslaved African people were introduced to the region by the Dutch West India Company (WIC). Under the Dutch, most were imported from the Dutch Caribbean islands, while some came directly from Africa. Slave labor for agriculture and infrastructure (clearing land, building roads, etc.) was integral to the economy of New Netherland. Subsequently, private ownership of slaves was allowed, and they worked as domestics, famers, and craftsmen.

In 1644 the policy of "half freedom" was established when the WIC gave eleven enslaved males and their wives conditional freedom and land, contingent upon their paying an annual tribute and contributing labor as needed.

These half-free blacks settled along the Bowery in New Amsterdam where several had been granted land. Just before the Dutch handed New Netherland to the British, the government granted full freedom to these families and the right to their land. By 1664 about 300 half-free blacks gained full freedom.

By the end of the seventeenth century, free blacks tended to migrate out of the City, some to Old Tappan (Orange County), where in 1687 the Tappan land patent had been granted to three free blacks from the Bowery settlement, and to thirteen Dutchmen. Possibly they were motivated by policies of the British that were more restrictive than those of the Dutch. By the mid-eighteenth century, this community of free blacks appear to have lost their land. See "Crossroads or Settlement? The Black Freedman's Community in Historic Greenwich Village 1664–1855" by Thelma Wills Foote.

Both free and enslaved blacks are interred in the African Burial Ground (1690s–1794) in lower Manhattan, now a National Monument dedicated to the earliest Americans of African descent (*www.nps.gov/afbg*).

Slavery grew under English colonial rule (1664–1776) and was accompanied by a succession of laws to regulate slaves. In 1712 a slave rebellion in New York City led to panic and fierce retaliation; increasing penalties and restrictions were placed on slaves and free blacks during the years that followed. Nevertheless, another slave uprising occurred in 1741; it lasted more than six months and resulted in further harsh reprisals. Although slavery often imposed forced separation on spouses, children, and parents, slaves sought to maintain their family connections. Marriages between slaves were not granted legal recognition in New York State until 1809.

In 1756 the area that makes up today's New York City was home to 13,000 slaves, about 25 percent of the population. See the bibliography at the end of this section for Henry Hoff's "Researching African-American Families in New Netherland and Colonial New York and New Jersey," which traces the genealogy of 14 African-American families and provides valuable research advice.

Abolition of Slavery

During the American Revolution, African Americans fought for both the British and the patriots, although New York law prohibited the recruitment of slaves for the military. Many slaves escaped to fight for the British, enticed by promises of freedom. In 1781 the Patriot side issued a similar promise, stating that any slave who served in the military for three years would be freed. At the end of the war in 1783, almost 3,000 black loyalists left New York for Canada fearing re-enslavement.

Beginning in 1785 the New York State legislature passed a series of acts that led to a steady decline in the population of enslaved people. Census figures show that the slave population dropped from 20,903 in 1800 to 15,017 in 1810, and to 10,088 in 1820.

An act of April 12, 1785 (Law 1785, Chapter 68), included a provision prohibiting the sale of slaves brought from other states into New York and permitting slave owners to free their able-bodied slaves who were under the age of 50, without posting indemnification to the municipality.

An act of February 22, 1788 (L. 1788, C.40), reaffirmed both of those provisions, while banning the export and sale of slaves; however, this act also reaffirmed that all current slaves and the children of female slaves were to be slaves for life.

"An Act for the Gradual Abolition of Slavery," approved on March 29, 1799 (L. 1799, C. 62), provided that children born to a slave after July 4, 1799, would be deemed free, but indentured until reaching the age of 25 (females) or 28 (males).

"An Act Relevant to Slaves and Servants" of March 31, 1817 (L. 1817, C. 137), provided further regulations regarding gradual emancipation. It also included a provision that required indentured children to be taught to read before age 18 or released from servitude; this act effectively granted freedom to all remaining slaves in New York on July 4, 1827.

In the antebellum period, there were active political organizations dedicated to supporting southern slavery, and others to abolishing it. The economic connection of New

York City's port to slave-produced products meant that many merchant families had strong economic and personal ties to the southern states. But at the same time, a strong and growing minority of white New Yorkers joined black New Yorkers in the abolitionist movement.

New York State was an important route along the Underground Railroad for fugitive slaves. It had active stations in the following counties: Cayuga, Essex, Kings, Madison, Nassau, New York, Niagara, Onondaga, Oswego, Queens/Nassau, Madison, and Westchester. Harriet Tubman bought property in Auburn (Cayuga County) in 1859, where she eventually established a home for the aged. Frederick Douglass spent 25 years in Rochester (Monroe County) where he was editor of the abolitionist newspaper *The North Star*. The literature on the Underground Railroad and on New York's connection to the pro-slavery and anti-slavery movements is very extensive.

Civil War

During the Civil War, African Americans from New York fought in the 20th, 26th, and 31st Infantry Regiments of the U.S. Colored Troops (USCT). The New York City Draft Riots of 1863 were sparked by fear of labor competition from emancipated slaves and resentment of the inequalities of the draft law. African Americans were the victims of vicious retaliation over a five-day period, which included horrific violence and the destruction of homes and property, notably the Colored Orphan Asylum.

After the Civil War, migration to New York City from the southern states began building. See Marcy Sacks's book, *Before Harlem: The Black Experience in New York City before World War I*, and her chapter in *Slavery in New York*, edited by Ira Berlin and Leslie Harris.

Migration to New York

Beginning around 1910 many more blacks fled the South in an attempt to escape segregation and oppression. This "Great Migration," slowing only during the Depression era, lasted into the mid-1970s. In 1904 Philip Payton founded the Afro-American Realty Company to entice African Americans to move to New York City's Harlem, which spurred integration of the neighborhood.

In 1911 real estate entrepreneur John Nail and his pastor, Rev. Hutchens C. Bishop of St. Philip's Episcopal Church, invested more than one million dollars to purchase and develop property in Harlem for homes and businesses. Harlem became a center of African American community life by the 1920s, and gave rise to the artistic movement called the Harlem Renaissance. During this time Buffalo and Rochester also saw large increases in their African American populations.

The twentieth century saw a growing influx of black immigrants to New York State from the Caribbean. The U.S. census recorded 38,000 West Indian-born New Yorkers in 1920, a number which grew to 236,000 in 2000. Immigration from Haiti surged in the 1970s, and 55,000 Haitian-born New Yorkers were reported in the 1980 census, and 105,000 in the 2000 census.

Manhattan's Harlem (New York County) and Brooklyn (Kings County) have been a primary destination for black immigrants. In recent years there has been an influx of immigrants from African nations; in 2010 the African-born population of New York totaled 158,000.

Genealogical Resources

While African Americans will be found in records discussed elsewhere in this book, the resources below and those cited in the bibliography at the end of this section have specific relevance to researching African Americans in New York:

- The New York State Archives (NYSA) has produced the guide "Records Relating to African Americans" that describes records in its collections pertaining to slavery, military service, education, human rights, politics, performing arts, and more. The guide may be accessed at *www.archives.nysed.gov/a/research/res_topics_pgcafri_amer.pdf*.
- The summer 1997 issue of *Prologue*, published by the National Archives (NARA), was a special issue that focused on the use of federal records in African American historical and genealogical research across many subject areas. All of the articles may be accessed for free at *www.archives.gov/publications/prologue/1997/summer/index.html*.
- The Black History page of NARA's Archives Library Information Center describes resources from NARA and other federal and nonfederal sites that are especially pertinent to African American research at *http://archives.gov/research/alic/reference/black-history.html*.

Slavery

The NYSA holds several series that document government actions pertaining to slavery in colonial New York: Dutch colonial council minutes, 1638–1665 (A1809); New York Colony Council papers, 1664–1781 (A1894); and New York Colony Council minutes, 1668–1783 (A1895). It also holds ship manifests documenting the slave trade during the mid-eighteenth century (A3196). Other relevant records include wills and probate records (J0038, J0043, J0301), and records of the State Controller and State Comptroller from 1797–1820 (A087, A3211).

The New-York Society for the Manumission of Slaves was organized in 1785 to promote abolitionism and provide support to slaves seeking freedom. Included in the Society's records are meeting minutes, financial records, indentures, and a register of the manumission of slaves in New York City between 1816 and 1818. These records have been digitized by the New-York Historical Society (N-YHS) as part of its Manuscript Collections

Relating to Slavery and are accessible at *www.nyhistory.org/slaverycollections.*

Masters who believed that their slaves had escaped to New York often filed court cases in an attempt to reclaim the runaway slaves. Cases filed in the Southern District of New York (Dutchess, New York, Orange, Putnam, Rockland, Sullivan, and Westchester counties) are part of Record Group 21 at NARA-NYC. Part of Record Group 21, Records Relating to Fugitive Slaves, 1837–1860, has been microfilmed as publication M938.

Slave births were recorded by town or city clerks, and manumissions were recorded by town, city, and county clerks; many of those records have been published. See the bibliography at the end of this section, as well as in the individual County Guides.

Census Records

The 1790, 1800, and 1810 federal censuses identified the number, but not the names, of slaves owned by each household. In these early censuses, the names of the heads of households were given, and free blacks were listed as "Other Free Persons." Beginning in 1820, a section was included on the census documenting "Free Colored Persons." The 1830 and 1840 censuses give the number of "Free Colored Persons" in a household, classified by gender and age groups. The 1850 census is the first to list every member of a household by name.

The 1825, 1835, and 1845 New York state censuses collected the following data relevant to African Americans in a household: the whole number of persons in the same family, who are persons of color (not taxed); the whole number of persons of color, in the same family (taxed); and the whole number of persons of color in the same family (taxed and qualified to vote at elections for state and county officers). See also chapter 3, Census Records.

Immigration and Migration

NARA holds passenger and immigration lists. Many are on microfilm and are widely available. *Ancestry.com* has digitized and indexed many of NARA's immigration records, including passenger arrival records for the ports of New York (1820–1957). See chapter 4, Immigration, Migration, and Naturalization, for detailed information about what records exist and where they can be accessed.

There is a large body of literature on the Great Migration of African Americans out of the South to New York and other cities in the North, the Midwest, and the West. The most recent is Isabel Wilkerson's much acclaimed book, *The Warmth of Other Suns.* The New York Public Library's Schomburg Center for Research in Black Culture has produced the interactive website *In Motion: The African American Migration Experience,* which documents major migrations across the United States and immigrations, both

historical and contemporary, from Africa, the Caribbean, and Haiti. See *www.inmotionaame.org/home.cfm.*

City directories can be a valuable tool for tracing the movement of African Americans in New York, as they often denoted people of color by using an abbreviation, such as B. or Col., or by grouping names together in a separate section. Sometimes directories were produced that profiled African American people and businesses in a community. Examples include Rochester's *City Directory of Negro Business and Progress 1939–1940* and the *Negro Directory of the Niagara Frontier, 1958.* See also chapter 11, City Directories.

Military Records

The United States armed forces were not desegregated until 1948, although African Americans have served in every war, including the American Revolution. Edited by Eric Grundset and published by the National Society Daughters of the American Revolution (DAR), *Forgotten Patriots* documents the service of more than 6,600 African Americans and American Indians during the American Revolution and provides an exceptionally thorough bibliography. The 874-page volume may be downloaded for free from the DAR website at *dar.org.*

The NARA guide "Military Service in the United States Colored Troops during the Civil War, 1863–1866" describes the compiled military service records, pension records, and textual records available for African Americans that served during the Civil War. It is accessible at *www.archives.gov/dc-metro/know-your-records/genealogy-fair/2011/handouts/army-2of4-923-usct.pdf.* The NYSA has abstracts of Civil War muster rolls of the 20th, 26th, and 31st U.S. Colored Troops, which have been digitized and indexed. These records may be accessed from the free New York records page on *Ancestry.com*; a direct link is on the homepage of *NewYorkFamilyHistory.org.*

During World War I, the 369th Infantry was an African American regiment organized in New York State. Sometimes called the Harlem Hellfighters or the Black Rattlers, the 369th was the first African American Regiment to serve with the American Expeditionary Force. The NYSA's World War I Veterans' Service Data (1913–1919) records have been digitized and indexed and may be accessed from the free New York records page on *Ancestry.com.* See also chapter 8, Military Records, and the bibliography at the end of this section.

Business, Institutional, and Organizational Records

Numerous social service, business, and cultural organizations—formed at the local, regional, or national level—served African Americans in New York State. See also chapter 10, Business, Institutional, and Organizational Records, for guidance on how to identify and access such records.

Two years after its own founding, the New-York Society for the Manumission of Slaves established the African Free School to serve the city's free black population. The school had its first black principal in 1799, and its teaching staff eventually included many graduates of the school. In 1835 the school was absorbed into the city's public school system. Records of school for 1817–1832 are held by the N-YHS (see listing below), and an online exhibition is at *www.nyhistory.org/web/africanfreeschool*.

In 1808 the New York African Society for Mutual Relief was founded by a group of prominent members of New York City's free black community to provide financial, medical, and burial assistance to community members in need. Records of the Society for 1809–1949 are held by Long Island University in Brooklyn; a finding aid and collection description is at *www2.brooklyn.liu.edu/library/services/specialcol/findaid/ african.htm*. Microfilms of selected documents are at the New York Public Library's Schomburg Center for Research in Black Culture. (See the listing below.)

The Freedman's Savings and Trust Company was chartered in 1865 and catered to recently freed slaves. During the nine years of its existence, the bank opened 33 branches. Although most of the branches were in southern cities, one branch was opened in New York City. NARA holds depositor records, which give the name of the depositor, place of birth, age, complexion, current residence, occupation, parents' names, siblings' names, and the depositor's signature. The collection "Freedman's Bank Records, 1865–1871" can be accessed on *Ancestry.com*. See also Reginald Washington's article in *Prologue* on using these records for genealogical research at *www.archives.gov/publications/ prologue/1997/summer/freedmans-savings-and-trust.html*.

At NARA, Freedman's Savings and Trust records can be found in publications M816 (*Registers of Signatures of Depositors in Branches of the Freedman's Savings and Trust Company, 1865–1874*) and M817 (*Indexes to Deposit Ledgers in Branches of the Freedman's Savings and Trust Company, 1865–1874*). Not on microfilm are collections of records relating to liquidation of the bank and requesting payment after its failure, including some passbooks, loan papers, and bonds. These collections are "Letters Received by the Commissioners of the Freedman's Savings and Trust Company and by the Comptroller of the Currency, 1870–1914," "Letters Sent by the Commissioners of the Freedman's Savings and Trust Company and by the Comptroller of the Currency as Ex Officio Commissioners, 1874–1913" and "Dividend Payment Records, 1882–1889."

The National Negro Business League, founded by Booker T. Washington, was incorporated in New York State in 1901. A "Guide to the Records of the National Negro Business League" in the Archives of Tuskegee Institute and the Library of Congress may be accessed at *www.lexisnexis.com/documents/academic/ upa_cis/1559_natnegrobusleaguept1.pdf*. The League had 320 chapters throughout the country and many in New York State; its members included small business owners, doctors, farmers, craftsmen, and professionals. Chapters sometimes published directories of their members, such as the *Directory of the Negro Business League of Rochester, 1926* (*www.libraryweb. org/~digitized/miscdir/Directory_published_by_the_Negro_ Business_League_1926.pdf*).

Founded by in New York City in 1909, the National Association for the Advancement of Colored People (NAACP) established local chapters in Buffalo (1915), Rochester (1919), Queens (1927), Albany (1935), and elsewhere in New York State. The NAACP archives 1909–1972 are accessible through the ProQuest History Vault subscription database, which is available at many libraries.

Newspapers

The first African American-owned and operated newspaper in the United States was *Freedom's Journal*, which was published in New York City from 1827–1829. The celebrated *North Star* was first published in 1847 in Rochester, NY; in 1851 it became known simply as *Frederick Douglass's Paper*. The Proquest Historical Newspapers Black Newspapers database, which is accessible at many libraries, includes full text of the *New York Amsterdam News* (1922–1993).

The Chronicling America website of the Library of Congress offers the U.S. Newspaper Directory (1690–present), which may be searched by ethnicity and location to identify African American newspaper titles from New York, and details on where to access them (*chroniclingamerica.loc.gov/search/titles*).

The New York State Library's list of New York newspapers at *www.nysl.nysed.gov/nysnp/title4.htm* provides holdings information for more than 10,000 newspaper titles that have been published in New York State. See also chapter 12, Newspapers, for information on how to identify and where to access newspapers, including abolitionist and anti-slavery papers written for both black and white readers.

Religious Records

During the colonial era, free blacks and slaves often attended the churches of the European population, although this was not always reflected in the church records. Many do appear in the early records of the Dutch Reformed and Lutheran churches, as Henry Hoff shows in his article "Researching African-American Families in New Netherland and Colonial New York and New Jersey."

After the American Revolution free blacks began to form their own congregations. The Abyssinian Baptist Church, founded in 1808 in what is now Harlem, was the first African American Baptist church in New York State. There had been African American worshippers at Trinity Church on Wall Street for a century, before members left to found the Free African Church of St. Philip in 1809. Also in New York City, Peter Williams and other black members left the John Street Methodist Church to form a congregation; in 1821 it became the independent denomination African Methodist Episcopal Zion Church (AMEZ).

Black Jews were present in Harlem in the early 1900s, and the Commandment Keepers Ethiopian Hebrew Congregation was founded in there in 1924; its records for 1923–1991 are held by the New York Public Library's Schomburg Center for Research in Black Culture. See also chapter 15, Religious Records.

Selected Repositories, Societies, and Websites
The African Atlantic Genealogical Society (TAAGS)

TAAGS Inc. • PO Box 7385 • Freeport NY 11520-0757
(516) 572-0730 • Email: taags.aam@gmail.com • *aagsinc.net*

TAAGS publishes a bimonthly newsletter and has two chapters in New York which hold regular meetings and present workshops and lectures. One meets at the Macon Library, Brooklyn; the other meets at the African American Museum of Nassau County in Freeport, where members can schedule genealogical research consultations. The website has an online questionnaire to help researchers conduct family interviews.

AfriGeneas

afrigeneas.com

AfriGeneas is an online research community focused on African ancestry in the Americas. It offers scheduled online forums and chats on a range of topics; online databases created by volunteers include a surname index of marriages and deaths.

Afro American Historical Association of the Niagara Frontier

PO Box 63 • Buffalo, NY 14207 • *aahanf.org*

The Association preserves the history of, and promotes research and scholarship on, African Americans in Western New York. It publishes a biannual interdisciplinary journal, *Afro American New York Life and History*. An index of past issues is available on the website.

Afro-American Historical and Genealogical Society, Jean Sampson Scott Greater New York Chapter

PO Box 1050 • New York, NY 10116-1060
(212) 330-7882 • *aahgs-newyork.org*

The chapter holds monthly meetings at the Central Harlem Senior Citizens Center, 34 West 134th Street, at which members and guest lecturers offer presentations on topics related to genealogy and history. Regional committees on research areas— Carolinas, Mid-Atlantic, and Caribbean—support individual and collaborative research. Experienced members also conduct onsite consultations for both new and advanced researchers. The Society's most recent publication is the book, *Family Legacies: A Three Generation Project*, in which 15 chapter members tell the stories of their ancestors.

Afro-American Historical and Genealogical Society (AAHGS), National

PO Box 73067 • Washington, DC 20056-3067
(202) 234-5230 • *aahgs.org*

The largest genealogical society devoted to African American families, the AAHGS has chapters in 17 states and the District of Columbia. It has published the biannual *Journal of the Afro-American Historical and Genealogical Society* since 1980 and a bimonthly newsletter. The AAHGS produces a multi-day national conference annually.

African American Historical Society of Rockland County (AAHS)

PO Box 464 • Piermont, NY 10968 • (845) 362-2126
Email: AAHSrockland@gmail.com • *aahsofrockland.org*

The AAHS is focused primarily on the experiences of African Americans in Rockland County and New York State. In addition to partnering on the Rockland African Diaspora Heritage Center, it has established *Rootswork-The AAHS Family History Institute*, which offers educational programs on family history research at the Nyack Library.

Buffalo Genealogical Society of the African Diaspora

PO Box 155 • Buffalo, NY 14209-0155
Email: BGSAD@verizon.net
www.rootsweb.ancestry.com/~nybgsad

The Society's collections include over 7,000 funeral programs. The website has an index of current research projects, with contact information for each researcher, surnames, and research locations and dates. Meetings are held at the Merriweather Library.

Gilder Lehrman Institute of American History

49 West 45th Street, 6th Floor • New York, NY 10036
(646) 366-9666 • Email: reference@gilderlehrman.org
gilderlehrman.org

The Gilder Lehrman Institute is dedicated to the improvement of history education. Its archive of more than 60,000 letters, diaries, maps, pamphlets, printed books, newspapers, photographs, and ephemera includes an outstanding collection of primary source material related to slavery. Many items in the collection have been digitized and are accessible on the Institute's website, along with reference guides, essays, videos, and timelines. Teachers K–12 enjoy free access; the general public is charged a modest subscription fee. The online magazine *History Now* may be accessed for free. Qualified researchers may apply in advance for permission to use the collection, which is housed at the N-YHS.

New-York Historical Society

170 Central Park West • New York, NY 10024 • (212) 873-3400

Email: info@nyhistory.org (general information)
or reference@nyhistory.org (research inquiries)

nyhistory.org

The New-York Historical Society holds extensive manuscript collections relating to slavery, many of which have been digitized as part of the New York Heritage Digital Collections project and may be accessed for free from *nyheritage.org* or *newyorkhistory.org*. The online collections include records of the New York Manumission Society, the African Free School, and the Association for the Benefit of Colored Orphans (Colored Orphan Asylum). Finding aids to these collections may be accessed at *www.nyhistory.org/library/findingaids/manuscripts#s*.

New York Public Library: Schomburg Center for Research in Black Culture

515 Malcolm X Blvd. at 135th Street • New York, NY 10037

(212) 491-2200 • *www.nypl.org/locations/schomburg*

Founded in 1925, the Schomburg Center is the world's leading repository focused on documenting the history and cultural development of peoples of African descent worldwide. It collects, preserves, and provides access to research resources, and promotes the study and interpretation of the history and culture of African peoples. The Center's collections total more than ten million items. The Jean Blackwell Hutson Research and Reference Division is of primary utility for genealogy research; its holdings include books, periodicals, newspapers, microforms, and online databases. The Manuscripts, Archives, and Rare Books Division holds personal and family papers; records of organizations and institutions; some religious records of churches and synagogues; literary and scholarly manuscripts; typescripts; ephemera; and rare books. The Moving Image and Recorded Sound Division manages an active oral history program.

Selected Bibliography and Further Reading

Afro-American Historical Association of the Niagara Frontier. *Afro-Americans in New York Life and History.* 1977–present. Online index at *aahanf.org*.

Afro-American Historical and Genealogical Society, Jean Sampson Scott Greater New York Chapter Writers Group. *Family Legacies: A Three Generation Project.* New York: AAHGS-NY, 2012.

Alexander, Leslie M. *African or American?: Black Identity and Political Activism in New York City, 1784-1861.* Urbana, IL: University of Illinois Press, 2008.

Andrews, Charles C. *The History of the New York African Free-Schools: From Their Establishment in 1787 to the Present Time, Embracing a Period of More Than Forty Years; Also a Brief Account of the Successful Labors of the New York Manumission Society, with an Appendix.* 1830. Reprint, New York: Negro Universities Press, 1969.

Armstead, Myra Beth Young. *A Heritage Uncovered: The Black Experience in Upstate New York, 1800–1925.* Elmira, NY: Chemung County Historical Society, 1988.

Bahn, Gilbert S. *Slaves and Nonwhite Free Persons in the 1790 Census of New York.* Baltimore: Clearfield Co., 2000.

Barnett, Enid. *Education for African Americans in New York State 1800–1860.* Kingston, ON: Harbinger House Press, 2003.

Berlin, Ira, and Leslie M. Harris. *Slavery in New York.* Published in conjunction with the N-YHS. New York: The New Press, 2005.

Brooks-Bertram, Peggy. *Uncrowned Queens: African American Women Community Builders of Western New York.* Buffalo: Uncrowned Queens Publishing, 2005.

Burroughs, Tony. *Black Roots: A Beginner's Guide to Tracing the African American Family Tree.* New York: Simon and Schuster, 2001.

Byers, Paula K., ed. *African American Genealogical Sourcebook.* New York: Gale Research, Inc., 1995.

Cannon, Essie W. *Negro Directory of the Niagara Frontier, 1958–1959.* Buffalo: Niagara Negro Sales Service, 1958.

Coles, Howard W., comp. *City Directory of Negro Business and Progress 1939–1940.* Rochester: Howard W. Coles, 1939. A digital version may be accessed on the website of the Monroe County Public Library at *http://www.libraryweb.org/~digitized/miscdir/City_Directory_of_Negro_Business_and_Progress_1939-1940.pdf*.

Dodson, Howard, Christopher Moore, and Roberta Yancy, *The Black New Yorkers: 400 Years of African American History.* New York: Wiley & Sons, 2000.

Eichholz, Alice, and James M. Rose. *Free Black Heads of Households in the New York State Federal Census, 1790–1830.* Gale Genealogy and Local History Series, Vol. 14. Detroit: Gale Research Co., 1981.

———. "New York State Manumissions." *NYG&B Record,* vol. 108 (1977) no. 4: 221–225; vol. 109 (1978) no. 1: 22–24, no. 2: 71–74, no. 3: 145–149, no. 4: 229–233; vol. 110 (1979) no. 1: 39–42, no. 2: 66. [NYG&B eLibrary]

———. "Slave Births in Castleton, Richmond County, New York." *NYG&B Record,* vol. 110, no. 4 (1979): 196–197. [NYG&B eLibrary]

———. "Slave Births in New York County [City]." *NYG&B Record,* vol. 111, no. 1 (1980): 13–17. [NYG&B eLibrary]

Entzminger, Thomas A. *Genealogies of African-American Families in Southwestern New York State, 1830–1955.* Aurora, CO: Thaaron Publications, 2002.

Foner, Eric. *Gateway to Freedom: The Hidden History of the Underground Railroad.* New York: W.W. Norton & Co., 2015 (projected publication date).

Foote, Thelma W. *Black and White Manhattan: The History of Racial Formation in Colonial New York City.* New York: Oxford University Press, 2004.

— — —. "Crossroads or Settlement? The Black Freedmen's Community in Historic Greenwich Village 1664-1855." In *Greenwich Village: Culture and Counterculture*, by Rick Beard and Leslie Berlowitz, eds. New Brunswick, N.J.: Published for the Museum of the City of New York by Rutgers University Press, 1993.

Freeman, Rhoda G. *The Free Negro in New York City in the Era before the Civil War.* New York: Garland Publishing, 1994.

Gates, Henry Louis, Jr. *Life upon These Shores: Looking at African American History, 1513–2008.* New York: Knopf Doubleday Publishing Group, 2011.

Gates, Henry Louis, Jr., and Evelyn Brooks Higginbotham, eds. *African American National Biography.* 12 vols. New York: Oxford University Press, 2008.

— — —. *African American National Biography Supplement 2008–2012.* 2 vols. New York: Oxford University Press, 2013.

Grundset, Eric G. et al. "New York." In *Forgotten Patriots: African American and American Indian Patriots in the Revolutionary War: A Guide to Service, Sources and Studies.* Washington: National Society Daughters of the American Revolution, 2008: 311–371. Available for free download, along with a supplement, at *dar.org*.

Harris, Leslie M. *In the Shadow of Slavery: African Americans in New York City, 1626–1863.* Chicago: University of Chicago Press, 2003.

Hodges, Graham Russell, ed. *The Black Loyalist Directory: African Americans in Exile after the American Revolution.* New York: Garland Publishing, 1966. Reprinted in association with the New England Historic Genealogical Society, 1996.

Hodges, Graham Russell. *David Ruggles: A Radical Black Abolitionist and the Underground Railroad in New York City.* Chapel Hill, NC: University of North Carolina Press, 2013.

— — —. *Root & Branch: African Americans in New York and East Jersey, 1613–1863.* Chapel Hill: University of North Carolina Press, 1999.

Hoff, Henry B. "Researching African-American Families in New Netherland and Colonial New York and New Jersey." *NYG&B Record*, vol. 136, no. 2 (2005): 83–95. [NYG&B eLibrary]

Johnson, James W. *Black Manhattan.* New York: Da Capo Press, 1991.

Journal of the Afro-American Historical and Genealogical Society. Washington: 1980–present. An index is available at *aahgs.org*.

Kobrin, David. *The Black Minority in Early New York.* Albany: New York State American Bicentennial Commission, 1975.

Lepore, Jill. *New York Burning: Liberty, Slavery, and Conspiracy in Eighteenth-Century Manhattan.* New York: Alfred A. Knopf, 2005.

Mabee, Carleton. *Black Education in New York State: From Colonial to Modern Times.* Syracuse: Syracuse University Press, 1979.

Matthews, Harry Bradshaw. *A Guide to Local Abolitionists and Resource Materials Identifying African American Soldiers of the Civil War from New York and Other States: A Tribute to the United States Colored Troops Commemorative Symposium of Delaware and Otsego Counties, New York, 1997–1998.* Oneonta, NY: n.p., 1997.

— — —. *Honoring New York's Forgotten Soldiers: African Americans of the Civil War with Research Examples A–Z. A Case Study in Historiographic Genealogy.* Oneonta, NY: H. B. Matthews, 1997.

— — —. *Voices from the Front Line: New York's African American Statesmen of the Underground Railroad Freedom Trail and the United States Colored Troops Organized in the Empire State, 1863–1865: Roll Call, Men of the 20th USCT and 26th USCT: Introductory Essay and Research Guide.* Oneonta, NY: Hartwick College, 2000.

McManus, Edgar J. *History of Negro Slavery in New York.* Syracuse: Syracuse University Press, 1966.

Merrill, Arch. *The Underground: Freedom's Road and Other Upstate Tales.* 1963. Reprint, Rochester: Creek Books, 1978.

Newman, Debra L., comp. *List of Black Servicemen Compiled from the War Department Collection of Revolutionary War Records, Special List 36.* Washington: National Archives and Records Service, 1974. Accessible on the website of the Allen County Public Library Genealogy Center at *www.genealogycenter.info/nara/speciallists/search_narasl36.php*.

New York State Archives. "Records Relating to African Americans." Information Leaflet Number 8. 1997. *www.archives.nysed.gov/a/research/res_topics_pgc_afri_amer.pdf*

O'Neill, Terri Bradshaw. "Manumissions and Certificates of Freedom in the New York Secretary of State Deeds," *NYG&B Record*, vol. 139, no. 1 (2008): 72–73. [NYG&B eLibrary]

Penn, Lisha. "Documenting African Americans in the Records of Military Agencies." *Prologue*, vol. 29, no. 2 (1997). *www.archives.gov/publications/prologue/1997/summer/military-agencies.html*

Peterson, Carla L. *Black Gotham: A Family History of African Americans in Nineteenth-Century New York City*. New Haven, CT: Yale University Press, 2011.

Petty, James W. "Black Slavery Emancipation Research in the Northern States." *National Genealogical Society Quarterly*, vol. 100, no. 4 (2012): 293–304.

Priebe, Paula J. "The Allen A. M. E. Church, Jamaica, NY, 1834–1900: The Role of the Black Church in a Developing 19th Century Community." *Afro-Americans in New York Life and History*, vol. 16, no. 1 (1992).

Rose, James M. *Black Genesis: A Resource Book for African-American Genealogy*. Baltimore: Genealogical Publishing Co., 2003.

Sacks, Marcy S. *Before Harlem: The Black Experience in New York City before World War I*. Philadelphia: University of Pennsylvania Press, 2006.

Sammons, Jeffrey T., and John H. Morrow, Jr. *Harlem's Rattlers and the Great War: The Undaunted 369th Regiment and the African American Quest for Equality*. Lawrence, KS: University Press of Kansas, 2014.

Scott, Kenneth. "Manumissions in Kings County, N.Y." *National Genealogical Society Quarterly*, vol. 65, no. 3 (1977): 177–180.

— — —. "Slave Births in Kings County, After 1800." *National Genealogical Society Quarterly*, Vol. 66, no. 2 (1978): 97–103.

Seraile, William. *Angels of Mercy: White Women and New York's Colored Orphan Asylum*. New York: Fordham University Press, 2011.

— — —. *New York's Black Regiments during the Civil War*. New York: Routledge, 2001.

Sernett, Milton C. *North Star Country: Upstate New York and the Crusade for African American Freedom*. Syracuse: Syracuse University Press, 2002.

Smith, Franklin Carter, and Emily Anne Croom. *A Genealogist's Guide to Discovering Your African-American Ancestors*. Cincinnati: Betterway Books, 2003.

Stevens-Acevedo, Anthony, Tom Weterings, and Leonor Alvarez Frances. *Juan Rodriguez and the Beginnings of New York City*. New York: Dominican Studies Research Monograph Series, City College of New York, 2013.

Walker, George E. *The Afro-American in New York City, 1827–1860*. New York: Garland Publishing, 1993.

Washington, Reginald. "The Freedman's Savings and Trust Company and African American Genealogical Research." *Prologue*, vol. 29, no. 2 (1997). *www.archives.gov/publications/prologue/1997/summer/freedmans-savings-and-trust.html*

Weidman, Budge. "Preserving the Legacy of the United States Colored Troops." *Prologue*, vol. 29, no. 2 (1997). *www.archives.gov/education/lessons/blacks-civil-war/article.htm*

White, Shane. *Somewhat More Independent: The End of Slavery in New York City, 1770–1810*. Athens, GA: University of Georgia Press, 1991.

— — —. *Stories of Freedom in Black New York*. Cambridge, MA: Harvard University Press, 2002.

Wilder, Craig S. *In the Company of Black Men: The African Influence on African American Culture in New York City*. New York: New York University Press, 2001.

Wilkerson, Isabel. *The Warmth of Other Suns: The Epic Story of America's Great Migration*. New York: Random House, 2010.

Wilson, Sherrill D. *New York City's African Slaveowners: A Social and Material Culture History*. New York: Garland Publishing, 1994.

Woodson, Carter G. *Free Negro Heads of Families in the United States in 1830*. Washington: The Association for the Study of Negro Life and History, 1918.

American Indian

Introduction

Names, terminology, and spelling variations used to describe American Indians have evolved over time, and today reflect a deeper and more accurate understanding of their languages and cultures than existed previously. This reflects current usage which may differ in some ways from the colloquial usage likely to be found in family stories, letters, old newspapers, and other documents. The same individuals, for example, may have been identified by their primary language family, Algonquian (Algonquin, Algonkian); by their dialect, Munsee (also known as Delaware); or by their group affiliation, Mahican (or Mohican, but not to be confused with Mohegan). In describing groups of Indians, the distinction in meaning between the terms nation, people, band, or tribe is ambiguous. However, the word "tribe" is used less frequently today, and the word "nation" may sometimes be an umbrella for many subgroups.

There are currently eight Indian nations in New York State that are federally recognized as self-governing entities: Cayuga Nation of New York, Oneida Nation of New York, Onondaga Nation of New York, Saint Regis Mohawk Tribe (formerly the Saint Regis Band of Mohawk Indians of New York), Seneca Nation of New York, Shinnecock Indian Nation, Tonawanda Band of Seneca Indians of New York, and Tuscarora Nation of New York. The Tonawanda and the Tuscarora are also recognized by New York State, as is the Unkechaug Nation.

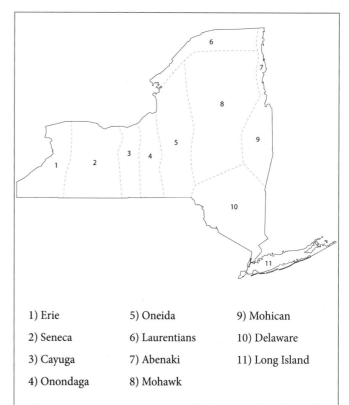

1) Erie	5) Oneida	9) Mohican
2) Seneca	6) Laurentians	10) Delaware
3) Cayuga	7) Abenaki	11) Long Island
4) Onondaga	8) Mohawk	

This map is an approximation of Indian tribal lands in the area that is now New York State before the arrival of Europeans. The arrival of European settlers radically altered the boundaries, which had always been very fluid. The map does not show all past or present Indian tribes. See table 2 for a list of current and dissolved reservations in New York State.

Recognized, Unrecognized, and Departed Tribes

Algonquian Peoples of Long Island

Before the seventeenth century there were a large number of different native communities. Historical literature lists the Canarsees, the Corchaugs, the Manhassets, the Massapequas, the Matinecocks, the Mericokes, the Nissequaqs, the Rockaways, the Secatagues, and the Setaukets. These are exonyms derived from the geographic place names the communities inhabited. Many spelling variations exist for these groups. Two of the tribes, Shinnecock and Unkechaug (also known as Patchogue or Patchoag), have reservations in Suffolk County. The Montaukett or Montauk are not recognized by the federal or state government; they have cultural ties to the Shinnecock and Unkechaug peoples. Descendants of other groups that survived can be found largely in Ontario, Quebec, Oklahoma, and Wisconsin, as well as on Long Island (but living without any tribal affiliation).

The Brothertown Indians were a group of Christian Indians from New England and Long Island that settled in Oneida County in the late-1700s. Pressure from incoming settlers led to a reluctant move to Wisconsin. In 1821 the Brothertown, with Stockbridge and Oneida Indians, purchased 860,000 acres in that state. To avoid being moved again—this time to Kansas—the Brothertown applied for United State citizenship. This was granted in 1839, and they were able to retain their lands in Wisconsin but lost their status as a sovereign nation. They have been denied federal recognition as a tribe because they attained citizenship through a congressional act.

Algonquian Peoples of the Hudson Valley and New York City

When the Dutch arrived at the beginning of the seventeenth century, there were many native communities in the mid- and lower Hudson Valley. All spoke what is now called the Munsee dialect of Delaware in the Algonquian language family. The Esopus Indians resided in what is now Ulster County. The Hackensacks lived along the Hackensack River Valley from today's Rockland County to Staten Island, and had communities both in New York and New Jersey. The neighboring Tappans sold their land in the 1670s and do not appear on later records. In 1683 the Wappinger sold land in present-day Dutchess County to the Rombout family; by 1822 the Wappinger descendants were relocated to a reservation set aside for the Oneida near Green Bay, Wisconsin. Other eighteenth-century communities in this region were the Siwanoys, Wiechquaskecks, and Kitchawanks. Today descendants of the Hudson Valley Indians reside in Munceytown and Moraviantown, Ontario, and in Delaware communities in Kansas, Oklahoma, and Wisconsin.

At the time of European contact, Indian residents of Manhattan, Staten Island, western Long Island, northern New Jersey, and southeastern New York state all spoke the Munsee language and were culturally indistinguishable. The term "Lenape" is often used to identify these people, although this Algonquian word is a general term for "real people." By the early 1700s, those who survived the effects of European arrival were forced to leave. Some joined together to form the short-lived Delaware Nation in the Ohio Valley. Descendants are in the Ramapough Lenape Indian Nation and the Nanticoke Lenni-Lenape Indians of New Jersey (both tribes are recognized by the State of New Jersey); the Delaware Nation of Oklahoma; and the Delaware Tribe of Indians (both located in Oklahoma and federally recognized).

The Mahicans (Mohicans) resided in the upper Hudson Valley, as well as in present-day Vermont, western Massachusetts, and far northeastern Connecticut. Most descendants are now part of the Stockbridge-Munsee Band of Mohican Indians in Wisconsin.

Iroquoian Peoples of Upstate New York

Commonly called the Iroquois League, the Haudenosaunee or Ganonsyoni (meaning roughly the "People of the Longhouse") was an association of Iroquoian-language family nations in what is now upstate New York. In the seventeenth century the Five Nations (Mohawk, Oneida, Onondaga, Cayuga, and Seneca) formed a "Covenant Chain" alliance with other native groups and European colonies in the Northeast to preserve trade through peace and stable relations. In 1722 the Tuscarora, also of the Iroquoian-language family, came north from present-day North Carolina to seek refuge among the Haudenosaunee and accepted an invitation to become the sixth nation. The Haudenosaunee's traditional territory spanned most of present-day upstate New York from the Hudson Valley to the Genesee River in western New York.

Today, all six nations are federally recognized, and only the Cayuga lack a reservation in New York State. After the Revolutionary War, significant numbers of Iroquois moved west into Ontario, Canada, Oklahoma, and Wisconsin. A federally recognized tribe of Oneidas was formed in Wisconsin, and a joint Seneca-Cayuga tribe in Oklahoma. The Erie lived in western New York, along the south-eastern shores of the Lake Erie. They lost their territory to the Iroquois by the mid-1650s, and were absorbed into the neighboring Seneca tribe.

Records and Resources

Census records for American Indians are incomplete for many reasons. There is a long history of strained relations between native peoples and federal/state governments which has an impact on participation in censuses. Many American Indians believe that the federal census impinges on their sovereignty and eschew it. Sometimes people refuse to respond, and sometimes people who self-identify as native are excluded from census rolls for various reasons.

Some native peoples of New York base membership on matrilineal descent: Cayuga, Mohawk (Saint Regis), Oneida, Onondaga, Seneca, Shinnecock, and Tuscarora. Therefore, the mother must be enrolled for the child to be enrolled. This means that if the father was an American Indian, but the mother was not, the family may not appear in records pertaining to American Indians. The majority of the neighboring Nations in New England base membership on patrilineal descent.

Federal Censuses

No American Indians were identified as such in the 1790–1840 censuses. The 1850 census was the first to list all family members and record information about each person. The American Indians who were enumerated in the population schedules had renounced tribal rule and were taxed. Surnames were often adopted for the census, sometimes in honor of a revered person; names were frequently changed upon converting to Christianity, marrying a non-Indian, or entering an American school. In both the 1850 and 1860 censuses, people were identified as white, black, or mulatto, and occasionally as Indian (usually with the notation "Ind" or "In"). In 1870 and 1880 census takers were instructed to identify Indians in the general population in column six (color). American Indians are sometimes listed incorrectly as "Mulatto" or "Black." American Indians that were nomadic or living on reservations were not taxed, so they were not included in the population schedules. However, special agents were used to count/estimate the number of untaxed Indians.

Nearly all of the 1890 census schedules were destroyed in the 1921 fire at the Department of Commerce. However, there was a special report complied in 1892 on the social conditions of the "Six Nations of New York" using data obtained by the eleventh census (1890). This report, produced under the direction of Thomas Donaldson, is published and also online at *Archive.org* where it can be found by searching for "Indians: The Six Nations of New York." The six nations are: Cayuga, Mohawk (Saint Regis), Oneida, Onondaga, Seneca, and the Tuscarora. The report does not provide a complete listing of individual reservation residents, but it does list Union soldiers and sailors from each nation and provides images of some individuals.

Beginning with the 1900 census, Indians are enumerated on reservations as well as in the general population. In 1900 and 1910 a special Indian schedule added additional questions to the general schedule; these special schedules are usually found at the end of the county, but sometimes grouped together on last roll of microfilm for the state. Indians living with non-Indian families outside of reservations continued to be enumerated on the general schedule with those families. There were no special

Table 3: Current and Dissolved Reservations in New York State.

Reservation	Years	Nation	County/Location*
Akwesasne (Saint Regis)	1796–present	Mohawk	Franklin
Allegany	1797–present	Seneca	Cattaraugus
Big Tree	1797–1826	Seneca	Livingston
Buffalo Creek	1797–1842	Seneca and others	Erie
Canadaway	1797–1802	Seneca	Chautauqua
Canawaugus	1797–1826	Seneca	Livingston
Caneadea	1797–1826	Seneca	Livingston
Cattaraugus	1797–present	Seneca	Erie, Chautauqua, and Cattaraugus
Cayuga	1789–1795	Cayuga	Near Cayuga Lake
Gardeau	1797–1826	Seneca	Livingston and Wyoming
Little Beard's Town	1797–1802	Seneca	Livingston
Oil Spring	1797–present	Seneca	Cattaraugus and Allegany
Oneida	1788–present	Oneida	Madison
Onondaga	1788–present	Onondaga	Onondaga
Poospatuck	1859–present	Unkechaug	Suffolk
Shinnecock	1859–present	Shinnecock	Suffolk
Squakie Hill	1797–1826	Seneca and descendants of Fox Indians	Livingston
Tonawanda	1797–present	Seneca	Genesee, Erie, and Niagara
Tuscarora	1797–present	Tuscarora	Niagara

*County locations provide approximate present day geographical locations

Indian schedules with the censuses of 1920 and 1930. However, the 1930 census sometimes notes the degree of Indian blood in column 19 and the tribe in column 20. The National Archives (NARA) summary "Native Americans in the Federal Decennial Censuses, 1790–1930," is available as an online PDF at *archives. gov/research/Native-americans/reference-reports/indians-in- decennial-census.pdf.*

American Indian Census Rolls, Conducted by the Bureau of Indian Affairs (BIA)

An act of July 4, 1884, required federal agents or superintendents in charge of Indian reservations to submit census information to the Commissioner of Indian Affairs; the data was to be collected annually. The rolls usually provide the English and/or Indian name of the person, roll number, age or date of birth, sex, and relationship to head of family. The data from 1885 to 1940 can be found in NARA Microfilm Publication M595, Indian Census Rolls. The federally recognized tribes for New York State were the Cayuga, Saint Regis (Mohawk), Oneida, Onondaga, Allegany and Cattaraugus Seneca, Tonawanda Seneca, and Tuscarora. Not all the censuses were conducted annually, and not all survive; there are records for New York tribes from 1885 to 1924.

These censuses are also online at *Archive.org, Fold3.com,* and *Ancestry.com,* and on microfilm at the Family History Library (FHL). NARA has a detailed publication about the Indian Census Rolls, 1885–1940, which is available as an online PDF at *archives.gov/research/microfilm/m595.pdf.*

New York State Censuses

From 1845 the New York state censuses enumerated American Indians living on reservations in New York except for those on Long Island. Sometimes the reservations are listed at the end of the state census (after Yates County) as in 1915, and sometimes the reservations are listed separately in the relevant county/ counties (e.g., 1905 and 1925) as they are in the decennial federal censuses. (See chapter 3, Census Records, for a table of 1855–1925 New York state censuses.)

The 1845 census for Indian Reservations is on microfilm at the New York State Archives, No. (N-Ar) A1832 and accessible online at *http://iarchives.nysed.gov/PubImageWeb/listCollections.jsp?id=6000*. It includes the following reservations: Allegany (Seneca), Cattaraugus (Seneca), Cattaraugus (Cayuga), Oneida, Onondaga, Saint Regis Mohawk, Tonawanda, and Tuscarora. It also includes a census of the Buffalo Creek reservation (Seneca) even though it was dissolved in 1842. (The Seneca later repurchased some of this land.)

New York State Indian Annuity Rolls

The NYSA holds "Indian Census Rolls" 1881–1950 (series A0742) for residents of reservations in New York entitled to receive annuities. The rolls are very incomplete in coverage, and the information in them essentially duplicates that found in the federal records described below.

1841–1949 Annuity Payrolls

These records are also part of Record Group 75 at NARA in Washington, DC. The payments recorded here were the result of treaties between the United States government and American Indian tribes. Annuity payments were made to individual Indians to compensate for land or the sale of materials. Some were single payments, and others were periodic annuity payments. Rolls list the names of those who were entitled to receive payment and may contain information such as age, sex, tribal affiliation, degree of Indian blood, and relationship to head of family. The series "Kansas Claims of New York Indians, 1901–1904" includes annuity payrolls for the sale of lands in Kansas to New York Indians which were never completed. The New York tribes were Brothertown, Oneida, Onondaga, Saint Regis (Mohawk), Seneca (and Cayuga), Stockbridge, Munsee, and Tuscarora.

1855 Bounty-Land Warrants for Military Service

These were extended to American Indians who fought in the Revolutionary and Indian Wars of 1818 and 1836. American Indian veterans could procure land promised upon completion of military service. The records are located at NARA in Washington, DC. Forms for requesting these documents can be downloaded at *archives.gov*.

The applications for bounty land are part of Record Group 15 of the Records of the Veterans Administration. Although the majority of the applications are from members of the so-called "Five Civilized Tribes" (Creek, Choctaw, Seminole, Chickasaw, and Cherokee), they also include New York tribes such as the Oneida, Onondaga, Seneca, Tonawanda, and Tuscarora. Other records created by the BIA (NARA Record Group 75) include information about the veterans' families.

Indian School Censuses and Records

Off-reservation boarding schools were set up by the federal government as a way to assimilate American Indian children by taking them away from their tribal lands. The Carlisle Indian Industrial School, in Pennsylvania, set up in 1879, was the first of these Indian boarding schools and was the model for the others. The majority of these Indian schools were much further west, which does not mean that Indian children were not sent there from New York.

NARA Record Group 75 (BIA) includes Indian School Records and the Annual School Census Reports 1912–1939; none of the schools was located in New York State. These records are in Washington, DC. School censuses created at individual school level or by region are held at the NARA facility that covers the states in which these censuses were created—most likely Kansas City, Fort Worth, Denver, or Chicago. Microfilms of many of these records are available at the FHL.

Numerous Indian children (aged 6 to 18) traveled from New York to attend Carlisle during its 39-year history, including children from the Cayuga, Oneida, Onondaga, Seneca, and Shinnecock tribes. NARA has more records for Carlisle than any other Indian school, as well as an online research guide to the collection; it also has an online PDF that lists all the students 1890–1918 for which NARA has records, by name, file number, tribe, and state of origin: *archives.gov/dc-metro/know-your-records/genealogy-fair/2010/handouts/carlisle-school-records.pdf*. Barbara Landis has a website about the Carlisle school and resources for doing research, including a student enrollment list (1879–1918) showing the number of students from each tribe at *http://home.epix.net/~landis*.

The Tunesassa Indian School was a Quaker school in Cattaraugus County that non-Quakers also attended. It was separate from government sanctioned Indian boarding schools. Records, ca. 1879–1938, can be found in the Haverford College Library Quaker Collection, *http://trilogy.brynmawr.edu/speccoll/hv/pymindian.xml*.

The Thomas Indian School was run by New York State. It began as The Thomas Asylum for Orphan and Destitute Indian Children in 1855, and became a school for children through grade seven, ca. 1905–1957. Records of the Thomas Indian School (restricted to protect personal privacy) are held by the NYSA.

Religious Records

Missionaries from the Catholic Church and various Protestant denominations interacted extensively with American Indians, so in many cases church records of marriages and baptisms may exist. A Moravian mission to American Indians was established at Shekomeko in Dutchess County in 1740. Extensive records for 1742–1746 survive and are held at the Archives of the Moravian Church in Bethlehem, Pennsylvania (*www.moravianchurcharchives.org*). An inventory is at *www.moravianchurcharchives.org/documents/IndianMissions.pdf*. See also chapter 15, Religious Records.

Manuscript Material

Journals, diaries, letters, and logs related to missionaries, traders, general store owners, Indian agents, and others can be a valuable source of information. These frequently pre-date any BIA or civil records, but also continue into the nineteenth and twentieth centuries. An exceptional manuscript collection is the Stockbridge Indian Papers, 1739–1915, which reside at Cornell University. A finding aid to the collection is available at *http://rmc.library.cornell.edu/EAD/htmldocs/RMM09185.html*.

Indian Nations in New York State

Before contacting an Indian nation for assistance, it is important to complete genealogical research that establishes a connection between an Indian nation and one's ancestor.

Cayuga Nation

Cayuga Nation • PO Box 803 • 2540 SR-89
Seneca Falls, NY 13148 • (315) 568-0750 • *cayuganation-nsn.gov*

The Cayuga Nation records the genealogy of each enrolled member going back to the early nineteenth century. Research requests should be sent to the Nation's office.

Oneida Indian Nation

Oneida Indian Nation • 2037 Dream Catcher Plaza
Oneida, NY 13421 • Email: info@oneida-nation.org
oneidaindiannation.com

Website offers information on the history of the Oneidas. The Nation Library is located at the Ray Elm Children and Elders Center, 5000 Skenondoa Way, Oneida.

Onondaga Nation

The Onondaga Nation Waterworks • Genealogy Request
PO Box 85 • Route 11A • Via-Nedrow, NY 13120
(315) 492-1922
Email: admin@onondaganation.org • *onondaganation.org*

The Onondaga Nation provides a genealogy search for a fee; a request form is available online at *onondaganation.org/aboutus/lineage.html*.

Saint Regis Mohawk Tribe

412 State Route 37 • Akwesasne, NY 13655 • (518) 358-2272
Email: publicinformation@srmt-nsn.gov • *srmt-nsn.gov*

Genealogical research inquiries should be sent to Saint Regis Mohawk Tribal Clerk's Office. Research forms, instructions, and information on fees may be requested by phone. The website has information on the history and culture of the tribe.

Seneca Nation

Seneca Nation • PO Box 231 • Salamanca, NY 14779
(716) 945-1790 • *sni.org*

The Seneca Nation provides genealogical research for a fee; as much information as possible should be included in a request, such as full name, date of birth, date of death, and maiden name. Requests may be sent to the attention of the Clerk's Office.

Shinnecock Indian Nation

PO Box 5006 • Southampton, NY 11969 • (631) 283-6143
Email: sination@optonline.net • *shinnecocknation.com*

Tribal departments include an Enrollment and Vital Records Office. The website has detailed information on the history and culture of the Shinnecock Nation.

Tonawanda Band of Senecas Council of Chiefs

7027 Meadville Road • Basom, NY 14013 • (716) 542-4244
Fax: (716) 542-4008

Unkechaug Nation

Poospatuck Reservation • Mastic, NY 11950 • (631) 281-7583
Email: unkechaugenroll@gmail.com

The Unkechaug Nation's Vital Records and Enrollment Office was created in 2010 to maintain enrollment records, past and present.

Relocated Nations

The following are websites for nations and tribes that were formerly located in present-day New York. They contain historical accounts and information about tribal enrollment.

- Delaware Nation (Oklahoma): *delawarenation.com*
- Delaware Tribe of Indians (Oklahoma): *delawaretribe.org*
- Ganienkeh Mohawk Settlement: *ganienkeh.net*
- Huron-Wendat Nation (Quebec): *wendake.ca*
- Oneida Tribe of Indians of Wisconsin: *oneidanation.org*
- Seneca-Cayuga Tribe of Oklahoma: *sctribe.com*
- Stockbridge-Musee Band of Mohican Indians (Wisconsin): *mohican-nsn.gov*

Selected Major Repositories and Resources
The Bureau of Indian Affairs (BIA)

1849 C Street, N.W. • Washington, DC 20240
(202) 208-5116 • *bia.gov*

The BIA, known before 1947 alternately as the Indian Bureau, the Indian Department, the Indian Office, and the Indian Service, was established in 1824. The New York Agency, originally known as the Six Nations Agency, was established in 1792 after the "Ordinance for the Regulation of Indian Affairs," enacted by Congress on August 7, 1786. It remained in operation, either as an agency or sub-agency, until 1949.

The BIA has collected information on the residents of Indian Reservations as well as on some American Indians who lived outside reservations but were affiliated with tribes recognized by the United States. (See the previous section on the American Indian Census Rolls conducted by the BIA.) Select records of the

New York Indian Agency (1829–1880) have been microfilmed and are available at NARA and the Family History Library. Researchers typically must know the tribe and residence of individuals in order to locate them in the records.

The BIA website has an online PDF which explains that it cannot help with genealogical inquiries, that it holds current rather than historic tribal membership enrollment lists, and that it does not maintain current or historic records of all individuals who possess some degree of American Indian blood. It provides helpful information on where to find records and further information, in particular the following record groups at NARA:

- Record Group 29: Records of the Bureau of the Census
- Record Group 48: Records of the Office of the Secretary of the Interior
- Record Group 75: Records of the Bureau of Indian Affairs, 1973–1989

The Interior Department's "Guide to Tracing American Indian & Alaska Native Ancestry" notes that BIA regional offices may have information on a person if:

- The estate was probated through the BIA because the person had land in trust or received income from land in trust with the BIA
- The person's name is on a tribe's base membership rolls
- The person is on a judgment distribution roll as part of a tribal claim settlement

Today the Eastern Cherokee Agency of the BIA serves the Cayuga Nation, Oneida Indian Nation, Onondaga Indian Nation, Seneca Nation of Indians, Saint Regis Band of Mohawk Indians, Tonawanda Band of Seneca, and Tuscarora Nation; and the Eastern Regional Office serves the Shinnecock Nation of Indians:

Eastern Cherokee Agency
Bureau of Indian Affairs • Highway 441 North
Cherokee, NC 28719 • (828) 497-9131
bia.gov/WhoWeAre/RegionalOffices/Eastern/WeAre/Cherokee/index.htm

Eastern Regional Office
Bureau of Indian Affairs • 545 Marriott Drive, Suite 700
Nashville, TN 37214 • (615) 564-6700
bia.gov/WhoWeAre/RegionalOffices/Eastern/index.htm

National Archives and Records Administration (NARA)
NARA has a large number of records from the BIA. Records are mostly located in Washington, DC, and include reports from field offices about the activities on reservations, correspondence between field agents and the United States government, individual history cards, and the American Indian Census Rolls conducted by the BIA. NARA-NYC has very limited administrative records from 1938 to 1949. The website (*archives. gov*) has a full listing of the holdings.

Smithsonian Institution, National Museum of the American Indian – New York
Smithsonian Institution National Museum of the American Indian
Alexander Hamilton U.S. Custom House • One Bowling Green
New York, NY 10004 • (212) 514-3700 • *nmai.si.edu*

The New York annex to the museum in Washington, DC, offers a permanent gallery covering the history of native peoples across the Americas, temporary exhibits, public educational programs, and a resource center with library to conduct scholarly research. The museum holds no genealogical records, but the resource center does offer assistance and guidance to help get started. The SNMAI website offers a searchable, digitized record collection at *nmai.si.edu/searchcollections/home.aspx*. This museum and NARA-NYC are in the same building.

Selected Other Repositories and Resources
American Philosophical Society
Library: 105 South Fifth Street • Philadelphia, PA 19106-3386
(215) 440-3400 • *amphilsoc.org*

The APS Library's collections include extensive holdings of manuscript collections and rare printed materials relating to the history, culture, and languages of the native peoples of New York. Materials from the seventeenth to nineteenth centuries include vocabularies of Iroquoian, Algonkian, and other languages, and records of interactions between Indians of the region and white settlers and diplomats. Materials from the twentieth century onward primarily come from the papers of linguists, anthropologists, and ethnologists, and include extensive visual and audio resources, in addition to manuscripts and printed materials. An annotated subject guide exists on the website for materials accessioned into the collections through 1982. Subsequently accessioned material can be located through the Library's online catalog.

Akwesasne Library & Cultural Center
321 State Route 37 • Hogansburg, NY 13655-3114
(518) 358-2240 • Email: akwlibr@nc3r.org
akwesasneculturalcenter.org

The Center maintains one of the largest collections of American Indian cultural materials in northern New York. Holdings include books and pamphlets, newspapers, photographs, and videos.

Neto Hatinakwe Onkwehowe
Niagara Arts and Cultural Center • 1201 Pine Avenue
Niagara Falls, NY 14301 • *netobuffalo.org*

The organization hosts programs, collections, and exhibitions on the art, history, and culture of the indigenous people of western New York.

Six Nations Indian Museum

1462 County Route 60 • Onchiota, NY 12989 • (518) 891-2299

Email: info@sixnationsindianmuseum.com

sixnationsindianmuseum.com

Holdings include artifacts, artwork, and documents detailing the history of the Iroquois from pre-Columbian times to the present.

Iroquois Indian Museum

324 Caverns Road • PO Box 7 • Howes Cave, NY 12092

(518) 296-8949 • Email: info@iroquoismuseum.org

iroquoismuseum.org

The museum is self-described as "an anthropological institution . . . informed by research on archaeology, history, and the common creative spirit of modern artists and craftspeople." The website has links to related sites, provides Iroquois history, and has a short guide to finding American Indian genealogical information.

Iroquois Studies Association

28 Zevan Road • Johnson City, NY 13790

(607) 729-0016 • *otsiningo.com*

The Association hosts events and programs on the history and culture of American Indians, particularly the Haudenosaunee (Iroquois), and publishes a semiannual newsletter, the *Otsiningo Circle*, which details events and exhibits on American Indians that take place within 200 miles of Binghamton, NY. The Association merged with the Otsiningo American Indian Project, which provides programs on the Indians of the lower Chenango River Valley, in 1996.

Selected Online Resources

U.S. Department of the Interior. "Guide to Tracing Your American Indian Ancestry." Available online at *bia.gov/cs/ groups/public/documents/text/idc002656.pdf*.

Ancestry.com maintains a forum for American Indian genealogy; the same forums can also be accessed via *Rootsweb. com* at *http://boards.ancestry.netscape.com/topics.ethnic. natam.nations/mb.ashx* and *http://boards.rootsweb.com/ topics.ethnic.natam.nations/mb.ashx*

A search for "American Indian" on *Cyndislist.com* will reveal numerous resources that are useful for American Indian genealogical research.

Genealogy.com has a separate set of forums dedicated to American Indian family history research: *http://genforum. genealogy.com/ai*

Based in Minnesota, the organization Native Languages of the Americas works to preserve the languages of American Indians. The New York section of its website, *native-languages.org/york.htm*, provides information about language resources and other helpful links.

Selected Bibliography and Further Reading

Bakel, John C., comp. *Long Island Indian Affairs: 1664–1681.* Huntington, NY: Town of Huntington, 1993. Compiled from documents in Huntington's Court Records.

Barclay, Henry. *Register of Baptisms, Marriages, Communicants & Funerals, 1734–1746.* Albany: New York State Library, 1919. Includes many Mohawks.

Bowman, Fred Q. "Vital Record Postings of an Indian Missionary in Western New York." *NYG&B Record*, vol. 117, no. 1 (1986): 20–26. [NYG&B eLibrary]

Byers, Paula K., ed. *Native American Genealogical Sourcebook.* New York: Gale Research, 1995.

Cook, Joyce, and Maureen Davis, eds. *Researching Native Americans in New York State.* Syracuse: New York State Council of Genealogical Organizations, 2007.

Donaldson, Thomas. *Extra Census Bulletin. Indians. The Six Nations of New York. Cayugas, Mohawks (Saint Regis), Oneidas, Onondagas, Senecas, Tuscaroras.* Washington: United States Printing Office, 1892.

Dunn, Shirley W. *The Mohican World, 1680–1750.* Fleischmanns, NY: Purple Mountain Press, 2000.

— — —. *The River Indians: Mohicans Making History.* Fleischmanns, NY: Purple Mountain Press, 2009.

Dunn, Shirley W., ed. *Mohican Seminar 1: The Continuance, an Algonquian Peoples Seminar: Selected Research Papers, 2000.* Albany: University of the State of New York, State Education Department, 2004.

— — —. *Mohican Seminar 2: The Challenge, an Algonquian Peoples Seminar.* Albany: University of the State of New York, State Education Department, 2005.

— — —. Mohican Seminar 3: *The Journey, an Algonquian Peoples Seminar.* Albany: University of the State of New York, State Education Department, 2009.

Engelbrecht, William A. *Iroquoia: The Development of a Native World.* Syracuse: Syracuse University Press, 2003.

Found, Mary. *Native American Records of Western New York.* FamilySearch CD-ROM no. 3464.

Frazier, Patrick. *The Mohicans of Stockbridge.* Lincoln: University of Nebraska Press, 1992.

Grumet, Robert S. *Historic Contact: Indian People and Colonists in Today's Northeastern United States in the Sixteenth through Eighteenth Centuries.* Norman, OK: University of Oklahoma Press, 1995.

———. *The Lenapes.* New York: Chelsea House Publishers, 1989. Focused on the Delaware (Lenape) of southern NJ and eastern PA, not the Delaware (Munsees) of southeastern NY and northern NJ.

———. *Manhattan to Minisink: American Indian Place Names in Greater New York and Vicinity.* Norman: University of Oklahoma Press, 2013.

———. *The Munsee Indians: A History.* Norman: University of Oklahoma Press, 2009.

Grundset, Eric G., et al. *Forgotten Patriots: African American and American Indian Patriots in the Revolutionary War: A Guide to Service, Sources and Studies.* Washington: National Society Daughters of the American Revolution, 2008.

Houghton, Frederick. "The History of the Buffalo Creek Reservation." *Publications of the Buffalo Historical Society*, vol. 24, 1920.

Jones, Gertrude H. *Vital and Miscellaneous Records of the Cattaraugus (Seneca Indians) Reservation of New York.* FHL Microfilm: 924,554.

———. *Vital Statistics (about 1833–1940) of the Cattaraugus Reservation, New York.* FHL Microfilm: 962,208.

Joslyn, Roger D. "The 1795 Census of Brothertown Indians, Oneida County." *NYG&B Record*, vol. 141, no. 3 (2010): 213–218. [NYG&B eLibrary]

Lankes, Frank J. *An Outline of West Seneca History.* West Seneca, NY: West Seneca Historical Society, 1962.

———. *Reservation Supplement: A Collection of Memorabilia Related to Buffalo Creek Reservation.* West Seneca, NY: West Seneca Historical Society, 1966.

Morrow, Mary Frances. "Indian Bounty Land Applications." *Prologue*, vol. 25, no. 3 (1993). *www.archives.gov/pu blications/prologue/1993/fall/indian-bounty-land-applications.html*

Mortensen, Hyrum K. *Indian Records of the Cumorah Mission.* Salt Lake City: Filmed by the Genealogical Society of Utah, 1974. FHL Microfilm: 924,575. Contains part of the Seneca Indian rolls, census records, from the Cattaraugus and Allegany Indian Reservations.

New York Indian Census, Volume 1: 1866–1899. Bowie, MD: Heritage Press, 2001.

Prevost, Toni Jollay. *Indians from New York, Volumes 1–3.* Bowie, MD: Heritage Press, 1995.

Sivertsen, Barbara J. *Turtles, Wolves and Bears, A Mohawk Family History.* Bowie, MD: Heritage Books, 1993.

Snow, Dean R. *The Iroquois.* New York: Blackwell, 1994.

Starna, William A. *From Homeland to New Land: A History of the Mahican Indians, 1600–1830.* Lincoln: University of Nebraska Press, 2013.

Strong, John A. *The Montaukett Indians of Eastern Long Island.* Syracuse: Syracuse University Press, 2001.

———. *The Unkechaug Indians of Eastern Long Island: A History.* Norman: University of Oklahoma Press, 2011.

Sturtevant, William C., ed. *Handbook of North American Indians: Volume 15: Northeast.* Washington: Smithsonian Institution, 1978.

Tiro, Karim. *The People of the Standing Stone: The Oneida Nation from the Revolution through the Era of Removal.* Amherst: University of Massachusetts Press, 2011.

Venables, Robert W., ed. *The Six Nations of New York: The 1892 United States Extra Census Bulletin.* Ithaca, NY: Cornell University Press, 1996.

Vescey, Christopher, and William A. Starna. *Iroquois Land Claims.* Syracuse: Syracuse University Press, 1988.

Austro-Hungarian (and related, but distinct ethicities)

Historical Overview

The diverse peoples and places of Austria-Hungary were previously part of the Holy Roman Empire and had long been under the rule of the Habsburg family. In 1867, following Austria's expulsion from the German Confederation, the Austrian Empire and the Kingdom of Hungary were joined under one ruler—Franz Joseph I, Emperor of Austria and King of Hungary—to form the Austro-Hungarian Empire. The empire spanned many distinct ethnic groups and included Germans, Magyars, Czechs, Poles, Ruthenians, Romanians, Croats, Serbs, Slovaks, Slovenes, and Italians. See also other sections in this chapter which provide detailed information on German, Italian, Jewish, Polish, and Russian peoples of New York.

The revolutions of 1848 that swept through Europe affected many of the ethnic groups within the empire and spurred immigration to the United States. The first Hungarians arrived in New York City in small numbers and were political refugees, mostly ethnic Magyars who were male, educated, and financially better off than the large waves of immigrants that would follow. A Hungarian glee club was established there in 1851. The Hungarian revolutionary leader Lajos Kossuth was lavishly feted in New York in 1852. Unlike other ethnic groups in Eastern Europe that were often present in multiple countries, virtually all Magyars emigrated from Hungary.

In 1855 political refugees from what is now the Czech Republic and what was then Bohemia founded the Suffolk County hamlet of Bohemia. A larger wave of Czech immigration to New York occurred during the 1860s, and large Czech communities developed in New York City, Chicago, and Cleveland. Slovaks from northern Hungary arrived in New York, as did Germans from Hungary, Romanians, and Croats in smaller numbers. There were concentrations of Austro-Hungarian immigrants on both the Upper East Side and Lower East Side of New York City, as well as in the cities of Buffalo, Syracuse, and Yonkers.

In the aftermath of 1879 legislation that required all men under the age of 50 to remain in Hungary for fulfillment of military service, the number of women emigrants increased greatly. Emigration from Austria-Hungary grew during the 1880s and surged during the years 1890–1914, largely triggered by economic conditions. Despite a severely restrictive emigration law that was enacted in Hungary in 1903, that year alone more than 200,000 Austro-Hungarians immigrated to the United States. The 1910 federal census reported a total of 1.1 million Austrian-born and 495,000 Hungarian-born residents in the United States. The population identified as Austrian was about one-quarter Polish; one-sixth Bohemian and Moravian; and close to one-tenth each German, Jewish, or Slovenian. The Hungarians were comprised of nearly one-half Magyars, one-fifth Slovaks, and one-seventh Germans. The counts for New York residents in 1910 identify 245,000 New Yorkers born in Austria and 96,000 born in Hungary, but do not specify the various ethnicities.

The peak years of Austro-Hungarian immigration to the United States brought huge numbers of people from rural areas, many of whom migrated to rural areas of New York, Pennsylvania, and Ohio, and to other states, especially in the Midwest. These immigrants often accepted low-paying jobs in heavy labor, manufacturing, and agriculture. Immigration between Austria-Hungary and the United States ceased during World War I.

The end of World War I in 1918 brought the collapse of the Austro-Hungarian Empire, which triggered another wave of immigration. Immigration slowed as stability in Europe recovered and the United States imposed strict immigration quotas. Immigration slowed after World War II and the imposition of Communist regimes over almost all of the former empire. The unsuccessful Hungarian revolt in 1956 brought refugees to New York, and, in more recent times, politics, war, and economics have triggered significant immigration to New York by Bosnians, Czechs, Slovaks, Serbians, and Ukrainians.

Genealogical Resources

The resources below have specific relevance to researching Austro-Hungarian immigrants to New York. However, Austro-Hungarian immigrants will also be found in records discussed elsewhere in this book.

Immigration

The National Archives at New York City (NARA-NYC) has microfilm copies of passenger arrival records of immigrants to the Port of New York for the years 1820–1957. *Ancestry.com* has digitized and indexed the full collection; portions of the records are also available elsewhere online. The selected bibliography at the end of this section includes books containing lists of Austro-Hungarian immigrants which may help fill in gaps in the records, whose availability varies with the time period. Researchers are advised to consult original records when available rather than rely solely on indexes and transcriptions. See chapter 4, Immigration, Migration, and Naturalization, for detailed information about records for New York and where they can be accessed.

Census

Because of European border changes following World War I, enumerators of the 1920 federal census were tasked with recording the province or city of origin for immigrants and their descendants who came from the former Austro-Hungarian Empire. Other foreign-born residents were required to name only their country of birth. See also chapter 3, Census Records.

Religious Records

The largest numbers of Austro-Hungarian immigrants to New York were Roman Catholic. German- and Italian-speakers often joined existing Catholic congregations. Distinct Hungarian, Slovak, Bohemian, Croatian, Polish, and Slovene parishes were formed in New York. Eastern Rite Catholic congregations were formed by Hungarians, Romanians, Ruthenians, Slovaks, and Ukrainians. Orthodox congregations were formed by Serbians, Russians, and Ukrainians. The Presbyterian Church in New York conducted extensive mission outreach to members of the Austro-Hungarian community and established several churches that served Slovaks, Hungarians, and Bohemians in New York City.

Austro-Hungarian immigrants also formed congregations in other Protestant denominations, including Reformed, Lutheran, and Baptist. The Hungarian Catholic Mission provides a list of current Hungarian Catholic and Protestant congregations at *hungariancatholicmission.com*. Jewish immigrants from Austria-Hungary often formed and/or joined congregations organized around a shared place of origin. See also chapter 15, Religious Records.

A smaller, Protestant denomination that is deeply rooted in the Austro-Hungarian Empire, the Moravian Church, was organized in 1457 in Bohemia by followers of Czech reformer Jan Hus. Despite persecution, the church spread to Moravia, Poland, Saxony, and North America, where Moravian missionaries ministered to slaves and American Indians. Moravian missionaries came to the Caribbean in 1732, the colony of Georgia in 1735, and later to New York. A Moravian mission to American Indians was established at Shekomeko in Dutchess County in 1740.

Moravian churches were organized in New York City in 1748 and about the same time on Staten Island, most of the members being local converts. Marriages have been published in the *NYG&B Record*. (See "Marriages in the First Moravian Church, New York, 1751–1801" by Harry Macy, Jr. and Lauren Maehrlein, and a second installment covering marriages 1802–1832; Harry Macy's introduction in the first installment provides historical background to the Moravian Church and sources for further information.) The Archive of the Moravian Church in Bethlehem, Pennsylvania (*moravianchurcharchives.org*) holds extensive records of Moravian Missions among American Indians, including its mission in New York. An inventory is at *moravianchurcharchives.org/documents/IndianMissions.pdf*; microfilm of the collection is at several locations, including the New York Public Library (NYPL) and the New York State Library (NYSL). An inventory of New York congregational records is at *moravianchurcharchives.org/documents/ChReg.pdf*.

Newspapers

New York's first Hungarian-language newspaper was the short-lived *Szamuzottek Lapja* (*Hungarian Exiles Journal*), which appeared in 1853. Newspapers in the various other languages of the Austro-Hungarian Empire emerged in the 1880s. The Chronicling America website of the Library of Congress offers the U.S. Newspaper Directory (1690–present), which may be searched by ethnicity, language, location, and keywords, to provide newspaper titles and details on where to access them at *chroniclingamerica.loc.gov/search/titles*. Titles may also be identified through the NYSL's list of more than 10,000 newspaper titles that have been published in New York State at *www.nysl.nysed.gov/nysnp/title4.htm*. See also chapter 12, Newspapers, for information on how to identify and where to access newspapers.

Selected Repositories, Societies, and Websites

For resources pertinent to researching Jewish immigrants from the Austro-Hungarian Empire, see the section on Jewish records in this chapter.

American Hungarian Foundation

300 Somerset Street • PO Box 1084 • New Brunswick, NJ 08903
(732) 846-5777 • Email: info@ahfoundation.org
ahfoundation.org

The Foundation preserves and interprets the history of Hungarians in America since colonial times through a museum and a library, affiliated with Rutgers University, which houses over 60,000 volumes. In addition, it maintains an archive of rare books and documents of historical significance, which pertain to Hungarian immigrants and the social, religious, and political institutions they founded. At the present time the archives have yet to be digitized and access is limited to serious researchers.

American Hungarian Library and Historical Society

Hungarian House • 215 East 82nd Street • New York, NY 10028
(212) 744-5298 • *americanhungarianlibrary.org*

The Society fosters research in and appreciation of Hungarian and Hungarian American history and culture. It maintains a reference library and a lending library; collects books, archives, and artifacts; and produces cultural and education programs.

Archives of Czechs and Slovaks Abroad (ACASA)

University of Chicago • Regenstein Library, Room 263
1100 East 57th Street • Chicago, IL 60637 • (773) 702-8456
Email: jpf3@uchicago.edu
www.lib.uchicago.edu/e/su/slavic/acasa.html

The Archives holds resources relating to immigrants who settled throughout North America, including many periodicals. The holdings are currently being cataloged online.

Bohemia Historical Society

PO Box 67 • Bohemia, New York 11716

Email: bohistsocny@aol.com • *bohemiahistoricalsocietyny.org*

The Society preserves and interprets the history of the community of Bohemia, which was settled in 1854 by Czech immigrants. It maintains a local museum with a photograph and book collection, runs educational and cultural programs, hosts monthly meetings, and publishes a newsletter for members.

Bukovina Society of the Americas

PO Box 81 • Ellis, Kansas 67637

Email: info@bukovinasociety.org • *bukovinasociety.org*

Through its museum and library the Society explores the immigration of Germans from Bukovina, a land at the frontier of Austria-Hungary, in the late–1800s to early–1900s. Its website has extensive resources concerning the genealogy of Bukovina Germans.

Carpatho-Rusyn Genealogy Web Site

rusyn.com

The website gathers genealogical resources relevant to research on Carpatho-Rusyns, who have also been known as Rusyns, Rusins, Rusnaks, Ruthenes, Ruthenians, Carpatho-Russians, Carpatho-Ruthenians, Carpatho-Ukrainians, and Lemkos and lived in the northeastern part of the Empire, now western Ukraine. Some information is also pertinent to other ethnic groups from the region, including Polish, Slovak, Hungarian, Ukrainian, German, and Jewish.

Carpatho-Rusyn Knowledge Base

carpatho-rusyn.org

The website collects and shares a broad range of resources on Carpatho-Rusyn history and culture. Its genealogy page provides links to articles and research advice.

Croatian Genealogy Newsletter

www.durham.net/facts/crogen

This online newsletter is published annually and covers topics related to genealogy within and outside Croatia. The website provides an index and direct access to past issues, as well as a listing of research resources.

Czechoslovak Genealogical Society International (CGSI)

PO Box 16225 • St. Paul, MN 55116-0225

Email: info@cgsi.org • *cgsi.org*

The CGSI provides resources for the genealogical study of ethnic groups of the former Czechoslovakia, including Czech, German-Bohemian, Hungarian, Moravian, Ruthenian, Silesian, Slovakian, and Jewish people. Its website offers instructional guides for conducting research, genealogical queries, a message board, and links to other resources. The Society's extensive library collection is housed at the Minnesota Genealogical Society Library; fee-based research services are available. The CGSI has published the quarterly journal, *Nase rodina*, since 1989.

Foundation for East European Family History Studies (FEEFHS)

PO Box 321 • Springville, UT 84663

Email: conference@feefhs.org • *feefhs.org*

The FEEFHS promotes family history research rooted in Eastern and Central Europe. Its website gathers and presents extensive information on research resources for individual ethnic groups in the region and offers an online map library, a calendar of events of relevant organizations, and a newsfeed on Eastern Europe Genealogy. It organizes the annual Eastern European Research Workshop in Salt Lake City, presents educational workshops, and produces an e-newsletter. Formerly, it published the annual *FEEFHS Journal* (1993–2008), and an index is on the website. In 2014 it announced a focus on indexing and other record discovery projects.

Genealogy of Halychyna /Eastern Galicia

halgal.com

The website provides information and links to resources for conducting family history research on emigrants from Halychyna, eastern Galicia, and western Ukraine.

Gesher Galicia

geshergalicia.org

The organization provides online resources for genealogical research relating to Galicia, a province of the former Austro-Hungarian Empire, which is today part of eastern Poland and southwestern Ukraine. With a focus on digitizing archival records of Galicia, its website has a database of more than 200,000 records covering 600,000 people, a digital map room, and instructional information. The organization also publishes the quarterly journal, *The Galitzianer*.

Gottscheer Heritage & Genealogy Association

gottschee.org

The Association assists researchers to explore the culture, history, and genealogical records of Gottscheers and Gottschee in today's Slovenia. It has published the journal, the *Gottschee Tree*, quarterly since 1987. Its website provides access to useful information for researchers, including a family and surname database, a genealogical queries page, and links to other resources for Gottscheer research.

Leo Baeck Institute (LBI)

Center for Jewish History • 15 West 16th Street
New York, NY 10011 • (212) 744-6400 • *lbi.org*

The LBI is dedicated to the study of the history and culture of German-speaking Jewry. The Austrian Heritage Collection documents the history of Austrian-Jewish émigrés who settled in the United States during the Nazi years. An online catalog, digital collections, and finding aids can be accessed at *cjh.org*. See chapter 16 for detailed information about the extensive genealogical resources of the Center for Jewish History, which is home to the LBI and four other Jewish repositories.

Moravian Heritage Society

czechusa.com

Founded in 1994, the Society promotes the history and culture of Moravia, the eastern half of today's Czech Republic. It publishes the quarterly newsletter *Morava Krasna*, maintains a database of Moravian immigrants to the United States, and offers genealogical research services to its members.

National Czech & Slovak Museum & Library

1400 Inspiration Place SW • Cedar Rapids, IA 52404

(319) 362-8500 • *ncsml.org*

The Museum encourages the appreciation of Czech and Slovak culture and the contributions of its immigrants to the United States. The genealogy page of the website provides lists of useful resources and links to other Czech and Slovak genealogy websites. The library's collection includes some cultural archives and oral histories accessible online.

New York Public Library (NYPL)

Stephen A. Schwarzman Building • Fifth Avenue at 42nd Street
New York, NY 10018-2788 • *nypl.org*

The New York Public Library has extensive holdings of Slavic and East European materials, dating from the fourteenth century to the present. A collection description is at *www.nypl.org/locations/tid/36/node/138855*. See chapter 16 for detailed information about the NYPL's extensive genealogical resources.

Romanian Genealogy Society

1185 N. Concord Street, Suite 218 • South St. Paul, MN 55075
Email: info@romaniangenealogy.com • *romaniangenealogy.com*

The Society fosters interest in Romanian genealogy and develops resources for researchers. Its growing library collection is housed at the Minnesota Genealogical Society Library. Members receive the quarterly newsletter, *Romanian Roots*, and may request research and translation services.

Slovak Heritage and Folklore Society International

151 Colebrook Drive • Rochester, NY 14617

(716) 342-9383 • *slovakpride.homestead.com*

The Society publishes *Slovakia* magazine for its members. Its website offers access to a database of more than 25,000 ancestral surnames from Slovakia and neighboring regions.

Slovenian Genealogical Society International

sloveniangenealogy.org

The Society assists its members in conducting their own genealogy research. It has published the *Linden Tree* newsletter quarterly since 1987 and maintains a website with online indexes and a discussion board. Its library is open by appointment to members and is located at the Slovenian Museum and Archives (see listing below).

Slovenian Museum and Archives (SMA)

6407 St. Clair Avenue • Cleveland, Ohio 44103

(216) 347-9888 • *smacleveland.org*

The SMA seeks to preserve and share the history of Slovenians in America, their immigrant experience, and family histories. In partnership with the Slovenian Studies Center at Cleveland State University, it offers services to historians, researchers, students and genealogists.

Selected Bibliography and Further Reading

Balch, Emily Greene. *Our Slavic Fellow Citizens*. New York: Arno Press, 1969.

Brandt, Edward R. *Contents and Addresses of Hungarian Archives: With Supplementary Material for Research on German Ancestors from Hungary*. Baltimore: Clearfield Publishing Co., 1998.

Capek, Thomas. *The Čech (Bohemian) Community of New York, with Introductory Remarks on the Čechslovaks in the United States*. New York: America's Making, 1921.

Centennial History Book Committee. *A History of Bohemia, Long Island*. Saylorville, NY: Weeks & Reichel Printing, 1985.

Church of Jesus Christ of Latter-day Saints. "The Austro-Hungarian Empire Boundary Changes and Their Effect on Genealogical Research." Series C, No. 18. [*books.FamilySearch.org*]

Fedor, Helen. "The Slovaks in America." *www.loc.gov/rr/european/imsk/slovakia.html*

Jerin, Robert. *Searching for Your Croatian Roots: A Handbook*. Shaker Heights, OH: R. M. Jerin, 2002.

Kovtun, George. "The Czechs in America." *www.loc.gov/rr/european/imcz/ndl.html*

Macy, Harry, Jr. (introduction) and Lauren Maehrlein (transcription). "Marriages in the First Moravian Church, New York, 1751–1801." *NYG&B Record*, vol. 134, no. 1: 22–26 (2003); 1802–1832 by an unidentified transcriber, vol. 141, no. 2 (2010): 121–128. [NYG&B eLibrary]

Miller, Olga K. *Genealogical Research for Czech and Slovak Americans*. Detroit: Gale Research Co, 1978.

Orenstein, Marie S., and Adam S. Eterovich. *Croatians and Serbians in New York City*. 1912. Reprint, San Carlos, CA: Ragusan Press, 1983.

Pallen, Condé B., ed. *A Memorial of Andrew J. Shipman, His Life and Writings*. New York: Encyclopedia Press, 1916. Includes essays on Hungarian Catholics, Greek Catholics, Eastern Rite Catholics, Poles, Slavs, and other immigrants in the United States.

Perlman, Robert. *Bridging Three Worlds: Hungarian-Jewish Americans, 1848–1914*. Amherst, MA: University of Massachusetts Press, 2009.

Pihach, John D. *Ukrainian Genealogy: A Beginner's Guide*. Edmonton, Alberta: Canadian Institute of Ukrainian Studies Press, 2007.

Schlyter, Daniel M. *A Handbook of Czechoslovak Genealogical Research*. Buffalo Grove, IL: Genun Publishers, 1985.

Senekovic, Dagmar. *Handy Guide to Austrian Genealogical Records*. Logan, Utah: Everton Publishers, 1979.

Shelley, Thomas J. *Slovaks on the Hudson: Most Holy Trinity Church, Yonkers, and the Slovak Catholics of the Archdiocese of New York, 1894–2000*. Washington: Catholic University of America Press, 2002.

Shmelev, Anatol. *Tracking a Diaspora: Émigrés from Russia and Eastern Europe in the Repositories*. Binghamton, NY: Haworth Information Press, 2006.

Smith, Clifford Neal. *Reconstructed Passenger Lists for 1851 via Hamburg: Emigrants from Germany, Austria, Bohemia, Hungary, Poland, Russia, Scandinavia, and Switzerland to Australia, Brazil, Canada, Chile, the United States, and Venezuela*. McNeal, AZ: Westland Publications, 1986.

Stipanovich, Joseph. *Slavic Americans: A Study Guide and Source Book*. San Francisco: R&E Research Associates, 1977.

Suess, Jared H. *Handy Guide to Hungarian Genealogical Records*. Logan, Utah: Everton Publishers, 1980.

Tajtak, Ladislav. "Slovak Emigration and Migration in the Years 1900-1914." *Studia Historica Slovaca*, vol. 10 (1978): 43–86.

Tanzone, Daniel F. *Slovaks of Yonkers, New York*. Middletown, PA: Jednota Printery, 1975.

Wellauer, Maralyn A. *Tracing Your Czech and Slovak Roots*. Milwaukee: The Author, 1980.

Wertsman, Vladimir. *Romanians in the United States and Canada: A Guide to Ancestry and Heritage Research*. North Salt Lake, UT: HeritageQuest, 2002.

———. *The Ukrainians in America, 1608–1975: A Chronology & Fact Book*. Dobbs Ferry, NY: Oceana Publications, 1976.

Chinese

Historical Overview

Some Chinese traders and sailors came to the United States during the China Trade that flourished from the 1780s through the first half of the nineteenth century, as clipper ships transported tea, textiles, porcelain, and other products from Canton (now known as Guangzhou) to seaports in New York and New England. It is estimated that about 150 Chinese men lived in New York City in the 1850s including sailors, peddlers, servants, merchants, and students.

Immigration to California by large numbers of Chinese began in the mid-nineteenth century. The United States drew immigrants seeking economic opportunity, largely from the provinces of Guangdong and Fujian. Many were brought to the United States as laborers to help build the railroads and other infrastructure, such as irrigation projects in major cities; others were enticed by the Gold Rush. By 1880 there were approximately 74,000 Chinese-born immigrants residing in California.

Following the completion of the Transcontinental Railroad in 1869, the number of manual labor jobs declined; some Chinese migrated eastward to seek employment and to escape growing anti-Chinese discrimination that was exacerbated by fear of labor competition. In New York State a large number of Chinese found employment in restaurants and laundries. An influx of about 300 Chinese who were brought from California to New Jersey to work in a Belleville, New Jersey laundry spurred many of them to migrate to New York. Chinese-owned hand laundries soon proliferated and numbered an estimated 2,000 in New York City by 1890 and spread to other locations in New York State. The Albany city directory for 1877 listed one Chinese laundry; by 1920 the directory listed 24. There were reportedly 40 Chinese laundries operating in or near Buffalo in 1902.

Some Chinese workers arrived by way of Cuba to work in New York City's cigar industry. New York City's Chinatown took root in its present location in the 1870s, as Chinese-owned businesses, social clubs, and benevolent societies were established there. Chinese workers, however, frequently lived nearby or on the premises of their workplaces, which were scattered throughout the city. Federal census figures report that by 1880 there were 1,015 Chinese-born residents of New York State; this number grew to 6,880 in 1900, and 7,512 in 1930. The city of Buffalo had 102 Chinese-born residents in 1920.

The Chinese community in New York is often described as a bachelor society, as it was comprised overwhelmingly of single men. Male immigrants from China, often temporary workers who intended to return home, had always outnumbered females. This trend was reinforced by the Page Act of 1875, whose clause prohibiting the entry of prostitutes from China was often broadly applied to all Chinese women. Consequently, Chinese men sometimes married outside their race, and marriages with Irish American women were not uncommon.

Successive discriminatory laws against Chinese immigrants were enacted at the local and federal levels, culminating in the 1882 Chinese Exclusion Act, the first federal law to severely restrict immigration based on nationality. The act prohibited the immigration of Chinese laborers to the United States and prevented Chinese immigrants from obtaining citizenship. The Chinese Exclusion Act was extended in 1892 in the form of the Geary Act and made permanent from 1902 to 1943. Legal immigration from China was limited to merchants, teachers, and consular officials—their wives and children—and the children of Chinese American citizens. Travel by Chinese who were resident in the United States before 1882 was allowed, but required registration and substantial documentation.

Many Chinese immigrants chose to bypass the Exclusion Act by entering the United States across New York's Canadian border, which did not have federal immigration stations until 1895. At the turn of twentieth century, "Chinese jails" for the purpose of detaining illegal immigrants existed in New York State in Malone (Franklin County), Massena (St. Lawrence County), Plattsburgh (Clinton County), and Port Henry (Essex County). Chinese American citizens sometimes assisted other immigrants to enter the United States through the creation of "paper families," facilitating an individual's immigration by claiming to be parents or spouses.

Restrictions on Chinese immigration were relaxed slightly in 1943 when the Magnuson Act was passed, introducing a quota allowing 105 Chinese immigrants annually. The Refugee Relief Act of 1953 allowed refugees from the Chinese Communist Revolution to immigrate. Finally, in 1965 the Immigration and Nationality Services Act removed discriminatory quotas based on country of origin and encouraged immigration by family members of citizens and permanent residents, as well as by professionals. The number of Chinese-born New Yorkers grew from 22,000 in 1960 to 300,000 in 2000. Today the New York City neighborhoods of Elmhurst and Flushing in Queens and Sunset Park in Brooklyn have very large Chinese populations, and growing numbers of Chinese Americans have settled in Nassau county and other suburbs of New York City. In 2010 New Yorkers of Chinese ancestry totaled an estimated 1,600 in Syracuse, 1,200 in Albany, and 950 in Buffalo.

Naming Customs

Variations in name forms and spellings for Chinese Americans in records abound, complicating the family research process. While it is Chinese tradition for the surname to precede the given name, the surname often appears as the given name in American records. The limited number of Chinese surnames poses an added challenge; it is estimated that more than 70 percent of China's population shares 100 common surnames

from a total of about 4,000. There is greater variety among given names, which convey special meaning for each individual. An individual might have multiple given names—formal, informal, Western—and use a different given name on different occasions. It should be noted that counterfeit genealogies with false names were often used to create "paper families." Individuals who successfully entered the United States under false names generally retained the false names. Some individuals eventually resumed their original names after participating in the Chinese Confession Program, which was introduced in 1956 and encouraged "paper families" to rectify their illegal status.

Spelling variations are common and can be attributed not only to American officials unfamiliar with the Chinese language, but to evolving transliteration methods. The Pinyin system of transcribing Chinese characters to the Roman alphabet, based on Mandarin pronunciation and developed in the 1950s, is the international standard today. Guangdong Romanization, developed in 1960, addresses Cantonese and other southern dialects.

The free Chinese Surname pages at *http://freepages.family. rootsweb.ancestry.com/~chinesesurname* offer a variety of useful information for genealogical research, including a surname list with both the Pinyin transliteration and the Chinese characters for each name. Recording family histories has long been of cultural importance in China, and *FamilySearch.org* has digitized and made freely accessible more than twelve million Chinese genealogies in its collection China, Collection of Genealogies, 1239–2013 at *https://familysearch.org/search/ collection/1787988*. Clicking on the browse option will reveal a list of names with both Chinese characters and Western translations. Occasionally, these records may include Chinese American family members.

Genealogical Resources

The resources below have specific relevance to researching Chinese immigrants to New York. However, Chinese immigrants will also be found in records discussed elsewhere in this book.

Immigration

The federal legislation restricting Chinese immigration created a large body of unique records that are rich in genealogical information. The National Archives (NARA) reference guide "Chinese Immigration and the Chinese in the United States" describes the extensive range of available records and identifies the collections held by each of its regional repositories; it may be accessed at *www.archives.gov/research/chinese-americans/ guide.html*.

The New York Chinese Exclusion Index to over 18,500 case files, created by the New York District Office of the Immigration and Naturalization Service from 1882 to 1960, is available at *Ancestry.com*. The case files document entry of Chinese aliens into the United States and the reentry of American citizens of Chinese ancestry. The index includes names, often both English and Chinese, and case numbers. Most entries include information about age, birthplace, town of origin, occupation, name of wife, children, and sponsor, and whether the case file includes a photograph, as well as comments. The original records are held by NARA at New York City (NARA-NYC). See the NARA entry in chapter 16.

The *Ancestry.com* database U.S. Chinese Immigration Case Files, 1883–1924 provides links to images of case file records from the Western District Court of Texas at El Paso (1892–1915), the INS District No. 4 Regional Office at Philadelphia (1900–1923), and San Francisco, California (ca. 1883–ca. 1916). Other relevant databases may be found by clicking the catalog tab and searching on the keyword "Chinese."

NARA holds passenger and immigration lists. Many are on microfilm and are widely available. *Ancestry.com* has digitized and indexed many of NARA's immigration records, including passenger arrival records for the ports of New York (1820–1957) and California (1882–1959), as well as Canadian border crossings to New York (1895–1956). The collection "California, Passenger and Crew Lists, 1882–1959" includes records from the Angel Island Immigration Station where Chinese immigrants were detained between 1910 and 1940. See also chapter 4, Immigration, Migration, and Naturalization.

Newspapers

New York's first Chinese-language newspaper was the *Chinese American*, a short-lived weekly published in New York City by the journalist and activist Wong Chin Foo in 1883. The holdings of the Museum of Chinese in America include several Chinese newspapers published in New York. The Chronicling America website of the Library of Congress offers the U.S. Newspaper Directory (1690–present), which may be searched by ethnicity, language, location, and keywords, to provide newspaper titles and details on where to access them at *chroniclingamerica.loc.gov/search/titles*. Chinese titles may also be identified through the New York State Library's list of more than 10,000 newspaper titles that have been published in New York State at *www.nysl.nysed.gov/nysnp/title4.htm*. See also chapter 12, Newspapers, for information on how to identify and where to access newspapers.

Religious Records

Chinese immigrants to New York brought with them a variety of belief systems, including Buddhism, Confucianism, and Taoism. Christian missionaries from various denominations had been active in China since the early-nineteenth century, and Christian missions in New York City ministered to the Chinese community from its earliest days, providing English language instruction as well as religious education. A Methodist mission was established in 1854, followed by Presbyterian, Baptist, Episcopal, and other missions. As the Chinese population grew, some missions gave rise to churches with Chinese

congregations. In 1910 the First Chinese Presbyterian Church of New York City was organized, and the Reverend Huie Kin installed as its first pastor. The First Chinese Baptist Church was established in 1926. More recently, Chinese congregations have formed among various evangelical Protestant denominations. See also chapter 15, Religious Records.

Cemetery Records

Traditionally, the remains of deceased Chinese were returned to their families in China for permanent burial after a temporary interment at a local cemetery. Chinese mutual aid societies provided burial repatriation services to their members. Interments of Chinese took place at the New York Bay Cemetery in the Greenville section of Jersey City, New Jersey, in the early-nineteenth century, and subsequently at Brooklyn's Green-Wood Cemetery. In the latter part of the nineteenth century, a large number of Chinese burials took place at the Evergreens Cemetery in Brooklyn, in an area called Celestial Hill. Not all Chinese interments were temporary, however. Terry Abraham has compiled a list of cemeteries with a significant number of Chinese burials at *http://webpages.uidaho.edu/special-collections/papers/ch_cem.htm*. See also chapter 9, Cemetery Records.

Mutual Aid Societies

To provide financial assistance, temporary food and lodging, and social, cultural, and business opportunities for immigrants, individuals in the Chinese community formed a variety of mutual aid societies, including family associations of individuals that shared a common surname; village associations of individuals from the same district in China (*hui guan* or *guang suo*); and merchant guilds. Many of these groups are constituent members of the Chinese Consolidated Benevolent Association (CCBA), an umbrella organization established in 1883 that plays a leadership role in coordinating charitable, cultural, education, commercial, and social activities among New York City's Chinese American community (see listing below). See also chapter 10, Business, Institutional, and Organizational Records.

Selected Repositories, Societies, and Websites
The China Institute
125 East 65th Street • New York, NY 10065
(212) 744-8181 • *chinainstitute.org*

Founded in 1926 by leading American and Chinese educators, the China Institute promotes Chinese cultural appreciation through language classes, education programs, exhibitions, and film screenings. A membership organization, the Institute makes digital educational resources available through its *china360online.org* website.

Chinese Consolidated Benevolent Association
62 Mott Street • New York, NY 10013 • (212) 226-6280
Email: ccbany@yahoo.com • *ccbanyc.org*

The Chinese Consolidated Benevolent Association is the oldest service organization in New York City's Chinatown, the parent of the Chinese Community Center, and home to the New York Chinese School, which was founded in 1909. Its membership comprises 60 Chinese American societies that are based on kinship, place of origin, or occupation; a listing of CCBA members is at *http://ccbanyc.org/emember.html*.

Chinese Historical Society of America (CHSA)

965 Clay Street • San Francisco, CA 94108 • (415) 391-1188

Email: info@chsa.org • *chsa.org*

Founded in 1963 the CHSA is the oldest and largest organization dedicated to the documentation, study, and presentation of Chinese American history through exhibitions, education programs, and publications. Its website provides online exhibitions and access to the Him Mark Lai Digital Archive Project, with over 200 published and unpublished works by Chinese American historian Him Mark Lai at *himmarklai.org*. The Society has published the journal *Chinese America: History & Perspectives* annually since 1987.

Chinese Historical Society of New England

China Trade Center • 2 Boylston Street, G-3 • Boston, MA 02116 (617) 338-4339 • Email: info@chsne.org • *chsne.org*

The Society preserves and interprets the contributions of Chinese immigrants in New England through education programs, exhibitions, publications, and collections. Its growing archival collection documents the Chinese experience in New England.

Museum of Chinese in America (MOCA)

215 Centre Street • New York, NY 10013 • (212) 619-4785

Email: info@mocanyc.org • *mocanyc.org*

The museum preserves and presents the history, heritage, culture, and experiences of Chinese Americans through exhibitions and education programs, including a core exhibition on 160 years of Chinese American history. Its growing collections of artifacts, photographs, oral histories, and archival and library materials document the Chinese immigrant experience in America. Museum members may research the collection for free; fees apply for nonmembers. A research application is on the website. Questions about conducting archival research may be emailed to collections@mocanyc.org. The museum's website provides access to a timeline of Chinese American history, summaries of key legislation and court cases between 1850 and 1943 that affected Chinese immigration, and online collections.

Selected Bibliography and Further Reading

Barde, Robert. "An Alleged Wife: One Immigrant in the Chinese Exclusion Era." *Prologue*, vol. 36, no. 1 (2004). *www.archives. gov/publications/prologue/2004/spring/alleged-wife-1.html*

Beck, Louis J. *New York's Chinatown: An Historical Presentation of Its People and Places.* New York, 1898.

Bonner, Arthur. *Alas! What Brought Thee Hither? The Chinese in New York, 1800–1950.* Madison, NJ: Fairleigh Dickinson University Press, 1997.

— — —. Arthur Bonner Papers (1980–1996). New York, Manuscripts and Archives Division, The New York Public Library. The collection contains transcripts and facsimile images of original material used to write the foregoing book.

Byers, Paula K., ed. *Asian American Genealogical Sourcebook.* Detroit: Gale Research, 1995.

Chao, Sheau-yueh J. *In Search of Your Asian Roots: Genealogical Research on Chinese Surnames.* Baltimore: Genealogical Publishing Co., 2000.

Cowan, Alison Leigh. "53 Questions That a Life May Depend On." *New York Times*, July 17, 2009, *http://cityroom.blogs. nytimes.com/tag/chinese-exclusion-act*.

Hall, Bruce. *Tea That Burns: A Family Memoir of Chinatown.* New York: Free Press, 1998.

Hsu, Madeline S. *Dreaming of Gold, Dreaming of Home: Transnationalism and Migration between the United States and South China, 1882–1943.* Stanford, CA: Stanford University Press, 2000.

Kane, Alice. "Chinese-American Genealogy." New England Historic Genealogical Society. *www.americanancestors.org/ chinese-american-guide*

Kwong, Peter. *Chinatown, New York: Labor and Politics, 1930– 1950.* New York: Monthly Review Press, 1979.

— — —. *The New Chinatown.* New York: Hill & Wang, 1987.

Lai, Him Mark. *Becoming Chinese American: A History of Communities and Institutions.* Walnut Creek, CA: Alta Mira Press, 1994.

Lau, Estelle T. *Paper Families: Identity, Immigration Administration, and Chinese Exclusion.* Durham, NC: Duke University Press, 2007.

Lee, Erika. *At America's Gates: Chinese Immigration during the Exclusion Era, 1882–1943.* Chapel Hill: University of North Carolina Press, 2003.

Lee, Lai T. *Early Chinese Immigrant Societies: Case Studies from North America and British Southeast Asia.* Singapore: Heinemann Asia, 1988.

Lo, Karl, and H. M. Lai. *Chinese Newspapers Published in North America, 1854–1975.* Washington: Center for Chinese Research Materials, Association of Research Libraries, 1977.

Low, Jeanie W. Chooey. *China Connection: Finding Ancestral Roots for Chinese in America.* 2nd edition. San Francisco: J. W. C. Low, 1993.

New York Correction History Society. "Ledgers of the Essex County Jail: Operating Expenses Audit Book, 1904–1931." Provides information about the detention in New York State of illegal Chinese immigrants who attempted to cross the Canadian border at the turn of the twentieth century. *www.correctionhistory.org/html/chronicl/essex/essexnyjailledgers02.html*

New York State Archives. "Legacies Project: Chinese and Latino Community Histories and Document Based Questions." *www.archives.nysed.gov/projects/legacies/bufchinese/history1.shtml*

Nicola, Patricia Hackett. "Chinese Exclusion Act Records: A Neglected Genealogical Source," *APGQ*, vol. 21 (March 2006): 25–30. *http://home.comcast.net/~btnicola/APGQMar06.pdf*

Peffer, George Anthony. *If They Don't Bring Their Women Here: Chinese Female Immigration before Exclusion.* Chicago: University of Illinois Press, 1999.

Salyer, Lucy. *Laws Harsh as Tigers: Chinese Immigrants and the Shaping of Modern Immigration Law.* Chapel Hill: University of North Carolina Press, 1995.

Seligman, Scott D. *The Remarkable Life of Wong Chin Foo.* Hong Kong, China: Hong Kong University Press, 2013. Biography of the nineteenth-century journalist and activist who moved to New York City in 1874.

She, Colleen. *A Student's Guide to Chinese American Genealogy.* Phoenix: Oryx Press, 1996.

Siener, William H. "Through the Back Door: Evading the Chinese Exclusion Act along the Niagara Frontier, 1900 to 1924." *Journal of American Ethnic History*, vol. 27, no. 4 (2008): 34–70.

Sung, Betty Lee. "Archival Records of Chinese Immigrants in New York." *Chinese America: History and Perspectives*, vol. 13 (1999): 80–84.

Tchen, John Kuo Wei. *Chinese American: Exclusion/Inclusion.* New York: New-York Historical Society, 2014.

———. *New York before Chinatown: Orientalism and the Shaping of American Culture, 1776–1882.* Baltimore: Johns Hopkins University Press, 2001.

Van Norden, Warner M. *Who's Who of the Chinese in New York.* New York: The Author, 1918. Includes short biographies and addresses of Chinese men, business listings, and societies in New York City.

Wang, Xinyang. *Surviving the City: The Chinese Immigrant Experience in New York City 1890–1970.* Lanham, MD: Rowman & Littlefield Publishers, 2001.

Dutch

Historical Overview

Between 1624 and 1664, when New Netherland was conquered by the English, it received a steady stream of immigrants from the Netherlands, but that influx largely ceased after the conquest. The next wave of Dutch immigration, which began in about 1840, was directed mostly to the midwestern states. Since World War II there has been some immigration to the United States, including New York, from the Netherlands and its former colonies. However, most Americans or Canadians who have New York Dutch ancestry trace that ancestry to the New Netherland immigrants.

The New Netherland Dutch Community

In the seventeenth century the successful Dutch war for independence from Spain led to the Dutch Golden Age, during which that small nation became one of the world's major economic powers, famous for its culture and tolerance. As such, it attracted immigrants from all over Europe, some seeking religious freedom and others pursuing a better life. While Dutch and Frisians from the Dutch Republic (the modern Netherlands) constituted a majority of the European immigrants to New Netherland, the "Dutch" community that emerged from New Netherland was actually a melting pot that also included Flemings and Walloons from the southern or Spanish Netherlands (modern Belgium and northernmost France); Huguenots from France; people from the many parts of the German Empire; Danes, Norwegians, and Swedes; and a few individuals from many other European countries, as well as North Africa.

Some of the English, Irish, Scots, and Welsh who settled in New Netherland also became part of this community, as did several French migrants from New France (Québec), and a little native Indian blood was also added to the mix. The process that created a community from these disparate strands was the result of innumerable marriages across ethnic lines and the use of Dutch as a common language. The Dutch Reformed Church also helped bind these peoples together.

Clues to the colonists' places of origin abound in the civil and religious records of New Netherland, and in European archives. Except for most of the English settlers, the European immigrants who came to New Netherland sailed from the port of Amsterdam, but some went first to other Dutch colonies, especially northeastern Brazil, which the Dutch lost to Portugal in 1654; the East Indies (modern Indonesia); and the West Indian islands of Curaçao and St. Eustatius. These alternate migration routes are mentioned in New Netherland records of those immigrants.

The Dutch community formed a majority of the population of New York until sometime in the eighteenth century, when the English became the majority group. Also in that century the English language slowly replaced Dutch. By the mid-nineteenth century some of the oldest members of the community could still speak their native tongue, and it survived in a few remote pockets until the beginning of the twentieth century. As the Dutch community became English-speaking, the number of marriages to non-Dutch spouses increased, and today, while the New Netherlanders have millions of descendants, few of those descendants have ancestry that can be traced entirely to the old Dutch colony.

Locations of the earliest Dutch settlements and later migrations from those settlements are discussed in chapter 1, Colonial Era, and chapter 4, Immigration, Migration, and Naturalization. From their initial settlements the Dutch spread into all of colonial New York's counties, and also migrated on a large scale into New Jersey, with a few going further west and south. At the end of the American Revolution some Loyalist New York Dutch went to Nova Scotia/New Brunswick and Upper Canada (Ontario), and they have numerous descendants in both the United States and Canada. The Dutch from eastern New York and from New Jersey also migrated into central and western New York State as those regions opened to settlement, but they settled in communities where they were almost always a small minority, and they soon lost their separate identity.

Low and High Dutch

Researchers may encounter the terms "Low Dutch" and "High Dutch," particularly in eighteenth-century records. When the Palatines and other Germans arrived in eighteenth-century New York, English-speaking New Yorkers usually called them Dutch (from *Deutsch*). To distinguish them from the Netherlanders, the latter were often called Low Dutch (people from the Low Countries or *Nederlanden*), while immigrants from the German states were called High Dutch. In the nineteenth century "Holland Dutch" was often used for the same purpose. Nowadays in the United States, except for the "Pennsylvania Dutch," Germans are called Germans, and plain "Dutch" is understood to mean the people of the Netherlands.

Naming Customs

Successful research into the families of New Netherland and their descendants for many generations requires an understanding of Dutch naming customs, which were adopted by all of the peoples absorbed into the Dutch community and were quite different from naming practices of the English and other groups. For a long time these customs were not fully understood by American genealogists, causing numerous errors in early published genealogies, some of which are yet to be corrected.

Basically, Dutch tradition required that the first two sons and first two daughters be named for the four grandparents, and subsequent children named for great-grandparents or for

aunts and uncles (who often bore the same names as the great-grandparents). When a child died, the next child of that sex was often given the same name, especially if it was the name of a grandparent. A widow or widower who remarried would name a child for their deceased spouse. If an aunt or uncle died before their time, the next child in the family might be named for them, even before the grandparents were honored. Children were only rarely given names from outside the family. Until the nineteenth century, most New York Dutch families observed these customs.

Many seventeenth-century men and women from the Netherlands, Scandinavia, and northern Germany arrived in New Netherland without permanent surnames, being known only by patronymics (their father's name) which changed with every generation. Thus the children of a Willem Janszen (Willem son of Jan) would be called Willemszen, not Janszen. After the English conquest it became clear that this could cause confusion in the new legal system, especially with regard to identifying heirs or tracing property titles; by 1700 most of these people had adopted fixed surnames, though some continued to use at least a patronymic initial to help distinguish them from others of the same name. The adopted surnames might be the family's current patronymic; a "van" name with their European place of origin; a surname that the family had used in the old country, sometimes on the mother's side; or a surname based on an occupation or physical characteristic. In some cases brothers or first cousins adopted different surnames, even though they had a common male ancestor.

Dutch women traditionally did not assume their husbands' surnames after marriage, retaining their own surnames or patronymics. In some records what appears to be a woman's patronymic actually indicates the name of her husband, for example, Marytje Pieters the wife of William Janszen might be called Marytje Willems. These practices also caused confusion after the English took over—an English clerk might record Marytje Pieters as Mary Johnson, mistaking her husband's patronymic for a surname—so it is not surprising that these practices died out. The naming customs are well covered in papers by Rosalie Bailey and Kenn Stryker-Rodda (see bibliography).

Genealogical Resources

The resources below have specific relevance to researching Dutch immigrants to New York. However, Dutch immigrants will also be found in records discussed elsewhere in this book.

Immigration

A collection of early passenger lists, *Ship Passenger Lists, New York and New Jersey 1600–1825*, was published in 1978 compiled by Carl Boyer. The lists for 1654–1664 can also be found in the 1902 *Year Book* of the Holland Society of New York, available at *HathiTrust.org*.

Ancestry.com has the following searchable databases for nineteenth- and twentieth-century Dutch immigration, which are based on information extracted by Robert Swierenga from passenger list records held by the National Archives (NARA): *Dutch Immigrants to America, 1820–1880: Records from NARA Passenger Lists of Vessels Arriving at New York, New York, 1820–1897* and *Dutch Immigrants to America: New York Passenger Lists, 1881–1894*. Information includes name, gender, age, occupation, port of embarkation, port of arrival, date of arrival, intended destination, family status, country of origin, birthplace, occupation, and ship accommodations.

Passenger Lists of the Holland-America Line 1900–1940, a microfiche publication of records in the Municipal Archives of Rotterdam, provides information on that company's ships departing from Dutch ports. Many of the passengers on these ships were Dutch citizens (but not all were immigrants). The microfiche publication is available at the New York Public Library (NYPL) and from the Family History Library (FHL). See also chapter 4, Immigration, Migration, and Naturalization.

Census Records

Natives of the Netherlands living in New York State in the mid-nineteenth century are identified in Robert Swierenga's *Dutch Households in U.S. Population Censuses, 1850, 1860, 1870*. See also chapter 3, Census Records.

Religious Records

At the time New Netherland was settled, the Dutch relied on their churches to keep their vital records, making religious records perhaps the most important single source for tracing the early generations of their families. In New Netherland only the Dutch Reformed Church was permitted to hold public worship services, except in the colony's English settlements. Regardless of their religious background, settlers in the Dutch communities came to the Reformed Church to be married or have their children baptized, and to be buried. The church deacons also cared for the poor of the community.

While there are gaps in the records of some congregations, an amazing number of church records have survived. The early baptismal records usually name the witnesses to the baptism, who more often than not were relatives. Early marriage and membership records often indicate places of birth or origin, as well as married women's maiden names or patronymics.

When searching for a Dutch family in church records, the Reformed Church records should be checked first. For the eighteenth or nineteenth centuries, if there are Lutheran, Moravian, Anglican, or Presbyterian records for the same area they should also be searched. When checking records of English churches, some creativity may be needed to recognize Dutch names which the recorder may have attempted to spell in phonetic English. (See also chapter 15, Religious Records.)

Getting Started

To begin research on a New Netherland Dutch family, Henry Hoff's article "Researching New York Dutch Families: A Checklist Approach" identifies the principal sources that may be utilized. David Riker's *Genealogical and Biographical Directory to Persons in New Netherland, from 1613 to 1674* is an attempt to identify every known immigrant to New Netherland through 1674, giving an outline of that individual's marriage and children and listing both original and derivative sources to be checked for further information.

There are other, predominantly older, works that attempt to cover all of the Dutch families in a given community, and these will be found listed in the County Guides in Part Two.

Compiled Genealogies

Best practices in genealogy require documentation from original sources. However, if someone else has compiled a genealogy of the family, it is worthwhile to consult his or her work. Genealogies of many New Netherland families have been published as separate books or in collections of genealogies, or as articles in periodicals, or they are available in manuscript collections. All of these possibilities need to be explored. Compiled genealogies may contain errors and need to be verified in original sources. Articles in the major journals, which have been either written or edited by professional genealogists and subjected to peer review, often provide the most reliable compilation of a family. Riker identifies many of them.

The periodicals with the most coverage of New Netherland families are the *New York Genealogical and Biographical Record*, the *Genealogical Magazine of New Jersey*, and *New Netherland Connections*. Among other periodicals to check are *The American Genealogist* and *The Genealogist*. Riker cites some of these articles, but researchers should also consult indexes to the individual periodicals, as well as the various overall periodical indexes such as PERSI. Henry B. Hoff, while coeditor of the *NYG&B Newsletter* (now *New York Researcher*), compiled a series of articles identifying Dutch and other New York families in both published and manuscript collective genealogies. Another series of *NYG&B Newsletter* articles by Hoff identifies genealogies of Dutch and other New York families in the major journals (other than the *NYG&B Record*, which has its own indexes at *NewYorkFamilyHistory.org*). Hoff's articles may be found in the Research Aids collection at *NewYorkFamilyHistory.org* and also in its eLibrary. See also chapter 17, Reference Shelf.

Land Records

In addition to the above mentioned records, there are land records. The Dutch West India Company (WIC) granted small farms and city lots to settlers, and their directors were authorized to privately finance the purchase and settlement of larger territories known as patroonships. The first patroonship,

Rensselaerswijck, was begun in 1629, and originally encompassed all of present-day Albany and Rensselaer counties. When the English took over in 1664, Rensselaerswijck was the only patroonship still in existence; it was later called Van Rensselaer Manor and lasted until 1839.

Most of the WIC land grants are abstracted by Charles Gehring in the Land Papers volume of New York Historical Manuscripts: Dutch (see chapter 7, Land Records). The New York State Library (NYSL) houses the Van Rensselaer Manor Papers; some have been added to the NYSL's Digital Collections for the colonial period (*www.nysl.nysed.gov/scandocs/colonial.htm*), including "Contract of Sale of Land Along the Hudson River From the Mahican Indians to Kiliaen Van Rensselaer, 6 August 1630, Correspondence of Maria van Rensselaer 1669–1689, Patent for the Manor of Rensselaerwyck" and maps of Rensselaerswijck.

The Holland Land Company (HLC) was organized by a group of bankers in the Netherlands after the American Revolutionary War. The HLC purchased its first land tract in 1792. The HLC purchased land from the Indians and then sold parcels to settlers. Some of those who bought land from the Company were descendants of the early New York Dutch, but few were new immigrants from the old country. Early purchases included what later became Cazenovia, in Madison County, New York, and land along the upper Black River (the Oldenbarneveld Settlement, now Trenton, Oneida County, New York), but most of the land was in western New York. See chapter 7, Land Records.

Resources in the Netherlands

In the Netherlands genealogy is just as popular as in the United States—if not more so. There are numerous genealogical societies, publications, and websites. The largest national genealogical collection is that of the Centraal Bureau voor Genealogie at The Hague (*cbg.nl*). The Bureau recently published the research guide *Dutch Roots: Finding your Ancestors in the Netherlands*. The country also has impressive archives—national, provincial, regional and municipal—many of which are making their holdings accessible online. Issues of the *New York Genealogical and Biographical Record* (in the NYG&B eLibrary) and the former *New Netherland Connections*, which can be found at *americanancestors.org*, contain many articles that show the value of Netherlands resources in tracing the ancestry of New Netherland settlers. For descendants of later Dutch immigrants their value is even greater.

The Work of New Netherland Historians

As historian Joyce Goodfriend explains in her introduction to *Revisiting New Netherland*, and in the Holland Society's journal *de Halve Maen*, histories of the United States written in the nineteenth and early-twentieth centuries tended to distort or totally ignore the contributions of New Netherland and its people to American history. Since the 1970s a school of New Netherland historians has developed, with the goal of correcting this bias, and genealogists who work on New Netherland

families will write more meaningful family histories if they are familiar with the work of these scholars. They might start with academic works like Jaap Jacobs' excellent overall history, *The Colony of New Netherland*, and Janny Venema's *Beverwijck*, a more detailed study of a typical community (modern Albany), or works written for a wider audience such as Firth Fabend's *New Netherland in a Nutshell* and Russell Shorto's very popular *The Island at the Center of the World*.

Articles by many of the historians will be found in *A Beautiful and Fruitful Place* and *Revisiting New Netherland* and in the Holland Society's journal *de Halve Maen*. Checking the names of the historians in online library catalogs will reveal their many books as well.

Selected Repositories, Societies, and Websites
The Dutch Settlers Society of Albany
dutchsettlerssociety.org
Email: president@dutchsettlerssociety.org

The society is a membership organization for descendants of settlers under the jurisdiction of "The Court of Rensselaerswijck before 1665, or in Esopus (Kingston, NY) before 1661." It preserves and documents the early Dutch history of Albany (1624–1664). It publishes the *Dutch Settlers Society Yearbook* (1924–present) of genealogies and historical studies focused on early history of the Hudson River Region. Henry Hoff's "Using *The Dutch Settlers Society of Albany Yearbook*" lists source records and genealogies found in the journal. Newsletters are available on the website.

Family History Library (FHL) and FamilySearch.org
The Family History Library has one of the largest collections of Netherlands genealogy and genealogical sources in the world. The collection is being digitized and added to the free digital resources at *FamilySearch.org*. See chapter 16 for detailed information about the FHL's collections and the online resources at *FamilySearch.org*.

Finding Your New Netherland Roots
The New York Genealogical and Biographical Society, the Holland Society of New York, and the New York Public Library copresented the two-day workshop, Finding Your New Netherland Roots, in 2009. The syllabus has been digitally published as a Research Aid at *NewYorkFamilyHistory.org* and includes papers on New Netherland history and sources for genealogical research on both sides of the Atlantic.

The Holland Society of New York
20 West 44th Street, 5th Floor • New York, NY 10036
(212) 758-1675 • Email: info@hollandsociety.org
hollandsociety.org

Established in 1885, the society collects and preserves documents concerning early Dutch communities in New York and New Jersey. It publishes transcriptions and original material. The society's quarterly journal, *de Halve Maen*, focuses on the latest research in New Netherland studies and has been published since 1922. Henry Hoff's article "Using *de Halve Maen*" lists articles of genealogical interest published up to 1991. The library, which is open to nonmembers for a nominal fee, includes regional histories and approximately 3,000 family histories and genealogies. The website has an online catalog searchable by title, author, keyword and subject. There is also an online list of almost 900 surnames—those most readily documented among the approximately 1,400 known to have appeared in New Netherland.

Library of Congress (LOC)

An extensive guide to the Library's Dutch-American history and genealogy titles is available online at *www.loc.gov/rr/genealogy/bib_guid/Dutch_Bibliography.pdf*. Included are land records, church records, and individual family histories of early Dutch settlers for the areas of present-day New York State and New Jersey. See chapter 16 for detailed information about the vast collections of the LOC.

New Netherland and Beyond

rootsweb.ancestry.com/nycoloni

This website provides annotated links to documents, including Fernow's abstracts of Albany wills from 1626 to 1836; minutes of the courts of Rensselaerswijck, Fort Orange, Beverwyck, the Orphanmasters, and the court of Burgomasters and Schepens; and other colonial records. There are online transcriptions for some documents, e.g., the Van Rensselaer Bowier Manuscripts.

The New Netherland Research Center (NNRC)

New York State Library, 7th Floor, Cultural Education Center
222 Madison Avenue • Albany, NY 12220 • (518) 486-4815
Email: nyslfnn@mail.nysed.gov • *newnetherlandinstitute.org*

In 1974 Dr. Charles T. Gehring, a scholar of Netherlandic studies, began translating seventeenth-century documents from Dutch New Netherland held at the NYSL and the New York State Archives (NYSA). His groundbreaking work became known as the New Netherland Project (NNP). The NNP developed into the NNRC; and the support group, the Friends of New Netherland, has become the New Netherland Institute, which continues to support New Netherland-related projects including the work of the NNRC.

In 2010 the NNRC opened at the NYSL where the work continues, and the public can consult published works, e.g., translations and monographs. The original manuscripts of Dutch New Netherland held by the NYSL and NYSA can be accessed through the research room in the Cultural Education Center. The new transcriptions and translations to date have been made by Dr. Gehring and Dr. Janny Venema. The NNRC continues to work on the 12,000 pages of the Dutch Colonial Manuscripts collection held by the NYSA. The major collections that have been translated include the Dutch Colonial Council Minutes.

Some Dutch colonial and early American documents have been digitized and are available on the NYSL website, *nysl.nysed.gov*, including *http://nysl.nysed.gov/uhtbin/cgisirsi.exe/?ps=dTfKEU Uzal/NYSL/322390065/9*. The Institute's website, *newnetherlandinstitute.org*, includes an online exhibit on the Van Rensselaer Manor Papers; finding aids to its collection of Dutch-American family papers; and a searchable Citations Database of the Center's articles, monographs, and other documents relating to the seventeenth-century Dutch in America.

New York Genealogical and Biographical Society (NYG&B)

36 West 44th Street • New York NY 10036 • (212) 755-8532
Email: education@nygbs.org • *NewYorkFamilyHistory.org*

The NYG&B website contains Dutch Reformed church records especially those of the New Amsterdam/New York City Church, the New Amsterdam Orphanmasters Court records, the *NYG&B Record*, and the *New York Researcher*, all in the eLibrary, and the Research Aids online. See chapter 16 for a full description of the NYG&B.

Rensselaer Polytechnic Institute: Archives and Special Collections (RPI)

110 8th Street • Troy, NY 12180-3590 • (518) 276-8340
Email through website • *archives.rpi.edu*

The Archives at RPI include the Stephen van Rensselaer III Collection, 1752–1851. The collection (MC-27) includes documents related to Rensselaerswijck under its ninth patroon, Stephen van Rensselaer III, relating to both his personal and business life.

The Society of Daughters of Holland Dames

308 Tunbridge Road • Baltimore, MD 21212-3803
info@hollanddames.org • *hollanddames.org*

Incorporated in 1895, the Society collects and preserves genealogical and historical documents and encourages research relating to the Dutch in America. A list of ancestral names of Society members and links to other resources are available on the website. See chapter 16 for more details.

Van Rensselaer Manor Papers at the New York State Library

The collection includes letters, contracts, ledgers, bonds, account books, and other documents. A guide can be found online at: *www.nysl.nysed.gov/mssc/vrm/index.html*. They have also been digitized as part of a project by the New Netherland Research Center at *www.newnetherlandinstitute.org/research/online-publications*.

Wie Was Wie (Who Was Who)

www.wiewaswie.nl

This website for genealogical research is the result of a collaboration among more than 20 archival institutions, including the National Archives of the Netherlands and The Hague Municipal Archives. It includes records of Dutch settlers of New York (New Amsterdam until 1674). It also has early Netherlands parish records and inheritance declarations. All pages are offered in English, as well as in Dutch.

Selected Bibliography and Further Reading

See also the bibliographies in chapter 1, Colonial Era, and chapter 15, Religious Records: Reformed Churches.

Bailey, Rosalie Fellows. *Dutch Systems in Family Naming, New York – New Jersey*. Genealogical Publications of the National Genealogical Society, No. 12, 1954.

———. *Pre-Revolutionary Dutch Houses and Families in Northern New Jersey and Southern New York*. New York: W. Morrow & Co., 1936.

A Beautiful and Fruitful Place: Selected Rensselaerswijck Seminar Papers, vol. 1 (1979–1987), ed. Nancy McClure Zeller. Albany: New Netherland Publishing, 1991. Also online at *www.nnp.org*. Vol. 2 (1988–1997), edited by Elisabeth Paling Funk and Martha Dickinson Shattuck. Albany: New Netherland Institute and SUNY Press, 2011.

Boyer, Carl. *Ship Passenger Lists, New York and New Jersey (1600–1825)*. 2 vols. Newhall, CA: C. Boyer, 1978. Vol. 1: National and New England; vol. 2: New York and New Jersey.

Davis, Natalie Zemon, et al. *Dutch New York Between East & West, the World of Margarieta van Varick*, edited by Deborah L. Krohn, Peter N. Miller, and Marybeth De Filippis. New York: Bard Graduate Center, 2009.

Dering, Maria A. *Researching Your Dutch Ancestors: A Practical Guide*. Baltimore: The Society of Daughters of Holland Dames, 2011.

Dilliard, Maud Esther. *An Album of New Netherland*. New York: Twayne, 1963.

Epperson, Gwenn F. *New Netherland Roots*. Baltimore: Genealogical Publishing Co., 1994. Pre-Internet, but still an excellent introduction to tracking New Netherland families to their European roots.

Fabend, Firth Haring. *New Netherland in a Nutshell: A Concise History of the Dutch Colony in North America*. Albany: New Netherland Institute, 2012.

Goodfriend, Joyce D., ed. *Revisiting New Netherland, Perspectives on Early Dutch America*. Leiden, The Netherlands and Boston, MA: Brill, 2005. Papers delivered at 2001 conference in New York cosponsored by New Netherland Project, Holland Society, and NYG&B Society.

Hoff, Henry B. "Researching New York Dutch Families: A Checklist Approach," *NYG&B Newsletter* (now *New York Researcher*) vol. 7 (Summer 1996): 12–14. Also a Research Aid at *NewYorkFamilyHistory.org*. [NYG&B eLibrary]

———. "Researching Dutch Families in New York and New Jersey." *de Halve Maen*, vol. 82, no. 4, (2009).

———. "Using *de Halve Maen*." *NYG&B Newsletter* (now *New York Researcher*), vol. 2 (Fall 1991): 28–29. Also a Research Aid at *NewYorkFamilyHistory.org*.

———. "Using *The Dutch Settlers Society of Albany Yearbook*." *NYG&B Newsletter* (now *New York Researcher*), vol. 7 (Fall 1996): 27. Also a Research Aid at *NewYorkFamilyHistory.org*.

Hoffman, William J. *An Armory of American Families of Dutch Descent*. New York: New York Genealogical and Biographical Society, 2010. [NYG&B eLibrary]

Jacobs, Jaap. *New Netherland: A Dutch Colony in Seventeenth-Century America*. Leiden and Boston: Brill, 2005. A shorter version is *The Colony of New Netherland: A Dutch Settlement in Seventeenth-Century America*. Ithaca, NY: Cornell University Press, 2009.

Kelly, Arthur C. M. *Names, Names, and More Names: Locating Your Dutch Ancestors in Colonial America*. Orem, UT: Ancestry, 1999.

Kenney, Alice. *Stubborn for Liberty: The Dutch in New York*. Published for the New York State American Revolution Bicentennial Commission. Syracuse: Syracuse University Press, 1975.

Kilpatrick, William Heard. *The Dutch Schools of New Netherland and Colonial New York*. Washington: G. P. O., 1912.

Klooster, Wim. *The Dutch in the Americas 1600–1800*. Providence, RI: The John Carter Brown Library, 1997.

Koenig, Dorothy, A., ed. *New Netherland Connections*. 15 vols. Berkeley, CA. 1996–2010.

Macy, Harry, Jr. "375th Anniversary of the *Eendracht and Nieuw Nederland*." NYG&B Newsletter vol. 10 (Winter 1999): 3–4. Also a Research Aid at *NewYorkFamilyHistory.org*. The article identifies the families known to have come on the first ships.

———. "Focus on New Netherland." Ongoing feature of *New York Researcher* beginning Spring 2011. [NYG&B eLibrary]

O'Callaghan, Edmund Bailey. *Papers Relating to the First Settlement of New York by the Dutch: Containing a List of the Early Immigrants to New Netherland 1657–1664*. 2 vols. (1888) Edinburgh: Privately printed. Information taken from *Documentary history of the State of New-York*, and *Wassenaers's Historie van Europa*.

Reynolds, Helen Wilkinson. *Dutch Houses in the Hudson Valley before 1776.* New York: The Holland Society, 1929.

Riker, David M. *Genealogical and Biographical Directory to Persons in New Netherland, from 1613 to 1674.* 4 vols. Salem, MA: Higginson Book Co., 1999, and Supplement, 2004.

Scheltema, Gajus, and Heleen Westerhuijs. *Exploring Historic Dutch New York: New York City, Hudson Valley, New Jersey, and Delaware.* New York: Museum of the City of New York, Dover Publications, 2011

Stryker-Rodda, Kenn. "New Netherland Naming Systems and Customs." *NYG&B Record,* vol. 126, no. 1 (1995): 35–45. [NYG&B eLibrary]

Swierenga, Robert, P. *Dutch Households in U.S. Population Censuses, 1850, 1860, 1870: An Aalphabetical Listing by Family Heads.* Wilmington, DE: Scholarly Resources, 1987.

———. comp. *Dutch Immigrants in U.S. Ship Passenger Manifests, 1820–1880: An Alphabetical Listing by Household Heads and Independent Persons.* Wilmington, DE: Scholarly Resources, 1983

Van Drie, Rob. *Dutch Roots: Finding your Ancestors in the Netherlands.* Translated by Suzanne Needs. The Hague: Centraal Bureau voor Genealogie, 2012. Kindle edition.

Venema, Janny. *Beverwijck, A Dutch Village on the American Frontier, 1652–1664.* Albany: SUNY Press, 2003.

English

Historical Overview

A few Englishmen were in New Netherland as early as 1635, and over the next three decades English settlers established several towns within the Dutch colony, though they remained a minority of the population. In 1639 Lion Gardiner claimed the island which bears his name at the east end of Long Island, and in the following years the English settled towns on Long Island from Oyster Bay eastward which were outside the Dutch jurisdiction. When the English colony of New York was created in 1664, it included all of these settlements. By the time the first census was taken in 1698, roughly forty percent of the population of the colony was English, with the largest concentrations in the two Long Island counties, Queens and Suffolk. (Nassau County was not formed until the late-nineteenth century.)

Although the earliest English settlers were almost all born in England, they did not come directly from England. Before settling in New Netherland or eastern Long Island, most of them had lived in the New England colonies. Some settlers arrived after brief stays in other English colonies such as Virginia, Bermuda, and Barbados, while still others came by way of the Netherlands. From 1664, when the English took over New Netherland, to the end of the colonial period, there was immigration to New York directly from England, though not on a large scale. Those immigrants are not always easily identified, as there are virtually no passenger lists, and they did not require naturalization.

The eighteenth century marked the beginning of a larger migration into New York from New England, primarily into parts of the Hudson Valley not already well settled by the Dutch. At the same time many native-born New Yorkers of English descent also migrated from Long Island into the Hudson Valley counties, while others moved west into New Jersey. At the close of the American Revolutionary War some who remained loyal to Britain left New York, most of them going to Canada.

After the Revolution, as northern, central, and western New York opened for settlement, those areas attracted a massive migration from New England, which historians have called both the Yankee Exodus and the Yankee Invasion, depending on their points of view (see bibliography at the end of this section). New Englanders came to form a majority of the population in most of the state's new counties, and they also moved in large numbers into the rapidly growing cities of New York and Brooklyn. Native-born New Yorkers of English descent also moved into the new counties and the cities. Many of these people did not remain in New York, but moved on to other parts of the country as those areas opened to settlement.

During the first half of the nineteenth century the English were also the third-largest foreign immigrant group in New York, after the Irish and Germans. Immigration from England has continued to the present day, though on a smaller scale.

In the nineteenth and twentieth centuries there has also been a migration of English-Canadians into New York, particularly from Ontario, which shares a long border with the state. Some of these Canadians were descendants of Loyalists with New York roots. Like the immigrants from England, they quickly assimilated into the native-born population.

By 1790 it has been estimated that slightly over half of the state's population was of English descent. The percentage rose with the subsequent New England migration, but in the second half of the nineteenth century it receded with the rise of non-English immigration, leaving no single group with a majority in New York.

Genealogical Resources

Aside from religious records there are almost no sources specific to the English population of New York, and they will be found in all the other types of records described elsewhere in this guide.

The origins and early generations of many early New York English families have been covered in numerous genealogies published in books and articles. Families where the first or second American generation settled in New Netherland or colonial New York (and some who immigrated later) have been the subject of many articles in the *New York Genealogical and Biographical Record*, while families that came to New York later from New England are more likely to be found in the *New England Historical and Genealogical Register* and other New England journals. Articles in *The American Genealogist* and, more recently, *The Genealogist*, cover both types of families.

Henry B. Hoff has written a number of articles for the *NYG&B Newsletter* (now the *New York Researcher*) which list New York families covered in all the major journals past and present; he lists other articles which identify New York families in various collective genealogies, both in print and manuscript, which may not show up in library catalog searches.

Immigration

The origins of many English immigrants have been discovered over the years, and the growing online access to English records from *findmypast.com*, for example, should bring many more such discoveries. An excellent introduction to such resources will be found in the publications of the International Society for British Genealogy and Family History.

It should be noted that some immigrants from England were of non-English ancestry, being descendants of earlier immigrants to England. These included descendants of Huguenots and Walloons who fled to England from France and the Southern Netherlands in the sixteenth and seventeenth centuries. Some immigrants from Scotland and Ireland sailed from English ports.

The most reliable accounts of those English settlers who came to New England from 1620 through 1635 will be found in Robert C. Anderson's *Great Migration* volumes, and should be checked before accepting any other published accounts of those settlers and their immediate families. While only a very small percentage of the settlers themselves came to New Netherland or New York, the descendants of many others migrated into New York in later years.

The National Archives (NARA) holds passenger and immigration lists. Many are on microfilm and are widely available. *Ancestry.com* has digitized and indexed many of NARA's immigration records, including passenger arrival records for the ports of New York (1820–1957). The subscription website *findmypast.co.uk* has passenger lists of people leaving the British Isles 1890–1960, and a register of passport applications 1851–1903. See chapter 4, Immigration, Migration, and Naturalization, for detailed information about what records exist and where they can be accessed.

Religious Records

New Yorkers of English descent are to be found in the records of a wide variety of religious denominations. Researchers should not assume that every English family had only one religious preference. If they lived near more than one English-speaking congregation, regardless of denomination, all of those congregations' records need to be checked. This applies to English families who came over in the nineteenth and twentieth centuries, as well as those who came earlier.

Most of the English who settled in New Netherland or eastern Long Island were Puritans who considered themselves members of the Church of England, a position that was strengthened when Oliver Cromwell rose to power in the old country in the 1640s. After the Restoration of Charles II in 1660, Puritans in England who refused to change their beliefs were expelled from the Church as Nonconformists, but this action had no immediate effect in New York. A small Anglican chapel was established within the Fort on Manhattan Island, attended mainly by the Governor and his entourage, and the Puritans continued to control the other English churches in the colony.

The Church of England was the official state religion in England, and there were many in authority who wanted to see all English New Yorkers brought into the Anglican fold. At the end of the 1600s, the Church of England was made the established church in four counties—New York, Queens, Richmond, and Westchester. The inhabitants of those counties henceforth were taxed to support the Anglican clergy. There was widespread opposition to the tax, and Anglican attempts to take over the existing English churches caused considerable unrest, especially in Queens County.

To protect their churches against an Anglican takeover, the English congregations on Long Island and in Westchester could have declared themselves self-governing Independent or Congregational churches, like their counterparts in New England. Feeling the need for greater protection, they instead became Presbyterian, under the umbrella of the Presbytery of Philadelphia and the Church of Scotland. Some New Englanders who migrated into the colony in later years did form Congregational churches, but they more often affiliated with the Presbyterians. The Anglican Church still attracted many communicants among the English population of New York, though the Presbyterians outnumbered them.

The earliest English settlers also included Separatists who had left the Church of England. Separatists were particularly evident in Gravesend and the towns of future Queens County, and when the first Quaker missionaries appeared in 1657, they found ready converts among that part of the population. The Quakers soon became a major faction in New York. This is a boon for genealogists, as the Quakers kept excellent vital records. There also were Baptists and Quakers, especially from Rhode Island, among the New Englanders who came into New York in the eighteenth and nineteenth centuries.

In the colonial period English people will also appear occasionally in records of non-English denominations such as the Reformed, Lutheran, or Moravians, sometimes with their names spelled phonetically in Dutch or German.

Immediately after the American Revolutionary War, the Methodists began converting New Yorkers, particularly those of English descent, on such a large scale that by the middle of the nineteenth century they were the largest Protestant denomination in the state. Many Anglicans had been loyalists and left the country after the Revolution. In 1789 those who remained formed the Protestant Episcopal Church, which was independent of the Church of England's hierarchy and loyalty to the British Monarchy. After the Revolution and through the nineteenth and twentieth centuries, English immigrants might appear in records of any of these denominations and others, including the Roman Catholic Church after 1784, when the ban on Catholic priests was abolished. (See also chapter 15, Religious Records.)

Selected Repositories, Societies, and Websites

Unlike others who came to the United States, the English assimilated so easily that they have sometimes been called the "invisible immigrants." They rarely formed separate neighborhoods, or felt the need to form their own churches or societies, or publish their own newspapers. The St. George's Society (*stgeorgessociety.org*), founded in 1770, and the Daughters of the British Empire in the State of New York (*dbeny.org*), founded in 1909, are primarily charities and social organizations. See the bibliography for the St. George's Society publication listing members from 1786 to 1913.

International Society for British Genealogy and Family History (ISBGFH)

PO Box 350459 • Westminster, CO 80035

Email: president@isbgfh.org • *isbgfh.org*

ISBGFH offers help to those researching British ancestors. It holds programs, provides research trips to Britain, and holds an annual British Institute at Salt Lake City; it published a newsletter from 1979 to 2000, and since 2000 has published a journal, *British Connections*. The website has an interactive surname database where anyone can make inquiries to surname researchers, links to useful resources, and a blog. Members can access past and current issues of the newsletter and journal.

The Society of Mayflower Descendants in the State of New York

20 West 44th Street, Rm. 505 • New York, NY 10036-6603

(212) 759-1620 • Email: director@mayflowernewyork.org

mayflowernewyork.org

The Mayflower library and research center is at the headquarters in Plymouth, MA, with a website at *themayflowersociety.com*. Both websites have lists of the Mayflower passengers and links to related websites.

Selected Bibliography and Further Reading

Anderson, Robert C. *The Great Migration Begins: Immigrants to New England 1620–1633*. 3 vols. Boston: New England Historic Genealogical Society, 1995–1996. The most reliable accounts of over 900 colonists; the review in the *NYG&B Record*, vol. 128, p. 71 (1997) identifies 35 who came to New Netherland, Long Island, or New York (or had close relatives who did).

———. *The Great Migration: Immigrants to New England 1634–1635*. 7 vols. Boston: New England Historic Genealogical Society, 1999–2011. Accounts of some 1,400 colonists; the review in the *NYG&B Record*, vol. 143, pp. 76–78 (2012) identifies 89 who came to New Netherland, Long Island, or New York (or had close relatives who did).

Coldham, Peter Wilson. *American Migrations 1765–1799 . . . .* Baltimore: Genealogical Publishing Co., 2000. [*Ancestry.com*]

———. *American Wills & Administrations in the Prerogative Court of Canterbury, 1610–1857*. Baltimore: Genealogical Publishing Co., 1989. [*Ancestry.com*]

———. *American Wills Proved in London, 1611–1775*. Baltimore: Genealogical Publishing Co., 1992. [*Ancestry.com*]

———. *English Estates of American Colonists: American Wills and Administrations in the Prerogative Court of Canterbury, 1800–1858*. Baltimore: Genealogical Publishing Co., 1981. [*Ancestry.com*]

———. *More English Adventurers and Emigrants 1625–1777: Abstracts of Examinations in the High Court of Admiralty with Reference to Colonial America.* Baltimore: Genealogical Publishing Co., 2002.

Davenport, David Paul. "The Yankee Settlement of New York." *Genealogical Journal [of the Utah Genealogical Association]*, vol. 17 (1988–1989): 63–88.

Ellis, David M. "The Yankee Invasion of New York." In *A Short History of New York State*. Ithaca, NY: Cornell University Press and the New York State Historical Association, 1957.

———. "The Yankee Invasion of New York, 1783–1830." In: Wendell Edward Tripp, ed., *Coming and Becoming: Pluralism in New York State History*. Cooperstown, NY: NYSHA, 1991.

Erickson, Charlotte. *Invisible Immigrants: The Adaptation of English and Scottish Immigrants in Nineteenth-Century America*. London: Weidenfeld and Nicolson, 1972.

Fischer, David Hackett. *Albion's Seed*. New York: Oxford University Press, 1989.

Glazier, Ira A. *Emigration from the United Kingdom to America: Lists of Passengers Arriving at U.S. Ports*. 18 vols. Lanham, MD: Scarecrow Press, 2006–2012. Volumes 1–18 cover 1870–81; the names are extracted from NARA's passenger lists. As with any compiled work, readers are advised to carefully assess lists for accuracy and completeness, and to consult original records where possible.

Hoff, Henry B. *English Origins of American Colonists from the New York Genealogical and Biographical Record*. Baltimore: Genealogical Publishing Co., 1991.

Holbrook, Stewart H. *The Yankee Exodus, an Account of Migration from New England*. New York: Macmillan, 1950, and Seattle: University of Washington Press, 1968.

Hotten, John Camden, ed. *The Original Lists of Persons of Quality; Emigrants; Religious Exiles; Political Rebels; Serving Men Sold for a Term of Years; Apprentices; Children Stolen; Maidens Pressed; and Others Who Went from Great Britain to the American Plantations, 1600-1700 . . . .* New York: Empire State Book Company, 1874.

Johnson, Stanley C. *A History of Emigration from the United Kingdom to North America, 1763–1912*. New York: E. P. Dutton and Co., 1913.

Leclerc, Michael J., ed. *Genealogist's Handbook for New England Research*. Boston: New England Historic Genealogical Society, 2012.

Lloyd's Register of British and Foreign Shipping. Fiche edition. LaCrosse, WI: Brookhaven Press, 1981. If the ship's name is known, this work may provide helpful details including the ports of departure and arrival.

Scott, Kenneth. *British Aliens in the United States during the War of 1812*. Baltimore: Genealogical Publishing Co., 1979.

St. George's Society. *A History of St. George's Society of New York from 1770 to 1913*. New York: Federal Printing Company, 1913. List of members 1786–1913 and biographies of officers.

French and French-Speaking

Historical Overview

The first European settlers of New Netherland were Walloons, inhabitants of the Southern Netherlands, which included today's Belgium (the region now called Wallonia) and those parts of France just south of the present Belgian border. The Walloons spoke a Romance language similar to French, which the Dutch called *Waalsch* or *Wals*. In the sixteenth century, when the Southern Netherlands was under Spanish rule, many Walloons became Protestants, but the Spanish authorities ordered them to return to the Catholic church or leave the country.

From that point on, for many decades, there was a large-scale migration of Walloons to Protestant countries, including the Dutch Republic, and between 1624 and 1664 many migrated to New Netherland, where it has been estimated that they constituted between five and ten percent of the population. After New Netherland became New York, there was a new influx of Walloons in the 1670s, many from a refugee community at Mannheim in the Pfalz or Palatinate on the Rhine; some of them founded the New York settlement which they called New Paltz in memory of their former home.

The Protestant Walloons were members of the Calvinist or Reformed branch of Protestantism. In some cities of the Dutch Republic they were numerous enough to form their own churches, which were called both Walloon and French. In New Netherland they became members of the Dutch Reformed Church. While the New Amsterdam church conducted services in both Dutch and French for a few years, the Walloons were gradually integrated into the larger Dutch community. Also joining that community were a few fellow Calvinists from France, known as Huguenots.

During the sixteenth-century Protestant Reformation, Calvinism attracted a large following in France, leaving the country deeply divided between Catholics and Huguenots. This led to a series of religious wars, and caused many Huguenots to leave the country. The conflict ended in 1598 with the Edict of Nantes, promulgated by King Henry IV, who himself had been a Huguenot until he inherited the throne.

The Edict brought about a semblance of peace between the two sides, making the Huguenots more comfortable to remain in France, though some continued to leave. Over the following decades the situation in France gradually deteriorated, leading in 1685 to the Revocation of the Edict of Nantes by King Louis XIV. There was a massive emigration of Huguenots, and quite a few of the refugees found their way to New York. While the few Huguenots who arrived before 1680 had become part of the Walloon and Dutch communities, those who came after were numerous enough to create their own communities, in New York City, New Rochelle, and Staten Island, which later merged into the English-speaking population.

French scholar Bertrand Van Ruymbeke has stressed that the term Huguenot should be applied only to subjects of the French king, which would exclude the Walloons. Some Walloons did come under French rule beginning in 1659, but that was after the New Netherland/New York settlers had left the region. Those French Protestants who arrived in New York between 1680 and 1700 were Huguenots, while those French-speaking Protestants who arrived earlier were Walloons, unless there is specific evidence that they originated in France and not the Spanish Netherlands.

New York records of the seventeenth century sometimes refer to the "French and Walloons," an indication that they recognized two distinct groups, but in modern times Huguenot societies in the United States have ignored that distinction and lumped the two together as Huguenots. Even the street containing the oldest houses in the predominantly Walloon settlement of New Paltz is now called Historic Huguenot Street (a National Historic Landmark District and museum).

While these Protestants were settling in New Netherland and New York, a much larger French Catholic community was developing to the north, in New France, a vast territory that included the present-day Canadian provinces of Québec and Ontario, parts of the future New York, and vast territories north of the Ohio River and west of the Mississippi. France had sent expeditions to explore North America beginning in 1524, and colonization began in earnest with Samuel de Champlain's founding of Québec as a fur trading settlement in 1608.

In what is now northern and western New York State, French soldiers, traders, and Jesuit priests set up forts (including Fort Niagara in Youngstown and Fort Carillon in Ticonderoga), trading posts, and missions. The French and Indian War (1754–1763), the North American counterpart of Europe's Seven Years' War (1756–1763), pitted France and her American Indian allies against the British, and resulted in all of France's colonial holdings east of the Mississippi being turned over to Britain, except for Saint-Pierre and Miquelon.

Although Britain gained control of French Canada in 1760, the French-Canadian population continued to grow dramatically, and in Québec it continued to outnumber the English-speaking population. During the colonial period, a few French from Québec found their way to Albany and other Hudson Valley settlements but were absorbed into the local Protestant population. Further north, some French Catholic settlers may have remained after 1763 in what eventually became part of New York, as reflected in the 1790 census.

Beginning in 1779 France supplied more than 10,000 ground troops to support the patriot cause during the American Revolution, and some of them remained in the United States.

Prior to the Battle of Yorktown, Virginia, General Rochambeau led 4,000 French troops to George Washington's New York camp at White Plains in Westchester County.

Several thousand refugees from the French Revolution—variously constitutionalists, monarchists, and republicans—immigrated to the United States during the 1790s, many settling in New York City, and others migrating north. The settlement of Castorland was established in 1792 with twenty French families near present-day Watertown.

The 1791–1803 slave revolt in Saint-Domingue (Haiti) caused French families to flee that island, and many came to the United States. Their names appear in the records of New York City's first Catholic Church (St. Peter's), and in issues of the *Gazette Française et Americaine*, published in New York City 1795–1799; see the bibliography for Kenneth Scott's extracts from this newspaper.

Many French-Canadians assisted the American side during the Revolutionary War, and some moved to New York in the years immediately after. These early migrants settled primarily in the areas that are today the northeastern counties of Clinton, Essex, and Franklin, with some drifting as far south as Warren and Washington counties. The reason for the popularity of these areas is simple: they were easily accessed via waterways from populated areas of Québec, following the Saint Lawrence River, or moving down rivers to Lake Champlain. In 1788 many French from Québec and Nova Scotia were granted land in the area that today comprises the towns of Champlain, Coopersville (formerly Corbeau), and Rouse's Point, Clinton County.

As the nineteenth century progressed, agricultural and economic conditions in Québec worsened, triggering increased emigration. Many French-Canadians came to the United States to fight for the Union during the Civil War and remained when the war was over. Many more came with the advance of the Industrial Revolution in the latter half of the nineteenth century. It was not uncommon for French-Canadians to move back and forth between New York and Québec over many years or to return to Québec after having spent decades working in New York. Such families might have births, marriages, deaths, and burials occurring on both sides of the border. When records cannot be found in New York, they can potentially be found in Canada.

Spelling variations among French-Canadian names abound. Names were often anglicized phonetically, which frequently meant the final consonant was lost, or by translation. French-Canadians frequently used "dit" names: nicknames or sobriquets that followed the surname and were used interchangeably. Thus one might find an individual named Jean Hervé dit Laliberté where one record says the last name is Hervé (or Harvey) and another that shows the surname as Laliberté (or Laliberty). A comprehensive list of dit names is at *afgs.org*, the website of the American-French Genealogical Society.

During the nineteenth and twentieth centuries, there was a small immigration to New York State from France, the number of French-born residents ranging from 21,000 in the 1860 census to 28,000 in 1950, with a peak of 32,000 in both 1920 and 1930. Political and economic issues in other Francophone countries have spurred contemporary immigration to New York. The number of Haitian-born New Yorkers climbed from 445 in 1950, to 55,000 in 1980, and to 125,000 in 2000. In recent years French-speaking immigrants from West Africa have come to New York City in increasing numbers. The neighborhood Le Petit Sénégal in Manhattan's Harlem is home to several thousand immigrants from Sénégal, Cote d'Ivoire, and other countries.

Genealogical Resources

The resources below have specific relevance to researching French-speaking immigrants to New York. However, French-speaking immigrants will also be found in records discussed elsewhere in this book.

Immigration

Many French and Walloons appear in published lists of passengers arriving in New Netherland. Others are identified in works such as Baird's *History of the Huguenot Emigration*. For the refugees of the 1790s from Haiti, see Scott's "New York's French Newspaper." Smith's *Emigrants from France* identifies some nineteenth century immigrants from Alsace.

The National Archives (NARA) holds passenger and immigration lists. Many are on microfilm and are widely available.

Ancestry.com has digitized and indexed many of NARA's immigration records, including passenger arrival records for the port of New York (1820–1957) and Canadian border crossings to New York and other states (1895–1956). The Family History Library (FHL) has microfilm of the Canadian border crossings in the collection "Manifests of Passengers Arriving in the St. Albans, Vermont, District through Canadian Pacific and Atlantic Ports."

Until 1895 people moved freely across the border, and early border crossing records were restricted to large transit (trains and ships). Those who traveled by private conveyance (walking, horse and buggy, cars) are not captured in the records. See chapter 4, Immigration, Migration, and Naturalization, for detailed information about what records exist and where they can be accessed.

The selected bibliography at the end of this section includes books that contain lists of French-speaking immigrants which may help fill in gaps in the records, whose availability varies with the time period. Researchers are advised to consult original records when available rather than rely solely on indexes and transcriptions. See also chapter 4, Immigration, Migration, and Naturalization.

Military Records

The enlistment records for the French regiments that came to the United States in 1780 with General Rochambeau are available on microfilm in the Sons of the American Revolution Library in Louisville, Kentucky (*library.sar.org*). The Lafayette GenWeb page, *http://memorial-genweb.org/~lafayette-genweb/depouillement.php*, is building a database of the soldiers and sailors who served in the French army and navy during its 1778–1783 American alliance. Further information about French participants in the American Revolution is available at the website of the National Washington-Rochambeau Revolutionary Route Association at *http://w3r-us.org/history/rosters/rosterfr.htm*. The Society of the Cincinnati (*societyofthecincinnati.org*), founded in 1783 by American and French officers who served in the American Revolution, has a chapter in France. See the entry under Lineage Societies in chapter 16 for a description of their resources.

Newspapers

One of the earliest French-language newspapers published in New York City, 1795–1799, was the *Gazette Française et Americaine*. A number of other French language newspapers were published in New York and can be located by searching the U.S. Newspaper Directory, 1690–present, on the Library of Congress's Chronicling America website *chroniclingamerica.loc.gov*. The New York State Library's list of New York newspapers at *www.nysl.nysed.gov/nysnp/title4.htm* provides holdings information for more than 10,000 newspaper titles that have been published in New York State. See also chapter 12, Newspapers.

Religious Records

As noted above, the early Walloon and Huguenot settlers attended Dutch Reformed churches. A separate Huguenot church was founded in New York City in 1682, soon followed by a church at New Rochelle, while a French church was formed on Staten Island for both the Huguenot and Walloon inhabitants. The New York City church still exists, as L'Église du Saint-Esprit, but it has been an Episcopal church since 1804. The New Rochelle congregation split in the eighteenth century, half going over to the Episcopal Church and half to the Presbyterians. The Staten Island church also ceased to exist in the early 1700s, and its members were absorbed by the island's other churches. Extensive records exist for the New York City church, and some survive for the church at New Rochelle, but all records of the Staten Island church are lost.

Apart from a brief period in the 1680s, colonial New York was hostile to Catholics. Some French Catholics who came into the Hudson Valley during the colonial period were absorbed into the Protestant community. Before the French territories in upstate New York fell to the British in 1763, French Catholics were free to practice their faith. French missionary priests from lower Canada ministered to the Catholics in northern New York and attempted to convert the American Indians there, particularly the Hurons, Iroquois, and Mohawks. However, sacramental records of baptism, marriage, and burial for Catholics in northern New York are rare before the 1840s. The Northern New York American-Canadian Genealogical Society has published many of these registers, as well as parish censuses and cemetery transcriptions. (See the Society's listing below.) Many records can be found in the parishes of Québec located near the border, such as St. Jean Chrysostôme in Châteauguay County.

Québec civil law followed the custom of Paris, which required churches to register births, marriages, and deaths, and send a copy to the civil government. As a result, there is very little record loss for parish registers in Québec. The Drouin Collection, which is accessible at *Ancestry.com*, includes more than 15 million records of Catholic and Protestant churches in Canada. Its database "Early U.S. French Catholic Church Records 1695–1954" contains vital records of French Canadians and French immigrants living in New York, New England, and other United States locations with significant French populations. See also chapter 15, Religious Records.

Notary Records

French-Canadians used notaries to handle all kinds of contracts, including wills, administrations, land transfers, and marriage contracts. One might easily find New York residents in the records of the notaries in the towns and villages from which they originated in Québec. They may have returned there, especially to continue the tradition of the marriage contract, which carried with it legal repercussions. Post-1800 notarial records are in the process of being digitized and made available on *FamilySearch.org*. Some can also be found on the Bibliothèque at Archives Nationales du Québec website, *banq.qc.ca*.

Selected Repositories, Societies, and Websites

The American-Canadian Genealogical Society
4 Elm Street • Manchester, NH 03108 • (603) 622-1554
Email: acgs@acgs.org • *acgs.org*

Holdings include local history books, family histories, and church records for New York (particularly Albany, Clinton, Rensselaer, Saratoga, and Washington counties), New England, and Canada. Full listings are available by selecting "Resources" under the Library section of the website.

The American-French Genealogy Society (AFGS)
78 Earle Street • Woonsocket, RI 02895 • (401) 765-6141
Email: database@afgs.org • *afgs.org*

The AFGS is devoted to researching and studying people of French Canadian descent. The Society's collection includes records from the entire United States; records from New York are largely parish records with a focus on Clinton, Essex, and Franklin counties. An index of library holdings is available online.

Bibliothèque et Archives Nationales du Québec (BAnQ)

Main library: 475, boulevard De Maisonneuve Est
Montréal, Québec H2L 5C4 Canada • AnQ Vieux-Montréal
Main Archives: Édifice Gilles-Hocquart 535, Avenue Viger Est
Montréal, Québec H2L 2P3 • (514) 873-1100 • *banq.qc.ca*

BAnQ is the provincial library and archives for Québec. Original records are kept in the Grande Bibliothèque in Montreal or one of nine regional repositories around the province. Library collections include compiled genealogies, local histories, newspapers, and other published work. Archives collections include original government documents, including older civil registration records, notarial records, land grants, military records, photographs, maps, and more. Holdings also include many collections of private papers.

Historic Huguenot Street (The Huguenot Historical Society)

88 Huguenot Street • New Paltz, NY 12561 • (845) 255-1660
Email: info@huguenotstreet.org • *huguenotstreet.org*

Holdings include approximately 2,500 titles of published and unpublished works on Huguenot and local history and genealogy; 200 cubic feet of archival and manuscript materials, including personal and family papers, family Bibles, and organizational records; and 100 cubic feet of Historic Huguenot Street's own organizational records and memorabilia. A name index of genealogy files is accessible on the website.

The Huguenot Society of America

20 West 44th Street, # 510 • New York, NY 10036
(212) 755-0592 • Email: hugsoc@verizon.net
huguenotsocietyofamerica.org

This lineage society collects and preserves documents, presents lectures, and publishes books relating to Huguenot history and genealogy. The website has a list of the names of Huguenots who left France prior to the promulgation of the Edict of Toleration on November 28, 1787. The Society's library is open for research by members and nonmembers; the collection includes books, monographs, manuscripts, and other materials on the Huguenots.

National Huguenot Society (NHS)

7340 Blanco Road, Suite 104 • San Antonio, TX 78216-4970
(210) 366-9995 • Email access on website
huguenot.netnation.com/general

The NHS is the governing body for more than 40 state societies. The website has information and links to online resources to help genealogists research their Huguenot heritage; it also has a searchable surname index. The NHS publishes *The Cross of Languedoc*, a semiannual journal; back issues from 2002 to the present are available on the website.

The Northern New York American-Canadian Genealogical Society

40 Emmons Street • Dannemora, NY 12981 • (518) 492-4142
Email: nnyacgs@gmail.com • *nnyacgs.com*

The Society has published the journal *Lifelines* since 1984, as well as abstracts and transcriptions of religious, cemetery, and vital records of the surrounding area, as well as of Québec, Canada. The website includes family history queries and completed genealogies.

Selected Bibliography and Further Reading

Baird, Charles. *The History of the Huguenot Emigration to America.* 2 vols. New York: Dodd, Mead & Company, 1885. The classic work on the subject, but subject to revision, particularly by Jon Butler (see below). Both volumes by Baird were reprinted by Heritage Books, Berwyn Heights, MD, in 2011.

Ballard, Frank W. *The Huguenot Settlers of New York City, and Its Vicinity.* New York: n.p., 1989. Reprint from Valentine's Manual for 1862, pp. 743–761.

Bayer, Henry G. *The Belgians: First Settlers in New York and in the Middle States, with a Review of the Events Which Led to Their Immigration.* New York: Devin-Adair Co., 1925. See Van Ruymbeke's paper below for comments on this work.

Bosher, J. F. "Huguenot Merchants and the Protestant International in the Seventeenth Century." *William and Mary Quarterly*, Third Series, vol. 52, no 1 (1995).

Boudreau, Dennis. *Beginning Franco-American Genealogy.* Pawtucket, RI: American-French Genealogical Society, 1993.

Briére, Eloise A. *J'aime New York: A Bilingual Guide to the French Heritage of New York State—Guide bilingue de l'héritage français de l'état de New York.* 2nd edition. Albany: State University of New York/Excelsior Editions, 2012.

Butler, Jon. *The Huguenots in America: A Refugee People in New World Society.* Cambridge, MA: Harvard University Press, 1983.

Carlo, Paula Wheeler. *Huguenot Refugees in Colonial New York: Becoming American in the Hudson Valley.* Portland, OR: Sussex Academic Press, 2005.

Clarke, T. Wood. *Émigrés in the Wilderness.* New York: Macmillan, 1941.

Gannon, Peter Steven. *Huguenot Refugees in the Settling of Colonial America.* New York: The Huguenot Society of America, 1985.

Gentile, Nancy. *Historic Huguenot Street and Its Founding Families.* New Paltz, NY: Huguenot Historical Society, 2004.

Geyh, Patricia Kenney, et al. *French-Canadian Sources: A Guide for Genealogists.* Orem, UT: Ancestry Publishing, 2002.

Goodfriend, Joyce D. "The Protestants of Colonial New York City: A Demographic Profile." In Bertrand Van Ruymbeke and Randy J. Sparks, eds. *Memory and Identity: The*

Huguenots in France and the Atlantic Diaspora, Columbia, SC: University of South Carolina Press, 2003.

Griffis, William Elliott. *The Story of the Walloons*. New York: Houghton Mifflin, 1923. See Van Ruymbeke's paper below for comments on this work.

Hill, Glenna S. *Huguenot Ancestors Documented by the Huguenot Society of New Jersey, Inc.* Bloomfield, NJ: The Society, 1975.

Hoff, Henry B. "New York Families and Sources in Some Genealogical Journals." *NYG&B Newsletter* (now *New York Researcher*), Winter 1995. Includes references to articles in the *Huguenot Historian*, 1980–1984, edited by Glenna See Hill. Also a Research Aid at *NewYorkFamilyHistory.org* [NYG&B eLibrary]

Huguenot Society of New Jersey. *The Huguenot Historian*. Cranford, NJ: The Society, 1982–present.

Kallal, Jeannine S. *Register of Qualified Huguenot Ancestors of the National Huguenot Society*, 5th Edition. San Antonio, TX: The National Huguenot Society, Inc., 2012.

Le Fevre, Ralph. *History of New Paltz, New York, and Its Old Families (from 1678 to 1820): Including the Huguenot Pioneers and Others Who Settled in New Paltz Previous to the Revolution; with an Appendix Bringing Down the History of Certain Families and Some Other Matter to 1850.* Albany: Fort Orange Press, 1909.

Les combattants Français de la guerre Américaine, 1778–1783. Washington: Government Printing Office, 1905. Reprinted, Baltimore: Genealogical Publishing Co., 1969. Text in French and English.

Letourneau, Armand, comp. *Reference and Guide Book for the Genealogist: Prepared Especially for the Franco-Americans.* Woonsocket, RI: American-French Genealogical Society, 2003.

Lindenfeld, Jacqueline. *The French in the United States: An Ethnographic Study.* Westport, CT: Bergin & Garvey, 2000.

Miller, Douglas J. *Miller's Manual: A Research Guide to the Major French-Canadian Genealogical Resources, What They Are, and How to Use Them.* Pawtucket, RI: Quintin Publications, 1997.

National Huguenot Society. *Cross of Languedoc.* San Antonio, TX: The Society, 1960–present.

Picard, Marc. *Dictionary of Americanized French-Canadian Names: Onomastics and Genealogy.* Baltimore: Clearfield Publishing Co., 2013.

Pilcher, Edith. *Castorland: French Refugees in the Western Adirondacks, 1793–1814.* Harrison, NY: Harbor Hill Books, 1985.

Publications of the Huguenot and Historical Association of New Rochelle, N.Y. Vol. 1, part 1. New Rochelle, NY: The Association, 1924. Includes essays on schools from "commencement" to 1856.

Pula, James S. *The French in America, 1488–1974: A Chronology and Factbook.* Dobbs Ferry, NY: Oceana Publications, 1975.

Scott, Kenneth. "New York's French Newspaper, 1795–1799, Genealogical Data." *NYG&B Record*, vol. 120 (1989) no. 4: 207–210; vol. 121 (1990) no. 1: 25–28; no. 2: 101–103; no. 3: 150–153. [NYG&B eLibrary]

Seacord, Morgan H. *Biographical Sketches and Index of the Huguenot Settlers of New Rochelle, 1687–1776.* New Rochelle, NY: Huguenot and Historical Association of New Rochelle, 1941.

Smith, Clifford Neal. *Emigrants from France (Haut-Rhin Department) to America. Part 1 (1837–1844) and Part 2 (1845–1847).* Baltimore: Genealogical Publishing Co., 2004. Haut-Rhin is the southern half of Alsace.

Van Ruymbeke, Bertrand. "The Walloon and Huguenot Elements in New Netherland and Seventeenth-Century New York: Identity, History, and Memory." In *Revisiting New Netherland, Perspectives on Early Dutch America*, edited by Joyce D. Goodfriend, 41-54. Leiden and Boston: Brill, 2005.

Vermilye, A. G. *The Huguenot Element among the Dutch.* Schenectady, NY, 1877.

Wyer, James Ingersoll. "Later French Settlements in New York State, 1783–1800." In *Proceedings of the New York State Historical Association*, vol. 15 (1916): 175–189.

German

Historical Overview

Prior to 1871 Germany did not exist as a unified nation, but was comprised of numerous independent states. The unified German nation included almost all German-speaking people in Europe outside Austria and Switzerland. See also the section on immigrants from the Austro-Hungarian Empire in this chapter.

Although there were some Germans living among the Dutch in New Netherland, the first German settlements in New York were founded in the early-eighteenth century by refugees from the Palatinate (southwestern Germany) who fled the economic deprivations that accompanied armed conflicts. (See Philip Otterness's book, *Becoming German: The 1709 Palatine Migration to New York*.) A group of about 55 Germans, led by the minister Joshua Kocherthal, arrived in December 1708 and settled along the Hudson River in present-day Newburgh (Orange County) in the spring of 1709. A much larger wave of settlers followed in the summer of 1710 when 2,800 German refugees, who had first immigrated to England, set out for New York in ten ships, the largest group of immigrants to enter the colony before the American Revolution.

By 1711 seven German Palatine villages were established on the Livingston Manor land tract in present-day Columbia County. During the 1700s the Palatines established themselves in the Mohawk Valley (Schenectady, Montgomery, Fulton, Oneida, and Herkimer counties) and the Schoharie Valley (consisting of Middleburgh, Schoharie, Fultonham, and Breakabeen in Schoharie County). Large numbers of Germans continued to move to Columbia County, in addition to Albany, Dutchess, and Ulster counties. Some of the original Palatine settlers left New York for Pennsylvania and New Jersey. Throughout the eighteenth century a small but steady stream of German immigrants settled in New York City.

During the Revolutionary War the British hired 32,000 German mercenaries from Hesse, Braunschweig, Ansbach-Beyreuth, Waldeck, and Anhalt-Zerbst to fight for the Loyalists. About 7,000 men settled in the United States after the war.

In the mid-1800s a new wave of German immigration was triggered by several factors, including mass unemployment; crop failures; and new inheritance laws that required property to be divided equally among heirs, causing many families to lose money and land. The Revolutions of 1848 prompted some political refugees to leave the German states for America—the so-called "Forty-Eighters." By 1860 more than 250,000 Germans had emigrated from Prussia, Baden, Bavaria, Hesse, Nassau, and Württemberg. German immigration to the United States was at its highest during the years 1840 to 1880; peak years were 1851,

Many Germans disembarked in New York City and did not leave. The heavily German-speaking community of Kleindeutschland ("Little Germany") was established on Manhattan's Lower East Side in the 1840s and was the first major ethnic enclave in the United States. It was home to two-thirds of New York City's German population in the 1840s and 1850s. By 1880 only Berlin and Vienna had larger German-speaking populations than New York City.

The Kleindeutschland community was struck by one of the worst tragedies in New York City's history on June 15, 1904. St. Mark's Evangelical Lutheran Church had organized a boat trip on the PS *General Slocum* for its annual picnic. More than 1,000 passengers—mostly women and children—perished when the steamboat caught fire. This precipitated the move of many Germans to Yorkville (also called Germantown) on the Upper East Side of Manhattan, which became the new center of German culture in New York City. Brooklyn's Williamsburg also became home to many German immigrants.

Those who left New York City and Brooklyn tended to move to other urban centers. From the mid-1800s an increasing number of Germans moved into the state of New Jersey, especially to Hudson County across the Hudson River, and to Newark (Essex County). Large numbers moved into other parts of New York State, namely Albany (Albany County), Buffalo (Erie County), Rochester (Monroe County), Syracuse (Onondaga County), Troy (Rensselaer County), and Utica (Oneida County), as well as Rockland County. In 1890, about 80 percent of ethnic Germans living in New York State lived in one of these cities. In 1920 Germans were the second largest ethnic group living in Buffalo and Rochester, and the third largest in Albany and Utica.

German immigration to New York slowed in the 1890s, increased in 1920s, and then surged during the 1930s and 1940s. Following World War II large numbers of ethnic Germans from Germany and Eastern Europe, as well as German Jews, were resettled in the United States.

German immigrants often faced severe discrimination during World Wars I and II, which accelerated their efforts to assimilate. Some businesses renamed themselves. Notably, New York City's Germania Life Insurance became the Guardian Life Insurance Company, and Buffalo's German-American Bank became the Liberty Bank. The production of German-language newspapers greatly decreased, and many German social organizations curtailed their activities.

Genealogical Resources

The resources below have specific relevance to researching German immigrants to New York. However, German immigrants will also be found in records discussed elsewhere in this book.

Immigration

The National Archives (NARA) holds passenger and immigration lists. Many are on microfilm and are widely available. *Ancestry.com* has digitized and indexed many of NARA's immigration records, including passenger arrival records for the ports of New York (1820–1957). See chapter 4, Immigration, Migration, and Naturalization, for detailed information about what records exist and where they can be accessed.

The selected bibliography at the end of this section includes books that contain lists of German immigrants which may help fill in gaps in the records, whose availability varies with the time period. Researchers are advised to consult original records when available rather than rely solely on indexes and transcriptions.

The NARA index "Germans to America Passenger Data File, 1850–1897" may be accessed at *http://aad.archives.gov/aad/series-list.jsp?cat=SB301&bc=sb*. The index covers about four million passenger names from ships on which 80 percent or more of the passengers were reputedly German. The database is derived from data compiled by the Balch Institute for Ethnic Studies, which was published in a multivolume series edited by Ira Glazier and P. William Filby. See also Gordon Remington's article "Feast or Famine: Problems in the Genealogical Use of *The Famine Immigrants* and *Germans to America*" for an evaluation of the index.

In December 1917, after the United States declared war on Germany, the *Herald* newspaper published the names and addresses of noncitizen German males between 16 and 50 years of age living in New York City; it also indicated whether they had submitted first papers for citizenship. The newspaper obtained the names from a "Military Census and Inventory" conducted by New York State; the registers are at county clerk's offices, which are listed in the County Guides in Part Two. The German Enemy Aliens database of 26,000 names is on the website of the German Genealogy Group (GGG) at *http://germangenealogygroup.com/records-search/german-enemy-aliens.php*.

During World War II approximately 11,000 individuals of German birth or heritage were interned in the United States as "enemy aliens." NARA holds records of the World War II Enemy Alien Control Program; an index to the WWII Alien Enemy Detention and Internment Case Files is at *archives.gov*. The Defense Security Service (DSS) Form 304, "Alien Personal History and Statement," was completed by noncitizens eligible for military service; statements are four pages long and rich in genealogical detail. The GGG website has an index of Alien Statements for New York State residents, which gives the corresponding file and box numbers at NARA.

Religious Records

Germans were members of many Christian denominations, including Lutheran, Catholic, Reformed, and Moravian, and often formed or joined congregations that offered services in German; see chapter 15, Religious Records. Richard Haberstroh provides information on 400 German churches in New York City in *The German Churches of Metropolitan New York: A Research Guide*. German Jews also immigrated to New York in large numbers, arriving as early as the 1650s; see the section on Jewish people in this chapter, as well as the Jewish section of chapter 15, Religious Records.

Rev. Franz Josef Schneider was an independent Lutheran minister who emigrated from Germany to New York City and performed nearly 20,000 marriage ceremonies, many for couples of mixed cultures and religions. His collection of marriage records for the years 1869 to 1906 are in the Manuscripts and Archives Division of the New York Public Library. His baptismal registers for the same years have been digitized and are in the NYG&B eLibrary.

Newspapers

New York's first German-language newspaper was *New-Yorker Plattdütshe Post*, which was published as a weekly from 1833 to 1930 in New York City. (*Plattdütshe* refers to the language of northern Germany.) By 1851 New York City had seven German-language newspapers; Buffalo and Rochester each had one, and other cities soon followed. Many German American newspapers (including the large number of German-language newspapers) published in New York can be identified on the Library of Congress's Chronicling America website *chroniclingamerica.loc.gov*. Listings of German-language newspapers in North America can also be found on the website of the German-North American Resources Partnership: *http://wessweb.info/index.php/German-Language_Newspaper_Access_in_North_America*.

Two Rochester newspapers, *Der Rochester Beobachter* (1864–1870) and *Der Rochester Taglicher Beobachter* (1871–1883), have been digitized as part of the Google News Archive and are accessible at *news.google.com/newspapers*. See also chapter 12, Newspapers.

Selected Repositories, Societies, and Websites
Leo Baeck Institute (LBI)

Center for Jewish History • 15 West 16th Street
New York, NY 10011 • (212) 744-6400 • *lbi.org*

The Institute is dedicated to the study of the history and culture of German-speaking Jewry. Its extensive collections are accessible to the public without charge and include more than 80,000 books; archives comprising family papers, community histories, personal correspondence, genealogical materials, and business and public records; memoirs; photographs; and an Austrian Heritage Collection. An online catalog is at *search.cjh.org*. The

LBI presents lectures and exhibitions; its website also has digital collections. The LBI is one of the constituent organizations of the Center for Jewish History, which is described in detail in chapter 16.

Cazoo.org German-American Cultural Center

cazoo.org

This website provides numerous links to German American resources in New York and beyond, including such social and cultural societies as the Federation of German American Societies, the German-American Club of Albany, the German American Club of Binghamton, the German American Society of Central New York, the Troy German Hall Association, and the German Society of the City of New York.

Donauschwaben Villages Helping Hands

dvhh.org

This online volunteer group helps descendants of the German ethnic group "Danube Swabian" discover their ancestral roots, history, culture, and lifestyles. The group maintains, preserves, and shares a unique, free collection of Donauschwaben resources on its website, with an extensive list of research links and research support.

German-American Heritage Foundation of the USA

719 6th Street NW • Washington, DC 20001

(202) 467-5000 • *gahmusa.org*

This national membership organization has a quarterly newsletter and website covering issues, programs, reports and research important to German Americans. The foundation established the German-American Heritage Museum in 2010, an art and multimedia museum; it collects, records, preserves, and exhibits the cultural legacy of German, Swiss, Austrian, and Slovakian Americans. Permanent and temporary exhibits feature the history of German immigration and migration across the United States. The foundation also offers lectures and educational programs designed for students of all ages.

German American Internee Coalition (GAIC)

PO Box 714 • New London, NH 03257

info@gaic.info • *gaic.info*

The German American Internee Coalition was founded in 2005 by former internees and their families. The website provides detailed information about internment camps and internee records and includes maps, photographs, biographies, and a historical timeline.

German American National Congress (DANK)

4740 N. Western Avenue, Suite 206 • Chicago, IL 60625

(773) 275-1100 • (888) USA-DANK

Email: office@dank.org • *dank.org*

The German American National Congress (*Deutsch Amerikanischer National Kongress*) works to preserve German culture, heritage, and language in the United States. A membership organization with numerous chapters, DANK publishes a bimonthly national newspaper, the *German-American Journal*. Its website provides links to digital resources and a blog which posts about German news, culture, and music.

German Genealogy Group (GGG)

PO Box 1004 • Kings Park, NY 11754

germangenealogygroup.com

The German Genealogy Group is a membership organization that assists people with German family history research. The GGG offers mentoring, translation services, and a lending library; produces a monthly newsletter; and holds monthly meetings which feature education programs and research assistance. The GGG website is free to all and has vital records and immigration databases of broad interest. German resources include databases of Bavarian Emigration; German Enemy Aliens from World War I; Alien Statements from World War II; a List of Dead and Missing from the PS *General Slocum*; and Surnames of Gottschee (1890–1941.) See also chapter 2, Vital Records, for a description of its indexes to vital records of New York City and locations on Long Island.

Germanic Genealogy Society

PO Box 16312 • St. Paul, MN 55116-0312 • *ggsmn.org*

This all-volunteer organization holds conferences and workshops in Germanic family history research. It collects and publishes genealogical, biographical, and historical material relating to German genealogy worldwide including a quarterly journal, e-newsletter, and books. The society's collection of genealogy material is housed at Concordia University, Saint Paul, Minnesota, where society members offer services in research and translation. A list of the collection is available on the website.

German Information Center, USA

www.germany.travel/en/ms/german-originality/heritage/ genealogy/genealogy.html

This German travel website has a Timeline of Emigration which provides detailed information about emigration from 1600 to the present; a tool for locating German American clubs by state; maps; and a genealogy page with links to numerous resources.

Immigrant Genealogical Society (IGS)

PO Box 7369 • Burbank, CA 91510-7369

(818) 848-3122 • *immigrantgesoc.org*

The IGS was founded in 1982 to help Americans trace their ancestors' origins, particularly in the German-speaking areas of Europe and the places in the world to which they migrated.

The society maintains a genealogical research library with a collection of materials related to German and American genealogy, publishes two periodical journals, and offers searches of its holdings to users worldwide.

Palatines to America National German Genealogy Society (PALAM)

PO Box 141260 • Columbus, OH 43214 • (614) 267-4700

palam.org

The society has chapters in seven states, including New York, and assists people researching their German-speaking ancestors. The website provides online databases, an interactive map, a list of links for genealogical research, and other resources. Collections include 700 family histories, family group charts, and a unique manuscript collection. PALAM offers research and translation services and publishes a quarterly journal, the *Palatine Immigrant*, and a newsletter. The society's books are housed as a special collection in the Columbus Municipal Library in Columbus, Ohio. PALAM sponsors an annual genealogical conference that takes place in rotating locations.

Steuben Society of America

One South Ocean Avenue • Patchogue, NY 11772

(631) 730-5111 • *steubensociety.org*

The Steuben Society is an educational, fraternal, and patriotic organization of American citizens of German background. It has published the *Steuben News* since 1929, and its website offers historical information on German American history with links to other resources.

Yorkville/Kleindeutschland Historical Society

yorkville-kleindeutschlandhistoricalsociety.com

The society works to preserve the history of Yorkville and Kleindeutschland in New York City. It currently offers programs and exhibits as well German-language classes on the Upper East Side of Manhattan. Its goal is to establish a Yorkville/Kleindeutschland Museum and research library in Yorkville.

Selected Bibliography and Further Reading

Ancestors in German Archives: A Guide to Family History Sources. Baltimore: Genealogical Publishing Co., 2004.

Baxter, Angus. *In Search of Your German Roots: A Complete Guide to Tracing Your Ancestors in the Germanic Areas of Europe.* Baltimore: Genealogical Publishing Co., 2008.

Biebel, Frank A. *Index to Marriage and Death Notices in the New-Yorker Staats-Zeitung, 1836–1870.* New York: New York Genealogical and Biographical Society, 2000. [NYG&B eLibrary]

Camann, Eugene W. *Background of Prussian Lutherans Who Settled in Wheatfield, Niagara County, New York, in 1843 and Reasons for Leaving Prussia.* Bergholz, NY: Historical Society of North German Settlements in Western New York, 1983.

Cobb, Sanford H. *The Story of the Palatines: An Episode in Colonial History.* New York & London: G. P. Putnam's Sons, 1897.

Evjen, John O. "Appendix IV: German Immigrants in New York, 1630–1674." In *Scandinavian Immigrants to New York 1630–1674.* Minneapolis: K. C. Holter, 1916. 390–437.

Glazier, Ira A., and P. William Filby. *Germans to America: Lists of Passengers Arriving at U.S. Ports.* Wilmington: Scholarly Resources, 1988–2002. Series I, 67 vols., Series II, 7 vols. The books cover 1850–1897 and includes passenger lists for ships on which 80 percent or more of the passengers were reputedly German. Data from these volumes can be accessed online in the National Archives "Germans to America Passenger Data File, 1850–1897." See also the article by Gordon Remington below. *http://aad.archives.gov/aad/series-list.jsp?cat=SB301&bc=sb*

Haberstroh, Richard. *The German Churches of Metropolitan New York: A Research Guide.* New York: New York Genealogical and Biographical Society, 2000. [NYG&B eLibrary]

Henry, Marian S. "Early Palatine Families of New York." New England Historic Genealogical Society. *www.americanancestors.org/early-palatine-families-of-new-york*

Jones, Henry Z, Jr. *The Palatine Families of New York: A Study of the German Immigrants Who Arrived in Colonial New York in 1710.* 2 vols. Universal City, CA: H. Z Jones, 1985.

———. *More Palatine Families: Some Immigrants to the Middle Colonies 1717–1776 and Their European Origins Plus New Discoveries on German Families Who Arrived in Colonial New York in 1710.* Universal City, CA: H. Z Jones, 1991.

Jones, Henry Z, Jr., and Lewis Bunker Rohrbach. *Even More Palatine Families: 18th Century Immigrants to the American Colonies and Their German, Swiss, and American Origins.* 3 vols. Rockport, ME: Picton Press, 2002.

Just, Michael. *Auswanderung und Schiffahrtsinteressen: Little Germanies in New York, Deutschamerikanische Gesellschaften.* Stuttgart: F. Steiner, 1992.

Kapp, Friedrich. *Die Deutschen im Staate New York während des achtzehnten Jahrhunderts.* New York: E. Steiger, 1884. The title translates to Germans in New York State during the 18th century.

Kaufmann, Wilhelm. *The Germans in the American Civil War: With a Biographical Directory.* Carlisle, PA: John Kallmann, 1999. Originally published in 1911 by Munich Publisher R. Oldenbourg in the German language.

Lohr, Otto. *The First Germans in North America and the German Element of New Netherland.* New York: G.E. Stechert & Co., 1912.

MacWethy, Lou D. *The Book of Names Especially Relating to the Early Palatines and the First Settlers in the Mohawk Valley*. Baltimore: Genealogical Publishing Co., 2007.

Manning, Barbara. *Genealogical Abstracts from Newspapers of the German Reformed Church, 1830–1839*. Bowie, MD: Heritage Books, 1992.

Minert, Roger P. *Germans to America and the Hamburg Passenger Lists: Coordinated Schedules*. Westminster, MD: Heritage Books, 2007.

Nadel, Stanley. *Little Germany: Ethnicity, Religion, and Class in New York City, 1845–80*. Urbana, IL: University of Illinois Press, 1990.

Otterness, Philip. *Becoming German: The 1709 Palatine Migration to New York*. Ithaca, NY: Cornell University Press, 2004. See a review of this book in the July 2005 issue of the *NYG&B Record*.

Reimer, Thomas. *Index to the Deaths Found in the New Yorker Volks-Zeitung, 1878–1920*. Bowie, MD: Heritage Books, 2000.

Remington, Gordon. "Feast or Famine: Problems in the Genealogical Use of *The Famine Immigrants* and *Germans to America*." *National Genealogical Society Quarterly*, vol. 78, no. 2 (1990): 135–146. The article provides an evaluation of the Balch index to help researchers understand the criteria for inclusion and what may be missing.

Rosengarten, J. G. *The German Soldier in the Wars of the United States*. Philadelphia: J. B. Lippincott, 1890.

Rupp, I. Daniel. *A Collection of Upwards of Thirty Thousand Names of German, Swiss, Dutch, French, and Other Immigrants in Pennsylvania from 1727 to 1776 . . . .* Philadelphia: IG. Kohler, 1876.

Schlegel, Carl. *German American Families in the United States*. 4 vols. New York: The American Historical Society, 1916–1926. Reprinted 2003 by Genealogical Publishing Co. The biographies are taken from many sources; these kinds of compilations should be used with caution—but may provide useful clues on some families.

Simmendinger, Ulrich. *True and Authentic Register of Persons . . . Who in the Year 1709, . . . Journeyed from Germany to America . . . .* Pamphlet, n.p., 1717. Reprints: St. Johnsville, NY: The Enterprise & News, 1934; later Kinship Books, *Authentic Register of Persons from Germany to America 1709, Columbia, Dutchess, Greene, Schoharie Counties, NY circa 1717*.

Smith, Clifford Neal. *German Mercenary Expatriates in the United States and Canada*. Baltimore: Reprinted for Clearfied Publishing Co. by Genealogical Publishing Co., 2006.

— — —. *Nineteenth-Century Germans to America: A Consolidation of Six Pamphlets Identifying Emigrants from Baden-Wuerttemberg, Hamburg, Bremen, Nordrhein-Westfalen, Rheinland-Pfalz, and Schleswig-Holstein*. Baltimore: Clearfield Publishing Co., 2005.

— — —. *Reconstructed Passenger Lists for 1851 via Hamburg: Emigrants from Germany, Austria, Bohemia, Hungary, Poland, Russia, Scandinavia, and Switzerland to Australia, Brazil, Canada, Chile, the United States, and Venezuela*. McNeal, AZ: Westland Publications, 1986.

Thode, Ernest. *German-English Genealogical Dictionary*. Baltimore: Genealogical Publishing Co., 1992.

Tolzmann, Don Heinrich. *The First Germans in America: With a Biographical Directory of New York Germans*. Bowie, MD: Heritage Books, 1992.

— — —. *German-Americans in the World Wars*. 5 vols. Münich; New Providence, NJ: K.G. Saur, 1995–1998.

Wolfert, Marion. *German Immigrants: Lists of Passengers Bound from Bremen to New York with Places of Origin 1868–1871*. 4 vols. Baltimore: Genealogical Publishing Co., 1993. Reprint 2006.

Zimmerman, Gary J., and Marion Wolfert. *German Immigrants: Lists of Passengers Bound from Bremen to New York with Places of Origin*. 3 vols. Baltimore: Genealogical Publishing Co., 1985–1988. Reprint 2006. Vol. 1: 1847–1854; vol. 2: 1855–1862; vol. 3: 1863–1867.

Hispanic

Historical Overview

The term Hispanic is broadly applied to a diverse range of Spanish-speaking peoples and cultures throughout the Caribbean and the Americas. The first nonindigenous permanent settler in the area that came to be New Netherland is said to have been Juan Rodriguez, a free man of African and Hispanic descent who was born on the island of Hispaniola. He served on the Dutch ship *Jonge Tobias*, which arrived on what is now Manhattan Island in 1613, and remained to set up a trading post. (See also the section on African American people in this chapter.)

Spanish exploration of the Western Hemisphere dates to the late-fifteenth century and was quickly followed by colonization. The first Spanish settlement in North America was Santo Domingo, founded in 1496 on the island of Hispaniola. By 1512 Spain had established colonies on the islands of Cuba, Jamaica, and Puerto Rico. Spanish explorers arrived in present-day Florida in 1513, and the Spanish conquest of Mexico began in 1519. The Spanish empire relied heavily on slave labor to operate gold and silver mines and sugar, coffee, and tobacco farms and mills. Initially, Spain enslaved indigenous people it had conquered; Spain began to import enslaved Africans to Hispaniola as early as 1501 and extended this practice to its other colonies in the Caribbean and South America. Intermarriage between Spaniards, indigenous peoples, people of African descent, and other immigrants added a distinctive multiracial component to Hispanic societies.

Some Spanish-speaking immigrants settled in New York in small numbers during the colonial period and subsequent years. Immigration by Hispanic merchants increased after 1824, when Spain allowed Puerto Rico and Cuba to engage in foreign trade. The Cuban-Puerto Rican Benevolent Merchants Association was founded in 1830 in New York City. Foreign-born New Yorkers identified in the 1870 census included 1,824 from Cuba; 49 from Central America; 442 from South America; 1,303 from all parts of the West Indies; and 818 from Spain.

Although Spain had lost control of all its other colonies in the region by 1825, Cuba and Puerto Rico struggled for independence throughout the nineteenth century. Beginning in the mid-1800s New York City became a haven for exiled Hispanic independence leaders, such as José Martí of Cuba and Ramón Betances and Eugenio María de Hostos of Puerto Rico. Political exiles and activists formed organizations to support the cause of independence for Cuba and Puerto Rico, including the Republican Society of Cuba and Puerto Rico (1865); Las Dos Antillas (1892), which was co-founded by Arturo Schomburg; and the Puerto Rican Revolutionary Committee (1895).

By 1900 it is estimated that half of the Spanish-speaking immigrants in New York City were from the Caribbean. Many were employed in the tobacco manufacturing industry; in 1894 there were approximately 1,000 cigar factories in New York City. Other immigrants were artisans, skilled and unskilled laborers, and small business owners.

As an outcome of the Spanish-American War in 1898, Puerto Rico came under rule by the United States; Cuba gained its independence in 1902. A Supreme Court ruling in 1904 allowed Puerto Ricans to enter the United States freely and not as immigrants. Immigration to New York by Cubans and Puerto Ricans increased, and by 1910 the number of Cuban-born New Yorkers had climbed to 17,400. (A comparable figure is not available for Puerto Ricans, who were no longer identified on the census as foreign-born.) United States citizenship was granted to Puerto Ricans in 1917, along with the obligation to register for the draft; 20,000 Puerto Ricans served in World War I, in units on the Western Front and the Panama Canal.

Beginning in about 1900 in New York City, the neighborhood around West 14th Street between Seventh and Eighth Avenues was a center of Spanish and Hispanic life that was for several decades known as Little Spain. The *New York Times* estimated in 1924 that New York City's Spanish-speaking community numbered about 30,000 Manhattan and Brooklyn residents with origins in Spain, Mexico, Central America, South America, and the West Indies.

In the 1930s East Harlem became a center of Puerto Rican life in New York City and would eventually be known as Spanish Harlem, or El Barrio. After World War II the numbers of Puerto Ricans coming to New York for economic opportunity increased greatly in a wave that lasted until the 1960s. Puerto Ricans form the largest Hispanic subgroup in New York City, numbering more than 700,000 in 2010, according to the U.S. Census Bureau.

Immigration from the Dominican Republic increased dramatically beginning in the 1960s; subsequent political and economic upheaval fueled continued immigration. The number of New York state residents born in the Dominican Republic grew from 9,600 in 1960 to 52,700 in 1970 and 408,000 in 2000. Dominicans settled in large numbers in the Washington Heights and Inwood neighborhoods of Manhattan, where they have a large presence and form the city's second largest Hispanic subgroup.

The Greater New York area is home to one of the larger concentrations of Cubans outside Florida. Politics and economics have been triggers for Cuban emigration. The number of Cuban-born New York State residents totaled 30,600 in1960 and peaked at 72,200 in 1970, after the Cuban government allowed Cubans to reunite with family members who had previously immigrated to the United States.

Beginning in the 1990s immigrants from Mexico, Ecuador, Colombia, Honduras, El Salvador, and other Central and South

American countries began to arrive in unprecedented numbers. In 2000 there were 726,000 New York residents who were born in Central and South America, as compared to 24,000 in 1950. Their combined total population now exceeds that of the city's Puerto Rican community.

While New York's Hispanic population is concentrated in New York City and its suburbs, about eleven percent of Hispanics in New York now live upstate, with a sizeable representation in the cities of Albany, Buffalo, and Rochester and the towns of Amsterdam (Montgomery County), Jamestown (Chautauqua County), and Watertown-Fort Drum (Jefferson County).

Genealogical Resources

The resources below have specific relevance to researching Hispanic immigrants to New York. However, Hispanic immigrants will also be found in records discussed elsewhere in this book.

Immigration

NARA holds passenger and immigration lists. Many are on microfilm and are widely available. *Ancestry.com* has digitized and indexed many of NARA's immigration records, including passenger arrival records for the ports of New York (1820–1957) and Florida (1898–1951), as well as Mexican border crossings (1895–1964). See chapter 4, Immigration, Migration, and Naturalization, for detailed information about what records exist and where they can be accessed.

The New York State Archives (NYSA) is actively documenting Latin American communities in the state as part of an initiative called the "Latino Heritage Documentation Project." Information on the project is at *www.archives.nysed.gov*. NYSA's Publication No. 66, "A Preliminary Guide to Historical Records Sources on Latinos in New York State," was produced in 2000 and is very comprehensive; it is accessible at *www.archives. nysed.gov/a/records/mr_pub66.pdf*.

Between 1930 and 1959, more than 47,000 identification cards were issued by the Bureau of Employment Identification and the Labor Department of Puerto Rico, Migration Division. These applications were voluntary. Information on the application includes name, photograph, permanent address, date of birth, and place of birth. A small selection has been digitized by Hunter College's Center for Puerto Rican Studies and is accessible at *http://centropr.hunter.cuny.edu/archives/ prdiaspora/introduction*. Researchers may also search through the names of applicants or request a copy of an application.

Census

Starting in 1910 the inhabitants of Puerto Rico have been enumerated on the United States decennial census. The 1900 census recorded only United States armed forces in Puerto Rico. *Ancestry.com* and *findmypast.com* have indexes and images for all decennial federal censuses except 1890. *FamilySearch.*

org has indexes for all available years and images for some years. Microfilm for all available years is at the National Archives (NARA). A special census of Puerto Rico was taken in 1935, and the Social and Population Schedules are accessible at *Ancestry.com* and on microfilm at NARA; the Agricultural Schedules are on microfilm at NARA. See also chapter 3, Census Records.

Military

Beginning in 1917 Puerto Ricans were subject to the draft. World War I draft registration cards for Puerto Rico are on NARA microfilm M1509; World War II registrations (4th registration) are not on microfilm but can be accessed online at *Ancestry.com*. See also chapter 8, Military Records.

Newspapers

New York's first Spanish American newspaper was *El Mensangero Semanal de Nueva York* (1828–1831). Early newspapers often had a strong political focus. The socialist monthly *La Hacienda* was first published in 1905 in Buffalo. The first and largest Spanish-language daily is *El Diario—Il Prensa*, whose roots date to 1913. The Chronicling America website of the Library of Congress offers the U.S. Newspaper Directory (1690–present), which may be searched by ethnicity, language, location, and keywords, to provide newspaper titles and details on where to access them (*chroniclingamerica.loc.gov/search/ titles*). See also chapter 12, Newspapers, for information on how to identify and where to access newspapers.

Religious Records

Most Hispanic immigrants have been Roman Catholic; more recently a growing number have belonged to various Protestant denominations. Apart from a brief period in the 1680s, colonial New York was hostile to Catholics, and the first Catholic church in New York was not established until 1785. In earlier years Hispanic Catholics may have attended Protestant congregations. See chapter 15, Religious Records.

Selected Repositories, Societies, and Websites

El Museo del Barrio

1230 Fifth Avenue • New York, NY 10029 • (212) 831-7272
Email: info@elmuseo.org • *elmuseo.org*

Through its collections, exhibitions, and education programs, El Museo del Barrio preserves and interprets the culture and history of people and places in Latin America and the Caribbean. The museum has a small reference library of books and catalogues on Latin American and Latino artists and installation slides of every el Museo exhibition since the 1980s.

Hispanic Genealogical Society of New York

Grand Central Station • PO Box 3007 • New York, NY 10163
(212) 340-4659 • Email: info@hgsny.com
hispanicgenealogy.com

The society organizes meetings, international research trips, instructional forums, and seminars on Hispanic genealogical research. Its website has an online Hispanic reference library drawn from genealogical resources from all over Latin America and Spain. The Society is in the process of establishing a library and research center to house its reference collection. It publishes the newsletter *Nuestra Herencia* and maintains two websites. Its Puerto Rico Roots website, *prroots.com*, provides online resources with a focus on Puerto Rican Genealogy.

Hispanic Society of America

613 W 155th Street • New York, NY 10032 • (212) 926-2234
hispanicsociety.org

Founded in 1904, the Hispanic Society of America has an extensive collection of paintings, sculptures, textiles, decorative arts, and photographs from Spain, Portugal, and Latin America housed in its impressive headquarters. The society's reference library contains more than 250,000 books and periodicals and almost 200,000 manuscripts from the twelfth century through the present day; it includes many historic and modern works in the Spanish language produced in the Americas.

The Hunter College Center for Puerto Rican Studies

Hunter College's East Building at 68th Street and Lexington Avenue, 14th floor • New York, NY 10065 • (212) 772-5688
centropr.hunter.cuny.edu

The center's Centro Library has more than 25,000 books, 2,500 dissertations and theses, 200 historical newspapers and periodicals, 600 audio recordings, and 500 videos and DVDs, and numerous archival collections of organizations and individuals relating to Puerto Rico and its diaspora. An archives database is currently available onsite only. A digital archive, online exhibits, and collections guide may be accessed at *http://centropr.hunter.cuny.edu/archives/general/digital-archives*.

New York Public Library: Schomburg Center for Research in Black Culture

515 Malcolm X Blvd. • New York, NY 10037 • (212) 491-2200
www.nypl.org/locations/schomburg

The Schomburg Center is named for Arturo Alfonso Schomburg, the Puerto Rican-born scholar who pioneered the study of African Caribbean, African American, and African Latin American history and culture. His personal collections formed the original core of the center's collections. See chapter 16 for a detailed description of the resources of the Schomburg Center.

Nueva York

nuevayork-exhibition.org

In September 2010 the New-York Historical Society (N-YHS) and el Museo del Barrio co-presented the groundbreaking exhibition, *Nueva York*, which documented Spanish and Latin American influences on New York's development from 1613 through 1945. The online exhibition provides a detailed narrative and images of historical maps, letters, paintings, and objects from the original exhibition. The accompanying catalog, which was edited by Edward Sullivan, is cited in the bibliography at the end of this section.

The Puerto Rican/Hispanic Genealogical Society, Inc., Digital Archive

www.rootsweb.ancestry.com/~prhgs

This website includes back issues of the society's newsletter (1996–2004) and links to online articles and data. The society disbanded as a separate organization in 2009 and is now part of the Hispanic Genealogical Society of New York.

Long Island Studies Institute, Hispanic/Latino Collection

www.hofstra.edu/Library/libspc/libspc_lisi_main.html

The Hispanic/Latino Collection, a cooperative endeavor of Hofstra University and Nassau County, documents the experience of Hispanic immigrants to Long Island, including their social life, customs, and culture. A detailed finding aid the collection is at *www.hofstra.edu/pdf/library/libspc_lisi_hlc_fa.pdf*.

Selected Bibliography and Further Reading

Byers, Paula K. *Hispanic American Genealogical Sourcebook*. New York: Gale Research, 1995.

Fernández-Shaw, Carlos M. *The Hispanic Presence in North America from 1492 to Today*. New York: Facts on File, 1999.

Hanson-Sanchez, Christopher. *New York City Latino Neighborhoods Databook*. New York: Institute for Puerto Rican Policy, 1960.

Harris, Stephen L. *Harlem's Hell Fighters: The African-American 369th Infantry in World War I*. Washington: Brassey's, Inc., 2003.

Haslip-Viera, Gabriel, and Angelo Falcónand Félix Matos Rodríguez, eds. *Boricuas in Gotham: Puerto Ricans in the Making of Modern New York City: Essays in Memory of Antonia Pantoja*. Princeton, NJ: Markus Wiener Publishers, 2005.

Hendricks, Glenn L. *The Dominican Diaspora: From the Dominican Republic to New York City—Villagers in Transition*. New York: Teachers College Press, Columbia University, 1974.

Hispanics and the Civil War from Battlefield to Homefront. Washington: National Park Service, U.S. Department of the Interior, 2011. Excerpts available online at *www.nps.gov/resources/story.htm?id=300*.

Hispanic Genealogy Workbook. New York: Hispanic Genealogical Society of New York, 2000.

Kanellos, Nicolás. *Introduction of Hispanic Periodicals in the United States, Origins to 1960: A Brief History and Comprehensive Bibliography*. Houston: Arte Público Press, 2000. Digital book.

Kanellos, Nicolás, and Fabregat C. Esteva. *Handbook of Hispanic Cultures in the United States*. Houston: Arte Público Press, 1993.

Laó-Montes, Augustín, and Arlene Dávila, eds. *Mambo Montage: The Latinization of New York*. New York: Columbia University Press, 2001.

New York State Archives. "A Preliminary Guide to Historical Records Sources on Latinos in New York State." Publication No. 66. 2000. *www.archives.nysed.gov/a/records/mr_pub66.pdf*

Nuestra Herencia: A Hispanic Genealogical Society of New York, Inc., Publication. New York: Hispanic Genealogical Society New York, 1997.

Ryskamp, George R. *Finding Your Hispanic Roots*. Baltimore: Genealogical Publishing Co., 1997.

Saenz, Julio. *Rochester's Latino Community*. Charleston, SC: Arcadia Publishing, 2011.

Sánchez Korrol, Virginia. *From Colonia to Community: The History of Puerto Ricans in New York City, 1917–1948*. Westport, CT: Greenwood Press, 1983.

Stevens-Acevedo, Anthony, Tom Weterings, and Leonor Alvarez Frances. *Juan Rodriguez and the Beginnings of New York City*. New York: Dominican Studies Research Monograph Series, City College of New York, 2013.

Sullivan, Edward J., ed. *Nueva York, 1613–1945: New York and the Spanish-Speaking World Book*. London: Scala, 2010.

Irish

Historical Overview

A small number of Irish immigrants lived in New Netherland, and the number increased when the British took control of the colony in 1664. During the British colonial era, the largest numbers of Irish immigrants to New York were Protestants of Scottish descent from the province of Ulster. (See also the section on Scots and Scots-Irish in this chapter.) There were some Irish Catholics in colonial New York, notably Thomas Dongan, New York's governor from 1682 to 1688. However, immigration to New York by Irish Catholics did not outpace that of Irish Protestants until the 1820s.

The largest colonial Irish community was in New York City. Scots-Irish communities were established in Orange and Ulster counties in the 1720s and 1730s. Irish landowners in the Mohawk Valley in the mid-1700s encouraged other Irish immigrants to settle in present-day Essex, Montgomery, Otsego, Schenectady, and Washington counties.

Sir William Johnson (originally of County Meath, Ireland) arrived in the Mohawk Valley in 1738 and established a settlement with 12 Scots-Irish families. He became one of the largest landowners in the state, acquiring property in Fulton, Herkimer, Oneida, and Otsego counties, including 90,000 acres in 1765 known as the Kingsland Grant. He encouraged settlement on his lands by Irish Protestants and Catholics. In 1791 three prosperous Irish merchants (Daniel McCormick, William Constable, and Alexander Macomb) formed a land syndicate that purchased 3.6 million acres in present-day St. Lawrence, Lewis, Jefferson, Franklin, Herkimer, and Oswego counties and attracted Irish settlers.

From the 1730s to the early 1770s, there was an active trade between New York and Ireland, as flaxseed was exported to Irish cities, and linen goods manufactured in Ireland were sold in New York. During the pre-Famine period (prior to 1845), Irish New Yorkers were a mix of merchants, professionals, farmers, soldiers, and seamen, as well as unskilled laborers and domestic servants. They were also religiously and politically diverse. Though the Presbyterian denomination was by far the largest, there were also Irish Anglicans (Episcopalians), Methodists, Quakers, and Catholics, despite New York's anti-Catholic laws, which banned Catholic worship until 1784, and were not fully lifted until 1806. The Irish numbered among both Patriots and Loyalists during the American Revolutionary War.

Irish immigration to New York increased in the 1800s; it surged in 1827 when the British government repealed the Passenger Acts, which had inflated the cost of emigration to the United States. Irish immigrant laborers played a significant role in building the infrastructure of New York State. More than 3,000

Irishmen were employed building the Erie Canal (1817–1825), its extensions, and its expansion, and workers settled along the canal route in cities such as Buffalo, Rome, Rochester, Syracuse, Troy, and Utica. Many Irish immigrants were also employed on the Croton Water System (1837–1842), which transported water from Westchester County to New York City, and on railways throughout the state, beginning with the Mohawk and Hudson Railroad (1826).

During and after the Great Famine (1845–1852), immigration by Irish Catholics to New York increased exponentially. By 1860 New York's population had grown to 3.8 million and included 500,000 Irish-born New Yorkers, nearly twice the number of German-born, and nearly five times the number of English-born. These Irish immigrants largely came from farms but settled in urban areas, such as New York City, the City of Brooklyn, and cities in Albany, Erie, and Rensselaer counties, where they could find work as unskilled laborers. Although they filled many gaps in the workforce and were employed in factories, on the docks, as day laborers, and as domestics, Irish Catholics faced severe discrimination on many fronts.

Irish women and girls often came to New York alone during and after the years of the Great Famine to seek work as live-in domestic help. They saved their salaries and sent money home to pay for other family members to emigrate—who would then do the same for additional family members; this process, known as chain migration, played an important role in Irish immigration.

The Irish quickly grew to be one of the largest ethnic populations in New York and transformed the political landscape. New York City's Tammany Society, a powerful political organization founded in 1786, was under Irish control from the mid-1800s to the 1920s. It had a major influence over Democratic Party nominations and mayoral elections. Known from the early-nineteenth century as Tammany Hall, the Society was an important source of support to Irish immigrants; it steered public sector jobs to them, especially ones in the police force and the fire department, in exchange for votes. This was a strong motivation for Irish immigrants to become citizens as soon after their arrival in New York as possible.

Political and economic conditions in Ireland fueled continued immigration, and the number of Irish-born New Yorkers did not drop below 400,000 until 1910. Recent Irish immigrants to New York have settled principally in New York City and its surrounding suburbs. Among New York's larger Irish enclaves are Woodlawn and North Riverdale, the Bronx; Woodside, Belle Harbor, and Breezy Point, Queens; Marine Park and Gerritsen Beach, Brooklyn; and the area around McLean Avenue, Yonkers.

Genealogical Resources

The resources below have specific relevance to researching Irish immigrants to New York. However, Irish immigrants will also be found in records discussed elsewhere in this book.

Immigration

The National Archives (NARA) holds passenger and immigration lists. Many are on microfilm and are widely available. *Ancestry.com* has digitized and indexed many of NARA's immigration records, including passenger arrival records for the ports of New York (1820–1957), Philadelphia (1800–1948), and Boston (1820–1954), as well as Canadian border crossings to New York (1895–1956). See chapter 4, Immigration, Migration, and Naturalization, for detailed information about what records exist and where they can be accessed.

The selected bibliography at the end of this section includes books that contain lists of Irish immigrants which may help fill in gaps in the records, whose availability varies with the time period. Researchers are advised to consult original records when available rather than rely solely on indexes and transcriptions.

The Famine Irish Entry Project, conducted at the Balch Institute for Ethnic Studies, resulted in eight volumes that were co-edited by Ira Glazier and Michael Tepper. The data from these volumes forms the basis of NARA's database, "Records for Passengers Who Arrived at the Port of New York during the Irish Famine, created 1977–1989, documenting the period 1/12/1846–12/31/1851," which may be accessed at *aad.archives.gov/aad/series-list.jsp?cat=GP44*. About 70 percent of the indexed names were emigrants from Ireland and 30 percent from other countries. See Gordon Remington's article "Feast or Famine: Problems in the Genealogical Use of *The Famine Immigrants* and *Germans to America*" for an evaluation of the index.

The Irish Emigrant Aid Society was founded in 1841 to promote the welfare of Irish immigrants; it led to the founding of the Emigrant (Industrial) Savings Bank in 1850 to help immigrants protect their savings and assist them to safely send money home to other family members. Test Books, which recorded questions and answers that were used to confirm the identity of the depositor for transactions, survive for 66,756 accounts. They are rich in genealogical data not always found elsewhere, and often include the birthplace in Ireland, the arrival date and ship name, and information about children, siblings, and parents, in addition to basic details such as address, spouse, and occupation.

The Test Books (1850–1868) are held by the New York Public Library (NYPL), which also holds an Index of Depositors (1850–1880); Transfer, Signature, and Test Books (1850–1883); Deposit-Account Ledgers; Real Estate Books (1851–1923); and Minutes of the Society's Board of Trustees (1841–1933). Kevin Rich has transcribed numerous records of the Emigrant Savings Bank in his multivolume work, *Irish Immigrants of the Emigrant Industrial Savings Bank*. The NYPL has a user's guide at *archives.nypl.org/uploads/collection/pdf_finding_aid/emigrant.pdf*. Many of the records are online at *Ancestry.com* and on microfilm at the Family History Library (FHL) and other locations.

The Mission of Our Lady of the Rosary for the Protection of Irish Immigrant Girls was established in 1883 to provide assistance to Irish girls arriving in New York City. The following year a residence and a chapel were established at Seven State Street, known then as Watson House; the church continues today as Our Lady of the Rosary and Shrine of St. Elizabeth Ann Seton (*setonshrine.com*). Five bound ledger books for the years 1897–1940 that record 35,000 arrivals have been digitized and indexed; they may be viewed at the Irish Mission at Watson House website, *watsonhouse.org*, which also has an online exhibition about the Mission's history.

Institutional Records

Particularly during the Famine years, many Irish immigrants were destitute. Irish names appear frequently in the records of almshouses, poorhouses, and potter's fields, as well as in court records—often for vagrancy, but also for other crimes, real or imagined, especially during times when anti-Irish sentiment ran high. See chapter 10, Business, Institutional, and Organizational Records, for information on how to access these records.

Newspapers

New York's first Irish American newspaper was the *Shamrock or Hibernian Chronicle* (1810–1817), and many others have followed. One of the most successful, the *Irish-American*, was published weekly from 1849 to1915. The Chronicling America website of the Library of Congress offers the U.S. Newspaper Directory (1690–present), which may be searched by ethnicity, language, location, and keywords, to provide newspaper titles and details on where to access them (*chroniclingamerica.loc. gov/search/titles*). A list of historical Irish American newspapers published in New York City is included in Joseph Buggy's recent book, *Finding Your Irish Ancestors in New York City*. See also chapter 12, Newspapers, for information on how to identify and where to access newspapers.

"Information Wanted" advertisements were placed in newspapers by people looking for relatives and friends; these advertisements are a rich source of genealogical information; they vary greatly, but often include place of birth, date of emigration, and occupation. Two volumes of ads from the *Truth Teller*, New York's first Catholic newspaper, and the *Irish-American* have been compiled by Laura Murphy DeGrazia and Diane Fitzpatrick Haberstroh. A database compiled from the book *The Search for Missing Friends: Irish Immigrant Advertisements Placed in The Boston Pilot 1831–1920* is at *AmericanAncestors.org* and contains over 40,000 newspaper ads published in the *Boston Pilot*. Much of the data is also available at *infowanted.bc.edu*.

Religious Records

During the colonial era, the largest numbers of Irish immigrants were Protestant; of those, Presbyterians, who belonged to the Church of Scotland, outnumbered Anglicans, who belonged to the Church of Ireland. Irish Quakers and Baptists were present in the colonies from the 1600s. Irish Methodists arrived in New York as early as 1760. Philip Embury, an Irish Palatine, led the first service of the John Street Methodist congregation in New York City in 1766.

Although Jesuit missionaries were active in several areas of upstate New York in the 1600s and 1700s, open worship by Catholics was outlawed in New York until 1784. Irish immigration was a catalyst for the rapid growth of the Catholic Church in the 1800s and the establishment of Catholic schools, hospitals, orphanages, social service organizations, and cemeteries. See chapter 15, Religious Records, for information on how to access sacramental and institutional records for the Catholic Church and other denominations.

Selected Repositories, Societies, and Websites

The American Irish Historical Society

991 Fifth Avenue • New York, NY 10028 • (212) 288-2263
Email: aihs@aihs.org • aihs.org

Founded in 1897, the Society presents lectures and concerts and publishes a journal, the *Recorder*. Its library is open to researchers and includes more than 10,000 volumes, which forms the most complete private collection of Irish and American Irish history and literature in the United States. Its holdings include newspapers, manuscripts, personal papers, rare books, and organization archives, as well as a small genealogical collection.

Archives of Irish America at New York University

The Tamiment Library • Bobst Library
70 Washington Square South • New York, NY 10012
(212) 998-3478 • *www.nyu.edu/library/bobst/research/aia*

The Archives of Irish America (AIA) is part of New York University's Tamiment Library, which is open to the public. The Archives collects material about the Irish immigration experience, its connection to the labor movement, and the Irish impact on American social and cultural development. Its growing collections include organization records, personal papers, photographs, and oral histories. Digital exhibits and selected documents may be viewed on the website. A list of collections and finding aids is at *http://www.nyu.edu/library/bobst/research/tam/fa_index.html#aia*.

The Buffalo Irish Center

buffaloirishcenter.com

The Buffalo Irish Genealogical Society (BIGS)

245 Abbott Road • Buffalo, NY 14220 • (716) 662-1164
bigs.limewebs.com

The Buffalo Irish Center houses the Gaelic American Athletic Association (GAAA) Irish Library and the collections of the Buffalo Irish Genealogical Society, which include general books about Ireland, various research resources for Irish American genealogy, and an index of burials at local cemeteries. The BIGS holds regular meetings, presents genealogical workshops, and encourages inter-member networking. It maintains a list of surnames being researched by its members and accepts inquiries from nonmembers.

Irish American Heritage Museum

370 Broadway • Albany, NY 12207 • (518) 427-1916
irish-us.org

The Museum presents exhibitions and programs about Irish contributions to American history and culture and offers genealogical workshops and consultations. Its Paul O'Dwyer Library contains the personal papers and books of New York politician Paul O'Dwyer (1907–1998); many volumes related to Irish history and culture; and some national historical records of the Ancient Order of Hibernians. The library is open to the public for onsite research, and its circulating material is available through the Capital District Library Council's Interlibrary Loan Program.

The Irish Ancestral Research Association (TIARA)

2120 Commonwealth Avenue • Auburndale, MA 02466
tiara.ie

TIARA publishes a quarterly newsletter, organizes annual research trips to Ireland, and presents a lecture series. Its website includes a surname database, which includes some immigrants to New York, and other helpful links.

The Irish Family History Forum (IFHF)

John Rowane Memorial Library: LDS Family History Center
Washington Avenue • Plainview, NY 11803 • *ifhf.org*
Monthly meetings: Bethpage Public Library
47 Powell Avenue • Bethpage, NY 11714 • (516) 931-3907

The IFHF supports the Irish family research efforts of members through monthly meetings with specialist speakers, a bimonthly newsletter with the latest developments in Irish research, the IFHF Surname Inquiry List, where members exchange their research, and a list of links to other Irish genealogical resources. The IFHF's John Rowane Memorial Library contains over 300 publications on various topics in Irish genealogy, history, and culture. The collection can be consulted by nonmembers, but only members may borrow materials.

The Irish Genealogical Society International, Inc. (IGSI)

1185 Concord Street North, Suite 218
South St. Paul, MN 55075 • questions@IrishGenealogical.org
irishgenealogical.org

The IGSI assists members and the general public in conducting Irish genealogical research. It has a large, noncirculating library collection which is housed in the Minnesota Genealogical Society Library and Research Center, and is searchable through an online catalog. The Society publishes a quarterly journal, the *Septs*, and a newsletter; it offers classes, research trips, and writing groups. The website hosts a blog and offers members a surname search, message board, maps, and information on Irish counties.

The New York Irish History Roundtable

Email: roundtable@irishnyhistory.org • *irishnyhistory.org*

The New York Irish History Roundtable promotes the research of people of Irish heritage in New York City from the colonial period to the present. It presents lectures, field trips, walking tours, special projects, museum exhibitions, and genealogy workshops, and publishes a newsletter and an annual journal, *New York Irish History*.

The Society of the Friendly Sons of Saint Patrick

Three West 51st Street, Room 604 • New York, NY 10019
(212) 269-1770 • *friendlysonsnyc.com*

The Society was founded in 1784 by prosperous Irish New Yorkers to promote cooperation among the Irish and to aid Irish in need. Its website has a complete list of past presidents and a few digitized historical documents. Membership rolls for various years are at *Archive.org*. An extensive history was published in 1962.

The Troy Irish Genealogy Society (TIGS)

452 Broadway • Troy, NY 12180 • (518) 326-3994
www.rootsweb.ancestry.com/~nytigs

The Troy Irish Genealogy Society promotes the heritage of Troy-area Irish families through monthly meetings, a website with research links, members' surname research, local history information, and opportunities to connect with other members. A significant amount of data is on the website.

Selected Bibliography and Further Reading

Almeida, Linda Dowling. *Irish Immigrants in New York City, 1945–1995*. Bloomington: Indiana University Press, 2001.

Anbinder, Tyler. "Moving Beyond Rags to Riches: New York's Irish Famine Immigrants and Their Surprising Savings Accounts." *Journal of American History*, vol. 99, no. 3 (2012): 741–770.

Ardolina, Rosemary Muscarella. *Old Calvary Cemetery: New Yorkers Carved in Stone*. Bowie, MD: Heritage Books, 1996.

— — —. *Second Calvary Cemetery: New Yorkers Carved in Stone*. Floral Park, NY: Delia Publications, 2000.

Bayor, Ronald H., and Timothy J. Meagher, eds. *The New York Irish*. Baltimore: Johns Hopkins University Press, 1996.

Brownstein, Robin, and Peter Guttmaker. *The Scotch-Irish Americans*, The Peoples of North America Series. New York: Chelsea House Publishers, 1988.

Buggy, Joseph. *Finding Your Irish Ancestors in New York City*. Baltimore: Genealogical Publishing Co., 2014.

Crowley, John, William J. Smyth, and Mike Murphy, eds. *Atlas of the Great Irish Famine, 1845–1852*. Cork, Ireland: Cork University Press, 2012.

DeGrazia, Laura Murphy, and Diane Fitzpatrick Haberstroh, comps. *Irish Relatives and Friends: From "Information Wanted" Ads in the* Irish-American, *1850–1871*. Baltimore: Genealogical Publishing Co., 2001.

———, comps. *Voices of the Irish Immigrant: Information Wanted Ads in the* Truth Teller, *New York City, 1825–1844*. New York: New York Genealogical and Biographical Society, 2005. [NYG&B eLibrary].

Diner, Hasia. *Erin's Daughters in America, Irish Women in the Nineteenth Century*. Baltimore: Johns Hopkins University Press, 1983.

Dobson, David. *Irish Emigrants in North America 1670–1830*. 7 vols. Baltimore: Genealogical Publishing Co., 1998–2008.

———. *Ships from Ireland to Early America, 1628–1850*. Baltimore: Genealogical Publishing Co., 2004.

Dunkak, Harry M. *Freedom, Culture, Labor: The Irish of Early Westchester County, New York*. New Rochelle, NY: Iona College Press, 1994.

Ellis, Eilish. *Emigrants from Ireland, 1847–1852: State-Aided Emigration Schemes from Crown Estates in Ireland*. Baltimore: Genealogical Publishing Co., 1993.

Glazier, Ira A. *Emigration from the United Kingdom to America: Lists of Passengers Arriving at U.S. Ports, 1870–1897*. 18 vols. Lanham, MD: Scarecrow Press, 2006–2012.

Glazier, Ira A., and Michael Tepper. *The Famine Immigrants: Lists of Irish Immigrants Arriving at the Port of New York, 1846–1851*. 8 vols. Baltimore: Genealogical Publishing Co., 1983–1986. The data from these volumes forms the basis of NARA's database, "Records for Passengers Who Arrived at the Port of New York during the Irish Famine, Created 1977–1989, Documenting the Period 1/12/1846–12/31/1851," which may be accessed at *aad.archives.gov/aad/series-list.jsp?cat=GP44*.

Harris, Ruth-Ann M., Donald M. Jacobs, Dominique M. Pickett, and B. Emer O'Keeffe, eds. *The Search for Missing Friends: Irish Immigrant Advertisements Placed in the* Boston Pilot. 7 vols. Boston: New England Historic Genealogical Society, 1989–1993.

Kelly, Mary C. *The Shamrock and the Lily: The New York Irish and the Creation of a Transatlantic Identity, 1845–1921*. New York: Peter Lang, 2005.

Lundrigan, Margaret. *Irish Staten Island*. Charleston, SC: Arcadia Publishing, 2009.

Maher, James P. *Index to Marriages and Deaths in the New York Herald, 1835–1876*. 4 vols. Baltimore: Genealogical Publishing Co., 1987–2006. More than 15,000 Irish places of origin are listed.

McDonnell, Frances. *Emigrants from Ireland to America, 1735–1743: A Transcription of the Report of the Irish House of Commons into Enforced Emigration to America*. Baltimore: Genealogical Publishing Co., 1992.

Miller, Kerby A. *Emigrants and Exiles: Ireland and the Irish Exodus to North America*. New York: Oxford University Press, 1985.

Mitchell, Brian. *Irish Emigration Lists, 1833–1839, Lists of Emigrants Extracted from the Ordnance Survey Memoirs for Counties Londonderry and Antrim*. Baltimore: Genealogical Publishing Co., 1989. Identifies New York as the destination for many of the names listed.

———. *Irish Passenger Lists, 1803–1806*. Baltimore: Genealogical Publishing Co., 1995.

———. *Irish Passenger Lists 1847–1871: Lists of Passengers Sailing from Londonderry to America on Ships of the J.& J. Cooke Line and the McCorkell Line*. Baltimore: Genealogical Publishing Co., 2001.

Moorhouse, B-Ann. "Researching the Irish-Born of New York City." *NYG&B Record*, vol. 112, no. 2 (1981). [NYG&B eLibrary] Updated by NYG&B staff April 2014 and published as a Research Aid on *NewYorkFamilyHistory.org*.

Murphy, Richard C., and Lawrence J. Mannion, *History of the Society of the Friendly Sons of Saint Patrick in the City of New York, 1784 to 1955*. New York: n.p., 1962.

O'Grady, Joseph. *How the Irish Became Americans*. The Immigrant Heritage of America Series. New York: Twayne Publishers, Inc., 1973.

Radford, Dwight A., and Kyle J. Betit. *A Genealogist's Guide to Discovering Your Irish Ancestors*. Cincinnati: Betterway Books, 2001.

Remington, Gordon. "Feast or Famine: Problems in the Genealogical Use of *The Famine Immigrants* and *Germans to America*." *National Genealogical Society Quarterly*, vol. 78, no. 2 (1990): 135–146.

Rich, Kevin J. *Irish Immigrants of the Emigrant Industrial Savings Bank*. 3 vols. Massapequa, NY: Broadway-Manhattan Co., 2001.

Ruddock, William T. *Linen Threads and Broom Twines: An Irish and American Album and Directory of the People of the Dunbarton Mill, Greenwich, New York, 1879–1952*. Bowie, MD: Heritage Books, 1997.

Salvato, Richard. "A User's Guide to the Emigrant Savings Bank Record." New York: New York Public Library Manuscripts and Archives Division, 1997. *archives.nypl.org/uploads/collection/pdf_finding_aid/emigrant.pdf*

Schlegel, Donald M. *Passengers from Ireland: Lists of Passengers Arriving at American Ports Between 1811 and 1817.* Baltimore: Genealogical Publishing Co., 2007.

Shea, Ann M., and Marion R. Casey. *The Irish Experience in New York City: A Select Bibliography.* New York: New York Irish History Roundtable, 1995.

Silinonte, Joseph M. *Bishop Loughlin's Dispensations, Diocese of Brooklyn: Genealogical Information from the Marriage Dispensation Records of the Roman Catholic Diocese of Brooklyn: Kings, Queens and Suffolk Counties.* Brooklyn, NY: The Author, 1996.

———. *Tombstones of the Irish Born: Cemetery of the Holy Cross, Flatbush, Brooklyn.* Westminster, MD: Heritage Books, 2006.

Italian

Historical Overview

The first Italian settler recorded in New York was Pietro Caesar Alberto, who is said to have arrived in New Amsterdam by 1639. His 1642 marriage record indicates that he was from Venice, and as "Pieter Cesar Italiaen" he was granted a farm in the Wallabout section of Brooklyn in 1647. Small numbers of Italians would continue to immigrate to New York during and after the colonial era.

By 1860 the number of Italian-born New Yorkers totaled just 1,862. Early Italian immigrants were often skilled workers, merchants, craftsmen, artisans, musicians, or artists; most came from the north of Italy and lived in New York City, though some migrated elsewhere in the state. Utica's first Italian resident arrived in 1815, and Rochester's first Italian resident was recorded in the early 1860s. Both cities eventually became home to large Italian communities.

Following the unification of Italy in 1861, severe economic conditions and political problems caused the exodus of large numbers of Italians from the southern regions of Abruzzo, Apulia, Basilicata, Calabria, Campania, Lazio, Molise, Naples, and Sicily. These largely rural regions suffered from a dearth of good farmland and a lack of natural resources, which was exacerbated by overpopulation, disease, and natural disasters.

After 1900 the United States outpaced South America as the preferred destination of most westward-bound Italians. More than 4.1 million Italians entered the United States between 1880 and 1920. The number of Italian-born residents in New York climbed from 15,000 in 1880 to 182,000 in 1900 and to 629,000 in 1930. Throughout the period 1910–1970, Italians were the largest foreign-born population in New York State.

During the peak immigration years 1880–1920, three quarters of Italian immigrants to the United States were men, many of whom were temporary seasonal workers, they went back and forth between the two countries for years before settling permanently in the United States or returning to Italy for good. Often called "birds of passage," a large number of these were married men who came to New York to earn money to send to their families in Italy. They often found employment as manual laborers and migrated throughout New York State working on heavy construction projects, such as laying railroad or streetcar tracks, paving roads, building bridges, repairing canals, or constructing universities, hospitals, and other public buildings.

While New York City had the highest concentration, Italians also settled in towns and cities throughout the state along the path of construction projects and manufacturing jobs in the Hudson Valley, Albany, Troy, Schenectady, Utica, Syracuse,

Rochester, and Buffalo. By 1920 significant Italian communities had also developed in Amsterdam (Montgomery County), Auburn (Cayuga County), Binghamton (Broome County), Elmira (Chemung County), Jamestown (Chautauqua County), Mount Vernon and New Rochelle (Westchester County), Newburgh (Orange County), Niagara Falls (Niagara County), and Poughkeepsie (Dutchess County). Less commonly, Italians settled in agricultural communities, such as Canastota (Madison County).

There was a prevalence of Italians among certain industries and occupations, such as bricklayer, stonemason, quarry worker, construction worker, carpenter, barber, dockworker, shoemaker, tailor, waiter, garment worker, fisherman, grocer, and street vendor. This gave rise to numerous Italian-owned small businesses that employed family members and other Italian immigrants. In the 1930s an estimated 10,000 grocery stores in New York City were owned by Italians.

Generally, Italian men deferred becoming citizens—sometimes until twenty years after first arriving in the United States. When the decision was eventually made to stay in America and the rest of the family emigrated, wives used their maiden names on passenger arrival records, while children used their father's name. Women in Italy have traditionally used their maiden names for legal purposes.

Italian immigrants often formed close-knit communities in urban centers that came to be called "Little Italy." New York City's Little Italy, centered on Mulberry Street on the Lower East Side of Manhattan, is the best known, but many other "Little Italies" and Italian enclaves exist. Also in New York City are Belmont (also known as Arthur Avenue), Morris Park, and Pelham Bay in the Bronx; Bath Beach, Bensonhurst, and Carroll Gardens in Brooklyn; East Harlem in Manhattan; Howard Beach and Middle Village in Queens; and Rosebank (formerly Peterstown) on Staten Island. Elsewhere in New York State are Dante Place (formerly Canal Street) in Buffalo, East Rochester in the City of Rochester, and neighborhoods known as Little Italy in the cities of Albany, Niagara Falls, Poughkeepsie, Syracuse, and Utica.

Immigration to New York by Italians has continued to the present day. According to the 2000 census, there were 147,000 New Yorkers born in Italy, the highest number of any European country of origin. The New York counties with the highest concentrations of people of Italian descent were Putnam (32 percent), Suffolk (29 percent), Nassau (24 percent), Dutchess (22 percent), Schenectady (22 percent), and Westchester (21 percent).

Genealogical Resources

The resources below have specific relevance to researching Italian immigrants to New York. However, Italian immigrants will also be found in records discussed elsewhere in this book.

Immigration

The National Archives at New York City (NARA-NYC) has microfilm copies of passenger arrival records for the Port of New York for the years 1820–1957. *Ancestry.com* has digitized and indexed the full collection; portions of the records are also available elsewhere online. See chapter 4, Immigration, Migration, and Naturalization, for detailed information about records for New York and where they can be accessed.

The selected bibliography at the end of this section includes books containing lists of Italian immigrants which may help fill in gaps in the records, whose availability varies with the time period. Researchers are advised to consult original records when available rather than rely solely on indexes and transcriptions.

The National Archives (NARA) index "Italians America Passenger Data File, 1855–1900" may be accessed at *http://aad.archives.gov/aad/series-list.jsp?cat=SB301&bc=sb*. The index covers about 845,000 passenger names and contains data compiled by the Balch Institute for Ethnic Studies, which was published in a multivolume series edited by Ira Glazier and P. William Filby.

Although Italians in the United States actively supported the American war effort during World War II, hundreds of Italians were designated by the United States government as enemy aliens and interned in camps between 1941 and 1945. The index to WWII Alien Enemy Detention and Internment Case Files held by NARA can be searched at *archives.gov/research/japanese-americans/internment-files.html*; paper copies of the Case Files may be ordered.

Newspapers

New York's first Italian-language newspaper was *L'Eco d'Italia* (1849). The popular daily *Il Progresso Italo-Americano* was published from 1880 to1988; microfilm of the years 1889–1976 is at the Calandra Italian American Institute at Queens College in New York City. Many other Italian-language newspapers were published in New York. The Chronicling America website of the Library of Congress offers the U.S. Newspaper Directory (1690–present), which may be searched by ethnicity, language, location, and keywords, to provide newspaper titles and details on where to access them at *chroniclingamerica.loc.gov/search/titles*. The New York State Library's list of New York newspapers at *www.nysl.nysed.gov/nysnp/title4.htm* provides holdings information for more than 10,000 newspaper titles that have been published in New York State. See also chapter 12, Newspapers.

Religious Records

Most Italian immigrants to New York were Roman Catholic and usually continued as active Catholics after arrival. Open worship by Catholics was outlawed in New York until 1784. The establishment of Catholic churches, as well as schools, hospitals, social service organizations, and cemeteries, rapidly spread throughout the state in the 1800s. See chapter 15, Religious Records, for information on how to access religious records and religious institutional records.

The Waldensians, who broke with the Catholic Church in the twelfth century, survived in the northwest corner of Italy despite much persecution. Some of them made their way to New York in the nineteenth century; two congregations in New York City merged in 1951 but are no longer active. Today there is a union in Italy between the Waldensians and the Methodists.

Selected Repositories, Societies, and Websites

The American Italian Heritage Association and Museum

1227 Central Avenue • Albany, NY 12205 • (518) 435-1979
aiha-albany.org

The Association records and preserves Italian heritage and culture. It produces a newsletter, cultural programs, and genealogy and language classes, and it operates the American Italian Heritage Museum. Photographs of current and past exhibitions are on the website.

Belmont Library and Enrico Fermi Cultural Center of the New York Public Library (NYPL)

610 East 186th Street • Bronx, NY 10458 • (718) 933-6410
www.nypl.org/locations/tid/10/about

This NYPL branch is located in the Bronx's Little Italy. It has a collection dedicated to Italian American heritage and offers special programming and exhibits related to Italian and Italian American culture, language, and history.

The John D. Calandra Italian American Institute

25 West 43rd Street • New York, NY 10036 • (212) 642-2094
Email: calandra@qc.edu • *http://qcpages.qc.edu/calandra*

Affiliated with Queens College but based in Manhattan, the Institute seeks to foster higher education among and about Italian Americans and serves as a cultural and research center. It publishes the journal *Italian American Review* and books about the Italian American experience. Its library collections include books, journals, magazines, and newspapers pertaining to Italian American and Italian history and culture.

Center for Migration Studies

27 Carmine Street • New York, NY 10014 • (212) 337-3080
Email: *archives@cmsny.org* • *cmsny.org/archives*

The Center's archives are particularly strong in Italian American material. Its collections include case histories of immigrants who received assistance from agencies on Ellis Island; papers of selected individual immigrants who achieved notable success; records of the National Catholic Welfare Conference, Bureau of Immigration; and photographs that document the immigrant experience.

The Italian Genealogical Group (IGG)

PO Box 626 • Bethpage, NY 11714-0626
Email: info@italiangen.org • *italiangen.org*

This prodigious Long Island genealogical group holds monthly meetings with guest speakers on Italian culture, history, and genealogy; publishes a newsletter; and has a lending library. Its website includes a surname database, also searchable by town, province or region of Italy, and a database of Italian town names. It offers other resources that are not limited to Italian immigrants, including databases of indexes to vital and naturalization records for New York City and Nassau and Suffolk counties, which have been indexed by volunteers of the IGG, the German Genealogy Group, and other organizations.

The Italian Genealogical Society of America

PO Box 3572 • Peabody, MA 01961-3572 • *italianroots.org*

The Society supports genealogical research through newsletters, meetings, and lectures at conferences and connects members with the same research interests through a yearly membership directory.

National Italian American Foundation (NIAF)

1860 19th Street, NW • Washington, DC 20009 • (202) 387-0600
Email: Information@niaf.org • *niaf.org*

The Foundation promotes appreciation of Italian American cultural heritage through a variety of activities, including education programs and grants. Its website resources provide demographic, historical, and biographical information that relates to Italian Americans, as well as a timeline of milestones of the Italian American experience.

The Order Sons of Italy in America (National)

219 E Street, NE • Washington, DC 20002 • (202) 547-2900
osia.org

OSIA is the largest and oldest national organization promoting Italian heritage in the United States, with 650 chapters nationwide. Its mission includes encouraging the study of Italian language and culture in American schools and universities and preserving Italian American traditions, culture, history, and heritage.

The Order Sons of Italy in America, Grand Lodge of New York

2101 Bellmore Avenue • Bellmore, NY 11710-5605
(516) 785-4623 • *nysosia.org*

The Grand Lodge of New York includes 96 statewide New York chapters of the national organization that preserves Italian culture through cultural, social, charitable, educational, patriotic, and civic programs and activities.

Westchester Italian Cultural Center

One Generoso Pope Place • Tuckahoe, NY 10707

(914) 771-8700 • *wiccny.org*

The Westchester Italian Cultural Center celebrates Italian history and culture through exhibitions, events, and education programs, including language classes and genealogy workshops.

Selected Bibliography and Further Reading

Accardi, Leonard. *Italian Contributions to Albany in the Nineteenth Century*. Schenectady: Franklin Print Shop, 1941.

Bean, Philip A. *La Colonia: Italian Life and Politics in Utica, New York, 1860–1960*. Utica, NY: Utica College, Ethnic Heritage Studies Center, 2004.

———. *The Urban Colonists: Italian American Identity and Politics in Utica, New York*. Syracuse: Syracuse University Press, 1910.

Briggs, John W. *An Italian Passage: Immigrants to Three American Cities, 1890–1930*. (Rochester, NY; Utica, NY; and Kansas City, MO) New Haven, CT: Yale University Press, 1978.

Brown, Mary Elizabeth. *Churches, Communities, and Children: Italian Immigrants in the Archdiocese of New York, 1880–1945*. Staten Island, NY: CMS, 1995.

Cannistraro, Philip V., ed. *The Italians of New York: Five Centuries of Struggle and Achievement*. New York: New-York Historical Society and John D. Calandra Italian American Institute, 1999.

Carmack, Sharon DeBartolo. *Italian-American Family History: A Guide to Researching and Writing About Your Heritage*. Baltimore: Genealogical Publishing Co., 1997.

Cole, Trafford R. *Italian Genealogical Records: How to Use Italian Civil, Ecclesiastical & Other Records in Family History Research*. Salt Lake City: Ancestry, 1995.

Colletta, John Philip. *Finding Italian Roots: The Complete Guide for Americans*. 2nd edition. Baltimore: Genealogical Publishing Co., 2003.

Daniels, Roger. *Coming to America: A History of Immigration and Ethnicity in American Life*. New York: Harper Perennial, 1991.

Eula, Michael J. *Between Peasant and Urban Villager: Italian-Americans of New Jersey and New York, 1880–1980: The Structures of Counter-Discourse*. New York: P. Lang, 1993.

Ewen, Elizabeth. *Immigrant Women in the Land of Dollars: Life and Culture on the Lower East Side 1890–1925*. New York: Monthly Review Press, 1985.

Federal Writers Project. *Gli Italiani di New York, speciale sezione commemorativa del XX anniversario dell Unione dei Dressmakers Italiani, Locale 89 - I.L.G.W.U.* New York: Labor Press, 1939.

———. *The Italians of New York*. New York: Arno Press, 1969.

Glazier, Ira A., and P. William Filby. *Italians to America: Lists of Passengers Arriving at U.S. Ports, 1880–1905*. 28 vols. Wilmington, DE: Scholarly Resources, 1992–2012.

Halsall, Paul. "Waldensians in New York City," digitally published at *www.fordham.edu/halsall/medny/halsall6.html*.

Iorizzo, Luciano J. "The Impact of World War I and World War II on Italian Americans in Oswego, New York: A Preliminary View." *Oswego Historian*. Posted July 19, 2011. Originally delivered at a conference April 1, 1992. *http://oswegohistorian.org/2011/07/impact-world-war-1-and-world-war-2-italian-americans-oswego-new-york*

LaGumina, Salvatore J. *Long Island Italians*. Charleston, SC: Arcadia Publishing, 2000.

Mangione, Jerre, and Ben Morreale. *La Storia: Five Centuries of the Italian American Experience*. New York: HarperCollins, 1992.

Nelson, Lynn. *A Genealogist's Guide to Discovering Your Italian Ancestors: How to Find and Record Your Unique Heritage*. Cincinnati: Betterway Books, 1997.

Paolo Busti Cultural Foundation Executive Committee, ed. *The Legacy of Italian-Americans in Genesee County, New York*. Interlaken, NY: Heart of Lakes Publishing, 1992.

Pascucci, Robert R. *Electric City Immigrants: Italians and Poles of Schenectady, N.Y., 1880–1930*. State University of New York at Albany, 1984. *www.schenectadyhistory.org/resources/pascucci/index.html*

Pyrke, Berne A. "Long Island's First Italian, 1639." *Long Island Forum*, 1943. *http://longislandgenealogy.com/FirstItalian.pdf*

Rochester Italian Directory, 1931. Rochester: North Printing Company, 1931. A digital version may be accessed on the website of the Monroe County Public Library at *http://www.libraryweb.org/~digitized/miscdir/Italian_directory_1931.pdf*.

Salamone, Frank A. *Italians in Rochester, New York, 1900–1940*. Lewiston, NY: Edwin Mellen Press, 2000.

Sowell, Thomas. *Migrations and Cultures, A World View*. New York: Basic Books, a Division of Harper Collins Publications, Inc., 1996.

Woolf, Stuart Joseph. *A History of Italy 1700–1860: The Social Constraints of Political Change*. London, UK: Routledge, 1991.

Jewish

Historical Overview

When the Jewish population was expelled from Spain in 1492 and from Portugal in 1496, the exiles fled to the Netherlands, Italy, Greece, Turkey, German principalities, and Poland. These individuals belong to a cultural group known as Sephardic Jews or the Sephardim. Many later migrated to "New World" colonies in South America and to islands in the Caribbean. When a colony was held by the Dutch or the English, Jews were tolerated and their communities grew. However, if Spain or Portugal captured a colony, the Inquisition and its persecution of "heretics" followed.

The first Jewish immigrants to form a permanent settlement in continental North America came to New Amsterdam from Recife, Brazil, in September 1654, when the Dutch lost their colony to the Portuguese. Twenty-three individuals managed to find their way to Dutch-controlled New Amsterdam. Despite the colony's Director-General Pieter Stuyvesant's reluctance to admit Jews to the colony, the group survived and prospered. Within a few years they had purchased ground for a cemetery, and by 1730 Congregation Shearith Israel was able to build the first synagogue in the future United States on Mill Street in Manhattan. From the earliest days, Jews were able to obtain "denization" which gave them certain rights, including the right to trade and practice their professions within the city. In 1727 British laws changed, enabling non-Christians to be naturalized within the colonies.

Prior to 1737 several individuals were naturalized under the British system, taking advantage of transferring their allegiance to the British crown. Permissions for full citizenship followed in 1740. During the 1750s and 1760s strong anti-loyalist sentiments began to rise within the community, and most Jewish households seem to have been in favor of the American patriot cause. However, when the War for Independence broke out, Jewish families in New York seemed to be equally divided on the issues, with some of the largest and most influential families remaining loyal to the crown.

By 1776 one-quarter of the approximately 2,000 Jews living in America lived in New York where, in 1777, they were granted almost equal treatment under New York law. Other early communities closely tied genealogically to New York could be found in Newport, Philadelphia, Savannah, Charleston, and Montreal (Trois-Rivières).

While the Sephardic Jews of Congregation Shearith Israel dominated the religious landscape in early America, the largest Jewish cultural group in the United States and Canada today are the Ashkenazim, who trace their Jewish ancestry to Northern and Eastern Europe (Germany, Austria-Hungary, Poland, and the Russian "Pale of Settlement"). The first Ashkenazi congregation in the United States was B'nai Jeshrun, a community that split off from Shearith Israel in New York in 1825.

The first Russian Jewish congregation, Beth Hamidrash, was formed in New York City in 1852. Although there was a Jewish business presence upstate (Albany, Kingston, and Westchester) as early as 1658, strong Jewish communities developed after 1820, as the Erie Canal and railroads opened up with new congregations organizing prior to the Civil War in Albany (1838), Syracuse (1839), Rochester (1843–1850), and Buffalo (1847).

The majority of Ashkenazim arrived in America during the "Great Wave" (1881–1924), when an estimated two million Jews entered through the port of New York; research will rely on nineteenth- and twentieth-century New York City and State immigration and vital records. The primary languages for genealogical records within this cultural group are English, Yiddish, Hebrew, German, Russian, Polish, Hungarian, and other Eastern European languages. Information pertinent to twentieth-century Jewish immigrants from Austria-Hungary, Germany, Poland, and Russia will also be found in other sections of this chapter.

Other Jewish cultural groups such as Mizrachi from North Africa, the Middle East, and the Arabian Peninsula (including Morocco, Tunisia, Egypt, Syria, Lebanon, Iran, and Yemen) are generally twentieth- and twenty-first-century immigrants.

Genealogical Resources

The resources below have specific relevance to researching Jewish immigrants to New York. However, Jewish immigrants will also be found in records discussed elsewhere in this book.

Immigration

Since 1654 New York has been the primary port of entry for Jews coming to North America. Consequently, extensive records relating to immigration and other genealogical events are available in New York repositories. Jewish genealogy is well served by a number of excellent local and international organizations and a wealth of record research—much of which is freely available. A thorough overview of these resources can be found in *Genealogical Resources in New York*, edited by Estelle M. Guzik.

Particularly for nineteenth- and twentieth-century families, records detailing the immigration and assimilation experiences through social service agencies and cultural organizations often will reveal more than records of specific congregational involvement. Therefore it is helpful to discover and understand both the Jewish cultural group that most closely reflects a family's ancestry at the time the earliest immigrant ancestor arrived in the United States, and its institutional community affiliations beyond a congregation. Genealogically pertinent records may be found in the archives of aid agencies (HIAS and Joint Distribution Committee, for example), social, volunteer, and service organizations (B'nai B'rith, Hadassah), and societies based on communities of origin—burial societies and mutual aid groups, including the landsmanshaftn formed by immigrants from Central and Eastern Europe.

The Yiddish Writers Study Group of the Federal Writers Project of the Works Progress Administration (WPA) undertook a survey of the Jewish hometown associations (landsmanshaftn), mutual aid societies, workers organizations, fraternal societies, and family circles in New York City, which was published in two volumes in Yiddish in 1938 and 1939. A partial index in English is on the website of the Jewish Genealogy Group at *www.jgsnydb.org/landsmanshaft/wpa.htm*. An English version of the survey was edited by Hannah Kliger and published in 1992. See also Daniel Soyer's *Jewish Immigrant Associations and American Identity in New York, 1880–1939*.

See also chapter 4, Immigration, Migration, and Naturalization, and other sections in this chapter on various Peoples of New York which include Jewish populations.

Cemetery Records

Jewish ritual burial practices are very specific, and hundreds of cemeteries were established throughout New York State to serve local Jewish communities. However, as smaller groups and congregations died off or migrated out of the urban centers, many formerly active Jewish cemeteries have been left in a state of suspension. In particular, there is a large group of Jewish burial sites (tens of thousands of graves) that line the border between the boroughs of Brooklyn and Queens. Records for "abandoned" cemeteries like these often now reside with Jewish funeral homes or social service agencies. For New York City, New Jersey, and Long Island cemeteries, researchers should consult Appendix G of *Genealogical Resources in New York*; the Jewish Genealogical Society of New York's cemetery directory and burial society database at *jgsny.org*; and the Museum of Family History's Cemetery Project at *http://museumoffamilyhistory.com/cp-main.htm* (see below).

For other cemeteries around the state, see the website of the International Jewish Cemetery Project, *iajgsjewishcemeteryproject.org*, or contact local congregations or the local office of the United Jewish Appeal Federation (UJA). The website *1654society.org* for America's first Jewish congregation, Shearith Israel, has a timeline and a complete, graphically interactive database covering all burials in their Manhattan cemeteries. See also chapter 9, Cemetery Records.

Religious Records

Unlike many other religions, there is no central repository of Jewish synagogue records. There have been thousands of large and small worship and study communities within New York, and it is generally advisable to contact the congregation or school directly regarding records in their archives. See chapter 15, Religious Records, for further information about locating Jewish sacramental and congregational records.

Selected Repositories, Societies, and Websites

The following repositories specialize specifically in Jewish records. Most have research collections of global relevance. For New York research repositories and local records in New York City and Albany, refer to Estelle Guzik's *Genealogical Resources in New York*.

Ackman & Ziff Family Genealogy Institute

Center for Jewish History • 15 West 16th Street
New York, NY 10011 • (917) 606-8217 • Email: gi@cjh.org
genealogy.cjh.org

The Genealogy Institute's website gives an overview of its resources and services, research guides on various subjects in local and international Jewish genealogy, and indexes to a selection of genealogically relevant archival collections from the collections of the five partner organizations of the Center for Jewish History (see below). Its resources for onsite research include numerous microfilms of New York vital record indexes from the Family History Library (FHL). Other FHL microfilms may be ordered at *FamilySearch.org* and viewed at the Institute.

Agudath Israel of America Orthodox Jewish Archives

84 William Street • New York, NY 10038 • (212) 797-9000

Holdings include Jewish immigration records from 1900, the work of Vaad Hatzala (Orthodox Jewish Rescue Committee), and newspapers and periodicals covering Jewish life in Eastern Europe prior to World War II.

American Gathering of Jewish Holocaust Survivors

(212) 239-4230 • *amgathering.org*

The society documents holocaust survivors worldwide. Its database has over 180,000 names of survivors and their children, including current contact information.

American Jewish Historical Society (AJHS)

Center for Jewish History • 15 West 16th Street
New York, NY 10011 • (212) 294-6160 • *ajhs.org*

The AJHS provides access to more than 25 million documents and 50,000 books, photographs, art, and artifacts that reflect the history of the Jewish presence in the United States from 1590 to the present.

American Jewish Joint Distribution Committee Archives (JDC)

(212) 687-6200 • *archives.jdc.org*

Holdings include a collection of information on Jewish rescue efforts, displaced person camps, and other subjects; these include the 1914 pogroms in Eastern Europe through the Holocaust era and into the late-twentieth century efforts to save individuals and communities around the world (not just Jewish). Online resources include a names database, an extensive, indexed image database, and finding aids to the collections.

American Sephardi Federation (ASF)

Center for Jewish History • 15 West 16th Street
New York, NY 10011 • (212) 294-8350
americansephardifederation.org

The ASF is one of the partner organizations at Center for Jewish History. Its book collection is available through the CJH library, and exhibits are mounted occasionally at the 16th Street facility. In 2011/12 the organization started a database of repositories in the northeast United States that house research materials of Sephardic import and interest.

Avotaynu, Inc.

794 Edgewood Avenue • New Haven, CT 06515
(475) 202-6575 • *avotaynu.com*

Avotaynu is a leading publisher of books and other resources for researching Jewish genealogy, Jewish family trees, or Jewish roots, including the journal *AVOTAYNU, The International Review of Jewish Genealogy*, which has been published quarterly since 1985. The website offers a "Five-minute Guide to Jewish Genealogical Research" and hosts the Consolidated Jewish Surname Index, which can search nearly 700,000 names across 42 separate databases.

Center for Jewish History (CJH)

15 West 16th Street • New York, NY 10011 • (212) 294-8301
cjh.org

The Lillian Goldman Main Reading Room of the CJH library serves the holdings from five organizations (American Jewish Historical Society, the American Sephardi Federation, the Leo Baeck Institute, the Yeshiva University Museum, and the YIVO Institute for Jewish Research). About 100 million archival documents, 500,000 books, and other artifacts and photographs are included. The Center is the largest Jewish repository outside of Israel. The Center's Ackman & Ziff Genealogy Institute has a family history reference book collection, excellent research database access, and a full-time staff to help. The Jewish Genealogical Society, Inc., partnered with the Genealogical Institute, makes National Archives and LDS microfilms of Jewish records available onsite. From the homepage of *cjh.org* it is possible to search across the collections of all five partners and to access a list of genealogical databases. (See also the separate entries for the CJH resident organizations in this section.)

Hebrew Union College–Jewish Institute of Religion (HUC-JIR)

The Klau Library • 3101 Clifton Avenue
Cincinnati, OH 45220-2488 • (212) 824-2258
http://huc.edu/libraries/CN

The Klau Library collections comprise 140,000 volumes, including portions of microfilm holdings of the American Jewish Archives in Cincinnati. The website gives access to an online catalog, as well as finding aids and collection descriptions.

Hebrew Immigrant Aid Society (HIAS), Immigrant Records & Location Services

HIAS Location Service • 333 Seventh Avenue, 16th Floor
New York, NY 10001-5004 • (212) 613-1409
Email: location@hias.org • *hias.org*

HIAS was founded in 1881 to aid Jewish refugees from Russia and Eastern Europe, and its mission has grown to serve refugees—Jewish and non-Jewish—from all parts of the world. It offers a Location Service to help refugees regain contact with family and friends. Its collections include arrival cards, case files, and photographs of refugee ships and other records. Arrival records 1909–ca.1978 and case files 1905–1960s are located at the YIVO Institute (see below).

JewishGen.org

Museum of Jewish Heritage • 36 Battery Place
New York, NY 10280 • (646) 437-4326
Email: info@jewishgen.org • *jewishgen.org*

The JewishGen website contains an extensive list of worldwide resource links for Jewish genealogy and hosts more than 20 million records. Links include online communities where members share family trees, a database of worldwide burial records, and databases of various genealogical records based on ancestry from specific countries.

Jewish Genealogical Society, Inc.

PO Box 631 • New York, NY 10113-0631 • (212) 294-8318
Email: info@jgsny.org • *jgsny.org*

The Jewish Genealogical Society website has a detailed list of repositories and cemeteries in the New York City metro area. These resource centers are listed by borough. There is also a list of LDS Family History Library microfilms on permanent loan at the Center for Jewish History (sponsored by the JGS), and databases of New York metropolitan area burial societies and Brooklyn naturalization records. Access to this website is free, although there are additional databases and benefits available to JGS members.

Jewish Genealogical Society of Long Island

37 Westcliff Drive • Dix Hills, NY 11746 • *jgsli.org*

The Jewish Genealogical Society of Long Island is a membership organization that presents lectures and genealogy workshops, conducts several volunteer projects, and produces the newsletter *LIneage*. Meetings are usually held at the Mid-Island Y-JCC (*miyjcc.org*) in Plainview.

JewishLink.net

JewishLink.net/genealogy.html

The website *JewishLink.net* contains numerous helpful links concerning Jewish genealogy all over the world.

The Jewish Theological Seminary of America Library (JTS)

3080 Broadway • New York, NY 10027 • (212) 678-8081
jtsa.edu/library

The JTS Library's collections comprise a vast number of books, manuscripts, rare books, microfilms, periodicals, and video records concerning Jewish life.

Leo Baeck Institute (LBI)

Center for Jewish History • 15 West 16th Street
New York, NY 10011 • (212) 744-6400 • *lbi.org*

The Leo Baeck Institute is the foremost research institute devoted to the history of German-speaking Jews. Its 80,000-volume library and extensive archival and art collections represent the most significant repository of primary source material and scholarship on the Jewish communities of Central Europe over the past five centuries.

Museum of Family History

museumoffamilyhistory.com

The Museum of Family History is a virtual museum which provides online exhibitions and education resources that preserve and interpret Jewish history and culture. Its Cemetery Project page includes a directory of New York metropolitan area Jewish cemeteries and lists of unique surnames for more than 200 towns and cities (and a few nonaffiliated organizations) that have society burial plots in more than 30 Jewish cemeteries in New York and New Jersey. Its Synagogues of New York City page features comprehensive lists of former synagogues in each of the boroughs.

Museum of Jewish Heritage-Holocaust Archive

36 Battery Place • New York, NY 10280 • (212) 968-1800
mjhnyc.org

The Museum's Holocaust Archive contains materials from the former Center for Holocaust Studies, Documentation, and Research in Brooklyn. The Archive includes more than 8,000 books, periodicals, journals, and pamphlets.

New York Public Library (NYPL)

Stephen A. Schwarzman Building
Fifth Avenue at 42nd Street, New York, NY 10018-2788
nypl.org • Dorot Jewish Division • (212) 930-0601
Email: freidus@nypl.org
www.nypl.org/locations/schwarzman/jewish-division
Slavic and East European Collections
www.nypl.org/locations/tid/36/node/138855

Of particular interest for Jewish research are the world-class holdings of the Dorot Jewish Division, and the Slavic and East European Collections, which may be accessed through the Rose Main Reading Room. See the NYPL entry in chapter 16 for detailed information about the NYPL's resources.

One-Step Webpages by Stephen P. Morse

stevemorse.org

This free website provides valuable tools that allow optimal searching of passenger lists, census records, and vital records from many different online sources; conversion tools for calendars (including Jewish) and foreign alphabets (including Hebrew); and other applications and resources for genealogy research. See chapter 16 for a detailed description of resources.

Safe Haven Museum and Education Center

Two East Seventh Street • Oswego, NY 13126 • (315) 342-3003
Email: safehaven@cnymail.com • *safehavenmuseum.com*

The Museum documents the experience of nearly 1,000 World War II refugees who were housed at Fort Ontario, the only designated refugee camp in the United States. A list of the refugees, most of whom were Jewish, is on the website.

Yeshiva University: Mendel Gottesman Library: Special Collections

2520 Amsterdam Avenue • New York, NY 10033
(212) 960-5451 • Email: archives@yu.edu
yu.edu/libraries/about/special-collections

The Library's collections include rare books, manuscripts, and archival records that document Jewish history in the United States and abroad, as well as Jewish religious, literary and cultural heritage.

YIVO Institute for Jewish Research

Center for Jewish History • 15 West 16th Street
New York, NY 10011 • (212) 246-6080 • *yivoinstitute.org*

YIVO Institute's Library and Archives concentrate on four main areas: East European Jewish history; the American Jewish immigrant experience; Yiddish language, literature, and culture; and the Holocaust. There are over 360,000 printed books and 10,000 linear feet of archives, including records, manuscripts, correspondence, printed materials, photographs, films, videotapes, and sound recordings.

Young Men's and Young Women's Hebrew Association Archives

92nd Street Y • 1395 Lexington Avenue • New York, NY 10128 (212) 415-5542 • *http://92y.org/archives*

The 92nd Street Y Archives contain a variety of Jewish and secular genealogical reference materials, as well as records for the Young Men's and Women's Hebrew Association, the Clara de Hirsch Home for Working Girls 1902–1962, the Surprise Lake Camp of the Educational Alliance and YMHA 1902–1976, and the Holy Society of the City of New York 1849–1968.

Selected Bibliography and Further Reading

Abelow, Samuel P. *History of Brooklyn Jewry*. Brooklyn, NY: Scheba Publishing Company, 1937.

Abromovitich, Ilana, et al. *Jews of Brooklyn*. Hanover, NH: University Press of New England for Brandeis University Press, 2002.

AVOTAYNU, The International Review of Jewish Genealogy. Bergenfield, NJ: Avotaynu, published quarterly since 1985.

Bernard, Jacqueline. *The Children You Gave Us: A History of 150 Years of Service to Children*. New York: Jewish Child Care Association of New York, 1973.

Bogen, Hyman. *The Luckiest Orphans: A History of the Hebrew Orphan Asylum of New York*. Urbana: University of Illinois Press, 1992.

Dorot: The Quarterly Journal of the Jewish Genealogical Society. New York: Jewish Genealogical Society, published since 1979.

Engel, Herbert M. *Shtetl in the Adirondacks: The Story of Gloversville and Its Jews*. Fleischmanns, NY: Purple Mountain Press, 1991.

Grinstein, Hyman Bogomolny. *The Rise of the Jewish Community of New York, 1654–1860*. Fleischmanns, NY: Purple Mountain Press, 1991.

Goldin, Eva Effron Acker. *The Jewish Community of Poughkeepsie, New York: An Anecdotal History*. Place and publisher not identified, 1982.

Gurock, Jeffrey S. *When Harlem Was Jewish, 1870–1930*. New York: Columbia University Press, 1979.

Guzik, Estelle M. *Genealogical Resources in New York*. New York: Jewish Genealogical Society, 2003.

———. *Resources for Jewish Genealogy in the New York Area*. New York: Jewish Genealogical Society, 1985.

Hershkowitz, Leo. *Wills of Early New York Jews, 1704–1799*. New York: American Jewish Historical Society, 1967. The volume presents facsimiles of forty-one wills that were originally published in three installments in the *American Jewish Historical Quarterly*, 1966.

Israelowitz, Oscar. *Synagogues of New York City: History of a Jewish Community*. Brooklyn, NY: Israelowitz Publishing, 2000.

The Jewish Communal Register of New York City, 1917–1918. Austin, TX: Booklab Inc., 1994.

Kliger, Hannah, ed. *Jewish Hometown Associations and Family Circles in New York: The WPA Yiddish Writers' Group Study*. Bloomington and Indianapolis: Indiana University Press, 1992.

Kohn, Solomon. *The Jewish Community of Utica, New York, 1847–1948*. New York: American Jewish Historical Society, 1959.

Kranzler, George C. *Williamsburg, A Jewish Community in Transition: A Study of the Factors and Patterns of Change in the Organization and Structures of a Community in Transition*. New York: P. Feldheim, 1961.

Levitt, Ellen. *The Lost Synagogues of Brooklyn* (2009); *The Lost Synagogues of the Bronx and Queens* (2011); *The Lost Synagogues of Manhattan* (2013). Bergenfield, NJ: Avotaynu, Inc.

Markel, Howard. *Quarantine! East European Jewish Immigrants in New York City and the Epidemics of 1892*. Baltimore: Johns Hopkins University Press, 1999.

Mitchell, William E. *Mishpokhe: A Study of New York City Jewish Family Clubs*. The Hague: Mouton, 1978.

Mokotoff, Gary. *Getting Started in Jewish Genealogy*. Bergenfield, NJ: Avotaynu, 2013.

Mokotoff, Gary, and Sallyann Amdur Sack, eds. *Avotaynu Guide to Jewish Genealogy*. Bergenfield, NJ: Avotaynu, 2004

Moore, Deborah Dash, ed. *City of Promises: A History of the Jews of New York*. 3 vols. New York: New York University Press, 2012.

The Old East Side: An Anthology. Philadelphia: Jewish Publication Society of America, 1969.

O'Neill, Terri B. "Birth and Death Records in New York Conveyances, 1687–1704: Early New York City Jewish Families." *NYG&B Record*, vol. 140, no. 4 (2009): 272–283. [NYG&B eLibrary]

Oppenheim, Samuel. *The Early History of the Jews in New York, 1654–1664: Some New Matter on the Subject*. New York: American Jewish Historical Society, 1909.

Pool, David de Sola. *An Old Faith in the New World: Portrait of Shearith Israel, 1654–1954*. New York: Columbia University Press, 1955.

———. *Portraits Etched in Stone: Early Jewish settlers, 1682–1831*. New York: Columbia University Press, 1952.

Rischin, Moses. *The Promised City–New York's Jews 1870–1914*. Cambridge: Harvard University Press, 1962.

Rosenbaum, Edward L. *Jewish Cemeteries in the New York City and Northern New Jersey Area*. New York: New York State Department of State, 1999.

Shargel, Baila. *The Jews of Westchester: A Social History*. Fleischmanns, NY: Purple Mountain Press, 1994.

Siegel, Stephen, ed. *Eleventh Summer Seminar on Jewish Genealogy: The New York Jewish Experience*. New York City, July 26–31, 1992, syllabus. New York: Jewish Genealogical Society, 1992.

Soyer, Daniel. *Jewish Immigrant Associations and American Identity in New York, 1880–1939*. Cambridge: Harvard University Press, 1997.

Tango, Jenny. *The Jewish Community of Staten Island*. Charleston: Arcadia, 2004.

Wolfman, Ira, and Ronda Small. *Jewish New York: Notable Neighborhoods and Memorable Moments*. New York: Universe Publishing, 2003.

Zollman, Joellyn. "Jewish Immigration to America: Three Waves. Sephardic, German, and Eastern European Immigrants Each Contributed to the Formation of American Jewry." *www.myjewishlearning.com/history/Modern_History/1700-1914/Emigration/To_America.shtml*

Polish

Historical Overview

In the late 1700s the Polish Commonwealth was partitioned by its neighbors—Russia, Prussia, and Austria—losing its sovereignty for more than 100 years. It was not until 1918 that Poland was formally reconstituted as a nation, and subsequently its boundaries continued to fluctuate. During World War II Poland was invaded by the Soviet Union and Germany, and after the war it lost its eastern provinces to the Soviets, but acquired new western provinces from Germany. From 1952 to 1989 it was officially known as the People's Republic of Poland and was governed by a communist regime.

There were some Poles present in New York State as early as the seventeenth century. However, large numbers of Polish immigrants began to arrive after failed insurrections against the partitions of Poland, which took place throughout the nineteenth century. Political and cultural oppression, as well as economic conditions, were major factors in the emigration of Poles. The number of Polish-born New Yorkers climbed from 4,000 in 1870 to 22,000 in 1890, and peaked at 350,000 in 1930.

The earliest Polish communities in New York were located in the cities of Albany, Buffalo (Erie County), New York, and Troy (Rensselaer County), as well as mill towns along the Erie Canal. By the end of the nineteenth century, significant Polish communities also existed in Amsterdam (Montgomery County), Dunkirk (Chautauqua County), Elmira (Chemung County), Rochester (Monroe County), and Schenectady. The Greenpoint neighborhood of Brooklyn is sometimes called Little Poland and has been a center of New York City's Polish community since the 1890s. Polish families also settled further east on Long Island, where many of them worked on, and eventually owned, farms. The Maspeth neighborhood of Queens is home to a large Polish community.

Most Polish immigrants were Catholic, but there also many who were Jewish; see the Jewish sections of this chapter and chapter 15, Religious Records, for information pertinent to Polish Jews. Those from German (Prussian) Poland tended to settle in New York City, Brooklyn, or Buffalo, while those from Austrian or Russian Poland were more scattered. Polish immigrants generally worked as laborers in manufacturing, textile mills, shoe factories, or the leather or steel industries. Women also worked as domestics or in factories. The poor economic condition of Polish families often meant that families took in boarders, and children left school at an early age. The economic status of Polish-Americans improved during the 1960s.

During World War II many scholars seeking refuge left Poland for the United States. In the post-war years, over 250,000 Polish refugees arrived in America. Another wave occurred after

1965, and a third after Communist rule ended in 1991. The post-World War II and Cold War refugees sought economic opportunity and political freedom in the United States.

Genealogical Resources

The resources below have specific relevance to researching Polish immigrants to New York. However, Polish immigrants will also be found in records discussed elsewhere in this book.

Immigration

The National Archives (NARA) holds passenger and immigration lists. Many are on microfilm and are widely available. *Ancestry.com* has digitized and indexed many of NARA's immigration records, including passenger arrival records for the ports of New York (1820–1957). The database "U.S. Immigrants Arriving at New York from Poland, Austria, and Galacia (sic) 1890–1891" at *Ancestry.com* is an index to arrival records of passengers who identified themselves as citizens of Austria, Galicia, or Poland.

The selected bibliography at the end of this section includes books that contain lists of Polish immigrants, which may help fill in gaps in the records; their availability varies with the time period. Researchers are advised to consult original records when available rather than rely solely on indexes and transcriptions. See chapter 4, Immigration, Migration, and Naturalization, for detailed information about what records exist, and where they can be accessed.

Newspapers

New York State's first Polish-language newspaper was the weekly *Echo z Polski*, which first appeared around 1863; several others have followed. The Chronicling America website of the Library of Congress offers the U.S. Newspaper Directory (1690–present), which may be searched by ethnicity, language, location, and keywords, to provide newspaper titles and details on where to access them at *chroniclingamerica.loc.gov/search/titles*. Titles may also be identified through the New York State Library's list of more than 10,000 newspaper titles that have been published in New York State at *www.nysl.nysed.gov/nysnp/title4.htm*. The Polish Genealogical Society of New York State (PGSNYS) is compiling a database of death notices from the Buffalo newspaper *Dziennik Dla Wsystkich*, which currently includes the years 1911–1941, and is working on a project to digitize all pages of the newspaper for those years. More information can be found on their website *pgsnys.org*. See also chapter 12, Newspapers, for information on how to identify and where to access newspapers.

Religious Records

Roman Catholicism is the prevalent religion in Poland and of Polish immigrants. Poles in New York State have often formed or joined Polish congregations in their communities. The website of the Polish Genealogical Society of New York State (see below) has a list of links to more than 40 Polish parishes in western New York State, most of which are Roman Catholic. The Polish National Catholic Church (*pncc.org*) was founded in the United States in 1897 following a rupture with the Roman Catholic Church. It has numerous parishes throughout New York State, which are listed on its website, as well as some cemeteries.

Some Poles have followed other Christian denominations, such as Eastern Orthodox, Lutheran, and Baptist. The First Polish Baptist Church (*firstpolishbaptistchurchny.org*) dates to the 1905 in New York City. Many Polish Jews have immigrated to New York and often formed and/or joined congregations organized around a shared place of origin. See also chapter 15, Religious Records.

Selected Repositories, Societies, and Websites
Buffalo & Erie County Public Library: Grosvenor Room
Central Library • One Lafayette Square • Buffalo, NY 14203
(716) 858-8900 • Email access on website
www.buffalolib.org/content/grosvenor

The Library's Grosvenor Room houses the Michael Drabik Memorial Library Collection of the Polish Genealogical Society of New York State. The Library's research guide "Polish Genealogy: Selected Sources in the Grosvenor Room" may be accessed at *www.buffalolib.org/sites/default/files/pdf/genealogy/subject-guides/PolishGenealogy.pdf*.

Foundation for East European Family History Studies (FEEFHS)
(formerly Federation of East European Family History Societies)
PO Box 321 • Springville, UT 84663
Email: conference@feefhs.org • *feefhs.org*

The FEEFHS promotes family history research rooted in Eastern and Central Europe. Its website gathers and presents extensive information on research resources for individual ethnic groups in the region and offers an online map library, a calendar of events of relevant organizations, and a newsfeed on Eastern Europe Genealogy. The Foundation organizes the annual Eastern European Research Workshop in Salt Lake City, presents educational workshops, and produces an e-newsletter. Formerly, it published the annual *FEEFHS Journal* (1993–2008), and an index is on the website. In 2014 the Foundation announced a commitment to focusing on indexing and other record discovery projects.

Gesher Galicia
geshergalicia.org

The Gesher Galicia website has a database of more than 200,000 records covering 600,000 people and a digital map room pertaining to the former Austro-Hungarian province of Galicia, which includes parts of Poland. The organization also publishes a quarterly journal, *The Galitzianer*.

Internet Polish Genealogical Source (IPGS)

ipgs.us

The IPGS provides a variety of online resources for researching Polish families both in Poland and in the United States. A list of parish histories for 18 largely Polish congregations in New York State is at *www.ipgs.us/usstates/parishhistories.html.*

Polish Genealogical Society of America

984 N. Milwaukee Avenue • Chicago, IL 60642-4101 • *pgsa.org*

The Society assists members in their genealogical research by providing books, newsletters, bulletins, printed information, regular Society meetings, and an annual workshop. The website offers a number of databases which include: an index for the obituaries found in the *Dziennik Chicagoski*; indexes of parish Jubilee Books from Polish parishes in a number of United States cities; an index of insurance claims for the Polish Roman Catholic Union of America; and marriages at Polish parishes in Chicago. The Society encourages members to communicate with each other and share leads, research sources, and any other information that may prove mutually beneficial. A part-time volunteer staff provides limited research services.

Polish Genealogical Society of Connecticut and the Northeast

8 Lyle Road • New Britain, CT 06053-2104 • (860) 229-8873 *pgsctne.org*

The Society organizes courses and lectures on Polish genealogy and publishes research materials with an emphasis on the Northeast, including a biannual newsletter; an index to the newsletter is on the website. The website offers a variety of online resources, and the Society is in the process of compiling a searchable database of parish and community histories, Polish cemetery inscriptions, and various regional data.

Polish Genealogical Society of New York State (PGSNYS)

PO Box 984 • Cheektowaga, NY 14225 • *pgsnys.org*

The PGSNYS promotes the study of Polish genealogy in the Western New York and Southern Ontario areas and beyond. Website research tools include a surname database of names currently being researched by members, other unique Polish records, and links to online resources. A member newsletter, *Searchers*, is published three times a year. The Society is in the process of creating an online database of surnames found in two directories of Buffalo's Polish community, to be called the *Przewodnik Handlowy Database*. The Society's library collection is housed at the Buffalo & Erie County Public Library (see above).

The Polish Heritage Society of Rochester (PHSR)

3690 East Avenue • Rochester, NY 14618 • (585) 248-0152 *polishheritagerochester.org*

The PHSR promotes and preserves Rochester's Polish heritage by producing and sponsoring lectures, exhibitions, and cultural presentations. The website includes a list of Rochester sites of historical significance to the Polish community.

Polish Roots: The Polish Genealogy Source

polishroots.org

The website provides useful information and many valuable links for conducting Polish family history research, as well as a free monthly e-newsletter, the *Gen Dobry*.

University at Buffalo Libraries: Polish Room

Lockwood Library, Room 517 • Buffalo, NY 14260-2200
(716) 645-2820 • Email: library@buffalo.edu
http://library.buffalo.edu/polish-room

The genealogical resources of the Polish Room include handbooks, geographical resources, armorials, biographies, and research guides; a description is on the website, as are some digital collections. The *Album Pamiątkowe: A Guide to Buffalo's Polonia from 1906*, may be downloaded for free from the website. The Polish Room is accessible to the public by appointment.

Selected Bibliography and Further Reading

Bukowczyk, John J. *And My Children Did Not Know Me: A History of the Polish-Americans.* Bloomington: Indiana University Press, 1987.

— — —. *Polish Americans and Their History: Community, Culture, and Politics.* Pittsburgh: University of Pittsburgh Press, 1996.

Chorzempa, Rosemary A. *Polish Roots.* Baltimore: Genealogical Publishing Co., 1993.

Drzewieniecki, Walter M. *Polonica Buffalonensis: Annotated Bibliography of Source and Printed Materials Dealing with the Polish-American Community in the Buffalo, New York, Area.* Buffalo: Buffalo and Erie County Historical Society, 1976.

Glazier, Ira A. *Migration from the Russian Empire: Lists of Passengers Arriving at the Port of New York.* 6 vols. Baltimore: Genealogical Publishing Co., 1995–1998. Lists from January 1875 to June 1891. Data from these volumes (which include Poland after 1867) can be accessed online in the National Archives "Russians to America Passenger Data File, 1834–1897." *http://aad.archives.gov/aad/series-list.jsp?cat=SB301&bc=sb*

Haiman, Mieczysław. *Poles in New York in the 17th and 18th Centuries.* Chicago: Polish R. C. Union of America, 1938.

Hart, Anne. *Tracing Your Baltic, Scandinavian, Eastern European, & Middle Eastern Ancestry Online . . . .* New York: ASJA Press, 2005.

Moser, Geraldine. *Hamburg Passengers from the Kingdom of Poland and the Russian Empire: Indirect Passage to New York, 1855–June 1873*. Washington: Landsmen Press, 1996. Many Polish immigrants left from German ports such as Bremen and Hamburg because Poland's ports—Gdańsk/Danzig and Szczecin/Stettin—were freight ports.

Pascucci, Robert R. *Electric City Immigrants: Italians and Poles of Schenectady, N.Y., 1880–1930*. State University of New York at Albany, 1984. *www.schenectadyhistory.org/resources/pascucci/index.html*.

Pogonowski, Iwo. *Poland: A Historical Atlas*. New York: Hippocrene Books, 1987. Maps provide an outline of changes in Poland's borders over the centuries.

Pula, James S. *Polish Americans: An Ethnic Community*. New York: Twayne Publishers, 1995.

Renkiewicz, Frank. *The Poles in America, 1608–1972; A Chronology & Fact Book*. Dobbs Ferry, NY: Oceana Publications, 1973.

Silverman, Marlene. *Poles and Russians in the 1870 Census of New York City: Full Alphabetical Index for the Second Enumeration, with Partial Index for the First Enumeration*. Washington: Landsmen Press, 1993.

Smith, Clifford Neal. *Reconstructed Passenger Lists for 1851 via Hamburg: Emigrants from Germany, Austria, Bohemia, Hungary, Poland, Russia, Scandinavia, and Switzerland to Australia, Brazil, Canada, Chile, the United States, and Venezuela*. McNeal, AZ: Westland Publications, 1986.

Urbanic, Kathleen. *Shoulder to Shoulder: Polish Americans in Rochester, New York, 1890–1990*. Rochester: Polonia Civic Center, 1991.

Wellauer, Maralyn A. *Tracing Your Polish Roots*. Milwaukee: The Author, 1991.

Russian (and related, but distinct ethnicities)

Historical Overview

Reaching its greatest extent before World War I, the Russian Empire encompassed present-day Azerbaijan, Belarus, Estonia, Finland, Georgia, Kazakhstan, Kyrgyzstan, Latvia, Lithuania, Moldova, Tajikistan, Turkmenistan, Ukraine and Uzbekistan, and parts of Armenia and Poland. Not surprisingly, there was wide variation in ethnic, cultural, and religious background among people from the Russian Empire who settled in the United States. See also other sections in this chapter which provide detailed information on immigrants from the Austro-Hungarian Empire, as well as German, Jewish, Polish, and Scandinavian peoples of New York.

Russian immigration to New York State began around 1870. By 1880 there were 5,400 Russian-born New York residents; this number grew to 550,000 by 1910. The majority of Russian immigrants were Jewish, and most settled in New York City, with large concentrations on the Lower East Side of Manhattan, as well as Harlem and Washington Heights; Brownsville and Williamsburg in Brooklyn; and parts of the Bronx. The cities of Buffalo and Rochester also had Russian-Jewish communities. The primary language spoken by Russian Jewish immigrants was Yiddish, although Russian was also spoken. The desire to escape religious persecution and poverty influenced Russian-Jewish immigration. Many early immigrants found employment in building trades and clothing factories. The Hebrew Immigrant Aid Society was founded in 1881 in New York City to assist Russian-Jewish immigrants.

Non-Jewish Russians emigrated in far smaller numbers, and by 1914 it is estimated that only 50,000 had settled in the United States. These were generally working-class people seeking better economic conditions, and many returned to Russia after a temporary stay. The Russian Orthodox Christian Immigrant Society of North America was founded in 1908 in New York City. Some Germans from Russia (Volga Germans) settled in New York. In 1888 a group of Volga Germans found employment in Orange County, where they later established the hamlet of Pine Island. In 1911 a group of Volga Germans settled in the town of Stuyvesant Falls in Columbia County.

The Bolshevik Revolution of 1917 prompted thousands of middle- and upper-class Russians to immigrate to New York. These immigrants included some aristocrats and many professionals, who once in New York were not always able to pursue their original careers. The Federation of Russian Organizations in America was founded in New York City in 1917 and the Russian Collegiate Institute in 1919.

A new wave of Russian immigration began around 1947 and consisted largely of World War II refugees, including prisoners of war, forced laborers, Russians who had unsuccessfully sought safety in other parts of Europe, and Estonian, Latvian and Lithuanian refugees whose countries had been independent between the wars but were now absorbed by the Soviet Union. Large émigré communities were established in the cities of Albany, Poughkeepsie, Schenectady, Syracuse, and Utica, as well as the villages of Nyack and Spring Valley (Rockland County), in addition to the preexisting communities in New York City, Rochester, and Buffalo.

The Soviet Union imposed severe restrictions on emigration, but in the 1970s began to allow Soviet Jews to emigrate. By the end of that decade, an estimated 110,000 Soviet Jews had arrived in New York and received refugee status. These immigrants settled within the five boroughs of New York City, forming Russian enclaves in Rego Park and Forest Hills (Queens); Washington Heights (Manhattan); Kings Highway, Boro Park, Midwood, and Brighton Beach/Little Odessa (Brooklyn).

Since the break-up of the Soviet Union in 1991, more than one million immigrants were admitted to the United States from countries of the former Soviet Union, with the largest numbers coming from Ukraine. Among the five Central Asian republics, Uzbekistan has sent the most immigrants, followed by Kazakhstan. A significant number of immigrants from the Central Asian republics appear to have been ethnic Russians, as was true of immigrants from Ukraine and Belarus. There is a sizable community of Bukharan Jews from the Central Asian republics in the Forest Hills and Rego Park neighborhoods of Queens.

Genealogical Resources

The resources below have specific relevance to researching Russian immigrants to New York. However, Russian immigrants will also be found in records discussed elsewhere in this book.

Immigration

The National Archives (NARA) holds passenger and immigration lists. Many are on microfilm and are widely available. *Ancestry.com* has digitized and indexed many of NARA's immigration records, including passenger arrival records for the ports of New York (1820–1957). The data file "Russians to America Passenger Data File, 1834–1897" may be accessed on NARA's website at *http://aad.archives.gov/aad/series-list.jsp?cat=SB301&bc=sb*.

Selected records of the Russian Consulates are available at NARA. Among the documents in the collection from the New York City consul are passport applications from 1910 to1914 and estate records from 1903 to 1915. A complete description can be found on the NARA website at *www.archives.gov/research/microfilm/m1486.pdf*.

The selected bibliography at the end of this section includes books that contain lists of immigrants which may help fill in gaps in the records; availability varies with the time period. Researchers are advised to consult original records when available rather than rely solely on indexes and transcriptions. See also chapter 4, Immigration, Migration, and Naturalization, for detailed information about what records exist and where they can be accessed.

Newspapers

One of the earliest Slavic-language newspapers published in New York was the *Russian News*, which began in 1892 as a weekly in New York City. The Ukrainian-language *Svoboda* (*Freedom*) published in nearby Jersey City, has been in publication since 1893. Founded in 1910, the *Novoye Russkoye Slovo*, or *New Russian Word*, is still in publication. The Chronicling America website of the Library of Congress offers the U.S. Newspaper Directory (1690–present), which may be searched by ethnicity, language, location, and keywords, to provide newspaper titles and details on where to access them, *chroniclingamerica.loc.gov/search/titles*. The New York State Library (NYSL) has a list of New York newspapers at *www.nysl.nysed.gov/nysnp/title4.htm* providing holdings information for more than 10,000 newspaper titles that have been published in New York State. See also chapter 12, Newspapers.

Religious Records

Jewish immigrants from the former Russian empire and the former Soviet Union have settled in New York in huge numbers and have often formed and/or joined congregations organized around a shared place of origin. Most Christian immigrants from the Russian empire were Eastern Orthodox, and the first Russian Orthodox chapel was formed in 1870 in New York City. There were attempts to unify the Orthodox Church into one entity, but linguistic, cultural, and political differences between different Orthodox communities made this impossible, and two major branches resulted: the Orthodox Church of America (previously known as Metropolia) and the Russian Orthodox Church Outside of Russia. Ukrainian Christians may be Orthodox or Roman or Eastern Catholic. Russians may be found among various Protestant denominations, including Baptist and Lutheran. See also chapter 15, Religious Records.

Selected Repositories, Societies, and Websites

As noted previously, a majority of immigrants to New York from Russia have been Jewish. For resources pertinent to researching Jewish immigrants from Russia, see the section on Jewish records in this chapter.

American Historical Society of Germans from Russia (AHSGR)

AHSGR International Headquarters • 631 D Street
Lincoln, NE 68502-1199 • (402) 474-3363 • *ahsgr.org*

The AHSGR is an international organization headquartered in Lincoln, NE, with local chapters nationwide. Its mission is to promote the cultural heritage and genealogy of Germanic settlers in the Russian Empire and their descendants from multiple regions, including Volhynia, Black Sea, Volga, Ukraine, Poland, Bessarabia, and Caucasus. Through their website, members can access the digital collection called SOAR (Saving Our Ancestral Records, *ahsgrsoar.org*), which contains obituaries, census and cemetery records, family group cards, maps, newspapers, photographs, reference books, surname charts, and ASHGR publications including newsletters and journals. The headquarters building includes a lending library for many of their holdings. Some research and translation support is available.

The Bakhmeteff Archive of Russian and East European History and Culture at Columbia University

Butler Library, 6th Floor East • 535 West 114th Street
New York, NY 10027 • (212) 854-3986
http://library.columbia.edu/indiv/rbml/units/bakhmeteff.html

The Bakhmeteff Archive at Columbia University is the second largest depository of Russian émigré materials outside Russia. More than 1,680,000 literary, artistic, political, military, and religious items in 1,500 collections serve to document and preserve Russian and East European heritage from the 1400s to the present day, with a primary focus on the twentieth century. The archive includes historical photographs, drawings, newspapers, and memoirs of both prominent and everyday people within four main areas: Prominent Literary Figures of the Russian Emigration, Institutions and Organizations, Historical Holdings, and Eastern Europe. Most of the material is in Russian, with some in English and Eastern European languages.

Foundation for East European Family History Studies (FEEFHS)

(formerly Federation of East European Family History Societies)
PO Box 321 • Springville, UT 84663
Email: conference@feefhs.org • *feefhs.org*

The FEEFHS promotes family history research rooted in Eastern and Central Europe. Its website gathers and presents extensive information on research resources for individual ethnic groups in the region and offers an online map library, a calendar of events of relevant organizations, and a newsfeed on Eastern Europe Genealogy. The Foundation organizes the annual Eastern European Research Workshop in Salt Lake City, presents educational workshops, and produces an e-newsletter. Formerly, it published the annual *FEEFHS Journal* (1993–2008), and an index is on the website. In 2014 the Foundation announced a commitment to focusing on indexing and other record discovery projects.

Germans from Russia Heritage Society

1125 West Turnpike Avenue • Bismarck, ND 58501
(701) 223-6167 • *grhs.org*

The Society collects and catalogs published materials and personal documents about European migrations to the United States and Canada, as well as of pioneer life on the plains. Collections include pedigree charts; obituaries; passenger lists; family, church, and county histories; Polish land records; German newspapers and resettlement papers on microfilm; and more than 5,000 letters written between 1800 and 1850—many requesting information on a lost relative or sending greetings to family and friends. Collections can be accessed at their library, and some materials and information are online. The website includes a Surname Exchange List of member supplied family research and links to other helpful resources. Its publications include the *Heritage Review* and national and chapter newsletters. Some research and translation support is available.

New York Public Library (NYPL)

Stephen A. Schwarzman Building • Fifth Avenue at 42nd Street
New York, NY 10018-2788 • *nypl.org*

The New York Public Library has extensive holdings of Slavic and East European materials, dating from the fourteenth century to the present. A collection description is at *www.nypl.org/locations/tid/36/node/138855*. The records of the Federation of Russian Organizations in America (1917–1924) are held by the Manuscripts and Archives Division. See chapter 16 for detailed information about the NYPL's extensive genealogical resources.

Ukrainian Academy of Arts and Sciences in the U.S., Inc. (UVAN)

206 West 100th Street • New York, NY 10025 • (212) 222-1866
Email: contact@uvan.org • *uvan.org*

The UVAN houses the most extensive Ukraine-related archive outside Ukraine. The collection includes material on individuals of cultural, historical, or political importance. One of the collections, the Volodymyr Vynnychenko Archive, is located in the Bakhmeteff Archive (see above).

Ukrainian American Archives & Museum of Detroit (UAAMD)

11756 Charest Street • Hamtramck, MI 48212 • (313) 366-9764
ukrainianmuseumdetroit.org

The Archives & Museum preserves and interprets the heritage of Ukrainian Americans through its collections and exhibitions. Its archives and library, which contains 20,000 books, document the Ukrainian immigrant experience in the United States.

The Ukrainian Historical and Educational Center of New Jersey

135 Davidson Avenue • Somerset NJ 08873 • (732) 356-0132
ukrhec.org

The center maintains collections and documents relating to the Ukrainian American immigrant experience. Access to the library is free and research assistance is available; the library has an online catalog on its website. Finding aids to the archival collections, which include personal papers and organizational records, are at *http://ukrhec.org/collections/archives/archival-collections.*

The Ukrainian Museum

222 East Sixth Street • New York, NY 10003 • (212) 228-0110
ukrainianmuseum.org

The museum presents exhibitions and education programs about Ukrainian culture. Its collections include photographs and materials documenting the past one hundred years of Ukrainian immigration to the United States.

Selected Bibliography and Further Reading

Baselt, Fonda D. *Russian-Germans in the 1910 New York Census: Orange County.* Champaign, IL: The Author, 1994. *www.albertwisnerlibrary.org/Factsandhistory/History/Genealogy/PineIsland1910census.htm*

Davis, Jerome. *The Russian Immigrant.* New York: MacMillan, 1922.

Glazier, Ira. A., ed. *Migration from the Russian Empire.* 6 vols. The books contain transcripts of 1875–1891 passenger lists. Baltimore: Genealogical Publishing Co., 1995–1998.

Kipel', Vitaŭt. *Belarusans in the United States.* Lanham, MD: University Press of America, 1999.

Kishinevsky, Vera. *Russian Immigrants in the United States: Adapting to American Culture.* New York: LFB Scholarly Publishing, 2004.

Koch, Fred C. *The Volga Germans: In Russia and the Americas, from 1763 to the Present.* University Park, PA: Pennsylvania State University Press, 1977.

Markowitz, Fran. *A Community in Spite of Itself: Soviet Jewish Émigrés in New York.* Washington: Smithsonian Institution Press, 1993.

Moser, Geraldine. *Hamburg Passengers from the Kingdom of Poland and the Russian Empire: Indirect Passage to New York, 1855–June 1873.* Washington: Landsmen Press, 1996.

Orleck, Annelise. *The Soviet Jewish Americans.* Westport, CT: Greenwood Press, 1999.

Pihach, John D. *Ukrainian Genealogy: A Beginner's Guide.* Edmonton, Toronto: Canadian Institute of Ukrainian Studies Press, 2007.

Silverman, Marlene. *Poles and Russians in the 1870 Census of New York City: Full Alphabetical Index for the Second Enumeration with Partial Index for the First Enumeration.* Washington: Landsmen Press, 1993.

Smith, Clifford Neal. *Reconstructed Passenger Lists for 1851 via Hamburg: Emigrants from Germany, Austria, Bohemia, Hungary, Poland, Russia, Scandinavia, and Switzerland to Australia, Brazil, Canada, Chile, the United States, and Venezuela.* McNeal, AZ: Westland Publications, 1986.

Stipanovich, Joseph. *Slavic Americans: A Study Guide and Source Book.* San Francisco: R&E Research Associates, 1977.

Stokoe, Mark, and the Very Rev. Leonid Kishkovsky. *Orthodox Christians in North America (1794–1994).* *http://oca.org/history-archives/orthodox-christians-na*

Tracking a Diaspora: Émigrés from Russia and Eastern Europe in the Repositories. Binghamton, NY: Haworth Information Press, 2006.

Wertsman, Vladimir. *The Russians in America: A Chronology & Fact Book.* Dobbs Ferry, NY: Oceana Publications, 1977.

———. *The Ukrainians in America, 1608–1975: A Chronology & Fact Book.* Dobbs Ferry, NY: Oceana Publications, 1976.

Scandinavian

Historical Overview

Scandinavia is generally understood to encompass the present-day countries of Denmark, Finland, Norway, and Sweden. For nearly 500 years most of Finland was ruled by Sweden (1323–1809); it was an autonomous Grand Duchy of Russia from 1809 to 1917 when it became an independent country. Norway was governed by the Danes from the Middle Ages until 1814 when Denmark surrendered Norway to Sweden. Norway was then part of Sweden, with a separate constitution and some autonomy until it became fully independent in 1905. In 1952 the geopolitical "Nordic Council" was formed; by 1984 it included Denmark, Finland, Iceland, Norway, Sweden, the Faroe Islands and Greenland (as part of the Danish delegation), and Åland (part of the Finnish delegation).

Data from the U.S. Census Bureau shows that Norwegians, Swedes, and Danes were enumerated separately on the federal census from 1850 (when the question on birthplace was first asked), the Finnish from 1900, and Icelanders from 1930. The greatest number of Scandinavian immigrants to the United States came from Norway and Sweden. Immigration peaked with 665,000 Swedes and 403,000 Norwegians reported on the 1910 U.S. census, of which 53,000 Swedes and 25,000 Norwegians lived in New York State.

It can be difficult to determine the specific nationality of many Scandinavians; for example, someone may be identified as a Dane or Swede who was Norwegian at a time when Norway was under Danish or Swedish rule. Names, too, can be challenging, as patronymic—and sometimes matronymic—naming was prevalent among all Scandinavian countries. Though common in Iceland today, the practice was gradually replaced by the use of fixed surnames in the other Scandinavian countries, with Norway being the last to make fixed surnames compulsory in 1925. The use of an additional surname that reflected a farm name, a place name, or an occupation, which might change over time, was also common.

Most early Swedish and Finnish immigrants to America came to settle in the colony of New Sweden. It which was established in 1638 along the banks of the Delaware River (present-day New Jersey, Delaware, and Pennsylvania) and became part of New Netherland in 1655. The early Scandinavian immigrants that came to present-day New York sailed from the port of Amsterdam under the Dutch, and settled mainly in New Amsterdam. Norwegians also settled in Rensselaerswijck (Rensselaer County). One of the earliest settlers was Jonas Bronck, who lent his name to the Bronx River, from which the New York City borough takes its name. He was a Swedish sea captain who settled near the Harlem River in 1639 with Danish,

Dutch, and German servants. The Bergen family in Brooklyn was of Norwegian descent, and Hans Hansen Bergen received a patent for his farm from the Dutch. As more Dutch documents from the colonial era have been translated, more Scandinavian history in New Amsterdam and New Netherland has been revealed. Scandinavians have been emigrating to Holland and on to New Amersdam/New York City, because of maritime trade, from the Dutch colonial era to the early-twentieth century.

There were relatively few Scandinavian immigrants during the 1700s. On October 9, 1825, the Norwegian sloop *Restaurationen* docked in New York Harbor with 53 passengers and marked the beginning of an increase in the number of Norwegian immigrants in New York State, which peaked in 1930 with 44,000. Bay Ridge and Red Hook in Brooklyn (Kings County) continued to be home to the most prominent Norwegian communities through the mid-twentieth century. When the Fourth Avenue subway opened in 1915, it was nicknamed the Norwegian-American line, because it ran through many of these neighborhoods from Red Hook and downtown Brooklyn to Bay Ridge. In the 1950s and 1960s there was a surge in the number of immigrants from southern Norway who also came to live in these same parts of Brooklyn.

Initially maritime occupations were an important source of employment to Scandinavians. As the shipyards gradually began moving to Brooklyn, Swedish immigrants moved from Manhattan to settle in neighborhoods there alongside Norwegians; Atlantic Avenue in Brooklyn was once known as "Swedish Broadway." This move is reflected by the establishment dates and locations of churches and social institutions that were built along the coast. Churches in Brooklyn established sister churches in Staten Island, as many Scandinavians moved to live across the Narrows. Around the turn of the twentieth century many Swedes also worked in industries, as well as in American homes. In 1930 there were 61,000 Swedish-born residents in New York State.

In addition to taking new jobs created by the maritime and naval industries, Danes also worked as craftsmen or laborers, while Swedish immigrants were noted for their woodwork and metalwork. Both the Norwegians and the Swedes had engineers' societies in Brooklyn. Beyond the New York City area, the largest Swedish enclaves developed in Albany (City and County), Buffalo (Erie County), Jamestown (Chautauqua County), and Rochester (Monroe County). The majority of Scandinavian immigrants moved on to settle in the Midwest (particularly in North Dakota and Minnesota), and in some cases in the Pacific Northwest.

The major immigration from Finland to America took place between 1870 and 1930. Most Finnish immigrants came from impoverished rural areas in Ostrobothnia. In addition to stories of land that could easily be made arable, Finns were encouraged to move to the United States by professional recruiters employed by shipping and mining companies. Such recruiters were banned by federal legislation in the late 1880s. In 1890 the Finnish Evangelical Lutheran Church of America was established in Calumet, Michigan. This was another factor that encouraged Finnish migration in the late nineteenth century. Most Finns in America now live in Michigan or Florida.

Danish immigration surged in the 1880s and peaked in 1920. The largest concentrations of Danes in New York State were in Bay Ridge, Brooklyn (Kings County), and in Chautauqua, Rensselaer, and Yates counties.

Genealogical Resources

The resources below have specific relevance to researching Scandinavian immigrants to New York. However, Scandinavian immigrants will also be found in records discussed elsewhere in this book.

Immigration

The National Archives (NARA) holds passenger and immigration lists. Many are on microfilm and are widely available. *Ancestry.com* has digitized and indexed many of NARA's immigration records, including passenger arrival records for the ports of New York (1820–1957) and other cities, which were often entry points for immigrants who later migrated to New York. See chapter 4, Immigration, Migration, and Naturalization, for detailed information about what records exist and where they can be accessed.

The selected bibliography at the end of this section includes books that contain lists of Scandinavian immigrants, which may help fill in gaps in the records, whose availability varies with the time period. Researchers are advised to consult original records when available rather than rely solely on indexes and transcriptions.

Newspapers

Many newspapers in New York have served the Scandinavian community, including the Swedish-language *Nordstjernan* (*nordstjernan.com*), which has been published continuously since 1872. The Norwegian-language *Nordisk Tidene* was published in Brooklyn from 1891 to 1983 and survives today as the *Norwegian American Weekly* (*blog.norway.com*); there have been numerous other New York newspapers in various Scandinavian languages. The Chronicling America website of the Library of Congress offers the U.S. Newspaper Directory (1690–present), which may be searched by ethnicity, language, location, and keywords, to provide newspaper titles and details on where to access them: *chroniclingamerica.loc. gov/search/titles*. See also chapter 12, Newspapers, for other resources.

Religious Records

Most Scandinavian immigrants were Lutheran, and they often established ethnicity-based Lutheran congregations which moved as communities dispersed. Information about historical Scandinavian congregations, see the *Inventory of Church Archives in New York City: Lutherans*, produced by the Historical Records Survey of the Work Projects Administration (WPA) in 1940. This volume provides substantial detail about Scandinavian congregations and social service institutions in New York City, as well as broader historical context about the evolution of Scandinavian congregations and synods. See chapter 15, Religious Records, for information about obtaining religious records of Lutheran churches and other denominations. Microfilmed records of many Scandinavian churches across New York State are held by the Swenson Center (see entry below).

The Seafarers and International House (*sihnyc.org*) began in New York City in 1873 as a mission of the Church of Sweden and continues today as a Lutheran social services organization. Other Scandinavian Seamen's Churches are "churches abroad" that fall under the jurisdiction of the home country's national church administration. The first Norwegian Seamen's Church in New York was established in Brooklyn in 1878 to minister to sailors from Norwegian ships and the larger Norwegian immigrant community. It survives today as King Olav V Church (*http:// sjomannskirken.no/newyork*), and is based in Manhattan. The Swedish Seamen's Church (*www.svenskakyrkan.se/newyork*) is now based in Manhattan and more commonly known as the Church of Sweden. The Danish Seamen's Church (*dankirkeny. org*) in New York is based in Brooklyn. These churches also serve as cultural and social centers.

Scandinavians belonged to, and sometimes established congregations in, other denominations. The *Bethel Ship John Wesley* was a floating Methodist mission that ministered to Scandinavian seamen and immigrants in New York from 1832 until 1876. It led to the founding of three churches in the 1870s: the Swedish Methodist Episcopal Church (Manhattan), the Immanuel Swedish Methodist Church (now the Immanuel and First Spanish United Methodist Church in Brooklyn), and the Bethelship Norwegian Methodist Episcopal Church in Brooklyn (now the Bethelship Norwegian United Methodist Church).

There were also Scandinavian Baptist congregations in New York. The First Swedish Baptist Church of New York was founded in 1867 in Manhattan and continued to provide services in Swedish until 1942 when it was renamed Trinity Baptist Church (*trinityny.org*). The First Norwegian-Danish Baptist Church in Brooklyn was founded in 1903.

Selected Repositories, Societies, and Websites
American-Scandinavian Foundation
58 Park Avenue • New York, NY 10016 • (212) 779-3587
amscan.org

An American nonprofit organization founded in 1911, the American-Scandinavian Foundation (ASF) fosters cultural understanding and exchange between the United States and Scandinavia. It presents a variety of cultural programs and has published the magazine *Scandinavian Review* (previously the *American-Scandinavian Review*) continuously since 1913. Its library offers some genealogical resources.

American Swedish Historical Museum (ASHM)

1900 Pattison Avenue • Philadelphia, PA 19145 • (215) 389-1776
americanswedish.org

Founded in 1926 on land that was part of a seventeenth-century land grant from Queen Christina of Sweden, the ASHM is the oldest Swedish museum in the United States. Two of its galleries document the history of the colony of New Sweden. A list of finding aids to its archival collections is on the website of the Philadelphia Area Consortium of Special Collections Libraries (PACSCL) *http://dla.library.upenn.edu/dla/pacscl/index.html*.

Danish Archives North East (DANE)

Danish Home • 855 New Durham Road • Edison, NJ 08817
(732) 287-6445 • Email: danenj@aol.com
www.rootsweb.ancestry.com/~njdane/index.html

DANE collects records, books, letters, genealogical information, and sociological data relating to Danish heritage in the northeastern United States. The organization publishes a newsletter; holds monthly meetings; presents programs and exhibitions; and assists with genealogical research. The website has back issues of the newsletter, a research exchange, and links to a large number of useful websites and online resources.

Danish Emigration Archives

udvandrerarkivet.dk

The Archives is based in Denmark, and its website has a free online database with information on 394,000 people who emigrated from Denmark from 1868 to 1908. Called the Copenhagen Police Emigration Protocols, the database can be searched by destination. The searchable digital collection called Emigration Archives contains more than 500,000 letters and images.

Danish Immigrant Museum

4210 Main Street • PO Box 249 • Elk Horn, IA 51531-0249
(712) 764-7008 • *danishmuseum.org*

The Museum produces exhibits that explore Danish American history, as well as events, publications, and online media tools. Its research library, the Family History & Genealogy Center (FHGC), holds a significant collection of family history resources and provides assistance with genealogical research and translation. The website offers an extensive list of links to other genealogical resources and the Digital Library of Danish American Newspapers and Journals.

Finnish American Heritage Center

435 Quincy Street • Hancock, MI 49930 • (906) 487-7347
Email: archives@finlandia.edu • *finlandia.edu*

The Archive at the Heritage Center is the largest collection of Finnish-North American materials in the world. Holdings include microfilmed Finnish church records dating to the late-sixteenth century, Finnish American church records, local cemetery and funeral home records, historic photographs, church and temperance calendars, family histories, books, newspapers, and obituary clippings. The collections include some New York-pertinent material; a guide to the Archive and finding aids are on the website.

Gjenvick-Gjønvik Archives

gjenvick.com

Among the free online resources offered by this website are selected passenger lists of the Norwegian American Line (Den Norske Amerikalinje, 1927–1937), the Swedish American Line (Svenska Amerika Linien, 1932–1950), and the Scandinavian American Line (Skandinavien Amerika Linien, 1905–1921).

National Danish-American Genealogical Society (NDAGS)

3030 West River Parkway South • Minneapolis, MN 55406
Email: ndags.mpls@gmail.com • *danishgenealogy.org*

The Society holds regular meetings for its members who provide research assistance to each other, presents programs on genealogical research topics, and publishes the quarterly newsletter, *Beech Tree*. In 2004 it produced *Searching for Your Danish Ancestors: A Guide to Danish Genealogical Research in the United States and Denmark*, which is available for purchase.

Norwegian-American Genealogical Center & Naeseth Library (NAGC)

415 West Main Street • Madison, WI 53703-3116
(608) 255-2224 • *nagcnl.org*

The Norwegian-American Genealogical Center and Naeseth Library is a leading research resource for Norwegian American genealogy and family history. The library is open to the public, and its catalog is online. Membership benefits include a subscription to the NAGC's newsletter, discounts on publications and seminars, ability to borrow books and microfilms, and reduced rates on staff-conducted research and translation services.

Norwegian-American Historical Association

1510 St. Olaf Avenue • Northfield, MN 55057-1097
(507) 786-3221 • Email: naha@stolaf.edu • *naha.stolaf.edu*

The Association has published nearly one hundred books and maintains a research library and archive on the campus of St. Olaf College. Genealogical materials include family histories, oral histories, congregational publications, a manuscripts, biographical directories, microfiche emigration lists, and maps. A guide to the collections, which include some New York-pertinent material, is on the website. Member benefits include a subscription to a quarterly newsletter.

Norwegian Immigration Association (NIA)

Research Center: King Olav V Church • 317 East 52nd Street
New York, NY 10022 • Email: niahistoryonline@yahoo.com
niahistory.org

The Norwegian Immigration Association documents the history of the Norwegian immigrant community of Greater New York. It has a digital collection at *niaresearchcenter.cdmhost.com* and a research center at the Inger and William Ginsberg Library of the Norwegian Seamen's Church (King Olav V Church), with books, files, and clippings. The NIA presents exhibitions at Heritage Hall at the Norwegian Christian Home and Health Center, 1250-67th Street, Brooklyn, NY 11219.

Scandinavian East Coast Museum

440 Ovington Avenue • Brooklyn, NY 11209 • (718) 748-5950
scandinavian-museum.org

The Scandinavian East Coast Museum (formerly the Norwegian-American Collection) holds bimonthly meetings, publishes a quarterly newsletter, and sponsors cultural events and educational programs. Its archive and library are open to the public; their virtual museum preserves archival, cultural, and intellectual resources provided by their members.

Sons of Norway

sofn.com

A fraternal and cultural organization, Sons of Norway is the largest Norwegian American organization in the country. Its local lodges offer social and cultural programs, including language classes and occasional genealogy workshops.

Swedish-American Historical Society

3225 W. Foster Avenue, Box 48 • Chicago, IL 60625
(773) 583-5722 • *swedishamericanhist.org*

The Society records and explores the full range of the Swedish American experience in North America through publications, including the journal *Swedish-American Historical Quarterly* (formerly the *Swedish Pioneer Historical Quarterly*); education programs; and a research collection; it also administers grants to support research. Its research collection, the Swedish-American Archives of Greater Chicago, is housed at North Park University. While focused on organizations and individuals in the Chicago area, it also includes some material of broader interest; a finding aid to manuscripts is online, as is a digital book collection which includes the *Guide to Swedish-American Archival and Manuscript Sources in the United States*.

Swedish Ancestry Research Association (SARA)

PO Box 70603 • Worcester, MA 01607-0603
www.members.tripod.com/~SARAssociation/sara/SARA_Home_Page.htm

The Swedish Ancestry Research Association collects and preserves genealogical records, including church records and obituaries. Members may register and share their research through a database. SARA publishes a newsletter and a journal and conducts education programs in Massachusetts and other locations throughout New England.

Swenson Swedish Immigration Research Center

Augustana College • 639 38th Street
Rock Island, IL 61201-2296 • (309) 794-7204
Email: sag@augustana.edu • *augustana.edu*

The Swenson Center is a national archives and research institute providing resources for the study of Swedish immigration to North America. It publishes the quarterly journal *Swedish American Genealogist*, conducts academic research, collects Swedish American archival and library materials, and assists people researching their Swedish American genealogy. Among its holdings are microfilm records of many Scandinavian churches in New York State; an index of more than one million emigrants from Sweden; Swedish American newspapers; and Swedish American lodge records. The website has finding aids to the collections, an online catalog, and issues of the *Swedish American Genealogist* for the years 1981–2007.

Vasa Order of America

vasaorder.com

Vasa is a Swedish American fraternal organization. Local lodges offer a variety of social and cultural activities, which sometimes include genealogical workshops.

Selected Bibliography and Further Reading

General

Evjen, John Oluf. *Scandinavian Immigrants in New York, 1630–1674. With Appendices on Scandinavians in Mexico and South America, 1532–1640, Scandinavians in Canada, 1619–1620, Some Scandinavians in New York in the Eighteenth Century, German Immigrants in New York, 1630–1674.* Minneapolis: K. C. Holter Publishing Co., 1916. The digital version of the book at *www.rootsweb.ancestry.com/~nycoloni/evjen/evjtitle.html* has an added name index with direct links to biographical profiles in the book. Reprint, Baltimore: Genealogical Publishing Co., 1972.

Historical Records Survey. *Inventory of Church Archives in New York City: Lutherans.* New York: Work Projects Administration, 1940. [NYG&B eLibrary]

Oppedal, Haldor O. *Scandinavian Newspaper Directory: Giving a Complete List, Together with a Synopsis of the History of the Scandinavian Newspapers in America.* Chicago: Thomas Brown, 1894.

Denmark

Barekman, June B., and Ruth Barekman. *Passenger List of the Steamship, Guiding Star, from Copenhagen, Denmark to New York City, June 29, 1869.* Chicago: n.p. 1970.

Carlberg, Nancy Ellen. *Beginning Danish Research.* Anaheim, CA: Carlberg Press, 1992.

Christensen, Carlo. *De Første Danske i New York.* Kjøbenhavn: Nyt nordisk forlag, 1953. Danish-language book about Danes in colonial New York.

Hale, Frederick. *Danes in North America.* Seattle: University of Washington Press, 1984.

Finland

Hoglund, A. William. *Finnish Immigrants in America, 1880–1920.* Madison: University of Wisconsin Press, 1960.

Norway

Brooklyn Historical Society. "First Norwegian Baptist Church." *Baptist Churches of Brooklyn Publications and Ephemera.* Collection description at: *http://brooklynhistory.org/library/wp/baptist-churches-of-brooklyn-publications-and-ephemera-1840-1957.*

Culbertson, Carol A., and Jerry Paulson. *A Research Guide for Norwegian Genealogy.* 6th edition. Madison, WI: Norwegian American Genealogical Center & Naeseth Library, 2013.

Hoover, Knight. "Norwegians in New York." *Norwegian-American Studies,* vol. 24 (1970): 221-235. *www.naha.stolaf.edu/pubs/nas/volume24/vol24_9.html*

Jorgenson, H. G. *A History of the First Norwegian Baptist Church.* Brooklyn: n.p., 1953.

Lovoll, Odd Sverre. *Norwegian Newspapers in America: Connecting Norway and the New Land.* St. Paul: Minnesota Historical Society Press, 2010.

Mauk, David C. *The Colony that Rose from the Sea: Norwegian Maritime Migration and Community in Brooklyn, 1850–1910.* Staten Island, NY: Norwegian-American Historical Association, 1997.

Naeseth, Gerhard B. *Norwegian Immigrants to the United States: A Biographical Directory, 1825–1850.* Decorah, IA: Anundsen Publishing Co., 1997.

Rygg, A. N. *Norwegians in New York 1825–1925.* Brooklyn, NY: Norwegian News Co., 1925.

———. *The Norwegian Seamen's Church: The Story of the New York Station for 81 Years–from 1867 to 1948.* Brooklyn, NY: n.p., 1948.

Wellauer, Maralyn A. *Tracing Your Norwegian Roots.* Milwaukee, WI: The Author, 1979.

Sweden

Berger, Vilhelm. *Svenskarne i New York.* New York: Adams & Co, 1918. Swedish-language book about the Swedish in New York.

Clemensson, Per. *Your Swedish Roots: A Step By Step Handbook.* Provo, UT: Ancestry, 2004.

Craig, Peter S. *1671 Census of the Delaware.* Philadelphia: Genealogical Society of Pennsylvania, 1999. This book identifies inhabitants of the former New Sweden and shows connections between them and New Netherland/New York.

Moe, M. Lorimer. *Saga from the Hills, A History of the Swedes of Jamestown.* Jamestown, NY: Fenton Historical Society, 1983.

Olsson, Nils William. *Tracing Your Swedish Ancestry.* Stockholm: Ministry for Foreign Affairs, 1987.

Olsson, Nils William, and Erik Wikén. *Swedish Passenger Arrivals in the United States, 1820–1850.* Stockholm: The Royal Library of Sweden, 1995. This volume consolidates information from two earlier versions with new information.

Whyman, Henry C. *The Hedstroms and the Bethel Ship Saga: Methodist Influence on Swedish Religious Life.* Carbondale: Southern Illinois University Press, 1992.

Wulff, Reinhold. *Die Anfangsphase der Emigration aus Schweden in die USA, 1820–1850: Gesamtdarstellung anhand der amerikanischen Passagierlisten sowie Detailanalyse der Emigration aus Kisa in Östergötland: mit Bibliographie.* Frankfurt am Main, New York: P. Lang, 1987. German-language book on Swedish immigration into the USA with passenger lists 1820–1850.

Scots and Scots-Irish

Historical Overview

Immigration by individual Scots to colonial New Netherland and New York occurred throughout the seventeenth century. Scottish merchants were among the first settlers to arrive in the early 1600s, and Scots were also employed by the Dutch trading companies at Fort Orange (present-day Albany) and elsewhere.

William Lord Alexander, later known as the first Earl of Stirling, established an unsuccessful colony of Scots in Canada, after which he received a grant in 1635 for lands that included Long Island. However, he was unable to establish a Scottish settlement there or to fully enforce his claim; it was through him that Lion Gardiner acquired Gardiners Island.

Most colonial-era Scots immigrants to New York sought economic opportunity, and it is estimated that about one-half were either farmers or skilled workers and the rest a mix of merchants, professionals, and unskilled workers. Early Scottish immigrants also included groups of transported religious, political, and criminal prisoners destined for indentured servitude and other exiles who were forced to emigrate. Scottish immigration to New York increased after British restrictions on Scottish trade and settlement were partially lifted beginning in 1669, and lifted altogether following the political union of England and Scotland in 1707.

Scots-Irish is an American term for Ulster Scots, whose ancestors left the Scottish lowlands (and sometimes the English side of its border) to become tenant farmers in Ulster in the north of Ireland. Ulster then comprised nine counties: Antrim, Armagh, Down, Fermanagh, Londonderry, and Tyrone (which today make up Northern Ireland) and Cavan, Donegal, and Monaghan (which are now part of the Irish Republic). Beginning in 1609, when land leases in Ulster first enticed Scots Lowlanders, the population grew steadily for about a century. Immigrants from elsewhere in Scotland also came to Ulster to escape poverty, political unrest, and, at times, famine.

However, as a result of a major rent increase in 1710, thousands of farmers were evicted. This triggered an exodus from Ulster, with an estimated 250,000 Scots-Irish immigrating to America between 1717 and the 1770s. By the 1730s groups of Scots-Irish could be found in present-day Albany, Fulton, Orange, Otsego, Rensselaer, Saratoga, Schenectady, Sullivan, Warren, and Washington counties. Scots-Irish communities were also established in Dutchess, Montgomery, Putnam, Rockland, and Ulster counties. County gazetteers often list the names of early settlers and their countries of origin; gazetteer titles will be found in the bibliographies for individual counties in Part Two.

The largest wave of Scots-Irish immigration took place during the eighteenth century, when Philadelphia was often the main port of entry; large numbers of Scots-Irish settled in Pennsylvania before migrating further inland. The collapse of the Ulster linen industry in 1771–1772 spurred the last big wave of Scots-Irish immigration. The Scots-Irish strove to develop an identity that separated them from Irish Catholic immigrants, especially in the second half of the nineteenth century. (See also the section on the Irish in this chapter.)

New York's governor offered land to Protestant Scots Highlanders in 1735, but did not honor the claims when more than 400 settlers arrived in the following years. Many of these Highlanders settled in Orange and Washington counties, and in 1764 nearly 50,000 acres in the Argyle Patent were distributed to some of those families.

In the 1760s land in present-day Essex County was given to Scots veterans of the French and Indian War. A group of 400 Catholic Highlanders settled in Fulton County in 1773, although many of those settlers later emigrated to Canada. Groups of Scots immigrants also established communities in Saratoga County around the same time.

During the American Revolutionary War, Scots fought on both sides. After the War, many Scots Loyalists left for Canada. It is estimated that in 1790 about seven percent of New York's population was of Scots descent.

Scots immigration grew to include many families who were displaced during the potato famine that struck the Highlands in the 1840s, and by the Clearances, which largely took place between the 1770s and 1850s. The Clearances evicted tenant farmers (crofters) from their land to make way for more profitable sheep farming in the Highlands and beyond. Often these Scots moved first to Ireland and then to Canada or the United States.

In the first half of the nineteenth century, many Scots textile workers, supplanted by industrialization, immigrated to America and were employed as carpenters, skilled workers, tradesmen, farmers, and factory workers. The cities of Albany, Brooklyn, Buffalo, Elmira, New York, Schenectady, and Syracuse became home to large numbers of Scots. A resurgence of Scots emigration occurred in the 1920s, with the majority of twentieth-century immigrants coming from Glasgow and central Scotland.

Genealogical Resources

The resources below have specific relevance to researching Scots and Scots-Irish immigrants to New York. However, Scots and Scots-Irish immigrants will also be found in records discussed elsewhere in this book.

Immigration

The National Archives (NARA) holds passenger and immigration lists. Many are on microfilm and are widely available. *Ancestry.com* has digitized and indexed many of NARA's immigration records, including passenger arrival records for the ports of New York (1820–1957) and Philadelphia (1800–1948), as well as Canadian border crossings to New York (1895–1956). See chapter 4, Immigration, Migration, and Naturalization, for detailed information about what records exist and where they can be accessed.

Official recordkeeping of passenger arrivals in the United States and border crossings to New York from Canada, a frequent entry point for Scots and Scots-Irish, began after the peak years of Scots and Scots-Irish immigration during the 1700s. The selected bibliography at the end of this section includes books that contain lists of Scottish and Scots-Irish immigrants which may help fill in gaps in the records, whose availability varies with the time period. Researchers are advised to consult original records when available rather than rely solely on indexes and transcriptions.

Newspapers

The Scots and Scots-Irish in New York established fewer newspapers than many other ethnic groups. The *Scottish American Journal* began in New York City as a weekly newspaper in 1857; it was succeeded in 1886 by the *Scottish American* and published until 1925. The Historical Society of Pennsylvania has the full run for the years 1865 to 1925 on microfilm; holdings information for other libraries may be obtained by searching the U.S. Newspaper Directory, 1690–Present, at the Chronicling America website of the Library of Congress at *chroniclingamerica.loc.gov/search/titles*.

The New York State Library's list of New York newspapers at *www.nysl.nysed.gov/nysnp/title4.htm* has holdings information in New York for the *Scottish American* and three other Scots titles. See also chapter 12, Newspapers, for information about how to identify and where to access newspapers.

Religious Records

The largest numbers of Scots and Scots-Irish immigrants to New York had belonged to the Church of Scotland, which is Presbyterian and helped establish Presbyterian congregations in the colonies in the early 1700s. There were also Catholics, Methodists, and Quakers among the Scots and Scots-Irish in New York. See chapter 15, Religious Records, for information on how to access records of these and other denominations.

Selected Repositories, Societies, and Websites

Council of Scottish Clans and Associations (COSCA)

PO Box 427 • Pinehurst, NC 28370 • (980) 333-4686
cosca.scot

The COSCA's primary purpose is to preserve and promote the customs, traditions, and heritage of the Scottish people and serve as a clearing house for Scottish American activities throughout the United States. They are in the process of developing genealogical resources.

New York Caledonian Club

PO Box 4542, Grand Central Station • New York, NY 10163-4542
(212) 662-1083 • *nycaledonian.org*

The New York Caledonian Club, established in 1856, provides Scots, Scottish Americans, and anyone with an interest in Scotland with opportunities for fellowship, cultural expression, and learning. The club's membership and history are documented in the New York Caledonian Club Records 1856–2007, which are held by the New-York Historical Society (N-YHS); a finding aid is at *http://dlib.nyu.edu/findingaids/html/nyhs/caledonian/caledonian.html*.

St. Andrew's Society of the State of New York

150 East 55th Street, 3rd Floor • New York, NY 10022
(212) 223-4248 • *standrewsny.org*

The St. Andrew's Society of the State of New York was founded in 1756 to provide financial assistance to Scots and people of Scottish descent; it has long served as a center for the Scottish community in New York and promotes the appreciation of Scottish cultural heritage. A comprehensive history of the Society is available on its website and includes biographies of all its presidents and a listing of Officers, Managers, and Committees (1756–2006).

Scottish American Society

5679 Sherwood Forest Drive • Akron, OH 44319
(330) 882-0342 • *scottishamericansociety.org*

The Society supports events that provide opportunities to share Scottish heritage and culture. Members have access to a genealogist, and research is shared on the website.

Ulster-Scots Society of America (USSA)

PO Box 3969 • Amarillo, TX 79116
Email: ulsterscotgp@yahoo.com • *ulsterscotssociety.com*

The Society presents educational and social programs related to Scots-Irish heritage. The website has articles about the Scots-Irish experience in the United States and provides links to other resources for research, as well as a discussion board.

Selected Bibliography and Further Reading

Brownstein, Robin and Peter Guttmaker. *The Scotch-Irish Americans: The Peoples of North America Series*. New York: Chelsea House Publishers, 1988.

Dobson, David. *Directory of Scots Banished to the American Plantations, 1650–1775*. Baltimore: Genealogical Publishing Co., 2003. [*Ancestry.com*]

———. *Directory of Scottish Settlers in North America, 1625–1825*. Baltimore: Genealogical Publishing Co., 1993. [*Ancestry.com*]

———. *The Original Scots Colonists of Early America, 1612–1783*. Baltimore: Genealogical Publishing Co., 1989. [*Ancestry.com*]

———. *The Original Scots Colonists of Early America Supplement: 1607–1707*. Baltimore: Genealogical Publishing Co., 1998. [*Ancestry.com*]

———. *Scots in the U.S.A. and Canada, 1825–1875*. Baltimore: Genealogical Publishing Co., 2004. [*Ancestry.com*]

———. *Scottish Emigration to Colonial America*. Athens: University of Georgia Press, 2004.

———. *Scottish Quakers and Early America, 1650–1700*. Baltimore: Genealogical Publishing Co., 1998. [*Ancestry.com*]

———. *Scottish Soldiers in Colonial America*. 4 vols. Baltimore: Genealogical Publishing Co., 1995–2012. [*Ancestry.com*]

———. *The Scottish Surnames of Colonial America*. Baltimore: Genealogical Publishing Co., 2003. [*Ancestry.com*]

———. *Ships from Scotland to America*. Baltimore: Genealogical Publishing Co., 2004.

Erickson, Charlotte. *Invisible Immigrants: The Adaptation of English and Scottish Immigrants in Nineteenth-Century America*. Coral Gables, FL: University of Miami Press, 1972.

Falley, Margaret Dickson. *Irish and Scotch-Irish Ancestral Research: A Guide to the Genealogical Records, Methods and Sources in Ireland*. 2 vols. Evanston, IL.: The author, 1962. Reprint, Baltimore: Genealogical Publishing Co., 1984.

Farrell, Charles. "Pew Rentals in the Scotch Presbyterian Church, New York City, 1785–1798." *NYG&B Record*, vol. 129, no. 4 (1998): 249–259. [NYG&B eLibrary]

Glazier, Ira A. *Emigration from the United Kingdom to America: Lists of Passengers Arriving at U.S. Ports, 1870–1897*. 18 vols. Lanham, MD: Scarecrow Press, 2006–2012.

Leyburn, James G. *The Scotch-Irish, A Social History*. Chapel Hill: University of North Carolina Press, 1962.

MacLean, John Patterson. *An Historical Account of the Settlements of Scotch Highlanders in America, Prior to the Peace of 1783: Together with Notices of Highland Regiments and Biographical Sketches*. Cleveland: Helman-Taylor Company, 1900.

McKnight, Mark. *Blue Bonnets O'er the Border: The 79th New York Cameron Highlanders*. Shippensburg, PA: White Mane Books, 1998.

Mijers, Esther. "Between Empires and Cultures: Scots and New Netherland and New York." *Journal of Scottish Historical Studies*, vol. 33, no. 2 (2013): 165–195. *euppublishing.com/doi/pdfplus/10.3366/jshs.2013.0076*

Millett, Stephen M. *The Scottish Settlers of America: The 17th and 18th Centuries*. Baltimore: Clearfield Company, 2004. [*Ancestry.com*]

O'Callaghan, Edmund Bailey. "Early Highland Immigration to New York." *The Historical Magazine and Notes and Queries Concerning the Antiquities, History and Biography of America*, vol. 5, no. 10 (1861): 301–304.

Porter, H. Leonard. *Destiny of the Scotch-Irish: An Account of a Migration from Ballybay, Ireland to Washington County, New York; Abbeville District, South Carolina; Pittsburgh, Pennsylvania; Preble County, Ohio; Randolph County, Illinois and the Central Illinois Prairie, 1720–1853*. Winter Haven, FL: Porter Co., 1985.

Remington, Gordon. "Feast or Famine: Problems in the Genealogical Use of *The Famine Immigrants* and *Germans to America*." *National Genealogical Society Quarterly*, vol. 78, no. 2 (1990): 135–146.

Scotch-Irish Settlers in America, 1500s–1800s. Baltimore: Genealogical Publishing Co., 2001. CD-ROM.

St. Andrew's Society of the State of New York. *Biographical Register of the St. Andrew's Society of the State of New York, 1756–1856*. 2 vols. New York: For the Society, 1923.

Whatley, Harlan Douglas, comp. and ed., and Duncan A. Bruce and Randall Lenox Taylor, eds. *Two Hundred Fifty Years: The History of Saint Andrew's Society of the State of New York, 1756–2006*. New York: Saint Andrew's Society of the State of New York, 2008. *http://standrewsny.org/sites/default/files/files/History%20Book%20as%20of%2022609_reduced.pdf*

Whyte, Donald. *A Dictionary of Scottish Emigrants to the U.S.A.* Baltimore: Genealogical Publishing Co., 2009.

Introduction

Religious records are valuable tools for New York genealogical research for many reasons. To begin with, they are key vital records substitutes in a state in which vital record keeping began very late. Religious records also help trace family migration across New York State and provide especially helpful cultural and historical context for families through the generations, sometimes linking them to origins in other parts of the world. Depending on the denomination and the era, record type and availability vary, but may include records for baptism, confirmation/coming of age, and marriage; burial records; membership records that document when people arrive and leave a congregation; meeting minutes; and correspondence. See also chapter 9, Cemetery Records.

This chapter describes genealogically-pertinent records collected by twelve religious groups in New York State:

- Baptist
- Catholic
- Congregational
- Eastern Rite Catholic and Eastern Orthodox
- Episcopal
- Jewish
- Lutheran
- Methodist
- Mormon (Latter-day Saints)
- Presbyterian
- Quaker (Society of Friends)
- Reformed (including Dutch, German, and French or Huguenot)

For each denomination, a historical overview is provided, along with a description of records and repositories that reflects the various ways religious groups maintain and preserve records, and a selected bibliography.

Historical Overview

The establishment of religious denominations and congregations in New York State has a fascinating and complex history. Although there was much religious and ethnic diversity in New Netherland, aside from the English Puritans, the only Christian denomination allowed to worship publicly was the Dutch Reformed Church. Thus, many marriages and baptisms took place in the Dutch churches of New Netherland among people of other faiths. New York's first Jewish congregation, Shearith Israel, which still exists today, was formed during the Dutch colonial period. It remained the only Jewish congregation in New York City until 1825.

When the English took over New Netherland in 1664, they extended religious tolerance to the several Protestant denominations already present, and more gradually to the one Jewish congregation, with the result that the Anglican Church became the dominant religion in only a few places. There was no tolerance of Roman Catholicism under the English, however, and although New York State's first constitution in 1777 assured general religious freedom, in practice it singled out Roman Catholics for discrimination. Despite colonial and early state efforts to suppress it, the Roman Catholic Church grew to be the largest denomination by far in New York, fueled by the influx of millions of Catholic immigrants during and after the Great Famine (1845–1852) and the "Great Wave" of American immigration (1880s–1920s).

The nineteenth century also saw the growth of Protestant denominations—notably Methodist, Baptist, and Presbyterian—especially in newly settled areas of New York State. During the first half of the century a series of religious revival meetings took place in central and western New York, which became known as the "Burned-over District" because of the fire-and-brimstone style of preaching that was dispensed there. Revivalism spurred the growth of existing evangelical denominations, as well as the founding of new religious movements, none more successful than the Church of Jesus Christ of Latter-day Saints, which was organized in Seneca County in 1830.

While some ethnic groups may have a particularly strong association with a single religious denomination, there is surprising variety among ethnic affiliations. For example, New York has been home to Italian, Norwegian, and Polish Baptist churches; Chinese, French, and Hungarian Presbyterian churches; and African American synagogues. Extensive descriptions of churches and missions that ministered to various ethnic groups are included in the 1920 report of the Joint Legislative Committee, which is cited below. See chapter 14, Peoples of New York, for additional information about locating religious records that pertain to particular ethnic groups. Jewish records are treated in two places in this book. This chapter describes Jewish sacramental records; chapter 14 provides more detail on resources for Jewish family history research, including cemetery records.

Transcribed, Published, and Digitized Church Records

The literature that describes religious denominations and local congregations is vast, and records of myriad churches across New York have been transcribed by intrepid individuals and groups of volunteers. Therefore, the bibliographies for each denomination in this chapter only scratch the surface of available records. Online library catalogs like *WorldCat.org* can assist in targeted searches to identify record transcriptions that have been compiled in books and typescripts. Many titles have been digitized—especially those produced before 1923—and are freely accessible at *Archive.org*, *HathiTrust.org*, and other digital book providers.

Since 1913 members of the Daughters of the American Revolution (DAR) have transcribed many thousands of unpublished records throughout New York, including numerous church records. The reports are at the DAR Library in Washington, DC; copies are at the New York State Library (NYSL) and the New York Public Library (NYPL). The DAR has a searchable name index to all the GRC reports at *http://services.dar.org/Public/DAR_Research/search/?Tab_ID=6*. See Jean Worden's index for a listing by county of the New York record sets that were transcribed by the DAR before 1998.

The individual County Guides in Part Two of this book present a selection of typescripts, books, and online databases of religious records for each county. Digitized transcriptions of religious records are available on the websites of various historical and genealogical societies and on the NYGenWeb pages of many counties. Royden Woodward Vosburgh, who became archivist and historian of the NYG&B in 1913, compiled more than 100 volumes of transcribed records from Protestant churches across New York State. See the bibliography for an inventory of his transcriptions, whose reliability is highly regarded. The NYG&B eLibrary collection of Religious Records includes transcribed records—many by Mr. Vosburgh—from more than 50 churches of various denominations across New York State.

Both *Ancestry.com* and *FamilySearch.org* have a large selection of religious records for New York State accessible online. The records on *Ancestry.com* are generally specific to particular churches and time periods, and most are classified in the "Birth, Marriage & Death" and "Schools, Directories & Church Histories" sections of the online card catalog.

FamilySearch.org allows for a search across all records, but a focused search of New York collections can sometimes be more fruitful. Starting at the Historical Record Collections page, *https://familysearch.org/search/collection/list*, then choosing the United States, New York, and finally the collection "Birth, Marriage & Death" will produce a list of New York-specific collections. Only a few of the collection titles actually contain the word church; religious records will also be found in the databases "New York, Marriages, 1686–1980" and "New York, Births & Christenings, 1640–1962."

The online catalog at *FamilySearch.org* will search the huge numbers of religious records that have been microfilmed by the Family History Library (FHL); the microfilms can be ordered on the website for use at any Family History Center. Generally, they are organized by individual church and are not included in the vital records index. An initial search by place will reveal all the collections for a county, including the category Church Records. Individual church records held by the FHL can be found by searching the card catalog for a church's name, denomination, or location in the "Place Name," "Titles," "Subjects," or "Keywords" sections of the catalog.

Locating Religious Records

Regardless of the denomination, religious records are usually kept at the most local level—the parish or the congregation. If a parish or a congregation has closed or merged, its records may have gone to the successor congregation or parish or to an archive, religious or secular. Researchers should begin by identifying the individual church, meeting house, or synagogue that their subject is likely to have attended, and guidance is provided for each denomination in the sections that follow in this chapter. In addition, city directories and newspapers can be a valuable source of information about churches and synagogues in a community, as well as their members, clergy, and staff. See also chapter 11, City Directories, and chapter 12, Newspapers.

The Historical Records Survey of the Work Projects Administration (WPA) produced a series of very useful guides to churches and their record holdings in New York State circa 1940. The two-volume *Guide to Vital Statistics Records of Churches in New York State (exclusive of New York City)* is organized by county and denomination and gives the name and location of the church, a brief history, and a list of what historical records were available at the time the survey was completed.

New York City churches and synagogues were addressed in the five-volume *Guide to Vital Statistics in the City of New York* and in a series of individual volumes for various denominations, which are listed in the relevant bibliographies in this chapter.

The Study Center for Early Religious Life in Western New York was created by Ithaca College in 1978 to document religious life in the first half of the nineteenth century during a period of religious revivalism. The collection of primary sources, mainly on film, is now at Cornell University and includes a variety of church records—minute books, membership registers, Sunday School records, and circuit books—among other material. Counties covered include Cayuga, Cortland, Erie, Genesee, Livingston, Monroe, Onondaga, Ontario, Oswego, Schuyler, Seneca, Steuben, Tompkins, Wayne, Wyoming, and Yates. A collections guide, with links to a list of holdings for each county, is at *http://rmc.library.cornell.edu/EAD/htmldocs/RMM06000.html.*

Religious records will sometimes be found in the archives of a religious institution or in the local history collections of a library, historical society, or college. The Historical Documents Inventory (HDI), conducted between 1978 and 1993 by the New York Historical Resources Center at Cornell University, surveyed the manuscript and archival holdings of more than 2,500 repositories across New York State. It resulted in the publication of the series *Guides to Historical Resources in Repositories* for every county except Nassau and Suffolk, which are available online only. The NYSL provides instructions on where to obtain HDI volumes at *www.nysl.nysed.gov/hdi.htm.* Titles in the series will be found in the individual county bibliographies in Part Two of this book; many have been digitized and are available at *books.FamilySearch.org.*

The New York Genealogical and Biographical Society conducted its own survey of church records in New York State at the turn of the twentieth century. More than 200 churches (some in New Jersey and Connecticut) completed questionnaires that asked about the records held, the church's history, and other denominations nearby. The surveys and an index are in the NYG&B eLibrary.

Errors and Omissions

Readers who find errors or omissions in any section in this book are encouraged to inform the editors by sending an email to *NYGuide@nygbs.org.* By submitting additions and corrections, all researchers consulting future editions of this book will benefit.

Selected Bibliography and Further Reading

The resources below provide broad coverage of religions in New York State. Bibliographies specific to each religion appear at the end of each section in this chapter. Gazetteers and local histories often provide information about the religions present in a community; see the Introduction to Part Two of this book

for a bibliography of state gazetteers, and the individual County Guides for county gazetteers and local histories.

Atwood, Craig D., Samuel S. Hill, and Frank S. Mead. *Handbook of Denominations in the United States.* Nashville: Abingdon Press, 2010.

Balmer, Randall Herbert. *A Perfect Babel of Confusion: Dutch Religion and English Culture in the Middle Colonies.* Oxford: Oxford University Press, 2002.

Barkun, Michael. *Crucible of the Millennium: The Burned-Over District of New York in the 1840s.* Syracuse: Syracuse University Press, 1986.

Cross, Whitney R. *The Burned-Over District: The Social and Intellectual History of Enthusiastic Religion in Western New York, 1800–1850.* 1950. Reprint, Ithaca, NY: Cornell University Press, 2009.

Des Grange, Jane. *Long Island's Religious History.* Stony Brook, NY: Suffolk Museum, Port Washington, NY, 1963.

Historical Records Survey. *Guide to Vital Statistics in the City of New York: Churches.* 5 vols. New York: Work Projects Administration, 1942. A separate volume was produced for each borough. [Brooklyn and Queens, NYG&B eLibrary]

Historical Records Survey. *Guide to Vital Statistics Records of Churches in New York State (Exclusive of New York City).* 2 vols. Albany: Work Projects Administration, 1942. [NYG&B eLibrary]

Johnson, Curtis D. *Islands of Holiness: Rural Religion in Upstate New York, 1790–1860.* Ithaca, NY: Cornell University Press, 1989.

New York Genealogical and Biographical Society. "The Vosburgh Collection of New York Church Records." *NYG&B Newsletter* (now *New York Researcher*), (Fall 1998). Also a Research Aid at *NewYorkFamilyHistory.org.*

New York Historical Resources Center. *Guide to Historical Resources in New York, Repositories.* Ithaca, NY: Cornell University, 1978–1993. 60 vols. Several vols. at *books.FamilySearch.org.*

New York State Legislature. Joint Legislative Committee Investigating Seditious Activities. "Citizenship Training in the State of New York." In *Revolutionary Radicalism, Its History, Purpose and Tactics with an Exposition and Discussion of the Steps Being Taken and Required to Curb It . . . Filed April 24, 1920, in the Senate of the State of New York.* Part II, "Constructive Movements and Measures in America," vols. 3 and 4. Albany: J. B. Lyon, 1920. See especially Chapter 6, Churches, pp. 2701–2947.

Pointer, Richard W. *Protestant Pluralism and the New York Experience: A Study of Eighteenth-Century Religious Diversity.* Bloomington: Indiana University Press, 1988.

Procter-Smith, George L. *Religion and Trade in New Netherland; Dutch Origins and American Development.* Ithaca, NY: Cornell University Press, 1973.

Stump, Roger W. "Religion." In *Encyclopedia of New York,* edited by Peter Eisenstadt. Syracuse: Syracuse University Press, 2005.

Worden, Jean D. "Book 1, Subject Index." In *Revised Master Index to the New York State Daughters of the American Revolution Genealogical Records Volumes.* Zephyrhills, FL: J. D. Worden, 1998. The Subject Index includes a listing by county of church and other records transcribed by the DAR.

Baptist

Introduction

"Baptist" describes a group of diverse Christian organizations. Beliefs and worship styles among various kinds of Baptists vary widely, making general statements about the Baptist faith difficult. However, common among almost all Baptists is the belief that only the professed faithful (who would necessarily not be infants) should be baptized, and that the baptism should be performed by complete immersion in water. Each congregation is largely independent, though churches often form associations for the purposes of fellowship.

Historical Overview

The Baptist denomination arose on the European continent during the Protestant Reformation, when it was also called by other names, including Anabaptist. The first Baptist churches in New England were founded in 1639 in Rhode Island. The Providence church was established by Roger Williams, who had been compelled to leave Puritan Massachusetts and who is remembered as a champion of religious liberty.

In New Netherland in 1645, Lady Deborah Moody, a friend of Roger Williams, and, like him, opposed to infant baptism, was granted a patent by Governor Kieft to form a community at Gravesend, Long Island. Even though some of her views were not compatible with those of the Dutch Church, the patent stated that the people of Gravesend were to enjoy free "liberty of conscience," and Kieft's successors did not disturb them. However, when a Rhode Island Baptist minister attempted to hold worship services in Flushing in 1656, he was thwarted by the Dutch authorities. After the British took over from the Dutch in 1664, Baptists were tolerated, but there is little evidence of any organized congregations during the rest of the seventeenth century.

Baptist churches began appearing in New York City in the early-eighteenth century. The early churches tended to struggle, fail, and occasionally experience renewal. These renewals were especially prevalent during the First Great Awakening, a religious movement that occurred in the mid-eighteenth century. It was characterized by religious revivals and impassioned preaching, and often led to the establishment of Baptist congregations. One, organized in 1724, struggled, failed, and revived by the 1760s when, as the First Baptist Church, it built a stone house of worship on Gold Street in Manhattan. Membership in this church, and others, was small.

Baptist meetings were held in Oyster Bay on Long Island by 1700. Before the American Revolution, small Baptist communities were established upstate as far away as present-day Otsego and Oneida counties. Some consisted of just a few families. The

New York Baptist Association was formed in 1791 and included churches in Oyster Bay, Manhattan, and Staten Island. By 1794 Baptist historian John Asplund reported that there were 84 Baptist churches, 109 Baptist ministers, and about 5,300 church members in New York State. These included churches in present-day Chenango, Delaware, Herkimer, Montgomery, Putnam, and Saratoga counties, among others. Many of the Baptists in the upstate counties had come from New England, especially Rhode Island.

Stimulated by the revival movements of the time, including the Second Great Awakening of the early-nineteenth century, by 1825 many more Baptist churches were founded in New York State; New York City became one of the leading centers for Baptist worship in the United States. The membership was largely working class. Many different types of Baptists congregations emerged throughout New York State.

The issue of slavery split the northern and southern Baptists in the mid-1840s, and the Southern Baptist Convention was formed. The northern churches maintained their decentralized organization until 1907, when the Northern Baptist Convention was created. Charles Evans Hughes, governor of New York, was the first president. The name was changed in 1950 to the American Baptist Convention (ABC).

In addition to the Northern/American Baptist Convention, there were many other smaller Baptist denominations in New York. In 1832 the Baptists in New York separated into Primitive and Missionary Baptists. Primitive or "Old School" Baptists declined "modern" institutions such as missions, Sunday schools, and anything for which precedent could not be found in the Bible. Missionary or "New School" Baptists embraced such changes. Other groups included the Free Will Baptists, Seventh Day Baptists, Landmark Baptists, Reformed Baptists, and others, who had their own churches. The nature of the Baptist church, with the focus on the congregation and lack of hierarchical structure, allowed these individual factions to form.

African American Churches

African American members of the First Baptist Church in New York City, offended by the racial segregation of the congregation, left to form the Abyssinian Baptist Church in 1808, on Anthony (now Worth) Street in downtown Manhattan. (In the 1920s the church moved uptown to Harlem.) It was the first African American Baptist church in New York State. See the recent history of the church by Genna Ray McNeil, et al.

In 1840 African American Baptists from New York and other mid-Atlantic states formed the American Baptist Missionary Convention. By the 1860s it had evolved to become the Consolidated American Baptist Convention. The national black conventions united as the National Baptist Convention by 1895.

Records

Records from Baptist churches are sparse, though not as sparse as is sometimes supposed. Baptist churches are essentially autonomous and are not governed by a centralized authority. Each church has its own record-keeping policies and maintains its own archives. The lack of formal structure of the church network means that there is no central repository for records.

Records for marriages, which Baptists do not consider a sacrament, were not regularly kept except by ministers who maintained their own logs.

Since baptism was not performed for infants, the date of the baptism cannot be a reliable proxy for a date of birth. Information often recorded for infant baptism in other denominations, such as names of parents, is not part of the Baptist records. However, if the minutes of a local church survive, they can be of particular value to the family historian, as they record members joining or leaving the congregation, and also the steps taken to discipline members who did not live up to the prescribed rules of behavior.

Locating Records

Despite their desire for autonomy, Baptist churches founded regional associations and kept minutes of their meetings. The first association formed in 1707 and included churches in the Philadelphia area, and eventually some New York Baptist congregations joined. The New York Baptist Association was formed in 1793. Today there are 18 Baptist associations in New York State; contact information and descriptions are online at the American Baptist Churches of New York State website at *abc-nys.org*. The Empire State Fellowship of Regular Baptist Churches at *efrbc.org* is a fundamentalist organization founded in 1942 and includes nearly 200 churches in New York State. There are a number of other Baptist church associations representing a variety of theological points of view.

The WPA's Public Archives Inventory and Church Archives Inventory can be consulted for records of Baptist churches. (These are online at *NewYorkFamilyHistory.org*.) Histories of Baptist churches, volumes of published records, the association minutes, transcriptions of records in genealogical publications, and the records themselves, if they exist, may be available in libraries and at local historical societies, in libraries with manuscript collections, and at the individual churches themselves, if they are still functioning.

For example, the New York Public Library (NYPL) holds several versions of the marriage register (1805–1855) of the Rev. Marmaduke Earle of Oyster Bay, Long Island, who married Baptist and also non-Baptist couples; the NYPL also holds a list of marriages (1841–1854) performed by the Rev. Marmaduke Earle's son, the Rev. Samuel H. Earle of the Baptist church in Cold Spring Harbor. The Oyster Bay Historical Society has a transcript of the Cold Spring Harbor's membership records and minutes dating from 1769. For details of these and other records, see Harry Macy Jr.'s article "Religious Records of Queens and Nassau Counties" on the NYG&B website, *NewYorkFamilyHistory.org.*

A collection of church records from upstate New York is at the library of Cornell University. The archive, described on its website, includes the records of more than fifty Baptist churches in Cayuga, Cortland, Erie, Monroe, Onondaga, Ontario, Schuyler, Seneca, Steuben, Wayne, and Yates counties.

Other libraries offer Baptist records, though finding them can be difficult. Repositories close to the church's location should be checked first. For example, the records of Ellery Baptist Church (1817–1977) in Ellery Center, New York, are at the Reed Library of SUNY Fredonia.

Extensive New York church records, and diaries and account books of some New York Baptist ministers, can be found in the archives of the American Baptist Historical Society (ABHS), founded in Philadelphia in 1853. The ABHS publishes a journal, the *American Baptist Quarterly.* Online finding aids are at *abhsarchives.org.* Records are listed by name of town (not county) and name of church. The earliest records date from the 1790s and extend well into the twentieth century. The catalog to these records and the records themselves are not online. The ABHS will answer specific queries and welcomes researchers who visit by appointment.

Many sources reference Baptist records collections in Rochester, NY. The ABHS collection was moved from Philadelphia to Rochester in 1955, and combined with another large collection of Baptist records that had ended up at the Colgate Rochester Divinity School in 1896. In 2008 the combined archive and the ABHS moved from Rochester to Mercer University in Atlanta, Georgia. The archives of the American Baptist Mission Center, once located at Valley Forge, Pennsylvania, is also at the ABHS facility in Atlanta. The Rochester repository no longer exists.

Researchers pursuing Primitive or Old School Baptists should consult the Primitive Baptist Library in Carthage, IL. The *Signs of the Times* has been published since 1832 and contains information on Primitive or "Old School" Baptists. The Primitive Baptist Library has the largest collection of the periodical. Other archives and special collections exist for various Baptist groups; see Repositories & Resources below.

A somewhat inexact but still useful bibliography of works about Baptist churches is online at *Baptisthistoryhomepage.com.* The search function allows the user to focus on New York material. Note that the bibliography often refers to chapters in a book rather than the book itself.

Selected Repositories and Resources

American Baptist Historical Society (ABHS)
2930 Flowers Road, South, Suite 150 • Atlanta, GA 30341
(678) 547-6680 • *abhsarchives.org*

As the archive of the American Baptist Churches USA, the Society publishes the oldest Baptist journal, the *American Baptist Quarterly.* Archival holdings include original missionary correspondence, records of Baptist organizations and societies, official denominational minutes and publications, documents from the Baptist World Alliance, and personal papers and ephemera of Baptist leaders. The archive holds only a few original church records, and those churches were all affiliated with the American Baptist Churches, USA (formerly the Northern Baptist Convention), the Free Will Baptist General Conference, and the Danish Baptist General Conference of America.

Baptist General Conference History Center
Bethel University • Seminary Library • 3949 Bethel Drive
Room 216 • St. Paul, MN 55112 • (651) 638-6184
bethel.edu/bgc-archives

The archives contain manuscripts, photographs, archival papers, published material, and ephemera relating to the denomination. Access is by appointment. A selection of materials from the Baptist General Conference Collection can be accessed online via the Bethel University Digital Library Collections at *cdm16120.contentdm.oclc.org/cdm/landingpage/collection/bapgecoco.*

Baptist History Homepage
Baptisthistoryhomepage.com

This useful website links to digitized Baptist documents. The website currently boasts links to 462 Baptist books, 75 Baptist magazines and journals, and more from various online sources, as well as a collection of digitized published Baptist histories, including 16 histories of Baptist organizations and congregations in New York State.

Cornell University Library
Division of Rare and Manuscript Collections
2B Carl A. Kroch Library • Cornell University
Ithaca, NY 14853 • (607) 255-3530
Email: rareref@cornell.edu • *rmc.library.cornell.edu*

Cornell University Library has a large collection of religious records pertaining to upstate New York in a collection entitled Records of the Ithaca College Study Center for Early Religious Life in Western New York, 1978–1981. The collection contains the records of 51 Baptist churches in Cayuga, Cortland, Erie, Monroe, Onondaga, Ontario, Schuyler, Seneca, Steuben, Wayne, and Yates counties. The records of four more Baptist churches located in Tompkins County are held elsewhere in the manuscript division.

Free Will Baptist Historical Collection

University of Mount Olive • Moye Library

634 Henderson Street • Mt. Olive, NC 28365 • (919) 658-7869

umo.edu/library/freewillbaptist

The Collection contains manuscripts, personal papers, photographs, pamphlets, bulletins, and ephemera related to the denomination. Many of the items in the collection are included in the Moye Library's online catalog. There are several searchable databases online, including a map of Free Will Baptist churches.

Herrick Memorial Library: Alfred Collection

Alfred University • One Saxon Drive • Alfred, NY 14802

(607) 871-2385 • Email: herricklibrary@alfred.edu

http://herr.alfred.edu/special/collections/alfred_collection.cfm

The library holds material on the Seventh Day Baptists, especially focused on the Seventh Day Baptist community that founded Alfred, New York and its university. A catalog of holdings is available on the library website.

North American Baptist (NAB) Conference Heritage Commission

2100 S Summit Ave • Sioux Falls, SD 57105-2729

(605) 274-2731 • Email: nabarchives@sfseminary.edu

nabarchives.org

The North American Baptist Conference Heritage Commission manages the archives, which consists of a large number of historical periodicals and publications associated with the conference. They have original records of NAB churches and provide research assistance.

Primitive Baptist Library

416 Main St • Carthage, IL 62321 • (217) 357-3723

carthage.lib.il.us/community/churches/primbap/pbl.html

The Primitive Baptist Library holds a large collection of church records, periodicals, minutes of church organizations, photographs, obituaries, books, and biographies, including the most complete collection of the Primitive Baptist publication, *Signs of the Times*. The library also has a partial index of the letters and obituaries that appear in that publication.

Seventh Day Baptist Historical Society

PO Box 1678 • Janesville, WI 53547 • (608) 752-5055

Email: sdbhist@seventhdaybaptist.org • *sdbhistory.org*

The Historical Society maintains the records of Seventh Day Baptist churches and members. The website contains an interactive map of current and extinct Seventh Day Baptist churches, as well as a surname, subject, and place index to more than 200,000 records.

Selected Bibliography and Further Reading

Baldwin, Evelyn Briggs. "The First Stanford (Baptist) Church at Bangall, Dutchess Co., N.Y." *NYG&B Record*, vol. 37 (1906) no. 3: 174–178, no. 4: 314–316; vol. 38 (1907) no. 2: 95–98, no. 3: 206–208. [NYG&B eLibrary]

Baptist Church of Oyster Bay. "The Church Book of the Oyster Bay Baptist Church [1774–1866]." Transcript Oyster Bay Historical Society, manuscript file #146, Oyster Bay, New York.

Eltscher, Susan M. *The Records of American Baptists in New York and Related Organizations*. Rochester, NY: American Baptist Historical Society, 1982.

Foster, Emma J. "Inscriptions from the Old Baptist Burying Ground, Carmel, N.Y." *NYG&B Record*, vol. 35, no. 1 (1904): 56–60. [NYG&B eLibrary]

Gardner, Robert. *Baptists of Early America: A Statistical History, 1639–1790*. Atlanta: Georgia Baptist Historical Society, 1983.

Greater New York Federation of Churches. *The Negro Churches of the Borough of Queens: A Study Made in 1931, by George H. Hobart, Survey Secretary of the Greater New York Federation of Churches*. New York: The Federation, 1931.

———. *The Negro Churches of the Borough of Richmond* [now Staten Island]: *A Study Made in 1931, by George H. Hobart, Survey Secretary of the Greater New York Federation of Churches*. New York: The Federation, 1931.

———. *The Negro Churches of The Bronx: A Study Made in 1931, by George H. Hobart, Survey Secretary of the Greater New York Federation of Churches*. New York: The Federation, 1931.

———. *The Negro Churches of Manhattan: A Study Made in 1930*. New York: The Federation, 1930.

Haberstroh, Richard. *The German Churches of Metropolitan New York: A Research Guide*. New York: NYG&B Society, 2000. Includes a number of Baptist churches. [NYG&B eLibrary]

Haight, Michael G. "The Ancestry of Elder Henry Hait, Primitive Baptist Preacher of Connecticut and New York." *NYG&B Record*, vol. 145 (2014), no. 1: 25–38, no. 3: 202–206. [NYG&B eLibrary]

Hansell, George H. *Reminiscences of Baptist Churches and Baptist Leaders in New York City and Vicinity: From 1835–1898*. Philadelphia: American Baptist Publication Society, 1899.

A History of the Stanton Street Baptist Church, in the City of New York: With a Sketch of Its Pastors, and a Register of the Entire Membership. New York: Sheldon & Co., 1860.

Macy, Harry, Jr. "Brooklyn/Kings County Church Records Since 1783." *NYG&B Newsletter* (now *New York Researcher*), Summer 2000. Updated June 2011 and published as a Research Aid on *NewYorkFamilyHistory.org*. [NYG&B eLibrary]

———. "Records of Other Protestant Denominations of New York City (Manhattan)." *NYG&B Newsletter* (now *New York Researcher*), Spring 1996. Updated May 2011 and published as a Research Aid on *NewYorkFamilyHistory.org*. This Research Aid includes a list of published Baptist records, including, for example, the history of the Stanton Street Baptist Church noted above. [NYG&B eLibrary]

———. "Religious Records of Queens and Nassau Counties." *NYG&B Newsletter* (now *New York Researcher*), Spring 2003. Updated June 2011 and published as a Research Aid on *NewYorkFamilyHistory.org*. [NYG&B eLibrary]

McNeil, Genna Rae, Houston Bryan Roberson, Quinton Hosford Dixie, and Kevin McGruder. *Two Hundred Years of African-American Faith and Practice at the Abyssinian Baptist Church of Harlem, New York*. New York: Wm. B. Eerdmans Publishing Company, 2013.

Stryker-Rodda, Kenneth. "Marriages by a Brooklyn Baptist Minister 1866–1887." *NYG&B Record*, vol. 116 (1985) no. 2: 94–99, no. 3: 132–140, no. 4: 220–228. [NYG&B eLibrary]

Catholic

Historical Overview

This section pertains to religious records of the Roman Catholic Church. Eastern Rite Catholic Churches are treated together with Eastern Orthodox churches elsewhere in this chapter.

The sweeping religious and political unrest in Europe during the sixteenth century left its mark on many Protestants immigrating to North America, who arrived with strong and sometimes virulent anti-Catholic sentiments. Roman Catholic immigrants to New Netherland and colonial New York were unable to practice their faith openly without reprisals throughout most of the colonial era, and widespread anti-Catholic discrimination endured well into the nineteenth century.

Outside the borders of colonial New York, the areas of northern and western New York State did not come under British rule until after the French and Indian War (1754–1763). Following the founding of Quebec in 1608, French traders crossed the border from Canada, accompanied by Jesuit missionaries, and the Catholic religion was freely practiced by French settlers seeking to convert and minister to American Indians. Jesuit missions were established among all five Iroquois nations, but there was great resistance by some tribes. The Catholic Church has conferred sainthood on Father Isaac Jogues and two of his Jesuit contemporaries who were killed at the Mohawk village of Ossernenon (Auriesville, NY) between 1642 and 1646. The Catholic Church also conferred sainthood on the American Indian Kateri Tekakwitha, who was born there in 1656.

There was a short reprieve for Catholics in colonial New York under the leadership of Governor Thomas Dongan (1682–1688), an Irish Catholic, who worked diligently to enact the New York Charter of Liberties and Privileges in 1688, which granted religious freedom to all Christians. That year three English Jesuits opened a school and celebrated the first Mass in New York City. But by 1688 Governor Dongan was removed during heightened political unrest in England and the colonies, which had strong anti-Catholic implications. These events put an end to Catholic tolerance in the colony of New York.

Throughout the British Isles, England had long imposed a series of harsh penal laws against Catholics. These laws were soon mirrored in New York. In 1700 a law was passed that threatened Catholic priests who entered the colony with life imprisonment. In 1718 the vote was denied to Catholics. During the eighteenth and much of the nineteenth centuries the political and social climate in New York was hostile to Catholics, who were barred from citizenship and public office, and denied access to education and admission into certain professions.

Although New York's first constitution in 1777 assured general religious freedom, it imposed a religious test that effectively barred the naturalization of Catholics and their election to public office; these barriers were not lifted until 1789 and 1806 respectively. The anti-priest law was repealed in 1784, paving the way for Catholics to worship openly in New York State. St. Peter's Roman Catholic Church, established in 1785 in lower Manhattan on the site that it still occupies today, was the first Catholic Church in New York State. St. Mary's Church, the state's second oldest Catholic church, was established in Albany in 1797. Brooklyn saw its first Catholic church established in 1822.

John Carroll, first Bishop of Baltimore, estimated in the 1780s that there were 1,500 Catholics in New York State. In the 1790s the Catholic population increased when many French and French West Indian refugees arrived in New York City, fleeing the 1789 French Revolution and the slave rebellion in Haiti.

However, the single greatest factor in the explosive growth of the Catholic Church in New York State was Irish immigration. Though Irish immigrants had arrived in New York State throughout the colonial period, most of the earlier immigrants were Protestants, mainly Presbyterians. The number of Irish Catholics immigrating to New York began to grow after 1800, surged by the 1830s, and increased exponentially during and after the Great Famine (1845–1852). By 1860 New York's population had grown to 3.8 million and included 500,000 Irish-born New Yorkers. The Catholic Church played a central role in the lives of Irish Catholics.

Most Italian immigrants were Catholic, and throughout the period 1910–1970 Italians were the largest foreign-born population in New York State. There were also large numbers of Catholics among Austro-Hungarian, German, Hispanic, Polish, French and other French-speaking immigrants to New York. See the sections on each of these populations, as well as the Irish, in chapter 14, Peoples of New York.

Organization

The local unit of organization in the Catholic Church is the parish, of which there are more than 1,200 in New York State, each headed by a pastor who is a priest. An inventory of active parishes in New York State (and all states) can be searched at *thecatholicdirectory.com* or at *ParishesOnline.com*. Parishes in New York State are organized into eight dioceses, each headed by a bishop, that together constitute the Ecclesiastical Province of New York. Today, the Ecclesiastical Province of New York is contiguous with the boundaries of New York State except for Fishers Island (Suffolk County), which is in the Diocese of Norwich, Connecticut.

An archdiocese is essentially a diocese that is larger or historically more important than a typical diocese, and it is headed by the archbishop who has authority of a kind over the other dioceses in his province. The original Diocese of New York has been, since 1850, an archdiocese. The formation of dioceses in New York is shown in table 1.

Table 1: The Catholic Dioceses of New York State			
Diocese	Created in	Formed from	Coverage
New York (Archdiocese since 1850)	1808	Archdiocese of Baltimore	Bronx, Dutchess, New York (Manhattan), Orange, Putnam, Richmond (Staten Island), Rockland, Sullivan, Ulster, and Westchester counties
Albany	1847	Diocese of New York	Albany, Columbia, Delaware, Fulton, Greene, Montgomery, Otsego, Rensselaer, Saratoga, Schenectady, Schoharie, Warren, Washington, and parts of Hamilton and Herkimer counties
Brooklyn	1853	Diocese of New York	Kings (Brooklyn) and Queens counties
Buffalo	1847	Diocese of New York	Allegany, Cattaraugus, Chautauqua, Erie, Genesee, Niagara, Orleans, and Wyoming counties
Ogdensburg	1872	Diocese of Albany	Clinton, Essex, Franklin, Jefferson, Lewis, St. Lawrence, and parts of Hamilton and Herkimer counties
Rochester	1868; enlarged 1896	Diocese of Buffalo	Cayuga, Livingston, Monroe, Ontario, Seneca, Tompkins, Wayne, Yates, and since 1896, Chemung, Schuyler, Steuben and Tioga counties
Rockville Centre	1957	Diocese of Brooklyn	Nassau and Suffolk counties
Syracuse	1886	Diocese of Albany	Broome, Chenango, Cortland, Madison, Oneida, Onondaga, and Oswego counties

Records of Parishes

There is no central record-keeping system in New York State for Catholic records pertaining to individual church members and their families. Existing records in New York State are kept at the parish level with few exceptions. In addition to sacramental registers, parishes generally hold historical church records, pastors' records, financial records, and records of parish schools.

Therefore it is necessary to identify the relevant parish church attended by the subject family. Most people attended the parish in the neighborhood in which they lived, and so locating the address of the subject family's home is the recommended starting point. In addition to neighborhood locality, ethnicity and language were also factors in parish choices. Complicating the search, however, is that parishes are closed from time to time, and new ones are created. In most cases, records for closed and merged parishes are transferred to a nearby parish, not to the archivist or diocese. There are some exceptions in most dioceses that are noted in the Archival Resources, table 2.

Most New York dioceses now make lists of active and closed parishes available on their websites, or they provide a "parish finder" tool. Additionally, the New York State Catholic Conference website, *nyscatholic.org*, provides links to the websites of individual dioceses. See the introduction to this chapter for information about the WPA Guide to Vital Statistics Records of Churches in New York State, which inventoried all the churches in New York State from 1936 to 1942. See also chapter 11, City Directories, as directories frequently contained listings of churches in a given community.

Family records and memorabilia are important sources that may indicate an ancestor's parish. Cemetery records, funeral cards, obituaries, a family Bible, marriage invitations and photos, and even decorative certificates that commemorate communion, confirmation, or Catholic school graduation can provide the name of an ancestor's parish.

Sacramental Records

The primary records of genealogical interest for Catholics are sacramental registers. Canon law requires every parish to permanently keep records of baptism, confirmation, and marriage. In particular, baptismal and marital records may be rich in information, including parents' names, mother's maiden name, addresses, place of birth, country of origin, occupations, and names of the godparents (sponsors) and witnesses. Since about 1909–1910 the parish of marriage has been required to record the parish of baptism of the bride and groom. Dispensation records might exist for couples who required special permission to marry, such as when one partner was non-Catholic. Many parishes also retain records of first communion and funerals, especially German ethnic parishes.

Sacramental records in the Catholic Church are private, but most parishes elect to cooperate with genealogists seeking family records. Policies and procedures vary regarding how to access records and information. It is advisable to contact the parish for specific information. Parish records are usually filed in chronological order, recorded as each sacramental event took place in the parish, and are sometimes also indexed by name. Older records are contained in ledger books that may be fragile and written in faded or illegible script.

At the time of this publication, the Family History Library (FHL) held microfilm of records of 385 Catholic churches throughout New York State. These records include some parish histories, some indexes to parish records, and some sacramental records. A search using the catalog option at *FamilySearch.org* by place (United States, New York) and by author, corporate name (Catholic Church) reveals a list of church names and locations. For information on how to access the microfilms, see the Family History Library entry in chapter 16, National and Statewide Repositories & Resources. Other published collections of sacramental records may be identified through *WorldCat.org*.

Institutional and Organizational Records

The rapid growth of the Catholic Church throughout the nineteenth century in New York spurred the establishment of a wide network of Catholic schools, hospitals, orphanages, social service organizations, and cemeteries. Catholic Charities of the Archdiocese of New York was founded in 1920 to help provide support to the more than 200 individual charities operating in the diocese at the time. A Guide to the Archives of the Archdiocese of New York Catholic Charities Collection is at *http://archnyarchives.org/wp-content/uploads/2013/05/GuidetotheCatholicCharitiesCollection.pdf*. Today each diocese has its own Catholic Charities bureau.

Anti-Catholic policies in the public schools sparked the creation of Catholic schools throughout New York beginning in the mid-1800s. Parochial school records are held at the parish level or sometimes by the diocese if the school has closed. See table 2 in this section for information about parochial school and other institutional records available at the diocesan level. The archives of independent Catholic schools, colleges, and universities, as well as hospitals and other charities that were founded and operated by religious orders, are generally held by the school or institution itself or by the religious order.

The Historical Documents Inventory (HDI) conducted between 1978 and 1993 to document the location of all of the manuscript and archive collections in repositories in each county of New York State can be a valuable tool for locating the archives of Catholic organizations, benevolent societies, and religious orders. See the bibliography in the introduction to this chapter for details on how to access the HDI. See also chapter 9, Cemetery Records; chapter 10, Business, Institutional, and Organizational Records; and chapter 14, Peoples of New York.

The Knights of Columbus, founded in 1882, is the world's largest Catholic fraternal organization and has more than 1.8 million members today. It was founded as a benevolent society to provide assistance to Catholics in financial need. Its archives are housed at its headquarters in New Haven, CT, and include officers' papers and correspondence, publications and other materials that document the history of the Order, and materials that relate to state and local councils. The archives are accessible by appointment, and a description of the collections and some digitized examples are at *www.kofcmuseum.org/en//index.html*.

Diocesan Research Resources

Each diocese is required to establish its own collections policy, which varies from diocese to diocese. However, archives at the diocesan level generally include records of the management of the diocese itself, such as diocesan personnel records; materials that document the history of the diocese and the parishes within it; and, often, records of closed parishes, schools, institutions, and diocesan newspapers. Table 2 provides a summary of the collections held by each diocese in New York State. Appointments to visit diocesan archives are mandatory.

Other Research Resources

Both Fordham University and the New York Public Library (NYPL) possess excellent and comprehensive collections of books, periodicals, and journals for Catholic history and church records. See the NYPL entry in chapter 16, National and Statewide Repositories & Resources, and the Fordham University entry in the Bronx Borough Guide.

Selected Bibliography and Further Reading

The literature about the history of Catholics and the Catholic Church in New York State is vast. This bibliography demonstrates the range of published material relevant to the researcher.

Ardolina, Rosemary Muscarella. *Old Calvary Cemetery: New Yorkers Carved in Stone*. Bowie, MD: Heritage Books, 1996. The cemetery is in Queens, NY, where large numbers of Irish are buried; headstone transcriptions list the place of origin in Ireland.

———. *Second Calvary Cemetery: New Yorkers Carved in Stone*. Floral Park, NY: Delia Publications, 2000.

Arlotta, Jack M. "Before Harlem: Black Catholics in the Archdiocese of New York and the Church of St. Benedict the Moor." *Dunwoodie Review*, vol. 16 (1992–1993): 69–108.

Bayley, James R. *A Brief Sketch of the Early History of the Catholic Church on the Island of New York*. New York: The Catholic Publication Society, 1870.

Beal, John P. "The Historical Archives." In *New Commentary on the Code of Canon Law*. Mahwah, NJ: Paulist Press, 2000: 644–645.

Becker, Martin J. *A History of Catholic Life in the Diocese of Albany, 1609–1864*. New York: U.S. Catholic Historical Society, 1975.

Bennett, William Harper. *Catholic Footsteps in Old New York*. New York: United States Catholic Historical Society, 1909.

Brown, Mary Elizabeth. *Churches, Communities, and Children: Italian Immigrants in the Archdiocese of New York, 1880–1945*. New York: Center for Migration Studies, 1995.

Buggy, Joseph. *Finding Your Irish Ancestors in New York City*. Baltimore: Genealogical Publishing Co., 2014. Includes a complete list of Catholic parishes in all five boroughs.

The Catholic Church in the United States of America: Undertaken to Celebrate the Golden Jubilee of His Holiness, Pope Pius X. Volume 3: The Province of Baltimore and the Province of New York, Section 1: Comprising the Archdiocese of New York and the Diocese of Brooklyn, Buffalo and Ogdensburg, Together with Some Supplementary Articles on Religious Communities of Women. New York: The Catholic Editing Company, 1914.

Cohalan, Florence D. *A Popular History of the Archdiocese of New York*. Yonkers, NY: United States Catholic Historical Society, 1983. 2nd edition, 1999.

de Courcy, Henry, and John Gilmary Shea. *The Catholic Church in the United States: A Sketch of Its Ecclesiastical History*. New York: Edward Dunigan and Brother, 1857.

Dolan, Jay P. *The Immigrant Church: New York's Irish and German Catholics 1815–1865*. Baltimore: The Johns Hopkins University Press, 1975.

Haberstroh, Richard. *The German Churches of Metropolitan New York: A Research Guide*. New York: New York Genealogical and Biographical Society, 2000. [NYG&B eLibrary]

Henry, Marian S. "John and Mary (Berberich) Hans, Nineteenth Century German Immigrants in Upstate New York." *American Ancestors Journal, Third Annual Supplement to the New England Historical and Genealogical Register*, vol. 165, no. 4 (2011): 358–367. The article concerns a German Catholic family in Rochester and cites online sources of marriage and cemetery records.

Historical Records Survey. *Inventory of the Church Archives in New York City: Roman Catholic Church, Archdiocese of New York*. New York: Work Projects Administration, 1941. [NYG&B eLibrary]

Karcher, Gerard C. "Roman Catholic Parishes in Brooklyn, New York." *Irish Family History Forum Newsletter*, vol. 6, no.4 (1996): 2–6.

O'Donnell, John Hugh. *The Catholic Hierarchy of the United States, 1790–1922*. Washington: 1922.

Table 2: Archival Resources in the Catholic Dioceses of New York

Diocesan Archives	Archival Resources
Archdiocese of New York 201 Seminary Avenue Yonkers, NY 10704 (914) 968-6200 *archnyarchives.org*	The Archives does not hold sacramental records or school records. The website provides a list of its collections which document the history of the diocese, its charitable institutions, and its parishes, with links to some finding aids and a parish finder tool. A list of locations of records of closed parishes is at *http://archnyarchives.org/wp-content/uploads/2013/05/ArchNY-Closed-Parishes.pdf.* Research by appointment only.
Albany 40 North Main Street Albany, NY 12203 (518) 453-6600 *rcda.org*	A search tool for finding diocesan parish records, institutional records, and closed parishes is available at *www.rcda.org/parishes.asp?type=ir.* Archival holdings include historical records for the diocese; older issues of *The Evangelist* Catholic newspaper; records of closed parishes not merged with existing ones; and institutional records including St. Clare's Hospital (Albany), St. Vincent's Female Orphan Asylum (Troy), Brady Hospital (Albany), St. Joseph's Infant Home (Troy), St. Vincent's Home (Albany), St. John's Church (Rensselaer), and St. Mary's Church founded 1797 (Albany). Research by appointment only; some records may be sent by mail.
Brooklyn 310 Prospect Park West Brooklyn, NY 11215 (718) 399-5900 *dioceseofbrooklyn.org*	Holdings include sacramental registers of nine closed parishes; records of 125 closed schools, three closed hospitals, and two closed orphanages; several series pertaining to marriage dispensations from 1854 to 1964; parish histories; deceased priest personnel files; and diocesan directories. The website has a Genealogical FAQ page that provides a helpful orientation to finding religious records at the diocese and elsewhere; parish lists for Brooklyn 1820–present, and for Queens 1843–present; and a list of record locations for schools formerly located in Brooklyn and Queens. Very strong photographic collection documenting the diocese's churches and schools. Full run of the *Tablet*, 1908—present, paper only. Genealogical research via written request only.
Buffalo 795 Main Street Buffalo, NY 14203 (716) 847-5500 *buffalodiocese.org*	Archival collections include parish histories, diocesan directories, older closed parish records, records of bishops, and papers relating to Father Baker and Our Lady of Victory Basilica. The collection of local Catholic newspapers in print or on microfilm includes: • *The Buffalo Catholic Sentinel,*1858–1860, various years • *Catholic Union and Times,* 1872–1939 • *Catholic Union and Echo,* 1915–1964 • *The Echo,* 1915–1937 • *The Magnificat,* 1964–1973 • *Our Sunday Visitor,* 1978 • *Catholic News of Western NY,* 1973–1974 • *Western New York Catholic,* 1974–present Research by appointment only.
Ogdensburg 622 Washington Street Ogdensburg, NY 13669 (315) 393-2920 *dioogdensburg.org*	Archival holdings include historical records of the diocese, bishops, and parishes (but not sacramental records); record abstracts for diocesan/parish lands and transfers; deeds for diocesan cemeteries. Closed parish records have been scanned; merged parishes' sacramental records are held by parishes. A history of the Diocese of Ogdensburg is online at *http://northcountrycatholic.org/welcome/history.html.* A full run of *North Country Catholic,* a diocesan newspaper, March 3, 1946–present, is online at *http://nyshistoricnewspapers.org.*
Rochester 1150 Buffalo Road Rochester, NY 14624 (585) 328-3210 *dor.org*	Archival holdings include the papers of all bishops who have served the diocese 1868–present; historical records for all parishes and diocesan schools, institutions and agencies; biographical information on diocesan priests; published works by diocesan authors; the historical records of St. Bernard's and St. Andrew's Seminaries; and archives of Fulton J. Sheen, Bishop of Rochester 1966–1969. Reference and research assistance by appointment only.
Rockville Centre 50 North Park Avenue Rockville Centre, NY 11571 (516) 678-5800 *drvc.org*	The Archives holds no sacramental records or registers—these are at the parish where the sacrament took place. Researchers should contact parishes directly to obtain sacramental records. If the parish name is unknown, they may contact the Diocesan Archivist for help narrowing down its geographic area and deciding which parishes to contact. Archival holdings include a clippings subject file and the original photographs file of the diocesan newspaper, the *Long Island Catholic,* begun in 1962. The newspaper transitioned into a magazine format in 2012 and past issues can be viewed online at *http://licatholic.org/past-issues-of-li-catholic-magazine.* Research by appointment only.
Syracuse 240 East Onondaga Street Syracuse, NY 13202 (315) 470-1493 *syracusediocese.org*	The Diocese collects material of historical value relating to the Diocese and its parishes, but does not hold sacramental records. Archival collections include parish histories and documents from various diocesan institutions; records of schools, religious orders, and noteworthy individuals; rare books; scrapbooks; and special collections from the 1950s to the 1990s; and a collection of the *Catholic Sun,* the official newspaper of the diocese, founded 1892. A museum, library, and records workroom are open to researchers by appointment.

The Official Catholic Directory. Multiple volumes. New Providence, NJ: P. J. Kenedy & Sons, 1817–present.

Pointer, Philip J. "Religious Life in New York during the Revolutionary War." *New York History*, vol. 66, no.4 (1985): 357–373.

Records of the Church of St. Peter's, New York City 1787–1908. Microform, 4 reels. New York: 1965. Includes baptismal records 1787–1908 and marriage registers 1802–1908. Available only at NYPL. A history of the church is at *stpetersrcnyc.org.*

Reuss, Francis X. *Biographical Cyclopedia of the Catholic Hierarchy of the United States, 1784–1898.* Milwaukee: M. H. Wiltzius & Co., 1898.

Ryan, Leo R. *Old St. Peter's: The Mother Church of Catholic New York.* New York: United States Catholic Historical Society, 1935.

Shea, John Gilmary, ed. *The Catholic Churches of New York City.* New York: Lawrence C. Goulding and Co., 1878.

Shelly, Thomas J. *The Bicentennial History of the Archdiocese of New York, 1808–2008.* Strasbourg, France: Éditions du Signe, 2007.

— — —. *Empire State Catholics: A History of the Catholic Community in New York State.* Strasbourg, France: Éditions du Signe, 2007.

Silinonte, Joseph M. *Bishop Loughlin's Dispensations, Diocese of Brooklyn: Genealogical Information from the Marriage Dispensation Records of the Roman Catholic Diocese of Brooklyn: Kings, Queens and Suffolk Counties, 1859–1866.* Brooklyn: The Author, 1996.

— — —. *Tombstones of the Irish Born: Cemetery of the Holy Cross, Flatbush, Brooklyn.* Westminster, MD: Heritage Books, 2006.

Taylor, Sr. Mary Christine. *A History of Catholicism in the North Country.* Camden, NY: A. M. Farnsworth Sons, 1972.

Congregational (also Independent)

Historical Overview

The Congregational church is a Protestant denomination in which each congregation operates autonomously, a key feature which differentiates it from most other denominations. Today most churches in the denomination affiliate with the United Church of Christ; others affiliate with the National Association of Congregational Christian Churches or the Conservative Christian Conference. All three groups are represented in New York State today.

Congregationalism has its roots in the reformed Protestant movement led by John Calvin (1509–1564) in Geneva, Switzerland. Their values and theological viewpoint led their founders to separate from Anglican and Catholic churches in the sixteenth century.

In North America the denomination flourished in New England since the founding of the Plymouth and Massachusetts Bay colonies. Harvard and Yale universities, and many of the older colleges in New England (including Dartmouth, Bowdoin, Middlebury, Williams, and Amherst) were founded by Congregationalists. In Connecticut, areas of Maine, Massachusetts, and New Hampshire, the Congregational Church was the largest Christian denomination, and, since it was supported by tax revenue, was practically the state church.

Long Island Beginnings

The earliest English settlements on Long Island established churches that were largely independent of any ecclesiastic structure and followed the New England Congregationalist model. Most of the settlers had resided in New England before moving to Long Island and also recruited many of their ministers from there. The Southold congregation, arguably the oldest in Suffolk County, was formed of settlers from the New Haven Colony. While the oldest congregations eventually became Presbyterian, in the earliest days of settlement they were largely independent or Congregationalist, with no real structure or hierarchy, until shortly before the first Presbytery of Long Island was formed in 1718.

The First Great Awakening in the middle of the eighteenth century was characterized by religious revivals, impassioned evangelical preaching, and dissociation from ceremony, hierarchy, and ritual within the church. On Long Island, this movement spawned the creation of new congregations that favored this emotional brand of preaching and lack of church structure, or even caused the conversion of entire congregations and churches. This movement caused some Long Island congregations to identify themselves as Congregationalists. The "First Strict Congregational Church of Southold" was organized in 1758. Known as the "Mother Church," it produced additional churches on Long Island before the Revolution.

Congregationalists reached out to American Indian communities on Long Island, especially the Shinnecock from the Bridgehampton area. Peter John, a Shinnecock Congregationalist preacher, had converted during the First Great Awakening and received ordination from the Strict Congregationalists of Connecticut. Peter John established American Indian Congregationalist congregations in Long Island at Canoe Place, Islip, Poosepatuck, and Wading River by the late 1790s. His work was continued by his grandson, Rev. Paul Cuffee, who continued to minister to the area. Long Island was the bastion of Congregationalism in New York before the American Revolution, and its Long Island adherents made their way into New York City. Congregationalists did not have a significant presence in New York City until about the mid-nineteenth century. The Broadway Tabernacle, founded in 1840, was the first formal, denominational Congregational church in New York City.

Expansion into Upstate and Western New York

The largest numbers of Congregationalists were New Englanders moving west after the conclusion of the American Revolution; they spread mainly to upstate and western New York. As settlers moved into previously unsettled territories in western New York, they were typically widely scattered and unable to support a local congregation for at least a few years or even generations. As early as 1784, Congregationalist church organizations from Connecticut sent visiting ministers to see to the needs of these settlers in the wilderness. These ministers typically had regular congregations in Connecticut, and records of early Congregationalist settlers in thinly populated areas of New York may be found among the records of these Connecticut ministers.

In 1798 the Connecticut Missionary Society was formed, and it continued to minister to Congregationalists in areas of New York too sparsely populated to form a congregation. Typically, once enough settlers had established themselves in an area, a congregation became established in a county or region, which would draw in further Congregationalist settlers, and then multiple congregations sprang up in large numbers, as many as 20 or more in a single county. The First Congregational Church of Canandaigua, the seat of Ontario County, was formed in 1799 and is still in existence.

The Changing Face of Congregationalism

The blending of Congregationalists and Presbyterians continued into the nineteenth century, both lay and clerical. In 1801 a plan to unite the two denominations developed in New York, only to fail later in the century. The Second Great Awakening, which lasted from the end of the eighteenth century through the mid-nineteenth century, contributed to the growth of the Congregational church, especially in the formation of missionary societies. Church histories often show churches beginning as one denomination, shifting to the other, and then changing back again, especially in eastern Long Island.

Regional associations of Congregational churches formed in the early-nineteenth century; the Oneida and Ontario county associations were formed in 1800. The first denominational association of statewide Congregationalist churches was formed in 1834. Later, more associations formed in several upstate regions, on Long Island, and in New York City. By 1871 a National Council had formed, providing for the first time a formal denominational structure for Congregationalists.

Records

Necessary to researching Congregationalists families is determining the church(es) to which they were likely to have belonged. Richard Taylor's series of books on Congregational churches by region contains detailed indexes of church names, mergers and name changes, and closings.

Published church histories are found at the churches themselves, if they still exist, and in local and regional libraries throughout New York State.

The best general single source of archives and published histories is the Congregational Library and Archives in Boston (*14beacon.org*). The collection, which has an online catalog, contains extensive New York materials. The site also offers an "obituary database" for nearly 30,000 Congregationalist ministers. The database is a sortable list with instructions for finding the full text obituary elsewhere.

The records collection of the Congregational Library and Archives contains mostly material from Congregational churches that have closed. The online description of their records, prepared by professional archivists, is superb. Three examples of its holding are:

- Records of the First Congregational Church of Fulton (Oswego County), founded in 1881. This church also operated as the First Congregational Church of Oswego Falls and First Congregational Church of Volney. The collection contains records of births, deaths, baptisms, marriages, confirmations, and various church activities.
- The Summer Hill Congregational Church (formerly East Locke Congregational Society of Locke, Cayuga County) was formed in 1827 and closed in 1974. The files contain records of baptisms and marriages, correspondence, pledge books, photographs, records of some auxiliary groups, and meeting minutes.
- The Lisle Collection contains material from churches and conferences all over New York State including Brooklyn and Manhattan. It includes some items from the New York Congregational Church History Society, which existed briefly in the early-twentieth century. Newton Whitmarsh Bates' short study of western New York Congregationalism was published by the CCHS in 1906.

The minutes of the National Council of Congregations Churches (meeting triennially) are digitized and online at *Archive.org*. These minutes, beginning in 1865 (six years prior to the actual formation of the National Council), are very lengthy and contain a great deal of valuable genealogical information. The 1865 volume, for example, contains 553 pages and reports hundreds of clergy names with their town of residence, the place of their birth, and even the places of birth of their parents.

The library at Cornell University has records, mostly on microfilm, of 27 congregational churches in various upstate counties, as shown in table 3. It might be the single largest collection of congregational church records in New York State. However, there were hundreds of congregational churches in New York State, and so this archive is far from comprehensive.

The Vosburgh Collection of New York State Church Records includes eighteenth- and nineteenth-century Congregational church records from five churches in Saratoga, Oneida, and Columbia counties.

Selected Repositories and Resources

The United Church of Christ maintains an archive, but has records only from 1957. A description of their holdings and relationship with other relevant collections is on their website (*UCC.org*).

The Family History Library, the New York State Library, and the New York Public Library, among other repositories, are rich in New York Congregational Church histories.

Congregational Library & Archives

14 Beacon Street • Boston, MA 02108

(617) 523-0470 • *14beacon.org*

The Library contains manuscripts, church records, biographies, town histories and an online obituary database for Congregational ministers and missionaries from the 1600s to the present. Electronic finding aids are available on the website.

Table 3: Congregational Church Records at Cornell University Library		
County	**Church**	**Time Period of Records**
Broome	First Congregational Church of Maine	1819–1916
Cayuga	First Congregational Church, Sennett Congregational Church, Summer Hill Congregational Church, Moravia	1827–1887 1805–1886 1825–1887
Cortland	Union Congregational Church, Cincinnatus and Solon	1819–1972 (Record book)
Erie	First Congregational Church, Eden	1817–1890
Genesee	First Congregational Church, Bergen	1807–1892
Monroe	First Congregational Church, Parma and Greece First Congregational Church, Perinton Congregational Church, Henrietta Union Congregational Church, Churchville First Congregational Church, Riga	1819–1867 1824–1910 1833–1868 (Record book) 1852–1893 1830–1965
Oswego	Congregational Church, New Haven First Congregational Society, Richland (Pulaski)	1817–1943 1811–1934
Ontario	First Congregational Church, Rushville Congregational Church of Reed's Corners, Gorham First Congregational Church, Bristol First Congregational Church, East Bloomfield First Congregational Church, Canandaigua First Congregational Church, Honeoye Congregational Society of Victor	1802–1898 1843–1949 1800–1913 1796–1895 1799–1978 1843, 1862–1914 1799–1896
Steuben	Congregational Church, Prattsburg	1804–1877
Tompkins	First Congregational Church, Christ, Danby Congregational Church, West Groton First Congregational Church, Ithaca	1807–1878 1817–1900 1830–1946
Wayne	First Congregational Church, Marion	1808–1946

Cornell University Libraries

Ithaca, NY 14853 • (607) 255-4144 • *cornell.edu/libraries*

Cornell's large collection of religious records from western New York State includes Congregational Churches, see table 3. Lists of churches may be found at *http://rmc.library.cornell.edu/eguides/lists/churchlist1.htm* and *http://rmc.library.cornell.edu/eguides/lists/churchlist2.htm*.

Selected Bibliography and Further Reading

Bates, Newton W. *Historical Gleanings in Western New York Congregationalism*. West Bloomfield, NY: Congregational Church History Society, 1906.

Brown, Russell K. "Records of the Congregational Church, Orient, Long Island." *NYG&B Record*, vol. 136, no. 3 (2005): 173–182. [NYG&B eLibrary]

Calkins, H., Jr. "An Exact Copy of the Records of the Congregational Church of Greenfield, Saratoga Co., N.Y." *NYG&B Record*, vol. 34 (1903) no. 2: 141–143, no. 3: 212–216, no. 4: 284–288; vol. 35 (1904) no. 1: 29–33. [NYG&B eLibrary]

Cray, Robert E., Jr. "More Light on a New Light: James Davenport's Religious Legacy, Eastern Long Island, 1740–1840." *New York History*, vol. 73, no. 1 (1992): 4–27.

Pearson, Samuel C. "From Church to Denomination: American Congregationalism in the Nineteenth Century." *Church History*, vol. 30, no. 1 (1969).

Prime, Nathaniel S. *A History of Long Island: From Its First Settlement by Europeans to the Year 1845, with Special Reference to Its Ecclesiastical Concerns*. New York: R. Carter, 1845.

Taylor, Richard Henry. *Plan of Union and Congregational Churches of Christ in the Middle Atlantic States*. Madison, WI: Richard H. Taylor, 2009.

Von Rohr, John. *The Shaping of American Congregationalism 1620–1957*. Cleveland: Pilgrim Press, 1992.

Walker, Williston. *Creeds and Platforms of Congregationalism*. New York: Pilgrim Press, 1991. Reprint of the 1893 edition.

Eastern Rite Catholic and Eastern Orthodox

Historical Overview

Eastern Christian churches—both Catholic and Orthodox—trace their roots to the eastern portion of the Holy Roman Empire and the earliest days of Christianity. The Great Schism (1054 CE) led to the separation of the Roman Catholic Church from the Eastern Christian churches, which had already undergone a variety of smaller schisms. As the Greek language was prevalent among early Eastern Christians, the term Greek is often used to describe Eastern churches in general and does not necessarily refer to the ethnicity of their adherents.

An excellent presentation of the complicated history of Eastern Christian churches in the United States is provided in the introduction to the *Inventory of the Church Archives in New York City: Eastern Orthodox Churches and the Armenian Church in America*, produced in 1940 by the Historical Records Survey of the Work Projects Administration (WPA). This volume not only provides information about Eastern churches in the five boroughs of New York City, but also provides information for many Eastern churches elsewhere in New York State.

Eastern Rite Catholic Churches

The Catholic Church headed by the Pope in Rome is in fact comprised of 23 particular churches. By far the largest of these churches is the Latin Rite, commonly referred to as Roman Catholic. The 22 other churches are primarily concentrated in Eastern Europe and the Middle East, and have small, ethnically-homogenous populations. The adherents of these churches are collectively called Eastern Rite Catholics. Some of these churches, like the Melkite and Ukrainian Greek Catholic Churches, were at one time part of the Orthodox communion, but now recognize the authority of the Pope and are called Uniate. Others, like the Maronite Church, were never separated from the Pope, but developed their own liturgy over centuries of relative geographic isolation.

Before the late-nineteenth century few immigrants to the United States came from Eastern Rite Catholic communities. However, as large numbers of immigrants arrived from the former empires of Austria-Hungary and Russia, ethnic communities began to establish their own parishes alongside those of Roman Catholics. Today the various Eastern Rite Catholic churches maintain their own hierarchies separate from, but in communion with, Rome.

Eastern Rite Catholic churches are centered around the parish, and it is at this level that the majority of records can be found pertaining to sacraments, such as baptism and marriage, as well as administrative issues. Unlike the Roman Catholic Church, in which the sacraments of baptism, first holy communion, and confirmation are administered at different times in a person's life, in most Eastern Rite Churches these sacraments are all conferred in infancy.

Of the 22 Eastern Rite churches worldwide, only ten have eparchies (equivalent to a diocese) in the United States, and only eight have parishes in New York State. If a parish closed, its records may be held at a nearby parish or by the eparchy; the chancellor of the eparchy has responsibility for its archives. Directories of Roman Catholic churches and dioceses sometimes include Eastern Rite parishes, but to identify Eastern Rite parishes, it is best to consult the website of the eparchy. (See table 4.) In the absence of an Eastern Rite Catholic parish, Eastern Rite Catholics would often participate in a Roman Catholic parish or an Eastern Orthodox parish. See the section on Catholic Religious Records in this chapter for information on locating records of Roman Catholic churches.

Eastern Orthodox Churches

Eastern Christian churches that are not in papal communion are called Orthodox churches. While many Orthodox churches hold the same basic theological principles of early Christianity and are in communion with each other, they do not share a unified hierarchy and are generally organized around ethnicity and language.

Orthodox Christians arrived in North America as early as 1794, when eight Russian missionaries landed at Kodiak, Alaska, then a Russian colony. New York first saw significant numbers of Orthodox Christians arrive in the late-nineteenth century from the former empires of Austria-Hungary and Russia. Although these immigrants formed various worship communities based on ethnic background, at the start almost

Table 4: Eastern Rite Catholic Denominations in New York State

Denomination	Parishes in New York	Eparchy	Eparchy Contact Information
Armenian Catholic Church	Manhattan	Armenian Catholic Church—Eparchy of the United States and Canada	1510 East Mountain St, Glendale, CA 91207 *armeniancatholic.org*
Maronite Church	Brooklyn, Olean, Sleepy Hollow, Utica, Watervliet, Williamsville	Eparchy of St. Maron of Brooklyn	109 Remsen Street, Brooklyn, NY 11201 (718) 237-9913 · *stmaron.org* Email: chancerystmaron@verizon.net
Melkite Greek Catholic Church	Brooklyn, Rochester, Utica, Yonkers	Eparchy of Newton	3 VFW Parkway, West Roxbury, MA 02132 (617) 323-9922 · *melkite.org*
Romanian Church United with Rome	Queens	Eparchy of St. George in Canton	1121 44th Street NE Canton, OH 44714 (330) 493-9355 · *romaniancatholic.org* Email: ovim@rcdcanton.org
Ruthenian Catholic Church	Binghamton, Endicott, Granville, Manhattan, Olean, Peekskill, Smithtown, Westbury, White Plains, Yonkers	Eparchy of Passaic	445 Lackawanna Avenue, Woodland Park, New Jersey 07424 (973) 890-7777 · *eparchyofpassaic.com*
Syro-Malabar Catholic Church	Bronx, Brooklyn, Cortlandt Manor, West Hempstead	Eparchy of Saint Thomas the Apostle of Chicago	372 South Prairie Avenue, Elmhurst, Illinois 60126 (630) 279-1383 · *stthomasdiocese.org*
Syro-Malankara Catholic Church	Elmont, New Rochelle	Apostolic Exarchate of United States of America (Syro-Malankarese)	1500 De Paul Street, Elmont, NY 11003 (516) 233-1656 · *syromalankarausa.org*
Ukrainian Catholic Church	Amsterdam, Auburn, Bronx, Brooklyn, Buffalo, Campbell Hall, Cohoes, Elmira Heights, Fresh Meadows, Glen Spey, Hempstead, Hudson, Hunter, Johnson City, Kenmore, Kerhonkson, Lackawana, Lancaster, Lindenhurst, Manhattan, Mt. Kisco, Niagara Falls, Queens, Riverhead, Rochester, Rome, Spring Valley, Staten Island, Syracuse, Troy, Utica, Watervliet, Yonkers	Eparchy of Stamford	161 Glenbrook Road, Stamford, CT 06902 (203) 324-7698 · *stamforddio.org*

all were united in a single North American diocese of the Russian Orthodox Church, known as the Metropola. Greek Orthodox parishes operated as independent congregations until the formation in 1921 of the Greek Orthodox Archdiocese of North and South America.

The twentieth century brought dramatic expansion and structural change to Christian Orthodoxy. The Russian Revolution of 1917 and subsequent events precipitated a series of schisms that resulted in numerous self-governing jurisdictions of Orthodox Christians, based largely on ethnic composition and affiliation with a Patriarch, the highest-ranking bishop in Eastern Orthodoxy.

Today there are ten, self-governing canonical jurisdictions of Orthodox Christians in the United States, with a combined total of about 200 congregations in New York State. (See table 5.) By far the two most populous branches of Eastern Orthodoxy in New York State are the Greek Orthodox and Russian Orthodox. Other cultures represented include Bulgarian, Carpatho-Russian, Georgian, Romanian, Serbian, and Ukrainian.

The Calendar—Julian and Gregorian

All Orthodox churches adhered to the Julian calendar before May 1923, when a congress of many—but not all—Orthodox churches proposed to adopt the Gregorian or "New" calendar that had already been in use in much of the world for centuries and in New York since 1752. A consensus among the churches was not reached. The Russian and Serbian churches continue to adhere to the Julian or "Old Calendar." Other Orthodox churches gradually transitioned to the New Calendar, the Bulgarian being the most recent in 1968. However, almost all Orthodox churches continue to calculate Easter based on the Julian calendar. An informative article on this complex subject is at *www.goarch.org/ourfaith/ourfaith7070*. To understand the impact of the calendar change on genealogical records, see the section on the calendar transition in chapter 1, Colonial Era.

Russian Orthodox

Russian Orthodox Christians are no longer united within a single church. The Metropola—the original Russian Orthodox diocese—changed its name in 1970 to the Orthodox Church in America (OCA); a helpful history is on the OCA's website at *http://oca.org/history-archives*. Some churches chose not to join the OCA at that time and instead formed the Russian Orthodox Church in the USA, which is administered by the Patriarch of Moscow. A third jurisdiction, the Russian Orthodox Church Outside of Russia (ROCOR), was organized in 1920. These three jurisdictions are now all in communion with each other and with the other canonical jurisdictions. However, there are several smaller, unaffiliated Russian Orthodox churches in the United States that have remained schismatic.

The WPA inventory provides detailed information about record keeping of the Eastern Orthodox churches. Until 1917—with the exception of Greek Orthodox churches—all Eastern Orthodox churches kept records in the Russian language and sent one copy to the archdiocese and kept one set on file at the local parish. However, conflicts and schisms during the twentieth century resulted in many parishes being relocated or closed after affiliating with a different branch of Russian Orthodoxy. Consequently, some parish records have been lost or misplaced in transition. Records of closed parishes and copies of missing parish records may be held by the diocese. A list of current parishes can be found on the website of the diocese. (See table 5.)

Greek Orthodox Church

The first Greek Orthodox congregation in New York was formed in the 1890s in New York City. Fueled by an influx of immigrants from Greece between 1890 and 1930, many more congregations formed across the state. Currently, there are 62 parishes in New York State affiliated with the Greek Orthodox Archdiocese, which recognizes the Ecumenical Patriarch of Constantinople. Not all Greek Orthodox churches in New York are affiliated with the archdiocese.

Most records are kept at the parish level, and may be found in the custody of the congregation that generated them. A directory of parishes is on the website of the archdiocese at *goarch.org*. Records of births, marriages, and deaths can be found in most churches. Some churches also maintain collections of minutes of meetings, church newsletters, or photographs. The records of defunct churches are usually kept by the archdiocese. Early records are likely to have been written in Greek. After the archdiocese founded a seminary in Connecticut in 1937, there was a rise in English-speaking, American-trained priests.

Armenian Apostolic Church

The Armenian Church is part of the Oriental Orthodoxy, a group of churches—including Coptic, Ethiopian, Eritrean, and Syrian—that split off from other Eastern Orthodox churches after the Council of Chalcedon (451 CE). Armenians began to immigrate in growing numbers to the United States in the 1880s to escape persecution by the Ottoman Empire. A schism within the American church began in the 1920s and eventually resulted in two divisions, both headquartered in New York City. The diocese of the Armenian Church of America includes ten Armenian parishes across New York State, the first of which, St. Peter's Armenian Apostolic Church, was established in Troy in 1899. The Eastern Prelacy of the Armenian Apostolic Church of America includes five churches in New York State. Records should be sought at the parish level, and parishes may be identified on the website of both organizations. (See table 6.)

Table 5: Eastern Orthodox Canonical Jurisdictions in the United States

Jurisdiction	Patriarchate Affiliation	Parishes in NY	Website	Contact Information
American Carpatho-Russian Orthodox Diocese of the USA	Ecumenical Patriarchate of Constantinople	9	acrod.org	312 Garfield Street, Johnstown, PA 15906 (814) 539-9143
Antiochian Orthodox Christian Archdiocese of North America	Patriarchate of Antioch	13	antiochian.org	PO Box 5238, Englewood, NJ 07631-5238 (201) 871-1355 · Email: archdiocese@antiochian.org
Bulgarian Eastern Orthodox Diocese of the USA, Canada, and Australia	Patriarchate of Bulgaria	2	www.bulgarian diocese.org	50-A West 50th Street, New York, NY 10019 (212) 246-4608 Email: metropolitan.joseph@verizon.net
Greek Orthodox Archdiocese of America	Ecumenical Patriarchate of Constantinople	62	goarch.org	8 East 79th Street, New York, NY 10075-0106 (212) 570-3517 · Email: archives@goarch.org
Orthodox Church in America	Formerly, Patriarchate of Moscow	49	oca.org	Archives of the Orthodox Church in America PO Box 675, Syosset, NY 11791 (516) 922-0550, ext. 121 http://oca.org/history-archives/about-archives
Romanian Orthodox Archdiocese in the Americas	Patriarchate of Romania	7	www.romarch.org	5410 N. Newland Ave, Chicago, IL 60656-2026 (773) 774-1677 · Email: contact@romarch.org
Russian Orthodox Church in the USA	Patriarchate of Moscow	4	mospatusa.com	Patriarchal Parishes in the USA 454 Outwater Lane, Garfield NJ 07026 (973) 930-3514 · Email: chancellor@mospatusa.com
Russian Orthodox Church Outside of Russia (ROCOR)	Patriarchate of Moscow	5	www.synod.com/ synod/indexeng. htm	55 East Third Street, Howell, NJ 07731 (732) 961-1917 · Email: eadiocese@gmail.com
Serbian Orthodox Church in North and South America	Patriarchate of Serbia	3	www.serborth.org	Diocese of Eastern America 138 Carriage Hill Drive, Mars, PA 16046 (724) 772-8866 · www.easterndiocese.org
Ukrainian Orthodox Church of the USA	Ecumenical Patriarchate of Constantinople	17	uocofusa.org	Metropolia Center 135 Davidson Avenue, Somerset, NJ 08873 (732) 356-0090 · Email: consistory@uocofusa.org

Table 6: Armenian Churches

Division	Affiliation	Parishes in NY	Website	Contact Information
Armenian Apostolic Church of America	Catholicate of the See of Cilicia (Antelias, Lebanon)	5	armenianprelacy.org	Eastern Prelacy of the Armenian Apostolic Church of America 138 East 39th Street New York, NY 10016 (212) 689-7810 Email: email@armenianprelacy.org
Armenian Church of America	Catholicate of All Armenians (The Mother See of Holy Etchmiadzin)	10	armenianchurch-ed.net	Eastern Diocese of the Armenian Church of America 630 Second Avenue New York, NY 10016 (212) 686-0710

Additional Online Resources

Assembly of Canonical Orthodox Bishops of the United States of America

assemblyofbishops.org

The assembly comprises all the active, canonical Orthodox bishops in the United States of every canonical jurisdiction and seeks to contribute to the unity of the Orthodox Church. It is one of 13 such regional assemblies throughout the world. The website provides links to the websites of each jurisdiction, as well as an online database of Orthodox parishes in the United States.

Krikor and Clara Zohrab Information Center

630 Second Avenue • New York, NY 10016-4885

(212) 686-0710 • *www.zohrabcenter.org*

Housed at the Eastern Diocese of the Armenian Church of America, the Zohrab Center's holdings include extensive information on the Armenian Church, as well as Armenian history, politics, and culture. The website provides access to an online library catalog and some digitized books.

The Sophia Institute: International Center for Orthodox Thought and Culture

sophiainstitutenyc.org

Located on the Campus of Union Theological Seminary, in New York City, the Sophia Institute is an independent foundation that explores the historical culture and ethical outreach of Orthodox Christianity. It organizes an annual conference and publishes the proceedings, as well as books, under the imprint of Theotokos Press New York.

Selected Bibliography and Further Reading

Armenian Church Magazine. New York: Diocese of the Armenian Church of America (Eastern), 1958–present.

Efthimiou, Miltiades B., et al., eds. *History of the Greek Orthodox Church in America.* New York: Greek Orthodox Archdiocese of North and South America, 1984.

Erickson, John H. *Orthodox Christians in America.* New York: Oxford University Press, 1999.

Historical Records Survey. *Inventory of the Church Archives in New York City: Eastern Orthodox Churches and the Armenian Church in America.* New York: Work Projects Administration, 1940. [NYG&B eLibrary]

Krindatch, Alexei D. *Atlas of American Orthodox Christian Churches.* Brookline, MA: Holy Cross Orthodox Press, 2011.

Pereira, Matthew J. *Philanthropy and Social Compassion in Eastern Orthodox Tradition: Papers of the Sophia Institute Academic Conference, New York, Dec. 2009.* New York: Theotokos Press, 2010.

Stokoe, Mark, and Leonid Kishkovsky. *Orthodox Christians in North America 1794–1994.* Syosset, NY: Orthodox Christian Publications Center, 1995.

Tarasar, Constance J. *Orthodox America, 1794–1976: Development of the Orthodox Church in America.* Syosset, NY: Orthodox Church in America, Department of History and Archives, 1975.

Zirogiannis, Marc. *Greek Orthodox Parishes of New York State, A Photo Tour.* vol. 1 N.p: *Lulu.com*, 2010.

Episcopal

Historical Overview

The Episcopal Church is a Protestant denomination whose origins date to sixteenth-century England, when King Henry VIII parted company with the Catholic Church in Rome, for political rather than theological reasons, and was declared the Supreme Head of the Church of England. The Church of England, later called the Anglican Church, became the established state church in England and Ireland. Anglican congregations were formed in the American colonies by settlers from the British Isles.

Under the articles of capitulation when the English took over the city from the Dutch in 1664, it was expressly stated that the Dutch should retain their freedom of worship and other customs; the English subsequently extended freedom of worship to the colony's other denominations. While the new government would have liked to make the Church of England the colony's established church, the bulk of the population ignored any moves in that direction, and the Anglican Church never became the exclusive church in New York. For many years the Anglican community was limited to a chaplain at the Fort in New York City who ministered to the governor, his entourage, the military garrison, and a few other communicants.

In 1697 Trinity Church (Wall Street) became the first parish and church in New York City, and its ministry was financed through a tax levied on all inhabitants. The tax resulted from the Ministry Act of 1693, which also led to a similar arrangement in Richmond, Westchester, and Queens counties. These counties were chosen because each had a diverse population with no denomination in the majority.

Trinity Church, like the Reformed Church, had a number of satellite churches, which the Anglicans called chapels of ease, meaning ease of access for people who lived at a certain distance from the Wall Street church. St. Paul's Chapel is one of these chapels of ease still in operation. There were a number of others, such as St. George's Chapel, St. John's Chapel, and St. Agnes' Chapel. Over the years, some of them eventually became independent parishes; most have been closed and their records may be at Trinity or at the Diocesan Archives, or at both. Trinity was involved, by grant-making, in the establishment of many new parishes in New York City and State, and its archives naturally contain records relating to these parishes.

While the authorities would have preferred to make the Church of England the established church of the entire colony, that was not feasible in counties like Puritan/Presbyterian Suffolk County, Dutch Reformed Kings County, or the Hudson Valley counties where most of the population was Dutch Reformed

or Lutheran. Parishes in New York, Richmond, Westchester, and Queens counties were organized and maintained with the assistance of the Society for the Propagation of the Gospel in Foreign Parts (SPG) in London.

Although over half the signatories to the Declaration of Independence were Anglicans, many church members remained loyal to the Crown and chose to leave New York at the end of the Revolutionary War to settle in Canada or England. After the American Revolution, the British monarch was no longer head of the church in the United States, and English bishops were no longer in control of the Church in America.

The Rev. Samuel Seabury was rector of St. Peter's Church, Westchester County, when he traveled to Aberdeen, Scotland in 1784 to be consecrated by Scottish bishops. (In Scotland, he was not required to swear allegiance to the crown.) He was the first bishop consecrated for the American church and became the first Bishop of Connecticut.

The Protestant Episcopal Church was founded in Philadelphia in 1789 (the "Protestant" was not officially dropped until 1967); its constitution was changed, but the church continued to use the Anglican *Book of Common Prayer*. Today, the Episcopal Church is one of 30 autonomous national churches in various parts of the world that are part of the Anglican Communion.

Like the Catholic Church, the Episcopal Church is organized at the local level in parish churches headed by a priest; each parish belongs to a diocese headed by a bishop. In New York State there are now six dioceses. The dioceses are unified by a national administration headquartered in New York City.

Records

Before the English took over New Netherland from the Dutch in 1664, some English names appear in the Dutch Reformed records. These English probably all considered themselves members of the Church of England, but most of them were Puritans who would be expelled from the Church as Nonconformists after the Restoration of Charles II in 1660. Between 1664 and 1697 there were still relatively few Anglicans in New York City, and no church records exist for this period.

Records about pre-Revolutionary Anglican congregations may be found in the Lambeth Palace Library, in the records of missionary activities, and in the Fulham papers of the bishops of London, as well as in the London Metropolitan Archives (LMA), as the Bishop of London took responsibility for Anglican congregations overseas without an appointed bishop. Extracts from these and other sources will be found in the seven volumes of *Ecclesiastical Records, State of New York*, which illustrate some of the problems that accompanied the attempt to introduce the Anglican Church into New York.

Diocesan Records

Many, but not all, records are held at the diocesan level. See table 7 in this section for a list of the counties in each diocese of New York.

From 1785 to 1838 the Diocese of New York covered all of the territory that encompasses the current state of New York. For administrative reasons the diocese divided several times:

- 1838: Diocese of New York divided into two, creating the new Diocese of Western New York
- 1868: Diocese of Western New York divided, creating the Diocese of Central New York
- 1868: Diocese of New York divided again, this time creating the Diocese of Albany and the Diocese of Long Island
- 1931: The Diocese of Central New York divided, creating the Diocese of Rochester

Table 7 provides information on archives held by the dioceses. Many records have been transcribed by the Work Projects Administration (WPA) and the Daughters of the American Revolution (DAR). An increasing number of records can be found at *FamilySearch.org* and *Ancestry.com*. Researchers can also visit the county pages of Rootsweb and USGenWeb, as there have been many local projects digitizing the records of individual churches. The NYG&B collection at the Milstein Division of the New York Public Library (NYPL) includes an inventory of parish registers held by the archives of the Episcopal Diocese of New York. For published or transcribed records of New York City (Manhattan, Brooklyn, and Queens) and Nassau County, see Harry Macy Jr.'s research papers in the selected bibliography of this section. Note that especially in the eighteenth and nineteenth centuries, many non-Episcopalians appear in the Episcopalian records.

The Episcopal Church does not have a central repository for its sacramental and vestry records, nor does it have any major indexes of these records. Records of baptism, marriage, and burial may be at the church or at the diocesan level. Additional records may have also been kept by individual ministers. There are, however, several ways a researcher can try to locate a specific church.

Parish Records

The Episcopal Church has a website with a Parish Finder search engine to help researchers locate churches near a family address at *ecdplus.org/parish*. It also has national clergy directories, which can also lead to the specific church, available online at *ecdplus.org/clergy*.

According to Episcopal Church guidelines, each parish should have a card file or database program which records each family. These guidelines were put into place at the beginning of the twentieth century, but they were not universally adopted. Information included varies with the date of the creation of the card, but more modern records should include the names,

addresses, telephone numbers, head of household and spouse, the names and dates of birth of all children; how and when received into communion (transferred or confirmed); status (baptized, confirmed, or communicant) of each family member; the occupation of head of household; the date of marriage; and whether removed by transfer or death and date. Unfortunately, few of these "card indexes" survive.

Selected Repositories and Resources

Lambeth Palace Library

Lambeth Palace Library • London, SE1 7JU, UK
+44 (0)20 7898 1400 • Email: archives@churchofengland.org
lambethpalacelibrary.org

The Fulham papers and the records of missionary activity held at the Lambeth Palace Library deal with the American colonies. The Fulham papers are the papers of several bishops of London which were formerly held in Fulham Palace.

London Metropolitan Archives

London Metropolitan Archives • 40 Northampton Road
London, EC1R 0HB, UK • +44 (0)20 7332 3820
Email: ask.lma@cityoflondon.gov.uk • *lma.gov.uk*

The archives hold the papers of the Diocese of London. The Bishop of London had responsibility for Anglican congregations overseas where no bishop had been appointed. The archives hold a number of records relating to the early church in North America. While the LMA does have an agreement with *Ancestry.com* to digitize their records, as of this printing, the collections relating to the early church in North America had not been digitized.

National Episcopal Church Archives

The Archives of the Episcopal Church • 606 Rathervue Place
PO Box 2247 • Austin, TX 78768 • (212) 602-9687
Email: research@episcopalarchives.org
episcopalarchives.org/genealogy.html

The Archives hold the personal papers and records of clergy. Sacramental and vital records are not held in this location.

Trinity Wall Street Archives

Parish of Trinity Church • 74 Trinity Place, 4th Floor
New York, NY 10006 • (212) 602-9687
Email: archives@trinitywallstreet.org • *trinitywallstreet.org*

An online database contains the records of the Parish of Trinity Church and its chapels, including St. Paul's. Collections include baptismal records 1769–1885, marriage records 1746–1886, and burial records 1777–2003. Seventeenth-century and many eighteenth-century records were lost in fires.

Table 7: Episcopal Dioceses of the State of New York

Diocesan Archives	Counties Served; Contents of Archives
Albany 62 South Swan Street, Albany, NY 12210 (518) 465-4737 Email: diocese@albanydiocese.org_ *albanyepiscopaldiocese.org*	Albany, Clinton, Columbia, Delaware, Essex, Franklin, Fulton, Greene, Hamilton, Herkimer, Montgomery, Otsego, Rensselaer, Saratoga, Schenectady, Schoharie, St. Lawrence, Warren, Washington The Diocese holds the records of some extinct churches in the Diocese. The records are not open to the public, and there is currently no complete list of holdings. For a fee, the Diocese will conduct searches on behalf of researchers.
Central New York 310 Montgomery Street, Suite 200, Syracuse, NY 13202 (315) 652-3350 Email: office@cny.anglican.org *cnyepiscopal.org/Archives.aspx*	Broome, Cayuga, Chemung, Chenango, Cortland, Jefferson, Lewis, Madison, Oneida, Onondaga, Oswego, Seneca, Tioga, Tompkins Archives contain parish records (active and closed), service registers, and vestry minutes; confirmations, marriages, and burials; photographs, scrapbooks, and source materials of every episcopate since 1868.
Long Island The George Mercer Jr. Memorial School of Theology 65 Fourth Street, Garden City, NY 11530 (516) 248-4800, ext 39 Email: merceroffice@dioceseli.org *dioceselongisland.org*	Kings (Brooklyn), Nassau, Queens, Suffolk Archives comprise the records of all extinct churches (and some current churches) in the diocese, including sacramental registers (confirmations, marriages, deaths, etc.) beginning in the eighteenth century. Archives also hold records of religious schools and charities. Each church/mission has its own file with records, historical data, parish journals, and photographs of events.
New York 1047 Amsterdam Avenue, New York, NY 10025 (212) 316-7419 Email: archives@dioceseny.org *dioceseny.org*	Bronx, New York (Manhattan), Richmond (Staten Island), Dutchess, Orange, Putnam, Rockland, Sullivan, Ulster, Westchester The archives contain some 2,000 boxes of historical records, including some records for over 400 congregations and all of the original cathedral records. Sacramental records for about 80 congregations, including the cathedral, can also be found there, as well as the personal papers of the bishops and all manner of diocesan business files.
Rochester Diocesan House 935 East Avenue, Rochester, NY 14607 (585) 473-2977 Email: communications@episcopaldioceseofrochester.org *episcopalrochester.org*	Allegany, Livingston, Monroe, Ontario, Schuyler, Steuben, Wayne, Yates Most records date from 1931, but also cover 1785–1838 for this area when it was under the jurisdiction of the original Diocese of New York. Collections include parish registers of closed congregations, journals, official papers (including those relating to the Woman's Auxiliary and the Girl's Friendly Society), photographs, and newspapers of the diocese from 1947 to present (online index available).
Western New York 1064 Brighton Road, Tonawanda, NY 14150 (716) 881-0660 Email: archives@episcopalwny.org *episcopalwny.org/archives/diocesan-archives*	Cattaraugus, Chautauqua, Erie, Genesee, Niagara, Orleans, Wyoming Archives contain records from all closed diocesan churches, including sacramental registers (marriages, deaths, etc.) from the 1850s to the 1990s.

Selected Bibliography and Further Reading

DeMille, George E. *The Diocese of Western New York: A History.* Albany, NY: J. H. Smith. 1969.

———. *A History of the Diocese of Albany, 1704–1923.* Philadelphia, PA: Church Historical Society, 1946.

———. *Saint Thomas Church in the City and County of New York 1823–1954.* Austin, TX: Church Historical Society, 1958. Baptisms 1823–1827, marriages 1824–1827, burials 1824–1827.

Ecclesiastical Records, State of New York. 7 vols. Albany: J. B. Lyon, State Printer, 1901–1916.

Goodwin, Aaron, comp. "Church Records Held at the Archives of Christ & St. Stephen's Episcopal Church, New York City." Digitally published as a Research Aid by the NYG&B, 2011. *NewYorkFamily History.org*

Haberstroh, Richard. *The German Churches of Metropolitan New York: A Research Guide.* New York: New York Genealogical and Biographical Society, 2000. Includes many Episcopal churches. [NYG&B eLibrary]

Hayes, Charles W. *The Diocese of Western New York: History and Recollections.* Rochester, NY: Scrantom, Wetmore & Co, 1905.

— — —. *Inventory of Church Archives of New York City: Protestant Episcopal Church in the United States of America, Diocese of New York.* Historical Records Survey, Division of Professional and Service Projects, Work Projects Administration, 1940. Covers all Protestant Episcopal Churches that were in Manhattan, the Bronx, and Staten Island since colonial times. This WPA Guide includes a list of the sacramental registers found in each parish, or found elsewhere if the parish was closed prior to 1940. The Appendix includes a dated chronology by borough, as well as a street location index. [NYG&B eLibrary]

— — —. *Inventory of Church Archives of New York City: Protestant Episcopal Church in the United States of America, Diocese of Long Island: Vol. 2, Protestant Episcopal Churches in Brooklyn and Queens Counties.* Historical Records Survey, Division of Professional and Service Projects, Work Projects Administration, 1940. [NYG&B eLibrary]

— — —. *Inventory of the Church Archives of New York State Exclusive of New York City: Protestant Episcopal Church Diocese of Rochester.* Historical Records Survey, Division of Professional and Service Projects, Work Projects Administration, 1941. [NYG&B eLibrary]

— — —. *Inventory of the Church Archives of New York State Exclusive of New York City: Protestant Episcopal Church Diocese of Western New York.* Historical Records Survey, Division of Professional and Service Projects, Work Projects Administration, 1939.

Kelly, Arthur C. M. *Baptismal Records of St. Peter's Episcopal Church, Albany, N.Y. 1756–1899, and Marriage Record of St. Peter's Episcopal Church, Albany, N.Y. 1756–1899.* Rhinebeck, NY: Kinship, 2007.

Lindsley, James Elliot. *This Planted Vine: A Narrative History of the Episcopal Diocese of New York.* New York: Harper & Row, 1984. Includes appendix of dates of parish formations.

Macy, Harry, Jr. "Brooklyn/Kings County Church Records Since 1783." *NYG&B Newsletter* (now *New York Researcher*), Summer 2000. Updated June 2011 and published as a Research Aid on *NewYorkFamilyHistory.org.*

— — —. "Episcopal Records of New York City (Manhattan)." *NYG&B Newsletter* (now *New York Researcher*), Spring 1995. Updated May 2011 and published as a Research Aid on *NewYorkFamilyHistory.org.* Researchers are referred to this Research Aid for a list of Episcopal Church records published in the *NYG&B Record* or online in the eLibrary. These include, but are not limited to:

> Barber, Gertrude A., comp. *Records of St. Mark's Church in the Bowery, New York City.* Typescript. Digitally published by the NYG&B, 2011. Lists baptisms 1799–1842, marriages 1813–1842, interments 1836–1841. [NYG&B eLibrary]

Goodwin, Aaron, comp. "Coloured Communicants at St. Stephen's Episcopal Church, New York City, ca.1809–1815," *NYG&B Record*, vol. 141, no. 1 (2010): 39–40. [NYG&B eLibrary]

— — —. "Marriages Recorded at St. Stephen's Episcopal Church, New York City, 1814–1850." *NYG&B Record*, vol. 140 (2009) no. 3: 215–229, no. 4: 308–314. [NYG&B eLibrary]

Vosburgh, Royden Woodward, ed. *Records of Christ Protestant Episcopal Church in New York City.* 2 vols. Typescript, 1919. Vol. 1: baptisms 1793–1811, 1805–1846, 1822–1848; communicants 1833–1836; burials 1833–1835. Vol. 2: marriages 1794–1804, 1805–1848. [NYG&B eLibrary]

— — —. "Religious Records of Queens and Nassau Counties." *NYG&B Newsletter* (now *New York Researcher*), Spring 2003. Updated June 2011 and published as a Research Aid on *NewYorkFamilyHistory.org.*

Map of the Local Boundaries of the Protestant Episcopal Churches of the City of New York. W. Endicott & Co., ca. 1850. [NYPL Digital Gallery]

"New York City Church of the Holy Apostles: Records 1845–1862." Transcript. New York: Mary Murray Chapter, N.S., D.A.R., 1947. Lists of families 1845–1862, marriages 1847–1862, baptisms 1845–1855, burials 1847–1849.

Wilson, The Rev. James Grant. *Centennial History of the Diocese of New York 1785–1885.* New York: D. Appleton and Company, 1886. Book includes summary parish histories.

Jewish

Introduction

The following section addresses Jewish sacramental and synagogue records. A more detailed historical overview and descriptions of an extensive range of resources for researching Jewish immigrants to New York are provided in chapter 14, Peoples of New York.

The Congregation Shearith Israel, founded in 1654 in New Amsterdam by a group of Sephardic Jews, was the first Jewish congregation established in North America. Despite the early objections of the colony's Director-General Pieter Stuyvesant, Jews in colonial New York under both Dutch and English rule were allowed to practice their faith openly. Shearith Israel served both Sephardic and Ashkenazi members and was the only Jewish congregation in New York City until 1825, when the first Ashkenazi congregation, B'nai Jeshrun, was formed. Strong Jewish communities developed outside New York City after 1820—with the opening of the Erie Canal and railroads—and congregations were formed in Albany (1838), Syracuse (1839), Rochester (1843), and Buffalo (1847).

As Jewish immigration to New York increased in the nineteenth century, so did the formation of congregations, which were often organized by groups of people who shared a common hometown. Congregations frequently established a cemetery before a synagogue, and one synagogue often served multiple congregations. Jewish ritual burial practices are very specific, and hundreds of cemeteries were established throughout New York State to serve local Jewish communities. See the Jewish section of chapter 14, Peoples of New York, for information about Jewish the records that might be available; see also chapter 9, Cemetery Records.

Records of Congregations

Most Jewish congregations in New York—regardless of whether they follow orthodox, conservative, or reform schools—are locally and independently organized. And while congregations will often belong to a larger denominational organization or federation, they are ultimately self-governing. Generally, Jewish congregations keep their own records, although what records are kept varies among congregations. It is advisable to identify the congregation a research subject belonged to, and contact the congregation for information about their records.

Synagogue and congregation records often include books of minutes of congregational, board, and other meetings; account books containing lists of members; congregational and communal histories; and vital records: birth, circumcision, bar and bat mitzvah (coming of age ceremony), marriage, and death records. However, not all congregations kept or preserved these sorts of records. Occasionally, records will remain in the possession of the rabbis rather than their congregations, and move with them from location to location. For congregations that have ceased to exist, their records may have been transferred to another synagogue or to a Jewish organization, archive, or historical society.

Locating a Congregation or Synagogue

City directories (see chapter 11), newspapers (see chapter 12), and local genealogical and historical societies can all be tools to identify congregations and synagogues in a community. The Center for Jewish History research guide "U.S. Synagogue Records" provides valuable guidance for identifying congregations, synagogues, and rabbis; it can be accessed at *http://researchguides.cjh.org/USSynagogueRecords.pdf*. The Buffalo and Erie Library has a finding aid to the Jewish Archives of Greater Buffalo, Synagogue Records, 1884–1986.

The Historical Records Survey (1935–1943) of the Work Projects Administration (WPA) undertook an inventory of the records of churches and synagogues throughout New York State, much of which has been published in individual volumes. The *WPA Guide to Vital Statistics, Records of Churches in New York State (Exclusive of New York City)* is organized by county, and provides basic information about Jewish congregations and the records available at the time for the 57 counties outside New York City. Each borough was treated in a seperate volume. See the bibliography in the introduction to this chapter for a complete citation.

The WPA inventory of synagogues in the five boroughs of New York City remains unpublished. However, the completed survey forms are held by the New York City Municipal Archives (see chapter 16, National and Statewide Repositories & Resources) and may be accessed on microfilm there. The Jewish Genealogy Society of New York has created an online index of the synagogues that includes the date of organization, alternate names, and form and card numbers; it may be accessed at *www.jgsnydb.org/landsmanshaft/synagogues.htm*.

The online Museum of Family History's webpage "The Synagogues of New York City" provides a listing of former synagogues in each of the five boroughs, which includes the name and address of the congregation, and, often, the associated hometown; it may be accessed at *www.museumoffamilyhistory.com/erc-syn-nyc.htm*.

The online resource "Remembrance of Synagogues Past: The Lost Civilization of the Jewish South Bronx" provides information on more than 300 defunct synagogues, as well as current synagogues, in the Bronx; it may be accessed at *www.bronxsynagogues.org/ic/bronxsyn/index.html*.

Selected Repositories and Resources

The following list provides a selection of repositories whose holdings include records of some New York congregations and synagogues. It is representative, not exhaustive. For relevant books, articles and other references, see the Selected Bibliography and Further Reading list in the Jewish section of chapter 14, Peoples of New York.

American Jewish Archives, Jacob Rader Marcus Center

Hebrew Union College-Jewish Institute of Religion

101 Clifton Avenue • Cincinnati, OH 45220

(513) 221-1875 • *americanjewisharchives.org*

The extensive holdings of the American Jewish Archives include records of Congregation Beth Emeth (Albany), 1843–1907, Congregation Beth El (Albany), 1847–1885, and Congregation Beth Jacob (Newburgh), 1861–1924, and some other New York congregations. An online catalog, finding aids, and some digital collections are accessible on the website.

Center for Jewish History (CJH)

American Jewish Historical Society • *ajs.org*

American Sephardi Federation • *americansephardifederation.org*

Leo Baeck Institute • *lbi.org*

Yeshiva University Museum • *yumuseum.org*

YIVO Institute for Jewish Research • *yivoinstitute.org*

15 West 16th Street • New York, NY 10011

(212) 294-8301 • *cjh.org*

The largest Jewish repository outside of Israel, the CJH is home to the five constituent organizations above, as well as the Lillian Goldman Reading Room and the Ackman & Ziff Genealogy Institute. From the homepage of the website it is possible to search across the collections of all five partners and to access genealogical databases. The American Jewisg Historical Society (AJHS) holds the historical records of a number of New York congregations. An online catalog, finding aids, and digital collections are on the website. For a more detailed description, see the separate entries for the CJH and its resident organizations in chapter 14, Peoples of New York.

Congregation Shearith Israel

8 West 70th Street • New York, NY 10023

(212) 873-0300 • *shearithisrael.org*

The Congregation's website provides a detailed history that begins with its founding in 1654. A guide to its archival collections, which are held by the American Jewish Historical Society, is at *http://findingaids.cjh.org/Congregation ShearithIsrael.html*.

Early New York Synagogue Archives

synagogues.cjh.org

The website provides access to digitized collections from 1730 until the beginning of the 20th century of five historic Jewish communities in New York City: Congregation Shearith Israel, Congregation B'nai Jeshrun, Congregation Ansche Chesed, the Kane Street Synagogue, and the Eldridge Street Synagogue. It is a collaboration of the Library of the Jewish Theological Seminary, the American Jewish Historical Society, and the Center for Jewish History.

Jewish Theological Seminary Library: Archives of Conservative Judaism

3080 Broadway • New York, NY 10027 • (212) 678-8869

www.jtsa.edu/The_Library/Collections/Archives.xml

The Archives holds records of several conservative congregations and rabbis, comprising marriage, membership lists, cemetery lots, meeting minutes, and other materials. Among the New York congregations are Beth El (Rochester), 1915–1990, and several New York City congregations. An online catalog and finding aids are accessible on the website.

Museum at Eldridge Street

12 Eldridge Street • New York, NY 10002

(212) 219-0888 • *eldridgestreet.org*

Located on the Lower East Side of New York City the Eldridge Street Synagogue was built by Eastern European Jews in 1887. Following a major architectural restoration, the synagogue building today operates as a museum and education center and is also home to a small Orthodox congregation. Its archival holdings include administrative records, burial records, marriage records, wills, deeds, insurance policies, as well as letters from some parishioners. Some records have been digitized and are accessible on the website. A finding aid to Eldridge Street congregation archives held by the American Jewish Historical Society is accessible at *http://digifindingaids. cjh.org/?pID=365400#a1*.

Lutheran

Historical Overview

The Lutheran church is a Protestant denomination that was formed by the followers of Martin Luther (1483–1546), a German theologian who attempted to reform the Catholic Church. Many early German and Scandinavian settlers on the island of Manhattan in the colonial period were Lutheran, as were a small percentage of the large Dutch population. Lutherans had been allowed to worship relatively freely in the Netherlands, but in New Amsterdam that was not the case. Public church services were generally restricted to Dutch Reformed and other Calvinist congregations, and Lutheran pastors sent to New Amsterdam from Europe were forbidden to serve their congregations until the English conquest in 1664. However, the first Lutheran parish of New Netherland, with congregations in both Albany and New Amsterdam, was recognized by the consistory in Amsterdam, Holland, as early as 1649.

A Lutheran church appears to have finally been built in New York City under British rule, with services conducted in Dutch. It was replaced by Trinity Church which was built on Broadway in 1671 (just south of the location of the Episcopal Trinity Church built in 1698). By 1749, to serve the many new German immigrants that were arriving in the eighteenth century, a new German-language congregation was formed called Christ Church.

After the Revolutionary War and the destruction of Trinity Lutheran Church by fire, the two congregations merged and worshipped, mostly in German and partially in English, in Christ Church under the name of the United German Lutheran Congregations in the City of New York (*Die Vereinigten Deutsch-Lutherischen Gemeinden in der Stadt New York*). The English speakers attending Christ Church (i.e., United German Lutheran) continued to grow in number. In 1797 some of them formed the separate English Lutheran Church of New York City, which was never recognized by the governing synod and in 1810 became Zion Episcopal Church. In 1821 another group of English speakers left to form St. Matthew's Church on Walker Street near Broadway. Though founded as an English-language church, St. Matthew's soon came to be dominated by new German immigrants.

The history of the Lutheran church in upstate New York began essentially at the same time as in New York City. Ebenezer Lutheran Church, with services held in Dutch, was founded in Albany within New Netherland in 1649. It is considered the oldest Lutheran congregation in the United States (and initially part of the same parish as the pastorless and churchless congregation in New Amsterdam). While initially Dutch was used for worship, this congregation later adopted German, and then English in 1808. The congregation began to use the name First Lutheran Church in 1871.

Palatine immigration in the early eighteenth century fueled the establishment of German Lutheran churches in more rural areas. Congregations formed in the upper Hudson Valley: Loonenburg (1706) and New Town (1711); in the central Hudson Valley: East Camp (1711) and Rhinebeck (1715); and in the Mohawk and Schoharie Valley: Schoharie (1714) and Stone Arabia (1729). See also chapter 14, Peoples of New York, German.

As the German population in these areas grew throughout the eighteenth century, the older congregations were gradually joined by new ones. Recognizing the need for organization of the disparate Lutheran congregations in the colonies, in 1748 Reverend Heinrich Melchior Mühlenberg united the congregations in Maryland, New Jersey, New York, and Pennsylvania into what came to be called the Ministerium of Pennsylvania. Synods were formed in New York in 1786 to facilitate church governance.

In the first half of the nineteenth century, German immigration to the United States, and New York State in particular, exploded. Many of the new immigrants joined German communities in New York City and other established cities and towns in the state; others settled relatively undeveloped parts of the state, especially along the Erie Canal which had opened in 1825. There were clusters of the German populace and their churches around Buffalo and Rochester, as well as other urban centers and the eastern shore of Lake Ontario. The oldest of these nineteenth-century congregations was founded in Eggertsville (Amherst, east of Buffalo) in 1827, just two years after the opening of the canal.

Later in the nineteenth century, when immigration from Scandinavia increased dramatically, new Lutheran churches were established to serve these populations, especially where larger numbers settled in ethnic enclaves, such as in New York City and Brooklyn. A less well-known Lutheran group was that of the Slovaks, whose rise in immigration near the end of the nineteenth century spurred the establishment of a few Slovak-language Lutheran churches, primarily in larger urban areas in New York. The disparate Lutheran churches in the United States have attempted to consolidate many times, and each attempt at unification has resulted in separate splinter groups and churches. The two largest Lutheran bodies in the United States are the Evangelical Lutheran Church in America and the Lutheran Church-Missouri Synod, both of which have large congregations in New York.

Records

Surviving records for baptisms, marriages, burials, and communicants do not begin for the Lutheran church in New York City until 1704. After that date they are mostly complete and are still retained by St. Matthew's Lutheran Church, the successor to the earlier congregations in the city. Transcripts of the earliest records have been published in the Holland Society's 1903 *Year Book*, and in the *NYG&B Record*. Manuscript transcripts at the Holland Society and the New York Public Library (NYPL), the latter in the NYG&B collection, include additional records and are also available on Family History Library (FHL) microfilm. Two different filmings of the original records, extending at least in part into the twentieth century, are also at the NYPL and FHL, but researchers should be warned that the early records on these films can be extremely difficult to read due to the condition of the originals and the fact that many are written in German or Dutch and in the old script.

The records of New York City's short-lived English (English language) Lutheran Church are at the New-York Historical Society and have been partially published in the *NYG&B Record*.

The surviving records for First Lutheran (Ebenezer) Church in Albany are widely dispersed, with some held by the New York State Museum, some at the offices of the Upstate New York Synod, and the bulk still held by the church, both on and off-site. Some vital records beginning in 1774 have appeared in published form (see bibliography in this section for Vosburgh's transcription). For the best overview of the history of the church, the many names used since its founding, and the locations of its various records, researchers should consult *Swan of Albany . . .*, published by the church in 1976.

The records for many of the rural colonial churches can be found in the FHL microfilm collection, either as filmed manuscripts or in some published form. Beyond that, originals may still exist in the existing successor congregations, at the repository of the governing body or synod, or the New York State Library, in manuscript and special collections departments of area libraries. Early records of the Loonenburg-Athens church will be found in the *NYG&B Record*, and records of many Hudson, Mohawk, and Schoharie Valley churches have been published by Kinship (check library catalogs for compiler Arthur C. M. Kelly).

Many of the records of nineteenth-century Lutheran churches in New York City have been microfilmed or digitized by the FHL. Two important exceptions are St. Mark's from Manhattan's Lower East Side (now located on East 84th Street) which holds its own records, and St. Luke's on the west side of Manhattan. Records from St. Luke's from 1850–1976 are held by the NYG&B; a finding aid is at *NewYorkFamilyHistory.org*.

Archives holding some church registers, primarily for defunct congregations, exist for both the Evangelical Lutheran Church in America (ELCA), and the Lutheran Church—Missouri Synod (LC–MS). These two denominations represent the overwhelming majority of all Lutheran churches existing in New York State today.

For a detailed list of original, published, and microfilmed records from Lutheran churches in New York City, see Harry Macy Jr.'s "Lutheran Records of New York City (Manhattan)," as well as *The German Churches of Metropolitan New York* by Richard Haberstroh.

Selected Repositories and Resources
Evangelical Lutheran Church in America (ELCA) Archives
321 Bonnie Lane • Elk Grove Village, IL 60007 • (847) 690-9410
Email access on website • *elca.org/archives*

The Archives catalog contains finding aids for processed collections, as well as brief records for unprocessed materials. Some records are now indexed and available online through a partnership with *Archives.com*.

Lutheran Archives Center at Philadelphia
(Northeast Regional Archives of the Evangelical Lutheran Church in America) • Lutheran Archives Center
7301 Germantown Avenue • Philadelphia, PA 19119
(215) 248-6383 • mtairyarchives@ltsp.edu
http://ltsp.edu/academics/the-ltsp-experience/the-community/the-lutheran-archives-center-at-philadelphia/

The materials in the archive pertain only to upstate New York (that is, excluding the Metropolitan New York City area and surrounding counties), eastern Pennsylvania, New Jersey, and New England. The archives hold personal papers of clergy, archives of church organizations, and the records of congregations, both extinct and active.

Lutheran Church—Missouri Synod (LC–MS)
Concordia Historical Institute • 804 Seminary Place
Saint Louis, MO 63105-3014 • Email: chi@lutheranhistory.org
lutheranhistory.org

Holdings include baptismal, wedding, and funeral records of defunct and active churches in New York. Their archive and manuscript holdings are listed online, with some finding aids available on their website.

St. Matthew's Lutheran Church
The Cornerstone Center • 178 Bennett Avenue
New York, NY 10040 • (212) 567-5948
Email: stmatthewnyc@aol.com • *stmatthewnyc.org/about/archives*

The archives cannot be consulted on-site; however the website contains lists of all their records. The records have been microfilmed and are available at the NYPL; most of the pre-1800 records have been published by the Holland Society and the NYG&B; many are also online at *Ancestry.com*. In addition, records of baptisms, confirmations, and marriages (1787–1841) have been indexed by the Mid-Atlantic German Society (MAGS) and can be searched online at *magsgen.com/recordindexes.html*.

Sutter Memorial Archives

(Archives of the Metropolitan New York Synod of the Evangelical Lutheran Church in America) Horrmann Library
Wagner College • Staten Island, NY 10301
Email access on website • *sutterarchives.org*

Materials in this archive date to the beginning of the New York Ministerium in 1786. Holdings include parish records (baptisms, confirmations, marriages, membership, deaths, burials, communion, pastors, council, photos, and minutes) of all defunct and some active congregations in Bronx, Kings (Brooklyn), Nassau, New York (Manhattan), Queens, Richmond (Staten Island), Suffolk, Sullivan, and Westchester counties.

Selected Bibliography and Further Reading

"Baptismal Records of Zion Lutheran Church, Loonenburg, Now Athens, Greene County, New York." *NYG&B Record*, vol. 82 (1951) no. 1: 15–31, no. 2: 81–88, no. 3: 161–173, no. 4: 227–243; vol. 83 (1952) no. 1: 24–40, no. 2: 109–116, no. 3: 132–145, no. 4: 240–245; vol. 84 (1953) no. 1: 16–26, no. 2: 82–97, no. 3: 149–159; vol. 85 (1954) no. 1: 13–17, no. 2: 73–83, no. 3: 140–153. [NYG&B eLibrary]

Ecclesiastical Records, State of New York. 7 vols. Albany: J. B. Lyon, State printer, 1901–1916.

Haberstroh, Richard. *The German Churches of Metropolitan New York: A Research Guide.* New York: NYG&B Society, 2000. [NYG&B eLibrary]

Hart, Simon, Sibrandina Geertruid Hart-Runeman, and John P. Dern, eds. *The Albany Protocol: Wilhelm Christoph Berkenmeyer's Chronicle of Lutheran Affairs in New York Colony, 1731–1750.* Ann Arbor, MI: The Editors, 1971.

Hart, Simon, and Harry J. Kreider, eds. *Protocol of the Lutheran Church in New York City 1702–1750.* New York: United Lutheran Synod of New York and New England, 1958.

Heins, Henry H. *Swan of Albany: A History of the Oldest Congregation of the Lutheran Church in America.* Albany: First Lutheran Church, 1976.

Historical Records Survey. *Inventory of the Church Archives in New York City: Lutheran.* The Historical Records Survey, Division of Professional and Service Projects, Work Projects Administration, 1940. Entry 128 in this work (St. Matthew's) outlines the history of the earliest Lutheran churches.

Kreider, Harry J. *The Beginnings of Lutheranism in New York.* New York: United Lutheran Synod of New York, 1949.

———. *Lutheranism in Colonial New York.* New York: Arno Press, 1972.

———, Simon Hart, United Lutheran Synod of New York and New England, and Staatsarchiv Hamburg (Germany). *Lutheran Church in New York and New Jersey, 1722–1760: Lutheran Records in the Ministerial Archives of the Staatsarchiv, Hamburg, Germany.* New York: United Lutheran Synod of New York and New England, 1962.

Macy, Harry, Jr. "Lutheran Records of New York City (Manhattan)." *NYG&B Newsletter* (now *New York Researcher*), Fall 1996. Updated May 2011 and published as a Research Aid on *NewYorkFamilyHistory.org*. [NYG&B eLibrary]

Scholz, Robert F. *Press Toward the Mark: History of the United Lutheran Synod of New York and New England, 1830–1930.* Philadelphia: American Theological Library Association, 1995.

United Lutheran Synod of New York. Committee on Documentary History. *The Lutheran Church in New York, 1649–1772: Records in the Lutheran Church Archives at Amsterdam, Holland.* New York: New York Public Library, 1946.

Vosburgh, Royden Woodward. *Records of the First Lutheran Church in the City of Albany, N.Y.* 2 vols. New York: New York Genealogical & Biographical Society, 1917 [NYG&B eLibrary]. Reprinted as *Vital Records of First Lutheran Church, Albany, N.Y. 1774–1842.* Rhinebeck, NY: Kinship, 1993.

Weiser, Frederick, ed. "Parish Registers of Christ Evangelical Lutheran Church." Transcript, 6 vols. Included in the transcribed registers are baptismal records 1868–1918, marriages 1868–1887, burials 1868–1946. The typewritten volumes are at the NYPL.

Wenner, George Unangst. *The Lutherans of New York: Their Story and Their Problems.* New York: The Petersfield Press, 1918.

Methodist

Historical Overview

The Methodist Church began as an evangelical revival movement within the Church of England in the 1730s. Its early leader, John Wesley, was an ordained minister in the Church of England who had served as chaplain to the colony of Georgia (1735–1736). Back in England in 1739, he drew up a set of general rules for societies of Methodists who would meet together regularly for Bible study and fellowship. In 1766 a group of New York City Methodists formed a society led by Philip Embury; they dedicated the Wesley Chapel in 1768, which survives today as the John Street Methodist Church.

In 1784 John Wesley ordained the first Methodist ministers in America, which led to the organization of the Methodist Episcopal Church as an independent denomination. (In England a full break from the Church of England did not occur until 1795.) In New York marriage and baptismal registers in the Methodist Church date to 1784; prior to this date, sacraments were administered in Anglican churches. After 1784 Methodism spread to all parts of New York, and membership grew rapidly. By the mid-1800s it was the largest Protestant denomination in the state.

The formation of the United Methodist Church in 1968 brought together two Methodist branches—the traditional Methodist Church and the Evangelical United Brethren, which had originated among the German population of Pennsylvania. This was the end result of an evolution shaped by several splits and mergers that are traced in table 8. The names and dates associated with the various offshoots can be important to researchers.

African Americans were welcomed by Methodists as early as 1758 when John Wesley baptized two slaves; in 1784 he ordained the first two African American preachers, Richard Allen and Absalom Jones. However, discrimination and segregation of African Americans led Richard Allen to organize the first black Methodist congregation in Philadelphia in 1794. Several black Methodist congregations from Delaware, Maryland, New Jersey, and Pennsylvania joined together in 1816 to form the African Methodist Episcopal Church (AME) as an independent denomination. In New York City, Peter Williams and other black members of the John Street Methodist Church formed their own congregation, which in 1821 became the independent denomination African Methodist Episcopal Zion Church (AMEZ). The AME (*ame-church.com*) and the AMEZ (*amez.org*) are two distinct denominations with numerous congregations throughout New York State.

Records

Each local church is responsible for keeping its own records, including baptismal, marriage, and funeral records, and lists of local preachers. When one church merges with another, the records go to the new church. The United Methodist Church (UMC) divides the country into "regional conferences," each one of which has its own archives (see tables 9 and 10). If a church closes and there is no successor church, the records are usually transferred to the archives of that church's conference. The UMC recommends starting any search at the conference archives for the appropriate region. The archives or conference staff can assist in locating churches in the region.

Researchers interested in New Yorkers who were ordained ministers or missionaries can consult the General Commission on Archives and History, located in Madison, NJ; records may also be available at the regional conferences. The staff at the Madison center will create a list of the churches served by ordained ministers for a fee. Usually information on missionaries, including copies of correspondence, will be found. Researchers are welcome to visit the Madison archive center and do their own research. Early Methodist preachers often were lay preachers who had not been ordained; any surviving records will only be found at the local churches where they preached.

For Methodist records in New York City, researchers can consult "Methodist Records of New York City (Manhattan)" by Harry Macy Jr. In this article he observes that many of the people

Table 8: Methodist Church Evolution					
Methodist Episcopal Church (est. 1784)			United Brethren in Christ 1800–1946	Evangelical Association 1803–1922	United Evangelical Church 1894–1922
Methodist Episcopal Church (1784–1939)	Methodist Protestant Church (1828–1939)	Methodist Episcopal Church South (1844–1939)		Evangelical Church 1922–1946	
Methodist Church 1939–1968			Evangelical United Brethren 1946–1968		
United Methodist Church 1968–present					

attracted to Methodism were of the working class, less likely to have their marriages published in newspapers, and so the Methodist church records are particularly important to genealogists. New York City researchers are also able to consult the Work Projects Administration (WPA)'s *Inventory of the Church Archives of New York City: The Methodist Church.* This inventory lists surviving records for every Methodist Episcopal church that existed in Manhattan at the time of publication.

Harry Macy's research aids for Brooklyn/Kings, Queens, and Nassau list published or transcribed Methodist records for those counties.

The New York Public Library (NYPL) has a large collection of Methodist church records for New York City and other locations in New York State. The New York City collection "Methodist Episcopal Church records, 1791–1945" consists of 486 volumes of original records which were acquired from the former Methodist Historical Society and have been microfilmed. While they were still at the Historical Society, many of those records were transcribed for the New York Genealogical and Biographical Society (see Harry Macy Jr.'s "Methodist Records of New York City"); the NYG&B collection is now also at the NYPL.

Before 1838 most baptisms and marriages in New York City's Methodist Episcopal churches were recorded in a joint citywide register; after 1838 each church maintained its own registers. *New York City Methodist Marriages 1785–1893,* by William Scott Fisher provides an index to the 41,000 marriages that were in the NYG&B Methodist collection and are now at the NYPL.

FamilySearch.org has Methodist church records online, but there are many more available through the Family History Library (FHL) on microfilm. The FHL has an extensive collection of New York Methodist records on microfilm, including the NYG&B collection and some of the transcriptions undertaken by the Daughters of the American Revolution (DAR) and the WPA. Some of these records have been posted to *FamilySearch.org.*

A source for records in western and central New York is microfilm held by the Buffalo and Erie Library (*buffalolib.org*). There is a detailed list of the churches, records types, and years covered on their website. They cover eleven counties in addition to Erie.

New York is divided into the New York Conference and the Upper New York Conference (UPNYC). The UPNYC was created in 2010 from four smaller regional conferences. The UPNYC began to reorganize its regional repositories in 2010, and that project is ongoing at the time of this publication.

Table 9: Methodist Church Archives: Upper New York Conference	
Regional Archives	**Counties and areas included:**
Andrews Memorial UM Church, 106 Church Street North Syracuse, NY 13212 (315) 458-0890 E-mail:office@andrewsmemorial_umc.org (Former North Central New York Archives)	Cayuga; Chemung; Chenango (only the villages of Otselic and South Otselic and the portion of the county north and west of Route 26); Cortland (except towns of Lapeer, Marathon, and Willet); Franklin (except towns of Altamont, Brighton, Franklin, Harrietstown, and the south half of Santa Clara); Fulton (only towns of Stratford and Oppenheim and the hamlet of Lassellsville in the Town of Ephratah); Hamilton (only the Town of Morehouse); Herkimer; Jefferson; Lewis; Madison; Montgomery (only Town of St. Johnsville); Oneida; Onondaga; Ontario (only towns of Canandaigua, Farmington, Naples and all the towns east of them); Oswego; Otsego (only towns of Cherry Valley, Plainfield, Richfield, and Springfield); St. Lawrence; Steuben (only towns of Avoca, Bath, Chocoton and Woodhull and towns east of them); Schuyler; Seneca; Tompkins; Wayne (Marion, Palmyra, and Williamson and all towns east of them) and Yates.
Saratoga Office of the UPNYC of the United Methodist Church Troy Conference Center, Archives, 396 Louden Road Saratoga Springs, NY 12866 (518) 584-8214, ext. 4; (Former Troy Archives and the New York material of the former Wyoming Archives)	Albany (except towns of Coeymans, Rensselaerville, Westerlo); Broome; Chenango (except the villages of Otselic and South Otselic and the portion of the county north and west of Route 26); Clinton; Columbia (only the hamlets of Chatham Center, Niverville, and North Chatham); Cortland (only the towns of Lapeer, Marathon, and Willet); Delaware (only the towns of Davenport, Hancock, Masonville, and Sidney and the village of Hale Eddy); Essex; Franklin (only the towns of Altamont, Brighton, Franklin, Harrietstown, and the south half of Santa Clara); Fulton (except towns of Oppenheim and Stratford and the hamlet of Lassellsville in the Town of Ephratah); Hamilton (except the Town of Morehouse); Montgomery (except the Town of St. Johnsville); Otsego (except the towns of Cherry Valley, Plainfield,); Rensselaer; Saratoga; Schenectady; Schoharie (except the towns of Blenheim, Broome, Conesville, Fulton, Gilboa, Jefferson, and Summit); Tioga; Warren; and Washington.
University UM Church 410 Minnesota Avenue, Buffalo, NY 14215 (716) 307-0797 (Former Western New York Archives)	Alleghany; Cattaraugus; Chautauqua; Erie; Genesee; Livingston; Monroe; Niagara; Ontario (only towns of Bristol, East Bloomfield, South Bristol, and Victor and all towns west of them); Orleans; Steuben (only towns of Canisteo, Dansville, Fremont, Howard, Jasper, Troupsburg, and Wayland and all the towns west of them); and Wyoming.

Table 10: Methodist Church Archives: New York Conference	
Archive	Counties and Areas Included:
Archives of the New York Conference of the Methodist Church C. Wesley Christman Archives New York Annual Conference Center, 20 Soundview Avenue, White Plains, NY 10606 (914) 997-1570 Email: archives@nyac.com *http://www.nyac.com/archives*	In Connecticut: all of the state west of the Connecticut River. In New York: the counties of Albany (only towns of Coeymans, Rensselaerville, and Westerlo); Bronx; Columbia (except the towns of Chatham Center, Niverville, and North Chatham); Delaware (except the towns of Davenport, Hancock, Masonville , Sidney, and the village of Hale Eddy); Dutchess; Greene; Kings; Nassau; New York; Putnam; Queens; Richmond; Rockland (west of the Ramapo River and including all of the village of Sloatsburg); Schoharie (only towns of Blenheim, Broome, Conesville, Fulton, Gilboa, Jefferson, and Summit); Suffolk; Sullivan (except the Towns of Highland and Lumberland Townships); Ulster; Westchester.

See the table 9 for locations covered by the three archives of the UPNYC. Some church records may be located at other repositories such as local historical societies or libraries.

Selected Repositories and Resources

General Commission on Archives and History for The United Methodist Church

United Methodist Archives and History Center

36 Madison Avenue (New Jersey Route 124) • PO Box 127

Madison, New Jersey 07940 • (973) 408-3189

Email: research@gcah.org • gcah.org

The Center holds the collection of the General Commission on Archive and History, an agency of the United Methodist Church that is charged with the documentation of Methodist history, as well as the Wesley and Methodist Collections of Drew University. Holdings include books, pamphlets, documents, manuscripts, printed records of early churches, personal papers, and photographs. There is material on ordained ministers, and on missionaries and their families at the Center.

Selected Bibliography and Further Reading

Additional transcribed or published Methodist records may be listed in the County Guides; check also library catalogs for transcripts by Arthur Kelly and others. This bibliography is representative of the available resources for Methodist history and congregations.

Biebel, Frank A. *Methodist Protestants and the Union Cemeteries of Brooklyn (1844–1894)*. New York: New York Genealogical and Biographical Society, 2007. Published as a CD. History of churches of the Methodist Protestant denomination in New York City and Brooklyn, and lists of burials in the Union Cemeteries which they founded. [NYG&B eLibrary]

Fisher, William Scott. *New York City Methodist Marriages 1785–1893*. Camden, ME: Picton Press, 1994

Haberstroh, Richard. *The German Churches of Metropolitan New York: A Research Guide*. New York: New York Genealogical and Biographical Society, 2000. Includes

Methodist churches and churches of the former Evangelical United Brethren and its predecessors. [NYG&B eLibrary]

Historical Records Survey. *Inventory of the Church Archives of New York City: The Methodist Church*. Historical Records Survey, Division of Professional and Service Projects, Work Projects Administration, 1940. Lists surviving records for every Methodist Episcopal church that existed in Manhattan at the time of publication. [NYG&B eLibrary]

———. *Inventory of the Church Archives of New York State Exclusive of New York City*. 2 vols. Historical Records Survey, Division of Professional and Service Projects, Work Projects Administration, 1939. [NYG&B eLibrary]

Kelly, Arthur C. M. *Vital Records of the First Methodist Church, Albany, New York*. Rhinebeck, NY: Kinship, 2012. Marriages 1806–1884, baptisms 1848–1882.

Lee, Jesse. *A Short History of the Methodists in the United States of America: Beginning in 1766, and Continued till 1809, To Which is Prefixed, a Brief Account of Their Rise in England in the Year 1729, & Co*. Baltimore: Magill and Clime, 1810.

Macy, Harry, Jr. "Brooklyn/Kings County Church Records Since 1783." *NYG&B Newsletter* (now *New York Researcher*), Summer 2000. Updated June 2011 and published as a Research Aid on *NewYorkFamilyHistory.org*.

———, ed. "Burials at the Methodist Church, John Street, New York City, 1785–1787." *NYG&B Record*, vol. 133, no. 2 (2002): 114–115. [NYG&B eLibrary]

———. "Methodist Records of New York City (Manhattan)." *NYG&B Newsletter* (now *New York Researcher*), Winter 1993. Updated 2011 and published as a Research Aid on *NewYorkFamilyHistory.org*.

———. "Religious Records of Queens and Nassau Counties." *NYG&B Newsletter* (now *New York Researcher*), Spring 2003. Updated June 2011 and published as a Research Aid on *NewYorkFamilyHistory.org*.

Methodist Episcopal Church. *Minutes of the Annual Conferences of the Methodist Episcopal Church, for the Years 1773–1828*. New York: T. Mason and G. Lane, 1840.

Pettingell, George H. *History of Methodism in Guilderland, Albany County, New York, and of the First Methodist Episcopal Church of Hamilton*. Salt Lake City: Filmed by the Genealogical Society of Utah. 1941. Microfilm of manuscript and newspaper clippings in possession of the New York State Library, Albany, New York.

Priebe, Paula J. "The Allen A. M. E. Church, Jamaica, NY, 1834–1900: The Role of the Black Church in a Developing 19th Century Community." *Afro-Americans in New York Life and History*, vol. 16, no. 1, 1992.

Sammis, A. Higbee. "Records of the First Methodist Episcopal Church of Flushing." *NYG&B Record*, vol. 125 (1994) no. 1: 24–29, no. 2: 93–95, no. 3: 167–169; A/C vol. 126, no. 4 (1995): 247. [NYG&B eLibrary]

Seaman, Samuel A. *Annals of New York Methodism, Being a History of the Methodist Episcopal Church in the City of New York from A.D. 1766 to A.D. 1890*. New York: Hunt & Eaton: 1892.

Totten, John Reynolds, ed. "Graveyard Inscriptions, Methodist Churchyard, Mekeels Corners, Putnam County, N.Y." *NYG&B Record*, vol. 55, no. 3 (1924): 240–241. [NYG&B eLibrary]

Mormon (Latter-day Saint)

Historical Overview

The Church of Jesus Christ of Latter-day Saints is the official name of the religion sometimes known as the "Mormon Church" or the "LDS Church." The Church was founded by Joseph Smith (1805–1844), a Vermont native who migrated west with his parents and settled in Palmyra (then Ontario, now Wayne County) in upstate New York. Mormons believe that an angel led Joseph Smith to a buried book written on golden plates; his translation of the plates became the *Book of Mormon*. The Church of Jesus Christ of Latter-day Saints was organized in April 1830 at Fayette, Seneca County, New York. It is now the fourth largest Christian denomination in the United States.

An important doctrine of the faith is that family relationships can continue beyond death if certain ordinances are completed on earth. Mormons trace their family trees to find the names of ancestors who died without baptism into the faith. For members of the Church, genealogy is a way to connect with family members and to strengthen family ties, stretching back to the past and forward to the future. That is the theological background to the LDS Church's very deep commitment to family history.

The LDS Church has copied and made available vast quantities of genealogically relevant records on a global scale. They are available at the Family History Library (FHL) in Salt Lake City and at the many Family History Centers around the world. A growing collection is online at *FamilySearch.org*. For more information on New York records available at the FHL and FamilySearch, see their entries in chapter 16, National and Statewide Repositories & Resources.

Church Organization and Records

A *temple* is not a regular house of worship but exists for sacred purposes that are central to the LDS doctrine. In New York there are two temples, one in Palmyra (2000) where the LDS Church originated, and the other in Manhattan (2004).

Typical, local LDS congregations are *wards*; smaller congregations are *branches*. A group of wards and/or branches forms a *stake*. Potential stakes in an embryotic state are *districts*. New York has 15 stakes. The oldest was established in 1934 in New York City. The second oldest was established in Rochester in 1962. Clearly, the re-establishment of the LDS Church in New York State is relatively recent, and, as a consequence, so are the records.

Complete information on locating records of LDS congregations can be found online at *http://familysearch.org/learn/wiki/en/LDS_Church_Records*.

Records created in New York prior to 1948 are available if they exist. Many of these have been microfilmed and are cataloged at the FHL. Some records after 1948 have been filmed. Records created after 1983 are restricted to the church members and their immediate families.

Records submitted annually by wards and/or branches to stakes (called Form E records) contain baptisms, confirmations, priesthood ordinations, marriages, divorces, excommunications, deaths, and information about missionaries arriving and departing. Some of this information may be restricted.

Some New York material from LDS congregations can be found in the online FHL catalog, but it may require patient searching. Examples of material online are family group sheets from the New York City stake submitted in 1965 and Form E reports from 1935 to 1948 for some locations, including Albany, Schenectady, and Queens County.

These records are found in the FHL catalog by searching for the place name. Note that some records described in the catalog may also be found in records of the Eastern States Mission (which included New York) and the New York-Philadelphia District.

Presbyterian

Historical Overview

The Presbyterian Church, a Protestant Christian denomination, traces its origins to the theologian John Calvin (1509–1564) and his Scottish follower John Knox (ca. 1514–1572). Their brand of religious reform, shared also by Dutch Reformed, German Reformed, and Huguenot communities, was adopted in parts of Europe, and, importantly to American and New York family history, in Scotland and Ireland. Unlike the Anglican Church of England, the Church of Scotland was established on a Presbyterian basis. The Scots-Irish, who immigrated to North America in large numbers, mainly from Ulster, in the eighteenth and nineteenth centuries, brought their Presbyterian faith to these shores, joining other Presbyterians who had preceded them.

The denomination's name reflects the governing structure of "presbyteries," or representative assemblies. This differentiates it from the Congregationalists, for whom each church is self-governing, and the Anglican and Catholic churches, which are managed by a hierarchy of bishops.

The first presbytery in North America was founded in Philadelphia in 1706; the first synod followed in 1716, and Philadelphia was essentially the "capital" of Presbyterianism during the colonial period.

At the end of the seventeenth century the Anglican church became the established church in four New York counties, and there was concern that this establishment might be extended to the entire province. The English churches on Long Island and in Westchester, founded years before as Puritan congregations of the Church of England, had long since left the Anglican fold and no longer had a higher governing body to protect them against this new establishment. Being sympathetic to Presbyterianism, they affiliated with the Philadelphia Presbytery. Thus New York's oldest English churches, some founded as early as the 1640s, have now been Presbyterian for some 300 years.

Francis Makemie (born in Ireland and educated in Scotland) conducted Presbyterian worship services in a private house in New York City in 1707. He was imprisoned for it by the royal governor, a strong Anglican partisan. By 1716, however, Presbyterians were permitted to worship openly, and the first Presbyterian church in New York City was formed.

During the remainder of the colonial period, more Presbyterian churches were founded in New York, and a New York synod formed in 1745. This expansion was due in part to Scots and Scots-Irish immigration, as well as the migration of descendants of the older English population into newly-settled areas.

Table 11: Records of Churches Held at Cornell University Library

County	Church	Time Period of Records
Cayuga	First Presbyterian Church, Springport Presbyterian Church, Cayuga First Presbyterian Church, Aurora First Presbyterian Church, Auburn	1801–1927 1819–1909 1818–1947 1801–1912 (Registers)
Cortland	Presbyterian Church, Virgil Presbyterian Church, Freetown First Presbyterian Church, Truxton First Presbyterian Church, Preble Presbyterian Church, Cortland Village	1805–1823 (Record book) 1809–1885 1811–1840 1827–1875 1824–1901
Erie	First Congregational Church, Eden	1817–1890
Livingston	Presbyterian Church, Dansville First Presbyterian Church, Livonia	1861–1889 1806–1872 (Registers)
Madison	Cazenovia Presbyterian Church	1798–1953 (various years)
Monroe	First Presbyterian Church, Wheatland Presbyterian Church, West Mendon First Presbyterian Church, Clarkson Presbyterian Church, Webster Presbyterian Church, Ogden First Presbyterian Church, Gates First Presbyterian Church, Pittsford	1832–1905 1831–1926 1816–1903 1820–1929 1811–1880 1828–1902 1811–1914
Onondaga	First Presbyterian Church, Syracuse First Presbyterian Church, Skaneateles	1823–1852 1801–1917
Ontario	First Presbyterian Church, Geneva First Presbyterian Church, Naples First Presbyterian Church, Canandaigua First Presbyterian Church, Manchester First Presbyterian Church, East Vienna (Phelps) Presbyterian Congregation, West Bloomfield. First Presbyterian Church, Oak's Corners (Phelps)	1808–1884 1840–1923 1870–1899 (Minutes) 1857–1900 1831–1869 1830–1841 (Minutes) 1801–1915
Schuyler	First Presbyterian Church, Havana (Montour Falls) First Presbyterian Church, Hector	1829–1888 1809–1924
Seneca	First Presbyterian Church, Romulus Second Presbyterian Church, Fayette in Canoga First Presbyterian Church, Waterloo First Presbyterian Church, Seneca Falls	1802–1824 1825–1859 1917–1835 1807–1879
Steuben	First Presbyterian Church, Corning First Presbyterian Church, Bath Second Presbyterian Church of Bath, Kennedyville (Kanona) Presbyterian Church, Hammondsport Presbyterian Church, Pulteney Presbyterian Church, Howard	1834–1915 1808–1893 1831–1874 1831–1880 (Record book) 1817–1880 1815–1975
Tompkins	First Presbyterian Church, Ulysses, Trumansburg First Presbyterian Church, Ithaca First Presbyterian Church, Cayuta (Newfield)	1853–1903 1801–1980 1817–1879
Wayne	First Presbyterian Church, Galen First Presbyterian Church, East Palmyra First Presbyterian Church, Lyons Presbyterian Church, Newark Presbyterian Church, Fairville	1838–1896 1817–1900 1799–1946 1824–1925 1860–1944
Yates	First Presbyterian Church, Dundee Presbyterian Church, Bellona Third Presbyterian Society of Starkey (Rock Stream)	1832–1887 (Minutes) 1811–1931 1813–1914

In 1789 church leaders created the General Assembly of the Presbyterian Church in the United States of America. The New York synod was one of four that were formed in the new nation.

Like the Congregational church, the Presbyterian church spread into upstate New York along with the migration of people coming from New England and elsewhere. During the nineteenth century, western New York was the scene of revival movements and intense religious fervor, becoming known as the "Burned-Over District." Congregationalists and Presbyterians flourished in that culture and were often blended, and in 1801 there was a "plan of union" to unite them. Eventually, that movement failed, and as the nineteenth century wore on, the two churches became differentiated, established denominations.

Splits and Reunions

The history of the Presbyterian denomination is one of continual splits and reunions, from the eighteenth century to the present era, and far too complex even to summarize. Disagreements and splits over the issue of revivals date from the First Great Awakening, and involved many New York congregations. Some Presbyterian congregations moved to other religions during the emotional upheavals of the First and Second Great Awakenings. Other important and divisive issues followed, including slavery, the secession of southern states, theological disagreements of various kinds, relationships between the church and state, the distribution of power among various economic classes, and temperance. Some divisions began in Scotland and were brought to New York by eighteenth century Scots immigrants. A good introduction to the complexities of Presbyterian Church history is on the website of the Presbyterian Historical Society (PHS) at *history.pcusa.org*.

Records

The PHS, located in Philadelphia, collects, preserves, and organizes Presbyterian Church records, among other activities. The PHS curates thousands of cubic feet of church records, including records relevant to dozens of churches in New York State, many of them no longer active. The PHS also has an extensive library of printed books and personal papers, among other resources. Some indexes are available on the PHS website, as are a list of churches, contact information, and notes on the disposition of their records.

Among the churches with records at PHS are the First Presbyterian of Poughkeepsie and Central Presbyterian of Rochester, and over 40 churches from Manhattan and some from the other New York City boroughs. The Family History Library (FHL) has many of these records on microfilm, as well as the original records of New York City's First Presbyterian Church and records of seven former churches now housed at the First Church. For further details see Harry Macy's research aids and Richard Haberstroh's book, listed in the bibliography below.

The FHL also has Presbyterian Church records from other sources, as do the larger research libraries in New York, including the Cornell University Library, the New York State Library (NYSL), and the New York Public Library (NYPL).

The Cornell University Library has records for over 50 Presbyterian churches in upstate New York, as listed in table 11.

Transcriptions

Transcriptions of religious records can be very useful for genealogical research if the originals are unavailable. The Vosburgh Collection of New York Church Records consists of transcribed church documents. The NYPL, the FHL, and the New England Historic Genealogical Society (NEHGS) are among the libraries that have microfilm of the Vosburgh Collection of New York Church Records. Though this collection is far from covering every single Presbyterian church in New York, nearly 30 Presbyterian churches are included, from Albany, Columbia, Delaware, Fulton, Greene, Montgomery, Oneida, Oswego, Otsego, Rensselaer, Saratoga, and Washington counties. The NYG&B eLibrary has transcribed records for 16 Presbyterian churches across New York State, most of them from the Vosburgh collection. Records of many Presbyterian churches have also been published in journals, particularly in the *NYG&B Record*, also available in the eLibrary; consult the *NYG&B Record* subject indexes at *NewYorkFamilyHistory.org*. Researchers should also check online for individual church records that have been transcribed and posted (e.g., First Presbyterian Church of Olean at *www.rootsweb.ancestry.com/~nycattar/towns/Olean/presbyterianchurchrecords.htm*).

Research Aids

Harry Macy Jr.'s Research Aids on New York City (Manhattan), Brooklyn/Kings, and Queens and Nassau (see bibliography) identify published or transcribed Presbyterian records for those counties. Many churches have published histories—some have several histories in print—and are far too numerous to list here; and synods publish minutes of their meetings. These records are easily located in library catalogs and, in the case of churches that are still in existence, by contacting the churches themselves.

Selected Repositories and Resources
Presbyterian Historical Society (PHS)

425 Lombard Street • Philadelphia, PA 19147 • (215) 627-1852
Email: refdesk@history.pcusa.org • *history.pcusa.org*

The PHS has a very useful website with a variety of tools to help users locate the churches attended by ancestors, as well as an online catalog to their holdings. Finding aids to some archival collections are also available online. A genealogy search service is available.

Table 12: Church Record Transcriptions Digitized by the NYG&B	
County	Church
Albany	First Presbyterian Church, Albany
Columbia	First Presbyterian Church, Canaan
Delaware	First Presbyterian Church, Stamford Presbyterian Church, Harpersfield
Fulton	First Presbyterian Church, West Galway, Perth
Montgomery	United Presbyterian Church, Florida
New York	Canal Street Presbyterian Church
Oneida	First Presbyterian Church, Whitesboro
Oswego	First Presbyterian Church, Oswego
Otsego	First Presbyterian Church, Cooperstown
Queens	First Presbyterian Church, Newtown (Elmhurst)
Rensselaer	First Presbyterian Church, Lansingburgh First Presbyterian Church, Troy Second Street Presbyterian Church, Troy
Saratoga	United Presbyterian Church, West Charlton
Washington	Presbyterian Church, Cambridge

Selected Bibliography and Further Reading

Additional transcribed or published Presbyterian records may be listed in the County Guides; check also library and archive catalogs for original, transcribed or published records, which abound in New York State.

Farrell, Charles. "Pew Rentals in the Scotch Presbyterian Church, New York City, 1785–1798." *NYG&B Record*, vol. 129, no. 4 (1998): 249–259. [NYG&B eLibrary]

Fish, John Dean. "History and Vital Records of Christ's First Presbyterian Church of Hempstead, Long Island, New York." *NYG&B Record*, vol. 53 (1922) no. 3: 235–257, no. 4: 381–392; vol. 54 (1923) no. 1: 30–42, no. 2: 138–150. [NYG&B eLibrary]

Goodfriend, Joyce. "A New Look at Presbyterian Origins in New York City." *American Presbyterians*, vol. 67, no. 3 (1989): 199–207.

Haberstroh, Richard. *The German Churches of Metropolitan New York: A Research Guide*. New York: NYG&B Society, 2000. [NYG&B eLibrary]

Hall, Russell E. "American Presbyterian Churches–A Genealogy 1706–1982." *Journal of Presbyterian History*, vol. 60, no. 2 (1982): 95–128.

Historical Records Survey. *Inventory of the Church Archives of New York City: Presbyterian Church in the United States of America*. Historical Records Survey, Division of Professional and Service Projects, Work Projects Administration, 1940. [NYG&B eLibrary]

Macy, Harry, Jr. "Brooklyn/Kings County Church Records Since 1783." *NYG&B Newsletter* (now *New York Researcher*), Summer 2000. Updated June 2011 and published as a Research Aid on *NewYorkFamilyHistory.org*.

———. "Presbyterian Records of New York City (Manhattan)." *NYG&B Newsletter* (now *New York Researcher*), Fall 1995. Updated May 2011 and published as a Research Aid on *NewYorkFamilyHistory.org*. This article identifies all Manhattan Presbyterian churches with records that have been published or microfilmed for the FHL, including many now at PHS.

———. "Religious Records of Queens and Nassau Counties." *NYG&B Newsletter* (now *New York Researcher*), Spring 2003. Updated June 2011 and published as a Research Aid on *NewYorkFamilyHistory.org*.

"Records of the First and Second Presbyterian Churches in the City of New York," *NYG&B Record*, vols. 4–14 (1873–1883). Births and Baptisms 1722–1783, Marriages 1756–1807 in the city's two oldest Presbyterian churches. For more records of these and other churches see Harry Macy Jr.'s *Presbyterian Records of New York City*, above.

Quaker (Society of Friends)

Historical Overview

The Religious Society of Friends was started in the mid-seventeenth century in England by George Fox (1624-1691), who believed that Christians could have a relationship with Christ without ordained clergy, religious hierarchy, and creeds; this set Quakers apart from the Church of England and other emerging Protestant groups. Fox was persecuted and even imprisoned for his views, but the movement quickly spread to Scotland, Ireland, and North America.

The term *Quaker* was first used to ridicule Fox's warning that his persecutors should *tremble* with the fear of the Lord.

Emigration of Friends to North America began in the mid-seventeenth century, and Friends were tolerated in Rhode Island, and, most notably, in Pennsylvania, as William Penn himself was an adherent. Quakers came to New Amsterdam in 1657; at first, they were persecuted, and then tolerated.

The New York Yearly Meeting was established in 1695. Previous to this, Friends in New York fell under the jurisdiction of the New England Yearly Meeting. See chapter 1, Colonial Era, for a note about the Flushing Remonstrance—a landmark in the history of religious freedom.

The Quakers have always been a small sect, but with influence far out of proportion to their numbers. Consequently the literature about Quakers is very extensive.

Quaker Meetings

Preparative meetings, where preparations for the monthly meeting are discussed, are the local administrative unit in the Society of Friends. Made up of individuals from one community, these meetings are held to worship and perform administrative tasks on a local level. Monthly meetings are made up of several local (preparative) meetings; the site of the monthly meeting rotates among the preparative meetings on a regular schedule. It is at the monthly meeting level that the records most useful for genealogists are kept. The Flushing Monthly Meeting, whose records began in1694, was the first in New York State.

Quarterly meetings are made up of several monthly meetings from the same area and are largely focused on business, as is the yearly meeting, drawing together Friends at the regional or state level.

Between 1828 and 1955 the yearly meeting separated into different divisions several times (see table 13). With the "Hicksite Split" in 1828, the yearly meeting was separated into two divisions, the Hicksite/Friends General Conference, and the Orthodox/Friends United Meeting. See Loren Fay's *Quaker Census of 1828*. Other separations took place, establishing many yearly meetings within New York State until the groups were reunited in 1955 as the New York Yearly Meeting.

Record Keeping

Quakers have no clergy; records were instead maintained by an appointed record keeper. Records of monthly meetings are the most pertinent, as they contain genealogical information for pre-1850 Quakers. After 1850 records are frequently less detailed. Quaker records often refer to months by number rather than name; however, the Gregorian calendar was not adopted until 1752, before which the year began in March (March was the first month and February the twelfth). See chapter 1, Colonial Era, for more detail on the calendar change, including the Quaker calendar traditions.

George Fox set out instructions for record keeping in an epistle written in 1653. A "registrar of sufferings" was to be appointed to maintain registers, separate from the meeting minutes. Many meetings recorded birth and death information from the beginning, but it was required under the Discipline of 1810.

Meeting Registers, usually kept by the clerk of the monthly meeting, were:

- Register of Births and Deaths. While deaths were recorded, burials were not, and it was not until 1852 that tombstones were permitted in Quaker cemeteries.
- Register of Marriages and Removals. Marriages were usually announced in both men's and women's meetings for two months prior to the ceremony. (Researchers should also check the minutes of the Preparative meetings.) Certificates of Removal recorded in the register gave permission for the transfer of families between meetings.

Table 13: The Divisions and Reunions of the Society of Friends in New York			
New York Yearly Meeting (1695)			
Hicksite/Friends General Conference (1828)	Orthodox/Friends United Meeting (1828)		
	Gurneyites (1840s–1850s)		Wilburites (1840s–1850s)
	Conservative (late-1800s)	Progressive (late-1800s)	
New York Yearly Meeting (1955)			

Men and women met separately, although they worshipped together. Minutes of their individual meetings are recorded in separate books, and the same event may be mentioned in both volumes. Included in the minutes are requests for membership to the Society and requests to marry (also in the registers).

Additional information kept in meeting minutes included the formation of committees, disownment of a Friend from the Society, and reinstatements to the Society. Extensive minutes recording business and administrative tasks also exist for many meetings.

Quakers were required to marry within the Society, and marriage between a Quaker and someone from another religion ("marriage out of unity") often resulted in the Quaker being disowned. This meant that the disowned parties could not financially support the religion, nor could they be on committees, and their children were not birthright members. They could, however, attend service. Only members of the Society would be mentioned in the minutes, so a person could be absent from the records after disownment, then reappear later if they were reinstated.

Also notable are the certificates necessary for a member or family to switch meetings (often called a "certificate of removal"); these allow movement of Quakers to be tracked. Within the United States, a common migration pattern emerged over time, with the earliest meetings in New York moving up the Hudson Valley, then west through the Mohawk Valley.

Finding the name of an ancestor's meeting is the first step to researching Quaker records. Names of meetings are often recorded in local histories, and finding the name of a person in the membership to a preparative meeting will often mention the monthly meeting to which that person belonged. Finding a family in the monthly meeting vital records register will open to the door to the monthly meeting records. It is important to note the following regarding names of meetings:

- Monthly and quarterly meetings may have the same name.
- Names of meetings changed over time.
- Names of meetings were often duplicated within a region.
- Yearly meetings may have either had a smaller or larger jurisdiction than suggested by the name—for example, the New York Yearly Meeting may not have covered the entire state in a given year. In fact, in the 1850s, more than three Yearly meetings existed with the name "New York Yearly Meeting."

Research Aids

Suzanne McVetty's Research Aid online at *NewYorkFamilyHistory.org*, "Records of the Society of Friends (Quakers), New York Yearly Meeting," is an excellent article for those beginning their research. Researchers may then want to consult James Hazard's index to New York Yearly Meeting records, on the website of the Friends Historical Library, which indicates each local meeting record where an individual is named. The NYG&B Research

Aid "Records of the Society of Friends (Quakers), New York Yearly Meeting: Microfilmed Copies in the NYG&B Collection and Family History Library" identifies the film numbers for those records in both the Family History Library (FHL) and the NYG&B Collection now at New York Public Library (NYPL).

Selected Repositories and Resources

Friends Historical Library

Swarthmore College • 500 College Avenue • Swarthmore, PA
(610) 328-8496 • Email: friends@swarthmore.edu
www.swarthmore.edu/academics/friends-historical-library.xml

The central repository for records of Friends meetings in New York is located at Swarthmore College as part of the Friends Historical Library. They were previously held at the Haviland Records Room at the Friends Seminary in New York City (until 1997). Holdings include:

- Records of the New York Yearly Meeting and the Genesee Yearly Meeting, as well as various quarterly, monthly, and preparative meetings. Detailed online finding aids are available at *www.swarthmore.edu/library/friends/NYYM/NYYMindex.htm*; index to collection available at *www.swarthmore.edu/library/friends/hazard*.
- Records of national Quaker organizations, such as the Friends General Conference (1867–present) and the Joint Committee of Indian Affairs (1836–1850).
- Records of New York based Quaker organizations, such as the Friends Literary and Library Association (1880–1906), the Friends Temperance Union (1876–1905), the New York Association of Friends for the Relief of those Held in Slavery (1839–1844), and the New York Female Association (1798–1988).
- Personal and family papers of Quakers, including journals, correspondence, and property records.

Microfilm copies of Swarthmore's collection are available at the New York State Library, NYPL, SUNY Buffalo Library, and Rutgers University Library (New Brunswick, NJ), and many are also available from the FHL.

Haverford College: Quaker Collections

370 Lancaster Avenue • Haverford, PA 19041-1392
(610) 896-1161 • Email: hc-special@haverford.edu
www.haverford.edu/library/special

Images of meetinghouses (many digitized and accessible online), family papers, and records of New Jersey and Pennsylvania meetings. Finding aids available at *www.haverford.edu/library/special/aids*.

Quaker Corner

www.rootsweb.ancestry.com/~quakers

Contains surname index, list of historic meetinghouse locations, guide to terminology found in Quaker records, and information on the historic Quaker calendar.

Selected Bibliography and Further Reading

Barbour, Hugh, et al., eds. *Quaker Crosscurrents: Three Hundred Years of Friends in the New York Yearly Meetings.* Syracuse: Syracuse University Press, 1995. Includes useful maps and lists of meetings as of 1828.

Berry, Ellen Thomas, and David Allen Berry. *Our Quaker Ancestors: Finding Them in Quaker Records.* Baltimore: Genealogical Publishing Co., 1987.

Bowden, James. *The History of the Society of Friends in America.* 2 vols. London, 1850, 1854, reprinted New York: Arno Press, 1972.

Cox, John, Jr. *New York City Church Archives. Religious Society of Friends. A Catalog of the Records in Possession of, or Relating to, the Two New York Yearly Meetings of the Religious Society of Friends and Their Subordinate Meetings.* New York: Historical Records Survey, Work Projects Administration, 1940. Useful for determining the origin of each meeting as well as the extent of its records.

— — —. "Quaker Records in New York." *NYG&B Record*, vol. 45 (1914) no. 3: 263–269, no. 4: 366–373. [NYG&B eLibrary]

— — —. *Quakerism in the City of New York 1657–1930.* New York: Privately Printed, 1930. Reprinted, Bowie, MD: Heritage Books, 2000.

Fay, Loren V. *Quaker Census of 1828: Members of the New York Yearly Meeting, the Religious Society of Friends (in New York, Ontario, Vermont, Connecticut, Massachusetts, and Quebec) at the time of the separation of 1828.* Rhinebeck, NY: Kinship Books, 1989. An alphabetized transcript of members' names may include parents' names and children's names and ages, as well as the meeting to which they belonged. A state map provides meeting locations.

Hazard, James E. *Abstracts of the Records of Monthly Meetings of New York Yearly Meeting.* 31 Vols. Swarthmore, PA: Friends Historical Library, 2000–. See the index on the website of the Friends Historical Library (the library is listed above).

Hinshaw, William Wade. *The Encyclopedia of American Quaker Genealogy.* 6 vols. Ann Arbor, MI: Edwards Brothers, 1936–1950.

Index to the Encyclopedia of American Quaker Genealogy. Baltimore: Genealogical Publishing Co., 1999.

McVetty, Suzanne. "Records of the Society of Friends (Quakers), New York Yearly Meeting." *NYG&B Newsletter* (now *New York Researcher*), Fall 1997. Updated and published as a Research Aid on *NewYorkFamilyHistory.org.*

Moorhouse, B-Ann. "Returns of Quakers in New York City Tax Assessment Books, 1810–1819." *NYG&B Record*, vol. 110 (1979) no. 3: 164–172, no. 4: 216–221. [NYG&B eLibrary]

Naylor, Natalie A. *"The People Called Quakers," Records of Long Island Friends 1671–1703.* Hempstead, NY: Long Island Studies Institute, Hofstra University, 2001.

Quaker History. Journal of the Friends Historical Association, Haverford College, 1906-present.

Underhill, Abraham S. "Records of the Society of Friends of the City of New York and Vicinity, from 1640 to 1800." *NYG&B Record*, vol. 3 (1872) no.4: 184–190; vol. 4 (1873) no. 1: 32–40, no. 2: 94–98, no. 4: 190–195; vol. 5 (1874) no. 1: 38–41, no. 2: 102–107, no. 4: 186–190; vol. 6 (1875) no. 2: 97–107, no. 4: 192–193; vol. 7 (1876) no. 1: 39–43, no. 2 85–90. [NYG&B eLibrary]

Reformed (Dutch, Huguenot, German, Christian)

The Dutch Reformed Church

Historical Overview

During the sixteenth century numerous congregations in the Netherlands affiliated with Calvinist Protestantism, leading to the formation of the *Nederlands Hervormde Kerk*, or Dutch Reformed Church. This was the church of most of the leaders of the Dutch war for independence from Spain, as well as the directors of the West India Company (WIC), which created the colony of New Netherland.

Until the colony was taken over by the English in 1664, the Dutch Reformed Church was the only Christian denomination permitted to hold public worship, except in the English settlements. Therefore, regardless of religion or nationality, in Dutch settlements marriages and baptisms were conducted by a Dutch Reformed minister.

Jonas Michaëlius organized the first congregation at Fort Amsterdam on Manhattan Island in 1628, which still continues as the Collegiate Church of New York City; its records exist from 1639. The second congregation was established at Fort Orange in 1642 and is now the First Church of Albany; its marriage and baptismal records do not begin until 1683, but there are deacons' records from 1652. By 1664 there were also churches at Midwout (Flatbush), Breuckelen (Brooklyn), and Wiltwyck (Kingston), and in subsequent years more Dutch churches were formed in western Long Island, Staten Island, the Hudson and Mohawk Valleys, and across the Hudson River in New Jersey.

By the end of the eighteenth century most of the churches had abandoned the use of the Dutch language in their services and records, in favor of English. This change began in New York City and later spread into the rural areas. After the Revolution, the American churches established their independence from the Church in the Netherlands. In 1819 the denomination was incorporated as the Reformed Protestant Dutch Church, but in 1867 it dropped the "Dutch" and assumed its present name of Reformed Church in America (RCA).

Records

In 1766 the Church founded Queen's College in New Brunswick, later renamed Rutgers College and now Rutgers, the State University of New Jersey. The college educated the sons of many early Dutch American families, and its seminary trained ministers for the Church. When the Church cut its ties to the college, it retained the New Brunswick Theological Seminary, which today also houses the RCA Archives.

The Archives have a superb collection with records from the seventeenth century to the present, primarily covering Dutch Reformed congregations in New York, New Jersey, and parts of the Midwest. They also hold records of the denomination and its staff offices, mission records from overseas and domestic mission areas, some personal papers and sermons of ministers, and an extensive pamphlet collection about pastors and congregations. The Archives works to maintain information about Dutch church records in other repositories, as well as transcriptions and publications. For details of the Archives' holdings see *Guide to Local Church Records in the Archives of the Reformed Church in America*. Some of the records at New Brunswick are also available on film through the Family History Library (FHL).

In New York City, as additional Dutch Reformed churches were created in the eighteenth century, they formed a "collegiate" system, sharing pastors and keeping a common set of records. In present-day Manhattan four Reformed churches (Marble Collegiate, Middle Collegiate, West End Collegiate, and Fort Washington Collegiate) are still organized as the Collegiate Church Corporation within the RCA. While they use "Collegiate" rather than "Reformed" in their individual church names, they collectively are still known as the Reformed Protestant Dutch Church of the City of New York.

The Collegiate Church Corporation has its own archives, including the original records of the collegiate churches dating back to the seventeenth century. The Archives are not open to the public; research queries may be sent to the Consistory of the collegiate Church. For a summary of holdings of records that may be of use to genealogists, see *Inventory of the Church Archives of New York City: Reformed Church in America*, which also lists nineteenth-and twentieth-century records of individual noncollegiate churches in the five boroughs, many of which are now in the RCA Archives at New Brunswick.

The Holland Society of New York has one of the largest collections of copies of New York Dutch Reformed records, handwritten transcripts made for the Society more than a century ago, many of them by Dingman Versteeg, a talented transcriber and native Dutch speaker. These transcripts are available in the Society's Manhattan library, and have been filmed for the FHL and now form a database on *Ancestry.com* titled "U.S. Dutch Reformed Church Records from Selected States." (See the bibliography of this section for a cautionary note about using this database.) The Society's *Year Book* for 1912 is available at *HathiTrust.org* and contains an inventory of the transcripts and a map showing the locations of all the early Reformed churches that they cover. This map is extremely useful for identifying neighboring Dutch churches that a family might have used in addition to their own.

The Society published records of the Albany and Bergen (NJ) churches in multiple issues of the *Year Book*, and those records have been consolidated into single volumes reprinted by the Genealogical Publishing Company and Clearfield Company. In its Collections series the Holland Society published the records of the New Paltz church, and the Hackensack and Schraalenburg (NJ) churches, where many New Yorkers migrated. More recently the Society published new transcriptions/translations of the Flatbush and Brooklyn churches.

The New York Genealogical and Biographical Society began publishing records of the New Amsterdam/New York City Dutch Reformed Church in the *NYG&B Record* in 1874, and reprinted the marriages and baptisms in their Collections series in 1890 and 1901–1902. These records, which begin in 1639 and are the earliest church records of any denomination in New York, are now available in the NYG&B eLibrary. Records of other Dutch Reformed churches will also be found in the *NYG&B Record*.

The collection of church records transcribed by Royden W. Vosburgh for NYG&B and now at the New York Public Library (NYPL) covers many Dutch Reformed churches, especially in the Hudson Valley. Available Dutch Reformed records for New York City (Manhattan), Kings (Brooklyn), Queens, and Nassau counties, as well as those in the Vosburgh Collection, are identified in research aids by Harry Macy Jr. (see bibliography), and indexes to the *NYG&B Record* will reveal other such records. In recent years many additional transcripts have been published by Arthur C. M. Kelly (through Kinship publishers of Rhinebeck, NY) and the late Jean Worden. Searching the New York State Library, the NYPL, or the FHL online catalogs will reveal the works of these and many other transcribers.

The Huguenot Churches
Historical Overview

Huguenots were Protestants from France. In the early-sixteenth century they were attracted to the works of John Calvin, and by the mid-sixteenth century they were known as Huguenots. The rest of the sixteenth century in France was marked by religious wars between the Catholics (who were in the majority) and the Huguenots; the Huguenots suffered considerable persecution, most infamously the St. Bartholomew's Day Massacre on August 24, 1572, when thousands of them were killed throughout France. In these years some Huguenots left France for more tolerant countries.

The Edict of Nantes in 1598 granted some religious freedom to the Huguenots, including the right to hold public worship (except in Paris). But over the next 80 years conditions gradually deteriorated, and Huguenots continued to leave the country. By 1680 it was apparent that they were no longer going to be tolerated, and in 1685 the Edict of Fontainebleau revoked the Edict of Nantes, after which Protestantism was forbidden, Huguenot "temples" (as they called their churches) were destroyed, those wanting to marry had to become Catholic, and children had to be baptized in Catholic churches. Though the Revocation also made it illegal to leave the country, a massive

exodus began, and over the next hundred years some 300,000 Huguenots escaped to Protestant countries of Europe, and to North America. In France it was not until 1787 that the Edict of Versailles, known as the Edict of Tolerance, allowed non-Catholics freedom of religion.

Among the French-speaking settlers of New Netherland and colonial New York before 1680, only a small number were Huguenots from France, the great majority being Walloons from the Southern Netherlands. There were not enough French-speakers to form separate churches, so both Huguenots and Walloons attended Dutch Reformed churches and were absorbed into the Dutch population.

The exodus from France in the latter half of the seventeenth century led to the establishment of Huguenot churches in New York City in 1682, and New Rochelle (Westchester County) in 1686. A French church was also established on Staten Island to serve both Huguenots and Walloons. New Paltz (Ulster County) was settled in 1678 primarily by Walloon immigrants who are often referred to as Huguenots; their church affiliated with the Dutch Reformed. None of the Huguenot churches survived.

Early in the eighteenth century the New Rochelle congregation divided, creating separate Episcopal (Anglican) and Huguenot (Reformed) churches, the latter eventually becoming Presbyterian.

Not long afterwards, the Staten Island church closed and its members scattered to that island's other churches, particularly St. Andrew's (Anglican).

The New York City church, known as the Eglise du Saint-Esprit, became an Episcopal church in 1804 and still exists under that name. See the section on the French and French-speaking people in chapter 14, Peoples of New York, for further information, particularly about the Walloons.

Records

The early records of the New York City church were published by the Huguenot Society of America, and a transcription of later records is at the NYPL; Historic Huguenot Street in New Paltz (a National Historic Landmark District and museum) and the New-York Historical Society (N-YHS) have some of the original records. The Holland Society and the NYPL have transcripts of the records of the New Rochelle church. The records of the Staten Island church are lost. Earliest records of the New Paltz church are at the church and Historic Huguenot Street, and were also published by the Holland Society and others.

The German Reformed Church
Historical Overview

Many early members of New York State's Dutch Reformed churches were Germans who were absorbed into the Dutch community, but German immigration in the eighteenth century led to the creation of separate German Reformed churches in both New York City and the Hudson Valley. Although these churches used the German language, they were affiliated with the Dutch Reformed denomination. This was also true of the German Reformed churches that developed in colonial Pennsylvania. After the Revolution the Pennsylvania churches severed their ties with the Dutch church and formed the German Reformed Church.

In 1869 "German" was dropped, and the denomination became the Reformed Church in the United States (RCUS). The great nineteenth-century German migration to New York led to the creation of many new German Reformed churches in the state, which affiliated with the RCUS. In 1934 the RCUS merged with the Evangelical Synod of North America to form the Evangelical and Reformed Church, and in 1958 that denomination merged with the Congregational Christian Churches to form today's United Church of Christ or UCC. This is not to be confused with the Evangelical Church, which merged in 1946 with the United Brethren in Christ to form the Evangelical United Brethren Church, and is now part of the United Methodist Church.

Records

New York City's first German Reformed Church no longer exists, but its earliest records are at the N-YHS (with a transcript at the NYPL, partly published in the NYG&B Record). Its later records and those of some other German Reformed churches are at the RCA Archives, while others are held by the Evangelical and Reformed Historical Society in Lancaster, PA. Records of some early churches in the Hudson Valley have been transcribed by authors such as Royden Vosburgh and Arthur Kelly. Richard Haberstroh's *German Churches of Metropolitan New York: A Reseach Guide* identifies the German Reformed churches in the five boroughs and their records, and explains the series of mergers that led the German church into the UCC.

The Christian Reformed Church
Historical Overview

Over the years there were a number of minor schisms in the Dutch Reformed Church, such as one that created the True Dutch Reformed Churches in 1822. A more serious division arose in the mid-nineteenth century, when the Dutch Reformed Church received a new wave of immigrants from the Netherlands, many of whom settled in the Midwest. This influx, and differing views on theology, led to several congregations seceding from the then-named Reformed Dutch Church and the formation in 1857 of the Christian Reformed Church in North America (CRC), with congregations in the East and the Midwestern states of Michigan, Wisconsin, Illinois, and Iowa.

In 1882 more congregations moved from the RCA to the CRC. The CRC has, or has had, congregations in more than 20 New York communities, ranging from upstate Baldwinsville to West Sayville, Long Island. The first congregations in New York were formed during the 1870s, and in 1890 the churches of the True Dutch Reformed Church joined the CRC.

Records

The denominational archives at Calvin College in Grand Rapids, MI, hold the minutes, membership records, and other historical material from most of the congregations. The material on the True Dutch Reformed Church goes back to the 1820s, but the bulk is from the 1870s forward.

Edward Corwin's *Manual of the Reformed Church in America . . . 1628–1921* includes the history of these different denominations, biographies of ministers, and a list of churches.

Selected Repositories and Resources
The Archives of the Reformed Church of America

21 Seminary Place • New Brunswick, NJ 08901
(732) 246-1779 • *www.rca.org/archives*

The RCA archives have a superb collection with records from the seventeenth century to the present, primarily covering Dutch Reformed congregations in New York, New Jersey, and parts of the Midwest. They also hold records of the denomination and its staff offices, mission records from overseas and domestic mission areas, some personal papers and sermons of ministers, and an extensive pamphlet collection about pastors and congregations. The Archives works to maintain information about Dutch church records in other repositories, as well as transcriptions and publications. For works on Reformed Church history see *rca.org/series*.

Calvin College

3201 Burton SE • Grand Rapids, MI 49546
(616) 526-6000 • Email: crcarchives@calvin.edu
www.calvin.edu/hh/crc_archives.htm

The denominational archives at Calvin College hold the minutes, membership records, and other historic material from most of the Christian Reformed Church congregations.

The Collegiate Church Corporation

500 Fifth Avenue, Suite 1710 • New York, NY 10110
(212) 233-1960 • Email: contact@collegiatechurch.org
www.collegiatechurch.org

Records that may be of use to genealogists include unpublished baptismal, marriage, and membership records for Collegiate Church Corporation 1695–1973; marriage and baptismal journals 1822–1923; and Map Collection of the Collegiate Church 1807–1956. Archives are not open the public; research queries may be sent to the Consistory of the Collegiate Church.

The Evangelical and Reformed Historical Society

Philip Schaff Library • Lancaster Theological Seminary
555 West James Street • Lancaster, PA 17603 • (717) 290-8734
Email: erhs@lancasterseminary.edu • *www.erhs.info/Home.html*

The Society holds the personal and pastoral records of clergy as well as an assortment of donated church records, including churches from ten New York counties.

Historic Huguenot Street

88 Huguenot Street • New Paltz, NY 12561 • (845) 255-1660
Email: info@huguenotstreet.org • *huguenotstreet.org*

Collections include family genealogies, church, cemetery and Bible records, wills and deeds, census records, genealogical periodicals, county histories, and publications relating to Huguenot, Walloon, and Dutch ancestry.

Huguenot Society of America

20 West 44th Street, Suite 510 • New York, NY 10036
(212) 755-0592 • Email: hugsoc@verizon.net
huguenotsocietyofamerica.org

The library of the Huguenot Society of American contains materials from the sixteenth century to the present, and covers all aspects of Huguenot scholarship, including theology, history, politics, and families. The library is open by appointment, and the catalog is available only on-site. Prospective researchers may wish to consult *Collections of the Huguenot Society of America* (volume 1), published by the Society in 1886.

Selected Bibliography and Further Reading

Balmer, Randall H. *A Perfect Babel of Confusion: Dutch Religion and English Culture in the Middle Colonies*. New York: Oxford University Press, 1989.

Cabaret, J. A. *Notice Historique sur l'Eglise Evangélique Française de New-York (Presbytérienne)*. Lausanne, Switzerland: Georges Bridel & Cie, 1897.

Corwin, Charles E. *A Manual of the Reformed Church in America, (formerly Reformed Protestant Dutch Church) 1628–1922*. 5th edition, 1922.

De Jong, Gerald F. *The Dutch Reformed Church in the American Colonies*. Grand Rapids, MI: Wm. B. Eerdmans Publishing Co., 1978.

Ecclesiastical Records, State of New York. 7 vols. Albany: J. B. Lyon, State Printer, 1901–1916.

Fabend, Firth H. *Zion on the Hudson—Dutch New York and New Jersey in the Age of Revivals*. Piscataway, NJ: Rutgers University Press, 2000.

Gasero, Russell L., ed. *Chronological List of Congregations 1628–2000*. Provides establishment dates and locations for congregations/churches. Digital version at *rca.org*.

— — —. *Guide to Local Church Records in the Archives of the Reformed Church in America and to Genealogical Resources in the Gardner Sage Library, New Brunswick Theological Seminary*. New Brunswick, NJ: Historical Society of the Reformed Church in America, 1979. The information is organized alphabetically by state, and includes details of records (type and date range) for 172 churches across the state of New York. Digital version at *rca.org*.

Gasero, Russell L. *Historical Directory of the Reformed Church in America, 1628–2000*. Grand Rapids, MI: Wm. B. Eerdmans Publishing Co., 2001.

Giuseppi, M. S., ed. *Naturalizations of Foreign Protestants in the American and West Indian Colonies*. London: Huguenot Society Publishing, 1921. The name database is on *Ancestry.com*.

Haberstroh, Richard. *The German Churches of Metropolitan New York: A Research Guide*. New York: New York Geneaological and Biographical Society, 2000. Includes churches of the former Evangelical and Reformed denomination and its German Reformed and Evangelical predecessors. [NYG&B eLibrary]

Historical Records Survey. *Inventory of the Church Archives of New York City: Reformed Church in America*. Historical Records Survey, Division of Professional and Service Projects, Work Projects Administration, 1939. [NYG&B eLibrary]

Hoes, Roswell Randall, ed. *Baptismal and Marriage Records of the Old Dutch Church at Kingston, Ulster County, New York*. New York: 1891.

Hoff, Henry B. "Some Thoughts About the New York Dutch Reformed Church Records." *NYG&B Newsletter* (now *New York Researcher*), vol 11, no. 2 (2000) 47, 55. [NYG&B eLibrary]

Holland Society of New York, ed. *Records of the Reformed Dutch Church of Albany, New York, 1683–1809: Marriages, Baptisms, Marriages, Etc.* Baltimore: Genealogical Publishing Co., 1978. Consolidated from the Year Books of the Holland Society for 1904–1908, and 1922/23 and 1926/27.

Macy, Harry, Jr. "Brooklyn/Kings County Church Records Since 1783." *NYG&B Newsletter* (now *New York Researcher*), Summer 2000. Updated June 2011 and published as a Research Aid on *NewYorkFamilyHistory.org*. See sections on the Dutch Reformed Church.

— — —. "Dutch Reformed Records of New York City (Manhattan)." *NYG&B Newsletter* (now *New York Researcher*), Spring 1994. Updated May 2011 and published as a Research Aid on *NewYorkFamilyHistory.org*.

— — —. "Kings County's Colonial Church Records." *NYG&B Newsletter* (now *New York Researcher*), Winter 1997. Updated May 2011 and published as a Research Aid on *NewYorkFamilyHistory.org*.

— — —. "Records of Other Protestant Denominations of New York City (Manhattan)." *NYG&B Newsletter* (now *New York Researcher*), Spring 1996. Updated May 2011 as a Research Aid at *NewYorkFamilyHistory.org*. Lists available German Reformed and French Reformed (Huguenot) records.

— — —. "Religious Records of Queens and Nassau Counties." *NYG&B Newsletter* (now *New York Researcher*), Winter 2003. Updated June 2011 and published as a Research Aid on *NewYorkFamilyHistory.org*.

— — —. "Researching the People of New Netherland and Their Descendants: How to Identify and Make Best Use of the Available Sources." *Finding Your New Netherland Roots*. Digitally published by the NYG&B, 2011. Appendix E is a bibliography of published Reformed church records that begin before 1700.

— — —. "The Vosburgh Collection of New York Church Records." *NYG&B Newsletter* (now *New York Researcher*), Fall 1998. Updated August 2011 and published as a Research Aid on *NewYorkFamilyHistory.org*. [NYG&B eLibrary] Of the 94 churches in this collection, 42 are Reformed. The Collection is also partially available online at *NewYorkFamilyHistory.org,* and other sites.

Maynard, John A. F. *The Huguenot Church of New York: A History of the French Church of Saint Esprit*, New York: n.p., 1938.

U.S., Dutch Reformed Church Records from Selected States, 1660–1926. Database online at *Ancestry.com*. Transcriptions of original data from Dutch Reformed Church Records from New York, New Jersey, and Pennsylvania. It also contains a few New York Lutheran and German Reformed churches and the New Rochelle French (Huguenot) church. This database contains records copied by the Holland Society of New York and others. Researchers should use it with caution and in conjunction with the Holland Society's Church Records Collection, a multivolume collection described in detail in the 1912 *Year Book*, as mentioned in the text above. (The Holland Society catalogues each church separately online.) *Ancestry.com*'s database requires judicious exploration, because the way it is presented does not reveal its full contents, and some churches are not correctly named. Microfilm of this collection is at the FHL.

Verheyden, Alphonse L. E. *Le Conseil des Troubles. Liste des Condamnés*. Bruxelles: Palais des Académies, 1961. List of people condemned by the Conseil des Troubles in the Netherlands and Belgium during the Spanish Inquisition.

Weintrob, Lori, and Philip Papas. *When New York State Spoke French: The Huguenots and Walloons of Staten Island: A Research Guide*. This publication, sponsored by the NYG&B, is nearing completion and will be added to the NYG&B eLibrary when finished.

"Research Guide to Staten Island's Huguenot History." This project, sponsored by the NYG&B, is nearing completion and will be added to the NYG&B eLibrary when finished.

Introduction

This section reviews some of the principal sources of information about New York families which pertain to the entire state, or close to it. Regional and county resources are addressed in the individual county research guides. Those focused on particular types (e.g., newspapers, military records) are listed in the sections pertaining to those subjects. Space does not permit describing every repository and website in New York State, which the editors regret.

This section is organized as follows:

- Government Repositories and Libraries
- Repositories, Libraries, Museums, and Genealogical Societies
- University and College Libraries
- Online Providers of Information
- Lineage Societies

Government Repositories and Libraries

National Archives and Records Administration (NARA), Washington, DC

700 Pennsylvania Avenue, NW • Washington, DC 20408-0001
(202) 357-5000 • *archives.gov*

The NARA website provides a detailed orientation to records of major genealogical significance. These include, but are certainly not limited to:

- Census records. NARA hold original federal census records and have microfilm for public use, although other repositories have copies of the microfilm. See chapter 3, Census Records. The website provides information on identifying the reels of film for each available census year and how to get free access to online subscription census data onsite at NARA facilities.
- Ship Passenger Arrival Records. NARA data on microfilm generally range from 1820 to 1955; the records are arranged by port. The online catalog identifies appropriate reels.

There are *partial* indexes to New York arrivals records. The website, however, provides detailed information on published data and indexes, including online sources. Naturalization records for New York are *not* at NARA in Washington, DC. See below, NARA in New York City.

- Land Records. New York was not a public land state, and therefore NARA is not the ideal place to look for New York land records. See chapter 7, Land Records.
- Military Records. NARA's military records are very extensive; the website provides a detailed guide. An introduction is at *www.archives.gov/research/military/index.html*. Generally speaking, records created before 1912 are in Washington, DC, and records after that date are at the National Personnel Records Center in St. Louis, Missouri. Records exist for the Army, Navy, Coast Guard, and Marines. Confederate military records are also at NARA. For more details see chapter 8, Military Records.
- Passport Applications. Applications made before 1925 are at NARA.

National Archives at New York City (NARA-NYC)

Alexander Hamilton U.S. Customs House
One Bowling Green, 3rd Floor • New York, NY 10004
(866) 840-1752 • Email: newyork.archives@nara.gov
www.archives.gov/nyc

NARA-NYC is located at the U.S. Customs House, a historic and architectural landmark and well worth a visit whether research is an objective. The building also houses the National Museum of the American Indian (see *nmai.si.edu*). NARA-NYC facilities include a Welcome Center with exhibits, a Learning Center, and an ample and comfortable Research Center.

NARA-NYC holds federal agency and court records from New Jersey, New York, Puerto Rico, and the United States Virgin Islands dating from 1685 to the present; holdings include documents, photographs, maps, and drawings. The NARA-NYC website provides detailed finding aids for the collections in New York which include, but are certainly not limited, to:

- New York Passenger Arrival Records, 1820–1957; indexes 1820–1846 and 1897–1948. Records of the U.S. Customs Service (Record Group 36) includes microfilm series M237, Passenger Lists of Vessels Arriving at New York, New York, 1820–1897; and series M261, Index to Passenger Lists of Vessels Arriving at New York, New York, 1820–1846.
- Naturalization Records: Federal Courts (U.S. District and Circuit Courts) in New York, New Jersey, and Puerto Rico and federal, state, and local Courts in New York City, 1792–1906. This collection includes dexigraphs of local and state court records in addition to federal records.
- Naturalization Records for Clinton and Essex Counties, New York. An index to this collection may be accessed at *GermanGenealogyGroup.com* and *ItalianGen.org*.

NARA-NYC is one of ten repositories in New York State with a microfiche copy of the New York State Department of Health Vital Records Indexes. These indexes, covering all of New York State except New York City, are not available online. See chapter 2, Vital Records.

Researchers are advised to search the catalog in advance of a visit, as some holdings are stored offsite and require several days advance notice. A researcher card is necessary for access to original records. The facility provides free access to online resources including *Ancestry.com*, *Fold3.com*, *HeritageQuest*, and *ProQuest*.

New York City Municipal Archives (MUNI)

New York, NY • *nyc.gov/html/records/html/home/home.shtml*

MUNI, part of the Department of Records, preserves records of New York City government, including vital records. For a detailed description of MUNI's vital records holdings see chapter 2, Vital Records; for court record holdings, see chapter 5, Court Records; for a concise description of all of MUNI's holdings, see the introductory section to the boroughs of New York City in Part Two.

New York County Clerk, Division of Old Records

See chapter 5, Court Records and the Manhattan Borough Guide

New York State Archives (NYSA)

Cultural Education Center
222 Madison Avenue, Empire State Plaza • Albany, NY 12230
(518) 474-8955 • Email: archref@mail.nysed.gov
www.archives.nysed.gov

The NYSA is a division of the New York State Education Department. The holdings of the NYSA are extensive and include records relating to almost every aspect of New York history. Through a partnership with *Ancestry.com*, many of these records have been digitized. New York residents may view them for free on *Ancestry.com*; see the entry for *Ancestry.com* below for details. The online catalog, Excelsior, includes summary information on the holdings of the NYSA and of the New York State Library (NYSL). The NYSA website also features various guides, fact sheets, and finding aids organized by record type. *A Guide to Records in the New York State Archives* (1993) is available in printed form only, although much of its content is now online scattered across appropriate categories of records.

Those records that are most likely to be of interest to local history and genealogy researchers include but are certainly not limited to:

- Vital records indexes (as distinct from the records themselves) beginning in 1880–1881 for the entire state of New York, except New York City; for the cities of Albany, Buffalo, and Yonkers, marriage records begin in 1908 and birth and death records begin in 1914 (see chapter 2, Vital Records)
- New York State census records (some years have been digitized and are available on *Ancestry.com*)
- American Indian records including the 1845 Population Census of Indian Reservations (microfilm) and Indian Census and Annuity Rolls 1881–1950 (partly restricted)
- Summary war service records from the War of 1812 through World War I, including town and city registers of Civil War service, Civil War muster rolls abstracts, and cards summarizing Spanish-American War and World War I service. (Revolutionary War records were largely destroyed in the 1911 Capitol fire in Albany, but intact records are indexed on the NYSA website.) The NYSA offers a War Records Search Service.
- Court records including Court of Chancery (1704–1847), Supreme Court of Judicature (1797–1847), and probate records of the Prerogative Court (1664–1783) and the Court of Probates (1778–1823)
- Alien depositions of intent to become U.S. citizens, 1825–1913
- Land grants by the Colony and State of New York (1664–present) and applications for grants
- Manuscript maps from the eighteenth century to the present
- Tax Assessment Records of Real and Personal Estates, 1799–1804 (except New York City)
- Census of Inmates in Almshouses and Poorhouses, 1875–1921 (digitized by *Ancestry.com*)
- Prison and reformatory records including cards, case files, and registers from the nineteenth and twentieth centuries (many restricted)

In addition to original records, materials created by the Works Progress Administration (WPA) Historical Records Survey for materials outside New York City are kept at the NYSA.

New York State Library (NYSL)

Cultural Education Center

222 Madison Avenue, Empire State Plaza • Albany, NY 12230

(518) 474-5161 • *www.nysl.nysed.gov/research.htm*

The NYSL's local history and genealogy holdings encompass all of the United States, but its collection of materials from New York, New England, New Jersey, and Pennsylvania are particularly strong. The NYSL's online catalog, Excelsior, shared with the NYSA, can be searched by individual surnames and/or geographic locations, as well as by title, subject, and author. The website includes a guide to genealogy research resources at the NYSL (*www.nysl.nysed.gov/gengen.htm*). The NYSL provides onsite access to number of online databases and full text eJournals related to genealogy and local history (*www.nysl.nysed.gov/gate/esubject.htm*), and a page of links to various online information sources relevant to New York research and to general genealogical research (*www.nysl.nysed.gov/reference/generef.htm*).

The NYSL's Digital Collections consist of more than 65,000 documents and images. Historical materials in the collections date from the eighteenth century and include almanacs, books, broadsides, diaries, drawings, letters, manuscripts, illustrations, maps, records, newspapers, pamphlets, and photographs relating to Native Americans, colonial New York, the Revolutionary and Civil Wars, local history, New York State government, religious history, and women's history. The Digital Collections are accessible and searchable at *www.nysl.nysed.gov/scandocs*.

Holdings of the NYSL that are most likely to be of interest to local history and genealogy researchers include, but are not limited to:

- Census records on microfilm include federal census 1790–1930; New York state census, 1825–1925, though not every year is available for every county (see the NYSL website for details); New York Indian census 1886–1924 available through an onsite database
- City directories, telephone books, and county directories on microfiche/microfilm with card file index; see NYSL website for a complete list
- National Society Daughters of the American Revolution (DAR) Genealogical Records Committee (GRC) collections for New York including, Bible Records (1924–present, 266 volumes); Cemetery, Church, and Town Records (1926–present, 650 volumes); DAR Patriot Index; Family Histories (1979–present, 13 volumes); Genealogical Data: New Project (1960–present, 145 volumes); Graves of Revolutionary Soldiers in New York (1922–1955, 15 volumes); Lineage Books (1890–1921, 166 volumes)
- Family genealogies
- Local histories of counties, towns, and villages in New York, New England, and the mid-Atlantic states
- Maps including digitized Sanborn Insurance Maps, 1867–1970

- Extensive collection of newspapers on microfilm
- Reference books on genealogical methodology, genealogical sources, personal names, epitaphs, heraldry, peerage and royal houses, coats of arms, and flags
- Card file indexes to NYSL holdings including a Surname Index, Vital Records Index, Local History Index, New Project Genealogical Data Index, and Revolutionary War Soldiers Index

A significant resource accessible through the NYSL is the Historical Document Inventory (HDI) described at *www.nysl.nysed.gov/hdi.htm*. The HDI is the product of a survey of New York State manuscripts and archival materials, representing more than 2,500 public repositories (historical agencies, libraries, museums, and colleges and universities) that was conducted between 1978 and 1993 by the New York Historical Resources Center at Cornell University. The purpose of the survey was to create an easily useable statewide finding aid to research materials in New York. Cornell published the HDI as a series of individual county guides under the name *Guide to Historical Resources in [Name of County]*. These guides (sometime referred to as the "Red Books") are available in the reference section of the State Library and at many other libraries. The HDI can be accessed through Excelsior, the NYSL's online catalog. The instructions are at *www.nysl.nysed.gov/hdi.htm*.

New York State Department of Health (NYSDOH)

Departmental Headquarters: Corning Tower • Empire State Plaza
Albany, NY 12237 • *www.health.ny.gov/vital_records*
Walk-In Vital Records Service: 800 North Pearl Street
2nd Floor, Room 200 • Menands, NY 12204

The NYSDOH is the repository for New York State's vital records for births, marriages, and deaths for all of New York State except New York City. This department is the source for certified and uncertified copies of vital records. Generally the NYSDOH has birth and death (1881–present), marriage (1880–present), and divorce (1963–present) certificates. See chapter 2, Vital Records, for details and exceptions which can be complicated. Instructions for obtaining the certificates are on the NYSDOH website. The following repositories each hold a copy of the New York State vital records index (made available over the years by the state in accordance with their regulations), of which only a small part is available online:

- New York State Archives, Albany, Albany County
- Broome County Public Library, Binghamton, Broome County
- Steele Memorial Library, Elmira, Chemung County
- Buffalo & Erie County Public Library, Buffalo, Erie County
- Roswell P. Flower Memorial Library, Watertown, Jefferson County
- Rochester Public Library, Rochester, Monroe County
- National Archives at New York City, New York County (Manhattan)

- Onondaga County Public Library, Syracuse, Onondaga County
- Patchogue-Medford Library, Patchogue, Suffolk County
- Crandall Public Library, Glens Falls, Warren County

Repositories, Libraries, Museums, and Genealogical Societies

There are many dozens of genealogical and historical societies in New York State; a comprehensive listing of societies with links to their websites is available at *New York Family History. org*. Regional genealogical societies include the Central New York Genealogical Society (see below), the Capital District Genealogical Society (see the Albany County Guide in Part Two of this book), and the Western New York Genealogical Society (see the Erie County Guide).

Center for Jewish History (CJH)

15 West 16th Street • New York, NY 10011
(212) 294-8301 • *cjh.org*
- American Jewish Historical Society • *ajhs.org*
- American Sephardi Federation • *americansephardifederation.org*
- Leo Baeck Institute • *lbi.org*
- Yeshiva University Museum • *yumuseum.org*
- YIVO Institute for Jewish • *yivo.org*

The largest Jewish repository outside Israel, the CJH is home to the five constituent organizations above, as well as the Lillian Goldman Reading Room and the Ackman & Ziff Genealogy Institute. An online catalog, finding aids, and digital collections are available on their website, and researchers can search across the collections and access genealogical databases of all five partners. For a more detailed description, see the separate entries for the CJH and its resident organizations in chapter 14, Peoples of New York. The CJH also functions as a Family History Center and has a permanent collection of microfilm from the Family History Library (FHL); for details, see the FHL entry below.

Central New York Genealogical Society (CNYGS)

PO Box 104 • Colvin Station • Syracuse, NY 13205
Email: CNYGS@yahoo.com
http://rootsweb.ancestry.com/~nycnygs

Since 1961 the Society has produced *Tree Talks*, a quarterly journal featuring abstracts of original records (including census and church records); guides to genealogical research; and publication reviews. Special Collection County Packets include all the *Tree Talks* data that CNYGS has published on 49 counties. Indexes to these abstract packets have been compiled by Arthur C. M. Kelly and published by Kinship Books. Online name indexes (to *Tree Talks* articles 1961–2006/09) organized by county, are available on the society's website for Allegany, Chenango, Clinton, Delaware, Erie, Franklin, Greene, Hamilton, Madison, Orleans, St. Lawrence,

and Wyoming Counties. Name indexes to recent years of *Tree Talks* (2006–2013) are on the website, which also features the Society's Surname Project, an index of surnames currently being researched by its members; tax lists; cemetery lists; and guides to genealogy research in central New York by county. The County Packets, compilations of census records, and other source material featured in *Tree Talks* are for sale on the website.

Family History Library (FHL)

35 North West Temple Street • Salt Lake City, UT 84150-3400
(801) 240-2584 • *FamilySearch.org*

The FHL genealogical library in Salt Lake City is the largest of its kind in the world. Operated by FamilySearch, the genealogical division of the LDS Church, the library is free and open to the public. (See also the *FamilySearch.org* entry under the Online Providers of Information section in this chapter.)

The library contains extensive amounts of New York material in print, microform, and digital media which can be identified by place name and other criteria in the online catalog at *https://familysearch.org/catalog-search*. Family History Library Catalog records, and live links to full text, have recently been loaded into the *WorldCat.org* database. The FHL, in partnership with a consortium of organizations, has made available more than 150,000 text-searchable digital books in and out of copyright at *books.FamilySearch.org*.

Microfilm from the FHL may be ordered and used at Family History Centers (FHC) provided or authorized by the LDS Church. To locate a FHC in New York State and elsewhere, go to *https://familysearch.org/locations/centerlocator*. Not all of these are Mormon church facilities; some are libraries or repositories partnering with FamilySearch. In Manhattan, for example, the Center for Jewish History (CJH) functions like an FHC. Some centers maintain a permanent collection of film. The microfilm library at the CJH has more than 2,000 reels and is listed at *www.cjh.org/p/34#microloans*. The CJH collection is mostly European (eastern, western, and Russian) and is very strong in passenger lists. The FHC in Manhattan at Lincoln Center has a permanent collection of 3,000 reels that is listed at *www.nynyfhc.blogspot.com*.

Federation of Genealogical Societies (FGS)

PO Box 200940 • Austin, TX 78720-0940 • fgs.org

The FGS holds an annual conference with topics for individuals, as well as societies, sometimes including New York specific lectures. A number of New York societies are members of FGS.

Franklin D. Roosevelt Presidential Library and Museum

Hyde Park, NY • *fdrlibrary.marist.edu*

This is the nation's first presidential library and the only one located in New York State. See the Dutchess County Guide in Part Two for a description of its holdings.

Library of Congress (LOC)

Thomas Jefferson Building • 10 First Street SE

Washington, DC 20540 • (202) 707-8000 • *loc.gov*

The LOC is the largest library in the world. Needless to say, it includes large amounts of information of interest to New York researchers. The online catalog and guides to collections are comprehensive, but because of the sheer size of the LOC, the researcher cannot expect to zero in immediately on targeted material.

Two research tips:

1. The LOC website tends to steer the internet visitor to digitized material when actually the vast majority of LOC resources are not online.
2. The LOC website is very large, and navigation is not intuitive, and so it is helpful to keep a record of relevant URLs in order to find them again quickly.

The following list covers collections that contain significant amounts of genealogically-relevant New York material, but is far from exhaustive.

Selected Research Resources at the LOC

- Online catalog, searchable by author, title, keyword, family name, place name, etc. Focused searches, or searches using unusual terms or uncommon family names, can be fruitful in this very large catalog (*http://catalog.loc.gov*).
- Maps arranged by state and locality with detailed cataloging data: *www.loc.gov/topics/maps.php*. A large selection of New York maps is available online. The majority of maps at the LOC, however, are not online. Some topics within the map division that include New York maps are separately described on the LOC website, such as Railroad Maps (1828–1900); the Rochambeau Map Collection (1715–1795); Panoramic Maps (1860–2000).
- Local History and Genealogy: county and local histories; family histories and genealogies, published and unpublished; vertical files (with searchable online index); family and regional newsletters (with searchable online index). See *www.loc.gov/rr/genealogy* and *http://lcweb2.loc.gov/ammem/awhhtml/awgc1/genealogies.html*.
- Manuscripts: though rich in papers of U.S. presidents and people of historical prominence, the majority of papers are of individuals and families. Many of the manuscript collections have detailed finding aids which produce results in a search, which can be especially important for collections which are not digitized. This department is at *www.loc.gov/rr/mss*.

- Newspapers: for information about New York newspapers at the LOC, see chapter 12, Newspapers. Information on the LOC's vast newspaper collection is at *www.loc.gov/topics/content.php?cat=5*.
- Periodicals: this collection includes many New York town, city, and county directories, newsletters (such as the *New York Suffrage Newsletter*); and professional registers (such as medical registers), to name a few.
- Prints and Photographs: the collections of photographs contain thousands of images from New York State: *www.loc.gov/rr/print*. The photograph archive has its own online catalog; many images are digitized. The Guide Records page gives access to summary finding aids to collections of photographs: *www.loc.gov/pictures/collection/guide*. A collection called Groups of Images organizes photographs that are related: *www.loc.gov/pictures/collection/coll*. Some collections, containing New York images, are separately described, including, but not limited to: Panoramic Photographs of Cities Collection; Frances Benjamin Johnston (1864–1952) Collection (mostly buildings and open spaces); Harris and Ewing Collection (news photos and studio portraits); Carol M. Highsmith Archive (architecture); Gottscho-Schleisner Collection (architecture, with an emphasis on New York buildings)

Selected Additional Collections

- Rare Books and Special Collections is at *www.loc.gov/rr/rarebook*; the website has a list of specialized collections such as the African-American Pamphlet Collection 1822–1909 and the American Almanacs Collection (1809–present)
- American Folklife Center, mostly sound recordings
- Frederick Douglass Papers, *www.loc.gov/collection/frederick-douglass-papers*
- Civil War Collection of photos, prints, and drawings. *www.loc.gov/pictures/collection/civwar*
- Early Films of New York (1898–1906). The collection contains 45 films listed at *www.loc.gov/collection/early-films-of-new-york-1898-to-1906/about-this-collection*
- Lamb Studios Archive. The well-known New Jersey company, still in existence, produced stained glass windows for many churches, mausoleums, and schools, many in New York State. *www.loc.gov/pictures/collection/lamb*.
- The Historic American Buildings Survey (HABS), the Historic American Engineering Record (HAER), and the Historic American Landscapes Survey (HALS) contain mainly photographs and measured drawings: *www.loc.gov/pictures/collection/hh*

National Genealogical Society (NGS)

3108 Columbia Pike, Suite 300 • Arlington, VA 22204-4370

(703) 525-0050 • Email: ngs@ngsgenealogy.org • *ngsgenealogy.org*

The annual NGS Family History Conference features over 150 experts and scholars in the field as speakers, and usually includes a New York track sponsored by the NYG&B. Publications include the *National Genealogical Society Quarterly* (*NGSQ*), *NGS Magazine*, Laura Murphy DeGrazia's *NGS Research in the States Series: New York City, Long Island and Westchester County*, and the online "NGS Standards and Guidelines" for genealogy research, writing, and publication. The NGS Library Collection of family histories, local histories, and abstracts is held by the St. Louis Library (*slcl.org/genealogy*). The website has back issues of the *NGSQ*, 1912–present, *NGS Magazine*, 2005–present, and indexes. Members can access databases of Bible records and member ancestry records.

New England Historic Genealogical Society (NEHGS)

99–101 Newbury Street • Boston, MA 02116 • (617) 536-5740
americanancestors.org

While the society's main focus is on New England, it offers access to New York State material. This entry focuses on the NEHGS's website; however, the NEHGS is also a large and expanding repository and library. The society's library is in Boston, and its catalog is online at *http://library.nehgs.org*. The NEHGS's online databases include New York State collections and are accessible to members and subscribing libraries. The society's quarterly magazine, *American Ancestors*, regularly covers New York subjects, and the *New England Historical and Genealogical Register*, a distinguished scholarly quarterly, incorporates the *American Ancestors Journal* as an annual supplement that focuses on New York.

An up-to-date list of the NEHGS's New York material is on the website. Of particular interest to researchers of New York families on the society's website are:

- Articles on researching various subjects related to record groups, places, and ethnic groups.
- Digitized data, including the Eardeley collection of abstracts of New York probate material from the Brooklyn Historical Society's manuscript collection and the published index (widely available on paper, with brief abstracts) to Albany County Deeds, 1630–1894, which records 250,000 land transactions.
- Searchable publications, including the multivolume series entitled *Settlers of the Beekman Patent*, by Frank Doherty, and the issues of *New Netherland Connections*, published from 1996 to 2010, which focused on the Dutch colonial period (1624–1664) in New York and New Jersey.

New Netherland Research Center (NNRC)

Albany, NY • *newnetherlandinstitute.org*

See section on the Dutch in chapter 14, Peoples of New York.

New York Genealogical and Biographical Society (NYG&B)

36 West 44th Street, 7th Floor • New York, NY 10036-8105
(212) 755-8532 • Email: education@nygbs.org
NewYorkFamilyHistory.org

The NYG&B, founded in 1869, is the oldest and largest genealogical society in New York, and the only one that is statewide. The NYG&B publishes two quarterlies: the *New York Genealogical and Biographical Record*, a peer-reviewed scholarly journal of great distinction in continuous publication since 1870, and the *New York Researcher*, a magazine that provides helpful information of interest to researchers of New York family history. Subscriptions to both are benefits of membership. The Society has also published numerous books, including this one. Its blog gathers news items about resources pertinent to New York research.

The NYG&B is the co-founder (with the Central New York Genealogical Society) of the New York State Family History Conference, a statewide genealogical conference. The Society offers educational programs under the banner "New York Family History School," often in partnership with the New York Public Library (NYPL), NARA-NYC, and MUNI. The NYG&B's library and archival collections were donated to the NYPL; see the NYPL entry in this chapter.

The Society's website, *NewYorkFamilyHistory.org*, features numerous research aids written by subject-matter experts and an eLibrary with important data sets essential to anyone doing New York research. Among them are:

- The complete run from 1870 to the present of the *NYG&B Record*, which forms the largest single collection of published material on families that lived in New York. For more than 140 years, the *NYG&B Record* has published compiled genealogies; transcriptions of original records and other source material from throughout New York State; works that solve genealogical problems; and reviews of important scholarship in the field. A search engine, which covers more than 1,000,000 names, and indexes (to subjects, places, titles, and authors) assists readers in mining the rich body of information in the *NYG&B Record*.
- The complete run of the *New York Researcher* (formerly the *NYG&B Newsletter*)
- A large collection of transcribed records from churches, cemeteries, and other sources across New York State
- Digitized images and a fully searchable transcription of Manhattan's 17th ward of the 1855 census, that is not available elsewhere in print, online, or on microfilm
- American Bible Society Family Records Collection
- Full-text searchable books published by the NYG&B
- A large digital collection of church archives inventories and public records inventories from the WPA Historical Records Survey

New York Public Library (NYPL)

Steven A. Schwarzman Building • Fifth Avenue and 42nd Street
New York, NY 10018 • Contact information: *www.nypl.org/research-collections* • *nypl.org*

The NYPL, one of the great research libraries in the world, is a large and multifaceted institution. A complete description of the library is online at *nypl.org*. This section highlights the departments of the NYPL of greatest interest to genealogists. The NYPL also operates branch libraries in Manhattan, Staten Island, and the Bronx, where patrons can find access to online subscription databases and genealogical reference books. Some branch libraries contain specialized collections; for example, the Belmont Library in the Bronx contains a good collection relating to Italian history and culture. (The NYPL branches are in Manhattan, Staten Island, and the Bronx; the public libraries of Queens and Brooklyn are independently-operated systems.)

Except for the Library for the Performing Arts and the Schomburg Center, all departments described in this section are located in the Schwarzman building in Manhattan. The General Research Division, centered in the monumental Rose Reading Room, is not noted separately here. However, it holds open-shelf reference works and collections of importance to people researching family history. Other resources not separately noted here are the Microform Reading Room, the Photographs Collection, the Prints Collection, and the DeWitt Wallace Periodical Room.

The New York Genealogical and Biographical Society Collection

The New York Genealogical and Biographical Society donated its library and archival collections to the New York Public Library in 2008. The NYG&B collections have been integrated into the NYPL catalog and retain "NYGB" as part of their call numbers. Books and microfilm are in the Irma and Paul Milstein Division of United States History, Local History and Genealogy; maps are in the Lionel Pincus and Princess Firyal Map Division. Archival material donated by the NYG&B—including research papers; family, locale, and subject files; records; and transcriptions—may be found both in the Manuscript Division and the Milstein Division. A directory of finding aids created by NYPL staff to the NYG&B archival collections is on the NYG&B website *New York Family History.org*.

The Irma and Paul Milstein Division of United States History, Local History and Genealogy
(212) 930-0828 • *www.nypl.org/milstein*

The Milstein Division houses one of the country's premier genealogical and historical collections. Its holdings document all periods in American history, and from all levels from local to national. Its genealogical holdings include the entire United States and some foreign countries, especially the British Isles, Ireland, Western Europe, Canada, and Latin America. Its reading room includes the most heavily used reference volumes and periodicals on open shelves.

The collection ranges from published books and periodicals to unpublished transcriptions of records and manuscripts on individual families. It also holds visual resources, including photographs and postcards. Notable among these collections is *Photographic Views of New York City, 1870s–1970s*, which is searchable by street name and viewable on the NYPL Digital Gallery. Other collections hold local history ephemera, including pamphlets, leaflets, and broadsides; and extensive microfilm collections, including census, directories, and vital records indexes, which are kept in its Microfilm Room.

Holdings of the Division are searchable through the library's online catalog. Use of the "Classic Catalog" is recommended. Free access to subscription databases including *Ancestry.com* (Library Edition), *AmericanAncestors.org*, *Fold3.com*, *HeritageQuest*, *ProQuest*, *America's Historical Newspapers*, the *New York Times*, and the *Washington Post* is available on site. (Note that not all data offered by these companies may be available through the NYPL.) Researchers may also submit research requests through email and letter; more extensive research requests are accepted for a fee by the NYPL Research Services. The Division's page on the NYPL website includes extensive resources, including guides to researching genealogy at the Library and on the internet.

Manuscripts and Archives Division
(212) 930-0801
www.nypl.org/locations/schwarzman/manuscripts-division

The Division's holdings, measured in miles of shelving, include paper documents, photographs, recordings, and video. It includes individual and family papers from New York and the region, along with collections covering the American Revolution, the New Nation period, and the Civil War. It houses the papers of the Schuyler family, Fiorello H. LaGuardia, Robert Moses, the Emigrant Savings Bank, and the enormous United States Sanitary Commission collection, to name only five. The Division also contains the records of major New York publishers including Farrar, Strauss & Giroux, Alfred A. Knopf, and the *New Yorker*. The Division now includes significant collections of family papers donated by the NYG&B. A special archives search engine for the holdings of this division is online at *archives.nypl.org*. Visiting the Division requires registration.

Lionel Pincus and Princess Firyal Map Division
(212) 930-0587
www.nypl.org/locations/schwarzman/map-division

This collection of more than 400,000 maps and 20,000 books is especially strong in New York State and New York City material. A guide to the thousands of maps which have been digitized is on the Division's main webpage. The antiquarian maps collection includes many early maps of New Netherland, colonial New York, and early New York State. Its architecturally splendid reading room offers reference books about maps on open shelves.

Maps are found in the library's main catalog at *http://catalog. nypl.org*. Many digitized maps are available in the Division's "Digital Gallery." An online guide to map holdings is at *www. nypl.org/node/80186*. The Division does advanced work in comparing historical and contemporary maps digitally, benefiting family history researchers. See *http://maps.nypl. org/warper*. See chapter 7, Land Records and Maps, for more information about maps at the NYPL.

Dorot Jewish Division

(212) 930-0601

www.nypl.org/locations/schwarzman/jewish-division

This Division collects globally and is especially strong in Jewish history in the United States and New York City during the late-nineteenth and early-twentieth centuries, when immigrants came in large numbers. The Division has a notable collection of Jewish newspaper backfiles and immigrant association publications.

Schomburg Center for Research in Black Culture (SCRBC)

515 Malcolm X Boulevard • New York, NY 10037-1801

(917) 275-6975 • *www.nypl.org/locations/schomburg*

A description of the SCRBC can be found in the African American section of chapter 14, Peoples of New York. The divisions of this center are:

- The Research and Reference Division holds books, microforms, serial publications, and black newspapers.
- The Manuscripts, Archives, and Rare Books Division holds rare books, manuscripts, and sheet music.
- The Art and Artifacts Division holds painting, sculpture, textiles, and works on paper, especially works from the period of the Harlem Renaissance and the Great Depression.
- The Photographs and Prints Division holds images of black leaders in all fields, black life in Africa and the period of enslavement in North America, and work by prominent photographers.
- The Moving Image and Recorded Sound Division holds recorded music, oral history, moving pictures, and radio broadcasts.

Library for the Performing Arts (LPA)

Dorothy and Lewis B. Cullman Center

40 Lincoln Center Plaza • New York, NY 10023

(917) 275-6975 • *www.nypl.org/locations/lpa*

The LPA holds collections about music, dance, and theater, and works of individuals, companies, or groups, in all media, both published and unpublished. Resources include rare books and manuscripts; photographs; sheet music; audio, video and film recordings; and ephemera and memorabilia of all kinds.

Rare Books Division

(212) 642-0110

www.nypl.org/locations/schwarzman/brooke-russell-astor-reading-room/rare-books-division

The collection includes Americana, especially books printed before 1801, broadsides, and American newspapers printed before 1865. Visitors to this division must register onsite or online.

New York State Historical Association (NYSHA)

State Route 80 • Cooperstown, NY 13326 • (607) 547-1470

Email: info@nysha.org (general information) or library@nysha.org (Research Library) • *nysha.org*

NYSHA, not to be confused with the New-York Historical Society, was founded in 1899 and is nongovernmental. It is an educational organization that offers exhibitions, programs, and publications, among other activities. The association's library has significant historical and genealogical collections, including New York State genealogies and histories; books and periodicals; business, assessment, cemetery, census, school, poorhouse, military, and church records; directories, atlases, and biographical reviews. The Local History Collection, focusing on central New York counties, includes county and town histories, city and county directories, newspapers, maps and atlases, books, church and town records, diaries, and postcards. Special collections, consisting of rare books and manuscripts, account books, diaries, maps, broadsides, and ephemera, include many family papers and images, as well as nearly 1,000 family files pertaining to genealogy and local history. It also holds more than 200,000 photos of everyday life in the region from the mid-nineteenth to the mid-twentieth centuries.

The library's online catalog is at *http://pathfinder.nysha.org/ search~S2*. Also online are detailed bibliographies for Delaware, Greene, Otsego, and Schoharie counties arranged by community, and a detailed bibliography about the Erie Canal. The library holds a newspaper collection from Delaware and Otsego counties, with a very detailed online inventory.

New-York Historical Society (N-YHS)

170 Central Park West • New York, NY 10024 • (212) 873-3400

Email: info@nyhistory.org (general information) or reference@nyhistory.org (research inquiries) • *nyhistory.org*

The N-YHS was founded in 1804, and is a museum of history, a museum of art, an educational institution, and a research library. (In the eighteenth and early-nineteenth centuries, "New York" was usually written with a hyphen, and that form is preserved in the society's name.) The Patricia D. Klingenstein Library is organized into four parts, which are clearly described on the website at *www.nyhistory.org/library/collections*.

- Printed Collection (books, pamphlets, newspapers, broadsides, maps and atlases)
- Manuscript Collection (family papers, organizational records, and business records)
- Graphic Collection (prints, photographs, and architectural drawings)
- Digital Collections

Holdings particularly relevant to genealogical researchers include business records, New York City directories, genealogies, local histories, maps, New York military records, newspapers (print and microfilm), photographs, probate abstracts, records of religious institutions and charitable organizations, and records of slavery in New York City.

The online library catalog, Bobcat, permits searches of the N-YHS collection, and, if desired, also the collections of the libraries of New York University, The New School University, Cooper Union, Brooklyn Historical Society, and New York School of Interior Design.

The N-YHS museum collections are searchable on the website, which also gives access to some digitized collections.

The Gilder Lehrman Institute of American History is located at the N-YHS and has its own website (*gilderlehrman.org*). It offers a searchable archive of historical documents, many of which are relevant to New York family history research.

New York State Military Museum and Veterans Research Center

Saratoga Springs, NY • *dmna.state.ny.us/historic/mil-hist.htm*

See chapter 8, Military Records, for a description of the Center's resources.

University and College Libraries
City University of New York (CUNY)

cuny.edu

The CUNY network of colleges extends over 20 campuses across the five boroughs and includes more than 21 libraries. Collections of particular genealogical interest are noted in the relevant subject and borough guide bibliographies and in the listing Citywide Repositories and Resources for New York City in Part Two.

Columbia University Libraries

535 West 114th Street, M.C. 1127 • New York, NY 10027
(212) 854-5590 • *library.columbia.edu*

The Columbia University library system, national and international in scope, includes 22 libraries. These are likely to be of most interest to genealogists:

Rare Book & Manuscript Library (RBML)

Butler Library • 535 West 114th St. • New York, NY 10027
(212) 854-5590 • Email: rbml@libraries.cul.columbia.edu
library.columbia.edu/locations/rbml.html

The collection is huge, incorporating printed books and fourteen miles of manuscripts, personal papers, and records. Of particular interest to family historians are newspapers from New York State, 1725 to the present; Columbia University Archives, containing documents regarding former students and faculty; and the online Archival Collections Portal, which provides access to descriptions and finding aids for collections including personal papers, diaries, institutional records, organizational records, and corporate archives. The RBML's webpages provides links to finding aids for archival collections, including an online Guide to New York City Documents.

Columbia Center for Oral History (CCOH)

801 Butler Library • 535 West 114th Street
New York, NY 10027 • (212) 854-7309
Email: oralhist@libraries.cul.columbia.edu
libraries.columbia.edu/locations/ccoh.html

CCOH's archive of recorded history, with over 8,000 interviews, is one of the world's largest. Most interviews have been transcribed. The archive has its own search engine for oral and written records in this library.

Avery Architectural & Fine Arts Library

300 Avery Hall • 1172 Amsterdam Avenue
New York, NY 10027 • (212) 854-619
Email: avery@libraries.cul.columbia.edu
library.columbia.edu/locations/avery

The library, international in scope, includes printed matter on architecture, historic preservation, art history, city planning, and real estate; maps and atlases of New York City and other places, including many which are digitized; and a very large architectural archive including drawings, blueprints, photographs, and correspondence, including a collection on the New York State Capitol (1866–1870). The Old York Library (a collection of 10,000 books, 3,000 photographs, 20,000 postcards, and assorted maps and pamphlets related to New York City, collected by real estate developer Seymour Durst) came to the Avery Library in 2012.

Burke Library at Union Theological Seminary

Union Theological Seminary • 3041 Broadway
New York, NY 10027 • (212) 851-5606
Email: burke@libraries.cul.columbia.edu
libraries.columbia.edu/locations/burke.html

One of the largest theological libraries in North America, Burke's holdings include material about individuals who have participated in, or influenced, theological education, ministry, and history. The Library also holds personal papers and institutional records.

Cornell University Libraries

Ithaca, NY 14853 • (607) 255-4144 • *cornell.edu/libraries*

The website offers a guide for genealogists at *http://olinuris.lib rary.cornell.edu/ref/genpage.htm*, and a comprehensive, detailed, and easy-to-navigate guide to its extensive manuscripts and rare books collections at *http://rmc.library.cornell.edu*. Most of Cornell University's genealogical material can be accessed through the online catalog. Holdings include genealogies, business papers, family papers, histories, bibliographies, censuses, city directories, colonial and state records, maps and atlases, newspapers, parish, and other local registers.

Of particular interest is a large collection of religious records from western New York State. These include records of several hundred churches in upstate New York. A description of this collection is at *http://rmc.library.cornell.edu/eguides/lists/churchlist1.htm* and *http://rmc.library.cornell.edu/eguides/lists/churchlist2.htm*. See the sections on Presbyterians and Congregationalists in chapter 15, Religious Records, for examples of church records held at Cornell.

The regional collection of the Division of Rare and Manuscript Collections documents the history of upstate New York. Holdings include family papers and genealogies; business, church, and school records; cemetery inscriptions; death and marriage notices; land holdings; alumni records; photographs, broadsides, and maps. Records relating to the Holland Land Company can be found there. See chapter 7, Land Records.

The Cornell Library also offers material that has been digitized. A description of the Historical Monographs Collection is at *http://ebooks.library.cornell.edu/c/cdl*. Within that collection is a section called "New York State Historical Literature." (Titles can be ordered from *Amazon.com* by print-on-demand—an interesting feature of this collection.) Titles may be browsed by region at *http://ebooks.library.cornell.edu/n/nys/browse/geography/index.html*.

New York University (NYU) Libraries

Elmer Holmes Bobst Library • New York University

70 Washington Square South • New York, NY 10012

(212) 998-2500 • *library.nyu.edu*

NYU operates a network of ten libraries, with the Elmer Holmes Bobst Library most likely to be of most interest to family historians. Special collections (described at *http://library.nyu.edu/collections/archives.html*) at the Bobst Library include the Fales Library, with archives of various people, places, and communities significant in the history and culture of New York City; the NYU Archives and the archives of the New York Polytechnic School of Engineering; and the Tamiment Library and Robert F. Wagner Labor Archives.

The Tamiment Library holds some of the most important collections in the United States relating to labor and social history, the history of the Left, women's history, and immigrant history. Tamiment preserves the history of working-class New York through its collection of archival records and publications of neighborhood associations, fraternal and ethnic societies, political organizations, and labor unions. It includes a collection pertaining to the Irish in America.

In 2008 Tamiment acquired the Leo Hershkowitz Collection of New York City historical documents. Of note are a collection of Judaica—early records of B'nai Jeshurun synagogue, estate records, property inventories, and business records documenting the activities of eighteenth and nineteenth-century Jewish merchants; Coroner's inquest records, many relating to the deaths of African American freedmen; and records of the New York State Supreme Court, mid-nineteenth to twentieth century.

State University of New York (SUNY)

The SUNY system (*suny.edu*) includes 64 campuses enrolling half a million students. See table 1 for research facilities of greatest interest to genealogists. Its special collections are referenced in other parts of this book, as outlined in the table.

Table 1: Selected SUNY Campuses		
Campus Libraries at:	**Unique Strengths:**	**Referenced In:**
SUNY Albany	Modern Political Archive (state government); German and Jewish Intellectual Émigré collection	Albany County Chapter 14, German Chapter 14, Jewish
SUNY Binghamton	Local history	Broome County
SUNY Buffalo	Jewish Buffalo Archives Project	Erie and Niagara counties Chapter 14, Jewish
SUNY Fredonia	Records of the Holland Land Company	Chautauqua and Cattaraugus counties Chapter 7, Land Records
SUNY Geneseo	Genesee Valley Historical Collection; records of the Phelps and Gorham Purchase	Livingston County Chapter 7, Land Records
SUNY Stony Brook	Local history	Nassau and Suffolk counties

Syracuse University Library

Bird Library • 222 Waverly Avenue • Syracuse, NY 13244
(315) 443-2093 • Email: libref@syr.edu • *library.syr.edu*

The special collections contain material about the history of upstate New York including central New York, the Mohawk Valley, the Adirondacks, and the Thousand Island region. The collection features newspapers, business records, diaries, pamphlets, serials, broadsides, maps, and ephemera. It also contains the archive of Genesee College, which no longer exists.

Vassar College Libraries

Archives & Special Collections • 124 Raymond Avenue
Poughkeepsie, NY 12604-0020 • (845) 437-5799
Email: spcoll@vassar.edu • *specialcollections.vassar.edu*

Vassar College was founded in 1861. This library is strong in local history, family papers, the papers of hundreds of people connected with Vassar College, and particularly the history of women. The digital archive offers selections from the collection and all of the college's newspapers since 1872.

Online Providers of Information

Ancestry.com

Most of the records on *Ancestry.com* are available only to individual subscribers and institutional subscribers (such as public libraries), and constitute a list of New York material too long to provide here. Online users can sort the various databases a number of ways, including by county.

Through a partnership with *Ancestry.com* and the NYSA, several large collections of New York State records have been digitized and may be viewed for free by New York State residents on *Ancestry.com*. A New York State zip code is required to register for a free account. The portal to free New York records on *Ancestry.com* is easily accessed through a direct link on the homepage of *NewYorkFamilyHistory.org*; it can also be reached through the NYSA website at *www.archives.nysed.gov*. New York material includes, but is by no means limited to:

- New York state census, various years
- Menands, New York, Albany Rural Cemetery Burial Cards 1791–2011
- New York Marriages 1600–1785
- New York Military Equipment Claims, War of 1812
- New York, Census of Inmates in Almshouses and Poorhouses 1830–1920
- New York, Town Clerks' Registers of Men Who Served in the Civil War ca. 1861–1865
- New York, World War I Veterans' Service Data 1913–1919
- New York, World War II Enlisted Men Cards 1940–1945
- Salina, New York, Records 1805–1969

In 2014 *Ancestry.com* added the indexes (not the records themselves) for New York City vital records at MUNI; these indexes were created by volunteers from the Italian Genealogical Group and the German Genealogy Group, and are also online elsewhere. Once a vital record is identified, it can be ordered from MUNI. See chapter 2, Vital Records.

CastleGarden.org

Castle Garden (now Castle Clinton National Monument) is in lower Manhattan. From 1855 to 1890 it was a state-run immigration center, processing eleven million people. The website offers information about individuals who passed through Castle Garden. Steve Morse offers a one-step search at *http://stevemorse.org/ellis/cg.htm*. See chapter 4, Immigration, Migration, and Naturalization.

Cyndi's List

CyndisList.com

Cyndi's List is a free website that categorizes online family history sources and provides links to information that exists on the internet, including both free and fee-based sites. The New York category offers researchers over 5,000 links to online sources of New York material.

FamilySearch

FamilySearch.org

FamilySearch is one of the largest, fastest growing, and most wide-ranging genealogical online databases in the world, and is free. The New York Wiki (*http://familysearch.org/learn/wiki/en/New_York_Introduction*) provides information on genealogical records kept by FamilySearch and by other repositories, as well as bibliographies and links to other sources.

Guides to researching New York places and topics are online in the Wiki section. These guides cover a very broad range of subjects to varying degrees of completeness.

The catalog of the FHL is also accessible through this website. See the entry for the FHL earlier in this chapter.

Online records for New York include immigration and naturalization, the New York state census, probate records (at least some for nearly all counties), church records, military records, land records, and vital records. It is best to explore the New York online records frequently to see what is added, and to subscribe to the NYG&B eNews and newsletters which regularly report additions to FamilySearch. These include Dick Eastman's popular blog at *blog.eogn.com* (free) and the e-zine of *Avotaynu.com* (subscription), to name two.

To see the New York online data in one place, click on "search" from the homepage, then click on the United States on the map and select "New York." There are several dozen data sets on *FamilySearch.org*. The larger ones include, for example:

- New York Passenger and Crew Lists 1909; 1925–1957 (NARA)
- New York, Passenger Lists 1820–1891 (NARA)
- Ellis Island Passenger Arrival Lists, 1892–1924 (NARA)

- New York Probate Records (extending over four centuries)
- New York State Census (1855–1925)
- United States Famine Irish Passenger Index, 1846–1851 (NARA)
- Naturalizations from New York County Courts
- New York Land Records (extending over four centuries)

Most collections on *FamilySearch.org* are indexed and therefore searchable by name or other criteria. Unindexed collections may be browsed. Large, browsable collections segmented by county include New York, Land Records, 1630–1975; New York, Probate Records, 1629–1971; various church and naturalization records; and a passenger list index.

Findmypast
findmypast.com

This very fast-growing website contains a significant amount of United States genealogical information, including United States federal census, passenger lists, military records, and newspapers, including New York newspapers. The PERiodical Source Index (PERSI) has 2.5 million entries from historical and genealogical publications. An important project is underway to link full-text articles to the index entries, including articles from the *NYG&B Record*. *Findmypast.com* requires a subscription, or payment per record. The website is part of a network of data sources that is located in the United Kingdom and provides vast amounts of data of particular interest to people researching immigrants from the British Isles. In 2014 Findmypast acquired Mocavo (see separate listing).

Fold3
Fold3.com

This site (owned by *Ancestry.com* and once known as *Footnote.com*) is an online database of American military records covering all states, and is available to individual and institutional subscribers. Popular datasets include Revolutionary War Service Records, Revolutionary War Pension Records, War of 1812 Pension Files, Civil War Widows Pensions, and registration data for both World Wars. There is some non-military material on this site, including city directories for Brooklyn (1862–1913), Buffalo (1828, 1861–1923), New York City (1786–1922), and Rochester (1861–1889). Selected databases are free to non-subscribers.

German Genealogy Group and Italian Genealogical Group
GermanGenealogyGroup.com • *ItalianGen.org*

These websites, created by volunteers assembled by the German Genealogy Group (Kings Park, New York) and the Italian Genealogical Group (Bethpage, New York), offer indexes to large collections of records. (See the sections on Germans and Italians in chapter 14, Peoples of New York.) Both organizations are membership organizations, but the indexes are free to nonmembers. Some indexes to vital records created by these two groups are also available on *Ancestry.com*. Data offered expands

regularly and verified corrections are rapidly incorporated by the volunteers. A complete list and descriptions of each resource are online. Most indexes are on both sites, and each site has unique offerings. At present, indexes held in common include, but are not limited to:

- Births, marriages, and deaths for the pre-1898 cities of New York and Brooklyn and other municipalities of Kings and Queens counties, and for the five boroughs of New York City after the modern city was organized in 1898; see chapter 2, Vital Records
- Naturalizations at NARA-NYC. And local courts of Nassau, Suffolk, and Westchester counties and local New York City courts; see chapter 4, Immigration, Migration, and Naturalization
- Fresh Pond Crematory and Columbarium, Queens County, beginning in 1884; see chapter 9, Cemetery Records
- Alien statements from the Selective Service System
- Veteran discharge records from Nassau and Suffolk counties (1924–2005)

The German Genealogy Group has indexes to various cemetery records and church records, including some Catholic parishes, as well as information about German family history. The Italian Genealogical Group offers articles from its newsletters relating to Italian genealogy.

HeritageQuest
HeritageQuestOnline.com

This subscription database includes the federal census; full text searchable books and serial publications including many New York titles; data from the records of the Freedman's Bank, which existed from 1865 to1874 and had a branch in New York City; and Revolutionary War pension records. PERSI (see *findmypast.com*) is available on this site, but is not the current version.

Italian Genealogical Group
See above, German Genealogy Group and Italian Genealogical Group.

Mocavo
Mocavo.com

This site offers free access to large amounts of highly unusual books, directories, yearbooks, military records, local histories and the like, plus some genealogical services. An enormous amount of material is offered from New York. A subscription provides additional benefits. In 2014 this site was acquired by Findmypast (see separate listing).

MyHeritage
MyHeritage.com

MyHeritage has become one of the largest commercial data providers in the genealogical world, with an emphasis on social networking and sharing family trees. The company's roots are in Europe and Israel. Recently it became a partner with FamilySearch to digitize records from the Family History Library, as did *Ancestry.com*. Little New York-specific information is on this website, other than the federal census, but that will likely change.

New Horizons Genealogy

newhorizonsgenealogicalservices.com

This website provides a miscellaneous collection of transcribed data and links, much of which pertains to New York.

New York Genealogy

newyork-genealogy.com

This free website offers an extensive list of links to data arranged by county and then by town. It does not offer any data on the site itself. Links connect to many familiar sources of information such as USGenWeb, the FHL, Find a Grave, and *Ancestry.com*. The benefit of the site is that the links are sorted by place, and some obscure sources are included among those which are well known.

New York Heritage Digital Collections

nyheritage.org

New York Heritage is supported by the NY 3Rs Association, Inc. (*ny3rs.org*) and is part of the New York State Board of Regent's New York Digital Collection Initiative. This site is experimental, but at present provides the researcher with access to a range of digital material about New York history and culture from more than 200 participating libraries, historical societies, and cultural organizations throughout New York State.

New York History Blog

newyorkhistoryblog.org

The New York History Blog posts news and articles about subjects related to New York history, as well as announcements about programs, conferences, books, and exhibitions.

New York History Net

NYHistory.com

This private site, operated by an individual, is an excellent collection of links to sources of information about New York history, including links to many libraries and repositories some of which are not included in this book.

New York Roots and Genealogical Trails

NewYorkRoots.org • GenealogyTrails.com/ny

These sites offer small, organized collections of genealogical source material that varies in depth and range from topic to topic.

NYCnuts.net—New York City Attractions—New York City Genealogy

NYCnuts.net

This commercial website contains a vast number of links to New York genealogical sources of all types, particularly New York City.

One-Step Webpages

SteveMorse.org

This website provides accelerated access to records that might require multi-step searches; the applications are called "One-Step Webpages." The list of One-Step applications is a long one. The following list covers New York material searchable through this site. New York material is not limited to this list.

- Ellis Island passengers, manifests, ship lists
- Castle Garden passengers, manifests, ship lists
- Searching Ellis Island and Castle Garden combined
- NARA and FHL film numbers for New York ship arrivals; film numbers for NYC vital records
- Canadian border crossings
- Enumeration Districts in large cities (U.S. Census)
- Assembly District/Election Districts for selected New York State censuses
- New York naturalization records
- New York City birth and death records
- New York City bride and groom indexes
- Long Island marriage index

Online Searchable Death Indexes, Records & Obituaries

deathindexes.com

This site, maintained as a service by an individual, aggregates links to death-related records for the entire country. There are extensive links for New York State and New York City (separate webpages for each); the New York State material is arranged by county and includes cemetery listings and some probate-related material. Other links relate to naturalizations, the New York State census, passenger lists, and New York data on *Ancestry.com*. Most of these links appear elsewhere in this book.

Rootsweb

rootsweb.ancestry.com

Rootsweb is a free genealogical community on a site owned by *Ancestry.com*. New York material is found throughout the site. Searching takes patience but can be amply rewarded.

Miscellaneous information has been posted on USGenWeb (*usgwarchives.org*) by individuals. The New York page is at *http://usgwarchives.net/ny/nyfiles.htm*.

The easiest way to find county-specific sites is to search NYGenWeb [county name]. These sites are managed by volunteers, and the quality varies widely. Examples of their content include transcriptions of local records, digitized maps of the towns or the county, and digitized county and town histories.

Listed below are examples of New York material found on this large and rambling website.

- Websites hosted by Rootsweb related to New York, *www.rootsweb.ancestry.com/~websites/usa/newyork.html*
- The Northern New York Tombstone Transcription Project, covering Clinton, Essex, and Franklin counties at *http://freepages.genealogy.rootsweb.ancestry.com/~frgen/index.htm*
- The New York Tombstone Transcription Project covering all counties is at *www.usgwtombstones.org/newyork/newyork.html*
- Data relevant to New Netherland is at *www.rootsweb.ancestry.com/~nycoloni*

Sampubco

Sampubco.com

This is a commercial site offering genealogical data for many states. New York data is offered in these categories: wills, guardianships, naturalizations, letters of administration, letters testamentary, surrogate's records and probate files, and cemetery burials. In each category, the data is sorted by county. Searching the indexes is free, but obtaining the records themselves requires payment.

Statue of Liberty-Ellis Island Foundation (SOLEIF)

libertyellisfoundation.org

The website of the Statue of Liberty-Ellis Island Foundation allows researchers to look for names of immigrants with a simple or advanced search. Twenty-two million passengers came through Ellis Island between 1892 and 1924, so this database is huge. (Ellis Island passengers may also be searched at *FamilySearch.org*.) Steve Morse offers a one-step search at *http://stevemorse.org/ellis/cg.htm*.

The database recently expanded to cover the years 1925 to 1957, adding about forty million records. This added about three million immigrants, and the rest Americans returning from visits to places outside the United States including heavily visited vacation destinations.

Tourists can visit—by boat—the remarkable American Family Immigration History Center and the Ellis Island Immigration Museum for a hands-on experience of Ellis Island and its database.

USGenNet

USGenNet.org

This is a hosting service for websites and for miscellaneous data posted by individuals.

- New York websites: *www.usgennet.org/search/ny.html*
- New York data: *www.us-data.org/ny*

4getmenotancestry.com

This website contains the archived radio interviews on "The Forget-Me-Not Hour" originating in the Hudson River Valley and hosted by Jane E. Wilcox. Genealogical subjects include ethnic topics, church records, land records, New York history, local archives, historic places, reports from genealogical conferences, and many others. The program archive is at *www.blogtalkradio.com/janeewilcox*.

Lineage Societies

Researchers may find lineage societies to be important resources even if membership is not sought. Many have libraries and websites that are available to nonmembers. There are hundreds of lineage societies. (For a list, see *hereditary.us*.) A short list of societies rooted in New York is on the website of the NYG&B at *http://newyorkfamilyhistory.org/research-discover/research-tools/selected-hereditary-lineage-societies*. Some societies are mainly social or charitable in nature and are not included in this chapter.

Colonial Dames

There are three organizations calling themselves *Colonial Dames*: the National Society of Colonial Dames, the Colonial Dames of America, and the National Society Colonial Dames XVII Century. The first two of these have national headquarters facilities in New York City. The third is located in Washington, DC and has chapters in New York State.

The National Society of Colonial Dames (NSCD)

215 East 71st Street • New York, NY 10021 • (212) 744-3572
Email: info@nscdny.org • *nscda.org* (National site)
nscdny.org (New York site)

The NSCD is a lineage society for women who descend from leaders in the colonial period. Established in 1891, it collects and preserves materials from American history and promotes education and patriotism. The New York chapter houses a genealogical and historical library. The *Catalog of the Genealogical and Historical Library of the National Society of Colonial Dames in the State of New York* was published by the society in 1912 and reprinted in 1971 (available on Google Books). References to data about the National Society of Colonial Dames and its members and their lineages are searchable in the FHL catalog (*FamilySearch.org*). The website of the New York chapter (*nscdny.org*) does not offer genealogical data except for short biographies of Colonial era ancestors. The website of the national organization *nscda.org* features a useful "Ancestor Bibliography Register," with bibliographies for hundreds of colonial ancestors, arranged by surname.

Colonial Dames of America (CDA)

Mount Vernon Hotel Museum & Garden • 421 East 61st Street
New York, NY 10065 • (212) 838-6878 • *cdany.org*

The CDA, founded in 1890, is a society of women whose ancestors were leaders in colonial America. The organization advocates for education and historic preservation. The CDA owns and operates the Mount Vernon Hotel Museum & Garden (formerly known as the Abigail Adams Smith Museum) in New York City. That facility is both the national headquarters and the home of the New York chapter.

National Society Colonial Dames XVII Century

1300 New Hampshire Avenue, NW • Washington, DC 20036-1502
(202) 293-1700 • *colonialdames17c.org*

As its name implies, the members trace their lineages to the seventeenth century. The Washington headquarters has a library which nonmembers may use. The website has contact information for the state chapters.

DAR

See below, National Society Daughters of the American Revolution (NSDAR).

Daughters of the Cincinnati

20 West 44th Street #508 • New York, NY 10036 • (212) 991-9945
office@daughters1894.org • *daughters1894.org*

The Daughters of the Cincinnati, founded in 1894, is a membership organization for women descended from the officers who served in the Continental Army during the Revolutionary War. The website offers a roster of soldiers with their ranks and home states who may be represented by members. See Society of the Cincinnati below.

Holland Society of New York

20 West 44th Street, 5th Floor • New York, NY 10036
(212) 758-1675 • Email: info@hollandsociety.org
hollandsociety.org

The Holland Society is an important resource for documents relating to early Dutch communities in New York and New Jersey. Membership in the Holland Society is open to men who descend in a direct male line from a settler of New Netherland; others interested in the purposes of the Society may affiliate as "Friends." Founded in 1885, the Society has published many volumes relating to New Netherland, New York, and New Jersey history and genealogy, and its quarterly, *de Halve Maen*, is the leading scholarly journal devoted to New Netherland and Dutch-American history.

The Holland Society has also supported publication of the New Netherland Documents and New York Historical Manuscripts series. The library, open to nonmembers, includes an impressive collection of histories and genealogies. The website offers a searchable catalog and a surname list of many New Netherland families. See the section on the Dutch in Chapter 14, Peoples of New York.

Huguenot Society of America (HSA)

20 West 44th Street, Suite 510 • New York, NY 10036
(212) 755-0592 • Email: hugsoc@verizon.net
huguenotsocietyofamerica.org

The Society was founded in 1883 to keep alive the memory of the Huguenot settlers in America and to stand for religious freedom. The library at its headquarters location is open by appointment. The catalog is not online. The website offers a list of Huguenot ancestors from whom members have descended. See also the listing for the National Huguenot Society in the section on the French, in chapter 14, Peoples of New York.

National Society Daughters of the American Revolution (NSDAR)

1776 D St. NW • Washington, DC 20006-5303 • (202) 628-1776
dar.org • *nydar.org*

Founded in 1890, the DAR is a membership organization for women who are descended from a patriot who served the American cause in the Revolution. There are almost 200,000 members. The Washington, DC, headquarters houses one of the leading genealogical libraries in America. Information about the library's resources is at *dar.org/library*. The DAR published a book, *American Genealogical Research at the DAR, Washington, D.C.*, by Eric G. Grundset, the Society's librarian, in 1997. Applications to join the DAR, which include detailed lineages, are searchable and downloadable (for a fee) from *dar.org*.

There is a New York State DAR organization with a website at *nydar.org*. It offers three useful grave-marking databases: Real Daughters (that is, actual daughters of Revolutionary War patriots who were DAR members), Patriot Marked Graves, and DAR Member Marked Graves. Within New York State, there are many chapters, with a well-organized list at *www.nydar.org/ny-chapters.html*.

In 2012 the DAR published Eric Grundset's astoundingly comprehensive *New York in the American Revolution: A Source Guide for Genealogists and Historians*. This book is a complete reference for sources about the place and period. It is available only from the DAR and may be purchased as a searchable e-book or in hard copy.

The NYSL and the NYPL have large collections of DAR material on their shelves, including *Genealogical Records Committee Reports* (1913–present) providing data from thousands of typescript volumes, including Bible, cemetery, and town records.

See also chapter 17, Reference Shelf, for a detailed description of important DAR research, which is increasingly accessible online.

Note that there used to be another national organization called Daughters of the Revolution (D of R). While it no longer exists, its records are housed at the Suffolk County Historical Society in Riverhead, New York. (See *suffolkcountyhistoricalsociety.org*.) The index of D of R applications is online at the website of the German Genealogy Group (*GermanGenealogyGroup.com*).

National Society Sons of the American Revolution

1000 South Fourth Street • Louisville, KY 40203

(502) 589-1776 • *sar.org*

The National Society of the Sons of the American Revolution was organized in 1889. The members are men who are descended from a patriot at the time of the American Revolution. The national headquarters, and its impressive research library, are in Louisville, Kentucky. Applications submitted to the SAR from 1889 to 1970 are online at *Ancestry.com*. These provide a rich source of genealogical information, some of which is documented, and some not.

Society of Colonial Wars in the State of New York

20 West 44th Street, Room 502 • New York, NY 10036

(212) 755-7082 • Email: nyscw@verizon.net

colonialwarsny.org

The General Society of Colonial Wars was formed in New York City in 1893. Members are men who are descendants of persons engaged in armed conflict in any of the Colonies before 1775. The General Society is online at *gscw.org*. The website has some historical background to colonial wars and militias. The New York Chapter has its own website at *colonialwarsny.org*. Neither website offers genealogical data.

Society of Daughters of Holland Dames (SDHD)

Email: info@hollanddames.org • *hollanddames.org*

The SDHD was founded in 1895. Its members are women who are descended from a person who resided in the colony of New Netherland or who was connected to its defense and maintenance. The Society is involved in supporting scholarship and projects that preserve and document the Dutch heritage in New Netherland. In 2011, the SDHD sponsored the publication of Maria Dering's *Researching Your Dutch Ancestors: A Practical Guide*. For the citation, see the section on the Dutch in chapter 14, Peoples of New York. The society's papers are a planned gift to the N-YHS. See also Holland Society above.

Society of Mayflower Descendants in the State of New York

20 West 44th Street, Room 505 • New York, NY 10036-6603

Email: director@mayflowernewyork.org

mayflowernewyork.org

The General Society of Mayflower Descendants (GSMD) and its various chapters perpetuate the story of the Mayflower passengers and their principles of civil and religious liberty. The New York Chapter is very active, publishes a newsletter, sponsors programs, and offers research assistance to prospective mem-

bers. All fifty states have chapters. The national headquarters is in Plymouth, MA, where there is a research library; the society is online at *themayflowersociety.com*; the national society also sponsors a DNA project at Family Tree DNA, which includes New York participants.

Society of the Cincinnati

2118 Massachusetts Avenue, NW • Washington, DC 20008

(202) 785-2040 • *societyofthecincinnati.org*

The Society was founded in 1783 by American and French officers who served in the American Revolution. The national headquarters is in Washington, DC; there are chapters in 13 states, including New York, and one in France. Generally, membership is limited to one male direct-line descendant of each officer, though where there is no male descendant, a collateral line may apply. There is some variability of membership policies among the chapters.

The extensive library at the Washington headquarters focuses on the eighteenth century and especially on the American Revolution. The catalog is online, and there is a small, but growing, body of digitized material, some of it specific to New York, that can be downloaded or viewed online at its new and impressive website, *societyofthecincinnati.org*. The library itself is open to researchers by appointment.

The website of the New York chapter is at *nycincinnati.org*; the headquarters is at Mount Gulian Historic Site in Beacon, New York. The New York chapter has published useful books: *The New York State Society of the Cincinnati* by John Schuyler (1886, reprinted 1998), containing biographical sketches of the original members of the New York State Society. *New York State Society of the Cincinnati Biographies of the Original Members & Other Continental Officers* (2004) and *Histories of New York Regiments of the Continental Army* (2008) were written by Francis J. Sypher, Jr. These books may be purchased by contacting the Beacon headquarters at *mountgulian.org*.

Sons of the American Revolution in the State of New York (SR)

Fraunces Tavern Museum • 54 Pearl Street

New York, NY 10004 • (212) 425-1776 • *sonsoftherevolution.org*

The organization owns, and is located in, the historic Fraunces Tavern Museum in lower Manhattan. The chapter provides guidance to people establishing their genealogical credentials for membership, but does not provide data. This organization is distinctly separate from the National Society Sons of the American Revolution (see above).

Introduction

As this book clearly shows, researchers of New York history and families have a wealth of resources to consult. New York's history is long and complicated, and, as a consequence, a seemingly endless body of literature exists and continues to grow.

Not all researchers are exploring all time periods and places. However, professional genealogists and experienced researchers who have a general interest in New York families have, in the course of preparing this book, purposefully identified a short list of familiar and reliable references they routinely consult, some on a daily basis. In order to be consistently successful, the New York researcher, and others needing general knowledge of the subject—such as, for example, reference librarians—must have a working knowledge of these references.

Research Guides: New York City

Rosalie Fellows Bailey's *Guide to Genealogical and Biographical Sources for New York City (Manhattan), 1783–1898* was first published in the *New England Historical and Genealogical Register* (1952–1954) and then in book form in 1954; that edition is now online at *books.FamilySearch.org*. In 1998 it was reprinted with a new introduction by Harry Macy Jr. He notes that while access to records has changed dramatically since 1954, Ms. Bailey's source descriptions are still very valuable. Much of her comprehensive bibliographical material is not duplicated elsewhere, so that "thorough research in the nineteenth-century city cannot be done without reference to this part of the guide."

In 1989 the Jewish Genealogical Society (JGS) published the award-winning *Genealogical Resources in the New York Metropolitan Area*, edited by Estelle Guzik; she included New York City, Long Island, Westchester County, and some of New Jersey. This was the precursor to her *Genealogical Resources in New York*, published in 2003. This book focused on New York

City and included some key repositories in Albany. Though out of print, the 2003 edition is still easily obtainable, including from the JGS.

The most recent addition to the New York City research guides is Laura Murphy DeGrazia's *NGS Research in the States Series: New York City, Long Island, and Westchester County*. Published in 2013, it covers the five boroughs of New York City, as well as Nassau, Suffolk, and Westchester counties.

Often overlooked are the Research Aids covering all of New York State on the NYG&B's website, *NewYorkFamilyHistory.org*. These guides are mentioned frequently in various chapters of this book where relevant; however, as a body of work, they cover most topics of importance to New York researchers and are often more up to date than the books listed here. The Research Aids were written by subject matter experts wellknown to experienced New York researchers—the majority by Harry Macy Jr., and others by Henry B. Hoff, Roger Joslyn, Leslie Corn, B-Ann Moorhouse, and Frank Biebel, among others.

Research Guides: New York State and City

Roger Joslyn's New York entry in *Red Book: American State, County and Town Sources* provides 20 pages of concise, excellent research guidance.

The New York Research Outline created at the Brigham Young University Family History Library is online at *http://net.lib.byu. edu/fslab/researchoutlines/US/NewYork.pdf*. It contains over 180 pages of references to New York research sources variously arranged, including by county and subject. This reference, which does not have a publication date, provides Family History Library (FHL) microfilm numbers, call numbers for books, and some links to online resources. This publication is the basis for its replacement reference, the FamilySearch wiki, but the document that exists is still useful, and may be downloaded. Its successor, the FamilySearch wiki, is at *https://familysearch.org/learn/wiki/en/New_York*.

Two encyclopedias are particularly useful. These are Peter Eisenstadt's *Encyclopedia of New York State*, published in 2005, and Kenneth Jackson's *Encyclopedia of New York City*, first published in 1995 with a second edition in 2010. Both of these volumes are weighty tomes with contributions from hundreds of experts.

Selected References

Early vital records of New York State are few and far between. Fred Bowman and Thomas Lynch together published two books and an article on New York vital records substitutes drawn from newspapers. Bowman published a number of other books of similar nature covering most of New York State, including his series of three *10,000 Vital Records of [Region] New York State*. A complete list of these books is in chapter 12, Newspapers and Periodicals.

When researching in upstate New York, see Marian Henry's *New York Essays: Resources for the Genealogist in New York State Outside New York City*, published in 2007. She writes about the Historic Documents Inventory (HDI), the Vosburgh Collection of Church Records, and the works of Fred Bowman, which are among the works listed in this chapter. She is also particularly strong on land records and offers a thorough chapter on the New York state census.

A significant resource accessible through the New York State Library (NYSL) is the HDI mentioned above and described at *www.nysl.nysed.gov/hdi.htm*. The HDI, conducted between 1978 and 1993 by the New York Historical Resources Center at Cornell University, surveyed the manuscript and archival holdings of repositories across New York State. It resulted in the publication of the series *Guides to Historical Resources in Repositories* for every county except Nassau and Suffolk. Many titles in the series have been digitized and are available at *books.FamilySearch.org*. All items and collections that were recorded by the HDI—including those in the unpublished inventories for Nassau and Suffolk— have been cataloged by the NYSL. Instructions on how to use the NYSL online catalog to identify and locate material recorded by the HDI are at *www.nysl.nysed.gov/hdi.htm*.

Despite the title, Eric Grundset's *New York in the American Revolution: A Source Guide for Genealogists and Historians* is not just for researchers studying families during the Revolutionary War period. It has broad utility for other periods and subjects as well. Essentially it is a carefully organized bibliography of over 600 pages, and many of its entries are heavily annotated. Published by the National Society Daughters of the American Revolution (DAR) in 2012, this book is available in hard copy and in e-book format, only from the DAR (*dar.org*.)

The DAR's Genealogical Research System (GRS) is a collection of databases of information drawn from applications and supplemental applications for membership in the DAR, and other DAR sources. It also covers many time periods and continues to expand on a daily basis. Entry to the GRS is online at *dar.org*. The DAR Library's online catalog is also included as part of the GRS. Databases include:

- "Ancestor," which contains data from verified applications
- "Descendants," an index of the names found on the lineage page of almost 900,000 applications
- "GRC," or *Genealogical Records Committee Reports* (1913–present), which incorporates data from thousands of typescript volumes, including Bible and cemetery records. There are 1,100 volumes of New York DAR records; the index to the New York records is online.
- "Resources," which includes the "Library Analytical Card Index" and the "Revolutionary War Pension Index"

John Homer French's *Gazetteer of the State of New York*, published in 1860, is a comprehensive guide to New York places and is still in print. The 1998 edition contains a supplementary index to place names found in the text and in the footnotes that were not in French's place name index. Also useful is the *All-Name Index to the 1860 Gazetteer of New York State*, published in 1993.

Donald Lines Jacobus' index to genealogical periodicals is included in the Reference Shelf List, which follows, but researchers are encouraged to see chapter 12 in this book for additional finding aids to periodical titles with New York material.

Finally, two titles on two particularly important subjects stand out.

Gordon L. Remington's *New York State Probate Records: A Genealogist's Guide to Testate and Intestate Records* describes the history of probate in New York, an understanding of which is critical to successfully finding records, and provides a detailed review of microfilmed records at the FHL, organized by county. The book also notes—on a county-by-county basis—material of relevance to its topic published in the *NYG&B Record* and *Tree Talks*, as well as other sources. It is important to use the second edition.

William Dollarhide's *New York State Censuses & Substitutes* is the most comprehensive reference book about the New York state census. It goes far beyond describing the various censuses by including county-by-county guides to census *substitutes*. Many of these guides refer to valuable but often overlooked sources.

The Reference Shelf List

Bailey, Rosalie Fellows. *Guide to Genealogical and Biographical Sources for New York City (Manhattan), 1783–1898*. New York: The Author, 1954. [*books.FamilySearch.org*] Reprinted with new introduction by Harry Macy Jr. Baltimore: Clearfield Co., 1998.

Bowman, Fred Q., and Thomas Lynch. Bowman's books, and books jointly prepared by Fred Bowman and Thomas Lynch, are listed in chapter 12, Newspapers and Periodicals. As noted, see Marion Henry's chapter on these books in *New York Essays*.

Daughters of the American Revolution (DAR) Genealogical Research System (GRS). Online at *dar.org*.

DeGrazia, Laura Murphy. *NGS Research in the States Series: New York City, Long Island, and Westchester County*. Arlington, VA: National Genealogical Society, 2013.

Doherty, Frank J. *Settlers of the Beekman Patent, Dutchess County, New York*. 11 vols. to date. Pleasant Valley, NY and Orlando, FL: The Author, 1990–2013. [Some of the titles are offered online at *AmericanAncestors.org*]

Dollarhide, William. *New York State Censuses & Substitutes*. North Salt Lake, UT: Heritage Creations, 2005.

Eardeley, William A. D. "Abstracts of Wills, Administrations and Guardianships in NY State, 1787–1835." Original manuscript in Eardeley Genealogy Collection: New York State Abstracts of Wills, Brooklyn Historical Society. [*AmericanAncestors.org*]

Eisenstadt, Peter E., ed. *Encyclopedia of New York State*. Syracuse: Syracuse University Press, 2005.

Epperson, Gwenn F. *New Netherland Roots*. Baltimore: Genealogical Publishing Co., 1994.

Family History Research New York Wiki. *https://FamilySearch.org/learn/wiki/en/New_York*

Foley, Janet Wethy. *Early Settlers of New York State: Their Ancestors and Descendants*. Originally published serially in nine volumes: Akron, NY: T. J. Foley, 1934–1942. Reprint, Baltimore: Genealogical Publishing Co., 2006.

French, John Homer. *Gazetteer of the State of New York*. Syracuse: Pearsall Smith, 1860. Reprint, Baltimore: Genealogical Publishing Co., 1998. See below for Walter Steesy's index to French's gazetteer.

Genealogical Department of The Church of Jesus Christ of Latter-day Saints. *County Formations and Minor Civil Divisions of the State of New York, Series B, No. 4*. Salt Lake City: The Department, 1978.

General Peter Gansevoort Chapter. *Revised Master Index to New York State Daughters of the American Revolution Genealogical Records Volumes*. 2 vols. Zephyrhills, FL: Jean Worden, 1998.

Grundset, Eric G. *New York in the American Revolution: A Source Guide for Genealogists and Historians*. Washington: National Society Daughters of the American Revolution, 2012.

Guzik, Estelle M., ed. *Genealogical Resources in New York*. New York: Jewish Genealogical Society, 2003.

Henry, Marian S. *New York Essays: Resources for the Genealogist in New York State Outside New York City*. Boston: New England Historic Genealogical Society, 2007.

Historic Documents Inventory (HDI). This source is described above, and more fully on the website of the New York State Library at *www.nysl.nysed.gov/hdi.htm*.

Jackson, Kenneth, ed. *Encyclopedia of New York City*. New Haven, CT: Yale University Press, revised edition, 2010.

Jacobus, Donald L. *Index to Genealogical Periodicals [1858–1952]*. Originally published in 3 vols. New Haven, CT: The Author, 1932–1952. Revised edition by Carl Boyer, 3rd merges the three volumes into one. Rockport, ME: Picton Press, 1995.

Joslyn, Roger D. "New York." In *Red Book: American State, County and Town Sources*, edited by Alice Eichholz, 472–492. 3rd edition. Provo, UT: Ancestry, 2004.

Livsey, Karen E. *Western New York Land Transactions, 1804–1835, Extracted from the Archives of the Holland Land Company*. 2 vols. Baltimore: Genealogical Publishing Co., 1991–1996.

[Munsell's] *Index to American Genealogies: And to Genealogical Material Contained in All Works, Such as Town Histories, County Histories, Local Histories, Historical Society Publications, Biographies, Historical Periodicals and Kindred Works*. Albany: J. Munsell's Sons, 1900. And *Supplement, 1900–1908 to the Index to Genealogies Published in 1900*. Albany: J. Munsell's Sons, 1908. Both volumes reprinted, Baltimore: Genealogical Publishing Co., 1997.

New York Genealogical and Biographical Record. New York: New York Genealogical and Biographical Society, 1870–present. Published quarterly, the *Record* forms the largest single collection of published genealogical material on New York families. [NYG&B eLibrary]

New York Genealogical and Biographical Society. *Research Aids*, online at *NewYorkFamilyHistory.org*. More than 100 articles written by subject matter experts on key topics in New York research comprise the *Research Aids* collection.

New York Genealogical and Biographical Society Family Files. One of several archival collections given to the NYPL by the NYG&B, these files contain genealogical research notes, Bible records, correspondence, legal document such as deeds and wills, and genealogical charts relating principally to families of New York City and State. Most material relates to the nineteenth and twentieth centuries. The detailed finding aid, organized by family name, describes the material relating to each family. The files are located at the NYPL's Manuscripts Division. See the online finding aid at *www.nypl.org/sites/default/files/archivalcollections/pdf/18274_2.pdf*. A list of finding aids to other archival collections of the NYG&B at the NYPL is at *NewYorkFamilyHistory.org*.

New York Research Outline. Provo, UT: Brigham Young University Family History Library, n.d. *http://net.lib.byu.edu/fslab/researchoutlines/US/NewYork.pdf*.

Pelletreau, William S. *Abstracts of Wills on File in the Surrogate's Office, City of New York [1665–1800]*. 17 vols. Collections of The New-York Historical Society 1892–1908. Wills 1665–1787 are from all counties, 1787–1800 from New York County only. [*FamilySearch.org*]

Remington, Gordon L. *New York State Probate Records: A Genealogist's Guide to Testate and Intestate Records*. Boston: New England Historic Genealogical Society, 2nd edition, 2011.

———. *New York State Towns, Villages, and Cities: A Guide to Genealogical Sources*. Boston: New England Historic Genealogical Society, 2002. Some of the content of this book is offered online at *AmericanAncestors.org*.

Riker, David M. *Genealogical and Biographical Directory to Persons in New Netherland, From 1613 to 1674*. 4 vols. Mechanicsburg, PA: The Author, 1999 and Salem, MA: Higginson Book Co., 1999 and Supplement, 2004. Vols. 1–4 also published as *New Netherland Vital Records, 1600s* on CD-ROM by Family Tree Maker (1999), available by subscription to *genealogy.com*.

Seversmith, Herbert F., and Kenn Stryker-Rodda. *Long Island Genealogical Source Material, A Bibliography*. Washington, DC: National Genealogical Society, 1962.

Steesy, Walter W. *All-Name Index to the Historical and Statistical Gazetteer of New York State, 1860 by J. H. French, and a Listing of Geographical Names Missing in the Original Index*. Interlaken, NY: Heart of the Lakes Publishing, 1993.

Thorne, Kathryn Ford, comp. John H. Long, ed. *New York Atlas of Historical County Boundaries*. New York: Simon and Schuster, 1993.

Tree Talks. Syracuse: Central New York Genealogical Society, 1961–present. Some indexes are online. [*www.rootsweb.ancestry.com/~nycnygs/publications.htm*] Kinship Books has published an index to 49 *Tree Talks* packets; see chapter 12, Newspapers and Periodicals, for citation.

Vosburgh Collection. Royden Woodward Vosburgh, who became archivist and historian of the NYG&B in 1913, compiled more than 100 volumes of transcribed records from Protestant churches across New York State; their reliability is highly regarded. The NYG&B eLibrary collection of Religious Records includes transcribed records—many by Mr. Vosburgh—from more than 50 churches of various denominations across New York State. See New York Genealogical and Biographical Society, "The Vosburgh Collection of New York Church Records." *NYG&B Newsletter* (now *New York Researcher*), Fall 1998. Also a Research Aid at *NewYorkFamilyHistory.org*.

Wilt, Richard A. *New York Soldiers in the Civil War: A Roster of Military Officers and Soldiers Who Served in New York Regiments in the Civil War*. 2 vols. Bowie, MD: Heritage Books, 1999.

Part Two

County Guides, including Gazetteers

Guides to each of the 62 counties of New York State comprise Part Two of this book. While much of Part Two will be intuitive, reading this introduction will increase its utility. An understanding of the government units that generate records in New York State is fundamental.

Counties, cities, towns, and villages are the only entities that generate official records in New York State. So the meaning of these terms must be understood to search effectively for records and to cite sources correctly. In New York State, researchers may need to check at the county, town, and village level for vital records, so it is important to know the county in which a town is located, and the town in which a village is located.

Formation of Counties

The history of county divisions is important to genealogists, because it affects the location of records. County records are generally retained by the county in which they were created, even if a municipality has left the jurisdiction of a county. However, sometimes the records might move with a municipality to its new county or to some other repository.

In 1683, after the British took over New Netherland from the Dutch and renamed it New York, the colony was divided into twelve counties, ten of which exist today and are often referred to as "the ten original counties."

Albany	Queens
Dutchess	Richmond
Kings	Suffolk
New York	Ulster
Orange	Westchester

Colonial-era counties and county names that were short-lived are listed in table 1.

Table 1: New York Counties and County Names No Longer in Existence

County	Created	Ended	Disposition
Cornwall	1683	1687	Became part of Maine
Dukes	1683	1692	Became part of Massachusetts
Cumberland	1766	1777	Became part of Vermont
Gloucester	1770		
Tryon	1772	1784	Renamed Montgomery
Charlotte	1772	1784	Renamed Washington

Over the years, as settlement expanded and the population grew, the ten original counties were subdivided by acts of the state legislature to form "daughter counties," and many daughter counties were further subdivided until there were 62 counties. Bronx County, the most recent, was formed in 1914.

Definition of Terms

Colonial New York also had cities and towns—divisions that continued to exist after the American Revolution when municipal organization in New York was simplified. The village, as a unit of government, appeared in the 1790s.

Other Colonial-era divisions, such as patroonships, manors, districts, precincts, and ridings, are now obsolete, and records that they generated may be found in municipal, public, or private repositories and collections.

More information on the structure of local government, and a note on citing records generated by municipalities, can be found in Harry Macy Jr.'s "Units of Local Government in New

York State." A very detailed description of the various levels of local government is in the New York Department of State *Local Government Handbook*.

Cities

In New York, a city is a municipality with its own individual charter. A city is defined by the way it is organized, not by its size; some cities are huge—most obviously, New York City itself—while others are smaller than some villages. Sherrill, a city in Oneida County, has a population of about 3,500. Other than New York City, cities are subordinate to the counties in which they are located. Today there are 62 cities in New York State, a number which is only coincidentally the same as the number of counties in New York. Not every county has a city within its boundaries. Cities are never subdivided into towns or villages, but may be subdivided into wards, districts, or other civil boundaries.

Since 1898 New York City has consisted of five boroughs—the Bronx, Brooklyn, Manhattan, Queens, and Staten Island (officially called Richmond until 1975)—which are today coterminous with Bronx, Kings, New York, Queens, and Richmond counties. New York County—the original New York City, and now the Borough of Manhattan—was never subdivided into cities, towns, or villages as the other four boroughs were. Former municipal place names are shown on the maps in the Guides for these boroughs.

Towns

When the Dutch ceded New Netherland to the British in 1664, there were 17 towns in existence. These towns were recognized by the British who began the process of codifying the structure of town government. Today, other than cities and Indian reservations, the entire state of New York is divided into nearly 950 towns, which are municipal corporations. A town may include villages that are subordinate to it. (The word "township" may exist in the vernacular, but is not a government entity in New York State.)

Villages

Like towns, most of the 550 or so villages in New York State are incorporated, while some operate under special charters. Villages pay taxes to the town in which they are located, raise taxes themselves, provide services to themselves, and receive services provided by towns. Villages can exist in more than one county and more than one town, and town and village boundaries can be coterminous.

Unincorporated Settlements:
Hamlets, Neighborhoods, and Census-Designated Places

Within towns, cities, and even villages, there are many named places that have no governmental structure and do not create official records. Such unincorporated settlements are often called hamlets in rural and suburban areas, and neighborhoods in urban areas or cities. These place names may be recognized by the United States Post Office, delineate a school district, or appear in the federal census as Census-Designated Places (CDP).

Postal Addresses

Postal addresses in New York State do not always reflect the name of the municipality in which a person resides. In the case of some communities near a border, they often use the name of a neighboring town or village. Occasionally, a mailing address simply uses the name of a neighborhood. For example, this has been a traditional practice for all locations in the Borough of Queens and for the neighborhood of Riverdale in the Borough of the Bronx.

Navigating the County Guides

The guides to genealogical research in the 62 counties have several clearly differentiated parts.

Cover Page

The cover page provides the formation date, other key details of the county, and an original map. The map shows current town and city boundaries and the location of Indian reservations; it does not show current villages and hamlets, or obsolete divisions such as manors and patents.

Gazetteer

The purpose of the gazetteer is to help the researcher identify the location of records. Each gazetteer inventories historical and contemporary names of every city, town, and village in a county—all of which are, or have been, units of government, and as such have generated official records. Many—but not all—unincorporated settlements have also been identified, following a more subjective methodology weighted toward historical significance and name recognition.

- **Column One.** Lists every city and town—present and past—alphabetically and provides a brief chronology of key events and place name changes that impact the availability and location of records. Existing municipalities are in blue; former ones are in black. Place names marked with an asterisk have a corresponding note in column three.
- **Column Two.** Lists place names associated with the town in column one. Current incorporated or chartered villages appear in blue and are denoted (v); villages that were incorporated but later dissolved are denoted (v) but appear in black.
- **Column Three.** Provides notes that apply to places mentioned in columns one and two. Places are listed in alphabetical order. "inc." is an abbreviation for "incorporated."

Readers should note that the names of almost all municipalities were in use long before their incorporation date, and that some places were called villages even if they were not incorporated as such. Furthermore, villages frequently moved from the jurisdiction of one town to another; in such cases the village will be listed under both its town of origin and its current town.

Table 2: Key to Gazetteers	
Blue text	Current city, town, and villages
Black text	Other past and present place names
(v)	Incorporated or chartered village
*	Links a place name in column 1 to a note in column 3

Place names in the gazetteers were sourced from state and local histories, eighteenth- and nineteenth-century gazetteers, county and local gazetteers, journal articles, and maps. Genealogists, municipal county, town, and village historians, and leaders of genealogical and historical societies provided edits and suggestions to this list. Contemporary resources consulted include the Geographic Names Information System (GNIS).

Researchers will benefit by consulting the statewide gazetteers listed in the bibliography at the end of this section, as well as the local gazetteers found in the bibliographies for the County Guides. Many of these are rich in genealogically relevant information. There is significant variation in the spelling of place names. Many of the variants have been noted. However, in general, names in this gazetteer conform to the United States Postal Service (USPS) convention, e.g. no apostrophes.

Repositories and Resources
Records Held by Municipal Cerks

For each county an annotated list is provided of government offices, repositories, societies, and organizations holding records and collections useful to genealogists, or offering research services or resources. Hours of operation, restrictions on access, and other details which change frequently should be obtained from the organization itself.

The location of various types of records can vary widely from place to place. Vital records (births, marriages, and deaths) can be found with the county, city, town, or village clerk, depending on the where the event occurred. Exceptions are the four counties (Chemung, Monroe, Onondaga, and Tompkins) that are "consolidated districts," where most vital records are kept at the county level.

County clerks are the record keepers for their respective Supreme and County courts. Outside New York City, county clerks are the recorders and holders of land records. They also may hold original records of censuses and naturalizations. County clerks may also have other kinds of records, such as voter registration records or military discharge records.

Most counties started preserving tax assessment records from the mid-nineteenth century. These, and earlier records if available, may be found with the county treasurer or fiscal officer. But in some cases, original records from municipalities (for example,

early vital records created in the late 1840s and early 1850s) have been transferred to local historical societies, public libraries, or other repositories.

See Part One of this book for detailed information about the major record types useful for genealogical research in New York.

Selected Print and Online Resources

Essentially, this section in each guide offers *selected* bibliographies. Since the literature on most counties is very extensive, it is not possible to be exhaustive, or even close to it.

Many listed publications, particularly if they are out of copyright, can be found online at *Archive.org, Hathitrust.org, books.google. com, Ancestry.com*, or *books.FamilySearch.org*. If a source is unique, its location is given; if it is online at a lesser known website, the URL is provided.

Selected Bibliography and Further Reading
Gazetteers

A number of statewide gazetteers track the development of place names through the nineteenth century. These titles are listed below in chronological order. The full-length titles are given as a way to differentiate their content. County and local gazetteers are listed in the respective county bibliographies.

1813

Spafford, Horatio Gates. *A Gazetteer of the State of New York: Carefully Written From Original and Authentic Materials, Arranged in a New Plan on Three Parts Comprising: First—A Comprehensive Geographical and Statistical View of the Whole State, Conveniently Disposed under Separate Heads. Second— An Ample General View of Each County in Alphabetical Order with Topographical and Statistical Tables, Showing the Civil and Political Divisions, Population, Post-offices, &C. Third—A Very Full and Minute Topographical Description of Each Town or Township, City, Borough, Village . . . As Also Its Lakes, Rivers, Creeks . . . Forming a Complete Gazetteer or Geographical Dictionary of the State of New-York. With an Accurate Map of the State.* Albany: H. C. Southwick, 1813.

1824

Spafford, Horatio Gates. *A Gazetteer of the State of New York: Embracing An Ample Survey and Description of Its Counties, Towns, Cities, Villages, Canals, Mountains, Lakes, Rivers, Creeks, and Natural Topography Arranged in One Series Alphabetically. . . With an Appendix Embracing the New Counties and Towns Erected 1823, 2. A Concise Geography of the State with All Its Civil Divisions to Jan. 1 1824; 3. A Table of All the Post-Offices in the State to Jan. 1, 1824.* Albany: B. D. Packard, 1824; Troy, NY: The Author, 1824.

1836

Gordon, Thomas F. *Gazetteer of the State of New York: Comprehending Its Colonial History, General Geography,*

Geology, and Internal Improvements, Its Political State, a Minute Description of Its Several Counties, Towns, and Villages, Statistical Tables, Exhibiting the Area, Improved Lands, Population, Stock, Taxes, Manufactures, Schools, and Cost of Public Instruction, in Each Town: With a Map of the State, and a Map of Each County, and Plans of the Cities and Principal Villages. Philadelphia: T. K. and P. G. Collins, 1836.

1842

Disturnell, John, and Orville Luther Holley. *A Gazetteer of the State of New-York: Comprising Its Topography, Geology, Mineralogical Resources, Civil Divisions, Canals, Railroads and Public Institutions, Together with General Statistics, the Whole Alphabetically Arranged. Also Statistical Tables Including the Census of 1840.* Albany: J. Disturnell, 1842 (1st edition); Albany: C. Van Benthuysen & Co., 1843 (2nd edition).

1860

French, John Homer. *Gazetteer of the State of New York: Embracing a Comprehensive View of the Geography, Geology, and General History of The State, and a Complete History and Description of Every County, City, Town, Village, and Locality. With Full Tables of Statistics.* Syracuse: R. Pearsall Smith, 1860. Reprint, Baltimore: Genealogical Publishing Co., 1998. The 1998 edition contains a supplementary index to place names found in the text and footnotes that were not in French's place name index. See also *All-Name Index to the 1860 Gazetteer of New York State.* Interlaken, NY: Heart of the Lakes Publishing, 1993.

1872

Hough, Franklin B. *Gazetteer of the State of New York: Embracing a Comprehensive Account of the History and Statistics of the State, with Geological and Topographical Descriptions, and Recent Statistical Tables Representing the Present Condition of Each County, City, Town and Village in the State.* Albany: Andrew Boyd, 1872.

Other Resources

See also chapter 7, Land Records and Maps, for additional resources.

Atlas of Historical County Boundaries. Newberry Library, Dr. William M. Scholl Center for American History and Culture. [*http://publications.newberry.org/ahcbp*] This interactive site shows graphically the boundary status of counties for New York from the late-seventeenth century to 2000, and provides detailed timelines on boundary changes for each county. Data may be downloaded in several formats.

Geographic Names Information System (GNIS). U.S. Board on Geographic Names and the United States Geological Survey. [http://geonames.usgs.gov/domestic/] This database of federally recognized place names can be searched by state and county to identify populated places, as well as topographical features.

Macy, Harry, Jr. "Units of Local Government in New York State." Published as a Research Aid, 2011, at *NewYorkFamilyHistory.org.*

New York City Department of City Planning. Community Portal. http://www.nyc.gov/html/dcp/html/neigh_info/nhmap.shtml#. The website provides access to an interactive map of the five boroughs, which provides present-day boundaries of the Community Districts and adjacent neighborhoods, and a list of place names in each.

New York State Department of Health (NYSDH). *New York State Gazetteer.* Albany, 2007. *https://health.data.ny.gov/api/assets/991FD0D8-73AF-4573-96F1-437E33D24BCA?download=true* This publication lists New York State cities, towns, villages, hamlets, and boroughs that are recognized by the NYSDH.

New York Department of State. *Local Government Handbook.* 6th edition. Albany, 2009. Reprinted, 2011. *www.dos.ny.gov/lg/ publications/Local_Government_Handbook.pdf*

Thorne, Kathryn Ford. *Atlas of Historical County Boundaries: New York.* Edited by John H. Long. New York: Simon and Schuster, 1993.

Corrections, Additions, and Omissions

The amount of detail in Part Two of this book is vast. Despite the input from dozens of informed people in every county, it undoubtedly contains omissions and errors. Corrections will appear in this book's next edition and online.

The editors of this book are particularly interested in identifying locations of original records for future editions. Corrections, additions, and omissions may be sent to NYGuide@nygbs.org, with the sincere thanks of the editors.

Albany County

Formed November 1, 1683

Parent County   Original county
Daughter Counties Cumberland 1766 • Gloucester 1770
                       Montgomery 1772 (as Tryon) • Washington 1772 (as Charlotte)
                       Columbia 1786 • Rensselaer 1791 • Saratoga 1791
                       Schoharie 1795 • Greene 1800 • Schenectady 1809
County Seat   City of Albany

Major Land Transactions
See chapter 7, Land Records
Rensselaerswijck 1629

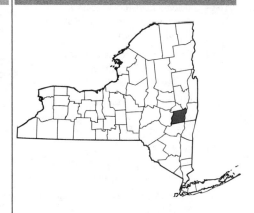

Town Boundary Map
★ - County seat

Towns (and Cities)	Villages and other Settlements	Notes
Albany (city) * Longest continuously chartered city in the U.S. 1614 Trading post (Fort Nassau) established on Castle/Westerlo Island (see Bethlehem) 1624 Dutch West India Company establishes Fort Orange (north of Westerlo Island) 1629 Kiliaen van Rensselaer acquires patroonship of Rensselaerswijck, surrounding Fort Orange 1652 Settlement surrounding Fort removed from Rensselaerswijck and named Beverwyck 1664 English rule, Beverwyck renamed New Albany 1673 Dutch return, New Albany renamed Willemstad(t) 1674 English rule resumed, name New Albany restored but "New" gradually discarded 1685 Rensselaerswijck given status of English manor; Van Rensselaers renounce all claims to Albany 1686 Charter incorporates City of Albany 1797 Made state capital 1815 Town of Colonie dissolved and divided between City of Albany and Town of Watervliet 1870 Annexed North Albany from Town of Watervliet; annexed large part of Normansville from Town of Bethlehem 1916 Annexed Groesbeck and Kenwood from Bethlehem 1926 Annexed Westerlo Island from Town of Bethlehem 1967 Annexed Hurstville and Karlsfeld from Town of Bethlehem	Arbor Hill Beverwyck Buckingham Pond Center Square Colonie Delaware Dunes Eagle Hill Groesbeck Helderberg Hurstville Karlsfeld Kenwood Melrose New Albany Normansville North Albany Pastures Pine Hills Washington Park Westerlo Island	* Albany known colloquially as Sturgeonville in the mid-1800s • Groesbeck in Town of Bethlehem before 1916 • Hurstville and Karlsfeld in Town of Bethlehem before 1967 • Kenwood in Town of Bethlehem before 1916 • Normansville formerly Upper Hollow • North Albany in Town of Watervliet before 1870 • Westerlo Island in Town of Bethlehem before 1926
Ballston * In Albany County 1775–1791		* See Saratoga County
Berne 1750 Settled by German immigrants 1795 Formed from Rensselaerville 1822 Daughter town Knox formed	Bern(e) Thompson Lake East Berne Warners Lake Myrtle West Berne Reidsville Wolf Hill South Berne	• Bern(e) formerly Beaver Dam, Berneville, and Torys Hole • East Berne formerly Philadelphia • West Berne formerly Peoria; on Knox town line
Bethlehem 1614 Fort Nassau established by the New Netherland Trading Company on Castle Island 1793 Formed from Town of Watervliet	Beckers Corners Clarksville Bethlehem Delmar Bethlehem Center Elsmere Bethlehem Heights Feura Bush Callanans Corners Font Grove Cedar Hill Glenmont	• Bethlehem Center also Babcock Corners • Callanans Corners and Clarksville in Town of New Scotland from 1832 • Delmar formerly Adams Station, Adamsville • Feura Bush in Town of New Scotland from 1832 (Bethlehem continued on next page)

Towns (and Cities)	Villages and other Settlements		Notes
Bethlehem (continued) 1832　Daughter town New Scotland formed 1870　Ceded large section north of Normansville to City of Albany 1916　Ceded Groesbeck and Kenwood to City of Albany 1926　Ceded Westerlo Island to City of Albany 1967　Ceded Hurstville and Karlsfeld to City of Albany	Groesbeck Houcks Corners Hurstville Jericho Karlsfeld Kenwood Mallorys Corners Meyers Corners Normansville North Bethlehem	Selkirk Selkirk Yards Slingerlands South Albany South Bethlehem Spawn Hollow Unionville Van Wies Point Wemple Westerlo Island	• Groesbeck ceded to City of Albany 1916 • Hurstville (also known as The Log Cabin) and Karlsfeld ceded to City of Albany 1967 • Kenwood also Lower Hollow; ceded to City of Albany 1916 • Normansville formerly Upper Hollow • Slingerslands formerly Normans Kill and Red Hook • South Bethlehem formerly Jaynes Corners and Kimmeys Corners • Unionville in Town of New Scotland from 1832 • Westerlo Island ceded to City of Albany
Cambridge ＊ In Albany County 1772–1791			＊ See Washington County
Canaan ＊ In Albany County as Kings District 1772–1786			＊ See Columbia County
Catskill ＊ In Albany County 1772–1798			＊ See Greene County
Claverack ＊ In Albany County 1772–1786			＊ See Columbia County
Coeymans 1636　Settlers from Utrecht 1791　Formed from Town of Watervliet 1815　Daughter town Westerlo formed	Alcove Alcove Reservoir Aquetuck Coeymans Coeymans Hollow Indian Fields	Keefer(s) Corners Mossy Hill Ravena (v) Roah Hook Stephensville Hollow	• Alcove formerly Stephensville • Coeymans formerly Coeymans Landing • Village of Ravena inc. 1914; also Coeymans Junction
Cohoes (city) 1869　Formed from Village of Cohoes in Town of Watervliet ＊	Simmons Island Van Schaick Island		＊ City bill passed 1869 and took effect 1870
Colonie 1791–1815 *See City of Albany and Town of Watervliet* 1791　Incorporated as a municipality in Town of Watervliet 1804　Village of Colonie incorporated 1808　Formed as town 1815　Divided and merged into City of Albany and Town of Watervliet			
Colonie 1895　Formed from Town of Watervliet	Boght Corners Colonie (v) Crescent Station Dunsbach Ferry Emerick Karner Latham	Lisha Kill Loudonville Maplewood Maywood Menands (v) Newtonville	• Boght Corners formerly in Town of Watervliet • Village of Colonie inc. 1921 • Lisha Kill formerly in Town of Watervliet • Loudonville was Ireland(s) Corners until 1871; formerly in Town of Watervliet • Village of Menands inc. 1924 • Newtonville formerly in Town of Watervliet

(Colonie continued on next page)

Towns (and Cities)	Villages and other Settlements		Notes
Colonie (continued)	Roessleville Schuyler Flatts Shakers Shaker Settlement Stanford Heights Verdoy West Albany		• Shakers and Shaker Settlement formerly in Town of Watervliet; Shaker Settlement now known as Watervliet Shaker Historic District • Stanford Heights shared with Town of Niskayuna, Schenectady County • West Albany formerly in Town of Watervliet
Coxsackie * In Albany County 1772–1800			* See Greene County
Duanesburg(h) * In Albany County 1765–1809			* See Schenectady County
Easton * In Albany County 1789–1791			* See Washington County
Freehold * In Albany County 1790–1800			* See Town of Durham in Greene County
Germantown * In Albany County as East Camp District 1775–1786			* See Columbia County
Green Island 1896 Formed from Village of Green Island when Town of Watervliet was dissolved and divided	Green Island (v)		• Village of Green Island inc. 1853; coterminous with Town of Green Island (both governments working together from 1896 to the present)
Guilderland 1803 Formed from Town of Watervliet 1871 Annexed land from Town of Watervliet	Altamont (v) Altamont Orchards Dunnsville Fort Hunter Frenchs Mills Fuller(s) Guilderland Guilderland Center	Guilderland Station Hartmans Corners McCormacks Corners McKownville Meadowdale Parkers Corners West Guilderland Westmere	• Village of Altamont inc. 1890; formerly Knowersville • Dunnsville formerly Hardscrabble • Fuller(s) also Fuller Station • Guilderland formerly Douwsburgh, Glass House, Hamiltonville, and Sloane • Guilderland Center formerly Bangall
Halfmoon * In Albany County 1772–1791			* See Saratoga County
Hillsdale * In Albany County 1782–1786			* See Columbia County
Hoosick * In Albany County 1772–1791			* See Rensselaer County
Hudson (city) * In Albany County 1785–1786			* See Columbia County
Kinderhook * In Albany County 1772–1786			* See Columbia County
Knox Settled by Germans before American Revolution 1822 Formed from Berne	East Township Knox West Berne West Township		• Knox formerly Knoxville which was formerly known as Union Street and locally called The Street • West Bern formerly Peoria; on Berne town line

Towns (and Cities)	Villages and other Settlements		Notes
Livingston * In Albany County 1772–1786			* See Columbia County (Livingston Manor in Albany County from 1717; Livingston district formed 1772 which became town of Livingston 1788)
New Scotland c. 1660 Settled 1832 Formed from Bethlehem	Callanans Corners Clarksville Feura Bush Helderberg Jerusalem New Salem New Scotland New Scotland Depot	Oniskethau Salem Hills Stony Hill Union Church Unionville Voorheesville (v) Wolf Hill	• Callanans Corners (also Callans Corners), in Town of Bethlehem until 1832 • Clarksville called Bethlehem until 1833 and was in the Town of Bethlehem • Feura Bush in Town of Bethlehem until 1832 • Oniskethau also Tarrytown • Unionville in Town of Bethlehem until 1832 • Village of Voorheesville inc. 1899
Pittstown * In Albany County 1761–1791			* See Rensselaer County
Princetown * In Albany County 1798–1809			* See Schenectady County
Rensselaerville Settlers from New England following the American Revolution 1790 Formed from Town of Watervliet 1795 Daughter town Berne formed 1815 Daughter town Westerlo formed	Connorsville Cooksburg(h) Crystal Lake Medusa Potters Hollow	Preston Hollow Rensselaerville Shoefelt Corners Smith(s) Corners Williamsburgh	• Cooksburg(h) settled 1840 • Medusa formerly Halls Hollow and Halls Mills
Rensselaerwyck (district) *See chapter 7, Land Records* 1629 Kiliaen van Rensselaer granted patroonship of Rensselaerswijck covering all of future Albany and Rensselaer counties, excepting Fort Orange 1652 Village of Beverwyck created around the Fort, separated from Rensselaerswijck 1665 English recognize Dutch patroonship and grant patent 1685 Rensselaerswijck given status of English manor 1772 Rensselaerswyck becomes a district 1779 Rensselaerswyck divided into East and West Districts 1784 Daughter town Stephentown formed from East District 1788 West District becomes Town of Watervliet 1791 Rensselaer County formed including remainder of East District 1839 Manor ceased to exist following death of Stephen Van Rensselaer III			

Towns (and Cities)	Villages and other Settlements		Notes
Saratoga * In Albany County 1772–1791			* See Saratoga County
Schaghticoke * In Albany County 1772–1791			* See Rensselaer County
Schenectady (town then city) * In Albany County 1684–1809			* See Schenectady County
Schoharie * In Albany County 1772–1795			* See Schoharie County
Stephentown * In Albany County 1784–1791			* See Rensselaer County
Stillwater * In Albany County 1788–1791			* See Saratoga County
Watervliet (city) 1896 Formed as City of Watervliet from the Village of West Troy when Town of Watervliet was dissolved and divided			
Watervliet (town) 1788–1896 1788 Formed as a town replacing the West District of Rensselaerswyck; includes all present day Albany County except the city 1790 Daughter town Rensselaerville formed 1791 Daughter town Coeymans formed 1793 Daughter town Bethlehem formed 1803 Daughter town Guilderland formed 1809 Daughter town Niskayuna formed in Schenectady County 1815 Town of Colonie dissolved and divided between Town of Watervliet and City of Albany 1869 Village of Cohoes became city 1870 Ceded North Albany to City of Albany 1871 Ceded land to Town of Guilderland 1895 Town of Colonie formed to avoid being part of City of Watervliet as plans for the new city were developed 1896 Town dissolved and divided into City of Watervliet and Town of Green Island	Boght Boght Corners Cohoes (v) Colonie (v) Crescent Station Gibbonsville (v) Green Island (v) Guilderland Hamiltonville Lishas Kil Loudonville Newtonville	Niskayuna North Albany Port Schuyler Shakers Shaker Settlement Tivoli Hollow Town House Corners Washington Watervliet Watervliet Center West Albany West Troy (v)	• Boght Corners now part of Town of Colonie • Village of Cohoes inc. 1848; became City of Cohoes 1869 • Village of Colonie inc. 1804; became Town of Colonie 1808–1815 • Village of Gibbonsville inc. 1804; became part of Village of West Troy in 1836 • Village of Green Island inc. 1853; see Town of Green Island after 1896 • Lishas Kil also LishasKil, now Lisha Kill in Town of Colonie • Loudonville formerly Ireland(s) Corners and now in Town of Colonie • Newtonville now in Town of Colonie • North Albany ceded to City of Albany 1870 • Port Schuyler became part of Village of West Troy in 1836 • Shakers and Shaker Settlement now in Town of Colonie • West Albany also Spencerville, now in Town of Colonie • Village of West Troy inc. 1836; became City of Watervliet 1896
Westerlo Settled before American Revolution 1815 Formed from towns of Coeymans and Rensselaerville	Bramans Corners Chesterville Dormansville Lambs Corners	Newry South Westerlo Van Leuvens Corners Westerlo	• Dormansville first settled 1795 • Van Leuvens Corners formerly Prestons Corners and Sackets Corners • Westerlo hamlet formerly Chesterville

Note on Early Censuses

For 1697 and 1790 censuses, see entries by Munsell and Scott in Abstracts, Indexes & Transcriptions below.

NEW YORK STATE CENSUS RECORDS

See also chapter 3, Census Records

County originals at Albany County Hall of Records: 1855, 1865, 1875, 1892, 1905, 1915, 1925 (1825, 1835, 1845 are lost)

State originals at the NYSA: 1915, 1925

Microfilm at the FHL, NYPL, and NYSL; many years are online at *FamilySearch.org* and *Ancestry.com*.

NATIONAL/STATEWIDE REPOSITORIES & RESOURCES

See chapter 16

The New York State Archives, the New York State Library and the New York State Department of Health are located in Albany; see the entries in chapter 16.

COUNTYWIDE REPOSITORIES & RESOURCES

Albany County Clerk

County Court House Room 128 • 16 Eagle Street
Albany, NY 12207-1077 • (518) 487-5100
(518) 487-5148 (Research and historical information)
Email: countyclerk@albanycounty.com • *www.albanycounty.com/clerk*

Records include court records 1793–present, adoptions 1886–1971, convictions 1896–present, deeds and mortgages 1630–present, divorces 1890–present, federal liens 1966–present, index to incompetents 1963–present, judgments 1877–present, military discharges 1917–present, patents 1784–present, and selected wills (1691–1833, 1895–1976).

Albany County – City, Town, and Village Clerks

Birth, marriage, and death records are maintained by the clerk of the municipality in which the event occurred; see Introduction to County Guides for details of other records which may also be held by municipal clerks. See municipal websites for contact information.

Unlike most city clerks, Albany City Clerk holds some vital records not available at the New York State Department of Health; see listing below and also chapter 2, Vital Records.

Albany County Surrogate's Court

Albany County Family Court Building • 30 Clinton Avenue
Albany, NY 12207 • (518) 285-8585

Holds probate records 1787–present and estate proceedings from the mid-1700s to the present. The NYSA holds most probate records prior to 1787. Also see chapter 6, Probate Records, including Harry Macy Jr.'s "New York Probate Records Before 1787."

Albany County Hall of Records

95 Tivoli Street • Albany, NY 12207 • (518) 487-5148
Email: achor@albanycounty.com • *www.albanycounty.com/achor*

Holds records of both the city and county of Albany, including: census records 1855–1925, court records 1652–1961, surrogate's court records 1800–1840, declarations of intention and naturalization 1827–1991, death records 1880–1947, marriage records for City of Albany 1870–1954, church records 1756–1997, cemetery records 1787–1997, deeds 1654–1894, mortgages 1752–1980, index to public records property transactions 1630–1940, index to wills and letters of administration 1780–1895, Civil War

allotment and correspondence 1861–1899, slave manumission register 1800–1829, Albany city directories 1830–1990, and atlases 1860–1941. See PDF on website, "Index to Historical Records," for a complete list of holdings.

Website includes finding aids to special research collections, court records, searchable online indexes including index to naturalization records 1821–1991; and records of the Constitutional Era 1783–1815, as well as a guide to researching genealogy at the Albany County Hall of Records.

Albany County Public Libraries

Albany is part of the Upper Hudson Library System; access each library at *www.uhls.org*. Information about special collections in each library relating to local history, genealogy, and archival materials can be found at *www.uhls.org/niche/Libraries.htm*. Albany Public Library, Bethlehem Public Library, Guilderland Public Library, and William K. Sanford Town Library have particularly strong collections and are listed below. The New York State Library is located in Albany; see chapter 16 for details.

Albany County Historian

Albany County Office Building • Office of the Albany County Historian
112 State Street, Room 825 • Albany, NY 12207 • (518) 447-7040

Albany County – All Municipal Historians

While not authorized to answer genealogical inquiries, county, city, town, and village historians can provide historical information and research advice; some maintain collections with genealogical material, e.g. the Town of Bethlehem historian. Some have webpages which may include transcribed records, local histories, etc. See contact information at the Albany County website *www.albanycounty.com/About/HistoricAlbanyCounty.aspx* or the website of the Association of Public Historians of New York State at *www.aphnys.org*.

REGIONAL REPOSITORIES & RESOURCES

Bard College Archives and Special Collections

See listing in Dutchess County Guide

Capital District Genealogical Society

Empire State Plaza Station • PO Box 2175 • Albany, NY 12220
www.capitaldistrictgenealogicalsociety.org

The Society documents the genealogy and history of Albany, Columbia, Fulton, Greene, Montgomery, Rensselaer, Saratoga, Schenectady, Schoharie, and Washington counties. Volunteers from the Society offer genealogy research services at the New York State Library. The *Capital District Genealogical Society Newsletter* has been published quarterly since 1982. Meetings are held at the Town of Colonie Library, Loudonville.

Fulton-Montgomery Community College Evans Library: The Kenneth R. Dorn Regional History Study Center

See listing in Fulton County Guide

The Underground Railroad History Project of the Capital Region

PO Box 10851 • Albany, NY 12201 • (518) 432-4432
Email access on website • *http://undergroundrailroadhistory.org*

Conducts original research on historical figures of the Underground Railroad.

University at Albany, SUNY

1400 Washington Avenue • Albany, NY 12222

(518) 437-3935 • http://library.albany.edu/archive
http://library.albany.edu/speccoll/albany.htm (Albany-specific collections)

M. E. Grenander Department of Special Collections and Archives has holdings on Albany, Rensselaer, and Schenectady counties. They include manuscript and archival collections, photograph collections, books and printed material. A complete list and selected digitized records are available on the University's website.

LOCAL REPOSITORIES & RESOURCES
Alphabetized by location

Albany City Clerk and Vital Statistics

City Hall • Albany, NY 12207 • (518) 434-5090

Email: cityclerk@ci.albany.ny.us • www.albanyny.org

Birth and death records for the City of Albany from September 1, 1870 to the present. Records from 1870–1913 are only available at this repository. See Albany County Hall of Records for marriage records 1870–1946. Records of births and deaths 1914–present, and marriages 1908–present, are also available at the New York State Department of Health in Albany.

Albany Institute of History & Art

125 Washington Avenue • Albany, NY 12210

(518) 463-4478 • Email: library@albanyinstitute.org
www.albanyinstitute.org

Holdings include documentary material, including photographs, architectural renderings, maps, ephemera, manuscripts, and periodicals from the 1600s–present. A complete list of holdings, research guides, and finding aids are available on the Institute's website.

Albany Public Library, Main Branch:
Pruyn Collection of Albany History

161 Washington Ave. • Albany, NY 12210 • (518) 427-4300

www.albanypubliclibrary.org/research/history/local

Holdings include microform copies of censuses, city directories, and newspapers, as well as photographs, books and pamphlets. The contents of the Pruyn Collection are not available online, but titles are searchable through the Albany Public Library's catalog.

Town of Berne Historical Society

Historical Center • Main Street • PO Box 34 • Berne, NY 12023

(518) 872-0212 • www.bernehistory.org

Website includes list of local cemeteries, list of local churches, maps, transcriptions of selected census and vital records, and family file name index.

Bethlehem Public Library: Local History

451 Delaware Avenue • Delmar, NY 12054 • (518) 439-9314
Email: information@bethlehempubliclibrary.org
www.mybethlehem.org/localhistory/index.asp

Holdings include indexes of cemetery records, Bethlehem families, and obituaries; local history files; and information on historic buildings. Selected records are available on the library's website, along with a list of microfilm holdings and links to local history organizations.

Guilderland Public Library: The Guilderland Room

2228 Western Avenue • Guilderland, NY 12084-9071

(518) 456-2400 • Email: info@guilpl.org • www.guilpl.org

Website's extensive collection of digitized local history materials can be searched and viewed online. The *Knowersville Enterprise* 1884–

1888, and its successor the *Altamont Enterprise & Albany County Post* 1884–2008, are online at http://historicnewspapers.guilpl.org. The Guilderland Room includes original documents and the book collection of former town historian Arthur B. Gregg.

William K. Sanford Town Library: Genealogy and Local History

629 Albany-Shaker Road • Loudonville, NY 12211-1196 • (518) 458-9274
www.colonie.org/library/digitalLibrary/materials/genealogy.html

Holdings include local histories, city directories on microfilm (selected years 1861–present), federal census on microfilm (1790–1930), and newspapers on microfilm (*Times-Union* 1976–present).

Ravena-Coeymans Historical Society and Museum

Ravena Village Hall • 15 Mountain Road • PO Box 324
Ravena, NY 12143 • Email: genealogy@coeymanshistory.org
www.coeymanshistory.org

Offers assistance with genealogical research.

Rensselaerville Historical Society

PO Box 8 • Rensselaerville, NY 12147 • (518) 797-5154

Holdings include genealogies, business records, school records, deeds, and cemetery records. Society publishes a quarterly newsletter, *Rensselaerville Press*. Located in the Grist Mill Museum.

New Scotland Historical Association and Museum

7 Old New Salem Road • PO Box 541 • Voorheesville, NY 12186
(518) 765-4652 • Email: newscotlandhistoricalassoc@gmail.com
www.newscotlandhistoricalassociation.org/museum.html

Website contains a list of its genealogy resources, which include cemetery records, family and local histories, religious records, and town records. Association publishes the *Sentinel*, a quarterly newsletter.

The Dutch Settlers Society of Albany

Address of current registrar on website

Email: president@dutchsettlerssociety.org • www.dutchsettlerssociety.org

Membership organization for descendants of settlers under the jurisdiction of "The Court of" Rensselaerswijck before 1665, or in Esopus (Kingston, NY) before 1661. Preserves and documents the Dutch history of Albany 1624–1664. Annual Yearbook publication of genealogies and historical studies focused on the Hudson River Region.

SELECTED PRINT & ONLINE RESOURCES

Below is a selection of resources relevant for research in this county. The list is representative, not exhaustive. Additional titles—particularly of abstracts, indexes, transcriptions, and local histories—are available; consult the introduction to Part Two for further information. For guidance on how to identify and locate community directories and local newspapers, see chapter 11, City Directories, and chapter 12, Newspapers, in Part One of this book.

Abstracts, Indexes & Transcriptions

Albany County (NY). *Index to the Public Records of the County of Albany, State of New York, 1630–1894*. 39 vols. Albany County: Argus Co., 1902–1917. Includes grantors, grantees, mortgagors, lis pendens, and maps.

Christoph, Florence A. *Upstate New York in the 1760s: Tax Lists and Selected Militia Rolls of Old Albany County, 1760–1768*. Camden, ME: Picton Press, 1992. Book includes index.

———. *Vital Records of Jerusalem Reformed Church, Feura Bush, Albany County, NY: Baptisms 1792–1886, Marriages 1822–1885, Deaths 1851–1890*. Rhinebeck, NY: A. C. M. Kelly, 1987.

Christoph, Florence A., and Peter R. Christoph. *Records of the People of the Town of Bethlehem, Albany County, New York, 1698–1880.* Selkirk, NY: Bethlehem Historical Association, 1982.

Cook, William B. "Transcript of the Baptismal and Marriage Records of the Reformed Protestant Dutch Church of the Boght, Albany County, NY." Typescript, 1954. NYPL, New York.

Conway, Martin D. *Surrogate's Court, County of Albany: Index to Wills and Letters of Administration, 1780–1895.* Albany, 1894. Organized by probate date.

County of Albany Abstracts. Syracuse: Central New York Genealogical Society, 2000. Abstracts for a range of genealogical records originally published in the quarterly *Tree Talks.*

Crounse, Appalona, comp. "Record of Deaths, Albany County, 1736–1897 (some notables included who died elsewhere …)." Typescript, 1994. NYPL, New York.

Daughters of the American Revolution, comps. *New York DAR Genealogical Records Committee Report.* Since 1913 DAR volunteers have transcribed many thousands of unpublished cemetery, church, and town records throughout New York. The reports are at the DAR Library; copies are at the NYSL and the NYPL. The DAR has a searchable name index to all the GRC reports at *http://services.dar.org/Public/DAR_Research/search/?Tab_ID=6.* See Jean Worden's index below for a listing by county of the New York record sets that were transcribed by the DAR before 1998.

Donhardt, Pat. *Second Dutch Reformed Church of Berne, Albany County, New York (Thompsons Lake Reformed Church): Church Records from March 1826 to May 1891.* Collierville, TN: Donhardt and Daughters Publishers, 1997.

Fernow, Berthold. *Calendar of Wills on File and Recorded in the Offices of the Clerk of the Court of Appeals, of the County Clerk at Albany, and of the Secretary of State, 1626–1836.* Baltimore: Genealogical Publishing Co., 1967. Reprint of 1896 ed.

First Reformed Protestant Dutch Church, Albany, New York. *Records of the Reformed Dutch Church of Albany, New York, 1683–1809: Marriages, Baptisms, Members, etc.* Baltimore: Genealogical Publishing Co., 1978. First published in the Year Books of the Holland Society of New York for 1904–1908 and 1922/23–1925/27.

Fitzgerald, Edward. *A Hand Book for the Albany Rural Cemetery, with an Appendix on Emblems.* Albany, 1871. Book includes list of officers of the Albany Cemetery Association and biographical information on people interred; arranged by section of cemetery.

Gehring, Charles T., trans. and ed. *Fort Orange Court Minutes, 1652–1660.* Syracuse: Syracuse University Press, 1990.

———, trans. and ed. *Fort Orange Records, 1656–1678.* Syracuse: Syracuse University Press, 2000.

Gehring, Charles T., and Janny Venema, trans. and ed. *Fort Orange Court Records, 1654–1679.* Syracuse: Syracuse University Press, 2009.

Hannay, William V. *Early Albany County, NY, Death Records, 1654–1883.* Rhinebeck, NY: Kinship, 2000. Book includes deacon's accounts, churchmaster's accounts, sexton's accounts, funeral information, and list of Albany pioneers/settlement dates.

Keefer, Donald A. *Marriages by the Rev. Harmanus Van Huysen, Minister of the United Dutch Reformed Congregations [sic] of Helderberg (Guilderland), Jerusalem (Feura Bush), and Salem (New Salem), Albany County, New York, from 1794 to 1825.* Rhinebeck, NY: Kinship, 1993.

Kelly, Arthur C. M. *Eighteenth-Century Persons of Albany City and County, New York: 1726–circa 1762.* Rhinebeck, NY: Kinship, 2005. Book includes indexed census substitute lists for Albany City/County.

———. *Index to Tree Talks County Packet, Albany County, NY: 1733–1936.* Rhinebeck, NY: Kinship, 2002.

———. *Marriage Records of St. Paul's Lutheran Church, Albany City, Albany County, NY, 1841–1899.* Rhinebeck, NY: Kinship, 2006.

———. *Vital Records of the Hamilton Union Church, Guilderland, Albany, New York, 1829–1899.* Rhinebeck, NY: Kinship, 1994.

Luckhurst, Charlotte T. "Cemetery at South Bethlehem, Albany County, NY." Typescript, 1929. NYPL, New York. [NYG&B eLibrary]

———. *Coeymans Cemetery Records.* Albany: The Author, 1928.

Munsell, Joel. "A List of the Heads of Families." In vol. 9, *The Annals of Albany.* Albany: J. Munsell, 1858. Contains 1697 census.

Pearson, Jonathan. *Early Records of the City and County of Albany, and Colony of Rensselaerswyck.* 4 vols. Albany: University of the State of New York, 1869–1919. Translated from the original Dutch. Vols. 2–4 edited by Arnold Johann Ferdinand van Laer; vol. 1 published by J. Munsell of Albany, NY. Vol. 1 contains Fort Orange records, vol. 2 contains deeds, vol. 3 contains notarial records, vol. 4 contains mortgages and wills.

Piwonka, Ruth. "Tax Lyste van d Stadt en County van Albany 1708/9 (Tax List of the City and County of Albany)." *NYG&B Record,* vol. 139, no. 1 (2008): 55–62. [NYG&B eLibrary]

Rankin, Russell B. "Gravestone Records from the Nicoll-Sill Burying Ground, Albany County, N.Y." *NYG&B Record,* vol. 58, no. 2 (1927): 151–153. [NYG&B eLibrary]

"Records of the Reformed Church of Bethlehem and of Reformed Church at Coeymans, Albany County, NY." Typescript, 1951. NYPL, New York.

Scott, Kenneth, comp. *New York: State Census of Albany County Towns in 1790.* Baltimore: Genealogical Publishing Co., 1975. Transcription of rescued portion of New York state census for Albany conducted in the same year as federal census.

Van Laer, Arnold Johann Ferdinand, trans. and ed. *Minutes of the Court of Albany, Rensselaerswyck and Schenectady, 1668–1685.* 3 vols. Albany: University of the State of New York, 1926–1932. Vol. 1 is a continuation of the *Minutes of the Court of Fort Orange and Beverwyck.*

———, trans. and ed. *Minutes of the Court of Fort Orange and Beverwyck.* 2 vols. Albany: University of the State of New York, 1920–1923.

———, trans. and ed. *Minutes of the Court of Rensselaerswyck, 1648–1652.* Albany: University of the State of New York, 1922.

———, trans. and ed. *Van Rensselaer Bowier Manuscripts, Being the Letters of Kiliaen Van Rensselaer, 1630–1643, and Other Documents Relating to the Colony of Rensselaerswyck.* Albany: University of the State of New York, 1908. Includes Van Laer's "Settlers of Rensselaerswyck 1630–1658."

Venema, Janny, trans. and ed., *Deacons' Accounts 1652–1674 First Dutch Reformed Church of Beverwyck/Albany, New York.* Grand Rapids, MI: Wm. B. Eerdmans Publishing Co., 1998.

Vosburgh, Royden Woodward, ed. "Records of the First Lutheran Church in the City of Albany." 2 vols. Typescript, 1917. NYPL, New York. Includes records 1774–1901.

———, ed. "Records of the Presbyterian Church of New Scotland in the Town of New Scotland, Albany County, NY." Typescript, 1919. NYPL, New York.

———, ed. "Records of the Reformed Dutch Church of the Beaver Dam in the Town of Berne, Albany County, NY." Typescript, 1918. NYPL, New York. [NYG&B eLibrary]

———, ed. "Records of St. Paul's Evangelical Lutheran Church in the Town of Berne, Albany County, NY." Typescript, 1916. NYPL, New York. [NYG&B eLibrary]

Worden, Jean D. "Albany County, New York: Rensselaerville Presbyterian (or Congregational) Church, 1794–1920; Rensselaerville Cemetery, Trinity Church Cemetery, Coeymans Reformed Church; Greene County, New York: Prattsville Church; Cairo Presbyterian Church." Typescript, 1993. NYPL, New York.

———. "Book 1, Subject Index." In *Revised Master Index to the New York State Daughters of the American Revolution Genealogical Records Volumes.* Zephyrhills, FL: J. D. Worden, 1998. The Subject Index includes a listing by county of the cemeteries and other sources of records transcribed by the DAR.

Other Resources

Beers, S. N. *New Topographical Atlas of the Counties of Albany and Schenectady, New York: From Actual Surveys by S. N. and D. G. Beers and Assistants.* Philadelphia: Stone & Stewart Publishers, 1866. [NYPL Digital Gallery]

Burr, David H. *Map of the Counties of Albany and Schenectady.* engd. by Rawdon, Clark & Co., Albany, & Rawdon, Wright & Co., New York, 1829. [NYPL Digital Gallery]

Child, Hamilton. *Gazetteer and Business Directory of Albany and Schenectady Co., NY, for 1870–71.* Syracuse: Printed at the Journal Office, 1870.

City Atlas of Albany, New York: From Official Records, Private Plans and Actual Surveys, Based Upon Plans Deposited in the Department of Surveys. Philadelphia: G. M. Hopkins & Co., 1876. [NYPL Digital Gallery]

Clark, Rufus W. *Heroes of Albany: A Memorial of the Patriot-Martyrs of the City and County of Albany, Who Sacrificed Their Lives During the Late War in Defence [sic] of Our Nation, 1861–1865 . . . and also Brief History of the Albany Regiments.* Albany: S. R. Gray, 1866. Book includes biographical sketches of more than one hundred men.

Cuyler, Reynolds. *Albany Authors: A List of Books Written by Albanians, Contained in the Collection of the Albany Institute and Historical and Art Society 1902. With Biographical Data.* Albany: The Institute, 1902.

Dutch Settlers Society of Albany Yearbook. Published by the Dutch Settlers Society, Albany, NY (irregular 1926–present). [*www.dutchsettlerssociety.org*]

Eddlemon, Sherida K. *Our Ancestors of Albany County, New York.* Bowie, MD: Heritage Books, 2004. Book includes information from Albany County censuses, city directories, and records of school meetings and fraternal orders from the late 1700s to the early 1900s.

Fay, Loren. V. *Albany County, New York, Genealogical Research Secrets.* Albany: L. V. Fay, 1983.

Giddings, Edward D. *Coeymans and the Past.* Rensselaer, NY: Tri-Centennial Committee of the Town of Coeymans, 1973. Indexed: Coner, Charles E. *Index, Coeymans and the Past.* Mukilteo, WA: C. E. Coner, 1986.

Gregg, Arthur B. *Old Hellebergh: Historical Sketches of the West Manor of Rensselaerswyck, Including an Account of the Anti-Rent Wars, the Glass House, and Henry R. Schoolcraft.* Altamont, NY: Altamont Enterprise, 1936. Index available from the Berkshire Family History Association.

Grimm, Tracy B. *World Our Fathers Made: A Survey of the Records of Local Governments in the County of Albany, New York, During the Constitutional Era, 1783–1815.* Albany: Albany County Hall of Records, 1988.

Historical Records Survey, New York State. *Inventory of the County Archives of New York State (Exclusive of the Five Counties of New York City) No. 1, Albany County.* Albany: Work Projects Administration, Historical Records Survey, 1937. [NYG&B eLibrary]

Hoff, Henry B. "Using the Dutch Settlers Society of Albany Yearbook." *NYG&B Newsletter* (now *New York Researcher*), Fall 1996. Published 2011 as a Research Aid on *NewYorkFamilyHistory.org.*

Hotchkiss, Jacob I. *The Diverse Backgrounds of Old Albany: A Concise History of Nationality Groups from Albany's Beginnings to the Erie Canal.* Albany: The Institute, 1964.

Howell, George R., and Jonathan Tenney. *Bi-Centennial History of Albany: History of the County of Albany, NY, from 1609 to 1886, with Portraits, Biographies and Illustrations.* New York: W. W. Munsell & Co., 1886.

Kelly, Arthur C. M. *The Capital.* Rhinebeck, NY: Kinship, quarterly 1986–1998; annually 1999–2001.

———. *Valley Quarterlies.* Directory of articles (vols. 1–15) and every-name index to the *Capital,* the *Columbia,* the *Mohawk,* and the *Saratoga.* Rhinebeck, NY: Kinship, CD-ROM, 2000.

Loveless, Richard W. *Genealogies of the Ancient Helleberg Escarpment and the Village of Guilderland, Albany County, New York: Including the Families of Evert Dirckse Terwilliger (c.1625–1711), Titus Tolles (c.1745–c.1805), and Simon Larrowa (1640–1711) and Two Hundred Related Families, 1623–1800.* Salt Lake City: Historical Publications, 1990.

Macy, Harry, Jr. "New York Probate Records Before 1787," in chapter 6, Probate Records.

Martin, David K. "The Districts of Albany County, New York, 1772–1784." *NYG&B Newsletter* (now *New York Researcher*), Fall 1990. Published 2011 as a Research Aid on *NewYorkFamilyHistory.org.*

Masten, Arthur H. *The History of Cohoes, New York, from its Earliest Settlement to the Present Time.* Albany: Joel Munsell, 1877.

Munsell, Joel. *The Annals of Albany.* 10 vols. Albany: J. Munsell, 1850–1859. Includes bibliographical references and indexes.

———. *Collections on the History of Albany: From its Discovery to the Present Time, with Notices of its Public Institutions, and Biographical Sketches of Citizens Deceased.* 4 vols. Albany: J. Munsell, 1864. Book includes government and religious records, genealogies, transportation, newspapers, politics, etc.

New York Historical Resources Center. *Guide to Historical Resources in Albany County, New York, Repositories.* Ithaca, NY: Cornell University, 1984.

Parker, Amasa J. *Landmarks of Albany County, New York*. Syracuse: D. Mason, 1897. Book includes biographical and family sketches.

Pearson, Jonathan. *Contributions for the Genealogies of the First Settlers of the Ancient County of Albany, from 1630 to 1800*. Albany: J. Munsell, 1872.

———. *A History of the Schenectady Patent in the Dutch and English Times: Being Contributions Toward a History of the Lower Mohawk Valley*. Albany: J. Munsell's Sons, 1883. Book includes bibliographical references and indexes.

Prominent People of the Capital District. Albany: Fort Orange Recording Bureau, Inc., 1923.

Rittner, Don. *Albany Revisited*. Charleston, SC: Arcadia, 2008.

———. *Remembering Albany: Heritage on the Hudson*. Charleston, SC: History Press, 2009.

Van Laer, Arnold Johan Ferdinand. *Settlers of Rensselaerswyck, 1630–1658*. Baltimore: Genealogical Publishing Co., 1965. First published 1908 by New York State Library, Albany.

Venema, Janny. *Beverwijck: A Dutch Village on the American Frontier, 1652–1664*. Albany: State University of New York Press, 2003.

Weise, Arthur J. *The History of the City of Albany, New York: From the Discovery of the Great River in 1524, by Verrazzano, to the Present Time*. Albany: E. H. Bender, 1884. Book includes colonial settlement, Native Americans, frontier history, trade, wealth, churches, newspapers, local politics, changed names of streets, Freemasons, censuses, etc.

Additional Online Resources

AlbanyCounty.com: Historic Albany County
www.albanycounty.com/About/HistoricAlbanyCounty.aspx
    Research guides to historic and genealogical records, historical overview, and links to relevant websites from the official Albany County website.

Albany Hill Towns
www.albanyhilltowns.com
    Provides historical information on the Helderberg Hilltowns of Albany County: Berne, Knox, Rensselaerville, and Westerlo. Wiki includes biographies, maps, general history, military history, family histories and genealogy, photographs, and information on land divisions, churches, cemeteries, schools, organizations, businesses, and communities.

Ancestry.com
    There are vast numbers of records on *Ancestry.com* that pertain to people who have lived in New York State. See chapter 16 for a description of Ancestry.com's resources and its partnership with the New York State Archives. A search of the online card catalog by county may reveal lesser known resources that pertain to a locality, such as town records, abstracts, transcriptions, city directories, and local histories.

Capital District Library Council
www.cdlc.org
    The Council is the service provider for the Capital District Region of the Documentary Heritage Program. Its online Directory of Repositories provides a comprehensive list of organizations in the region (including Albany County) that hold historical records. It includes collection details, location and contact information, as well as links to websites.

Connors Genealogy
http://connorsgenealogy.com/Albany
    The website provides transcriptions of Albany County naturalizations 1836–1864 for many Irish-born residents and an online surname registry (lists surname, year arrived/moved to Albany, last known Albany address, and current contact information of the researcher).

FamilySearch.org
    A detailed description of resources is found in chapter 16, National and Statewide Repositories & Resources. FamilySearch has extensive collections of New York records, including religious records, which are searchable by name and location, but not by county. For land records in Albany County, search in both Albany County and the "all counties" database; this is necessary because of cataloging errors made by FHL.

    For Probate records, many counties' records may be listed under Albany County; see Remington and Macy in chapter 6, Probate Records.

The New Netherland Research Center
www.nysl.nysed.gov/newnetherland/nnp.htm
    The center's New Netherland Project transcribes, translates, and publishes seventeenth-century documents from Dutch New Netherland that are held in New York repositories. Holdings of the NYSL that have been transcribed and translated by the Project include: Dutch Colonial Council Minutes, Van Rensselaer Manor Papers, and Holland Land Company Records. (For full listing see chapter 14, Peoples of New York, Dutch.)

New York State Museum exhibit: People of Colonial Albany Live Here
www.nysm.nysed.gov/albany
    This interactive web exhibit of the Colonial Albany Social History Project presents material relating to residents of the city of Albany born before 1800; includes articles, biographies, family pages, images, maps, wills, and information on Albany militia, businesses, churches, ethnic groups, land divisions, laws, and cemeteries.

World Our Fathers Made: A Survey of the Records in the County of Albany During the Constitutional Era 1783–1815.
www.albanycounty.com/Government/Departments/AlbanyCountyHallofRecords.aspx
    This online finding aid on the Hall of Records website identifies published and unpublished records and indexes to records of Albany County, including those held by the county clerk. Print version available at NYSL.

Allegany County

Formed April 7, 1806

Parent County   Genesee
Daughter Counties   None
County Seat   Village of Belmont, Town of Amity

Major Land Transactions
See chapter 7, Land Records
Phelps and Gorham Purchase 1788
Morris Reserve 1791
Holland Land Company Purchase 1792–1796

Indian Territories
See chapter 14, Peoples of New York, American Indian
Seneca Nation: Oil Springs Reservation (1797–present)

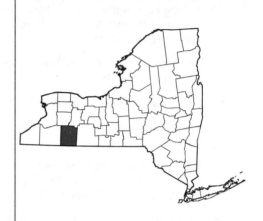

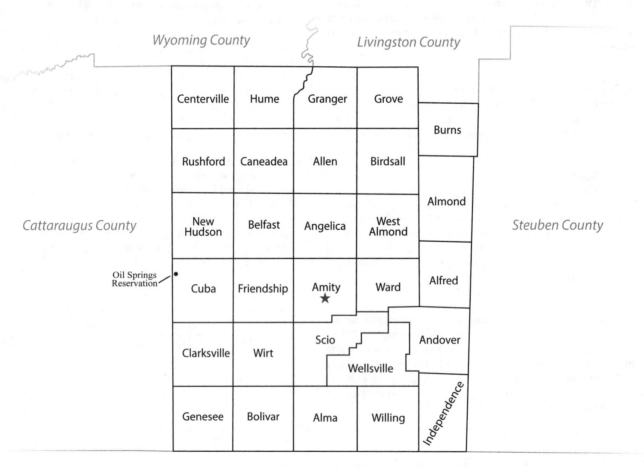

Town Boundary Map
★ - County seat

Towns (and Cities)	Villages and other Settlements	Notes
Alfred 1807 Settled 1808 Formed from Town of Angelica 1816 Annexed land from Angelica 1821 Daughter towns Almond and Harrison (now Independence) formed 1833 Daughter town West Almond formed 1856 Daughter town Ward formed	Alfred (v) Alfred Center Alfred Station Five Corners Tinkertown Tip Top Vandemark	• Village of Alfred inc. 1881 • Alfred Station formerly Bakers Bridge
Allen 1800 Settled 1823 Formed from Town of Angelica 1829 Daughter town Birdsall formed	Allen Bakers Creek Allen Center West Allen Aristotle	
Alma 1833 Settlers from Quebec 1854 Formed from Town of Willing	Allentown Honeoye Creek Alma Pike(s)ville Ford Brook Vosburg	• Alma formerly Honeoye Corners, Honeoye, and Shongo • Vosburg on Bolivar town line
Almond 1796 Settlers from Pennsylvania at Karr Valley 1821 Formed from Town of Alfred 1829 Daughter town Birdsall formed 1833 Daughter town West Almond formed	Almond (v) Karr Valley Bishopville North Almond Center Almond North Almond Valley Karrdale West Almond	• Village of Almond inc. 1821; shared with Town of Hornellsville, Steuben County • West Almond in Town of West Almond after 1833
Amity 1804 Settled near Belvidere 1830 Formed from towns of Angelica and Scio 1856 Daughter town Ward formed	Belmont (v) Belvidere Belvidere Station Withey	• Belmont inc. 1853 as Village of Philipsville (formerly Phillipsburgh); name changed to Belmont in 1870s; village became county seat in 1859, alternating with Angelica until 1892
Andover 1795–96 Settlers from Pennsylvania and Connecticut at Elm Valley 1824 Formed from Town of Harrison (now Independence) 1855 Daughter town Wellsville formed	Andover (v) Elm Valley	• Village of Andover inc. 1892 • Elm Valley formerly Shoemakers Corners; on Wellsville town line
Angelica 1802 Settled at Angelica Village 1805 Formed in Genesee County from Town of Leicester * 1806 Transferred to new county of Allegany 1808 Daughter towns Alfred, Caneadea, and Nunda formed 1816 Ceded land to Town of Alfred 1823 Daughter towns Allen and Scio formed 1830 Daughter town Amity formed 1833 Daughter town West Almond formed	Angelica (v) Aristotle County House Shoemakers Corners State Road	* Town of Leicester now in Livingston County • Village of Angelica inc. 1835; was the sole county seat 1806–1859; courts alternated with Belmont 1859–1892; in 1892 Belmont became the sole county seat

Towns (and Cities)	Villages and other Settlements		Notes
Belfast 1803 Settlers from Pennsylvania on Genesee River 1824 Formed as Orrinsburgh from Town of Caneadea 1825 Name changed to Belfast	Belfast Rockville Summer Valley Transit Bridge		
Birdsall 1816 Settled 1829 Formed from towns of Allen and Almond	Birdsall Birdsall Center Grove	Hiltonville Scholes	• Grove on Grove town line
Bolivar 1819 Settlers from Otsego County 1825 Formed from Town of Friendship 1838 Daughter town Wirt formed	Bolivar (v) Hoben Kossuth Richburg (v)	Sawyer South Bolivar Vosburg	• Village of Bolivar inc. 1882 • Village of Richburg inc. 1882; shared with Town of Wirt • South Bolivar also Honeoye Forks and Honeoye Corners • Vosburg on Alma town line
Burns 1805 Settled at Whitney Valley 1826 Formed from Town of Ossian, Livingston County	Burns Burns Station Canaseraga (v) Garwood(s)	Garwoods Station Gas Spring Mastin Corners Moraine Whitneys Crossing(s)	• Burns also Burns Village, formerly DeWittsburgh, DeWitts Valley, and DeWittsville • Village of Canaseraga inc. 1892; formerly Whitney Valley
Caneadea 1800 Settlers from Pennsylvania 1808 Formed from Town of Angelica 1815 Daughter town Friendship formed 1816 Daughter town Rushford formed 1824 Daughter town Orrinsburgh (now Belfast) formed	Caneadea Houghton Houghton Creek Oramel (v)		• Houghton also Jockey Street • Village of Oramel inc. 1856 and dissolved 1925
Centerville 1808 Settlers from Rhode Island 1819 Formed from Town of Pike	Centerville Fairview	Higgins Welsh Settlement	• Fairview on Rushford town line
Church Tract Name for Town of Grove 1827–1828			
Clarksville 1822 Settlers from Warsaw, Wyoming County 1835 Formed from Town of Cuba	Clarksville Clarksville Corners Germantown	North Clarkstown Obi West Clarksville	• North Clarkstown also North Clarksville • Obi on Genesee town line
Cuba * 1817 Settled 1822 Formed from Town of Friendship 1830 Daughter town Genesee formed 1835 Daughter town Clarksville formed	Cadysville Cuba (v) Cuba Summit	North Cuba South Cuba	* Cuba also known as Town of Oil Creek • Village of Cuba inc. 1850 • North Cuba also Seymour
Eagle * In Allegany County 1823–1846			* See Wyoming County

Towns (and Cities)	Villages and other Settlements		Notes
Friendship 1806 Settlers from Kingston, Ulster County 1815 Formed from Town of Caneadea 1822 Daughter town Cuba formed 1825 Daughter town Bolivar formed 1838 Daughter town Wirt formed	Friendship (v) Higgins Nile		• Friendship established as fire district in 1881, village legally dissolved 4/4/1977 • Nile also South Branch; on Wirt town line
Genesee 1823 Settlers from Rensselaer County on Genesee Creek 1830 Formed from Town of Cuba	Bowler Ceres Coon Hollow Deer Creek Dodges Creek Little Genesee	Obi Prosser Rock City Salt Rising Sanford Wolf Creek	• Obi on Clarksville town line
Granger 1816 Settlers from Vermont and Otsego County 1838 Formed as West Grove from Town of Grove 1839 Name changed to Granger	East Granger Granger Hickory Swale Short Tract		
Grove 1818 Settlers from Herkimer County 1827 Formed as Church Tract from Town of Nunda 1828 Name changed to Grove 1838 Daughter town West Grove (now Granger) formed	Brewer Corners Chautauque Valley Grove Grove Center Rosses Swain Van Nostrand Crossing		• Grove on Birdsall town line • Rosses shared with Town of Nunda, Livingston County • Swain formerly Swain Station, Swainsville, and Swin
Haight Name for Town of New Hudson 1825–1837			
Harrison Name for Town of Independence 1821–1827			
Hume 1807 Settlers from Montgomery County at Mills Mills 1822 Formed from Town of Pike	Cold Creek Fillmore (v) Hume Mills Mills	Mixville Rossburg Wiscoy	• Village of Fillmore inc. 1924 and dissolved 1/13/1994 • Rossburg formerly Mixville Landing and Wiscoy Landing
Independence 1819 Settlers from Madison County at Whitesville 1821 Formed as Harrison from Town of Alfred 1824 Daughter town Andover formed 1827 Name changed to Independence 1851 Daughter town Willing formed	Fulmer Valley Green(s) Corners Independence Spring Mills Whitesville		
New Hudson 1820 Settlers from Waterbury, VT 1825 Formed as Haight from Town of Rushford 1837 Name changed to New Hudson	Bellville Black Creek Lyons Corners Marshall	McGrawville New Hudson New Hudson Corners Rawson	• Bellville formerly North Valley

Towns (and Cities)	Villages and other Settlements		Notes
Nunda * In Allegany County 1808–1846			* See Livingston County
Orrinsburgh (Name for Town of Belfast 1824–1825)			
Ossian * In Allegany County 1808–1856			* See Livingston County
Pike * In Allegany County 1818–1846			* See Wyoming County
Portage * In Allegany County 1827–1846			* See Livingston County
Rushford 1808 Settlers from Vermont 1816 Formed from Town of Caneadea 1825 Daughter town Haight (now New Hudson) formed	Balcom Beach East Rushford Fairview Hardy Corners	Hillcrest Kellogville Rushford	• Fairview on Centerville town line
Scio 1805 Settlers from Oneida County 1823 Formed from Town of Angelica 1830 Daughter town Amity formed 1851 Daughter town Willing formed 1855 Daughter town Wellsville formed	Knight(s) Creek Norton Summit Petrolia Scio		
Ward 1817 Settlers from Ontario County 1856 Formed from towns of Alfred and Amity	Philips Creek Vandermark Creek		
Wellsville 1800 Settled 1855 Formed from towns of Andover, Scio, and Willing	Elm Valley Genesee Stannards Wellsville (v)		• Elm Valley formerly Dyke and Shoemakers Corners; on Andover town line • Stannards on Willing town line • Village of Wellsville inc. 1857
West Almond 1833 Formed from towns of Alfred, Almond, and Angelica	Bennetts West Almond		• West Almond in Town of Almond before 1833
West Grove Name for Town of Granger 1838–1839			
Willing 1825 Settlers from Brookfield, Madison County 1851 Formed from towns of Independence and Scio 1854 Daughter town Alma formed 1855 Daughter town Wellsville formed	Beanville Graves Elmwood Hallsport Hawk(e)s Mapes	Paynesville Shongo Stannards Stone Dam York Corners	• Elmwood also MacDougall's Stand • Shongo formerly Honeoye • Stannards formerly Stannards Corners, also Stanard; on Wellsville town line
Wirt 1812 Settlers from Amsterdam, Montgomery County 1838 Formed from towns of Bolivar and Friendship	Inavale Nile Richburg (v)	Utopia West Notch Wirt	• Nile also South Branch; on Friendship town line • Village of Richburg inc. 1881; shared with the Town of Bolivar • Wirt also Wirt Center

NEW YORK STATE CENSUS RECORDS

See also chapter 3, Census Records

County originals at Allegany County Clerk's Office: 1855, 1865*, 1875, 1892, 1905, 1915, 1925 (1825, 1835 and 1845** are lost)

State originals at the NYSA: 1915, 1925

Microfilm at the FHL, NYPL, and NYSL; many years are online at *FamilySearch.org* and *Ancestry.com*.

* For 1865 transcription of all towns, see Burton in Abstracts, Indexes & Transcriptions; and for online transcriptions for the towns of Friendship and Genesee, see Barrett in Abstracts, Indexes & Transcriptions.

** 1845 census is lost except for the original for Belfast and an index for Genesee. Original for Town of Belfast at Belfast Public Library. For the index for Genesee, see DeGroff in Abstracts, Indexes & Transcriptions.

NATIONAL/STATEWIDE REPOSITORIES & RESOURCES

See chapter 16

COUNTYWIDE REPOSITORIES & RESOURCES

Allegany County Clerk

7 Court Street, Room 18 • Belmont, NY 14813
(585) 268-9270 • *www.alleganyco.com*

Federal censuses for Allegany County 1850, 1870, 1880, New York state censuses for Allegany County 1855, 1865, 1875, 1892, 1905, 1915, 1925, civil court records 1806–present, deeds and mortgages, military discharges, land records 1806–present, marriages 1908–1935, and 19th-century naturalizations.

Allegany County – Town and Village Clerks

Birth, marriage, and death records are maintained by the clerk of the municipality in which the event occurred; see Introduction to County Guides for details of other records which may also be held by municipal clerks. See list of town/village clerks at *www.alleganyco.com*.

Allegany County Surrogate's Court

7 Court Street • Belmont, NY 14813 • (585) 268-5815

Holds probate records from 1807 to the present. Also see chapter 6, Probate Records.

Allegany County Public Libraries

Allegany is part of the Southern Tier Library System; see *www.stls.org/libraries* to access each library. Many hold genealogy and local history collections, including maps and newspapers. For example, Andover Free Library has digitized the *Andover Advertiser*, 1867–1978, available on their website *www.andoverfreelibrary.org*; Belmont's local history collection includes the *Belmont Dispatch*, 1900–1966. Also see listings below for the Bolivar Free and David Howe Libraries.

Allegany County Historical Society

PO Box 588 • Wellsville, NY 14895 • (585) 268-7428
Email: alleganychs@gmail.com • *www.alleganycountynylocalhistory.org*

Census transcripts 1810, 1850, 1865; veterans' information; obituaries; cemetery information; and burial lists. The Genealogy Research Center & Offices are located at the David A. Howe Public Library, see listing below. Website contains an extensive collection of digitized materials, including biographies, census transcriptions, obituaries, select genealogies, and lists of online resources.

Allegany County Historian

7 Court Street • Belmont, NY 14813 • (585) 268-9293
Email: historian@alleganyco.com • *www.gahwny.org/p/allegany.html*

Allegany County – All Municipal Historians

While not authorized to answer genealogical inquiries, county, town and village historians can provide historical information and research advice; some maintain collections and webpages which may include transcribed records, local histories, and other genealogical material. See contact information at the Government Appointed Historians of Western New York at *www.gahwny.org/p/allegany.html* or at the website of the Association of Public Historians of New York State at *www.aphnys.org*.

Alfred State College: Jean B. Lang Western New York Historical Collection

Hinkle Memorial Library • 10 Upper College Drive
Alfred, NY 14802 • (607) 587-4313
Email: library@alfredstate.edu • *www.alfredstate.edu/library*

Collection includes census microfilm and abstracts, newspapers, books, archives, histories, atlases and maps, photographs, artifacts, and costumes. The collection of the Alfred Historical Society is housed here, see listing below.

Alfred University: Herrick Memorial Library: Alfred Collection

Alfred University • One Saxon Drive • Alfred, NY 14802
(607) 871-2385 • Email: herricklibrary@alfred.edu
http://herr.alfred.edu/special/collections/alfred_collection.cfm

Holds genealogical and historical material of local interest, publications by local authors, and material on Seventh Day Baptists. A catalog of holdings is available on the Library website.

The Bolivar-Richburg-Allentown-Genesee Historical Preservation Society (B.R.A.G.)

Bolivar Free Library • 390 Main Street • Bolivar, NY 14715
(585) 928-2659 • Email address on website • *www.brag.4mg.com*

Census records (including Indian census), the *Bolivar Breeze* newspaper on microfiche 1895–1965, genealogies, a computerized family name database, obituaries, military records, local cemetery records, and vital records. Society publishes quarterly newsletter, *Blast From the Past*.

REGIONAL REPOSITORIES & RESOURCES

Milne Library at SUNY Geneseo: Special Collections: Genesee Valley Historical Collection

See listing in Livingston County Guide

Painted Hills Genealogy Society

Email: paint@paintedhills.org • *www.paintedhills.org*

Website provides transcribed records: Bible records (Cattaraugus and Steuben only); cemetery listings with some transcriptions; death notices and obituaries; vital records; wills; censuses; religious records (Allegany only); biographies, family histories, and genealogies; military information, including Civil War soldiers lists; city directories (Cattaraugus only); newspaper clippings including the *Cattaraugus Republican*; school records; property maps (Steuben only); postcards, scrapbooks, and photographs; maps of Allegany, Cattaraugus, Chautauqua, and Steuben Counties.

SUNY Fredonia: Daniel A. Reed Library:
Archives & Special Collections
See listing in Chautauqua County Guide

University of Rochester: Rare Books, Special Collections,
and Preservation: Manuscript and Special Collections:
Rochester, Western New York, and New York State
See listing in Monroe County Guide

Western New York Genealogical Society
See listing in Erie County Guide

Western New York Heritage Press
See listing in Erie County Guide

LOCAL REPOSITORIES & RESOURCES
Alphabetized by location

Alfred Historical Society
PO Box 1137 • Alfred, NY 14802 • (607) 587-8358

Society's collection is located at the Hinkle Library, Alfred State College. It includes genealogies of Alfred residents and local Seventh Day Baptist families.

Allegany Area Historical Association
25 North Second Street • PO Box 162
Allegany, NY 14706 • Email access on website
www.allegany.org/town.php?AlleganyAreaHistoricalAssociation

The Association is headquartered in the former United Methodist Church in Allegany village. Holdings include business records, city directories, genealogies, journals and diaries, local histories, and scrapbooks. A complete list of families whose histories are documented by the Association is available on its website. The Association publishes a newsletter; issues 2004–present are on the website.

Almond Historical Society
7 Main Street • Almond, NY 14804 • (607) 276-6324
Email: AlmondHistoricalSociety@gmail.com
http://almondhistory.wordpress.com

Holdings include local family files, marriage certificates, pictures, scrapbooks, cemetery indexes, and yearbooks. Society publishes quarterly newsletter.

Town of Hume Museum
10842 Claybed Road • Hume, NY 14735
(585) 567-8399 • Email: museum@humetown.org
www.humetown.org/HISTORYMAIN.html

Holdings include index of local marriages, obituaries, and special events.

David A. Howe Public Library: Genealogy Resources
155 North Main Street • Wellsville, NY 14895
Email: wellsville@stls.org • *www.davidahowelibrary.org/genealogy.htm*

Microfilm holdings include federal census for Allegany County, 1810–1880, and many county and local newspapers, including *Allegany County Reporter*, 1874–1930, *Allegany County Republican*, 1879–1898, *Allegany County Democrat* (various years). Website has online catalog of its historical and genealogical records and links to online resources. The Genealogy Research Center & Offices of the Allegany County Historical Society are also located in the library.

SELECTED PRINT & ONLINE RESOURCES

Below is a selection of resources relevant for research in this county. The list is representative, not exhaustive. Additional titles—particularly of abstracts, indexes, transcriptions, and local histories—are available; consult the introduction to Part Two for further information. For guidance on how to identify and locate community directories and local newspapers, see chapter 11, City Directories, and chapter 12, Newspapers, in Part One of this book.

Abstracts, Indexes & Transcriptions

Barber, Gertrude Audrey. "Gravestone Inscriptions in Allegany County, New York: Including Cemeteries in Granger, East Caneadea, Allen Center, Hume, Houghton, and Centerville." Typescript, 1933. NYPL, New York. [*Ancestry.com*]

———. "Gravestone Inscriptions of Allegany County, New York, including Cemeteries in Filmore and Hume, NY." Typescript, 1932. NYPL, New York. [*NYG&B eLibrary*]

———. "Gravestone Inscriptions of Until the Day Dawns Cemetery, Angelica, NY; Pine Grove Cemetery, Filmore, NY; All in Allegany County." Typescript, 1933. NYPL, New York. [*PaintedHills.org*]

Barrett, Charlie. "1865 New York State Census - Friendship, Allegany County." NYGenWeb Project. *www.rootsweb.ancestry.com/~nyallega/Friendship1865.html*.

———. "1865 New York State Census - Genesee, Allegany County." NYGenWeb Project. *www.rootsweb.ancestry.com/~nyallega/Genesee1865.html*.

Burton, Mrs. Charles. "1865 Census Index of Allegany County, New York." Manuscript, n.d. Western New York Genealogical Society Library, Buffalo, New York.

County of Allegany Abstracts. Syracuse: Central New York Genealogical Society, 2000. Abstracts for a range of genealogical records originally published in the quarterly *Tree Talks*.

Daughters of the American Revolution, comps. *New York DAR Genealogical Records Committee Report.* Since 1913 DAR volunteers have transcribed many thousands of unpublished cemetery, church, and town records throughout New York. The reports are at the DAR Library; copies are at the NYSL and the NYPL. The DAR has a searchable name index to all the GRC reports at *http://services.dar.org/Public/DAR_Research/search/?Tab_ID=6*. See Jean Worden's index below for a listing by county of the New York record sets that were transcribed by the DAR before 1998.

DeGroff, Jerald S. "Index to the 1845 State Census for the Town of Genesee, Allegany Co." Western New York Genealogical Society Journal, vol. 14, no. 2 (September 1987): 64–65.

Kelly, Arthur C. M. *Index to Tree Talks County Packet: Allegany County.* Rhinebeck, NY: Kinship, 2002.

Mountford, Sharon. "1855 New York State Census: Friendship, Allegany, New York." NYGenWeb Project. *www.rootsweb.ancestry.com/~nyallega/1855friend.html*.

Samuelsen, W. David. *Allegany County, New York, Willbook Index, 1836–1906.* Salt Lake City: Sampubco, 1992.

Sanford, Ilou M., and Frank L. Greene. *First Alfred Seventh Day Baptist Church Membership Records, Alfred, New York, 1816–1886.* Bowie, MD: Heritage Books, 1995.

Western New York Genealogical Society Journal. Hamburg, NY: Western New York Genealogical Society, 1974–present. An index to journal articles is at *wnygs.org.*

Wood, C. B., and Archie H. Eldridge, comps. "Some Cemeteries of Allegany County." Typescript, n.d. Onondaga County Public Library, Syracuse. [NYG&B eLibrary]

Worden, Jean D. "Book 1, Subject Index." In *Revised Master Index to the New York State Daughters of the American Revolution Genealogical Records Volumes.* Zephyrhills, FL: J. D. Worden, 1998. The Subject Index includes a listing by county of the cemeteries, churches, towns, and other sources of records transcribed by the DAR.

Other Resources

Beers, D. G. & Co. *Atlas of Allegany County, New York: From Actual Survey and Official Records.* New York, 1869.

Beers, F.W. & Co. *History of Allegany County, New York: With Illustrations Descriptive of Scenery, Private Residences, Public Buildings, Fine Blocks, and Important Manufactories from Original Sketches by Artists of the Highest Ability, and Portraits of Old Pioneers and Prominent Residents.* New York, 1879.

Child, Hamilton. *Gazetteer and Business Directory of Allegany County, NY, for 1875.* Syracuse, 1875.

Colombo, Robert N. *To Save the Union: Volunteers in the Civil War from Centerville, Hume, and Granger Townships, Allegany County, New York.* Westminster, MD: Heritage Books, 2007.

Fay, Loren V. *Allegany County, New York, Genealogical Research Secrets.* Albany: L. V. Fay, 1983.

Foley, Janet W. *Early Settlers of New York State: Their Ancestors and Descendants.* 9 vols. Akron, NY: 1934–1942. Reprint, 2 vols. Baltimore, Genealogical Publishing Co., 1993.

French, Robert. *History of Allegany County, New York, 1806-1879: A Name Index.* Interlaken, NY: Heart of the Lakes Publishing, 1978.

Minard, John S. *Allegany County and Its People: A Centennial Memorial History of Allegany County, New York. Also Histories of the Towns of the County.* Edited by Georgia Drew Merrill. Alfred, NY, 1896.

———. *Hume Pioneer Sketches: A History of Early Times, First Settlers, Pioneer Experiences and Hardships, Our Predecessors, the "Six Nations," etc.* Fillmore, NY, 1888.

Newman, Lucile Thornton. *Centennial, St. Paul's Episcopal Church, Angelica, New York, Diocese of Western New York: A Short History of the Parish, 1827–1927.* Angelica, NY: n.p. 1927.

New York Historical Resources Center. *Guide to Historical Resources in Allegany County, New York, Repositories.* Ithaca, NY: Cornell University, 1983.

Thomson, Mrs. Howard B. *A History of the Town of Wirt and Village of Richburgh, New York.* Wirt, NY: The Author, 1963.

Additional Online Resources

AlfredNY.Biz
www.alfredny.biz/about_alfred.htm
Website provides links to genealogical and historical information for the Town of Alfred and for Allegany County; including links to countywide repositories and a wide range of online records.

Ancestry.com
There are vast numbers of records on *Ancestry.com* that pertain to people who have lived in New York State. See chapter 16 for a description of *Ancestry.com*'s resources and its partnership with the New York State Archives. A search of the online card catalog by county may reveal lesser known resources that pertain to a locality, such as town records, abstracts, transcriptions, city directories, and local histories.

FamilySearch
FamilySearch has extensive collections of New York records, including religious records, which are searchable by name and location, but not by county. The following collections include record images (browsable, but not searchable) that are organized by county:

- "New York, Land Records, 1630–1975." Includes land and property records. *familysearch.org/search/collection/2078654*
- "New York, Probate Records, 1629–1971." Includes wills, letters of administration, and guardianship papers. *familysearch.org/search/collection/1920234*

For both collections, choose the browse option and then select Allegany to view the available records sets.

A detailed description of *FamilySearch.org* resources, which include the catalog of the Family History Library, is found in chapter 16.

NYGenWeb Project: Allegany County
www.rootsweb.ancestry.com/~nyallega
Part of the national, USGenWeb volunteer initiative, the website provides information and resources for county research.

Old Fulton New York Postcards
www.FultonHistory.com
The website provides free access to a vast collection of digitized New York newspapers, including 13 titles for Allegany County.

Painted Hills Genealogy Society, Allegany County, New York Index Page
www.paintedhills.org/allco.html
The county webpage of this regional society has direct links to numerous records transcriptions of cemeteries for the county as well as census information, family histories, and other historical resources.

Broome County

Formed March 28, 1806

Parent County   Tioga
Daughter Counties   None
County Seat   City of Binghamton

Major Land Transactions
See table in chapter 7, Land Records
Boston Ten Towns 1787

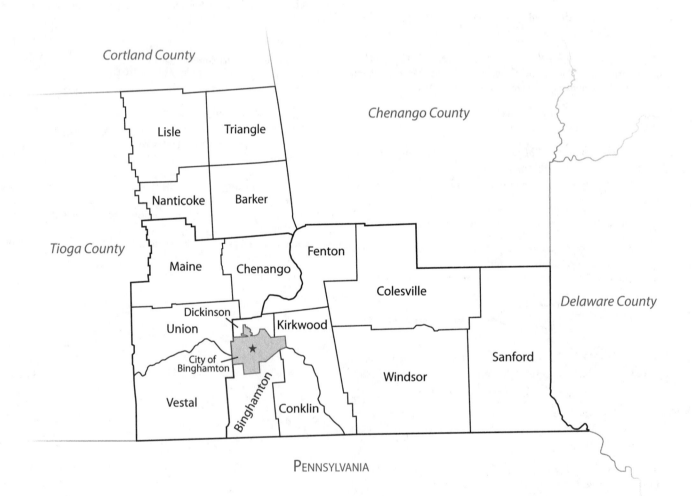

Town Boundary Map
★ - County seat

Towns (and Cities)	Villages and other Settlements		Notes
Barker 1791 Settlers from Connecticut 1831 Formed from Town of Lisle 1840 Annexed land from Town of Greene, Chenango County	Adams Settlement Barker Chenango Forks Hydeville Itaska		• Southern part of Chenango Forks in Town of Chenango; Chenango Forks in Chenango County before 1840 • Hydeville also Hyde Settlement
Berkshire * In Broome County 1808–1822			* See Tioga County
Binghamton (city) * 1813 Incorporated as Village of Chenango Point in Town of Chenango 1855 Transferred to Town of Binghamton as Village of Binghamton 1867 Village became City of Binghamton			* County seat at Binghamton 1806–present: 1806–1813 as hamlet of Chenango Point; 1813–1855 as Village of Chenango Point; 1855–1867 as Village of Binghamton, and from 1867 as City of Binghamton
Binghamton (town) 1787 Settlers from New England 1855 Formed from Town of Chenango 1867 Village of Binghamton became City of Binghamton 1890 Daughter town Dickinson formed	Binghamton (v) Hawleyton Park Terrace Port Dickinson (v) Summit Hill		• Village of Binghamton inc. 1813 as Village of Chenango Point in Town of Chenango; name changed 1834; in Town of Binghamton from 1855; became City of Binghamton in 1867 • Port Dickinson was Carmansville in Town of Chenango before 1855; inc. 1876 as Village of Port Dickinson in Town of Binghamton; 1890 transferred to Town of Dickinson
Chenango 1787 Settled 1791 Formed in Tioga County 1806 Transferred to new county of Broome 1807 Daughter town Windsor formed 1808 Annexed land from Town of Union 1824 Daughter town Conklin formed 1855 Daughter towns Binghamton and Port Crane (now Fenton) formed	Carmansville Castle Creek Castle Farm Chenango Chenango Bridge Chenango Forks Chenango Point (v)	Glen Castle Hinmans Corners Kattelville Newmans Corner Nimmonsburg West Chenango	• Carmansville now Village of Port Dickinson in Town of Dickinson • Chenango Forks mostly in Town of Barker • Village of Chenango Point inc. 1813; renamed Binghamton 1834; moved to Town of Binghamton 1855; became City of Binghamton 1867 • Kattelville also Cattellville and Kettleville
Colesville 1785 Settlers from Connecticut 1821 Formed from Town of Windsor	Belden Belden Hill Center Village Colesville Doraville Fish Island Harpursville New Ohio Nineveh	North Colesville Ouaquaga Sanitaria Springs Susquehanna Tunnel Unitaria Vallonia Springs West Colesville	• Doraville formerly Dora • Harpursville also Harpersville and Harpurville • Sanitaria Springs formerly Osborne(s) Hollow
Conklin 1788 Settled 1824 Formed from Town of Chenango 1859 Daughter town Kirkwood formed	Conklin Conklin Center Conklin Forks Conklin Station	Corbettsville Kirkwood Millburn	

Towns (and Cities)	Villages and other Settlements		Notes
Dickinson 1890 Formed from Town of Binghamton	Chenango Shores Port Dickinson (v)	Stella Sunrise Terrace	• Village of Port Dickinson inc. 1876 in Town of Binghamton; reincorporated 1890 in Town of Dickinson; before 1855 was Carmansville in Town of Chenango
Fenton 1788 Settled 1855 Formed as Port Crane from Town of Chenango 1867 Name changed to Fenton	Hillcrest North Fenton Pleasant Hill	Port Crane Quinneville Wyman Corner	• North Fenton also Ketchums Corners
Kirkwood 1859 Formed from Town of Conklin	Brookvale Five Mile Point Kirkwood Kirkwood Center Langdon	Popes Ravine Riverside Standley Hollow South Osborne Hollow	• Standley Hollow formerly South Osborne
Lisle 1791 Settlers from New England 1801 Formed in Tioga County from Town of Union 1806 Transferred to new county of Broome 1827 Ceded land to Town of Union 1831 Daughter towns Barker, Nanticoke, and Triangle formed	Center Lisle Killawog Lisle (v) Manningville Millville		• Center Lisle formerly Yorkshire • Killawog formerly Union Village • Village of Lisle inc. 1866
Maine 1797 Settled 1848 Formed from Town of Union	Arbutus Bowers Corners East Maine Maine	New Ireland North Maine Tiona	
Nanticoke 1793 Settlers from Luzerne County, PA 1831 Formed from Town of Lisle	Glen Aubrey Lambs Corners Nanticoke Nanticoke Springs		
Owego * In Broome County 1813–1822			* See Tioga County (Owego called Tioga 1806–1813)
Port Crane Name for Town of Fenton 1855–1867			
Sanford 1787 Settlers from New Hampshire 1821 Formed from Town of Windsor	Cuif Summit Danville Deposit (v) Gulf Summit Howes	McClure Mount Carmel North Sanford San(d)ford Vallonia Springs	• Village of Deposit inc. 1811; shared with Town of Deposit, Delaware County • McClure formerly McClure Settlement • San(d)ford also Creek Settlement
Tioga * In Broome County 1806–1813			* See Town of Owego in Tioga County
Triangle 1791 Settlers from Massachusetts at Whitney Point 1831 Formed from Town of Lisle	Barnes Corners Clarks Corners Hazzard Corners Penelope	Triangle Upper Lisle Whitney Point (v)	• Village of Whitney Point inc. 1871

Towns (and Cities)	Villages and other Settlements	Notes
Union 1785 Settled 1791 Formed in Tioga County 1793 Daughter towns Norwich and Oxford formed 1798 Daughter town Greene formed in Chenango County 1800 Daughter town Tioga formed in Tioga County 1801 Daughter town Lisle formed in Tioga County 1806 Transferred to new county of Broome 1808 Ceded land to Town of Chenango 1823 Daughter town Vestal formed 1827 Annexed land from Town of Lisle 1848 Daughter town Maine formed	Ashery Corners Oakdale Choconut Center Owego Endicott (v) Parkview Endwell Union (v) Finch Hollow Union Center Hooper West Corners Johnson City (v) West Endicott Westover	* Towns of Norwich and Oxford in Chenango County after 1798 * Town of Tioga called Owego from 1813 • Choconut Center in Town of Vestal after 1823 • Village of Endicott inc. 1906 • Village of Johnson City inc. 1892 as Lestershire, renamed Johnson City in 1916 • Owego now Village of Owego in Town of Owego, Tioga County • Village of Union inc. 1871 and dissolved c. 1921; became part of the Village of Endicott in 1964
Vestal 1785 Settlers from New England 1823 Formed from Town of Union	Castle Gardens Twin Orchards Choconut Center Vestal Four Corners Vestal Center Ross Corners Vestal Hills South Vestal Willow Point Tracy Creek	• Choconut Center in Town of Union before 1823 • Vestal also Cranes Ferry • Vestal Center also Vestal Corner
Windsor 1786 Settlers from Connecticut on the Susquehanna 1807 Formed from Town of Chenango 1821 Daughter towns Colesville and Sanford formed	Bartonville Mount Carmel Blatchley Occanum Cascade Valley Randolph Center Damascus South Windsor Dunbar State Line East Windsor Stillson Hollow Edson Tuscarora Flowers Wake Hazzardville West Windsor Lester Windsor (v)	• Village of Windsor inc. 1897

NEW YORK STATE CENSUS RECORDS

See also chapter 3, Census Records

County originals at Broome County Clerk's Office: 1825*, 1835, 1845, 1855, 1865, 1875, 1892, 1905, 1915, 1925

State originals at the NYSA: 1915, 1925

Microfilm at the FHL, NYPL, NYSHA, and NYSL; many years are online at *FamilySearch.org* and *Ancestry.com*.

*1825 originals are incomplete; they include statistics for all towns; complete population schedules for towns of Lisle and Windsor; and partial population schedules for the towns of Chenango, Colesville, Conklin, Sanford, and Union.

NATIONAL/STATEWIDE REPOSITORIES & RESOURCES
See chapter 16

COUNTYWIDE REPOSITORIES & RESOURCES

Broome County Clerk
Edwin L. Crawford County Office Building, 3rd Floor
PO Box 2062 • Binghamton, NY 13902 • (607) 778-2256
Email: clerkinfo@co.broome.ny.us • *www.gobroomecounty.com/clerk*

Court records, land records, military records, naturalization records 1850–1994, marriage records 1908–1934, New York state censuses for Broome County 1825–1925. Documents 1964 to present available online.

Broome County – City, Town, and Village Clerks
Birth, marriage, and death records are maintained by the clerk of the municipality in which the event occurred; see Introduction to County Guides for details of other records which may also be held by municipal clerks. For contact information, see *www.bclibrary.info/townclerks.htm*. For information on obtaining vital records in Broome County, see *www.gobroomecounty.com/clerk/vital*.

Broome County Surrogate's Court
92 Court Street • Binghamton, NY 13901 • (607) 778-2111

Holds probate records from 1806 to the present. See also chapter 6, Probate Records.

Broome County Public Libraries
Broome is part of the Four County Library System; see *www.4cls.org* to access each library. See listing below for Broome County Local History and Genealogy Center which is located on the 2nd floor of the Broome County Public Library. Many hold genealogy and local history collections. For example, Vestal Public Library holds local yearbooks and 20th-century newspapers and the Mary Wilcox Memorial Library holds yearbooks and the *Whitney Point Reporter*, 1897–2008.

Broome County Local History and Genealogy Center
Broome County Public Library, 2nd Floor • 185 Court Street
Binghamton, NY 13901 • (607) 778-3572
Email: localhistory@bclibrary.info • *www.bclibrary.info/history.htm*

Holds a copy of the New York State Department of Health vital records indexes. Regional censuses on microfilm with finding aid on website, abstract of 1925 New York state census online for all of Broome County, manuscripts, maps, military lists, name index called the Woodward file of 225,000 cards of abstracted information 1790–1895, business ledgers, deeds (Hotchkiss and Joshua Whitney collections), diaries, funeral records, manuscripts, maps, newspapers (more than 30 local papers), obituaries,

orphanage records, photographs, vertical files.

Website has online resources and research guides, lists of Broome County historical societies, town clerks, and municipal historians. Selection of records available online.

Broome County Historical Society
Local History and Genealogy Center
Broome County Public Library, 2nd Floor • 185 Court Street
Binghamton, NY 13091 • (607) 778-3572
www.bclibrary.info/brocohist.htm

Society's collections located at the Broome County Local History and Genealogy Center. Society has published the *Broome County Historical Society Bulletin* semi-annually since 1954.

Broome County Historian
Local History and Genealogy Center
Broome County Public Library, 2nd Floor • 185 Court Street
Binghamton, NY 13901 • (607) 778-2076
www.gobroomecounty.com/historian

Broome County – All Municipal Historians
While not authorized to answer genealogical inquiries, city, town, and village historians can provide valuable historical information and research advice; some maintain collections and webpages which may include transcribed records, local histories, and other genealogical material. For contact information see the Directory of Officials at *www.gobroomecounty.com*, *www.bclibrary.info/munihist.htm* or the website of the Association of Public Historians of New York State at *www.aphnys.org*.

Broome County Military History Collection:
Old Stone House Museum
22 Chestnut Street • Windsor, NY 13865-4105 • (607) 655-1491

Civil War Military History Collection includes lists of soldiers, registers of deaths, a memorandum book, copies of surgeons' certificates, information on regiment reunions 1906–1909, clippings, diaries, letters, maps, pamphlets.

REGIONAL REPOSITORIES & RESOURCES

Binghamton University SUNY: Glenn G. Bartle Library
PO Box 6012 • Vestal Parkway East • Binghamton, NY 13902
(607) 777-2194 • Email: refquest@binghamton.edu
www.binghamton.edu/libraries

Collections include Civil War diaries, letters, photographs, postcards, and ephemera; maps, local history ephemera, theater programs, oral history interviews, and papers of the Broome County Medical Society. Holds census returns for New York and Pennsylvania on microfilm and CD ROM. Website provides genealogy subject guide.

Central New York Genealogical Society
See listing in Onondaga County Guide

Southern Tier Genealogical Society
PO Box 680 • Vestal, NY 13850 • Email access on website
www.rootsweb.ancestry.com/~nystgs

Genealogical group focused primarily on researching Broome, Chenango, and Tioga counties of New York; and Bradford and Susquehanna counties of Pennsylvania. Monthly meetings are held in the Vestal Public Library. The Society maintains a card catalog of names previously researched, as well as a computer based list of names currently researched by members. Contact via email on website to inquire about research assistance. The Society has published a newsletter three times a year since 1977.

LOCAL REPOSITORIES & RESOURCES
Alphabetized by location

Binghamton City Clerk
Binghamton City Hall, 1st Floor • 38 Hawley St.
Binghamton, NY 13901 • (607) 772-7005 • Email contact on website
www.binghamton-ny.gov/departments/city-clerk/city-clerk

Records include marriage records 1885–present. For birth and death records, see the Office of Vital Statistics below.

Binghamton Office of Vital Statistics
Binghamton City Hall • 38 Hawley St. • Binghamton, NY 13901
(607) 772-7029 • Email contact on website
www.binghamton-ny.gov/departments/city-clerk/city-clerk

Holdings for the City of Binghamton include records of births and deaths occurring within the city since 1884. Genealogical records are available according to the conditions on the website.

Chenango Schoolhouse Museum
Office: corner of River Rd. and Patch Rd. • Kattelville, NY 13901
Mail: 1529 State Route 12 • Binghamton, NY 13901 • (607) 648-9650
Email: historian@townofchenango.com • *www.townofchenango.com*

A local history center and the office of the Chenango town historian are in the museum building. Holdings include genealogies and histories, census materials, cemetery records, maps, photographs, and books.

Old Onaquaga Historical Society and Colesville/Windsor Museum
St. Luke's Church • PO Box 318 • Harpursville, NY 13787
(607) 693-1222 • *www.townofcolesville.org*

Museum has a library containing family files and church records.

Town of Kirkwood Historical Society and Museum
Old Schoolhouse • Veterans River Park • Main Street
Kirkwood, NY 13795 • (607) 775-0811 • *www.townofkirkwood.org*

Holds books, photographs, manuscripts, and school yearbooks. Library includes books, family histories, and local photographs.

SELECTED PRINT & ONLINE RESOURCES
Below is a selection of resources relevant for research in this county. The list is representative, not exhaustive. Additional titles—particularly of abstracts, indexes, transcriptions, and local histories—are available; consult the introduction to Part Two for further information. For guidance on how to identify and locate community directories and local newspapers, see chapter 11, City Directories, and chapter 12, Newspapers, in Part One of this book.

Abstracts, Indexes & Transcriptions
Card, Lester. "Broome County Surrogate Records, 1811–1843." Typescript, 1930. NYPL, New York.

County of Broome Abstracts. Syracuse: Central New York Genealogical Society, 2000. Abstracts for a range of genealogical records originally published in the quarterly *Tree Talks.*

Daughters of the American Revolution, comps. *New York DAR Genealogical Records Committee Report* Since 1913 DAR volunteers have transcribed many thousands of unpublished cemetery, church, and town records throughout New York. The reports are at the DAR Library; copies are at the NYSL and the NYPL. The DAR has a searchable name index to all the GRC reports at *http://services.dar.org/Public/DAR_Research/search/?Tab_ID=6.* See Jean Worden's index below for a listing by county of the New York record sets that were transcribed by the DAR before 1998.

Elliott, Letti. "Broome County, New York, Cemetery Records." Microfilm of typescript, 1940. NYPL, New York.

Kelly, Arthur C. M. *Index to Tree Talks County Packet: Broome County.* Rhinebeck, NY: Kinship, 2002.

Sawyer, Ray C. "Death Notices Published in the Broome County Republican, a Weekly Newspaper of Binghamton, New York, 1831–1870." Typescript, 1942. NYPL, New York. [NYG&B eLibrary]

———. "Marriage Announcements in the Broome County Republican, a Weekly Newspaper of Binghamton, New York." Typescript, 1941. NYPL, New York. [NYG&B eLibrary]

———. "Record of the First Presbyterian Church of Chenango Point, Broome County, New York, Later Changed to Binghamton, NY." Typescript, 1944. NYPL, New York. Includes lists of pastors and members, marriages, deaths, and baptisms.

Worden, Jean D. "Book 1, Subject Index." In *Revised Master Index to the New York State Daughters of the American Revolution Genealogical Records Volumes.* Zephyrhills, FL: J. D. Worden, 1998. The Subject Index includes a listing by county of the cemeteries, churches, towns, and other sources of records transcribed by the DAR.

Other Resources
Aswad, Ed, and Suzanne M. Meredith. *Broome County: 1850–1940.* Charleston, SC: Arcadia Publishing, 2002. Includes history of settlement, local commerce and community, war, and folklore.

Biographical Review Publishing Company. *Biographical Review: This Volume Contains Biographical Sketches of the Leading Citizens of Broome County, New York.* Boston, 1893.

Child, Hamilton. *Gazetteer and Business Directory of Broome and Tioga Counties, NY, for 1872–3.* Syracuse, 1872.

Everts, Ensign & Everts. *Combination Atlas Map of Broome County, New York.* Philadelphia, 1876. [NYPL Digital Gallery]

Fay, Loren V. *Broome County, New York, Genealogical Research Secrets.* Albany: L.V. Fay, 1982.

Hinman, Marjory Barnum. *Bingham's Land, Whitney's Town: A Documentary History of the First Half-Century in the Development of Binghamton, New York and Vicinity, 1794–1845.* Binghamton, NY: Broome County Historical Society, 1996

Historical Records Survey, New York State. *Inventory of the County Archives of New York State (Exclusive of the Five Counties of New York City) No. 3. Broome County.* Albany: Work Projects Administration, Historical Records Survey, 1938.

Lawyer, William S. *Binghamton, Its Settlement, Growth, and Development, and the Factors in Its History, 1800–1900.* Binghamton, NY, 1900.

McGuire, Ross, and Nancy Grey Osterud. *Working Lives, Broome County, New York, 1800–1930: A Social History of People at Work in Our Region.* Binghamton, NY: Roberson Center for the Arts and Sciences, 1980.

New York Historical Resources Center. *Guide to Historical Resources in Broome County, New York, Repositories.* Ithaca, NY: Cornell University, c. 1984. [books.FamilySearch.org]

Revolutionary War Veterans in Broome County. Binghamton, NY: Sons of the American Revolution, Chapter of the Empire State Society, 1960. Book includes statistics, list of pensioners, town and cemetery directories, and descriptions of grave markers.

Seward, William F. *Binghamton and Broome County, New York: A History*. New York: Lewis Historical Publishing Co., 1924.

Smith, Gerald R. *Partners All: A History of Broome County, New York*. Virginia Beach, VA: Donning Company Publishers, 2006. Book includes Native American history.

———. *The Valley of Opportunity: A Pictorial History of the Greater Binghamton Area*. Norfolk, VA: Wallsworth Publishing Company, 1988.

Smith, H. P. *History of Broome County, With Illustrations and Biographical Sketches of Some of its Prominent Men and Pioneers*. Syracuse, 1885.

Thomas, Carol LeVan. *Naming the Hills and Hollows of Broome County*. The Author, 1999.

Wilkinson, J. B. *The Annals of Binghamton, and of the County Connected with It: From the Earliest Settlement*. Binghamton, NY, 1872.

Additional Online Resources

Ancestry.com

There are vast numbers of records on *Ancestry.com* that pertain to people who have lived in New York State. See chapter 16 for a description of *Ancestry.com*'s resources and its partnership with the New York State Archives. A search of the online card catalog by county may reveal lesser known resources that pertain to a locality, such as town records, abstracts, transcriptions, city directories, and local histories.

FamilySearch

FamilySearch has extensive collections of New York records, including religious records, which are searchable by name and location, but not by county. The following collections include record images (browsable, but not searchable) that are organized by county:

- "New York, Land Records, 1630–1975." Includes land and property records. *familysearch.org/search/collection/2078654*

- "New York, Probate Records, 1629–1971." Includes wills, letters of administration, and guardianship papers. *familysearch.org/search/collection/1920234*

For both collections, choose the browse option and then select Broome to view the available records sets.

A detailed description of *FamilySearch.org* resources, which include the catalog of the Family History Library, is found in chapter 16.

Macri's Early Families of Broome County, New York
http://freepages.genealogy.rootsweb.ancestry.com/~marcri

Website includes transcribed land, church, orphanage, vital, and military records and lists of early settlers and families in Broome County.

NYGenWeb Project: Broome County
www.rootsweb.ancestry.com/~nybroome

Part of the national, USGenWeb volunteer initiative, the website provides information and resources for county research.

Old Fulton New York Postcards
www.FultonHistory.com

The website provides free access to a vast collection of digitized New York newspapers, including eight titles for Broome County.

Cattaraugus County

Formed March 11, 1808

Parent County Genesee
Daughter Counties None
County Seat Village of Little Valley

Major Land Transactions
See chapter 7, Land Records
Holland Land Company Purchase 1792–1796

Indian Territories
See chapter 14, Peoples of New York, American Indian
Seneca Nation: Allegany, Cattaraugus, and Oil Springs Reservations (1797–present)

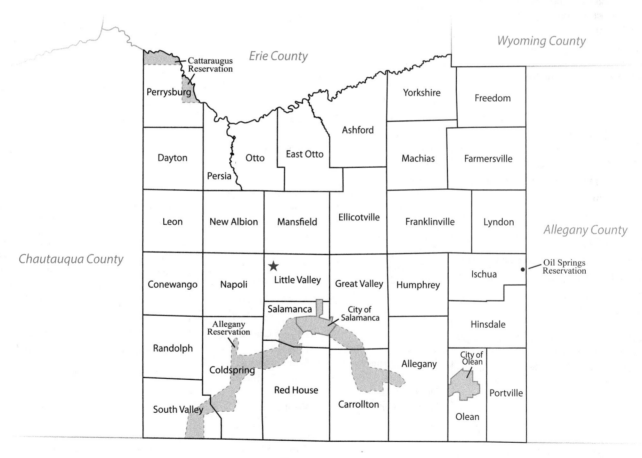

Town Boundary Map
★ - County seat

Towns (and Cities)	Villages and other Settlements		Notes
Allegany 1820 Settlers from Connecticut 1831 Formed as Burton from Town of Great Valley 1836 Daughter town Humphrey formed 1851 Name changed from Burton to Allegany	Allegany (v) Chipmunk Crestview Five Mile Run Four Mile Harrisburg Knapp Creek	Pumpkin Hollow Rock City Rockview St. Bonaventure Vandalia Wing Hollow	• Village of Allegany inc.1906 • Chipmunk also Chipmonk • Knapp Creek also Knapps Creek
Ashford 1816 Settlers from Columbia Co., Herkimer Co., and Massachusetts 1824 Formed from Town of Ellicottville 1835 Annexed land from Town of Otto	Ashford Ashford Hollow Ashford Junction Beaver Siding Bellow Corners Edies Siding	Fox Riceville Riceville Station Riverville Thomas Corners West Valley	• Ashford Junction also Ashford Station • Edies Siding on East Otto town line • Riceville formerly East Ashford
Bucktooth (see Town of Salamanca)			
Burton (see Town of Allegany)			
Carrollton 1814 Settled 1842 Formed from Town of Great Valley 1847 Annexed land from Allegany Reservation	Carrollton Carrolton Station Irvine Mills Limestone (v) New Ireland	Riverside Junction South Carrollton South Vandalia Tuna Vandalia	• Irvine Mills also Ervine Mills • Limestone formerly Fullersburg; Village of Limestone inc. 1877, dissolved 2010
Cecelius (see Town of Mansfield)			
Cold Spring (see Town of Napoli)			
Coldspring 1818 Settlers from Susquehanna, PA 1837 Formed from Town of Napoli 1847 Daughter town South Valley formed 1965 Absorbed Town of Elko	Bunker Hill Cold Spring Hardscrabble Lebanon Price Corners Quaker Bridge	Quaker Run Steamburg Ten Mile Spring Underwood Corner Wolf Run	• Quaker Bridge, Quaker Run, and Wolf Run formerly in Town of Elko which was absorbed by Town of Coldspring in 1965
Conewango * 1816 Settled near Rutledge 1823 Formed from Town of Little Valley 1826 Daughter town Randolph formed 1832 Daughter town Leon formed	Ax(e)ville Clear Creek Con(n)ewango Conewango Station Conewango Valley East Randolph	Elm Elm Creek Pope Randolph Rutledge The Hollow	* Conewango spelling officially changed from Connewango May 1899 • Conewango Station formerly Olds Corners • East Randolph and Randolph in Town of Randolph from 1826; small part of East Randolph remained in Connewango • Rutledge also Rudledge
Dayton 1810 Settlers from Otsego County 1835 Formed from Town of Perrysburg	Cottage Dayton Dexter Corners East Leon Howards Corners Judd Corners Markham	Meyers Corners Pine Valley Skunks Corner South Dayton (v) Wesley West Dayton	• Markham formerly Markhams Corners • Village of South Dayton inc. 1915 • Wesley formerly Sociality
East Otto 1816 Settled 1854 Formed from Town of Otto	Brooklyn East Otto East Otto Corners Edies Siding	Otto Corners Plato Whiteford Hollow	• Edies Siding on Ashford town line • Whiteford Hollow also Whitford Hollow
Elgin (see Town of Lyndon)			

Towns (and Cities)	Villages and other Settlements		Notes
Elko 1890–1965 1890 Town of Elko formed from Town of South Valley 1965 Elko absorbed into Town of Coldspring when the Kinzua Dam was built on the Allegheny River	Old Town Quaker Bridge Quaker Run Tunesassa Wolf Run		
Ellicottville 1815 Settlers from Oneida County and Massachusetts 1820 Formed from Town of Ischua (now Franklinville) 1824 Daughter town Ashford formed	Ashford Ash Park Ashford Junction Bryant Hill	Devereaux Ellicottville (v) Fancy Tract Plato	• Devereaux on Franklinville town line • Village of Ellicottville inc. 1837; county seat 1817–1867 • Fancy Tract on Franklinville and Machias town lines
Farmersville 1815–17 Settled 1821 Formed from Town of Ischua (now Franklinville)	Fairview Farmersville Farmersville Center	Farmersville Station Hardy Corners Laidlaw	
Franklinville 1806 Settlers from Vermont 1812 Formed as Hebe from Town of Olean 1814 Daughter town Perry (now Perrysburg) formed 1816 Name changed from Hebe to Ischua 1820 Daughter towns Ellicottville, Freedom, and Yorkshire formed 1821 Daughter town Farmersville formed 1824 Name changed from Ischua to Franklinville 1829 Daughter town Lyndon formed	Cadiz Devereaux Devereaux Station Fancy Tract Fitch Franklinville (v) The Narrows		• Devereaux on Ellicottville town line • Fancy Tract on Ellicottville and Machias town lines • Village of Franklinville inc. 1874; formerly McLuer Settlement
Freedom 1811 Settlers from New Hampshire and Vermont 1820 Formed from Town of Ischua (now Franklinville) 1844 Ceded land to Town of Yorkshire	Beaver Lake Crystal Lake Elton Elton Station	Fairview Freedom Sandusky	• Crystal Lake formerly Fish Lake • Elton formerly Coles Settlement
Great Valley 1812 Settled 1818 Formed from Town of Olean 1831 Daughter town Burton (now Town of Allegany) formed 1842 Daughter town Carrollton formed 1847 Ceded land to Allegany Reservation	Bradford Junction Chamberlainville Great Valley Great Valley Station Horseshoe Bend	Kill Buck Peth Sugartown Willoughby	• Sugartown also Sugar Town; on Humphrey town line
Hebe (see Town of Franklinville)			

Towns (and Cities)	Villages and other Settlements		Notes
Hinsdale 1806 Settled 1820 Formed from Town of Olean 1846 Daughter town Rice (now Ischua) formed	Haskel(l) Flat(s) Hinsdale Jollytown Maplehurst		• Maplehurst formerly Scott Corners
Humphrey 1815 Settled 1836 Formed from Town of Burton (now Town of Allegany)	Chapellsburg Five Mile Humphrey	Humphrey Center Sugartown	• Sugartown also Sugar Town; on Great Valley town line
Ischua (see Town of Franklinville)			
Ischua 1812 Settlers from Massachusetts 1846 Formed as Rice from Town of Hinsdale 1855 Name changed from Rice to Ischua	Abbotts Cuba Lake Fitch Ischua		• Ischua formerly Rice
Leon 1819 Settled on Mud Creek 1832 Formed from Town of Connewango	East Leon Kendall Corners Leon Leon Center Leon Mills	Meyers Corners Millmans Corners Peace Vale Rays Corners Thompsonville	• East Leon formerly Pleasant Grove
Little Valley 1807 Settled but many left during War of 1812 1818 Formed from Town of Perrysburg 1823 Daughter towns Cold Spring (now Napoli) and Connewango formed 1830 Daughter towns Cecelius (now Mansfield) and New Albion formed 1854 Daughter town Bucktooth (now Salamanca) formed	Elkdale Little Rock City Little Valley (v) Little Valley Center Little Valley Creek Little Valley Depot Salamanca		• Little Valley county seat from 1867; county seat at Ellicottville 1817–1867; Village of Little Valley inc. 1876
Lyndon 1808 Settled 1829 Formed from Town of Franklinville 1857 Name changed from Lyndon to Elgin 1858 Name changed back to Lyndon	Elgin Hopkins Lyndon Lyndon Center Rawson		
Machias 1813 Settlers from Maine 1827 Formed from Town of Yorkshire 1847 Annexed land from Town of Yorkshire	Bakerstand Bird Brewer Corners Fancy Tract Leek	Lime Lake Machias Machias Junction Summit Station	• Fancy Tract on Ellicottville and Franklinville town lines
Mansfield 1817 Settled 1830 Formed as Cecelius from Town of Little Valley 1831 Name changed from Cecelius to Mansfield	Eddyville Eddyville Corners Five Points Hencoop	Maples North Valley Orlando	• Maples also Union Corners

Towns (and Cities)	Villages and other Settlements	Notes
Napoli 1818 Settled 1823 Formed as Cold Spring from Town of Little Valley 1828 Name changed from Cold Spring to Napoli 1837 Daughter town Coldspring formed	Enchanted Lake Napoli Napoli Corners Peaslee Hollow	
New Albion 1818 Settled 1830 Formed from Town of Little Valley	Cattagaurus (v) Champlain Corners New Albion	• New Albion formerly Horths Corners • Village of Cattaraugus inc. 1882
Olean (city) 1854 Incorporated as village in Town of Olean 1893 Formed as city from Village of Olean	Cherry Hill Seneca Heights	
Olean (town) Settled before 1805 1808 Formed as town; initially encompassed all of Cattaraugus County 1812 Daughter town Hebe (now Franklinville) formed 1814 Daughter town Perry (now Perrysburg) formed 1818 Daughter town Great Valley formed 1820 Daughter town Hinsdale formed 1837 Daughter town Portville formed 1893 Village of Olean became City of Olean	Baldwin Heights Barnum Boardmanville Camel Back East Olean Four Mile Haydenville Haymaker Homer Hill North Olean Olean (v) Olean Station	• Village of Olean inc. 1854; became City of Olean in 1893
Otto 1816 Settled on Cattaraugus Creek 1823 Formed from Town of Perrysburg 1835 Ceded land to Town of Ashford 1854 Daughter town East Otto formed	North Otto Otto Zoar	• Otto formerly Waverly
Perry (see Town of Perrysburg)		
Perrysburg 1814 Formed as Perry from towns of Hebe (now Franklinville) and Olean 1818 Name changed from Perry to Perrysburg 1818 Daughter town Little Valley formed 1823 Daughter town Otto formed 1835 Daughter towns Dayton and Persia formed	Balltown North Perrysburgh Perrysburg (v) Versailles West Perrysburg	• Village of Perrysburg inc. 1916 and dissolved 2011
Persia 1811 Settlers from Vermont 1835 Formed from Town of Perrysburg	Allens Switch Persia Darby Flats Point Peter Gowanda (v) Snyders Corners Hidi	• Gowanda formerly Aldrichs Mills and Lodi; Village of Gowanda inc. 1848, shared with Town of Collins, Erie County

Towns (and Cities)	Villages and other Settlements		Notes
Portville 1805 Settled 1837 Formed from Town of Olean	Bedford Corners Carroll Gordon Station Haydenville Lake View Terrace Maine Main Settlement	Mill Grove Portville (v) Toll Gate Corner Weston Mills Westonville White House	• Village of Portville inc. 1895

Randolph
1820   Settlers from Oneida County
        at Randolph
1826   Formed from Town of
        Connewango
1847   Daughter town South Valley
        formed
	Bowen
	Carr Corners
	East Randolph (v)
	Mud Creek
	Randolph (v)
	Valentine
			• Village of East Randolph inc. 1881 and
			dissolved 2011
			• Village of Randolph inc. 1867 and
			dissolved 2011

Red House 1827 Settled 1869 Formed from Town of Salamanca	Freck(s) Hall Hidecker Palmer Summit Percival Red House Red House Creek	Red House Station Schoonmaker Stevens Stoney Brook Junction Yeager Junction Zellif Mill	
Rice (see Town of Ischua)			

Salamanca (city) *
1878   Incorporated as village in Town
        of Salamanca
1913   Formed as city from Village of
        Salamanca
			* City of Salamanca, with the exception of
			a northern spur along U.S. Route 219,
			is part of the Seneca Nation's Allegany
			Reservation

Salamanca (town)
1830   Settled
1854   Formed as Bucktooth from Town
        of Little Valley
1862   Name changed from Bucktooth
        to Salamanca
1869   Daughter town Red House formed
	Bucktooth
	Bucktooth Run
	East Salamanca
	Jimerson Town
	Kill Buck
		Page
		Salamanca (v)
		Shongo
		West Salamanca
			• Village of Salamanca inc. 1878; became
			the City of Salamanca in 1913

South Valley
1825   Settled
1847   Formed from towns of Cold
        Spring and Randolph
1890   Daughter town Elko formed
        (dissolved 1965)
	Highbanks
	Onoville
	Onoville Station		

Yorkshire
1810   Settlers from Vermont
1820   Formed from Town of Ischua
        (now Franklinville)
1827   Daughter town Machias formed
1844   Annexed land from Town of
        Freedom
1847   Ceded land to Town of Machias
	Delevan (v)
	McKinstry
	McKinstrys Hollow
	Sillimans Corners
	The Forks
	West Yorkshire
	Yorkshire
			• Village of Delevan inc. 1915; formerly
			Yorkshire Center

Note about Cattaraugus County

Though Cattaraugus was formed in 1808, it was administered 1808–1817 from Buffalo, Niagara County. For 1810 federal census information, see the Town of Olean under Niagara County. From 1812 to 1817 the eastern part of the county was administered from Angelica, Allegany County.

NEW YORK STATE CENSUS RECORDS

See also chapter 3, Census Records

County originals at Cattaraugus County Clerk's Office: 1825, 1835, 1845, 1855, 1865, 1875, 1892, 1905, 1915, 1925

State originals at the NYSA: 1915, 1925

Microfilm at the FHL, NYPL, and NYSL; many years are online at *FamilySearch.org* and *Ancestry.com*.

For 1835 and 1865 census abstracts and indexes see Barnello and NY GenWeb Project, respectively, in Abstracts, Indexes & Transcriptions below.

NATIONAL/STATEWIDE REPOSITORIES & RESOURCES

See chapter 16

COUNTYWIDE REPOSITORIES & RESOURCES

Cattaraugus County Clerk

303 Court Street • Little Valley, NY 14755 • (716) 938-9111
www.co.cattaraugus.ny.us/tag/department-clerks-office

New York state censuses for Cattaraugus County 1825–1925, naturalization records 1840s–1950s, court records, and land records. Many records are held off-site at the Records Retention Center. Requests for these records must be made to the County Clerk's office.

Cattaraugus County – City, Town, and Village Clerks

Birth, marriage, and death records are maintained by the clerk of the municipality in which the event occurred; see Introduction to County Guides for details of other records which may also be held by municipal clerks. For contact information on municipal clerks in Cattaraugus County see "Directory of Officials" at *www.cattco.org*.

Cattaraugus County Surrogate's Court

303 Court Street • Little Valley, NY 14755 • (716) 938-9111

Holds probate records from 1830 to the present and probate indexes from 1800 to the present. Also see chapter 6, Probate Records.

Cattaraugus County Treasurer's Office

303 Court Street • Little Valley, NY 14755
(716) 938-9111 ext. 2286 • *www.cattco.org/treasurers-office*

Tax records generated more than four years ago are held off-site at the Records Retention Center. Requests for these records must be made to the County Treasurer's office.

Cattaraugus County Public Libraries

Cattaraugus is part of the Chautauqua-Cattaraugus Library System; see *www.cclslib.org* to access each library. For example, Delevan-Yorkshire Public Library has the *Arcade Herald/Ashford Gazette* on microfilm 1892–1998. Also see listings below for Olean Public Library and Randolph Free Library.

Cattaraugus County Historical Museum and Research Library

9824 Route 16 • PO Box 352 • Machias, NY 14101
(716) 353-8200 • *www.cattco.org/museum*

County histories and genealogies, vital statistics 1847–1849, marriage records 1908–1925, county censuses 1820–1880, federal censuses 1892–1925, cemetery stone abstracts, obituary abstracts 1984–present, surrogate's court records, maps, deeds, and Civil War information.

Cattaraugus County Historian

(716) 938-9111 ext. 440 • (716) 353-8200 ext. 4721

Historian's office is located in the Cattaraugus County Historical Museum.

Cattaraugus County – All Municipal Historians

While not authorized to answer genealogical inquiries, county, city, town, and village historians can provide valuable historical information and research advice; some maintain collections and webpages which may include transcribed records, local histories, and other genealogical material. Contact information at Government Appointed Historians of Western New York at *www.gahwny.org/p/cattaraugus.html* or the Association of Public Historians of New York State at *www.aphnys.org*.

REGIONAL REPOSITORIES & RESOURCES

Painted Hills Genealogy Society

See listing in Allegany County Guide

SUNY Fredonia: Daniel A. Reed Library: Archives & Special Collections

See listing in Chautauqua County Guide

University of Rochester: Rare Books, Special Collections, and Preservation: Manuscript and Special Collections: Rochester, Western New York, and New York State

See listing in Monroe County Guide

Western New York Genealogical Society

See listing in Erie County Guide

Western New York Heritage Press

See listing in Erie County Guide

LOCAL REPOSITORIES & RESOURCES

Alphabetized by location

Allegany Area Historical Association

25 North Second Street • PO Box 162 • Allegany, NY 14706
Email: oeph31@verizon.net • *www.allegany.org*

Business records, city directories, genealogies, journals and diaries, local histories, and scrapbooks. A complete list of families whose histories are documented by the Association is available on the website. The Association publishes a newsletter; issues 2004–present are on the website. Note: the town and village of Allegany are in Cattaraugus County.

Cattaraugus Area Historical Society and Museum

23 Main Street • Cattaraugus, NY 14719 • (716) 257-3971
www.enchantedmountains.com/place/cattaraugus-area-historical-society

Holdings include records documenting local military, industrial and general history, and genealogy.

East Otto Historical Museum

Reed Hill Road • East Otto, NY 14729 • (716) 257-3337
www.enchantedmountains.com/place/east-otto-historical-museum

Holdings include artifacts and genealogical information such as compiled family histories and cemetery records.

Ischua Valley Historical Society

The Miner's Cabin, 9 Pine Street • PO Box 153 • Franklinville, NY 14737
(716) 676-2590 • Email: info@ischuavalleyhistoricalsociety.org
www.ischuavalleyhistoricalsociety.org

Family files, books, local histories, cemetery records, school censuses (1840s), business records, scrapbooks, newspapers, obituaries, diaries, directories, letters, ledgers, military material, photographs and postcards, and yearbooks documenting history of Farmersville, Franklinville, Ischua, Lyndon, and Machias.

Seneca Nation of Indians Library: Cattaraugus Territory

3 Thomas Indian School Drive • Irving, NY 14081 • (716) 532-9449
http://senecanationlibrary.wordpress.com

Includes Native American Room with special collection.

Leon Historical Society and Museum

Route 62 • Leon, NY 14751 • (716) 296-5709
Email access on website • *www.leonhistoricalsociety.webs.com*

Holdings include artifacts and genealogies.

Olean Public Library: Genealogy Resources

134 North 2nd Street • Olean, NY 14760 • (716) 372-0200
Email: reference@oleanlibrary.org • *www.oleanlibrary.org*

Local newspapers 1850s–present; obituary index (searchable online); city directories 1882–present (1882–1915 available online); federal census microfilm for select counties 1810–1930; NYS census indexes online for Olean 1855, 1865, 1875; cemetery records available online; and local histories.

Perrysburg Historical Museum

Perrysburg Town Hall • Perrysburg, NY 14129 • (716) 532-1558
www.enchantedmountains.com/place/perrysburg-historical-museum

Holdings include memorabilia and genealogy library.

Portville Historical and Preservation Society

17 Maple Avenue • Portville, NY 14770
Email: contactus@portvillehistory.org • *www.portvillehistory.org*

Local histories and genealogies, books and pamphlets, obituaries, census indexes, cemetery records, newspapers (*Portville Review* and *Portville Star* 1900–present), and maps. The Society shares its headquarters with the Chestnut Hill Cemetery Association.

Randolph Free Library: Local History Room

26 Jamestown Street • Randolph, NY 14772-1121 • (716) 358-3712
Email: randolphlib@gmail.com • *www.randolphfreelibrary.org*

Genealogies and histories, gazetteers, school yearbooks, and material relating to Chamberlain Institute and Randolph Children's Home.

Randolph Historical Society

PO Box 143 • Randolph, NY 14772
Email address on website • *www.randolphhistoricalsociety.org*

Ongoing projects include Century Homes Project (a research project of historic Randolph homes) and oral history project.

Salamanca Public Library

155 Wildwood Avenue • Salamanca, NY 14779 • (716) 945-1890
Email address on website • *www.salmun.com/dept/library/library.htm*

Holdings include *Salamanca Press* on microfilm 1867–2009, family files, and obituary indexes.

Salamanca Historical Society and Museum

125 Main Street • Salamanca, NY 14779 • (716) 945-2946
Email: salhistorical@verizon.net
www.enchantedmountains.com/place/salamanca-historical-museum

Family histories, cemetery records, city directories, church histories and local history books.

Ashford Historical Society Museum

5380 School Street • West Valley, NY 14171 • (716) 942-3885
www.enchantedmountains.com/place/ashford-historical-society-museum

Holdings include family files, local death notices, a hotel ledger containing names of patrons (including American Indians), personal letters, family Bibles, and newspapers from the nineteenth century. Assists with genealogical inquiries.

SELECTED PRINT & ONLINE RESOURCES

Below is a selection of resources relevant for research in this county. The list is representative, not exhaustive. Additional titles—particularly of abstracts, indexes, transcriptions, and local histories—are available; consult the introduction to Part Two for further information. For guidance on how to identify and locate community directories and local newspapers, see chapter 11, City Directories, and chapter 12, Newspapers, in Part One of this book.

Abstracts, Indexes & Transcriptions

Barber, Gertrude Audrey. "Gravestone Inscriptions in Cattaraugus County, NY: Including Cemeteries in and near the Towns of Freedom, Franklinville, and Yorkshire." Typescript, 1930. NYPL, New York. [*Ancestry.com*]

———. "Silome Cemetery in the Town of Freedom, Cattaraugus County, New York and Farmersville Center Cemetery, in the Town of Farmersville Center, Cattaraugus County, New York." Typescript, 1930–1931. NYPL, New York.

———. "Gravestone Inscriptions in Cattaraugus County, NY: Of Riceville Cemetery, Ashford, NY Thomas Corners Cemetery, Ashford, NY." Typescript, 1933. NYPL, New York.

———. "Gravestone Inscriptions, Sundry Cemeteries in Cattaraugus, Erie and Wyoming Counties, New York." Typescript, 1934. NYPL, New York. [*NYG&B eLibrary*]

Barnello, Kathleen. *Cattaraugus County: Abstract of the 1835 New York State Census with the 1825 New York State Census for the Town of Ellicottville*. Syracuse: Central New York Genealogical Society, 1997. Originally published in *Tree Talks*, vol. 37, no. 4 (December 1997).

"Cemetery Inscriptions, Cattaraugus County, New York." Typescript, 1932. NYPL, New York. [*NYG&B eLibrary*]

County of Cattaraugus Abstracts. Syracuse: Central New York Genealogical Society, 2000. Abstracts for a range of genealogical records originally published in the quarterly *Tree Talks*.

Daughters of the American Revolution, comps. *New York DAR Genealogical Records Committee Report*. Since 1913 DAR volunteers have transcribed many thousands of unpublished cemetery, church, and town records throughout New York. The reports are at the DAR Library; copies are at the NYSL and the NYPL. The DAR has a searchable name index to all the GRC reports at *http://services.dar.org/Public/DAR_Research/search/?Tab_ID=6*. See Jean Worden's index below for a listing by county of the New York record sets that were transcribed by the DAR before 1998.

Kelly, Arthur C. M. *Index to Tree Talks County Packet, Cattaraugus County, NY: 1810–1941*. Rhinebeck, NY: Kinship, 2003.

NYGenWeb Project, Cattaraugus County. "Index to the 1865 New York State Census for Cattaraugus County." *www.rootsweb. ancestry.com/~nycattar/census.htm#1865*.

Radlinski, William A. *Ellicott Street Cemetery, Salamanca, New York: Gravestone Inscriptions; With Burial Records from St. Patrick Parish, 1872–1912 and Death Records from Holy Cross Parish, 1896–1912*. Herndon, VA: The Author, 1997.

Sager, Ida M., comp. *Cemetery Records, Town of New Albion and Village of Cattaraugus, New York: Cemeteries: Liberty Park, New Albion, Lower, Rumsey, Snyder Hill, Tug Hill*. Cattaraugus, NY: Cattaraugus-New Albion Historical Society, 1961.

Stahley, Susan E. *Cattaraugus County, New York: Surrogate Court Abstracts*. Westminster, MD: Heritage Books, 2008. Book includes abstracts of the records of the first 78 boxes in the Cattaraugus County Surrogate's Court. Includes guardianship records from early 1800s to 1920s arranged alphabetically by surname, with name, date of birth, and names of relatives.

Worden, Jean D. "Book 1, Subject Index." In *Revised Master Index to the New York State Daughters of the American Revolution Genealogical Records Volumes*. Zephyrhills, FL: J. D. Worden, 1998. The Subject Index includes a listing by county of the cemeteries and other sources of records transcribed by the DAR.

Other Resources

Adams, William. *Historical Gazetteer and Biographical Memorial of Cattaraugus County, NY*. Syracuse: Lyman, Horton and Co., 1893.

Atlas of Cattaraugus County, New York: From Actual Surveys and Official Records. New York: D. G. Beers & Co., 1869.

Barden, Virginia W. "Genealogical Research in the Southern Tier (Chautauqua, Cattaraugus, and Allegany counties)." *Tree Talks*, vol. 25, no. 2 (1985): 23–31.

A Book to Commemorate the Golden Jubilee of Holy Name of Mary Church, Ellicottville, New York, 1909–1959: and the 109th Anniversary of the Founding of the Parish, 1850–1959 . . . . Ellicottville, NY: n.p., 1985.

Cattaraugus County Sesquicentennial Corporation. *The Sesquicentennial of Cattaraugus County, 1808–1958: To Be Held in Ellicottville, August 10–16, 1958*. Ellicottville, NY: n.p., 1958. [*Ancestry.com*]

Donovan, Michael C. *Historical Review of Cattaraugus*. N.p., 1959.

Doty, William J., Charles E. Congdon, and Lewis H. Thornton. *The Historic Annals of Southwestern New York*. New York: Lewis Historical Publishing Co., 1940.

Ellis, Franklin and Eugene Arus Nash. *History of Cattaraugus County, New York: Illustrations and Biographical Sketches of Some of its Prominent Men and Pioneers*. Philadelphia: L. H. Everts, 1879.

Fay, Loren V. *Cattaraugus County, New York, Genealogical Research Secrets*. Albany: L. V. Fay, 1984.

Historical Records Survey, New York State. *Inventory of the County Archives of New York State (Exclusive of the Five Counties of New York City) No. 4. Cattaraugus County*. Albany: Work Projects Administration, Historical Records Survey, 1939. [NYG&B eLibrary]

Manley, John, ed. *Cattaraugus County: Embracing its Agricultural Society, Newspapers, Civil List, Biographies of the Old Pioneers (with portraits), Colonial and State Governors of New York; Names of Towns and Post Offices, with the Statistics of Each Town*. Little Valley, NY: J. Manley, 1857.

New York Historical Resources Center. *Guide to Historical Resources in Cattaraugus County, New York, Repositories*. Ithaca, NY: Cornell University, 1984. [*books.FamilySearch.org*]

Olson, Marlynn McNallie. *A Guide to Burial Sites, Cemeteries, and Random Stones in Cattaraugus County, New York*. Randolph, NY: Register Graphics Inc., 1996.

Turner, Orasmus. *Pioneer History of the Holland Purchase of Western New York . . . .* Buffalo: Jewett, Thomas & Co., 1849.

Western New York Genealogical Society Journal. Hamburg, NY: Western New York Genealogical Society, 1974–present. [*wnygs.org*]

Additional Online Resources

Ancestry.com

There are vast numbers of records on Ancestry.com that pertain to people who have lived in New York State. See chapter 16 for a description of *Ancestry.com*'s resources and its partnership with the New York State Archives. A search of the online card catalog by county may reveal lesser known resources that pertain to a locality, such as town records, abstracts, transcriptions, city directories, and local histories.

FamilySearch.org

A detailed description of resources is found in chapter 16, National and Statewide Repositories & Resources. FamilySearch has extensive collections of New York records, including religious records, which are searchable by name and location, but not by county. The following collections include record images (browsable, but not searchable) that are organized by county:

- "New York, Land Records, 1630–1975." Includes land and property records. *familysearch.org/search/collection/2078654*

- "New York, Probate Records, 1629–1971." Includes wills, letters of administration, and guardianship papers. *familysearch.org/search/collection/1920234*

For both collections, choose the browse option and select Cattaraugus in the county listing.

A detailed description of *FamilySearch.org* resources is found in chapter 16.

NYGenWeb Project: Cattaraugus
www.rootsweb.ancestry.com/~nycattar

Part of the national USGenWeb volunteer initiative, the website provides information and resources for county research.

Old Fulton New York Postcards
www.FultonHistory.com

The website provides free access to a vast collection of digitized New York newspapers, including nine titles for Cattaraugus County.

Cayuga County

Formed March 8, 1799

Parent County   Onondaga
Daughter Counties   Seneca 1804 • Tompkins 1817
County Seat   City of Auburn

Major Land Transactions
See chapter 7, Land Records
All present day Cayuga County was part of the New Military Tract

Town Boundary Map
★ - County seat

Towns (and Cities)	Villages and other Settlements	Notes
Auburn (city) * 1795 Settled as Hardenburgh Corners 1805 Settlement name changed to Auburn 1815 Incorporated as village in Town of Aurelius 1823 Formed as town from Town of Aurelius 1848 Incorporated as city from Town of Auburn 1869 Annexed Clarksville from Town of Aurelius	Clarksville	* Auburn (city, village, and hamlet) has been county seat since 1808; county seat at Aurora, Town of Scipio 1799–1808 • Clarksville in Town of Aurelius before 1869
Auburn (town) 1823 Formed from, and coterminous with, Village of Auburn, Town of Aurelius 1848 Incorporated as a city	Auburn (v)	• Village of Auburn inc. 1815, became city in 1848
Aurelius * 1788 Settled at Cayuga Village 1789 Formed in Montgomery County 1791 Transferred to new county of Herkimer 1794 Transferred to new county of Onondaga 1799 Transferred to new county of Cayuga 1802 Daughter towns Brutus, Cato, Jefferson (now Mentz), and Owasco formed 1823 Daughter towns Auburn, Fleming, and Springport formed 1859 Daughter town Throop formed 1869 Ceded Clarksville to City of Auburn	Auburn (v) Aurelius Aurelius Station Cayuga (v) Clarksville Elmhurst Fosterville Half Acre Mud Lock Relius	* Aurelius was the name of one of the 28 Military Tract townships • Village of Auburn inc. 1815, became coterminous with new Town of Auburn in 1823; became City of Auburn in 1848; county seat since 1808 • Village of Cayuga inc. 1857, reincorporated 1874 • Clarksville ceded to City of Auburn 1869
Brutus * 1800 Settled 1802 Formed from Town of Aurelius 1827 Daughter town Sennett formed	Centerport North Weedsport Weedsport (v)	* Brutus was the name of one of the 28 Military Tract townships • Village of Weedsport inc. 1831
Cato * 1800 Settled 1802 Formed from Town of Aurelius 1812 Daughter town Sterling formed 1821 Daughter towns Conquest, Ira, and Victory formed 1824 Annexed land from Town of Ira	Brick Church Cato (v) Meridian (v)	* Cato was the name of one of the 28 Military Tract townships • Village of Cato inc. 1880; shared with Town of Ira • Village of Meridian inc. 1854, formerly Cato Four Corners
Conquest 1800 Settled 1821 Formed from Town of Cato	Conquest Howland Cottage Corners Mosquito Point Emerson Pineville Hard Point Spring Lake	• Hamlet of Conquest formerly Conquest Center • Emerson formerly The Pepper Mill • Pineville took name of earlier settlement • Spring Lake called Pineville before 1874

Towns (and Cities)	Villages and other Settlements		Notes
Dryden * In Cayuga County 1803–1817			* See Tompkins County
Fayette * In Cayuga County 1800–1804			* See Seneca County
Fleming **1790-91** Settled **1823** Formed from Town of Aurelius	Fleming Mapleton Owasco Lake Station	Sherlock Corners Shumaker Crossing Wyckoff	• Owasco Lake Station also Owasco Lake; on Scipio town line • Wyckoff formerly Wyckoff Station
Genoa **1791** Settled at Northville (now King Ferry) **1789** Formed in Montgomery County as Milton * **1791** Transferred to new county of Herkimer **1794** Transferred to new county of Onondaga **1799** Transferred to new county of Cayuga **1802** Daughter town Locke formed **1808** Name changed from Milton to Genoa **1817** Daughter town Lansing formed in Tompkins County	Atwaters Belltown Bowers Corners Clear View East Genoa Five Corners Forks of the Creek Genoa Goodyear Corners	Goosetree Jump Corners King(s) Ferry King Ferry Station Little Hollow McQuiqqin Corners Sills Corners Weekes Corner	* Milton was the name of one of the 28 Military Tract townships • Goodyear Corners also Goodyear • King Ferry formerly Northville; name changed c. 1879
Hector * In Cayuga County 1802–1804			* See Schuyler County
Ira **1800** Settled **1821** Formed from Town of Cato **1824** Ceded land to Town of Cato	Benton Corners Bethel Bethel Corners	Cato (v) Floridaville Ira	• Village of Cato inc. 1880; shared with Town of Cato • Hamlet of Ira formerly Ira Center
Jefferson Name for Town of Mentz 1802–1808			
Junius * In Cayuga County 1803–1804			* See Seneca County
Ledyard **1789** Settled at Aurora **1823** Formed from Town of Scipio	Aurora (v) Barber(s) Corners Black Rock Bunker Chapel Corners Cooney Corners	Ellsworth Ledyard Levan(n)a Prospect Corners Turney Corners Willet(s)	• Aurora county seat 1799–1808; village inc. 1837; in Town of Scipio before 1823 • Ledyard also Talcotts Corners; on Venice town line
Locke * **1790** Settled **1802** Formed from Town of Milton (now Genoa) **1817** Daughter town Division (now Groton) formed in Tompkins County **1831** Daughter town Plato (now Summerhill) formed	Centerville Chipman Corners Locke Satterly Corners Shaw Corners Toll Gate Corners		* Locke was the name of one of the 28 Military Tract townships • Hamlet of Locke formerly Milan

Towns (and Cities)	Villages and other Settlements		Notes
Mentz 1797 Settled 1802 Formed as Jefferson from Town of Aurelius 1808 Name changed to Mentz 1859 Daughter towns Montezuma and Throop formed	Centerport High Bridge Montezuma (v) North Port Byron Port Byron (v) Troopsville		• Village of Montezuma inc. 1866 and dissolved 1889; in Town of Montezuma after 1859 • Village of Port Byron inc. 1837; formerly Bucksville
Milton Name for Town of Genoa 1789–1808			
Montezuma 1798 Settled 1859 Formed from Town of Mentz	Fox Ridge Free Bridge Corners Montezuma (v)	Montezuma Station Willow Grove	• Village of Montezuma inc. 1866 and dissolved 1889; in Town of Mentz before 1859
Moravia 1791 Settled at Moravia Village 1833 Formed from Town of Sempronius	Court(w)right Corners Folts Corners Four Town Corners Indian Grove Montville Moravia (v) Morse Mills	Owasco Hill Owasco Valley Perkins Corners Southeast Owasco Toll Gate Corners Wilson Corners	• Village of Moravia inc. 1837 • Owasco Hill on Venice town line
Niles 1793 Settled 1833 Formed from Town of Sempronius	Austin Conklin(s) Cove Globe Hotel Corners Gregory Landing Kelloggsville Koenigs Point New Hope	Niles Nine Corners Omro Partello Corners Rice Point Twelve Corners West Niles	• Koenigs Point formerly Conklins Point
Ovid * In Cayuga County 1799–1804			* See Seneca County
Owasco 1792 Settled 1802 Formed from Town of Aurelius	Baptist (Four) Corners Degroff Highland Beach Koenigs Point	Melrose Park Owasco Petty Corner Valentines Corners	
Romulus * In Cayuga County 1799–1804			* See Seneca County
Scipio * 1790 Settled 1794 Formed in Onondaga County 1799 Transferred to new county of Cayuga; daughter town Sempronius formed 1823 Daughter towns Ledyard, Springport, and Venice formed	Ashland Aurora (v) Bolts Corners Botsford Corners Cascade Casowasco Corey Corners Edgewater Elmwood Ensenore Ensenore Point	Kings Corners Merrifield Number One Owasko Lake Station Richardson Square Scipio Scipio Center Scipioville Sherwood Woods Mill	* Scipio was the name of one of the 28 Military Tract townships • Aurora county seat 1799–1808; village inc. 1837; in Town of Ledyard after 1823 • Ensenore Point formerly Culvers Point • Owasco Lake Station also Owasco Lake; on Fleming town line • Richardson Square formerly The Square • Scipioville formerly Fitchs Corners and Mechanicsville • Sherwood also Sherwoods Corners
Sempronius * 1794 Settled 1799 Formed from Town of Scipio 1833 Daughter towns Moravia and Niles formed	Dresserville Glen Haven Hardy Corners Morse Hill Murphy Corner(s) North Summer Hill	Sayles Corners Sempronius Sempronius Hill Vansville Wards Corner(s)	* Sempronius was the name of one of the 28 Military Tract townships

Towns (and Cities)	Villages and other Settlements		Notes
Sennett 1794 Settled 1827 Formed from Town of Brutus 1859 Daughter town Throop formed	McMasters Corners Sennett Soule Wicks Corners		• Hamlet of Sennett formerly Fellows Corners
Springport 1800 Settled 1823 Formed from towns of Aurelius and Scipio	Cayuga Junction Cross Roads Station Farley(s) Oakwood	Powers Corner(s) Springport Station Union Springs (v)	• Village of Union Springs inc. 1848
Sterling * 1805 Settled 1812 Formed from Town of Cato	Crocketts Fair Haven (v) Fintches Corners Martville McKnight Corners Moon Beach Nine Mile Point	North Fairhaven North Sterling North Victory Sterling Sterling Station Sterling Valley Whiting Corners	* Sterling was the name of one of the 28 Military Tract townships • Crocketts formerly Sterling Valley Station • Village of Fair Haven inc. 1880 • Hamlet of Sterling also Sterling Center • Sterling Valley also Coopers Mills
Summerhill 1797 Settled 1831 Formed as Town of Plato from Town of Locke 1832 Name changed from Plato to Summerhill	Como Four Town Corners Halls Corners Summerhill		
Throop 1790 Settled 1859 Formed from towns of Aurelius, Mentz, and Sennett	Cold Spring Polk(s) Corners Sawyers Corner(s) Throop Throopsville		
Ulysses * In Cayuga County 1799–1817			* See Tompkins County
Venice 1800 Settled 1823 Formed from Town of Scipio	Ashland Bruton Corners Cascade East Venice Holley Corners Ledyard Levanna Owasco Hill	Poplar Ridge Rafferty Corners South Venice Stewarts Corners Tait Corners Venice Venice Center Wheeler Corners	• Ledyard also Talcotts Corners; on Ledyard town line • Owasco Hill on Moravia town line • Stewarts Corners also Stuart(s) Corners
Victory 1800 Settled 1821 Formed from Town of Cato	Ira Corner(s) K Cat Corner(s) North Victory Victory Westbury		• Westbury shared with Butler, Wayne County

NEW YORK STATE CENSUS
See also chapter 3, Census Records

County originals at Cayuga County Records Management: 1855, 1865*, 1875, 1892, 1905, 1915, 1925 (1825, 1835, and 1845 are lost)

State originals at the NYSA: 1915, 1925

Microfilm at the FHL, NYPL, and NYSL; many years are online at *FamilySearch.org* and *Ancestry.com*.

*For 1865 census index for towns of Owasco and Victory, see NYGenweb Project in Abstracts, Indexes & Transcriptions.

NATIONAL/STATEWIDE REPOSITORIES & RESOURCES
See chapter 16

COUNTYWIDE REPOSITORIES & RESOURCES

Cayuga County Clerk
County Office Building, 1st Floor • 160 Genesee Street
Auburn, NY 13021 • (315) 253-1271 • *www.cayugacounty.us*

Court records, land records, New York state censuses for Cayuga County 1855, 1865, 1875, 1892, 1905, federal censuses, and naturalization records 1799–1952. The website includes a map of Cayuga County with links to city, town, and village websites.

Cayuga County – City, Town and Village Clerks
Birth, marriage, and death records are maintained by the clerk of the municipality in which the event occurred; see Introduction to County Guides for details of other records which may also be held by municipal clerks. For contact information on Cayuga County clerks, see *www.cayugacounty.us*.

Cayuga County Surrogate's Court
154 Genesee Street • Auburn, NY 13021 • (315) 237-6210

Holds probate records from 1799 to the present. See also chapter 6, Probate Records.

Cayuga County Records Management
12 Court Street • Auburn, NY 13021
(315) 253-1037 • Email: ccrecords@co.cayuga.ny.us
www.cayugacounty.us/LivingWorking/RecordsRetention.aspx

Military records (Revolutionary and Civil Wars), census records 1800–1925, maps and atlases, marriage records 1908–1936, naturalization records 1799–1952, property assessments 1840–1985, and surrogate's court records 1799–2003. A complete list of holdings can be found in the Collection Overview on the website. A selection of records is available on the Records Management website.

Cayuga County Public Libraries
Cayuga is part of the Finger Lakes Library System; see *www.flls.org* to access each library. Many hold genealogy and local history collections. Also see listings below for Hazard Library and Seymour Public Library.

Cayuga County Historian
Historic Old Post Office Building, 3rd Floor
57 Genesee Street • Auburn, NY 13021 • (315) 253-1300
Email: historian@cayugacounty.us
www.cayugacounty.us/LivingWorking/Historian.aspx

Books, pamphlets, and periodicals, church and cemetery records, DAR records, family files (including Bible records, census transcriptions, family charts, newspaper obituaries, correspondence, etc.), maps (1853, 1859, 1875, 1904), newspapers (50+ titles: 1811–1813, 1816–

present), obituaries (1969–present), photographs, and town records. A complete list of surnames included in the Family Files is available on the Historian's website.

Cayuga County – All Municipal Historians
While not authorized to answer genealogical inquiries, county, city, town and village historians can provide valuable historical information and research advice; some maintain information and research advice; some maintain collections and webpages which may include transcribed records, local histories, and other genealogical material. For contact information, see *www.cayugacounty.us* or the website of the Association of Public Historians of New York State at *www.aphnys.org*.

Cayuga County Community College: Bourke Memorial Library
197 Franklin Street • Auburn, NY 13021
(315) 255-1743 • *www.cayuga-cc.edu/library*

Library contains a local history room with books, census indexes, and newspapers.

Cayuga Museum of History and Art and Case Research Lab Museum
203 Genesee Street • Auburn, NY 13021 • (315) 253-8051
Email: cayugamuseum@roadrunner.com • *http://cayugamuseum.org*

Business records, family histories, letters, and artifacts tracing the history of Auburn and Cayuga County, including Auburn Prison and the Case Research Lab.

REGIONAL REPOSITORIES & RESOURCES

Central New York Genealogical Society
See listing in Onondaga County Guide

State University of New York at Oswego: Local History Collection
See listing in Oswego County Guide

LOCAL REPOSITORIES & RESOURCES
Alphabetized by location

Seymour Public Library: Mary Van Sickle Wait History Room
176-178 Genesee Street • Auburn, NY 13021 • (315) 252-2571
Email: localhistory@seymourlibrary.org
www.seymourlibrary.org/seymour-library

Wait History Room contains a collection of books on state and local history, newspapers, and genealogical records. Holdings also include extensive information about Harriet Tubman and the Auburn Correctional Facility.

Genoa Historical Association and Rural Life Museum
920 State Route 34B • PO Box 316 • King Ferry, NY 13081
(315) 364-8202 • Email: genoahistorical@gmail.com
www.genoahistorical.org

Society's records room is located in the Rural Life Museum. It contains family histories and books; birth and death information; church, cemetery, school, and military records; and newspapers (100 years of the *Genoa Tribune*).

Montezuma Historical Society: Historic Mentz Church
Mentz Church and McDonald Roads • PO Box 476
Montezuma, NY 13117 • (315) 776-4656 • Email access on website •
www.montezumahistoricalsociety.org

The Society documents Erie Canal heritage, has an ongoing online genealogical and biographical database, and offers free access to family records. Provides indexes, photos, maps, timeline and a canal slide show.

Cayuga-Owasco Lakes Historical Society and Museum
14 West Cayuga Street • PO Box 247 • Moravia, NY 13118-0247
(315) 497-3906 • www.colhs.org

Society's focus is on the southeastern towns of Cayuga County, and President Millard Fillmore who was born in Moravia. Holdings include atlases and maps, Bible records, books and gazetteers, cemetery records (267 cemeteries), census information (including 1828 Quaker census), church information and booklets, family files, newspaper abstracts 1819–1865, photographs and scrapbooks, town histories, and several vital records indexes. A complete list of holdings can be found on the Society's website, along with a list of surnames featured in its family files.

Hazard Library: Local History Collection
Route 34B • PO Box 2487 • Poplar Ridge, NY 13139-0003
(315) 364-7975 • Email: Librarian@hazardlibrary.org
www.hazardlibrary.org/local-history

Holdings include autobiographies, biographies, and memoirs; genealogies; history of local places, churches, libraries, museums, and schools; vertical files of clippings and ephemera; and maps. Website includes Guide to Local History and Genealogy Resources.

The Lock 52 Historical Society of Port Byron
73 Pine Street • PO Box 528 • Port Byron, NY 13140
(315) 776-4027 • Email available on website
www.rootsweb.ancestry.com/~nycayuga/Lock52/index.html

Documents the history of the Town of Mentz and the Village of Port Byron. Website includes detailed information about how to find records in Mentz and Port Byron.

Sterling Historical Society and Museum
PO Box 114 • Sterling, NY 13156 • (315) 564-6721
Email: info@SterlingHistoricalSociety.org
www.sterlinghistoricalsociety.org

Website includes list of local historical markers, sites, and veterans from Sterling.

Old Brutus Historical Society
8943 North Seneca Street • PO Box 516 • Weedsport, NY 13166
(315) 834-9342 • www.rootsweb.ancestry.com/~nycayuga/obhs

Society documents the local history of the Town of Brutus and Village of Weedsport. Holdings include family data files, cemetery records, census materials (1840 and 1855), books, the Cayuga County Biographical Review, and county and local maps (1859 and 1885).

SELECTED PRINT & ONLINE RESOURCES

Below is a selection of resources relevant for research in this county. The list is representative, not exhaustive. Additional titles—particularly of abstracts, indexes, transcriptions, and local histories—are available; consult the introduction to Part Two for further information. For guidance on how to identify and locate community directories and local newspapers, see chapter 11, City Directories, and chapter 12, Newspapers, in Part One of this book.

Abstracts, Indexes & Transcriptions
Barber, Gertrude Audrey. "Abstract of Wills of Cayuga County, NY." Typescript, 1947. NYPL, New York. Copied from the original records at the Surrogate's Office, Auburn, NY.

———. "Marriages and Deaths from the "Cayuga Patriot": A Newspaper Published Every Wednesday at Auburn, Cayuga County, New York, from June 29, 1825 to March 19, 1834." Typescript, 1947. NYPL, New York.

County of Cayuga Abstracts. Syracuse: Central New York Genealogical Society, 2000. Abstracts for a range of genealogical records originally published in the quarterly Tree Talks.

Daughters of the American Revolution, comps. New York DAR Genealogical Records Committee Report. Since 1913 DAR volunteers have transcribed many thousands of unpublished cemetery, church, and town records throughout New York. The reports are at the DAR Library; copies are at the NYSL and the NYPL. The DAR has a searchable name index to all the GRC reports at http://services.dar.org/Public/DAR_Research/search/?Tab_ID=6. See Jean Worden's index below for a listing by county of the New York record sets that were transcribed by the DAR before 1998.

DeLawyer, Mark W. Deaths at Auburn Prison, Cayuga County, New York, 1888–1937. Bowie, MD: Heritage Books Inc., 2003. Book includes records of 700 inmates who died at Auburn Prison, including biographical information, crime and sentence, cause of death, names and residences of relatives. Arranged chronologically.

Kelly, Arthur C. M. Index to Tree Talks County Packet: Cayuga County. Rhinebeck, NY: Kinship, 2002.

Lester, Claud F. "Gravestone Inscriptions, Cayuga County, NY." NYG&B Record, vol. 54 (1923) no. 1: 49–59, no. 3: 227–240. Includes Venice (Stewart's Corners); Port Byron; Village Cemetery, Genoa. [NYG&B eLibrary]

———. "Gravestone Inscriptions, Cayuga County, NY. East Venice Cemetery; Baker Cemetery; Locke Cemetery." NYG&B Record, vol. 53, no. 4 (1922): 307–325. [NYG&B eLibrary]

McKay, Janet. "Port Byron, Cayuga County, N.Y. Gravestone Inscriptions." NYG&B Record, vol. 54, no. 1 (1923): 59–62. [NYG&B eLibrary]

NYGenWeb Project. "Indexes to the 1865 New York State Census for the Towns of Owasco and Victory." www.rootsweb.ancestry.com/~nycayuga/census/censusin.html

Smith, Mrs. W. Arthur. "Scipio Monthly Meeting of the Religious Society of Friends, 1795–1834." Typescript. NYPL, New York. [NYG&B eLibrary]

"St. Peter's Church, Auburn, N.Y. Baptismal Records, 1801–1863." Typescript, 1952. NYPL, New York. Transcribed from parish book registers 1 and 2 by New York Genealogical and Biographical Society. [NYG&B eLibrary]

Worden, Jean D. "Book 1, Subject Index." In Revised Master Index to the New York State Daughters of the American Revolution Genealogical Records Volumes. Zephyrhills, FL: J. D. Worden, 1998. The Subject Index includes a listing by county of the cemeteries, churches, towns, and other sources of records transcribed by the DAR.

Other Resources
Allen, Henry M. A Chronicle of Auburn from 1793 to 1955: Being a Chronicle of Early Auburn and Auburn Consolidated. Auburn, NY: H. M. Allen, 1955.

Anderson, Scott W. "Entrepreneurs and Place in Early America: Auburn, New York, 1783–1880." PhD diss., Syracuse University, 1997.

Beers, F. W. *County Atlas of Cayuga, New York: From Recent and Actual Surveys and Records under the Superintendence of Beers.* New York, 1875. [NYPL Digital Gallery]

Bellafaire, Judith. "Kith, Kin, and Community: Pioneer Networking in Cayuga County, New York, 1800–1860." PhD diss., University of Delaware, 1984.

Biographical Review Publishing Company. *Biographical Review: This Volume Contains Biographical Sketches of the Leading Citizens of Cayuga County, New York.* Boston, 1894.

Child, Hamilton. *Gazetteer and Business Directory of Cayuga County, NY, for 1867–68.* Syracuse, 1868.

Cutter, William R. *Genealogical and Family History of Central New York: A Record of the Achievements of Her People in the Making of a Commonwealth and the Building of a Nation.* New York: Lewis Historical Publishing Co., 1912.

Ellis, Janet. *Cayuga County: A Bibliography of Local History.* Albany: Department of Librarianship, New York State College for Teachers, 1941.

Fay, Loren V. *Cayuga County, New York, Genealogical Research Secrets.* Albany: L. V. Fay, 1981.

Galpin, William F. *Central New York, an Inland Empire, Comprising Oneida, Madison, Onondaga, Cayuga, Tompkins, Cortland, Chenango Counties and their People.* New York: Lewis Historical Publishing Co., 1914. Contains biographies. Index available from Berkshire Family History Association.

Gero, Anthony, and Roger Sturcke. *Cayugans in the Field, 1793–2003: Citizen Soldiers of Cayuga County, New York.* Auburn, NY: Jacobs Press, 2004.

History of Cayuga County. New York; Compiled from Papers of the Archives of the Cayuga County Historical Society, with Special Chapters by Local Authors from 1775 to 1908. Auburn, NY: Cayuga County Historical Society, 1908.

Monroe, Joel H. *Historical Records of a Hundred and Twenty Years, Auburn, NY.* Geneva, NY: W. F. Humphrey, 1913.

New York Historical Resources Center. *Guide to Historical Resources in Cayuga County, New York, Repositories.* Ithaca, NY: Cornell University, 1980. [books.FamilySearch.org]

O'Hara, Ward. *South of Auburn.* Auburn, NY: W. O'Hara, 1988.

Records of the Ithaca College Study Center for Early Religious Life in Western New York, 1978–1981. Division of Rare and Manuscript Collections, Cornell University Library. A description of the holdings for each county is at *http://rmc.library.cornell.edu/eguides/lists/churchlist1.htm*.

Seymour, Mary L. *Historical Sketch of Cayuga Asylum for Destitute Children, Auburn, NY: With Statistics from Organization.* Auburn, NY, 1893.

Snow, Dorothy E. *Early Cayuga Days: Folk Lore and Local History of a New York County.* New York: Genoa Historical Association, 1993.

Storke, Elliot G. *History of Cayuga County, New York: With Illustrations and Biographical Sketches of Some of its Prominent Men and Pioneers.* Syracuse, 1879.

Van Sickle, John. *The Cayuga Indian Reservation and Colonel John Harris.* Ithaca, NY: DeWitt Historical Society of Tompkins County, 1965.

Wait, Mary Van Sickle. *Brigham Young in Cayuga County, 1813–1829.* Ithaca, NY: DeWitt Historical Society of Tompkins County, 1964

Yawger, Rose N. *The Indian and the Pioneer: An Historical Study.* Syracuse, 1893.

Additional Online Resources

Ancestry.com

There are vast numbers of records on *Ancestry.com* that pertain to people who have lived in New York State. See chapter 16 for a description of *Ancestry.com*'s resources and its partnership with the New York State Archives. A search of the online card catalog by county may reveal lesser known resources that pertain to a locality, such as town records, abstracts, transcriptions, city directories, and local histories.

FamilySearch

FamilySearch has extensive collections of New York records, including religious records, which are searchable by name and location, but not by county. The following collections include record images (browsable, but not searchable) that are organized by county:

• "New York, Land Records, 1630–1975." Includes land and property records. *familysearch.org/search/collection/2078654*

• "New York, Probate Records, 1629–1971." Includes wills, letters of administration, and guardianship papers. *familysearch.org/search/collection/1920234*

For both collections, choose the browse option and then select Cayuga to view the available records sets.

A detailed description of *FamilySearch.org* resources, which include the catalog of the Family History Library, is found in chapter 16.

Following the Freedom Trail in Auburn and Cayuga County, NY
www.auburncayugafreedomtrail.com

A cultural resources survey of sites relating to the Underground Railroad, Abolitionism, and African American life in Auburn, and Cayuga County, New York, sponsored by the City of Auburn Historic Resources Review Board and Cayuga County, New York.

NYGenWebProject: Cayuga County
www.rootsweb.ancestry.com/~nycayuga

Part of the national, USGenWeb volunteer initiative, the website provides information and resources for county research.

Old Fulton New York Postcards
www.FultonHistory.com

The website provides free access to a vast collection of digitized New York newspapers, including 39 titles for Cayuga County.

Chautauqua County

Formed March 11, 1808

County Name	Officially changed from Chautauque to Chautauqua in 1859
Parent County	Genesee
Daughter Counties	None
County Seat	Village of Mayville, Town of Chautauqua

Major Land Transactions

See table in chapter 7, Land Records

Holland Land Company Purchase 1792–1796

Indian Territories

See chapter 14, Peoples of New York, American Indian

Seneca Nation: Cattaraugus Reservation (1797–present)

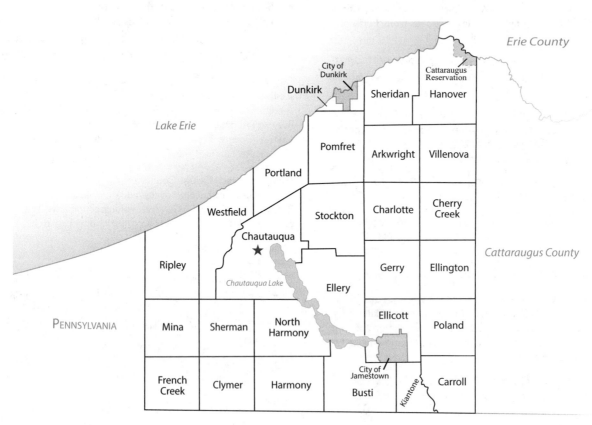

Town Boundary Map

 - County seat

Towns (and Cities)	Villages and other Settlements		Notes
Arkwright 1807 Settled 1829 Formed from towns of Pomfret and Villenova 1830 Annexed land from Town of Pomfret	Abbey Arkwright Arkwright Summit Black Corners	Cowdens Corner Griswold Town Corners	• Arkwright also Arkwright Center • Arkwright Summit also Chicken Tavern • Griswold also Burhams Hollow
Busti 1810 Settlers from Herkimer County 1823 Formed from towns of Ellicott and Harmony 1845 Ceded land to Town of Ellicott	Ashville Ashville Bay Boomertown Busti Cottage Park	Lakewood (v) Loomises Maple Point Shermans Bay Vukote	• Ashville in Town of Harmony before 1823; on North Harmony town line from 1918 • Boomertown also Ashville Station • Busti formerly Busti Corners • Village of Lakewood inc. 1893; also Cowings
Carroll 1807 Settlers from Rensselaer County 1825 Formed from Town of Ellicott 1845 Ceded land to Ellicott 1853 Daughter town Kiantone formed	Carroll Connewango Dodge Fentonville Frewsburg(h) Ivory State Line		• Carroll formerly Sears and Searsburg; after 1853 see Kiantone in Town of Kiantone • Ivory formerly Pope Hollow
Charlotte 1809 Settlers from Oneida County 1829 Formed from Town of Gerry	Charlotte Charlotte Center Luce Hill Moons	Pettit Corners Pickett Corners Pulaski Sinclairville (v)	• Moons on Stockton town line • Pickett Corners also Holdenville • Pulaski also Pickett • Village of Sinclairville inc. 1887; shared with Town of Gerry, formerly Gerry, Saint Clairsville, and Sinclearville
Chautauqua 1804 Settled at Mayville 1804 Formed in Genesee County from Town of Batavia 1808 Transferred to new county of Chautauqua; daughter town Pomfret formed 1813 Daughter town Portland formed 1816 Daughter town Harmony formed 1821 Daughter towns Clymer, Ellery, and Stockton formed	Chautauqua Cottage Park Dean Dewittville Hartfield Hewes Lakeside Park Lighthouse Point Magnolia Mayville (v)	Orchard Terrace Peacock Lodge Pleasantville Point Chautauqua Prospect Station Shorelands Summerdale Wahmeda Wooglin	• Chautauqua also Fair Point • Chautauqua Institution (founded 1874) located here • Dewittville formerly De Wittville and Tinkertown • Magnolia also Whitneys Landing • Mayville county seat 1811 to present; village inc. 1830 • Pleasantville on Stockton town line • Prospect Station on Portland town line
Cherry Creek 1812 Settlers from Rensselaer County 1829 Formed from Town of Ellington	Cherry Creek (v) Gates Corners Kings School Corner Shattucks Corners	Shattucks Creek Shattuck School Thornton	• Village of Cherry Creek inc. 1893; also Cherrycreek and Puckrum • Gates Corners on Ellington town line • Kings School Corner on Ellington town line • Thornton on Ellington town line
Clymer 1820 Settled 1821 Formed from Town of Chautauqua 1824 Daughter town Mina formed 1829 Daughter town French Creek formed	Clymer Clymer Center Clymer Hill Clymer Station Jaquins	Kings Corners North Clymer Panama Station Wickwire Corners	• Jaquins also Hurlburt Switch

Towns (and Cities)	Villages and other Settlements		Notes
Dunkirk (city) 1837 Incorporated as Village of Dunkirk in the Town of Pomfret 1859 Village became part of new Town of Dunkirk 1880 Village incorporated as a city			
Dunkirk (town) 1859 Formed from Town of Pomfret	Chadwicks Bay Dunkirk (v) Gratiotsville		• Village of Dunkirk inc. in Town of Pomfret 1837; village in Town of Dunkirk from 1859; became City of Dunkirk 1880
Ellery 1806 Settlers from Rensselaer County 1821 Formed from Town of Chautauqua 1850 Ceded land to Town of Stockton	Alden Corners Bayview Belleview Bemus Point (v) Chedwel Colburns Driftwood Ellery Ellery Center Giffords Greenhurst Griffith(s) Jones Corners Maple Springs Midway Park	Oriental Park Phillips Mills Point Stockholm Red Bird Sheldon Hall Shore Acres Starr Farm Sunnyside Sunset Bay Towerville (Corners) Union Ellery Waterman Corners West Ellery Whitesides Willow Brook	• Village of Bemus Point inc. 1911 • Red Bird also Redbird • Towerville (Corners) on Gerry town line
Ellicott 1806 Settled at Chautauque Lake 1812 Formed from Town of Pomfret 1823 Daughter town Busti formed 1825 Daughter town Carroll formed 1832 Daughter town Poland formed 1845 Annexed land from towns of Busti and Carroll	Bonila Celoron (v) Dexterville East Oak Hill Elmhurst Fairbanks Falconer (v) Falconer Junction Fluvanna	Jamestown (v) Kennedys Mills Kimball Stand Levant Ross Mills Ross Station Tiffanys West Ellicott Works Mills	• Bonila also Bonita • Village of Celoron inc. 1896 • Village of Falconer inc. 1891; formerly Worksburg • Village of Jamestown inc. 1827; became City of Jamestown 1886 • Kennedys Mills in Town of Poland from 1832 • Kimball Stand on Gerry town line • Ross Mills on Gerry town line
Ellington 1814 Settled 1824 Formed from Town of Gerry 1829 Daughter town Cherry Creek formed	Bates Clear Creek Conewango Valley Ellington	Gates Corners Kings School Corner Thornton Waterboro	• Gates Corners on Cherry Creek town line • Kings School Corner on Cherry Creek town line • Thornton on Cherry Creek town line • Waterboro on Poland town line
French Creek 1812 Settlers from Oswego County 1829 Formed from Town of Clymer	Cutting French Creek Marks Corners	Marvin Morgan Corners Pekin Hill	• Marks Corners on Mina town line
Gerry 1811 Settled 1812 Formed from Town of Pomfret 1824 Daughter town Ellington formed 1829 Daughter town Charlotte formed	Gerry Kimball Stand Ross Mills	Sinclairville (v) Sinclairville Station Towerville (Corners)	• Gerry formerly Bucklins Corner and Vermont • Kimball Stand on Ellicott town line • Ross Mills on Ellicott town line • Village of Sinclairville inc. 1887; shared with Town of Charlotte formerly Gerry, Saint Clairsville, and Sinclearville • Towerville (Corners) on Ellery town line

Towns (and Cities)	Villages and other Settlements		Notes
Hanover 1797 Settled 1812 Formed from Town of Pomfret 1823 Daughter town Villenova formed 1827 Daughter town Sheridan formed	Balltown Cattaraugus Creek/Village Dennison Corners Fayette Forestville (v) Hanford Bay Hanover Hanover Center Irving	Keaches Corners Kensington Nashville Oak Hill Old Irving Parcells Corners Silver Creek (v) Smiths Mills Sunset Bay West Irving	• Village of Forestville inc. 1849; also Walnut Creek and Walnut Falls, formerly Hanover • Irving formerly Cattaraugus Village (Lower Village) and La Grange (Upper Village); also Acasto and South Irving • Kensington see East Sheridan in Town of Sheridan after 1827 • Nashville also Webster Settlement • Village of Silver Creek inc. 1848
Harmony 1806 Settlers from Otsego County 1816 Formed from Town of Chautauqua 1823 Daughter town Busti formed 1918 Daughter town North Harmony formed	Ashville Bemus Blockville Brokenstraw Cherry Hill Grant Harmony Niobe	Niobe Junction North East Junction Panama (v) Panama Rocks Panama Station Stedman Watts Flats	• Ashville in Town of Busti after 1823 • Niobe formerly Grant Station • Village of Panama inc. 1861 • Stedman in Town of North Harmony from 1918
Jamestown (city) 1827 Incorporated as a village in the Town of Ellicott 1886 Village incorporated as a city			
Kiantone 1807 Settled 1853 Formed from Town of Carroll	Findley Goulds Corners James Hall	Kiantone Stillwater	• Kiantone in Town of Carroll before 1853 as Carroll, Sears, and Searsburg
Mina 1816 Settled by Irish from Pennsylvania 1824 Formed from Town of Clymer 1832 Daughter town Sherman formed	Findley(s) Lake Friends Marks Corners	Mina Minaboro West Mina	• Marks Corners on French Creek town line • Mina formerly Mina Corners
North Harmony 1918 Formed from Town of Harmony ✳	Ashville Cheneys Point Connelly Park Elm Tree Hadley Bay Little America Long View Mentor	Niets Crest Open Meadows Quigley Park Stebbins Corners Stedman Stow Victoria Woodlawn	✳ Act passed Dec. 19, 1918, to take effect Jan. 1, 1919 • Ashville on Busti town line • Mentor also Fishers Corners • Stebbins Corners on Sherman town line • Stedman in Town of Harmony before 1918
Poland 1805 Settlers from Pennsylvania at Connewango Creek 1832 Formed from Town of Ellicott	Clark Clarks Corners Dry Brook Ivesville Kennedy	Mud Creek (Corners) Poland Center Schermerhorn Corners Waterboro	• Kennedy formerly Falconer, Kennedys Mills, and Kennedyville; see Kennedys Mills in Town of Ellicott before 1832 • Waterboro on Ellington town line

Towns (and Cities)	Villages and other Settlements		Notes
Pomfret 1804 Settlers from Pennsylvania at Fredonia 1808 Formed from Town of Chautauqua 1812 Daughter towns Ellicott, Gerry, and Hanover formed 1827 Daughter town Sheridan formed 1829 Daughter town Arkwright formed 1830 Ceded land to Town of Arkwright 1859 Daughter town Dunkirk formed	Brigham Cascade Cordova Dunkirk (v) Fredonia (v) Lamberton Laona	Lil(l)y Dale Morians Nortons Switch Reed Corners Shumla Van Buren Bay Van Buren Harbor	• Cordova also Millville, formerly Crosby Ville • Village of Dunkirk inc. 1837; formerly Chadwicks Bay; became part of Town of Dunkirk in 1859, and a city in 1880 • Village of Fredonia inc. 1829; also Canadaway (Village) • Lamberton formerly Little Canadaway, West Milford, and Milford
Portland 1805 Settled 1813 Formed from Town of Chautauqua 1817 Daughter town Ripley formed 1829 Daughter town Westfield formed	Broc(k)ton (v) Elm Flat Greencrest Green Hills North Portland Portland	Portland Center Prospect Station Skinners Switch Van Buren Point Vineyard West Portland	• Village of Broc(k)ton inc. 1894; formerly Salem, Salem Cross Roads, and Salem-on-Erie • Portland also Centerville • Prospect Station on Chautauqua town line • Vineyard formerly Grapes
Ripley 1804 Settled at Quincy 1817 Formed from Town of Portland 1829 Daughter town Westfield formed	East Ripley East Ripley Corners Forsyth Minnegar Corners Raters Corners Ripley (v)	Ripley Hill Sheldon Corners Shore Haven South Ripley State Line Wattlesburg	• Forsyth also Forsyth Crossing • Village of Ripley formerly Quincy
Sheridan 1804 Settlers from Massachusetts 1827 Formed from towns of Pomfret and Hanover	Center Corners Cook Corners East Sheridan	Hawkins Corner Sheridan South Sheridan	• Center Corners also Havilah • East Sheridan see Kensington in Town of Hanover before 1827 • Sheridan also Sheridan Center and Orrington
Sherman 1824 Settled 1832 Formed from Town of Mina	Centre Sherman Pleasant Valley North Sherman Sherman (v)	Sherman Center Slab City Stebbins Corners Wait(s) (Corners)	• Village of Sherman inc. 1890; also Kipville and Millerville • Stebbins Corners on North Harmony town line
Stockton 1810 Settlers from Saratoga County 1821 Formed from Town of Chautauqua 1850 Annexed land from Town of Ellery	Burnhams Cassadaga (v) Centralia Coes Corners Denton Dentons Corners Kabob	Kelly Corners Moons Oregon Pleasantville South Stockton Stockton	• Village of Cassadaga inc. 1921 • Moons on Charlotte town line • Pleasantville on Chautauqua town line • Stockton also Stockton Corners, formerly Delanti
Villenova 1810 Settled 1823 Formed from Town of Hanover 1829 Daughter town Arkwright formed	Balcom Balcom Corners Hamlet Pope Hill	Skunks Corners Villenova Wango Wrights Corners	• Hamlet also Omar
Westfield 1801 Settlers from Pennsylvania 1829 Formed from towns of Portland and Ripley	Barcelona Fairbanks Lombard Nettle Hill	Rogersville Volusia Westfield (v)	• Barcelona also Portland Harbor • Lombard also Lombard Corners • Village of Westfield inc. 1833; formerly The Crossroads

Note about Chautauqua County

Chautauqua County was created in 1808 but was administered from Buffalo, Niagara County until 1811. The 1810 federal census for the towns of Chautauque and Pomfret are under Niagara County.

NEW YORK STATE CENSUS RECORDS

See also chapter 3, Census Records

County originals at Chautauqua County Clerk's Office: 1825, 1835, 1845, 1855, 1865*, 1875, 1892, 1905, 1915, 1925

State originals at the NYSA: 1915, 1925

Microfilm at the FHL, NYPL, and NYSL; many years are online at *FamilySearch.org* and *Ancestry.com*.

*For 1865 transcription and index, see Barris in Abstracts, Indexes & Transcriptions below.

NATIONAL/STATEWIDE REPOSITORIES & RESOURCES

See chapter 16

COUNTYWIDE REPOSITORIES & RESOURCES

Chautauqua County Clerk

1 North Erie Street • PO Box 170 • Mayville, NY 14757

(716) 753-4331 • *chautauqua.ny.us/departments/clerk/Pages/default.aspx*

Archives date from 1811 and include land records, court records, census records (county originals of New York State censuses 1825–1925 inclusive), naturalization records 1811–1972, marriage records 1908–1935, military discharges (sealed), incorporation records 1880–present, business certificates 1900–present, and maps. Most historical records are in the care of the county historian (in the same building) who serves as Records Manager. A selection of 20th- and 21st-century records is online and searchable through the county clerk's website. The website also has more than 4,000 images of maps (1820s–present).

Chautauqua County – City, Town, and Village Clerks

Birth, marriage, and death records are maintained by the clerk of the municipality in which the event occurred; see Introduction to County Guides for details of other records which may also be held by municipal clerks. For contact information, see municipal directory at *www.co.chautauqua.ny.us*.

Chautauqua County Surrogate's Court

Gerace Office Building Courthouse • PO Box C
Mayville, NY 14757 • (716) 753-4339

Holds probate records from 1811 to the present. See also chapter 6, Probate Records.

Chautauqua County Public Libraries

Chautauqua is part of the Chautauqua-Cattaraugus Library System; see *www.cclslib.org* to access each library. Many hold genealogy and local history collections, such as local newspapers. Also see listing below for James Prendergast Library.

Chautauqua County Historical Society and McClurg Museum

Moore Park • NYS Rts. 394 & 20 • PO Box 7
Westfield, NY 14787 • (716) 326-2977
Email: mcclurg@fairpoint.net • *www.mcclurgmuseum.org*

The McClurg Museum is the headquarters of the Chautauqua Historical Society and houses the Society's archives and library. The Museum hosts regular exhibits and events. Its website has digitized records, including Chautauqua County Civil War muster rolls, biographies of local people, and the papers of Elial T. Foote, a 19th-century Chautauqua County historian. Foote's extensive collection of papers include genealogical information, real estate and land transactions, newspaper clippings, military information, letters, and documents.

Chautauqua County Historian

One North Erie Street • PO Box 170 • Mayville, NY 14757
(716) 753-4857 • Email address on website
http://chautauqua.ny.us/172/Historians

The historian's office has many of the original county records including censuses, naturalizations, court minute books, and marriage records; see county clerk listing for dates. The historian also has city directories; and indexes and microfilm of many records including those held by the County Clerk. The microfilm collections include tax assessment records ca.1850–1970. The website contains a complete list of municipal historians and historical societies in Chautauqua County with addresses and contact information.

Chautauqua County – All Municipal Historians

While not authorized to answer genealogical inquiries, city, town and village historians can provide valuable historical information and research advice; some maintain collections and webpages which may include transcribed records, local histories, and other genealogical material. For contact information, see the Government Appointed Historians of Western New York at *www.gahwny.org/p/chautauqua.html* or the website of the Association of Public Historians of New York State at *www.aphnys.org*.

Chautauqua County Genealogical Society

D. R. Barker Museum • Corner of Route 20 (Main Street) and Day Street
PO Box 404 • Fredonia, NY 14063 • (716) 672-2114
www.chautgen.org

Society's website features a list of surnames currently being researched by its members and a list of the Society's publications. Has published the *Chautauqua Genealogist*, quarterly, since 1977.

Chautauqua Institution: Smith Memorial Library & Archives

21 Miller Avenue • PO Box 1093 • Chautauqua, NY 14722
(716) 357-6332 or 357-6306 • Email address on website
www.ciweb.org/education-archives

Website includes an online "Archives Finding Aid" which can be searched by keyword, with or without images.

REGIONAL REPOSITORIES & RESOURCES

Painted Hills Genealogy Society

See listing in Allegany County Guide

SUNY Fredonia: Daniel A. Reed Library:
Archives & Special Collections

Fredonia, NY 14063 • (716) 673-3184
www.fredonia.edu/library/special_collections

Special collections include: Local History (state census microfilm, cemetery records, church records, vital records, newspapers, and histories); an American Indian Collection; and records and maps of the Holland Land Company. Website includes a PDF, "Guide to Chautauqua County holdings."

University of Rochester: Rare Books, Special Collections, and Preservation: Manuscript and Special Collections: Rochester, Western New York, and New York State
See listing in Monroe County Guide

Western New York Genealogical Society
See listing in Erie County Guide

Western New York Heritage Press
See listing in Erie County Guide

LOCAL REPOSITORIES & RESOURCES
Alphabetized by location

Harmony Historical Society
1943 Open Meadows Road • PO Box 127 • Ashville, NY 14710
(716) 782-3074 • Email: info@harmonyhistoricalsociety.org
www.harmonyhistoricalsociety.org

The Society maintains a library for genealogical and historical research. Holdings include artifacts, photographs, maps, and other records relating to local history.

Dunkirk Historical Society and Museum
513 Washington Ave. • Dunkirk, NY 14048 • (716) 366-3797
Email: contact@dunkirkhistoricalmuseum.org
www.dunkirkhistoricalmuseum.org

Website provides Chautauqua County timeline and historical information.

Historical Museum of the Darwin R. Barker Library Association
Mail: 7 Day Street• Fredonia, NY 14063 • *Museum:* 20 East Main Street Fredonia, NY 14063 • (716) 672-2114 • Email: barker@netsync.net
www.cclslib.org/fredonia/barker_historical_museum_main.htm

The Association maintains a museum, library, and archives. Publishes a quarterly newsletter and occasional papers.

Fenton History Center: Museum and Research Center
67 Washington Street • Jamestown, NY 14701 • (716) 664-6256
Email: information@fentonhistorycenter.org
www.fentonhistorycenter.org

The Center's collections of historical and genealogical material include archives, Jamestown city directories 1875–2000, county census microfilm and indexes, federal census microfilm for Chautauqua and Cattaraugus counties, genealogies, manuscripts, newspaper clippings, photographs, postcards, and family files. Its focus is on Jamestown and southern Chautauqua County. Its library catalog is searchable through its website. Publishes a quarterly newsletter and annual report.

James Prendergast Library
509 Cherry Street • Jamestown, NY 14701 • (716) 484-713
Email: prendergastlibrary@yahoo.com • *www.prendergastlibrary.org*

Collection includes federal census microfilms for Chautauqua and Cattaraugus counties and local newspapers. Select Jamestown city directories, 1875–1916, are accessible on the library's website. Obituary searches will be performed for a fee.

Valley Historical Society
Main at Lester Streets • PO Box 1045 • Sinclairville, NY 14782
(716) 962-8520

Holdings include records of local cemeteries, churches, businesses, and material about the Grange (Fredonia #1), the oldest dues-paying Grange in the world.

SELECTED PRINT & ONLINE RESOURCES

Below is a selection of resources relevant for research in this county. The list is representative, not exhaustive. Additional titles—particularly of abstracts, indexes, transcriptions, and local histories—are available; consult the introduction to Part Two for further information. For guidance on how to identify and locate community directories and local newspapers, see chapter 11, City Directories, and chapter 12, Newspapers, in Part One of this book.

Abstracts, Indexes & Transcriptions

Barden, Virginia W. *Earliest Holland Land Company Sales in Chautauqua County, New York.* Fredonia, NY: Chautauqua Family Genealogical Society, 1990.

Barris, Lois, comp. *Holland Land Company Delinquent Contracts in Chautauqua County, NY.* Fredonia, NY: Chautauqua County Genealogical Society, 1991.

Barris, Lois, and Norwood Barris. *Selected Information from the 1865 New York State Census for the County of Chautauqua.* Fredonia, NY: Chautauqua County Genealogical Society, 1991.

Cohen, Minnie. "Gravestone Inscriptions from Chautauqua County, NY, Cemeteries: Including Chautauqua Cemetery, Chautauqua, NY, Hunt Family Private Cemetery, Chautauqua, NY, Magnolia Cemetery, Magnolia Springs, NY, Bemus Point Cemetery, Bemus Point, NY." Typescript, 1932. NYPL, New York. [*Ancestry.com*]

— — —. "Gravestone Inscriptions of Fluvannah [sic] Cemetery, Fluvannah, [sic] NY; Burrows Private Cemetery, Mayville, NY; Mayville Cemetery, Mayville, NY: All in Chautauqua County." Typescript, 1932. NYSL, New York. [*Ancestry.com*]

County of Chautauqua Abstracts. Syracuse: Central New York Genealogical Society, 2000. Abstracts for a range of genealogical records originally published in the quarterly *Tree Talks.*

Daughters of the American Revolution, comps. *New York DAR Genealogical Records Committee Report.* Since 1913 DAR volunteers have transcribed many thousands of unpublished cemetery, church, and town records throughout New York. The reports are at the DAR Library; copies are at the NYSL and the NYPL. The DAR has a searchable name index to all the GRC reports at *http://services.dar.org/Public/DAR_Research/search/?Tab_ID=6.* See Jean Worden's index below for a listing by county of the New York record sets that were transcribed by the DAR before 1998.

Griswold, Glenn E., and Charles D. Townsend. *Chautauqua County, New York, Cemetery Inscriptions and County and Town History.* Sarasota, FL: Aceto Bookmen, 1995. Book includes transcriptions copied by Glenn Griswold around 1931.

Jamestown Directory, 1879–80: Containing the Names of the Inhabitants of Jamestown: Together with a Business Directory of Brocton, Broken Straw, Busti, Cassadaga, Clymer, Corry, Delanti, Dunkirk, Forestville, Fredonia, Frewsburg, Kennedy, Mayville, Panama, Randolph, Ripley, Sherman, Smith's-Mills, Sinclairville, and Westfield. Jamestown, 1879.

Kelly, Arthur C. M. *Index to Tree Talks County Packet: Chautauqua County.* Rhinebeck, NY: Kinship, 2002.

Lamb, Frank B. "Mayville, N.Y., Cemetery Inscriptions." *NYG&B Record,* vol. 58, no. 4 (1927): 371–381. [NYG&B eLibrary]

Starr, L. N. *Alphabetical Directory of the Village of Fredonia, 1899.* Fredonia, NY, 1899.

Worden, Jean D. "Book I, Subject Index." In *Revised Master Index to the New York State Daughters of the American Revolution Genealogical Records Volumes*. Zephyrhills, FL: J. D. Worden, 1998. The Subject Index includes a listing by county of the cemeteries, churches, towns, and other sources of records transcribed by the DAR.

"Yorker Cemetery Record, Sherman, New York." Typescript, 1987. NYSL, New York. [*Ancestry.com*]

Other Resources

Anderson, Arthur W. *The Conquest of Chautauqua: Jamestown and Vicinity in the Pioneer and Later Periods as Told by Pioneer Newspapers and Persons*. Jamestown, NY: Printed by Journal Press, Inc., 1932.

Barden, Virginia W., Lois Barris, and Norwood Barris. *A Guide to Chautauqua County, New York, Cemeteries and Burial Sites*. Fredonia, NY: Chautauqua County Genealogical Society, 1992.

Beers, F.W., & Co. *Illustrated Historical Atlas of the Co. of Chautauqua, New York*. New York, 1881.

Burgess, Chalon. *The Churches and Clergy of the Pioneer Period in Chautauqua County*. N.p., 1902.

Centennial History of Chautauqua County: A Detailed and Entertaining Story of One Hundred Years of Development. Jamestown, NY: Chautauqua History Co., 1904.

Child, Hamilton, comp. *Gazetteer and Business Directory of Chautauqua County, NY, for 1873–4*. Syracuse, 1872.

Downs, John P. *History of Chautauqua County, New York, and Its People*. Boston: American Historical Society Inc., 1921.

Edson, Obed. *Biographical and Portrait Cyclopedia of Chautauqua, with a Historical Sketch of the County*. Edited by Butler F. Dilley. Philadelphia, 1891. Book includes hundreds of biographies of local people with portraits. Excerpted and alphabetized index by Annabelle Hiller published 1974 by Fenton Genealogical Library.

— — —. *History of Chautauqua County, New York*. Edited by D. Georgia. 2 vols. Boston, 1894.

— — —. *History of Evergreen Cemetery: Sinclairville, Chaut. Co., NY, and Other Burial Grounds in Its Laws, Rules, Regulations, Names of Lot-Owners and Map*. Sinclairville, NY, 1890.

Fay, Loren V. *Chautauqua County, New York, Genealogical Research Secrets*. Albany: L. V. Fay, 1983.

Foley, Janet W. *Early Settlers of New York State: Their Ancestors and Descendants*. 9 vols. Akron, NY: 1934–1942. Reprint, 2 vols. Baltimore: Genealogical Publishing Co., 1993.

Historical Records Survey, New York State. *Inventory of the County Archives of the New York State (Exclusive of the Five Counties of New York City) No. 6, Chautauqua County*. Albany: Works Progress Administration, Historical Records Survey, 1938. [NYG&B eLibrary]

Kaufman, Joanne. "Place Names in Chautauqua County." *Chautauqua Genealogist*, vol. 19, no.3 (August 1996): 1, 46–56. *www.chautgen. org/sadmin/pdfs/960800.pdf*

Kurtz, E. T., and Loraine C. Smith. *Names and Places in Chautauqua County, New York*. Portland, NY: E.T. Kurtz Sr., 2001.

Leet, Ernest D., ed. *History of Chautauqua County, New York, 1938–1978*. Westfield, NY: Chautauqua County Historical Society, 1980.

McMahon, Helen G. *Chautauqua County, A History*. Buffalo: Stewart Publishers, 1958.

Morrison, Wayne E., and Hamilton Child. *A History of Chautauqua County, New York, 1808–1874*. Clyde, NY: Wayne E. Morrison, 1969.

New York Historical Resources Center. *Guide to Historical Resources in Chautauqua County, New York Repositories: Update No. 1*. Ithaca, NY: Cornell University, 1988. [*books.FamilySearch.org*]

Peterson, A. Bartholdi. *"Lest We Forget," The Record of Chautauqua County's Own. A History*. Jamestown, NY: Chautauqua County Post American Legion, 1920. Book includes history of Chautauqua County soldiers in World War I.

Stewart, W. M. *New Topographical Atlas of Chautauqua County, New York: From Actual Surveys Especially for this Atlas*. Philadelphia, 1867. [NYPL Digital Gallery]

Warren, Emory F. *Sketches of the History of Chautauqua County*. Jamestown, NY, 1846.

Western New York Genealogical Society Journal. Hamburg, NY: Western New York Genealogical Society, 1974–present. [*wnygs.org*]

Young, Andrew W. *History of Chautauqua County, New York: From its First Settlement to the Present Time, with Numerous Biographical and Family Sketches*. Buffalo, 1875.

Additional Online Resources

Ancestry.com

There are vast numbers of records on *Ancestry.com* that pertain to people who have lived in New York State. See chapter 16 for a description of *Ancestry.com*'s resources and its partnership with the New York State Archives. A search of the online card catalog by county may reveal lesser known resources that pertain to a locality, such as town records, abstracts, transcriptions, city directories, and local histories.

Chautauqua County Historical Society: Italian Newspaper Collection
www.mcclurgmuseum.org/collection/archives/italian_newspapers/italian_ newspapers.html

Many issues of the Chautauqua County Italian-language newspaper *Il Risveglio*, 1921–1953, have been digitized and are accessible on the website.

FamilySearch.org

FamilySearch has extensive collections of New York records, including religious records, which are searchable by name and location, but not by county. The following collections include record images (browsable, but not searchable) that are organized by county:

- "New York, Land Records, 1630–1975." Includes land and property records. *familysearch.org/search/collection/2078654*
- "New York, Probate Records, 1629–1971." Includes wills, letters of administration, and guardianship papers. *familysearch.org/ search/collection/1920234*

For both collections, choose the browse option and then select Chautauqua to view the available records sets.

A detailed description of *FamilySearch.org* resources, which include the catalog of the Family History Library, is found in chapter 16.

Holland Land Company Collection at the Reed Library at the State University of New York at Fredonia
www.fredonia.edu/library/collections/archives/holland.asp

The website provides a description of the Reed Library's collection and information about Holland Land Company records in other libraries. A guide to "Genealogical Research and Holland Land Company Records" is at *www.fredonia.edu/library/special_ collections/HLC/genealogical.pdf*.

New York Heritage Digital Collections: Chautauqua-Cattaraugus Library System
http://cdm16694.contentdm.oclc.org/cdm/landingpage/collection/VXU
    The digital collection includes selected city directories for Jamestown and Olean and selected Westfield newspapers.

New York Heritage Digital Collections: Holland Land Company Maps
http://nyheritage.org/collections/holland-land-company-maps
    More than 1,000 maps pertaining to the Holland Land purchase in Western New York and held by the Reed Library at the State University of New York at Fredonia have been digitized and are accessible at this website, which also provides links to related online resources.

New York Heritage Digital Collections: New York State Newspaper Project
www.nyheritage.org/newspapers
    The website provides links to digital newspapers collections in 26 counties (currently) made accessible through New York Heritage, New York State Historic Newspapers, HRVH Historical Newspapers, and other providers.

NYGenWeb Project: Chautauqua County
www.rootsweb.ancestry.com/~nychauta
    Part of the national, USGenWeb volunteer initiative, the website provides information and resources for county research.

Old Fulton New York Postcards
www.FultonHistory.com
    The website provides free access to a vast collection of digitized New York newspapers, including 13 titles for Chautauqua County.

Painted Hills Genealogy Society, Chautauqua County, New York Index Page
www.paintedhills.org/chautco.html
    The county webpage of this regional society has direct links to numerous records transcriptions of cemeteries for the county as well as census information and historical resources.

Chemung County

Formed March 29, 1836

Parent County   Tioga
Daughter County   Schuyler 1854
County Seat   City of Elmira

Major Land Transactions
See table in chapter 7, Land Records
Watkins and Flint Purchase 1794

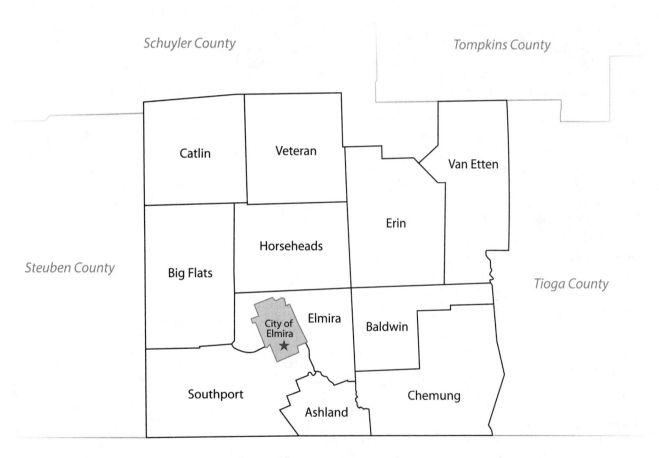

Town Boundary Map
★ - County seat

Towns (and Cities)	Villages and other Settlements		Notes
Ashland 1738 Settled 1867 Formed from towns of Chemung, Elmira, and Southport	Lowman Lowmanville Wellsburg(h) (v)		• Lowman on Chemung town line • Village of Wellsburg(h) inc. 1872; in Town of Southport before 1867
Baldwin 1813 Settled 1856 Formed from Town of Chemung	Hicks North Chemung		• North Chemung formerly Hammonds Corners
Big Flats 1787 Settled 1822 Formed in Tioga County from Town of Elmira 1836 Transferred to new county of Chemung	Big Flats Fisherville Fitch Bridge Golden Glow Heights Grooms Corners Harris Hill Manor North Big Flats		• Golden Glow Heights also Hendry Creek
Catharine * In Chemung County 1836–1854			* See Schuyler County
Catlin 1816 Settled 1823 Formed in Tioga County from Town of Catharine 1835 Daughter town Dix formed 1836 Transferred to new county of Chemung	Catlin Center Chambers Fero Kendall Martins Hill	Pine Valley Post Creek Smith Corners Tompkins Corners West Catlin	• Tompkins Corners formerly Catlin
Chemung 1788 Settled at Breckville 1789 Formed in Montgomery County 1791 Transferred to new county of Tioga 1792 Daughter town Elmira formed 1822 Daughter town Erin formed 1836 Transferred to new county of Chemung 1856 Daughter town Baldwin formed 1867 Daughter town Ashland formed	Amot Baldwin Beantown Breckville Chemung Lowman Owens Mills		• Beantown formerly Chemung Center • Lowman on Ashland town line
Dix * In Chemung County 1836–1854			* See Schuyler County
Elmira (city) * 1828 Village of Elmira formed in Town of Elmira 1864 Village incorporated as a city from Village of Elmira and land from Town of Southport	Southport Station		* County seat at Elmira from 1836 when Chemung County was formed; Elmira was one of Tioga's county seats 1792–1836
Elmira (town) 1788 Settled 1792 Formed in Tioga County as Newtown from Town of Chemung 1798 Daughter town Catharine formed	Carr Corners East Elmira Elmira (v)	Elmira Heights (v) Reception Center West Elmira	• Village of Elmira inc. 1828; became City of Elmira 1864; county seat from 1836 • Village of Elmira Heights inc. 1896; shared with Town of Horseheads

(Elmira continued on next page)

Towns (and Cities)	Villages and other Settlements		Notes
Elmira (town) (continued) 1808 Name changed from Newtown to Elmira 1822 Daughter towns Big Flats and Southport formed 1836 Transferred to new county of Chemung 1854 Daughter town Horseheads formed 1864 Daughter city Elmira formed from Village of Elmira and Town of Southport 1867 Daughter town Ashland formed			
Erin 1817 Settled 1822 Formed in Tioga County from Town of Chemung 1836 Transferred to new county of Chemung 1854 Daughter town Van Etten formed	Erin Herrington Corners Park Park Station Rodbournville South Erin State Road		
Horseheads 1788 Settled 1854 Formed from Town of Elmira	Breesport Elmira Heights (v) Horseheads (v) Horseheads Station	North Elmira Orchard Knoll Slabtown	• Village of Elmira Heights inc. 1896; shared with Town of Elmira • Village of Horseheads incorporated as Fairport in 1837; name changed to Horseheads in 1845 • Slabtown was on Veteran town line
Newtown Name for Town of Elmira 1792–1808			
Southport 1788 Settled 1822 Formed in Tioga County from Town of Elmira 1836 Transferred to new county of Chemung 1864 Daughter city Elmira formed 1867 Daughter town Ashland formed	Bulkhead Elmira Hendry Creek Pine City Rosstown Sagetown Seely Creek	Southport State Line Junction Webb(s) Mills Wells Wellsburg(h) Wells Station	• Wellsburg(h) in Town of Ashland from 1867
Van Etten 1795 Settled 1854 Formed from towns of Cayuta and Erin *	Cayuta Lockwood Radburn Station Rodbourn Swartwood	Swartwood Station Van Etten (v) Van Etten Junction Van Ettenville	* Town of Cayuta in Schuyler County • Village of Van Etten inc. 1876
Veteran 1800 Settlers from Connecticut and Pennsylvania 1823 Formed in Tioga County from Town of Catharine 1836 Transferred to new county of Chemung	East Grove Lower Pine Valley Midway Millport (v) Pine Grove Pine Valley	Rush Run Slabtown Sullivanville Terry Corners Veteran	• Village of Millport inc. 1923 • Slabtown was on Horseheads town line

Notes on Chemung County

While Chemung is a daughter county of Tioga, Chemung holds the deed and mortgage records for both counties from 1790 to 1835.

Chemung is one of four "County Registration Districts," which have consolidated the administration of birth and death records. These civil records are kept at the Chemung County Vital Records office; see details below. Civil birth and death records earlier than 1881 may still be found with city, town, or village clerks.

NEW YORK STATE CENSUS RECORDS
See also chapter 3, Census Records

County originals at Chemung County Historian's Office: 1845, 1855, 1865*, 1875, 1892, 1905, 1915, 1925

State originals at the NYSA: 1915, 1925

Microfilm at the FHL, NYPL, and NYSL; many years are online at *FamilySearch.org* and *Ancestry.com*.

*1865 census for the Town of Horseheads, Chemung County, includes the maiden names of all married women.

NATIONAL/STATEWIDE REPOSITORIES & RESOURCES
See chapter 16

COUNTYWIDE REPOSITORIES & RESOURCES
Chemung County Clerk
210 Lake Street • PO Box 588 • Elmira, NY 14902-0588
(607) 737-2920 • *www.chemungcounty.com*

Court records; deeds 1836–present; mortgages; naturalization records 1860–1906; declarations of intention 1907–1949; and bound copies of the New York state censuses for Chemung County 1855, 1865, 1892, and 1905 (for 1875 state census, see County Historian below). County clerk holds Tioga County deeds and mortgages 1790–1835. Marriage records are kept by town clerks; Chemung County Vital Records holds birth and death records; vital records in New York State are typically kept by the town clerk.

Chemung County – City, Town, and Village Clerks
Marriage records are maintained by the clerk of the municipality in which the event occurred; see Introduction to County Guides for details of other records which may also be held by municipal clerks. For contact information, see the Directory of County, Town, City & Village Officials at *www.chemungcounty.com*.

Chemung County Surrogate's Court
224 Lake Street • PO Box 588 • Elmira, NY 14902-0588

Holds probate records 1836 to the present. See also chapter 6, Probate Records.

Chemung County Vital Records
103 Washington Street • PO Box 588 • Elmira, NY 14902
(607) 737-2018 • *www.chemungcountyhealth.org*

Holds births and death records for all municipalities in Chemung County.

Chemung County Public Libraries
Chemung is part of the Southern Tier Library System; see *www.stls.org/libraries* to access each library. Many hold genealogy and local history collections. Also see listing below for Steele Memorial Library.

Steele Memorial Library:
Chemung County Library District Genealogy Department
101 East Church Street • Elmira, NY 14901 • (607) 733-9173
www.steele.lib.ny.us (Steele Memorial Library)
Email access on website • *www.ccld.lib.ny.us/genealogy.htm* (Chemung County Library District Genealogy Department)

Holds a copy of the New York State Department of Health vital records index. Books and periodicals, city directories 1857–present, yearbooks, histories and genealogies, surname files, local history files; microfilm collection includes censuses (federal and New York State), local newspapers 1835–present, mortality schedules, religious records (Catholic church records for Chemung County, 1848–1910), cemetery records of Steuben County. Website includes online obituary index from local newspapers 1898–1960, yearbooks 1909–1938 (gaps), maps and atlases, and links to useful websites/resources. Genealogy queries may be submitted for a fee.

Chemung County Historical Society, Chemung Valley Museum, and Mrs. Arthur W. Booth Library
415 East Walter Street • Elmira, NY 14901
(607) 734-4167 ext. 207 • Email: cchs@chemungvalleymuseum.org
archivist@chemungvalleymuseum.org • *www.chemungvalleymuseum.org*

The Booth Library contains the Chemung County Historical Society's collection of books, manuscripts, church records (including membership records of the First Baptist Church of Elmira), photographs, maps, and architectural records. The newspaper collection begins in the 1810s (some digitized), and includes the *Elmira Gazette*, 1830–1832 (transcripts online at *www.joycetice.com/clippings/elgz1830.htm*), and the *Elmira Republican*, 1832–1834 (marriages and deaths were extracted and online at *www.joycetice.com/clippings/el1832.htm*). A list of holdings is available on the museum website, along with online research services and a list of local historians. Society has published the quarterly *Chemung Historical Journal*, since 1955.

Chemung County Historian
415 East Water Street • Elmira, NY 14901 • (607) 734-4167
Email: historian@chemungvalleymuseum.org

Holdings include the originals of the New York state census 1845, 1855, 1865, 1875, 1892, 1905, 1915, and 1925; documents; ledgers; minutes; correspondence; photographs; historic maps; newspapers beginning in the early-1800s; and original membership records of the First Baptist Church of Elmira.

Chemung County – All Municipal Historians
While not authorized to answer genealogical inquiries, city, town, and village historians can provide valuable historical information and research advice; some maintain collections and webpages which may include transcribed records, local histories, and other genealogical material. For contact information, see *www.joycetice.com/articles/chistlis.htm* or the website of the Association of Public Historians of New York State at *www.aphnys.org*.

REGIONAL REPOSITORIES & RESOURCES
Central New York Genealogical Society
See listing in Onondaga County Guide

Erin Historical Society Museum
53 Fairview Road • Erin, NY 14838 • (607) 739-0242

Holdings include tax records and marriage certificates dating to the 19th century.

Lowman Historical Society

PO Box 7 • Lowman, New York 14861
Email: chalecogus@aol.com • Email: info@lowmanhistoricalsociety.com
www.lowmanhistoricalsociety.com

Society maintains a historic schoolhouse; website has a presentation on the historic architecture of the Lowman/Chemung area. Inquiries should be mailed.

Southport Historical Society

Laurel Street • PO Box 146 • Pine City, NY 14871
www.joycetice.com/towns/soutport.htm

Website includes cemetery and tax records, and census abstracts and transcriptions.

LOCAL REPOSITORIES & RESOURCES

Alphabetized by location

Elmira City Clerk

City Hall First Floor • 317 E. Church Street • Elmira, NY 14901
(607)737-5672 • *www.cityofelmira.net/city-clerk*

Holds marriage records 1876–present. For births and deaths, see Chemung County Vital Records above.

Big Flats Historical Society

258 Hibbard Road • PO Box 232 • Big Flats, NY 14814
(607) 562-7460 • *www.bigflatsny.gov/historical-society*

Articles available on website.

SELECTED PRINT & ONLINE RESOURCES

Below is a selection of resources relevant for research in this county. The list is representative, not exhaustive. Additional titles—particularly of abstracts, indexes, transcriptions, and local histories—are available; consult the introduction to Part Two for further information. For guidance on how to identify and locate community directories and local newspapers, see chapter 11, City Directories, and chapter 12, Newspapers, in Part One of this book.

Abstracts, Indexes & Transcriptions

Barber, Gertrude Audrey. "Abstracts of Wills of Chemung County, NY, from 1836–1850: Copied from Original Records at the Surrogate's Office, Elmira, NY." Typescript, 1941. New York State Library, Albany. [*Ancestry.com*]

County of Chemung Abstracts. Syracuse: Central New York Genealogical Society, 2000. Abstracts for a range of genealogical records originally published in the quarterly *Tree Talks.*

Daughters of the American Revolution, comps. *New York DAR Genealogical Records Committee Report.* Since 1913 DAR volunteers have transcribed many thousands of unpublished cemetery, church, and town records throughout New York. The reports are at the DAR Library; copies are at the NYSL and the NYPL. The DAR has a searchable name index to all the GRC reports at *http://services.dar.org/Public/DAR_Research/search/?Tab_ID=6.* See Jean Worden's index below for a listing by county of the New York record sets that were transcribed by the DAR before 1998.

Kelly, Arthur C. M. *Index to Tree Talks County Packet: Chemung County.* Rhinebeck, NY: Kinship, 2002.

List of Confederate Soldiers Buried in Woodlawn Cemetery, Elmira, New York. Elmira, NY: Chemung County Historical Society, 1980.

Sheldon, Nellie M. *Name Index, History of Tioga, Chemung, Tompkins and Schuyler Counties, New York: Compiled by H.B. Peirce and D. Hamilton Hurd, Published by Everts and Ensign, 1879.* N.p: The Author, 1965.

Worden, Jean D. "Book 1, Subject Index." In *Revised Master Index to the New York State Daughters of the American Revolution Genealogical Records Volumes.* Zephyrhills, FL: J. D. Worden, 1998. The Subject Index includes a listing by county of the cemeteries, churches, towns, and other sources of records transcribed by the DAR.

Other Resources

A Biographical Record of Chemung County, New York. New York: S. J. Clarke Publishing Co., 1902.

Beers, F. W. *Atlas of Chemung County, New York: From Actual Surveys by and under the Direction of F.W. Beers, Assisted by Geo. P. Sanford & Others.* New York, 1869. [NYPL Digital Gallery]

Byrne, Thomas E. *Chemung County, 1890–1975.* Elmira, NY: Chemung County Historical Society, 1976.

Chemung Historical Society. *Chemung County Memories: The Early Years.* Staten Island, NY: Pediment Group, ca. 2001.

Child, Hamilton. *Gazetteer and Business Directory of Chemung and Schuyler Counties, NY, for 1868–9.* Syracuse, 1868.

Historical Records Survey, New York State. *Inventory of the County Archives of the New York State (Exclusive of the Five Counties of New York City) No. 7, Chemung County.* Albany: Works Progress Administration, Historical Records Survey, 1937. [NYG&B eLibrary]

Hoiland, Doris R. *Pioneers of the Southern Tier; Chemung County.* N.p. 1974.

Inventory of the County Archives of New York State: Chemung County. Albany: The Historical Records Survey, 1939. [NYG&B eLibrary]

New York Historical Resources Center. *Guide to Historical Resources in Chemung County, New York, Repositories.* Ithaca, NY: Cornell University, 1982. [*books.FamilySearch.org*]

Peirce, Henry B., and D. Hamilton Hurd. *History of Tioga, Chemung, Tompkins and Schuyler Counties, New York: With Illustrations and Biographical Sketches of Some of Its Prominent Men and Pioneers.* Philadelphia, 1879. See above for a name index by Nellie Sheldon.

Sexton, John L., Jr. *An Outline History of Tioga and Bradford Counties in Pennsylvania; Chemung, Steuben, Tioga, Tompkins, and Schuyler in New York . . . .* Elmira, NY, 1885.

Towner, Ausburn. *A Brief History of Chemung County, for the Use of Grade Schools.* New York: A. S. Barnes, 1907.

———. *Our County and Its People: A History of the Valley and County of Chemung, from the Closing Years of the Eighteenth Century.* Syracuse, 1892.

Wilson, Amy H. *Chemung County: An Illustrated History.* Montgomery, AL: Community Communications, 1999.

Additional Online Resources

Ancestry.com

There are vast numbers of records on *Ancestry.com* that pertain to people who have lived in New York State. See chapter 16 for a description of *Ancestry.com*'s resources and its partnership with the New York State Archives. A search of the online card catalog by county may reveal lesser known resources that pertain to a locality, such as town records, abstracts, transcriptions, city directories, and local histories.

Chemung County Atlases

www.newyorkheritage.org

The Steele Memorial Library has digitized two atlases of Chemung County for 1869 and 1904 and two atlases of the City of Elmira for 1876 and 1896.

Chemung County New York Archives

www.usgwarchives.net/ny/chemung/chemung.htm

The website has links to a selection of transcribed cemetery records, wills, and indexes. See below for the current NYGenWeb site for Chemung County.

FamilySearch.org

FamilySearch has extensive collections of New York records, including religious records, which are searchable by name and location, but not by county. The following collections include record images (browsable, but not searchable) that are organized by county:

- "New York, Land Records, 1630–1975." Includes land and property records. *familysearch.org/search/collection/2078654*
- "New York, Probate Records, 1629–1971." Includes wills, letters of administration, and guardianship papers. *familysearch.org/search/collection/1920234*

For both collections, choose the browse option and then select Chemung to view the available records sets.

A detailed description of *FamilySearch.org* resources is found in chapter 16.

Tri-Counties Genealogy and History

www.joycetice.com/jmtindex.htm

This website, which is operated by Joyce M. Tice, serves as the NYGenWeb site for Chemung County and provides free access to numerous transcriptions and links to other resources.

Chenango County

Formed March 15, 1798

Parent Counties   Herkimer • Tioga
Daughter County   Madison 1806
County Seat   City of Norwich

Major Land Transactions
See table in chapter 7, Land Records
Vermont Sufferers Tract 1786
Chenango Twenty Townships 1789–1794

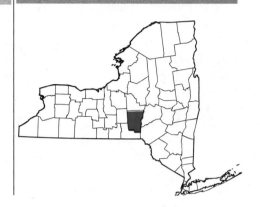

Town Boundary Map
★ - County seat

Towns (and Cities)	Villages and other Settlements		Notes
Afton 1786 Settlers from Connecticut and Vermont 1857 Formed from Town of Bainbridge	Afton (v) Afton Center Bennettsville Bettsburg East Afton Middle Bridge	Nineveh Nineveh Junction North Afton South Bainbridge Stumptown Hill	• Village of Afton inc. 1891 • Bennettsville and Middle Bridge (Middlebridge), in Town of Bainbridge before 1857 • North Afton formerly Ayreshire
Bainbridge 1785 Settlers from Connecticut and Vermont 1791 Formed in Tioga County as Jericho 1793 Daughter towns Norwich and Oxford formed 1798 Daughter town Greene formed 1798 Transferred to new county of Chenango 1814 Name changed to Bainbridge 1857 Daughter town Afton formed	Bainbridge (v) Bennettsville East Bainbridge Middlebridge Newton Newtown Hollow North Bainbridge South Bainbridge Union Valley West Bainbridge		• Village of Bainbridge inc. 1829 • Bennettsville formerly Bainbridge Center • Bennettsville and Middle Bridge (Middlebridge) in Town of Afton from 1857 • West Bainbridge formerly Turnpike
Brookfield * In Chenango County 1798–1806			* See Madison County
Cazenovia * In Chenango County 1798–1806			* See Madison County
Columbus 1791 Settled 1805 Formed from Town of Brookfield * 1807 Annexed land from Town of Norwich	Button City Columbus Columbus Center Columbus Corners Columbus Quarter	Lambs Corners Sodom South Edmeston Station Sweets Tallette	* Town of Brookfield in Madison County from 1806 • Tallette formerly Gooseville
Coventry 1785 Settled 1806 Formed from Town of Greene 1843 Annexed land from towns of Greene and Oxford	Blackesley Corner Bobell Hill Church Hollow Coventry	Coventry Station Coventryville West Coventry	• Bobell Hill also Bowbell Hill • Hamlet of Coventry formerly Union
DeRuyter * In Chenango County 1798–1806			* See Madison County
Eastern Name for Town of Guilford 1813–1817			
German 1795 Settlers from Oneida County 1806 Formed from Town of DeRuyter * 1817 Daughter town Otselic formed 1823 Daughter town Lincklaen formed 1827 Daughter town Pitcher formed	Brackel East German German German Five Corners German Four Corners Livermores Corners		* Town of German also Brakel Township * Town of DeRuyter in Madison County from 1806 • Brackel in Town of Pitcher after 1827
Greene 1792 Settled 1798 Formed from Town of Union, Tioga County, and Jericho (now Bainbridge) *	Brisben Chenango Forks Cowles Old Stand East Greene Fickles Corner	Genegantslet Greene (v) Lower Genegantslet Corner	* Town of Union in Broome County from 1806 • Brisben formerly Tinkerville • Chenango Forks in Broome County after 1840 **(Greene continued on next page)**

Towns (and Cities)	Villages and other Settlements		Notes
Greene (continued) 1806 Daughter town Coventry formed 1808 Daughter town Smithville formed 1840 Ceded land to Town of Barker, Broome County 1843 Ceded land to Town of Coventry	Page Brook Quinne(y)ville Read Sacketts Harbor	Upper Genegantslet Corner Willard Station	• Fickles Corner also Ficals Corner • Genegantslet formerly Greens Corners • Village of Greene inc. 1842 • Quinne(y)ville formerly Three Corners
Guilford 1787 Settled 1813 Formed as Eastern from Town of Oxford 1817 Name changed to Guilford	Batterson Bridge Coburns East Guilford Fayette Godfrey Corners Guilford Guilford Center High Bridge Ives Settlement Knappsburg Lathams Corners Mount Hope Mount Upton New Berlin Junction	North Guilford North Guilford Corners Parker Parker Station Rockdale Rockwells Mills Shavers Corners Shilton Corners Trestle Trestle Corners Union Van Burens Corners Windsor Corners Yaleville	• East Guilford formerly Gospel Hill • Hamlet of Guilford formerly Bear Wallow • Mount Hope formerly Grecian Bend
Hamilton * In Chenango County 1798–1806			* See Madison County
Jericho Name for Town of Bainbridge 1791–1814			
Lancaster Name for Town of New Berlin 1821–1822			
Lincklaen 1796 Settled 1823 Formed from Town of German 1827 Daughter town Pitcher formed 1833 Ceded land to Town of Pitcher	Burdick Settlement Catlin Settlement Lincklaen Lincklaen Center	Mariposa North Lincklaen Rhode Island West Lincklaen	• Rhode Island on Otselic town line; also Rhode Island Settlement
MacDonough 1795 Settled 1816 Formed from Town of Preston	Corbin(s) Corners East Macdonough	Galetown Macdonough	
New Berlin Settled before Revolutionary War 1807 Formed as New Berlin from Town of Norwich 1821 Name changed to Lancaster 1822 Name changed back to New Berlin 1852 Ceded land to Sherburne	Ambler Settlement Amblerville Chenango Lake Davis Crossing Five Corners Great Brook Holmesville New Berlin (v)	New Berlin Center New Berlin Center Station New Berlin Station North New Berlin Sage Corners Sages Crossing South New Berlin Turks Corners	• Village of New Berlin inc. 1816 • South New Berlin formerly Boyes Corners and Crandalltown; shared with towns of Butternuts and Morris, Otsego County
North Norwich * 1794 Settled 1849 Formed from Town of Norwich	Burwell Corners Galena German Hollow King(s) Settlement	North Norwich Plasterville Sherburne Four Corners Whaupaunaucau	* County seat alternated between towns of Oxford and North Norwich 1806–1809 • King(s) Settlement in Town of Norwich before 1849 • Sherburne Four Corners shared with towns of Plymouth, Sherburne, and Smyrna

Towns (and Cities)	Villages and other Settlements		Notes
Norwich (city) * 1816 Incorporated village in Town of Norwich 1914 Incorporated as a city from Village of Norwich			* County seat at Norwich (village and city) from 1809; for county seat 1798–1809 see Oxford and North Norwich
Norwich (town) 1788 Settled 1793 Formed in Tioga County from towns of Union and Jericho (now Bainbridge) 1798 Transferred to new county of Chenango 1806 Daughter towns Pharsalia, Plymouth, and Preston formed 1807 Daughter towns Columbus and New Berlin formed; ceded land to Town of Columbus 1808 Annexed land from Town of Preston 1820 Ceded land to Town of Preston 1849 Daughter town North Norwich formed 1915 Village of Norwich incorporated as a city	Barbers Barbers Crossings Barburs Barburs Station East Norwich Hawley Corners Haynes Holmesville King(s) Settlement North Guilford Corners	North Norwich Norwich (v) Palkville Polkville Springvale Webb Corners White Store Woods Corners Woods Corners Station Woods Station	* Town of Union in Broome County from 1806 • King(s) Settlement and North Norwich in Town of North Norwich after 1849 • Village of Norwich inc. 1816, became City of Norwich 1915; county seat 1809–present
Otselic 1800 Settled 1817 Formed from Town of German	Beaver Meadow Otselic Otselic Center Rhode Island Seventh Day Hollow	South Otselic Stanbro Tallette Upper Beaver Meadow	• Hamlet of Otselic also The Flats • Rhode Island on Lincklaen town line; also Rhode Island Settlement • South Otselic formerly Bowens Settlement, Sugar Hollow, and The Burg
Oxford * 1790 Settled 1793 Formed in Tioga County from towns of Union and Jericho (now Bainbridge) * 1798 Transferred to new county of Chenango 1813 Daughter town Guilford formed 1843 Ceded land to Town of Coventry	Cheshireville Cork Island Coventry Station Hayes Ingraham Corners Northrups Corners Oklahoma Oxford (v)	Oxford Station Oxfordville Puckerville (Corners) Robinson Mills South Oxford Summit Walker(s) Corners	* County seat 1798–1806 alternated between Oxford and Hamilton (now in Madison County), 1806–1809 alternated between Oxford and North Norwich * Town of Union in Broome County from 1806 • Hayes also Hayes Junction • Village of Oxford inc. 1808
Pharsalia 1797 Settlers from Stonington, CT 1806 Formed as Stonington from Town of Norwich 1808 Name changed to Pharsalia	Cranes Corners Cranesville East Pharsalia North Pharsalia Northwest Corners	Pharsalia Pharsalia Hook Skunk Hollow Waldron Corners	• East Pharsalia formerly Podunk, Skunks Misery • Waldron Corners on Pitcher town line
Pitcher 1794–95 Settled 1827 Formed from towns of German and Lincklaen 1833 Annexed land from Town of Lincklaen	Brackle Chandler(s) Corners Hydes Mills Hydeville North Pitcher Pitcher	Pitcher Springs South Pitcher Ufford Corners Union Valley Waldron Corners West Pitcher	• Brackle in Town of German before 1827 • Waldron Corners on Pharsalia town line

Towns (and Cities)	Villages and other Settlements		Notes
Plymouth 1794 Settled by some French families 1806 Formed from Town of Norwich	Ireland Mills Kirk Perrytown Plymouth	Sherburne Four Corners South Plymouth Stuart Corners	• Hamlet of Plymouth formerly Franklinville, Frenchtown, and Frenchville • Sherburne Four Corners shared with towns of North Norwich, Sherburne, and Smyrna • South Plymouth formerly Frinkville • Stuart Corners also Stewarts Corners
Preston 1787 Settled on Fly-Meadow Creek 1806 Formed from Town of Norwich 1808 Ceded land to Town of Norwich 1816 Daughter town Macdonough formed 1820 Annexed land from Town of Norwich	Bogusville Nortons Corners Preston Preston Center Preston Corners		• Preston Corners also Masons Corners
Sangerfield * In Chenango County 1798–1804			* See Oneida County
Sherburne 1792 Settled 1795 Formed in Herkimer County from Town of Paris 1798 Transferred to new county of Chenango 1808 Daughter town Smyrna formed 1852 Annexed land from Town of New Berlin	Earlville (v) Harrisville Quarter Sherburne (v) Sherburne Four Corners		* Town of Paris in Oneida County 1798–present • Small part of Village of Earlville inc. 1887; shared with Town of Hamilton in Madison County • Village of Sherburne inc. 1830 • Sherburne Four Corners shared with towns of North Norwich, Plymouth, and Smyrna
Smithville 1797 Settlers from Ireland 1808 Formed from Town of Greene	Adams Corner Black Falls Buckley Hollow Corbin Corner Dibble Corner East Smithville Lakeview Lakeville	Smithville Center Smithville Corners Smithville Flats Teertville Three Taverns Tyner Wilcox Corner	• Smithville Flats formerly Big Flats • Tyner formerly Sod
Smyrna 1792 Settled 1808 Formed as Stafford from Town of Sherburne; name changed to Smyrna one month after formation	Beaver Meadow Bonney Flat Iron Ireland Mills Sherburne Four Corners	Smyrna (v) Smyrna Center Upperville West Smyrna Wilburs Station	• Sherburne Four Corners shared with towns of North Norwich, Plymouth, and Sherburne • Village of Smyrna inc. 1829
Stonington Name for Town of Pharsalia 1806–1808			
Sullivan * In Chenango County 1803–1806			* See Madison County

NEW YORK STATE CENSUS RECORDS

See also chapter 3, Census Records

County originals at Chenango County Clerk's Office: 1855, 1865, 1875, 1905, 1915, 1925 (1825, 1835, 1845, and 1892 are lost)

State originals at the NYSA: 1915, 1925

Microfilm at the FHL, NYPL, and NYSL; many years are online at *FamilySearch.org* and *Ancestry.com*.

NATIONAL/STATEWIDE REPOSITORIES & RESOURCES

See chapter 16

COUNTYWIDE REPOSITORIES & RESOURCES

Chenango County Clerk

5 Court Street • Norwich, NY 13815-1671 • (607) 337-1450
Email: countyclerk@co.chenango.ny.us • *www.co.chenango.ny.us/clerk*

Holdings include land records, court records, naturalization records 1857–1991, and New York state censuses for Chenango County 1855, 1865, 1875, and 1905.

Chenango County – City, Town, and Village Clerks

Birth, marriage, and death records are maintained by the clerk of the municipality in which the event occurred; see Introduction to County Guides for details of other records which may also be held by municipal clerks. For contact information on Chenango County clerks see *www.co.chenango.ny.us/clerk/documents/co.pdf* for details.

Chenango County Surrogate's Court

5 Court Street #2 • Norwich, NY 13815-1695 • (607) 337-1827

Holds probate records from 1798 to the present. See also chapter 6, Probate Records.

Chenango County Public Libraries

Chenango is part of the Four County Library System; see *www.4cls.org* to access each library. Many hold genealogy and local history collections such as local newspapers. See listing below for Guernsey Memorial Library.

Chenango County Historical Society, Museum, and Research Center

43/45 Rexford Street • Norwich, NY 13815-1121 • (607) 334-9227
Email: countyhistorian@co.chenango.ny.us • *www.chenangohistorical.org*

The James S. Flanagan History Research Center is operated by the Chenango County Historical Society and the Chenango County Historian's Office; collections include vital statistics, histories, genealogies, DAR records, will directories (index to deceased and some name abstracts), and family files. The Chenango Historical Museum also issues a newsletter.

Chenango County Historian

43 Rexford Street • Norwich, NY 13815-1221
(607) 337-1845 • Email: countyhistorian@co.chenango.ny.us
www.co.chenango.ny.us/historian

Located in the Research Center (see above). Holdings include cemetery records, family files, local histories, photographs, Revolutionary and Civil War collections, and computerized will indexes.

Chenango County– All Municipal Historians

While not authorized to answer genealogical inquiries, city, town, and village historians can provide valuable historical information and research advice; some maintain collections and webpages which may include transcribed records, local histories, and other genealogical material. For contact information, see *freepages.genealogy.rootsweb.ancestry.com/~rsaft/ccgr.html* or the website of the Association of Public Historians of New York State at *www.aphnys.org*.

REGIONAL REPOSITORIES & RESOURCES

Central New York Genealogical Society

See listing in Onondaga County Guide

Lorenzo State Historic Site

See listing in Madison County Guide

LOCAL REPOSITORIES & RESOURCES

Alphabetized by location

Afton Historical Society

Society: 335 State Highway 41 • *Museum:* 116 Main Street
Afton, NY 13730 • (607) 639-2720 • Email: info@sidneyonline.com
www.aftonmuseum.org

Collections include genealogical and historical material relating to the Iroquois Confederacy, early settlers (including Vermont Sufferers and Revolutionary War Veterans), religious movements of the "burned-over district" of Western New York, and the towns of Afton, Bainbridge (formerly Jericho), and Coventry. As the founding period of the Mormon Church occurred in the area, there are unique holdings related to Joseph Smith and the Mormon Church.

Bainbridge Historical Society and Museum

PO Box 146 • Bainbridge, NY 13733
(607) 967-8546 • (607) 967-7159 (town historian)

Holdings include family file folders, scrapbooks, historical photographs of the town, American Indian artifacts from the area, and histories of several Bainbridge churches.

Coventry Town Museum Association

3075 State Highway 206 • 115 County Rt. 27
Coventryville, NY 13733-3117 • (607) 639-4073
Email: crimsoncloaks@aol.com

Holdings include books, deeds, diaries, maps, photographs, memorabilia, scrapbooks, and artifacts from pre-settlement to the present. Collections trace the history of Coventry, Coventryville and surrounding towns including Afton, Bainbridge, Coventry, Harpursville, and Oxford. Onsite research services provided.

Town of Greene Historical Society and Museum

Moore Memorial Library, 2nd Floor • 59 Genesee Street
PO Box 412 • Greene, NY 13778 • (607) 656-4981 or 656-8314
Email access through website
www.greenenylibrary.org/index.php/museum

Holdings include census and vital record materials, newspapers (*Chenango American*), and artifacts.

Guilford Historical Society and Klee House

PO Box 201 • Guilford, NY 13780 • (607) 895-6532
www.guilfordhistoricalsociety.blogspot.com

Society maintains a collection of documents, photos, indexed scrapbooks, and obituaries. They are currently working to document and transcribe cemetery headstones in Guilford. The Society works with the town historian on research projects.

Mount Upton Historical Society and Unadilla Valley Historical Museum
Route 8 • PO Box 135 • Mount Upton, NY 13809 • (607) 764-8375

Holdings of the society include scrapbooks, yearbooks, photographs, and artifacts.

Guernsey Memorial Library:
The Otis A. Thompson Local History Room
3 Court Street • Norwich, NY 13815 • (607) 334-4034
www.4cls.org/webpages/members/norwich/LHframes.html

Genealogies, family files, cemetery records, census materials, city directories, vital records, an indexed obituary collection, and the Glen Buell Newspaper Collection, comprised of the *Saturday Utica Globe*, 1909–1916.

Oxford Historical Society and Historical Museum
One Depot Street • PO Box 57 • Oxford, NY 13830
(607) 821-1223 • Email: Museum@OxfordNY.com
www.oxfordny.com/community/groups/historical.php

Collections include books, photographs, and artifacts.

SELECTED PRINT & ONLINE RESOURCES

Below is a selection of resources relevant for research in this county. The list is representative, not exhaustive. Additional titles—particularly of abstracts, indexes, transcriptions, and local histories—are available; consult the introduction to Part Two for further information. For guidance on how to identify and locate community directories and local newspapers, see chapter 11, City Directories, and chapter 12, Newspapers, in Part One of this book.

Abstracts, Indexes & Transcriptions

Barber, Gertrude Audrey. "Index of Wills of Chenango County, New York, from 1797–1875." Typescript, 1935. [*Ancestry.com*]

Chenango County Federal Census Transcript, 1810. Syracuse: Central New York Genealogical Society, 1979.

Chenango County, NYG&B Church Surveys Collection. NYG&B, New York. [NYG&B eLibrary]

County of Chenango Abstracts. Syracuse: Central New York Genealogical Society, 2000. Abstracts for a range of genealogical records originally published in the quarterly *Tree Talks*. A name index is on the CNYGS website.

Daughters of the American Revolution, comps. *New York DAR Genealogical Records Committee Report*. Since 1913 DAR volunteers have transcribed many thousands of unpublished cemetery, church, and town records throughout New York. The reports are at the DAR Library; copies are at the NYSL and the NYPL. The DAR has a searchable name index to all the GRC reports at *http://services.dar.org/Public/DAR_Research/search/?Tab_ID=6*. See Jean Worden's index below for a listing by county of the New York record sets that were transcribed by the DAR before 1998.

Genealogical Research Notes and Lists of Baptisms from Three Congregations: The Reformed Dutch Church of Cortlandtown, Westchester County, NY; the Dutch Reformed Church of Conowago, Adams County, PA; and the Second Calvinistic Congregational Society of Sherburne, Chenango County, NY, 1741–1830. Manuscript. N.d. NYPL, New York.

Kelly, Arthur C. M. *Index to Tree Talks County Packet: Chenango County*. Rhinebeck, NY: Kinship, 2002.

Meola, Mrs. J. B. "Chenango County, New York: Church and Cemetery Records." Typescript, 1934. NYPL, New York.

Smith, Gertrude M. "Marriages Performed by David Cutler, Pastor of the Baptist Church of New Berlin, Chenango County, NY, 1830–1873." Typescript, 1954. New York State Historical Association, New York.

Smith, Mrs. Arthur W. "Records of the Congregational Church Formed 1805 in German and Lincklaen, Chenango County, New York." Typescript, n.d. NYPL, New York.

Smith, Mrs. Edwin P. and Mrs. Ryland H. Hewitt. *Vital Records of Chenango County, New York, Before 1880: Marriages, Births, Deaths from Original Sources*. Norwich, NY: Printed by the Chenango County Board of Supervisors, 1972.

Thomas, Ethel B. "Marriage Records for Years 1847–9, Found in City Hall, Norwich, NY." Typescript, 1953. New York State Historical Association, Cooperstown, NY.

Worden, Jean D. "Book 1, Subject Index." In *Revised Master Index to the New York State Daughters of the American Revolution Genealogical Records Volumes*. Zephyrhills, FL: J. D. Worden, 1998. The Subject Index includes a listing by county of the cemeteries, churches, towns, and other sources of records transcribed by the DAR.

Other Resources

Bagg, Leona. *History of South New Berlin, Holmesville, and Great Brook*. Bainbridge, NY: RSG Publishing, 1976.

Bickford, Catherine E. *History of the Town of Coventry, 1905–1975*. 1975. Written by the town historian.

Biographical Publishing Company. *Biographical Review: Biographical Sketches of Leading Citizens of Chenango County, NY*. Buffalo, 1898.

Chenango County Planning Board. *Inventory of Historic Resources in Chenango County*. Norwich, NY: The Board, 1975.

Child, Hamilton. *Gazetteer and Business Directory of Chenango County, NY, for 1869–70*. Syracuse, 1868.

Clark, Hiram C. *History of Chenango County, Containing the Divisions of the County and Sketches of the Towns; Indian Tribes and Titles*. Norwich, NY, 1850.

Cochrane, Mildred E. *From Raft to Railroad: A History of the Town of Greene, Chenango County, New York, 1792–1867*. Ithaca, NY: Cayuga Press, 1967.

Danforth, Edward. *Stones from the Walls of Jericho: The Official Bicentennial History of Bainbridge, New York*. Deposit, NY: Valley Offset, Inc., 1986.

Doing, Maude P. B. *History of the Town of Plymouth, NY*. Norwich, NY: n.p., 1954.

Fay, Loren V. *Chenango County, New York, Genealogical Research Secrets*. Albany: L. V. Fay, 1981.

Galpin, Henry J. *Annals of Oxford, New York: With Illustrations and Biographical Sketches of Some of Its Prominent Men and Early Pioneers*. Oxford, NY: H. J. Galpin, 1906.

Galpin, William F. *Central New York, an Inland Empire, Comprising Oneida, Madison, Onondaga, Cayuga, Tompkins, Cortland, Chenango Counties and Their People*. New York: Lewis Historical Publishing Co., 1914. Contains biographies. Index available from Berkshire Family History Association.

Gomph, John P. *Sherburne Illustrated: A History of the Village of Sherburne, NY* . . . . Utica, NY, 1896.

Gridley, Lou Ella E. *Folklore of Chenango County*. Chenango County: Chenango County Historical Society, 1969.

Hagen, Mabel B. *Pages from the Past: Story of Pitcher Springs*. Norwich, NY: Chenango Union Printing, 1996. First published 1956 by author.

Hanford, George. *Directory of Chenango County, NY*. Elmira, NY: Advertiser Association, 1902.

Hatch, Joel. *Reminiscences, Anecdotes, and Statistics of the Early Settlers and the 'Olden Time' in the Town of Sherburne, Chenango County, N.Y.* Utica, NY: Curtiss & White, 1862.

Hayes, Carlton J. H. *Story of Afton: A New York Town on the Susquehanna*. Deposit, NY: Valley Offset, Inc., 1976.

Hyde, John. *Historical Sketches of Old New Berlin*. New Berlin, NY: Unadilla Valley Historical Society, 1907.

Judd, Oliver P. *History of the Town of Coventry from the First White Man's Log Hut: With All the Most Important Events, Down to the Present Time*. Oxford, NY: The Oxford Review, 1912.

Lynch, Carrie F. *History of Chenango County: And Surroundings of Pioneer Life, 1778–1929*. Chenango County, NY: C. F. Lynch, 1929.

Munson, George A. *Early Years in Smyrna and Our First Old Home Week*. Bainbridge, NY: RSG Publishing, 1905.

New York Historical Resources Center. *Guide to Historical Resources in Chenango County, New York, Repositories*. Ithaca, NY: Cornell University, 1982. [books.FamilySearch.org]

Next Stop Galena! A Historical Perspective of North Norwich, New York, 1849–1999. North Norwich, NY: Sesquicentennial Book/Planning Committee, 1999.

Nichols, Beach. *Atlas of Chenango County, New York*. Philadelphia, 1875. [NYPL Digital Gallery]

Oxford Then & Now: A Pictorial History of Oxford, Chenango County, NY. Oxford, NY: Sunshine Press, 1976.

Palen, Ida T. *North Guilford Pioneers*. New York: The Hobson Book Press, 1946.

Phillips, Albert, and Goldie Phillips. *Annals of Norwich*. 2 vols. Norwich, NY: Chenango County Historical Society, 1964–1965.

Smith, James H. *History of Chenango and Madison Counties, New York, with Illustrations and Biographical Sketches of Some of Its Prominent Men and Pioneers*. Syracuse, 1880. Includes American Indian history, early civil divisions, genealogy, newspapers, early courts, criminal calendar, Revolutionary War, town histories, schools, and more. Separate index by John Tyne (1974).

Stafford, Charlotte, comp. *A Chronology of Oxford Happenings, 1788–1950*. Oxford, NY: sponsored by the Town and Village of Oxford, 2002.

Tiffany, Nelson B., Dale Storms, and Patricia E. Evans. *History of Woods Corners, Town Of Norwich, Chenango County, NY*. Norwich, NY: Chenango County Historical Society, 2010.

———. *Revolutionary War Veterans, Chenango County, New York*. Bowie, MD: Heritage Books, 1998. Includes detailed biographical information on each veteran.

Additional Online Resources

Ancestry.com

There are vast numbers of records on *Ancestry.com* that pertain to people who have lived in New York State. See chapter 16 for a description of *Ancestry.com*'s resources and its partnership with the New York State Archives. A search of the online card catalog by county may reveal lesser known resources that pertain to a locality, such as town records, abstracts, transcriptions, city directories, and local histories.

Chenango County Historic Districts

www.chenangocounty.org/historic-districts.php

County website has lists of historic districts, historic sites, and historic cemeteries in Chenango. It also offers historical information on the county and links to useful repositories and resources.

FamilySearch.org

FamilySearch has extensive collections of New York records, including religious records, which are searchable by name and location, but not by county. The following collections include record images (browsable, but not searchable) that are organized by county:

- "New York, Land Records, 1630–1975." Includes land and property records. *familysearch.org/search/collection/2078654*
- "New York, Probate Records, 1629–1971." Includes wills, letters of administration, and guardianship papers. *familysearch.org/search/collection/1920234*

For both collections, choose the browse option and then select Chenango to view the available records sets.

A detailed description of *FamilySearch.org* resources is found in chapter 16.

NYGenWeb Project: Chenango County

www.rootsweb.ancestry.com/~nychenan

Part of the national, USGenWeb volunteer initiative, the website provides information and resources for county research.

Clinton County

Formed March 7, 1788

Parent County   Washington
Daughter Counties   Essex 1799 • St. Lawrence County 1802 • Franklin 1808
County Seat   City of Plattsburgh

Major Land Transactions
See chapter 7, Land Records
Beekmantown Patent 1769
Canadian and Nova Scotia Refugee Tract 1784
Old Military Tract 1786

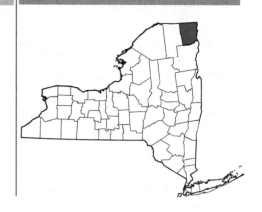

Town Boundary Map
★ - County seat

Cities and Towns	Villages, Settlements, Neighborhoods		Notes
Altona 1800 Settled 1857 Formed from Town of Chazy	Alder Bend Altona Crowley Corners Dannemora Crossing Ellenburg Depot Forest	Ingraham Irona Jericho Jersalem Purdy(s) Mill Robinson	• Ingraham on Beekmantown and Chazy town lines
Au Sable * 1786 Settled 1839 Formed from Town of Peru	Arnold Hill Au Sable Chasm Birmingham Falls Clintonville Ferrona Hallock Hill Harkness	Keese Corners Keeseville (v) New Sweden Rogers The Union Thomasville Verona	* Au Sable also Ausable • Au Sable (Ausable) Chasm shared with Town of Chesterfield, Essex County • Birmingham Falls was shared with Town of Chesterfield, Essex County • Village of Keeseville inc. 1878; was Anderson Falls until 1812; shared with the Town of Chesterfield, Essex County
Beekmantown 1783 Settled at Point Au Roche 1820 Formed from Town of Plattsburgh 1854 Daughter town Dannemora formed	Beartown (Corners) Beekmantown East Beekmantown Gilroy Corners Ingraham	Lawless Corners Point Au Roche Rand Hill West Beekmantown Whig Hollow	• Ingraham on Altona and Chazy town lines • Lawless Corners also Lawliss Corners; on Plattsburgh town line
Black Brook 1825 Settled at Au Sable Forks 1839 Formed from Town of Peru	Au Sable Forks Black Brook Clayburg Cold Brook Dean Chase Settlement Devins Corners Disco East Kilns Garlick Falls Goodrich Mills Hawkeye Middle Kilns	Palmer Hill Riverview Rome Silver Lake Stevens Landing Swastika Thomasville Union Falls Upper Kilns West Kilns Williamsburg	• Au Sable (Ausable) Forks shared with Town of Jay, Essex County
Champlain Settled after Revolution 1788 Formed as a town 1799 Daughter town Chateaugay formed 1804 Daughter towns Chazy and Mooers formed	Champlain (v) Coopersville Corbeau Fort Montgomery	Perry Mills Rouses Point (v) Scales Point Twin Bridges	• Village of Champlain inc. 1873 • Village of Rouses Point inc. 1877
Chateaugay * In Clinton County 1799–1808			* See Franklin County
Chazy 1763 Settled 1804 Formed from Town of Champlain 1857 Daughter town Altona formed	Chazy Chazy Junction Chazy Landing Chazy Lodge Ingraham	Northern Landing Lodge Sciota (Village) Suckertown West Chazy	• Chazy Landing also Saxes Landing • Ingraham on Altona and Beekmantown town lines
Clinton Settled at Old Military Road 1845 Formed from Town of Ellenburg	Churubusco Clinton Mills Frontier	Gibson Corners Saranac Wrightsville	• Frontier also The Frontier

Cities and Towns	Villages, Settlements, Neighborhoods		Notes
Constable * In Clinton County 1807–1808			* See Franklin County
Crown Point * In Clinton County 1788–1799			* See Essex County
Dannemora **1838** Settled **1854** Formed from Town of Beekmantown	Bradley Point Kiln Chazy Lake Chazy Lake House Chazy Lake Station Dannemora (v) Ducharm Ledger Corners	Lyon Mountain Ralph Rogersfield Standish Station The Junction Thomas Upper Chateaugay Lake	• Village of Dannemora inc. 1901; shared with Town of Saranac; site of Clinton Prison (1845), still exists as Clinton Correctional Facility
Elizabethtown * In Clinton County 1798–1799			* See Essex County
Ellenburg **1800** Settlers from Vermont **1830** Formed from Town of Mooers **1845** Daughter town Clinton formed	Brandy Brook Dannemora Crossing Ellenburg Ellenburg Center Ellenburg Corners Ellenburgh Depot	Gibson Corners Hammonds Corners Harrigan (Corners) Merrill Shelden Star	• Merrill also The Forge
Harrison * In Clinton County 1805–1808			* See Town of Malone in Franklin County
Jay * In Clinton County 1798–1799			* See Essex County
Lisbon * In Clinton County 1801–1802			* See St. Lawrence County
Mooers **1796** Settled **1804** Formed from Town of Champlain **1830** Daughter town Ellenburgh formed	Angellville Canaan Cannon Corners Centerville Green Valley Mooers	Mooers Forks Mooers Junction (v) Thorn Corners Twin Bridges Whitney Corners Wood(s) Falls	• Mooers Forks formerly Centerville • Mooers Junction and Mooers village incorporated 1899 as Village of Mooers Junction; village dissolved 3/31/1994
Peru **1772** Settled by Scots **1792** Formed from towns of Willsboro (Essex County) and Plattsburgh **1822** Ceded land to Town of Jay, Essex County **1839** Daughter towns Au Sable and Black Brook formed	Au Sable Baggs Clark Corners Coffey Corners Cromie Corners Goshen Lapham Lapham(s) Mills	Peasleeville Peru Peru Landing Port Jackson South Junction The Union Valcour Valcour Island(s)	• Lapham(s) Mills formerly Bartonville, also Travis Forge • Valcour formerly Port Valcour
Plattsburgh (city) * **1815** Incorporated as a village in Town of Plattsburgh **1902** Incorporated as city			* County seat at Plattsburgh (hamlet, village, and city) from 1788 when Clinton County was formed

Cities and Towns	Villages, Settlements, Neighborhoods		Notes
Plattsburgh (town) 1785 Settled 1785 Formed as a town in Washington County 1788 Transferred to new county of Clinton 1792 Daughter town Peru formed 1820 Daughter town Beekmantown formed 1824 Daughter town Saranac formed 1848 Daughter town Schuyler Falls formed 1902 Village of Plattsburgh established as City of Plattsburgh	Bluff Point Cadyville Champlain Park Cliff Haven Cumberland Head Elsinor(e) Freydenburgh Falls Halseys Corners Lawless Corners Military Turnpike Morrisonville	North Plattsburgh Plattsburgh (v) Pleasant Ridge Corners Rocky Point Salmon River Schuyler Falls South Junction South Plattsburgh Treadwells Mills Wallace Hills West Plattsburgh	• Cadyville in Town of Schuyler Falls after 1848 • Lawless Corners also Lawliss Corners; on Beekmantown town line • Morrisonville on Schuyler Falls town line • Village of Plattsburgh inc. 1815, became City of Plattsburgh 1902; county seat 1788–present • Schuyler Falls in Town of Schuyler Falls after 1848
Saranac 1802 Settled 1824 Formed from Town of Plattsburgh	Clayburg Dannemora (v) Elsinore Hard Scrabble High Bank Irondale Lobdell Moffitsville	Pickett(s) Corners Redford Riverview Russia Russia Station Saranac Saranac Hollow Standish	• Village of Dannemora inc. 1901; shared with Town of Dannemora
Schuyler Falls 1797 Settled 1848 Formed from Town of Plattsburgh	Banker Corners Cadyville Fanlon Corners Irish Settlement Morrisonville	Norrisville Rock Corners Schuyler Falls Woods Mill(s)	• Cadyville in Town of Plattsburgh before 1848 • Morrisonville on Plattsburgh town line • Schuyler Falls in Town of Plattsburgh before 1848
Willsboro * In Clinton County 1788–1799			* See Essex County

NEW YORK STATE CENSUS RECORDS
See also chapter 3, Census Records

County originals at Clinton County Clerk's Office: 1892, 1905, 1915, 1925 (1825, 1835, 1845, 1855*, 1865, and 1875 are lost)

State originals at the NYSA: 1915, 1925

Microfilm at the FHL, NYPL, and NYSL; many years are online at *FamilySearch.org* and *Ancestry.com*.

* Most of the 1855 New York state census for Clinton County is lost; the information for the Town of Clinton was published by Valley Quarterlies in *The Capital*, vol. 4, no. 2, 1989.

An earlier draft had Kinship as the publisher, but Valley Quarterlies is a trademark of Kinship.

NATIONAL/STATEWIDE REPOSITORIES & RESOURCES
See chapter 16

COUNTYWIDE REPOSITORIES & RESOURCES

Clinton County Clerk
Clinton County Government Center, First Floor • 137 Margaret Street
Plattsburgh, NY 12901 • (518) 565-4700
www.clintoncountygov.com/departments/cc/CountyClerkHome.html

Court records; land records 1788–present; New York state censuses for Clinton County 1892 and 1905; marriage records 1908–1936; and naturalization records 1840–1900.

Clinton County – City, Town, and Village Clerks
Birth, marriage, and death records are maintained by the clerk of the municipality in which the event occurred; see Introduction to County Guides for details of other records which may also be held by municipal clerks. For contact information on Clinton County clerks, see *www.clintoncountygov.com*.

Clinton County Surrogate's Court
137 Margaret Street • Plattsburgh, NY 12901 • (518) 565-4630

Probate records 1790 to the present. See also chapter 6, Probate Records.

Clinton County Public Libraries
Clinton is part of the Clinton-Essex-Franklin Library System; see *www.cefls.org* to access each library. Many hold genealogy and local history collections. Also see listing below for Plattsburgh Public Library.

Clinton County Historian
Clinton County Government Center, Suite 105
137 Margaret Street • Plattsburgh, NY 12901
(518) 565-4749 • Email: historian@co.clinton.ny.us
www.clintoncountygov.com/departments/historian/historianhomepage.html

Holdings include many local genealogies and family files. The historian's website contains a list of helpful links for those pursuing genealogical and historical research in Clinton County, a list of town historians (see below), and a list of museums, galleries, and libraries.

Clinton County – All Municipal Historians
While not authorized to answer genealogical inquiries, city, town, and village historians can provide valuable historical information and research advice; some maintain collections and webpages which may include transcribed records, local histories, and other genealogical material. See contact information at *www.nnyacgs.com/bisuals.html*, *www.clintoncountygov.com/departments/historian/HistorianPicturePage.*

html or at the website of the Association of Public Historians of New York State at *www.aphnys.org*.

Clinton County Historical Association and Museum
98 Ohio Avenue • Plattsburgh, NY 12903 • (518) 561-0340
www.clintoncountyhistorical.org

The museum's holdings range from the 1600s to the present, and include maps and fine art. The website includes collection highlights, a gallery of glass negative portraits, a list of historic sites, a list of local historians, listings of glass negative portraits, and online publications. Publishes *North Country Notes*, quarterly, 1960–present, and the *Antiquarian*, annually, 1984–present.

Northern New York American-Canadian Genealogical Society/Clinton County Genealogical Society
Headquarters: Village of Dannemora Offices • 44 Emmons Street
Dannemora, NY • (518) 492-4142
Library: Keeseville Civic Center, 2nd Floor • 17 Vine Street
Keeseville, NY • (518) 561-5728 • *www.nnyacgs.com*

Library holdings include family histories, local histories, vital records, census microfilms, church records, genealogical discs, and other records ranging from the early-1600s to the present, and encompassing Clinton, Essex, and Franklin counties, nearby counties in Vermont, and sections of Quebec and Ontario. Its collection of French-Canadian genealogy is particularly strong. Website includes contact information for local historians, a digitized photograph collection, family trees, and journal articles.

REGIONAL REPOSITORIES & RESOURCES

Adirondack Genealogical-Historical Society
See listing in Franklin County Guide

Adirondack Museum Library
See listing in Hamilton County Guide

Saranac Lake Free Library: The William Chapman White Memorial Room: Adirondack Research Center
See listing in Franklin County Guide

SUNY Plattsburgh: Special Collections
101 Broad Street • Plattsburgh, NY 12901 • (518) 564-5206
www.plattsburgh.edu/library/specialcollections

Holds archival materials focused on the north country of New York State, including Clinton, Essex, and Franklin Counties, and Adirondack and Champlain Valley regions. Its website features guides to the College Archives, Manuscript Collections, the Rockwell Kent Collection, and the Clinton County Cemetery Index. A full description of holdings is available on the website.

LOCAL REPOSITORIES & RESOURCES
Alphabetized by location

Champlain Memorial Library
148 Elm Street • PO Box 279 • Champlain, NY 12919 • (518) 298-8620 • Email: champlib@primelink1.net
Holdings include cemetery records and local histories.

Alice T. Miner Museum: Colonial Collection
9618 Route 9 (Main Street) • PO Box 628 • Chazy, NY 12921
(518) 846-7336 • Email: director@minermuseum.org
www.minermuseum.org

A "Colonial Revival museum" that houses the collection of Alice T. Miner. Highlights from the collection are viewable on the museum's website. Archives include books, documents, letters, and photographs; a selection is viewable online.

Anderson Falls Heritage Society
1790 Route 22 Suite 3/4 • Keeseville, NY 12944 • (518) 834-7342

Holdings include books, maps, memorabilia, maps, and artifacts.

Plattsburgh Public Library
19 Oak Street • Plattsburgh, NY 12901-2810
(518) 563-0921 • www.plattsburghlib.org

Holdings include family files, scrapbooks, maps, cemetery records, and other printed materials relating to local history.

SELECTED PRINT & ONLINE RESOURCES

Below is a selection of resources relevant for research in this county. The list is representative, not exhaustive. Additional titles—particularly of abstracts, indexes, transcriptions, and local histories—are available; consult the introduction to Part Two for further information. For guidance on how to identify and locate community directories and local newspapers, see chapter 11, City Directories, and chapter 12, Newspapers, in Part One of this book.

Abstracts, Indexes & Transcriptions

County of Clinton Abstracts. Syracuse: Central New York Genealogical Society, 2000. Abstracts for a range of genealogical records originally published in the quarterly Tree Talks. A name index is on the CNYGS website.

Daughters of the American Revolution, comps. New York DAR Genealogical Records Committee Report. Since 1913 DAR volunteers have transcribed many thousands of unpublished cemetery, church, and town records throughout New York. The reports are at the DAR Library; copies are at the NYSL and the NYPL. The DAR has a searchable name index to all the GRC reports at http://services.dar.org/Public/DAR_Research/search/?Tab_ID=6. See Jean Worden's index below for a listing by county of the New York record sets that were transcribed by the DAR before 1998.

Kelly, Arthur C. M. Index to Tree Talks County Packet: Clinton County. Rhinebeck, NY: Kinship, 2002.

Samuelsen, W. David. Clinton County, New York, Will Testators Index. Salt Lake City: Sampubco, 1995.

Worden, Jean D. "Book 1, Subject Index." In Revised Master Index to the New York State Daughters of the American Revolution Genealogical Records Volumes. Zephyrhills, FL: J. D. Worden, 1998. The Subject Index includes a listing by county of the cemeteries, churches, towns, and other sources of records transcribed by the DAR.

Other Resources

Allan, Helen W., et al. Clinton County: A Pictorial History. Norfolk, VA: The Donning Co., 1988.

Averill, Henry K. A New Geography and History of Clinton County, New York: Compiled from Original Manuscripts, Surveys, and Other Reliable Sources. Plattsburgh, NY, 1885.

Beers, F. W. Atlas of Clinton County, New York: From Actual Surveys by and under the Direction of F. W. Beers, Assisted by Geo. P. Sanford and Others. New York, 1869. [NYPL Digital Gallery]

Biographical Review Publishing Company. Biographical Review: This Volume Contains Biographical Sketches of Leading Citizens of Clinton and Essex Counties, New York. Boston, 1896. Index available from Berkshire Family History Association.

Child, Hamilton. Gazetteer and Directory of Franklin and Clinton Counties: With an Almanac for 1862–3, Embracing the Names of Business Men, County Officers, Distances, Interest Tables, Census Returns, and Much Other Valuable Statistical Information. Ogdensburg, NY, 1862.

Ciborski, James R. A Guide to the Clinton County, New York, Historical Archive. Plattsburgh, NY: Clinton County Historian's Office, 1993.

Everest, Allan S. Briefly Told: Plattsburgh, New York, 1784–1984. Burlington, VT: Clinton County Historical Association, 1984.

Fay, Loren V. Clinton County, New York, Genealogical Research Secrets. Albany: L. V. Fay, 1983.

Frost, Richard B. Plattsburgh, New York: A City's First Century. Virginia Beach, VA: The Donning Co., 2002.

Hurd, Duane H. History of Clinton and Franklin Counties, New York: With Illustrations and Biographical Sketches of Its Prominent Men and Pioneers. Plattsburgh, NY: Clinton County American Revolution Bicentennial Commission, 1978. First published 1880. Book includes Iroquois history and coverage of land grants.

Kellogg, David S. Recollections of Clinton County and the Battle of Plattsburgh, 1800–1840: Memoirs of Early Residents from the Notebooks of Dr. D. S. Kellogg. Plattsburgh, NY: Clinton County Historical Association, 1964.

New York Historical Resources Center. Guide to Historical Resources in Clinton County, New York, Repositories. Ithaca: Cornell University, 1987. [books.FamilySearch.org]

Northern New York Library Network. Directory of Archival and Historical Document Collections. 2011–2013 edition; published digitally at http://nny.nnyln.org/archives/ArchivalDirectory.pdf. Online indexes at http://nny.nnyln.org/archives/page01.html. Describes collections held by organizations in Clinton, Essex, Franklin, Jefferson, Lewis, Oswego, and St. Lawrence counties.

Pratt, Anastasia L. Clinton County. Charleston, SC: Arcadia Publishing, 2010.

Sullivan, Nell J. B., and David K. Martin. A History of the Town of Chazy, Clinton County, New York. Burlington, VT: George Little Press, 1970. Reprint, 1994.

Additional Online Resources
Ancestry.com

There are vast numbers of records on Ancestry.com that pertain to people who have lived in New York State. See chapter 16 for a description of Ancestry.com's resources and its partnership with the New York State Archives. A search of the online card catalog by county will reveal lesser known resources that pertain to a locality, such as town records, abstracts, transcriptions, city directories, and local histories. In addition, the Drouin Collection: Early U.S. French Catholic Church Records 1695–1954 contains some records pertaining to Clinton, Franklin, St. Lawrence, and Essex counties.

Bigelow Society
www.bigelowsociety.com/slic/dann1.htm

The website provides information and images about the history of Dannemora and Clinton Prison and links to additional online resources.

Clinton County Naturalization Records, 1865–1906
www.italiangen.org
> Volunteers of the Italian Genealogical Group have created a searchable database of these records, which is accessible for free on their website.

FamilySearch.org
> FamilySearch has extensive collections of New York records, including religious records, which are searchable by name and location, but not by county. The following collections include record images (browsable, but not searchable) that are organized by county:
>
> - "New York, Land Records, 1630–1975." Includes land and property records. *familysearch.org/search/collection/2078654*
> - "New York, Probate Records, 1629–1971." Includes wills, letters of administration, and guardianship papers. *familysearch.org/search/collection/1920234*
>
> For both collections, choose the browse option and then select Clinton to view the available records sets.
>
> A detailed description of *FamilySearch.org* resources is found in chapter 16.

New York Heritage Digital Collections: New York State Newspaper Project
www.nyheritage.org/newspapers
> The website provides links to digital newspapers collections in 26 counties (currently) made accessible through New York Heritage, New York State Historic Newspapers, HRVH Historical Newspapers, and other providers.

NYGenWeb Project: Clinton County
www.rootsweb.ancestry.com/~nyclinto
> Part of the national, USGenWeb volunteer initiative, the website provides information and resources for county research.

Columbia County

Formed April 4, 1786

Parent County   Albany
Daughter Counties   None
County Seat   City of Hudson

Major Land Transactions
See table in chapter 7, Land Records
Rensselaerswijck 1629
Livingston Manor 1686

Town Boundary Map
★ - County seat

Towns (and Cities)	Villages and other Settlements		Notes
Ancram 1740s Settled by Scots 1803 Formed as Gallatin from Town of Livingston 1814 Name changed to Ancram 1830 Daughter town Gallatin formed	Ancram Ancram Center Ancramdale Ancram Leadmines Barton Corners Boston Corner(s) Boswell Corners	Chestnut Ridge Halstead Hot Ground Tanners Weed Mine(s) Whitehouse Crossing	• Ancram Center formerly Black Rock and Scotchtown • Weed Mine(s) on Copake town line
Austerlitz 1745–50 Settlers from Connecticut and Massachusetts 1818 Formed from towns of Canaan, Chatham, and Hillsdale	Austerlitz Morehouse Center Morehouse Corners	Red Rock Spencertown State Line Station	• Hamlet of Austerlitz also Upper Green River • Red Rock also Pilfershire; on Canaan town line
Canaan 1756 Settled 1772 Formed as Kings District in Albany County 1786 Transferred to new county of Columbia 1788 Name changed to Canaan and recognized as a town by the State of New York 1795 Daughter town Chatham formed 1818 Daughter towns Austerlitz and New Lebanon formed	Canaan Canaan Center Canaan Shakers Canaan Shakers Station Canaan Station East Chatham Edwards Park Flatbrook Frisbee Street Queechy Queechy Lake Red Rock State Line		• Hamlet of Canaan also Canaan Four Corners • Queechy Lake formerly Whitings Pond • Red Rock also Pilfershire; on Austerlitz town line
Chatham 1725 Dutch settlers from Kinderhook 1795 Formed from towns of Canaan and Kinderhook 1818 Daughter towns Austerlitz and Ghent formed	Chatham (v) Chatham Center East Chatham Malden Bridge New Concord Niverville	North Chatham Old Chatham Rayville Riders Mills Rock City White Mills	• Village of Chatham inc. 1869; shared with Town of Ghent; formerly Chatham Four Corners and Groats Corners • Old Chatham formerly Federal Stores • Riders Mills also Moshers Mills
Claverack Settled in early 1700s 1772 Formed as a district in Albany County 1782 Daughter district Hillsdale formed 1785 Daughter city Hudson formed 1786 Transferred to new county of Columbia 1788 Recognized as a town by the State of New York 1818 Daughter town Ghent formed	Brick Tavern Buttermilk Falls Churchtown Claverack Harlemville Highland Mills Hoffmans Gate Hollowville	Humphreysville Martindale Mellenville Philmont (v) Red Mills South Bend Mills Upper Hollowville	• Claverack was county seat 1786–1805 • Hollowville formerly Smoky Hollow • Martindale formerly Martindale Depot • Village of Philmont inc. 1892; formerly Factory Hill
Clermont Settled by German Palatines in mid-1700s 1787 Formed from Livingston District (see Town of Livingston) 1858 Ceded land to Germantown	Clermont Nevis Pleasantvale Viewmonte		• Viewmonte on Germantown town line

Towns (and Cities)	Villages and other Settlements		Notes
Copake Settled in mid-1700s 1824 Formed from Town of Taghkanick	Black Grocery Copake Copake Falls Copake Iron Works	Copake Station Craryville Weed Mine(s) West Copake	• Hamlet of Copake formerly Copake Flats • Craryville formerly Baines Corner, Baines Station, and North Copake • Weed Mine(s) on Ancram town line • West Copake formerly Andersons Corners
Gallatin *			* Name for Town of Ancram 1803–1814
Gallatin Settled by Dutch and Germans in mid-1700s 1830 Formed from Town of Ancram	Elizaville Gallatinville Jacksons Corners Silvernails Snyderville	Spaulding Furnace Suydam Union Corners Weaver Hollow	• Elizaville also Ellerslie; on Livingston town line • Gallatinville also Gallatin • Jacksons Corners was shared with Town of Milan, Dutchess County • Union Corners formerly Harrisons Corners and Pleasant Vale; on Livingston town line
Germantown 1710 Settled as East Camp by German Palatines 1775 East Camp District (also known as German Camp) formed in Albany County * 1786 Transferred to new county of Columbia 1788 Recognized as Town of Germantown by the State of New York 1858 Annexed land from Town of Clermont	Annsberg Cheviot Germantown Germantown Station Haysburgh Hunterstown North Germantown Queensbury Sharps Landing Viewmonte		* East Camp District formed from Livingston Manor • Cheviot formerly East Camp and East Camp Landing • Viewmonte on Clermont town line
Ghent 1735 Dutch and German settlers 1818 Formed from towns of Chatham, Claverack, and Kinderhook 1833 Daughter town Stockport formed	Arnolds Mill Buckleys Corner Buckleyville Chatham (v) Ghent	Omi Pulvers Pulvers Station West Ghent	• Village of Chatham inc. 1869; shared with Town of Chatham; formerly Groats Corners • Hamlet of Ghent formerly Moffats Stores
Granger *			* Name for Town of Taghkanic 1803–1814
Greenport Settled in mid-1700s 1837 Formed from City of Hudson	Buckleyville Greendale Greenport Center		• Greendale formerly Catskill Station, Oak Hill, and Oak Hill Landing
Hillsdale Settlers from Massachusetts and Holland in mid-1700s 1782 Formed as a district from District of Claverack in Albany County 1786 Transferred to new county of Columbia 1788 Recognized as a town by the State of New York 1818 Daughter town Austerlitz formed	East Hillsdale Green River Harlemville Hillsdale Hillside Murray Corners North Hillsdale		• Hamlet of Hillsdale formerly Nobletown

Towns (and Cities)	Villages and other Settlements		Notes
Hudson (city) * Settled under Dutch government 1785 Incorporated as a city in Albany County from Claverack District * 1786 Transferred to new county of Columbia 1833 Daughter town Stockport formed 1837 Daughter town Greenport formed			* Hudson known as Claverack Landing when still a settlement in Claverack District * City of Hudson also Hudson District until 1788 * County seat 1805–present; 1786–1805 at Claverack
Kinderhook Settled under Dutch government 1772 Formed as a district in Albany County 1786 Transferred to new county of Columbia 1788 Recognized as a town by the State of New York 1795 Daughter town Chatham formed 1818 Daughter town Ghent formed 1823 Daughter town Stuyvesant formed	Columbiaville (v) Kinderhook (v) Niverville Valatie (v) Valatie Colony		• Village of Columbiaville inc. 1812 dissolved 1833; now in Town of Stockport, in Town of Stuyvesant 1823–1833; in Town of Kinderhook before 1823 • Village of Kinderhook inc. 1838 • Niverville formerly Kinderhook Station • Village of Valatie inc. 1856; formerly Millville
Kings District *			* Name for Town of Canaan 1772–1788
Livingston 1686 Livingston Manor granted to Robert Livingston; land in Dutchess County * 1717 Albany County annexed land from Dutchess County 1772 Livingston District formed from part of Livingston Manor 1786 Transferred to new county of Columbia 1787 Daughter town Clermont formed 1788 Recognized as a town by the State of New York 1803 Daughter towns Ancram and Taghkanic(k) formed	Bakers Mills Bells Pond Bingham Mills Blue Store Burden Elizaville Glenco Mills Linlithgo Linlithgo Mills	Linlithgo Station Livingston Livingston Station Manor Church Manorton Schooderhook Viewmonte Union Corners Walker(s) Mills	* Livingston Manor granted by colonial Governor of New York • Elizaville also Ellerslie; on Gallatin town line • Glenco Mills also Sober • Hamlet of Livingston also Johnstown • Union Corners formerly Harrisons Corners and Pleasant Vale; on Gallatin town line
New Lebanon 1760 Settlers from Connecticut and Massachusetts 1818 Formed from Town of Canaan	Adams Crossing Darrow Lebanon Springs New Britain	New Lebanon New Lebanon Center Shaker Village West Lebanon	• Darrow also Mount Lebanon • Lebanon Springs also Montepoale; formerly New Lebanon Springs • Hamlet of New Lebanon formerly Tildens • West Lebanon formerly Moffats Store
Stockport Settled by Dutch as part of Rensselaerswijck in mid-1600s 1833 Formed from City of Hudson and towns of Ghent and Stuyvesant	Chittenden(s) Falls Columbiaville (v) Gould Rossman Rossman Station	Smith Corners Stockport Stockport Center Station Stottville	• Village of Columbiaville inc. 1812 dissolved 1833; in Town of Stuyvesant 1823–1833; in Town of Kinderhook before 1823 • Stottville also Springville

Towns (and Cities)	Villages and other Settlements	Notes
Stuyvesant Settled by Dutch in late 1600s 1823 Formed from Town of Kinderhook 1833 Daughter town Stockport formed	Columbia Mills Columbiaville (v) Newton Hook Poelsburg Stuyvesant Stuyvesant Falls Sunnyside	• Village of Columbiaville inc. 1812 dissolved 1833; now in Town of Stockport, in Town of Stuyvesant 1823–1833; in Town of Kinderhook before 1823 • Newton Hook formerly Coxsackie, Coxsackie Station, and Nutten Hook • Hamlet of Stuyvesant also Stuyvesant Landing
Taghkanic Part of Livingston Manor settled by Dutch and Germans in late 1600s 1803 Formed as Granger from Town of Livingston 1814 Name changed to Taghkanic(k) 1824 Daughter town Copake formed	Churchtown East Taghkanic New Forge Pumpkin Hollow Taghkanic West Taghkanic	• West Taghkanic formerly Laphams and Millers Corners

NEW YORK STATE CENSUS RECORDS

See also chapter 3, Census Records

County originals at Columbia County Clerk's Office: 1845*, 1855, 1865, 1875, 1905, 1915, 1925 (1825, 1835, and 1892 are lost)

State originals at the NYSA: 1915, 1925

Microfilm at the FHL, NYPL, and NYSL; many years are online at *FamilySearch.org* and *Ancestry.com*.

*1845 census is lost except for the City of Hudson; NYSL has microfilm.

NATIONAL/STATEWIDE REPOSITORIES & RESOURCES

See chapter 16

COUNTYWIDE REPOSITORIES & RESOURCES

Columbia County Clerk

560 Warren Street • (518) 828-3339
www.columbiacountyny.com/depts/ctyclerk

Court records, dissolution of marriage records, estate tax releases, executions, naturalization records 1845–1940s, judgments, land records, liens, maps, mortgages, notary records, wills and probate inventories; New York state census for Columbia County 1845 (Hudson City only), 1855, 1865, 1875, 1905, 1915, 1925.

Columbia County – City, Town, and Village Clerks

Birth, marriage, and death records are maintained by the clerk of the municipality in which the event occurred; see Introduction to County Guides or details of other records which may also be held by municipal clerks. For contact information, see *www.columbiacountyny.com/town.html*.

Columbia County Surrogate's Court

Columbia County Courthouse • 401 Union Street
Hudson, NY 12534 • (518) 828-0414

Holds probate records from 1787 to the present. Also see chapter 6, Probate Records.

Columbia County Historical Society, Museum, and Library

5 Albany Avenue • PO Box 311 • Kinderhook, NY 12106
(518) 758-9265 • Email: cchs@cchsny.org • *www.cchsny.org*

Church and cemetery record transcriptions, census indexes, city and county directories, family genealogies, local history and genealogy books, family surname files, and photographs. Index to deaths, marriages, and births from county papers 1800–1930. Website contains index to cemetery books and catalog of manuscripts held in research library. Will answer genealogy research requests for a fee.

Columbia County Public Libraries

Columbia is part of the Mid-Hudson Library System; see *www.midhudson.org* to access each library. Many hold genealogy and local history collections. For example, Chatham Public Library has a local history collection that includes old photographs and cemetery records, and Roecliff Jansen Community Library holds cemetery records, church histories, and vital records. Also see listing below for Hudson Area Library.

Columbia County Historian

Livingston History Barn • 490 County Route 10
Germantown, NY 12526 • (518) 828-3442

Columbia County – All Municipal Historians

While not authorized to answer genealogical inquiries, city, town, and village historians can provide valuable historical information and research advice; some maintain collections and webpages which may include transcribed records, local histories, and other genealogical material. See contact information at *www.cchsny.org/coll_links_resources.html* or at the website of the Association of Public Historians of New York State at *www.aphnys.org*.

Clermont State Historic Site

One Clermont Avenue • Germantown, NY 12526 • (518) 537-4240
www.nysparks.com/historic-sites/16/details.aspx • (518) 537-6622
Email: info@friendsofclermont.org • *www.friendsofclermont.org*

Family papers and genealogical material documenting Chancellor Robert R. Livingston, the Livingston family, Robert Fulton, and Hudson River steamboat transportation.

Shaker Museum and Library

North Family, Mount Lebanon Shaker Historic Site
202 Shaker Road • New Lebanon, NY 12125
Library and Administrative Offices: 88 Shaker Museum Road
Old Chatham, NY 12136 • (518) 794-9100
Email: contact@shakerml.org • *www.shakermuseumandlibrary.org*

Manuscripts, documents, photographs, and printed materials. Official repository for records of discontinued Shaker communities.

Livingston Manor

Archival material related to Livingston Manor and the Livingston and related families are held in various locations including Columbia University, Butler Library: Livingston Family Papers, 1787–1893; N-YHS: several Livingston collections; University of Michigan, Clements Library: Wilson Family Papers, 1704–1884 (agents); Princeton University, Firestone Library: Edward Livingston Papers; Gilder Lehrman Institute: Livingston, Family Paper . . . Livingstone-Redmond Papers; NYPL: Gilbert Livingston Papers, 1711–1862; NYSL: Henry Livingston Collection, 1751–1833. Some may be found on microfilm.

REGIONAL REPOSITORIES & RESOURCES

Capital District Genealogical Society

See listing in Albany County Guide

Bard College Archives & Special Collections

See listing in Dutchess County Guide

LOCAL REPOSITORIES & RESOURCES

Alphabetized by location

Austerlitz Historical Society and Museum

1550 State Route 22 • PO Box 144 • Austerlitz, NY 12017
(518) 392-0062 • Email: oldausterlitz@fairpoint.net
www.oldausterlitz.org

Holdings include artifacts, photographs, and memorabilia. Quarterly newsletter.

Roeliff Jansen Historical Society and Museum

8 Miles Road • PO Box 172 • Copake Falls, NY 12517 • (518) 329-0652
Email: roeliffjansenhs@gmail.com • *www.roeliffjansenhs.org*

Documents history of Ancram, Copake, Gallatin, Hillsdale, and Taghkanic. Website contains historic photographs and postcards. Newsletter available.

Germantown History Department

51 Maple Avenue • Germantown, NY 12526 • (518) 537-3600
Email: germantownhistory@gmail.com • *www.germantownnyhistory.org*

Genealogies, local history, cemetery records, Civil War letters, maps and atlases, photographs, religious records, Germantown Central School yearbooks (some online), veterans records, and wills. Resources for Palatine family research.

Hudson Area Library: History Room

400 State Street • Hudson, NY 12534 • (518) 828-1792
www.hudsonarealibrary.org/history-room

Holdings document history of City of Hudson, Columbia County, and New York State and include sets of city directories, yearbooks, magazines, periodicals, and photographs. Books are searchable through online catalog.

Robert Jenkins House

National Society of the Daughters of the American Revolution, Hendrick Hudson Chapter • 113 Warren Street
Hudson, NY 12534 • (518) 828-9764

Library includes books, family histories, and local photographs, including contributions from Hudson City historian.

Livingston History Barn

County Route 19 • Livingston, NY 12541 • (518) 851-7637
Email: livingstonhistorybarn@hotmail.com
www.livingstontown.com/history.html

Genealogy, photographs, and information on local agriculture, economy, and military involvement.

Riders Mills Historical Association and Schoolhouse

142 Riders Mills Road • PO Box 1 • Old Chatham, NY 12136
(518) 794-7146 • Email: info@ridersmillsschoolhouse.org
www.ridersmillsschoolhouse.org

The schoolhouse was built in the late 1790s and closed in 1953; archives include school records and school photographs.

SELECTED PRINT & ONLINE RESOURCES

Below is a selection of resources relevant for research in this county. The list is representative, not exhaustive. Additional titles—particularly of abstracts, indexes, transcriptions, and local histories—are available; consult the introduction to Part Two for further information. For guidance on how to identify and locate community directories and local newspapers, see chapter 11, City Directories, and chapter 12, Newspapers, in Part One of this book.

Abstracts, Indexes & Transcriptions

Barber, Gertrude Audrey. "Abstracts of Wills of Columbia County, New York." Typescript, 1935–1947. 8 vols. Information taken from Surrogate's Court original records (1786–1851) at Hudson, NY. Indexed. Vols. 1–4 (1786–1828). [*books.FamilySearch.org*]

———. *Index to Abstracts of Wills of Columbia County, New York, Volumes 1-4, 1787-1827*. Pittsfield, MA: Berkshire Family History Association, 2001.

Barber, Gertrude Audrey, and Minnie Cohen. *Gravestone Inscriptions in Columbia County, NY*. 12 vols. New York, 1935–1941. Includes inscriptions from Reformed Dutch Church Cemetery at Claverack, NY; Reformed Church Cemetery of West Ghent, NY; and Hudson City Cemetery. [*Ancestry.com* (vols. 1–3 only)]

Berkenmeyer, Wilhelm C., and Justus Falckner. *Baptismal Register from the New York Lutheran Church Book*. Athens, NY: 1936. Includes baptismal, marriage and death records 1704–1737 from Ancram, Claverack, East Camp and Queensbury (now Germantown), Kinderhook, and Taghkanick.

Bussing, Carol W. "Records of the Reformed Church of Linlithgo in the Town of Livingston, Columbia County, New York." Typescript, 1949. DAR Library, Washington, D.C.

Columbia County, NYG&B Church Surveys Collection. NYG&B, New York. [NYG&B eLibrary]

County of Columbia Abstracts. Syracuse: Central New York Genealogical Society, 2000. Abstracts for a range of genealogical records originally published in the quarterly *Tree Talks*.

Daughters of the American Revolution, comps. *New York DAR Genealogical Records Committee Report*. Since 1913 DAR volunteers have transcribed many thousands of unpublished cemetery, church, and town records throughout New York. The reports are at the DAR Library; copies are at the NYSL and the NYPL. The DAR has a searchable name index to all the GRC reports at *http://services.dar.org/Public/DAR_Research/search/?Tab_ID=6*. See Jean Worden's index below for a listing by county of the New York record sets that were transcribed by the DAR before 1998.

Divine, Albert L. *Columbia County, NY, Gravestone Inscriptions: A Guide to Understanding Them, with a Comprehensive Family Name Index*. Rhinebeck, NY: Kinship, 1991.

Divine, Gerda E. *Old Tombstones and Unusual Cemeteries in Columbia County, New York: A Collection of Inscriptions from Old Tombstones, and Descriptions of Hard-to-Find and Unusual Cemeteries in Columbia County, New York State*. Hillsdale, NY: Graphos, 1973.

Herrick, Margaret E. *Marriage Notices, Dutchess and Columbia County, New York, 1859–1936: Notices Compiled from the Red Hook Journal, Red Hook Times-Journal, Red Hook Advertiser, and Rhinebeck Gazette*. Rhinebeck, NY: Kinship, 1991.

Hudson Monthly Meeting (Society of Friends). *Quaker Records of the Hudson Monthly Meeting, Columbia County, NY, 1793+*. Rhinebeck, NY: Kinship, 1999. Indexed by Arthur C. M. Kelly.

Kelly, Arthur C. M. *The Columbia*. Rhinebeck, NY: Kinship, quarterly 1986–1998, annually 1999–2001.

———. *Deaths, Marriages, and Miscellaneous from Hudson, New York, Newspapers: The Balance and Columbian Repository, 1802–1811 [and] the Rural Repository or Bower of Literature, 1824–1851*. 2 vols. Rhinebeck, NY: The Author, 1980.

———. *Index to Tree Talks County Packet: Columbia County*. Rhinebeck, NY: Kinship, 2002.

———. *Old Gravestones of Columbia County, New York*. Rhinebeck, NY: Kinship, 1996.

———. *Valley Quarterlies*. Directory of articles (vols. 1–15) and every-name index to the *Capital*, the *Columbia*, the *Mohawk*, and the *Saratoga*. Rhinebeck, NY: Kinship, CD-ROM, 2000.

Losee, John. *Death Notices, Dutchess and Columbia County, New York, from Red Hook Newspapers*. Rhinebeck, NY: Kinship, 1992.

Luckhurst, Charlotte T. "Columbia County, New York, Cemetery Records. Albany, NY, 1931." Typescript, 1931. NYPL, New York.

Phillips, Ralph D. "Inscriptions from the Graveyards in the Northern Part of Columbia County, New York, in the Vicinity of Chatham, New Britain, Malden Bridge, etc." Typescript, 1936. [Ancestry.com]

Thomas, Milton. Gravestone Inscriptions, Columbia County, New York. 5 vols. Troy, NY: M. H. Thomas, 1920.

Vosburgh, Royden Woodward, ed. "Records of the First Presbyterian Church of New Canaan." Typescript, 1920. NYPL, New York. [NYG&B eLibrary]

———, ed. "Records of St. John's Evangelical Lutheran Church at Manorton, in the Town of Livingston, Columbia County, NY." Vol. 2. Typescript. NYPL, New York. [NYG&B eLibrary]

———, ed. "Records of the Congregational Church and Society of New Canaan at Canaan Four Corners in the Town of Canaan, Columbia County, NY." Typescript. NYPL, New York. [NYG&B eLibrary]

———, ed. "Records of the Reformed Dutch Church of Kinderhook in Kinderhook, Columbia County, NY." Typescript. NYPL, New York. [NYG&B eLibrary] 2 vols.

Worden, Jean D. "Book 1, Subject Index." In Revised Master Index to the New York State Daughters of the American Revolution Genealogical Records Volumes. Zephyrhills, FL: J. D. Worden, 1998. The Subject Index includes a listing by county of the cemeteries, churches, towns, and other sources of records transcribed by the DAR.

Other Resources

Beers, D. G. Atlas of Columbia County, New York: From Actual Surveys and Official Records. Philadelphia, 1872. [NYPL Digital Gallery]

Biographical Review Publishing Company. Biographical Review: This Volume Contains Biographical Sketches of the Leading Citizens of Columbia County, New York. Boston, 1894.

Bradbury, Anna R. History of the City of Hudson, New York: With Biographical Sketches of Henry Hudson and Robert Fulton. Hudson, NY: Record Print and Publishing Co., 1908. Book includes biographical sketches of other prominent residents.

Capital District Genealogical Society Newsletter. Albany: Capital District Genealogical Society, 1982–present. [capitaldistrictgenealogicalsociety.org]

Child, Hamilton. Gazetteer and Business Directory of Columbia County, NY, for 1871–2. Syracuse, 1870.

Collier, Edward A. A History of Old Kinderhook from Aboriginal Days to the Present Time; Including the Story of the Early Settlers, Their Homesteads, Their Traditions, and Their Descendants; with an Account of Their Civic, Social, Political, Educational, and Religious Life. New York: G. P. Putnam's Sons, 1914.

Columbia County History & Heritage. Kinderhook, NY: Columbia County Historical Society, 2002.

Ellis, Franklin. History of Columbia County, New York: With Illustrations and Biographical Sketches of Some of Its Prominent Men and Pioneers. Philadelphia, 1878.

Foley, Janet W. Early Settlers of New York State: Their Ancestors and Descendants. 9 vols. Akron, NY: 1934–1942. Reprint, 2 vols. Baltimore, Genealogical Publishing Co., 1993.

Hacklett, W. V. The Hudson City and Columbia County Directory of the Year: With an Appendix Containing a Record of the Soldiers of the City and County, and a Variety of Useful Information. Albany: W. V. Hacklett, 1862–1901. Published annually, not all years survive.

Howell, Mary. Livingston: Then and Now. Ghent, NY: Published by the Town of Livingston, 1988. Book includes family history.

Hudson River Valley Review: A Journal of Regional Studies. Poughkeepsie, NY: Hudson River Valley Institute at Marist College, 2002–present. [hudsonrivervalley.org]

Hughes, Thomas P. American Ancestry: Giving the Name and Descent, in the Male Line, of Americans Whose Ancestors Settled in the United States Previous to the Declaration of Independence, A.D. 1776; Vol. 2 (local series): Columbia County, State of New York, 1887. Albany, 1887.

Hunt, Thomas. A Historical Sketch of the Town of Clermont. Hudson, NY: The Hudson Press, 1928. Reprint, Rhinebeck, NY: Palatine Transcripts, 1984.

Kelly, Arthur C. M. Settlers and Residents [of Germantown/ Clermont/ Livingston]. 3 vols. Rhinebeck, NY: Kinship, 1973-1989.

Lant, J. H. Columbia County Directory, 1878–9: Containing the Names and Post Office Address of the Inhabitants of the County, Together with a Business Directory of the City of Hudson, and Other Miscellaneous Information. Hudson, NY, 1878.

Lawrence & Co.'s Columbia County Directory for 1880–1 . . . . Newburgh, NY, 1880.

Maynard, Mary S. A Guide to Local History and Genealogical Resources in Columbia County, New York, at Public Libraries and Other Locations. Brookville, NY: M. S. Maynard, 1979.

New York Historical Resources Center. Guide to Historical Resources in Columbia County, New York, Repositories. Ithaca, NY: Cornell University, 1987. [books.FamilySearch.org]

Piwonka, Ruth. A Portrait of Livingston Manor, 1686–1850. Clermont, NY: Friends of Clermont, 1986.

Raymond, William. Biographical Sketches of the Distinguished Men of Columbia County: Including an Account of the Most Important Offices They Have Filled in the State and General Governments and in the Army and Navy. Albany, 1851.

Saums, Dorothy D. A History of the Roeliff Jansen Area: A Historical Review of Five Townships in Columbia County, New York. New York: Roeliff Jansen Historical Society, 1900. The Roeliff Jansen Area consists of Ancram, Copake, Gallatin, Hillsdale, and Taghkanic.

Silvernail, Peter. Southern Columbia County, New York, Families: A Genealogy. Rhinebeck, NY: Kinship, 1996.

Smith, Henry P. Columbia County at the End of the Century: A Historical Record of Its Formation and Settlement, Its Resources, Institutions, Its Industries, and Its People. 3 vols. Hudson, NY: Record Printing and Publishing Co., 1900.

Additional Online Resources

Ancestry.com

There are vast numbers of records on Ancestry.com that pertain to people who have lived in New York State. See chapter 16 for a description of Ancestry.com's resources and its partnership with the New York State Archives. A search of the online card catalog by county may reveal lesser known resources that pertain to a locality, such as town records, abstracts, transcriptions, city directories, and local histories.

Columbia County, NY History
www.berkshire.net/OnlineArchives/columbia

The website provides access to a selection of searchable archives, transcribed records, gazetteer excerpts, historical photographs, bibliographies, and other links.

FamilySearch.org

FamilySearch has extensive collections of New York records, including religious records, which are searchable by name and location, but not by county. The following collections include record images (browsable, but not searchable) that are organized by county:

- "New York, Land Records, 1630–1975." Includes land and property records. *familysearch.org/search/collection/2078654*

- "New York, Probate Records, 1629–1971." Includes wills, letters of administration, and guardianship papers. *familysearch.org/search/collection/1920234*

For both collections, choose the browse option and then select Columbia to view the available records sets.

A detailed description of *FamilySearch.org* resources is found in chapter 16.

Hudson River Valley Heritage (HRVH)
www.hrvh.org/cdm

The HRVH website provides free access to digital collections of historical material from more than 40 organizations in Columbia, Greene, Dutchess, Ulster, Sullivan, Rockland, Orange, Putnam, and Westchester counties.

NYGenWeb Project: Columbia County
www.rootsweb.ancestry.com/~nycolumb

Part of the national, USGenWeb volunteer initiative, the website provides information and resources for county research.

Cortland County

Formed April 8, 1808

Parent County   Onondaga
Daughter Counties   None
County Seat   City of Cortland

Major Land Transactions
See chapter 7, Land Records
New Military Tract 1782–1791
Boston Ten Towns 1787

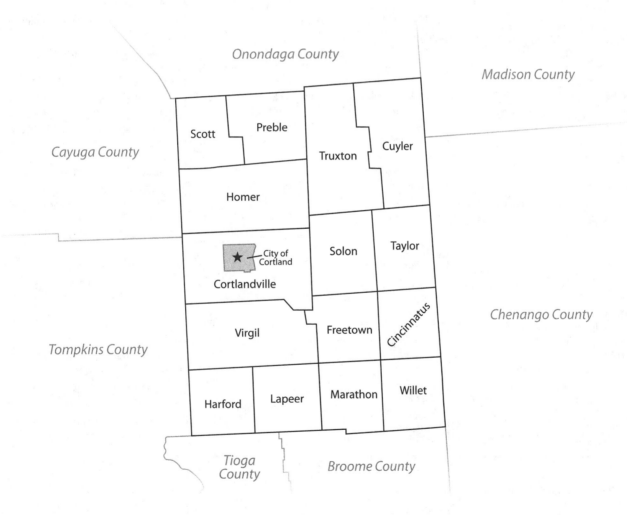

Town Boundary Map
★ - County seat

Towns (and Cities)	Villages and other Settlements	Notes
Cincinnatus * 1795 Settlers from Lenox, MA, and Salem, NY 1804 Formed in Onondaga County from Town of Solon 1808 Transferred to new county of Cortland 1818 Daughter towns Freetown, Harrison (now Marathon), and Willett formed	Cincinnatus Gee Brook Lower Cincinnatus Taylor Texas Valley	* Cincinnatus was the name of one of the 28 Military Tract townships • Taylor on Solon town line before 1849; on Taylor town line after 1849 • Texas Valley shared by towns of Freetown and Marathon after 1818
Cortland (city) 1900 Incorporated as a city from Village of Cortland Village		* County seat from 1808 as hamlet, village, and city
Cortlandville 1792 Settlers from New Jersey 1829 Formed from Town of Homer and a small northeastern part of Town of Virgil 1900 City of Cortland formed from Cortland Village	Blodgett Mills Loring (Crossing) Camp Tioughnioga McGraw (v) Cortland Village (v) McGrawville Gracie Munsons Corners Homer (v) Polkville Hoxies Gorge South Cortland	• Cortland Village, formerly Cortlandville, in Town of Homer until 1829; village established 1853, rechartered 1864; became City of Cortland in 1900; county seat from 1808 • Village of Homer inc. 1835, mostly within Town of Homer • Village of McGraw inc. 1869
Cuyler 1794–95 Settled 1858 Formed from Town of Truxton	Cowles Settlement Keeney Cowles Station New Boston Settlement South Cuyler Cuyler Tripoli Cuyler Hill	• Cowles Settlement formerly part of Town of Fabius, Onondaga County • Cuyler and Keeney (also Keeney(s) Settlement) in Town of Truxton before 1858
Freetown 1795 Settled 1818 Formed from Town of Cincinnatus 1850 Annexed land from Town of Virgil	East Freetown Galatia Freetown Texas Valley Freetown Corners	• Galatia on Marathon town line • Texas Valley on Marathon town line; in Town of Cincinnatus before 1818
Harford 1803 Settled 1845 Formed from Town of Virgil	Harford Harford Mills South Harford	
Harrison Name for Town of Marathon 1818–1827		
Homer * 1791 Settled 1794 Formed as town in Onondaga County 1798 Daughter town Solon formed 1804 Daughter town Virgil formed 1808 Transferred to new county of Cortland 1829 Daughter town Cortlandville formed	Carpenterville Cortlandville East Homer East River Homer (v) Little York Port Watson Pratt Corners Scott	* Homer was the name of one of the 28 Military Tract townships • Cortlandville in Town of Cortlandville from 1829; county seat from 1808 • Small part of Village of Homer, inc. 1835, in Town of Cortlandville
Lapeer 1799 Settled 1845 Formed from Town of Virgil	Hunt(s) Corners Lapeer State Bridge Station	

Towns (and Cities)	Villages and other Settlements		Notes
Marathon 1794 Settled 1818 Formed as Harrison from Town of Cincinnatus 1827 Name changed to Marathon	Galatia Marathon (v) Texas Valley		• Galatia on Freetown town line • Village of Marathon inc. 1861 • Texas Valley on Freetown town line; in Town of Cincinnatus before 1818
Preble 1796–98 Settled 1808 Formed from Town of Tully, Onondaga County 1815 Daughter town Scott formed	Baltimore Cummings Crossing Preble	Preble Center Preble Corners Slab City	
Scott 1799 Settlers from Massachusetts and Vermont 1815 Formed from Town of Preble	East Scott Fair Haven Grout Mill Scott		• East Scott also Scott Corners • Fair Haven also Glen Haven • Scott also Scott Center
Solon * 1796 Settlers from Canterbury, CT 1798 Formed in Onondaga County from Town of Homer 1804 Daughter town Cincinnatus formed 1808 Transferred to new county of Cortland 1811 Ceded land to Town of Truxton 1849 Daughter town Taylor formed	East Solon Maybury Mills Solon Solon Pond Taylor Union Valley		* Solon was the name of one of the 28 Military Tract townships • Maybury Mills also Mayberry Mills • Taylor and Union Valley in Town of Taylor after 1849; Taylor on Cincinnatus town line
Taylor 1793 Settled 1849 Formed from Town of Solon	Mount Roderick Potter Hill Taylor Taylor Center	Taylor Valley Taylorville Union Valley	• Taylor and Union Valley in Town of Solon before 1849; Taylor on Cincinnatus town line • Taylorville formerly Bangall
Truxton 1795 Settled 1808 Formed from Town of Fabius, Onondaga County 1811 Annexed land from Town of Solon 1858 Daughter town Cuyler formed	Cheningo Crain(s) Mills Cuyler Keeney Settlement	Manchester Mills Truxton Tubville	• Cuyler and Keeney Settlement see Town of Cuyler after 1858
Virgil * 1792 Settled 1804 Formed in Onondaga County from Town of Homer 1808 Transferred to new county of Cortland 1829 Ceded small amount of land to formation of Town of Cortlandville 1845 Daughter towns Harford and Lapeer created 1850 Ceded land to Town of Freetown	East Virgil Franks Corners Messengerville State Bridge Virgil		* Virgil was the name of one of the 28 Military Tract townships
Willett 1793 Settlers from Barrington, MA 1818 Formed from Town of Cincinnatus	Burlingames Mills Dyersville Georgetown Georgetown Heights	Lakeview Penelope Willet	

NEW YORK STATE CENSUS RECORDS

See also chapter 3, Census Records

County originals at the Cortland County Clerk's Office: 1825*, 1835, 1845**, 1855, 1865, 1875, 1892, 1905, 1915, 1925

State originals at the NYSA: 1915, 1925

Microfilm at the FHL, NYPL, and NYSL; many years are online at *FamilySearch.org* and *Ancestry.com*.

*For 1825 census abstract, see Eisenberg, et al., in Abstracts, Indexes & Transcriptions.

**1845 New York state census for Cortland County is lost with the exception of the towns of Scott, Solon, and Willett

NATIONAL/STATEWIDE REPOSITORIES & RESOURCES

See chapter 16

Cortland County Clerk

Cortland County Courthouse • 46 Greenbush Street, Suite 105
Cortland, NY 13045 • (607) 753-5021
www.cortland-co.org/cc/index.htm

Holdings include mortgages and deeds 1808–present, New York state censuses for Cortland County 1825, 1835, 1856, 1855, 1865, 1875, 1892, 1905; marriages 1908–1933; naturalization records 1816–1960s; and court records. A selection of recent documents is viewable online through the clerk's website.

Cortland County – City, Town, and Village Clerks

Birth, marriage, and death records are maintained by the clerk of the municipality in which the event occurred; see Introduction to County Guides for details of other records which may also be held by municipal clerks. For contact information, see *www.cortland-co.org*.

Cortland County Surrogate's Court

Cortland County Courthouse • 46 Greenbush Street, Suite 301
Cortland, NY 13045-2725 • (607) 753-5355

Holds probate records from 1808 to the present. See also chapter 6, Probate Records.

Cortland County Public Libraries

Cortland is part of the Finger Lakes Library System; see *www.flls.org* to access each library. Many hold genealogy and local history collections such as local newspapers. Also see listing below for Cortland Free Library.

Cortland County Historical Society, Suggett House Museum, and Kellogg Memorial Research Center

25 Homer Avenue • Cortland, NY 13045 • (607) 756-6071
Email: info@CortlandHistory.com • *www.cortlandhistory.com*

Cemetery listings for each town, DAR records and volumes, city directories, children's home records, farm records, military records (Cortland County Civil War regiments), newspaper clippings (birth, marriage, and death announcements), published and unpublished family histories and genealogies, scrapbooks, surname family files, town records, vital record information, and an index of federal census records (all years) and New York state census records (1825, 1835, 1855, 1865, 1875, 1905, 1915, 1925) for Cortland County. *Cortland County Historical Society Bulletin*, 1983–present, contains some genealogical material.

Cortland County Historian

60 Central Avenue • Cortland, NY 13045
(607) 753-5360 • *www.cortland-co.org/Historian*

The Cortland County Historian oversees the Cortland Record Center. The Historian's website contains a list of municipal historians and a list of historic sites in Cortland County. The Historian's Facebook page provides news and trivia related to the history of Cortland County and information on the historian's projects; visitors can ask research questions.

Cortland County – All Municipal Historians

While not authorized to answer genealogical inquiries, city, town, and village historians can provide valuable historical information and research advice; some maintain collections and webpages which may include transcribed records, local histories, and other genealogical material. See contact information at *www.cortland-co.org/Historian* or at the website of the Association of Public Historians of New York State at *www.aphnys.org*.

REGIONAL REPOSITORIES & RESOURCES

Central New York Genealogical Society

See listing in Onondaga County Guide

LOCAL REPOSITORIES & RESOURCES

Alphabetized by location

Taylor Historical Society

3245 Chenango Solon Pond Road • Cincinnatus, NY 13040
Email: info@taylorhistoricalsociety.com • *www.taylorhistoricalsociety.com*

The Society has undertaken an oral history project and is planning to make oral histories available on its website. Its publication, *Taylor Town History*, documents the town's history and genealogy. Select photographs can be viewed on the website.

Cortland Free Library

32 Church Street • Cortland, NY 13045 • (607) 756-6071
Email: cortlandlib-ref@twcny.rr.com • *www.flls.org/cortlandlib*

Library maintains a local history section, including local directories (beginning in the 19th century), the *Cortland Standard* on microfilm (beginning in the early 1900s), and yearbooks.

Glen Haven Historical Society

7325 Fair Haven Road • PO Box 293 • Homer, NY 13077
Email: glen_haven_historical@hotmail.com
www.glenhavenhistoricalsociety.org

Holdings include family files, photographs, books, and manuscripts.

McGraw Historical Society and History Room

5 Main Street • PO Box 537 • McGraw, NY 13101
(607) 836-6537 • Email: mcgrawhistoricalsociety@yahoo.com
www.mcgrawhistoricalsociety.com

Society's Local History Room is located at the Lamont Memorial Free Library. Holdings include scrapbooks, newspapers, photographs, postcards, and memorabilia. Special collections include New York Central College Archives and the collection of Daniel S. Lamont who was NYS Governor, Secretary of War, and personal friend to President Cleveland.

SELECTED PRINT & ONLINE RESOURCES

Below is a selection of resources relevant for research in this county. The list is representative, not exhaustive. Additional titles—particularly of abstracts, indexes, transcriptions, and local histories—are available; consult the introduction to Part Two for further information. For guidance on how to identify and locate community directories and local newspapers, see chapter 11, City Directories, and chapter 12, Newspapers, in Part One of this book.

Abstracts, Indexes & Transcriptions

Cortland County Historical Society. *Cortland County Chronicles: Being Papers from the Collections of the Cortland County Historical Society.* 3 vols. Cortland, NY: Cortland County Historical Society, 1957.

Cortland County Historical Society. "Family Records." Typescript, n.d. NYPL, New York.

Cortland County, NYG&B Church Surveys Collection. NYG&B, New York. [NYG&B eLibrary]

County of Cortland Abstracts. Syracuse: Central New York Genealogical Society, 2000. Abstracts for a range of genealogical records originally published in the quarterly *Tree Talks.*

Crutts, Katherine W. "*Cortland County Cemetery Records, 1932–1933.*" Typescript, n.d. NYPL, New York. Includes cemeteries in Blodgett Mills, Cincinnatus, Cortland, Cortlandville, Cuyler, DeRuyter, East Freetown, Harford, Homer, Lapeer, Marathon, Preble, Scott, Solon, Taylor, Truxton, and Virgil.

Daughters of the American Revolution, comps. *New York DAR Genealogical Records Committee Report.* Since 1913 DAR volunteers have transcribed many thousands of unpublished cemetery, church, and town records throughout New York. The reports are at the DAR Library; copies are at the NYSL and the NYPL. The DAR has a searchable name index to all the GRC reports at *http://services.dar.org/Public/DAR_Research/search/?Tab_ID=6.* See Jean Worden's index below for a listing by county of the New York record sets that were transcribed by the DAR before 1998.

Dexter, Mary L., Shirley G. Heppell, and Carolyn T. Ibbotson. *Residents of Cortland County, NY, 1800–1810: A Finding List Compiled from Local Records.* Cortland, NY: Cortland County Historical Society, 1971.

Eisenberg, Marcia J., Robert Vasalius Moyer, [and members of the Central New York Genealogical Society]. *Abstract of the 1825 New York State Census of Cortland County, New York.* Syracuse: Central New York Genealogical Society, 1985. Originally published in *Tree Talks,* vol. 25, no. 4 (1985): 1–26. Introduction, content and maps: i–xii. No index.

Kelly, Arthur C. M. *Index to Tree Talks County Packet: Cortland County.* Rhinebeck, NY: Kinship, 2002.

Worden, Jean D. "Book 1, Subject Index." In *Revised Master Index to the New York State Daughters of the American Revolution Genealogical Records Volumes.* Zephyrhills, FL: J. D. Worden, 1998. The Subject Index includes a listing by county of the cemeteries, churches, towns, and other sources of records transcribed by the DAR.

Other Resources

Albertson, J. Donald, and Mrs. Clarence J. Varian. *Historic Van Cortlandtville.* Van Cortlandtville, NY: Van Cortlandtville Historical Society, 1976.

Biographical Publishing Company. *Book of Biographies: This Volume Contains Biographical Sketches of Leading Citizens of Cortland County, NY.* Buffalo, 1898.

Blodgett, Bertha E. *Stories of Cortland County.* Cortland, NY: Cortland County Historical Society, 1975. Book includes American Indian history, Military Tract, early settlers, education, historical developments.

Child, Hamilton. *Gazetteer and Business Directory of Cortland County, NY, for 1869.* Syracuse, 1869.

Cornish, Cornelia B. *The Geography and History of Cortland County.* Ann Arbor, MI: Edwards Bros., 1935.

Cutter, William R. *Genealogical and Family History of Central New York: A Record of the Achievements of Her People in the Making of a Commonwealth and the Building of a Nation.* New York: Lewis Historical Publishing Co., 1912.

Everts, Ensign & Everts. *Combination Atlas Map of Cortland County, New York.* Philadelphia, 1876.

Fay, Loren V. *Cortland County, New York, Genealogical Research Secrets.* Albany: L. V. Fay, 1981.

Foley, Janet W. *Early Settlers of New York State: Their Ancestors and Descendants.* 9 vols. Akron, NY: 1934–1942. Reprint, 2 vols. Baltimore: Genealogical Publishing Co., 1993.

Galpin, William F. *Central New York, an Inland Empire, Comprising Oneida, Madison, Onondaga, Cayuga, Tompkins, Cortland, Chenango Counties and Their People.* New York: Lewis Historical Publishing Co., 1914. Contains biographies. Index available from Berkshire Family History Association.

Goodwin, Hermon C. *Pioneer History, or Cortland County and the Border Wars of New York: From the Earliest Period to the Present Time.* New York, 1859. Book includes American Indian, French, and English history in the area; natural history; border wars and Sullivan's campaign; migrations, Revolutionary War, Military Tract, institutions, town and county organization, legends, and biographical sketches.

Kurtz, D. Morris. *Past and Present A Historical and Descriptive Sketch of Cortland, N.Y.* Binghamton, NY, 1883.

McFall, Francis M. *1821–1921, History of the First Methodist Episcopal Church of Cortland, New York.* Cortland, NY: The First Methodist Episcopal Church, 1921.

New York Historical Resources Center. *Guide to Historical Resources in Cortland County, New York, Repositories.* Ithaca, NY: Cornell University, 1981. [*books.FamilySearch.org*]

Records of the Ithaca College Study Center for Early Religious Life in Western New York, 1978–1981. Division of Rare and Manuscript Collections, Cornell University Library. A description of the holdings for each county is at *http://rmc.library.cornell.edu/eguides/lists/churchlist1.htm.*

Smith, H. P., ed. *History of Cortland County: With Illustrations and Biographical Sketches of Some of its Prominent Men and Pioneers.* Syracuse, 1885. Book includes natural history, American Indian history, European exploration and settlement, formation of county, military history, newspapers, local societies, town histories, biographical sketches and portraits.

Souvenir Book: Cortland County Sesquicentennial Celebration, July 20–26, 1958. Cortland, NY: Cortland County Historical Society, 1958.

Welch, E. L. "*Grip's*" *Historical Souvenir of Cortland.* Cortland, NY, 1899.

Additional Online Resources

Ancestry.com

There are vast numbers of records on *Ancestry.com* that pertain to people who have lived in New York State. See chapter 16 for a description of *Ancestry.com*'s resources and its partnership with the New York State Archives. A search of the online card catalog

by county may reveal lesser known resources that pertain to a locality, such as town records, abstracts, transcriptions, city directories, and local histories.

Cortland Connection
www.cortlandny.com/1-genealogy.htm
The website posts genealogical queries and provides links to resources relevant for Cortland research.

FamilySearch.org
FamilySearch has extensive collections of New York records, including religious records, which are searchable by name and location, but not by county. The following collections include record images (browsable, but not searchable) that are organized by county:

- "New York, Land Records, 1630–1975." Includes land and property records. *familysearch.org/search/collection/2078654*
- "New York, Probate Records, 1629–1971." Includes wills, letters of administration, and guardianship papers. *familysearch.org/search/collection/1920234*

For both collections, choose the browse option and then select Cortland to view the available records sets.

A detailed description of *FamilySearch.org* resources is found in chapter 16.

NYGenWeb Project: Cortland County
www.rootsweb.ancestry.com/~nycortla
Part of the national, USGenWeb volunteer initiative, the website provides information and resources for county research.

Old Fulton New York Postcards
www.FultonHistory.com
The website provides free access to a vast collection of digitized New York newspapers, including 22 titles for Cortland County.

Delaware County

Formed March 10, 1797

Parent Counties   Otsego • Ulster
Daughter Counties   None
County Seat   Village of Delhi

Major Land Transactions
See table in chapter 7, Land Records
Hardenbergh Patent 1708

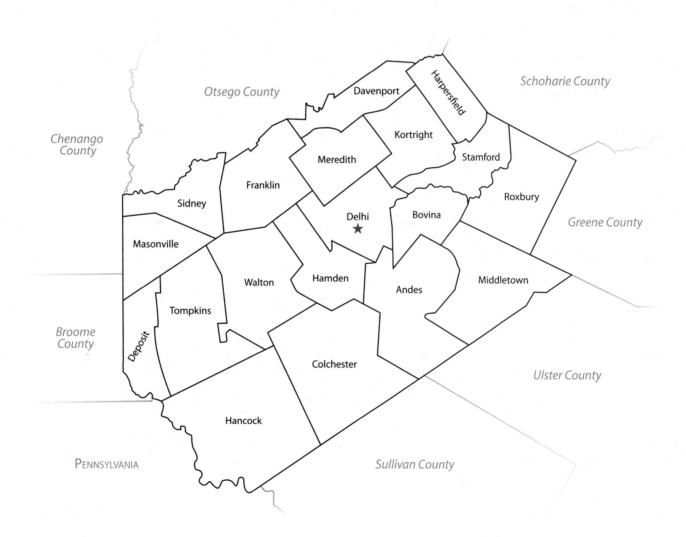

Town Boundary Map
★ - County seat

Towns (and Cities)	Villages and other Settlements		Notes
Andes 1784 Settled 1819 Formed from Town of Middletown	Andes (v) Barkaboom Bussey Hollow Cabin Hill Canada Hollow Davis Hollow Dingle Hill Fall Clove Gladstone	Jacksonburg Lake Hill Palmer Hill Pleasant Valley Shavertown Tremper(s) Kil(l) Union Grove Wolf Hollow	• Village of Andes inc. 1888, dissolved 2004 • Shavertown also Shaver Hollow; lost to Pepacton Reservoir flooding 1942–1955 • Union Grove lost to Pepacton Reservoir flooding 1942–1955
Bovina 1792 Settled 1820 Formed from towns of Delhi, Middletown, and Stamford	Bovina Bovina Center Bovina Valley	Lake Delaware Mountain Brook	• Hamlet of Bovina locally known as Butt End c. 1860 • Bovina Center formerly Brushland
Colchester 1774 Settled 1792 Formed in Ulster County from Town of Middletown * 1797 Transferred to new county of Delaware 1799 Ceded land to Town of Walton 1806 Daughter town Hancock formed 1827 Annexed land from the Town of Walton	Barney Hollow Berry Brook Brooklyn Butternut Grove Colchester Coles Clove Cook(s) Falls Corbett	Downsville (v) Gregorytown Horton Pepacton Shinhopple Springbrook Tel(l)ford Hollow Wilson Hollow	* Town of Middletown in Delaware County from 1797 • Colchester also Pawpacton • Village of Downsville inc. 1921, dissolved 9/21/1950 • Pepacton lost to Pepacton Reservoir flooding 1942–1955
Davenport 1786 Settled at Davenport Center 1817 Formed from towns of Maryland (Otsego County) and Kortright	Butts Corners Davenport Davenport Center Fergusonville Hoseaville	Pindars Corners Pumpkin Hollow Simpsonville West Davenport	• Davenport formerly East Davenport
Delhi 1785 Settled 1798 Formed from towns of Kortright, Middletown, and Walton 1812 Ceded land to Town of Walton 1820 Daughter town Bovina formed 1825 Daughter town Hamden formed	Checkerville Delhi (v) East Delhi Fraser Glen Burnie West Delhi		• County seat at Delhi from 1798; Village of Delhi inc. 1821
Deposit 1880 Formed from Town of Tompkins	Barbourville China Deposit (v) Dickerson City	Hale(s) Eddy Hamblettville Stilesville Upper Barbourville	• Barbourville and Hale(s) Eddy in Town of Tompkins before 1880 • Village of Deposit inc. 1811; in Town of Tompkins before 1880; shared with Town of Sanford, Broome County, after 1852 • Dickerson City also The City

Towns (and Cities)	Villages and other Settlements		Notes
Franklin 1785 Settled 1792 Formed in Otsego County from Town of Harpersfield 1797 Transferred to new county of Delaware; daughter town Walton formed 1800 Daughter town Meredith formed 1801 Daughter town Sidney formed 1822 Daughter town Huntsville (now Otego, Otsego County) formed	Arabia Bartlett Hollow Bennett Hollow Brooklyn Cobine Franklin (v) Leonta Merrickville Northfield Station North Franklin Summit Treadwell		• Arabia formerly South Franklin • Village of Franklin inc. 1874 • Treadwell formerly Croton and East Franklin
Hamden 1795 Settled 1825 Formed as Hampden from Towns of Delhi and Walton 1826 Name changed to Hamden	Basin Clove Chambers Hollow Church Lot Covert Hollow Delancey Gregory Hollow	Hamden Hawley(s) Mundale North Hamden Terry Clove	• Delancey formerly Lansingville • Hamlet of Hamden formerly Lansing • North Hamden formerly Stoodley Hollow
Hancock Settled before Revolution and abandoned during the war 1806 Formed from Town of Colchester	Basket Station Beaverkill Burnwood Cadosia Cadosia Valley Centerville Chiloway Craryville Douglass (v) East Branch Elk Brook Fish(s) Eddy French Woods Gould(s) Hancock (v) Harvard Kerry Siding Kerryville	Kilgore Spur Long Flat(s) Lord(s)ville Luzerne Martin Flat Methol Partridge Island Pea Brook Peakville Peas Eddy Readburn Read Creek Rock Valley Stockport Trout Brook Tylers Switch Westfield Flats	• Village of Douglass inc. 1867 and later dissolved • Fish(s) Eddy formerly Fishers Eddy and Partridge Island • Village of Hancock inc. 1888; formerly Chehocton or Shohakin • Kerryville on Tompkins town line • Stockport on Pennsylvania state line • Tylers Switch formerly Catlin Hollow
Harpersfield 1782 Settled 1788 Formed in Montgomery County 1791 Transferred to new county of Otsego 1792 Daughter town Franklin formed 1793 Daughter town Kortright formed 1797 Transferred to new county of Delaware 1834 Ceded land to Town of Stamford	Harpersfield Harpersfield Center North Harpersfield Quaker Hill Stamford (v)		• Village of Stamford inc. 1870; shared with Town of Stamford, formerly Devils Halfacre

Towns (and Cities)	Villages and other Settlements	Notes
Kortright Settled and abandoned before Revolution; settled by families from Dutchess County, Connecticut, and Scotland after Revolution 1793 Formed in Otsego County from Town of Harpersfield 1797 Transferred to new county of Delaware 1798 Daughter town Delhi formed 1800 Daughter town Meredith formed 1817 Daughter town Davenport formed 1834 Ceded land to Town of Stamford	Bloomville Doonan Corners Kiffville Kortright Kortright Center North Kortright South Kortright Sturges Corner West Harpersfield West Kortright	• South Kortright formerly Almeda; on Stamford town line after 1834
Masonville 1795 Settlers from Massachusetts at Cockburns Gore 1811 Formed from Town of Sidney	Arctic Masonville Cockburns Gore Tacoma East Masonville Whitman Ivanhoe	
Meredith 1787 Settled 1800 Formed from towns of Franklin and Kortright	East Meredith Ouleout Meredith West Meredith Meridale	• East Meredith formerly Brier Street • Hamlet of Meredith also Meredith Square • Meridale formerly Meredith Hollow
Middletown 1762–63 Settlers from Ulster County; abandoned during Revolution 1789 Formed in Ulster County from towns of Rochester and Woodstock 1792 Daughter town Colchester formed 1797 Transferred to new county of Delaware 1798 Daughter town Delhi formed 1819 Daughter town Andes formed 1820 Daughter town Bovina formed	Arena Grant Mills Arena Heights Halcottsville Arkville Hanley Corners Clovesville Kelly(s) Corners Denver Margaretville (v) Dry Brook Settlement New Kingston Dunraven Solitude Fleischmanns (v) Spruceville	• Arena formerly Lumberville; lost to the Pepacton Reservoir 1954, some houses moved to newly named Arena Heights • Arkville formerly Deans Corner • Clovesville formerly Clothesville and Franceville; also Covesville • Dunraven formerly Clarks Factory • Village of Fleischmanns inc. 1913; formerly Griffins Corners • Village of Margaretville inc. 1875
Pinefield Name for Town of Tompkins 1806–1808		
Roxbury 1786 Settled at Mores Settlement 1799 Formed from Town of Stamford	Batavia Little Falls Batavia Kil Roxbury (v) Bedell Stratton(s) Falls Grand Gorge Vega Hardscrabble West Settlement Hubbel Corners	• Bedell formerly Red Kill • Grand Gorge formerly Mores Settlement and Moresville • Village of Roxbury incorporated c. 1825 dissolved 4/18/1900; formerly Beaver Dam • Vega also Shackville
Sidney 1773 Settled, abandoned during Revolutionary War 1801 Formed from Town of Franklin 1811 Daughter town Masonville formed	Barrett Hollow Sidney Center Crookerville South Unadilla East Sidney Wattles Ferry Franklin Depot Youngs Sidney (v)	• Franklin Depot formerly Smith Settlement • Village of Sidney inc. 1888; formerly Sidney Plains • Youngs formerly Tripoli

Towns (and Cities)	Villages and other Settlements		Notes
Stamford 1773 Settlers from Scotland and New England, especially from Stamford, CT 1792 Formed in Ulster County as Stamford * 1797 Transferred to new county of Delaware 1799 Daughter town Roxbury formed 1820 Daughter town Bovina formed 1834 Annexed land from towns of Harpersfield and Kortright	Hobart (v) South Kortright Stamford (v)		* Town of Stamford known as New Stamford before 1792 • Village of Hobart inc. 1888; formerly Tinkertown and Waterville • South Kortright formerly Almeda; in Town of Kortright before 1834; on Kortright town line after 1834 • Village of Stamford inc. 1870; formerly Devils Halfacre, shared with Town of Harpersfield
Tompkins 1787 Settled 1806 Formed as Pinefield from Town of Walton 1808 Name changed to Tompkins 1880 Daughter town Deposit formed	Apex Barbourville Cannonsville Cleaver Cookhouse Deposit (v) Dickinsons Station Granton Hales Eddy	Kerryville Kelsey Little Cokeose Loomis Piersons Rock Rift Rock Royal Trout Creek	• Barbourville and Hales Eddy in Town of Deposit after 1880 • Village of Deposit inc. 1811; in Town of Deposit after 1880; shared with Town of Sanford, Broome County, after 1852 • Granton formerly Carpenters Eddy • Kerryville on Hancock town line • Loomis formerly Little York; on Walton town line • Rock Rift and Rock Royal submerged by Cannonsville Reservoir; Rock Royal formerly Sherruck or Shurock • Trout Creek formerly Teedville
Walton 1785 Settled 1797 Formed from Town of Franklin 1798 Daughter town Delhi formed 1799 Annexed land from Town of Colchester 1806 Daughter town Pinefield (now Tompkins) formed 1812 Annexed land from Town of Delhi 1825 Daughter town Hamden formed 1827 Ceded land to Town of Colchester	Beerston East Brook Loomis Northfield Ogdens Pine(s)ville Walton (v) West Brook Woodford		• Loomis formerly Little York; on Tompkins town line • Northfield formerly New Road • Pine(s)ville formerly Pine Brook • Pinesville took name of earlier settlement • Village of Walton inc. 1851

NEW YORK STATE CENSUS RECORDS

See also chapter 3, Census Records

County originals at Delaware County Clerk's Office: 1845*, 1855, 1865**, 1875, 1892, 1905, 1915, 1925 (1825 and 1835 are lost)

State originals at the NYSA: 1915, 1925

Microfilm at the FHL, NYPL, NYSHA, and NYSL; many years are online at *FamilySearch.org* and *Ancestry.com*.

*1845 New York State census for Delaware County is lost except for the Town of Masonville. See Goerlich in Abstracts, Indexes & Transcriptions below.

**1865 Searchable transcriptions for the Towns of Andes and Bovina and an index for Town of Davenport at *www.dcnyhistory.org*. See Additional Online Resources below.

NATIONAL/STATEWIDE REPOSITORIES & RESOURCES

See chapter 16

COUNTYWIDE REPOSITORIES & RESOURCES

Delaware County Clerk

Court House Square • PO Box 426 • Delhi, NY 13753
(607) 746-2123 • *www.co.delaware.ny.us/departments/clerk/clerk.htm*

Court records, land records 1797–present, naturalization records 1810–1950, births and deaths 1847–1848, marriages 1847–1848, 1874–1881, 1909–1935, and New York state censuses for Delaware County 1845 (Town of Masonville only), 1855, 1865, 1875, 1892, 1905.

Delaware County – Town, and Village Clerks

Birth, marriage, and death records are maintained by the clerk of the municipality in which the event occurred; see Introduction to County Guides for details of other records which may also be held by municipal clerks. For contact information, see *www.dcnyhistory.org/hist.html*.

Delaware County Surrogate's Court

Delaware County Courthouse • 3 Court Street • Delhi, NY 13753
(607) 746-2126

Holds probate records 1797 to the present. See also chapter 6, Probate Records.

Delaware County Public Libraries

Delaware is part of the Four County Library System; see *www.4cls.org* to access each library Many hold genealogy and local history collections, including maps and newspapers. For example, Deposit Free Library holds the *Deposit Courier*, to 1849, and Skene Memorial Library holds a collection of local history books and ephemera. Some, like Bovine Public Library, offer genealogy assistance. The Louise Adelia Read Memorial Library performs obituary search requests and is home to a local history museum. Also see listing below for Stamford Village Library.

Delaware County Historical Association and Suggett House Museum

46549 State Highway 10 • Delhi, NY 13753 • (607) 746-3849
Email: dcha@delhi.net • *www.dcha-ny.org*
Civil War list: *www.dcha-ny.org/civilwarsoliderlist.pdf*

Association maintains historic buildings, galleries, and a research library and archives. Holdings include church records, diaries, family Bibles, genealogies, land records, newspapers, school records, town histories, and photographs dating largely from the mid-1900s. Holdings related to the Civil War include letters, diaries, roster sheets, and Grand Army of the Republic Post records. The website contains research guides, as well as a list of several thousand Delaware County Civil War soldiers with unit, census district, age, and biographical notes. Publishes a newsletter, *Headwaters of History*.

Delaware County Historian

One Court House Square, Suite 1 • Delhi, NY 13753
(607) 746-8660 • Email: hist@co.delaware.ny.us
www.co.delaware.ny.us/departments/hist/hist.htm

Holdings include cemetery records and photographs.

Ontario County Surrogate's Court

While not authorized to answer genealogical inquiries, town and village historians can provide valuable historical information and research advice; some maintain collections and webpages which may include transcribed records, local histories, and other genealogical material. See contact information at *www.dcnyhistory.org/hist.html* or at the website of the Association of Public Historians of New York State at *www.aphnys.org*.

LOCAL REPOSITORIES & RESOURCES

Alphabetized by location

Bovina Historical Society

Main Street • Bovina, NY • Email: bovinahistorian@gmail.com
http://bovinanyhistory.blogspot.com

Holdings include cemetery records, photographs, and Civil War records.

Davenport Historical Society

Town Hall, Route 23 • PO Box 88 • Davenport Center, NY 13751
(607) 278-5149 • *www.dcnyhistory.org/Fact_Fancy/about.htm*

Publications of the Society include a cemetery guide, indexes to *History of Delaware County* . . . and biographical sketches, church and school histories, and alumni profiles of 20th-century Davenport High School graduates.

Deposit Historical Society and Museum

145 Second Street • Deposit, NY 13754 • (607) 467-4422
Email: curator@DepositHistoricalSociety.org or depositsoc@aol.com
www.deposithistoricalsociety.org

Museum collections include local history artifacts, letters, and photographs. Newsletters 2003–present available on website.

Colchester Historical Society

Colchester Town Hall • 72 Tannery Road • PO Box 112
Downsville, NY 13755 • (607) 363-7196 • Email address on website
www.colchesterhistoricalsociety.org

Holdings include documents, genealogies, and artifacts. An index of family histories housed by the Society (Genealogy Surname files) and a gallery of artifacts are available on its website.

Hobart Historical Society

PO Box 11 • Hobart, NY 13788 • Email access through website
www.hobarthistoricalsociety.org

Society's website contains transcriptions from Hobart cemeteries and a gallery of photographs.

Historical Society of Middletown
778 Cemetery Rd. • Margaretville, NY 12455
Email access through website • www.mtownhistory.org

Website contains place histories, photographs, a transcribed railroad directory, and a transcribed newspaper clipping of a Civil War unit reunion. Collections include farm diaries, hotel ledgers, glass plate negatives, and school yearbooks.

Meredith Historical Society
PO Box 26 • Meridale, NY 13806 • (607) 746-8083
Email access through website • www.meredithhistory.org

Society's holdings include documents, photographs, and maps which are stored at the Hanford Mills Museum Archive. Photographs, cemetery burial lists, and a list of Meredith Civil War veterans are available online.

Roxbury Library Association: Irma Mae Griffin History Room
53742 State Highway 30 • PO Box 186 • Roxbury, NY 12474-0186
(607) 326-7901 • www.roxburylibraryonline.com/category/historyroom

Holdings include genealogies and newspapers, including the *Roxbury Times* on microfilm.

Sidney Historical Association and Museum
Sidney Civic Center • 21 Liberty Street, Second Floor, Room 218
Sidney, NY 13838 • (607) 967-7369
Email: sidneyhistorical@stny.rr.com • www.sidneyonline.com/sha.htm

Holdings include microfilm copies of the *Sidney Record*, *Sidney Enterprise*, and *Tri-Town News*, 1882–present; genealogical materials; obituaries; yearbooks; maps; and photographs.

The Maywood Historical Group of Sidney Center and Museum
O&W Depot • PO Box 298 • Sidney Center, NY 13839
Email: info@mhgonline.org • www.mhgonline.org

Group is headquartered in an old railroad depot. Holdings include records and photographs; the Group also sells books on local history.

Stamford Village Library Historical Room
117 Main Street • Stamford, NY 12167-1029 • (607) 652-5001
http://libraries.4cls.org/stamford

Family histories (multiple counties and New York State), cemetery records, business and organization records, land records, maps 1860s–1960s, photographs and postcards, Daughters of the American Revolution minutes, and vital records (1800s).

Walton Historical Society
9 Townsend Street • Walton, NY 13856 • (607) 865-5895
Email: whs@waltonhistoricalsociety.org
www.waltonhistoricalsociety.org

Headquartered in the 19th-century home of Henry and Kate G. Eells. Collections include scrapbooks, diaries, ledgers, *Walton Reporter*, from 1881 (paper copies and on CDs), cemetery records, etc. Appointments can be made for help with genealogical research.

SELECTED PRINT & ONLINE RESOURCES

Below is a selection of resources relevant for research in this county. The list is representative, not exhaustive. Additional titles—particularly of abstracts, indexes, transcriptions, and local histories—are available; consult the introduction to Part Two for further information. For guidance on how to identify and locate community directories and local newspapers, see chapter 11, City Directories, and chapter 12, Newspapers, in Part One of this book.

Abstracts, Indexes & Transcriptions

Barber, Gertrude Audrey. "Deaths Taken from the Delaware Gazette (1819–1895)." 4 vols. Typescript, 1934. NYPL, New York. [vols. 2–4 (1844–1895) on *Ancestry.com*]

———. "Letters of Administration of Delaware County, New York: Copied from the Original Records at the Courthouse, Delhi, NY." Typescript, 1939. Microfiche, NYSL, Albany, New York. [*Ancestry.com*]

———. "Marriages Taken from the Delaware Gazette (1819–1879)." Typescript, 1939. NYPL, New York.

———. "Marriages Taken from the Delaware Gazette (1880–1895)." Typescript, 1939. NYPL, New York.

Brush, Grace L. "Whitlock and Others: Some Old Cemeteries Near Stamford, Delaware County, New York." Typescript, 1930. Salt Lake City: Filmed by the Genealogical Society of Utah, 1971.

County of Delaware Abstracts. Syracuse: Central New York Genealogical Society, 2000. Abstracts for a range of genealogical records originally published in the quarterly *Tree Talks*. A name index is on the CNYGS website.

Daughters of the American Revolution, comps. *New York DAR Genealogical Records Committee Report*. Since 1913 DAR volunteers have transcribed many thousands of unpublished cemetery, church, and town records throughout New York. The reports are at the DAR Library; copies are at the NYSL and the NYPL. The DAR has a searchable name index to all the GRC reports at *http://services.dar.org/Public/DAR_Research/search/?Tab_ID=6*. See Jean Worden's index below for a listing by county of the New York record sets that were transcribed by the DAR before 1998.

Delaware County Potter's Field Burials, 1885–1956. Delhi, NY: The Delaware County Times, 1984. Indexed by John Raitt, 1985.

Delaware County, NYG&B Church Surveys Collection. NYG&B, New York. [NYG&B eLibrary]

Goerlich, Shirley B. *Data Collected by the New York City Board of Water Supply During the Relocation of Graves as Part of the Construction of the Cannonsville and Pepacton Reservoirs in Delaware County, New York*. Hamilton, NY: n.p., 1985.

———. *Delaware County Land Records. Series A: A Calendar of the H. Fletcher Davidson of Land Records at the Delaware County Historical Association*. Hamilton, NY: n.p., 1986.

———. *Delaware County, New York: Raw Materials from the Past*. Bainbridge, NY: RSG Publishing, 1994. Book includes boundary and town changes, maps, deaths and marriages from local newspapers (1819–1900) with index, 144th Regiment of Volunteers.

———. *New York State Census, Town of Masonville, Delaware County, New York, 1845*. Bainbridge, NY: RSG Publishing, 1998.

Goodrich, Victor B. "Index to Delaware County, New York, Probate Files for Persons Dying 1900 or Earlier." Typescript, 1989. New York Historical Association Library, Cooperstown, NY. Online transcription available at *dcnyhistory.org*.

———. *Miscellaneous Genealogical Data Pertaining to Residents of Delaware County, New York*. Hamilton, NY: n.p., 1987–1991. Published in three parts.

"Guardianship Records, Delaware County, NY: Transcribed from a Volume Marked on the Spine 'Index of Guardians,' and Located in the Delaware County Surrogate's Office, Delhi, NY." Typescript, n.d.

New York State Historical Association Library, Cooperstown, NY. These records continue those published in *Tree Talks*, 1963–1966.

Kelly, Arthur C. M. *Index to Tree Talks County Packet: Delaware County.* Rhinebeck, NY: Kinship, 2002.

Oman, Kitty R. Hilton. *The 1850 Census of Delaware County, New York.* Vancouver, WA : K. R. Oman, 1988.

Vosburgh, Royden Woodward, ed. "Records of the First Presbyterian Church of Stamford in the Village and Town of Stamford, Delaware County, NY." Typescript, 1921. NYPL, New York. [NYG&B eLibrary]

———, ed. "Records of the Presbyterian Congregation of Harpersfield, in the Town of Harpersfield, Delaware County, NY." Typescript, 1921. NYPL, New York." [NYG&B eLibrary]

Worden, Jean D. "Book 1, Subject Index." In *Revised Master Index to the New York State Daughters of the American Revolution Genealogical Records Volumes.* Zephyrhills, FL: J. D. Worden, 1998. The Subject Index includes a listing by county of the cemeteries, churches, towns, and other sources of records transcribed by the DAR.

Other Resources

Adams, Arthur G., ed. *The Catskills: An Illustrated Historical Guide with Gazetteer.* New York: Fordham University Press, 1990. First published 1975 by Sun Publishing Company.

Beers, F. W. *Atlas of Delaware County, New York: From Actual Surveys and Under the Direction of F.*

W. Beers, Assisted by A. B. Prindle and Others. New York, 1869. [NYPL Digital Gallery]

Biographical Review Publishing Company. *Biographical Review: This Volume Contains Biographical Sketches of the Leading Citizens of Delaware County, New York.* Boston, 1895.

Delaware County Bicentennial Book Committee. *The Spirit of Delaware County: A Look Back from 1976.* Delhi, NY: The Committee, 1976.

DeNatale, Douglas. *Two Stones for Every Dirt: The Story of Delaware County, New York.* Fleischmanns, NY: Purple Mountain Press, 1987.

De Vine, John F. *Three Centuries in Delaware County: The Story of a Picturesque and Progressive Section of the Empire State and Its Leading Citizens.* New York: Swiss Alps of Delaware, 1933.

Duerden, Tim. *A History of Delaware County, New York: A Catskill Land and Its People, 1797–2007.* Fleischmanns, NY: Purple Mountain Press, 2007.

Foley, Janet W. *Early Settlers of New York State: Their Ancestors and Descendants.* 9 vols. Akron, NY: 1934–1942. Reprint, 2 vols. Baltimore, Genealogical Publishing Co., 1993.

Goodrich, Victor B. *Any News from Walton? Family Data and Local History.* 6 vols. Hamilton, NY: n.p., 1981–1995.

Gould, Jay. *History of Delaware County, and Border Wars of New York, Containing a Sketch of the Late Anti-Rent Difficulties in Delaware, with Other Historical and Miscellaneous Matter, Never Before Published.* Roxbury, NY, 1856. Book includes American Indian history, early settlers, Revolutionary War, growth and development, religion, issues over land, obituaries, newspapers, social organizations and fraternal orders, education, and more.

History of Delaware County, NY: With Illustrations, Biographical Sketches, and Portraits of Some Pioneers and Prominent Residents. New York, 1880.

Houck, Shirley A. *The Evolution of Delaware County, New York: Being a History of Its Land.* Nashville, TN: Express Media, 1995.

Meagley, James G., comp. *A Look Back at Hobart, NY, On the 125th Anniversary of the Village Incorporation, 1888–2013.* Hobart, NY: Hobart Historical Society, 2014.

Monroe, John D. *Chapters in the History of Delaware County, New York.* Delaware, NY: Delaware County Historical Association, 1949.

Munsell, W. W. *History of Delaware County, N.Y., 1797–1880: With Illustrations, Biographical Sketches and Portraits of Some Pioneers and Prominent Residents.* Ithaca, NY: Filmed by Photo Science of Cornell University, 1974. Index published by the Davenport Historical Society.

Murray, David. *Delaware County, New York: History of the Century, 1797–1897. Centennial Celebration, June 9 and 10, 1897.* Delhi, NY, 1898. Book includes list of sources, maps, Native American history, natural history, early settlements, pioneer experiences, Revolutionary War, organization of the county, anti-rent troubles, Civil War, industries, transportation, education, churches, early physicians, biographical sketches, town histories, and many illustrations.

New York Historical Resources Center. *Guide to Historical Resources in Delaware County, New York, Repositories.* Ithaca, NY: Cornell University, 1980.

North, Arthur W. *Handbook and History of the Delaware County, NY: Being an Intimate Sketch of the Erection and Development of One of the Earliest County Units of the Legion.* New York: Organization of the American Legion, 1925.

Reynolds, Paul E. *Geographical Names in Delaware County, NY.* Cooperstown: New York State Historical Association, 1983.

Rockwell, Charles. *The Catskill Mountains and the Region Around.* Saugerties, NY: Hope Farm Press, 1973. First published 1869.

Spaulding, Helim G. *Spaulding's Business Directory of Delaware County for 1895.* Sidney, NY: The Sidney Advocate, 1986.

Walton Reporter. *Some Early History of Delaware County, NY.* Walton, NY: n.d.

Additional Online Resources

Ancestry.com
There are vast numbers of records on *Ancestry.com* that pertain to people who have lived in New York State. See chapter 16 for a description of *Ancestry.com*'s resources and its partnership with the New York State Archives. A search of the online card catalog by county may reveal lesser known resources that pertain to a locality, such as town records, abstracts, transcriptions, city directories, and local histories.

Delaware County, NY, Genealogy and History Site
www.dcnyhistory.org/index2.html
This volunteer-run website coordinates the NYGenWeb Project for Delaware County and provides access to cemetery transcriptions, census indexes, deed abstracts 1797–1808, school records, obituaries, tax roll abstracts, will abstracts, digitized newspapers and photographs, and links to other resources for county research.

FamilySearch.org

FamilySearch has extensive collections of New York records, including religious records, which are searchable by name and location, but not by county. The following collections include record images (browsable, but not searchable) that are organized by county:

- "New York, Land Records, 1630–1975." Includes land and property records. *familysearch.org/search/collection/2078654*

- "New York, Probate Records, 1629–1971." Includes wills, letters of administration, and guardianship papers. *familysearch.org/search/collection/1920234*

For both collections, choose the browse option and then select Delaware to view the available records sets.

A detailed description of *FamilySearch.org* resources is found in chapter 16.

New York Heritage Digital Collections: New York State Newspaper Project
www.nyheritage.org/newspapers

The website provides links to digital newspapers collections in 26 counties (currently) made accessible through New York Heritage, New York State Historic Newspapers, HRVH Historical Newspapers, and other providers.

Dutchess County

Formed November 1, 1683

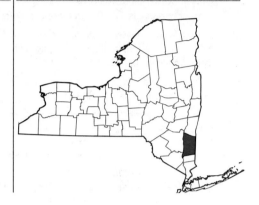

Parent County	Original county
Daughter County	Putnam 1812
County Seat	City of Poughkeepsie

Major Land Transactions
See chapter 7, Land Records

Rombout Patent 1685 • Beekman Patent 1697 • Great Nine Partners Patent 1697
Highland (Philipse) Patent 1697 • Kipsburgh Manor-Rhinebeck Patent 1697
Little Nine Partners Patent 1706 • Oblong (tract) 1731

Town Boundary Map
★ - County seat

Towns (and Cities)	Villages and other Settlements	Notes
Amenia Part of Great Nine Partners Patent and the Oblong tract 1711 Settled 1719 Included in North Ward and Middle Ward * 1737 Part of new Crum Elbow Precinct 1762 Formed as a precinct from Crum Elbow 1788 Recognized as a town by the State of New York 1823 Ceded northern part of town to Town of North East	Amenia Amenia Union Amenia Village Ameniaville Leedsville Sharon Station Smithfield South Amenia Wassaic	* Colonial Act of June 24, 1719 divided the county into the North, Middle, and South wards; the eastern boundaries were not defined but these wards probably extended to the Oblong tract/ Connecticut line • Amenia Union also Hitchcock Corners • Sharon Station on Northeast town line • Smithfield formerly The City • Wassaic also Washiack; formerly known as the Steel Works
Beacon (city) 1913 Incorporated as a city from Fishkill Landing and Matteawan in Town of Fishkill	Fishkill Landing Matteawan	
Beekman Part of Beekman Patent 1710 Settled 1719 Included in Middle Ward and South Ward * 1737 Patent renamed Beekman precinct 1743 Precinct extended east across the Oblong tract 1768 Daughter precinct Pawling formed 1788 Recognized as a town by the State of New York 1821 Town of Freedom (now LaGrange) formed from towns of Beekman and Fishkill 1827 Town of Union Vale formed from towns of Beekman and LaGrange	Beekman Beekmanville Clove Valley Freemanville Garner Hollow Green Haven Oswego Poughquag Spellmans Sylvan Lake	* See note for 1719, Town of Amenia • Clove Valley formerly Beekman Furnace • Freemanville also known as Guinea, an African-American settlement • Oswego in Town of Freedom (now LaGrange) 1821–1827, then called Waterbury Hill in Town of Union Vale
Carmel * In Dutchess County 1795–1812		* See Putnam County
Charlotte (precinct) Part of Great Nine Partners Patent 1719 Included in North Ward and Middle Ward * 1761/2 Formed as Charlotte precinct from Crum Elbow precinct 1786 Divided into Clinton and Washington precincts		* See note for 1719, Town or Amenia
Clinton Part of Great Nine Partners Patent and several smaller patents 1719 Included in North Ward and Middle Ward * 1737 Part of Crum Elbow and Rhinebeck precincts	Beaman Bull(s) Head Clinton Corners Clinton Hollow Clinton Point Dewitt Mills Frontier Frost Mills	* See note for 1719, Town of Amenia

(Clinton continued on next page)

Towns (and Cities)	Villages and other Settlements		Notes
Clinton (continued) 1762 Part of Charlotte precinct, which was formed from Crum Elbow and Rhinebeck precincts 1786 Formed as Clinton precinct from Charlotte and Rhinebeck precincts 1788 Recognized as a town by the State of New York 1821 Daughter towns Hyde Park and Pleasant Valley formed	Glen Rock Hibernia Kansas Lent LeRoy Mills Pleasant Plains	Schultzville Slate Quarry Hill Sleights Corner Sodom Corners Travers Corners	• Hibernia settled by Irish
Crum Elbow (precinct) Part of Great Nine Partners Patent 1719 Included in North Ward and Middle Ward * 1737 Great Nine Partners Patent renamed Crum Elbow precinct 1762 Divided into Charlotte and Amenia precincts			* See note for 1719, Town of Amenia
Dover Part of Beekman Patent and Oblong tract; settled by Dutch before 1770 1807 Formed from Town of Pawling	Bains Corner Chestnut Ridge Dogtail Corners Dover Dover Furnace Dover Plains Grants Corner	Oniontown Preston Mountain South Dover Webatuck Wing(s) Station Wingdale	• Chestnut Ridge on Union Vale town line • Oniontown's name was a misunderstanding of "Younguntown" a name created by Keats due to the neighborhood's high number of children
East Fishkill Part of Rombout Patent 1730 Settled 1849 Formed from Town of Fishkill	Adriance Arthursburg(h) Clove Branch Junction Co(u)rtlandville East Fishkill Fishkill Furnace Fishkill Furnace Hook Fishkill Furnace Plains Fishkill Hook Fishkill Plains Gayhead Hackensack	Hillside Lake Hopewell Hopewell Junction Johnsontown Johnsville Leetown Lomala Peck(s)ville Shenandoah Shenandoah Corners Stormville Wiccopee	• Arthursburg(h) on LaGrange town line • East Fishkill on Fishkill town line • Shenandoah and Wiccopee in Town of Fishkill before 1849
Fishkill * Part of Rombout Patent 1682 Settled 1685 Rombout Patent granted 1719 Included in Middle Ward and South Ward * 1737 Rombout Patent renamed Rombout precinct, later Fishkill precinct 1788 Recognized as a town by State of New York 1806 Annexed land from Town of Philipstown * 1821 Town of Freedom (now LaGrange) formed from towns of Fishkill and Beekman	Baxtertown Brinckherhoff Brinkerhoffville Brockway Byrnsville Carthage Landing Chelsea Didell Dutchess Junction Fishkill (v) Fishkill Hook Fishkill Landing (v)	Fishkill-on-Hudson Franklindale Franklinville Glenham Groveville Hughsonville Johnsville Low Point Station Matteawan Melinzgah Middlebush	* Town of Fishkill formerly Vis-Kill * Middle and South wards, see note for 1719, Town of Amenia * Philipstown in Putnam County after 1812 • Byrnsville also Tioranda • Didell in Town of Wappinger after 1875 • Dutchess Junction was in Town of Philipstown before 1806 • Village of Fishkill inc. 1899 • Village of Fishkill Landing (inc. 1864) and Matteawan formed the City of Beacon in 1913 • Hughsonville in Town of Wappinger after 1875 • Johnsonville on East Fishkill town line

(Fishkill continued on next page)

Towns (and Cities)	Villages and other Settlements		Notes

Fishkill (continued)
1849   Daughter town East Fishkill
         formed
1875   Daughter town Wappinger formed
1913   Fishkill Landing and Matteawan
         became the City of Beacon
	Myer(s) Corners
	New Hackensack
	Rocky Glen
	Shenandoah
	Swartoutville
	Tioranda Mills
	Wappingers Falls (v)
	Wiccopee
			• Myers Corner(s) and New Hackensack
			  in Town of Wappinger after 1875
			• Shenandoah and Wiccopee in Town of
			  East Fishkill after 1849
			• Swartoutville in Town of Wappinger
			  after 1875
			• Village of Wappingers Falls inc. 1871;
			  shared with Town of Poughkeepsie; in
			  Town of Wappinger after 1875

Franklin * In Dutchess County 1795–1812			* See Town of Patterson in Putnam County
Frederickstown * In Dutchess County 1772–1795, as Fredericksburgh precinct 1772–1788			* See Putnam County
Frederick * In Dutchess County 1795–1812			* See Town of Kent in Putnam County
Freedom Name for Town of LaGrange 1821–1828			

Hyde Park
Part of Great Nine Partners, Pawling,
and Fauconnier/Hyde Park patents
1720   Settled by Dutch
1737   Part of Crum Elbow and
         Rhinebeck precincts
1762   Part of Charlotte and Rhinebeck
         precincts
1821   Formed from Town of Clinton
	Campton
	Conklin Store
	Cream Street
	Crum Elbow
	DeCantillon Landing
	East Park
	Eel Pot
	Haviland
		Hyde Park
		Hyde Park Landing
		Knob Street
		Lower Corners
		Staatsburg(h)
		Stoutenburgh
		Upper Corners
		Victory Lake
			• Conklin Store formerly Wilkes Dock
			• Crum Elbow on Pleasant Valley town line
			• East Park formerly Union Corners

LaGrange
Part of Rombout and Beekman patents,
later Fishkill and Beekman precincts
1800   Settled by Society of Friends
1821   Formed as Freedom from towns
         of Beekman and Fishkill
1827   Town of Union Vale formed
         mostly from Town of Beekman
         and partly from Town of
         Freedom (LaGrange)
1828   Name changed from Freedom
         to LaGrange
	Arthursburg(h)
	Berbank
	Billings
	Billings Gap
	Briggs Station
	Freedom Plains
	LaGrangeville
	Manchester Bridge
	Meddaugh
		Moores Mill(s)
		Noxon
		Oswego
		Overlook
		Potters Corners
		Rombout Ridge
		Sprout Creek
		Titusville
			• Arthursburg(h) on East Fishkill town line
			• LaGrangeville formerly Moreys Corners
			• Manchester Bridge on Poughkeepsie
			  town line
			• Oswego in Town of Beekman until 1821;
			  in Town of Union Vale from 1827, now
			  Waterbury Hill
			• Potters Corners on Union Vale town line

Livingston Manor
1686   Patent granted to Robert
         Livingston by Gov. Dongan
1717   Land annexed by Albany County
         from Dutchess County *
			* Livingston Manor in new county of
			  Columbia from 1786

Milan
Part of Little Nine Partners Patent
1760   Settled
1818   Formed from Town of North East
	Cases Corner
	Enterprise
	Jackson(s) Corners
	La Fayetteville
	Locke
	Maplehurst
		Milan
		Rock City
		Shookville
		Straw Hudson
		Thornville
			• Cases Corner also Caseys Corner
			• Jackson(s) Corners was shared with
			  Town of Gallatin, Columbia County
			• Milan formerly Milanville and West
			  Northeast

Towns (and Cities)	Villages and other Settlements	Notes
North East * Part of Great Nine Partners Patent, the Little Nine Partners Patent, and the Oblong tract 1719 Included in North Ward * 1725–30 Settlers from Connecticut 1737 Little Nine Partners Patent renamed North precinct; Great Nine Partners Patent renamed Crum Elbow precinct 1743 Boundary extended east across the Oblong tract 1746 North precinct renamed Northeast precinct 1788 Recognized as a town by the State of New York 1818 Daughter town Milan formed 1823 Annexed northern part of Town of Amenia; daughter town Pine Plains formed	Boston Corner Coleman Station Federal Store Indian Pond Irondale Millerton (v) Mount Riga Northeast Northeast Center Oblong Ogdensville Perry Corners Sichem Sharon Station Shekomeko Spencer(s) Corners State Line State Line Station Whitehouse Crossing Winchell Station	* North East also Northeast * North Ward, see note for 1719, Town of Amenia • Village of Millerton inc. 1875 • Sharon Station on Amenia town line • Shekomeko in Town of Pine Plains after 1823 • Spencer Corners also Clearing • Winchell Station also Winchels and Winchels Station; in Town of Pine Plains after 1823
Oblong (tract) * 1731 Opened to settlement 1743 Divided between Beekman, Crum Elbow, North, and South precincts		* Boundary between New York and Connecticut was contested until 1731 when the Oblong tract was granted to New York
Patterson * In Dutchess County 1795–1812, as Philips precinct 1772–1788		* See Putnam County
Pawling Part of Beekman Patent and the Oblong tract 1719 Included in Middle Ward and South Ward * 1720–30 Settled by Quakers from Long Island and Westchester County at Quaker Hill 1768 Formed as a precinct from Beekman precinct 1788 Recognized as a town by the State of New York 1807 Daughter town Dover created	Baker Corner Reynoldsville Station Campbellville Stone House Farmers Hill Storm House Holmes Toffeys Corners Hurd Corners West Pawling Mizzentop West Pawling Station Pawling (v) Whaley Lake Quaker Hill Woodinville Reville Summit	* See note for 1719, Town of Amenia • Holmes also Reynoldsville and Reynoldsville Station • Village of Pawling inc. 1893
Philipstown * In Dutchess County 1772–1812, as Philips predinct 1772–1788		* See Putnam County
Pine Plains Part of Little Nine Partners Patent 1740 Settled by German Palatines 1823 Formed from Town of North East	Bethel Pachin Mills Hammertown Pine Plains Hicks Hill Pulvers Corner Husted Shekomeko Mount Ross Winchels	• Shekomeko and Winchels (also Winchels Station and Winchells Station) in Town of Northeast before 1823

Towns (and Cities)	Villages and other Settlements		Notes
Pleasant Valley Part of Great Nine Partners Patent **1737–62** Settled by Presbyterians and Quakers **1821** Formed from Town of Clinton	Bloomvale Clark Heights Crow Hill Crum Elbow Gretna Hope Farm Netherwood	Pleasant Valley (v) Ruskey Salt Point Timothy Heights Tinkertown Wards Mill Washington Hollow	• Clark Heights on Pleasant Valley town line • Potters Corners on LaGrange town line • Village of Pleasant Valley inc. 1814 and dissolved 5/22/1926 • Washington Hollow formerly Pit(t)sburg(h) and Pit(t)sber(r)y; on Washington town line
Poughkeepsie (city) * **1799** Formed as a village in the Town of Poughkeepsie **1854** Incorporated as a city			* Poughkeepsie (hamlet, village, and city) has been the county seat since 1717; Kingston, Ulster County, was the county seat for Dutchess and Ulster counties 1684–1717
Poughkeepsie (town) * Part of Schuyler and Sanders & Harmanse patents **1660s** Settled by Dutch **1717** Made county seat **1719** Included in Middle Ward * **1737** Formed as Poughkeepsie precinct **1788** Precinct recognized as a town by the State of New York **1854** Daughter city Poughkeepsie formed from Village of Poughkeepsie	Arlington Barnegat Brewsters Corner Bulls Head Camelot Channingville Clark Heights Colonial Heights Crown Heights East Poughkeepsie Edamville Fairview Freertown Locust Glen	Macdonnell Heights Manchester Manchester Bridge New Hamburg(h) Poughkeepsie (v) Red Oaks Mill Rochdale Rudco Spackenkill Stoneco Van Keurens Van Wagner Wappingers Falls (v)	* Spelled Picipsi, Pokipsi, and Pooghkepesingh in early documents * Middle Ward, see note for 1719, Town of Amenia • Camelot formerly Milton Ferry and Lewis Ferry • Channingville in Village of Wappingers Falls • Clark Heights on Pleasant Valley town line • Manchester Bridge on LaGrange town line • New Hamburg(h) formerly Hook Landing and Wappingers Landing • Village of Poughkeepsie inc. 1799, became the City of Poughkeepsie in 1854; county seat from 1717 • Rochdale formerly Wippleville • Stoneco formerly Clinton Point • Village of Wappingers Falls inc. 1871; shared with Town of Fishkill until 1875 and Town of Wappinger after 1875
Red Hook Part of Schuyler Patent **1713–27** Settlements by Dutch **1812** Formed from Town of Rhinebeck	Anandale Annadale-on-Hudson Barrytown Barrytown Corners Cedar Hill Cokertown College Park Elmendorph Corner Fraleighs Kerleys Corners	Linden Acres Lower Red Hook Madalin Red Hook (v) Red Hook Mills Spring Lake(s) Spring Lake Station Tivoli (v) Upper Red Hook	• Barrytown formerly Lower Red Hook Landing • Lower Red Hook formerly Hardscrabble • Madalin formerly Mechanicsville and Myersville • Village of Red Hook inc. 1894 • Village of Tivoli inc. 1872; also Madalin, formerly Upper Red Hook Landing
Rhinebeck * Part of several small patents including Kipsburgh alias Rhinebeck **1713** Became known as Rhinebeck **1719** Included in North Ward * **1737** Formed as Rhinebeck precinct **1786** Ceded southern portion to Clinton precinct **1788** Recognized as a town by the State of New York **1812** Daughter town Red Hook formed	Eighmyville Ellerslie Kipsbergen Kirchehock Monterey Rhinebeck (v) Rhinebeck Flatts Rhinebeck Station Rhinecliff Weys Corners Würtemburg		* Rhinebeck spelled Rhinebeek, Reinebaik, and Ryn Beck in early documents * North Ward, see note for 1719, Town of Amenia • Village of Rhinebeck inc. 1834 • Weys Corners also Weys Crossing • Würtemburg formerly the Whitaberger Land

Towns (and Cities)	Villages and other Settlements		Notes
Rombout (patent and precinct) *			* See Town of Fishkill
Southeast * In Dutchess County 1772–1812			* See Putnam County
South(ern) (precinct) * Formed 1737 in Dutchess County, in 1722 it was divided into Phillips, Fredericksburgh, and Southeast precincts			* See Putnam County
Stanford Part of Great Nine Partners 1793　Formed from Town of 　　　Washington	Ansons Crossing Attlebury Bangall Hulls Mills Huns Lake Lenihan Market McIntyre	Old Attlebury Separate Stanfordville Stewarts Corner Stissing Upton Lake Willow Brook	• Market formerly Bare Market and Bear Market (Corner) • Stissing formerly Stissingville
Union Vale Part of Beekman Patent 1827　Formed mostly from Town of 　　　Beekman and partly from Town 　　　of Freedom (now LaGrange)	Camby Chestnut Ridge Clove Crouse(s) Store Hoxie Corner Lamoree Mansfield North Clove	Pleasant Ridge Potters Corners Quaker City Verbank Verbank Station Verbank Village Waterbury Hill	• Chestnut Ridge on Dover town line • Moores Mill also Moores Mills Station • Potters Corners on LaGrange town line • Waterbury Hill formerly Oswego Village, see Town of Beekman before 1821, and Town of Freedom (now LaGrange) 1821–1827 • Quaker City formerly part of Oswego
Wappinger Part of Rombout Patent 1875　Formed from Town of Fishkill	Castle Point Chelsea Didell Hughsonville Marlorville	Myers Corner(s) New Hackensack Swartoutville Wappingers Falls (v)	• Chelsea also Low Point or Carthage Landing • Didell, Hughsonville, Myers Corner(s), New Hackensack, and Swartoutville in Town of Fishkill before 1875 • Village of Wappingers Falls inc. 1871; shared with Town of Poughkeepsie
Washington Part of Great Nine Partners Patent 1719　Included in North Ward and 　　　Middle Ward * 1737　Part of new Crum Elbow precinct 1762　Part of new Charlotte precinct 1786　Formed as Washington precinct 　　　from Charlotte Precinct 1788　Precinct recognized as a town by 　　　the State of New York 1793　Daughter town Stanford formed	Coffins Summit Four Corners Lithgow Littlerest Mabbettsville Mechanic Millbrook (v)	Mutton Hollow Nine Partners Oak Summit Shunpike South Millbrook Washington Washington Hollow	* See note for 1719, Town of Amenia • Mabbettsville formerly Filkinville • Village of Millbrook inc. 1896; formerly Harts Village and Hartsville • South Millbrook formerly The Cross Roads, The Four Corners, and Washington Four Corners • Washington Hollow formerly Pit(t)- sburg(h) and Pit(t)sber(r)y; on Pleasant Valley town line

Notes about Dutchess County

Use of Dutchess County records before 1788 requires an understanding of the county's early subdivisions.

1683 County created, but sparsely populated and administered as part of Ulster County. County seat at Kingston. Thirteen patents granted to individuals, but little settlement.

1717 Dutchess County government established at Poughkeepsie

1719 Divided into North, Middle, and South wards, with boundaries set only along the Hudson where most of the population concentrated

1731 Narrow Oblong tract along eastern border, previously disputed with Connecticut, is ceded to New York and opened to settlement

1737 Wards replaced by precincts following many of the earlier patent boundaries and called Rhinebeck, North, Crum Elbow, Poughkeepsie, Rombout, Beekman, and South precincts

1743 Oblong tract divided between North, Crum Elbow, Beekman, and South precincts

1746–1786 Some precincts divided, re-divided, or renamed, as indicated in column one of the gazetteer

1788 Precincts converted into towns by New York State legislature

The first settlers were Dutch and other northern Europeans who settled along the Hudson. Beginning in 1709 they were joined, especially in the north, by Palatine Germans. All these people migrated east as land became available, and were joined by New Englanders moving west and English and Dutch families moving north from other New York counties.

Notes on Early Censuses and Lists

See O'Callaghan in Abstracts, Indexes & Transcriptions for 1714 and 1740 lists and 1755 census of slaves; Meyers for 1740 index; and Buck for tax lists 1718–1787.

See also *The Dutchess*, vol. 3, no. 3, for a list of inhabitants and slaves in 1714.

NEW YORK STATE CENSUS RECORDS

See also chapter 3, Census Records

County originals at Dutchess County Archives and Records Management: 1865, 1875, 1892, 1915, 1925 (1825, 1835, 1845, 1855, and 1905 are lost)

State originals at the NYSA: 1915, 1925

Microfilm at the FHL, NYPL, and NYSL; many years are online at *FamilySearch.org* and *Ancestry.com*.

NATIONAL/STATEWIDE REPOSITORIES & RESOURCES

See chapter 16

COUNTYWIDE REPOSITORIES & RESOURCES

Dutchess County Clerk

22 Market Street • Poughkeepsie, NY 12601 • (845) 486-2120
www.co.dutchess.ny.us

Court records, land records, maps 1822–present, marriage records 1908–1926 with indexes to 1935, divorce records (closed), naturalization records 1800–present. Most older records are kept at the Dutchess County Archives (see below) but accessed through the County Clerk's Research Room in this building.

Dutchess County – City, Town, and Village Clerks

Birth, marriage, and death records are maintained by the clerk of the municipality in which the event occurred; see Introduction to County Guides for details of other records which may also be held by municipal clerks. Contact information on clerks in Dutchess County at *www.co.dutchess.ny.us*.

Dutchess County Surrogate's Court

10 Market Street • Poughkeepsie, NY 12601 • (845) 431-1770

Holds probate records, early 1700s–present. The NYSA holds most probate records prior to 1787. Many probate records have been filmed and are accessible at *FamilySearch.org*; see Additional Online Resources. Abstracts have been published in *The Dutchess* and in books by Canfield, Cowen, Sypher, and others. See also chapter 6, Probate Records.

Dutchess County Archives & Records Management

170 Washington Street • Poughkeepsie, NY 12601 • (845) 486-3677

Documents stored at the archives include the state census for Dutchess County 1865, 1875, 1892, 1915, and 1925; the Supervisors tax lists 1717–1779; early county court records 1721–1862 including the Ancient Documents collection of loose case papers for the Court of Common Pleas, General Sessions, and 18th century court records—including arrest warrants, debts statements, bonds, naturalizations, and jury lists. Most of the court records have been microfilmed by the FHL and much is now online at *FamilySearch.org* (browsable images—not indexed). See *The Dutchess* for a surname index published in more than 50 installments, starting with vol. 21, no. 2. See Clifford Buck in bibliography for index for to 18th century tax lists. Requests to view the collections must be made at the County Clerk's Research Room on Market Street (see above).

Dutchess County Public Libraries

Dutchess is part of the Mid-Hudson Library System; see *www.midhudson.org* to access each library. Many hold genealogy and local history collections including maps and newspapers. For example, Grinnell Library Association, Howland Public Library, and Millbrook Free Library hold local history collections including photographs, and Amenia Free Library holds the *Harlem Valley Times*, 1913–1988 (with gaps). Also see listings below for Akin Free Library, Consortium of Rhinebeck History, and Poughkeepsie Public Library District.

Poughkeepsie Public Library District: Genealogy Room and Local History Room

Adriance Memorial Library • 93 Market Street
Poughkeepsie, NY 12601 • (845) 485-3445
Email access on website • *www.poklib.org*

Central library of the Mid-Hudson Library System. Local History Room and Genealogy Room hold collections 1700s–present and include books and periodicals; census materials; church records; histories and genealogies; immigration records; newspapers (*Poughkeepsie Journal*, 1785–present); maps; records of local organizations; obituary index; Supervisors tax lists microfilm (1717–1719); Ancient Documents on microfilm and the index published in *The Dutchess*. Access to the Local History Collection is by appointment only.

Dutchess County Historian

22 Market Street • Poughkeepsie, NY 12601 • (845) 486-2381
www.co.dutchess.ny.us/CountyGov/Departments/History/HSindex.htm

Works in conjunction with county clerk to help maintain and research county-level collections, including a rich collection of court records, tax rolls, deeds, etc. In-person research is conducted from the County Clerk's reading room. The historian will field inquiries from the general public, and help guide individuals to the correct county department or specialist when needed.

Dutchess County – All Municipal Historians

While not authorized to answer genealogical inquiries, city, town, and village historians can provide valuable historical information and research advice; some maintain collections and webpages which may include transcribed records, local histories, and other genealogical material. See contact information at *www.co.dutchess.ny.us* or at the website of the Association of Public Historians of New York State at *www.aphnys.org*.

Dutchess County Historical Society (DCHS)

The Clinton House • Franklin A. Butts Research Library
549 Main Street • PO Box 88 • Poughkeepsie, NY 12602
(845) 471-1630 • Library: Email: dchistorical@verizon.net
www.dutchesscountyhistoricalsociety.org

Materials date from the 1600s to the present and include Bible, cemetery, and church records; architecture and landscape survey of Dutchess County 1600s–1940; county and family histories; genealogy files; maps and atlases; Justice of the Peace records; photographs and postcards; wills; artifacts; and yearbooks. Its published Collections include church and cemetery records and newspaper extracts. The Society publishes the *DCHS Year Book* of local history scholarship, 1914–present, and the newsletter *Dutchess Historian*, 1976–present. Website has an index to journal articles, a description of holdings, and lists of local historians, historical societies, and historical sites.

Dutchess County Genealogical Society

204 Spackenkill Road • PO Box 708 • Poughkeepsie, NY 12602
(845) 462-4168 • Email: dcgsinfo@aol.com • *www.dcgs-gen.org*

The Society's library shares space with the local LDS Family History Center. Archival and published holdings include vital records; census microfilms; church records; cemetery transcriptions; immigration records; military records; tax lists; county, town, and village records; city directories; newspaper clippings; obituaries 1849–1949; records of Dutchess Quaker Meetings; family histories and biographies; gazetteers, atlases and maps; histories of Palatines and Huguenots; local histories of Dutchess and Putnam counties; reference books; research guides; and bibliographies. An extensive catalog of holdings is on the website. Publishes *The Dutchess*, 1973–present, a quarterly journal of essential genealogical information with indexes to state and federal census records and court records, including the Ancient Documents; transcribed town records; abstracts of vital records from churches, newspapers, Bibles, and family records; residency records from store ledgers, tax lists, and membership lists of churches. Accepts name search requests of its collections.

REGIONAL REPOSITORIES & RESOURCES

Bard College Archives and Special Collections

Stevenson Library Archives and Special Collections • One Library Road
Annandale-on-Hudson, NY 12504 • (845) 758-7396
Email: archives@bard.edu • *www.bard.edu/archives*

Categories include Hudson Valley Archives (local history materials), Tivoli Photograph Collection, historical journals, and Bard College history. Complete list of holdings available on website.

Franklin D. Roosevelt Presidential Library and Museum

4097 Albany Post Road • Hyde Park, NY 12538
(845) 486-7763 or (845) 486-7743
Email: Roosevelt.Library@nara.gov • *www.fdrlibrary.marist.edu*

Holdings include papers of the Hall, Delano, Livingston, and Roosevelt families; 17th–20th century papers on the Quackenbush, Van Gaasbeek, Van Wyck, Depew, DePeyster, and other families; the Coxsackie Town Record of Freeborn Slaves and some town records of New Paltz. A detailed finding aid is accessible at *www.fdrlibrary.marist.edu/archives/collections/pdfs/histmaterials.pdf*.

Historic Hudson Valley (HHV)

www.hudsonvalley.org

See full listing in Westchester County Guide. Holds papers related to the Delafield Family and their Montgomery Place estate.

Hudson River Valley Institute

Marist College • 3399 North Road • Poughkeepsie, NY 12601-1387
(845) 575-3052 • Email: hrvi@marist.edu • *www.hudsonrivervalley.org*

Publishes the semi-annual journal, *Hudson River Valley Review*, and manages a digital library of regional resources. Coverage area includes Albany, Columbia, Delaware, Dutchess, Fulton, Greene, Orange, Putnam, Rensselaer, Rockland, Saratoga, Schenectady, Sullivan, Ulster, Washington, and Westchester counties, as well as New York City. A menu of article, books, bibliographies, and historic documents is accessible on the website.

Princeton University: Firestone Library: Department of Rare Books and Special Collections

One Washington Road • Princeton, NJ 08544-2098 • (609) 258-4820
Email: rbsc@princeton.edu • *http://library.princeton.edu/libraries/firestone*

The Edward Livingston Papers collection contains extensive material pertaining to the Livingston, Beekman, Montgomery, Davezac, Barton, Hunt, and Delafield families, as well as John Cox, Jr. and Benjamin French, and their land holdings in Dutchess County. The Dyckman and Martine Family Papers also include material relevant to Dutchess County.

Vassar College Libraries: Archives & Special Collections

124 Raymond Avenue • PO Box 20 • Poughkeepsie, NY, 12604-0020
(845) 437-5799 • Email: spcoll@vassar.edu
http://specialcollections.vassar.edu/findingaids

Manuscript holdings include Dutchess County Loyalists Papers, 1776–1922; Federal Writers Project Records for Dutchess County; and various family papers, business records, correspondence, land records, and maps. Digital collections are accessible on the website.

LOCAL REPOSITORIES & RESOURCES

Alphabetized by location

Amenia Historical Society

Main Street • PO Box 22 • Amenia, NY 12501 • (845) 373-9376
Email addresses on website
http://ameniany.gov/community/historical-society.html

Books and pamphlets; information files; Amenia Precinct record book 1762–1800; Amenia District Poll Lists (District 1, 1876 and 1896; District 2, 1896); assessor's records 1860, 1870, 1880, 1890, 1900, 1910; Amenia Town Supervisor's Book 1888–1915; Amenia Precinct Book for the Poor 1760–1797; Town Clerk's Record Book 1755–1809; indentures 1799–1830; Town Accounts 1817–1820; mortgages 1850–1912; Registry of Electors 1894, 1900, 1910, 1911, 1914, 1915; and family files.

Beacon Historical Society

Howland Cultural Center • 477 Main Street • PO Box 89
Beacon, NY 12508 • (845) 831-0514
Email: info@beaconhistoricalsociety.org
www.beaconhistoricalsociety.org

Documents history of Beacon, Fishkill Landing, Matteawan, and surrounding areas. Website includes photographs. Monthly newsletter.

Town of Hyde Park Historical Society and Museum
4389 Albany Post Road (Route 9) • PO Box 182
Hyde Park, NY 12538 • (845) 229-2559
www.townofhydeparkny-historicalsociety.org

Holdings include local history artifacts and books. Society does not offer genealogical services but possesses some material that may be relevant to genealogy researchers.

Akin Free Library
97 Old Quaker Hill Road • Pawling, NY 12564 • (845) 855-5099
http://akinfreelibrary.blogspot.com

Holdings date from the 1700s and include family histories and genealogies, books and periodicals, land records and maps, rare books and ledgers, newspapers, photographs, and Quaker records (Quaker Hill, Oblong Monthly Meeting, and more).

The Historical Society of Quaker Hill and Pawling
John Kane House • 126 East Main Street • Pawling, NY 12562
(845) 855-5355 • *www.pawling-history.org*

The Society is custodian of three historic sites. Its research collections are held at the Akin Free Library (see above).

Little Nine Partners Historical Society (L9PHS)
PO Box 243 • Pine Plains, NY 12567 • Email: LNPHS@hotmail.com
www.rootsweb.ancestry.com/~nylnphs

The society documents the history of the Little (or Upper) Nine Partners Patent of 1706, which lies in the vicinity of Milan, Pine Plains and the northern part of Northeast. Holdings include Richter/Righter family papers, hotel registers, newspaper clippings, and vertical files. A catalog is on the website, as are a bibliography of research resources, select genealogies and histories, maps, and photographs. The society is custodian of the Historic Graham-Brush House. The website provides some information pertaining to the Great (or Lower) Nine Partners Patent of 1697 (Clinton, Pleasant Valley, Stanford, Washington, Amenia, Hyde Park beyond the Crum Elbow Creek, and the southern part of Northeast), but the society does not assist with research on this subject.

City of Poughkeepsie: City Clerk
62 Civic Center Plaza • Poughkeepsie, NY 12601 • (845) 451-4276
Email on website • *www.cityofpoughkeepsie.com/city-information/contact*

Holdings for the City of Poughkeepsie include birth and death records 1882–present and marriage records 1882–present.

Beekman Historical Society
Society: PO Box 235 • Poughquag, NY 12533 • Email: ush78@aol.com
www.beekmanhistory.com
Collections: Beekman Library • 11 Town Center Blvd.
Hopewell Junction, NY 12533 • (845) 724-3414
Email: beeklib@beekmanlibrary.org

The Society's collections are held at the Beekman Library and include vertical file of articles, clippings, programs, pamphlets, and copies of documents; maps; photographs; and the records of the Beekman Bicentennial Committee. The website is maintained by the town historian and has information on the town's history, historic sites, individuals, and cemetery transcriptions.

Egbert Benson Historical Society of Red Hook
7562 North Broadway • PO Box 397 • Red Hook, NY 12571-0397
(845) 758-1920 • Email: redhookhistory@gmail.com
www.redhookhistory.com

Maintains the Rosemary Coons Archives Room. Church records 1767–present, birth, death and marriage records 1860–1914,

cemetery records, and all the volumes on Palatine families of New York by Henry Z Jones.

Consortium of Rhinebeck History
Starr Library • 68 West Market Street • Rhinebeck, NY 12572-1419
(845) 876-4030 • Email: kinship@hvc.rr.com • *www.rhinebeckhistory.org*

This consortium of local history organizations operates a Local History and Genealogy Research Center at the Starr Library and manages a digital archives that is freely accessible on the website and draws from the collections of the DAR Livingston Chapter, Egbert Benson Historical Society, Museum of Rhinebeck History, Rhinebeck Historical Society, Rhinebeck Reformed Church, Rhinebeck Town Historian, Rhinebeck Town Records, Southlands Foundation, United Methodist Parish, and Wurtemburg Lutheran Church. Also online are searchable databases of cemetery records; Rhinebeck settlers and tenants; newspaper abstracts; maps; and postcards.

Rhinebeck Historical Society
Society: PO Box 291 • Rhinebeck, NY 12572
Email: info@rhinebeckhistoricalsociety.org
www.rhinebeckhistoricalsociety.org
Collections: Starr Library • 68 West Market Street
Rhinebeck, New York 12572 • (845) 876-4030
Email: kinship@hvc.rr.com

Holdings date from the 1700s and include books, maps, photographs, and town hall records. The society's collections are at the Local History and Genealogy Research Center at the Starr Library.

Wilderstein Historic Site: Library and Archives
330 Morton Road • PO Box 383 • Rhinebeck, NY 12572
(845) 876-4818 • Email: curator@wilderstein.org • *www.wilderstein.org*

Holdings range from the 1700s to the mid-1900s and include personal and business papers of the Suckley family, maps, indentures, architectural drawings, and photographs. Some material has been digitized and is accessible on the website. Research is by appointment only.

Mills Mansion State Historic Site, Archives
75 Mills Mansion Drive • Staatsburg, NY 12580 • (845) 889-8851
http://millsmansion.org

The historic mansion and its grounds are preserved as a history museum and state park. Archival holdings include papers related to the Livingston, Lewis, and Beekman families.

Wappingers Historical Society and Brewer-Mesier Homestead
7 East Main Street, Junction Route 9D • PO Box 174
Wappingers Falls, NY 12590 • (845) 430-9520
Email: info@wappingershistoricalsociety.org
www.wappingershistoricalsociety.org

Website includes local history articles and digitized historic photographs.

PRINT & ONLINE RESOURCES
Below is a selection of resources relevant for research in this borough. The list is representative, not exhaustive. Additional titles—particularly of abstracts, indexes, transcriptions, and local histories—are available; consult the introduction to Part Two for further information. For guidance on how to identify and locate community directories and local newspapers, see chapter 11, City Directories, and chapter 12, Newspapers, in Part One of this book.

Abstracts, Indexes & Transcriptions
Baldwin, Evelyn Briggs. "Dutchess County (N.Y.) Cemetery Inscriptions." Typescript, n.d. NYPL, New York. With an index by Beverly Kane. [FHL microfilm]

Barber, Gertrude A. "Index of Wills of Dutchess County, New York: 1812–1832." Typescript, 1950. [*Ancestry.com*]

———. "Index of Wills of Dutchess County, New York: 1834–1839." Typescript, 1944. NYPL, New York.

Buck, Clifford M., and William McDermott. *Eighteenth-Century Documents of the Nine Partners Patent, Dutchess County, New York.* Vol. 10, Collections of the Dutchess County Historical Society. Baltimore: Gateway Press, 1979.

Buck, Clifford M., Arthur C. M. Kelly, and William W. Reese. *Dutchess County, New York, Tax Lists, 1718–1787: With Rombout Precinct by William Willis Reese.* Rhinebeck, NY: Kinship Books, 1990. Index to the tax lists for all wards and precincts.

Buys, Barbara Smith. *Old Gravestones of Putnam County, New York, Together with Information from Ten Adjacent Dutchess County Burying Grounds: Eleven Thousand Eight Hundred Inscriptions of Persons Born up to and Including 1850.* Baltimore: Gateway Press, 1975. Index available from Berkshire Family History Association.

Canfield, Amos. "Abstracts of Wills Recorded at Poughkeepsie, Dutchess Co., New York." *NYG&B Record,* vol. 61 (1930) no. 1: 6–13, no. 2: 119–126, no. 3: 257–263, no. 4: 381–386; vol. 62 (1931) no. 1: 58–59. Covers Libers A and AA (1752–1805)." [NYG&B eLibrary]

Cowen, Minnie. "Abstracts of Wills of Dutchess County, New York." 13 vols. 1752–1839. Typescript, 1939–1941. [*Ancestry.com*]

Daughters of the American Revolution, comps. *New York DAR Genealogical Records Committee Report.* Since 1913 DAR volunteers have transcribed many thousands of unpublished cemetery, church, and town records throughout New York. The reports are at the DAR Library; copies are at the NYSL and the NYPL. The DAR has a searchable name index to all the GRC reports at *http://services.dar.org/Public/DAR_Research/search/?Tab_ID=6.* See Jean Worden's index below for a listing by county of the New York record sets that were transcribed by the DAR before 1998.

Daughters of the American Revolution. Enoch Crosby Chapter, Helen G. Daniels, Florence D. Hopkins, and Harriet Akin Ferris. "Historical Records of Enoch Crosby Chapter; Putnam, Dutchess and Westchester Counties, New York." 3 vols. Typescript, 1944–1959. DAR Library, Washington, DC. Includes indexes. [Microfilm at FHL]

Doherty, Frank J. "Col. Jacobus Swartwout's Dutchess County Regiment of Minute Men." *NYG&B Record,* vol. 120 (1989) no. 2: 65–71, no. 3: 165–169, no. 4: 226–228; vol. 121 (1990) no. 1: 38–45, no. 2: 83–86, no. 3: 153–156, no. 4: 212–215. [NYG&B eLibrary]

Dutchess County. "Ancient Documents (Dutchess County, New York), 1721–ca. 1862." Manuscript of original records in the Dutchess County Courthouse. Poughkeepsie, New York. [Microfilm FHL] Online at *FamilySearch.org.* Includes probate records, warrants for arrest, court cases, statements of debt, and bonds.

Dutchess County. *Book of the Supervisors of Dutchess County, N.Y. A.D. 1718–1722.* Poughkeepsie, NY, 1907.

Dutchess County. *Old Miscellaneous Records of Dutchess County (the Second Book of the Supervisors and Assessors).* Poughkeepsie, NY: Vassar Brothers Institute, 1909. Apprentices contracts, assessor's assessments (tax lists for three wards 1718–1736), administration, elections, treasurers' receipts, roads, supervisors' proceedings, wills, Great Nine Partners Patent documents, and more. Index available from Berkshire Family History Association.

Dutchess County Historical Society. *Collections of the Dutchess County Historical Society.* 13 vols. Poughkeepsie, NY: The Society, 1924–1992. Record abstracts include gravestone transcriptions; town records for Clinton and Hyde Park; newspaper notices of marriages and deaths; Reformed Dutch Church (Hackensack) records; Nine Partners Patent, Rombout Patent and Precinct, Town of Fish Kill, and Crum Elbow Precinct.

Earderley, William Applebie. "Dutchess County, New York, Cemeteries: 1733–1907." Typescript, 1917. NYPL, New York. [Microfilm at various libraries] Book includes marriage notices, church records, and other material.

Fisher, Floyd. *They All Rest Together: Burial Sites of Early Settlers—Southern Dutchess and Putnam Counties.* Holmes, NY: n.p., 1972.

Frost, Josephine C. *Quaker Meeting Records, State of New York: Ulster County, Columbia County, Albany County, Clinton County.* Brooklyn: The Author, n.d. Includes Dutchess County records of the Oblong Monthly Meeting (Quaker Hill), Nine Partners Monthly Meeting (Washington), and the Creek Monthly Meeting (Clinton). [*books. FamilySearch.org*]

Grundset, Eric G. "Officials of Poughkeepsie Precinct, Dutchess County, New York, 1775–1783." *NYG&B Record,* vol. 143, no.2 (2012): 147–153. [NYG&B eLibrary]

Herrick, Margaret E. *Marriage Notices, Dutchess and Columbia County, New York, 1859–1936, Compiled from the Red Hook Journal, Red Hook Times-Journal, Red Hook Advertiser, and Rhinebeck Gazette.* Rhinebeck, NY: Kinship, 1991.

Kelly, Arthur C. M. *Dutchess County, NY, Probate Records, 1787–1865: Registers of Wills and Letters Testamentary and of Administration in the Surrogate's Office, Poughkeepsie, NY.* Rhinebeck, NY: Kinship, 1997. Index of wills and letters of administration.

———. *Early Records of Matteawan Methodist Church, Beacon, Dutchess County, N.Y., 1862–1920: Members 1862–1920.* Rhinebeck, NY: Kinship, 2006.

———. *Early Records of North East Baptist Church, Millerton, New York, Dutchess County, 1751–1910.* Rhinebeck, NY: Kinship, 2008.

———. *Marriage Record of the Four Reformed Congregations of Old Rhinebeck, Dutchess County, New York, 1731–1899.* Rhinebeck, NY: Kinship, 1971.

———. *Records of Lutheran Churches of Rhinebeck, Dutchess County, NY Area: Members, Confirmands, & Family Lists, 1734–1889.* Rhinebeck, NY: Kinship, 2000.

———. *Red Hook Undertaker's Records, Dutchess County, NY, 1874–1936.* Rhinebeck, NY: Kinship, 1999.

———. *Vital Records of Presbyterian Church, Pleasant Valley, New York, Dutchess County, 1793–1947: Baptisms 1793–1830, 1869–1947: Marriages 1793–1947.* Rhinebeck, NY: Kinship, 2007.

———. *Vital Records of Smithfield Presbyterian Church, Amenia, Dutchess County, NY, 1787–1942: Baptisms 1810–1937, Marriages 1823–1891, Deaths 1890–1893, Members 1787–1942.* Rhinebeck, NY: Kinship, 2004.

Koehler, Linda. *Dutchess County, New York, Churches and Their Records, an Historical Directory.* Rhinebeck, NY: Kinship, 1994. Churches listed by denomination and chronology of Dutchess County patents and civil divisions.

Losee, John. *Death Notices, Dutchess and Columbia County, New York, from Red Hook Newspapers*. Rhinebeck, NY: Kinship, 1992.

Meyers, Carol M. *Early New York State Census Records, 1663–1772*. Gardena, CA: RAM Publishers, 1965. Has an index to the 1740 census.

New York Genealogical and Biographical Society. "Baptisms of the Dutch Reformed Church of Rhinebeck, Dutchess County, New York." *NYG&B Record*, vol. 94 (1963) no. 1: 51–54; vol. 96 (1965) no. 1: 28–39. [NYG&B eLibrary]

New York Genealogical and Biographical Society. "Baptisms of the Dutch Reformed Church of Rhinebeck Flats, Dutchess County, New York." *NYG&B Record*, vol. 84 (1953) no. 1: 40–52; vol. 88 (1957) no. 1: 22–34. [NYG&B eLibrary]

New York Genealogical and Biographical Society. "Baptisms of the German Reformed Church of Rhinebeck, Now St. Paul's Lutheran Church, Red Hook, N.Y." *NYG&B Record*, vol. 96 (1965), no. 2: 102–115; vol. 100 (1969) no. 2: 119–122, no. 3: 154–160. [NYG&B eLibrary]

O'Callaghan, Edmund B. *Documentary History of the State of New York*. 4 vols. Albany, 1849–1851. Vol. 1: 368–369, list of inhabitants and slaves, 1714; vol. 4: 205–208, list of freeholders, 1740; vol. 3: 851–852, 1755 census of slaves.

Poucher, J. Wilson, and Helen W. Reynolds. *Old Gravestones of Dutchess County, New York: Nineteen Thousand Inscriptions*. 1924. Vol. 2 of Collections of the Dutchess County Historical Society. [books.FamilySearch.org] Reprinted with new index, Poughkeepsie, NY: Dutchess County Historical Society, 1998.

Reynolds, Helen W. *Notices of Marriages and Deaths, about 4,000 in Number, Published in Newspapers Printed at Poughkeepsie, New York, 1778–1825*. Vol. 4 of Collections of the Dutchess County Historical Society. Poughkeepsie, NY: The Society, 1930. Index available from Berkshire Family History Association.

Roosevelt, Franklin D., ed. *Records of Crum Elbow Precinct: Dutchess County, New York, 1738–1761, Together with Records of Charlotte Precinct, 1762–1785, Records of Clinton Precinct, 1786–1788, and Records of the Town of Clinton, 1789–1799*. Vol. 3 of Collections of the Dutchess County Historical Society. Poughkeepsie, NY: The Society, 1928.

St. Paul's Lutheran Church (Wurtemburg, New York). "Records of the Evangelical Lutheran Church called St. Paul's in Wurtemburg, Rhinebeck, Dutchess County, State of New York, 1760–1874." Manuscript photocopy. NYSL, Albany, NY. [Microfilm at FHL]

Spies, Francis Ferdinand. "Inscriptions from Quaker Burying Grounds with Notes: Purchase, West Chester Co; Chappaqua, West Chester Co.; Pawling, Dutchess Co. (Quaker Hill); Bethel, Dutchess Co., Index." Typescript, 1923. [Ancestry.com]

Tower, Maria Bockée Carpenter, ed. *The Records of the Reformed Dutch Church of New Hackensack, Dutchess County, New York*. Vol. 5 of Collections of the Dutchess County Historical Society. Poughkeepsie, NY: The Society, 1932.

Van Alstyne, L. *Burying Grounds of Sharon, CT, Amenia and Northeast, NY: Abstract of Inscriptions from 30 Places of Burial*. Interlaken, NY: Heart of the Lakes Publishing, 1983. First published 1903 by Walsh, Griffen & Hoysradt, Printers.

Vosburgh, Royden Woodward, ed. *Round Top Lutheran Church in the Town of Pine Plains, Dutchess County, NY*. Transcribed and published by the New York Genealogical and Biographical Society, 1921.

Reprinted with an introduction by Isaac Hunnting in the *NYG&B Record*, vol. 114 (1983) no. 2: 66–69, no. 3: 164–172, no. 4: 216–220. [NYG&B eLibrary]

Wheeler, Glendon E. *Town Records: Frederickstown to Kent, 1788–1841, Dutchess/Putnam Counties, New York*. Rhinebeck, NY: Kinship, 2002.

Other Resources

Bailey, Henry D. B. *Dutchess County: Local Tales and Historical Sketches*. Fishkill Landing, NY, 1874.

Commemorative Biographical Record of the Counties of Dutchess and Putnam, New York: Containing Biographical Sketches of Prominent and Representative Citizens and of Many of the Early Settled Families. 2 vols. Chicago: J. H. Beers, 1897.

Conklin, Henry S. "Maps of Lots Sold by the New York Commissioners of Forfeitures, 1779–1786." Drafted by Henry Conklin, 1885, held by the Putnam County Historian, Brewster, NY.

Doherty, Frank J. *The Settlers of the Beekman Patent, Dutchess County, New York: An Historical and Genealogical Study of All the 18th-Century Settlers in the Patent*. 11 vols., ongoing. Boston: New England Historic Genealogical Society, 1990–2013. [www.beekmansettlers.com]

Dutchess County Genealogical Society. *The Dutchess*. Poughkeepsie, NY: The Society, 1973–present.

Dutchess County Historical Society. *Year Book*. Poughkeepsie, NY: The Society, 1914–present. An annual publication of scholarship on local history.

Fay, Loren V. *Dutchess County, New York, Genealogical Research Secrets*. Albany: L.V. Fay, 1984.

Finkel, Charlotte C. "Some Sources for Research on the History of Southern Dutchess County, New York." Typescript, 1962. [Ancestry.com]

Fredriksen, Beatrice. *The Role of Dutchess County during the American Revolution*. Poughkeepsie, NY: The Author, 1976.

Ghee, Joyce C., et al. *Transformations of an American County: Dutchess County, New York, 1683–1983: Papers of the Tercentenary Conference, April 23 and 24, 1983*. Poughkeepsie, NY: Published by Dutchess County Historical Society on Behalf of the Dutchess County Tercentenary Advisory Committee, et al., 1986.

Goldin, Eva Effron Acker. *The Jewish Community of Poughkeepsie, New York: An Anecdotal History*. Poughkeepsie, NY: Maar Print Service, 1982.

Herrick, Margaret E. *Early Settlements in Dutchess County, New York*. Rhinebeck, NY: Kinship, 1994.

Historical and Genealogical Record, Dutchess and Putnam Counties, New York. Poughkeepsie, NY: Oxford Publishing, 1912.

Hudson River Valley Institute at Marist College. *Hudson River Valley Review: A Journal of Regional Studies*. Poughkeepsie, NY: The Institute, 2002–present. [hudsonrivervalley.org]

Koehler, Linda C. *Dutchess County, NY, Churches and Their Records: An Historical Directory*. Rhinebeck, NY: Kinship, 1994.

MacCracken, Henry N. *Blithe Dutchess, the Flowering of an American County from 1812*. New York: n.p., 1958.

———. *Old Dutchess Forever! The Story of an American County*. New York: Hastings House, 1956.

Matthieu, Samuel A., and Frank Hasbrouck. *The History of Dutchess County, New York*. Poughkeepsie, NY: S. A. Matthieu, 1909. Index available from Berkshire Family History Association.

McDermott, William P. "Colonial Land Grants in Dutchess County, NY: A Case Study in Settlement." In *Hudson Valley Regional Review*. vol. 3.(September 1986) no. 2.

———. *Dutchess County's Plain Folks: Enduring Uncertainty, Inequality, and Uneven Prosperity, 1725–1875*. Clinton Corners, NY: Kerleen Press, 2004.

Morse, Howard H. *Historic Old Rhinebeck: Echoes of Two Centuries: A Hudson River and Post Road Colonial Town: When, Where, and by Whom Settled and Named, the Whys and the Wherefores, Who's Who and Was*. Rhinebeck, NY: The Author, 1908.

New York Genealogical and Biographical Society. *Dutchess County Church Surveys*. Digitally published by New York Genealogical and Biographical Society, 2012. Identifies records held by eleven churches in Dutchess County, ca. 1900. [NYG&B eLibrary]

New York Historical Resources Center. *Guide to Historical Resources in Dutchess County, New York, Repositories*. Ithaca, NY: Cornell University, 1990. [*books.FamilySearch.org*]

Polk's Poughkeepsie (Dutchess County, NY) City Directory . . . Including Arlington and Fairview: Containing an Alphabetical Directory of Business Concerns and Private Citizens, a Directory of Householders, Occupants of Office Buildings and Other Business Places, Including a Complete Street and Avenue Guide, and Much Information of a Miscellaneous Character: Also a Buyers' Guide and Complete Classified Business Directory. Boston: R. L. Polk, 1936–1948.

Reed, Thomas H. *Map of Putnam County*. Carmel, NY, 1876.

Smith, James H. *History of Duchess [sic] County, New York: With Illustrations and Biographical Sketches of Some of Its Prominent Men and Pioneers*. Syracuse, NY: D. Mason, 1882. Index published by Heart of the Lakes Publishing, 1980. [*FamilySearch.org*]

Smith, Philip H. *General History of Dutchess County from 1609 to 1876 Inclusive*. Pawling, NY, 1877.

Swain, Charles B. *Toward Equal Partnership: Black History in Dutchess County, 1683–1983*. Poughkeepsie, NY: Mid-Hudson Library System, Resource Center for Library Materials and Services, 1983.

Town of Stanford. "Town Book, Town of Stanford, Dutchess County, New York, 1793–1825." Typescript (carbon copy). NYPL, New York. [Microfilm at FHL]

United States. Census Office. *Special Schedules of the 11th Census (1890) Enumerating Union Veterans and Widows of Union Veterans of the Civil War New York, Bundle 109 (Columbia, Dutchess, Putnam, and Westchester Counties)*. Washington: National Archives, 1948.

Zimm, Louise Hasbrouck. *Southeastern New York: History of the Counties of Ulster, Dutchess, Orange, Rockland, and Putnam*. 3 vols. New York: Lewis Historical Publishing, 1946.

Additional Online Resources

Ancestry.com

There are vast numbers of records on *Ancestry.com* that pertain to people who have lived in New York State. See chapter 16 for a description of *Ancestry.com*'s resources and its partnership with the New York State Archives. A search of the online card catalog by county may reveal lesser known resources that pertain to a locality, such as town records, abstracts, transcriptions, city directories, and local histories.

FamilySearch.org

FamilySearch has extensive collections of New York records, including religious records, which are searchable by name and location, but not by county. The following collections include record images (browsable, but not searchable) that are organized by county:

- "New York, Land Records, 1630–1975." Includes land and property records. *familysearch.org/search/collection/2078654*

- "New York, Probate Records, 1629–1971." Includes wills, letters of administration, and guardianship papers. *familysearch.org/search/collection/1920234*

For both collections, choose the browse option and then select Dutchess to view the available records sets. The Wiki on Cemetery Abstracts for Dutchess County New York is very comprehensive *https://familysearch.org/learn/wiki/en/Cemetery_Abstracts_for_Dutchess_county_New_York*. A detailed description of *FamilySearch.org* resources is in chapter 16.

Hudson River Valley Heritage (HRVH)

www.hrvh.org/cdm

The HRVH website provides free access to digital collections of historical material from more than 40 organizations in Columbia, Greene, Dutchess, Ulster, Sullivan, Rockland, Orange, Putnam, and Westchester counties.

Kinship Books

www.kinshipny.com

Based in Rhinebeck and operated by Arthur C. M. Kelly, a prolific transcriber of New York records, Kinship Books has published more than 130 volumes of church, cemetery, newspaper, town, and other records. Dutchess County is extensively covered, and only a few representative titles have been included in this bibliography; a catalog is on the website.

New York Heritage Digital Collections:
New York State Newspaper Project

www.nyheritage.org/newspapers

The website provides links to digital newspapers collections in 26 counties (currently) made accessible through New York Heritage, New York State Historic Newspapers, HRVH Historical Newspapers, and other providers.

NYGenWeb Project: Dutchess County

www.usgennet.org/usa/ny/county/dutchess

Part of the national, USGenWeb volunteer initiative, the website provides information and resources for county research.

Old Fulton New York Postcards

www.FultonHistory.com

The website provides free access to a vast collection of digitized New York newspapers, including 16 titles for Dutchess County.

Erie County

Formed April 2, 1821

Parent County Niagara
Daughter Counties None
County Seat City of Buffalo

Major Land Transactions
See chapter 7, Land Records
Holland Land Company Purchase 1792–1796

Indian Territories
See chapter 14, Peoples of New York, American Indian
Seneca Nation: Cattaraugus Reservation (1797–present)
Tonawanda Band of Seneca Indians: Tonawanda Reservation (1797–present)

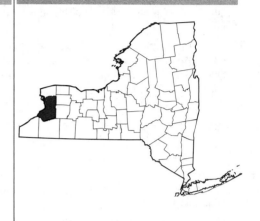

Town Boundary Map
★ - County seat

Towns (and Cities)	Villages and other Settlements	Notes
Alden 1810 Settled 1823 Formed from Town of Clarence 1853 Daughter town Marilla formed	Alden (v) Alden Center Crittenden Dellwood Mill Grove Peters Corners Reservation Town Line Town Line Station Wende West Alden West Wende	• Village of Alden incorporated by special charter in 1869 and reincorporated under village law in 1949 • Town Line and Town Line Station on Lancaster town line
Amherst 1804 Settlers from Massachusetts 1818 Formed in Niagara County from Town of Buffalo 1821 Transferred to new county of Erie 1839 Daughter town Chicktowaga (Cheektowaga) formed	Amherst Audubon East Amherst Eggertsville Getzville Jewettville North Bailey Snyder Sworm(s)ville West Amherst Westwood Williamsville (v)	• East Amherst also Transit Station; on Clarence town line • Snyder formerly Snyderville • Sworm(s)ville on Clarence town line • Village of Williamsville inc. 1850; shared with Town of Cheektowaga
Aurora 1803 Settled 1804 Formed in Genesee County as Willink from Town of Batavia 1808 Transferred to new county of Niagara; daughter towns Cambria and Clarence formed 1812 Daughter towns Concord, Eden, and Hamburgh formed 1818 Name changed from Willink to Aurora; daughter towns Holland and Wales formed 1821 Transferred to new county of Erie 1857 Daughter town Elma formed	Auroraville Blakeley East Aurora (v) Griffins Mills Jewettville South Wales West Falls Willink (v)	• Blakely also Osborn • Village of East Aurora inc. 1874; also see Willink • Griffins Mills formerly Smiths Mills • South Wales on Wales town line • Village of Willink reincorporated as Village of East Aurora in 1874; Willink p.o. continued until 1913
Black Rock 1839–1853 1839 Town of Buffalo, including the Village of Black Rock, reorganized as Town of Black Rock * 1853 Town of Black Rock became part of Buffalo City by charter	Black Rock (v) Eleysville	* Most of the Town of Buffalo had become the City of Buffalo seven years earlier • Village of Black Rock (formerly Buffalo Creek) incorporated in Town of Buffalo 1837; transferred to Town of Black Rock in 1839
Boston 1803 Settled 1817 Formed in Niagara County from Town of Eden 1821 Transferred to new county of Erie	Boston Creekside East Boston Hill North Boston Patchin	• Patchin also Boston Center and Boston Corners
Bran(d)t 1817 Settled 1839 Formed from towns of Collins and Evans	Bran(d)t Farnham (v) Irving Mill Branch	• Bran(d)t formerly Morses Corners and Samptown • Village of Farnham inc. 1892; formerly Saw Mill Station
Buffalo (city) * 1832 Incorporated as a city from part of Town of Buffalo including Village of Buffalo 1853 Town of Black Rock added to city by charter	Allentown Black Rock Buffalo Buffalo Plains Cold Springs Delevan East Buffalo Elmwood Village Fort Porter Hertel Kaisertown Kensington Lovejoy North Buffalo Old First Ward Polonia Red Jacket	* County seat from 1821 (village then city) when Erie County was formed; formerly county seat for Niagara County 1808–21 • Lovejoy also Iron Island

Towns (and Cities)	Villages and other Settlements		Notes
Buffalo (town) 1810–1839 1801 Laid out by the Holland Land Company called New Amsterdam 1808 New Amsterdam made county seat of Niagara County and name changed to Buffalo 1810 Formed in Niagara County as Town of Buffalo from Town of Clarence 1818 Daughter town Amherst formed 1821 Transferred to new county of Erie 1832 Part of the town, and the Village of Buffalo, incorporated as City of Buffalo 1836 Daughter town Tonawanda formed 1839 Remaining part of the town organized as Town of Black Rock	Black Rock (v) Buffalo (v) Springville		• Village of Black Rock (formerly Buffalo Creek) incorporated in Town of Buffalo 1837; transferred to Town of Black Rock 1839, becomes part of City of Buffalo 1853 • Village of Buffalo incorporated in Niagara County in 1813 and 1815; county seat from 1821; incorporated in Erie County 1822; Village of Buffalo becomes large part of the new City of Buffalo 1832
Cheektowaga * 1808 Settled 1839 Formed from Town of Amherst 1851 Daughter town West Seneca formed	Bellevue Cheektowaga Cleveland Hill Depew (v) Doyle Forks Four Mile Creek Haywood	Maryvale Pine Hill Sloan (v) South Cheektowaga U-Crest Walden Williamsville (v)	* Cheektowaga also Chictawauga and Chicktowaga • Village of Depew inc. 1894; shared with Town of Lancaster • Village of Sloan inc. 1896 • Village of Williamsville inc. 1850; shared with Town of Amherst
Clarence 1799 Settled at Clarence Hollow 1808 Formed in Niagara County from Town of Willink (now Aurora) 1810 Daughter town Buffalo created 1821 Transferred to new county of Erie 1823 Daughter town Alden created 1833 Daughter town Lancaster created	Clarence Clarence Center East Amherst East Clarence Harris Hill Hunts Corner(s) Mansfield Corners Millersport	North Clarence Rapids Shimmerville Smiths Corners Snearly Corners Sturnerville Sworm(s)ville Wolcott(s)burg	• Clarence also Clarence Hollow, Ransomville, and The Hollow • Clarence Center formerly Van Tines Corners • East Amherst formerly Transit Station; on Amherst town line • Sworm(s)ville on Amherst town line • Wolcott(s)burg formerly West Prussia
Colden 1810 Settled 1827 Formed from Town of Holland	Colden Glenwood		• Colden formerly Buffums Mills
Collins 1806 Settled at Taylors Hollow 1821 Formed from Town of Concord 1839 Daughter town Bran(d)t formed 1852 Daughter Town of Shirley formed (renamed North Collins 1853)	Angola Babbitch Corners Bagdad Black Hills Collins Collins Center Gowanda (v) Hide	Hutzenlaub Hill Iroquois Newton Taylor Hollow Tubtown Versailles Whites Corners Zoar	• Gowanda formerly Aldrichs Mills and Lodi; Village of Gowanda inc. 1848; shared with Town of Persia, Cattaraugus County; reincorporated 1878 to include Hide
Concord 1807 Settled 1812 Formed in Niagara County from Town of Willink (now Aurora) 1821 Transferred to new county of Erie; daughter towns Collins and Sardinia formed	Cascade Park Concord Concord Center East Concord Footes Fowlerville Hakes Bridge	Kahes Bridge Morton(s) Corners Springville (v) Waterville Corners Wheeler Hollow Woodside Wyandale	• Village of Springville inc. 1834 • Wyandale formerly Woodwards Hollow

Towns (and Cities)	Villages and other Settlements		Notes
East Hamburg(h) Name for Town of Orchard Park 1852–1934			
Eden 1809 Settled 1812 Formed in Niagara County from Town of Willink (now Aurora) 1817 Daughter town Boston formed 1821 Transferred to new county of Erie; daughter town Evans formed	Clarksburg(h) East Eden Eden Eden Valley Hills Corners Zoar		• Clarksburg(h) formerly Tubbs Hollow
Ellicott Name for Town of Orchard Park 1850–1852			
Elma 1857 Formed from towns of Aurora and Lancaster	Billington Heights Blossom Blossoms Mills East Elma Elma Elma Center	Jamison Jamison Road Jamison Station Spring Brook Spring Brook Station	• Blossom formerly Upper Ebenezer; on West Seneca town line • East Elma formerly Hemstreets Mills
Erie Name for Town of Newstead 1804–1831			
Evans 1804 Settled 1821 Formed from Town of Eden 1826 Annexed land from Town of Hamburgh 1839 Daughter town Bran(d)t formed	Angola (v) Angola-on-the-Lake Camp Lakeland Camp Pioneer Derby East Evans Evans Evans Beach Park Evans Center	Evans Center Station Grandview Bay Highland-on-the-Lake Jerusalem Corners Lake Erie Beach North Evans Pontiac Sturgeon Point St. Vincent de Paul	• Village of Angola inc. 1873 • Highland-on-the-Lake on Hamburg town line
Grand Island Settled before the War of 1812 1852 Formed from Town of Tonawanda	Ferry Village Grand Island Grandyle Village	Sheenwater White Haven	
Hamburg(h) 1812 Formed in Niagara County from Town of Willink (now Aurora) 1821 Transferred to new county of Erie 1826 Ceded land to Town of Evans 1850 Daughter town Ellicott (now Orchard Park) formed 1851 Daughter town Seneca (now West Seneca) formed	Abbott Road Station Abbott(s) Corners Amsdell Heights Armor Athol Springs Barkersville Bay View Bethford Big Tree Big Tree Corners Blasdell (v) Carnegie Clifton Heights Clover Bank Deerfield Heights Dewells Corners East Hamburgh Grand View Park Hamburg (v) Hamburg(h)-on-(the)-Lake Highland-on-the-Lake	Idlewood Idlewood Station Lake Shore Road Lake View Locksley Park Mount Vernon Mount Vernon-on-the-Lake New Scranton North Evans Pinehurst Roundtree Scranton Shaleton Walden Cliffs Wanakah Water Valley Weyer Willow Run Windom Woodlawn	• Armor on Orchard Park town line • Village of Blasdell inc. 1898 • Village of Hamburg inc. 1874; formerly Smiths Mills and Smithville; also Whites Corners • Hamburg(h)-on-(the)-Lake also West Hamburgh • Highland-on-the-Lake on Evans town line • Windom on Orchard Park town line • Woodlawn also Woodlawn Beach

Towns (and Cities)	Villages and other Settlements		Notes
Holland 1807 Settled 1818 Formed in Niagara County from Town of Willink (now Aurora) 1821 Transferred to new county of Erie 1827 Daughter town Colden formed	Coopers Mills Dutchtown East Holland Holland Protection		• Protection on Sardinia town line
Lackawanna (city) 1909 Incorporated as a city from Town of West Seneca			
Lancaster 1803 Settled 1833 Formed from Town of Clarence 1851 Daughter town Seneca (now West Seneca) formed 1857 Daughter town Elma formed	Bowmansville Dellwood Depew (v) East Lancaster Lancaster (v) Looneyville	Pavement Town Line Town Line Station Wilhelm Winspear	• Dellwood also Looneyville Station • Village of Depew inc. 1894; shared with Town of Cheektowaga • Village of Lancaster inc. 1849 • Town Line and Town Line Station on Alden town line
Marilla 1853 Formed from towns of Alden and Wales	Bush Gardens Iron Bridge Marilla	Porterville Williston	• Portville formerly Bartoos Mills and Shanty Town
Newstead 1804 Formed in Genesee County as Town of Erie from Town of Batavia 1808 Transferred to new county of Niagara 1821 Transferred to new county of Erie 1831 Name changed to Newstead	Akron (v) Akron Junction Falkirk Hawkins Corners Murrays Corner Sand Hill South Newstead Swift Mills		• Village of Akron inc. 1849
North Collins 1809 Settled 1852 Formed as Town of Shirley from Town of Collins 1853 Name changed to North Collins	Langford Lawtons Marshfield New Oregon	North Collins (v) Shirley West Branch	• Langford also Sippels Corners • Lawtons also Lawtons Station • Village of North Collins inc. 1911; also Kerrs Corners and Roses Corner
Orchard Park 1803 Settled 1850 Formed as Town of Ellicott from Town of Hamburgh 1851 Daughter town Seneca (now West Seneca) formed 1852 Name changed to East Hamburgh; later spelled East Hamburg 1934 Name changed to Orchard Park	Armor Duells Corner Ellicott Loveland Orchard Park (v) Webster Corners Windom		• Armor on Hamburg town line • Village of Orchard Park inc. 1921; formerly Potters Corners • Windom on Hamburg town line
Sardinia 1809 Settlers from Vermont 1821 Formed from Town of Concord	Chaffee Glenwood Johnstons Corners Matteson Corners Pratham	Protection Sardinia Scott Corners Shepards Corners	• Protection on Holland town line • Sardinia also Colegroves Corners
Shirley Name for Town of North Collins 1852–1853			

Towns (and Cities)	Villages and other Settlements		Notes
Tonawanda (city) 1903 Incorporated as a city from Village of Tonawanda in Town of Tonawanda	Bushes Bridge Tonawanda		
Tonawanda (town) 1805 Settled 1836 Formed from Town of Buffalo 1852 Daughter town Grand Island formed 1903 Daughter city Tonawanda formed	Brighton Green Acres Valley Kenilworth Kenmore (v) Midway	Old Town Parkview Sheridan Parkside Tonawanda (v)	• Village of Kenmore inc. 1899 • Village of Tonawanda inc. 1853; (included North Tonawanda, Town of Wheatfield, Niagara County 1853–1857); became City of Tonawanda 1903
Wales 1805 Settled 1818 Formed in Niagara county from Town of Willink (now Aurora) 1821 Transferred to new county of Erie 1853 Daughter town Marilla formed	Colegrave South Wales Wales Wales Center Wales Hollow		• South Wales on Aurora town line • Wales Center also Halls Center
West Seneca 1851 Formed as Town of Seneca from towns of Chicktowaga, Ellicott (now Orchard Park), Hamburgh, and Lancaster 1852 Name changed to West Seneca 1909 Daughter city Lackawanna formed	Blossom East Seneca Ebenezer French Quarters Gardenville Lower Ebenezer	New Ebenezer Reserve West Seneca West Seneca Center Winchester	• Blossom formerly Upper Ebenezer; on Elma town line • Ebenezer also Ebenezer Station and Graymont • Gardenville formerly Middle Ebenezer • West Seneca also Limestone Hill • Winchester also South Buffalo
Willink Name for Town of Aurora 1804–1818			

NEW YORK STATE CENSUS RECORDS

See also chapter 3, Census Records

County originals at Erie County Clerk's Office: 1855, 1865*, 1875, 1892, 1905, 1915, 1925 (1825, 1835, and 1845 are lost)

State originals at the NYSA: 1915, 1925

Microfilm at the FHL, NYPL, and NYSL; many years are online at *FamilySearch.org* and *Ancestry.com*.

*1865 New York state census index is in progress by the Western New York Genealogical Society, see listing in Regional Resources below.

NATIONAL/STATEWIDE REPOSITORIES & RESOURCES

See chapter 16

COUNTYWIDE REPOSITORIES & RESOURCES

Erie County Clerk

92 Franklin Street • Buffalo, NY 14202 • (716) 858-8865
Email: ErieCountyClerkOffice@erie.gov • *www2.erie.gov/clerk*

Website provides information on holdings, which include federal censuses 1850–1920; New York state censuses 1855–1925, marriages 1878–1935, divorces 1830–present, naturalizations 1827–1929, and City of Buffalo births 1881–1913. Selection of documents online including land records. Also holds Niagara County naturalization and land records (1808–1821).

Erie County – City, Town, and Village Clerks

Birth, marriage, and death records are maintained by the clerk of the municipality in which the event occurred; see Introduction to County Guides for details of other records which may also be held by municipal clerks. See municipal websites for details and contact information. Unlike most city clerks, Buffalo City Clerk holds some vital records not available at the New York State Department of Health; see full listing below.

Erie County Surrogate's Court

92 Franklin Street • Buffalo, NY 14202 • (716) 845-2560

Holds probate records from the early 1800s to the present. Also holds probate records (1808–1821) from Niagara County. See also chapter 6, Probate Records.

Erie County Public Libraries

Erie County maintains the Buffalo & Erie County Public Library System; see *www.buffalolib.org* to access each library. Many hold genealogy and local history collections including maps and newspapers. For more information visit the "Special Collections" section of the System's website. For example, the Frank E. Merriweather Library has an extensive African-American history collection. Also see listing below for the Buffalo & Erie County Public Library: Grosvenor Room.

Buffalo & Erie County Public Library: Grosvenor Room

Central Library • One Lafayette Square • Buffalo, NY 14203
(716) 858-8900 • Email access on website
www.buffalolib.org/content/grosvenor

Holds a copy of the New York State Department of Health vital records indexes. Census records on microfilm and census indexes for Western New York, local histories, scrapbooks, family files, city directories, newspapers, local church and cemetery records, maps, and rare books. Website contains a list of genealogy holdings, a genealogy

and local history blog, subject guides, digital projects, and databases. The Western New York Genealogical Society collection is located in the Grosvenor Room.

The Buffalo History Museum

One Museum Court • Buffalo, NY 14216 • (716) 873-9644
Email: library@buffalohistory.org • *www.buffalohistory.org*

Formerly the Buffalo and Erie County Historical Society. Local directories, local histories, biographies, census microfilm and indexes, microfilm of church and cemetery records, marriage index, military records, institution records, thousands of microfilms of newspapers, obituary index with over 99,000 names and family files. Online resources include Buffalo address books, Crystal Beach photographs, manuscripts and drawings from the War of 1812, and finding aids. Holdings include records for parent county (Niagara) pre-1821—before Erie County was formed. Website contains list of finding aids and collection inventories.

Erie County Historian

Buffalo & Erie County Public Library: Grosvenor Room, Central Library
One Lafayette Square • Buffalo, NY 14203
(716) 858-8900 • Email access on website
www.buffalolib.org/content/grosvenor/local-history/erie-county-historian

Office hours by appointment.

Erie County – All Municipal Historians

While not authorized to answer genealogical inquiries, city, town, and village historians can provide valuable historical information and research advice; some maintain collections and webpages which may include transcribed records, local histories, and other genealogical material. See contact information at the Government Appointed Historians of Western New York at *www.gahwny.org/p/erie-county-historian-c.html* or at the website of the Association of Public Historians of New York State at *www.aphnys.org*.

Erie County Historical Federation

11 Danforth Street • Cheektowaga, NY 14227
Email address on website • *http://echfwny.org* • Facebook page

Consortium of Erie County historic sites. Member list available online.

Niederlander Research Library and Archives

3755 Tonawanda Creek Road • Amherst, NY 14228 • (716) 689-1440
Email: amhmuseum@adelphia.net • *www.bnhv.org*

Library is located in the Buffalo Niagara Heritage Village/Amherst Museum. Extensive genealogy collection includes: ledgers, scrapbooks, certificates, newspapers, maps, and photographs. The *Amherst Bee* is available on microfilm, dating from 1879–present. The library's catalog is searchable online.

Afro American Historical Association of the Niagara Frontier

See listing in chapter 14, Peoples of New York, African American

Neto Hatinakwe Onkwehowe

See listing in chapter 14, Peoples of New York, American Indian

University at Buffalo: Polish Room

See listing in chapter 14, Peoples of New York, Polish

REGIONAL REPOSITORIES & RESOURCES

SUNY Fredonia: Daniel A. Reed Library:
Archives & Special Collections
See listing in Chautauqua County Guide

University of Rochester: Rare Books, Special Collections,
and Preservation: Manuscript and Special Collections:
Rochester, Western New York, and New York State
See listing in Monroe County Guide

Western New York Genealogical Society
Library: Buffalo and Erie County Public Library, Grosvenor Room
One Lafayette Square • Buffalo, NY 14203 • (716) 858-8900
Society: PO Box 338 • Hamburg, NY 14075-0338
Email: info@wnygs.org • www.wnygs.org

Documents genealogy and history of Allegany, Cattaraugus, Chautauqua, Erie, Genesee, Niagara, Orleans, and Wyoming counties. The June P. Zintz Memorial Library of the Western New York Genealogical Society is located in the Grosvenor Room of the downtown Central Branch of the Buffalo and Erie County Public Library and contains atlases and gazetteers; directories (including Buffalo City Directories 1832–present); histories; Bible, birth, baptism, church, marriage, burial, cemetery, and death records; a card file vital record index of early Western New York families; census materials for the eight Western New York counties (federal and state); ancestor charts, biographies, family histories, and genealogies; immigration lists and indexes; and military records.

The Society's projects include a Church and Cemetery Records Microfilming Program, which funds the microfilming of records from Western New York and makes them available to researchers at the Zintz Memorial Library. A complete list of records that have been microfilmed is available on the Society's website. The website also contains a list of surnames currently being researched by its members, partial indexes for the 1865 state census (*www.wnygs.org/census_index_Erie.html*), and a limited amount of transcribed records.

The Society has published the *Western New York Genealogical Society Journal* since 1974, which includes unpublished records, book reviews, and research advice. A list of article titles from 1998 to 2010 is available on the website.

Western New York Heritage Press
495 Pine Ridge Heritage Boulevard • Cheektowaga, NY 14225-2503
(716) 893-4011 • Email: emaillist@wnyheritagepress.org
www.wnyheritagepress.org

Publishes original research on Western New York, including *Heritage Magazine*.

LOCAL REPOSITORIES & RESOURCES
Alphabetized by location

Alden Historical Society and Museum
13213 Broadway • Alden, NY 14004
(716) 937-3700 • Email: AldenHistSoc@gmail.com
http://alden.erie.gov/historical_society.asp

Holdings include artifacts and documents relating to Native American, military, agricultural, and railroad history, as well as the history of daily life in the town of Alden.

Brant-Farnham Historical Society
1294 Brant-North Collins Road • Brant, NY 14027 • (716) 549-0282
Email address on website • *www.brantny.com/about.php*

Holdings include newspaper clippings and photographs.

Boston Historical Society and Museum
Old Pioneer Church • 9410 Boston State Road • PO Box 31
Boston, NY 14025 • (716) 941-5015
Email: historicalsociety@townofboston.com
www.townofboston.com/historical_info.html

Original deeds, mortgages, promissory notes dating to the early 1800s, and cemetery records. Website contains an in-depth history of the town of Boston with a bibliography.

Brant-Farnham Historical Society
1294 Brant-North Collins Road • Brant, NY 14027 • (716) 549-0282
Email address on website • *www.brantny.com/Historical%20Society.php*

Holdings include newspaper clippings and photographs.

Buffalo City Clerk and Records Management
City Clerk: 1308 City Hall • Buffalo, NY 14202 • (716) 851-5431
Records Management: 85 River Rock Drive, Suite 301 • Buffalo, NY 14207
(716) 874-6401 or 570-8721 • Email address on website
www.ci.buffalo.ny.us/Home/City_Departments

Holdings for the City of Buffalo include births 1878–present, marriages 1877–present, and deaths 1852–present. Birth and death records 1914–present, and marriage records 1908–present are also available at the New York State Department of Health in Albany.

Buffalo Genealogical Society of the African Diaspora
PO Box 155 • Buffalo, NY 14209-0155 • Email: BGSAD@verizon.net
www.rootsweb.ancestry.com/~nybgsad

Collection includes over 7,000 funeral programs. Website contains index of current research projects with contact information for each researcher; information includes surnames with research locations and dates. Meetings are held at the Merriweather Library.

Cheektowaga Historical Association and Museum
Alexander Community Center • 275 Alexander Avenue
3329 Broadway (museum) • Cheektowaga, NY 14227 • (716) 684-6544
Email: cheektowagahistory@yahoo.com • *www.cheektowagahistory.com*

The Association's collection of local history documents and artifacts dates from the 1850s. Publishes the *Cheektowaga Archival News*.

Clarence Historical Society, Museum, and Genealogy Library
Society: 10456 Main Street • *Genealogy Library:* 10871 Main Street
Clarence, NY 14031 • (716) 759-8575
Email: info@clarencehistory.com • *www.clarencehistory.com*

Holdings include genealogies and memoirs of local World War II veterans.

Elma Historical Society and Museum
3011 Bowen Road • PO Box 84 • Elma, NY 14059-0084
Email: elmahistory@aol.com • *www.elmanyhistory.com*

Website includes a town history and photograph collection.

Marilla Historical Society and Museum
1810 Two Rod Road • PO Box 36 • Marilla, NY 14102 • (716) 652-1827
Email address on website • *www.townofmarilla.com/historian.php*

Museum and the town historian's office are located in the Marilla Community Center. Holdings include cemetery records, newspapers, and tax records. The town historian accepts genealogy requests.

Concord Historical Society and Museum and
Lucy Bensley Center
23 North Buffalo Street • PO Box 425 • Springville, NY 14141
(716) 592-0094 • Email: bensley@localnet.com

Society maintains the Lucy Bensley Center, which is the site of the Society's office, its genealogy and history library, and the repository for Springville newspapers. Website includes a Concord history timeline (1800–1999).

Historical Society of the Tonawandas

113 Main Street • Tonawanda, NY 14150-2129 • (716) 694-7406
Email: tonahist@gmail.com • *www.tonawandashistory.org*

Documents the history of the two Tonawandas: the City of Tonawanda, Erie County, and the adjacent City of North Tonawanda, Niagara County. It maintains a research library, photo file, and extensive genealogical and historical collection. Holdings include cemetery records and gravestone inscriptions, church records, city directories, documents, local newspapers (*Tonawanda Herald, Evening News,* and *Tonawanda News*), local veterans information, maps, obituaries (1877–present), photographs, scrapbooks, yearbooks, artifacts, and information pertaining to local medical practice, entertainment, municipal history, Indian American history, transportation, and industry. Website includes articles and guide to research at the Society. It has a monthly newsletter, *The Lumber Shover.*

Tonawanda-Kenmore Historical Society and Museum

100 Knoche Road • Tonawanda, NY 14150 • (716) 873-5774
Email: lach@roadrunner.com • *www.buffaloah.com/a/knoche/100/tc.html*

Holdings include records of the St. Peter's (German) Evangelical Church Cemetery.

SELECTED PRINT & ONLINE RESOURCES

Below is a selection of resources relevant for research in this county. The list is representative, not exhaustive. Additional titles—particularly of abstracts, indexes, transcriptions, and local histories—are available; consult the introduction to Part Two for further information. For guidance on how to identify and locate community directories and local newspapers, see chapter 11, City Directories, and chapter 12, Newspapers, in Part One of this book.

Abstracts, Indexes & Transcriptions

Barber, Gertrude Audrey. "Erie County, New York Gravestone Inscriptions: Including Cemeteries in South Newstead and Sardinia." Typescript, 1930. Family History Library, Salt Lake City. [*books.FamilySearch.org*]

———. "Erie County, N.Y. Cemetery Inscriptions: Including Cemeteries in Protection, Sardinia, Holland and Wales." Typescript, 1931. NYPL, New York. [NYG&B eLibrary]

———. "Gravestone (Cemetery) Inscriptions, Erie County, New York." Typescript, 1932. NYPL, New York. Includes cemeteries in East Aurora, Wales, and Holland, NY. [NYG&B eLibrary]

———."Gravestone Inscriptions, Sundry Cemeteries in Cattaraugus, Erie and Wyoming Counties, New York." Typescript, 1934. NYPL, New York. Includes East Concord cemetery. [NYG&B eLibrary]

———. "Wales Hollow Cemetery, Wales Hollow, Erie County, NY." Typescript, n.d. NYPL, New York. [NYG&B eLibrary]

County of Erie Abstracts. Syracuse: Central New York Genealogical Society, 2000. Abstracts for a range of genealogical records originally published in the quarterly *Tree Talks.* A name index is on the CNYGS website.

Daughters of the American Revolution, comps. *New York DAR Genealogical Records Committee Report.* Since 1913 DAR volunteers have transcribed many thousands of unpublished cemetery, church,

and town records throughout New York. The reports are at the DAR Library; copies are at the NYSL and the NYPL. The DAR has a searchable name index to all the GRC reports at *http://services.dar.org/Public/DAR_Research/search/?Tab_ID=6.* See Jean Worden's index below for a listing by county of the New York record sets that were transcribed by the DAR before 1998.

Kelly, Arthur C. M. *Index to Tree Talks County Packet: Erie County.* Rhinebeck, NY: Kinship, 2002.

Reamy, Bill. *Erie County, New York Obituaries as Found in the Files of the Buffalo and Erie County Historical Society.* Finksburg, MD: Pipe Creek Publishing, 1992.

Worden, Jean D. "Book 1, Subject Index." In *Revised Master Index to the New York State Daughters of the American Revolution Genealogical Records Volumes.* Zephyrhills, FL: J. D. Worden, 1998. The Subject Index includes a listing by county of the cemeteries, churches, towns, and other sources of records transcribed by the DAR.

Zintz, June P. *Index of Marriages from Buffalo Newspapers, 1811–1884: From a File in the Buffalo and Erie County Historical Society, Supplemented with Additional Information from Erie County Hall.* Hamburg, NY: J. P. Zintz, 1999.

Other Resources

Beers, F. W. *Illustrated Historical Atlas of Erie Co., New York: From Actual Surveys and Records.* Evansville, IN: Whipporwill Publications, 1985. First published 1880. [NYPL Digital Gallery]

The Buffalo City and Erie County Register and Business Directory Including a Directory of Farmers. Rochester, 1870.

Clark, Donna K. *Erie County, New York, Genealogical Depositories of Local Records by TAD (The Ancestor Detective).* Arvada, CO: Ancestor Publishers, 1986.

Devoy, John. *A History of the City of Buffalo and Niagara Falls: From the Earliest Authentic Date to the Present Period; Biographical Sketches.* Buffalo, 1896.

Dunn, Walter S. *History of Erie County, 1870–1970.* Buffalo: Buffalo and Erie County Historical Society, 1972.

Eberle, Scott G., and Joseph A. Grande. *Second Looks: A Pictorial History of Buffalo and Erie County.* Norfolk: Donning Co, 1987.

Foley, Janet W. *Early Settlers of New York State: Their Ancestors and Descendants.* 9 vols. Akron, NY: 1934–1942. Reprint, 2 vols. Baltimore: Genealogical Publishing Co., 1993.

Hill, Henry W. *Municipality of Buffalo, New York: A History, 1720–1923.* 4 vols. New York: Lewis Historical Publishing Co., 1923. Book includes biographical sketches.

Johnson, Crisfield. *Centennial History of Erie County, New York: Being Its Annals from the Earliest Recorded Events to the Hundredth Year of American Independence.* Buffalo, 1876.

Ketchum, William. *An Authentic and Comprehensive History of Buffalo: With Some Account of Its Early Inhabitants, Both Savage and Civilized, Comprising Historic Notices of the Six Nations or Iroquois Indians, Including a Sketch of the Life of Sir William Johnson, and of Other Prominent White Men, Long Resident Among the Senecas, Arranged in Chronological Order.* 2 vols. Buffalo, 1864-1865.

Laughlin, John. *A Complete Pocket Guide of the City of Buffalo: Containing a Brief Sketch of the City, Descriptions of All Places of Interest, a Directory of Places of Amusement, Churches, Public*

Buildings, Parks, and a Classified Directory of Leading Business Firms to Which is Appended a Street Guide and Map of the City. Also a Guide to Niagara Falls, and a Thousand Facts Worth Knowing. Buffalo, 1894?

McNallie, Ridgway, and Henry P. Smith. *Early Settlers of Erie County, New York: Being a Complete Name Index to the History of the City of Buffalo and Erie County in Two Volumes.* Buffalo, 1950.

Memorial and Family History of Erie County, New York. Buffalo: The Genealogical Publishing Co., 1906–1908.

Men of Buffalo: A Collection of Portraits of Men Who Deserve to Rank as Typical Representatives of the Best Citizenship, Foremost Activities, and Highest Aspirations of the City of Buffalo. Chicago: A. N. Marquis & Co., 1902.

New York Historical Resources Center. *Guide to Historical Resources in Erie County, New York, Repositories.* Ithaca, NY: Cornell University, 1983. [books.FamilySearch.org]

Records of the Ithaca College Study Center for Early Religious Life in Western New York, 1978–1981. Division of Rare and Manuscript Collections, Cornell University Library. A description of the holdings for each county is at *http://rmc.library.cornell.edu/eguides/lists/churchlist1.htm*.

Smith, H. Perry. *History of the City of Buffalo and Erie County: With Illustrations and Biographical Sketches of Some of its Prominent Men and Pioneers.* Syracuse, 1884.

Stone & Stewart Publishers. *New Topographical Atlas of Erie Co., New York: From Actual Surveys Especially For This Atlas.* Philadelphia, 1866. [NYPL Digital Gallery]

Sweeney, Daniel J., comp. *History of Buffalo and Erie County, 1914–1919.* Buffalo: Committee of One Hundred, 1920.

Van Ness, Cynthia. "Is There a Buffalo in Your Family Tree?" *New York Researcher*, Spring 2006. Updated May 2011 and published as a Research Aid on *NewYorkFamilyHistory.org*.

Western New York Genealogical Society Journal. Hamburg, NY: Western New York Genealogical Society, 1974–present. [wnygs.org]

White, Truman C. *Our County and Its People: A Descriptive Work on Erie County, New York.* Boston, 1898.

Additional Online Resources

Ancestry.com
> There are vast numbers of records on *Ancestry.com* that pertain to people who have lived in New York State. See chapter 16 for a description of *Ancestry.com*'s resources and its partnership with the New York State Archives. A search of the online card catalog by county may reveal lesser known resources that pertain to a locality, such as town records, abstracts, transcriptions, city directories, and local histories.

Buffalo Folklore etc.
http://buffalolore.buffalonet.org/index.htm
> Collection of links and information relating to the folklore and local history of Buffalo.

Buffalo History Works
www.buffalohistoryworks.com
> Guide to Buffalo history and culture, including photographs.

The Buffalonian
www.buffalonian.com
> Buffalo and Western New York History. "Online community and archive," including genealogical "Peoples History Pages," forum, photographs, and articles.

BuffaloResearch.com
www.buffaloresearch.com
> Information, resources, and links to online materials relating to the history and genealogy of Buffalo, including city directories, maps, obituaries, images, vital records, cemetery, church, and probate records, and information about obtaining documents on microfilm, etc.

Erie County, New York Cemeteries Past and Present
http://members.tripod.com/~wnyroots
> Listing of Erie County, New York cemeteries by town.

FamilySearch.org
> FamilySearch has extensive collections of New York records, including religious records, which are searchable by name and location, but not by county. The following collections include record images (browsable, but not searchable) that are organized by county:
> • "New York, Land Records, 1630–1975." Includes land and property records. *familysearch.org/search/collection/2078654*
> • "New York, Probate Records, 1629–1971." Includes wills, letters of administration, and guardianship papers. *familysearch.org/search/collection/1920234*
> For both collections, choose the browse option and then select Erie to view the available records sets.
> A detailed description of *FamilySearch.org* resources, which include the catalog of the Family History Library, is found in chapter 16.

New York Heritage Digital Collections
Buffalo History Museum
http://nyheritage.nnyln.net/cdm/landingpage/collection/VTP003

Buffalo & Erie County Public Library
http://nyheritage.nnyln.net/cdm/landingpage/collection/VHB011
> Together, the two collections provide free access to more than 50 digitized city and family directories for Buffalo.

New York Heritage Digital Collections: New York State Newspaper Project
www.nyheritage.org/newspapers
> The website provides links to digital newspapers collections in 26 counties (currently) made accessible through New York Heritage, New York State Historic Newspapers, HRVH Historical Newspapers, and other providers.

NYGenWeb Project: Erie County
www.usgennet.org/usa/ny/county/erie1
> Part of the national USGenWeb volunteer initiative, the website provides information and resources for county research.

Old Fulton New York Postcards
www.FultonHistory.com
> The website provides free access to a vast collection of digitized New York newspapers, including 15 titles for Erie County.

Essex County

Formed March 1, 1799

Parent County	Clinton
Daughter Counties	None
County Seat	Elizabethtown, Town of Elizabethtown

Major Land Transactions
See chapter 7, Land Records
Totten and Crossfield Purchase 1771–1787
Old Military Tract 1786

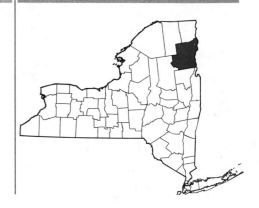

Town Boundary Map
★ - County seat

Towns (and Cities)	Villages and other Settlements		Notes
Chesterfield 1792 Settled 1802 Formed from Town of Willsboro	Adgate Falls Ausable Chasm Birmingham Falls Highland Irish Hill	Keeseville (v) Port Douglas(s) Port Kendall Port Kent	• Ausable Chasm and Birmingham Falls shared with Town of Au Sable, Clinton County • Village of Keeseville was Anderson Falls until 1812; inc. 1878; shared with the Town of Au Sable, Clinton County • Port Douglas(s) also Douglass
Crown Point 1731 Settled by French 1777 Crown Point district formed in Charlotte County * 1786 Town of Crown Point formed from Crown Point district in Washington County 1788 Transferred to new county of Clinton; daughter town Willsboro formed 1798 Daughter town Elizabethtown formed 1799 Transferred to new county of Essex 1804 Daughter towns Schroon and Ticonderoga formed 1808 Daughter town Moriah formed 1860 Annexed land from Town of Schroon	Breed Breed(s) Hill Burdick Crossing Burdicks Cold Spring Cold Spring Park Crown(e) Point Crown(e) Point Center Factoryville Gunnsons	Hammonds Corners Hammondville Ironville Meacham Corners Old Furnace Renne Corners Schuyler (Island) Sherman Corners Stanton Hill White Church	* Charlotte County renamed Washington County 1784 • Ironville also Irondale and Penfield(s)
Dansville Name for Town of Wilmington 1821–1822			
Elizabethtown 1792 Settled 1798 Formed in Clinton County from Town of Crown Point 1799 Transferred to new county of Essex 1808 Daughter towns Keene and Moriah formed 1815 Daughter town Westport formed 1844 Annexed land from towns of Jay and Lewis 1854 Annexed land from Town of Lewis	Elizabethtown (v) Euba Mills Meigsville New Russia Pine Grove The Kingdom Yaws Mills		• Village of Elizabethtown inc. 1875; dissolved 4/23/1981; formerly named Pleasant Valley and The Valley • Elizabethtown designated county seat by act passed 1807, courthouse built 1810; previously at Essex
Essex 1765 Settled 1805 Formed from Town of Willsboro 1860 Annexed land from Town of Schroon 1861 Annexed land from Town of Schroon	Boquet Brookfield Craterclub Essex	Split Rock Wessex Whallonburg(h) Whallon(s) Bay	• Boquet also Bouquet • Essex in Town of Willsboro before 1805; Essex was county seat from 1799, in 1807 county seat moved to Elizabethtown • Whallonburg(h) also Whal(l)onsburg, and Whalsonburgh • Whallon(s) Bay also Whal(l)onsburg Bay

Towns (and Cities)	Villages and other Settlements		Notes
Jay 1796 Settled 1798 Formed in Clinton County from Town of Willsboro 1799 Transferred to new county of Essex 1808 Daughter town Keene formed 1821 Daughter town Dansville (now Wilmington) formed 1822 Annexed land from Town of Peru, Clinton County 1844 Ceded land to Town of Elizabethtown	Au Sable Acres Au Sable Forks Flagg Green Street Jay Lower Jay North Jay Rocky Branch Rome Stickney Bridge Upper Jay		• Au Sable (Ausable) Forks shared with Town of Black Brook, Clinton County
Keene 1797 Settled 1808 Formed from towns of Elizabethtown and Jay 1849 Daughter town North Elba formed	Cascade Glenmore Keene Keene Center Keene Valley St. Hubert(s)		• Keene Valley formerly Keene Flat
Lewis 1796 Settled 1805 Formed from Town of Willsboro 1844, 1854 Ceded land to Town of Elizabethtown	Cross Crowningshield Deerhead Lewis	Lewis Towers Forge Spruce Mill Stowersville	• Stowersville also Towers Forge
Minerva 1804 Settled 1817 Formed from Town of Schroon 1828 Daughter town Newcomb formed 1870 Annexed land from Town of Schroon	Aiden Lair Balfour Boreas River Gosley Irishtown Iron Works Leonardsville Loch Muller	MacIntyre Iron Works Minerva Moose Pond Club Morse Corners Northwoods Club Olmstedville Pudding Hollow Stillwater	• MacIntyre Iron Works also Old MacIntyre Iron Works • Olmstedville formerly Olmsteadville
Moriah 1785 Settled 1808 Formed from towns of Crown Point and Elizabethtown 1828 Daughter town Newcomb formed 1848 Daughter town North Hudson formed 1849 Annexed land from Town of Westport	Belfry Hill Cheever Grover Hills Mineville Moriah Moriah Center Moriah Corners Pondsville Port Henry (v) Witherbee		• Belfry Hill also Belfrey Hill • Village of Port Henry inc. 1869
Newcomb 1816 Settled 1828 Formed from towns of Minerva and Moriah	Adirondack Adirondack Club Camp Santanoni Cheney Cobble Lake Arbutus	Lower Iron Works Newcomb Tahawus Tohawus Club Upper Iron Works	• Newcomb also Pendleton
North Elba 1800 Settled 1849 Formed from Town of Keene	Averyville Cascade Lake Placid (v) Newman North Elba	Ray Brook Saranac Lake (v) Timbuctoo Undercliff Whiteface	• Village of Lake Placid inc. 1900 • Village of Saranac Lake inc. 1892; shared with towns of Harrietstown (Franklin County) and St. Armand

Towns (and Cities)	Villages and other Settlements		Notes
North Hudson 1800 Settled 1848 Formed from Town of Moriah	Blue Ridge Deadwater North Hudson	Schroon River Underwood	• Deadwater formerly Dead Water Iron Works • Schroon River was on Schroon town line; some sources give Schroon River as a variant name for North Hudson
Schroon 1797 Settlers from New England 1804 Formed from Town of Crown Point 1817 Daughter town Minerva formed 1860 Ceded land to towns of Crown Point and Essex 1861 Ceded land to Town of Essex 1870 Ceded land to Town of Minerva	Charlie Hill Hoffman Loch Muller Paradox Schroon Schroon Falls	Schroon Lake Schroon River Severance Sola Bella South Schroon Woodwardsville	• Schroon River was on North Hudson town line; some sources give Schroon River as a variant name for North Hudson
St. Armand 1842 Settled 1844 Formed from Town of Wilmington	Bloomingdale (v) Saranac Lake (v) St. Armand Trudeau		• Village of Bloomingdale Inc. 1905, dissolved 2/26/1985 • Village of Saranac Lake inc. 1892; shared with towns of Harrietstown (Franklin County) and North Elba
Ticonderoga Settled by French soon after 1755 1804 Formed from Town of Crown Point	Baldwin Chilson Ticonderoga (v)	Ti Street Upper Falls	• Village of Ticonderoga inc. 1889, dissolved 5/1/1992 • Ticonderoga also Lower Falls
Westport Settled before Revolution 1815 Formed from Town of Elizabethtown 1849 Ceded land to Town of Moriah	Allen(s) Brainards Forge Graeffes Jacksonville Meigsville Merriams Forge	Raymond Mills Seventy-Five Stevenson Wadham Mills Station Wadhams Westport (v)	• Wadhams formerly Wadham(s) Mills • Village of Westport (formerly Bessboro and Northwest Bay) inc. 1907, dissolved 5/29/1992
Willsboro * 1784 Settled * 1788 Formed in Clinton County from Town of Crown Point 1792 Daughter town Peru formed 1798 Daughter town Jay formed 1799 Transferred to new county of Essex 1802 Daughter town Chesterfield formed 1805 Daughter towns Essex and Lewis formed	Essex Reber South Willsoboro Willsboro Willsboro Point Willsboro Station Willsborough Falls Willsborough Mountain		* Willsboro formed as Willsborough, spelling changed in the twentieth century * First settled 1765 but abandoned during Revolutionary War • Essex was county seat from 1799 when county was formed; from 1805 in Town of Essex • Willsboro also Willsborough
Wilmington Settled late 1700s 1821 Formed as Dansville from Town of Jay 1822 Name changed to Wilmington 1844 Daughter town St. Armand formed	Haselton High Falls Gorge Markhamville Whiteface Wilmington		

NEW YORK STATE CENSUS RECORDS

See also chapter 3, Census Records

County originals at Essex County Building in Elizabethtown: 1855, 1865, 1875, 1892, 1905, 1915, 1925 (1825, 1835, and 1845 are lost)

State originals at the NYSA: 1915, 1925

Microfilm at the FHL, NYPL, and NYSL; many years are online at *FamilySearch.org* and *Ancestry.com.*

NATIONAL/STATEWIDE REPOSITORIES & RESOURCES

See chapter 16

COUNTYWIDE REPOSITORIES & RESOURCES

Essex County Clerk

7559 Court Street • PO Box 247 • Elizabethtown, NY 12932
(518) 873-3601 • *www.co.essex.ny.us/cclerk.asp*

New York state censuses for Essex County 1855, 1865, 1875, 1892, 1905, 1915, and 1925; court records; deeds 1800s–present; marriages 1909–1912; births, deaths, and marriages (1847–1850 for towns of Crown Point, Keene, Moriah, Schroon, Ticonderoga, Westport, and Willsboro); probate records before 1915; and naturalization records 1799–1956.

Essex County – Town, and Village Clerks

Birth, marriage, and death records are maintained by the clerk of the municipality in which the event occurred; see Introduction to County Guides for details of other records which may also be held by municipal clerks. For contact information, see *www.co.essex.ny.us/downloads/townvillageclerks.pdf.*

Essex County Surrogate's Court

7559 Court Street • PO Box 217 • Elizabethtown, NY 12932
(518) 873-3384

Holds probate records from 1915 to the present. Records before 1915 are kept in the county clerk's office. Also see chapter 6, Probate Records.

Essex County Public Libraries

Essex is part of the Clinton-Essex-Franklin Library System; see *www.cefls.org* to access each library. Many hold genealogy and local history collections such as local newspapers. For example, Wadhams Library and Wilmington E. M. Cooper Memorial Library hold selected family files, and Hammond Library contains extensive information on the Bigelow family. Also see listings below for Keene Public Library, Keene Valley Library, Keeseville Public Library, Lake Placid Public Library, Sherman Free Library, and Wells Memorial Library.

Essex County Historical Society and Brewster Research Library & Archives

Adirondack History Center Museum: Brewster Library
7590 Court Street • PO Box 428 • Elizabethtown, NY 12932
(518) 873-6466 • Email: echs@adkhistorycenter.org (general information)
research@adkhistorycenter.org (research queries)
www.adkhistorycenter.org • *www.adkhistorycenter.org/res/guide.html* (Guide to Archival Resources)

Holdings include historical documents and manuscripts; cemetery index; census records (federal 1790–1910 on microfilm); Upper Jay, NY, U.S. Post Office Dept. records 1914–1949; newspapers, vertical files, and books. Website includes digital collections and a guide to Essex County archival resources. Publishes *Reveille.*

Essex County Historian

Brewster Memorial Library Adirondack History Center Museum
Court Street • PO Box 428 • Elizabethtown, NY 12932
(518) 873-6466 • Email: research@adkhistorycenter.org

Holdings include cemetery records and photographs.

Essex County – All Municipal Historians

While not authorized to answer genealogical inquiries, city, town, and village historians can provide valuable historical information and research advice; some maintain collections and webpages which may include transcribed records, local histories, and other genealogical material. See contact information at *www.co.essex.ny.us/Downloads/Historians.pdf* or at the website of the Association of Public Historians of New York State at *www.aphnys.org.*

REGIONAL REPOSITORIES & RESOURCES

Adirondack Genealogical-Historical Society

See listing in Franklin County Guide

Adirondack Museum Library

See listing in Hamilton County Guide

Northeastern New York Genealogical Society

See listing in Warren County Guide

Saranac Lake Free Library: The William Chapman White Memorial Room: Adirondack Research Center

See listing in Franklin County Guide

SUNY Plattsburgh: Special Collections

See listing in Clinton County Guide

LOCAL REPOSITORIES & RESOURCES

Alphabetized by location

Crown Point State Historic Site

21 Grand View Drive • Crown Point, NY 12928 • (518) 597-3666
www.nysparks.com/historic-sites/34/details.aspx

Books, manuscripts, records, and microfilm documenting 18th-century local history, especially military history.

Penfield Homestead Museum

703 Creek Road • Crown Point, NY 12928 • (518) 597-3804
Email: penfield@cptelco.net • *www.penfieldmuseum.org*

The museum's research library holdings range from 1790–present and include vital, church, cemetery, and census materials, over 1,600 family files, the records of the Crown Point Iron Company, and Civil War records. A list of local cemeteries and family names documented by the library's holdings can be found on the museum's website. Accepts genealogical research requests for a fee.

Essex Community Heritage Organization, Inc.

PO Box 250 • Essex, NY 12936 • Email: echo@essexny.org
www.essexny.org

Holdings include historic records of the Town of Essex 1880–1991, photographs, and books.

Keene Public Library

New York 73 Scenic • PO Box 206 • Keene, NY 12942
www.cefls.org/keene.htm

Holdings include albums, newspapers, photographs, and genealogical information.

Keene Valley Library Archives: Loomis Room
1796 NYS Rt. 73 • PO Box 86 • Keene Valley, NY 12943
(518) 576-4335 • Email: library@kvvi.net • archives@kvvi.net
www.keenevalleylibrary.org

Historical and genealogical material (including cemetery records, genealogies, and news clippings), the records of the Adirondack Mountain Preserve, and photographs.

Keeseville Free Library
1721 Front Street • Keeseville, NY 12944 • (518) 834-9054
Email: kesvlib@yahoo.com • *www.cefls.org/keeseville.htm*

Books, ledgers, and scrapbooks, marriage, and death records from local churches, as well as some family histories.

Lake Placid-North Elba Historical Society and Museum
242 Station Street • PO Box 189 • Lake Placid, NY 12946
(518) 523-1608 • Email: thehistorymuseum@verizon.net
www.lakeplacidhistory.com

Holdings include documents, photographs, and artifacts.

Lake Placid Public Library
2471 Main Street • Lake Placid, NY 12946 • (518) 523-3200
Email: librarian@lakeplacidlibrary.org • *www.lakeplacidlibrary.org*

Holdings include an Adirondack Collection, scrapbook collection 1926–1944, and Lake Placid Club Archives.

Minerva Historical Society and Museum
PO Box 906 • Minerva, NY 12851 • (518) 251-2229
Email address on website • *www.irishtown.org/society.html*

Holdings include genealogy and family files. Publishes a quarterly newsletter with historical information.

Sherman Free Library
20 Church Street • Port Henry, NY 12975 • (518) 546-7461
Email: flibrar1@nycap.rr.com • *www.shermanfreelibrary.org*

Books, family histories, maps, photographs and postcards, and scrapbooks compiled by local Reverend Woodbridge 1880s–1895 (including genealogical information from local newspapers).

Schroon-North Hudson Historical Society and Museum
PO Box 444 • Schroon Lake, NY 12870
(518) 532-7615 • Facebook page

Cemetery records, family histories, military records, photographs, school records, and artifacts.

Fort Ticonderoga/Thompson-Pell Research Center`
30 Fort Ti Road • PO Box 390 • Ticonderoga, NY 12883
(518) 585-2821 • Email: info@fort-ticonderoga.org
www.fortticonderoga.org

Holdings include Revolutionary era American and British newspapers, such as the *London Chronicle* and *Annual Register*; manuscripts, diaries, orderly books, maps, and photographs.

Ticonderoga Historical Society and Hancock House Museum
6 Moses Circle • Ticonderoga, NY 12883 • (518) 585-7868
Email: ths@capital.net • *http://ticonderogahistoricalsociety.org*

Research library contains historical and genealogical material relating to the history of Ticonderoga, New York State, and surrounding areas. Records date from the mid-1700s–present and include census materials, cemetery records, newspapers (*Ticonderoga Sentinel*, 1874–1982), obituaries, photographs, and vital records.

Wells Memorial Library
12230 NYS Route 9N • PO Box 57 • Upper Jay, NY 12987
(518) 946-2644 • Email: upperjaylibrary@whiteface.net
www.cefls.org/upperjay.htm

Genealogies, documents, and photographs; records of the Prime Brothers General Store 1880s–1910.

Willsboro Heritage Society, Inc.
6 Gilliland Lane • Willsboro, NY 12996 • Email: whs@willex.com
www.willsboroheritage.hostzi.com

Family files and cemetery transcriptions. Website includes cemetery transcriptions and surname index.

Wilmington Historical Society Collections
Wilmington Community Center • 7 Community Center Circle
Wilmington, NY 12997 • (518) 420-8370
Email: whs12997@hotmail.com • *www.wilmingtonhistoricalsociety.org*

Family history files, personal papers, census transcriptions, church records, maps, newspapers, photographs, school records, vital records, and the published series of Town of Wilmington records (transcriptions of school records 1822–1900, tax assessments 1850–1869, voting records 1860–1900, and more) compiled by Professor Harold Hinds (also see Hinds listing in Abstracts, Indexes & Transcriptions, below).

SELECTED PRINT & ONLINE RESOURCES

Below is a selection of resources relevant for research in this county. The list is representative, not exhaustive. Additional titles—particularly of abstracts, indexes, transcriptions, and local histories—are available; consult the introduction to Part Two for further information. For guidance on how to identify and locate community directories and local newspapers, see chapter 11, City Directories, and chapter 12, Newspapers, in Part One of this book.

Abstracts, Indexes & Transcriptions
County of Essex Abstracts. Syracuse: Central New York Genealogical Society, 2000. Abstracts for a range of genealogical records originally published in the quarterly *Tree Talks*.

Daughters of the American Revolution, comps. *New York DAR Genealogical Records Committee Report*. Since 1913 DAR volunteers have transcribed many thousands of unpublished cemetery, church, and town records throughout New York. The reports are at the DAR Library; copies are at the NYSL and the NYPL. The DAR has a searchable name index to all the GRC reports at *http://services.dar.org/Public/DAR_Research/search/?Tab_ID=6*. See Jean Worden's index below for a listing by county of the New York record sets that were transcribed by the DAR before 1998.

Essex County, NYG&B Church Surveys Collection. NYG&B, New York. [NYG&B eLibrary]

Haviland, Mrs. Frank. "Essex and Warren County Cemetery Records." Typescript, 1925. NYPL, New York

Hinds, Harold E. *Town of Wilmington, Essex County, New York: Transcribed Serial Records*. Bowie, MD: Willow Bend Books. Multiple volumes, 2004–2012. Book includes information transcribed from ledgers, census and schedules, tax assessment records, voting records, newspapers, and scrapbooks.

Jennings, Laura O. "Essex County Cemetery Inscriptions." Typescript, 1963. [*Ancestry.com*]

Kelly, Arthur C. M. *Index to Tree Talks County Packet: Essex County*. Rhinebeck, NY: Kinship, 2002.

Samuelsen, W. David. *Essex County, New York, Will Testators Index, 1803–1904.* Salt Lake City: Sampubco., 1996.

Worden, Jean D. "Book 1, Subject Index." In *Revised Master Index to the New York State Daughters of the American Revolution Genealogical Records Volumes.* Zephyrhills, FL: J. D. Worden, 1998. The Subject Index includes a listing by county of the cemeteries, churches, towns, and other sources of records transcribed by the DAR.

Other Resources

Bernstein, Burton. *The Sticks: A Profile of Essex County, New York.* New York: Dodd, Mead and Co., 1972.

Biographical Review: This Volume Contains Biographical Sketches of Leading Citizens of Clinton and Essex Counties, New York. Boston, 1896. Index available from Berkshire Family History Association.

Cook, Joseph. *Home Sketches of Essex County.* Keeseville, NY, 1858.

Edith E. Cutting. *Lore of an Adirondack County (Essex).* Ithaca, NY: Cornell Press, 1944.

Essex County Historical Society. *A Compendium of Local History, Being a Guide for the Educator and the Scholar to the History of Essex County, New York.* Elizabethtown, NY: The Society, 1986.

Fay, Loren V. *Essex County, New York, Genealogical Research Secrets.* Albany: L. V. Fay, 1983.

Gray, O. W. and Son. *New Topographical Atlas of Essex County, New York: From Official Records, Unpublished Maps and Plans, and Special Explorations and Surveys . . . .* Philadelphia, 1876. [NYPL Digital Gallery]

Hinds, Harold E., and Tina M. Didreckson. *A Basic Guide to Genealogical and Family History Resources for Essex County, New York.* Elizabethtown, NY: Essex County Historical Society, 2004.

New York Historical Resources Center. Guide to Historical Resources in Essex County, New York, Repositories. Ithaca, NY: Cornell University, 1987. [*books.FamilySearch.org*]

Northern New York Library Network. *Directory of Archival and Historical Document Collections.* 2011–2013 edition; published digitally at *http://nny.nnyln.org/archives/ArchivalDirectory.pdf.* Online indexes at *http://nny.nnyln.org/archives/page01.html.* Describes collections held by organizations in Clinton, Essex, Franklin, Jefferson, Lewis, Oswego, and St. Lawrence counties.

O. W. Gray & Son. *New Topographical Atlas of Essex County, New York.* Philadelphia, 1876.

Smith, Henry P. *History of Essex County (NY): With Illustrations and Biographical Sketches of Some if Its Prominent Men and Pioneers.* Syracuse, 1885.

Watson, Winslow C. *The Military and Civil History of the County of Essex, New York: And a General Survey of Its Physical Geography, Its Mines and Minerals, and Industrial Pursuits, Embracing an Account of the Northern Wilderness; and the Military Annals of the Fortresses of Crown Point and Ticonderoga.* Albany, 1869.

Additional Online Resources

Ancestry.com

There are vast numbers of records on *Ancestry.com* that pertain to people who have lived in New York State. See chapter 16 for a description of *Ancestry.com*'s resources and its partnership with the New York State Archives. A search of the online card catalog by county will reveal lesser known resources that pertain to a locality, such as town records, abstracts, transcriptions, city directories, and local histories. In addition, the Drouin Collection: Early U.S. French Catholic Church Records 1695–1954 contains some records pertaining to Clinton, Franklin, St. Lawrence, and Essex counties.

Essex County Naturalization Records, 1836–1906
www.italiangen.org or *www.germangenealogygroup.com*

Volunteers of the Italian Genealogical Group and German Genealogy Group have created a searchable database of these records, which is accessible for free on their website.

FamilySearch.org

FamilySearch has extensive collections of New York records, including religious records, which are searchable by name and location, but not by county. The following collections include record images (browsable, but not searchable) that are organized by county:

- "New York, Land Records, 1630–1975." Includes land and property records. *familysearch.org/search/collection/2078654*
- "New York, Probate Records, 1629–1971." Includes wills, letters of administration, and guardianship papers. *familysearch.org/search/collection/1920234*

For both collections, choose the browse option and then select Essex to view the available records sets.

A detailed description of *FamilySearch.org* resources is found in chapter 16.

New York Heritage Digital Collections: New York State Newspaper Project
www.nyheritage.org/newspapers

The website provides links to digital newspapers collections in 26 counties (currently) made accessible through New York Heritage, New York State Historic Newspapers, HRVH Historical Newspapers, and other providers.

NYGenWeb Project: Essex County
www.rootsweb.ancestry.com/~nyessex

Part of the national, USGenWeb volunteer initiative, the website provides information and resources for county research.

Franklin County

Formed March 11, 1808

Parent County	Clinton
Daughter Counties	None
County Seat	Village of Malone

Major Land Transactions
See chapter 7, Land Records
Old Military Tract 1786
Macomb Purchase 1792

Indian Territories
See chapter 14, Peoples of New York, American Indian
Mohawk Nation: Akwesasne Reservation (1796–present)
Also called St. Regis Mohawk Reservation

Town Boundary Map
★ - County seat

Towns (and Cities)	Villages and other Settlements		Notes
Altamont Name for Town of Tupper Lake 1890–2004			
Bangor 1806 Settled 1812 Formed from Town of Dickinson 1828 Daughter town Brandon formed	Baconville Bangor Bangor Station Cooks Corners	North Bangor (v) South Bangor West Bangor	• Cooks Corners on Fort Covington town line • Village of North Bangor, formerly Amador, inc. 1914 and dissolved 3/24/193
Bellmont * 1833 Formed from Town of Chateaugay 1836 Daughter town Franklin formed	Bannerhouse Bellmont Bellmont Center Brainardsville Bryants Mill Callsville Chateaugay Lake Middle Kilns	Mountain View Owls Head Popeville Porcaville Standish Upper Kilns West Bellmont Wolf Pond	* Bellmont also Belmont • Bellmont Center also Belmont Centre • Brainardsville also Crompville • Owls Head formerly Ringville
Bombay 1811 Settled 1833 Formed from Town of Fort Covington	Bombay Corners Bombay (Village) Bradley Corners Hogansburg	Irish Ridge Kavanaugh Corners South Bombay St. Regis	• Hogansburg formerly Grays Mills • Kavanaugh Corners also Cavanaugh Corners
Brandon 1820 Settled 1828 Formed from Town of Bangor 1888 Daughter town Santa Clara formed 1896 Ceded land to Town of Santa Clara	Beans Corners Brandon Brandon Center Reynoldston Skerry		
Brighton 1858 Formed from Town of Duane	Easy Street Gabriels Keese Mills Lower St. Regis Lake	McColloms Paul Smiths Rainbow Wardner	
Burke 1796–98 Settled 1844 Formed from Town of Chateaugay	Burke (v) Burke Center Burke Depot Burke Hollow Cooks Mill	Coveytown Corners North Burke Sun Thayer(s) Corners	• Village of Burke inc. 1922 • Burke Center also West Chateaugay • Burke Hollow also Andrewsville and Andrusville
Chateaugay 1796 Settled 1799 Formed in Clinton County from Town of Champlain 1805 Daughter town Harrison (now Malone) formed 1808 Transferred to new county of Franklin 1833 Daughter town Bellmont formed 1844 Daughter town Burke formed	Brayton Hollow Chateaugay (v) Chateaugay Chasm Earlville Ogdensburgh Plattsburgh West Chateaugay		• Village of Chateaugay inc. 1868; formerly Four Corners

Towns (and Cities)	Villages and other Settlements		Notes
Constable 1800 Settled 1807 Formed in Clinton County from Town of Harrison (now Malone) 1808 Transferred to new county of Franklin 1817 Daughter town Fort Covington formed 1829 Daughter town Westville formed	Constable East Constable Trout River		• Constable formerly West Constable
Dickinson 1808 Formed from Town of Harrison (now Malone) 1812 Daughter town Bangor formed 1828 Daughter town Moira formed 1880 Daughter town Waverly formed	Alburg Barnes Corners Barnesville Dickinson Dickinson Center East Dickinson	Heath Hill Corners Irish Corners McClelan Tebo Thomasville	• Hamlet of Dickinson formerly Annastown • Dickinson Center formerly Ives and Thomasville • Irish Corners on Moira town line
Duane 1823–24 Settlers from Schenectady 1828 Formed from Town of Malone 1841 Daughter town Harrietstown formed 1858 Daughter town Brighton formed	Ayers Deer River Falls Duane Duane Center	Kempton Meacham (Lake) Porcaville	
Ezraville Name for Town of Malone 1808–1812			
Fort Covington 1793 Settled 1817 Formed from Town of Constable 1833 Daughter town Bombay formed	Cooks Corners Fort Covington (v) Fort Covington Center Wolf Swamp		• Cooks Corners on Bangor town line • Village of Fort Covington, also French Mills, inc. 1889 and dissolved 1976
Franklin 1827 Settled at Franklin Falls 1836 Formed from Town of Bellmont	Alder Brook Alder Brook Farms Bloomingdale Calamount Chase Forestdale Franklin Falls Goldsmith Hartwell Station Inman Kushagua Lake Kushagua Loon Lake Merrickville Merrill(s)ville	Molasses Corners Onchiota Ozonia Plumadore Rainbow Station Roakdale Round Pond Station Slab Bridge Sugar Bush Tekane Two Brooks Union Falls Vermontville White Feathers	• Franklin Falls formerly McClenathans Falls • Lake Kushagua post office established 1894; name changed to Stony Wold 1954 • Merrill(s)ville post office called Hunters Home(s) 1858–1861

Towns (and Cities)	Villages and other Settlements		Notes
Harrietstown 1812 Settled on North West Bay Road 1841 Formed from Town of Duane	Algonquin Ampersand Axton Axton Landing Barlett Carry Barrymore Clear Pond Coreys Donnellys Corners Fish Creek Ponds Harrietstown Lake Clear Lake Clear Junction Lake Colby	McMasters Crossing Mount View Farm Rice Ridgewood Villa Rustig Lodge Saranac Club Saranac Lake (v) St. Regis Lake Tromblees Upper St. Regis Wawbeek Wawbeek Center Station	• Donnellys Corners formerly Works Corners • Lake Clear Junction formerly Saranac Junction • Village of Saranac Lake inc. 1892; shared with towns of North Elba and St. Armand, Essex County
Harrison Name for Town of Malone 1805–1808			
Malone 1802 Settlers from Vermont near Malone Village 1805 Formed in Clinton County as Town of Harrison 1807 Daughter town Constable formed 1808 Transferred to new county of Franklin; name changed to Ezraville; daughter town Dickinson formed 1812 Name changed to Malone 1828 Daughter town Duane formed	Chasm Falls Chasm Falls Station Clarks Corner Comet Fay Malone (v) Malone Junction Teboville Whippleville		• Chasm Falls formerly Titusville, also South Malone • Village of Malone inc. 1853; county seat from 1808 when county was formed • Teboville also Whippleville Station
Moira 1803 Settled 1828 Formed from Town of Dickinson	Alburg Brushton (v) Irish Corners	Moira Moira Corners	• Village of Brushton inc. 1925; formerly Brushs Mills • Irish Corners on Dickinson town line
Santa Clara 1888 Formed from Town of Brandon 1896 Annexed land from Town of Brandon	Bay Pond Brandon (Center) Ennis Everton Floodwood Keys Mill Kildare Leboeufs	Madawaska Meno Santa Clara Saranac Inn Spring Cove Walkers Wiedman	• Saranac Inn also Upper Saranac
Tupper Lake 1890 Formed as Altamont from Town of Waverly 1913 Annexed land from Town of Piercefield, St. Lawrence County 2004 Name changed to Tupper Lake	Big Tupper Big Wolfe Lake Cheltenham Childwood Station Derrick Faust Kildare Station	Litchfield Moody Sunmount Tupper Lake (v) Tupper Lake Junction Willis Pond	• Village of Tupper Lake inc. 1902
Waverly 1880 Formed from Town of Dickinson 1890 Daughter town Altamont (now Tupper Lake) formed	Bingotown Gile St. Regis Falls		
Westville 1800 Settlers from Vermont 1829 Formed from Town of Constable	Chapin Dustins Corners West Constable	Westville Center Westville	

NEW YORK STATE CENSUS RECORDS
See also chapter 3, Census Records

County originals at Franklin County Clerk's Office: 1855, 1875, 1905, 1915, 1925 (1825, 1835, 1845, 1865, and 1892 are lost)

State originals at the NYSA: 1915, 1925

Microfilm at the FHL, NYPL, and NYSL; many years are online at *FamilySearch.org* and *Ancestry.com.*

NATIONAL/STATEWIDE REPOSITORIES & RESOURCES
See chapter 16

COUNTYWIDE REPOSITORIES & RESOURCES

Franklin County Clerk and Records Management
355 West Main Street, Suite 248 • PO Box 70 • Malone, NY 12953
(518) 481-1681 • Email: rmdept@co.franklin.ny.us (records management)
www.franklincony.org

Land records 1808–present; court records 1918–present; and original copies of the New York state censuses for Franklin County 1855, 1875, 1905, 1915, and 1925 are at the county clerk's office. The Records Management website lists genealogy records available for research; these include birth and marriages 1847–1848, 1908–1935; cemetery records late 1700s–present; censuses 1800, 1810, 1820, 1845, 1875, 1905, 1915, 1925, and 1930; civil court records 1808–1917; baptismal and marriage records of St. Patrick's Church, Hogansburg 1820–1862; marriages performed by Reverend Ashbel Parmelee of Malone 1810–1862; marriage surname index 1908–1935; maps and atlases; military records (Revolutionary War–present) including a Civil War collection; naturalization surname index 1832–1957; criminal files; coroner's inquest; divorce records; declaration of intent from 1834; volunteer firemen's discharge certificates 1877–1934; homestead exemptions 1830s; historical reviews (Franklin County Historical Society's Collection); register of professions 1821–1888; and will index 1809–1919.

Franklin County – Town and Village Clerks
Birth, marriage, and death records are maintained by the clerk of the municipality in which the event occurred; see Introduction to County Guides for details of other records which may also be held by municipal clerks. See municipal website for details and contact information.

Franklin County Surrogate's Court
355 West Main Street • Malone, NY 12953 • (518) 481-1736

Probate records from the late 1800s to the present. See also chapter 6, Probate Records.

Franklin County Public Libraries
Franklin is part of the Clinton-Essex-Franklin Library System; see *www.cefls.org* to access each library. Many hold genealogy and local history collections (e.g., Goff-Nelson Memorial Library and Wead Library hold local newspapers and obituaries). Also see listings below for Saranac Lake Free Library and Akwesasne Library & Cultural Center.

Franklin County Historical and Museum Society
51 Milwaukee Street • PO Box 388 • Malone, NY 12953
(518) 483-2750 • Email: fchms@northnet.org
www.franklinhistory.org

Family histories and genealogies, Adirondack history, cemetery information, census materials, directories and phone books, early assessment rolls, maps, newspapers pre-1900, obituaries, scrapbooks, school yearbooks, and vital records. Special collections include the Clarence Kilburn Papers and 16th Regiment Civil War Papers. Annual journal, *Franklin Historical Review.*

Franklin County Historian
www.franklinhistorian.blogspot.com

The historian's office is located in the Franklin County Historical and Museum Society.

Franklin County – All Municipal Historians
While not authorized to answer genealogical inquiries, city, town, and village historians can provide valuable historical information and research advice; some maintain collections and webpages which may include transcribed records, local histories, and other genealogical material. See contact information at *http://nny.nnyln.org/archives/franklin_county.html* or at the website of the Association of Public Historians of New York State at *www.aphnys.org.*

REGIONAL REPOSITORIES & RESOURCES

Adirondack Genealogical-Historical Society
100 Main Street • Saranac Lake, NY 12983 • Email address on website
http://freepages.genealogy.rootsweb.ancestry.com/~adkghs

Region includes Clinton, Essex, and St. Lawrence counties. Offers research services, at the Saranac Lake Free Library: The William Chapman White Memorial Room: Adirondack Research Center, for a fee.

Adirondack Museum Library
See listing in Hamilton County Guide

Akwesasne Library & Cultural Center Western New York Historical Collection
See listing in chapter 14, Peoples of New York, American Indian

Saranac Lake Free Library: The William Chapman White Memorial Room: Adirondack Research Center
109 Main Street • Saranac Lake, NY 12983 • (518) 891-0807
Email: sllibrary@adelphia.net • *http://www.slfl.org*

Village of Saranac Lake shared with Essex County. Books, manuscripts, periodicals, newspapers, and pamphlets; federal and state census microfilm for Essex, Franklin, Clinton, and St. Lawrence counties 1850–1925; church records; obituary index; maps, gazetteers, and atlases 1869, 1876; photographs and postcards; cemetery inscriptions published by the Adirondack Genealogical and Historical Society; county, town, and municipal histories; genealogies and biographies; high school yearbooks and school attendance records; and early tuberculosis patient history from the Trudeau Sanatorium.

Six Nations Indian Museum
See listing in chapter 14, Peoples of New York, American Indian

SUNY Plattsburgh: Special Collections
See listing in Clinton County Guide

LOCAL REPOSITORIES & RESOURCES
Alphabetized by location

Chateaugay Historical Society
PO Box 123 • Chateaugay, NY 12920 • (518) 497-6685
Email: chathistsoc@gmail.com • www.chateaugayonline.com

Cemetery indexes, Catholic church records ca. 1863–1920, birth and marriage listings from Protestant churches, and histories of Franklin County. Society and archives are located in the Chateaugay Memorial Library.

Chateaugay Memorial Library
4 John St. • PO Box 10 • Chateaugay, NY 12920 • (518) 497-0400
Email: chatlib@gmail.com • www.cefls.org/chateaugay.htm

Books and pamphlets, Chateaugay records on microfilm 1881–1995, photographs, scrapbooks, and the collections of the Chateaugay Historical Society: genealogies, cemetery lists, church records, *Chateaugay Record* on microfilm, and photographs.

Town of Moira Historical Association
State Route 776 • PO Box 75 • Moira, NY 12957
(518) 529-7426 • Facebook page

Genealogies; information on local businesses, schools, and industries; military records; and postcards.

Historic Saranac Lake
89 Church Street, Suite 2 • Saranac Lake, NY 12983 • (518) 891-4606
Email: mail@historicsaranaclake.org • www.historicsaranaclake.org

Dedicated to the "restoration, preservation, and interpretation of the Saranac Lake region." Holdings include information on local historical buildings and sites. The online wiki, www.hsl.wikispot.org, is developed as an encyclopedia of local history. *Historic Saranac Lake News* published semi-annually.

Westville Historical Organization and Westville History Center
History Center: 3510 State Route 37 • Westville, NY 12937
Mailing address: PO Box 157 • Constable, NY 12926
Email: info@westvillehistory.net • www.westvillehistory.net

Genealogies (list of names on website), local history books, census materials 1800–1875, cemetery records, church records, maps, military records, school records, tax assessment books, and voter lists.

SELECTED PRINT & ONLINE RESOURCES

Below is a selection of resources relevant for research in this county. The list is representative, not exhaustive. Additional titles—particularly of abstracts, indexes, transcriptions, and local histories—are available; consult the introduction to Part Two for further information. For guidance on how to identify and locate community directories and local newspapers, see chapter 11, City Directories, and chapter 12, Newspapers, in Part One of this book.

Abstracts, Indexes & Transcriptions
Austin, John M. *In the Thanks of the Republic: Some Civil War Soldiers from Franklin Co. NY.* New York: The Author, 1998. Filmed by the Genealogical Society of Utah, 1999.

County of Franklin Abstracts. Syracuse: Central New York Genealogical Society, 2000. Abstracts for a range of genealogical records originally published in the quarterly *Tree Talks.* A name index is on the CNYGS website.

Daughters of the American Revolution, comps. *New York DAR Genealogical Records Committee Report.* Since 1913 DAR volunteers have transcribed many thousands of unpublished cemetery, church, and town records throughout New York. The reports are at the DAR Library; copies are at the NYSL and the NYPL. The DAR has a searchable name index to all the GRC reports at *http://services.dar.org/Public/DAR_Research/search/?Tab_ID=6.* See Jean Worden's index below for a listing by county of the New York record sets that were transcribed by the DAR before 1998.

Kelly, Arthur C. M. *Index to Tree Talks County Packet: Franklin County.* Rhinebeck, NY: Kinship, 2002.

Rabideau, Clyde, comp. *Obituaries, Franklin County, New York: 71 Years, 1887-1958, As Published in the Fort Covington Sun and Other Newspapers in Franklin Co.* Plattsburgh, NY: Heartnut Publishing, n.d.

Samuelsen, W. David. *Franklin County, New York, Will Testators Index, 1809–1919.* Salt Lake City: Sampubco., 1994.

Worden, Jean D. "Book 1, Subject Index." In *Revised Master Index to the New York State Daughters of the American Revolution Genealogical Records Volumes.* Zephyrhills, FL: J. D. Worden, 1998. The Subject Index includes a listing by county of the cemeteries, churches, towns, and other sources of records transcribed by the DAR.

Other Resources
Beers, D. G. *Atlas of Franklin County, New York: From Actual Surveys and Official Records.* Philadelphia, 1876. [NYPL Digital Gallery]

Child, Hamilton. *Gazetteer and Directory of Franklin and Clinton Counties: With an Almanac for 1862–3, Embracing the Names of Business Men, County Officers, Distances, Interest Tables, Census Returns, and Much Other Valuable Statistical Information.* Ogdensburg, NY, 1862.

Fay, Loren V. *Franklin County, New York, Genealogical Research Secrets.* Albany: L. V. Fay, 1984

Harder, Kelsie B., and Carol Payment Poole. *Place Names of Franklin County, New York: Their Origins and History.* Brushton, NY: TEACH Services, 2008.

Hough, Franklin B. *A History of St. Lawrence and Franklin Counties, New York, from the Earliest Period to the Present Time.* Albany, 1853. Index available from Berkshire Family History Association.

Hurd, Duane H. *History of Clinton and Franklin Counties: With Illustrations and Biographical Sketches of Its Prominent Men and Pioneers.* Philadelphia, 1880.

Landon, Harry F. *The North Country: A History, Embracing Jefferson, St. Lawrence, Oswego, Lewis and Franklin Counties, New York.* 3 vols. Indianapolis: Historical Publishing Co., 1932.

New York Historical Resources Center. *Guide to Historical Resources in Franklin County, New York, Repositories.* Ithaca, NY: Cornell University, 1987. [books.FamilySearch.org]

Northern New York Library Network. *Directory of Archival and Historical Document Collections.* 2011–2013 edition; published digitally at *http://nny.nnyln.org/archives/ArchivalDirectory.pdf.* Online indexes at *http://nny.nnyln.org/archives/page01.html.* Describes collections held by organizations in Clinton, Essex, Franklin, Jefferson, Lewis, Oswego, and St. Lawrence counties.

Seaver, Frederick J. *Historical Sketches of Franklin County and Its Several Towns, with Many Short Biographies.* Albany: J. B. Lyon, 1918.

Additional Online Resources
Ancestry.com
There are vast numbers of records on *Ancestry.com* that pertain to people who have lived in New York State. See chapter 16 for

a description of *Ancestry.com*'s resources and its partnership with the New York State Archives. A search of the online card catalog by county may reveal lesser known resources that pertain to a locality, such as town records, abstracts, transcriptions, city directories, and local histories.

FamilySearch.org

FamilySearch has extensive collections of New York records, including religious records, which are searchable by name and location, but not by county. The following collection includes record images (browsable, but not searchable) that are organized by county:

- "New York, Probate Records, 1629–1971." Includes wills, letters of administration, and guardianship papers. *familysearch.org/search/collection/1920234*

Choose the browse option and then select Franklin to view the available records sets in this collection.

A detailed description of *FamilySearch.org* resources is found in chapter 16

New York Heritage Digital Collections:
New York State Newspaper Project
www.nyheritage.org/newspapers

The website provides links to digital newspapers collections in 26 counties (currently) made accessible through New York Heritage, New York State Historic Newspapers, HRVH Historical Newspapers, and other providers.

NYGenWeb Project: Franklin County
www.usgennet.org/usa/ny/county/franklin

Part of the national, USGenWeb volunteer initiative, the website provides information and resources for county research.

Fulton County

Formed April 18, 1838

Parent County   Montgomery
Daughter Counties None
County Seat   City of Johnstown

Major Land Transactions
See table in chapter 7, Land Records
Kayaderosseras Patent 1708
Sacandaga Patent 1741
Kingsborough Patent 1753

Town Boundary Map
★ - County seat

Cities and Towns	Villages, Settlements, Neighborhoods		Notes
Bleecker 1800 Settlers from New England 1831 Formed in Montgomery County from Town of Johnstown 1838 Transferred to new county of Fulton 1841 Ceded land to Town of Johnstown 1842 Daughter town Caroga formed	Bleecker Bleecker Center Bowlers Corners Chase(s) Lake Lindsley Corners	Peck(s) Lake Peters Corners Pinnacle Woodworth Lake	
Broadalbin First settlement pre-Revolution 1793 Formed in Montgomery County from Town of Caughnawaga (now towns of Amsterdam, Broadalbin, Johnstown, and Mayfield) 1799 Daughter town Northampton formed 1838 Transferred to new county of Fulton 1842 Ceded land to Town of Perth	Beatty Corners Benedict Benedicts Corners Broadalbin (v) Fish House Fondas Bush Gorthey Corners Hill Corners Hoesville Honeywell Corners	Mills Corners North Broadalbin South Broadalbin Steele(s) Corners Stever Mill Union Mills Van Vranken Van Vranken Corners West Galway Church	• Village of Broadalbin inc. 1924; shared with Town of Mayfield • Fondas Bush formerly Rawsonville • North Broadalbin formerly Averys and Spencers Corners • Van Vranken Corners also Vanvranken Corners
Caughnawaga *			* See Montgomery County
Caroga c.1790 Settled 1842 Formed from towns of Bleecker, Johnstown, and Stratford	Auskerada Bradtville Canada Lake Caroga Lake Glasgow Mills Green Lake Knights	Newkirk Northbush Pine Lake Shaw Corners Sherman Stoner Lake(s) Wheelerville	• Bradtville on Ephratah town line • Glasgow Mills also Gloscow Mills and Glasco Mills • Newkirk formerly Newkirks Mills
Ephratah Settled mid-1700s 1827 Formed in Montgomery County from Town of Palatine 1838 Transferred to new county of Fulton	Bradtville Dempster Corners Ephratah Fecoe Corners Fical Corners	Garoga Lassellsville Rockwood Scotchbrush	• Bradtville on Caroga town line • Rockwood formerly Pleasant Valley • Scotchbrush also Scotchbush
Gloversville (city) 1853 Village of Gloversville incorporated in Town of Johnstown 1890 Village of Gloversville incorporated as City of Gloversville	Kingsboro Mills Settlement Settlement on the Hill		• Kingsboro also Kingsboro Settlement and Kingsborough; in Town of Johnstown before 1890
Johnstown (city) * 1808 Village of Johnstown incorporated in Town of Johnstown 1895 Village of Johnstown incorporated as City of Johnstown			* County seat in Village, then City of Johnstown

Cities and Towns	Villages, Settlements, Neighborhoods		Notes

Johnstown (town)

	Cities and Towns	Villages, Settlements, Neighborhoods		Notes

Johnstown (town)

1760   Settled

1793   Formed in Montgomery County from Town of Caughnawaga (now towns of Amsterdam, Broadalbin, Johnstown, and Mayfield)

1812   Daughter town Lake Pleasant formed *

1816   Ceded land to Town of Lake Pleasant, Hamilton County

1831   Daughter town Bleecker formed

1837   Daughter town Mohawk formed *

1838   Transferred to new county of Fulton

1841   Annexed land from Town of Bleeker

1842   Daughter town Caroga formed

1895   Village of Johnstown incorporated as City of Johnstown

Albany Bush   Kingsborough
Berkshire   Kingsboro Station
Bull Run   Meco
Cork   Pleasant Square
Dennies Crossing   Progress
Eppie Corners   Sammonsville
Gloversville (v)   Smith(s) Corners
Hale Mills   Sulphur Spa
Johnstown (v)   Sulphur Spa Junction
Keck(s) Center   West Bush

* Town of Lake Pleasant in Hamilton County from 1816

* Town of Mohawk in Montgomery County

• Village of Gloversville inc. 1853, became City of Gloversville 1890; called Stump City before 1853

• Village of Johnstown inc. 1808, became City of Johnstown 1895; county seat from 1838

• Kingsborough also Kingsboro; in City of Gloversville from 1890

• Meco formerly Bennets Corners and McEwens Corners

Mayfield

c. 1760   First settled as Philadelphia Bush

1793   Formed in Montgomery County from Town of Caughnawaga (now towns of Amsterdam, Broadalbin, Johnstown, and Mayfield)

1805   Daughter town Wells formed *

1812   Ceded land to Town of Wells *

1838   Transferred to new county of Fulton

1842   Ceded land to Town of Perth

1860   Daughter town Benson formed in Hamilton County

Broadalbin (v)   Munsonville
Broadalbin Junction   Red Bunch Corners
Closeville   Riceville
Cranberry Creek   Shawville
Dennies Hollow   Tolmantown
Jackson Summit   Vail(s) Mills
Mayfield (v)   Wilkins Corners
Mayfield Corners   Woodworths Corners
Mayfield Station

* Town of Wells in Hamilton County from 1816

• Village of Broadalbin inc. 1924; shared with Town of Broadalbin

• Cranberry Creek on Northampton town line

• Village of Mayfield inc. 1896

Northampton

c. 1765   Settled

1799   Formed in Montgomery County from Town of Broadalbin

1805   Daughter town Wells formed *

1838   Transferred to new county of Fulton

Carpenters Corners   Northville (v)
Cranberry Creek   Osbourne Bridge
Fairchilds Corners   Parkville
Fish House   Sacandaga
Newtons Corners   Sacandaga Park
Northampton   Sweets Crossing

* Town of Wells in Hamilton County from 1816

• Cranberry Creek on Mayfield town line

• Village of Northville inc. 1873

• Osbourne Bridge also Osborn(s) Bridge

Oppenheim

Settled pre-Revolution

1808   Formed in Montgomery County from Town of Palatine

1838   Transferred to new county of Fulton; daughter town St. Johnsonville formed in Montgomery County

Brockets Bridge   Kringsbush
Crum Creek   Lot(t)ville
Dolgeville (v)   Middle Sprite
Doxtater Corner   Oppenheim
Ingham(s) Mills   Phipps Corners
Irish Settlement   Rasbach Corner(s)

• Village of Dolgeville inc. 1881; shared with Town of Manheim in Herkimer County

Cities and Towns	Villages, Settlements, Neighborhoods	Notes
Perth Pre-Revolution settlers from Scotland 1831 Formed in Montgomery County from Town of Amsterdam 1838 Transferred to new county of Fulton 1842 Annexed land from towns of Broadalbin and Mayfield	Beyers Corners Perth Perth Center Stairs Corners West Galway West Perth	
Stratford 1800 Settled 1805 Formed in Montgomery County from Town of Palatine 1838 Transferred to new county of Fulton 1842 Daughter town Caroga formed	Bliss Corner Oregon Emmonsburg(h) Pleasant Lake Knappville Stewart Landing Middle Sprite Stratford Nicholsville Whitesburgh	

NEW YORK STATE CENSUS RECORDS

See also chapter 3, Census Records

County originals at Fulton County Clerk's Office: 1845, 1855, 1865, 1875, 1905, 1915, 1925 (1892 is lost)

State originals at the NYSA: 1915, 1925

Microfilm at the FHL, NYPL, and NYSL; many years are online at *FamilySearch.org* and *Ancestry.com*.

NATIONAL/STATEWIDE REPOSITORIES & RESOURCES

See chapter 16

COUNTYWIDE REPOSITORIES & RESOURCES

Fulton County Clerk

County Office Building • 223 West Main Street • Johnstown, NY 12095 (518) 736-5555 • *www.fultoncountyny.gov*

Land records; court records; naturalization records 1848–1903; and the New York state censuses for Fulton County 1845, 1855, 1865, 1875, 1905, 1915, and 1925. Website includes Fulton County Directory.

Fulton County – City, Town, and Village Clerks

Birth, marriage, and death records are maintained by the clerk of the municipality in which the event occurred; see Introduction to County Guides for details of other records which may also be held by municipal clerks. For contact information, see the County Directory at *www.fultoncountyny.gov*.

Fulton County Surrogate's Court

223 West Main Street • Johnstown, NY 12095 • (518) 736-5685

Holds probate records from 1838 to the present. See also chapter 6, Probates Records.

Fulton County Public Libraries

Fulton is part of the Mohawk Valley Library System; see *www.mvls. info* to access each library. Information on special collections relating to local history and genealogy can be found on a separate webpage at *www.mvls.info/lhg*. See also listings below for Gloversville, Johnstown, and Northville Public Libraries.

Fulton County Historian

County Office Building • 223 West Main Street • Johnstown, NY 12095 (518) 736-5667 • *www.fultoncountyny.gov*

Fulton County – All Municipal Historians

While not authorized to answer genealogical inquiries, city, town, and village historians can provide historical information and research advice; some maintain collections and webpages which may include transcribed records, local histories, and other genealogical material. See contact information at *www.fulton.nygenweb.net/resources/histrns.html* or at the website of the Association of Public Historians of New York State at *www.aphnys.org*.

Fulton County Historical Society and Museum

237 Kingsboro Ave • Gloversville, NY 12078 • (518) 725-2203 Email: fultoncohist@frontier.com • *www.fultoncountymuseum.com*

Website includes photo archive.

REGIONAL REPOSITORIES & RESOURCES

Adirondack Museum Library

See listing in Hamilton County Guide

Capital District Genealogical Society

See listing in Albany County Guide

Fulton-Montgomery Community College: Evans Library: The Kenneth R. Dorn Regional History Study Center

2805 State Highway 67 • Johnstown, NY 12095 • (518) 212-7685 Email: libinfo@fmcc.edu • *http://libguides.fmcc.edu/reghistory*

The Center's holdings, which are searchable through its online catalog, document history of the Mohawk Valley beginning in the colonial era. Website provides access to New York Heritage Digital Collections, which contain local directories, newspapers, maps, and yearbooks, the Capital District Library Council Digital Collections, and Fulton-Montgomery Photographic Archives.

Montgomery County Department of History and Archives

See listing in Montgomery County Guide

LOCAL REPOSITORIES & RESOURCES

Alphabetized by location

Bleecker Historical Society

575 County Highway 112 • Gloversville, NY 12078 Email: bleeckerhistoricalsociety@gmail.com *www.bleeckerhistoricalsociety.org*

Website includes links to information on cemeteries, town officials, and businesses and residents of Bleecker.

Gloversville Public Library: Historical Reference Room

58 East Fulton Street • Gloversville, NY 12078-3219 • (518) 725-2819 Email: gpl@sals.edu • *www.gloversvillelibrary.org/local-history*

Holdings include city directories 1864–present, high school yearbooks, cemetery records, and atlases. Regional holdings for Fulton, Montgomery, Schoharie, Saratoga, Albany, and Schenectady counties; the Mohawk Valley, and the Adirondacks region.

Johnstown Historical Society

17 North William Street • Johnstown, NY 12095-2115 (518) 762-7076 • *http://cityofjohnstown.ny.gov/city-historian*

Holdings include federal census materials, history of the Mohawk Valley since the mid-1700s, and women's suffrage history.

Johnstown Public Library: Local History Collection

38 South Market Street • Johnstown, NY 12095 • (518) 762-8317 *www.johnstownpubliclibrary.info*

Histories and genealogies, cemetery transcriptions, obituaries, and early newspapers with name index.

Northville Public Library: Genealogy

341 South Third Street • PO Box 1259 • Northville, NY 12134 (518) 863-6922 • Email: norlib@mvls.info *http://northville.mvls.info/genealogy.html*

Maintains Sacandaga Families database, cemetery transcriptions, and maps. Newsletters containing genealogical information are archived on website.

Town of Perth Historical Society

Route 6 • Amsterdam, NY 12010 • (518) 842-9497

Holdings include cemetery records, church records, genealogies, local history books, and information on old farms in the town and the families who owned them.

SELECTED PRINT & ONLINE RESOURCES

Below is a selection of resources relevant for research in this county. The list is representative, not exhaustive. Additional titles—particularly of abstracts, indexes, transcriptions, and local histories—are available; consult the introduction to Part Two for further information. For guidance on how to identify and locate community directories and local newspapers, see chapter 11, City Directories, and chapter 12, Newspapers, in Part One of this book.

Abstracts, Indexes & Transcriptions

Becker, Edith van Heusen (Mrs. Frank N. Becker). "Cemetery Inscriptions in Mayfield, NY, Fulton Co. and Hagaman, Amsterdam, NY, Montgomery Co." Typescript, n.d. NYPL, New York. [NYG&B eLibrary]

———. "Cemetery Inscriptions: In the Vicinity of Montgomery and Fulton Counties, NY." 5 vols. Typescript, 1923–1963. NYPL, New York.

County of Fulton Abstracts. Syracuse: Central New York Genealogical Society, 2000. Abstracts for a range of genealogical records originally published in the quarterly *Tree Talks.*

Daughters of the American Revolution, comps. *New York DAR Genealogical Records Committee Report.* Since 1913 DAR volunteers have transcribed many thousands of unpublished cemetery, church, and town records throughout New York. The reports are at the DAR Library; copies are at the NYSL and the NYPL. The DAR has a searchable name index to all the GRC reports at *http://services.dar.org/Public/DAR_Research/search/?Tab_ID=6.* See Jean Worden's index below.

Fulton County, NYG&B Church Surveys Collection. NYG&B, New York. [NYG&B eLibrary]

Kelly, Arthur C. M. *Index to Tree Talks County Packet: Fulton County.* Rhinebeck, NY: Kinship, 2002.

Vosburgh, Royden Woodward, ed. "Records of the First Presbyterian Church of West Galway in the Town of Perth, Fulton County, N.Y.: Originally the First Presbyterian Church in Galloway." Typescript, 1919. NYPL, New York. [NYG&B eLibrary]

———. "Records of the St. John's Episcopal Church in the Village of Johnstown, Fulton County, N.Y." Typescript, 1919. NYPL, New York. [NYG&B eLibrary]

Worden, Jean D. "Book 1, Subject Index." In *Revised Master Index to the New York State Daughters of the American Revolution Genealogical Records Volumes.* Zephyrhills, FL: J. D. Worden, 1998. The Subject Index includes a listing by county of the cemeteries, churches, towns, and other sources of records transcribed by the DAR.

Other Resources

Campbell, William W. *Annals of Tryon County: Or, the Border Warfare of New York, During the Revolution.* New York, 1831.

Capital District Genealogical Society Newsletter. Albany: Capital District Genealogical Society, 1982–present. [*capitaldistrictgene alogicalsociety.org*]

Child, Hamilton. *Gazetteer and Business Directory of Montgomery and Fulton Counties, NY, for 1869–70.* Syracuse, 1869.

Engel, Herbert M. *Shtetl in the Adirondacks: The Story of Gloversville and Its Jews.* Fleischmanns, NY: Purple Mountain Press, 1991.

Frothingham, Washington. *History of Fulton County: . . . With Town and Local . . . Fulton County Patriots.* Syracuse, 1891.

Greene, Nelson. *History of the Mohawk Valley, . . . 1614–1925; Covering the Six Counties of Schenectady, Schoharie, Montgomery, Fulton, Herkimer, and Oneida.* Chicago: S. J. Clarke, 1925.

History of Montgomery and Fulton Counties, NY: . . . Old Pioneers and Prominent Residents. Interlaken, NY: Heart of the Lakes Publishing, 1979.

Laird, Audrey, and Audrey Bowman. *Black Heritage in Fulton County.* Gloversville, NY: City of Gloversville Bicentennial of the U.S. Constitution Committee, 1990.

Morrison, James F. *A History of Fulton County in the Revolution.* Gloversville, NY: Fulton County Bicentennial History Committee, 1977.

New Century Atlas of Montgomery and Fulton Counties, New York. Philadelphia: Century Map Co., 1905.

New York Historical Resources Center. *Guide to Historical Resources in Fulton County, New York, Repositories.* Ithaca, NY: Cornell University, 1984. [*books.FamilySearch.org*]

Nichols, Beach. *Atlas of Montgomery and Fulton Counties, New York: From Actual Surveys by and under the Direction of B. Nichols.* New York, 1867. [NYPL Digital Gallery]

Palmer, Robert M. *Historical Fulton County, New York.* Johnstown, NY: Fulton County Publicity, 1960.

Additional Online Resources

Ancestry.com

See chapter 16 for a description of *Ancestry.com*'s resources and its partnership with the New York State Archives. A search of the online card catalog by county may reveal lesser known resources that pertain to a locality, such as town records, abstracts, transcriptions, city directories, and local histories.

FamilySearch.org

FamilySearch has extensive collections of New York records, including religious records, which are searchable by name and location, but not by county. The following collections include record images (browsable, but not searchable) that are organized by county:

- "New York, Land Records, 1630–1975." Includes land and property records. *familysearch.org/search/collection/2078654*
- "New York, Probate Records, 1629–1971." Includes wills, letters of administration, and guardianship papers. *familysearch.org/search/collection/1920234*

For both collections, choose the browse option and then select Fulton to view the available records sets.

A detailed description of *FamilySearch.org* resources is found in chapter 16.

NYGenWeb Project: Fulton County

fulton.nygenweb.net

Part of the national, USGenWeb volunteer initiative, the website provides information and resources for county research.

Old Fulton New York Postcards

www.FultonHistory.com

The website provides free access to a vast collection of digitized New York newspapers, including eight titles for Fulton County.

Schenectady Digital History Archive

www.schenectadyhistory.org/local/fulton-history.html

Links to libraries, archives, museums, and online projects for Fulton County, as well as other genealogical resources.

Genesee County

Formed March 30, 1802

Parent County	Ontario
Daughter Counties	Allegany 1806 • Cattaraugus 1808 • Chautauqua 1808
	Niagara 1808 • Livingston 1821 • Monroe 1821
	Orleans 1824 • Wyoming 1841
County Seat	City of Batavia

Major Land Transactions
See chapter 7, Land Records
Morris Reserve 1791
Holland Land Company Purchase 1792–1796

Indian Territories
See chapter 14, Peoples of New York, American Indian
Tonawanda Band of Seneca Indians: Tonawanda Reservation (1797–present)

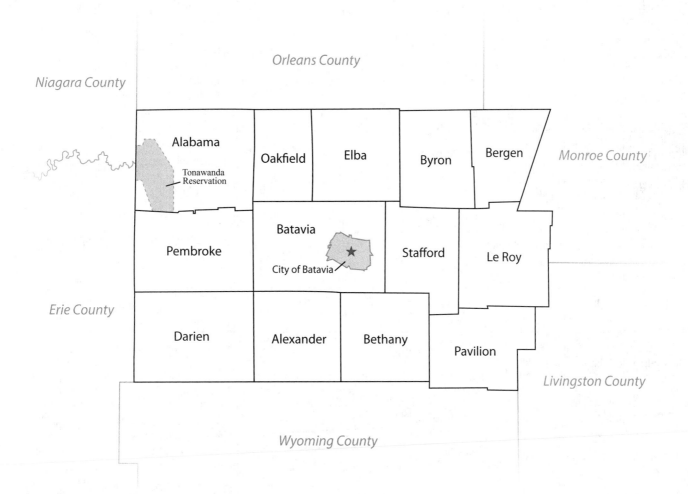

Town Boundary Map
★ - County seat

Towns (and Cities)	Villages and other Settlements		Notes
Alabama 1806 Settled 1826 Formed as Gerryville from towns of Shelby (Orleans County) and Pembroke 1828 Name changed to Alabama	Alabama Basom Brookville East Alabama Indian Falls	Meadeville South Alabama West Alabama Wheatville	• Alabama also Alabama Center • South Alabama formerly Smithville
Alexander 1802 Settled 1812 Formed from Town of Batavia	Alexander (v) Attica (v) Brookville Cady Station	East Alexander North Alexander Ray West Bethany	• Village of Alexander inc. 1834 • Village of Attica inc. 1837; most of village in Town of Attica, Town of Attica in Wyoming County after 1841 • West Bethany on Bethany town line
Angelica * In Genesee County 1805–1806			* See Allegany County
Attica * In Genesee County 1811–1841			* See Wyoming County
Barre * In Genesee County 1818–1824			* See Orleans County
Batavia (city) * 1823 Incorporated as a village in Town of Batavia 1915 Formed as a city from Village of Batavia			* County seat at Batavia (village and city) from 1802
Batavia (town) 1802 Formed as a town 1804 Daughter towns Chautauqua and Willink (now Aurora) formed 1808 Daughter towns Sheldon and Warsaw formed 1812 Daughter towns Alexander, Bethany, Pembroke, and Ridgeway formed * 1820 Daughter towns Elba and Stafford formed 1915 City of Batavia formed from Village of Batavia	Batavia (v) Bushville Brushville Crafts Station Daws Daws Corners	East Pembroke Five Corners Putnam Settlement Upton West Batavia	* French (1860) incorrectly includes Bergen as a daughter town in 1812 • Village of Batavia inc. 1823; formerly The Bend; became City of Batavia in 1915; county seat from 1802 • East Pembroke formerly Ellicott Mills; on Pembroke town line
Bellona Name for Town of Le Roy 1812–1813			
Bennington * In Genesee County 1818–1841			* See Wyoming County
Bergen 1805 Settled in Bergen Village 1804–10 Settled by 60 families from New Haven, CT 1813 Formed from Town of Murray * 1820 Daughter town Byron formed	Bergen (v) Bergen Corners East Bergen Jerico(n) Corners Little Boston North Bergen	Sheepskin Corners Stone Church Wardville West Bergen West Sweden	* French (1860) incorrectly gives Batavia as the parent town of Bergen in 1812 • Village of Bergen inc. 1877; formed from Bergen Corners, Lower Bergen, and Wardville • Bergen Corners also High Bergen; formerly Buells Corner • North Bergen called Lyme before 1840 • Wardville formerly Cork

Towns (and Cities)	Villages and other Settlements		Notes
Bethany 1803 Settled in northeast part of town 1812 Formed from Town of Batavia	Bethany Bethany Center Canada East Alexander East Bethany	Linden Little Canada Suicide Corners West Bethany West Bethany Mills	• Canada formerly Bennetts Settlement • Linden formerly Gad-Pouch • West Bethany on Alexander town line
Byron 1807 Settled 1820 Formed from Town of Bergen	Byron Byron Center Station Byron Station Lidke(s) Hill	Mosquito Point Pumpkin Hill South Byron Transit	• Byron formerly Byron Center • Pumpkin Hill also North Byron • South Byron formerly Brusselville • Transit was on Elba town line
Caledonia * In Genesee County 1802–1821			* See Livingston County
Castile * In Genesee County 1821–1841			* See Wyoming County
Chautauqua * In Genesee County 1804–1808			* See Chautauqua County
China * In Genesee County 1818–1841			* See Town of Arcade in Wyoming County
Clarendon * In Genesee County 1821–1824			* See Orleans County
Clarkson * In Genesee County 1819–1821			* See Monroe County
Covington * In Genesee County 1817–1841			* See Wyoming County
Darien 1803 Settled near Darien City 1832 Formed from Town of Pembroke	Corfu (v) Corfu Station Darien Darien Center Fargo	Griswold Lehigh Longwood North Darien Sawens	• Village of Corfu inc. 1868; also Longs Corners; shared with Town of Pembroke • Darien formerly South Pembroke in Town of Pembroke; also formerly Darien City • Darien Center formerly Kings Corners
Elba 1801 Settlers from Vermont at Daws Corners 1820 Formed from Town of Batavia 1842 Daughter town Oakfield formed	Daws East Elba Elba (v) Five Corners	Langton(s) Corners Oakfield Transit	• Daws formerly Daws Corners • East Elba also Mills Corners • Village of Elba inc. 1884; formerly Pine Hill • Five Corners also Newkirk • Langton(s) Corners also Lancktons Corner • Oakfield formerly Caryville, Gau-dak, and Plain Brook; in town of Oakfield after 1842 • Transit was on Byron town line
Gaines * In Genesee County 1816–1824			* See Orleans County
Gainesville * In Genesee County 1814–1841			* See Wyoming County
Gates * In Genesee County 1802–1821			* See Monroe County

Towns (and Cities)	Villages and other Settlements		Notes
Gerrysville Name for Town of Alabama 1826–1828			
Java * In Genesee County 1832–1841			* See Wyoming County
Leicester * In Genesee County 1802–1821			* See Livingston County
LeRoy 1797 Settled 1812 Formed as Town of Bellona from Town of Caledonia 1813 Name changed to LeRoy 1817 Daughter town Covington formed 1820 Daughter town Stafford formed 1842 Ceded land to Town of Pavilion	Asbury Corners Baileys Mills Beaver Meadow Dutchtown Fort Hill Gansons Jug City Laws Corners	LeRoy (v) Lime Rock Little Red Schoolhouse North Leroy North Woods Roanoke Union Corners	• Asbury Corners, Baileys Mills, Laws Corners, Little Red Schoolhouse, and Union Corners in Town of Pavilion after 1842 • Jug City also Southbridge and Tufts Mills • Village of LeRoy inc. 1834 • Lime Rock also Limerock • Roanoke formerly Orangeburgh; became part of Town of Stafford in 1820
Middlebury * In Genesee County 1812–1841			* See Wyoming County
Murray * In Genesee County 1808–1821			* See Orleans County
Newstead * In Genesee County 1804–1808			* See Erie County
Oakfield 1801 Settled 1842 Formed from Town of Elba	Caryville Dunhams Grove East Oakfield Five Corners	Mechanicsville North Oakfield Oakfield (v) Old Fort	• Caryville formerly Cary • Five Corners formerly Oakfield Corners • Village of Oakfield inc. 1858; formerly Plain Brook before 1837, and Caryville 1837–1858
Oak Orchard * In Genesee County 1822–1824			* See Town of Carlton in Orleans County
Ogden * In Genesee County 1817–1821			* See Monroe County
Orangeville * In Genesee County 1816–1841			* See Wyoming County
Parma * In Genesee County 1808–1821			* See Monroe County

Pavilion
1809   Settled
1841   Formed from Town of Covington,
         Wyoming County
1842   Annexed land from towns of
         LeRoy and Stafford
	Asbury Corners
	Baileys Mills
	Bennetts Corners
	Billyville
	Burleigh Hill
	Junction
	Laws Corners
	Madison Corners
		Pavilion
		Pavilion Center
		Phelps Corners
		Poplar Corners
		Red School House
		   Corners
		Union Corners
			• Asbury Corners, Baileys Mills, Laws Corners, and Union Corners in Town of LeRoy before 1842
			• Madison Corners also Swedes Corners
			• Pavilion Center formerly South Le Roy
			• Red Schoolhouse Corners formerly Little Red Schoolhouse; in Town of LeRoy before 1842

Pembroke 1804 Settled 1812 Formed from Town of Batavia	Airville Brick House Corners Cookville	Corfu (v) East Pembroke Indian Falls	• Airville settlement 1837–1845 • Village of Corfu inc. 1868; was Longs Corners before 1839; shared with Town of Darien

(Pembroke continued on next page)

Towns (and Cities)	Villages and other Settlements	Notes
Pembroke 1826 Daughter town Alabama formed 1832 Daughter town Darien formed from South Pembroke	North Pembroke Pembroke Pembroke Center Pembroke Station Prospect Hill South Pembroke	• East Pembroke formerly Ellicott Mills; settled c. 1806; on Batavia town line • Indian Falls, formerly Tonawanda Falls 1842–1866; site of Indian village until 1857 • North Pembroke formerly Mogadore • Pembroke settled c. 1804; also Richville before 1900 • Pembroke Center also Frog Hollow • Prospect Hill settlement 1840–1931; also Papermill • South Pembroke became Town of Darien 1832
Perry * In Genesee County 1814–1841		* See Wyoming County
Ridgeway * In Genesee County 1812–1824		* See Orleans County
Riga * In Genesee County 1808–1821		* See Monroe County
Shelby * In Genesee County 1818–1824		* See Orleans County
Sheldon * In Genesee County 1808–1841		* See Wyoming County
Stafford 1801 Settled 1820 Formed from towns of Batavia and LeRoy 1842 Ceded land to Town of Pavilion	Morganville Roanoke Stafford (Village)	• Morganville settled 1820, formerly Jake Town and Moss Town • Roanoke formerly Orangeburgh; in Town of LeRoy before 1820 • Stafford (Village) formerly Transit Storehouse then Transit; name changed to Stafford 1841
Southampton * In Genesee County 1802–1821		* See Town of Caledonia in Livingston County
Sweden * In Genesee County 1813–1821		* See Monroe County
Warsaw * In Genesee County 1808–1841		* See Wyoming County
Wethersfield * In Genesee County 1823–1841		* See Wyoming County
Willink * In Genesee County 1804–1808		* See Town of Aurora in Erie County
Yates * In Genesee County 1822–1824		* See Orleans County
York * In Genesee County 1819–1821		* See Livingston County

NEW YORK STATE CENSUS RECORDS

See also chapter 3, Census Records

County originals at Genesee County Clerk's Office: 1875, 1892, 1905, 1915, 1925 (1825, 1835, 1845, 1855, and 1865 are lost)

State originals at the NYSA: 1915, 1925

Microfilm at the FHL, NYPL, and NYSL; many years are online at *FamilySearch.org* and *Ancestry.com.*

NATIONAL/STATEWIDE REPOSITORIES & RESOURCES

See chapter 16

COUNTYWIDE REPOSITORIES & RESOURCES

Genesee County Clerk

County Building 1 • 15 Main Street • Batavia, NY 14020
(585) 344-2550 ext. 2243 • Email: coclerk@co.genesee.ny.us
www.co.genesee.ny.us/departments/countyclerk/index.html

Land records; deeds 1802–present; naturalization records 1834–1962; marriages 1908–1934; and the New York state censuses for Genesee County 1875, 1892, 1905.

Genesee County – City, Town, and Village Clerks

Birth, marriage, and death records are maintained by the clerk of the municipality in which the event occurred; see Introduction to County Guides for details of other records which may also be held by municipal clerks. For contact information, see *www.co.genesee.ny.us/departments/countyclerk/clerks.html.* For holdings of vital records in towns, see *www.rootsweb.ancestry.com/~nygags.*

Genesee County Surrogate's Court

Genesee County Courts Facility • One West Main Street
Batavia, NY 14020 • (585) 344-2550 ext. 2240

Probate records from 1802 to the present. See also chapter 6, Probate Records.

Genesee County Public Libraries

Genesee is part of the Nioga Library System; see *www.niogalibrary. org* to access each library. Many hold genealogy and local history collections, including books and newspapers. Also see listing below for Richmond Memorial Library.

Genesee County Historian and History Department

County Building 2, 3837 West Main Street Road • Batavia, NY 14020
(585) 344-2550 ext. 2613 • Email: history@co.genesee.us
Historian: *www.co.genesee.ny.us/departments/history/genesee_county_historians.html*
Collection: *www.co.genesee.ny.us/departments/history/collections.html*

Books; genealogy files; federal censuses 1810, 1820, 1830, 1840, 1850, 1860, 1870, and 1880; state census indexes 1905 and 1915 online; cemetery records; church records; directories 1869–1881; indentured servants records 1827–1899; maps and atlases 1854–1900s; marriages and divorces; military records and information; naturalization records 1849–1929; newspapers, *Daily News,* 1878–1974; photographs; obituaries 1891–1937, 1992–2007; slavery information; yearbooks; and deaths that occurred in the County Home. The historian's website includes a list of municipal historians. A selection of holdings from the Department's collection is available online.

Genesee County – All Municipal Historians

While not authorized to answer genealogical inquiries, city, town, and village historians can provide valuable historical information and research advice; some maintain collections and webpages which may include transcribed records, local histories, and other genealogical material. See contact information at *www.co.genesee.ny.us/departments/history/genesee_county_historians.html,* the Government Appointed Historians of Western New York at *www.gahwny.org/p/genesee.html,* or at the website of the Association of Public Historians of New York State at *www.aphnys.org.*

Genesee Area Genealogists

www.rootsweb.ancestry.com/~nygags

Meetings held at the Richmond Memorial Library. Website includes a list of surnames currently being researched by members.

Richmond Memorial Library: Local History

19 Ross Street • Batavia, NY 14020
(585) 343-9550 • Email: webbtv@nioga.org
www.batavialibrary.org/localhistory/localhistory.php

Books, periodicals, church records, tax records, census materials, directories, and newspapers. Holdings include cemetery records and photographs.

REGIONAL REPOSITORIES & RESOURCES

Milne Library at SUNY Geneseo: Special Collections: Genesee Valley Historical Collection

See listing in Livingston County Guide

SUNY Fredonia: Daniel A. Reed Library: Archives & Special Collections

See listing in Chautauqua County Guide

University of Rochester: Rare Books, Special Collections, and Preservation: Manuscript and Special Collections: Rochester, Western New York, and New York State

See listing in Monroe County Guide

Western New York Genealogical Society

See listing in Erie County Guide

Western New York Heritage Press

See listing in Erie County Guide

LOCAL REPOSITORIES & RESOURCES

Alphabetized by location

Tonawanda Reservation Historical Society

PO Box 516 • Basom, NY 14013 • (716) 542-4370

The Society offers genealogical research services for a fee.

Holland Land Office Museum

131 West Main Street • Batavia, NY 14020 • (585) 343-4727
Email: info@hollandlandoffice.com • *www.hollandlandoffice.com*

Museum is in a former office of the Holland Land Company and houses the artifact collection of the Holland Purchase Historical Society. No research holdings.

Byron Museum

6451 Mill Pond Road • 6405 Townline Road • Byron, NY 14422
(585) 548-2302 • Facebook page

Cemetery records, census materials, family Bibles, local organization membership lists, obituaries, phone books, photographs, tax books, and voter registration lists.

Pembroke Historical Association

1145 Main Road • Corfu, NY 14036 • (585) 599-4892 ext. 30
Email: historian@townofpembroke.org

History room with changing exhibitions. Pembroke historian's office located in building—has family files, genealogies, indexed birth, marriage, and death information extracted from local newspapers, and cemetery records.

Historical Society of Elba

Maple Avenue Ext. • PO Box 24 • Elba, NY 14058
(585) 757-9094 • Email: historicalsocietyofelba@yahoo.com
http://historicalsocietyofelba.wordpress.com

Holdings include family files.

LeRoy Historical Society, Historic LeRoy House, and Jell-O Museum/Gallery

23 East Mail Street • PO Box 176 • LeRoy, NY 14482 • (585) 768-7433
Email: jellodirector@frontiernet.net • www.leroyhistoricalsociety.org

The Society has a genealogical library containing files and archives.

Stafford Historical Society and Museum

6684 Randall Road • LeRoy, NY 14482-9316
www.staffordhistoricalsociety.org

Holdings include domestic and agricultural artifacts, school records, and documents.

Oakfield Historical Society

PO Box 74 • Oakfield, NY 14125 • (585) 948-5901
www.oakfield.govoffice.com

Holdings include census material, cemetery records, and family histories. The Society offers help with genealogical research in cooperation with the town historian. The society publishes a monthly newsletter.

Town of Alabama Historical Society and Museum

Alabama Town Hall • 2218 Judge Road, Route 63
South Alabama, NY 14125 • (716) 948-9773
www.rootsweb.ancestry.com/~nycalaba/Museum.html

Located in the former Alabama School House #12. Holdings include artifacts, diaries, photographs, school minute ledgers 1839–present, voter records, property assessment logs, and notes about the town (1880–1887 and 1910–1921). The Society does not accept genealogy research requests.

SELECTED PRINT & ONLINE RESOURCES

Below is a selection of resources relevant for research in this county. The list is representative, not exhaustive. Additional titles—particularly of abstracts, indexes, transcriptions, and local histories—are available; consult the introduction to Part Two for further information. For guidance on how to identify and locate community directories and local newspapers, see chapter 11, City Directories, and chapter 12, Newspapers, in Part One of this book.

Abstracts, Indexes & Transcriptions

Cooley, La Verne C. *Tombstone Inscriptions from the Abandoned Cemeteries and Farm Burials of Genesee County*. Batavia, NY: n.p., 1952. [*HathiTrust.org*]

County of Genesee Abstracts. Syracuse: Central New York Genealogical Society, 2000. Abstracts for a range of genealogical records originally published in the quarterly *Tree Talks*.

Daughters of the American Revolution, comps. *New York DAR Genealogical Records Committee Report*. Since 1913 DAR volunteers have transcribed many thousands of unpublished cemetery, church, and town records throughout New York. The reports are at the DAR Library; copies are at the NYSL and the NYPL. The DAR has a searchable name index to all the GRC reports at *http://services.dar.org/Public/DAR_Research/search/?Tab_ID=6*. See Jean Worden's index below for a listing by county of the New York record sets that were transcribed by the DAR before 1998.

Dows, Robert H., and Marjorie S. "Gravestone Inscriptions, E. Bergen Cemetery, Genesee Co., N.Y." Typescript, 1986. Central Library of Rochester and Monroe County, Rochester.

Kelly, Arthur C. M. *Index to Tree Talks County Packet: Genesee County*. Rhinebeck, NY: Kinship, 2002.

Russell, Marian A. *Cemetery Records, Genesee County, New York*. Salt Lake City: Filmed by the Genealogical Society of Utah, 1984.

Sutton, Leola Crane, and Charlotte L. Greening. *Elmwood Cemetery, Harvester Avenue, Batavia, NY, volumes I, II, III, IV*. New York: Daughters of the American Revolution, New York, 2006.

Worden, Jean D. "Book 1, Subject Index." In *Revised Master Index to the New York State Daughters of the American Revolution Genealogical Records Volumes*. Zephyrhills, FL: J. D. Worden, 1998. The Subject Index includes a listing by county of the cemeteries, churches, towns, and other sources of records transcribed by the DAR.

Other Resources

The Architectural Heritage of the Genesee County, New York. Batavia, NY: Landmark Society of Genesee County, 1988.

Beers, F. W. *Gazetteer, Biographical Record: Directory of Over 10,500 Names, Occupations, Genesee County, NY, 1788–1890*. Knightstown, IN: Bookmark, 1977. First published 1890.

Beers, S. N. *New Topographical Atlas of Genesee and Wyoming Counties, New York*. Philadelphia, 1866.

Child, Hamilton. *Gazetteer and Business Directory of Genesee County, NY, for 1869–70*. Syracuse, 1868.

Conklin, Susan. *A Guide to Genesee County, New York, Cemeteries and Burial Sites: Bicentennial Book, No. 2*. Batavia, NY: Genesee County History Department, 1997.

Everts, Ensign & Everts. *Combination Atlas Map of Genesee County, New York*. Philadelphia, 1876. [NYPL Digital Gallery]

Foley, Janet W. *Early Settlers of New York State: Their Ancestors and Descendants*. 9 vols. Akron, NY: 1934–1942. Reprint, 2 vols. Baltimore: Genealogical Publishing Co., 1993.

Genesee County Business Directory Embracing Common Business and Social Forms, and Containing Sketches of the Early Pioneers of the Holland Land Purchase. Buffalo, 1882.

Genesee County Rural Index and "Compass System" Map with Almanac. Ithaca, NY: Rural Directories, Inc., 1939.

Genesee Valley Historians Association (NY). *Genesee County, New York: 20th Century-in-Review and Family Histories*. Nashville: Turner Publishing Company, 2004.

Hedtke, James R. *Civil War Professional Soldiers, Citizen Soldiers, and Native American Soldiers of Genesee County, New York: Ordinary Men of Valor.* Lewiston, NY: Edwin Mellen Press, 2006.

McCulley, Mary, ed. *History of Genesee County, New York, 1890–1982.* Interlaken, NY: Heart of the Lakes Publishing, 1985.

McEvoy, Ruth, M. *History of the City of Batavia, 1915–1980.* Batavia, NY: Hodgins Print Co., 1993.

New Century Atlas of Genesee County, New York, with Farm Records. Philadelphia: Century Map Co., 1904.

New York Historical Resources Center. *Guide to Historical Resources in Genesee County, New York, Repositories.* Ithaca, NY: Cornell University, 1982. [books.FamilySearch.org]

North, Safford E. *Our County and Its People: A Descriptive and Biographical Record of Genesee County, New York.* Boston, 1899.

Noyes, J. O. *The Genesee Valley of Western New York: A Virtually Unknown, Rambling Account of Life and Times in Upstate New York.* Ovid, NY, 1857.

O'Keefe, Rose. *Historic Genesee County: A Guide to Its Lands and Legacies.* Charleston, SC: History Press, 2010.

Paolo Busti Cultural Foundation, ed. *The Legacy of Italian-Americans in Genesee County, New York.* Interlaken, NY: Heart of Lakes Publishing, 1992.

Rand McNally & Company's Map of Genesee County, New York. New York: Rand McNally & Co., ca. 1918.

Records of the Ithaca College Study Center for Early Religious Life in Western New York, 1978–1981. Division of Rare and Manuscript Collections, Cornell University Library. A description of the holdings for each county is at *http://rmc.library.cornell.edu/eguides/lists/churchlist1.htm.*

The Sesquicentennial of Genesee County, 1802–1952. Batavia, NY: Sesquicentennial Committee, 1952.

Western New York Genealogical Society Journal. Hamburg, NY: Western New York Genealogical Society, 1974–present. [wnygs.org]

Williamson, Charles., and Robert Munro. *A Description of the Genesee Country, in the State of New-York: In Which the Situation, Dimensions, Civil Divisions, Soil, Minerals, Produce, Lakes and Rivers, Curiosities, Climate, Navigation, Trade and Manufactures, Population, and Other Interesting Matters Relative to that Country, Are Impartially Described; To Which is Added, an Appendix, Containing a Description of Military Lands.* New York, 1804.

Additional Online Resources

Ancestry.com

There are vast numbers of records on *Ancestry.com* that pertain to people who have lived in New York State. See chapter 16 for a description of *Ancestry.com*'s resources and its partnership with the New York State Archives. A search of the online card catalog by county may reveal lesser known resources that pertain to a locality, such as town records, abstracts, transcriptions, city directories, and local histories.

FamilySearch.org

FamilySearch has extensive collections of New York records, including religious records, which are searchable by name and location, but not by county. The following collections include record images (browsable, but not searchable) that are organized by county:

- "New York, Land Records, 1630–1975." Includes land and property records. *familysearch.org/search/collection/2078654*
- "New York, Probate Records, 1629–1971." Includes wills, letters of administration, and guardianship papers. *familysearch.org/search/collection/1920234*

For both collections, choose the browse option and then select Genesee to view the available records sets.

A detailed description of *FamilySearch.org* resources, which include the catalog of the Family History Library, is found in chapter 16.

NYGenWeb Project: Genesee County
http://genesee.bettysgenealogy.org

Part of the national, USGenWeb volunteer initiative, the website provides information and resources for county research.

Old Fulton New York Postcards
www.FultonHistory.com

The website provides free access to a vast collection of digitized New York newspapers, including ten titles for Genesee County.

Town of Alabama, New York, Historian's Page
www.rootsweb.ancestry.com/~nycalaba/index.html

The website provides information and links relevant to genealogical research in Genesee County.

USGenWeb: Genesee County New York Archives
www.usgwarchives.net/ny/genesee/genesee.htm

The website provides access to a selection of transcribed records, including cemetery, land, census, and probate.

Greene County

Formed March 25, 1800

Parent Counties   Albany • Ulster
Daughter Counties None
County Seat   Village of Catskill

Major Land Transactions
See table in chapter 7, Land Records
Hardenbergh Patent 1708

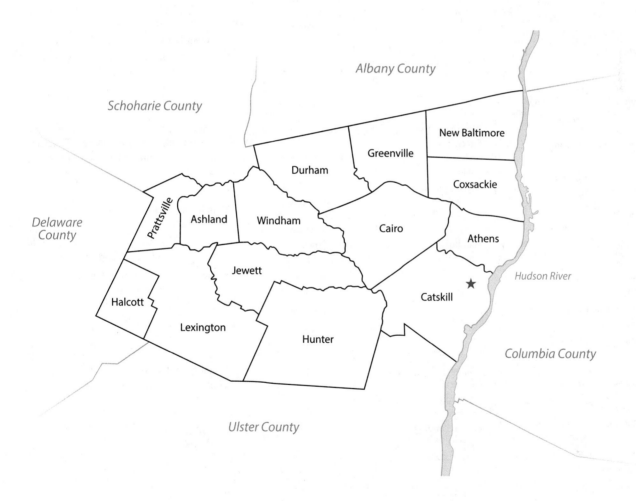

Town Boundary Map
★ - County seat

Towns (and Cities)	Villages and other Settlements	Notes
Ashland Dutch families from Schoharie County settled at Batavia Kil pre-Revolution 1848 Formed from towns of Prattsville and Windham	Ashland Batavia East Ashland Four Corners North Settlement Sutton Hollow West Settlement	• Ashland formerly Scienceville; in Town of Windham before 1848 • Batavia on Windham town line • North Settlement on Windham town line • Sutton Hollow also West Hollow • West Settlement formerly Richmond Corners
Athens 1685 Settled by Dutch in eastern part of town 1815 Formed from towns of Catskill and Coxsackie	Athens (v) Prentiss Athens Station Sleepy Hollow Limestreet West Athens	• Village of Athens inc. 1805; formerly Loonenburgh (1794) also Canisikek, Esperanzay, Looneberg, and Lunenburg • Limestreet also Lime Street
Cairo First settlement at Shinglekill pre-Revolution 1803 Formed as Town of Canton from towns of Catskill, Coxsackie, and Freehold (now Durham) 1808 Name changed to Cairo	Acra Round Top Cairo Sandy Plains Canton South Cairo Gayhead South Durham Indian Ridge The Forge Purling Woodstock	• Cairo formerly Shingle Kill or Shinglekill • Gayhead also Gay Head; on Greenville town line • Indian Ridge was a locality within Sandy Plains • Purling formerly Cairo Forge and The Forge • South Durham on Durham town line
Canton Name for Town of Cairo 1803–1808		
Catskill Dutch and German settlers in mid-1600s 1772 Part of Great Imboght District in Albany County 1788 Recognized as Town of Catskill in Albany County 1798 Transferred to new county of Ulster 1800 Transferred to new county of Greene 1803 Daughter town Canton (now Cairo) formed 1815 Daughter town Athens formed	Alsen Irvingsville Beachview Jefferson Belfast Mills Jefferson Heights Blivinville Kiskatom Cairo Junction Lawrence Station Catskill (v) Lawrenceville Cauterskill Leeds Great Falls Otis Junction Hamburg(h) Palen(s)ville High Falls Smith(s) Landing	• Catskill county seat (as hamlet and village)1800–present; Village of Catskill inc. 1806; formerly Het Strand (Dutch) and The Landing • Cauterskill also Cauters Kill • Jefferson Heights also Jefferson Flats and The Flats • Leeds also Madison, Mill Village, Old Catskill, Old Katskill, and Pasqoecq • Smith(s) Landing also Cementon after local cement factory
Coxsackie 1662 Settled by Dutch 1772 Formed as Coxsackie District 1788 Formed as a town in Albany County 1790 Daughter town Freehold (now Durham) formed 1800 Transferred to new county of Greene 1803 Daughter towns Canton (now Cairo) and Greenfield (now Greenville) formed 1811 Daughter town New Baltimore formed 1815 Daughter town Athens formed	Climax Coxsackie (v) Coxsackie Landing Earlton Lower Landing Upper Landing West Coxsackie	• Village of Coxsackie inc. 1867 • Earlton formerly Jacksonville and Urlton

Towns (and Cities)	Villages and other Settlements	Notes
Durham 1776 Settled 1790 Formed as Town of Freehold from Town of Coxsackie in Albany County 1800 Transferred to new county of Greene 1803 Daughter towns Canton (now Cairo) and Greenfield (now Greenville) formed; ceded land to Town of Windham 1805 Name changed to Durham 1836 Daughter town Conesville formed in Schoharie County	Centerville Cornwall(s)ville Dewittsburgh Durham Durso Corner East Durham East Windham Hamburg Hervey Street Oak Hill South Durham Sunside West Durham	• Durham also New Durham • East Durham formerly Winansville • Hamburg also Saybrook • South Durham on Cairo town line
Freehold Name for Town of Durham 1790–1805		
Greenfield Name for Town of Greenville 1803–1808		
Greenville 1750 Settled 1768 Land patented 1803 Formed as Town of Greenfield from towns of Coxsackie and Freehold (now Durham) 1808 Name changed to Freehold 1809 Name changed to Greenville	East Greenville O'Haras Corners Freehold Place(s) Corner(s) Gayhead Result Greenville Sanfords Corner(s) Greenville Center Surprise Newry(s) West Greenville Norton Hill	• Gayhead also Gay Head; on Cairo town line
Halcott 1790 Settled 1851 Formed from Town of Lexington	Halcott Center West Lexington	
Hunter c.1783 Settlers from Putnam County 1813 Formed as Town of Greenland from Town of Windham 1814 Name changed to Hunter 1849 Daughter town Jewett formed 1865 Ceded land to Town of Jewett	Catskill Mountain Kaaterskill Station Station Lanesville East Hunter Laurel House East Kill Laurel House Station Edgewood Mountain House Elka Park Mount House Haines Corners Onteora Park Haines Corners Station Platt(e) Cove Haines Falls Stony Clove Haines Falls Corners Stony Clove Station Haines Falls Station Sugarloaf Hunter (v) Tannerslate Indian Head Tannersville (v) Kaaterskill Tannersville Four Kaaterskill Falls Corners Kaaterskill Junction Twilight Park	• Village of Hunter inc. 1894; formerly Edwardsville • Village of Tannersville inc. 1895
Jewett 1783–84 Settlers from Scotland 1849 Formed from towns of Hunter and Lexington 1858 Ceded land to Town of Lexington 1865 Annexed land from Town of Hunter	Beach(e)s Corner Jewett Heights East Jewett Mill Hollow Goshen Street South Jewett Jewett West Jewett Jewett Center	• East Jewett also East Kill • Jewett formerly Lexington Heights

Towns (and Cities)	Villages and other Settlements		Notes
Lexington 1788 Settled 1813 Formed as Town of New Goshen from the Town of Windham; name changed to Lexington later that year 1849 Daughter town Jewett formed 1851 Daughter town Halcott formed 1858 Annexed land from Town of Jewett	Broadstreet Hollow Bushnell(s)ville East Lexington Forest Valley Lexington Lexington Heights Little Westkill	Mosquito Point North Lexington O'Hara House Sportsville Spruceton West Kill	• Lexington also Lexington Flats and The Flats • Little Westkill was on Prattsville town line • West Kill also Westkill
New Baltimore 1811 Formed from Town of Coxsackie	Deans Mill Grapeville Hannacroix Medway New Baltimore Otter Hook	Paradise Hill Roberts Hill Staco Stanton Hill Sylvandale	• Hannacroix also Hannecroix Kill and New Baltimore Station; variant spellings include Haanadrois, Haanakrois, Hairnadraus, Hanacroys, Hannacraus, Hanna Kress, Hannekraai, and Hennercroix Kill
Prattsville ✳ 1763–76 Settled by Dutch from Schoharie County; left during Revolution, returned after the war 1833 Formed from Town of Windham 1848 Daughter town Ashland formed	Huntersfield Little Westkill Prattsville (v) Red Falls		✳ Prattsville known as Schoharie Kill before 1830 • Little Westkill was on Lexington town line • Village of Prattsville inc. 1883 and dissolved 3/26/1900
Windham Settled pre-Revolution 1798 Formed in Ulster County from Town of Woodstock 1800 Transferred to new county of Greene 1803 Annexed land from Town of Freehold (now Durham) 1813 Daughter towns Greenland (now Hunter) and New Goshen (now Lexington) formed 1833 Daughter town Prattsville formed 1848 Daughter town Ashland formed	Batavia Brook Lynne Brooksburg East Windham Hensonville Maplecrest Mitchell Hollow Nauvoo North Settlement Scienceville Union Society Windham		• Batavia on Ashland town line • Maplecrest formerly Big Hollow • North Settlement on Ashland town line • Scienceville, see hamlet of Ashland in Town of Ashland after 1848 • Windham also Osbornville and Windham Center

NEW YORK STATE CENSUS RECORDS
See also chapter 3, Census Records

County originals at Greene County Clerk's Office: 1855, 1865, 1875, 1892, 1905, 1915, 1925 (1825, 1835, and 1845 are lost)

State originals at the NYSA: 1915, 1925

Microfilm at the FHL, NYPL, NYSHA, and NYSL; many years are online at *FamilySearch.org* and *Ancestry.com*.

NATIONAL/STATEWIDE REPOSITORIES & RESOURCES
See chapter 16

COUNTYWIDE REPOSITORIES & RESOURCES

Greene County Clerk
411 Main Street • Catskill, NY 12414 • (518) 719-3255
Email: countyadministrator@discovergreene.com
http://greenegovernment.com/departments/county-clerk

Land records, court records, naturalization records 1850–1994, and the New York state censuses for Greene County 1855, 1865, 1875, 1892, 1905, 1915, 1925. Complete list of holdings is available on the clerk's website. Greene County's digitized map collection can be accessed in the Records Room. No records are available online.

Greene County – Town and Village Clerks
Birth, marriage, and death records are maintained by the clerk of the municipality in which the event occurred; see Introduction to County Guides for details of other records which may also be held by municipal clerks. For contact information, see *www.greenegovernment. com/about-greene/municipalities*.

Greene County Surrogate's Court
Green County Courthouse • 320 Main Street Catskill, NY 12414
(518) 444-8750

Holds probate records from 1920 to the present. Earlier records are kept at the Vedder Library. The Surrogate's Court also has microfilm of these earlier records. See also chapter 6, Probate Records.

Greene County Public Libraries
Greene is part of the Mid-Hudson Library System; see *www. midhudson.org* to access each library. Many hold genealogy and local history collections, including local newspapers. For example, Catskill Public Library, Greenville Public Library, and Haines Falls Free Library all maintain local history collections.

Greene County Historian
71 Sutton Place • Coxsackie, NY • Email: gchistorian@gmail.com

Greene County – All Municipal Historians
While not authorized to answer genealogical inquiries, town and village historians can provide valuable historical information and research advice; some maintain collections and webpages which may include transcribed records, local histories, and other genealogical material. See contact information at *www.greenegovernment.com/ about-greene/municipalities* or at the website of the Association of Public Historians of New York State at *www.aphnys.org*.

Greene County Historical Society
90 County Route 42 • PO Box 44 • Coxsackie, NY 12051
(518) 731-6490 • Email: gchsvl@mhcable.com (Vedder Research Library)
www.gchistory.org

The Society maintains the Vedder Research Library (see below)

and publishes a quarterly journal, *Greene County Historical Journal* (indexes on the Vedder Library website).

Vedder Research Library
90 County Road 42 • Coxsackie, NY 12051• (518) 731-1033
Email: veddderlibrary@yahoo.com • *www.vedderlibrary.org*

The Vedder Library, maintained by the Greene County Historical Society, contains an extensive collection of genealogy and local history materials including genealogies, research guides, cemetery inscriptions, court records, military records, probate indexes 1800–1930, and vital records. A complete list of holdings is available online.

REGIONAL REPOSITORIES & RESOURCES

Capital District Genealogical Society
See listing in Albany County Guide

Bard College Archives and Special Collections
See listing in Dutchess County Guide

LOCAL REPOSITORIES & RESOURCES
Alphabetized by location

Ashland Historical Association
(518) 734-6432 • *www.ashlandny.com/historical.htm*

Holdings include cemetery records, photographs, postcards, and some vital records. The Association maintains the West Settlement Church.

Cairo Historical Society
PO Box 803 • Cairo, NY 12143
www.rootsweb.ancestry.com/~nygreen2/cairo_historical_society.htm

Projects include digitization of cemetery transcriptions.

Durham Center Museum
State Route 145 • PO Box 192 • East Durham, NY 12423
(518) 239-8461 • Email: DurhamCenterMu@aol.com
www.rootsweb.ancestry.com/~nygreen2/durham_center_museum.htm

Cemetery and church records, family Bibles and family files, and local ephemera. Records from Greene, Albany, Ulster, and Columbia counties; close to 1000 family files pertaining to both genealogy and local history; many out of print books; other hand written records.

Mountain Top Historical Society of Greene County
Route 23A • Haines Falls, NY 12436
Email: mttophistsoc@aol.com • *www.mths.org*

Society documents and preserves the history and culture of the Catskill Mountains of Greene County, including art, literature, folklore, and legends. It hosts historical events and programs, genealogical lectures, and produces a quarterly publication containing news and historical sketches. Holdings include photographs, books, and some family records.

Town of Lexington Historical Society
Church Street • PO Box 247 • Lexington, NY 12452
(518) 989-6476 ext. 16 • Email: lexingtonnyhistorian@hotmail.com
www.lexingtonny.com

Website includes "History of Lexington, NY," with select transcribed records documenting Lexington's history, including land transactions, an indenture record, government appointments, and various town documents.

Zadock Pratt Museum

Main Street • PO Box 333 • Prattsville, NY 12468 • (518) 299-3258
Email: prattmuseum@hotmail.com • Facebook page

Collections (1600s–present) were badly damaged by Hurricane Irene. They include scrapbooks, newspapers, and other genealogical records. Museum is the former home of tanner Colonel Zadock Pratt (1790–1871). Prattsville was one of the first planned communities in New York State. Staff will assist with genealogical inquiries.

SELECTED PRINT & ONLINE RESOURCES

Below is a selection of resources relevant for research in this county. The list is representative, not exhaustive. Additional titles—particularly of abstracts, indexes, transcriptions, and local histories—are available; consult the introduction to Part Two for further information. For guidance on how to identify and locate community directories and local newspapers, see chapter 11, City Directories, and chapter 12, Newspapers, in Part One of this book.

Abstracts, Indexes & Transcriptions

Barber, Gertrude Audrey. "Abstracts of WIlls of Greene County, New York, from Aug. 1803 to. . .[March 1838]" Typescript, 1932. New York State Library, New York.

Barber, Gertrude Audrey, Marjorie S. Dows, and Virginia Moscrip. *Index of Wills, Greene County, New York, 1803–1875*. Vol. 410 of *Cemetery, Church and Town Records of New York State*. Rochester, NY: Daughters of the American Revolution, New York, 1973–1974.

Bowman, Fred Q. *New York's Detailed Census of 1855: Greene County*. Rhinebeck, NY: Kinship, 1988.

Cohen, Minnie. "Gravestone Inscriptions of Catskill Village Cemetery: Catskill, Greene County, N.Y." 2 vols. Typescript, 1931. NYPL, New York. [*Ancestry.com*]

———. "Gravestone Inscriptions of Greene County, New York." 3 vols. Typescript, 1933. NYPL, New York.

County of Greene Abstracts. Syracuse: Central New York Genealogical Society, 2000. Abstracts for a range of genealogical records originally published in the quarterly *Tree Talks*. A name index is on the CNYGS website.

Daughters of the American Revolution, comps. *New York DAR Genealogical Records Committee Report*. Since 1913 DAR volunteers have transcribed many thousands of unpublished cemetery, church, and town records throughout New York. The reports are at the DAR Library; copies are at the NYSL and the NYPL. The DAR has a searchable name index to all the GRC reports at *http://services.dar.org/Public/DAR_Research/search/?Tab_ID=6*. See Jean Worden's index below for a listing by county of the New York record sets that were transcribed by the DAR before 1998.

Greene County Poor House Accounts, 1828–32 and 1849–84. Cooperstown, NY: Microfilmed by the New York State Historical Association, 1997.

Hoffman, William J., comp. "Baptismal Records of Zion Lutheran Church, Loonenburg, Now Athens, Greene County, New York." *NYG&B Record*, vol. 82 (1951) no. 1: 15–31, no. 2: 81–88, no. 3: 161–173, no. 4: 227–243; vol. 83 (1952) no. 1: 24–40, no. 2: 109–116, no. 3: 132–145, no. 4: 240–245; vol. 84 (1953) no. 1: 16–26, no. 2: 82–97, no. 3: 149–159; vol. 85 (1954) no. 1: 13–17, no. 2: 73–83, no. 3: 140–153. [NYG&B eLibrary]

Kelly, Arthur C. M. *Index to Tree Talks County Packet: Greene County*. Rhinebeck, NY: Kinship, 2002.

Sawyer, Ray C., comp. and ed. "Abstract of Wills of Greene County, N.Y." 3 vols. Typescript, 1933–1934. [*Ancestry.com*]

Vosburgh, Royden Woodward, ed. "History of the First Reformed Church of Coxsackie, in West Coxsackie, Greene County, N.Y." 3 vols. Typescript, 1919. NYPL, New York. [NYG&B eLibrary]

———, ed. "Records of the Protestant Reformed Dutch Church of Leeds, in the Town of Catskill, Greene County, N.Y." Typescript. NYPL, New York. [NYG&B eLibrary]

———, ed. "Records of the Reformed Dutch Church in Oak Hill in the Town of Durham, Greene County, N.Y." Typescript. NYPL, New York. [NYG&B eLibrary]

———, ed. "Records of the Reformed Dutch Church of Kiskatom in the Town of Catskill, Greene County, N.Y." Typescript. NYPL, New York. [NYG&B eLibrary]

———, ed. "Records of the Reformed Dutch Church of Wawarsing." Typescript, 1920. NYPL, New York. [NYG&B eLibrary].

Worden, Jean D. "Book 1, Subject Index." In *Revised Master Index to the New York State Daughters of the American Revolution Genealogical Records Volumes*. Zephyrhills, FL: J. D. Worden, 1998. The Subject Index includes a listing by county of the cemeteries, churches, towns, and other sources of records transcribed by the DAR.

Other Resources

Adams, Arthur G., ed. *The Catskills: An Illustrated Historical Guide with Gazetteer*. 2nd edition. New York: Fordham University Press, 1990.

Atkinson, Oriana. *Not Only Ours: A Story of Greene County, N.Y.* Cornwallville, NY: Hope Farm Press, 1974.

Beecher, Raymond. *Greene County: A Bicentennial Overview*. Catskill, NY: The Greene County Historical Society, 2000.

———. *Out to Greenville and Beyond: Historical Sketches of Greene County*. Cornwallville, NY: Hope Farm Press, 1977.

———. *Under Three Flags*. Hensonville, NY: Black Dome Press, 1991.

Beecher, Raymond, Harvey Durham, and Greene County Historical Society. *Around Greene County*. Dover, NH: Arcadia Publishing, 1997.

Beers, F. W. *Atlas of Greene County, New York: From Actual Surveys*. New York, 1867.

Biographical Review . . . Containing Life Sketches of Leading Citizens of Schenectady, Schoharie, and Greene Counties, New York. Boston, 1899.

Bush, Clesson S. *Episodes from a Hudson River Town: New Baltimore, New York*. New York: SUNY Press, 2011.

Bush, Jean M. *Historic Places in Greene County, New York*. Coxsackie, NY: Flint Mine Press, 2009.

Capital District Genealogical Society Newsletter. Albany: Capital District Genealogical Society, 1982–present. [*capitaldistrict genealogicalsociety.org*]

Gallt, Frank A. *Dear Old Greene County; Embracing Facts and Figures: Portraits and Sketches of Leading Men Who Will Live in Her History, Those at the Front To-day and Others Who Made Good in the Past*. Catskill, New York: n.p., 1915.

Geil, Samuel. *Map of Greene County, NY: From Actual Surveys*. Philadelphia, 1856.

The Greene County Directory. Catskill, NY: The Examiner, 1928.

History of Greene County, New York, with Biographical Sketches of Its Prominent Men. New York, 1884.

Horne, Field. *The Greene County Catskills: A History*. Hensonville, NY: Black Dome Press, 2000.

Hudson River Valley Review: A Journal of Regional Studies. Poughkeepsie, NY: Hudson River Valley Institute at Marist College, 2002–present. [hudsonrivervalley.org]

Morrow, Patricia, ed. *Greene Genes: A Genealogical Quarterly about Greene County, New York*. 1988–1999.

New York Historical Resources Center. *Guide to Historical Resources in Greene County, New York, Repositories*. Ithaca, NY: Cornell University, 1988.

Prout, Rev. Henry Hedges. *Old Times in Windham*. Cornwallville, NY: Hope Farm Press, 1970. First published Feb. 18, 1869 to Mar. 31, 1870.

Rockwell, Charles. *The Catskill Mountains and the Region Around*. Cornwallville, NY: Hope Farm Press, 1973. First published 1867.

Ross, Claire L., and Edward R. Kozacek. *Greene County, New York: '76 Bicentennial Overview: Beginnings and Background*. Catskill, NY: Catskill Enterprise, 1976.

Smith, Mabel P. *Greene County, New York: A Short History*. 7th edition. Catskill, NY: E and G Press, 1979.

Vedder, Jessie Van Vechten. *History of Greene County*. Catskill, NY: n.p., 1927.

Woodworth, Olive N. *East Kill Valley Genealogy: A Record of the Burials in Two Catskill Mountain Graveyards with Genealogical Information from 1620 to 1964*. Catskill, NY: Greene & Ulster Print. Co., 1964. Transcription available on Rootsweb.

Additional Online Resources

Ancestry.com

There are vast numbers of records on *Ancestry.com* that pertain to people who have lived in New York State. See chapter 16 for a description of *Ancestry.com*'s resources and its partnership with the New York State Archives. A search of the online card catalog by county may reveal lesser known resources that pertain to a locality, such as town records, abstracts, transcriptions, city directories, and local histories.

FamilySearch.org

FamilySearch has extensive collections of New York records, including religious records, which are searchable by name and location, but not by county. The following collections include record images (browsable, but not searchable) that are organized by county:

- "New York, Land Records, 1630–1975." Includes land and property records. *familysearch.org/search/collection/2078654*

- "New York, Probate Records, 1629–1971." Includes wills, letters of administration, and guardianship papers. *familysearch.org/search/collection/1920234*

For both collections, choose the browse option and then select Greene to view the available records sets.

A detailed description of *FamilySearch.org* resources is found in chapter 16.

Hudson River Valley Heritage (HRVH)
www.hrvh.org/cdm

The HRVH website provides free access to digital collections of historical material from more than 40 organizations in Columbia, Greene, Dutchess, Ulster, Sullivan, Rockland, Orange, Putnam, and Westchester counties.

USGenWeb Project: Greene County
www.hopefarm.com/geneatop.htm

Part of the national, USGenWeb volunteer initiative, the website provides information and resources for county research.

Hamilton County

Formed February 12, 1816

Parent County   Montgomery
Daughter Counties None
County Seat   Lake Pleasant, Town of Lake Pleasant

Major Land Transactions
See table in chapter 7, Land Records
Sacandaga Patent 1741
Totten and Crossfield Purchase 1771–1787

Town Boundary Map
★ - County seat

Towns (and Cities)	Villages and other Settlements	Notes
Arietta 1827 Settled 1836 Formed from Town of Lake Pleasant 1837 Daughter town Long Lake formed	Arietta Piseco Avery(s) Place Powley Place Clockmill Corners Rudeston(e) Higgins Bay Shaker Place Kenwells Spy Lake	• Kenwells on Inlet town line • Piseco also Pezceko
Benson 1860 Formed from Town of Mayfield (Fulton County) and Town of Hope	Benson Upper Benson	• Benson in Town of Hope before 1860 • Upper Benson also Benson Centre and Benson Center
Gilman 1839–1860 1839 Formed from Town of Wells 1858 Daughter town Indian Lake formed 1860 Town dissolved and divided between towns of Wells and Lake Pleasant	Gilman	• Hamlet of Gilman now Gilmantown in Town of Wells
Hope 1790 Settled 1818 Formed from Town of Wells 1847 Annexed land from Town of Lake Pleasant 1860 Daughter town Benson formed	Benson Benson Center Fayville Hope Hope Falls Hope Valley Maple Grove	• Benson and Benson Center in Town of Benson after 1860 • Hope also Hope Center
Indian Lake 1858 Formed from towns of Gilman, Long Lake and Wells 1861 Annexed land from Town of Lake Pleasant	Blue Mountain Lake Little Canada Cedar River Parkerville Eagle Nest Sabael Indian Lake Wilderness Lodge	
Inlet 1901 Formed from Town of Morehouse	Beecher Seventh Lake Inlet Uncas Road Kenwells	• Kenwells on Inlet town line
Lake Pleasant 1795 Settlers from Columbia County 1812 Formed in Montgomery County from Town of Johnstown * 1816 Transferred to new county of Hamilton; annexed land from Montgomery County (land from towns of Johnstown and Salisbury) * 1835 Daughter town Morehouse formed 1836 Daughter town Arietta formed 1837 Daughter town Long Lake formed 1847 Ceded land to Town of Hope 1858 Ceded land to Town of Wells 1860 Town of Gilman dissolved and divided between towns of Lake Pleasant and Wells 1861 Ceded land to Indian Lake	Lake Pleasant Speculator (v)	* Town of Johnstown now in Fulton County * Town of Salisbury now in Herkimer County • Part of hamlet of Lake Pleasant was called Sageville 1844–1897; county seat from 1816 • Village of Speculator inc. 1925; was Newtons Corners 1864–1896

Towns (and Cities)	Villages and other Settlements		Notes
Long Lake **1837** Formed from towns of Arietta, Lake Pleasant, Morehouse, and Wells **1858** Daughter town Indian Lake formed	Antlers Bog Lake Brandreth Lake Brightside Catlin Caugeville Deerland Golden Beach Hasbroucks Island House Keepawa Lake Lila	Long Lake Nehasane Partlow Raquette Lake Robinwood Rocky Point Sabattis (The) Sagamore Uncas Whitney(s) Woods	• Deerland formerly Grove • Hasbroucks also Hasbrooks • Raquette Lake also Racket • Sabattis was Long Lake West; burned 1908; named Sabattis in 1923
Morehouse **1833** Settled **1835** Formed from Town of Lake Pleasant **1837** Daughter town Long Lake formed **1901** Daughter town Inlet formed	Bethunville Hoffmeister Morehouseville Mountain Home		• Morehouseville also Morehouse
Wells **1798** Settled **1805** Formed in Montgomery County from towns of Mayfield and Northampton * **1812** Annexed land from Town of Mayfield * **1816** Transferred to new county of Hamilton **1818** Daughter town Hope formed **1837** Daughter town Long Lake formed **1839** Daughter town Gilman formed **1858** Daughter town Indian Lake formed; annexed land from Town of Lake Pleasant **1860** Town of Gilman dissolved and divided between towns of Wells and Lake Pleasant	Alvord Black Bridge Gilmantown Griffin Pickleville Pumpkin Hollow Wells Whitehouse Windfall		* Towns of Mayfield and Northampton now in Fulton County • Gilmantown formerly Gilman; in Town of Gilman before 1860

NEW YORK STATE CENSUS RECORDS

See also chapter 3, Census Records

County originals at Hamilton County Clerk's Office: 1825*, 1892, 1905, 1915, 1925 (1835, 1845, 1855, 1865, and 1875 are lost)

State originals at the NYSA: 1915, 1925

Microfilm at the FHL, NYPL, and NYSL; many years are online at *FamilySearch.org* and *Ancestry.com*.

*Although created in 1816, Hamilton County is included in the 1825 New York state census for Montgomery County. The towns (Hope, Lake Pleasant, and Wells) are enumerated separately and Hope and Lake Pleasant have been indexed by the Montgomery County Department of History and Archives.

NATIONAL/STATEWIDE REPOSITORIES & RESOURCES

See chapter 16

COUNTYWIDE REPOSITORIES & RESOURCES

Hamilton County Clerk

102 County View Drive • PO Box 204 • Lake Pleasant, NY 12108
(518) 548-7111 or 548-6204
Email: countyclerk@hamiltoncountyny.gov • *www.hamiltoncounty.com*

Land records; court records; naturalization records 1854–1906; and the New York state censuses for Hamilton County 1892, 1905, 1915, and 1925.

Hamilton County – Town and Village Clerks

Birth, marriage, and death records are maintained by the clerk of the municipality in which the event occurred; see Introduction to County Guides for details of other records which may also be held by municipal clerks. For contact information, see *www. hamiltoncounty.com*.

Hamilton County Surrogate's Court

Chief Clerk's Office • 79 White Birch Lane
PO Box 780 • Indian Lake, NY 12842 • (518) 648-5411

Holds probate records from the late 1800s to the present. Also see chapter 6, Probate Records.

Hamilton County Public Libraries

Hamilton is part of the Southern Adirondack Library System; many local libraries hold genealogy and local history collections. See *http://directory.sals.edu* to access each library.

Hamilton County Historian

102 County View Drive • PO Box 205 • Lake Pleasant, NY 12108
(518) 548-5526 • Email: historian@HamiltonCountyNY.gov

Holdings include genealogy and subject files, maps, and photographs.

Hamilton County – All Municipal Historians

While not authorized to answer genealogical inquiries, city, town, and village historians can provide valuable historical information and research advice to family historians; some maintain collections with genealogical material. For contact information, see *www.hamilt on.nygenweb.net/resources/index.html*.

REGIONAL REPOSITORIES & RESOURCES

Adirondack Museum Library

Rt. 28N & 30 • Blue Mountain Lake, NY 12812 • (518) 532-7311
Email: info@adirondackmuseum.org • *www.adkmuseum.org*

Books and manuscripts, audio recordings, periodicals, maps, serials, vertical files, and government documents. Collection may be searched via online catalog.

Fulton-Montgomery Community College: Evans Library: The Kenneth R. Dorn Regional History Study Center

See listing in Fulton County Guide

LOCAL REPOSITORIES & RESOURCES

Alphabetized by location

Morehouse Historical Museum

Route 8, Box 1 • Hoffmeister, NY 13353 • Email: BearPath@ntcnet.com
www.hamilton.nygenweb.net/MoreMus/museum.html

Museum is located in the old Methodist Church.

Indian Lake Museum

Corner of West Main Street and Crow Hill Road
Indian Lake, NY 12842 • (518) 648-5377
www.adirondackscenicbyways.org/resource/indian-lake-museum.html

Holdings include 19th-century photographs and information on history of American Indians in the area.

Inlet Historical Society

PO Box 473 • Inlet, NY 13360 • Email: info@InletHistoricalSociety.org
www.inlethistoricalsociety.org

Society's Archives are located above Inlet Post Office. Meetings held at Inlet Town Hall.

Long Lake Historical Society & Archives Building

1132 Deerland Road • PO Box 201 • Long Lake, NY 1284
(518) 524-5374 • Email: llarchives@frontiernet.net • Facebook page

Archives include photographs and family history records.

Piseco Lake Historical Society, Riley House and Tavern

Old Piseco Road • Piseco, NY 12139 • (518) 548-4920

Holdings include Town of Arietta census materials 1850–1925, letters 1836–1864, photographs, and artifacts.

Historical Society of Lake Pleasant & Speculator and Museum

PO Box 103 • Speculator, NY 12164 • (518) 548-4478
Email: lphistory@frontiernet.net • *www.lakespec.wordpress.com*

Museum and town historian's office are located in the former Lake Pleasant Town Hall. Holdings include photographs.

SELECTED PRINT & ONLINE RESOURCES

Below is a selection of resources relevant for research in this county. The list is representative, not exhaustive. Additional titles—particularly of abstracts, indexes, transcriptions, and local histories—are available; consult the introduction to Part Two for further information. For guidance on how to identify and locate community directories and local newspapers, see chapter 11, City Directories, and chapter 12, Newspapers, in Part One of this book.

Abstracts, Indexes & Transcriptions

Becker, Edith V., Melvin W. Lethbridge, and Leslie A. Frye. *Cemetery Records of Saratoga, Herkimer, and Hamilton Counties.* New York: Montgomery County (NY) Department of History and Archives, 1939. Includes index.

County of Hamilton Abstracts. Syracuse: Central New York Genealogical Society, 2000. Abstracts for a range of genealogical records originally published in the quarterly *Tree Talks*. A name index is on the CNYGS website.

Daughters of the American Revolution, comps. *New York DAR Genealogical Records Committee Report.* Since 1913 DAR volunteers have transcribed many thousands of unpublished cemetery, church, and town records throughout New York. The reports are at the DAR Library; copies are at the NYSL and the NYPL. The DAR has a searchable name index to all the GRC reports at *http://services.dar.org/Public/DAR_Research/search/?Tab_ID=6*. See Jean Worden's index below for a listing by county of the New York record sets that were transcribed by the DAR before 1998.

Deed Books, 1797–1901; Indexes to Deeds and Mortgages, 1797–1959. Salt Lake City: Filmed by the Genealogical Society of Utah, 1968. [

Estate Papers, Nos. 1–1468; 1861–1900s. Salt Lake City: Filmed by the Genealogical Society of Utah, 1968.

Fyvie, Helen B. *Cemeteries of Fulton and Hamilton Counties.* Salt Lake City, Utah: Filmed by the Genealogical Society of Utah, 1980.

Hamilton County Clerk. *Marriage Records, 1908–1936.* Salt Lake City: Filmed by the Genealogical Society of Utah, 1979.

Kelly, Arthur C. M. *Index to Tree Talks County Packet: Hamilton County.* Rhinebeck, NY: Kinship, 2002.

Kennedy, Jesse, and Lorraine Kennedy. "Cemetery Inscriptions from Fulton and Hamilton Counties, New York." Typescript, 1969–1970.

New York County Court (Hamilton County). *Naturalization Records, 1854–1906.* Salt Lake City: Filmed by the Genealogical Society of Utah, 1979. Includes index.

New York Supreme Court (Hamilton County). *Lis Pendens, No. 1, 1880–1902, with Index.* Salt Lake City: Filmed by the Genealogical Society of Utah, 1968.

New York Surrogate's Court (Hamilton County). *Probate Records, 1861–1934.* Salt Lake City: Filmed by the Genealogical Society of Utah, 1968. Includes index.

Worden, Jean D. "Book 1, Subject Index." In *Revised Master Index to the New York State Daughters of the American Revolution Genealogical Records Volumes.* Zephyrhills, FL: J. D. Worden, 1998. The Subject Index includes a listing by county of the cemeteries, churches, towns, and other sources of records transcribed by the DAR.

Other Resources

Aber, Ted, and Stella King. *The History of Hamilton County.* Lake Pleasant, NY: Great Wilderness Books, 1965.

———. *Tales from an Adirondack County.* Prospect, NY: Prospect Books, 1961.

Butler, B. C. *The New York Wilderness: Hamilton County and Adjoining Territory.* Albany, 1879.

Fay, Loren V. *Hamilton County, New York, Genealogical Research Secrets.* Albany: L.V. Fay, 1981.

Hamilton County, New York. Map. New York: Everts Publishing Company, 1911.

National Survey. *Highway Department Map of Hamilton County, New York.* Lake Pleasant, NY: Hamilton County Planning, Tourism, and Community Development, 1985.

New York Historical Resources Center. *Guide to Historical Resources in Hamilton County, New York, Repositories.* Ithaca, NY: Cornell University, 1984. [*books.FamilySearch.org*]

Northern New York Library Network. *Directory of Archival and Historical Document Collections.* 2011–2013 edition; published digitally at *http://nny.nnyln.org/archives/ArchivalDirectory.pdf.* Online indexes at *http://nny.nnyln.org/archives/page01.html.* Describes collections held by organizations in Clinton, Essex, Franklin, Jefferson, Lewis, Oswego, and St. Lawrence counties.

Southern Adirondack Library System. *Guide to Local Historical Materials: A Union List of Holdings of Public Libraries in Saratoga, Warren, Washington and Hamilton Counties.* Saratoga Springs, NY: Southern Adirondack Library System, 1977.

Additional Online Resources

Ancestry.com

There are vast numbers of records on *Ancestry.com* that pertain to people who have lived in New York State. See chapter 16 for a description of *Ancestry.com*'s resources and its partnership with the New York State Archives. A search of the online card catalog by county may reveal lesser known resources that pertain to a locality, such as town records, abstracts, transcriptions, city directories, and local histories.

FamilySearch.org

FamilySearch has extensive collections of New York records, including religious records, which are searchable by name and location, but not by county. The following collections include record images (browsable, but not searchable) that are organized by county:

- "New York, Land Records, 1630–1975." Includes land and property records. *familysearch.org/search/collection/2078654*
- "New York, Probate Records, 1629–1971." Includes wills, letters of administration, and guardianship papers. *familysearch.org/search/collection/1920234*

For both collections, choose the browse option and then select Hamilton to view the available records sets.

A detailed description of *FamilySearch.org* resources is found in chapter 16.

NYGenWeb Project: Hamilton County

www.hamilton.nygenweb.net

Part of the national, USGenWeb volunteer initiative, the website provides information and resources for county research.

Herkimer County

Formed February 16, 1791

Parent County   Montgomery
Daughter Counties Onondaga 1794 • Chenango 1798 • Oneida 1798
County Seat   Village of Herkimer

Major Land Transactions
See table in chapter 7, Land Records
Burnetsfield Patent 1725 • Cosby's Manor 1734 • Royal Grant 1765
Totten and Crossfield Purchase 1771–1787 • Macomb Purchase 1792

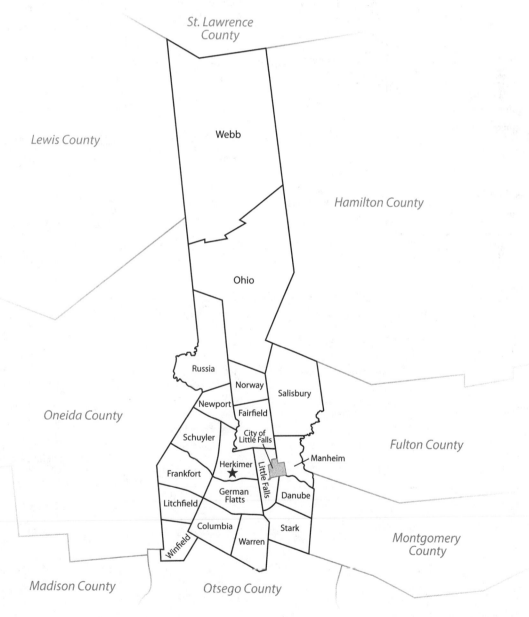

Town Boundary Map
★ - County seat

Towns (and Cities)	Villages and other Settlements		Notes
Aurelius * In Herkimer County 1791–1794			* See Cayuga County
Bridgewater * In Herkimer County 1797–1798			* See Oneida County
Brookfield * In Herkimer County 1795–1798			* See Madison County
Cazenovia * In Herkimer County 1795–1798			* See Madison County
Columbia Settled pre-Revolution at Coonrodstown 1812 Formed from Town of Warren	Cedarville Cedarville Station Columbia Center Coonrodsto(w)n Dennison Corners Elizabeth Town Getman Corners Kingdom McKoon(s) Crossing	Millers Mills Millers Mills Crossing North Columbia Orendorf Corners South Columbia Spinnerville Youngs Crossing Youngs Mills	• Cedarville on Litchfield and Winfield town lines • Columbia Center also Columbia and Petries Corners • Dennison Corners also Dennison and Whitmantown; on German Flatts town line • Kingdom on Warren town line
Danube 1780 Settled 1817 Formed from Town of Minden, Montgomery County 1828 Daughter town Stark formed	Davys Corners Finks Basin Indian Castle Indian Castle Station Newville Walrath Hollow		• Indian Castle also Danube
Fairfield 1770 German settlers 1796 Formed from Town of Norway 1806 Daughter town Newport formed 1829 Daughter town Little Falls formed	Barto Hill Countryman Countryman Station Dillenbeck Corners Eatonville	Fairfield Goodall Corners Middleville (v) Old City Welch Corners	• Eatonville on Herkimer and Little Falls town lines • Village of Middleville inc. 1890; shared with Town of Newport • Old City on Newport town line • Welch Corners on Newport town line
Floyd * In Herkimer County 1796–1798			* See Oneida County
Frankfort Settled pre-Revolution 1796 Formed from Town of German Flatts	Center Corrado Corners East Frankfort Frankfort (v) Frankfort Center Frankfort Hill Graefenberg Grand View Gulph Harbor	Harbor Barge Canal Harbor Station Jerusalem Hill Kinne(y) Corners McGowan New Graefenberg North Frankfort Stewart Corners West Frankfort	• East Frankfort on German Flatts town line • Village of Frankfort inc. 1863 • Frankfort Center formerly Howards Bush • Gulph on Litchfield town line • Jerusalem Hill was on Litchfield town line • Kinne(y) Corners was on German Flatts and Litchfield town lines • North Frankfort on Schuyler town line • West Frankfort formerly Four Mile Grocery

Towns (and Cities)	Villages and other Settlements	Notes
German Flatts 1722 Settled by German Palatines 1756 Settlements attacked and abandoned during French and Indian War 1772 Formed as Kingsland District in Tryon County (now Montgomery County) 1773 Exchanged names with German Flatts District 1788 Recognized as a town by State of New York 1791 Transferred to new county of Herkimer 1796 Daughter towns Frankfort, Litchfield, and Warren formed 1829 Daughter town Little Falls formed	Days Rock Dennison Corners East Frankfort Edicks Fort Herkimer German Flatts Ilion (v) Kinne(y) Corners Mohawk (v) North Ilion Paines Hollow South Ilion	• Dennison Corners also Dennison, and Whitmantown; on Columbia town line • East Frankfort on Frankfort town line • Village of Ilion inc. 1852; also Remington, Remington Corners, and The Corners • Kinne(y) Corners was on Frankfort and Litchfield town lines • Village of Mohawk inc. 1844 • Paines Hollow now in Town of Little Falls
Hamilton * In Herkimer County 1795–1798		* See Madison County
Herkimer 1722 Settled by German Palatines 1788 Formed in Montgomery County from Kingsland District and Town of German Flatts 1791 Transferred to new county of Herkimer 1792 Daughter towns Norway and Schuyler formed 1806 Daughter town Newport formed 1829 Daughter town Little Falls formed	Beacon Light Corners County House Station East Herkimer Eatonville Herkimer (v) Kast Bridge Kast Bridge Station Petrie Development Schells Bush West Herkimer	• Eatonville on Fairfield and Little Falls town lines • Village of Herkimer inc. 1807; formerly Stone Ridge; county seat 1798–present; 1791–1798 county seat in Whitesboro, Town of Whitestown (now in Oneida County)
Leyden * In Herkimer County 1797–1798		* See Lewis County
Litchfield 1789 Settled on Snow Hill 1796 Formed from Town of German Flatts 1816 Daughter town Winfield formed	Cedar Lake Cedarville Columbia(n) Springs Cranes Corners Days Corners Goodiers Corners Gulph Jerusalem Jerusalem Hill Kinne(y) Corners Litchfield North Litchfield Norwich Corners Parkers Corners Wheelock(s) Hill	• Cedarville on Columbia and Winfield town lines • Gulph on Frankfort town line • Jerusalem Hill was on Frankfort town line • Kinne(y) Corners was on Frankfort and German Flatts town lines • Wheelock(s) Hill also Whelocks Hill, formerly Snow Hill and Snows Bush
Little Falls (city) 1811 Incorporated as a village in the Town of Little Falls 1895 Formed as a city from Village of Little Falls		

Towns (and Cities)	Villages and other Settlements	Notes
Little Falls (town) 1722 Settled by German Palatines 1829 Formed from towns of Fairfield, German Flatts, and Herkimer 1868 Ceded land to Town of Stark 1895 Village of Little Falls incorporated as City of Little Falls	Bethel Deck Eatonville Jacksonburg Little Britain Little Falls (v) Paines Hollow Wrights Corners	• Deck on Stark town line • Eatonville on Fairfield and Herkimer town lines • Village of Little Falls inc. 1811; renamed Rockton in 1850, name restored 1852, also known as Rock City; became City of Little Falls in 1895 • Paines Hollow formerly in Town of German Flatts
Manheim 1736 German settlers 1797 Formed from Town of Palatine, Montgomery County 1817 Transferred to Herkimer County	Dolgeville (v) Ingham Mills Station East Creek Manheim Garlock Corners Manheim Center	• Village of Dolgeville inc. 1881; formerly Greens Bridge 1805–1826, Brocketts Bridge 1826–1881; shared with Town of Oppenheim in Fulton County • Ingham Mills Station formerly Ingham(s) Mills
Mexico * In Herkimer County 1792–1798		* See Oswego County
Milton * In Herkimer County 1791–1794		* See Town of Genoa in Cayuga County
Newport 1791 Settlers from Rhode Island 1806 Formed from towns of Fairfield, Herkimer, Norway, and Schuyler	Brayton(s) Corners Newport (v) Farrel Corner Newport Station Fenner Grove Station Old City Irish Settlement Poland (v) Martin(s) Corners Welch Corners Middleville (v)	• Village of Middleville inc. 1890; shared with Town of Fairfield • Village of Newport inc. 1857 • Old City on Fairfield town line • Village of Poland inc. 1890; shared with Town of Russia • Welch Corners on Fairfield town line
Norway 1786 Settlers from Rhode Island 1792 Formed from Town of Herkimer 1796 Daughter town Fairfield formed 1798 Daughter town Remsen formed in Oneida County 1806 Daughter towns Union (now Russia) and Newport formed 1823 Daughter town Ohio formed	Gray Hurricane Norway	• Gray also Graysville and Grayville; on Ohio town line
Ohio Settled pre-Revolution, abandoned during Revolution 1823 Formed as West Brunswick from Town of Norway 1836 Name changed to Ohio; daughter town Wilmurt formed 1896 Town of Wilmurt dissolved and divided between Town of Ohio and new Town of Webb	Atwell Nobleboro Bull Hill North Wilmurt Conklin Bridge Northwood Dutch Settlement Ohio Gray Ohio City Honnedaga Wilmurt McIntosh Bridge Wilmurt Corners	• Gray also Graysville and Grayville; on Norway town line
Paris * In Herkimer County 1792–1798		* See Oneida County
Pompey * In Herkimer County 1791–1794		* See Onondaga County

Towns (and Cities)	Villages and other Settlements		Notes
Rome * In Herkimer County 1796–1798			* See Oneida County
Russia 1792 Settlers from Connecticut 1806 Formed as Union from Town of Norway 1808 Name changed to Russia 1836 Daughter town Wilmurt formed	Cold Brook (v) Gang Mills Grant Gravesville Hinckley Northwood Pardeeville Corners	Poland (v) Prospect Russia Russia Corners Trenton Falls Station Wheelertown	• Village of Cold Brook inc. 1903 • Grant also Black Creek, Booth, Postville, and Potters Bush • Village of Poland inc. 1890; shared with Town of Newport
Sangerfield * In Herkimer County 1795–1798			* See Oneida County
Salisbury Settled pre-Revolution 1797 Formed in Montgomery County from Town of Palatine 1816 Ceded land to Town of Lake Pleasant, Hamilton County 1817 Town transferred to Herkimer County	Bungtown Burrell Corners California Curtis Curtis Corners Devereaux Diamond Hill Dutchtown Emmonsburg Fairview Corners Hopson District	Irondale Ives Hollow Jerseyfield Mexico Oak Mountain Paper Mill Corners Salisbury Salisbury Center Shedd Corners Stratford Woods Corners	• Emmonsburg formerly Harts Bridge and Whitesburgh • Salisbury also Salisbury Corners • Stratford also Nicholsville
Schuyler c. 1765 German settlers 1792 Formed from Town of Herkimer 1797 Daughter town Trenton formed 1798 Daughter town Deerfield formed in Oneida County 1806 Daughter town Newport formed	Baker Corners Carey Corners Chyle Croton Station Dutch Town East Schuyler Johnson Corners	Minott Corners North Frankfort Schuyler Junction Sheaf Corners West Schuyler Windfall	• Chyle formerly Youngsfield • North Frankfort on Frankfort town line
Sherburne * In Herkimer County 1795–1798			* See Chenango County
Stark Settled before 1775; broken up during Revolution, resettled later 1828 Formed from Town of Danube 1868 Annexed land from Town of Little Falls	Cramer Corners Deck Smith(s) Corners Starkville Van Hornesville Willse Four Corners		• Deck on Little Falls town line
Steuben * In Herkimer County 1792–1798			* See Oneida County
Trenton * In Herkimer County 1797–1798			* See Oneida County
Union Name for Town of Russia 1806–1808			
Warren Settled by Germans pre-Revolution 1796 Formed from Town of German Flatts 1812 Daughter town Columbia formed	Crains Corners Cullen Henderson Jordanville	Kingdom Pages Corners Warren	• Kingdom on Columbia town line • Warren also Little Lakes

Towns (and Cities)	Villages and other Settlements		Notes
Webb 1896 Formed from Town of Wilmurt when Wilmurt was dissolved	Beaver River Big Moose Bisby Lodge Brandreth Carter Station Eagle Bay Keepawa Little Rapids McKeever	Minnehaha Moshier Falls Mountain Lodge Old Forge (v) Rondaxe Stillwater Thendara Woods Lake	• Village of Old Forge inc. 1903, dissolved 10/21/1933
West Brunswick Name for Town of Ohio 1823–1836			
Western * In Herkimer County 1797–1798			* See Oneida County
Westmoreland * In Herkimer County 1792–1798			* See Oneida County
Whitestown * In Herkimer County 1791–1798			* See Oneida County
Wilmurt 1836–1896 * 1836 Formed from towns of Russia and West Brunswick (now Town of Ohio) 1896 Dissolved and divided between the Town of Ohio and the new Town of Webb			* In 1840 Wilmurt was the largest town in the state and had the lowest population—only 60 people in the 1840 census
Winfield 1792 Settled 1816 Formed from towns of Plainfield and Richfield (Otsego County), and Town of Litchfield	Birmingham Corners Cedarville Cedarville Station Chepachet East Winfield Hitching Corner	Meeting House Green North Winfield Sepachet West Winfield (v) Winfield Woods Corners	• Cedarville on Columbia and Litchfield town lines • Village of West Winfield inc. 1898

Note about Herkimer Early Records

Herkimer's county seat was in Whitestown 1791–1798; these records are with the Oneida County Clerk's office as Whitestown became part of Oneida County in 1798. Records 1798–1804 were lost in a courthouse fire. For records 1804–present, see Herkimer County Clerk below.

NEW YORK STATE CENSUS RECORDS

See also chapter 3, Census Records

County originals at Herkimer County Clerk's Office: 1825*, 1835, 1845, 1855, 1865, 1875, 1892, 1905, 1915, 1925

State originals at the NYSA: 1915, 1925

Microfilm at the FHL, NYPL, NYSHA, and NYSL; many years are online at *FamilySearch.org* and *Ancestry.com.*

* For 1825 census transcription and index, see Barnello, et. al., in Abstracts, Indexes & Transcriptions.

NATIONAL/STATEWIDE REPOSITORIES & RESOURCES

See chapter 16

COUNTYWIDE REPOSITORIES & RESOURCES

Herkimer County Clerk
Herkimer County Building • 109 Mary Street
Suite 1111 • Herkimer, NY 13350 • (315) 867-1129
www.herkimercounty.org/content/departments/View/12

Deeds 1804–present (for earlier records, see Oneida County); survey maps mid-1800s–present; atlases 1868–1906; incorporation records 1814–present; index to business names 1902–present; naturalization records 1818–1955; federal census records 1820–1920, Herkimer County originals of the New York state census 1825, 1835, 1845, 1855, 1865, 1875, 1892, 1905, 1915, and 1925.

Herkimer County – City, Town, and Village Clerks
Birth, marriage, and death records are maintained by the clerk of the municipality in which the event occurred; see Introduction to County Guides for details of other records which may also be held by municipal clerks. For contact information, see *www.herkimercounty. org/content/Generic/View/5.*

Herkimer County Surrogate's Court
Herkimer County Office and Court Facility
301 N. Washington Street • Herkimer, NY 13350 • (315) 867-1170

Holdings include probate records from 1791 to the present. See also chapter 6, Probate Records.

Herkimer County Public Libraries
Herkimer is part of the Mid-York Library System; see *http://myls.ent. sirsi.net* to access each library. Many hold genealogy and local history collections, including maps and newspapers. Also see listings below for the Ilion Free and Frank J. Basloe public libraries.

Herkimer County Historical Society
400 North Main Street • Herkimer, NY 13350 • (315) 866-6413
Email: herkimerhistory@yahoo.com
www.rootsweb.Ancestry.com/~nyhchs/index.html

Federal and New York state census records 1790–1930 (in print and on CD), business directories (1869–1995 with gaps), cemetery files, will index 1790–1900, newspapers, marriage, and obituary notices 1800s, *Evening Telegram*, 1900–1920, and *Herkimer/Ilion Citizen*, 1867–1921,

genealogies, gazetteers 1860 and 1875, county atlases 1868 and 1906, township/village publications, history books, and vertical files. Website includes contact information for town and village historians; family sketches taken from Hardin's 1893 *History of Herkimer County*; and town histories taken from Benton's 1856 *History of Herkimer County.* Publishes a journal, *Herkimer County Historical Crier.*

Herkimer County Historian
318 Margaret Street • Herkimer, NY 13350 • (315) 866-1398

Herkimer County – All Municipal Historians
While not authorized to answer genealogical inquiries, city, town and village historians can provide valuable historical information and research advice to family historians; some maintain collections with genealogical material. Some historians also have webpages with local histories, transcribed records, links to useful resources, and other genealogical information. For contact information, see *www.herkimer. nygenweb.net/histsocs.html.*

REGIONAL REPOSITORIES & RESOURCES

Adirondack Museum Library
See listing in Hamilton County Guide

Fulton-Montgomery Community College: Evans Library: The Kenneth R. Dorn Regional History Study Center
See listing in Fulton County Guide

SUNY at Oswego: Local History Collection
See listing in Oswego County Guide

LOCAL REPOSITORIES & RESOURCES
Alphabetized by location

The Dolgeville/Manheim Historical Society
74 South Main Street • Dolgeville, NY 13329
www.dolgeville-manheimhistoricalsociety.blogspot.com

Local history books, genealogies, newspapers, and photographs.

Frank J. Basloe Public Library: Genealogy Room
The Evelyn Dexter Arthur Collection • 245 N. Main Street
Herkimer, NY 13350 • (315) 866-1733
www.midyork.org/herkimer/genealogy.html

Obituary index from *Herkimer Evening Telegram* 1945–present, more than 600 genealogical research books, more than 100 binders of locality files and various publications, census on microfilm, private genealogical books of various town families, maps, and city directories.

Ilion Free Public Library
78 West Street • Ilion, NY 13357 • (315) 894-5028
www.midyork.org/ilion

Local histories, city directories, church files, business files, local newspapers on microfilm, photographs, obituary files, founding family files, genealogical books on local families, local directories, and yearbooks.

Town of Warren Historical Society
Main Street • PO Box 44 • Jordanville, NY 13407 • (315) 858-2874

Family files, newspaper clippings, photographs, and scrapbooks.

The Little Falls Historical Society Museum
319 South Ann Street • Little Falls, NY 13365 • (315) 823-0643
Email: lfhistor@ntcnet.com • www.LFHistoricalSociety.com

Materials, records, and artifacts that relate to local history and genealogy. Research services are available for a fee.

Kuyahoora Valley Historical Society
Newport History Center • 7435 Main Street
PO Box 445 • Newport, NY 13416 • (315) 845-8434
Email: newhisct@ntcnet.com • www.rootsweb.Ancestry.com/~nykvhs

Documents the history of the towns of Fairfield, Newport, Norway, Ohio, and Russia. Obituaries, cemetery records, artifacts, family files, yearbooks, pictures, postcards, souvenirs, biographies, town history, diaries, book and record indexes, historical house information, and wedding photos.

Newport History Center
7435 Main Street • Newport, NY 13416 • (315) 845-8434
Email: newhisct@ntcnet.com
www.rootsweb.Ancestry.com/~nynhc/index.htm

Books, documents, and genealogical information, 1796–present.

Norway Historical Society
1067 Newport Gray Road • Norway, NY 13416 • (315) 845-6650

Housed in the Norway Baptist Church, built in 1831. Holdings include records from the early-1800s to the present.

Town of Webb Historical Association and Goodsell Museum
Corner of Gilbert and Main Streets • PO Box 513
Old Forge, NY 13420 • (315) 369-3838
Email: director@webbhistory.org • www.webbhistory.org

Local newspapers 1926–present, maps, photographs and postcards, vertical files, yearbooks, artifacts, and more.

Salisbury Historical Society and 1805 Frisbie House
109 State Route 29A • Salisbury Center, NY 13454
(315) 429-3605 • Facebook page

Holdings include family files, photographs, and scrapbooks.

SELECTED PRINT & ONLINE RESOURCES

Below is a selection of resources relevant for research in this county. The list is representative, not exhaustive. Additional titles—particularly of abstracts, indexes, transcriptions, and local histories—are available; consult the introduction to Part Two for further information. For guidance on how to identify and locate community directories and local newspapers, see chapter 11, City Directories, and chapter 12, Newspapers, in Part One of this book.

Abstracts, Indexes & Transcriptions

American Agriculturist Farm Directory and Reference Book of Otsego and Herkimer Counties, New York, 1917; A Rural Directory and Reference Book Including a Road Map of Otsego and Herkimer Counties. New York: O. Judd Co., 1917.

Barnello, Kathleen, Joan Green, Joyce Mason, and Harold Witter. *Abstract of the 1825 New York State Census of Herkimer County, New York.* Syracuse: Central New York Genealogical Society, 1999. Originally published in *Tree Talks*, vol. 39, no. 4 (1999): 1–47. Index: 49–66, introduction: ii–vii.

Becker, Edith V., Melvin W. Lethbridge, and Leslie A. Frye. *Cemetery Records of Saratoga, Herkimer, and Hamilton Counties.* New York: Montgomery County (NY) Department of History and Archives, 1939. Includes index.

Cormack, Marie Noll, and Katherine A. Furman. *New York State Cemetery Inscriptions: Albany County, Herkimer County, Montgomery County, Saratoga County, Schenectady County.* Salt Lake City: Filmed by the Genealogical Society of Utah, 1967.

County of Herkimer Abstracts. Syracuse: Central New York Genealogical Society, 2000. Abstracts for a range of genealogical records originally published in the quarterly *Tree Talks*.

Daughters of the American Revolution, comps. *New York DAR Genealogical Records Committee Report.* Since 1913 DAR volunteers have transcribed many thousands of unpublished cemetery, church, and town records throughout New York. The reports are at the DAR Library; copies are at the NYSL and the NYPL. The DAR has a searchable name index to all the GRC reports at http://services.dar.org/Public/DAR_Research/search/?Tab_ID=6. See Jean Worden's index below for a listing by county of the New York record sets that were transcribed by the DAR before 1998.

Herkimer County Historical Society. *Index to the 1855 New York State Census of Herkimer County.* Syracuse: Hall & McChesney, 1980.

Herkimer County, NYG&B Church Surveys Collection. NYG&B, New York. [NYG&B eLibrary]

Kelly, Arthur C. M. *Baptism Record of German Flats Reformed Church.* Rhinebeck, NY: Arthur C. M. Kelly, 1983. Includes indexes.

———. *Baptism Record of Herkimer Reformed Church, 1801–1899.* Rhinebeck, NY: Arthur C. M. Kelly, 1983. Includes indexes.

———. *Index to Tree Talks County Packet: Herkimer County.* Rhinebeck, NY: Kinship, 2002.

———. *Marriage Records of German Flats and Herkimer Reformed Churches, German Flats & Herkimer, Herkimer County, New York, 1781–1899.* Rhinebeck, NY: Arthur C.M. Kelly, 1983.

Montgomery Department of History and Archives. *Index of Records Reformed Protestant Dutch Church of Herkimer.* 2 vols. New York: Montgomery Department of History and Archives, 1941.

"Records of the Dutch Reformed Church of Columbia, Herkimer County, New York, 1806–1836, and Columbia Dutch Reformed Church Cemetery, etc." Typescript, 1956. Family History Library, Salt Lake City.

Samuelson, W. David. *Herkimer County, New York, 1835 State Census Index.* Salt Lake City: Sampubco., 1994.

Unsel, Mary M. "Private Business Records: Oneida and Herkimer County." Typescript, 1982. NYPL, New York.

Vosburgh, Royden Woodward, ed. "Records of the Reformed Protestant Dutch Church of Herkimer in the Town of Herkimer, Herkimer County, N.Y." 3 vols. Typescript, 1918. NYPL, New York. [NYG&B eLibrary (vol 1)]

Wood, Ralph V. *Herkimer County, New York State: Federal Population Census Schedules, 1800, 1810, 1820; Transcripts and Index.* Cambridge, MA: n.p., 1965.

Worden, Jean D. "Book 1, Subject Index." In *Revised Master Index to the New York State Daughters of the American Revolution Genealogical Records Volumes.* Zephyrhills, FL: J. D. Worden, 1998. The Subject Index includes a listing by county of the cemeteries, churches, towns, and other sources of records transcribed by the DAR.

Other Resources

Barker, William V. H. *Early Families of Herkimer County, New York: Descendants of the Burnetsfield Palatines.* Baltimore: Genealogical Publishing Co., 1986.

Benton, Nathaniel S. *A History of Herkimer County: Including the Upper Mohawk Valley . . . the Palatine Immigrations into the Colony of New York, and Biographical Sketches of the Palatine Families, the Patentees of Burnetsfield in the Year 1725 . . . .* Albany: J. Munsell, 1856.

Central New York Library Resources Council. *Guide to Historical Organizations in Central New York.* (Onondaga, Herkimer, Oneida, Madison) Digitally published May 2009. *www.clrc.org/wp-content/uploads/2011/05/DHPHistGuide09b.pdf*

Child, Hamilton. *Gazetteer and Business Directory of Herkimer County, N.Y., for 1869–70.* Syracuse: Hamilton Child, 1869.

Cristman, Franklin W. *Herkimer County in the World War: 1916 to 1918.* Little Falls, NY: Press of the Journal & Courier Co., 1927.

Cutter, William R. *Genealogical and Family History of Central New York: A Record of the Achievements of Her People in the Making of a Commonwealth and the Building of a Nation.* New York: Lewis Historical Publishing Co., 1912.

Denton, Emily R. *Prayer and Praise: Churches in Herkimer County, 1723–1981.* Herkimer, NY: Herkimer County Historical Society, 1981.

Dieffenbacher, Jane W. *Herkimer County Valley Towns.* Charleston, SC: Arcadia, 2002.

Greene, Nelson. *History of the Mohawk Valley, Gateway to the West, 1614–1925; Covering the Six Counties of Schenectady, Schoharie, Montgomery, Fulton, Herkimer, and Oneida.* Chicago: S. J. Clarke, 1925.

Hardin, George A., and Frank Willard. *History of Herkimer County, NY: Illustrated with Portraits of Many of Its Citizens.* Syracuse, 1893.

Herkimer County Historical Society. *Herkimer County at 200.* Herkimer, NY: Herkimer County Historical Society, 1992.

History of Herkimer County, NY. New York, 1878. Index available from Berkshire Family History Association.

Krutz, David P. *Distant Drums: Herkimer County, New York, in the War of the Rebellion.* Utica, NY: North Country Books, 1997.

New York Historical Resources Center. *Guide to Historical Resources in Herkimer County, New York, Repositories.* Ithaca, NY: Cornell University, 1982. [*books.FamilySearch.org*]

Nichols, Beach. *Atlas of Herkimer County, New York.* New York, 1869.

Roback, Henry. *The Veteran Volunteers of Herkimer and Otsego Counties in the War of the Rebellion: Being a History of the 152nd N.Y.V. . . . the 34th N.Y., 97th N.Y., 121st N.Y. Heavy Artillery and 1st and 2nd N.Y. Mounted Rifles . . . .* Utica, NY, 1888.

Additional Online Resources

Ancestry.com

There are vast numbers of records on *Ancestry.com* that pertain to people who have lived in New York State. See chapter 16 for a description of *Ancestry.com*'s resources and its partnership with the New York State Archives. A search of the online card catalog by county may reveal lesser known resources that pertain to a locality, such as town records, abstracts, transcriptions, city directories, and local histories.

FamilySearch.org

FamilySearch has extensive collections of New York records, including religious records, which are searchable by name and location, but not by county. The following collections include record images (browsable, but not searchable) that are organized by county:

- "New York, Land Records, 1630–1975." Includes land and property records. *familysearch.org/search/collection/2078654*
- "New York, Probate Records, 1629–1971." Includes wills, letters of administration, and guardianship papers. *familysearch.org/search/collection/1920234*

For both collections, choose the browse option and then select Herkimer to view the available records sets.

A detailed description of *FamilySearch.org* resources is found in chapter 16.

NYGenWeb: Herkimer County

www.herkimer.nygenweb.net

Part of the national, USGenWeb volunteer initiative, the website provides information and resources for county research, including the Herkimer County Tombstone Inscriptions page which provides links to more than 100 cemetery and burial records databases for Herkimer County.

Jefferson County

Formed March 28, 1805

Parent County   Oneida
Daughter Counties   None
County Seat   City of Watertown

Major Land Transactions
See table in chapter 7, Land Records
Penet's Square 1788
Macomb Purchase 1792

Town Boundary Map
★ - County seat

Towns (and Cities)	Villages and other Settlements		Notes
Adams 1801 Settled 1802 Formed in Oneida County from Town of Mexico 1804 Daughter town Harrison (now Rodman) formed 1805 Transferred to new county of Jefferson	Adams (v) Adams Center Appling Butterville Coopers Corners Green(e) Settlement Honeyville Lisk Settlement	Lyon(s) Corner(s) North Adams Sanford Corners Smithville Smithville Post Office Talcott Corners Thomas Settlement	• Village of Adams inc. 1851; formerly Smiths Mills • Butterville on Henderson town line
Alexandria 1811 Settled 1821 Formed from towns of Brownville and Le Ray 1841 Daughter town Theresa formed	Alexandria Alexandria Bay (v) Alexandria Center Alexandria Station Bean Hill Bean Hill Crossing Browns Corners Cottage Edgewood Park Godfreys Corner Goose Bay	Ples(s)is Point Vivian Redwood Saxe Corner(s) Schnauber Corners Skinners Corners St. Lawrence Park Tanner Corners Westminster Westminster Park	• Village of Alexandria Bay inc. 1878 • Plessis formerly Flat Rock
Antwerp 1803 Settled at Ox Bow 1810 Formed from Town of Le Ray	Antwerp Antwerp (v) Bentleys Corners Bishops Corners East Antwerp Fort Drum Hall Corners Keenes Mills	Nauvoo New Connecticut Oxbow Rices Corners Spragues Corners Spragueville Steeles Corners Sterlingburg(h)	• Village of Antwerp inc. 1853 • Fort Drum Military Reservation includes land in the towns of LeRay, Philadelphia, and Wilna • Spragueville also Keenes
Brownville 1799 Settled 1802 Formed in Oneida County from Town of Leyden * 1805 Transferred to new county of Jefferson 1806 Daughter town Le Ray formed 1818 Daughter town Lyme formed 1819 Daughter town Pamelia formed 1821 Daughter towns Alexandria and Orleans formed	Adams Cove Brownville (v) Dexter (v) Dexter Junction Glen Park (v) Limerick Millville Perch River Pillar Point Reynolds Corner(s)		* Town of Leyden now in Lewis County • Village of Brownville inc. 1828 • Village of Dexter inc. 1855; formerly Fish Island • Village of Glen Park inc. 1893; shared with Town of Pamelia • Perch River formerly Moffatville • Reynolds Corner(s) on Clayton town line
Cape Vincent c. 1778 Fort built on Carlton Island 1801 Settled on mainland at Port Putnam 1849 Formed from Town of Lyme	Burnham Point Cape Vincent (v) Carl(e)ton Island Cedar Point Park Fox Island French Settlement Grenadier Island Kings Garden	Millen(s) Bay Ponds Corners Riverview Rosiere Saint Lawrence Sunnybank Warren Warren Settlement	• Village of Cape Vincent inc. 1853; formerly Gravelly Point • Carleton Island also Buck Island

Towns (and Cities)	Villages and other Settlements		Notes
Champion **1797–98** Settled **1800** Formed in Oneida County from Town of Mexico **1803** Daughter town Harrisburg(h) formed in Oneida County * **1805** Transferred to new county of Jefferson	Champion Champion Huddle Champion South Road(s) Great Bend South Champion West Carthage (v)		* Town of Harrisburg(h) now in Lewis County • Village of West Carthage inc. 1889
Clayton Includes part of Penet's Square (land tract) **1803** Settled **1833** Formed from towns of Lyme and Orleans	Bartletts Point Clayton (v) Clayton Center Corbins Corners Deforno Depauville Frontenac Grenell Grenell Island Grindstone	Grindstone Island Gunns Corners Murray Isle Port Metcalf Prospect Park Reynolds Corner(s) Smith Corners South Corners Thurso	• Village of Clayton inc. 1872; also Cornelia and French Creek • Depauville formerly Catfish Falls • Reynolds Corner(s) on Brownville town line
Ellisburg(h) **1797** Settled **1803** Formed in Oneida County from Town of Mexico **1805** Transferred to new county of Jefferson **1806** Daughter town Henderson formed	Belleville (v) Cobblestone Corners Cobbtown Ellisburg (v) Ellis Village Giddingsville Hammond(s) Corners Hossington Jefferson Park	Mannsville (v) Montario Point North Landing Pierrepont Manor Rural Hill Saxe Corner(s) Wardwell Woodville Woodville Post Office	• Village of Belleville inc. 1860; dissolved 4/20/1979 • Village of Ellisburg inc. 1895 • Village of Mannsville inc. 1879 • Rural Hill formerly Buck Hill
Harrison Name for Town of Rodman 1804–1808			
Henderson **1802** Settled **1806** Formed from Town of Ellisburgh	Alexander Corners Aspinall Corners Babbitt Corner(s) Bishop Street Butterville Clark Point Henderson (v)	Henderson Harbor Hungerford Corners Roberts Corner(s) Scotts Corners Smithville Stony Point	• Butterville on Adams town line • Village of Henderson inc. 1886; formerly Salisbury Mills; village was dissolved 5/23/1992 • Henderson Harbor formerly Naples
Hounsfield **1800** Settled **1806** Formed from Town of Watertown	Alverson(s) Baggs Corner Blanchards Corners Boulton Beach Camp(s) Mills Chamberlins East Hounsfield East Hounsfield Station Fields Settlement Jewettville Madison Barracks	Maxon Corners Paddy Hill Price Settlement Purpura Corners Robbins Settlement Sackets Harbor (v) Sackets Harbor Station Stony Island Stowell(s) Corner(s) Sulphur Springs	• Village of Sackets Harbor inc. 1814

Towns (and Cities)	Villages and other Settlements		Notes
LeRay * 1802 Settled 1806 Formed from Town of Brownville 1810 Daughter town Antwerp formed 1813 Daughter town Wilna formed 1821 Daughter towns Alexandria and Philadelphia formed	Black River (v) Calcium Doolins Crossing Dutch Settlement Evans Mills (v) Evans Station Five Corners Fort Drum Gould Corners Gracey Corners	Hall(s) Corners Le Raysville Pine Plains Sanford Station Sanford(s) Corners Sanfords Four Corners Slocumville West Le Ray Westwood Corners	* LeRay (current official town spelling) also Le Ray • Village of Black River inc. 1891; also Lockport; shared with Town of Rutland • Doolins Crossing and Le Raysville are part of Fort Drum Military Reservation; also see towns of Antwerp, Philadelphia, and Wilna • Village of Evans Mills inc. 1874; formerly Evansville • Pine Plains on Town of Philadelphia town line • Sanfords Corners also known as Jewetts Corners, Jewetts School-House, and Captain Jewetts
Lorraine 1802 Settled 1804 Formed in Oneida County as Malta from Town of Mexico 1805 Transferred to new county of Jefferson 1808 Name changed to Lorraine 1848 Daughter town Worth formed	Allendale Allen District Gould Corners Haights Corners Lorraine Washington Park Waterville Winona		• Hamlet of Lorraine formerly known as Lorraine Huddle or The Huddle
Lyme 1801 Settled 1818 Formed from Town of Brownville 1833 Daughter town Clayton formed 1849 Daughter town Cape Vincent formed	Chaumont (v) Cherry Island Clines Point Herrick Grove Long Point Park Millers Bay	Peninsula Point Peninsula Three Mile Bay Three Mile Bay Station Wells Settlement Wilcoxville	• Village of Chaumont inc. 1874
Malta Name for Town of Lorraine 1804–1808			
Orleans Includes part of Penet's Square (land tract) 1806 Settled 1821 Formed from Town of Brownville 1829 Ceded land to Town of Pamelia 1833 Daughter town Clayton formed	Barlows Corners Collins Landing De La Farge Corners Fineview Fishers Landing Getman Corners Grandview Park Grenell La Fargeville Moore Landing	Omar Orleans Corners Orleans Four Corners Penets Square Port Orleans Stone(s) Mills Strough Corners Thousand Island Park Upper Town Landing	• La Fargeville also Lafargeville, called Log Mills before 1823 • Omar formerly Mudges Mills • Orleans Four Corners formerly Shantyville • Stone Mills formerly Collins Mills
Pamelia Includes part of Penet's Square (land tract) 1799 Settled 1819 Formed from Town of Brownville 1824 Name changed to Leander and restored to Pamelia 1829 Annexed land from Town of Orleans 1869 Ceded land to new City of Watertown	Glen Park (v) Juhelville Knowlesville North Watertown Pamelia Center Pamelia Four Corners Pamelia Station Pamelia Village Scoville Corner		• Village of Glen Park inc. 1893; shared with Town of Brownville • Pamelia Center formerly Williamsville

Towns (and Cities)	Villages and other Settlements		Notes
Philadelphia 1804 Settled by Quakers from Pennsylvania and New Jersey 1821 Formed from Town of Le Ray	Fort Drum Philadelphia (v) Pine Plains Pogeland Rogers	Shurtleff Corners Sterlingville Sterlingville Station Strickland Corners Whitneys Corners	• Fort Drum Military Reservation includes Sterlingville formerly De Launeys Mill; also see towns of Antwerp, LeRay, and Wilna • Village of Philadelphia inc. 1872; also Quaker Settlement • Pine Plains on Town of LeRay town line
Rodman 1801 Settled 1804 Formed in Oneida County as Town of Harrison from Town of Adams 1805 Transferred to new county of Jefferson 1808 Name changed to Rodman; daughter town Pinckney formed in Lewis County	Babbits Corners Dillen East Rodman Rodman Ross Corners Tremaines	Tremaines Corners Unionville Whitesville Whitford Corners Zoar	• Ross Corners also Algona • Whitford Corners also Toad Hollow and West Rodman
Rutland 1799 Settled 1802 Formed in Oneida County from Town of Watertown 1805 Transferred to new county of Jefferson	Black River (v) Felts Mills Harpers Ferry Middleroad Church	Rutland Rutland Center South Rutland Tylersville	• Village of Black River inc. 1891; also Lockport; shared with Town of LeRay • Rutland Center also Brooksville
Theresa 1841 Formed from Town of Alexandria	Bartletts Corners Chapel Corners Chaulty Corners Cooper(s) Corners Douglass Crossing Hyde Lake Rivergate	Shurtleff Stills Corner Strough Stroughs Crossing Theresa (v) Theresa Station West Theresa	• Village of Theresa inc. 1871
Watertown (city) * 1816 Village of Watertown formed in Town of Watertown 1869 Incorporated as a city; formed from Village of Watertown and land annexed from Town of Pamelia			* County seat at Watertown (village and city) from 1805 when county was formed
Watertown (town) 1800 Settled and formed in Oneida County from Town of Mexico 1802 Daughter town Rutland formed 1805 Transferred to new county of Jefferson 1806 Daughter town Hounsfield formed 1869 Daughter city Watertown formed	Burrs Mills Burrville Dry Hill East Watertown Fields Settlement Huntingtonville North Watertown	Rices Rices Station Watertown (v) Watertown Center Watertown Junction	• Village of Watertown inc. 1816, became the City of Watertown in 1869; county seat from 1805

Towns (and Cities)	Villages and other Settlements		Notes
Wilna 1798 Settled at Carthage 1813 Formed from towns of Leyden, Lewis County, and Le Ray	Carthage (v) Clearwater (Station) Cowan Corner(s) Deferiet (v) DeVoice Corners Fargo Fort Drum Gates Corners Herring Station Herrings (v) Hewitt Park Hubbards Crossing Karter Karter Crossing Lewisburg (Corners)	Mons Corners Mt. Quillen Natural Bridge North Croghan North Wilna Ormistead Corners Pine Camp Pine Camp Junction Reed(s)ville Wilna Wilna Fargo Wilna Station Woods Mill(s) Wood(s) Settlement	• Village of Carthage inc. 1841; formerly Long Falls • Village of Deferiet inc. 1921 • Fort Drum (Pine Camp) annexed 70,000 acres in Jefferson County 1939–1941; in the Town of Wilna this includes: Fargo, Gates Corners, Hubbards Crossing, Lewisburg, North Wilna, Reedsville, and Woods Mills; also see towns of Antwerp, LeRay, and Philadelphia • Village of Herrings inc. 1921 • Pine Camp was a military training camp from 1908; 1939-1941 it was expanded; 1951 renamed Camp Drum; 1974 became Fort Drum Military Reservation
Worth 1802 Settled by an association from Litchfield, Herkimer County 1816–17 Settlement abandoned 1848 Formed from Town of Lorraine	Bullock Corners Diamond Frederick(s) Corners Klondike Seven by Nine Corners	Stears Corners Worth Worth Center Worthville	• Worth formerly Wilcoxs Corners

NEW YORK STATE CENSUS RECORDS
See also chapter 3, Census Records

County originals at Jefferson County Clerk's Office: 1825*, 1835, 1855, 1865, 1875, 1905, 1915, 1925 (1845 and 1892 are lost)

State originals at the NYSA: 1915, 1925

Microfilm at the FHL (1825, 1835, and 1855 at FHL only), NYPL, and NYSL; many years are online at *FamilySearch.org* and *Ancestry.com*.

*For 1825 census index, see *County of Jefferson Abstracts* and James in Abstracts, Indexes & Transcriptions, below.

NATIONAL/STATEWIDE REPOSITORIES & RESOURCES
See chapter 16

COUNTYWIDE REPOSITORIES & RESOURCES

Jefferson County Clerk and Records Management
Jefferson County Building • 175 Arsenal Street
Watertown, NY 13601 • (315) 785-5149 • *www.co.jefferson.ny.us*

Land records late 1700s–present; court records early 1800s–present; federal census 1850, 1860, 1870, 1880; New York state census for Jefferson County 1825, 1835, 1855, 1865, 1875, 1905, 1915, 1925; maps 1864, 1887; marriage records 1908–1935; military records 1800s–present; naturalizations 1825–1973; mortgages 1805–present; vital records; tax rolls 1935–2006; and town directories. Website has list of "inactive" records that are available to researchers.

Jefferson County – City, Town, and Village Clerks
Birth, marriage, and death records are maintained by the clerk of the municipality in which the event occurred; see Introduction to County Guides for details of other records which may also be held by municipal clerks. For contact information, see *www.co.jefferson.ny.us*.

Jefferson County Surrogate's Court
Jefferson County Court Complex • 163 Arsenal Street
Watertown, NY 13601 • (315) 785-3019

Probate records 1805–present, decedent's estates 1847–present. Some court records are searchable online. See also chapter 6, Probate Records.

Jefferson County Public Libraries
Jefferson is part of the North Country Library System; see *http://ncls. northcountrylibraries.org* to access each library. Many hold genealogy and local history collections, including maps and newspapers. For example, Philomathean Public Library's collection includes information on local institutions and Macsherry Library holds information on George Boldt, as well as the Cornwell family. Also see listings below for Bodman Memorial Library, Carthage Free Library, East Hounsfield Free Library, Theresa Free Library, and Roswell P. Flower Memorial Library.

Roswell P. Flower Memorial Library: Genealogy Department
229 Washington Street • Watertown, NY 13601 • (315) 785-7705
www.flowermemoriallibrary.org/genealogy.html

Holds a copy of the New York State Department of Health vital records index. Federal and New York state census microfilm 1810–1930 (Franklin, Herkimer, Jefferson, Lewis, Montgomery, Oneida, Onondaga, and Oswego counties); marriage records (French-Canadian); cemetery records; poorhouse records; information about Civil War veterans from 1890; and records of the Revolutionary War, the War of 1812, the Civil War, the Spanish-American War*, and World War I. Staff offer research services at no charge.

Jefferson County Historical Society
28 Washington Street • Watertown, NY 13601 • (315) 782-3491
Email: jchs@nnyonline.net • *www.jeffersoncountyhistory.org*

Manuscripts, local histories, account books and ledgers, family papers, land surveys, letters and diaries, maps, photographs, records of governments and organizations, First Presbyterian Church records, and more. A selection of collections is online. Semiannual, *Bulletin*, 1955–present.

Jefferson County Historian
Jefferson County Building • 175 Arsenal Street
Watertown, NY 13601 • (315) 785-5149

Jefferson County – All Municipal Historians
While not authorized to answer genealogical inquiries, city, town, and village historians can provide valuable historical information and research advice; some maintain collections and webpages which may include transcribed records, local histories, and other genealogical material. See contact information at *http://nny.nnyln.org/archives/ jefferson_county.html* or at the website of the Association of Public Historians of New York State at *www.aphnys.org*.

Jefferson County Genealogical Society
PO Box 6453 • Watertown, NY 13601 • Email: jcnygs@imcnet.net
http://jefferson.nygenweb.net/jeffsoc.htm

Published genealogies and indexes are available for purchase. Researchers may publish inquiries in the Society's newsletter at no cost. Bimonthly journal, *Informer*, 1999–present.

Jefferson County Community College:
Melvil Dewey Library Local History Room
1220 Coffeen Street • Watertown, NY 13601 • (315) 786-2225
www.sunyjefferson.edu

Books, periodicals, manuscripts, pamphlets, and clippings about Watertown and Jefferson County. Special collections include Fort Drum Steering Council Papers, Frank Augustine Papers, and Harold Sanderson Civil War Database, as well as the Jefferson Community College Archives.

REGIONAL REPOSITORIES & RESOURCES

The 4 River Valleys Historical Society
PO Box 504 • Carthage, NY 13619 • (315) 773-5133 • *www.4rvhs.org*

Documents the history of the Beaver, Black, Indian, and Deer River valleys, covering Jefferson County and part of Lewis County. It maintains the late Woolworth Memorial United Methodist Church, which includes a Heritage Room of documents. A selection of articles is available on the Society's website.

Annie P. Ainsworth Memorial Library: Genealogy
See listing in Oswego County Guide

SUNY at Oswego: Local History Collection
See listing in Oswego County Guide

LOCAL REPOSITORIES & RESOURCES
Alphabetized by location

Historical Association of South Jefferson
29 East Church Street • Adams, NY 13605 • (315) 232-2616
Email: hasouthjeff@yahoo.com • *http://hasjny.tripod.com*

Books, documents, genealogies, newspapers 1856–present, federal and Jefferson County census records, and other materials relating to the history of six towns (Adams, Ellisburg, Henderson, Lorraine, Rodman, and Worth).

Alexandria Township Historical Society
36 Market Street • PO Box 695 • Alexandria Bay, NY 13607
(315) 482-4586 • www.alexandriahistorical.com

Maps and charts, ledgers, books, photographs, postcards, historical documents, and ephemera.

Cape Vincent Historical Museum
175 North James Street • PO Box 302 • Cape Vincent, NY 13618
(315) 654-4400 or 654-3640

Holdings include marriage files and records, obituaries, scrapbooks, and artifacts.

Carthage Free Library: Heritage Room
412 Budd Street • Carthage, NY 13619 • (315) 493-2620
Email: carlib@nnyln.net • www.carthagefreelibrary.org

Histories and genealogies, cemetery records, census material, government records, historical society newsletters, local directories, local newspapers (1860–1885, 1905–2005), maps, and scrapbooks.

Thousand Island Museum
312 James Street • Clayton, NY 13624 • (315) 686-5794
Email: info@timuseum.org • www.timuseum.org

Documents the history of the Town of Clayton, the St. Lawrence River, and the Thousand Islands Region. Library holdings include books, documents, local histories, newspaper clippings, maps, and scrapbooks. Website includes a guide to resources and a list of Clayton veterans of World War I.

Henderson Historical Society and Museum
12581 County Route 72 • Henderson, NY 13650 • (315) 938-7163
Email: hendersonhist@yahoo.com • www.hendersonhistoricalsociety.com

Genealogies and local histories, cemetery records, maps, military records, photographs, and town records. Website includes historical information and details on ongoing projects.

Historical Society of Mannsville/Town of Ellisburg
110 Lilac Park Drive • PO Box 121 • Mannsville, NY 13661
(315) 465-4049

Holdings include genealogies, ledgers, local newspapers, photographs and pictures, and scrapbooks.

Bodman Memorial Library and Museum
8 Aldrich Street • Philadelphia, NY 13673 • (315) 642-3323 (Library)
642-5502 (Historian) • www.bodmanmemoriallibrary.org

Genealogies and histories, church records, photographs, scrapbooks, and school records.

Pickering-Beach Historical Museum
510 West Main Street • Sackets Harbor, NY 13685
(315) 646-1529 • Email: shvisit@gisco.net
www.usgennet.org/usa/ny/county/jefferson/hounsfield/pickeringmuseum.html

Holdings include almanacs, Bibles, journals, ledgers, schoolbooks, and artifacts.

Sackets Harbor Battlefield State Historic Site Library/
Sackets Harbor Battlefield Alliance
504 West Main Street • PO Box 27 • Sackets Harbor, NY 13685-0027
(518) 646-3634 • Email: mail@sacketsharborbattlefield.org
www.sacketsharborbattlefield.org

Documents the history of the Sackets Harbor Battlefield, the War of 1812, Sackets Harbor Naval Station 1810–1950s, and of the general area. Holdings include books, biographical information, letters, manuscripts and documents, maps, and artifacts.

Oxbow Historical Society
34542 County Route 22 • Theresa, NY 13691 • (315) 287-2293

Holdings include family histories and cemetery records, 1939 Jefferson County Farm Index, birth and death records 1880, and school information.

Theresa Free Library
301 Main Street • Theresa, NY 13691 • (315) 628-5972
www.northnet.org/theresalibrary

Historical museum is located on the second floor of the library. Holdings include family files, cemetery records, and histories.

Lyme Heritage Center
Old Grange Hall • 8718 County Route 5 • Three Mile Bay, NY 13693
(315) 649-5452 • www.jefferson.nygenweb.net/lyher.htm

Genealogies, family files, histories, diaries, cemetery records, census materials, ledgers, maps and atlases, news clippings, and vital records documenting history of the Town of Lyme.

East Hounsfield Free Library
19438 State Route 3 • Watertown, NY 13601 • (315) 788-0637
www.easthounsfieldlibrary.org

Captains' log books and shipping records (1860s), information on World War I military members from Jefferson County, family and local histories.

SELECTED PRINT & ONLINE RESOURCES

Below is a selection of resources relevant for research in this county. The list is representative, not exhaustive. Additional titles—particularly of abstracts, indexes, transcriptions, and local histories—are available; consult the introduction to Part Two for further information. For guidance on how to identify and locate community directories and local newspapers, see chapter 11, City Directories, and chapter 12, Newspapers, in Part One of this book.

Abstracts, Indexes & Transcriptions
Bartlett, Ellen. *Grooms and Brides of Jefferson County.* New York: E. and J. Bartlett, 1993.

— — —. *Town of Antwerp, Jefferson County, New York Cemetery Inscriptions.* Syracuse: The Author, 1997.

Bartlett, Ellen, John Bartlett, and A. E. Rogers. "Jefferson County Cemetery Inscriptions." The Bartlett Cemetery Inscriptions website provides free access to a large database of transcriptions from multiple cemeteries across Jefferson County. Print versions of the transcriptions are available from the authors, who are also known as the Gravestone Scribes. *http://jefferson.nygenweb.net/bartlett.htm*

County of Jefferson Abstracts. Syracuse: Central New York Genealogical Society, 2000. Abstracts for a range of genealogical records originally published in the quarterly *Tree Talks.* Includes abstracts of 1825 census for some towns.

Daughters of the American Revolution, comps. *New York DAR Genealogical Records Committee Report.* Since 1913 DAR volunteers have transcribed many thousands of unpublished cemetery, church, and town records throughout New York. The reports are at the DAR Library; copies are at the NYSL and the

NYPL. The DAR has a searchable name index to all the GRC reports at *http://services.dar.org/Public/DAR_Research/search/?Tab_ID=6*. See Jean Worden's index below for a listing by county of the New York record sets that were transcribed by the DAR before 1998.

James, Patricia R. *Genealogical Journal of Jefferson County, New York.* Boise, ID: Family Tree, 1989–2008. Issues from 1990–1999 include abstracts of 1825 state census for various towns in Jefferson County.

———. *Index to DAR Bible Records of Jefferson County, New York.* Boise, ID: Family Tree, 1993.

Kelly, Arthur C. M. *Index to Tree Talks County Packet: Jefferson County.* Rhinebeck, NY: Kinship, 2002.

New York Historical Resources Center. *Guide to Historical Resources in Jefferson County, New York, Repositories.* Ithaca, NY: New York Historical Resources Center, Olin Library, Cornell University, 1985.

Pierrepont, William C. *The Taming of the Wilderness in Northern New York: Records of the Land Purchases of Early Settlers for 1826 for Lands in Jefferson, Lewis, and Oswego Counties.* Sandy Creek, NY: Write to Print, 1993.

Rogers, A. E. *Town of [Alexandria, Cape Vincent, Hounsfield, Le Ray, Lyme, Theresa, Philadelphia] Jefferson County, New York Cemetery Inscriptions.* 7 vols. New York: J & E Bartlett, 1996.

Worden, Jean D. "Book 1, Subject Index." In *Revised Master Index to the New York State Daughters of the American Revolution Genealogical Records Volumes.* Zephyrhills, FL: J. D. Worden, 1998. The Subject Index includes a listing by county of the cemeteries, churches, towns, and other sources of records transcribed by the DAR.

Other Resources

Beers, S. N. *New Topographical Atlas of Jefferson County, New York: From Actual Surveys.* Philadelphia, 1864. [NYPL Digital Gallery]

Child, Hamilton. *Gazetteer and Directory of Jefferson County, New York, for 1866–7.* Watertown, NY, 1866.

———. *Geographical Gazetteer of Jefferson County, N.Y., 1684–1890.* Syracuse, 1890. Includes business directory of Jefferson County for 1890.

Coughlin, Jere, comp. *Jefferson County Centennial, 1905.* Watertown, NY: Hungerford-Holbrook, 1905.

DeLawyer, Mark W. *Troops Furnished by the Town of Adams, New York for Service During the War of the Rebellion, 1861–1865.* Bowie, MD: Heritage Books, 2002.

Eddy, Justus. *Our Early Local History (Embracing the Sixtown Area of Southern Jefferson County, State of New York).* Adams, NY: Historical Association of South Jefferson, 1998.

Emerson, Edgar C. *Our County and Its People: A Descriptive Work on Jefferson County, New York.* Boston, 1898.

Foley, Janet W. *Early Settlers of New York State: Their Ancestors and Descendants.* 9 vols. Akron, NY: 1934–1942. Reprint, 2 vols. Baltimore: Genealogical Publishing Co., 1993.

Gummer, Robert E. *The Sixtown Settlers.* New York: Historical Association of South Jefferson, 1988.

Haddock, John A. *The Growth of a Century: As Illustrated in the History of Jefferson County, New York, from 1793–1894.* Albany, 1895.

Hough, Franklin Benjamin. *History of Jefferson County in the State of New York, from the Earliest Period to the Present Time.* Albany, 1854.

James, Patricia R. *Genealogical Journal of Jefferson County, New York.* Boise, ID: Family Tree, 1989–2007.

———. *Index to the Genealogical Journal of Jefferson County, New York.* Boise, Idaho: Family Tree, 1997.

———. *Upstate New York Researcher: Principally for Research in Jefferson, Oneida, and St. Lawrence Counties.* Boise, ID: Family Tree, 1991.

Landon, Harry F. *The North Country: A History, Embracing Jefferson, St. Lawrence, Oswego, Lewis and Franklin Counties.* 3 vols. Indianapolis: Historical Publishing Co., 1932.

New York Historical Resources Center. *Guide to Historical Resources in Jefferson County, New York, Repositories.* Ithaca, NY: Cornell University, 1985. [books.FamilySearch.org]

Northern New York Library Network. *Directory of Archival and Historical Document Collections.* 2011–2013 edition; published digitally at *http://nny.nnyln.org/archives/ArchivalDirectory.pdf*. Online indexes at *http://nny.nnyln.org/archives/page01.html*.

Oakes, Rensselaer Allston. *Genealogical and Family History of the County of Jefferson, New York.* New York and Chicago: Lewis Publishing Co., 1905.

Peirce, Henry B., and Samuel W. Durant. *History of Jefferson County, New York: With Illustrations and Biographical Sketches of Some of Its Prominent Men and Pioneers.* Philadelphia, 1878.

Reeves, George W. *Jefferson County in the World War.* Watertown, NY: Hungerford-Holbrook, 1920.

Additional Online Resources

Adams, New York: History and Genealogy
http://adamsny.net/hist-adams.html
> The website provides free access to selected record transcriptions, family histories, and other information.

Ancestry.com
> There are vast numbers of records on *Ancestry.com* that pertain to people who have lived in New York State. See chapter 16 for a description of *Ancestry.com*'s resources and its partnership with the New York State Archives. A search of the online card catalog by county may reveal lesser known resources that pertain to a locality, such as town records, abstracts, transcriptions, city directories, and local histories.

Cape Vincent, New York: History
www.capevincent.org/history.asp
> Provides a detailed history of the town of Cape Vincent.

FamilySearch.org
> FamilySearch has extensive collections of New York records, including religious records, which are searchable by name and location, but not by county. The following collections include record images (browsable, but not searchable) that are organized by county:
> - "New York, Land Records, 1630–1975." Includes land and property records. *familysearch.org/search/collection/2078654*
> - "New York, Probate Records, 1629–1971." Includes wills, letters of administration, and guardianship papers. *familysearch.org/search/collection/1920234*

For both collections, choose the browse option and then select Jefferson to view the available records sets.

A detailed description of *FamilySearch.org* resources is found in chapter 16.

New York Heritage Digital Collections: New York State Newspaper Project
www.nyheritage.org/newspapers

The website provides links to digital newspapers collections in 26 counties (currently) made accessible through New York Heritage, New York State Historic Newspapers, HRVH Historical Newspapers, and other providers.

NYGenWeb Project: Jefferson County
www.jefferson.nygenweb.net

Part of the national, USGenWeb volunteer initiative, the website provides information and resources for county research.

Old Fulton New York Postcards
www.FultonHistory.com

The website provides free access to a vast collection of digitized New York newspapers, including seven titles for Jefferson County.

Town of Hounsfield: Genealogy
www.townofhounsfield-ny.gov/genealogy.htm

Provides links to a selection of transcribed census, Civil War, and other historical records for Hounsfield.

Lewis County

Formed March 28, 1805

Parent County   Oneida
Daughter Counties None
County Seat   Village of Lowville

Major Land Transactions
See table in chapter 7, Land Records
Macomb Purchase 1792

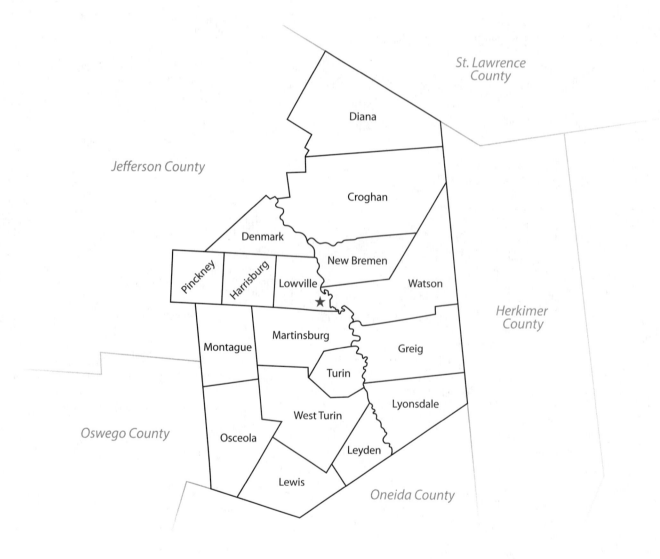

Town Boundary Map
 - County seat

Towns (and Cities)	Villages and other Settlements		Notes
Brantingham Name for Town of Greig 1828–1832			
Croghan 1830 Settled 1841 Formed from towns of Diana and Watson 1848 Daughter town New Bremen formed	Bear Town Beaver Falls Beaverton Belfort Bent Settlement Bishas Mill Croghan (v) Dutton Corners Edgebert Forest City Indian River	Jerden Falls Jordan Lyons Naumburg North Croghan North Croghan Crossing Rogers Crossing Soft Maple Texas Wisner	• Village of Croghan inc. 1906; shared with Town of New Bremen • Jerden Falls also Jordan Falls • Lyons formerly High Falls • Naumburg formerly locally known as the Prussian Settlement
Denmark 1800 Settled 1807 Formed from Town of Harrisburg(h)	Blodgett Landing Castorland (v) Copenhagen (v) Deer River	Deer River Station Denmark Kings Falls Runyans Landing	• Village of Castorland inc. 1929 • Village of Copenhagen inc. 1869; formerly Mungers Mills • Deer River formerly French Mills and Myers Mills

Diana
1830 Formed from Town of Watson
1841 Daughter town Croghan formed
	Aldrich Settlement
	Alpina
	Bartlett Corners
	Blanchard Corners
	Bonaparte
	Diana
	Diana Center
	Diana Station
	Fitzgerald
	Ford Clearing
	French Settlement
	Harrisville (v)
	Kimball Mill
		Lake Bonaparte
		Lake Bonaparte Station
		Lewisburg
		Middle Branch
		Middle Branch
		   Settlement
		Oswegatchie Corners
		Oswegatchie
		   Settlement
		Remington Corners
		Rices Corners
		Tinney Corners
			• Alpina also North Alpine
			• Diana Center also Blanchards Settlement
			• Village of Harrisville inc. 1892
			• Lewisburg formerly Louisburg and Sterlingbush; part of the Military reservation of Fort Drum

Greig 1792 Settled by French 1828 Formed as Brantingham from Town of Watson 1832 Name changed to Greig 1873 Daughter town Lyonsdale formed	Abb(e)yville Brantingham Brownville Donattsburg Eatonville Glenfield Greig	Hubbards Lyonsdale Otter Creek Palenville Partridgeville Port Leyden Rockville	• Donattsburg also Dannattsburg
Harrisburg(h) 1803 Formed in Oneida County from towns of Champion, Lowville, and Mexico * 1805 Transferred to new county of Lewis 1807 Daughter town Denmark formed 1808 Daughter town Pinckney formed	Bellwood Harrisburg(h) South Harrisburg(h)		* Town of Champion now in Jefferson County; Town of Mexico now in Oswego County • Harrisburg(h) formerly Windecker
High Market 1852–1973 (see West Turin) 1852 Formed from Town of West Turin 1973 Town of High Market dissolved, became a hamlet in the Town of West Turin	Byron Corners High Market		

Towns (and Cities)	Villages and other Settlements		Notes
Lewis 1800 Settled 1852 Formed from towns of Leyden and West Turin	Caufleys Corners Fey Mill Fish Creek Leisher Mill Mud Lake	Prussian Settlement Sunset Corners Swancott Mill(s) West Leyden Williams Settlement	• Williams Settlement also Yankee Settlement
Leyden 1794 Settled 1797 Formed in Herkimer County from Town of Steuben * 1798 Transferred to new county of Oneida 1802 Daughter town Brownville formed * 1805 Transferred to new county of Lewis; daughter town Boonville formed in Oneida County 1813 Daughter town Wilna formed in Jefferson County 1821 Daughter town Watson formed 1852 Daughter town Lewis formed	Barretts Corners Denley Station Kelpytown Leyden Hill Leyden Station Locust Grove Pasadena Port Leyden (v) Talcottville West Leyden		* Town of Steuben now in Oneida County * Town of Brownville now in Jefferson County • Village of Port Leyden inc. 1871; formerly Kelseys Mills; shared with Town of Lyonsdale • Talcottville formerly Leyden
Lowville 1797 Settled 1800 Formed in Oneida County from Town of Mexico * 1803 Daughter town Harrisburg(h) formed 1805 Transferred to new county of Lewis	Dadville Hamblins Corner Lowville (v) Lowville Landing Smith(s) Landing Stows Square Sulfur Springs West Lowville		* Town of Mexico now in Oswego County • Village of Lowville inc. 1847, charter adopted 1854; county seat from 1864; 1805–1864 county seat at Martinsburg(h)
Lyonsdale 1873 Formed from Town of Greig	Bucks Corner Fowler(s)ville Goulds Mill(s) Kosterville Lyons Falls (v) Lyonsdale	Moose River Phinney Settlement Port Leyden (v) Porters Corners Shuetown	• Village of Lyons Falls inc. 1899; formerly High Falls; shared with Town of West Turin • Phinney Settlement also Penny or Pinney Settlement • Village of Port Leyden inc. 1871; formerly Kelseys Mills; shared with Town of Leyden
Martinsburg(h) 1801 Settled 1803 Formed in Oneida County from Town of Turin 1805 Transferred to new county of Lewis 1823 Annexed land from Town of Turin	Centerville Chapel Hill East Martinsburg(h) Glendale Glenfield Glensville Station Goodrich Corners Graves Corner(s) Hoffman Hill Lanesburg Maple Ridge Martinsburg(h)	Martinsburg Station Martinsburgh Depot McGraw Corners Meadow Brooke North Martinsburg Pansey Hill Pitchers Settlement Sheldon Corners Tabolt Corners Tiffany Landing West Martinsburg(h) Wetmore	• Martinsburg(h) county seat from 1805 when county was formed; 1864 transferred to Village of Lowville • Sheldon Corners also Whetstone Gulf
Montague 1846 Settled 1850 Formed from Town of West Turin 1867 Annexed land from Town of Osceola	Boyd Gardner(s) Corners Hooker Liberty (Corners)	Montague Parkers Rector (Corners)	

Towns (and Cities)	Villages and other Settlements		Notes
New Bremen 1798 Settled 1848 Formed from towns of Croghan and Watson	Beach Hill Beaver Falls Beaverton Bushs Corners Cartonville	Croghan (v) Crystal Dale Kirschnerville New Bremen	• Village of Croghan inc. 1906; shared with Town of Croghan • New Bremen formerly Dayansville
Osceola 1838 Settled 1844 Formed from Town of West Turin 1867 Ceded land to Town of Montague	Monteola New Campbellwood Wye North Osceola Old Campbellwood Wye Osceola		
Pinckney 1804 Settled 1808 Formed from towns of Rodman (Jefferson County) and Harrisburg(h)	Barnes Corners Cronk(s) Corners New Boston Pinckney		
Turin 1798 Settled 1800 Formed in Oneida County from Town of Mexico * 1803 Daughter town Martinsburg(h) formed 1805 Transferred to new county of Lewis 1823 Ceded land to Town of Martinsburg(h) 1830 Daughter town West Turin formed	Burdicks Crossing Deweyville Glenfield Gomer Hill Gulf Head Gulf Head Station Houseville Turin (v) Welch Hill		* Town of Mexico now in Oswego County • Village of Turin inc. 1873
Watson 1815 Settled 1821 Formed from Town of Leyden 1828 Daughter town Brantingham (now Greig) formed 1830 Daughter town Diana formed 1841 Daughter town Croghan formed 1848 Daughter town New Bremen formed	Bushes Landing Chase(s) Lake Crandallville Dayansville Eagle Falls Independence River	Number Four Petrie(s) Corners Pine Grove Sperryville Watson	
West Turin 1796 Settled at Constableville 1830 Formed from Town of Turin 1844 Daughter town Osceola formed 1850 Daughter town Montague formed 1852 Daughter towns High Market and Lewis formed 1973 Annexed dissolved Town of High Market	Byron Corners Collinsville Constableville (v) Fish Creek High Market Lyons Falls (v)	Lyons Falls Station Michigan Mills Mohawk Hill Page Potters Corners Windmers	• Collinsville formerly High Falls Village • Village of Constableville inc. 1877 • Hamlet of High Market was Town of High Market 1852–1973 • Village of Lyons Falls inc. 1899; formerly High Falls; shared with Town of Lyonsdale

NEW YORK STATE CENSUS RECORDS

See also chapter 3, Census Records

County originals at Lewis County Clerk's Office: 1825*, 1835, 1855, 1865, 1875, 1892, 1905, 1915, 1925 (1845 is lost)

State originals at the NYSA: 1915, 1925

Microfilm at the FHL, NYPL, and NYSL; many years are online at *FamilySearch.org* and.

* For 1825 census transcription and index, see Barnello, et al., in Abstracts, Indexes & Transcriptions, below.

NATIONAL/STATEWIDE REPOSITORIES & RESOURCES

See chapter 16

COUNTYWIDE REPOSITORIES & RESOURCES

Lewis County Clerk

Lewis County Court House • 7660 State Street • Lowville, NY 13367
(315) 376-5333 • Email: clerk@lewiscountyny.org
www.lewiscountyny.org/content/Departments/View/24

Deeds 1805–present, some marriage and death records, naturalization records 1808–present, and Lewis County originals of New York state censuses for 1825, 1835, 1855, 1865, 1875, 1892, and 1905.

Lewis County – Town and Village Clerks

Birth, marriage, and death records are maintained by the clerk of the municipality in which the event occurred; see Introduction to County Guides for details of other records which may also be held by municipal clerks. For contact information, see *www.lewiscountyny.org*.

Lewis County Surrogate's Court

Lewis County Courthouse • 7660 State Street • Lowville, NY 13367
(315) 376-5368 or (315) 376- 5344

Holds probate records 1805 to the present; 1970–2000 available online. See also chapter 6, Probate Records.

Lewis County Public Libraries

Lewis is part of the North Country Library System; see *http://ncls. northcountrylibraries.org* to access each library. Many hold genealogy and local history collections, such as local newspapers and ephemera. For example, the William H. Bush Memorial Library holds scrapbooks and diaries. Also see listings below for Lyons Falls Free Library and Port Leyden Community Library.

Lewis County Historical Society

7552 South State Street • PO Box 446 • Lowville, NY 13367
(315) 376-8957 • Email: lewiscountyhistoricalsociety@gmail.com
www.lewiscountyhistory.org

Notebooks containing transcripts of church and cemetery records, genealogical charts, chronological lists of marriages by town and village, and obituary notes from newspapers 1933–1950; files on Lewis County families containing genealogies, narrative family histories, research notes, genealogical correspondence, copies of family records, articles, and clippings 1871–1985; Cutter's index (Coast Guard), farm records, immigration cards, military records, local newspapers on microfilm (*Northern Journal, Black River Gazette, Lewis County Democrat, Journal & Republican,* and *Adirondack Mountain Sun*), an obituary index, and photographs. The society publishes *Artifacts, Lewis County Historical Society Journal.*

**Lewis County Research Center
(formerly the Lewis County Historian's Office)**
See Lewis County Historical Society above

Lewis County – All Municipal Historians

While not authorized to answer genealogical inquiries, town and village historians can provide valuable historical information and research advice; some maintain collections and webpages which may include transcribed records, local histories, and other genealogical material. For contact information, see *www.rootsweb.ancestry.com/~nylewis/ historia.htm* or the website of the Association of Public Historians of New York State at *www.aphnys.org*.

REGIONAL REPOSITORIES & RESOURCES

The 4 River Valleys Historical Society
See listing in Jefferson County Guide

Adirondack Museum Library
See listing in Hamilton County Guide

SUNY at Oswego: Local History Collection
See listing in Oswego County Guide

LOCAL REPOSITORIES & RESOURCES

Alphabetized by location

Harrisville-Bonaparte History Association
8286 High Street • Harrisville, NY 13648

Holdings include an obituary index, selected birth records, and scrapbooks. Subjects documented include local pioneer family histories and community history.

Lyons Falls Free Library
3918 High Street • Lyons Falls, NY 13368 • *www.lyonsfallslibrary.org*

Holdings include local histories and genealogies, cemetery records, and photographs.

Lyons Falls History Association and Museum
PO Box 1 • Lyons Falls, NY 13368
Email address on website • *www.lyonsfallshistory.org*

Holdings include books, photographs, and artifacts. Website has articles on local history. The museum is located behind the Falls Pharmacy.

Martinsburg Historical Society
PO Box 17 • Martinsburg, NY 13404
(315) 376-0156 • *www.martinsburghistory.org*

Holdings include artifacts, photographs, scrapbooks, newspaper clippings, and town records.

Port Leyden Community Library
3145 Canal Street • PO Box 97 • Port Leyden, NY 13433
Email: plylib@ncls.org • *www.portleydenlibrary.org*

Holdings include local histories, cemetery records, maps, photographs, and scrapbooks.

SELECTED PRINT & ONLINE RESOURCES

Below is a selection of resources relevant for research in this county. The list is representative, not exhaustive. Additional titles—particularly of abstracts, indexes, transcriptions, and local histories—are available; consult the introduction to Part Two for further information. For guidance on how to identify and locate community directories and local newspapers, see chapter 11, City Directories, and chapter 12, Newspapers, in Part One of this book.

Abstracts, Indexes & Transcriptions

Barnello, Kathleen, Maria J. Eisenberg, Betty Emery, Harriet Hall, and Joyce Mason. *Abstract of the 1825 New York State Census of Lewis County, New York.* Syracuse: Central New York Genealogical Society, 1990. Originally published in *Tree Talks*, vol. 30, no. 4 (1990): 1–26, population enumeration abstract by Kathleen Barnello with Betty Emery, Harriet Hall, and Joyce Mason. Index, 27–34, introduction (by Marcia J. Eisenberg with Harriet Hall) and maps: iii–xii.

County of Lewis Abstracts. Syracuse: Central New York Genealogical Society, 2000. Abstracts for a range of genealogical records originally published in the quarterly *Tree Talks*.

Daughters of the American Revolution, comps. *New York DAR Genealogical Records Committee Report.* Since 1913 DAR volunteers have transcribed many thousands of unpublished cemetery, church, and town records throughout New York. The reports are at the DAR Library; copies are at the NYSL and the NYPL. The DAR has a searchable name index to all the GRC reports at *http://services.dar.org/Public/DAR_Research/search/?Tab_ID=6.* See Jean Worden's index below for a listing by county of the New York record sets that were transcribed by the DAR before 1998.

Kelly, Arthur C. M. *Index to Tree Talks County Packet: Lewis County.* Rhinebeck, NY: Kinship, 2002.

Pierrepont, William C. *The Taming of the Wilderness in Northern New York: Records of the Land Purchases of Early Settlers for 1826 for Lands in Jefferson, Lewis, and Oswego Counties.* Sandy Creek, NY: Write to Print, 1993.

Samuelsen, W. David. *Lewis County, New York, Will Testators Index, 1806–1870.* Salt Lake City: Sampubco, 1996.

Worden, Jean D. "Book 1, Subject Index." In *Revised Master Index to the New York State Daughters of the American Revolution Genealogical Records Volumes.* Zephyrhills, FL: J. D. Worden, 1998. The Subject Index includes a listing by county of the cemeteries, churches, towns, and other sources of records transcribed by the DAR.

Other Resources

Beers, D. G. *Atlas of Lewis County, New York: From Actual Surveys.* Philadelphia, 1875.

Bowen, G. Byron. *History of Lewis County, New York, 1880–1965.* Lowville, NY: Board of Legislators of Lewis County, 1970.

Child, Hamilton. *Gazetteer and Business Directory of Lewis County, N.Y., for 1872–3.* Syracuse, 1872.

Foley, Janet W. *Early Settlers of New York State: Their Ancestors and Descendants.* 9 vols. Akron, NY: 1934–1942. Reprint, 2 vols. Baltimore: Genealogical Publishing Co., 1993.

Hough, Franklin Benjamin. *A History of Lewis County, in the State of New York: From the Beginning of Its Settlement to the Present Time.* Albany, 1860.

———. *History of Lewis County, New York: With Biographical Sketches of Some of Its Prominent Men and Pioneers.* Syracuse, 1883.

Landon, Harry F. *The North Country: A History, Embracing Jefferson, St. Lawrence, Oswego, Lewis, and Franklin Counties.* 3 vols. Indianapolis: Historical Publishing Co., 1932.

New York Historical Resources Center. *Guide to Historical Resources in Lewis County, New York, Repositories.* Ithaca, NY: Cornell University, 1987. [*books.FamilySearch.org*]

Northern New York Library Network. *Directory of Archival and Historical Document Collections.* 2011–2013 edition; published digitally at *http://nny.nnyln.org/archives/ArchivalDirectory.pdf.* Online indexes at *http://nny.nnyln.org/archives/page01.html.* Describes collections held by organizations in Clinton, Essex, Franklin, Jefferson, Lewis, Oswego, and St. Lawrence counties.

Williams, Emily, and Ethel Evans Markham. *A History of Turin, Lewis County, New York.* Lakemont, NY: North Country Books, 1974.

Yousey, Arlene. *Strangers and Pilgrims: History of Lewis County Mennonites.* Croghan, NY: A. R. Yousey, 1987.

Additional Online Resources

Ancestry.com

There are vast numbers of records on *Ancestry.com* that pertain to people who have lived in New York State. See chapter 16 for a description of *Ancestry.com*'s resources and its partnership with the New York State Archives. A search of the online card catalog by county may reveal lesser known resources that pertain to a locality, such as town records, abstracts, transcriptions, city directories, and local histories.

FamilySearch.org

FamilySearch has extensive collections of New York records, including religious records, which are searchable by name and location, but not by county. The following collections include record images (browsable, but not searchable) that are organized by county:

- "New York, Land Records, 1630–1975." Includes land and property records. *familysearch.org/search/collection/2078654*
- "New York, Probate Records, 1629–1971." Includes wills, letters of administration, and guardianship papers. *familysearch.org/search/collection/1920234*

For both collections, choose the browse option and then select Lewis to view the available records sets.

A detailed description of *FamilySearch.org* resources is found in chapter 16.

New York Heritage Digital Collections: New York State Newspaper Project
www.nyheritage.org/newspapers

The website provides links to digital newspapers collections in 26 counties (currently) made accessible through New York Heritage, New York State Historic Newspapers, HRVH Historical Newspapers, and other providers.

NYGenWeb Project: Lewis County
www.rootsweb.ancestry.com/~nylewis

Part of the national, USGenWeb volunteer initiative, the website provides information and resources for county research.

Livingston County

Formed February 23, 1821

Parent Counties Genesee • Ontario
Daughter Counties None
County Seat Village of Geneseo

Major Land Transactions
See chapter 7, Land Records
Phelps and Gorham Purchase 1788
Morris Reserve 1791

Town Boundary Map
★ - County seat

Towns (and Cities)	Villages and other Settlements		Notes
Avon 1785 Settled 1789 Formed as Hartford in Ontario County 1808 Name changed to Avon 1818 Daughter town Rush formed * 1821 Transferred to new county of Livingston	Ashantee Avon (v) Avon Springs East Avon Littleville North Avon South Avon		* Town of Rush now in Monroe County • Village of Avon inc. 1853
Caledonia 1797 Settled by Danish 1802 Formed in Genesee County as Southampton 1806 Name changed to Caledonia 1812 Daughter town of Bellona (now Leroy) formed in Genesee County 1819 Daughter town York formed 1821 Transferred to new county of Livingston	Baker Caledonia (v) Canawaugus Maxwell Menzie Crossing Taylor Toggletown		• Village of Caledonia inc. 1891
Charleston Name for Town of Lima 1789–1808			
Conesus 1794–95 Settlers from Pennsylvania at Conesus Lake 1819 Formed in Ontario County as Freeport from towns of Groveland and Livonia 1821 Transferred to new county of Livingston 1825 Name changed to Bowersville in March, and changed to Conesus in April	Conesus Conesus Center Crocketts Corners Excelsior Springs Foots Corner(s) Sunny Shores Union Corners Walkleys Landing West Conesus		
Freeport Name for Town of Conesus 1819–1825			
Geneseo 1788–89 Settled near Geneseo village 1789 Formed in Ontario County 1821 Transferred to new county of Livingston	Cottonwood Cove Eagle Point Geneseo (v) Long Point	Long Point Cove Sacketts Harbor Sleggs Landing Wadsworth Cove	• Geneseo county seat from 1821 when county was formed; Village of Geneseo inc. 1832; formerly Big Tree
Groveland 1792 Settled by Germans at Williamsburgh 1812 Formed in Ontario County 1819 Daughter town Conesus formed 1821 Transferred to new county of Livingston	Cottonwood Point East Groveland Groveland Groveland Center Groveland Corners Groveland Station	Hampton Corners Hunts Corners Ross Corners Sonyea Williamsburgh	• Sonyea was site of Shaker settlement c.1837–1892
Hartford Name for Town of Avon 1789–1808			

Towns (and Cities)	Villages and other Settlements	Notes
Leicester 1789 Settled 1802 Formed in Genesee County as Lester from Town of Northampton 1805 Name changed to Leicester; daughter town Angelica formed * 1814 Daughter town Perry formed 1818 Daughter town Mount Morris formed 1819 Daughter town York formed 1821 Transferred to new county of Livingston	Big Tree Cuylerville Gibsonville Leicester (v) Little Beards Town Pine Tavern Corners Shaker Crossing Squakie Hill Teed Corners The Pines	* Town of Angelica now in Allegany County • Village of Leicester inc. 1907; formerly Moscow
Lima 1788 Settlers from Pennsylvania 1789 Formed in Ontario County as Charleston 1808 Name changed to Lima 1821 Transferred to new county of Livingston	Commins Corners Idaho Lima (v) North Bloomfield South Lima	• Village of Lima inc. 1867
Livonia 1792 Settlers from Connecticut 1808 Formed in Ontario County from Town of Pittstown * 1819 Daughter town Conesus formed 1821 Transferred to new county of Livingston	Bosley Corner Cedarcrest Glenville Hartson Point Hemlock Hemlock Lake Jacksonville Lakeville Livonia (v) Livonia Center Livonia Station McPherson Cove McPherson Point Old Orchard Point Sand Point South Livonia Tuxedo Park	* Town of Pittstown renamed Richmond in 1815 • Hemlock formerly Slab City • Jacksonville also Holdenville • Village of Livonia inc. 1882
Mount Morris 1784–85 Settled 1818 Formed in Ontario County from Town of Leicester 1821 Transferred to new county of Livingston	Brooks Grove Mount Morris (v) Murray Hill Ridge River Road River Road Forks St. Helena Tuscarora	• Village of Mount Morris inc. 1835; formerly Allens Hill and Richmond Hill
North Dansville 1795 Settlers from Pennsylvania at Dansville village 1846 Formed from Town of Sparta 1849 Annexed land from Town of Sparta	Cumminsville Dansville (v) Dansville Station Stone Falls	• Cumminsville formerly Commonsville, Comminsville, Cummingsville • Dansville in Town of Dansville, Steuben County, before 1822; in Town of Sparta 1822–1846; in Town of North Dansville after 1846; Village of Dansville inc. 1845
Nunda 1806 Settled near Nunda village 1808 Formed in Allegany County from Town of Angelica 1818 Daughter town Pike formed * 1823 Daughter town Eagle formed* 1827 Daughter towns Church Tract and Portage formed * 1846 Town transferred to Livingston County	Barkertown Cooper(s)ville Dalton East Hill Guys Corners Nunda (v) Nunda Junction Nunda Valley Rosses Sweetcake Hollow West Nunda Wilcox Corners	* Town of Pike now in Wyoming County * Town of Eagle now in Wyoming County * Church Tract now Town of Grove in Allegany County • Dalton formerly Nunda Station • Village of Nunda inc. 1839 • Rosses shared with Town of Grove, Allegany County

Towns (and Cities)	Villages and other Settlements	Notes
Ossian 1804 Settlers from New Jersey 1808 Formed in Allegany County from Town of Angelica 1826 Daughter town Burns formed in Allegany County 1856/7 Town transferred to Livingston County	Ossian State Park Westview	• Ossian also Ossian Center
Perry * In Livingston County 1814–1841		* See Wyoming County
Portage 1810 Settled 1827 Formed in Allegany County from Town of Nunda 1846 Town transferred to Livingston County; daughter town Genesee Falls formed in Wyoming County	Hunt Hunts Hollow Oakland Portage Portage Station Portageville	• Hunt also Hunts Station and Washington Hunt
Sparta 1789 Formed in Ontario County 1816 Daughter town Springwater formed 1821 Transferred to new county of Livingston 1822 Annexed land, including Dansville village, from Town of Dansville, Steuben County 1846 Daughter towns North Dansville and West Sparta formed 1849 Ceded land to Town of North Dansville	Dansville North Sparta Reed(s) Corners Ross Corners Scottsburg(h) Sparta White Bridge	• Dansville in Town of Dansville, Steuben County, before 1822; in Town of Sparta 1822–1846; in Town of North Dansville after 1846
Springwater 1807 Settlers from Connecticut 1816 Formed in Ontario County from towns of Naples and Sparta 1821 Transferred to new county of Livingston	Claytonville Springwater Valley East Springwater Tabor Corners Liberty Pole Webster(s) Crossing Springwater	• Springwater also Knowlesville
West Sparta 1795 Settled 1846 Formed from Town of Sparta	Byersville West Sparta Kysorville West Sparta Station McNair Station Wood(s)ville Union Corners	• Union Corners also Brushville
York 1800 Settled by Scottish 1819 Formed in Genesee County from towns of Caledonia and Leicester 1821 Transferred to new county of Livingston	Allens Corners Retsof Bows Corners Retsofs Corners Craigs Rippeys Corners Fowler(s)ville Root Corners Fraser South Greigsville Greigsville The Forks Greigsville Station Tryons Corners Inverness Wadsworth Linwood Walkers Corners McMillans Corners York Piffard York Center	• Piffard formerly Piffardinia

NEW YORK STATE CENSUS RECORDS

See also chapter 3, Census Records

County originals at Livingston County Clerk's Office: 1855, 1865, 1875, 1915, 1925 (1825, 1835, 1845, 1892, and 1905 are lost)

State originals at the NYSA: 1915, 1925

Microfilm at the FHL, NYPL, and NYSL; many years are online at *FamilySearch.org* and *Ancestry.com*.

NATIONAL/STATEWIDE REPOSITORIES & RESOURCES

See chapter 16

COUNTYWIDE REPOSITORIES & RESOURCES

Livingston County Clerk

6 Court Street, Room 201 • Geneseo, NY 14454
(585) 243-7010 or (585) 335-1712
www.co.livingston.state.ny.us/clerk.htm

Court records; land records 1821–present; naturalization records 1860s–1954; and county originals of New York state censuses 1855, 1865, 1875, 1915, 1925.

Livingston County – Town and Village Clerks

Birth, marriage, and death records are maintained by the clerk of the municipality in which the event occurred; see Introduction to County Guides for details of other records which may also be held by municipal clerks. For contact information for town clerks, see directory at *www.co.livingston.state.ny.us*.

Livingston County Surrogate's Court

2 Court Street • Geneseo, NY 14454 • (585) 243-7095

Probate records 1821– present. See also chapter 6, Probate Records.

Livingston County Public Libraries

Livingston is part of the Pioneer Library System; see *www.pls-net.org* or *www.owwl.org* to access each library. Many hold genealogy and local history collections.

Livingston County Historical Society and Museum

30 Center Street • Geneseo, NY 14454 • (585) 243-9147
Email: town@geneseony.org • *www.livingstoncountyhistoricalsociety.com*

Holdings include research materials and artifacts.

Livingston County Historian

5 Murray Hill Drive • Mount Morris, NY 14510
(585) 243-7955 or (585) 335-1730 • Email: Historian@co.livingston.ny.us
www.co.livingston.state.ny.us/departments.htm

Local histories; family files; cemetery survey conducted in 1885; census materials 1790–1930; directories; gazetteers; newspapers 1824–2000s; maps and atlases early 1800s to 1900s; military records; naturalization records 1821–1954; photographs and postcards. Website includes searchable records index. Publishes a quarterly newsletter.

Livingston County – All Municipal Historians

While not authorized to answer genealogical inquiries, town and village historians can provide valuable historical information and research advice; some maintain collections and webpages which may include transcribed records, local histories, and other genealogical material. See contact information at *www.co.livingston.state.ny.us*, *www.gahw ny.org/p/livingston.html* or at the website of the Association of Public Historians of New York State at *www.aphnys.org*.

REGIONAL REPOSITORIES & RESOURCES

Milne Library at SUNY Geneseo: Special Collections: Genesee Valley Historical Collection

One College Circle • Geneseo, NY 14454 • (585) 245-5194
www.geneseo.edu/library/special-collections-0

Documents the local histories of eight counties (Allegany, Genesee, Livingston, Monroe, Ontario, Orleans, Steuben, and Wyoming) and includes books, maps and atlases, videos and sound recordings, pamphlets and ephemera, and newspapers. Website includes Local History Subject Guide. Library houses Wadsworth Family Papers, Carl Schmidt Collection in Historic Architecture, and Walter Harding Collection.

LOCAL REPOSITORIES & RESOURCES

Alphabetized by location

Avon Preservation and Historical Society

23 Genesee Street • Avon, NY 14414 • (585) 226-2425 ext. 22
www.avonhistorical.org

Website includes a photograph collection, newsletter archive, and history of local schools.

Big Springs Historical Society Museum, Collection & Archives

3095 Main Street • Caledonia, NY 14423 • (585) 538-9880
Email: bigspringhistoricalsociety@yahoo.com
www.bigspringsmuseum.org

Holdings include photographs, genealogical material, and archives. Collections include military artifacts and memorabilia; American Indian artifacts; paintings and folk art; and costumes and textiles.

Lima Historical Society and Tenny Burton Museum

1850 Rochester Street • Lima, NY 14485 • (585) 624-1050
Email: president@limahistorical.com • *www.limahistorical.com*

Materials date back to the 1790s and include books, census materials, letters, maps, newspapers (*Livonia Gazette*, 1875–1965), town and village records, and yearbooks.

Livonia Area Preservation & Historical Society and Maurice F. Sweeney Museum

10 Commercial Street • Livonia, NY 14487 • (585) 346-4579
Email: laphs@localnet.com • *www.livonianyhistory.org*

Holdings include bound volumes of the *Livonia Gazette* (1875–1970), books, and artifacts. Published *Gazette News* quarterly.

Nunda Historical Society, Nunda Museum & Rose Shave Gallery

24 Portage Street • PO Box 341 • Nunda, NY 14517 • (585) 468-5420
Email: nundahs@localnet.com • *www.nundahistory.org*

Documents history of Nunda and Dalton. Website includes photographs, links to cemetery information, and some documents including Civil War letters, maps, military lists, and town meeting minutes.

Springwater-Websters Crossing Historical Society

PO Box 68 • Springwater, NY 14560 • (585) 669-2545
Email address on website • *www.townofspringwaterny.org*

Holdings include photographs of local families. The Society can assist with genealogical research.

SELECTED PRINT & ONLINE RESOURCES

Below is a selection of resources relevant for research in this county. The list is representative, not exhaustive. Additional titles—particularly of abstracts, indexes, transcriptions, and local histories—are available; consult the introduction to Part Two for further information. For guidance on how to identify and locate community directories and local newspapers, see chapter 11, City Directories, and chapter 12, Newspapers, in Part One of this book.

Abstracts, Indexes & Transcriptions

Cemetery Records of York, Livingston County, New York, and Togglestown, Livingston County, New York. Buffalo: 1933. Toggletown located in Town of Caledonia.

County of Livingston Abstracts. Syracuse: Central New York Genealogical Society, 2000. Abstracts for a range of genealogical records originally published in the quarterly *Tree Talks.*

Daughters of the American Revolution, comps. *New York DAR Genealogical Records Committee Report.* Since 1913 DAR volunteers have transcribed many thousands of unpublished cemetery, church, and town records throughout New York. The reports are at the DAR Library; copies are at the NYSL and the NYPL. The DAR has a searchable name index to all the GRC reports at *http://services.dar. org/Public/DAR_Research/search/?Tab_ID=6.* See Jean Worden below.

Decker, David E. *Gravestone Inscriptions: Town of Ossian, Livingston County, New York.* The Author, 1996.

— — —. "Oakland Cemetery, Town of Portage, Livingston County, New York." Typescript, 1997. Central Library of Rochester and Monroe County, Rochester, New York.

Douglas, Mary T. "Livingston County Cemetery Records, York Township." Typescript, 1928. Central Library of Rochester and Monroe County, Rochester, New York.

Dows, Marjorie S., and Virginia Moscrip. "Cemetery Inscriptions: Livingston County, New York State." Typescript, 1980. Central Library of Rochester and Monroe County, Rochester, New York.

Kelly, Arthur C. M. *Index to Tree Talks County Packet: Livingston County.* Rhinebeck, NY: Kinship, 2002.

Livingston County, NYG&B Church Surveys Collection. NYG&B, New York. [NYG&B eLibrary]

Steitz, Jessie H. "Inscriptions from Tombstones, in the South Avon Cemetery, Livingston County, New York." Typescript, 1943. Central Library of Rochester and Monroe County, Rochester, New York.

Worden, Jean D. "Book 1, Subject Index." In *Revised Master Index to the New York State Daughters of the American Revolution Genealogical Records Volumes.* Zephyrhills, FL: J. D. Worden, 1998. Includes listing of cemetery, church, towns and other records transcribed by the DAR.

Other Resources

American Agriculturist Farm Directory and Reference Book, Monroe and Livingston Counties, New York, 1917: A Rural Directory and Reference Book including a Road Map of Monroe and Livingston Counties. New York: O. Judd Co., 1917.

Beers, F. W. *Atlas of Livingston County, New York: From Actual Surveys.* New York, 1872.

Biographical Review: This Volume Contains Biographical Sketches of the Leading Citizens of Livingston and Wyoming Counties, New York. Boston, 1895.

Cook, William R. *Celebrating Our Past: Livingston County in the Twentieth Century.* Geneseo, NY: Q Publishing, 2000.

Doty, Lockwood L. *A History of Livingston County, New York: From Its Earliest Traditions, to Its Part in the War for Our Union, with an Account from the Seneca Nation of Indians, and Biographical Sketches of Earliest Settlers and Prominent Public Men.* Geneseo, NY, 1875.

Doty, Lockwood R. *What the Livingston County Historical Society Has Done in Collecting and Preserving County History.* Geneseo, NY, 1910.

Fay, Loren V. *Livingston County, New York, Genealogical Research Secrets.* Albany: L. V. Fay, 1983.

New York Historical Resources Center. *Guide to Historical Resources in Livingston County, New York, Repositories.* Ithaca, NY: Cornell University, 1981. [*books.FamilySearch.org*]

Pierce, Preston E. *Western New York Oral History Collections in Livingston County, Monroe County, Ontario County, Wayne County, Wyoming County.* Fairport, NY: Rochester Regional Library Council, 2009. *http://rrlc.org/wp-content/uploads/2013/02/dhp_ Oral-History-Inventory.pdf*

Records of the Ithaca College Study Center for Early Religious Life in Western New York, 1978–1981. Division of Rare and Manuscript Collections, Cornell University Library. A description of the holdings for each county is at *http://rmc.library.cornell.edu/ eguides/lists/churchlist1.htm.*

Root, Mary R. *History of the Town of York, Livingston County, New York.* Caledonia, NY: Big Springs Historical Society, 1940.

Smith, James H. *History of Livingston County, New York: With Illustrations and Biographical Sketches of Some of Its Prominent Men and Pioneers.* Syracuse, 1880.

Stetson, G. Emmet, comp. *New Gazetteer and Business Directory for Livingston County, N.Y. for 1868.* Geneva, NY, 1867.

Turner, Orasmus. *History of the Pioneer Settlement of Phelps and Gorhams Purchase and Morris' Reserve. . . .* Rochester, 1852.

Additional Online Resources

Ancestry.com

> See chapter 16 for a description of *Ancestry.com*'s resources and its partnership with the New York State Archives. A search of the online card catalog by county may reveal lesser known resources that pertain to a locality, such as town records, abstracts, transcriptions, city directories, and local histories.

FamilySearch.org

> FamilySearch has extensive collections of New York records, including religious records, which are searchable by name and location, but not by county. The following collections include record images (browsable, but not searchable):

- "New York, Land Records, 1630–1975." Includes land and property records. *familysearch.org/search/collection/2078654*
- "New York, Probate Records, 1629–1971." Includes wills, letters of administration, and guardianship papers. *familysearch.org/ search/collection/1920234*

> For both collections, choose the browse option and then select Livingston to view the available records sets. A detailed description of *FamilySearch.org* resources, which include the catalog of the Family History Library, is found in chapter 16.

NYGenWeb Project: Livingston County
www.rootsweb.ancestry.com/~nyliving

> Part of the national, USGenWeb volunteer initiative, the website provides information and resources for county research.

Old Fulton New York Postcards
www.FultonHistory.com

> The website provides free access to a vast collection of digitized New York newspapers, including 28 titles for Livingston County.

Madison County

Parent County   Chenango
Daughter Counties   None
County Seat   Village of Wampsville, Town of Lenox

Major Land Transactions
See table in chapter 7, Land Records
Chenango Twenty Towns 1789–1794

Indian Territories
See chapter 14, Peoples of New York, American Indian
Oneida Nation: Oneida Reservation (1788–present)

Town Boundary Map
★ - County seat

Towns (and Cities)	Villages and other Settlements		Notes
Brookfield 1791 Settled at Five Corners 1795 Formed in Herkimer County from Town of Paris (now in Oneida County) 1798 Transferred to new county of Chenango 1805 Daughter town Columbus formed in Chenango County 1806 Brookfield transferred to new county of Madison	Beaver Creek Brightman Neighborhood Brookfield (v) Brown District Burhyte District Button Falls Coons Corners DeLanc(e)y DeLancey Corners Five Corners Giles Corners Green Mills Guideboard Leonardsville Marsh Corners Moscow Hill	Nashville North Brookfield North Brookfield Station Northwest Settlement Puckerville Quaker Hill River Forks River Station Snow Corners South Brookfield Sweet Corners Unadilla Forks Waterman District West Brookfield West Edmeston West Side	• Beaver Creek post office 1820–1827 • Village of Brookfield inc. 1834, dissolved 1923; also Clark(s)ville, called Bailey Corners before 1834 • Coons Corners also Esquire Coons Corners and Coontown • DeLanc(e)y was Moscow before 1850 • Giles Corners also Giles Neighborhood • Green Mills formerly Mains Mills • Leonardsville shared with Town of Plainfield, Otsego County • South Brookfield formerly Babcock Mills and Southwest Settlement • West Edmeston formerly Coontown, Coonville; was shared with Town of Edmeston, Otsego County
Cazenovia 1793 Settled by Dutch 1795 Formed in Herkimer County from towns of Paris and Whitestown * 1798 Transferred to new county of Chenango; daughter town De Ruyter formed 1803 Daughter town Sullivan formed 1806 Transferred to new county of Madison 1807 Daughter towns Nelson and Smithfield formed 1823 Daughter town Fenner formed	Ballina Bingley Cazenovia (v) Cazenovia Station Chittenango Falls Constine Bridge Corkinsville Delphi Station Downersport Durfee District East Woodstock Floodport	Juddville Kiley Bridge New Woodstock North Cazenovia Perkins District Peth Rippleton Shelter Valley Union Webster (Station) West Woodstock	* Towns of Paris and Whitestown now in Oneida County • Bingley formerly Bingley Mills; on Fenner town line • Village of Cazenovia inc. 1810; county seat 1810–1817 • Rippleton also Pig City • West Woodstock formerly Bulls Corners and Woodstock Settlement
DeRuyter 1793 Settled 1798 Formed in Chenango County from Town of Cazenovia 1806 Transferred to new county of Madison; daughter town German formed in Chenango County 1815 Daughter town Georgetown formed	Burdick Settlement Crum(b) Hill DeRuyter (v) Puckerville Quaker Settlement Rakeville Sheds Sheds Corners Sheds Corners Station		• Village of DeRuyter inc. 1833; formerly Tromptown • Quaker Settlement also Quaker Basin
Eaton 1793 Settlers from Vermont and Massachusetts 1807 Formed from Town of Hamilton	Center Davis Corners Eagleville Eaton Eaton Center Gills Corners Hamilton Irish Settlement Morrisville (v) Morrisville Station	Pecksport Pecksport Station Pierceville Pine Woods Pratts Pratts Hollow Pratts Station West Eaton White Corners Williams Corners	• Eaton formerly Log City • Village of Morrisville inc. 1819; was Morris Flatts before 1819; county seat 1817–1907 • Morrisville Station also Midland • Pecksport also Pecks Basin • West Eaton formerly Leeville

Towns (and Cities)	Villages and other Settlements		Notes
Fenner 1793 Settled 1823 Formed from towns of Cazenovia and Smithfield	Bingley Bingley Station Blakeslee Chittenango Falls Christianson Corners Cody Corners	Fenner Milestrip Perryville Roberts Corners Rowan Corners	• Bingley formerly Bingley Mills; on Cazenovia town line • Cody Corner cemetery now Needham cemetery • Fenner also Fenner Corners • Milestrip also Mile Strip; on Lenox town line before 1896, on Lincoln town line after 1896 • Perryville formerly Blakeslee, Dykemans Mills, and New Chuckery; shared with towns of Lincoln and Sullivan
Georgetown 1804 Settled 1815 Formed from Town of De Ruyter	Browns Valley Georgetown Georgetown Station	Lazyville Mariposa Texas	• Georgetown formerly Slab City • Lazyville formerly Battle Creek
Hamilton 1792 Settlers from Massachusetts and Scotland 1795 Formed in Herkimer County from Town of Paris (now in Oneida County) 1798 Transferred to new county of Chenango 1806 Transferred to new county of Madison 1807 Daughter towns Eaton, Lebanon, and Madison formed	Beekman Corners Brooks Corner Canada Chemung Darts Corner(s) Earlville (v) Earlville Station East Hamilton Excell Corners Hamilton (v)	Hamilton Center Hamilton Station Hubbardsville Hubbardsville Station Loomis Corners Poolville Poolville Station Red City South Hamilton The Kingdom	• Village of Earlville inc. 1887; formerly Madison Forks, Teekyville, and The Forks; shared with Town of Sherburne, Chenango County • East Hamilton formerly Colchester Settlement • Village of Hamilton inc. 1816; formerly Paynes Corners, Paynes Hollow, Paynes Settlement, and Paynesville; courts held here and in Town of Lenox 1806–1810 • Hamilton Center also The Center • Hubbardsville formerly Dunbars Mills and Hubbards Corners
Lebanon 1792 Settlers from Vermont 1807 Formed from Town of Hamilton	Campbell Kenyon Corners Lebanon Lebanon Center	Middleport Niles Settlement Smiths Valley South Lebanon	• Campbell formerly Campbell Settlement • Hamlet of Lebanon also Toad Hollow • Smiths Valley formerly Randallsville
Lenox 1792 Settled 1809 Formed from Town of Sullivan 1836 Daughter town Stockbridge formed 1896 Daughter towns Lincoln and Oneida (now City of Oneida) formed	Bennetts Corners Campbells Corners Canastota (v) Clockville Durhamville Five Corners Lenox Lenox Basin Lenox Furnace Merrill(s)ville Messenger Bay Mile Strip Oneida (v) Oneida Creek Oneida Lake Oneida Lake Beach East Oneida Valley		• Bennetts Corners formerly Pine Bush; now in City of Oneida • Village of Canastota inc. 1835 • Clockville formerly Shippeville; now in Town of Lincoln • Durhamville see City of Oneida • Hamlet of Lenox formerly Lenox, Furnace, and Sullivan • Lenox Furnace now in Town of Lincoln • Merrill(s)ville formerly Cowaselon; now in Town of Lincoln • Mile Strip also Milestrip; in Town of Lincoln after 1896; on Fenner town line • Village of Oneida inc. 1848; in Town of Oneida 1896–1901; now City of Oneida • Oneida Valley formerly Wilsons Corners and State Bridge

(Lenox continued on next page)

Towns (and Cities)	Villages and other Settlements		Notes
Lenox (continued)	Pine Bush Quality Hill South Bay Union Corners Walkers Corners Wampsville (v) Whitelaw		• Union Corners formerly Rebel Corners • Village of Wampsville inc. 1907, called Wempsville before 1907; county seat 1907–present; 1806–1810 courts alternated between schoolhouses in Town of Sullivan (now Town of Lenox) and Hamilton village; 1810–1817 county seat at Village of Cazenovia and 1817–1907 at Village of Morrisville, Town of Eaton • Whitelaw formerly Ridgeville
Lincoln 1896　Formed from Town of Lenox	Alene Clockville Cottons Hoboken(ville) Lenox Furnace	Lenox Hill Merrill(s)ville Mile Strip Perryville	• Alene formerly Reynolds Corners • Clockville, Lenox Furnace, Merrill-(s)ville, and Mile Strip formerly in Town of Lenox • Perryville formerly Blakeslee, Dykemans Mills, and New Chuckery; shared with towns of Fenner and Sullivan
Madison 1793　Settled 1807　Formed from Town of Hamilton	Bouckville Durfee Corners Madison (v)	Madison Center Sig(s)by Corners Solsville	• Bouckville formerly Johnsville, McClures Settlement, and The Hook • Village of Madison inc. 1816; formerly also Madisons Corners • Solsville formerly Dalrymples Mill
Nelson 1794　Settled 1807　Formed from Town of Cazenovia	Argos Bucks Corners East Nelson Erieville	Hugh(e)s Corner Nelson Nelson Heights Pughs Corners	• Erieville formerly also Erietown • Nelson formerly Nelson Flats and Skunk Hollow
Oneida (city) 1901　Town of Oneida incorporated as the City of Oneida	Bennetts Corners Durhamville Eaton Corners	Five Corners Kenwood Oneida Heights	• Bennetts Corners and Durhamville formerly in Town of Lenox • Kenwood also Kenwood Station
Oneida (town) 1896–1901 1896　Formed from Town of Lenox including Village of Oneida 1901　Incorporated as a city	Oneida (v)		• Village of Oneida inc. 1848 in Town of Lenox, transferred to Town of Oneida 1896; dissolved when town became city
Smithfield 1795　Settled 1807　Formed from Town of Cazenovia 1823　Daughter town Fenner formed 1836　Daughter town Stockbridge formed	Bliss Corners Campbell District Eisaman(s) Corners Emburys Corners Green District	Ingalls District North Smithfield Peterboro Pleasant Valley Siloam	• Bliss Corners formerly Russ Corners • Pleasant Valley was Tinker Hollow before 1888 • Siloam formerly Ellenwood Hollow
Stockbridge 1791　Settled 1836　Formed from towns of Augusta, Lenox, Smithfield, and Vernon *	Bridges Corners Cole Settlement Daggetsville Five Chimneys Corner Knoxville Munns Munns Station	Munnsville (v) Munnsville Station New Stockbridge Stockbridge Stockbridge Hollow Stockbridge Station Valley Mills	* Towns of Augusta and Vernon in Oneida County • Village of Munnsville inc. 1915 • Hamlet of Stockbridge formerly Knoxville • Valley Mills formerly Cooks Corners

Towns (and Cities)	Villages and other Settlements		Notes
Sullivan 1790 Settled 1803 Formed in Chenango County from Town of Cazenovia 1806 Transferred to new county of Madison 1809 Daughter town Lenox formed	Blakeslee Blakeslee Station Bolivar Bridgeport Canaseraga Station Chittenango (v) Chittenango Springs Chittenango Station East Boston Fyler Settlement Gees Corner(s) Joslins Corners	Lakeport New Boston North Chittenango North Manlius Oneida Lake Beach West Oniontown Peck Corner(s) Perryville Sullivan (v) Sullivan Station Weaver Corner	• Bolivar formerly Barnesville, Chittenango Rifts, and The Rapids • Bridgeport formerly Barnesville • Village of Chittenango inc. 1842 • Chittenango Springs also Mount Washington and White Sulfur Springs • North Manlius formerly Matthews Mill; was shared with the Town of Manlius, Onondaga County • Perryville formerly Blakeslee, Dykemans Mills, and New Chuckery; shared with towns of Fenner and Lincoln • Sullivan was formerly Canaseraga and Canaseraga Flats; incorporated as Village of Sullivan 1823, dissolved c.1859 when name reverted to Canaseraga; 1891 name changed back to Sullivan though locals still call it Canaseraga

NEW YORK STATE CENSUS RECORDS
See also chapter 3, Census Records

County originals at Madison County Clerk's Office: 1855, 1865, 1875, 1892, 1905, 1915, 1925 (1825, 1835, and 1845 are lost)

State originals at the NYSA: 1915, 1925

Microfilm at the FHL, NYPL, NYSHA, and NYSL; many years are online at *FamilySearch.org* and *Ancestry.com*.

NATIONAL/STATEWIDE REPOSITORIES & RESOURCES
See chapter 16

COUNTYWIDE REPOSITORIES & RESOURCES

Madison County Clerk
138 North Court Street #4 • Wampsville, NY 13163
(315) 366-2261 • *www.madisoncounty.ny.gov/county-clerk*

New York state census for Madison County 1855, 1865, 1875, 1892, 1905, 1915, and 1925; court records; deeds and mortgages; naturalization records; school records; books; and miscellaneous records of Madison County. Also see Madison County History and Archives (below); the archives are located in the County Clerk's office.

Madison County – City, Town, and Village Clerks
Birth, marriage, and death records are maintained by the clerk of the municipality in which the event occurred; see Introduction to County Guides for details of other records which may also be held by municipal clerks. For contact information, see *www. madisoncounty.ny.gov*.

Madison County Surrogate's Court
138 North Court Street • PO Box 607
Wampsville, NY 13163 • (315) 366-2392

Holds probate records from 1806 to the present. See also chapter 6, Probate Records.

Madison County History and Archives
138 North Court Street #4 • Wampsville, NY 13163
Email address on website • *www.madisoncounty.ny.gov/historian/home*

The Archives are located in the County Clerk's office and include archival documents, census records 1800–1870, cemetery incorporations 1874–1951, court records 1853–1985, deeds 1806–1920, journals 1892–2005, marriage licenses 1908–1926, mortgages 1806–2008, naturalizations 1852–1953, school records 1826–1953, and military records. A selection of records (including naturalization index, some census, deeds, mortgages, and school records) and photographs is available on the website, along with abundant information on the county's history.

Madison County Public Libraries
Madison is part of the Mid-York Library System; see *http://myls.ent. sirsi.net* to access each library. Many hold genealogy and local history collections, including maps and newspapers. Also see listings below for Cazenovia Public Library, Earlville Free Library, and Oneida Public Library.

Madison County Historical Society, Cottage Lawn Museum, and Mary King Research Library
435 Main Street • Oneida, NY 13421 • (315) 363-4136 or 361-9735
Email: history@mchs1900.org • *www.mchs1900.org*

Library holdings include family histories, newspapers, and vital records.

A comprehensive list is available on the website, along with newsletter archives. Annual journal, *Heritage*, 1977–present.

Madison County Historian
PO Box 668 • Wampsville, NY 13163 • (315) 366-2453

The historian is located in the office of the Madison County Clerk (see above) and manages the Madison County History and Archives (see above).

Madison County – All Municipal Historians
While not authorized to answer genealogical inquiries, city, town, and village historians can provide valuable historical information and research advice; some maintain collections and webpages which may include transcribed records, local histories, and other genealogical material. See municipal websites for details and contact information or the website of the Association of Public Historians of New York State at *www.aphnys.org*.

REGIONAL REPOSITORIES & RESOURCES

Central New York Genealogical Society
See listing in Onondaga County Guide

Lorenzo State Historic Site
17 Rippleton Road • Cazenovia, NY 13035 • (315) 655-3200
www.lorenzony.org

Holdings include cemetery, land, and other records from Madison and Chenango counties.

SUNY at Oswego: Local History Collection
See listing in Oswego County Guide

LOCAL REPOSITORIES & RESOURCES
Alphabetized by location

Town of Brookfield Historical Society Museum and Giles School
Museum: 10556 Skaneateles Turnpike Road
Society: 10556 Main Street • PO Box 214 • Brookfield, NY 13314
(315) 899-3333 • Email: brookfieldhistorysociety@gmail.com
www.brookfieldnyhistory.org

Books and genealogies, cemetery records, maps, local newspapers 1875–present, paintings, and artifacts. The Society maintains the 19th-century Giles Schoolhouse.

Canasota Canal Town Museum
122 Canal Street • Canasota, NY 13032 • (315) 697-5002
www.canastota-canal.com

Holdings include memorabilia, art, and historical material, including newspapers (*Canasota Bee-Journal*).

Cazenovia Public Library: Archive Room and Museum
100 Albany Street (Route 20) • Cazenovia, NY 13055
(315) 655-9322 • Email: Cazenovia@midyork.org
www.cazenoviapubliclibrary.org/archives.php

Holdings of the Archive Room include family files, cemetery records, church records, maps, and newspapers the *Pilot*, 1808–present, and the *Republican*, 1854–present. The museum contains manuscripts and ephemera, papers and diaries, photographs, land deeds, maps, and artifacts from the Cazenovia area.

Erieville-Nelson Heritage Society

Town of Nelson Office Building • 4085 Nelson Road
Cazenovia, NY 13035 • (315) 655-8045
http://erieville-nelson.dyndns.org/~enca/heritagesociety.html

Genealogies and family histories, local histories and biographies, assessment records 1900–present, land records, newspaper indexes, photographs, maps, scrapbooks, town board minutes, and vital records 1845–1847 and 1887 to the present.

Town of Sullivan/Village of Chittenango Collection

Town of Sullivan Office Building • 7507 Lakeport Road
Chittenango, NY 13037 • (315) 633-5344

Genealogies and family files, census records 1890–1930, church records, government records, newspapers 1831–1850 and 1870–present, obituaries, photographs, and information on local historical businesses and industry. Town and village both have historians.

Tromptown Historical Society and DeRuyter Museum

712 Utica Street • PO Box 176 • DeRuyter, NY 13052
www.tromptown.comoj.com

Holdings include a collection of the local newspaper, the *DeRuyter Gleaner*. Website contains information on recent exhibits and local history books. The Society maintains the 19th-century Seventh Day Baptist Church of DeRuyter.

Earlville Free Library: Local History Collections

6 North Main Street • PO Box 120 • Earlville, NY 13332
(315) 691-5931 • Email: earlville@midyork.org
www.earlvillefreelibrary.org/local-history

Local histories, cemetery records, newspapers (*Saturday Utica Globe*, 1909–1916), obituary index, photographs, and scrapbooks. The library's local history and genealogical materials are searchable via its online catalog.

Colgate University Libraries: Special Collections and Archives

Case Library • Colgate University • 13 Oak Drive
Hamilton, NY 13346 • (315) 228-6175
http://exlibris.colgate.edu/speccoll/default.html

Extensive local collections, including family histories, family papers, letters, the Andrew J. Russell Photographs (Civil War), railroad collection, local newspapers on microfilm, American Indian collection, Victor B. Goodrich Collection (vital statistics, etc., for Madison County). Website contains digital collections.

Hamilton Historical Commission

Hamilton Public Library • 13 Broad Street • Hamilton, NY 13346
(315) 824-3060 • *www.midyork.org/hamilton* (library)

Holdings include local histories, census indexes, cemetery listings, newspapers, and photographs.

Fryer Memorial Museum

Route 46 and Williams Street • PO Box 177
Munnsville, NY 13409 • (315) 495-2586
www.rootsweb.ancestry.com/~nymadiso/bit-of-past/borg/fryer.htm

Family histories, Bible records, cemetery records, local American Indian history, newspapers, and obituaries.

Oneida Public Library: Local History Room

220 Broad Street • Oneida, NY 13421 • (315) 363-3050
www.midyorklib.org/oneida/local-history-room

Genealogies and histories, cemetery records, census microfilms, immigration records, local directories, material on the Oneida Community, maps, newspapers (*Oneida Daily Dispatch* and others,

1800s–present), photographs, and the genealogical collection of the Daughters of the American Revolution, Skenandoah Chapter (Oneida, NY).

Peterboro Area Historical Society and Museum

4608 Peterboro Road • PO Box 42
Peterboro, NY 13134 • (315) 684-9022

The museum building is the late-19th-century schoolhouse of the Madison County Home for Destitute Children; the Society maintains its records (1871–1926). Additional holdings include genealogies, Bible records, cemetery listings, church records, the *Freeholder* (selected issues, 1808–1811), school records, and veteran information.

SELECTED PRINT & ONLINE RESOURCES

Below is a selection of resources relevant for research in this county. The list is representative, not exhaustive. Additional titles—particularly of abstracts, indexes, transcriptions, and local histories—are available; consult the introduction to Part Two for further information. For guidance on how to identify and locate community directories and local newspapers, see chapter 11, City Directories, and chapter 12, Newspapers, in Part One of this book.

Abstracts, Indexes & Transcriptions

Atwell, Christine O. "Revolutionary Soldiers and Descendants of Madison County, New York State." Typescript, 1930. NYPL, New York.

Bracy, Isabel. *Records of Revolutionary War Veterans Who Lived in Madison County, New York.* Interlaken, NY: Heart of the Lakes Publishing, 1988.

County of Madison Abstracts. Syracuse: Central New York Genealogical Society, 2000. Abstracts for a range of genealogical records originally published in the quarterly *Tree Talks*. A name index is on the CNYGS website.

Daughters of the American Revolution, comps. *New York DAR Genealogical Records Committee Report.* Since 1913 DAR volunteers have transcribed many thousands of unpublished cemetery, church, and town records throughout New York. The reports are at the DAR Library; copies are at the NYSL and the NYPL. The DAR has a searchable name index to all the GRC reports at *http://services.dar.org/Public/DAR_Research/search/?Tab_ID=6.* See Jean Worden's index below for a listing by county of the New York record sets that were transcribed by the DAR before 1998.

Kelly, Arthur C. M. *Index to Tree Talks County Packet: Madison County.* Rhinebeck, NY: Kinship, 2002.

Madison County's Welcome Home for Her Sons and Daughters Who Served in the World War from 1917–1919: With a Complete Roster, a List of Golden Stars, and Special Articles. Oneida, NY: Madison County (N.Y.) Welcome Home Committee, 1919.

Meyer, Mary K, and Joyce C. Scott. *Cemetery Inscriptions of Madison County, NY.* Westminster, MD: Willow Bend Books, 1997.

Smith, Mrs. E. P., Joyce C. Scott, and Mary K. Meyer. *Deaths, Births, and Marriages from Newspapers Published in Hamilton, Madison County, NY, 1818–1886 Inclusive.* Mt. Airy, MD: Pipe Creek Publications, 1991.

Worden, Jean D. "Book 1, Subject Index." In *Revised Master Index to the New York State Daughters of the American Revolution Genealogical Records Volumes.* Zephyrhills, FL: J. D. Worden, 1998. The Subject Index includes a listing by county of the cemeteries, churches, towns, and other sources of records transcribed by the DAR.

Other Resources

Beers, D. G. *Atlas of Madison County, New York: From Actual Surveys.* Philadelphia, 1875. [NYPL Digital Gallery]

Biographical Review: This Volume Contains Biographical Sketches of the Leading Citizens of Madison County, New York. Boston, 1894.

Bracy, Isabel. *Immigrants in Madison County, New York, 1815–1860.* Interlaken, NY: Heart of the Lakes Publishing, 1990.

Central New York Library Resources Council. *Guide to Historical Organizations in Central New York.* (Onondaga, Herkimer, Oneida, Madison) Digitally published May 2009. [www.clrc.org/wp-content/uploads/2011/05/DHPHistGuide09b.pdf]

Child, Hamilton. *Gazetteer and Business Directory of Madison County, N.Y., for 1868–9.* Syracuse, 1868.

Cutter, William R. *Genealogical and Family History of Central New York: A Record of the Achievements of Her People in the Making of a Commonwealth and the Building of a Nation.* New York: Lewis Historical Publishing Co., 1912.

Fay, Loren V. *Madison County, New York, Genealogical Research Secrets.* Albany: L.V. Fay, 1981.

Foley, Janet W. *Early Settlers of New York State: Their Ancestors and Descendants.* 9 vols. Akron, NY: 1934–1942. Reprint, 2 vols. Baltimore: Genealogical Publishing Co., 1993.

Galpin, William F. *Central New York, an Inland Empire, Comprising Oneida, Madison, Onondaga, Cayuga, Tompkins, Cortland, Chenango Counties and Their People.* New York: Lewis Historical Publishing Co., 1941. Contains biographies. Index available from Berkshire Family History Association.

Giambastiani, Barbara J. *Country Roads Revisited: The Cultural Imprint of Madison County.* Oneida, NY: Madison County Historical Society, 1984.

Ingalls, Anita M. *Guide to Madison County Cemeteries.* Oneida, NY: Madison County Historical Society, 2009.

Lehman, Karl H. *Madison County Today.* Oneida Castle, NY: Karl H. Lehman, 1943.

Madison County Heritage. Oneida, NY: Madison County Historical Society. Annual publication of the Madison County Historical Society.

New York Historical Resources Center. *Guide to Historical Resources in Madison County, New York, Repositories.* Ithaca, NY: Cornell University, 1982. [books.FamilySearch.org]

Nichols, Claude A. *Sullivan in History: Interesting Events and People Contributing to the Development of the Township of Sullivan, Madison County, New York.* Chittenango, NY: McHenry Press, 1939.

Smith, James H. *History of Chenango and Madison Counties, New York: With Illustrations and Biographical Sketches of Some of Its Prominent Men and Pioneers.* Syracuse, 1880. Separate index by John Tyne, Interlaken, NY: Heart of the Lakes Publishing, 1974.

Smith, John E. *Our Country and Its People: A Descriptive and Biographical Record of Madison County, New York.* Boston, 1899.

Teeple, John B. *The Oneida Family: Genealogy of a 19th Century Perfectionist Commune, Containing Original Community Photographs and Drawings.* Oneida, NY: Oneida Community Historical Committee, 1985.

Tuttle, William H. *Madison County, New York Soldiers in the War of 1812.* Mt. Airy, MD: Pipe Creek Publications, 1994.

———. *Names and Sketches of the Pioneer Settlers of Madison County, New York.* Interlaken, NY: Heart of the Lakes Publishing, 1984.

Whitney, Luna M. Hammond. *History of Madison County, State of New York.* Syracuse, 1872. Index available from Berkshire Family History Association.

Additional Online Resource

Ancestry.com

There are vast numbers of records on *Ancestry.com* that pertain to people who have lived in New York State. See chapter 16 for a description of *Ancestry.com*'s resources and its partnership with the New York State Archives. A search of the online card catalog by county may reveal lesser known resources that pertain to a locality, such as town records, abstracts, transcriptions, city directories, and local histories.

Civil War Soldiers in Madison County

http://localhistory.morrisville.edu/sites/mad_bury/master.html
Sue Greenhagen, librarian at Morrisville State College, has created a database of more than 5,000 names: Civil War Soldiers in Madison County: A Constantly Expanding List of Those Men Who Served in the War or the Rebellion, 1861–1865, and Were Born in, Lived In, Enlisted In, Died In, and/or Are Buried in Madison County, New York. Information might include: name, age, where the soldier was from, rank and unit, brief details of service, and place of burial.

FamilySearch.org

FamilySearch has extensive collections of New York records, including religious records, which are searchable by name and location, but not by county. The following collections include record images (browsable, but not searchable) that are organized by county:

- "New York, Land Records, 1630–1975." Includes land and property records. *familysearch.org/search/collection/2078654*
- "New York, Probate Records, 1629–1971." Includes wills, letters of administration, and guardianship papers. *familysearch.org/search/collection/1920234*

For both collections, choose the browse option and then select Madison to view the available records sets.

A detailed description of *FamilySearch.org* resources is found in chapter 16.

Madison County, New York

www.home.comcast.net/~ingallsam/index.html
Extensive collection of useful links, online information and documents including: burial listings, genealogies, wills, family Bibles, local histories, and transcribed books including Claude Nicholls' *Sullivan in History* and William Tuttle's articles for the *Oneida Democratic Union*, which describe the families of the 1802 land purchase.

Madison County History Trail Guide

www.madisontourism.com/trail_history.pdf
Historical places and repositories with description of holdings, addresses, and contact information.

NYGenWeb Project: Madison County

www.rootsweb.ancestry.com/~nymadiso
Part of the national, USGenWeb volunteer initiative, the website provides information and resources for county research.

Old Fulton New York Postcards

www.FultonHistory.com
The website provides free access to a vast collection of digitized New York newspapers, including 12 titles for Madison County.

Monroe County

Formed February 23, 1821

Parent Counties	Genesee • Ontario
Daughter Counties	None
County Seat	City of Rochester

Major Land Transactions
See chapter 7, Land Records
Phelps and Gorham Purchase 1788
Morris Reserve 1791

Town Boundary Map
★ - County seat

Towns (and Cities)	Villages and other Settlements		Notes
Brighton 1790 Settled 1814 Formed in Ontario County from Town of Smallwood * 1821 Transferred to new county of Monroe 1834 Ceded land to city of Rochester 1839 Daughter town Irondequoit formed	Brighton South Park Tryon Twelve Corners West Brighton		* Town of Smallwood dissolved and divided into towns of Brighton and Pittsford
Chili 1792 Settled 1822 Formed from Town of Riga	Brookdale Brookdale Station Buckbees Corners Chili Chili Center Clifton	North Chili O'Connellsville South Chili West Chili Whites	• Clifton also Harmons Mills and Harmonsburg
Clarkson 1803 Settled 1819 Formed in Genesee County from Town of Murray 1821 Transferred to new county of Monroe 1852 Daughter town Union (now Hamlin) formed	Brockport (v) Clarkson Clarkson Corners East Clarkson Garland	Otis Redman Corners Redmond West Clarkson	• Village of Brockport inc. 1829; mostly in Town of Sweden • Clarkson Corners formerly Murray Corners; now a registered Historic District
East Rochester 1897 Village of Despatch established, shared between towns of Pittsford and Perinton 1906 Incorporated as Village of East Rochester 1981 Coterminous Village and Town of East Rochester formed from towns of Pittsford and Perinton	East Rochester (v)		• Village of East Rochester inc. 1906; formerly Despatch
Gates 1802 Formed in Genesee County as Town of Northampton 1808 Daughter towns Murray, Parma, and Riga formed * 1809 Settlers from Vermont 1812 Name changed from Northampton to Gates 1821 Transferred to new county of Monroe 1822 Daughter town Greece formed 1834 Village of Rochester incorporated as City of Rochester	Cold Water Elmgrove Gates Gates Center Gates-North Gates North Gates Rochester (v) West Gates		* Town of Murray in Orleans County 1825–present • Village of Rochester inc. 1817; formerly Rochesterville; county seat from 1821 when county was formed; became part of new City of Rochester in 1834

Towns (and Cities)	Villages and other Settlements		Notes
Greece 1792 Settled 1822 Formed from Town of Gates	Barnard Beatie Braddock Heights Charlotte (v) Elmgrove Grand View Beach Grandview Heights Greece Greece Center	Hanfords Landing Kirks Crossing Manitou Beach Mount Read North Greece Reads Corners South Greece West Greece	• Barnard also Barnard(s) Crossing • Village of Charlotte inc. 1869 dissolved 1916; became 23rd ward of City of Rochester in 1916; also called Charlottsburg and Port Genesee
Hamlin 1810 Settled 1852 Formed as Town of Union from Town of Clarkson 1861 Name changed to Hamlin	Beachwood Park Benedict Beach Bluff Beach Clarkson Center Hamlin Kendall(s) Mills Morton	North Hamlin Onteo Beach Sandy Harbor Beach Shore Acres Sunnyside Beach Troutburg Walker	• North Hamlin formerly Thomasville • Walker formerly North Clarkson; also East Hamlin
Henrietta 1806 Settled 1818 Formed in Ontario County from Town of Pittsford 1821 Transferred to new county of Monroe	Cedar Swamp East Henrietta Edgewood Station Henrietta Henrietta Station Mortimer Red Creek	Ridgeland Riverton West Hempstead West Henrietta West Henrietta Station	
Irondequoit * 1791 Settled 1839 Formed from Town of Brighton	Bayview Culver Meadows German Village Glen Haven Glen Haven Valley Irondequoit Lake Beach Laurelton	Newport Orchard Park Parkside Point Pleasant Sea Breeze Summerville White City Windsor Beach	* Irondequoit also known as Market Garden Town
Mendon 1790 Settlers from Vermont at Honeoye Falls 1812 Formed in Ontario County from Town of Bloomfield (now East Bloomfield) 1821 Transferred to new county of Monroe	Dann Corner East Mendon Ford Corner Honeoye Falls (v) Mendon (v) Mendon Center	Mendon Village Moran Corner(s) North Mendon Rochester Junction Sibleyville Tomlinson Corners	• Village of Honeoye Falls inc. 1838 as West Mendon; also Norton Mills • Village of Mendon inc. 1833 dissolved mid-1800s
Murray * In Monroe County 1821–1824			* See Orleans County
Northampton Name for Town of Gates 1802–1812			
Ogden 1802 Settlers from East Haddam, CT 1817 Formed in Genesee County from Town of Parma 1821 Transferred to new county of Monroe	Adams Basin Moreton Farm Ogden Ogden Center Spencerport (v) Town Pump		• Village of Spencerport inc. 1867; also Spencers Basin

Towns (and Cities)	Villages and other Settlements	Notes
Parma 1796 Settlers from Connecticut 1808 Formed in Genesee County from Town of Northampton (now Gates) 1817 Daughter town Ogden formed 1821 Transferred to new county of Monroe	Collamer Hilton (v) Hilton Beach Hinkleyville Lighthouse Beach Parma Center (re) Parma Corners	• Village of Hilton inc. 1885; formerly North Parma and Unionville • Hinkleyville also Hinckleyville • Parma Corners also Parma
Penfield 1791 Settlers from Vermont are not permanent; 1795 land repurchased and permanent settlement begins 1810 Formed in Ontario County from Town of Boyle 1821 Transferred to new county of Monroe 1840 Daughter town of Webster formed	East Penfield North Penfield Penfield Penfield Center Roseland West Penfield	• East Penfield also Lovetts Corners • Penfield also Mill Site
Perinton * 1790 Settled, then abandoned 1793 First permanent settler 1812 Formed in Ontario County from Town of Boyle * 1821 Transferred to new county of Monroe 1981 Daughter town East Rochester formed	Bushnell(s) Basin East Rochester (v) Egypt Fairport (v) Fullams Basin	* Perinton also Perrinton and Perrington * Town of Boyle renamed Smallwood in 1813 • Bushnell(s) Basin also Hartwells Basin • Village of East Rochester (formerly Despatch) inc. 1906; shared with Town of Pittsford until 1981; became coterminous with new Town of East Rochester • Village of Fairport inc. 1867; also Fullams and Fullam Town
Pittsford 1789 Settled 1814 Formed in Ontario County from Town of Smallwood * 1818 Daughter town Henrietta formed 1821 Transferred to new county of Monroe 1981 Daughter town East Rochester formed	Cartersville East Rochester (v) Irondequoit Mills Pittsford (v)	* Town of Smallwood dissolved and divided into towns of Brighton and Pittsford • Village of East Rochester (formerly Despatch) inc. 1906; shared with Town of Perinton until 1981; became coterminous with new Town of East Rochester • Village of Pittsford inc. 1827
Riga 1805–06 Settled 1808 Formed in Genesee County from Town of Northampton (now Gates) 1821 Transferred to new county of Monroe 1822 Daughter town Chili formed	Churchville (v) Five Points Riga	• Village of Churchville inc. 1852 • Riga also Riga Center

Towns (and Cities)	Villages and other Settlements		Notes
Rochester (city) * 1788–89 Settled 1834 Formed as a city from Village of Rochester (Town of Gates), and land from Town of Brighton	Beechwood Bethlehem Carthage Landing Charlotte	Genesee Rapids Kelseys Landing Lincoln Park	* County seat at Rochester (village and city) from 1821 when county was formed
Rush 1799 Settlers from New Hampshire 1818 Formed in Ontario County from Town of Avon * 1821 Transferred to new county of Monroe	East Rush Five Points Genesee Valley Junction Golah Industry	Manns Corner Meadow Wood North Rush Rush West Rush	* Town of Avon in Livingston County from 1821 • North Rush also Harts Corner • Rush also Websters Mills
Sweden 1807 Settled 1814 Formed in Genesee County from Town of Murray * 1821 Transferred to new county of Monroe; daughter Town of Clarendon formed in Genesee County *	Brockport (v) Sweden Center West Sweden		* Town of Murray in Orleans County from 1825 * Town of Clarendon in Orleans County from 1825 • Village of Brockport inc. 1829; small part of village in Town of Clarkson • Sweden Center and West Sweden also Sweden
Union Name for Town of Hamlin 1852–1861			
Webster 1805 Settled 1840 Formed from Town of Penfield	Forest Lawn Glen Edith Oakmonte	Union Hill Webster (v) West Webster	• Village of Webster inc. 1905
Wheatland 1786 Settlers from Pennsylvania 1821 Formed as Town of Inverness from Town of Caledonia, Livingston County; name changed to Wheatland later that year	Belcoda Beulah Garbutt Lehigh Junction Mumford	Scottsville (v) Scottsville Station Wheatland Wheatland Center	• Garbutt formerly Garbuttsville • Mumford formerly Mumfordville; also McKenzies Corners and Slab City • Village of Scottsville inc. 1914; also Oatka

Repositories and Resources

Note on Monroe County

Monroe is one of four "County Registration Districts" which have consolidated the administration of birth and death records. These civil records are kept at the Monroe County Department of Public Health, Office of Vital Records. See details below. Civil birth and death records earlier than 1881 may still be found with city, town, or village clerks.

NEW YORK STATE CENSUS RECORDS

See also chapter 3, Census Records

County originals at Monroe County Clerk's Office: 1855, 1865, 1875, 1892, 1905, 1915, 1925 (1825, 1835, and 1845 are lost)

State originals at the NYSA: 1915, 1925

Microfilm at the FHL, NYPL, and NYSL; many years are online at *FamilySearch.org* and *Ancestry.com*.

NATIONAL/STATEWIDE REPOSITORIES & RESOURCES

See chapter 16

COUNTYWIDE REPOSITORIES & RESOURCES

Monroe County Clerk
101 County Office Building • 39 West Main Street
Rochester, NY 14614 • (585) 753-1600
Email: mcclerk@monroecounty.gov
www.monroecounty.gov/clerk-index.php

Land records 1821–present; court records; naturalization records 1821–1950s; and Monroe County originals of the New York state censuses 1855, 1865, 1875, 1892, 1905, 1915, and 1925. Birth and death records are maintained by the Monroe County Health Department's Office of Vital Records. The Monroe County Clerk's Office does not issue marriage licenses and does not keep copies of marriage licenses; they are held by city, town, or village clerks.

Monroe County – City, Town, and Village Clerks
Marriage records are maintained by the clerk of the municipality in which the marriage occurred. For contact information, see *www. monroecounty.gov/government-index.php*. Unlike most city clerks, Rochester City Clerk holds some vital records not available at the New York State Department of Health; see listing for City of Rochester Municipal Archives.

Monroe County Surrogate's Court
99 Exchange Boulevard • Rochester, NY 14614 • (585) 371-3310

Holds probate records from the early 1800s to the present. See also chapter 6, Probate Records.

Monroe County Department of Public Health: Office of Vital Records
111 Westfall Road, Room 147 • Rochester, NY 14620
(585) 753-5141 • *www2.monroecounty.gov/health-VitalRecords.php*

Holdings include all birth and death records that occurred in Monroe County from 1880–present. Cities, towns, and villages forward their records to the county for this consolidated district. Copies can be ordered online.

Monroe County Records and Archives
City Place, 7th Floor • 50 West Main Street • Rochester, NY 14614
(585) 753-7367 • *www.monroecounty.gov/gis-records.php*

Holdings include record drawings of county construction projects

Monroe County

1870s to the present, topographic and land use maps, and aerial photographs of Monroe County.

Monroe County Public Libraries
For the Monroe County Library System, see *www3.libraryweb.org*. Most libraries have special collections and archival materials relating to local history and genealogy, including newspapers, maps, local histories, photographs, and ephemera. An overview of holdings can be found on the website. The Central Library, Henrietta Public Library, and Scottsville Free Library have particularly strong collections, and are listed below. A large selection of Monroe County city directories dating from the mid-1800s to the mid-1900s can be found online by searching the LibraryWeb catalog, and are available for download.

Central Library of Rochester and Monroe County: Local History and Genealogy Department
Rundel Memorial Library Building, 2nd Floor • 115 South Avenue
Rochester, NY 14604 • *www3.libraryweb.org*

Holds a copy of the New York State Department of Health vital records indexes. Census microfilms, newspapers, Civil War research collection, and photographs. Website includes a searchable Life Records Database (birth, death, and marriage indexes from City of Rochester newspapers 1900–present), genealogy indexes, local directories, Rochester Newspaper Index 1818–1903, Research Guide, and Genealogy Links. Publishes *Rochester History*, quarterly.

Monroe County Historian
St. John Fisher College • 3690 East Avenue • Rochester, NY 14618
(585) 385-8244 • *www.monroecounty.gov/history-index.php*

Monroe County – All Municipal Historians
While not authorized to answer genealogical inquiries, city, town, and village historians can provide valuable historical information and research advice; some maintain collections and webpages which may include transcribed records, local histories, and other genealogical material. See contact information at *http://mcnygenealogy.com/historians.htm*, the Government Appointed Historians of Western New York at *www.gahwny.org/p/monroe.html* or the website of the Association of Public Historians of New York State at *www.aphnys.org*.

Genealogical Roundtable of Monroe County
35 Country Lane • Penfield, NY 14526-1028

Has published collections of land records, school records, vital records culled from the 1865 census, and tax records.

SUNY: The College at Brockport: Rose Archives
Drake Memorial Library • 350 New Campus Drive
Brockport, NY 14420 • Email: archives@brockport.edu
www.brockport.edu/archives

Holdings document the history of the college, Town of Brockport, and western Monroe County.

Western Monroe County Genealogical Society and Ogden Farmers' Library
269 Ogden Center Road • Spencerport, NY 14559
www.wmcgs.blogspot.com

Holdings include the *Rural New Yorker*, 1858–1878.

REGIONAL REPOSITORIES & RESOURCES

Milne Library at SUNY Geneseo: Special Collections: Genesee Valley Historical Collection
See listing in Livingston County Guide

University of Rochester: Rare Books, Special Collections, and Preservation: Manuscript and Special Collections: Rochester, Western New York, and New York State
Rush Rhees Library • Second Floor, Room 225
University of Rochester • Rochester, NY 14627-0055
(585) 275-4477 • *www.lib.rochester.edu*

The University's collection of Rochester, Western New York, and New York State material includes local histories (more than 1,500 volumes), broadsides and circulars, Farmers' Library of Wheatland manuscripts 1805–1870, maps, newspapers 1820–1870, photographs and postcards, prints, stereo views, and upstate imprints.

LOCAL REPOSITORIES & RESOURCES
Alphabetized by location

East Rochester Department of Local History
901 Main Street • East Rochester, NY 14445 • (585) 381-3023
Email: historian@erhistory.com • *www.erhistory.com*

Collections include Board of Education 1927–2006; businesses 1898–2006; fire and police 1898–2006; newspapers (*East Rochester Herald*, 1943–2006); obituaries 1910–2006; school news 1932–2006; village politics 1897–2006; and weddings 1924–2006. Yearbooks 1928–2006 are viewable online.

Perinton Historical Society and Fairport Historical Museum
18 Perrin Street • Fairport, NY 14450 • (585) 223-3989
Email: info@PerintonHistoricalSociety.org
www.perintonhistoricalsociety.org

Archives include business and residential directories 1864–1966; cemetery information; census materials 1800–1915; maps, property records, and surveys; newspapers 1873–1990; obituaries 1980–present; Fairport High School Yearbooks 1926–2002; photographs and postcards; and local government documents. The museum documents history of local agriculture, architecture and commerce, industry, transportation, pioneer life, communications, and the Underground Railroad. Publishes a newsletter, *Perinton Historigram.*

Henrietta Public Library: Local History Collections
455 Calkins Road • Henrietta, NY 14623 • (585) 334-3401
Email: hplinfo@libraryweb.org • *http://hpl.org*

Collections include agricultural records; architecture; canal records; cemetery indexes (some online); census reports; church histories and records; suburban directories; gazetteers; government records; histories of Henrietta and Monroe counties; journals, diaries, and personal correspondence; maps; military records; American Indian records; local newspapers; obituaries; oral history; personal and family histories; school records; social life and customs; tax assessment rolls; transportation; and yearbooks. A list of holdings for each collection is available on the Library's website. Website also includes genealogy research tools, including how-to guides and tips, extensive digital collections, and numerous links.

Parma-Hilton Historical Society and Parma Historical Museum
1300 Hilton Parma Corners Road (Route 259), North Entrance
Hilton, NY 14468 • (585) 392-9496 • Email: curator@parmany.org
http://parmahiltonhistoricalsociety.com

Exhibits document local involvement in the Civil War, World War I and World War II, and the town's agricultural and domestic history.

City of Rochester: City Clerk
City Hall, Room 300A • 30 Church St. • Rochester, NY 14614
(585) 428-7421

Holdings for the City of Rochester include marriage records 1908–present. See City of Rochester Municipal Archives and Records Center listing for birth and death records.

City of Rochester Municipal Archives and Records Center
414 Andrews Street • Rochester, NY 14604 • (585) 428-7331
www.cityofrochester.gov/records

Holdings for the City of Rochester include marriages 1876–1943, with complete online bride/groom index, copies of original marriage licenses from the years 1908–1960 (can be obtained from onsite microfilm records); government records; archival materials; and photographic collection 1860–1970. (Birth and marriage records 1881–present and death records June 1880–present are available at the New York State Department of Health in Albany.)

Historic Brighton
PO Box 18525 • Rochester, NY 14618-0525
Email: info@historicbrighton.com • *www.historicbrighton.org*

Website provides history of agriculture, industry, and architecture in Brighton area, including maps and census information. Includes history of Buckland Farmstead, Brighton Brick, and the 17 existing brick structures in Brighton.

Irondequoit Historical Society and Historic Complex
1288-1290 Titus Avenue • Rochester, NY 14617 • (585) 266-5144
www.ggw.org/~ihsociety/index.htm

Website includes list of the Society's publications and photos of historic Irondequoit homes. Publications of the Society include local histories, biographies, cemetery records, letters, and maps.

Rochester Genealogical Society
PO Box 10501 • Rochester, NY 14610-0501
Email: rgsmembership@rochester.rr.com • *http://nyrgs.org*

Website includes list of surnames currently being researched by members, list of the Society's publications, selected church and cemetery records, and numerous links. Publishes a quarterly called *Hear Ye, Hear Ye.*

Rochester Historical Society
Rundel Memorial Building • 115 South Avenue • Rochester, NY 14604
(585) 428-8470 • Email: librarian@rochesterhistory.org
www.rochesterhistory.org

Architectural drawings, art and artifacts, books and manuscripts (genealogies and histories, correspondence, papers, and minute books), and prints and photographs. Publishes the *Observer* quarterly.

Scottsville Free Library:
Eugene Cox Memorial Local History Room
28 Main Street • Scottsville, NY 14546 • (585) 889-2023
www.libraryweb.org/scottsville/scohist.html

Books and documents, artifacts, cemetery index, genealogies and family files, letters, maps, photographs, and yearbooks.

Wheatland Historical Association
69 Main Street • PO Box 184 • Scottsville, NY 14546 • (585) 889-4574
www.townofwheatland.org/History

The Association maintains the Skivington Local History Room.

SELECTED PRINT & ONLINE RESOURCES

Below is a selection of resources relevant for research in this county. The list is representative, not exhaustive. Additional titles—particularly of abstracts, indexes, transcriptions, and local histories—are available; consult the introduction to Part Two for further information. For guidance on how to identify and locate community directories and local newspapers, see chapter 11, City Directories, and chapter 12, Newspapers, in Part One of this book.

Abstracts, Indexes & Transcriptions

American Agriculturist Farm Directory and Reference Book, Monroe and Livingston Counties, New York, 1917: A Rural Directory and Reference Book Including a Road Map of Monroe and Livingston Counties. New York: O. Judd Co., 1917.

Barber, Gertrude Audrey. "Abstracts of Wills of Monroe County, N.Y." Typescript, 1940–1941. University of Wisconsin, Madison. [*HathiTrust.org*]

Cohen, Minnie. "Abstracts of Wills of Monroe County, N.Y., from 1821–1841." Typescript, 1941. NYPL, New York.

County of Monroe Abstracts. Syracuse: Central New York Genealogical Society, 2000. Abstracts for a range of genealogical records originally published in the quarterly *Tree Talks.*

Daughters of the American Revolution, comps. *New York DAR Genealogical Records Committee Report.* Since 1913 DAR volunteers have transcribed many thousands of unpublished cemetery, church, and town records throughout New York. The reports are at the DAR Library; copies are at the NYSL and the NYPL. The DAR has a searchable name index to all the GRC reports at *http://services.dar.org/Public/DAR_Research/search/?Tab_ID=6.* See Jean Worden's index below for a listing by county of the New York record sets that were transcribed by the DAR before 1998.

Kabelac, Karl Sanford. *Index to Pictures of Rochesterians and Monroe Countians.* Rochester: Local History Committee, 1992.

Kelly, Arthur C. M. *Index to Tree Talks County Packet: Monroe County.* Rhinebeck, NY: Kinship, 2002.

Montgomery, George Washington. *Monroe County, New York, Marriage Records of Rev. George Washington Montgomery, 1846–1879, Founding Minister of the First Universalist Society of the City of Rochester.* Rochester: Rochester Genealogical Society, 1992.

Naukam, Lawrence W. *Monroe County, N.Y. Cemetery Record Index.* Rochester: Rochester Genealogical Society, 1984.

Worden, Jean D. "Book 1, Subject Index." In *Revised Master Index to the New York State Daughters of the American Revolution Genealogical Records Volumes.* Zephyrhills, FL: J. D. Worden, 1998. The Subject Index includes a listing by county of the cemeteries, churches, towns, and other sources of records transcribed by the DAR.

Other Resources

Beers, F. W. *Atlas of Monroe County, New York: From Actual Surveys.* New York, 1872.

Bragdon, George C. *Notable Men of Rochester and Vicinity: XIX and XX Centuries.* Rochester: D. J. Stoddard, 1902.

Calavano, Alan. *Rochester.* Charleston, SC: Arcadia Publishing, 2008.

Child, Hamilton. *Gazetteer and Business Directory of Monroe County, NY, for 1869–70.* Syracuse, 1868.

Clark, Donna K. *Monroe County, New York, Directory of Genealogical Records.* Arvada, CO: Ancestor Publishers, 1985.

Connors, Mary, and Jim Burlingame. *East Rochester, New York: One Hundred Years of History, 1897–1997.* Dallas: Taylor Publishing Co., 1997.

Du Bois, Eugene E. *The City of Frederick Douglass: Rochester's African-American People and Places.* Rochester: Landmark Society of Western New York, 1995.

Federal Writers' Project (NY). *Rochester and Monroe County.* Rochester: Scrantom's, 1937. [*Archive.org*]

Foley, Janet W. *Early Settlers of New York State: Their Ancestors and Descendants.* 9 vols. Akron, NY: 1934–1942. Reprint, 2 vols. Baltimore, Genealogical Publishing Co., 1993.

Halsey, Richard T. *Genealogical Guide to Monroe County, New York.* Rochester: Rochester Genealogical Society, 1985.

Hanford, Franklin, and E. H. T. Miller. *Name Sources of Townships of Monroe Co.* Scottsville, NY: n.p., 1930.

Hawley, Jesse, and Elisha Ely. *Early History of Rochester: 1810 to 1827, with Comparisons of Its Growth and Progress to 1860.* Rochester, 1860.

Hosmer, Howard C. *Monroe County, 1821–1971: The Sesquicentennial Account of the History of Monroe County, New York.* Rochester: Rochester Museum and Science Center, 1971.

Husted, Shirley C., and Ruth Rosenberg-Naparsteck. *Rochester Neighborhoods.* Charleston, SC: Aracadia, 2000.

Johnson, Paul E. *A Shopkeeper's Millennium: Society and Revivals in Rochester, New York, 1815–1837.* New York: Hill and Wang, 1978.

Lee, Florence. *The Founding of Monroe County.* Rochester: County of Monroe, 1965.

———. *Pleasant Valley: An Early History of Monroe County and Region, 1650–1850.* New York: Carlton Press, 1970.

MacNab, Margaret C. *First Footers: Settlers around Monroe County before 1820.* Rochester: The Author, n.d.

MacNab, Margaret Schmitt, Shirley C. Husted, and Katherine W. Thompson. *Northfield on the Genesee: Early Times in Monroe County, N.Y., with Town Minutes and Highway Records, 1796–1814, of Dr. John Ray and Samuel Kempton, Town Clerks, and Biographies of Nearly 500 Early Families.* Rochester: County of Monroe, 1981.

Marcotte, Robert. *Where They Fell: Stories of Rochester Area Soldiers in the Civil War.* Franklin, VA: Q. Publishing, 2002.

McIntosh, W. H. *History of Monroe County, New York: With Illustrations Descriptive of Its Scenery, Palatial Residences, Public Buildings, Fine Blocks, and Important Manufactories.* Philadelphia, 1877.

McKelvey, Blake. *Rochester in the Civil War.* Rochester: Rochester Historical Society, 1944.

———. *Rochester on the Genesee: The Growth of a City.* Syracuse: Syracuse University Press, 1973.

New York Historical Resources Center. *Guide to Historical Resources in Monroe County, New York, Repositories.* Ithaca, NY: Cornell University, 1988. [*books.FamilySearch.org*]

Osgood, Howard L. *The Struggle for Monroe County.* N.p., 1892.

Peck, William F. *History of Rochester and Monroe County, New York: From the Earliest Historic Times to the Beginning of 1907.* New York, Chicago: Pioneer Publishing Company, 1908.

———. *Semi-centennial History of the City of Rochester: With Illustrations and Biographical Sketches of Some of Its Prominent Men and Pioneers.* Syracuse, 1884.

Pierce, Preston E. *Western New York Oral History Collections in Livingston County, Monroe County, Ontario County, Wayne County, Wyoming County.* Fairport, NY: Rochester Regional Library Council, 2009. *http://rrlc.org/wp-content/uploads/2013/02/dhp_Oral-History-Inventory.pdf*

Preface to Tomorrow: Monroe County History Briefly Told and Illustrated. Rochester: County of Monroe, 1971.

Raines, Thomas, et al. *Landmarks of Monroe County, New York . . . : Followed by Brief Historical Sketches of the Towns of the County with Biography and Family History.* Boston, 1895.

Records of the Ithaca College Study Center for Early Religious Life in Western New York, 1978–1981. Division of Rare and Manuscript Collections, Cornell University Library. A description of the holdings for each county is at *http://rmc.library.cornell.edu/eguides/lists/churchlist1.htm.*

Slocum, George E. *Wheatland, Monroe County, New York: A Brief Sketch of Its History.* Scottsville, NY: I. Van Hooser, 1908.

Turner, Orsamus. *History of the Pioneer Settlement of Phelps and Gorham's Purchase, and Morris' Reserve . . . .* Rochester, 1851.

Additional Online Resources

Ancestry.com

There are vast numbers of records on *Ancestry.com* that pertain to people who have lived in New York State. See chapter 16 for a description of *Ancestry.com*'s resources and its partnership with the New York State Archives. A search of the online card catalog by county may reveal lesser known resources that pertain to a locality, such as town records, abstracts, transcriptions, city directories, and local histories.

FamilySearch.org

FamilySearch has extensive collections of New York records, including religious records, which are searchable by name and location, but not by county. The following collections include record images (browsable, but not searchable) that are organized by county:

- "New York, Land Records, 1630–1975." Includes land and property records. *familysearch.org/search/collection/2078654*

- "New York, Probate Records, 1629–1971." Includes wills, letters of administration, and guardianship papers. *familysearch.org/search/collection/1920234*

For both collections, choose the browse option and then select Monroe to view the available records sets.

A detailed description of *FamilySearch.org* resources is found in chapter 16.

The College at Brockport: Local History Resources
www.brockport.edu/archives/resources.html

This page provides links to online genealogical resources for Monroe and neighboring counties.

Monroe County Library System
www3.libraryweb.org

The website provides access to numerous digital collections of city directories, local histories, civil records and indexes, photographs, journals, and other material; pathfinders and research guides on topics of historical interest; and links to other resources for Monroe County research.

New York Heritage Digital Collections: New York State Newspaper Project
www.nyheritage.org/newspapers

The website provides links to digital newspapers collections in 26 counties (currently) made accessible through New York Heritage, New York State Historic Newspapers, HRVH Historical Newspapers, and other providers.

NYGenWeb Project: Monroe County
www.mcnygenealogy.com

Part of the national, USGenWeb volunteer initiative, the website provides information and resources for county research.

Old Fulton New York Postcards
www.FultonHistory.com

The website provides free access to a vast collection of digitized New York newspapers, including 14 titles for Monroe County.

Rochester Churches Indexing Project (RCIP)
www.rcip.info

The RCIP is a volunteer initiative that has produced a growing database of thousands of marriage and baptism record transcriptions from more than 30 churches in the Rochester area.

Montgomery County

Formed March 12, 1772

County Name   Originally named Tryon County; name changed to Montgomery April 2, 1784

Parent County   Albany

Daughter Counties   Ontario 1789 • Herkimer 1791 • Otsego 1791 Tioga 1791 • Hamilton 1816 • Fulton 1838

County Seat   Village of Fonda, Town of Mohawk

Major Land Transactions
See table in chapter 7, Land Records
Kayaderosseras Patent 1708
Stone Arabia Patent 1723

Town Boundary Map
★ - County seat

Towns (and Cities)	Villages and other Settlements		Notes
Amsterdam (city) 1885 Incorporated as a city from Village of Amsterdam in the Town of Amsterdam			
Amsterdam (town) 1793 Formed from Town of Caughnawaga 1831 Daughter town Perth formed 1885 Village of Amsterdam became City of Amsterdam	Amsterdam (v) Church Corners Crane Village Station Crane(s)ville Fort Johnson (v) Hagaman (v) Harrower	Manny(s) Corners Rockton South Amsterdam Tribes Hill Truax Station Wallins Corners	• Village of Amsterdam inc. 1830; formerly Vedersburgh; became City of Amsterdam in 1885 • Village of Fort Johnson inc. 1909 • Village of Hagaman inc. 1892; formerly Hagamans Mills
Aurelius * In Montgomery County 1789–1791			* See Cayuga County
Bleecker * In Montgomery County 1831–1838			* See Fulton County
Broadalbin * In Montgomery County 1793–1838			* See Fulton County
Canajoharie Settled mid-1700s 1772 Formed as a district 1788 Recognized as a town by State of New York 1791 Daughter town Cherry Valley formed in Otsego County 1798 Daughter town Minden formed 1823 Daughter town Root formed	Ames (v) Blaine Bowmans Creek Budd Hill Buel Canajoharie (v) Fort Plain (v)	Maple Hill Mapleto(w)n Marshville Seeber(s) Lane Sprout Brook Van Deusenville Waterville	• Village of Ames inc. 1924 • Village of Canajoharie inc. 1829 • Village of Fort Plain inc. 1832; shared with Town of Minden
Caughnawaga 1788–1793 * 1788 Formed as a town by State of New York 1793 Dissolved, land divided between towns of Amsterdam, Broadalbin, Johnstown, and Mayfield			* Town included Village of Caughnawaga— see Fonda in Town of Mohawk; Caughnawaga was a Mohawk village and also a French Jesuit mission 1668–1679
Charleston 1770 Stone Heap Patent granted 1793 Formed from dissolved Town of Mohawk 1823 Daughter towns Root and Glen formed	Burton(s)ville Carrytown Charleston Charleston Four Corners Davis Corners	Fox Corners Lib Corners Lost Valley Market Corners Oak Ridge Rockwell Corners	• Hamlet of Charleston formerly Eatons Corners, also Riders Corners
Chemung * In Montgomery County 1789–1791			* See Chemung County
Ephratah * In Montgomery County 1827–1838			* See Fulton County
German Flatts * In Montgomery County 1772–1791			* See Herkimer County
Florida 1793 Formed from dissolved Town of Mohawk	Fort Hunter Kline Lost Valley Mill Point	Miller(s) Corner(s) Minaville Morris Corners Mudge Hollow	• Fort Hunter also Lower Mohawk Castle • Minaville formerly Yankee Street (Florida continued on next page)

Towns (and Cities)	Villages and other Settlements		Notes
Florida (continued)	Port Jackson Scotch Bush Scotch Church Snooks Corners	South Amsterdam Wellsville Young(s) Corners	• Scotch Bush also Powder Spring
Glen 1722–26 Patents granted 1823 Formed from Town of Charleston	Auriesville Fultonville (v) Glen Mill Point	Square Barn Corners Stone Ridge Voorheesville	• Village of Fultonville incorporated 1848, reincorporated 1886; Fultonville formerly Van Epps Swamp
Harpersfield * In Montgomery County 1788–1791			* See Delaware County
Herkimer * In Montgomery County 1788–1791			* See Herkimer County
Johnstown * In Montgomery County 1793–1838			* See Fulton County
Lake Pleasant * In Montgomery County 1812–1816			* See Hamilton County
Mayfield * In Montgomery County 1793–1838			* See Fulton County
Milton * In Montgomery County 1789–1791			* See Town of Genoa, Cayuga County
Minden Settled early 1700s by Germans 1798 Formed from Town of Canajoharie 1817 Daughter town Danube (Herkimer County) formed	Brookman Corner(s) Charlesworth Corners Fordsborough Fordsbush Fort Plain (v) Freysbush Hallsville Hessville	Minden Mindenville Moyers Corners Ripple Corners Salt Springville Sand Hill Valley Brook	• Village of Fort Plain inc 1832; shared with Town of Canajoharie • Freysbush also Frey Bush
Mohawk 1772–1793 c.1725 Settled 1772 Formed in Tryon County (now Montgomery County) 1788 Recognized as a town by State of New York 1793 Dissolved, land divided between towns of Charleston and Florida			
Mohawk * French Jesuits at Caughnawaga in mid-1600s 1837 Formed from Town of Johnstown	Albany Bush Berryville East Stone Arabia Fonda (v) Fonda Sand Flats Tribes Hill Yost(s)		* This town formed 44 years after earlier Town of Mohawk was dissolved; same name slightly different location • East Stone Arabia on Palatine town line • Fonda county seat 1836–present; 1772–1836 county seat at Johnstown (now Fulton County); Village of Fonda inc. 1850, formerly Caughnawaga
Northampton * In Montgomery County 1799–1838			* See Fulton County

Towns (and Cities)	Villages and other Settlements		Notes
Oppenheim * In Montgomery County 1808–1838			* See Fulton County
Otsego * In Montgomery County 1788–1791			* See Otsego County
Palatine 1689 Settlers from Switzerland 1713 German Palatine settlers 1772 Formed as District of Stone Arabia 1773 Name changed to Palatine 1788 Recognized as a town by State of New York 1797 Daughter town Salisbury formed 1805 Daughter town Stratford formed 1808 Daughter town Oppenheim formed 1817 Daughter town Manheim formed in Herkimer County 1827 Daughter town Ephrata formed	Christmas Corners Cook Corners Cranes Landing East Stone Arabia McKinley Nelliston (v) Palatine Bridge (v) Palatine Church Sprakers Station Stone Arabia		• East Stone Arabia on Mohawk town line • Village of Nelliston inc. 1878 • Village of Palatine Bridge inc. 1867
Perth * In Montgomery County 1831–1838			* See Fulton County
Pompey * In Montgomery County 1789–1791			* See Onondaga County
Root 1823 Formed from towns of Canajoharie and Charleston	Brandys Corners Browns Hollow Bundys Corners Currytown Downing Station Flat Creek Kilmartin Corners Little Nose	Lykers Randall Root Root Center Rural Grove Sprakers Stone Ridge Sutphens Hollow	• Lykers formerly Lykers Corners • Randall formerly Yatesville; also Downing • Rural Grove formerly Leatherville • Sprakers formerly Sprakers Basin • Sutphens Hollow formerly Hamilton Hollow
Salisbury * In Montgomery County 1797–1817			* See Herkimer County
St. Johnsville 1776 Settled 1838 Formed from Town of Oppenheim	East Creek Fort House Klocks Field	St. Johnsville (v) West St. Johnsville	• Village of St. Johnsville inc. 1857 • West St. Johnsville also Upper St. Johnsville
Stone Arabia Name for Town of Palatine 1772–1773			
Stratford * In Montgomery County 1805–1838			* See Fulton County
Wells * In Montgomery County 1805–1816			* See Hamilton County
Whitestown * In Montgomery County 1788–1791			* See Oneida County

NEW YORK STATE CENSUS RECORDS

See also chapter 3, Census Records

County originals shared between Montgomery County Clerk's Office and Montgomery County Department of History and Archives (MCDHA): 1825*, 1835*, 1845*, 1855, 1865, 1875, 1892, 1905, 1915, 1925

State originals at the NYSA: 1915, 1925

Microfilm at the FHL, NYPL, and NYSL; many years are online at *FamilySearch.org* and *Ancestry.com*.

* 1825, 1835 and 1845 are incomplete censuses, they have been indexed by the MCDHA and only include the following towns, 1825: Canajoharie, Florida, Minden, Palatine, and Root; also the towns (now in Fulton County) of Johnstown, Oppenheim, and Stratford; and the towns (from Hamilton County) of Hope, Lake Pleasant, and Wells; 1835: Oppenheim; 1845: Towns of Minden and Oppenheim

NATIONAL/STATEWIDE REPOSITORIES & RESOURCES

See chapter 16

COUNTYWIDE REPOSITORIES & RESOURCES

Montgomery County Clerk
County Office Building • 64 Broadway • PO Box 1500
Fonda, NY 12068 • (518) 853-8124
www.co.montgomery.ny.us/sites/public/government/clerk/CountyClerk_Development/CountyClerk_contact.aspx

Court records, land records, naturalization records 1810–1955, and Montgomery County originals of the New York state censuses for 1825, 1835, 1845, 1855, 1865, 1875, 1892, 1905, 1915, and 1925.

Montgomery County – City, Town, and Village Clerks
Birth, marriage, and death records are maintained by the clerk of the municipality in which the event occurred; see Introduction to County Guides for details of other records which may also be held by municipal clerks. Some municipal websites contain historical and genealogical information, for example the Village of Fonda has online cemetery records, and information about former mayors and other prominent citizens. For contact information, see *www.co.montgomery.ny.us*.

Montgomery County Surrogate's Court
58 Broadway • PO Box 1500 • Fonda, NY 12068 • (518) 853-8108

Holdings include probate records from 1787 to the present. See also chapter 6, Probate Records.

Montgomery County Public Libraries
Montgomery is part of the Mohawk Valley Library System; see *www.mvls.info* to access each library. Many maintain local history and genealogy collections. A separate webpage provides detailed information at *www.mvls.info/lhg*. The Amsterdam Free Library holds city directories 1876–1988 (gaps), and Fort Plain Free Library holds cemetery and canal records. Also see listings below for Canajoharie Library and Art Gallery and Margaret Reaney Memorial Library.

Montgomery County Department of History and Archives, Heritage & Genealogical Society of Montgomery County, Montgomery County Historian
Old Court House • 9 Park Street • PO Box 1500
Fonda, NY 12068-1500 • (518) 853-8186
www.co.montgomery.ny.us (choose History & Archives from dropdown menu)

Collects information on all counties formerly in Montgomery County prior to their formation. Holdings include histories, biographies, cemetery records, census records, land records, directories and gazetteers, vital statistics, church records, civil records, military records, historical files, archives, newspapers, and pamphlets. Selected family genealogies are available on the website, along with a list of surnames. The Department operates an Underground Railroad Project.

Montgomery County – All Municipal Historians
While not authorized to answer genealogical inquiries, city, town, and village historians can provide valuable historical information and research advice; some maintain collections and webpages which may include transcribed records, local histories, and other genealogical material. See contact information at *http://montgomery.nygenweb.net/histsocs.html* or at the website of the Association of Public Historians of New York State at *www.aphnys.org*.

REGIONAL REPOSITORIES & RESOURCES

Capital District Genealogical Society
See listing in Albany County Guide

Fulton-Montgomery Community College: Evans Library: The Kenneth R. Dorn Regional History Study Center
See listing in Albany County Guide

LOCAL REPOSITORIES & RESOURCES

Alphabetized by location

Canajoharie Library and Art Gallery: Local History Room
2 Erie Boulevard • Canajoharie, NY 13317 • (518) 673-2314
Email: canlib@sals.edu • *www.clag.org*

Family files and genealogies, books and periodicals, newspapers on microfilm, and yearbooks. Website contains digital local history exhibits.

Charleston Historical Society
741 Corbin Hill Road • Esperance, NY 12066 • (518) 922-5867

Holdings include family histories for the Town of Charleston as well as some federal and state census materials. Publishes *Charleston Historical Society Newsletter*.

Fort Plain Museum and Historic Park
389 Canal Street • PO Box 324 • Fort Plain, NY 13339
(518) 993-2527 • Email: fortplainmuseum@yahoo.com
www.fortplainmuseum.org

Website includes information on the history and archaeology of Fort Plain, as well as maps, newsletters, photographs, and postcards.

Margaret Reaney Memorial Library & Museum
19 Kingsbury Avenue • St. Johnsville, NY 13452 • (518) 568-7822
Email: mrml@telenet.net • *margaretreaneylibrary.blogspot.com*

County and family histories; an obituary, marriage, and birth index; newspapers; cemetery records; and scrapbooks. The museum's collection includes fine art, sculpture, memorabilia, military artifacts, and period rooms with a focus on Mohawk Valley history from the pre-Revolutionary period to the present.

The Palatine Settlement Society and Nellis Homestead/Tavern
PO Box 183 • St. Johnsville, NY 13452
www.palatinesettlementsociety.org

Website includes issues of the Society's newsletter and information on the Nellis Family.

SELECTED PRINT & ONLINE RESOURCES

Below is a selection of resources relevant for research in this county. The list is representative, not exhaustive. Additional titles—particularly of abstracts, indexes, transcriptions, and local histories—are available; consult the introduction to Part Two for further information. For guidance on how to identify and locate community directories and local newspapers, see chapter 11, City Directories, and chapter 12, Newspapers, in Part One of this book.

Abstracts, Indexes & Transcriptions

Becker, Edith Van Heusen (Mrs. Frank N. Becker). "Abstracts of Wills, Montgomery County, N.Y." *NYG&B Record*, vol. 56 (1925) no. 2: 145–161, no. 4: 380–397; vol. 57 (1926) no. 2: 163–186, no. 3: 380–397. [NYG&B eLibrary]

———. "Cemetery Inscriptions in Mayfield, N.Y., Fulton Co. and Hagaman, Amsterdam, N.Y., Montgomery Co." Typescript, ca. 1938. NYPL, New York. [NYG&B eLibrary]

———. "Cemetery Inscriptions: In the Vicinity of Montgomery and Fulton Counties, N.Y." 5 vols. Typescript, 1923–1963. NYPL, New York.

———. "Cemetery Inscriptions, Montgomery County, New York." Typescript. NYPL, New York. [NYG&B eLibrary] Information overlaps with some of the transcriptions published in the NYG&B Record (see above citation) and pertains to several cemeteries in the Town of Florida, Montgomery County.

Becker, Edith Van Heusen (Mrs. Frank N. Becker) and Melvin W. Lethbridge. "Tombstone Inscriptions, Montgomery County, N.Y." *NYG&B Record*, vol. 56 (1925) no 4: 376–380; vol. 57 (1926) no. 2: 163–186, no. 3: 264–282; vol. 58 (1927) no. 1: 82–89, no. 2: 155–172; vol. 59 (1928) no. 1: 85–92, no. 2: 171–181, no. 3: 267–276, no. 4: 380–385; vol. 60 (1929) no. 1: 54–64, no. 2: 185–192, no. 3: 285–291, no. 4: 374–387; vol. 61 (1930) no. 1: 88–92, no. 2: 190–204, no. 3: 304–306, no. 4: 403–409; vol. 62 (1931) no. 1: 85–89, no. 3: 318–322, no. 4: 427–430; vol. 63 (1932) no. 1: 90–94, no. 4: 411–414; vol. 64 (1933) no. 1: 83–86, no. 2: 197–202, no. 4: 404–407; vol. 65 (1934) no. 3: 288–289, no. 4: 393–397; vol. 66 (1935) no. 1: 84–88, no. 2: 185–189, no. 3: 288–290, no. 4: 393–396; vol. 67 (1936) no 3: 281–284, no. 4: 388–390; vol. 68 (1937) no. 2: 182–186; vol. 69 (1938) no. 3: 292–295. Pertains to the Town of Florida. [NYG&B eLibrary]

Cormack, Marie N., and Katherine A. Furman. "New York State Cemetery Inscriptions: Albany County, Herkimer County, Montgomery County, Saratoga County, Schenectady County." Typescript, 1940. [microfilm at FHL, NYSL]

County of Montgomery Abstracts. Syracuse: Central New York Genealogical Society, 2000. Abstracts for a range of genealogical records originally published in the quarterly *Tree Talks*.

Daughters of the American Revolution, comps. *New York DAR Genealogical Records Committee Report*. Since 1913 DAR volunteers have transcribed many thousands of unpublished cemetery, church, and town records throughout New York. The reports are at the DAR Library; copies are at the NYSL and the NYPL. The DAR has a searchable name index to all the GRC reports at *http://services.dar.org/Public/DAR_Research/search/?Tab_ID=6*. See Jean Worden's index below for a listing by county of the New York record sets that were transcribed by the DAR before 1998.

Hartley, Robert M. *Marriage and Birth Records as Recorded by Rev. James Dempster, 1778–1803 …With a Complete Index of Names*. Alexandria, VA: Sleeper Co., 1995.

Keefer, Donald A. *Records of the First Reformed Protestant Dutch Church of the Town of Glen: Organized as the First Reformed Protestant Dutch Church of Charlestown (Charleston), Montgomery County, New York, on March 18, 1795*. Rhinebeck, NY: Kinship, 1990.

Kelly, Arthur C. M. *Index to Tree Talks County Packet: Montgomery County*. Rhinebeck, NY: Kinship, 2002.

Kelly, Arthur C. M., and Henry Barclay. *Vital Records of Queen Anne Chapel (Episcopal) Fort Hunter, N.Y., Town of Florida, Montgomery County, 1735–1746*. Rhinebeck, NY: Kinship, 2000.

Lethbridge, Melvin W. *Montgomery County, N.Y., Marriage Records: Performed by Rev. Elijah Herrick, 1795–1844; Also Records of Rev. Calvin Herrick, 1834–1876; Also Records of Rev. John Calvin Toll, 1803–1844*. St. Johnsville, NY: Enterprise and News, 1922.

Montgomery County Department of History and Archives. *Catalogue of Historical and Genealogical Material*. Fonda, NY, 1982.

Montgomery County, NYG&B Church Surveys Collection. NYG&B, New York. [NYG&B eLibrary]

Vosburgh, Royden Woodward, ed. "Records of the First Reformed Dutch Church at Glen in the Town of Glen, Montgomery County, N.Y.: Formerly the First Reformed Protestant Dutch Church at Charleston." Typescript, 1918. NYPL, New York. [NYG&B eLibrary]

———, ed. "Records of the Reformed Dutch Church of Stone Arabia: In the Town of Palatine, Montgomery County, N.Y." 3 vols. Typescript, 1916. NYPL, New York. [NYG&B eLibrary]

———, ed. "Records of the Reformed Protestant Dutch Church of Florida, in the Village of Minaville, Town of Florida, Montgomery County, NY and Records of the Reformed Protestant Dutch Church of Duanesburgh, 1798-1804." Typescript, n.d. NYPL, New York. [NYG&B eLibrary]

———, ed. "Records of the United Presbyterian Church in the Town of Florida, Montgomery County, N.Y." Typescript, n.d. NYPL, New York. [NYG&B eLibrary]

Wikoff, Helen Lyons. "Gravestone Inscriptions from Cemeteries in Montgomery and Otsego Counties, New York." Typescript, 1931. NYPL, New York.

Worden, Jean D. "Book 1, Subject Index." In *Revised Master Index to the New York State Daughters of the American Revolution Genealogical Records Volumes*. Zephyrhills, FL: J. D. Worden, 1998. The Subject Index includes a listing by county of the cemeteries, churches, towns, and other sources of records transcribed by the DAR.

Other Resources

Beers, F. W. *History of Montgomery and Fulton Counties*. New York, 1878.

Capital District Genealogical Society Newsletter. Albany: Capital District Genealogical Society, 1982–present. [*capitaldistrictgenealogicalsociety.org*]

Child, Hamilton. *Gazetteer and Business Directory of Montgomery and Fulton Counties, NY, for 1869–70*. Syracuse, 1870.

Dailey, William Nelson Potter. *The History of Montgomery Classis, R.C.A. To Which Is Added Sketches of Mohawk Valley Men and Events of Early Days, . . . Reformed Church in America, Doctrine and Progress, Revolutionary Residences, etc.* Amsterdam, NY: Recorder Press, 1916

Donlan, Hugh P. *Outlines of History, Montgomery County, State of New York, 1772–1972.* Bicentennial ed. Amsterdam, NY: Noteworthy Co., 1973.

Frothingham, Washington. *History of Montgomery County.* Syracuse, 1891.

Greene, Nelson. *History of the Mohawk Valley, Gateway to the West, 1614–1925; Covering the Six Counties of Schenectady, Schoharie, Montgomery, Fulton, Herkimer, and Oneida.* Chicago: S. J. Clarke, 1925.

Kelly, Arthur C. M. *The Mohawk.* Rhinebeck, NY: Kinship, quarterly 1986–1998, annually 1999–2001.

— — —. *Valley Quarterlies.* Directory of articles (vols. 1–15) and every-name index to the *Capital*, the *Columbia*, the *Mohawk*, and the *Saratoga*. Rhinebeck, NY: Kinship, CD-ROM, 2000.

New Century Atlas of Montgomery and Fulton Counties, New York. Philadelphia: Century Map Co., 1905.

New York Historical Resources Center. *Guide to Historical Resources in Montgomery County, New York, Repositories.* Ithaca, NY: Cornell University, 1983. [*books.FamilySearch.org*]

Nichols, Beach. *Atlas of Montgomery and Fulton Counties, New York: From Actual Surveys by and under the Direction of B. Nichols . . . .* New York, 1867. [NYPL Digital Gallery]

Simms, Jeptha R. *Frontiersmen of New York: The Frontiersmen of New York: Showing Customs of the Indians, Vicissitudes of the Pioneer White Settlers, and Border Strife in Two Wars.* Albany, 1882–1883.

Additional Online Resources

Ancestry.com

There are vast numbers of records on *Ancestry.com* that pertain to people who have lived in New York State. See chapter 16 for a description of *Ancestry.com*'s resources and its partnership with the New York State Archives. A search of the online card catalog by county may reveal lesser known resources that pertain to a locality, such as town records, abstracts, transcriptions, city directories, and local histories.

FamilySearch.org

FamilySearch has extensive collections of New York records, including religious records, which are searchable by name and location, but not by county. The following collections include record images (browsable, but not searchable) that are organized by county:

- "New York, Land Records, 1630–1975." Includes land and property records. *familysearch.org/search/collection/2078654*

- "New York, Probate Records, 1629–1971." Includes wills, letters of administration, and guardianship papers. *familysearch.org/search/collection/1920234*

For both collections, choose the browse option and then select Montgomery to view the available records sets.

A detailed description of *FamilySearch.org* resources is found in chapter 16.

NYGenWeb Project: Montgomery County

montgomery.nygenweb.net

Part of the national, USGenWeb volunteer initiative, the website provides information and resources for county research.

Nassau County

Formed January 1, 1899

Parent County   Queens
Daughter Counties   None
County Seat   Village of Mineola, Town of North Hempstead

Town Boundary Map

 - County seat

Towns (and Cities)	Villages and other Settlements	Notes
Glen Cove (city) 1668 Land purchased by English families, named Musquito Cove; part of Town of Oyster Bay 1683 Land included in new county of Queens 1834 Name changed to Glen Cove 1899 Transferred to new county of Nassau 1918 Unincorporated village of Glen Cove and some adjacent areas separated from Town of Oyster Bay and incorporated as City of Glen Cove *	Dosoris East Island Garvies Point The Landing North Country Colony The Orchard Red Spring	* BIll to create city passed June 8, 1917, city government installed January 1, 1918

| **Hempstead**
(See Queens County Guide for early history and former place-names 1639–1899)
1899   Town ceded from Queens County to new county of Nassau
1922   Village of Long Beach separated from town and incorporated as City of Long Beach | Alden Manor
Ancle Sea
Argo Village
Atlantic
Atlantic Beach (v)
Atlantic Beach Estates
Baldwin
Baldwin Harbor
Bank Plaza
Barnum Island
Bay Colony
Bay Park
Bellerose (v)
Bellerose Terrace
Bellmore
Bowling Green
Briar Park
Bryn Mawr
Cedarhurst (v)
Compton Park
East Atlantic Beach
East Garden City
East Hempstead
East Meadow
East Rockaway (v)
Ellisons Point
Elmont
Floral Park (v)
Floral Park Center
Floral Park Crest
Franklin Square
Freeport (v)
Garden City (v)
Garden City South
Gibson
Grant Park
Green Acres
Harbor Acres
Harbor Isle
Hempstead (v)
Hempstead Gardens
Hewlett
Hewlett Bay Park (v)

Hewlett Harbor (v)
Hewlett Neck (v)
Hewlett Point
Hingletown
Inwood
Island Park (v)
Lakeview
Lawrence (v)
Levittown
Lido Beach
Long Beach (v)
Long Beach North
Lynbrook (v)
Lynbrook Park
Malverne (v)
Malverne Park Oaks
Meadowmere Park
Merrick
Merrick Gables
Meyer Harbor
Mil(l)burn
Mineola (v)
Mitchel Field
Munson
New Hyde Park (v)
North Bellmore
North Lawrence
North Lynbrook
North Merrick
North Rockville Centre
North Valley Stream
North Wantagh
North Woodmere
Ocean Point
Oceanside
Point Lookout
Rockville Centre (v)
Roosevelt
Salisbury
Schodack
Seaford
Seaford Harbor | • Village of Atlantic Beach inc. 1962
• Bellerose shared with Queens Borough; Village of Bellerose inc. 1924 only in Nassau County
• Bellmore includes former New Bridge
• Village of Cedarhurst inc. 1910; Cedarhurst one of the "Five Towns" in southwest corner of Town of Hempstead, namely Cedarhurst, Inwood, Lawrence, Woodmere, and "the Hewletts" which include Woodsburgh
• Village of East Rockaway inc. 1900
• Elmont formerly Fosters Meadows
• Village of Floral Park inc. 1908; shared with Town of North Hempstead
• Floral Park Center was shared with Town of North Hempstead
• Village of Freeport inc. 1892
• Village of Garden City inc. 1919; small part in Town of North Hempstead
• Harbor Isle also Harbor Island
• Village of Hempstead inc. 1853
• Village of Hewlett Bay Park inc. 1928
• Village of Hewlett Harbor inc. 1925
• Village of Hewlett Neck inc. 1927
• Inwood one of "Five Towns" see Cedarhurst
• Village of Island Park inc. 1926
• Lakeview formerly Woodfield
• Village of Lawrence inc. 1897; one of "Five Towns" see Cedarhurst
• Levittown includes small part of former Jerusalem; formerly Island Trees
• Village of Long Beach inc. 1918 became City of Long Beach 1922
• Village of Lynbrook inc. 1911
• Village of Malverne inc. 1921, formerly Norwood
• Meadowmere Park part of Woodmere
• Village of Mineola inc. 1906, most of village in Town of North Hempstead
• Mitchel Field Army Air Corps Base during WWII

(Hempstead continued on next page) |

Towns (and Cities)	Villages and other Settlements	Notes
Hempstead (continued)	Short Beach Signal Smith Pond South Floral Park (v) South Hempstead South Valley Stream South Westbury Stewart Manor (v) Uniondale Valley Stream (v) Wantagh Westbury South West Hempstead Westwood Woodmere Woodsburgh (v) Wreck Lead	• Village of New Hyde Park inc. 1927; shared with Town of North Hempstead • North Bellmore formerly Smithville South • North Wantagh includes most of former Jerusalem • Village of Rockville Centre inc. 1893 • Roosevelt formerly Greenwich Point • Salisbury includes South Westbury (Westbury South) • Village of South Floral Park inc. 1925 • Village of Stewart Manor inc. 1927 • Village of Valley Stream inc. 1925 • Wantagh formerly Ridgewood • Village of Woodsburgh inc. 1912; one of "Five Towns" see Cedarhurst
Long Beach (city) 1918 Long Beach incorporated as a village in Town of Hempstead 1922 Long Beach village separated from town and incorporated as a city		
North Hempstead (See Queens County Guide for early history and former place-names 1639–1899) 1899 Town ceded from Queens County to new county of Nassau	Albertson Bar Beach Barkers Point Baxter Estates (v) Beacon Hill Bird Grove Brookdale Carle Place East Hills (v) East Shore East Williston (v) Elm Point Floral Park (v) Floral Park Center Flower Hill (v) Garden City (v) Garden City Park Glenwood Landing Great Neck (v) Great Neck Estates (v) Great Neck Gardens Great Neck Plaza Greenvale Greenwolde Harbor Hills Herricks Hillside Heights Hillside Manor Kensington (v) Kings Point (v) Lake Success (v) Manhasset Manhasset Hills Manorhaven (v) Merillon Avenue	• Barkers Point now in Village of Sands Point • Village of Baxter Estates inc. 1931 • Beacon Hill in Port Washington • Village of East Hills inc. 1931; small part in Town of Oyster Bay • Village of East Williston inc. 1926 • Elm Point now in Village of Kings Point • Village of Floral Park inc. 1908; shared with Town of Hempstead • Floral Park Center was shared with Town of Hempstead • Village of Flower Hill inc. 1931 • Village of Garden City inc. 1919; only small part in North Hempstead, mostly in Hempstead • Garden City Park formerly Clowesville • Glenwood Landing also formerly part of Village of Roslyn Harbor; on Oyster Bay town line • Village of Great Neck inc. 1921 • Village of Great Neck Estates inc. 1911 • Great Neck Gardens also Allenwood • Greenvale formerly North Roslyn; on Oyster Bay town line • Village of Kensington inc. 1921 • Village of Kings Point inc. 1924 • Village of Lake Success inc. 1927; formerly Lakeville • Manhasset formerly Tan Yard, Cow Neck • Village of Manorhaven inc. 1930 • Merillon Avenue neighborhood named for railroad station

(North Hempstead continued on next page)

Towns (and Cities)	Villages and other Settlements	Notes
North Hempstead (continued)	Mineola (v) Munsey Park (v) **New Cassel** New Hyde Park (v) North Hills (v) **North New Hyde Park** Old Westbury (v) Plandome (v) Plandome Heights (v) Plandome Manor (v) **Port Washington** Port Washington North (v) Roslyn (v) Roslyn Estates (v) Roslyn Harbor (v) **Roslyn Heights** Russell Gardens (v) Saddle Rock (v) **Saddle Rock Estates** Sands Point (v) **Searingtown** **South Glenwood Landing** **Stonington** **Strathmore** Thomaston (v) **University Gardens** Westbury (v) **West Williston** Williston Park (v)	• Village of Mineola inc. 1906; county seat 1899 to present; small part of village in Town of Hempstead • Village of Munsey Park inc. 1930 • Village of New Hyde Park inc. 1927; shared with Town of Hempstead • Village of North Hills inc. 1929 • North New Hyde Park includes former Plattsdale; extends into Borough of Queens • Village of Old Westbury inc. 1924; shared with Town of Oyster Bay • Village of Plandome inc. 1911 • Village of Plandome Heights inc. 1929 • Village of Plandome Manor inc. 1931 • Village of Port Washington North inc. 1932 • Village of Roslyn inc. 1932 • Village of Roslyn Estates inc. 1931 • Village of Roslyn Harbor inc. 1931; formed from parts of Roslyn and Glenwood Landing; shared with Town of Oyster Bay • Village of Russell Gardens inc. 1931 • Village of Saddle Rock inc. 1911 • Village of Sands Point inc. 1910 • Village of Thomaston inc. 1931 • Village of Westbury inc. 1932 • Village of Williston Park inc. 1926; formerly part of East Williston
Oyster Bay (See Queens County Guide for early history and former place-names 1639–1899) **1899** Town of Oyster Bay ceded from Queens County to the new county of Nassau **1917** Daughter city of Glen Cove formed	**Allens Point** **Arlyn Oaks** Bayville (v) **Bedelltown** **Bethpage** **Biltmore Shores** Brookville (v) Centre Island (v) **Cold Spring Harbor** Cove Neck (v) **Crown Village** **Dosoris** East Hills (v) **East Massapequa** **East Norwich** Farmingdale (v) **Fort Neck** **Glen Cove** **Glen Cove Landing** **Glen Head** **Glenwood Landing** **Greenvale** **Harbor Green** **Hicksville** **Jericho** Lattingtown (v) Laurel Hollow (v) **Lenox Hills** **Locust Grove**	• Village of Bayville inc. 1919 • Bedelltown now part of Bethpage • Bethpage until 1936 was Central Park and Old Bethpage was called Bethpage • Biltmore Shores part of Massapequa • Village of Brookville inc. 1931; formed from parts of Brookville and Jericho, and annexed Wheatley Hills in 1950s • Village of Centre Island inc. 1926 • Cold Spring Harbor also Cold Spring; mostly in Town of Huntington, Suffolk County; Oyster Bay portion now partly in Laurel Hollow • Village of Cove Neck inc. 1927 • Dosoris in City of Glen Cove from 1918 • Village of East Hills inc. 1931; mostly in Town of North Hempstead • East Massapequa eastern part includes West Amityville • East Norwich formerly included parts of Muttontown and other adjacent villages • Village of Farmingdale inc. 1904 • Glen Cove incorporated 1918 as City of Glen Cove • Glen Cove Landing part of City of Glen Cove from 1918

(Oyster Bay continued on next page)

Towns (and Cities)	Villages and other Settlements	Notes
Oyster Bay (continued)	Locust Valley Mannetto Hill Massapequa Massapequa Park (v) Matinecock (v) Mill Neck (v) Muttontown (v) Nassau Shores North Massapequa Old Bethpage Old Brookville (v) Old Ship Point Old Westbury (v) Oyster Bay Oyster Bay Cove (v) Pine Hollow Piping Rock Plainedge Plainview Roslyn Harbor (v) Sea Cliff (v) South Farmingdale Swedetown Village Syosset Upper Brookville (v) West Amityville Wheatley Wheatley Hills Woodbury	• Glenwood Landing also formerly part of Village of Roslyn Harbor and Glen Head; on North Hempstead town line • Greenvale on North Hempstead town line; included Old Brookville until 1929 • Jericho formerly included parts of villages of Brookville and Muttontown • Village of Lattingtown inc. 1931 • Village of Laurel Hollow inc. 1926; formerly Laurelton and part of Cold Spring Harbor • Locust Valley also traditional name for adjacent areas now in Lattingtown, Matinecock, and part of Mill Neck • Village of Massapequa Park inc. 1931 • Village of Matinecock inc. 1928 • Village of Mill Neck inc. 1925 • Village of Muttontown inc. 1931; includes part of Syosset • Nassau Shores part of East Massapequa • Old Bethpage formerly Bethpage • Village of Old Brookville inc. 1929; formerly part of Greenvale • Village of Old Westbury inc. 1924; shared with Town of North Hempstead; Oyster Bay portion includes part of Wheatley • Village of Oyster Bay Cove inc. 1931, also The Cove; includes part of Syosset • Village of Roslyn Harbor inc. 1931; shared with Town of North Hempstead; Oyster Bay portion formerly part of Glenwood Landing • Village of Sea Cliff inc. 1883 • Syosset formerly Little East Woods; parts now in villages of Muttontown and Oyster Bay Cove • Village of Upper Brookville inc. 1932 • West Amityville part of East Massapequa • Wheatley partly in Village of Old Westbury • Woodbury formerly East Woods
South Hempstead Name for Town of Hempstead 1784–1796		

Notes on Nassau County

Nassau County was created in 1899. For earlier records, see Queens County.

NEW YORK STATE CENSUS RECORDS

See also chapter 3, Census Records

County originals at Nassau County Clerk's Office: 1915, 1925 (1905 is lost)

State originals at the NYSA: 1915, 1925

Microfilm at the FHL, NYPL, and NYSL; both years are online at *FamilySearch.org* and *Ancestry.com*.

Notes about Early Censuses

For colonial censuses, see Queens County.

NATIONAL/STATEWIDE REPOSITORIES & RESOURCES

See chapter 16

COUNTYWIDE REPOSITORIES & RESOURCES

Nassau County Clerk

240 Old Country Road • Mineola, NY 11501 • (516) 571-2664
www.nassaucountyny.gov/agencies/Clerk

Land records 1899–present; naturalization records 1899–1987; county originals of the New York state censuses 1915 and 1925; marriage records 1907–1935; mortgages; and indexes. Land records and maps prior to 1899 from Queens County are available on microfilm; indexes on microfilm as well. Website has an extensive FAQ at *www. nassaucountyny.gov/agencies/clerk/clerkinfo/faq.html*.

Nassau County – City, Town, and Village Clerks

Birth, marriage, and death records are maintained by the clerk of the municipality in which the event occurred; see Introduction to County Guides for details of other records which may also be held by municipal clerks. For contact information, see *www.nassaucountyny.gov*.

Nassau County Surrogate's Court

262 Old Country Road • Mineola, NY 11501 • (516) 493-3800

Holds probate records, 1899–present. Onsite computerized index and ordering system. Also see chapter 6, Probate Records.

Nassau County Public Libraries

For the Nassau Library System, see *www.nassaulibrary.org*. Most libraries have special collections and archival materials relating to local history and genealogy, including newspapers, maps, local histories, photographs, scrapbooks, and pamphlets. Selected libraries with strong collections are listed below.

Nassau County Historian

240 Old Country Road • Mineola, NY 11501 • (516) 383-1557

Nassau County – All Municipal Historians

While not authorized to answer genealogical inquiries, city, town, and village historians can provide valuable historical information and research advice; some maintain collections and webpages which may include transcribed records, local histories, and other genealogical material. For example, the Oyster Bay town historian maintains a page on the town's website with selected Civil War and vital records. For contact information see *www.nassaucountyny.gov* or the website of the Association of Public Historians of New York State at *www.aphnys.org*.

Nassau County Historical Society

PO Box 207 • Garden City, NY 11530-0207 • (516) 538-7679
Email: webmaster@nassaucountyhistoricalsociety.org
www.nassaucountyhistoricalsociety.org

Society's collection is housed in the Long Island Studies Institute at Hofstra University (see below). Publishes an annual journal.

REGIONAL REPOSITORIES & RESOURCES

Hofstra University Library Special Collections Department: Long Island Studies Institute

Joan & Donald E. Axinn Library, Room 032 • 123 Hofstra University
Hempstead, NY 11549-1230 • (516) 463-6407
Email: lisi@hofstra.edu
www.hofstra.edu/Library/libspc/libspc_lisi_main.html

Holdings include Hofstra University Long Island Studies Institute collection, collection of the Nassau County Historical Society, reference collection of the Nassau County Museum, and James N. MacLean American Legion Memorial Collection. Materials include books and manuscripts, family papers, genealogies, local histories, census materials, government documents (including Queens and Nassau property records on microfilm), photographs, and newspapers. See the online catalog for descriptions and some specific finding aids for the Rare Books and Manuscript division.

Patchogue-Medford Library: Celia M. Hastings Local History Room

See listing in Suffolk County Guide

Stony Brook University: Special Collections & Archives

See listing in Suffolk County Guide

Stony Brook University: Center for Global and Local History

See listing in Suffolk County Guide

LOCAL REPOSITORIES & RESOURCES

Alphabetized by location

Baldwin Historical Society and Museum

1980 Grand Avenue • PO Box 762 • Baldwin, NY 11510
www.baldwinhistoricalsociety.com

Society's archives include letters, journals, newspapers, maps, postcards, and photographs. Provides research assistance.

Long Island University: C.W. Post Campus: B. Davis Schwartz Memorial Library: Cedar Swamp Historical Society Collection

Library: 720 Northern Blvd • Brookville, NY 11548 • (516) 299-2928
www.liucedarswampcollection.org
Society: PO Box 458 • Oyster Bay, NY 11771 • *www.cedarswamp.org*

Collections date from 1763 and include letters and deeds, maps, ephemera, books, and other records documenting the history of Cedar Swamp, the Society of Friends, and the Long Island Railroad.

The Historical Society of East Rockaway and Lynbrook

PO Box 351 • East Rockaway, NY 11518-0351 • (516) 887-9094
Email: hserl@optonline.net • *www.hserl.com*

Holdings include books about both communities, cemetery records, biographical files, and Davison genealogy.

Farmingdale-Bethpage Historical Society

PO Box 500 • Farmingdale, NY 11735 • Email: info@fbhsli.org
www.fbhsli.org

Documents history of the Bethpage Purchase (Bethpage, Farmingdale, Melville, North Massapequa, Old Bethpage, Plainedge, and Plainview). Website features photographs and historical articles.

Franklin Square Historical Society and Museum

John Street School, Nassau Boulevard • PO Box 45
Franklin Square, NY 11010 • (516) 352-1586
www.franklinsquarehistory.org

Maintains research library; also the George and Helen Christ Fosters Meadow Heritage Center, a collection of books and documents, genealogies, and photographs documenting the history of Fosters Meadow, a former German American farming community in Nassau County.

Freeport Historical Society and Museum

350 South Main Street • Freeport, NY 11520 • (516) 623-9632
Email: freeporthistoricalsociety@yahoo.com
www.freeporthistorymuseum.org

Cemetery records, Freeport census (1898 and 1912), 1911 Freeport High School Alumni Records, photographs, and theater playbills. Many records online.

Glen Cove Public Library: The Robert R. Coles Long Island History Collection

4 Glen Cove Avenue • Glen Cove, NY 11542-2885 • (516) 676-2130
Email: glencove@glencovelibrary.org
http://glencovelibrary.org/history/index.html

Map collection, photograph collection (including postcards and negatives, mid-1800s to present), history pamphlet file organized by subject, local newspapers on microfilm 1700s–present, documents, manuscripts, and records including family papers and diaries, 1665–present, periodicals; and artifacts and memorabilia.

Hempstead Village Historical Society

c/o Hempstead Public Library • 115 Nichols Court
Hempstead, NY 11550 • (516) 481-6990
Email: Hempstead@nassaulibrary.org

Holdings include newspaper articles, census materials, and local history.

Hicksville Public Library: Hicksville Historical Society Collection

Library: 169 Jerusalem Avenue • Hicksville, NY 11801 • (516) 931-1417
www.hicksvillelibrary.org
Society: PO Box 443 • Hicksville, NY 11802 • Facebook page

Society maintains a local history room in the library with census materials, maps, and estate information.

Jericho Public Library: Local History Collection

One Merry Lane • Jericho, NY 11753 • (516) 935-6790 ext. 28
www.jericholibrary.org

Books, family histories, periodicals, photographs, artwork, archival boxes (including clippings, diaries, letters, manuscripts, pamphlets, memorabilia, and documents), and oral histories 1700s–present.

Levittown Historical Society and Museum

Levittown Memorial Education Center • 150 Abbey Lane • PO Box 57
Levittown, NY 11756-0057 • (516) 731-5728
Email: Levhistsociety@aol.com • Facebook page

Holdings include local history, census materials, maps, and property information.

Locust Valley Historical Society: Julia Clark Historical Collection

Locust Valley Library • 170 Buckram Road • Locust Valley, NY 11560
Email: locustvalleyhistory@yahoo.com • *www.locustvalleyhistory.org*

Holdings include cemetery information and transcriptions, maps, records of local organizations and institutions, family papers, and genealogies. Subject guide online.

The Long Beach Historical and Preservation Society and Museum

226 West Penn Street • PO Box 286 • Long Beach, NY 11561
(516) 432-1192 • Email: info@longbeachhistory.org
www.longbeachhistory.org

Holdings include photographs, local newspapers, and census information.

Malverne Historical and Preservation Society and Museum

369 Ocean Avenue • PO Box 393 • Malverne, NY 11565
(516) 792-1910 • *www.malvernehistoricalsociety.org*

Holdings include local history and information about Malverne citizens, 1920s–present.

Historical Society of the Town of North Hempstead

220 Plandome Road • Manhasset, NY 11030 • (516) 627-3664
Email: nsai@optonline.net

Holdings include photographs and maps. Webpages hosted by *www.northshorearchitectureandinteriors.com*

Historical Society of the Massapequas

4755 Merrick Road • PO Box 211 • Massapequa, NY 11758
(516) 799-2023 • *www.massapequahistoricalsociety.org*

Maintains a library collection, the Old Grace Church and a local cemetery.

Mineola Historical Society

211 Westbury Avenue • PO Box 423 • Mineola, NY 11501
(516) 746-6722

Phone books, most years 1953–2008; high school yearbooks Mineola's *Signet*, 1923–1928, 1941–1952 (alumni office has additional years); Chaminade's *Crimson & Gold*, 1932–2010 (gaps). Over 1700 photographs and postcards, images include: village and street scenes, LIRR, early aviation, Nassau Hospital, courthouses, residences, schools, politicians, military (incl. Camp Mills), Mineola Fair, Mineola Theater, and the Vanderbilt Cup races; maps, pamphlets and booklets 1880s–present; vertical files relating to Mineola and the area, including theater programs 1930s–1960s, Corpus Christi parish records and school history. Book collection includes complete set of *North and South Hempstead Town Records* (1654–1880; see Hicks in Abstracts, Indexes & Transcriptions).

Oyster Bay Historical Society, Earle-Wightman House, and Angela Koening Center

20 Summit Street • PO Box 297 • Oyster Bay, NY 11771
(516) 922-1177 • Email: obhistory@aol.com
www.oysterbayhistorical.org

Maintains library of books, genealogies, almanacs, and catalogs. Collections include photographs and postcards (some are viewable online); maps and charts (also online); local newspapers; and manuscript archives. Holdings range 1680–present. Website includes articles on local history.

Raynham Hall Museum

20 West Main Street • Oyster Bay, NY 11771 • (516)-922-6808
www.raynhamhallmuseum.org

Historic home of Townsend family, with archives relating to Townsends and other local families.

Townsend Society of America

21 West Main Street • Oyster Bay, NY 11771• (516) 558-7092
Director@TownsendSociety.org • *www.townsendsociety.org*

Museum holds records and artifacts of the Townsend family and neighbors, 17th to 20th centuries. Society maintains an archive and publishes the *Townsend Genealogical Journal*.

Underhill Society of America

PO Box 712 • Oyster Bay, NY 11771-0712 • (516) 833-6724
Email: webmaster@underhillsociety.org • *www.underhillsociety.org*

Society, founded in 1892, holds an extensive collection of artifacts, books, manuscripts and records, images and photographs. Website includes collection catalogs. Appointments are necessary. Publishes annual *Bulletin* and *Underhill Genealogy*, now 8 vols.

The Cow Neck Peninsula Historical Society

336 Port Washington Boulevard • Port Washington, NY 11050-4530
(516) 365-9047 • Email: info@cowneck.org • *www.cowneck.org*

Holdings include maps, photographs, and postcards. Annual journal.

Port Washington Public Library: Local History Center

One Library Drive • Port Washington, NY 11050
(516) 883-4400 ext. 167 • Email: localhistory@pwpl.org
www.pwpl.org/localhistory

Books and periodicals, family files and family photographs, maps, postcards, oral history, scrapbooks; digitized collection on website. Oral histories (transcriptions, tapes, indexes and catalogue listings) are extensive and include African American, early aviation and seaplanes (PanAm Clipper), estate workers from the Gold Coast estates, fire fighters, maritime, and sand mining. Photography collections from Mason and Witmer.

The Bryant Library: Bryant Room Local History Collection

2 Paper Mill Road • Roslyn, NY 11576 • (516) 621-2240 ext. 1
www.bryantlibrary.org/local-history-v15-172/from-the-bryant-room

Holdings include Bryant Library Local History Collection (family papers, records, newspaper clippings, maps), diary collection 1849–1885, document collection 1636–1981, Grand Army of the Republic records 1862–1938, map collection ca. 1675–1984, photographs ca. 1860–1989, record book collection 1852–1902, Roslyn Cemetery records 1861–1984, Roslyn Grist Mill records 1850–1877, Roslyn High School yearbooks 1927–present, Roslyn Neighborhood Association records 1914–1952, *Roslyn News*, 1878–present, Roslyn Visiting Nurse Association records 1914–1969, telephone directories 1942–1943, 1957, 1968–present, and personal papers of local families.

Sea Cliff Village Museum

95 Tenth Avenue • Sea Cliff, NY 11579 • (516) 671-0090
Email: SeaCliffMuseum@aol.com • *www.seacliffmuseum.com*

Holdings include documents, photographs and postcards, and artifacts.

Historical Society of the Westburys

445 Jefferson Street • Westbury, NY 11590 • (516) 333-0176
www.villageofwestbury.org

Documents history of villages of Westbury and Old Westbury in the Town of North Hempstead, and the Village of Salisbury (South Westbury) in the Town of Hempstead. Holdings include documents and photographs, including school photographs from the early 1900s.

SELECTED PRINT & ONLINE RESOURCES

Below is a selection of resources relevant for research in this county. The list is representative, not exhaustive. Additional titles—particularly of abstracts, indexes, transcriptions, and local histories—are available; consult the introduction to Part Two for further information. For guidance on how to identify and locate community directories and local newspapers, see chapter 11, City Directories, and chapter 12, Newspapers, in Part One of this book.

See also the Queens Borough / Queens County guide and the Long Island Print and Online Resources fro additonal titles.

Abstracts, Indexes & Transcriptions

Barck, Dorothy C., ed. *Papers of the Lloyd Family of the Manor of Queens Village, Lloyd's Neck, Long Island, New York, 1654–1826*. 2 vols. Collections of The New-York Historical Society, vols. 59–60, 1926–1927

Bogart, Joseph H., and Walter K. Griffin, trans. "A Translation of the Baptismal Records and Marriage Entries of the Reformed Dutch Church of Oyster Bay, L.I. 1741–1835: The Wolver Hollow Church." Typescript, n.d. NYPL, New York. [*longislandgenealogy. com*] Baptisms 1741–1834 also in "Reformed Dutch Church of Wolver Hollow (Oyster Bay), Long Island." *NYG&B Record*, vol. 73 nos. 1–4, 1942.

Bowen, Constance G. "Soldiers of the American Revolution: Patriots and Founders of Our Country Interred in the Sands Family Burying Ground, Sands Point, Nassau County, Long Island, New York." Typescript, n.d. NYPL, New York.

Cocks, George W., trans. "Marriages on Long Island, New York, 1802–1855 [by Rev. Marmaduke Earle, Baptist Minister at Oyster Bay]." Copied by Josephine C. Frost. Typescript, 1914. NYPL, New York. A different version of the same marriages, by Charles T. Gritman, is at *longislandgenealogy.com*.

Combes, George D. A. "Births, Marriages, and Deaths, Hempstead, Long Island, N.Y., 1847, 1848, 1849." *NYG&B Record*, vol. 55 (1924) no. 3: 270–280, no. 4: 368–377; vol. 56 (1925) no. 1: 19–28. Records reported as required by 1847 state law, suspended in 1850. [*NYG&B eLibrary*]

Cox, John Jr., ed. *Oyster Bay Town Records [1653–1878]*. 8 vols. New York: The Town, 1916–1940.

Daughters of the American Revolution, comps. *New York DAR Genealogical Records Committee Report*. Since 1913 DAR volunteers have transcribed many thousands of unpublished cemetery, church, and town records throughout New York. The reports are at the DAR Library; copies are at the NYSL and the NYPL. The DAR has a searchable name index to all the GRC reports at *http://services.dar.org/Public/DAR_Research/search/?Tab_ID=6*. See Jean Worden's index below for a listing by county of the New York record sets that were transcribed by the DAR before 1998.

Fish, John Dean. "History and Vital Records of Christ's First Presbyterian Church of Hempstead, Long Island, New York." *NYG&B Record*, vol. 53 (1922) no. 3: 235–257, no. 4: 381–392; vol. 54 (1923) no. 1: 30–42, no. 2: 138–150. Baptisms 1805–1893, Deaths 1821–1890 (no earlier records exist). [*NYG&B eLibrary*]

———. "Inscriptions from Hempstead's Old Town Burying Ground [title varies]." *NYG&B Record*, vol. 54 (1923) no. 3: 201–209, no. 4: 335–345; vol. 55 (1924) no. 1: 72–77, no. 2: 154–161, no. 3: 243–250. [*NYG&B eLibrary*]

Frost, Josephine C., comp. "Baptisms from Reformed Dutch Church at Success [now Manhasset], Long Island, New York, 1742–1793." Typescript, 1913. NYPL, New York. [A more limited transcript by Dingman Versteeg at *Ancestry.com*]

Frost, Josephine C., and Henry Onderdonk Jr., comps. "Marriages Recorded at Reformed Dutch Church, Manhasset, Long Island." Typescript, 1913. NYPL, New York. Copied from the originals by Onderdonk, copied from Onderdonk manuscript by Frost. Includes marriages, 1785–1878 and 1826–1859, and a few deaths, 1841–1878.

———, comps. "Minutes of the Reformed Dutch Church at Success, Now Known as Manhassat [sic], Formerly Known as North Hempstead, Long Island, New York, 1731–1847." Typescript, 1913. NYPL, New York. Copied from the originals by Onderdonk, copied from Onderdonk manuscript by Frost.

Haight, Sylvanus J. *Adventures for God: A History of St. George's Episcopal Church, Hempstead, Long Island.* New York: J. S. Haight, 1932. History of St. George's Anglican/Episcopal Church, Hempstead, which also served Oyster Bay, with marriages 1725–1812, baptismal records 1725–1791.

Hammond, John E. *Birth, Marriage and Death Records 1847–1849.* Oyster Bay, NY: Town of Oyster Bay, 2008. Index of records reported—as required by a short-lived state law. [*oysterbaytown.com*]

———. *Civil War Records: Town of Oyster Bay.* Oyster Bay, NY: Town of Oyster Bay, 2011. [*oysterbaytown.com*]

———. *Historic Cemeteries of Oyster Bay-A Guide to Their Locations and Sources of Transcription Information.* Oyster Bay, NY: Town of Oyster Bay, 2007. Identifies 127 cemeteries (including Glen Cove), lists all known pre-1920 burials. [*oysterbaytown.com*]

———. *Index to Register of Deaths, Town of Oyster Bay (1881–1920).* Oyster Bay, NY: Town of Oyster Bay, 2007. Lists 9,421 deaths recorded 1881–1919. [*oysterbaytown.com*]

Hicks, Benjamin D., ed. "Records of St. George's Church, Hempstead, L.I." *NYG&B Record*, vol. 9 (1878) vol. 4: 182–187; vol. 10 (1879) no. 1: 16–19, no. 2: 89–92, no. 3: 133–139; vol. 11 (1880) no. 1: 47–51, no. 2: 88–93, no. 3: 133–136; vol. 12 (1881) no. 1: 45–46, no. 2: 78–83, no. 3: 141–145; vol. 13 (1882) no. 2: 93–95, no. 3: 116–118; vol. 15 (1884) no. 2: 77–80, no. 3: 111–113, no. 4: 176–177; vol. 24 (1893) no. 2: 79–80. Baptismal records 1725–1771, marriages 1725–1786. [NYG&B eLibrary]

———. *Records of the Towns of North and South Hempstead, Long Island, NY.* 8 vols. Jamaica, NY: Long Island Farmer Print, 1896–1904. Covers 1654–1880, but records after 1784 are for North Hempstead only. Original records microfilm NYSL. Hempstead Town Clerk has "Archival Holdings of the Town of Hempstead: Record of Bound Volumes" (1994).

Hinshaw, William W., and John Cox, Jr. *Encyclopedia of American Quaker Genealogy.* Ann Arbor, MI: Edwards Brothers, 1940. Vol. 3 (New York). Contains New York, Westbury and Jericho Monthly Meetings. Original records on microfilm FHL, NYPL. [*Ancestry.com, longislandgenealogy.com*]

Hood, Anthony, for the Nassau Genealogy Workshop. *Queens County Sentinel, Queens County, New York. Index of Birth, Marriage, and Death Announcements 1858–1878.* Bowie, MD: Heritage Books, 1991. The *Sentinel* was a Hempstead newspaper.

Macy, Harry, Jr. "Religious Records of Queens and Nassau Counties." *NYG&B Newsletter* (now *New York Researcher*), Spring 2003. Updated June 2011 and published as a Research Aid on *NewYorkFamilyHistory.org*. Identifies records not listed above under Abstracts, Indexes & Transcriptions.

Nassau County Church Surveys. Digitally published by New York Genealogical & Biographical Society, 2012. [NYG&B eLibrary]

Van Santvoord, Peter Luyster, and Herbert S. Hale. "A Complete Transcript of Monuments in Private and Abandoned Cemeteries in Oyster Bay Town, North, to which has been added A Transcript of All Eighteenth-Century Stones Now Remaining in Public Cemeteries Still in Use." Typescript, 1961. NYPL, New York.

Worden, Jean D. "Book 1, Subject Index." In *Revised Master Index to the New York State Daughters of the American Revolution Genealogical Records Volumes.* Zephyrhills, FL: J. D. Worden, 1998. The Subject Index includes a listing by county of the cemeteries, churches, towns, and other sources of records transcribed by the DAR.

Other Resources

Atlas of Nassau County, Long Island, N.Y. Complete in One Volume. Historical, Statistical. Based upon Maps on File at the County Seat in Mineola and upon Private Plans and Surveys Furnished by Surveyors and Individual Owners. New York: E. Belcher Hyde, 1914. [NYPL Digital Gallery]

Bailey, Paul. *Long Island: A History of Two Great Counties, Nassau and Suffolk.* New York: Lewis Historical Publishing, 1949.

Coles, Robert Reed, and Peter Luyster van Santvoord. *A History of Glen Cove 1668–1968.* Glen Cove, NY: Privately published, 1967.

Darlington, Oscar G. *Glimpses of Nassau County's History.* Mineola, NY: Nassau County Trust Co., 1949.

Hazelton, Henry Isham. *The Boroughs of Brooklyn and Queens, Counties of Nassau and Suffolk, Long Island, New York, 1609–1924.* 6 vols. New York: Lewis Historical Publishing, 1925.

History of Queens County, New York. New York, 1882.

Home Town Long Island: The History of Every Community on Long Island in Stories and Photographs. Melville, NY: Newsday, 1999.

Krieg, Joann P., and Natalie A. Naylor. *Nassau County: From Rural Hinterland to Suburban Metropolis.* Interlaken, NY: Empire State Books, 2000.

Merritt, Jesse. "The Historical Importance of Nassau County." *New York History*, vol. 21, no. 1 (January 1940): 15–30.

Nassau County Historical [Society] Journal [title varies]. 1937–present. Indexes 1937–1957 by Edward J. Smits (Spring 1958 issue, separate reprint 1989) and 1958–1988 by Jeanne M. Burke (1989).

Naylor, Natalie A. *The Roots and Heritage of Hempstead Town.* Interlaken, NY: Heart of the Lakes Publishing, 1994. Includes valuable bibliography of Long Island, Nassau County, and Hempstead sources. Among appendices are texts of Indian deeds and Kieft's patent, and Combes, George D. A., "The Fifty Original Proprietors of Hempstead," also published in *Nassau County Historical Journal*, vol. 18, no. 3, April 1957.

Smits, Edward J. *The Creation of Nassau County.* Mineola, NY: Nassau County Department of Public Works, 1960.

———. *Nassau: Suburbia, USA: The First Seventy-Five Years of Nassau County, New York, 1899 to 1974.* Syosset, NY: Friends of the Nassau County Museum, 1974.

Stoutenburgh, Henry A. *A Documentary History of Het (the) Nederduytsche Gemeente, Dutch Congregation of Oyster Bay, Queens County, Island of Nassau now Long Island.* Published in 10 parts. New York: Press of Eben Storer, 1902–1907.

Wanzor, Leonard, and Joshua Epstein. *Patriots of the North Shore: Great Neck, Cow Neck, Hempstead Harbor, Cedar Swamp, Wolver Hollow, Norwich, Oyster Bay, Jericho During the Revolutionary War.* N.p., [1976?].

Winsche, Richard A. *History of Nassau County Community Place-Names.* Interlaken, NY: Empire State Books and Hempstead, NY: Long Island Studies Institute, Hofstra University, 1999.

Additional Online Resources

Ancestry.com

There are vast numbers of records on *Ancestry.com* that pertain to people who have lived in New York State. See chapter 16 for a description of *Ancestry.com*'s resources and its partnership with the New York State Archives. A search of the online card catalog by county may reveal lesser known resources that pertain to a locality, such as town records, abstracts, transcription, city directories, and local histories.

Brooklyn Genealogy Information

http://bklyn-genealogy-info.stevemorse.org/LI/index.html

Contains information relating to New York City and Long Island, including links and tips for general genealogical research. Particular records relating to Nassau County include cemetery information, city directories (1868–1869 and 1909–1913), history of local post offices, wills (1691–1703), historic maps, military information, *Long Island Farmer*, *Long Island Press*, and *Newsday* extracts, and house of worship directories.

FamilySearch

FamilySearch has extensive collections of New York records, including religious records, which are searchable by name and location, but not by county. As of the publication date, neither land or probate records from the county formation in 1889 to present were available in the New York collections. See Queens for earlier records. A detailed description of *FamilySearch.org* resources, which include the catalog of the Family History Library, is found in chapter 16.

German Genealogy Group and Italian Genealogy Group

www.GermanGenealogyGroup.com or *www.ItalianGen.org*

The Nassau County Naturalization Project/Index. Searchable index of Nassau County Petitions for Naturalization and Declarations of Intention, 1899–1986; listing gives name, age, and birth year.

Also index to Nassau County marriages 1908–1935. See full listing in chapter 16, National and Statewide Repositories & Resources.

Suffolk Historic Newspapers

www.live-brary.com/historic-newspapers

This site has the *Long Islander* of Huntington 1839–1974 and *South Side Signal* of Babylon 1869–1920, which reported many Queens/Nassau County events.

Long Island Genealogy

See listing in Long Island Print and Online Resources

Nassau County Libraries Historic Newspaper Collections

longislandmemories.org

A program of the Long Island Library Regional Digitization Program, this database includes issues of *Bethpage Tribune*, *Farmingdale Observer*, *Daily Review of Nassau County*, *Freeport News*, *Garden City News*, *South Side Messenger*, *Queens County Review*, *Nassau County Review*, *Nassau Post*, and *The Leader*. Also accessible through *www.nyheritage.org/newspapers* which links to digital newspapers collections in 26 counties (currently).

NYGenWeb Project: Nassau County

www.rootsweb.ancestry.com/~nynassau

Part of the national, USGenWeb volunteer initiative, the website provides information and resources for county research.

Niagara County

Formed March 11, 1808

Parent County   Genesee
Daughter County   Erie County 1821
County Seat   City of Lockport

Major Land Transactions
See chapter 7, Land Records
Holland Land Company Purchase 1792–1796

Indian Territories
See chapter 14, Peoples of New York, American Indian
Tonawanda Band of Seneca Indians: Tonawanda Reservation (1797–present)
Tuscarora Nation Reservation (1797–present)

Town Boundary Map
 - County seat

Towns (and Cities)	Villages and other Settlements		Notes
Amherst * In Niagara County 1818–1821			* See Erie County
Aurora * In Niagara County 1808–1821			* See Erie County
Boston * In Niagara County 1817–1821			* See Erie County
Buffalo * In Niagara County 1810–1821			* See Erie County
Cambria c. 1800 Settled 1808 Formed from Town of Willink (now Aurora, Erie County) 1812 Daughter towns Hartland, Niagara, and Porter formed 1818 Daughter town Lewiston formed 1824 Daughter town Lockport formed	Cambria Cambria Center Cambria Station Comstock Corners Hickory Corners Molyneux Corners	Mount Cambria North Ridge Pekin Sanborn Streeters Corners Warrens Corners	• Hickory Corners on Lockport town line • Pekin, also Mountain Ridge and Perkin, on Lewiston town line • Sanborn on Lewiston town line • Warrens Corners on Lockport town line
Clarence * In Niagara County 1808–1821			* See Erie County
Concord * In Niagara County 1812–1821			* See Erie County
Eden * In Niagara County 1812–1821			* See Erie County
Hamburg(h) * In Niagara County 1812–1821			* See Erie County
Hartland 1803 Settled 1812 Formed from Town of Cambria 1817 Daughter town Royalton formed 1823 Daughter town Somerset formed 1824 Daughter town Newfane formed	Hartland Hartland Corners Jeddo Johnson(s) Creek	Middleport (v) North Hartland North Ridgeway	• Jeddo also Morehouses • Village of Middleport inc. 1859; shared with Town of Royalton
Holland * In Niagara County 1818–1821			* See Erie County
Lewiston Occupied by French intermittently until the British takeover in 1763; first permanent settlement c. 1800 1818 Formed from Town of Cambria	Colonial Village Devils Hole Dickersonville Escarpment Falcon Manor Johnsons Creek Lewiston (v) Lewiston Heights Lewiston Heights Station	Model City Model City Station Modeltown Niagara Junction Pekin Rumsey Ridge Sanborn South Pekin Stella Niagara	• Dickersonville also Hardscrable • Village of Lewiston inc. 1822 • Model City also Middletown and Modeltown • Pekin, also Mountain Ridge and Perkin, on Cambria town line • Sanborn on Cambria town line
Lockport (city) * 1865 Incorporated as a city from the Village of Lockport in Town of Lockport			* County seat at Lockport (village then city) from 1821; 1808–1821 county seat at Buffalo (now Erie County)

Towns (and Cities)	Villages and other Settlements		Notes
Lockport (town) 1805 Settled near Lockport village 1824 Formed from towns of Cambria and Royalton 1865 Village of Lockport became City of Lockport	Carlisle Gardens Hickory Corners Highland Park Lockport (v) Lockport Junction Lockport Junction Rapids Millardville Nottingham Estates Rapids	Raymond Raymond Hill Ridgelea Heights Shooktown South Lockport Warrens Corners West Lockport Wright Wright(s) Corners	• Hickory Corners on Cambria town line • Village of Lockport inc. 1829; became City of Lockport 1865; county seat from 1821 • Ridgelea Heights also Ridgelea • Warrens Corners on Cambria town line • Wright(s) Corners on Newfane town line
Newfane 1807 Settlers from Canada 1824 Formed from towns of Hartland, Somerset, and Wilson	Appleton Burt Coomer Corwin(s) Hess Road Newfane	Olcott Ridge Road Ridgewood Woodland Heights Wright(s) Corners	• Burt also Newfane Station • Newfane also Charlotte, Charlottesville, and New Fane • Olcott formerly Kempville • Woodland Heights on Wilson town line • Wright(s) Corners on Lockport town line
Newstead * In Niagara County 1808–1821			* See Erie County
Niagara 1678 Temporarily settled at La Salle 1759 Permanently settled at Schlosser 1812 Formed as Schlosser from Town of Cambria 1816 Name changed to Niagara 1827 Daughter town Pendleton formed 1836 Daughter town Wheatfield formed 1892 Daughter city Niagara Falls formed	La Salle Niagara Niagara City (v) Niagara Falls (v) Pendleton		• La Salle now in City of Niagara Falls • Village of Niagara City inc. 1854; also Suspension Bridge • Village of Niagara Falls inc. 1848; formerly Manchester and Schlosser • Villages of Niagara Falls and Niagara City form City of Niagara Falls in 1892 • Pendleton in Town of Pendleton after 1827
Niagara Falls (city) 1892 Incorporated as a city from Village of Niagara Falls and Village of Niagara City in Town of Niagara	Black Creek Village La Salle Love Canal Pletchers Corners		• La Salle formerly in Town of Niagara
North Tonawanda (city) 1897 Incorporated as a city from the Village of North Tonawanda in the Town of Wheatfield	Park Village Wurlitzer Park Village		
Pendleton 1805 Settled 1827 Formed from Town of Niagara	Beach Ridge Halls Station Hodgeville Hodgeville Station Hoffman Maple Street Mapleton	Mapleton Station Pendleton Pendleton Center Pendleton Center Station Picard Bridge Wendelville	• Hoffman also Hoffman Station, on Wheatfield town line • Pendleton in Town of Niagara before 1827
Porter French military and trading presence from late 1600s; permanently settled by early 1800s 1812 Formed from Town of Cambria 1818 Daughter town Wilson formed	Blairville Collingwood Estates East Porter Fillmore Chapel Fort Niagara Fort Niagara Beach Harrison Grove National Monument	Porter Porter Center Ransomville Towers Corners Tryonville Uneeda Beach Youngstown (v) Youngstown Estates	• Fort Niagara also Old Fort Niagara • Fort Niagara Beach also Rumsey Park • Village of Youngstown inc. 1854

Towns (and Cities)	Villages and other Settlements		Notes
Royalton 1803 Settled 1817 Formed from Town of Hartland 1824 Daughter town Lockport formed	Dysin(g)er Gasport Gilberts Corner(s) Leslie Locust Tree Mabee Marble Station McNalls	Middleport (v) Orangeport Reynales Basin Royalton Royalton Center South Royalton Terrys Corners Wolcott(s)ville	• McNalls formerly McNalls Corners • Village of Middleport inc. 1859; shared with Town of Hartland
Schlosser Name for Town of Niagara 1812–1816			
Somerset 1810 Settled 1823 Formed from Town of Hartland 1824 Daughter town Newfane formed	Barker (v) County Line Lake Road Millers	Somerset South Somerset Thirtymile Point West Somerset	• Village of Barker inc. 1908; also Barkers and Somerset Station • Somerset also Somerset Corners
Wales * In Niagara County 1818–1821			* See Erie County
Wheatfield 1802 Settled 1836 Formed from Town of Niagara	Berghol(t)z Hoffman Martinsville Nashville North Tonawanda (v)	Sawyer S(h)awnee St. Johnsburg(h) Walmore	• Berghol(t)z also New Berghol(t)z • Hoffman on Pendleton town line • North Tonawanda was part of the Village of Tonawanda, Erie County 1853–1857; Village of North Tonawanda inc. 1865; became City of North Tonawanda 1897
Wilson 1810 Settled 1818 Formed from Town of Porter 1824 Daughter town Newfane formed	Coolidge Beach Dorwood Park East Wilson Elberta Hopkins Beach Maple Street North Wilson Pleasant Corners	Randall Randall Road Roosevelt Beach South Wilson Sunset Beach Wilson (v) Woodland Heights	• Village of Wilson inc. 1858 • Woodland Heights on Newfane town line

Note about Niagara County

Niagara County was created in 1808; the county seat was at Buffalo until 1821, when Buffalo became part of Erie County. In 1821 the county seat moved to Lockport.

NEW YORK STATE CENSUS RECORDS

County originals at Niagara County Historian's Office: 1855, 1865*, 1875, 1892, 1905, 1915, 1925 (1825, 1835, and 1845 are lost)

State originals at the NYSA: 1915, 1925

Microfilm at the FHL, NYPL, and NYSL; many years are online at *FamilySearch.org* and *Ancestry.com*.

* For 1865 census index, see Niagara County Historian listing in Abstracts, Indexes & Transcriptions below.

NATIONAL/STATEWIDE REPOSITORIES & RESOURCES
See chapter 16

COUNTYWIDE REPOSITORIES & RESOURCES

Niagara County Clerk
Niagara County Court House, First Floor • PO Box 461
Lockport, NY 14095-0461 • (716) 439-7025
Email: niagaracounty.clerk@niagaracounty.com
www.niagaracounty.com/Departments/CountyClerk.aspx

Holdings include court and land records, 1821–present. Naturalization and land records 1808–1821 are held in Erie County.

Niagara County – City, Town, and Village Clerks
Birth, marriage, and death records are maintained by the clerk of the municipality in which the event occurred; see Introduction to County Guides for details of other records which may also be held by municipal clerks. See municipal websites for details and contact information.

Niagara County Surrogate's Court
175 Hawley Street • Lockport, NY 14094 • (716) 439-7130

Holds probate records 1821 to the present. Earlier records (1808–1821) are held in Erie County. Also see chapter 6, Probate Records.

Niagara County Public Libraries
Niagara is part of the Nioga Library System; see *www.niogalibrary.org* to access each library. Many hold genealogy and local history collections including books and newspapers. See listings below for the Lewiston, Lockport, Niagara Falls, and North Tonawanda Public Libraries.

Niagara County Historical Society
215 Niagara Street • Lockport, NY 14094 • (716) 434-7433
Email: history@niagaracounty.org • *www.niagarahistory.org*

Holdings include ephemera, memorabilia, and research materials documenting the history of Niagara County, the Erie Canal, and the Civil War. *Niagara County Genealogical Society Newsletter* published quarterly.

Niagara County Historian
Civil Defense Building • 139 Niagara Street • Lockport, NY 14094
(716) 439-7324 • Email: historian@niagaracounty.com
www.niagaracounty.com/Departments/Historian.aspx

Obituaries 1840s–present, marriage records 1908–1928, index of wills (prior to 1880), naturalization records (1833–1954); microfilm

and indexes at historian's office, physical records are in storage and are accessible through the historian; city directories 1856–present, veterans' files (French and Indian War to the present), church records, family scrapbooks, and the New York state censuses for Niagara County 1855–1925.

Niagara County – All Municipal Historians
While not authorized to answer genealogical inquiries, city, town, and village historians can provide valuable historical information and research advice; some maintain collections and webpages which may include transcribed records, local histories, and other genealogical material, for example, the Town of Porter historian at *www.townofporter.net/about/historian.shtml*. See contact information at the Government Appointed Historians of Western New York at *www.gahwny.org/p/niagara.html* or at the website of the Association of Public Historians of New York State at *www.aphnys.org*.

Niagara County Genealogical Society
215 Niagara Street, Second Floor • Lockport, NY 14094
(716) 433-1033 • Email: genealogy@niagaracounty.org
www.niagaragenealogy.org

Cemetery records, census records, and genealogies. Some material on other New York counties, Pennsylvania, New England, and Ontario, Canada. Publishes a newsletter quarterly.

REGIONAL REPOSITORIES & RESOURCES

Buffalo History Museum: Research Library
See listing in Erie County Guide

Old Fort Niagara Association Visitor Center
Fort Niagara State Park • One Quartermaster Court
Youngstown, NY 14174 • (716) 745-7611 • *www.oldfortniagara.org*

Cemetery records and military records (troop returns, service records, regimental rosters) from the 1750s to the 1900s.

SUNY Fredonia: Daniel A. Reed Library:
Archives & Special Collections
See listing in Chautauqua County Guide

University of Rochester: Rare Books, Special Collections, and Preservation: Manuscript and Special Collections: Rochester, Western New York, and New York State
See listing in Monroe County Guide

Western New York Genealogical Society
See listing in Erie County Guide

Western New York Heritage Press
See listing in Erie County Guide

LOCAL REPOSITORIES & RESOURCES
Alphabetized by location

Historical Association and Society of Lewiston and the Lewiston Museum
469 Plain Street • PO Box 43 • Lewiston, NY 14092
(716) 754-4214 • *www.historiclewiston.org*

Museum is located in the former St. Paul's Episcopal Church (built 1835). Website includes history of Lewiston, local history bibliography, and photographs. The Association has access to cemetery records, property tax records, town census record transcriptions (1860, 1865, 1885), and very limited marriage and death records.

Lewiston Public Library: Genealogy/History Room

305 South 8th Street • Lewiston, NY 14092
716) 754-4720 • www.lewistonpubliclibrary.org

Books, periodicals, newspapers, cemetery records, church records, court records, marriage records (including Niagara County marriages 1838–1841 and Suspension Bridge marriages 1886–1893), military records, published genealogies, vertical files, tax records, Town of Pendleton early vital records, school records, newspapers, obituaries, scrapbooks, personal papers, American Indian history, a family database of all Lewiston censuses until 1940. The library accepts research requests and has a monthly newsletter, *Historic Lewiston*.

Lockport Public Library: Local History Room

23 East Avenue • Lockport, NY 14094
(716) 433-5935 • www.lockportlibrary.org

Newspapers, Lockport High School yearbooks 1897–present, DeSales Catholic High School yearbooks 1950–1989, federal census microfilm 1820–1930, except 1890, and New York state census microfilm and print indexes for Niagara County 1855, 1865, 1875.

Niagara Falls Public Library: Local History Department

Earl W. Brydges Building • 1425 Main Street, Third Floor
Niagara Falls, NY 14305 • (716) 286-4899
www.niagarafallspubliclib.org/Pages/History.html

Newspapers and newspaper indexes 1854–present, DeVeaux School archives, photographs, and vital record index 1854–1930, 1980–2000.

North Tonawanda History Museum

54 Webster Street • North Tonawanda, NY 14120 • (716) 213-0554
Email: nthistorymuseum@aol.com • www.nthistorymuseum.org

Holdings include local, business, military, and family histories.

North Tonawanda Public Library: Local History Department

505 Meadow Drive • North Tonawanda, NY 14120 • (716) 693-4132
Email: ntwref@nioga.org • www.ntlibrary.org/wordpress/history

Books, census, maps, photographs, newspapers 1880–present, city directories 1892–present, cemetery directories, and memoirs.

Town of Porter Historical Society Museum

240 Lockport Street • PO Box 168 • Youngstown, NY 14174
(716) 745-1271 • www.townofporter.net

Newspaper clippings, obituaries, local census records (1830–present), town birth records (1888-1901), church records, genealogies, and veterans' records.

SELECTED PRINT & ONLINE RESOURCES

Below is a selection of resources relevant for research in this county. The list is representative, not exhaustive. Additional titles—particularly of abstracts, indexes, transcriptions, and local histories—are available; consult the introduction to Part Two for further information. For guidance on how to identify and locate community directories and local newspapers, see chapter 11, City Directories, and chapter 12, Newspapers, in Part One of this book.

Abstracts, Indexes & Transcriptions

County of Niagara Abstracts. Syracuse: Central New York Genealogical Society, 2000. Abstracts for a range of genealogical records originally published in the quarterly *Tree Talks*.

Daughters of the American Revolution, comps. *New York DAR Genealogical Records Committee Report*. Since 1913 DAR volunteers have transcribed many thousands of unpublished cemetery, church, and town records throughout New York. The reports are at the DAR Library; copies are at the NYSL and the NYPL. The DAR has a searchable name index to all the GRC reports at *http://services.dar.org/Public/DAR_Research/search/?Tab_ID=6*. See Jean Worden's index below for a listing by county of the New York record sets that were transcribed by the DAR before 1998.

Kelly, Arthur C. M. *Index to Tree Talks County Packet: Niagara County*. Rhinebeck, NY: Kinship, 2002.

Niagara County Historian. "Index: 1865 N. Y. State Census Niagara County." Manuscript, n.d. Western New York Genealogical Society Library, Buffalo.

Pettit, Ira S., and Jean P. Ray. *The Diary of a Dead Man: Letters and Diary of Private Ira S. Pettit, Wilson, Niagara County, New York . . . .* New York: Eastern Acorn Press, 1981.

Walck, Adam, Dorothy M. Rolling, and Donna M Barnes. *Niagara County Cemetery Directory*. New York: Niagara County Historian's Office, 1994.

Worden, Jean D. "Book 1, Subject Index." In *Revised Master Index to the New York State Daughters of the American Revolution Genealogical Records Volumes*. Zephyrhills, FL: J. D. Worden, 1998. The Subject Index includes a listing by county of the cemeteries, churches, towns, and other sources of records transcribed by the DAR.

Other Resources

Aiken, John, et al. *Outpost of Empires: A Short History of Niagara County*. Phoenix, NY: F. E. Richards, 1961.

Beers, D. G. *Atlas of Niagara and Orleans Counties, New York: From Actual Surveys and Official Records*. Philadelphia, 1875.

Boyd's Lockport City Directory: With a Business Directory of Niagara County and an Appendix. Lockport, NY, 1866.

Fierch, Frederick G. *Royalton, Middleport, and Hartland*. Charleston, SC: Arcadia Publishing, 2010.

Foley, Janet W. *Early Settlers of New York State: Their Ancestors and Descendants*. 9 vols. Akron, NY: 1934–1942. Reprint, 2 vols. Baltimore, Genealogical Publishing Co., 1993.

History of Niagara County, N.Y., with Illustrations Descriptive of Its Scenery, Private Residences, Public Buildings, Fine Blocks, and Important Manufactories, and Portraits of Old Pioneers and Prominent Residents. New York, 1878.

Kirwin, William H. *Kirwin's Directory of the City of Lockport and County of Niagara for the Year. . . .* Lockport, NY: W. H. Kirwin. Multiple years.

Kostoff, Robert D. *A History of Niagara County, New York*. Lewiston, NY: Edwin Mellen Press, 2001.

Lewis, Clarence O. *History of Lockport, New York*. Lockport, NY: Niagara County Court House, 1960. Revised 1964.

New York Historical Resources Center. *Guide to Historical Resources in Niagara County, New York, Repositories*. Ithaca, NY: Cornell University, 1982. [*books.FamilySearch.org*]

Percy, John W. *Tonawanda, the Way It Was: A History of the Town of Tonawanda from 1805–1903*. Kenmore, NY: Partners' Press, 1979.

Pool, William, ed. *Landmarks of Niagara County, New York*. Syracuse, 1897.

Records of the Ithaca College Study Center for Early Religious Life in Western New York, 1978–1981. Division of Rare and Manuscript Collections, Cornell University Library. A description of the holdings for each county is at *http://rmc.library.cornell.edu/eguides/lists/churchlist1.htm.*

Reed, Irving R. *100 Years Ago Today: Niagara County in the Civil War.* Lockport, NY: Niagara County Historical Society, 1966.

Souvenir History of Niagara County: Commemorative of the 25th Anniversary of the Pioneer Association of Niagara County. Lockport, NY: Lockport Journal, 1902.

Turner, Orsamus. *Pioneer History of the Holland Purchase of Western New York: Embracing Some Account of the Ancient Remains . . . .* Buffalo, 1849.

Wiley, Samuel T., and Winfield Scott Garner. *Biographical and Portrait Cyclopedia of Niagara County, New York.* Philadelphia, 1892.

Williams, Edward T. *Niagara County, New York: One of the Most Wonderful Regions in the World: A Concise Record of Her Progress and People, 1821–1921, Published During Its Centennial Year.* Chicago: J. H. Beers, 1921.

Additional Online Resources
Ancestry.com

There are vast numbers of records on *Ancestry.com* that pertain to people who have lived in New York State. See chapter 16 for a description of *Ancestry.com*'s resources and its partnership with the New York State Archives. A search of the online card catalog by county may reveal lesser known resources that pertain to a locality, such as town records, abstracts, transcriptions, city directories, and local histories.

FamilySearch

FamilySearch has extensive collections of New York records, including religious records, which are searchable by name and location, but not by county. The following collections include record images (browsable, but not searchable) that are organized by county:

- "New York, Land Records, 1630–1975." Includes land and property records. *familysearch.org/search/collection/2078654*

- "New York, Probate Records, 1629–1971." Includes wills, letters of administration, and guardianship papers. *familysearch.org/search/collection/1920234*

For both collections, choose the browse option and then select Niagara to view the available records sets.

A detailed description of FamilySearch.org resources, which include the catalog of the Family History Library, is found in chapter 16.

New York Heritage Digital Collections: New York State Newspaper Project
www.nyheritage.org/newspapers

The website provides links to digital newspapers collections in 26 counties (currently) made accessible through New York Heritage, New York State Historic Newspapers, HRVH Historical Newspapers, and other providers.

NYGenWeb Project: Niagara County
www.rootsweb.ancestry.com/~nyniagar

Part of the national, USGenWeb volunteer initiative, the website provides information and resources for county research.

Old Fulton New York Postcards
www.FultonHistory.com

The website provides free access to a vast collection of digitized New York newspapers, including six titles for Niagara County.

Oneida County

Formed March 15, 1798

Parent County   Herkimer
Daughter Counties   Jefferson 1805 • Lewis 1805 • Oswego 1816
County Seat   City of Utica

Major Land Transactions
See table in chapter 7, Land Records
Holland Patent 1769
Chenango Twenty Townships 1789–1794

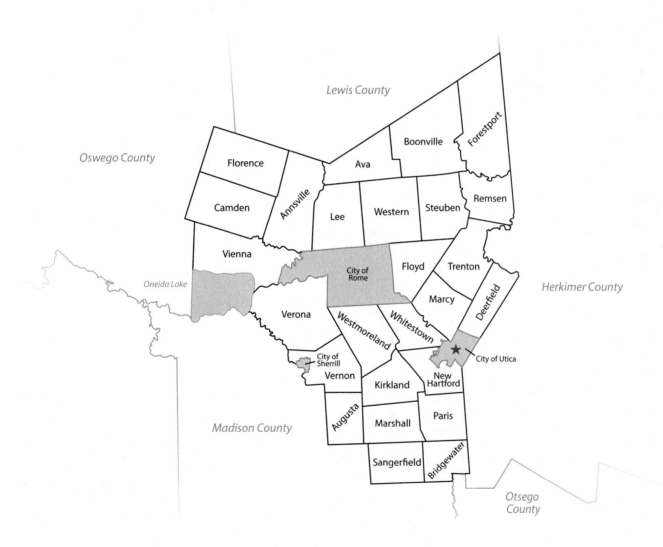

Town Boundary Map
★ - County seat

Towns (and Cities)	Villages and other Settlements		Notes
Adams * In Oneida County 1802–1805			* See Jefferson County
Annsville 1793 Settlers from New Jersey 1823 Formed from towns of Camden, Florence, Lee, and Vienna 1867 Ceded land to Town of Vienna	Annsville Blennes Corner Blossvale Connellsville Station Glenmore	McConnellsville McConnellsville Corners Pine Hill Taberg Taberg Station	• McConnellsville on Vienna town line
Augusta 1793 Settled 1798 Formed from Town of Whitestown 1802 Daughter town Vernon formed 1836 Daughter town Stockbridge formed in Madison County	Augusta Five Corners Knoxboro Lloyds Corners Newell Corners Oriskany Falls (v) Wells Corner		• Knoxboro formerly Knox Corners, also Cooks Corners • Village of Oriskany Falls inc. 1890
Ava 1798 Settled 1846 Formed from Town of Boonville	Ava Flint Town Redmond Corner		• Hamlet of Ava also Ava Corners
Bengal Name for Town of Vienna 1808–1816			
Boonville 1795 Settled 1805 Formed from Town of Leyden, Lewis County 1846 Daughter town Ava formed	Alder Creek Alder Creek Station Barnes Boonville (v)	Bucks Corners Forestport Hawkinsville Hurlbutville	• Village of Boonville inc. 1855 • Forestport (also Forest Port) on Forestport town line after 1869; on Remsen town line before 1869 • Hurlbutville also Hurbutville
Bridgewater 1788 Settled at Farwells Hill 1797 Formed in Herkimer County from Town of Sangerfield 1798 Transferred to new county of Oneida	Babcock Hill Bridgewater (v) Bridgewater Center Hobin Corners Mapledale North Bridgewater		• Village of Bridgewater inc. 1825
Brownville * In Oneida County 1802–1805			* See Jefferson County
Camden Settled late 1700s 1799 Formed from Town of Mexico 1805 Daughter town Florence formed 1807 Daughter town Vienna formed 1823 Daughter town Annsville formed	Brockway Corners Camden (v) Hillsboro Preston Hill West Camden Westdale		• Village of Camden inc. 1834 • Hillsboro also Hillsborough
Champion * In Oneida County 1800–1805			* See Jefferson County
Constantia * In Oneida County 1808–1816			* See Oswego County
Deerfield 1773 Settled 1798 Formed from Town of Schuyler, Herkimer County 1832 Daughter town Marcy formed	Deerfield Deerfield Heights Dewey Corners North Gage Walker Corners		• Deerfield also Deerfield Corners

(Deerfield continued on next page)

Towns (and Cities)	Villages and other Settlements		Notes
Deerfield (continued) 1891 Land ceded to City of Utica 1916 Southern end of town annexed to City of Utica			
Ellisburg(h) * In Oneida County 1803–1805			* See Jefferson County
Florence 1801 Settled 1805 Formed from Town of Camden 1823 Daughter town Annsville formed	East Florence Empeyville Florence Florence Hill	Forty-six Corners Hanifin Corners Malone Corners Thompson Corners	
Floyd 1790 Settled 1796 Formed in Herkimer County from Town of Steuben 1798 Transferred to new county of Oneida	Camroden East Floyd Floyd Steuben Valley The Punch Bowl		• Floyd also Floyd Corners • Steuben Valley on Steuben town line
Forestport 1869 Formed from Town of Remsen	Anos Siding Bellingertown Big Brook Enos Forestport (v) Forestport Station Holiday House Meekerville	Nichols Mills Nicholsville Otterlake White Lake White Lake Corners White Lake Station Woodgate Woodhull	• Village of Forestport (also Forest Port) inc. 1899; dissolved 6/18/1938, now the hamlet of Forestport; on Booneville town line; in Town of Remsen before 1869
Harrisburg(h) * In Oneida County 1803–1805			* See Lewis County
Harrison * In Oneida County 1804–1805			* See Town of Rodman in Jefferson County
Kirkland 1787 Settled by eight families 1827 Formed from Town of Paris 1829 Daughter town Marshall formed 1834 Ceded land to Town of New Hartford 1839 Annexed land from Town of Paris	Chuckery Corners Clark Mills Clinton (v) College Hill Farmers Mills Franklin Franklin Springs Kirkland		• Clark Mills on Westmoreland and Whitestown town lines • Village of Clinton inc. 1843 • Franklin Springs formerly Franklin Iron Works • Kirkland also Manchester
Lee 1790 Settled at Delta 1811 Formed from Town of Western 1823 Daughter town Annsville formed	Brookfield Delta Elmer Hill Hawkins Corner Lake Delta Lee	Lee Center Point Rock Stokes Corner West Branch West Lee	• Stokes Corner formerly Stokes, also Lee Corners and Nisbets Corners • West Branch in Town of Western before 1811
Leyden * In Oneida County 1798–1805			* See Lewis County
Lowville * In Oneida County 1800–1805			* See Lewis County
Malta * In Oneida County 1804–1805			* Town of Malta now Town of Lorraine in Jefferson County

Towns (and Cities)	Villages and other Settlements		Notes
Marcy 1793 Settled 1832 Formed from Town of Deerfield	Careys Corners Marcy	Maynard Stitt(s)ville	• Stitt(s)ville on Trenton town line
Marshall 1793 Settled 1829 Formed from Town of Kirkland	Brothertown Daytonville Deansboro Forge Hollow Hanover Hubbard Corners Lewis Corners	Marshall Marshall Station McConnell(s) Corners Moore Corners Peck(s) Corners Small Corners Waterville (v)	• Deansboro formerly Deansville • Village of Waterville inc. 1871; also The Huddle, formerly Skanawis; village shared with Town of Sangerfield
Martinsburg * In Oneida County 1800–1805			* See Lewis County
Mexico * In Oneida County 1798–1816			* See Oswego County
New Hartford 1788 Settled 1827 Formed from Town of Whitestown 1834 Annexed land from Town of Kirkland	Capron Chadwicks Middle Settlement New Hartford (v) New Hartford Station	New York Mills (v) New York Upper Mills Washington Mills Willowvale	• Village of New Hartford inc. 1870; also Chegaquatka • Village of New York Mills inc. 1922; shared with Town of Whitestown
New Haven * In Oneida County 1813–1816			* See Oswego County
Orange Name for Town of Vienna 1807–1808			
Paris 1789 Settled at Paris Hill 1792 Formed in Herkimer County from Town of Whitestown 1795 Daughter towns Brookfield, Cazenovia, Hamilton, Sangerfield, and Sherburne formed * 1798 Transferred to new county of Oneida 1827 Daughter town Kirkland formed 1839 Ceded land to Town of Kirkland	Cassville Chadwicks Mill Clayville (v) Dakins Corners East Sauquoit Greens Crossing Holman City Ludlow Corners	Paris Paris Furnace Paris Hill Paris Station Richfield Junction Sauquoit West Sauquoit	* Towns of Brookfield, Cazanovia, and Hamilton now in Madison County; Town of Sherburne now in Chenango County • Village of Clayville inc. 1887 • Paris also Ganundoglee and Paris Hill
Redfield * In Oneida County 1800–1816			* See Oswego County
Remsen 1792 Settled 1798 Formed from Town of Norway, Herkimer County 1809 Annexed land form Town of Steuben 1869 Daughter town Forestport formed	Bardwell Mill Forest Port Hinckley Honnedaga Honnedaga Station Ninety Six Corners Port Woodhull Remsen (v)		• Forest Port became Town of Forestport in 1869; on Booneville town line • Hinckley on Trenton town line • Village of Remsen inc. 1845; shared with Town of Trenton
Richland * In Oneida County 1807–1816			* See Oswego County

Towns (and Cities)	Villages and other Settlements		Notes
Rome (city) * 1870 Town of Rome incorporated as a city	Coonrod Fish Creek Landing Fort Bull Greene Corners Station Greens Corners Greenway Humaston Humaston Plains	Humaston Station Lorena North Rome Ridge Mills Rome Stanwix West Rome Wright Settlement	* Rome shared county seat with Utica until 1960 • Fish Creek Landing on Vienna town line
Rome (town) 1796–1870 **Pre-1755** Settled at the Carrying Place * 1796 Formed in Herkimer County from Town of Steuben 1798 Transferred to new county of Oneida 1870 Town incorporated as a city	Greens Corners North Rome Ridge Mills Rome (v) West Rome		* Carrying Place was between the Mohawk River and Wood Creek • Village of Rome inc. 1819; became part of City of Rome 1870; shared county seat with Village of Whitesborough, Town of Whitestown, 1798–1851 then with City of Utica 1851–1960; built on site of Fort Stanwix later Fort Schuyler
Rutland * In Oneida County 1802–1805			* See Jefferson County
Sangerfield 1791 Settlers from Massachusetts 1795 Formed in Herkimer County from Town of Paris 1797 Daughter town Bridgewater formed 1798 Transferred to new county of Chenango 1804 Transferred to Oneida County	Conger Corners Five Corners Pleasant Valley Sangerfield Stockwell Waterville (v)		• Sangerfield also Sangerfield Center and Skawanis • Stockwell also Stockwells Settlement • Village of Waterville inc. 1871; also The Huddle, formerly Skanawis; village shared with Town of Marshall
Scriba * In Oneida County 1811–1816			* See Oswego County
Sherrill (city) * 1916 Incorporated as a city from Town of Vernon			* City of Sherrill has the legal identity of a village under the jurisdiction of the Town of Vernon; the City Clerk maintains vital and marriage records
Steuben 1789 Settled 1792 Formed in Herkimer County from Town of Whitestown 1796 Daughter towns Floyd and Rome formed * 1797 Daughter towns Leyden and Western formed 1798 Transferred to new county of Oneida 1809 Ceded land to Town of Remsen	East Steuben Fink Hollow French Road Merrick Corner North Steuben Sixty Corners Steuben Steuben Station Steuben Valley		* Town of Rome now City of Rome • Steuben also Steuben Corners • Steuben Valley on Floyd town line
Trenton 1793 Settled by Dutch 1797 Formed in Herkimer County from Town of Schuyler 1798 Transferred to new county of Oneida	Barneveld (v) Barneveld Station Gang Mills Hinckley Holland Patent (v) Mapledale		• Village of Barneveld inc. 1819 as Oldenbarnevelt(t); name changed to Trenton 1833; reincorporated 1970; name changed to Barneveld 1975 • Hinckley on Remsen town line • Village of Holland Patent inc. 1885

(Trenton continued on next page)

Towns (and Cities)	Villages and other Settlements		Notes
Trenton (continued)	Prospect (v) Prospect Junction Prospect Station Remsen (v)	South Trenton Stitt(s)ville Trenton Falls Trenton Falls Station	• Village of Prospect inc. 1890 • Village of Remsen inc. 1845; shared with Town of Remsen • Stitt(s)ville on Marcy town line
Turin * In Oneida County 1800–1805			* See Lewis County
Utica (city) * 1832 Incorporated as a city from Town of Utica 1891 Land annexed from Town of Deerfield 1916 Annexed southern end of Town of Deerfield	Crooked Brook East Utica Station North Utica		* Utica shared county seat with Rome from 1851 to 1960 when Utica became sole county seat; 1798–1851 county seat shared between Rome and Whitestown • North Utica in Town of Deerfield before 1916
Utica (town) 1817–1832 Formerly part of Cosbys Manor; settled shortly after Revolution 1798 Incorporated as a village in Town of Whitestown 1817 Formed as town from Town of Whitestown 1832 Town incorporated as a city			
Vernon 1794–97 Settled 1802 Formed from towns of Westmoreland and Augusta 1836 Daughter town Stockbridge formed in Madison County 1916 Daughter City of Sherrill formed	Brewers Corner Oneida Castle (v) Sconondoa Turkey Street Vernon (v) Vernon Center		• Village of Oneida Castle inc. 1841 • Sconondoa also Skenandoa; on Verona town line • Village of Vernon inc. 1827
Verona 1792 Settled 1802 Formed from Town of Westmoreland	Agnes Corners Blackmans Corners Cagwin Corners Churchville Dams Corner Dumbarton Durhamville East Verona Fish Creek Fish Creek Station Goodrich Corners Grove Springs Higginsville	New London Oneida Depot Paradise Hill Sconondoa Stacy Basin Starks Landing State Bridge Verona Verona Beach Verona Depot Verona Mills Verona Springs Verona Station	• Dumbarton also Dunbarton • Sconondoa also Skenandoa; on Vernon town line • Stacy Basin also Staceys Basin • Hamlet of Verona also Teonatale, formerly Hands Village
Vienna 1798 Settled 1807 Formed as Town of Orange from Town of Camden 1808 Name changed to Bengal 1816 Name changed to Vienna 1823 Daughter town Annsville formed 1867 Annexed land from Town of Annsville	Brockway Corners Dibbletown Edgewater Beach Elpis Fish Creek Landing Hall Corners Jewell Long Crossing	Loomis Corners Maple Flats McConnellsville North Bay Pine Sylvan Beach (v) Thompson Corners Vienna	• Fish Creek Landing also in City of Rome • Jewell formerly West Vienna • McConnellsville on Annsville town line • Village of Sylvan Beach inc. 1971 • Hamlet of Vienna also Parkers Corners and South Corners

Towns (and Cities)	Villages and other Settlements		Notes
Volney * In Oneida County 1806–1816			* See Oswego County
Watertown * In Oneida County 1800–1805			* See Jefferson County
Western 1789 Settled 1797 Formed in Herkimer County from Town of Steuben 1798 Transferred to new county of Oneida 1811 Daughter town Lee formed	Beartown Big Brook Carmichael Hill Delta Dunn Brook Frenchville	Hillside Lake Delta North Western West Branch Westernville	• Beartown also Baretown • West Branch in Town of Lee after 1811
Westmoreland c. 1786 Settled 1792 Formed in Herkimer County from Town of Whitestown 1798 Transferred to new county of Oneida 1802 Daughter towns Verona and Vernon formed	Bartlett Clark Mills Dix Eureka Goodrich Corners Greenway Corners	Hecla Lairdsville Lowell South Church Spencer Settlement Westmoreland	• Clark Mills on Kirkland and Whitestown town lines • Dix formerly Republican • Hecla formerly Hecla Works • Westmoreland also Hampton
Whitestown 1784 Settled 1788 Formed as a town in Montgomery County 1791 Transferred to new county of Herkimer 1792 Daughter towns Mexico, Paris, Steuben, and Westmoreland formed 1795 Daughter town Cazenovia formed in Herkimer County * 1798 Transferred to new county of Oneida; daughter town Augusta formed 1817 Daughter town Utica formed 1827 Daughter town New Hartford formed	Clark Mills Coleman(s) Mills New York Mills (v) Oriskany (v) Pleasant Valley Utica (v) Walesville Whitesboro (v) Whitestown Yorkville (v)		* Town of Cazenovia now in Madison County • Clark Mills on Kirkland and Westmoreland town lines • Village of New York Mills inc. 1922; shared with Town of New Hartford • Village of Oriskany inc. 1914 • Village of Utica inc. 1798 became part of City of Utica 1832 • Village of Whitesboro inc. 1813, reinc. 1829; county seat for Herkimer County 1791–1798; shared Oneida county seat with Rome 1798–1851 • Village of Yorkville inc. 1902
Williamstown * In Oneida County 1804–1816			* See Oswego County

NEW YORK STATE CENSUS RECORDS

See also chapter 3, Census Records

County originals at the Utica Public Library: 1825*, 1835, 1855, 1865, 1875, 1915, 1925 (1845, 1892, and 1905 are lost)

State originals at the NYSA: 1915, 1925

Microfilm at the FHL, NYPL, NYSHA, and NYSL; many years are online at *FamilySearch.org* and *Ancestry.com*.

* 1825 New York state census—only the indexes for the Towns of Paris and Western survive. The originals for these indexes are held at the Utica Public Library. Microfilm is only available at the FHL.

NATIONAL/STATEWIDE REPOSITORIES & RESOURCES

See chapter 16

COUNTYWIDE REPOSITORIES & RESOURCES

Oneida County Clerk

Oneida County Office Building • 800 Park Avenue • Utica, NY 13501
(315) 798-5794 • Email: countyclerk@ocgov.net
http://ocgov.net/oneida/countyclerk

Court records, criminal files, mortgages and deeds, coroner's reports, and government records dating from the late 1700s–present are kept in the clerk's office and include early records for Herkimer County. The clerk also maintains naturalization records from 1805–present; these are kept on the eighth floor of the County Office Building. Some documents are kept in the Records Room of the Oneida County Office Building and others are at the Regional Records Center, Westmoreland.

Oneida County – City, Town, and Village Clerks

Birth, marriage, and death records are maintained by the clerk of the municipality in which the event occurred; see Introduction to County Guides for details of other records which may also be held by municipal clerks. For contact information, see municipal websites. Unlike most city clerks, Utica City Clerk holds some vital records not available at the New York State Department of Health; see listing below for City of Utica. For more information on obtaining historical records in Oneida County, see *www.ocgov.net/historicalrecords*.

Oneida County Surrogate's Court

Oneida County Office Building • 800 Park Avenue, 8th Floor • Utica, NY 13501• (315) 266-4550 (Utica Office) • (315) 266-4309 (Rome Office)

Holds probate records from the 1790s to the present. See also chapter 6, Probate Records.

Oneida County Public Libraries

Oneida is part of the Mid-York Library System; see *http://myls.ent.sirsi.net* to access each library. Many hold genealogy and local history collections including maps and newspapers. Also see listings below for Erwin Library, Jervis Public Library, Kirkland Town Library, Utica Public Library, and Woodgate Free Library.

Utica Public Library

303 Genesee Street • Utica, NY 13501 • (315) 735-2279
www.uticapubliclibrary.org

Local newspapers (*Utica Daily Press* and *Observer Dispatch*); city directories; land records; census records—including the originals of the New York state censuses for Oneida County 1835, 1855, 1865, 1875, 1915, and 1925; and indexes for the 1825 New York state census for the Towns of Paris and Western.

Oneida County – All Municipal Historians

While not authorized to answer genealogical inquiries, city, town, and village historians can provide valuable historical information and research advice; some maintain collections and webpages which may include transcribed records, local histories, and other genealogical material. For contact information, see the website of the Association of Public Historians of New York State at *www.aphnys.org*.

Oneida County Historical Society, Research Library & Museum

1608 Genesee Street • Utica, NY 13502 • (315) 735-3642
Email: ochs@oneidacountyhistory.org
historyinquiries@oneidacountyhistory.org (research requests)
www.oneidacountyhistory.org

Holdings document family, local, and American history, and include business archives; annual reports; family and genealogical files; census materials; demographic data for City of Utica and surrounding towns; county, city and village maps; military histories from American Revolution to Civil War; newspapers; books; photographs; and scrapbooks. Website includes historical sketches organized by subject and municipality. Published the *Oniota* quarterly.

REGIONAL REPOSITORIES & RESOURCES

Fulton-Montgomery Community College: Evans Library: The Kenneth R. Dorn Regional History Study Center

See listing in Fulton County Guide

SUNY at Oswego: Local History Collection

See listing in Oswego County Guide

LOCAL REPOSITORIES & RESOURCES

Alphabetized by location

Boonville Historical Club

Dodge-Pratt-Northam Arts & Cultural Center
106 Schuyler Street • Boonville, NY 13309 • (315) 942-4251
http://boonvillehistoricalclub.wordpress.com

Club's collections are distributed between the D-P-N Center (newspapers, photographs, and club history), Erwin Library (see below), and town clerk's office (genealogical information, biographies, and vital statistics).

Erwin Library and Institute

104 Schuyler Street • Boonville, NY 13309 • (315) 942-4834
http://midyorklib.org/boonville

Local historical books and files from the northern part of Oneida County, *Boonville Herald* on microfilm 1853–present, local history room, and cemetery records. Library maintains the Boonville Historical Club's collection of local history, Civil War history, newspapers, and photographs.

The Carriage House Museum of the Queen Village Historical Society

2 North Park Street • PO Box 38 • Camden, NY 13316 • (315) 245-4652

Family histories, local newspapers, photographs, and information on history of local businesses, churches, and schools. Offers research services. Open May–October.

Paris Historical Society

2241 Oneida Street • PO Box 62 • Clayville, NY 13322
(315) 737-8611 • Facebook page

Local histories, genealogies and family histories, census materials (1800, 1814, 1820, 1840, and 1860), cemetery records, postcards and photographs, scrapbooks, artifacts; also information on local businesses, industries, agriculture, and religious societies.

Clinton Historical Society, Museum, and Munson Library
One Fountain Street • PO Box 42 • Clinton, NY 13323
(315) 859-1392 • Email: clintonhistoricalsociety@yahoo.com
www.clintonhistory.org

Business files; church, cemetery, and census records; directories; family files; photographs; newsletters; newspapers (*Clinton Courier* and *Clinton Signal*), some originals, 1846–present on microfilm, and onsite online access to searchable digital copies; obituaries; school catalogs; scrapbooks; veterans' records; and information on local industry, transportation, and politics. Selected records, photographs, histories, and newsletter on website.

Hamilton College Library
198 College Hill Road • Clinton, NY 13323 • (315) 859-4479
Email: askref@hamilton.edu • *www.hamilton.edu/library*

In addition to college documents dating from 1786, archival collections cover local history, the Adirondacks, Civil War regimental histories (especially New York State), and a Communal Societies Collection (particularly the Shakers). Primary collections are being digitized and much is already online. The website includes detailed finding aids.

Kirkland Town Library
55½ College Street • Clinton, NY 13323 • (315) 853-2038
www.kirklandtownlibrary.org

Holdings include *Clinton Courier* on microfilm July 1846–2011 with print index, obituaries from the *Courier* 1928–2010 on DVD, and transcribed cemetery records for Village of Clinton.

Marshall Historical Society
PO Box 232 • Deansboro, NY 13328 • (315) 853-6887
Email address on website • *www.marshallhistsoc.org*

Family histories, cemetery records, census materials (for Marshall 1865), *Oriskany Valley Gazette* 1899–1900, local histories, deeds, atlases, and information on local industry, transportation, American Indians, and prominent figures. Monthly newsletter.

Deerfield Historical Society
6329 Walker Road • Deerfield, NY 13502 • (315) 724-0413
Email: OurDeerfieldHistory@gmail.com
http://townofdeerfield.org/content/History

Website includes historical photographs and map, as well as a short guide to research in Town of Deerfield.

New Hartford Historical Society
Village Point Apartment Building • 2 Paris Road • PO Box 238
New Hartford, NY • (315) 724-7258 • Email: historicalnh@yahoo.com
www.nhnyhistorical.com

Books, church records, directories 1853–1991, family files, maps, school records, and information on local businesses, industry, and agriculture. Website includes postcards of local buildings and sites. *Tally Ho*, quarterly newsletter.

New York Mills Historical Society and Museum
96 Main Street • PO Box 151 • New York Mills, NY 13417
(315) 736-0489/4532 • Email: nymhistoricalsociety@live.com
http://villageofnewyorkmills.org

Early village maps, high school yearbooks, photographs and postcards, histories, and World War II collection.

Oriskany Museum
420 Utica Street • PO Box 284 • Oriskany, NY 13424 • (315) 736-1227
Email access on website • *www.oriskanymuseum.com*

Holdings include records of Oriskany village and school, the USS *Oriskany*, and Battle of Oriskany (American Revolution).

Limestone Ridge Historical Society
223 Main Street • PO Box 383 • Oriskany Falls, NY 13425
(315) 821-8103 • Email: limestoneridge@juno.com

Holdings include local histories, cemetery records, and photographs.

Remsen-Steuben Historical Society
Stone Meeting House • 9793 Prospect Street • PO Box 254
Remsen, NY 13438 • (315) 831-8481
http://villageofremsen.org/content/Generic/View/5

Local histories, cemetery index, photographs and postcards, and information and memorabilia relating to local Welsh families. Research requests are handled by volunteers.

Jervis Public Library
613 North Washington Street • Rome, NY 13440 • (315) 336-4570
www.jervislibrary.org/lh_broch.html

Books and periodicals, cemetery records, city directories 1857–present, census microfilms, gazetteers, maps and atlases, and newspapers (*Rome Telegraph*, 1834–1837; *Rome Citizen*, 1840–1903 with gaps; *Rome Sentinel*, 1842–1883 with gaps; *Rome Observer*, 1993–present).

Rome Historical Society Museum
200 Church Street • Rome, NY 13440 • (315) 336-5870
Email: news01@artcom.com • *www.romehistoricalsociety.org*

Library collections include genealogies and local histories, maps, samplers, photographs, and exhibits documenting history of local Iroquois people, early European settlers, transportation, and industry. Archival collections and research facility include original documents from the Revolutionary and Civil Wars, business records, diaries, scrapbooks, and information on Griffiss Air Force Base. Research requests may be sent by mail or email.

City of Utica: City Clerk
Vital Records • One Kennedy Plaza • Utica, NY 13502
(315) 792-0113 • *www.cityofutica.com*

Holdings for the City of Utica include birth and death records 1876–present, and marriage records 1874–present. Records at the New York State Department of Health in Albany for the City of Utica do not begin until 1880.

Utica College: Frank E. Gannett Library
1600 Burrstone Road • Utica, NY 13502 • (315) 792-3041
Email: library@utica.edu • *www.utica.edu/academic/library*

Holdings include local newspapers (*Boonville Herald*) and census material.

Town of Verona Historical Association
6600 Germany Road • Historical Building • Verona, NY 13054
(315) 363-6799 ext. 8 • Email: veronahistoricalny@gmail.com
http://townverona.org

Holdings include local histories, family histories and genealogies, obituaries, and scrapbooks.

Waterville Historical Society

220 East Main Street • Waterville, NY 13480 • (315) 841-4018
Email: watervillehistoricalsociety@juno.com
www.watervilleny.com/WHS.htm

Holdings include *Waterville Times* archive and yearbooks 1850s to the present. Collection is held at Waterville Public Library.

Westmoreland Historical Society

50 Station Road • PO Box 200 • Westmoreland, NY 13490
(315) 853-8001 ext. 230 • Email: wessociety@roadrunner.com
http://town.westmoreland.ny.us

Genealogies and local histories, ledgers, letters, yearbooks, and information relating to local schools, businesses, industries, and the fire department.

Whitesboro Historical Society

Whitesboro Village Office • 10 Moseley Street •
Whitesboro, NY 13492 • (315) 736-1613
Email: whtboro@roadrunner.com
http://village.whitesboro.ny.us/content/History

Local histories, cemetery records, birth and death information, yearbooks, photographs, and information on local transportation, courts, sports, and fire department.

Woodgate Free Library: Local Genealogy

11051 Woodgate Road • Woodgate, NY 13494
(315) 392-4814 • *http://midyorklib.org/woodgate*

History room has newspapers and information on local history and families. Website includes online cemetery transcriptions, diaries, ledger abstracts, and newspaper clippings.

SELECTED PRINT & ONLINE RESOURCES

Below is a selection of resources relevant for research in this county. The list is representative, not exhaustive. Additional titles—particularly of abstracts, indexes, transcriptions, and local histories—are available; consult the introduction to Part Two for further information. For guidance on how to identify and locate community directories and local newspapers, see chapter 11, City Directories, and chapter 12, Newspapers, in Part One of this book.

Abstracts, Indexes & Transcriptions

Barber, Gertrude Audrey. "Abstracts of Wills of Oneida County, NY." Typescript, 1939. [Ancestry.com]

County of Oneida Abstracts. Syracuse: Central New York Genealogical Society, 2000. Abstracts for a range of genealogical records originally published in the quarterly *Tree Talks.*

Daughters of the American Revolution, comps. *New York DAR Genealogical Records Committee Report.* Since 1913 DAR volunteers have transcribed many thousands of unpublished cemetery, church, and town records throughout New York. The reports are at the DAR Library; copies are at the NYSL and the NYPL. The DAR has a searchable name index to all the GRC reports at *http://services.dar.org/Public/DAR_Research/search/?Tab_ID=6.* See Jean Worden's index below for a listing by county of the New York record sets that were transcribed by the DAR before 1998.

Hatcher, Patricia L. "Marriages by Rev. Israel Brainerd in and around Verona, Oneida County, 1807–1849." *NYG&B Record,* vol. 141 (2010), no. 3: 221–225, no. 4: 310–313. [NYG&B eLibrary]

Kelly, Arthur C. M. *Index to Tree Talks County Packet: Oneida County.* Rhinebeck, NY: Kinship, 2002.

"McConnellsville, Oneida Co., NY, Cemetery Inscriptions." Typescript, 1931. NYPL, New York. Transcribed and indexed by Kenn Stryker-Rodda for The Long Island Historical Society, 1955. [NYG&B eLibrary]

Pitcher, James S. *From the Files of the Town Historian: Ava, Boonville, West Leyden, Lewis.* Boonville, NY: Adirondack Communities Advisory League, 1995.

Vosburgh, Royden Woodward, ed. "Records of the First Presbyterian Church of Whitesboro in the Town of Whitestown, Oneida County, NY." Typescript, 1920. NYPL, New York. [NYG&B eLibrary]

———. "Records of the Paris Religious Society in the Town of Paris, Oneida County, NY." Typescript, 1921. NYPL, New York. [NYG&B eLibrary]

———. "Records of the Society of Clinton, a Congregational Church in the Village of Clinton, in the Town of Kirkland, Oneida County, NY." Typescript, 1921. NYPL, New York. [NYG&B eLibrary]

Williams, Richard L. *Oneida County Cemeteries.* New York: Oneida County Historians Association, 2005.

Worden, Jean D. "Book 1, Subject Index." In *Revised Master Index to the New York State Daughters of the American Revolution Genealogical Records Volumes.* Zephyrhills, FL: J. D. Worden, 1998. The Subject Index includes a listing by county of the cemeteries, churches, towns, and other sources of records transcribed by the DAR.

Other Resources

Beers, D. G. & Co. *Atlas of Oneida County, New York: From Actual Surveys and Official Records.* Philadelphia, 1874.

Bagg, M.M., M.D., ed. *Memorial History of Utica, NY: From Its Settlement to the Present Time.* Syracuse: D. Mason, 1892.

———. *The Pioneers of Utica: Being Sketches of Its Inhabitants and Its Institutions with the Civil History of the Place, from the Earliest Settlement to the Year 1825, the Era of the Opening of the Erie Canal.* Utica, NY: Curtiss and Childs, 1877. Index available from Berkshire Family History Association.

Brown, Dorothy W., and Francis W. Cunningham. *Oneida County.* Utica, NY: Oneida Historical Society, 1953.

Canfield, William W., and J. E. Clark. *Things Worth Knowing About Oneida County.* Utica, NY: T. J. Griffiths, 1909.

Central New York Library Resources Council. *Guide to Historical Organizations in Central New York.* (Onondaga, Herkimer, Oneida, Madison) Digitally published May 2009. *www.clrc.org/wp-content/uploads/2011/05/DHPHistGuide09b.pdf*

Child, Hamilton. *Gazetteer and Business Directory of Oneida County, NY, for 1869.* Syracuse, 1868.

Cookinham, Henry J. *History of Oneida County, New York: From 1700 to the Present Time.* Chicago: S. J. Clarke Publishing Co., 1912.

Cutter, William R. *Genealogical and Family History of Central New York: A Record of the Achievements of Her People in the Making of a Commonwealth and the Building of a Nation.* New York: Lewis Historical Publishing Co., 1912.

Durant, Samuel W. *History of Oneida County, New York: With Illustrations and Biographical Sketches of Some of Its Prominent Men and Pioneers.* Philadelphia, 1878.

Foote, Allan D. *Historical Guide to the Battle of Oriskany.* Whitesboro, NY: Mohawk Valley History Project, 1999.

Galpin, William F. *Central New York, an Inland Empire, Comprising Oneida, Madison, Onondaga, Cayuga, Tompkins, Cortland, Chenango Counties and Their People.* New York: Lewis Historical Publishing Co., 1914. Contains biographies. Index available from Berkshire Family History Association.

Greene, Nelson. *History of the Mohawk Valley, Gateway to the West, 1614–1925; Covering the Six Counties of Schenectady, Schoharie, Montgomery, Fulton, Herkimer, and Oneida.* Chicago: S. J. Clarke, 1925.

James, Patricia R. *Upstate New York Researcher: Principally for Research in Jefferson, Oneida, and St. Lawrence Counties.* Boise, ID: Family Tree, 1991.

Jones, Erasmus W. *The Early Welsh Settlers of Oneida County.* Westminster, MD: Heritage Books, 2004.

Jones, Pomroy. *Annals and Recollections of Oneida County.* Salem, MA, 1850.

Kessler, Glenn D. *Roadside Historical Markers around Oneida County: with an Expanded Story.* New York: G. D. Kessler, 1998.

Kohn, Solomon J. *The Jewish Community of Utica, New York, 1847–1948.* New York: American Jewish Historical Society, 1959.

New York Historical Resources Center. *Guide to Historical Resources in Oneida County, New York, Repositories.* Ithaca, NY: Cornell University, 1983. [*books.FamilySearch.org*]

Peck, Ada M., and Douglas Swarthout. *A History of the Hanover Society: The Early Settlers of the Town of Marshall, Oneida County, New York Together with a Genealogical Mention of Many Prominent Families.* Deansboro, NY: Berry Hill Press, 1995.

Wager, Daniel E. *Our County and Its People: A Descriptive Work on Oneida County, New York.* Boston, 1896. Index available from Berkshire Family History Association.

White, Donald F. *Exploring 200 Years of Oneida County History.* Utica, NY: Oneida County Historical Society, 1998.

Additional Online Resources

Ancestry.com

There are vast numbers of records on *Ancestry.com* that pertain to people who have lived in New York State. See chapter 16 for a description of *Ancestry.com*'s resources and its partnership with the New York State Archives. A search of the online card catalog by county may reveal lesser known resources that pertain to a locality, such as town records, abstracts, transcriptions, city directories, and local histories.

FamilySearch.org

FamilySearch has extensive collections of New York records, including religious records, which are searchable by name and location, but not by county. The following collections include record images (browsable, but not searchable) that are organized by county:

• "New York, Land Records, 1630–1975." Includes land and property records. *familysearch.org/search/collection/2078654*

• "New York, Probate Records, 1629–1971." Includes wills, letters of administration, and guardianship papers. *familysearch.org/search/collection/1920234*

For both collections, choose the browse option and then select Oneida to view the available records sets.

A detailed description of *FamilySearch.org* resources is found in chapter 16.

NYGenWeb Project: Oneida County
oneida.nygenweb.net
Part of the national, USGenWeb volunteer initiative, the website provides information and resources for county research.

Old Fulton New York Postcards
www.FultonHistory.com
The website provides free access to a vast collection of digitized New York newspapers, including 31 titles for Oneida County.

Onondaga County

Formed March 5, 1794

Parent Counties   Herkimer • Tioga
Daughter Counties   Cayuga 1799 • Cortland 1808 • Oswego 1816
County Seat   City of Syracuse

Major Land Transactions
See chapter 7, Land Records
New Military Tract 1782–1791

Indian Territories
See chapter 14, Peoples of New York, American Indian
Onondaga Nation: Onondaga Reservation **(1788–present)**

Town Boundary Map
★ - County seat

Towns (and Cities)	Villages and other Settlements		Notes
Aurelius * In Onondaga County 1794–1799			* See Cayuga County
Camillus * 1790 Settled 1799 Formed from towns of Marcellus and Onondaga 1829 Daughter town Elbridge formed 1834 Annexed land from Town of Onondaga	Amboy Amboy Station Belle Isle Bennetts Corners Camillus (v) Edgewood Garden Fairmount Garden Terrace Greenfield Village Hidden Knolls Newport North Belle Isle Orchard Village Oswego Bitter(s)	Parson Farms Pioneer Farms Scenic Hills Sherwood Knolls Stanley Manor Sweets Crossing Warners Weatheridge Wellington Westerlea West Genesee Terrace Westview Manor Wincrest Park	* Camillus was the name of one of the 28 Military Tract townships • Village of Camillus inc. 1852
Cicero * 1790 Settled 1807 Formed from Town of Lysander 1827 Daughter town Clay formed	Brewerton Bridgeport Brown Center Cicero Cicero Center Cicero Corners Forest Beach	Kraus Landing Lower South Bay North Syracuse (v) Plank Road Sandy Bay Valentines Beach	* Cicero was the name of one of the 28 Military Tract townships • Brewerton shared with Town of Hastings, Oswego County • Hamlet of Cicero formerly Codys Corners • Village of North Syracuse inc. 1925; formerly Centerville and Podunk; shared with Town of Clay • Plank Road was shared with Town of Clay
Cincinnatus * In Onondaga County 1804–1808			* See Cortland County
Clay 1793 Settled at Three River Point 1827 Formed from Town of Cicero	Bayberry Bear Villa Belgium Bel Harbor Briarwood Castle Nova Clay Dutch Settlement Elmcrest Euclid Fairway West Horseshoe Island	Iron Gate Morgan Settlement Moyers Corners Mufale Villa North Syracuse (v) Plank Road Quarry Pointe Rodger Corner Three Rivers Willow Stream Woodard Youngs	• Clay also West Cicero • Euclid also Clay Corners • Village of North Syracuse inc. 1925; formerly Centerville and Podunk; shared with Town of Cicero • Plank Road was shared with Town of Cicero • Three Rivers also Three Rivers Point
DeWitt 1789 Settlers from Dutchess County 1835 Formed from Town of Manlius 1926 Ceded Village of Eastwood to City of Syracuse	Collamer DeWitt East Syracuse (v) Eastwood (v)	Jamesville Lyndon Messina Springs	• Collamer formerly Britton Settlement • Hamlet of DeWitt formerly Hulls Landing, Orville, and Youngsville • Village of East Syracuse inc. 1881 • Village of Eastwood inc. 1895, dissolved 1926 and ceded to City of Syracuse

Towns (and Cities)	Villages and other Settlements		Notes
Elbridge 1793 Settled 1829 Formed from Town of Camillus	California Crossman Corners Elbridge (v) Eno Point Halfway Jacks Reef	Jordan (v) Junction Laird Corners Memphis Peru Skaneateles Junction	• Village of Elbridge inc. 1848 • Eno Point called Jones Point until c. 1984 • Jacks Reef on Lysander and Van Buren town lines • Village of Jordan inc. 1835 • Laird Corners formerly Crab Hollow • Memphis also Canton; mostly in Town of Van Buren • Skaneateles Junction formerly Hart Lot
Fabius * 1794 Settlers from Stockbridge, MA 1798 Formed from Town of Pompey 1803 Daughter town Tully formed 1808 Daughter town Truxton formed in Cortland County	Apulia Apulia Station Cowles Settlement Fabius (v)	Gooseville Gooseville Corners Keeney Settlement Vincent Corners	* Fabius was the name of one of the 28 Military Tract townships • Apulia Station also Summit Station • Cowles Settlement now in Town of Cuyler, Cortland County • Village of Fabius inc. 1880; formerly Franklinville; called Fabius Center c. 1812
Geddes 1794 Settled 1848 Formed from Town of Salina	Geddes (v) Lakeland Lakeside	Lindbergh Lawns Solvay (v) Westvale	• Village of Geddes inc. 1832; in Town of Salina before 1848; reincorporated in Geddes 1867, ceded to City of Syracuse in 1886 • Village of Solvay inc. 1894
Hannibal * In Onondaga County 1806–1816			* See Oswego County
Homer * In Onondaga County 1794–1808			* See Cortland County
LaFayette 1791 Settled 1825 Formed from towns of Onondaga and Pompey	Baileys Settlement Big Bend Cardiff Collingwood LaFayette	Linn Onativia Tully Valley Webb Hollow	
Lysander * 1793 Settled 1794 Formed as a town 1806 Daughter town Hannibal formed 1807 Daughter town Cicero formed	Baird Corners Baldwinsville (v) Belgium Cold Springs Jacks Reef Jacksonville Lamson	Little Utica Lysander Plainville Radisson Red Rock West Phoenix Wrights Corners	* Lysander was the name of one of the 28 Military Tract townships • Village of Baldwinsville inc. 1847; shared with Town of Van Buren • Jacks Reef on Elbridge and Van Buren town lines • Hamlet of Lysander also Betts Corners and Vickerys Settlement
Manlius * 1790 Settled 1794 Formed as a town 1798 Daughter town Onondaga formed 1809 Daughter town Salina formed 1835 Daughter town DeWitt formed	Eagle Village Erie Village Fayetteville (v) Fillmore Corner Franklin Park Fremont High Bridge Kirkville Manlius (v) Manlius Center	Matthews Mills Minoa (v) Mycenae North Manlius Oot Park Peck Hill Polkville Saintsville Schepps Corners Snyder(s) Crossing	* Manlius was the name of one of the 28 Military Tract townships • Village of Fayetteville inc. 1844 • Village of Manlius inc. 1813 • Village of Minoa inc. 1913; formerly Manlius Station • Mycenae formerly Hartsville • North Manlius was shared with the Town of Sullivan, Madison County

Towns (and Cities)	Villages and other Settlements		Notes
Marcellus * 1794 Formed as a town 1798 Daughter town Onondaga formed 1799 Daughter town Camillus formed 1806 Daughter town Otisco formed 1830 Daughter town Skaneateles formed 1840 Annexed land from Town of Spafford	Bumblebee City Clintonville Marcellus (v) Marcellus Falls Marietta Martisco	Pumpkin Hollow Rose Hill Shamrock Thorn Hill Tyler Hollow	* Marcellus was the name of one of the 28 Military Tract townships • Village of Marcellus inc. 1853 • Pumpkin Hollow was shared with Town of Onondaga
Milton * In Onondaga County 1794–1799			* Town of Milton now Town of Genoa in Cayuga County
Onondaga 1786 Settlers from New Hampshire 1798 Formed from towns of Manlius, Marcellus, and Pompey 1799 Daughter town Camillus formed 1809 Daughter town Salina formed 1825 Daughter town La Fayette formed 1834 Ceded land to Town of Camillus	Cards Corners Cedarvale Five Corners Griffins Corners Howlett Hill Ironsides Joshua Kellys Corners Loomis Hill Lords Corners Navarino Nedrow	Nichols Corners Onondaga Onondaga Castle Onondaga Hill Onondaga Valley Pumpkin Hollow Sentinel Heights South Onondaga Southwood Split Rock Taunton Wellington Corner	• Onondaga Hill county seat 1805–1829; also West Onondaga • Pumpkin Hollow was shared with Town of Marcellus
Onondaga Reservation *	Indian Village		* Onondaga Nation is self-governing; reservation established in 1788
Otisco 1801 Settlers from Northampton, MA 1806 Formed from towns of Marcellus, Pompey, and Tully	Amber Bay Shores Gamble Mill Heath Grove Maple Grove	Otisco Otisco Valley Rice Grove Williams Grove	• Otisco Valley formerly Spafford Hollow; shared with Town of Spafford
Ovid * In Onondaga County 1794–1799			* See Seneca County
Pompey * 1789 Settled 1789 Formed in Montgomery County 1791 Transferred to new county of Herkimer 1794 Transferred to new county of Onondaga 1798 Daughter towns Fabius and Onondaga formed 1825 Daughter town LaFayette formed	Atwell Corners Berwyn Buellville Clough Corners Delphi Delphi Falls Delphi Falls Park Hills Corners Jerome Corners	Oran Pompey Pompey Center Pompey Hill Pompey Hollow Salem Corner Swift Corner Watervale	* Pompey was the name of one of the 28 Military Tract townships • Pompey Center formerly Greens Corners
Romulus * In Onondaga County 1794–1799			* See Seneca County

Towns (and Cities)	Villages and other Settlements		Notes
Salina 1795 Settled at Liverpool 1809 Formed from towns of Manlius and Onondaga 1848 Daughter town Geddes formed; Village of Syracuse and Village of Salina incorporated as City of Syracuse	Elmcrest Galeville Geddes (v) Hinsdale Liverpool (v) Long Branch	Lyncourt Mattydale Pitcher Hill Salina (v) Syracuse (v)	• Village of Geddes inc. 1832; moved to Town of Geddes in 1848, ceded to City of Syracuse 1886 • Village of Liverpool inc. 1830 • Village of Salina inc. 1824; incorporated as part of City of Syracuse in December 1847 • Village of Syracuse inc. 1825; became county seat 1829; incorporated as City of Syracuse in December 1847
Scipio * In Onondaga County 1794–1799			* See Cayuga County
Skaneateles 1793–94 Settled 1830 Formed from Town of Marcellus 1840 Annexed land from Town of Spafford	Jones Beach Kelloggs Mills Long Bridge Mandana Mottville Shepard Settlement Skaneateles (v)	Skaneateles Falls Thornton Grove Thornton Heights Wicks Corners Willow Glen Winding Ways	• Village of Skaneateles inc. 1833
Spafford 1794 Settled 1811 Formed from Town of Tully 1840 Ceded land to towns of Marcellus and Skaneateles	Borodino Borodino Landing Bromley Edgewater Park Jenney Point Lader(s) Point Otisco Valley Pine Grove	Ripley Hill Shamrock South Spafford Spafford Spafford Landing Spafford Valley Ten Mile Point Woodland	• Edgewater Park also Five Mile Point • Otisco Valley formerly Spafford Hollow; shared with Town of Otisco • Hamlet of Spafford also Spafford Corners • Spafford Landing formerly Randalls Point
Solon * In Onondaga County 1798–1808			* See Cortland County
Syracuse (city) * 1784 Settled as Salt Point 1806 Named Bogardus Corners 1809 Name changed to Milan 1812 Name changed to South Salina 1814 Name changed to Cositts Corners 1817 Name changed to Corinth 1820 Name changed to Syracuse 1825 Incorporated as Village of Syracuse in Town of Salina 1847 Villages of Syracuse and Salina incorporated as City of Syracuse 1886 Annexed Village of Geddes from Town of Salina 1926 Annexed Village of Eastwood from Town of DeWitt	Barnes Bradford Hills Cityline Brook Clary-Meachem Coldbrook Court-Woodlawn Danforth DeWitt Downtown Syracuse Eastwood (v) Elmwood Franklin Square Geddes (v) Genesee Manor Hanover Square Hawley-Green Hopper Lincoln Hill	Lodi Lower Valley Drive Maciejowa Nob Hill-LaFayette Onondaga Hollow Onondaga Valley Outer Brighton Park Avenue Salina (v) Skytop South Midland South Salina Strathmore Valley Van Duyn Walton Tract Websters Landing Webster Pond	* County seat (village and city) from 1829; 1805–1829 county seat Onondaga Hill, Town of Onondaga; courts 1794–1805 "The first courts were held in barns and private residences at Onondaga, Levana, on the shore of Cayuga Lake, Cayuga co., and Ovid, Seneca co." (J. H. French 1860) • Eastwood formerly a village in Town of DeWitt; annexed by City of Syracuse in 1926 • Geddes formerly Village of Geddes formerly in Town of Salina; annexed by City of Syracuse in 1886 • Salina formerly a village in Town of Salina; became part of new City of Syracuse 1847

Towns (and Cities)	Villages and other Settlements		Notes
Tully * 1795 Settled 1803 Formed from Town of Fabius 1806 Daughter town Otisco formed 1808 Daughter town Preble formed in Cortland County 1811 Daughter town Spafford formed	Assembly Park Tully (v) Tully Center Tully Lake Park Tully Valley Vesper		* Tully was the name of one of the 28 Military Tract townships • Village of Tully inc. 1875
Van Buren c. 1792 Settled 1829 Formed from Town of Camillus	Baldwinsville (v) Bangall Crows Hollow Daboll Corners Ionia Jacks Reef Jones Point	Memphis Seneca Knolls Stiles Van Buren Van Buren Center Village Green Warners	• Village of Baldwinsville inc. 1847; shared with Town of Lysander • Bangall formerly Sand Spring • Ionia formerly Barns Corners • Jacks Reef on Elbridge and Lysander town lines • Memphis also Canton; on Camillus town line
Virgil * In Onondaga County 1804–1808			* See Cortland County

Notes on Onondaga County

Onondaga is one of four "County Registration Districts" which have consolidated the administration of birth and death records. These civil records are kept at the Onondaga County Office of Vital Statistics, see details below. Civil birth and death records earlier than 1880 may still be found with city, town, or village clerks.

NEW YORK STATE CENSUS RECORDS

See also chapter 3, Census Records

County originals at Onondaga County Clerk's Office: 1855, 1865, 1875, 1892, 1905, 1915, 1925 (1825, 1835, and 1845 are lost)

State originals at the NYSA: 1915, 1925

Microfilm at the FHL (1855 only at FHL), NYPL, and NYSL; many years are online at *FamilySearch.org* and *Ancestry.com*.

NATIONAL/STATEWIDE REPOSITORIES & RESOURCES

See chapter 16

COUNTYWIDE REPOSITORIES & RESOURCES

Onondaga County Clerk

Onondaga County Court House • 401 Montgomery Street, Room 200
Syracuse, NY 13202-2568 • (315) 435-2227
Archives and Microfilm Department: Basement Level, County Court House
(315) 435-2237
www.ongov.net/clerk/index.html

Holdings include directories 1861–present, judgments and liens, maps, mortgages and deeds 1794–present, naturalization records 1802–present, and the New York state censuses for Onondaga County 1855, 1865, 1875, 1892, 1905, 1915, and 1925. Marriage records: City of Syracuse 1908–1935 (these and later records with city clerk, City Hall; earlier records at the Onondaga County Office of Vital Statistics). Marriage records for towns in Onondaga County 1880–1935; later records with town/village clerks.

Onondaga County Office of Vital Statistics

Onondaga County Health Department
421 Montgomery Street, Room 20 (Basement) • Syracuse, NY 13202
(315) 435-3241 • *www.ongov.net/vital*

Maintains birth and death certificates for towns in Onondaga County 1883–present, and City of Syracuse 1873–present; also marriage records for City of Syracuse 1873–1907. Records before 1880 are not available at the New York State Department of Health.

Onondaga County – City, Town, and Village Clerks

Birth, marriage, and death records are maintained by the clerk of the municipality in which the event occurred; see Introduction to County Guides for details of other records which may also be held by municipal clerks. For contact information, see *www.ongov.net/clerk/clerks.html*. The City of Syracuse is one of the few cities in the state that holds some early birth and death records that are not available at the New York State Department of Health; see listing for Onondaga County Office of Vital Statistics.

Onondaga County Surrogate's Court

Onondaga County Courthouse • 401 Montgomery Street
Syracuse, NY 13202-2568 • (315) 671-2100

Holds probate records early-1800s to the present. Records are sparse for the mid-1880s. See also chapter 6, Probate Records.

Onondaga County Public Libraries

For the Onondaga County Public Library see *www.onlib.org*. Many hold genealogy and local history collections. Also see listings below for Baldwinsville Public Library, Fayetteville Free Library, Onondaga Public Library Central Branch, and Solvay Public Library.

Onondaga County Public Library: Local History and Genealogy Department

The Galleries of Syracuse • 447 South Salina Street
Syracuse, NY 13202 • (315) 435-1900
Email: reference@onlib.org • *www.onlib.org/web/lh/index.htm*

Holds a copy of the New York State Department of Health vital records indexes. Vital, military, census, land, and cemetery records; genealogies and histories; maps, directories, and newspapers from New York, New England, Pennsylvania, and New Jersey. Census holdings include transcripts, indexes, and microfilms of federal and New York state censuses for multiple counties, including: federal censuses for Onondaga County (1800, 1810, 1820, 1830, 1840, 1850, and 1860); and the New York state censuses for Onondaga County 1855 (index, transcript, and microfilm) and 1865, 1875, 1892, 1905, 1915, and 1925 (microfilm). Website includes finding aids, handouts, and list of collections.

Onondaga Historical Association Museum & Research Center

321 Montgomery Street • Syracuse, NY 13202
Phone: (315) 428-1864 • Email addresses on website
www.cnyhistory.org

Collection includes census records; family and biographical files; diaries; personal correspondence; photographs; local and military histories; newspapers; maps and atlases; directories; cemetery records; court trial information; information on churches, hospitals (1860s–present), hotels (1840s–present), schools (1840s–present), post offices (1830s–present), local industries, prisons (1850s–present), transportation, and the police force; local government proceedings (1850s–present); and society, club, and business records. Comprehensive finding aids online.

Onondaga County Historian

Onondaga County Courthouse, Room 220 • 401 Montgomery Street
Syracuse, NY 13202-2568 • (315) 435-2227

Onondaga County – All Municipal Historians

While not authorized to answer genealogical inquiries, city, town, and village historians can provide valuable historical information and research advice; some maintain collections and webpages which may include transcribed records, local histories, and other genealogical material, for example, the Town of Elbridge historian's page at *www.townofelbridge.com*. See contact information at *www.rootsweb.ancestry.com/~nyononda/towns.html* or at the website of the Association of Public Historians of New York State at *www.aphnys.org*.

Syracuse University Library

222 Waverly Avenue • Syracuse, NY 13244
(315) 443-2093 • *http://library.syr.edu*

Search collections for New York State and Ephemera, which includes the Oneida Community Collection (1811–1983). The library holds 415 New York manuscript collections including account books, church records, correspondence, daybooks, deeds, family papers, military material, and ship's log. Other manuscript collections contain New York material (e.g., Civil War, Military, and Politics). Website includes list of bibliographies and finding aids, publications, and digitized photographs.

REGIONAL REPOSITORIES & RESOURCES

Central New York Genealogical Society
PO Box 404 – Colvin Station • Syracuse, NY 13205
Email: cnygs@yahoo.com • www.rootsweb.ancestry.com/~nycnygs

The Society currently publishes information on 33 New York counties. Since 1961, it has produced *Tree Talks*, a quarterly journal featuring abstracts of records (including census and church records); guides to genealogical research; and publication reviews. Special collection County Packets include all the *Tree Talks* information CNYGS has published on 49 counties. Indexes to these abstract packets have been compiled by Arthur C. M. Kelly and published by Kinship Books. Name indexes (to *Tree Talks* articles 1961–2006/09) organized by county, are available on their website for Allegany, Chenango, Clinton, Delaware, Erie, Franklin, Greene, Hamilton, Madison, Orleans, St. Lawrence, and Wyoming counties. There are also online name indexes to recent years of *Tree Talks*, 2009–2013. The website features the Society's Surname Project, an index of surnames currently being researched by its members; tax lists; cemetery lists; and guides to genealogy research in central New York by county. The County Packets, compilations of census records, and other original sources featured in *Tree Talks* are for sale on the website.

State University of New York at Oswego: Local History Collection
See listing in Oswego County Guide

LOCAL REPOSITORIES & RESOURCES
Alphabetized by location

Baldwinsville Public Library: Local History Room
33 East Genesee Street • Baldwinsville, NY 13027-2575 • (315) 635-5631
Email: localhistory@bville.lib.ny.us • www.bville.lib.ny.us

Censuses, cemetery databases (covering towns of Lysander and Van Buren), directories, newspapers, maps and atlases, photographs, and yearbooks documenting Village of Baldwinsville and towns of Lysander, Van Buren, and Clay.

Camillus Historical Society
4600 West Genesee Street • Camillus, NY 13031
(315) 488-1234 (ask for Historical Society)
camillushistorical@townofcamillus.com

Database including family histories and photo archives.

Fabius Historical Society
PO Box 27 • Fabius, NY 13063
www.fabius-ny.gov/php-files/fabius_historical.php

Website includes some transcribed vital records, census materials, obituaries, and Civil War records.

Fayetteville Free Library
300 Orchard St. • Fayetteville, NY 13066 • (315) 637-6374
http://fflib.org

Biographical, school, and cultural and civic organization reference material; local newspapers on microfilm 1840–present; and yearbooks.

Village of Liverpool: Village Museum and Historian's Office
Gleason Mansion • 314 Second Street • Liverpool, NY 13088
(315) 451-7091 • Email: villageclerk@villageofliverpool.org
http://www.villageofliverpool.org/content/villagehistorian

Holdings include documents, photographs, and Liverpool cemetery records.

Manlius Historical Society, Historical Museum, and Cheney House Research Center & Library
Manlius Historical Museum: 101 Scoville Avenue
Research Center & Library: 109 Pleasant Street

Manlius, NY 13104 • (315) 682-6660
Email: ManliusHistory@gmail.com • www.manliushistory.org

Holdings include historical and genealogical material and photographs relating to Town of Manlius and surrounding area. Quarterly newsletter called the *Seraph*.

Town of Pompey Historical Society: William G. Pomeroy Museum and Research Center/Genealogy Research Center
Research Center: 8347 U.S. Route 20 • Manlius, NY 13104-9543
Society: 2944 Michael Avenue • Pompey Hill • Jamesville, NY 13078
(315) 682-4729 • Email: PompeyHistory@hotmail.com
http://www.pompeyhistorical.org/geneology.php

Local history publications, cemetery records, census materials including indexes to the New York state census for 1855 and 1865 for the Town of Pompey, church records, school records, maps and atlases, and diaries documenting history of Delphi Falls, Oran, Pompey Center, Pompey, and Watervale. The website has a comprehensive list of their research collection holdings.

Marcellus Historical Society
18 North Street • PO Box 165 • Marcellus, NY 13108
(315) 673-4839 • *http://mhs.villageofmarcellus.com*

Holdings include historical and genealogical material. Website features town maps and publications.

Town of Onondaga Historical Society & Museum
5020 Ball Road • Onondaga Hill, NY 13215 • (315) 214-2383
Email: tohsociety@yahoo.com • *http://onondagatownhist.org*

Family histories, historical maps, photographs, census materials, burial records, oral histories, and materials relating to history of town's poorhouse. Some records available on website.

Skaneateles Historical Society and Museum
28 Hannum Street • Skaneateles, NY 13152-1009 • (315) 685-1360
Email: skaneateleshistoricalsociety@verizon.net
www.skaneateleshistoricalsociety.org

Assessment books; maps (1852, 1860, 1875, and 1889); birth, marriage, and death indexes; biographical files; telephone books; old newspapers on microfilm; and collection of papers. Website includes online archives, including vital, census, and cemetery indexes and databases.

Solvay Public Library
615 Woods Road • Solvay, NY 13209 • (315) 468-2441
www.solvaylibrary.org

Histories and biographies, correspondence, maps, newsletters, photographs, school records and yearbooks, technical reports, and other records documenting history of Village of Solvay, Town of Geddes, Onondaga County, and New York State.

City of Syracuse: City Clerk
231 City Hall • 233 E. Washington Street • Syracuse, NY 13202
(315) 448-8216 • www.syracuse.ny.us/City_Clerk.aspx

The city clerk holds marriage records 1908–present. Birth and death records are available at the Onondaga Office of Vital Statistics.

SELECTED PRINT & ONLINE RESOURCES

Below is a selection of resources relevant for research in this county. The list is representative, not exhaustive. Additional titles—particularly of abstracts, indexes, transcriptions, and local histories—are available; consult the introduction to Part Two for further information. For guidance on how to identify and locate community directories and local newspapers, see chapter 11, City Directories, and chapter 12, Newspapers, in Part One of this book.

Abstracts, Indexes & Transcriptions

1938 Farm Register of All Farms in Onondaga County, New York: For Merchants, Manufacturers, and Professional Men. Ithaca, NY: Rural Directories, Inc., 1938.

Beauchamp, William Martin. *Revolutionary Soldiers Resident or Dying in Onondaga County, New York: With Supplementary List of Possible Veterans.* Syracuse: McDonnell Co., 1913.

County of Onondaga Abstracts. Syracuse: Central New York Genealogical Society, 2000. Abstracts for a range of genealogical records originally published in the quarterly *Tree Talks.*

Daughters of the American Revolution, comps. *New York DAR Genealogical Records Committee Report.* Since 1913 DAR volunteers have transcribed many thousands of unpublished cemetery, church, and town records throughout New York. The reports are at the DAR Library; copies are at the NYSL and the NYPL. The DAR has a searchable name index to all the GRC reports at *http://services.dar.org/Public/DAR_Research/search/?Tab_ID=6.* See Jean Worden's index below for a listing by county of the New York record sets that were transcribed by the DAR before 1998.

Humphryes, Frederick J., and Scott B Chase. *Birth, Marriage, and Death Records of Early Residents of the Skaneateles Area.* Rochester: N.p., 1984.

Kellogg, Minnie L. "Cemetery Inscriptions from Pompey Hill, Onondaga County, N.Y." *NYG&B Record,* vol. 44, no. 1 (1913): 69–87. [NYG&B eLibrary]

Kelly, Arthur C. M. *Index to Tree Talks County Packet: Onondaga County.* Rhinebeck, NY: Kinship, 2002.

Onondaga County, New York, Wills. Sauk Village, IL: Hanson Heritage Publications, 1981.

Scisco, Louis Dow. "Federal Census, 1800—Onondaga County." *NYG&B Record,* vol. 53 (1922) no. 3: 225–234, no. 4: 352–367. [NYG&B eLibrary]

———. "Onondaga County Records." *NYG&B Record,* vol. 30 (1899) no. 4: 237–242; vol. 31 (1900) no 1: 36–38, no. 2: 79–82, no. 3: 170–174, no. 4: 242–247; vol. 32 (1901) no. 1: 25–30, no. 2: 108–111, no. 3: 156–160, no. 4: 204–206; vol. 33 (1902) no. 1: 17–20, no. 2: 76–79, no.3: 76–79, no. 4: 242–246; vol. 34 (1903) no. 1: 44–47, no. 2: 93–97, no. 3: 206–210, no. 4: 263–267; vol. 35 (1904) no. 1: 17–19. [NYG&B eLibrary]

Town of Pompey Historical Society. "Indexes to the New York State Census for 1855 and 1865 for Pompey." Typescript, n.d. Town of Pompey Historical Society, Pompey, NY.

Worden, Jean D. "Book 1, Subject Index." In *Revised Master Index to the New York State Daughters of the American Revolution Genealogical Records Volumes.* Zephyrhills, FL: J. D. Worden, 1998. The Subject Index includes a listing by county of the cemeteries, churches, towns, and other sources of records transcribed by the DAR.

Other Resources

Bannan, Theresa. *Pioneer Irish of Onondaga (about 1776–1847).* New York and London: G. P. Putnam's Sons, 1911.

Barrett, Judy. *Bridgeport; Images of America.* Charleston, South Carolina: Arcadia Publishing, 2014.

Beauchamp, William M. "Major Moses DeWitt and His Relatives in Onondaga County." Typescript, 1918. [FamilySearch.org]

———. *Past and Present of Syracuse and Onondaga County* . . . . 2 vols. New York: S. J. Clarke Publishing, 1908. Includes biographical sketches.

Bruce, Dwight H. *Memorial History of Syracuse, N.Y.: From Its Settlement to the Present Time.* Syracuse, 1891.

———. *Onondaga's Centennial: Gleanings of a Century.* 2 vols. Boston, 1896.

Central New York Library Resources Council. *Guide to Historical Organizations in Central New York.* (Onondaga, Herkimer, Oneida, Madison) Digitally published May 2009. *www.clrc.org/wp-content/uploads/2011/05/DHPHistGuide09b.pdf*

Chase, Franklin H. *Syracuse and its Environs: A History.* New York and Chicago: Lewis Historical Publishing Co., 1924. [Ancestry.com]

Child, Hamilton. *Gazetteer and Business Directory of Onondaga County, N.Y., for 1868–9.* Syracuse, 1868.

Clark, Joshua V. H. *Onondaga or Reminiscences of Earlier and Later Times . . . With Notes on the Several Towns in the County, and Oswego.* 2 vols. Syracuse, 1849.

Clay Historical Association. *Welcome to Clay: Clay's History Compiled in Honor of Its Sesquicentennial (1827–1977).* Clay, NY: Clay Historical Association, 1978.

Clayton, W. W. *History of Onondaga County, New York, 1615–1878, with . . . Biographical Sketches* . . . . Syracuse, 1878.

Collins, George Knapp. *Mortuary Records with Genealogical Notes of the Town of Spafford, Onondaga County, New York.* Syracuse: Onondaga Historical Association, 1917.

———. *Spafford, Onondaga County, New York.* Syracuse: Onondaga Historical Association, 1917.

Cutter, William R. *Genealogical and Family History of Central New York: A Record of the Achievements of Her People in the Making of a Commonwealth and the Building of a Nation.* New York: Lewis Historical Publishing Co., 1912.

Fay, Loren V. *Onondaga County, New York, Genealogical Research Secrets.* Albany: L.V. Fay, 1981.

Galpin, William Freeman. *Central New York, an Inland Empire, Comprising Oneida, Madison, Onondaga, Cayuga, Tompkins, Cortland, Chenango Counties and Their People.* New York: Lewis Historical Publishing Co., 1941. Contains biographies. Index available from Berkshire Family History Association.

Hand, Marcus Christian. *From a Forest to a City: Personal Reminiscences of Syracuse, N.Y.* Syracuse, 1889.

Heffernan, Kathryn. *Nine Mile Country: The History of the Town of Marcellus, New York.* 2nd edition. N.p.: Visual Artis, 1979.

Hoff, Henry B. "Upstate New York Research: Skaneateles, Onondaga County, as an Example." *American Ancestor,* vol. 15, no. 1 (2014).

Jugan, Andy. *Onondaga County Bicentennial, 1794–1994.* Syracuse: Extra Points Unlimited, Onondaga County Department of Parks and Recreation, 1994.

Leslie, Edmund N. *Skaneateles: History of Its Earliest Settlement and Reminiscences of Later Times* . . . . New York: Press of A. H. Kellogg, 1902.

New York Historical Resources Center. *Guide to Historical Resources in Onondaga County, New York, Repositories*. Ithaca, NY: Cornell University, 1985. 3 vols. [*books.FamilySearch.org*]

Maxwell, Mary Ellis. *Among the Hills of Camillus; the Story of a Small Town*. Camillus, NY: n.p., 1952. Reprint, 1976.

Palmer, Jean B. "Researching in Syracuse: Central Library of Onondaga County." *NYG&B Newsletter* (now *New York Researcher*), Spring 2007. Updated May 2011 and published as a Research Aid on *NewYorkFamilyHistory.org*.

Parsons, Israel. *The Centennial History of the Town of Marcellus*. Marcellus, NY: Reed's Printing House, 1878.

Records of the Ithaca College Study Center for Early Religious Life in Western New York, 1978–1981. Division of Rare and Manuscript Collections, Cornell University Library. A description of the holdings for each county is at *http://rmc.library.cornell.edu/eguides/lists/churchlist1.htm*.

Scisco, Louis Dow. *Early History of the Town of Van Buren, Onondaga Co., N.Y.* Baldwinsville, NY, 1895.

Sims, Ralph H. *History of Camillus*. Camillus, NY: Marikar Press, 1999.

Smith, Carroll Earl. *Pioneer Times in the Onondaga Country . . . .* Syracuse: C. W. Bardeen, 1904.

Sneller, Anne Gertrude. *A Vanished World*. Syracuse: Syracuse University Press, 1964.

Sweet, Homer D. L. *Sweet's New Atlas of Onondaga Co., New York: From Recent and Actual Surveys and Records*. New York, 1874.

Syracuse and Onondaga County, New York: Pictorial and Biographical. New York: S. J. Clarke Publishing Co., 1908.

Syracuse-Onondaga County Planning Agency. *Onondaga Landmarks: A Survey of Historic and Architectural Sites in Syracuse and Onondaga County*. Syracuse: Cultural Resources Council of Syracuse & Onondaga County, 1975.

Additional Online Resources

Ancestry.com

There are vast numbers of records on *Ancestry.com* that pertain to people who have lived in New York State. See chapter 16 for a description of *Ancestry.com*'s resources and its partnership with the New York State Archives. A search of the online card catalog by county may reveal lesser known resources that pertain to a locality, such as town records, abstracts, transcriptions, city directories, and local histories.

FamilySearch.org

FamilySearch has extensive collections of New York records, including religious records, which are searchable by name and location, but not by county. The following collections include record images (browsable, but not searchable) that are organized by county:

- "New York, Land Records, 1630–1975." Includes land and property records. *familysearch.org/search/collection/2078654*

- "New York, Probate Records, 1629–1971." Includes wills, letters of administration, and guardianship papers. *familysearch.org/search/collection/1920234*

For both collections, choose the browse option and then select Onondaga to view the available records sets.

A detailed description of *FamilySearch.org* resources is found in chapter 16.

History of the Onondaga County Department of Corrections
www.ongov.net/correction/history.html
Gives brief history of the organization and photographs from the mid-1900s.

NYGenWeb Project: Onondaga County
www.rootsweb.ancestry.com/~nyononda/index.htm
Part of the national, USGenWeb volunteer initiative, the website provides information and resources for county research.

Old Fulton New York Postcards
www.FultonHistory.com
The website provides free access to a vast collection of digitized New York newspapers, including 39 titles for Onondaga County.

Ontario County

Formed January 27, 1789

Parent County   Montgomery

Daughter Counties   Steuben 1796 • Genesee 1802 • Livingston 1821
Monroe 1821 • Wayne 1823 • Yates 1823

County Seat   City of Canandaigua

Major Land Transactions

See chapter 7, Land Records
Phelps and Gorham Purchase 1788

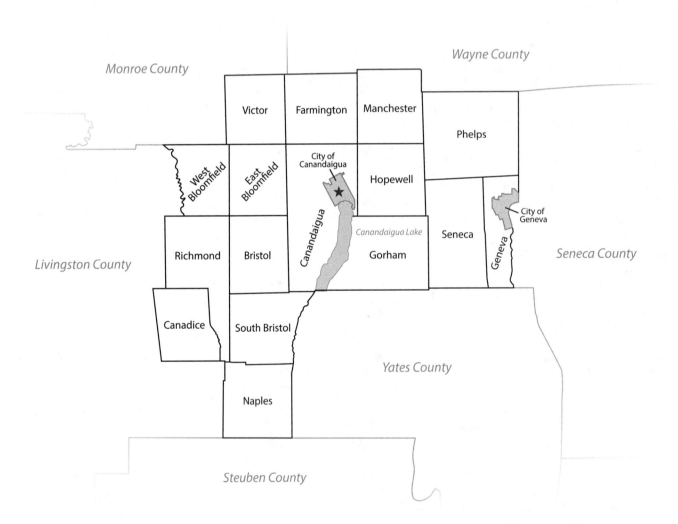

Town Boundary Map

 - County seat

Towns (and Cities)	Villages and other Settlements		Notes
Augusta * In Ontario County 1789–1823 (Named Middlesex 1808–present)			* See Town of Middlesex, Yates County
Avon (named Hartford 1789–1808) * In Ontario County 1789–1821			* See Town of Avon, Livingston County
Benton * In Ontario County 1803–1823			* See Yates County
Bloomfield Name for Town of East Bloomfield 1789–1833			
Boyle Name for Town of Smallwood 1808–1812			
Brighton * In Ontario County 1814–1821			* See Monroe County
Bristol 1788 Settled at Old Indian Orchard 1789 Formed from Montgomery County 1838 Daughter town South Bristol formed 1848 Ceded land to Town of Richmond 1852 Annexed land from Town of Richmond	Bristol Bristol Center Egypt Fletchers Corners Gladding Corner Mayweed Corner Old Indian Orchard Vincent		• Bristol also Baptist Hill • Vincent formerly Muttonville
Burt Name for Town of Manchester 1821–1822			
Canadice 1804 Settlers from Vermont 1829 Formed from Town of Richmond 1836 Ceded land to Town of Richmond	Canadice Corners Canadice Hollow West Canadice Corners		• Canadice Corners also Canadice
Canandaigua (city) * 1913 Village of Canandaigua incorpo- rated as City of Canandaigua			* County seat at Canandaigua from 1789 when county was formed
Canandaigua (town) 1788 Settled 1789 Formed from Montgomery County 1824 Ceded land to Town of Gorham 1913 Daughter city Canandaigua formed from Village of Canandaigua	Academy Arsenal Hill Canandaigua (v) Centerfield Chesire	Four Winds Corners Grange Landing McMillin Corners Padelford	• Village of Canandaigua inc. 1815; became City of Canandaigua in 1913; county seat from 1789
East Bloomfield 1789 Settled; formed as Town of Bloom- field from Montgomery County 1812 Daughter towns Mendon and Victor formed 1833 Name changed to East Bloomfield; daughter town West Bloomfield formed	Bloomfield (v) Brag Village East Bloomfield (v) East Bloomfield Station Griffiths Mills	Holcomb (v) Shepards Mills South Bloomfield Speaker(s) Corners	• Village of Bloomfield inc. 1990, created from East Bloomfield and Holcomb; earlier names still used by local residents • Village of East Bloomfield inc. 1917 be- came part of Village of Bloomfield 1990 • Village of Holcomb inc. 1917 became part of Village of Bloomfield 1990 • Shepards Mills also Shepherds Mills

Towns (and Cities)	Villages and other Settlements		Notes
Easton Name for Town of Gorham 1789–1806			
Farmington 1789 Settled by Quakers from Berkshire, MA; formed as a town from Montgomery County 1821 Daughter town Burt (now Manchester) formed	Blacksmith Corners Brown(s)ville East Farmington Farmbrook Farmington Farmington Station	Farmton Hathaway(s) Ingleside Corner Mertensia Mertensia Station Tuttle	• Brown(s)ville also Norton Mills • Farmington also New Salem and Pumpkin Hook • Mertensia formerly West Farmington
Freeport * In Ontario County 1819–1821			* See Town of Conesus in Livingston County
Geneseo * In Ontario County 1789–1821			* See Livingston County
Geneva (city) 1806 Village of Geneva incorporated in Town of Seneca 1872 Village of Geneva ceded to new Town of Geneva 1898 Village of Geneva incorporated as City of Geneva			
Geneva (town) 1872 Formed from Town of Seneca 1898 Daughter city Geneva formed from Village of Geneva	Billsboro Billsboro Corners Border City	Geneva (v) Lenox Park Pre-Emption	• Village of Geneva inc. 1806 in Town of Seneca; in Town of Geneva from 1872; became City of Geneva 1898
Gorham 1789 Settled at Reeds Corners; formed as Town of Easton from Montgomery County 1806 Name changed to Lincoln 1807 Name changed to Gorham 1822 Daughter town Hopewell formed 1824 Annexed land from Town of Canandaigua	Babbitt Corner Baldwin Corners Cottage City Crystal Beach Gooding Landing Gorham Granger	Green Green(s) Landing Greens Station Mead Corner Reed(s) Corners Rushville (v) Wilson Corners	• Gorham formerly Bethel • Village of Rushville inc. 1866, reincorp. 1876; shared with Town of Potter, Yates County
Groveland * In Ontario County 1812–1821			* See Livingston County
Henrietta * In Ontario County 1818–1821			* See Monroe County
Honeoye Name for Town of Richmond 1808–1815			
Hopewell 1789–90 Settled 1822 Formed from Town of Gorham, Montgomery County	Aloquin Beulah Chapin Ennerdale Ennerdale Station Hopewell	Hopewell Center Hopewell Station Lewis Littleville Ontario County Home	• Aloquin also Lewis Station • Chapin formerly Chapinville
Italy * In Ontario County 1815–1823			* See Yates County

Towns (and Cities)	Villages and other Settlements		Notes
Jerusalem * In Ontario County 1789–1823			* See Yates County
Lima * In Ontario County 1789–1821			* See Livingston County
Lincoln Name for Town of Gorham 1806–1807			
Livonia * In Ontario County 1808–1821			* See Livingston County
Lyons * In Ontario County 1811–1823			* See Wayne County
Manchester 1793 Settled 1821 Formed as Town of Burt from Town of Farmington 1822 Name changed to Manchester	Bunker Hill Clifton Springs (v) Coonsville Gypsum Littleville	Manchester (v) Manchester Center Port Gibson Shortsville (v)	• Village of Clifton Springs inc. 1859; on Phelps town line • Gypsum also Plainsville • Littleville formerly Parkers Mills • Village of Manchester inc. 1892; Hill Cumorah, in Manchester, is where Joseph Smith is said to have discovered the Golden plates which contained the writings later known as the Book of Mormon • Village of Shortsville inc. 1889
Mendon * In Ontario County 1812–1821			* See Monroe County
Middlesex * In Ontario County 1789–1823 (Named Augusta 1789–1808)			* See Yates County
Middletown Name for Town of Naples 1789–1808			
Milo * In Ontario County 1818–1823			* See Yates County
Naples 1779 Settled and known as Watkinstown 1789 Formed as Town of Middletown from Montgomery County 1808 Name changed to Naples 1815 Daughter town Italy formed 1816 Daughter town Springwater formed	Garlinghouse Hunt(s) Hollow Naples (v) Parish Se(a)mans Corners Suttons Settlement West Hollow		• Village of Naples inc. 1894
Northfield Name for Town of Smallwood 1792–1808			
Ontario * In Ontario County 1807–1823			* See Wayne County
Palmyra * In Ontario County 1789–1823			* See Wayne County

Towns (and Cities)	Villages and other Settlements		Notes
Penfield * In Ontario County 1810–1821			* See Monroe County
Perinton * In Ontario County 1812–1821			* See Monroe County
Phelps 1788–90s Part of townships 10 and 11 purchased from Phelps and Gorham; district called Sullivan; early settlers from Columbia County 1796 Formed as Town of Phelps 1823 Land ceded to Town of Lyons, Wayne County	Bennett Clifton Springs (v) Cuddeback Dobbins Corners East Crossing East Harvey East X Five Points Five Waters Corners Fort Hill Harvey Junius Knickerbocker Corner Melvin Hill	Mitchell N. C. Crossing Oaks Corners Orleans Outlet Station Phelps (v) Phelps Junction Phelps Station Pierson Corners Thompson Unionville Warner Corners West Junius	• Village of Clifton Springs inc. 1859; on Manchester town line • Village of Phelps inc. 1855; formerly Vienna, also Woodpecker City • Pierson Corners on Seneca town line
Pittsford * In Ontario County 1814–1821			* See Monroe County
Pittstown Name for Town of Richmond 1796–1808			
Richmond 1789 Settled 1796 Formed as Town of Pittstown 1808 Name changed to Honeoye; daughter town Livonia formed 1815 Name changed to Richmond 1829 Daughter town Canadice formed 1836 Annexed land from Town of Canadice 1848 Annexed land from towns of Bristol and South Bristol 1852 Ceded land to towns of Bristol and South Bristol	Allens Hill Curtis Corner Denison(s) Corner(s) Frost Hollow Honeoye Honeoye Lake Honeoye Park Richmond Center Richmond Mills Willow Beach		
Rush * In Ontario County 1818–1821			* See Monroe County
Seneca 1787 Settlers from New England on site of Indian village Kanadesaga 1793 Formed as a town 1872 Daughter town Geneva formed	Flint Geneva (v) Gorham Station Hall Kanadesaga	Pierson Corners Seneca Seneca Castle Stanley	• Flint formerly Flint Creek • Village of Geneva inc. 1806; in Town of Geneva after 1872; became City of Geneva 1898 • Hall formerly Halls Corners • Pierson Corners on Phelps town line • Seneca Castle also Castleton • Stanley formerly Stanleys Corners

Towns (and Cities)	Villages and other Settlements		Notes
Smallwood 1792–1814 1792 District of Northfield formed from seven townships northeast of Genesee River 1796 District of Northfield was organized as Town of Northfield 1808 Town of Northfield renamed Boyle 1810 Daughter town Penfield formed 1812 Daughter town Perinton formed 1813 Town of Boyle renamed Smallwood 1814 Smallwood dissolved and divided into towns of Brighton and Pittsford			
Sodus * In Ontario County 1789–1823			* See Wayne County
South Bristol 1789 Settlers from Massachusetts at Wilburs Point 1838 Formed from Town of Bristol 1848 Ceded land to Town of Richmond 1852 Annexed land from Town of Richmond	Boswells Corners Bristol Springs Cold Spring Covel Corners Frost Hill Gulick	Hickspoint Powell Hill Seneca Point South Bristol Woodville	• Seneca Point formerly Wilders Point
Sparta * In Ontario County 1789–1821			* See Livingston County
Springwater * In Ontario County 1816–1821			* See Livingston County
Victor 1789 Settlers from Stockbridge, MA 1812 Formed from Town of Bloomfield (now East Bloomfield)	Boughton Hill East Victor Fishers Fishers Station Fisherville Station Motts Corner(s)	Railroad Mills Thompson Corners Turners Hill Victor (v) Victor Station	• East Victor formerly Freedom and Scudderville • Village of Victor inc. 1879
Watkinstown Name for Town of Naples 1779–1789			
West Bloomfield 1789 Settled 1833 Formed from Town of East Bloomfieldf	Bush Corner Factory Hollow Ionia	North Bloomfield West Bloomfield West Bloomfield Station	• Iona formerly Millers Corners and Taylor(s)ville
Williamson * In Ontario County 1802–1823			* See Wayne County

NEW YORK STATE CENSUS RECORDS

See also chapter 3, Census Records

County originals at Ontario County Department of Records, Archives, and Information Management Services: 1845*, 1855*, 1865*, 1875, 1892, 1905, 1915, 1925 (1825 and 1835 are lost)

State originals at the NYSA: 1915, 1925

Microfilm at the FHL, NYPL, and NYSL; many years are online at *FamilySearch.org* and *Ancestry.com*.

* 1845 census is lost with the exception of schedules for the Town of Canandaigua. For online census index for 1845 (Canandaigua only), 1855, and 1865, see Ontario County Department of Records in Abstracts, Indexes & Transcriptions below.

NATIONAL/STATEWIDE REPOSITORIES & RESOURCES

See chapter 16

COUNTYWIDE REPOSITORIES & RESOURCES

Ontario County Clerk

20 Ontario Street • Canandaigua, NY 14424 • (585) 396-4200
www.co.ontario.ny.us

Website offers searchable index of land records and court filings. See holdings of the Ontario County Records and Archives Center below.

Ontario County – City, Town, and Village Clerks

Birth, marriage, and death records are maintained by the clerk of the municipality in which the event occurred; see Introduction to County Guides for details of other records which may also be held by municipal clerks. The Geneva City Clerk has cemetery records for Washington and Glenwood Cemeteries. For contact information, see the directory at *www.co.ontario.ny.us*.

Ontario County Surrogate's Court

27 North Main Street • Canandaigua, NY 14424 • (585) 396-4055
www.nycourts.gov/courts/7jd/courts/surrogates

Probate records 1789–1975 are held at the Ontario County Records and Archives Center. See also chapter 6, Probate Records.

Ontario County Records and Archives Center (Department of Records, Archives, and Information Management Services)

3051 County Complex Drive • Canandaigua, NY 14424
(585) 396-4376 • *www.raims.com*

Holdings include federal censuses 1790–1930 and New York state censuses 1845 (Canandaigua only), 1855–1925, inclusive. Online census indexes for 1845 (Canandaigua only), 1850, 1855, 1860, 1865, 1870, 1875, 1892. Other holdings include court records (jury lists 1800–1855, list of indentures 1827–1907, index to court records 1850–1899, and surrogate court records 1789–1965), civil commissions, land records 1789–1845, mortgages 1830–1870, marriage records 1908–1935, military records (Revolutionary and Civil Wars), naturalization records 1803–1956, probate and estate records 1789–1975, and town vital records; all of these records are indexed on the RAIMS website.

Ontario County Public Libraries

Ontario is part of the Pioneer Library System; see *www.pls-net.org* to access each library. Many hold genealogy and local history collections. Also see listing below for Geneva Public Library.

Ontario County Historical Society and Museum

55 North Main Street • Canandaigua, NY 14424 • (585) 394-4975
Email: ochs@ochs.org • *www.ochs.org*

Books and manuscripts; local histories, genealogies, and surname files; cemetery, church, and census materials; local directories; gazetteers and maps; ledgers and minute books; photographs, ephemera, and scrapbooks; vital statistics and records; and information on local military history, historic homes, businesses, and children's homes. A more detailed list of holdings is available on the Society's website. The Society will take research requests for a fee. Quarterly newsletter, the *Chronicle*, 1971–present.

Ontario County Historian

3051 County Complex Drive • Canandaigua, NY 14424
(716) 396-4034 • *www.co.ontario.ny.us/index.aspx?nid=105*

Website contains cemetery list and selected veteran burials. Monthly newsletter.

Ontario County – All Municipal Historians

While not authorized to answer genealogical inquiries, city, town, and village historians can provide valuable historical information and research advice; some maintain collections and webpages which may include transcribed records, local histories, and other genealogical material. For contact information, see *www.co.ontario.ny.us*, *http://ny-ontariocounty.civicplus.com/BusinessDirectoryII.aspx?lngBusinessCategoryID=36*, or the Association of Public Historians of New York State at *www.aphnys.org*.

Ontario County Genealogical Society

55 North Main Street • Canandaigua, NY 14424
(585) 394-4975 • *www.ocgsny.net*

The Society's meetings are held at the Ontario Historical Society and Museum. The Society does not take research requests (however, the Ontario County Historical Society does; see above). It holds regular programs on Ontario County genealogical research and tours of local cemeteries.

REGIONAL REPOSITORIES & RESOURCES

Hobart and William Smith Colleges: Warren Hunting Smith Library: Archives and Special Collections

300 Pulteney Street • Geneva, NY 14456 • (315) 781-3009
http://library.hws.edu/archives

Archives include family papers and genealogies.

Milne Library at SUNY Geneseo: Special Collections: Genesee Valley Historical Collection

See listing in Livingston County Guide

LOCAL REPOSITORIES & RESOURCES

Alphabetized by location

East Bloomfield Historical Society

8 South Avenue • PO Box 212 • East Bloomfield, NY 14443
(585) 657-7244 • Email: director@ebhs1838.org • *www.ebhs1838.org*

Includes genealogy records of residents from the town.

Geneva Historical Society and Museum

543 South Main Street • Geneva, NY 14456 • (315) 789-5151
Email: info@genevahistoricalsociety.com • *www.genevahistoricalsociety.com*

The Society maintains a museum, archives, and research library. Holdings include family files, church records, tax rolls, cemetery indexes, school and club records, newspapers on microfilm with indexes 1806–1914, city directories 1857–1999, federal and state census indexes 1790–1930, index to city hall vital records 1882–1957, funeral home records 1889–1985, monument ledgers 1913–1942, high school yearbooks, and indexes to the 1876 and 1893 published histories of Ontario County.

Geneva Public Library:
Local History and Genealogy Collection
244 Main Street • Geneva, NY 14456 • (315) 789-5303
Email: genevaref@pls-net.org • *http://genevapubliclibrary.net*

Books, histories, atlases, city directories, newspapers 1809–1977, and more documenting the history of Geneva and the surrounding area 1788–present.

Town of Gorham Historical Society and Museum
Museum: Gorham Free Library • 2264 State Route 245
Gorham, NY 14461 • *Society*: PO Box 176 • Gorham, NY 14461
Email: ghs@gorhamnyhistoricalsociety.org
www.gorhamnyhistoricalsociety.org

The Society's museum is located in the Gorham Free Library and includes historic maps and photographs. Quarterly newsletter, *New Age*.

Phelps Historical Society and Howe House Museum
66 Main Street • Phelps, NY 14532 • (315) 548-4940
Email: histsoc@fltg.net • *www.phelpsny.com/historical-society*

The Society will conduct local genealogy and cemetery research upon request.

SELECTED PRINT & ONLINE RESOURCES

Below is a selection of resources relevant for research in this county. The list is representative, not exhaustive. Additional titles—particularly of abstracts, indexes, transcriptions, and local histories—are available; consult the introduction to Part Two for further information. For guidance on how to identify and locate community directories and local newspapers, see chapter 11, City Directories, and chapter 12, Newspapers, in Part One of this book.

Abstracts, Indexes & Transcriptions

Burnisky, David L. *The Personalities of Melvin Hill Cemetery, Phelps, Ontario County, New York*. Bowie, MD: Heritage Books, 1995.

County of Ontario Abstracts. Syracuse: Central New York Genealogical Society, 2000. Abstracts for a range of genealogical records originally published in the quarterly *Tree Talks*.

Daughters of the American Revolution, comps. *New York DAR Genealogical Records Committee Report*. Since 1913 DAR volunteers have transcribed many thousands of unpublished cemetery, church, and town records throughout New York. The reports are at the DAR Library; copies are at the NYSL and the NYPL. The DAR has a searchable name index to all the GRC reports at *http://services.dar.org/Public/DAR_Research/search/?Tab_ID=6*. See Jean Worden's index below for a listing by county of the New York record sets that were transcribed by the DAR before 1998.

Grantor and Grantee Deeds Index, 1789–1958, Ontario County, NY. Microfilm of original records in the Ontario County Courthouse, Canandaigua, NY. Salt Lake City: Reproduction Systems for the Genealogical Society of Utah, 1969.

Kelly, Arthur C. M. *Index to Tree Talks County Packet: Ontario County*. Rhinebeck, NY: Kinship, 2002.

Naukam, Lawrence W. *Ontario County, NY, Cemetery Record Index*. Originally published privately in 1984 under title: *Union List of Cemetery Records Holdings, Ontario County, NY*. Includes index. Rochester: Rochester Genealogical Society, 1987.

Ontario County Records and Archives Center. "Historical Census Records for Ontario County." Census indexes, including 1845 (Canadaigua only), 1855, and 1865, are accessible at *http://ny-ontariocounty.civicplus.com/index.aspx?nid=612*.

———. *Inventory to the Naturalization Records of the Ontario County Clerk, 1803–1932*. Canandaigua, NY: Ontario County Records Center and Archives, 1988. An online index is at *http://ny-ontariocounty.civicplus.com/index.aspx?NID=370*.

Perinton Historical Society, comp. "Inscriptions from Farmington Cemetery (Friends Cemetery)." Typescript, 1950. New York State Library. [*Ancestry.com*]

Pierce, Preston E. *Index to the Burial Places of Revolutionary Patriots in and around Ontario County, New York*. Ontario County, NY: Ontario County Historian, Division of Human Services, 1986.

Wiles, Harriett M. "Abstract of Wills from Ontario County, New York, in the Courthouse, Canandaigua, NY, 1794–1812, Books I–IV." Typescript, 1949. NYPL, New York.

———. "Inscriptions Copied from Headstones in a Cemetery at Port Gibson, Ontario County, New York." Typescript, 1941. NYPL, New York.

———. "Inscriptions from Headstones in Washington Street Cemetery, Geneva, Ontario County, New York." Typescript, 1941. NYPL, New York.

Worden, Jean D. "Book 1, Subject Index." In *Revised Master Index to the New York State Daughters of the American Revolution Genealogical Records Volumes*. Zephyrhills, FL: J. D. Worden, 1998. The Subject Index includes a listing by county of the cemeteries, churches, towns, and other sources of records transcribed by the DAR.

Other Resources

Aldrich, Lewis C. *History of Ontario County, New York: With Illustrations and Family Sketches of Some of the Prominent Men and Families*. Syracuse, 1893.

Child, Hamilton. *Gazetteer and Business Directory of Ontario County, NY, for 1867–8*. Syracuse, 1867.

Childs, Robert E. *A History of the Town of Victor, Ontario County, New York: 1656–1898*. Canandaigua, NY, 1898.

Clark, Louis M. *A Book of Facts about the City of Canandaigua, Ontario County, New York, 1789–1991*. Canandaigua, NY: Ontario County Historical Society, 1991.

Foley, Janet W. *Early Settlers of New York State: Their Ancestors and Descendants*. 9 vols. Akron, NY: 1934–1942. Reprint, 2 vols. Baltimore, Genealogical Publishing Co., 1993.

Granger, J. Albert. *A History of (Early) Canandaigua*. Canandaigua, NY: Ontario County Historical Society, 1905.

Harford, Lucille M. *The Country Cousin: A Chronicle of the Town of Geneva, Ontario County, New York*. Newark, NY: Vanderbook Press, 1976.

McIntosh, W. H. *History of Ontario Co., NY: With Illustrations Descriptive of Its Scenery, Palatial Residences, Public Buildings, Fine Blocks, and Important Manufactories, with Original Sketches by Artists of the Highest Ability.* Ovid, NY: W. E. Morrison, 1976.

Milliken, Charles F. *A History of Ontario County, New York, and Its People.* 2 vols. New York: Lewis Historical Publishing Co., 1911.

New Century Atlas of Ontario County New York, with Farm Records. Philadelphia: Century Map Co., 1904.

New York Historical Resources Center. *Guide to Historical Resources in Ontario County, New York, Repositories.* Ithaca, NY: Cornell University, 1982. [*books.FamilySearch.org*]

Nichols, Beach. *Atlas of Ontario County, New York, from Actual Surveys.* Philadelphia, 1873.

Pierce, Preston E. *Western New York Oral History Collections in Livingston County, Monroe County, Ontario County, Wayne County, Wyoming County.* Fairport, NY: Rochester Regional Library Council, 2009. [*http://rrlc.org/wp-content/uploads/2013/02/dhp_Oral-History-Inventory.pdf*]

Records of the Ithaca College Study Center for Early Religious Life in Western New York, 1978–1981. Division of Rare and Manuscript Collections, Cornell University Library. A description of the holdings for each county is at *http://rmc.library.cornell.edu/eguides/lists/churchlist1.htm.*

Swartout, Barbara C. *Building Canandaigua: A Collection.* Rochester, NY: Ontario County Historical Society, 1997.

Additional Online Resources

Ancestry.com

There are vast numbers of records on *Ancestry.com* that pertain to people who have lived in New York State. See chapter 16 for a description of *Ancestry.com*'s resources and its partnership with the New York State Archives. A search of the online card catalog by county may reveal lesser known resources that pertain to a locality, such as town records, abstracts, transcriptions, city directories, and local histories.

Burr Cook Genealogy: Maps, Photographs, and Records of Ontario County

www.burrcook.com/history/ontario.htm

Includes cemetery transcriptions, directories, maps, journals, and links to Ontario County genealogy resources.

FamilySearch.org

FamilySearch has extensive collections of New York records, including religious records, which are searchable by name and location, but not by county. The following collections include record images (browsable, but not searchable) that are organized by county:

- "New York, Land Records, 1630–1975." Includes land and property records. *familysearch.org/search/collection/2078654*

- "New York, Probate Records, 1629–1971." Includes wills, letters of administration, and guardianship papers. *familysearch.org/search/collection/1920234*

For both collections, choose the browse option and then select Ontario to view the available records sets.

A detailed description of *FamilySearch.org* resources is found in chapter 16.

New York Heritage Digital Collections: New York State Newspaper Project

www.nyheritage.org/newspapers

The website provides links to digital newspapers collections in 26 counties (currently) made accessible through New York Heritage, New York State Historic Newspapers, HRVH Historical Newspapers, and other providers.

NYGenWeb Project: Ontario County

www.ontario.nygenweb.net

Part of the national, USGenWeb volunteer initiative, the website provides information and resources for county research.

Old Fulton New York Postcards

www.FultonHistory.com

The website provides free access to a vast collection of digitized New York newspapers, including 16 titles for Ontario County.

Orange County

Formed November 1, 1683

Parent County   Original county
Daughter County   Rockland 1798
County Seat   Village of Goshen

Major Land Transactions
See table in chapter 7, Land Records
Wawayanda Patent 1703
Minisink Patent 1704
Chesecock Patent 1707

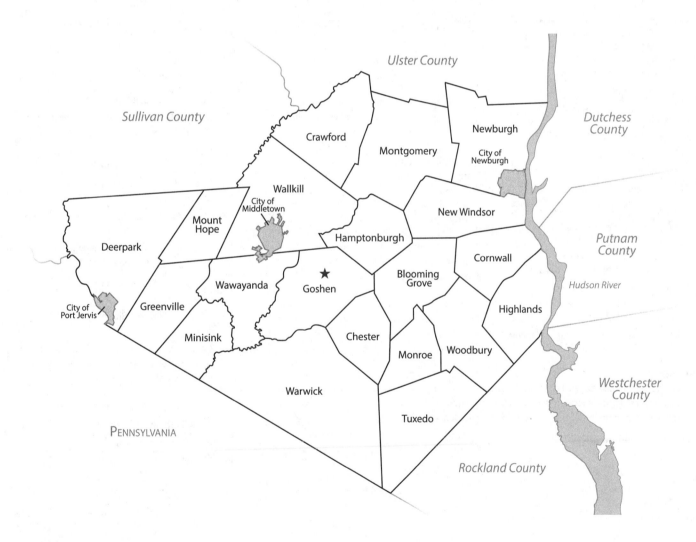

Town Boundary Map
★ - County seat

Towns (and Cities)	Villages and other Settlements		Notes
Blooming Grove 1735 Settled 1799 Formed from Town of Cornwall 1830 Daughter town Hamptonburgh formed 1845 Daughter town Chester formed	Beaverdam Lake Blooming Grove Blooming Grove Station Bull Mine Craig(s)ville Farmingdale Hope Chapel Merriewold Lake Mountain Lodge Park	Oxford Salisbury Mills Slatterlys Mills South Blooming Grove (v) Tomahawk Lake Washington Washingtonville (v) West Craigville West Craigville Station	• Oxford formerly Oxford Depot • Salisbury Mills on Cornwall town line • Village of South Blooming Grove inc. 2006 • Village of Washingtonville inc. 1895; formerly Little York and Matthews Field
Calhoun Name for Town of Mount Hope 1825–1833			
Chesecocks Name for Town of Monroe 1799–1801			
Chester 1716 Settlers from Long Island at Gray Court 1845 Formed from towns of Blooming Grove, Goshen, Monroe, and Warwick	Camp Laguardia Chester (v) East Chester Gray Court Station Greycourt	Salem Sugarloaf Surrey Meadows Walton Park West Chester	• Village of Chester inc. 1892; shared with Town of Goshen • Salem was on Warwick town line • Walton Park on Monroe town line
Clarkstown * In Orange County 1791–1798			* See Rockland County
Cornwall Part of Evans and Chesecock patents 1714 Included in Goshen Precinct 1720 Settled 1764 Formed as New Cornwall Precinct from Goshen Precinct 1788 Recognized as Town of New Cornwall by the State of New York 1797 Name changed to Cornwall 1799 Daughter towns Blooming Grove and Chesecocks (now Monroe) formed 1872 Daughter town Highlands formed	Bethlehem Buttermilk Falls Canterbury Canterbury Estates Canterbury Knolls Cornwall Heights Cornwall Landing Cornwall Oars Cornwall-on-Hudson (v) Cornwall Station Cornwall Woolen Mills Cozens Landing Endorlin Firthcliffe Firthcliffe Heights Fort Montgomery Highland Falls	Highlandville Houghton Farm Idlewild Iona Island Ketchamtown Meadowbrook Mountainville Orr(s) Mill(s) Riverside Roeville Salisbury Salisbury Mills Townsville West Cornwall West Cornwall Station West Point Willisville	• Buttermilk Falls in Town of Highlands after 1872 • Village of Cornwall-on-Hudson inc. 1884; formerly Cornwall, name changed 1978 • Firthcliffe also Montana; on New Windsor town line • Firthcliffe Heights on New Windsor town line • Fort Montgomery and Highland Falls in Town of Highlands after 1872 • Riverside also The Hollow and The Landing • Salisbury Mills on Blooming Grove town line • West Point United States Military Academy established in 1802; in Town of Highlands after 1872
Crawford Settled before 1779 1823 Formed from Town of Montgomery	Bullville Camp Maple Collabar Goldin Park Grahams Church Hopewell	Pine Bush Red Mills Searsville Thompson Ridge Union School Area Van Keuren	• Collabar formerly Collaburgh • Pine Bush also Crawford • Searsville also Searsburg • Thompson Ridge also Thomas Ridge

Towns (and Cities)	Villages and other Settlements		Notes
Deerpark 1690 Settled 1798 Formed from Town of Mamakating, Ulster County, and Town of Minisink * 1825 Daughter town Calhoun (now Mount Hope) formed 1907 Daughter city Port Jervis formed from Village of Port Jervis	Bolton Brooklyn Bushkill Cahoonzie Carpenters Point Cuddebackville Germantown Godeffroy Gumaers Huguenot Lower Neighborhood Magaghkemeck	Meyers Grove Paradise Port Clinton Port Jervis (v) Port Orange Prospect Hill Rio Rose(s) Point Shin Hollow Sparrow Bush Westbrookville	* Town of Mamakating now in Sullivan County; land annexed from Minisink known as Lower Neighborhood • Cuddebackville is located in the old "Neighborhood of Magaghkemeck" which dates from the early 1700s • Magaghkemeck also Machachemeck • Village of Port Jervis inc. 1853, became City of Port Jervis in 1907 • Rio formerly Quarry Hill • Sparrow Bush also Honesville and Sparrowbush
Goshen 1703 Included in Wawayanda Patent 1714 Included in Goshen Precinct, later formed as Goshen township 1764 Daughter precinct New Cornwall (now Cornwall) formed 1788 Recognized as a town by the State of New York; daughter towns Minisink and Warwick formed 1830 Daughter town Hamptonburgh formed 1845 Daughter town Chester formed	Big Island Cedarcrest Chester (v) County Farm Durlandville Finnegans Corner Florida (v) Goshen (v) Goshen Hills	Howells Jessup Switch Kipps Mapes Corners Maple Island Orange Farm Station Otter Kill Pellets Island Randelville	• Big Island on Warwick town line • Village of Chester inc. 1892; shared with Town of Chester • Village of Florida inc. 1946; shared with Town of Warwick • Village of Goshen inc. 1809; county seat at Goshen 1727–present • Kipps in Town of Hamptonburgh from 1830 • Pellets Island on Wawayanda town line
Greenville 1720–30 Settled 1853 Formed from Town of Minisink	Bushville Center Point Greenville Logtown	Smith(s) Corners Wood Woodsville	• Hamlet of Greenville also Minisink
Hamptonburg(h) 1719–20 Settled 1830 Formed from towns of Blooming Grove, Goshen, Montgomery, New Windsor, and Wallkill	Burnside Campbell Hall Campbell Hall Junction Deckers Four Corners Girade Hamptonburgh Kipps	LaGrange Lincolndale Maybrook (v) Neelytown Otter Kill Paradise Purgatory Stony Ford	• Burnside also Bushkirks Mills, Hunting Grove, and Otterville • Kipps in Town of Goshen before 1830 • LaGrange and Stony Ford on Wallkill town line • Village of Maybrook inc. 1925; shared with Town of Montgomery • Neelytown on Montgomery town line
Haverstraw * In Orange County 1719–1798			* See Rockland County
Highlands 1872 Formed from Town of Cornwall	Buttermilk Falls Cranson Station Forest of Dean Fort Montgomery Highland Falls (v)	Queensboro West Grove West Point West Point Station	• Buttermilk Falls and Fort Montgomery in Town of Cornwall before 1872 • Village of Highland Falls inc. 1906; in Town of Cornwall before 1872 • Queensboro was on Woodbury town line • West Point United States Military Academy established in 1802, in Town of Cornwall before 1872

Towns (and Cities)	Villages and other Settlements		Notes
Middletown (city) 1848 Village of Middletown incorporated in Town of Wallkill 1888 Village incorporated as City of Middletown 1968 Annexed Village of Amchir from Town of Wawayanda	Amchir (v)		• Amchir was Village of Amchir in Town of Wawayanda before 1968, now a neighborhood in City of Middletown
Minisink 1703 Included in Wawayanda Patent 1704 Minisink Patent granted 1788 Formed as a town from Town of Goshen 1798 Daughter town Deerpark formed 1825 Daughter town Calhoun (now Mount Hope) formed 1849 Daughter town Wawayanda formed 1853 Daughter town Greenville formed	Drowned Lands Gardner(s)ville Johnsons Meadville Millsburg(h) Rutgers Station Unionville (v) Waterloo Mills West Town		• Drowned Lands on Warwick town line • Gardner(s)ville also Garnerville; on Wawayanda town line • Johnsons also Smith Village • Millsburg(h) formerly Racine, also Wells Corner; on Wawayanda town line • Village of Unionville inc. 1871 • West Town also Westtown
Monroe 1707 Part of Chesecock Patent 1742 Settled 1799 Formed as Town of Chesecocks from Town of Cornwall 1801 Name changed to Southfield 1808 Name changed to Monroe 1845 Daughter town Chester formed 1863 Daughter town Woodbury formed 1865 Woodbury dissolved and returned to Monroe 1889 Daughter town Woodbury recreated 1890 Daughter town Tuxedo formed	Augusta Central Valley Eagle Valley Greenwood Greenwood Iron Works Greenwood Lake Harriman (v) Helm(s)burg(h) Highland Mills Kiryas Joel (v) Lake Sapphire Lower Smith Clove Marycrest Mombasha Lake Monroe (v) Monroe Works	Mountain House Newburgh Junction Queensborough Round Lake Seamanville Smiths Clove Southfield(s) Southfields Station Southfield Works Upper Village Walton Park Woodbury Woodbury Clove Woodbury Falls Woodbury Meadows	• Augusta in Town of Tuxedo from 1890 • Central Valley in Town of Woodbury from 1889 • Eagle Valley, Greenwood Iron Works, and Helm(s)burg(h) in Town of Tuxedo from 1890 • Village of Harriman inc. 1914; shared with Town of Woodbury; also called Centerville and Turner before 1914 • Village of Kiryas Joel inc. 1977 • Village of Monroe inc. 1894 • Newburgh Junction on Woodbury town line • Southfield(s) in Town of Tuxedo from 1890 • Walton Park on Chester town line • Woodbury (now Village of Woodbury) and Woodbury Falls in Town of Woodbury from 1889 • Woodbury Meadows on Woodbury town line
Montgomery 1694 Part of Evans Patent 1708 New land patents begin to be issued for former Evans Patent land * 1714 Included in Shawangunk Precinct 1743 Part of Wallkill Precinct 1772 Hanover Precinct formed from Wallkill Precinct in Ulster County 1782 Name changed to Montgomery Precinct 1788 Recognized as a town in Ulster County by the State of New York	Allard(s) Corners Beaver Dam Beaver Dams Station Berea Coldenham East Walden East Walden Station Goodwill Honey Pot Kaisertown Lake Osiris Colony Maybrook (v)	Maybrook Junction Mitchells Corners Momson Heights Montgomery (v) Morrison Heights Neelytown Scotts Corner(s) Scott Town Sloats Corners St. Andrew(s) Talbot Corners Walden (v)	∗ Evans Patent affected by Act for Breaking and Annulling Several Extravagant Grants of Land passed May 16, 1699 • Coldenham on Newburgh town line • Honey Pot on Wallkill town line • Kaisertown also Keisertown • Village of Maybrook inc. 1925; shared with Town of Hamptonburgh • Village of Montgomery (formerly Wards Bridge) formed by special charter 1810; incorporated by Village Law 1933 • Neelytown on Hamptonburgh town line • Village of Walden inc. 1855

(Montgomery continued on next page)

Towns (and Cities)	Villages and other Settlements		Notes
Montgomery (continued) 1798 Transferred to Orange County 1823 Daughter town Crawford formed 1830 Daughter town Hamptonburgh formed			
Mount Hope Settled pre-Revolution 1825 Formed as Town of Calhoun from towns of Deerpark, Minisink, and Wallkill 1833 Name changed to Mount Hope	Finchville Guymard Guymard Station Howells	Mount Hope New Vernon Otisville (v)	• Howells also Howells Depot; on Wallkill town line • Village of Otisville inc. 1921
Newburgh (city) * 1800 Village of Newburgh incorporated in Town of Newburgh 1865 Village inc. as City of Newburgh			* 1798–1970 Newburgh and Goshen shared the county seat
Newburgh (town) Part of Evans Patent and Highlands Precinct 1708–09 Settled by German Palatines 1762 Formed as Newburgh Precinct from Precinct of the Highlands in Ulster County 1772 Daughter precinct New Marlborough formed in Ulster County 1788 Recognized as a town in Ulster County by the State of New York 1798 Transferred to Orange County 1865 Daughter city Newburgh formed from Village of Newburgh	Balmville Belknaps Ridge Candlestick Hill Cedar Cliff Cedar Hill Coldenham Cronomer Valley DuBois Mills DuPont Park East Coldenham East Leptondale Fostertown Fostertown Heights Frozen Ridge Gardnertown Gidneytown Glenwood Park Hampton HyVue Terrace	Leptondale Meadow Hill Middle Hope Newburgh (v) Newburgh Gardens New Mills Orange Lake Powder Mills Rocky Forest Roseton Savilton Sherwood Forest The Dans Kamer The Glebe Union Grove Wedgewood Park West Newburgh Winona Lake	• Cedar Cliff also Cedarcliff • Coldenham on Montgomery town line • Leptondale also Liptondale and Luptondale • Middle Hope formerly Middletown • Village of Newburgh inc 1800; became City of Newburgh in 1865; from 1798 to 1970 Newburgh and Goshen shared county seat • Orange Lake formerly Moosepond • Savilton also Savil and Saville; formerly Rossville
New Cornwall Name for Town of Cornwall 1788–1797			
New Hampstead * In Orange County 1791–1798			* Called Hampstead 1797–1828; see Town of Ramapo in Rockland County
New Windsor Part of Highlands Precinct 1685–86 Settled by Scots at Plum Point 1762 Formed as New Windsor Precinct from Precinct of the Highlands in Ulster County 1788 Recognized as a town in Ulster County by the State of New York 1798 Transferred to Orange County 1830 Daughter town Hamptonburgh formed	Denniston Firthcliffe Firthcliffe Heights Lacey Field Little Britain Moodna Mortonville New Windsor New Windsor Station	Plum Point Ragville Rocklet Rock Tavern Vails Gate Vails Gate Junction Washington Lake Washington Square	• Firthcliffe also Montana; on Cornwall town line • Firthcliffe Heights on Cornwall town line • Moodna also Orangeville • Washington Square also The Square

Towns (and Cities)	Villages and other Settlements		Notes
Orangetown * In Orange County 1686–1798			∗ See Rockland County
Port Jervis (city) 1853 Village of Port Jervis incorporated in Town of Deerpark 1907 Village incorporated as City of Port Jervis			
Southfield Name for Town of Monroe 1801–1808			
Tuxedo 1890 Formed from Town of Monroe	Arden Arden House Augusta Eagle Valley Greenwood Iron Works Helmburg Indian Hill	Laurel Ridge Maplebrook Scottminis Southfield(s) Tuxedo Park (v) Tuxedo Station	• Augusta, Eagle Valley, Greenwood Iron Works, Helmburg, and Southfield(s) in Town of Monroe before 1890 • Village of Tuxedo Park inc. 1952
Wallkill Part of Minisink Patent 1743 Wallkill Precinct formed in Ulster County 1772 Daughter precinct Hanover (now Montgomery) formed 1788 Recognized as a town in Ulster County by the State of New York 1798 Transferred to Orange County 1825 Daughter town Calhoun (now Mount Hope) formed 1830 Daughter town Hamptonburgh formed 1888 Daughter city Middletown formed from Village of Middletown	Baileyville Bull Hack Circleville Crawford Junction Crystal Run Davistown East Middletown Fair Oaks Guinea Honey Pot Howells LaGrange Lockwoods Maple Glen Mechanicstown Michigan Michigan Corners	Middletown (v) Midway Park Millburn Millsburg Phil(l)ipsburg Pierce Valley Pilgrim Corners Pocatello Purdys (Station) Rockville Scotchtown Silver Lake Stony Ford Summit Grove Van Burenville Washington Heights	• Crystal Run also Crystalrun • Guinea settled by former slaves • Honey Pot on Montgomery town line • Howells also Howells Depot; on Mount Hope town line • LaGrange on Hamptonburgh town line • Mechanicstown also Mechanic Town • Village of Middletown (also South Middletown) inc. 1912, became City of Middletown 1888 • Stony Ford on Hamptonburgh town line
Warwick Part of Wawayanda Patent 1714 Included in Goshen Precinct 1719 First deed of sale in the town, area already known as Warwick 1788 Formed as a town from Town of Goshen 1845 Daughter town Chester formed	Amity Bellvale Big Island Blooms Corners Drowned Lands Durland Dutch Hollow Edenville Florida (v) Forest Knolls Furnace Brook Greenwood Lake (v) Indian Park Lakeville Lawton Liberty Corners Little York Mount Peter New Milford	Newport Pine Island Quaker Creek Salem Sanfordville Snufftown Sterling Forest Sterling Mines Sterling Works Stone Bridge Warwick (v) West Shore Greenwood Lake Wickham Knolls Wickham Lake Wickham Village Wilcox Wisner	• Big Island on Goshen town line • Drowned Lands on Minisink town line • Edenville formerly Postville • Village of Florida inc. 1946; shared with Town of Goshen • Village of Greenwood Lake inc. 1924 • Lakeville also Lake • Lawton also Lake Station • Salem was on Chester town line • Village of Warwick inc. 1867 • Wisner also Wisner Lake

Towns (and Cities)	Villages and other Settlements		Notes
Wawayanda Settled before 1700 1849 Formed from Town of Minisink 1968 Village of Amchir ceded to City of Middleton	Amchir (v) Breeze Hill Denton Gardner(s)ville Hampton Haunted House Kirbytown Millsburg(h)	New Hampton Pellets Island Ridgebury Slate Hill South Centerville Wawayanda Station Wells Corners	• Village of Amchir inc. 1964, dissolved and ceded to City of Middleton 1968 • Denton formerly The Outlet • Gardner(s)ville also Garnerville; on Minisink town line • Millsburgh formerly Racine; also Wells Corner; on Minisink town line • Pellets Island on Goshen town line • Slate Hill also Brookfield • South Centerville formerly Centerville
Woodbury 1863 Formed from Town of Monroe 1865 Town dissolved and returned to Monroe 1889 Town reestablished	Baileytown Central Valley Harriman (v) Highland Lake Estates Highland Mills Lebanon Newburgh Junction Queensboro Silver Maples Thevenet Hall Woodbury (v) Woodbury Falls Woodbury Meadows Woodbury Station		• Central Valley in Town of Monroe before 1889 • Village of Harriman inc. 1914; shared with Town of Monroe • Highland Mills is site of Smith Clove Quaker Meeting House built 1802 • Newburgh Junction on Monroe town line • Queensboro was on Highlands town line • Village of Woodbury inc. 2006; in Town of Monroe before 1889 • Woodbury Falls in Town of Monroe before 1889 • Woodbury Meadows on Monroe town line

Notes on Orange County Seat

1683–1702 Administered from New York County

1702–1727 County seat at Tappantown

1727–1798 Goshen shared county seat with Tappantown (Tappantown in Town of Orangetown, Rockland County after 1798)

1798–1970 Goshen shared county seat with Newburgh

1970–present Goshen sole county seat

NEW YORK STATE CENSUS RECORDS

See also chapter 3, Census Records

County originals at Orange County Courthouse: 1825, 1835, 1845, 1855, 1865*, 1875*, 1915, 1925 (1892 and 1905 are lost)

State originals at the NYSA: 1915, 1925

Microfilm at the FHL, NYPL, and NYSL; many years are online at *FamilySearch.org* and *Ancestry.com*.

* For an indexed compilation of marriages and deaths from the 1865 and 1875, censuses see Burrows in Abstracts, Indexes & Transcriptions

NATIONAL/STATEWIDE REPOSITORIES & RESOURCES

See chapter 16

COUNTYWIDE REPOSITORIES & RESOURCES

Orange County Clerk

The Parry Building • 4 Glenmere Cove Road • Goshen, NY 10924 (845) 291-2690 • *www.co.orange.ny.us*

Court records 1800s–present; bail records 1798–1813; federal census 1820, 1840, 1850, 1860; New York state census 1835, 1845, 1855, 1865, 1875, 1915, 1925; mortgages and deeds; indentures 1831–1845; maps; naturalization records 1802–present; and divorce records.

Orange County – City, Town, and Village Clerks

Birth, marriage, and death records are maintained by the clerk of the municipality in which the event occurred; see Introduction to County Guides for details of other records which may also be held by municipal clerks. For contact information, see *www.ocgsny.org/ historians/historians.htm*.

Orange County Surrogate's Court

30 Park Place • Goshen, NY 10924 • (845) 476-3655

Probate records 1830s–present. See also chapter 6, Probate Records.

Orange County Public Libraries

Orange is part of the Ramapo Catskill Library System; see *www.rcls.org* to access each library. Many libraries hold genealogical material such as local newspapers. For example, Cornwall Public Library's local history collection includes photographs, Goshen Public Library has an online obituary search, and Greenwood Lake Public Library and Tuxedo Park Library hold scrapbooks. Also see listings below for Newburgh Free Library and Middletown Thrall Library.

Orange County Genealogical Society

1841 Court House • 101 Main Street • Goshen, NY 10924 (845) 291-2327 or 291-2388 (historian) • *www.ocgsny.org*

Histories and genealogies, census microfilm (federal 1790–1880 with printed indexes and 1900–1930, and state 1825–1875), family files, church and cemetery records, local directories, deeds and mortgages, marriages 1908–1932, naturalization records, newspapers, maps, and military records (Revolutionary, Civil, and Mexican Wars). Website in-

cludes list of city, town, and village historians and a catalog of its publications, which include transcriptions of cemeteries in the towns of Chester, Hamptonburgh, and Minisink, as well as many other original records. Has published the *Orange County Genealogy Society Quarterly* since 1971.

Orange County Historian

101 Main Street • Goshen, NY 10924 • (845) 291-2388 *www.co.orange.ny.us/content/124/1338*

Holdings include court and naturalization records. Website includes information on military records.

Orange County – All Municipal Historians

While not authorized to answer genealogical inquiries, city, town, and village historians can provide valuable historical information and research advice; some maintain collections and webpages which may include transcribed records, local histories, and other genealogical material. For contact information, see *www.ocgsny.org/historians/historians.htm* or *www.aphnys.org*.

Orange County Historical Society

21 Clove Furnace Drive • PO Box 55 • Arden, NY 10910 (845) 351-4696 • Email: orangechs@optonline.net *www.orangecountyhistoricalsociety.org/OCHS/index.html*

Holds original documents and research materials on industries in the region; special collections for the Sterling Iron Railroad and iron mining in Orange County. Members-only access to records and documents.

REGIONAL REPOSITORIES & RESOURCES

Bard College Archives and Special Collections

See listing in Dutchess County Guide

LOCAL REPOSITORIES & RESOURCES

Alphabetized by location

Bull Stone House Genealogy and History

183 County Route 51 • Campbell Hall, NY 10916 (845) 496-BULL (2855) • Email: info@bullstonehouse.org *www.bullstonehouse.org*

Hosts reunion of Bull family descendants. Website includes information on Bull genealogy. Onsite genealogist available by appointment.

Hill-Hold and Brick House Museums

Hill-Hold Museum: 128 Route 416 • Campbell Hall, NY • (845) 291-2404 *Brick House Museum:* 850 Route 17K • Montgomery, NY (845) 457-4921 • *www.hillholdandbrickhouse.org*

Holdings include genealogies of early Orange County settlers.

Chester Historical Society:
Collections and 1915 Erie Station Museum

47 Main Street, above Village of Chester offices • Chester, NY 10918 (845) 469-2388 • Email: chester_historical@mac.com *www.chesterhistoricalsociety.com*

Selection of materials on website, including business records, diaries, indentures, inventories, ledgers, and wills.

New York Military Academy: Museum and Archives

78 Academy Avenue • Cornwall-on-Hudson, NY 12520 (888) ASK-NYMA (275-6962) • *www.nyma.org*

Official academy records, photographs, and yearbooks. Website features online exhibits.

The Neversink Valley Museum of History and Innovation: Collections and Library
D&H Canal Park, Route 209 • Cuddebackville, NY • (845) 754-8870
Email: nvam@frontiernet.net • www.neversinkmuseum.org

Categories include D&H Canal, blacksmithing and carpentry, farming, home furnishings, local history (1800–1900), and Westbrook family papers. Museum features exhibit of Orange County archaeology in collaboration with Orange County chapter of New York State Archaeology Society.

Town of Highlands Historical Society
Village Hall • 303 Main Street • Highland Falls, NY 10928
(845) 446-0400 • www.historichudsonhighlands.org

Family files, prints and photographs, memorabilia, and historic buildings register.

Woodbury Historical Society
543 Route 32 • PO Box 30 • Highland Mills, NY 10930
(845) 928-6770 • Email: historian@woodburyhistoricalsociety.org
www.woodburyhistoricalsociety.org

Local histories, photographs and postcards, and records of Cemetery of the Highlands.

Middletown Thrall Library
11-19 Depot Street • Middletown, NY 10940 • (845) 341-5454
Email: midhistory@rcls.org • www.thrall.org

Holdings include genealogies, church records, cemetery records, and directories.

City of Newburgh: City Clerk
83 Broadway • Newburgh, NY 12550 • (845) 569-7300
Email on website • www.cityofnewburgh-ny.gov/city-clerk

Holdings for the City of Newburgh include birth and death records 1865–present and marriage records 1865–present.

Historical Society of Newburgh Bay and the Highlands The Captain David Crawford House and Helen Gearn Memorial Library
189 Montgomery Street • Newburgh, NY 12550 • (845) 561-2585
Email: historicalsocietynb@yahoo.com
www.newburghhistoricalsociety.com

Books, documents, photographs, maps, and ephemera. Collection searchable through online database.

Newburgh Free Library:
Local History and Genealogy Research Room
124 Grand Street • Newburgh, NY 12550 • (845) 563-3601
http://guides.rcls.org/newburghhistory

Books, pamphlets, business records, city directories 1858–present, church records, cemetery records, census microfilm, family histories, land grants, maps, newspapers on microfilm, photographs and postcards, obituary indexes, town records, and scrapbooks.

Washington's Headquarters State Historic Site
84 Liberty Street • Newburgh, NY 12551 • (845) 562-1195
http://nysparks.com/historic-sites/17/details.aspx

Holdings include letters, journals, and personal documentation of families.

Minisink Valley Historical Society
Society Headquarters, Fort Decker Museum of History, and Robert Kleinstuber House: 125-133 West Main Street
Port Jervis, NY 12771 • (845) 856-2375
Library: Port Jervis Free Library, 2nd Floor • 138 Pike Street
Port Jervis, NY 12771 • (845) 856-7313 • www.minisink.org

Society's library located in Port Jervis Free Library. Holdings include cemetery records, church records, census materials, family Bibles, family files, obituary records, DAR Patriot Index and Records, NYG&B Index and the *Record*, maps and atlases, newspaper clippings, local directories, and local histories. Society will send copies of individual Surname Files to those who request them for a fee.

Sugar Loaf Historical Society
PO Box 114 • Sugar Loaf, NY 10981-0114
Email: info@sugarloafhistoricalsociety.com
www.sugarloafhistoricalsociety.com

Website includes maps, photographs, local folklore, and information on Society's projects.

Historical Society of Walden and Walkill Valley:
Jacob T. Walden House
34 North Montgomery Street • PO Box 48 • Walden, NY 12586
Email: HSWWV@adprose.org • www.thewaldenhouse.org

Holdings include digitized records of Walden Methodist Church (marriages 1866–1881; baptismal records 1866–1882). Publishes the *Walden House Tattler.*

Historical Society of the Town of Warwick
2–12 Maple Avenue • Warwick, NY 10990 • (845) 986-3236
Email: info@warwickhistoricalsociety.org
www.warwickhistoricalsociety.org

Holdings include documents, manuscripts, newspapers, photographs, and maps.

SELECTED PRINT & ONLINE RESOURCES

Below is a selection of resources relevant for research in this county. The list is representative, not exhaustive. Additional titles—particularly of abstracts, indexes, transcriptions, and local histories—are available; consult the introduction to Part Two for further information. For guidance on how to identify and locate community directories and local newspapers, see chapter 11, City Directories, and chapter 12, Newspapers, in Part One of this book.

Abstracts, Indexes & Transcriptions

Barber, Gertrude Audrey, comp. "Cemeteries Located in Orange County, N.Y. (Including Greenville, Mt. Hope, Wallkill and Crawford, NY." Typescript, 1932. NYPL, New York. [NYG&B eLibrary]

———, comp. "Graveyard Inscriptions of Orange County, NY." 4 vols. Typescript, 1930. [*Ancestry.com*]

———, comp. "Orange County Patriot: Orange County, New York, Marriages and Deaths from 1828–1831." Typescript, 1932. NYPL, New York.

Brennan, Robert W. *Goshen Independent Republican Marriage Notices, Volume One 1866–1883; Volume Two 1884–1903.* Goshen, NY: Orange County Genealogical Society, 2003–2006.

Burrows, Dan, comp. *Orange County Marriages and Deaths from the New York State 1865 and 1875 Censuses.* Goshen, NY: Orange County Genealogical Society, 2004.

Bush, Cornelia W. "1823 and 1825 Muster Rolls from Chester, Orange County." *NYG&B Record,* vol. 133, no. 3 (2002): 185–190. [NYG&B eLibrary]

Carey, C. R. "Town of Deer Park 1798 Assessment Records." *Orange County Historical Society Publication,* no. 8. (1978–1979): 13–25.

Coleman, Charles. *The Early Records of the Presbyterian Church in Goshen, NY, from 1767–1885*. Goshen, NY: The Democrat Print Co., 1934.

Coleman, James Cash. *Coleman's Orange County Tombstone Inscriptions*. Goshen, NY: Orange County Genealogical Society, 2011. Reprint of 1941 edition. Index by Joseph Lieby.

County of Orange Abstracts. Syracuse: Central New York Genealogical Society, 2000. Abstracts for a range of genealogical records originally published in the quarterly *Tree Talks*.

Daughters of the American Revolution, comps. *New York DAR Genealogical Records Committee Report*. Since 1913 DAR volunteers have transcribed many thousands of unpublished cemetery, church, and town records throughout New York. The reports are at the DAR Library; copies are at the NYSL and the NYPL. The DAR has a searchable name index to all the GRC reports at *http://services.dar.org/Public/DAR_Research/search/?Tab_ID=6*. See Jean Worden's index.

Dunning, Kenneth A. *Orange County Jury Lists, Volume 1, 1798–1825; Volume 2, 1826–1837*. Goshen, NY: Orange County Genealogical Society, 2010, 2013.

Gardner, George, and Virginia H. Gardner. *The Whig Press Death Notices 1851–1865*. Middletown, NY: Hartwell Associates, 1978. Includes over 15,000 entries.

Gardner, Virginia H. "Persons of Color, Town of Wallkill 1825 Census." Goshen, NY: 1977. *Orange County Genealogical Society Quarterly*, vol. 7, no. 3 (1977): 23.

———. *The Whig Press Marriage Notices 1851–1865*. Goshen, NY: Orange County Genealogical Society, 1986. Includes over 10,000 entries.

Joslyn, Roger D. "Indentures of the Poor Children of Orange County, 1829–1847, 1871, 1884, 1885." *NYG&B Record*, vol. 137 (2006) no. 4: 294–303; vol. 138 (2007) no. 2: 227–231, no. 3: 144–150. [NYG&B eLibrary]

Kelly, Arthur C. M. *Index to Tree Talks County Packet: Orange County*. Rhinebeck, NY: Kinship, 2002.

———. *Vital Records of St. Andrew's Episcopal Church, Walden, Orange County, New York, 1793–1906*. Rhinebeck, NY: Kinship, 2001.

Krish, Jeanne, and Lee Krish. *Official Vital Records from the Various Towns of Orange County, NY: Births, Deaths, and Marriages 1847–1849 with a Supplement of Additional Marriage and Death Returns*. Goshen, NY: Orange County Genealogical Society, 2003.

Leslie, Augusta, comp. *Record of Baptisms and Marriages, Copied From and Compared with the Original Entries in Stewards' Book, Newburgh, N.Y., Circuit of the Methodist Episcopal Church, 1789 to 1835*. Newburgh, NY: n.p., 1901.

Mapes, Clarence Eugene. "Burials in Howells Cemetery, Howells, Orange County, NY." Typescript, n.d. NYPL, New York. [NYG&B eLibrary]

Moffat, Almot S. *Old Churches of Orange County*. Goshen, NY: Orange County Genealogical Society, 1990. Reprint of 1927 edition. Includes histories of Goshen Presbyterian, Goodwill Presbyterian, Bethlehem Presbyterian, Blooming Grove Congregational, and Newburgh First Presbyterian with member lists from 1927.

New York Genealogical and Biographical Society, comp. "A Group of Orange County, NY, Cemeteries: Alphabetically Arranged." Typescript, 1922. NYPL, New York.

———. *Minisink Valley: Reformed Dutch Church Records, 1716–1830*. New York: New York Genealogical and Biographical Society, 1913.

O'Callaghan, Edmund B. *Documentary History of the State of New York*. 4 vols. Albany, 1849–1851. Contains 1702 Orange Co. census in vol. 4: 366–367, List of the Inhabitants of the County of Orange, 1702. Also transcribed in "1702 Orange Co. Census," *Orange County Genealogical Society Quarterly*, vol. 4, no. 3 (1974): 16.

Orange County Genealogical Society. *Cemeteries of Chester, NY*. Monroe, NY: Orange County Genealogical Society, 1980.

———. *Cemeteries of Hamptonburgh, NY*. Goshen, NY: Orange County Genealogical Society, 1980.

———. *Early Orange County Wills 1731–1830*. Goshen, NY: Orange County Genealogical Society, 1991.

Orange County Genealogical Society, and Edna D. Raymond. *Cemeteries of the Town of Minisink, NY*. Goshen, NY: Orange County Genealogical Society, 1988.

Orange County, NYG&B Church Surveys Collection. NYG&B, New York. [NYG&B eLibrary]

Proceedings to Determine Boundaries of the Wawayanda and Cheesecocks Patents Held in 1785 in Yelverton's Barn, Chester. Goshen, NY: Independent Republican Print Co., 1915. Book draws from records of the Orange County clerk that do not survive. Testimony of Orange County residents is given with their ages, dates of birth, and lengths of residence in the county.

Shepard, Elmer I. *Orange County, New York, Deaths: From the Independent Republican and the Goshen Democrat, Goshen, New York*. New York: S. Weller and R. H. Siemers, 1967.

Smeltzer-Stevenot, Marjorie. *Old Burying Grounds within Harriman and Bear Mountain State Parks*. Goshen, NY: Orange County Genealogical Society, 1998. Reprint of 1992 edition.

Stephens, John M. *1825 Census of Calhoun (now Mt. Hope) Township*. Goshen, NY: 1977. *Orange County Genealogical Society Quarterly*, vol. 7, no. 3 (1977): 24.

Thompson, Robert O. *Census of Neelytown*. Goshen, NY: 1975. *Orange County Genealogical Society Quarterly*, vol. 5, no. 1 (1975): 4–5. Transcribed by Helen Van Burgen, as noted in the brief introduction to the census.

Weller, Caroline S., and Raymond H. Siemers, comps. *Orange County, New York, Marriages: From the Independent Republican, Goshen, New York*. Kew Gardens, NY: R. H. Siemers, 1967.

Worden, Jean D. "Book 1, Subject Index." In *Revised Master Index to the New York State Daughters of the American Revolution Genealogical Records Volumes*. Zephyrhills, FL: J. D. Worden, 1998. The Subject Index includes a listing by county of the cemeteries, churches, towns, and other sources of records transcribed by the DAR.

Van Buren, Elizabeth R. "The Union Cemetery of the Presbyterian Parish of Middle Town." Typescript, n.d. NYPL, New York. [NYG&B eLibrary]

Other Resources

Beers, F. W. *County Atlas of Orange, New York: From Actual Surveys*. Chicago, 1875. [NYPL Digital Gallery]

Brennan, Robert W. *Genealogical History of Black Families of Orange County, New York*. 6 vols. Goshen, NY: Orange County Historical Society, 2001–2006.

Chapman Publishing Company. *Portrait and Biographical Record of Orange County, New York: Containing. . . Citizens of the County, . . .* New York: Chapman Publishing, 1895. Reprinted with index by Orange County Genealogical Society in 1995.

Clark, Donna K. *Orange County, New York, Field Trip Guide: Directory of Genealogical Depositories of Local Records.* Arvada, CO: Ancestor Publishers, 1987.

Clearwater, Alphonso T., ed. *The History of Ulster County, New York.* Kingston, NY: W. J. Van Deusen, 1907.

Corning, Amos E. *The Concise History of Orange County.* Saugerties, NY: Hope Farm Press, 1993.

Eager, Samuel W. *An Outline History of Orange County: With an Enumeration of the Names of Its Towns, Villages, . . . Local Traditions and Short Biographical Sketches of Early Settlers, etc.* Newburgh, NY: 1846. Indexed by Mildred Roberts and Samuel Eager in 1968. Reprinted by Orange County Genealogical Society, 1995.

Foley, Janet W. *Early Settlers of New York State: Their Ancestors and Descendants.* 9 vols. Akron, NY: 1934–1942. Reprint, 2 vols. Baltimore: Genealogical Publishing Co., 1993.

Greater Hudson Heritage Network. *History Keepers' Companion: Guide to Sites & Sources of the Lower Hudson Valley and Western Connecticut.* Fleischmanns, NY: Purple Mountain Press, 1998. The Greater Hudson Heritage Network is in the process of updating and creating an online version of this publication; information is at *www.greaterhudson.org/history-keepers-companion.html.*

Headley, Russel. *The History of Orange County, New York.* Middletown, NY: Van Deusen and Elms, 1908. Separate index published by Orange County Genealogical Society 1993.

Hudson River Valley Review: A Journal of Regional Studies. Poughkeepsie, NY: Hudson River Valley Institute at Marist College, 2002–present. [*hudsonrivervalley.org*]

Lathrop, J. M. *Atlas of Orange County, New York: Compiled and Drawn from Official Records, Public and Private Plans and Actual Surveys.* Philadelphia: H. A. Mueller, 1903.

Laws of New-York, from the Year 1691 to 1751, Inclusive: Published According to an Act of the General Assembly. New York, 1752.

Moffat, Almet S. *Orange County, New York: A Narrative History: Descriptive of Its Places of . . . Its Historic Churches with Biographies of Their Pastors . . . Its Statesmen, Historians, Poets, Writers, and Distinguished People of the Past . . .* Washingtonville, NY: n.p., 1928.

New York Historical Resources Center. *Guide to Historical Resources in Orange County, New York, Repositories.* Ithaca, NY: Cornell University, 1989.

Olde Ulster: An Historical and Genealogical Magazine. Kingston, NY: B. M. Brink, 1905.

Orange County: A Journey Through Time. A Text on Local History. Prepared by Orange-Ulster Board of Cooperative Educational Services. Goshen, NY: The Board, 1983.

Reamy, Martha, and Bill Reamy. *Pioneer Families of Orange County, New York.* Bowie, MD: Willow Bend Books, 2003.

Ruttenber, Edward M., and Lewis H. Clark. *History of Orange County, New York: With . . . Biographical Sketches . . . .* Philadelphia: Everts &

Peck, 1881. Reprinted by Orange County Genealogical Society in 2000. Separate index published by Orange County Genealogical Society in 1979.

Smith, Philip H. *Legends of the Shawangunk (Shon-Gum) and Its Environs, Including Historical Sketches, Biographical Notices, and Thrilling Border Incidents and Adventures Relating to Those Portions of the Counties of Orange, Ulster, and Sullivan Lying in the Shawangunk Region.* Pawling, NY, 1887.

Weygant, Charles H. *History of the One Hundred and Twenty-Fourth Regiment, New York State Volunteers.* Newburgh, NY, 1877.

Zimm, Louise H. *Southeastern New York: History of the Counties of Ulster, Dutchess, Orange, Rockland, and Putnam.* 3 vols. New York: Lewis Historical Publishing Co., 1946. Index available from Berkshire Family History Association.

Additional Online Resources

Ancestry.com

There are vast numbers of records on *Ancestry.com* that pertain to people who have lived in New York State. See chapter 16 for a description of *Ancestry.com*'s resources and its partnership with the New York State Archives. A search of the online card catalog by county may reveal lesser known resources that pertain to a locality, such as town records, abstracts, transcriptions, city directories, and local histories.

FamilySearch.org

FamilySearch has extensive collections of New York records, including religious records, which are searchable by name and location, but not by county. The following collections include record images (browsable, but not searchable) that are organized by county:

- "New York, Land Records, 1630–1975." Includes land and property records. *familysearch.org/search/collection/2078654*
- "New York, Probate Records, 1629–1971." Includes wills, letters of administration, and guardianship papers. *familysearch.org/search/collection/1920234*

For both collections, choose the browse option and then select Orange to view the available records sets.

A detailed description of *FamilySearch.org* resources is found in chapter 16.

Hudson River Valley Heritage (HRVH)
www.hrvh.org/cdm

The HRVH website provides free access to digital collections of historical material from more than 40 organizations in Columbia, Greene, Dutchess, Ulster, Sullivan, Rockland, Orange, Putnam, and Westchester counties.

New York Heritage Digital Collections: New York State Newspaper Project
www.nyheritage.org/newspapers

The website provides links to digital newspapers collections in 26 counties (currently) made accessible through New York Heritage, New York State Historic Newspapers, HRVH Historical Newspapers, and other providers.

NYGenWeb Project: Orange County
www.rootsweb.ancestry.com/~nyorange

Part of the national, USGenWeb volunteer initiative, the website provides information and resources for county research.

Orleans County

Formed November 12, 1824

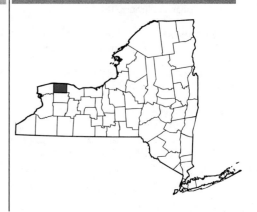

Parent County   Genesee
Daughter Counties   None
County Seat   Village of Albion

Major Land Transactions
See chapter 7, Land Records
Morris Reserve 1791
Holland Land Company Purchase 1792–1796

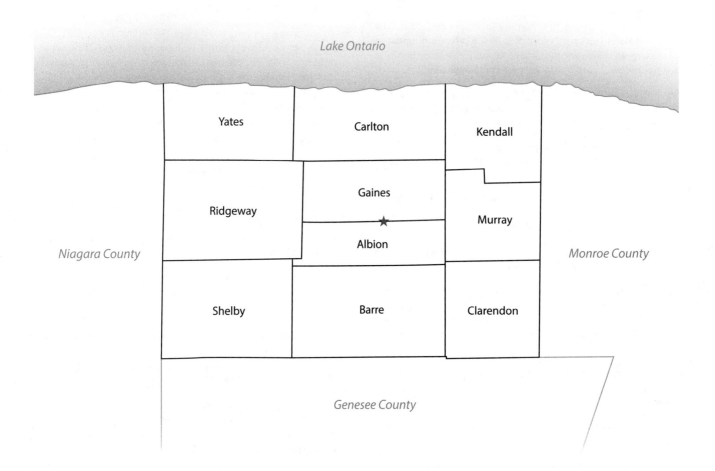

Lake Ontario

Yates

Carlton

Kendall

Gaines

Ridgeway

Murray

★

Albion

Niagara County

Monroe County

Shelby

Barre

Clarendon

Genesee County

Town Boundary Map
 - County seat

Towns (and Cities)	Villages and other Settlements		Notes
Albion 1875 Formed from Town of Barre, including Village of Albion	Albion (v) Eagle Harbor Eagle Harbor Station Oak Orchard Estates Richs Corners Salmon River South Albion		• Village of Albion incorporated in Town of Barre 1828; in new Town of Albion from 1875; rechartered 1879 and village enlarged to include a small part of Town of Gaines; county seat from 1827; 1824–1827 county seat in Gaines • Eagle Harbor in Town of Barre before 1875; on Gaines town line • Richs Corners in Town of Barre before 1875
Barre 1811 Settled 1818 Formed in Genesee County from Town of Gaines 1825 Transferred to new county of Orleans 1875 Daughter town Albion formed	Albion (v) Barre Center Braggs Corners Burma Woods Eagle Harbor	Farmington Richs Corners South Barre West Barre	• Village of Albion inc. 1828; called Newport before 1828; in Town of Albion from 1875 • Eagle Harbor and Richs Corners now in Town of Albion • West Barre also Jackson Corners
Carlton 1803 Settlers from Canada 1822 Formed in Genesee County as Oak Orchard from towns of Gaines and Ridgeway 1825 Transferred to new county of Orleans; name changed to Carlton	Ashwood Baldwin Corner Brice Brice Station Carlton Carlton Center Harris Road Jones Beach Kent Kenyonville Kuckville Lakeside	Lakeside Park Manilla Oak Orchard Harbor Oak Orchard on the Lake Point Breeze Rock Ledge Beach Sawyer Toms Landing Waterport Waterport Station	• Ashwood on Yates town line • Hamlet of Carlton formerly Two Bridges • Kent formerly East Carlton • Kuckville also West Carlton • Sawyer formerly Curtis Corners
Clarendon 1811 Settled at Clarendon village 1821 Formed in Genesee County from Town of Sweden * 1825 Transferred to new county of Orleans	Bennetts Corners Clarendon Honest Hill Manning		* Town of Sweden transferred to Monroe County in 1821 • Hamlet of Clarendon formerly Farwells Mills • Manning formerly Mudville and West Clarendon
Gaines Settled before 1809 1816 Formed in Genesee County from Town of Ridgeway 1818 Daughter town Barre formed 1822 Daughter town Carlton formed 1825 Transferred to new county of Orleans	Albion (v) Childs Eagle Harbor East Gaines Five Corners Gaines (v) Gaines Basin West Gaines		• Village of Albion in Town of Gaines from 1879 when village was enlarged; most of village in Town of Albion • Childs formerly Fair Haven and Proctors Corners • Eagle Harbor on Albion town line • Villiage of Gaines, inc. 1832, lost village charter in 1854 through lack of use; 1824–1827 county seat
Kendall 1812 Settlers from Vermont 1837 Formed from Town of Murray	Kendall Kendall Mills Morton West Kendall		• Kendall Mills formerly Webster Mills • Morton formerly Clarks Corners and East Kendall

Towns (and Cities)	Villages and other Settlements	Notes
Murray 1808 Formed in Genesee County from Town of Northampton (now Gates, Monroe County) 1813 Daughter towns Bergen and Sweden formed ∗ 1819 Daughter town Clarkson formed ∗ 1821 Transferred to new county of Monroe 1825 Transferred to new county of Orleans 1837 Daughter town Kendall formed	Brockville Fancher Hindsburg(h) Holley (v) Hu(l)berton Murray Murray Depot	∗ Towns of Clarkson and Sweden now in Monroe County; Bergen remained in Genesee County • Hindsburg(h) also Hinsberg and Hindsville • Village of Holley inc. 1850 • Hamlet of Murray also Sandy Creek
Northton Name for Town of Yates 1822–1823		
Oak Orchard Name for Town of Carlton 1822–1825		
Ridgeway 1809 Settlers from Madison County 1812 Formed in Genesee County from Town of Batavia 1816 Daughter town Gaines formed 1818 Daughter town Shelby formed 1822 Daughter towns Oak Orchard (now Carlton) and Northon (now Yates) formed 1825 Transferred to new county of Orleans	Jeddo Knowlesville Knowlesville Station Medina (v) North Ridgeway Oak Orchard Ridgeway West Ridgeway	• Village of Medina inc. 1832; small part in Town of Shelby • Ridgeway also Ridgeway Corners
Shelby 1810 Settlers from Rensselaer County 1818 Formed in Genesee County from Town of Ridgeway 1825 Transferred to new county of Orleans 1826 Daughter Town of Gerrysville (now Alabama, Genesee County) formed	East Shelby Medina (v) Millville Shelby Basin Shelby Center West Shelby	• Village of Medina inc. 1832; mostly in Town of Ridgeway • Shelby Center formerly Barnegat; also Shelby
Yates 1809 Settlers from Town of Adams, Jefferson County 1822 Formed in Genesee County as Northton from Town of Ridgeway 1823 Name changed to Yates 1825 Transferred to new county of Orleans	Ashwood County Line Lyndonville (v) Millers Platten Shadigee Yates Yates Center	• Ashwood on Carlton town line • Village of Lyndonville inc. 1903; also Lyndon • Yates Center formerly Northton

NEW YORK STATE CENSUS RECORDS

See also chapter 3, Census Records

County originals at Orleans County Clerk's Office: 1855, 1865*, 1875, 1892, 1905 (1825, 1835, and 1845 are lost)

State originals at the NYSA: 1915, 1925

Microfilm at the FHL, NYPL, and NYSL; many years are online at *FamilySearch.org* and *Ancestry.com.*

* For 1865 census indexes see NY GenWeb Project in Abstracts, Indexes & Transcriptions below.

NATIONAL/STATEWIDE REPOSITORIES & RESOURCES
See chapter 16

COUNTYWIDE REPOSITORIES & RESOURCES

Orleans County Clerk
3 South Main Street • Courthouse Square
Albion, NY 14411 • (585) 589-5334
www.orleansny.com/Departments/PublicRecords/CountyClerk.aspx

Citizenship oaths 1853–present, naturalization records 1830–1955, land records 1824–present, New York state census for Orleans County 1855, 1865, 1875, 1892, 1905, and United States federal census 1850, 1870, 1880.

Orleans County – Town and Village Clerks
Birth, marriage, and death records are maintained by the clerk of the municipality in which the event occurred; see Introduction to County Guides for details of other records which may also be held by municipal clerks. See municipal websites for details and contact information.

Orleans County Surrogate's Court
One South Main Street, Suite 3 • Albion, NY 14411-1497
(585) 589-4457

Holdings include probate records from 1845 to the present. See also chapter 6, Probate Records.

Orleans County Public Libraries
Orleans is part of the Nioga Library System; see *www.niogalibrary. org* to access each library. Many hold genealogy and local history collections including books and newspapers. Also see listings below for Hoag Library and Lee-Whedon Public Library.

Orleans County Historical Association
PO Box 181 • Albion, NY 14411 • *www.orleanshistory.org*
Website includes the Association's publications, list of local historians, antique postcards, links to Orleans County historical resources, and information about the Oral History Project.

Orleans County Historian
3070 Gaines Basin Road • Albion, NY 14411
(585) 589-4174 (office) (585) 589-9013 (museum)

Orleans County – All Municipal Historians
While not authorized to answer genealogical inquiries, town and village historians can provide valuable historical information and research advice; some maintain collections and webpages which may include transcribed records, local histories, and other genealogical material. For example, the Kendall Town Historian website contains place names, important dates, histories, and information on resources

available at the town hall. See contact information at *www.orleansny. com/Departments/PublicRecords/CountyClerk/Genealogy.aspx*, the Government Appointed Historians of Western New York at *www.gahwny. org/p/orleans.html*, or the Association of Public Historians of New York State at *www.aphnys.org.*

Orleans County Genealogical Society
Albion Town Hall • 3665 Clarendon Road • PO Box 103
Albion, NY 14411 • Email: ochomefront@yahoo.com
www.orleanscountygenealogicalsociety.org

Society conducts educational programs on the "Orphan Train," the mass relocation of orphans from New York City between 1854 and 1929. Meetings are held at the Pullman Memorial Universalist Church.

REGIONAL REPOSITORIES & RESOURCES

Milne Library at SUNY Geneseo: Special Collections: Genesee Valley Historical Collection
See listing in Livingston County Guide

SUNY Fredonia: Daniel A. Reed Library: Archives & Special Collections
See listing in Chautauqua County Guide

University of Rochester: Rare Books, Special Collections, and Preservation: Manuscript and Special Collections: Rochester, Western New York, and New York State
See listing in Monroe County Guide

Western New York Genealogical Society
See listing in Erie County Guide

Western New York Heritage Press
See listing in Erie County Guide

LOCAL REPOSITORIES & RESOURCES
Alphabetized by location

Hoag Library (Swan Library): Genealogy and History
134 South Main Street • Albion, NY 14411 • (585) 589-4246
www.swanlibrary.org/Departments.html

Local histories and genealogies, census indexes and microfilm (1830–1930), gazetteers, local directories and phone books, burial transcriptions for all cemeteries in Orleans County, newspapers on microfilm (1820–present; not indexed), oral histories, and more. Website includes "how-to" resources for researching genealogy and links.

Lee-Whedon Memorial Library
620 West Avenue • Medina, NY 14103 • (585) 798-3430
Email: info@medinalibrary.org • *http://leewhedon.org*

Local papers dating back to 1882, census microfilm, cemetery records, city directories, and oral histories.

Medina Historical Society and Museum
406 West Avenue • Medina, NY 14103 • (585) 798-3006
www.historicmedina.org

Holdings include military memorabilia and other artifacts.

SELECTED PRINT & ONLINE RESOURCES

Below is a selection of resources relevant for research in this county. The list is representative, not exhaustive. Additional titles—particularly of abstracts, indexes, transcriptions, and local histories—are available; consult the introduction to Part Two for further information. For guidance on how to identify and locate community directories and local newspapers, see chapter 11, City Directories, and chapter 12, Newspapers, in Part One of this book.

Abstracts, Indexes & Transcriptions

County of Orleans Abstracts. Syracuse: Central New York Genealogical Society, 2000. Abstracts for a range of genealogical records originally published in the quarterly *Tree Talks*. A name index is on the CNYGS website.

Daughters of the American Revolution, comps. *New York DAR Genealogical Records Committee Report*. Since 1913 DAR volunteers have transcribed many thousands of unpublished cemetery, church, and town records throughout New York. The reports are at the DAR Library; copies are at the NYSL and the NYPL. The DAR has a searchable name index to all the GRC reports at *http://services.dar.org/Public/DAR_Research/search/?Tab_ID=6*. See Jean Worden's index below for a listing by county of the New York record sets that were transcribed by the DAR before 1998.

Kelly, Arthur C. M. *Index to Tree Talks County Packet: Orleans County*. Rhinebeck, NY: Kinship, 2002.

"Marriages by Justice Ammon Blair, Orleans County, 1840–1850." *NYG&B Record*, vol. 140, no. 4 (2009): 285–286. [NYG&B eLibrary]

NYGenWeb Project, Orleans County. "Index to the 1865 New York State Census." *www.rootsweb.ancestry.com/~nyorlean/1865Cen.htm*

Sheldon, Nellie M. *Marriages 1826 to 1837, Murray, Orleans County, New York: Copied from the Original Manuscripts*. San Diego: Nellie M. Sheldon, 1964.

Worden, Jean D. "Book 1, Subject Index." In *Revised Master Index to the New York State Daughters of the American Revolution Genealogical Records Volumes*. Zephyrhills, FL: J. D. Worden, 1998. The Subject Index includes a listing by county of the cemeteries, churches, towns, and other sources of records transcribed by the DAR.

Other Resources

Beers, D. G. *Atlas of Niagara and Orleans Counties, New York: From Actual Surveys and Official Records*. Philadelphia, 1875. [NYPL Digital Gallery]

Child, Hamilton. *Gazetteer and Business Directory of Orleans County, NY, for 1869*. Syracuse, 1869.

Gardepe, Carol D., and Janice Dates Regester. *A History of the Town of Yates in Orleans County, New York*. Ann Arbor, MI: Edwards Bros, 1976.

Historical Album of Orleans County, NY: With Illustrations Descriptive of Its Scenery, Private Residences, Public Buildings, Fine Blocks, and Important Manufactories; and Portraits of Old Pioneers and Prominent Residents. New York: Press of W. E. Morrison & Co., 1979. First published 1879.

New Century Atlas of Orleans County, New York. Philadelphia: Century Map Co., 1913.

New York Historical Resources Center. *Guide to Historical Resources in Orleans County, New York, Repositories*. Ithaca, NY: Cornell University, 1982. [*books.FamilySearch.org*]

Signor, Isaac S. *Landmarks of Orleans County, New York*. Syracuse, 1893. Includes American Indian history, topography, early land divisions, early settlement, military, industries, businesses, transportation, Erie Canal, town histories, medicine, biographies, and family sketches.

Swart, Joseph. *Swart's Orleans County, NY, Directory, 1894 ....* Medina, NY, 1894.

Thomas, Arad. *Pioneer History of Orleans County, New York: Containing Some Account of the Civil Divisions of Western New York, with Brief Biographical Notices of Early Settlers, and of the Hardships and Privations They Endured, the Organization of the Towns in the Country, Together with Lists of Town and County Officers, Since the County Was Organized: With Anecdotes and Reminiscences, Illustrating the Character and Customs of the People*. Bowie, MD: Heritage Books, 1998. First published 1871. Includes American Indian history, pioneer life, Erie Canal, transportation, education, religion, town histories, and biographies of early settlers.

———. *Sketches of the Village of Albion: Containing Incidents of Its History and Progress, from Its First Settlement, and a Statistical Account of Its Trade, Schools, Societies, Manufactures, & c.* Albion, NY, 1853.

Western New York Genealogical Society Journal. Hamburg, NY: Western New York Genealogical Society, 1974–present. [*wnygs.org*]

Additional Online Resources

Ancestry.com

There are vast numbers of records on *Ancestry.com* that pertain to people who have lived in New York State. See chapter 16 for a description of *Ancestry.com*'s resources and its partnership with the New York State Archives. A search of the online card catalog by county may reveal lesser known resources that pertain to a locality, such as town records, abstracts, transcriptions, city directories, and local histories.

FamilySearch.org

FamilySearch has extensive collections of New York records, including religious records, which are searchable by name and location, but not by county. The following collections include record images (browsable, but not searchable) that are organized by county:

- "New York, Land Records, 1630–1975." Includes land and property records. *familysearch.org/search/collection/2078654*
- "New York, Probate Records, 1629–1971." Includes wills, letters of administration, and guardianship papers. *familysearch.org/search/collection/1920234*

For both collections, choose the browse option and then select Orleans to view the available records sets.

A detailed description of *FamilySearch.org* resources, which include the catalog of the Family History Library, is found in chapter 16.

New York Heritage Digital Collections: New York State Newspaper Project
www.nyheritage.org/newspapers

The website provides links to digital newspapers collections in 26 counties (currently) made accessible through New York Heritage, New York State Historic Newspapers, HRVH Historical Newspapers, and other providers.

NYGenWeb Project: Orleans County
www.rootsweb.ancestry.com/~nyorlean

Part of the national, USGenWeb volunteer initiative, the website provides information and resources for county research.

Oswego County

Formed March 1, 1816

Parent Counties Oneida • Onondaga
Daughter Counties None
County Seat City of Oswego

Major Land Transactions
See chapter 7, Land Records
New Military Tract 1782–1791
Macomb Purchase 1792
Scriba Patent 1794

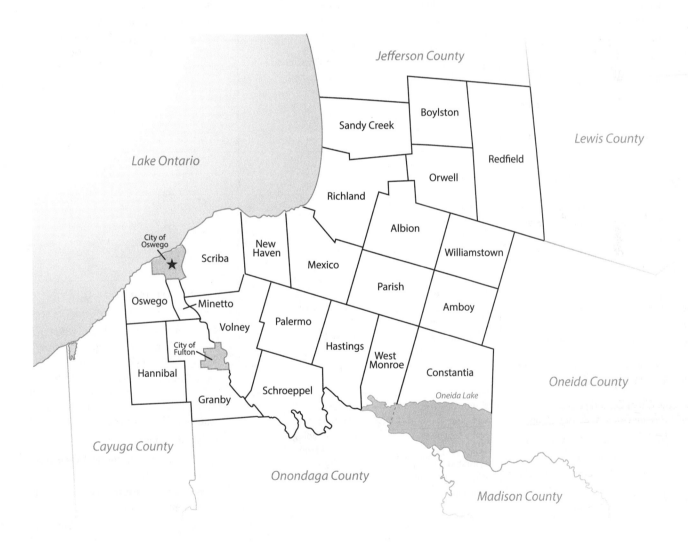

Town Boundary Map
★ - County seat

Towns (and Cities)	Villages and other Settlements		Notes
Albion 1812 Settled 1825 Formed from Town of Richland	Albion Center Altmar (v) Barber Corners Centerville Dugway Happy Valley	Howardville Maple Corners Mosher Corners Pineville South Albion Spruce	• Village of Altmar inc. 1876 as Sand Bank, name changed c. 1895; village dissolved 6/1/2013 • Centerville formerly New Centerville • Pineville also Salmon River • Spruce formerly Albion
Amboy 1805 Settlers from Connecticut 1830 Formed from Town of Williamstown	Amboy Center Carterville East Amboy Jami(e)son Corners	Mud Hill North Amboy West Amboy	
Boylston 1810–12 Settlers from Canajoharie, Otsego County 1828 Formed from Town of Orwell	Boylston Boylston Center Catholic Church Corners East Boylston	Hemlock District North Boylston Plantz Corners Smartville	• Boylston Center also Boylston Corner • Plantz Corners also LaPlant Corners
Constantia 1786 Settled by French 1808 Formed in Oneida County from Town of Mexico 1816 Transferred to new county of Oswego 1825 Daughter town Hastings formed 1839 Daughter town West Monroe formed	Bernhards Bay Carroll Corners Cleveland (v) Constantia (v) Constantia Center Doris Park	Dutcherville Gayville Kempwick Nicholsville North Constantia Panther Lake	• Village of Cleveland inc. 1857 • Village of Constantia called Rotterdam before 1798, originally known as New Rotterdam; village inc. 1836 and dissolved 1923
Fredericksburgh Name for Town of Volney 1806–1811			
Fulton (city) 1902 Incorporated as a city; formed from Village of Oswego Falls (Town of Granby) and Village of Fulton (Town of Volney)	Fulton Oswego Falls Volney		
Granby 1792 Settlers from Rensselaer County 1818 Formed from Town of Hannibal 1836 Ceded land to Town of Oswego 1902 Daughter City of Fulton formed from Village of Oswego Falls	Bowens Corners Dexterville Granby Center Lewis Corners Oswego Falls (v)	Pember Corners Six Mile Creek South Granby West Granby	• Bowens Corners named c. 1817 • Granby Center formerly Williams Corners • Village of Oswego Falls inc. 1853 and Village of Fulton (Town of Volney) became City of Fulton in 1902 • West Granby formerly Camps Mills
Hannibal * 1802 Settlers from Saratoga County 1806 Created in Onondaga County from Town of Lysander 1816 Transferred to new county of Oswego 1818 Daughter towns Granby and Oswego formed	Cains Corners Fairdale Halls Corners Hannibal (v) Hannibal Center Kinney(s) (Four) Corners	Mallory Mallorys Mills Metcalf Siding North Hannibal Oswego South Hannibal	* Hannibal was the name of one of the 28 Military Tract townships • Village of Hannibal inc. 1860, reinc. 1876 • North Hannibal formerly Wheeler(s) Corners • Oswego county seat from 1816; in Town of Oswego from 1818 • South Hannibal formerly Hulls Corners
Hastings 1789 Settled at Fort Brewerton 1825 Formed from Town of Constantia	Bardeen Corners Benders Corners Brewerton Carley Mills	Caughdenoy Central Square (v) Emmons Siding Fort Brewerton	• Brewerton shared with Town of Cicero, Onondaga County • Village of Central Square inc. 1890

(Hastings continued on next page)

Towns (and Cities)	Villages and other Settlements		Notes
Hastings (continued)	Gardners Corners	Mallory	• Little France formerly French Settlement
1789 Settled at Fort Brewerton	Hastings	Mallory Station	• Mallory also Mallorys Mills; formerly
1825 Formed from Town of Constantia	Hastings Center	McMahon Corners	Smiths Mills and Brewsterville
	Little France	Piguet Corners	
Mexico	Arthur		* Town of Camden in Oneida County
1792 Formed from Town of	Colosse		• Colosse formerly Mexico Four Corners
Whitestown in Herkimer County	Deweys Corners		• Maple View formerly Union Square
1798 Transferred to new county of	Graftons Square		• Village of Mexico inc. 1851
Oneida	Lambs Corners		• Prattham formerly Prattville
1799 Daughter town Camden formed *	Maple View		• Texas formerly Vera Cruz
1800 Daughter towns Champion and	Mexico (v)		• Wellwood also South Mexico
Watertown formed in Jefferson	North Church Corner		
County; Redfield in Oneida	Prattham		
County; Lowville and Turin in	Red Mill		
Lewis County	Texas		
1802 Daughter town Adams formed	Wellwood		
in Jefferson County			
1803 Daughter town Ellisburgh			
formed in Jefferson County			
1804 Daughter towns Malta (now			
Lorraine), formed in Jefferson			
County and Williamstown,			
Oneida County			
1806 Daughter town Fredericksburgh			
(now Volney) formed			
1808 Daughter town Constantia formed			
1813 Daughter town New Haven			
formed			
1816 Mexico transferred from Oneida			
County to new county of Oswego			
1828 Daughter town Parish formed			
1836 Annexed land from towns of			
New Haven and Richland			
Minetto	Minetto		• Minetto in Town of Oswego before 1916
1916 Formed from Town of Oswego	Minetto Station		
New Haven	Austin(s) Corners	New Haven	• Cummings Bridge also Cummings Mills
1798 First settled	Butterfly (Corners)	New Haven Station	• Hamlet of New Haven formerly Gay Head
1813 Formed in Oneida County from	Cheevers Mills	Pleasant Point (Crossing)	• Vermillion on Palermo town line
Town of Mexico	Cummings Bridge	Sala	
1816 Transferred to new county of	Demster	Shore Oaks	
Oswego	Demster Beach	South New Haven	
1836 Ceded land to Town of Mexico	Demster Grove	The Hollow	
	Hickory Grove	Vermillion	
	Johnsons Corners		
Orwell	Beecherville	Orwell	• Chateaugay formerly also Shatagee
1806 Settled	Bennett Bridges	Pekin	• Molino also Maline
1817 Formed from Town of Richland	Chateaugay	Pine	• Orwell also Orwell Corners; formerly
1828 Daughter town Boylston formed	Little America	Stillwater	Moscow
1844 Annexed land from Town of	Molino	Vorea	
Richland	New Scriba		

Towns (and Cities)	Villages and other Settlements		Notes
Oswego (city) * Site of British garrison during Revolutionary War 1828 Incorporated as a village in towns of Oswego and Scriba 1848 Enlarged and formed as a city from towns of Oswego and Scriba	Fort Ontario		* County seat from 1816 as hamlet, village, and city; 1816–1852 county seat shared with Village of Pulaski, Town of Richland
Oswego (town) 1797 Settlers from Connecticut 1818 Formed from Town of Hannibal 1836 Annexed land from Town of Granby 1848 Daughter city Oswego formed 1916 Daughter town Minetto formed	Fruit Valley Furniss Minetto Oswego (v) Oswego Beach Oswego Center Southwest Oswego		• Fruit Valley also Union Village • Minetto in Town of Minetto from 1916 • Village of Oswego in Town of Hannibal before 1818 (before incorp.); village inc. 1828; shared with Town of Scriba; est. as City of Oswego in 1848; county seat (see City of Oswego) • Oswego Beach formerly Burts Point • Oswego Center formerly Fitchs (Corners)
Palermo 1806 Settlers from Oneida county 1832 Formed from Town of Volney	Catfish Corners Clifford Cribbs Corner East Palermo Farley Corners Loomis Corner Morse Mungers Corners	Palermo Peat Corners Russ Mills Sayles Corners Suttons Corner Upson Corners Vermillion	• Clifford formerly Dentons Corners • East Palermo formerly Flints Corners • Hamlet of Palermo also Palermo Center; formerly Jennings Corners • Vermillion on New Haven town line
Parish 1803 Settlers from Otsego County 1828 Formed from Town of Mexico	East Parish Merritt Corners Parish (v) Parish Center	Parishville Vorhees Wrightston	• Village of Parish inc. 1883; also Parishville
Redfield 1795–98 Settlers from Connecticut at Redfield Square 1800 Formed in Oneida County from Town of Mexico 1816 Transferred to new county of Oswego	Center Square Greenboro Little John Settlement Otto Mills Redfield		• Hamlet of Redfield also Center Square, Central Square, and Redfield Square
Richland 1801 Settlers from Rome, NY 1807 Formed in Oneida County from Town of Williamstown 1816 Transferred to new county of Oswego 1817 Daughter town Orwell formed 1825 Daughter towns Albion and Sandy Creek formed 1836 Ceded land to Town of Mexico 1844 Ceded land to Town of Orwell	Daysville Daysville Corner Farmers Corners Fernwood Holmesville Port Ontario (v) Pulaski (v)	Rainbow Shores Ramona Beach Richland Sand Hill Selkirk Tylers Corner	• Holmesville also South Richland • Village of Port Ontario inc. 1837 and dissolved 1844 • Village of Pulaski inc. 1832; served as county seat with Village of Oswego 1816–1852; known as Village of Rich- land c. 1824 • Hamlet of Richland also Richland Station

Towns (and Cities)	Villages and other Settlements		Notes
Sandy Creek 1804 Settlers from Oneida County 1825 Formed from Town of Richland	East Sandy Creek Lacona (v) Pine Ridge	Sandy Creek (v) Sandy Pond The Elms	• Village of Lacona inc. 1878 • Village of Sandy Creek inc. 1878; also Washingtonville • Sandy Pond also Sandy Pond Corners
Schroeppel 1800 Settled at Phoenix 1832 Formed from Town of Volney	Bowen Corners Gilbert Mills Great Bear Siding Hinmansville Ingalls Crossing McMahon Corners Oak Orchard Peacock Corners	Pennellville Phoenix (v) Ro(o)sevelt Corners Sand Ridge Shepard Corners Stewart Corners Three Rivers Point	• Gilbert Mills also Gilbertsville • Hinmansville also Six Mile Creek • Ingalls Crossing in Town of Volney before 1832 • Village of Phoenix inc. 1848; formerly Three River Rifts
Scriba 1798 Settled 1811 Formed in Oneida County from Town of Fredericksburgh (now Volney) 1816 Transferred to new county of Oswego 1848 Daughter city Oswego formed	Hammonds Corner Klocks Corners Lakeview Lansing Lycoming North Scriba	Oswego (v) Pecks Corners Scriba South Scriba Walker	• Village of Oswego inc. 1828; shared with Town of Oswego, became part of new City of Oswego in 1848; before 1828 hamlet called East Oswego • Scriba also Scriba Center and Scriba Corners
Volney Settled temporarily in early 1700s 1793 Settled 1806 Formed in Oneida County as Town of Fredericksburgh from Town of Mexico 1811 Name changed to Volney; daughter town Scriba formed 1816 Transferred to new county of Oswego 1832 Daughter towns Palermo and Schroeppel formed 1902 Daughter city Fulton formed	Bell Bundy Crossing Drakes Corner Farley Corners Fulton (v) Ingalls Crossing Mount Pleasant North Volney Seneca Hill Vanburen Volney Whittemore		• Bundy Crossing also Bundyville • Fulton formerly Oswego Falls • Village of Fulton inc. 1835 (and Village of Oswego Falls, Town of Granby) became City of Fulton in 1902 • Ingalls Crossing in Town of Schroeppel from 1832 • Volney also Volney Center and Volney Corners
West Monroe 1806 Settled 1839 Formed from Town of Constantia	Gulf Bridge Jerry Little France Mud Settlement Phillips	Toad Harbor Union Settlement West Monroe Whig Hill	
Williamstown 1801 Settled 1804 Formed in Oneida County from Town of Mexico 1807 Daughter town Richland formed 1816 Transferred to new ounty of Oswego 1830 Daughter town Amboy formed	Checkered House (Corners) Fraicheur Happy Valley Kasoag Maple Hill	Ricard Stone Hill Wardville Williamstown Williamstown Mills	

NEW YORK STATE CENSUS RECORDS
See also chapter 3, Census Records

County originals at Oswego County Records Center: 1855, 1865, 1875, 1892, 1905, 1915, 1925 (1825, 1835, and 1845 are lost)

State originals at the NYSA: 1915, 1925

Microfilm at the FHL, NYPL, and NYSL; many years are online at *FamilySearch.org* and *Ancestry.com*.

NATIONAL/STATEWIDE REPOSITORIES & RESOURCES
See chapter 16

COUNTYWIDE REPOSITORIES & RESOURCES

Oswego County Clerk
46 East Bridge Street • Oswego, NY 13126
(315) 349-8621 • *www.oswegocounty.com/clerk.shtml*
Archival Index: *www.oswegocounty.com/clerk/archivalindextitlepage.pdf*

Holdings include land records and court records. Website includes history and timeline of Oswego County, list of local historians, historical attractions, Oswego County Archival Index (comprehensive guide to archives with locations and contact information, organized by municipality and record type), and research forms.

Oswego County – City, Town, and Village Clerks
Birth, marriage, and death records are maintained by the clerk of the municipality in which the event occurred; see Introduction to County Guides for details of other records which may also be held by municipal clerks. For contact information, see *www.rootsweb.ancestry. com/~nyoswego/townclerkoffices.html*.

Oswego County Surrogate's Court
Oswego County Courthouse • 25 East Oneida Street
Oswego, NY 13126 • (315) 349-3295

Holdings include probate records from 1836 to the present. See also chapter 6, Probate Records.

Oswego County Public Libraries
Oswego is part of the North Country Library System; see *http://ncls. northcountrylibraries.org* to access each library. Many hold genealogy and local history collections such as local newspapers. For example, Central Square Library holds local cemetery records and yearbooks. Also see listings below for Annie P. Ainsworth Memorial Library, Fulton Public Library, Oswego Public Library, Parish Public Library, and Pulaski Public Library.

Oswego County Records Center and County Historian
384 East River Road • Oswego, NY 13126 • (315) 349-8460
www.oswegocounty.com/clerk/inventory.html

Holdings include original copies of the New York state censuses for Oswego County 1855, 1865, 1875, 1892, 1905, 1915, and 1925 (1855 and 1865 are indexed), as well as federal census records 1820, 1850, 1860, 1870, 1880, 1900, 1910, and 1920; records for over 170 cemeteries; city directories 1869–present; civil court records; local histories; maps and atlases; marriages 1908–1935; naturalization records 1829–1957; town records; books; and genealogies.

Oswego County –All Municipal Historians
While not authorized to answer genealogical inquiries, city, town, and village historians can provide valuable historical information and research advice to family historians; some maintain collections with genealogical material. Some historians also have web-pages with

local histories, transcribed records, links to useful resources and other genealogical information. For contact information, see *http:// visitoswegocounty.com/historical-info/historians-historic-society*, *http:// nny.nnyln.org/archives/oswego_county.html* or the website of the Association of Public Historians of New York State at *www.aphnys.org*.

Oswego County Historical Society and Richardson-Bates House Museum
135 East Third Street • Oswego, NY 13126 • (315) 343-1342
Email: ochs@rbhousemuseum.org • *www.rbhousemuseum.org*

Diaries and family papers (Church-Douglas, Judson, Richardson, and Mary E. Walker), business records, cemetery records, photographs, maps, scrapbooks, Civil War collection (1850–1901), World War 1 collection, records of the Oswego County Health Association (1917–1952), and records of the Oswego Orphan Asylum (1852–1945). See Oswego Public Library for its former publication.

Heritage Foundation of Oswego County
143 West Third Street • PO Box 405 • Oswego, NY 13126
(315) 342-3354 • Email: president@oswegocountyheritage.com
www.oswegocountyheritage.org

Books, city directories, photographs, "Reconnaissance Level Architectural Survey of Oswego County (1999)," and other records relating to historic buildings.

Safe Haven Museum and Education Center
2 East Seventh Street • PO Box 486 • Oswego, NY 13126
(315) 342-3003 • Email: safehaven@cnymail.com
www.safehavenmuseum.com

Documents the history of the nearly 1,000 European refugees who came to live in Oswego during World War II. Website includes list of refugees.

REGIONAL REPOSITORIES & RESOURCES

Central New York Genealogical Society
See listing in Onondaga County Guide

SUNY at Oswego: Local History Collection
Penfield Library, Special Collections • Oswego, NY 13126
(315) 312-3537 • Email: archives@oswego.edu
www.oswego.edu/library/archives.html
Genealogy Resources: *www.oswego.edu/library/archives/Penfield_Library_ Genealogical_Resources.pdf*

Holdings include books and manuscripts, census indexes, diaries and correspondence, city records and directories, family papers (Millard Fillmore and Marshall Family), institutional records, government records, maps and gazetteers, military records, newspapers 1819–present, oral histories, periodicals, tax rolls (Oswego City 1925–1952, 1962, 1964, 1973, 1975) and vital record abstracts. Genealogical information is drawn from Cayuga, Herkimer, Jefferson, Lewis, Madison, Oneida, Onondaga, Oswego, Seneca, St. Lawrence, and Wayne Counties.

LOCAL REPOSITORIES & RESOURCES
Alphabetized by location

Hastings Heritage and History Club
196 County Route 33 • Central Square, NY 13036 • (315) 668-2178

Holdings include genealogies, histories, obituaries, photographs, and scrapbooks.

Fulton Public Library

160 South First Street • Fulton, NY 13069 • (315) 592-5159

Email: fullib@nnyln.net • *www.fultonpubliclibrary.info*

Holdings include local histories and genealogies, cemetery records, census records, local newspapers (*Fulton Times* and *Fulton Patriot*, 1881–1996), Fulton city directories (1886–2006), and local yearbooks.

Hannibal Historical Society and Museum

Hannibal Community Center • 162 Oswego Street • PO Box 150 Hannibal, NY 13074 • (315) 564-5471

www.rootsweb.ancestry.com/~nyoswego/towns/hannibal/hanhistsoc.html

Genealogy files (including surname list) and photographs (including a digitized collection). Website includes information on the Society's publications, 1854 map of Hannibal with names, family file index, cemetery index, and brief history of Hannibal.

Mexico Historical Society and Museum

South Jefferson Street • PO Box 331 • Mexico, NY 13114 (315) 963-8542 • Facebook page

Holdings include artifacts, maps, memorabilia, and photographs.

Williamstown Historical Society

584 County Route 64 • Mexico, NY 13114 • (315) 963-3144

Email: grams42@aol.com

Census materials, obituaries, cemetery records, maps, birth and death certificates, military books, and photographs. Towns of Albion and Amboy are also documented.

Oswego Public Library

120 East Second Street • Oswego, NY 13126

Email: oswegopl@northnet.org • *www.oswegopubliclibrary.org*

Books, cemetery records, city directories 1852–present, city newspapers 1819–present, *Oswego County Historical Journals* (some digitized copies online at *http://ochs.nnyln.org*), local government records, news clippings, phone books, scrapbooks, and some vital records. Website includes gazetteers, local history, and guide to local resources.

Oswego Town Historical Society

2320 County Route 7 • Oswego, NY 13126 • (315) 343-2586

Email: records@twcny.rr.com • *www.townofoswego.com/historical.html*

Website contains historical photographs and documents, links, and a genealogical research request form.

Scriba Town Historical Association

Scriba Municipal Building • 42 Creamery Road • Oswego, NY 13126 (315) 342-6420 • Email: history22@scribany.org

Holdings include cemetery records, diaries, genealogies, and more.

Parish Public Library

3 Church Street • Parish, NY 13131 • (315) 625-7130

www.parishpubliclibrary.org

Artifacts, genealogies, local histories, cemetery records, newspapers, photographs, scrapbooks (1880s–1940s), and yearbooks.

Pulaski Historical Society

3428 Maple Avenue • Pulaski, NY 13142 • (315) 298-4650

Email: phspulaski@aol.com

Local and family histories, business records, military records, school records, photographs, and scrapbooks.

Pulaski Public Library

4917 North Jefferson Street • Pulaski, NY 13142 • (315) 298-2717

Email: pullib@ncls.org • *www.pulaskinypubliclibrary.org*

Books, cemetery records, newspapers (*Pulaski Democrat*, 1834–1990), and yearbooks (1893–present).

Half-Shire Historical Society

1100 County Route 48 • PO Box 73 • Richland, NY 13144-0073 (315) 298-3620 • Email: info@halfshire.org • *www.halfshire.org*

Documents the history of the northern towns of Oswego County. Holdings include obituaries, photographs, and newspapers; website includes information on each town and its local historian, as well as historic maps. Quarterly journal, *Tug Hill Literary Review.*

Annie P. Ainsworth Memorial Library: Genealogy

6064 South Main Street • PO Box 69 • Sandy Creek, NY 13145 (315) 387-3732 • Email: ainsworth6064@yahoo.com

www.ainsworthmemoriallibrary.org

Local histories, cemetery records (northern Oswego and southern Jefferson counties), census materials (CD-ROM and transcriptions), photographs, and vital records.

Sandy Creek History Center

1992 Harwood Drive • PO Box 52 • Sandy Creek, NY 13145 (315) 387-5456 ext. 7 • Email: schistorian@frontiernet.net

www.sandycreeknyhistory.com

Genealogies and local histories, assessment records, cemetery records, census materials, maps, newspapers, marriage records, photographs, and more.

West Monroe Historical Society

2355 State Route 49 • PO Box 53 • West Monroe, NY 13167 (315) 676-7414 • *westmonroehistory.org*

Books, genealogies, business records, census materials, cemetery records, church records, maps, military records, newspapers (*Lakeside Press*, 1873–1900, *North Shore News*), photographs, school records, and vital records.

SELECTED PRINT & ONLINE RESOURCES

Below is a selection of resources relevant for research in this county. The list is representative, not exhaustive. Additional titles—particularly of abstracts, indexes, transcriptions, and local histories—are available; consult the introduction to Part Two for further information. For guidance on how to identify and locate community directories and local newspapers, see chapter 11, City Directories, and chapter 12, Newspapers, in Part One of this book.

Abstracts, Indexes & Transcriptions

County of Oswego Abstracts. Syracuse: Central New York Genealogical Society, 2000. Abstracts for a range of genealogical records originally published in the quarterly *Tree Talks.*

Daughters of the American Revolution, comps. *New York DAR Genealogical Records Committee Report.* Since 1913 DAR volunteers have transcribed many thousands of unpublished cemetery, church, and town records throughout New York. The reports are at the DAR Library; copies are at the NYSL and the NYPL. The DAR has a searchable name index to all the GRC reports at *http://services.dar.org/Public/DAR_Research/search/?Tab_ID=6.* See Jean Worden's index below for a listing by county of the New York record sets that were transcribed by the DAR before 1998.

Kelly, Arthur C. M. *Index to Tree Talks County Packet: Oswego County.* Rhinebeck, NY: Kinship, 2002.

Oswego County, NYG&B Church Surveys Collection. NYG&B, New York. [NYG&B eLibrary]

Vosburgh, Royden Woodward, ed. "Records Pertaining to the First Presbyterian Church in the City of Oswego, N.Y." Typescript, 1917. NYPL, New York. [NYG&B eLibrary]

Worden, Jean D. "Book 1, Subject Index." In *Revised Master Index to the New York State Daughters of the American Revolution Genealogical Records Volumes.* Zephyrhills, FL: J. D. Worden, 1998. The Subject Index includes a listing by county of the cemeteries, churches, towns, and other sources of records transcribed by the DAR.

Other Resources

Child, Hamilton. *Gazetteer and Business Directory of Oswego County, NY, for 1866–7.* Oswego, 1866.

Churchill, John C., H. P. Smith, and W. Stanley Child. *Landmarks of Oswego County, New York.* Syracuse, 1894. Includes biographies and family sketches.

Cutter, William R. *Genealogical and Family History of Central New York: A Record of the Achievements of Her People in the Making of a Commonwealth and the Building of a Nation.* New York: Lewis Historical Publishing Co., 1912.

Faust, Ralph M. *The Story of Oswego: With Notes about the Several Towns in the County.* Oswego, NY: The Author, 1934.

Johnson, Crisfield. *History of Oswego County, New York, 1789–1877. With Illustrations and Biographical Sketches of Some of Its Prominent Men and Pioneers.* Philadelphia, 1877.

Landon, Harry F. *The North Country: A History, Embracing Jefferson, St. Lawrence, Oswego, Lewis and Franklin Counties.* 3 vols. Indianapolis: Historical Publishing Co., 1932.

New York Historical Resources Center. *Guide to Historical Resources in Oswego County, New York, Repositories.* Ithaca, NY: Cornell University, 1982. [*books.FamilySearch.org*]

Northern New York Library Network. *Directory of Archival and Historical Document Collections.* 2011–2013 edition; published digitally at *http://nny.nnyln.org/archives/ArchivalDirectory.pdf.* Online indexes at *http://nny.nnyln.org/archives/page01.html.* Describes collections held by organizations in Clinton, Essex, Franklin, Jefferson, Lewis, Oswego, and St. Lawrence counties.

Parsons, David K. *Bugles Echo Across the Valley: Oswego County, New York, and the Civil War.* Sandy Creek, NY: Write to Print, 1994.

Pierrepont, William C. *The Taming of the Wilderness in Northern New York: Records of the Land Purchases of Early Settlers for 1826 for Lands in Jefferson, Lewis, and Oswego Counties.* Sandy Creek, NY: Write to Print, 1993.

Records of the Ithaca College Study Center for Early Religious Life in Western New York, 1978–1981. Division of Rare and Manuscript Collections, Cornell University Library. A description of the holdings for each county is at *http://rmc.library.cornell.edu/eguides/lists/churchlist1.htm.*

Slosek, Anthony M., and Helen M. Breitbeck. *Oswego and the War of 1812.* Oswego, NY: Heritage Foundation of Oswego, 1989.

———. *Oswego: Its People and Events.* Interlaken, NY: Heart of the Lakes Publishing, 1985.

Snyder, Charles M. *Oswego County, New York, in the Civil War.* Oswego, NY: Oswego County Historical Society, 1986. The Oswego County Civil War Centennial Committee Yearbook.

Stone, C. K. *New Topographical Atlas of Oswego County, New York: From Actual Surveys Especially for this Atlas.* Philadelphia, 1867. [NYPL Digital Gallery]

Wellman, Judith, ed. *Landmarks of Oswego County.* Syracuse: Syracuse University Press, 1988.

Additional Online Resources

Ancestry.com

There are vast numbers of records on *Ancestry.com* that pertain to people who have lived in New York State. See chapter 16 for a description of *Ancestry.com*'s resources and its partnership with the New York State Archives. A search of the online card catalog by county may reveal lesser known resources that pertain to a locality, such as town records, abstracts, transcriptions, city directories, and local histories.

FamilySearch.org

FamilySearch has extensive collections of New York records, including religious records, which are searchable by name and location, but not by county. The following collections include record images (browsable, but not searchable) that are organized by county:

- "New York, Land Records, 1630–1975." Includes land and property records. *familysearch.org/search/collection/2078654*
- "New York, Probate Records, 1629–1971." Includes wills, letters of administration, and guardianship papers. *familysearch.org/search/collection/1920234*

For both collections, choose the browse option and then select Oswego to view the available records sets.

A detailed description of *FamilySearch.org* resources is found in chapter 16.

New York Heritage Digital Collections: Oswego Public Library
http://cdm16694.contentdm.oclc.org/cdm/landingpage/collection/p16694coll19

The website provides access to two digital collections: Oswego City Directories 1852–1929, and the Safe Haven Collection, which documents the experience of Jewish refugees at the Safe Haven compound during 1944–1945.

NYGenWeb Project: Oswego County
www.rootsweb.ancestry.com/~nyoswego

Part of the national, USGenWeb volunteer initiative, the website provides information and resources for county research.

Otsego County

Formed February 16, 1791

Parent Counties   Montgomery
Daughter Counties   Schoharie 1795 • Delaware 1797
County Seat   Village of Cooperstown, Towns of Middlefield and Otsego

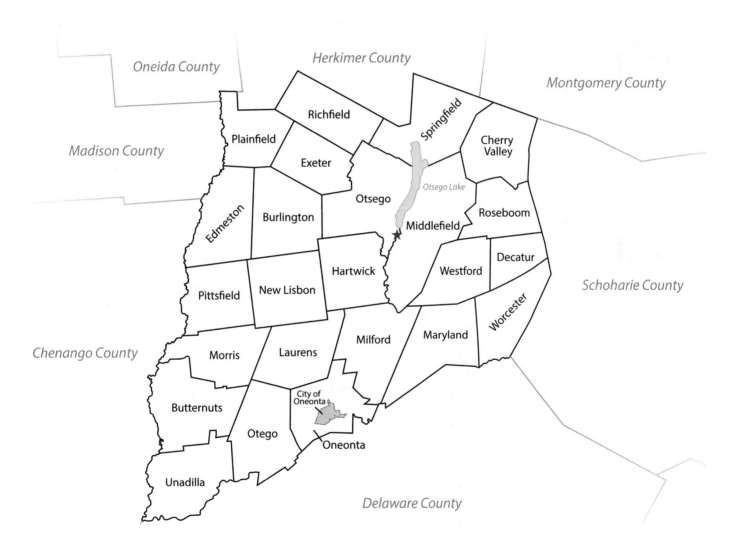

Town Boundary Map
★ - County seat

Towns (and Cities)	Villages and other Settlements		Notes
Burlington 1790 Settled 1792 Formed from Town of Otsego 1797 Daughter town Pittsfield formed 1808 Daughter town Edmeston formed	Barrett Corners Beverly Inn Corners Burlington Burlington Flats Chapinville	Methodist Hollow Patent West Burlington Wharton	• Hamlet of Burlington formerly Burlington Green • Burlington Flats formerly Walbridge Flats • Wharton also Hubbards Corners and Pecktown
Butternuts Settled before Revolution, abandoned during war 1787 Resettled 1796 Formed from Town of Unadilla 1849 Daughter town Morris formed 1857 Annexed land from Town of Unadilla	Church Corners Copes Corner Freer Corner Frog Harbour Gilbertsville (v) Heslops Corner	Hughston Corner Mallory Corner Maple Grove Rootville South New Berlin Toll Corner	• Church Corners on Morris town line • Village of Gilbertsville inc. 1896; also Butternuts • Maple Grove on Morris town line • South New Berlin was shared with Town of Morris, Otsego County, and Town of New Berlin, Chenango County • Toll Corner also Toll Center formerly Tole Center
Cherry Valley 1738–40 Settled by Irish and Scots 1791 Formed from Town of Canajoharie, Montgomery County 1792 Daughter town Dorlach (now Sharon, Schoharie County) formed * 1797 Daughter towns Middlefield, Springfield, and Worcester formed 1854 Daughter town Roseboom formed	Center Valley Cherry Valley (v) Salt Spring(s)ville		* Dorlach referred to as New Dorlach in some county supervisor's minutes • Center Valley on Roseboom town line after 1854 • Village of Cherry Valley inc. 1812 • Salt Spring(s)ville also Saltspringsville
Decatur 1780 Settled 1808 Formed from Town of Worcester	Decatur Furnaceville Gothicville		
Dorlach * In Otsego County 1792–1795			* See Town of Sharon in Schoharie County
Edmeston 1763–75 Settled, abandoned during Revolutionary War 1808 Formed from Town of Burlington	Amblers Crossing Coontown East Edmeston Edmeston Edmeston Manor Manchester Corners	North Edmeston Rutherford Hollow South Edmeston Taylor Hill West Edmeston	• Hamlet of Edmeston formerly Peet Hook, also Edmeston Center • Manchester Corners formerly Manchester Crossing • North Edmeston formerly Wrights Corners • West Edmeston shared with the Town of Brookfield, Madison County
Exeter 1789 Settled 1799 Formed from Town of Richfield	Angel Hill Brainard Corners Exeter Center Exeter Corner	Lidell Corners Mattesons Mills Schuyler(s) Lake West Exeter	• Exeter Center formerly Exeter
Franklin * In Otsego County 1792–1797			* See Delaware County

Towns (and Cities)	Villages and other Settlements		Notes
Harpersfield * In Otsego County 1791–1797			* See Delaware County
Hartwick 1761 Hartwick Patent granted 1802 Formed from Town of Otsego	Chase Clintonville Field Crossing Hartwick Hyde Park Index	Jones Crossing Perkins Crossing Scotch Hill South Hartwick Summit Crossing Toddsville	• Clintonville on Middlefield town line • Index formerly Hope, Hope Factory, and Hopeville; on Otsego town line • Toddsville in Town of Otsego before 1802; on Otsego town line after 1802
Huntsville Name for Town of Otego 1822–1830			
Kortright * In Otsego County 1793–1797			* See Delaware County
Laurens 1810 Formed from Town of Otsego	Butts Corners Laurens (v) Laurensville	Mount Vision Naylor Corners West Laurens	• Village of Laurens inc. 1834 • Mount Vision formerly Jacksonville • West Laurens formerly Sheepskin
Lisbon Name for Town of New Lisbon 1806–1808			
Maryland 1790 Settled 1808 Formed from Town of Worcester 1817 Daughter town Davenport formed in Delaware County	Chaseville Cooperstown Junction Elk Creek Maryland Schenevus (v)		• Chaseville formerly Roseville • Cooperstown Junction formerly South Milford; on Milford town line • Elk Creek also Elkcreek; on Westfield town line • Village of Schenevus formerly Jacksonboro; inc. 1870, dissolved 3/29/1993
Middlefield 1755 Settled by Irish and Scots, abandoned during Revolutionary War 1797 Formed from Town of Cherry Valley	Bower(s)to(w)n Clintonville Cooperstown (v) Lent(s)ville Middlefield Middlefield Center Phoenix Mills Westville Whig(s) Corners		• Clintonville on Hartwick town line • Village of Cooperstown shared with Town of Otsego; 1807 the unincorporated village of Cooperstown was incorporated as Village of Otsego; 1812 name changed back to Cooperstown; county seat from 1791 • Middlefield also Clark(s)ville • Middlefield Center formerly Newtown-Martin • Westville on Westford town line
Milford 1770 Settled, abandoned during Revolutionary War 1796 Formed as Suffrage from Town of Unadilla 1800 Name changed from Suffrage to Milford 1830 Land ceded to Town of Otego	Christian Hill Cliffside Collier(s)ville Cooperstown Junction Edson Corners	Emmons Station Milford (v) Milford Center Portlandville Spoonville	• Collier(s)ville also Colliers • Cooperstown Junction formerly South Milford, on Maryland town line • Village of Milford inc. 1890
Morris c. 1773 Settled, abandoned during Revolutionary War 1849 Formed from Town of Butternuts	Church Corners Collier Bridge Dimmick Hollow Elm Grove Filer Corners Maple Grove Morris (v) South New Berlin		• Church Corners on Butternuts town line • Maple Grove on Butternuts town line • Village of Morris inc. 1870; formerly Louisville • South New Berlin was shared with Town of Butternuts, Otsego County, and Town of New Berlin, Chenango County

Towns (and Cities)	Villages and other Settlements	Notes
New Lisbon 1775 Settled, abandoned during Revolutionary War 1806 Formed as Lisbon from Town of Pittsfield 1808 Name changed from Lisbon to New Lisbon	Fall Bridge Garrattsville Lena New Lisbon Stetsonville Stevens Corners Welcome	• New Lisbon also Noblesville • Stetsonville also Stitsonville • Welcome formerly New Lisbon Center
Oneonta (city) 1909 Formed as a city from Village of Oneonta		
Oneonta (town) 1796 Formed as Otego from Town of Unadilla 1830 Name changed to Oneonta (same year Town of Huntsville renamed Otego) 1909 City of Oneonta formed from Village of Oneonta	Alliger Hill Emmons Oneonta (v) Richardson Hill Southside West End West Oneonta	• Village of Oneonta inc. 1848; formerly MacDonalds Bridge, MacDonalds Mills, and Milfordville; became City of Oneonta 1909 • West End formerly Oneonta Plains
Otego Settled after Revolution 1822 Formed as Town of Huntsville from towns of Franklin, Delaware County and Unadilla 1830 Name changed to Otego; annexed land from Town of Milford	Center Brook Cooks Corners Hell Hollow Mill Creek Otego (v) Otsdawa	• Hell Hollow also The Perry District • Village of Otego inc. 1892
Otego Name for Town of Oneonta 1796–1830		
Otsego 1760s Settled, abandoned during Revolutionary War 1788 Formed as town in Montgomery County; originally included greater part of Otsego and Delaware counties 1791 Transferred to new county of Otsego 1792 Daughter towns Burlington, Richfield, and Unadilla formed 1802 Daughter town Hartwick formed 1810 Daughter town Laurens formed	Bourne Oak(s)ville Cattown Otsego Lake Cooperstown (v) Pail Shop Corners Fitch Hill Pierstown Fly Creek Snowdon Forkshop Corners Taylortown Index Toddsville Le Roy Twelve Thousand Metcalf Hill Wileytown	• Village of Cooperstown inc. 1807; shared with Town of Middlefield; see Middlefield for more details • Fly Creek also Flycreek • Index formerly Hope, Hopeville, and Hope Factory; on Hartwick town line • Toddsville on Hartwick town line after 1802
Pittsfield 1793 Settled 1797 Formed from Town of Burlington 1806 Daughter town Lisbon (now New Lisbon) formed	Briggs Corners Ketchum Cardtown New Berlin Finksville Pittsfield Hoboken	

Towns (and Cities)	Villages and other Settlements		Notes
Plainfield 1793 Settled 1799 Formed from Town of Richfield 1816 Daughter town Winfield, Herkimer County, formed	Huntly Corners Leonardsville Lloydsville Plainfield Center	Plainfield Hill Spooner(s) Corners Unadilla Forks	• Leonardsville shared with Town of Brookfield, Madison County
Richfield Settled before Revolution, abandoned during war 1787 Resettled 1792 Formed from Town of Otsego 1799 Daughter towns Exeter and Plainfield formed 1816 Daughter town Winfield, Herkimer County, formed	Brighton East Richfield Mayflower Richfield Richfield Springs (v) West Richfield		• Brighton also Brighton Corners • Hamlet of Richfield also Monticello • Village of Richfield Springs inc. 1861
Roseboom 1800 Settled 1854 Formed from Town of Cherry Valley	Butler Corners Center Valley Pleasant Brook	Roseboom South Valley Webster Corners	• Center Valley on Cherry Valley town line after 1854
Springfield 1762 Settled 1797 Formed from Town of Cherry Valley	East Springfield Grayville Middle Village Springfield	Springfield Center Springfield Four Corners	• Springfield Center formerly Hallsville and Mechanicsville
Suffrage Name for Town of Milford 1796–1800			
Unadilla Settled before Revolution, abandoned during war 1792 Formed from Town of Otsego 1796 Daughter towns Butternuts, Suffrage (now Milford), and Otego (now Oneonta) formed 1822 Daughter town Huntsville (now Otego) formed 1857 Land ceded to Town of Butternuts	Ayre Riverside Rogers Hollow Sand Hill Sidney Unadilla (v) Unadilla Center Wells Bridge		• Village of Unadilla inc. 1827 • Wells Bridge formerly East Unadilla
Westford 1787 Settled 1808 Formed from Town of Worcester	Centreville Elk Creek Maple Valley	Westford Westville	• Elk Creek also Elkcreek; on Maryland town line • Westville on Middlefield town line
Worcester 1788–90 Settled 1797 Formed from Town of Cherry Valley 1808 Daughter towns of Decatur, Maryland, and Westford formed	Center Valley Charlotteville East Worcester South Worcester Worcester		

NEW YORK STATE CENSUS RECORDS

See also chapter 3, Census Records

County originals at Otsego County Office Building: 1825*, 1855, 1865, 1874, 1892, 1905, 1915, 1925 (1835 and 1845** are lost)

State originals at the NYSA: 1915, 1925

Microfilm at the FHL, NYPL, NYSHA, and NYSL; many years are online at *FamilySearch.org* and *Ancestry.com*.

* For 1825 census transcription and index for Town of Otsego, see Barnello in Abstracts, Indexes and Transcriptions, below.

** For 1845, a handwritten transcript is at Huntington Memorial Library, see below.

NATIONAL/STATEWIDE REPOSITORIES & RESOURCES

See chapter 16

COUNTYWIDE REPOSITORIES & RESOURCES

Otsego County Clerk

197 Main Street • PO Box 710 • Cooperstown, NY 13326
(607) 547-4200 • *www.otsegocounty.com/depts/clk*

Holdings include land records 1791–present; naturalization records 1806–1889, 1895–1955; marriages 1908–Jan. 1935; census and court records.

Otsego County – City, Town, and Village Clerks

Birth, marriage, and death records are maintained by the clerk of the municipality in which the event occurred; see Introduction to County Guides for details of other records which may also be held by municipal clerks. For contact information, see vital records at *www. otsegocounty.com*.

Otsego County Surrogate's Court

197 Main Street • Cooperstown, NY 13326 • (607) 547-4213

Holdings include probate records from 1792 to the present. See also chapter 6, Probate Records.

Otsego County Public Libraries

Otsego is part of the Four County Library System; see *www.4cls.org* to access each library. Many hold genealogy and local history collections, including maps and newspapers. For example, Unadilla Public Library holds the *Unadilla Times*, 1857–1967. Also see listings below for Edmeston Free Library, Gilbertsville Free Library, and Huntington Memorial Library.

Otsego County Historian

197 Main Street • Cooperstown, NY 13326 • (607) 547-4281

Otsego County – All Municipal Historians

While not authorized to answer genealogical inquiries, city, town, and village historians can provide valuable historical information and research advice; some maintain collections and webpages which may include transcribed records, local histories, and other genealogical material. See contact information on municipal websites or at the website of the Association of Public Historians of New York State at *www.aphnys.org*.

REGIONAL REPOSITORIES & RESOURCES

Huntington Memorial Library: Genealogical Resources

62 Chestnut Street • Oneonta, NY 13820
(607) 432-1980 • *www.hmloneonta.org*

Holdings include family histories and biographies, cemetery records, census records (including a handwritten transcript of the 1845 New York state census for Otsego County), church and Bible records, court records, immigration records, maps and atlases, newspapers, probate records, and vital records. Breese Collection includes deeds. Also a Family History Center (*FamilySearch.org*). Research requests may be submitted for a fee.

New York State Historical Association (NYSHA)

Cooperstown, NY • *nysha.org*

Major repository in Otsego County for genealogical research including: genealogical name files, published and family genealogies, newspapers and newspaper indexes, church records, transcriptions of tombstone inscriptions; federal, state, and local census records; assessment records; school records; local histories, directories; abstracts of wills; Bible records, maps and atlases, and military records. Offers research services for a fee. See also the listing in chapter 16.

LOCAL REPOSITORIES & RESOURCES

Alphabetized by location

Burlington Historical Society

Municipal Building, Rt 51 • Burlington Flats, NY 13315
Email: burlingtonhistory@yahoo.com • Facebook page

Holdings include genealogical files and obituaries.

Town of Middlefield Historical Association

3698 County Highway 35 • PO Box 348 • Cooperstown, NY 13326
Email: tmhawebmail@gmail.com • *www.middlefieldhistorical.org*

Holdings include artifacts, printed materials, and photographs.

Edmeston Free Library and Museum

6 West Street • PO Box 167 • Edmeston, NY 13335-0167
(607) 965-8208 • *www.4cls.org/otsego.html*

Genealogical materials are held in the museum, which is maintained by the town historian.

Fly Creek Area Historical Society

208 Cemetery Road • PO Box 87 • Fly Creek, NY 13337-0087
(607) 547-2501 • Email: inthevalley@oecblue.com
http://fcahs.org/index.html

Holdings include family files and local family photographs.

The Gilbertsville Free Library: Local History Collection

17 Commercial Street • PO Box 332 • Gilbertsville, NY 13776
(607) 783-2832 • Email: archivist@gilbertsvillefreelibrary.org
www.gilbertsvillefreelibrary.org/records.html

Genealogies, histories, cemetery and funeral director records, census microfilm and transcriptions (federal and state), tax records, church records, maps and atlases, newspapers on microfilm (*Morris Chronicle*, 1865–1932, *Otsego Journal*, 1876–1965), photographs and postcards, school records, blueprints and scrapbooks, material on veterans (Revolutionary War and Civil War), town and village records, and more.

Hartwick Historical Society

3140 County Highway 11 • PO Box 1 • Hartwick, NY 13348
(607) 293-6600

Holdings include genealogy, family files, and photographs.

Greater Milford Historical Association
7 North Main Street • Milford, NY 13807 • (607) 286-7038

Holdings include business records, family records, and photographs.

Greater Oneonta Historical Society
183 Main Street • PO Box 814 • Oneonta, NY 13820
(607) 432-0960 or (607) 431-9509 • Email: info@oneontahistory.org
www.oneontahistory.org

Holdings include artifacts, photographs and postcards, and ephemera.

Hartwick College: The Paul F. Cooper Jr. Archives
Stevens-German Library • Yager Hall, Hartwick College
Oneonta, NY 13820 • (607) 431-4450
www.hartwick.edu/academics/stevens-german-library/library-services/archives

Holdings include City of Oneonta Archives, family papers, postcards, and more.

Otego Historical Association
6 River Street • PO Box 27 • Otego, NY 13825 • (607) 988-2225
Email: otegohistorical@gmail.com • http://otegohistoricalsociety.com

Holdings include photographs and artifacts; website includes digitized local history books. Meetings are held at the Harris House at 334 Main Street.

Richfield Springs Historical Association
PO Box 374 • Richfield Springs, NY 13439 • (315) 858-0027

Offers genealogical research services for a fee.

Town of Exeter Historical Society
Schuyler Lake, NY
www.rootsweb.ancestry.com/~nyotsego/exeterhistorical.htm

Website includes historic photographs, including school and family photographs with names.

Westford Historical Society
Town Hall • PO Box 184 • Westford, NY 13488 • (607) 638-9250

Holdings include newspapers and family, business, and education records.

SELECTED PRINT & ONLINE RESOURCES

Below is a selection of resources relevant for research in this county. The list is representative, not exhaustive. Additional titles—particularly of abstracts, indexes, transcriptions, and local histories—are available; consult the introduction to Part Two for further information. For guidance on how to identify and locate community directories and local newspapers, see chapter 11, City Directories, and chapter 12, Newspapers, in Part One of this book.

Abstracts, Indexes & Transcriptions

American Agriculturalist Farm Directory and Reference Book of Otsego and Herkimer Counties. New York: Orange Judd Co., 1917.

Aspinwall, Alice, and Lelah Smith. "Tombstone Records of Small Cemeteries in Otsego County." Typescript, n.d. New York State Historical Association Library, Cooperstown, NY.

Barber, Gertrude Audrey. "Abstracts of Wills of Otsego County, New York, 1794–1850, v. 1–5." Typescript, 1941. NYPL, New York. [Ancestry.com]

———. A Collection of Abstracts from Otsego County, New York, Newspaper Obituaries, 1808–1875. Westminster, MD: Willow Bend Books, 2002. Originally published: Waipahu, Hawaii: M. & W. Reamy, 1993.

———. "Deaths Taken from the Otsego Herald & Western Advertiser and Freeman's Journal." Typescript, 1939. NYPL, New York. [Ancestry.com]

———. "Index of Wills of Otsego County, New York: Filed in the Probate Office of the Surrogate at Cooperstown, NY." Typescript, 1934. NYPL, New York. [Ancestry.com]

———. "Lake View Cemetery at Richfield Springs, Otsego County, NY." Typescript. NYPL, New York. [NYG&B eLibrary]

———. "Marriages Taken from the Otsego Herald & Western Advertiser, and Freeman's Journal: Newspaper Kept at the Cooperstown Library, Cooperstown, Otsego County, NY." Typescript, 1932. NYPL, New York. [Ancestry.com]

———. "Tombstone Inscriptions in the Catholic Cemetery at Richfield Springs, N.Y. and also in the Exeter Cemetery at Exeter, N.Y.: Both Located in Otsego County, N.Y." Typescript, 1931. NYPL, New York [Ancestry.com]

Barnello, Kathleen. Abstract of the 1825 New York State Census of Otsego County, New York. Syracuse: Central New York Genealogical Society, 1995. Originally published in Tree Talks, vol. 35, no. 4 (1995): 1–17. Introduction and map: iii–vii, index: 18–22.

Butterfield, Roy L. The Land Patents of Otsego County. Cooperstown, NY: The Freeman's Journal, 1953.

County of Otsego Abstracts. Syracuse: Central New York Genealogical Society, 2000. Abstracts for a range of genealogical records originally published in the quarterly Tree Talks.

Daughters of the American Revolution. "Inscriptions Copied from Old Cemeteries in the Town of Springfield, Otsego County, NY." Typescript. NYPL, New York. [NYG&B eLibrary]

Daughters of the American Revolution, comps. New York DAR Genealogical Records Committee Report. Since 1913 DAR volunteers have transcribed many thousands of unpublished cemetery, church, and town records throughout New York. The reports are at the DAR Library; copies are at the NYSL and the NYPL. The DAR has a searchable name index to all the GRC reports at http://services.dar.org/Public/DAR_Research/search/?Tab_ID=6. See Jean Worden's index below for a listing by county of the New York record sets that were transcribed by the DAR before 1998.

Gage, Edith. "Cemetery Records of Otsego County." Typescript, 1962–1967. New York State Historical Association, New York. Also contains Bible records and cemetery records from other counties.

Haviland, Frank. Friends' Records of Butternuts (formerly Duanesburgh) Otsego County, New York: Births, 1788–1861: Deaths, 1809–1869. Brooklyn, NY: Long Island Historical Society, 1905.

Hawkins, Ethelyn E. Morse. "Deaths in the Year 1847." Typescript, 1967. New York State Historical Association, New York. As reported by all town clerks in Otsego County except Milford.

———. "Guardianship Records, 1803–1830, of Otsego County, New York State." Typescript, 1970. New York State Historical Association, New York.

———. "Otsego County Marriages of 1847 as Reported to the County Clerk by the Town Clerks." Typescript, 1970. New York State Historical Association, New York.

Kelly, Arthur C. M. Index to Tree Talks County Packet: Otsego County. Rhinebeck, NY: Kinship, 2002.

Otsego County, NYG&B Church Surveys Collection. NYG&B, New York. [NYG&B eLibrary]

The Roll of Honor for Otsego County: A Complete List of Soldiers, Sailors, Marines, and Red Cross Workers ... During the World War. Oneonta, NY: Oneonta Daily Star, 1919.

Vosburgh, Royden Woodward, ed. "Records of the First Baptist Church of Springfield in Springfield Center, Otsego County, NY." Typescript, 1920. NYPL, New York. [NYG&B eLibrary]

———, ed. "Records of the Presbyterian Church of Cooperstown in Otsego County, NY." Typescript, 1920. NYPL, New York. [NYG&B elibrary]

Wikoff, Helen L. "Gravestone Inscriptions from Cemeteries in Montgomery and Otsego Counties, New York." Typescript, 1931. NYPL, New York.

Worden, Jean D. "Book 1, Subject Index." In *Revised Master Index to the New York State Daughters of the American Revolution Genealogical Records Volumes.* Zephyrhills, FL: J. D. Worden, 1998. The Subject Index includes a listing by county of the cemeteries, churches, towns, and other sources of records transcribed by the DAR.

Other Resources

Bacon, Edwin F. *Otsego County, New York: Geographical and Historical: From the Earliest Settlement to the Present Time, with County and Township Maps from Original Drawings.* Oneonta, NY: The Oneonta Herald, 1902.

Beardsley, Levi. *Reminiscences: Personal and Other Incidents; Early Settlement of Otsego County; Notices and Anecdotes of Public Men; Judicial, Legal, and Legislative Matters; Field Sports; Dissertations and Discussions.* New York, 1852.

Beers. F. W. *Atlas of Otsego Co., New York: From Actual Surveys and Under the Direction of F. W. Beers, Assisted by F. S. Fulmer and Others.* New York, 1868. [NYPL Digital Gallery]

Biographical Review: This Volume Contains Biographical Sketches of the Leading Citizens of Otsego County, New York. Bowie, MD: Heritage Books, 1995. Originally published: Boston, 1893.

Butterfield, Roy L. *In Old Otsego: A New York County Views its Past.* Cooperstown, NY: Reprinted by The Freeman's Journal Co. for the Otsego County Board of Supervisors, 1959.

Card, Gene A. *Families of Otsego Co., NY, & Surrounding Areas: Bennett, Bentley, Boardman, Brown, Cass, Gardner, Potter, Seaver, Southern, Thurber.* Otsego County, NY: The Author, 2009.

Child, Hamilton. *Gazetteer and Business Directory of Otsego County, NY, for 1872–3.* Syracuse, 1872.

Compass System Map of Otsego County, New York: 1940 Special Classified Rural Register. Ithaca, NY: Rural Surveys, Inc., 1940.

Cooper, James F. *The Legends and Traditions of a Northern County.* Cooperstown: The Freeman's Journal Co., 1936.

Cutter, William R. *Genealogical and Family History of Central New York: A Record of the Achievements of Her People in the Making of a Commonwealth and the Building of a Nation.* New York: Lewis Historical Pub. Co., 1912.

Ellis, D. A. *Grand Army of the Republic: History of the Order in the U.S. by Counties: Otsego County Posts, Department of New York, Including a Complete Record of Soldiers Surviving and Buried in the County, with Company and Regiment ....* Otsego, NY, 1892.

Fay, Loren V. *Otsego County, New York, Genealogical Research Secrets.* Albany: The Author, 1981.

Fielder, Dorothy S. *Otsego County Postal History.* Walton, NY: Printed by the Reporter Co., 1994

Foley, Janet W. *Early Settlers of New York State: Their Ancestors and Descendants.* 9 vols. Akron, NY: 1934–1942. Reprint, 2 vols. Baltimore: Genealogical Publishing Co., 1993.

Frontier Days: Otsego County, 1776–1976. New York: Otsego County Bicentennial, Frontier Days Committee, 1976.

Gates, C. *Map of Otsego County, New York.* Philadelphia, 1856.

Hall, John. *School House John's Pictorial Collection of One Room Schools of Otsego County, NY.* Edited by Anita Harrison. Hartwick, NY: Hartwick Historical Society, 1997.

Hurd, D. Hamilton. *History of Otsego County, New York: With Illustrations and Biographical Sketches of Some of Its Prominent Men and Pioneers.* Philadelphia, 1878.

Matthews, Harry B. *The Abolitionist Movement and Reconstruction: Family Legacies in Cooperstown Village and Towns in Otsego County, New York. A Case Study in Historiographic Genealogy.* Oneonta, NY: The Author, 1995.

———. *A Guide to Local Abolitionists and Resource Materials Identifying African American Soldiers of the Civil War from New York and Other States: A Tribute to the United States Colored Troops Commemorative Symposium of Delaware and Otsego Counties, New York, 1997–1998.* Oneonta, NY: n.p., 1997.

New Century Atlas of Otsego County, New York: With Farm Records. Philadelphia: Century Map Co., 1903.

New York Historical Resources Center. *Guide to Historical Resources in Otsego County, New York, Repositories.* Ithaca, NY: Cornell University, 1982. [books.FamilySearch.org]

Reamy, Martha. *Early Families of Otsego County, New York.* Mount Airy, MD: Pipe Creek, 1995.

Reynolds, Paul E. *Geographical Names in Otsego County, New York.* Cooperstown, NY: Prepared for the New York State Historical Association, 1957–1959.

Roback, Henry. *The Veteran Volunteers of Herkimer and Otsego Counties in the War of the Rebellion: Being a History of the 152nd N.Y.V. with Scenes ... of the 34th N.Y., 97th N.Y., 121st N.Y. Heavy Artillery and 1st and 2nd N.Y. Mounted Rifles ... the 152nd N.Y. V. . . . .* Utica, NY, 1888.

Otsego County Planning Department. *Cemeteries of Otsego County: A Comprehensive Map of Active and Inactive Cemeteries in Otsego County, New York.* Cooperstown, NY: The Department, 2002.

Schull, Diantha D. *Landmarks of Otsego County.* Syracuse: Syracuse University Press, 1980.

Smith, Lelah. *Early Families of Otsego Co., NY.* 1955. Copied by John Potter. Mohawk, NY, 1982.

Additional Online Resources

Ancestry.com

There are vast numbers of records on *Ancestry.com* that pertain to people who have lived in New York State. See chapter 16 for a description of *Ancestry.com*'s resources and its partnership with the New York State Archives. A search of the online card catalog

by county may reveal lesser known resources that pertain to a locality, such as town records, abstracts, transcriptions, city directories, and local histories.

FamilySearch.org

FamilySearch has extensive collections of New York records, including religious records, which are searchable by name and location, but not by county. The following collections include record images (browsable, but not searchable) that are organized by county:

- "New York, Land Records, 1630–1975." Includes land and property records. *familysearch.org/search/collection/2078654*
- "New York, Probate Records, 1629–1971." Includes wills, letters of administration, and guardianship papers. *familysearch.org/search/collection/1920234*

For both collections, choose the browse option and then select Otsego to view the available records sets.

A detailed description of *FamilySearch.org* resources is found in chapter 16.

NYGenWeb Project: Otsego County
theusgenweb.org/ny/otsego

Part of the national, USGenWeb volunteer initiative, the website provides information and resources for county research.

www.FultonHistory.com

The website provides free access to a vast collection of digitized New York newspapers, including six titles for Otsego County.

Putnam County

Formed June 12, 1812

Parent County   Dutchess
Daughter Counties   None
County Seat   Carmel, Town of Carmel

Major Land Transactions
See chapter 7, Land Records
Highland (Philipse) Patent 1697
Oblong (tract) 1731

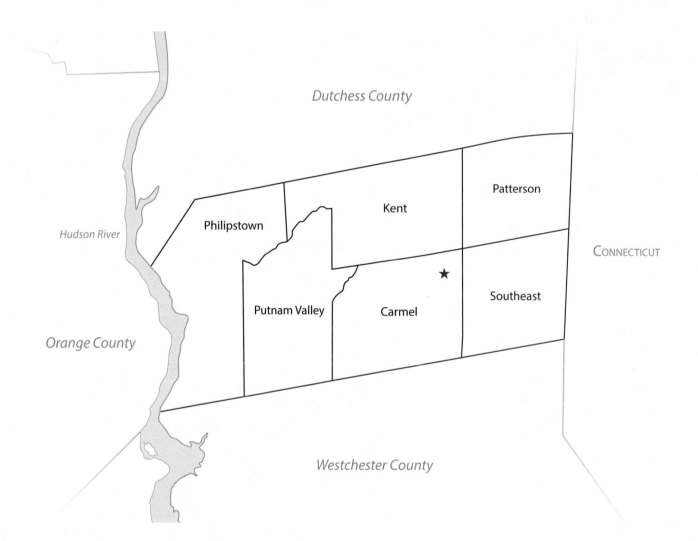

Dutchess County

Patterson

Kent

Philipstown

Hudson River

CONNECTICUT

★

Putnam Valley   Carmel   Southeast

Orange County

Westchester County

Town Boundary Map
★ - County seat

Towns (and Cities)	Villages and other Settlements		Notes
Carmel 1740 Settled 1795 Formed in Dutchess County from Town of Frederickstown * 1812 Transferred to new county of Putnam 1861 Ceded land west of Peekskill Hollow Creek to Putnam Valley	Baldwin Place Carmel Carmel Hills Crafts Hopkins Corners Houseman Corners Mahopac Mahopac Falls	Mahopac Mines Mahopac Point McLaughlin Acres Secor Corners Stillwater Tilly Foster Union Valley West Mahopac	* Town of Carmel came from the southwest quadrant of Frederickstown • Hamlet of Carmel county seat from 1812 • Mahopac Falls formerly Red Mills • Tilly Foster on Southeast town line
Franklin Name for Town of Patterson 1795–1808			
Frederick Name for Town of Kent 1795–1817			
Frederickstown 1788-1795 * Part of Highland/Philipse Patent 1719 Patent included in South Ward of Dutchess County 1737 Part of new Southern precinct 1772 Formed in Dutchess County as Fredericksburgh precinct from middle portion of Southern precinct 1788 Recognized as Town of Frederickstown in Dutchess County by State of New York 1795 Frederickstown divided into four towns: Carmel, Frederick (now Kent), Franklin (now Patterson), and Southeast *			* Frederickstown was Fredericksburgh precinct 1772–1788 * Town of Southeast's boundaries were changed; Southeast gained land from Frederickstown and gave land to Town of Franklin
Kent 1795 Formed in Dutchess County as Town of Frederick from Town of Frederickstown * 1812 Transferred to new county of Putnam 1817 Name changed from Frederick to Kent 1879 Annexed northwestern part of Town of Philipstown	Allen Corners Berkshire Terrace Boydsville Coles Mills Farmers Mills Foshays Corners Hortontown Kent Kent Cliffs	Kent Corners Kent Hills Kentwood Estates Lake Carmel Ludingtonville Meads Corners Richardsville Terry Corners Yale Corners	* Town of Frederick came from the northwest quadrant of Frederickstown • Farmers Mills also Milltown • Kent Cliffs formerly Boyds Corners • Richardsville formerly Dicktown
Oblong (tract) Boundary between New York and Connecticut was contested until 1731 when the Oblong tract was granted to New York 1731 Opened to settlement 1743 Southern portion annexed to Southern precinct			

Towns (and Cities)	Villages and other Settlements		Notes
Patterson 1795 Formed in Dutchess County as Town of Franklin from towns of Frederickstown and Southeast-town * 1808 Name changed to Patterson 1812 Transferred to new county of Putnam	Akins Corners Barnum Corners Big Elm Couch Corners Develville Fields Corners Haines Corners Haviland Hollow	Ice Pond Station Patterson Putnam Lake Steinbeck Corners Towners Towners Station Valleyville West Patterson	* The northern half of Southeasttown and the northeast quadrant of Frederick-stown formed Franklin * Southeastown see Town of Southeast • Big Elm also Elm Tree • Patterson also Patterson City • Towners also Towners Station
Philipstown Part of Highland/Philipse Patent **c. 1715** Settled 1719 Patent included in South Ward of Dutchess County 1737 Became part of new Southern precinct 1772 Formed in Dutchess County as Philips precinct from western part of Southern precinct 1788 Recognized as Town of Philipstown in Dutchess County by State of New York 1806 Ceded land in northwest corner to Town of Fishkill 1812 Transferred to new county of Putnam 1839 Daughter town Quincy (Putnam Valley) formed 1879 Ceded land (northeastern part of town) to Town of Kent	Breakneck Cold Spring (v) Constitution Island Continental Village Davenport Corners Denning Fahnestock Corners Forsonville Garrison(s) Garrison Four Corners Glenclyffe Graymoor Griffins Corners Highland Station Manitou MeKeel Corners Nelson Corners Nelsonville (v) North Highlands South Highlands Storm King Travis Corners		• Village of Cold Spring inc. 1846 • Constitution Island also Mart(e)laers Island • Continental Village on Putnam Valley town line • Garrison(s) formerly Garrisons Landing • Village of Nelsonville inc. 1855
Putnam Valley 1839 Formed as Quincy from Town of Philipstown 1840 Name changed to Putnam Valley 1861 Annexed land (west of Peekskill Hollow Creek) from Town of Carmel	Abele Park Adams Corners Amen Hill Bullet Hole Christian Corners Continental Village Croft(s) Corners Dennytown East Hill Gilbert Corners Indian Hill Indian Hill Road Lake Peekskill	Lawsonville Lookout Odel(l)town Oregon Oregon Corners Oscawana Corners Putnam Valley Roaring Brook Lake Sodom Sunnybrook Tom(p)kins Corners Wiccopee Wildwood	• Continental Village on Philipstown town line
Southeast * One of the first settled towns in the county 1772 Formed in Dutchess County as Southeast precinct from the Southern precinct; comprised land originally in the Oblong tract 1788 Recognized as Town of Southeasttown in Dutchess County by the State of New York	Brewster (v) Brewster Heights Brewster Hill Brewsters Station Brush Hollow Deans Corner Deforest Corners Doanesburg(h) Drewville Heights Dykeman(s)	Dykemans Station Foggingto(w)n Heddingville Milltown Peach Lake Sears Corners Sodom Southeast Center Tilly Foster	* Southeast also South East and South-East * Franklin renamed Patterson in 1808 • Village of Brewster inc. 1894 • Doanesburg(h) also Doansburg • Tilly Foster on Carmel town line

(Southeast continued on next page)

Towns (and Cities)	Villages and other Settlements	Notes
Southeast * (continued)		
1795 Name changed to Southeast; boundaries redrawn, ceded northern half to new Town of Franklin, and annexed southeast quadrant of former Town of Frederickstown *		
1812 Transferred to new county of Putnam		
Southern (precinct) *		* Southern precinct also called the South Precinct
1697 Highland/Philipse Patent in Dutchess County granted to Frederick Philipse		
1719 Patent included in South Ward of Dutchess County		
1737 Patent becomes Southern precinct of Dutchess County		
1743 Boundary extended east across the Oblong tract		
1772 Divided into three new Dutchess County precincts of Philips, Fredericksburgh, and Southeast		

Note about Putnam County

Putnam County was formed in 1812 after separating from Dutchess County. For earlier records, see Dutchess County.

NEW YORK STATE CENSUS RECORDS
See also chapter 3, Census Records

The state census for Putnam County is lost for all years 1825–1905, except 1825 Town of Patterson, county originals at Southeast Museum, Brewster; 1845 towns of Kent and Philipstown, county originals at the New-York Historical Society. See Glendon Wheeler's abstract for Kent.

State originals at the NYSA: 1915, 1925

Microfilm at the FHL, NYPL, and NYSL; many years are online at *FamilySearch.org* and *Ancestry.com*.

NATIONAL/STATEWIDE REPOSITORIES & RESOURCES
See chapter 16

COUNTYWIDE REPOSITORIES & RESOURCES

Putnam County Clerk
Putnam County Office Building • 40 Gleneida Avenue, Room 100
Carmel, NY 10512 • (845) 808-1142
www.putnamcountyny.com/county-clerk

Civil and criminal court records, deeds and mortgages, maps, judgment and lien dockets, and related books and documents. The county clerk has an index to naturalization records; actual records are kept at the Putnam County Archives (see below).

Putnam County – Town and Village Clerks
Birth, marriage, and death records are maintained by the clerk of the municipality in which the event occurred; see Introduction to County Guides for records generally held by municipal clerks. See municipal websites for details and contact information.

Putnam County Surrogate's Court
44 Gleneida Avenue • Carmel, NY 10512 • (845) 208-7860

Holds probate records from 1814 to the present. See also chapter 6, Probate Records.

Putnam County Archives and Putnam County Historian
68 Marvin Avenue • Brewster, NY 10509-1515 • (845) 808-1420
Email: historian@putnamcountyny.gov
www.putnamcountyny.com/countyhistorian

The office of the county historian holds both the County Archives of governmental records and the Historian's Collection of archival documents, derivative records, and other material. The County Archives includes census, court, probate, naturalization, tax, and town records. The Historian's Collection includes books, maps, photographs, and pamphlets; historical newspapers and periodicals; city directories; family histories; lineage books from the local DAR chapter; and clipping files; a detailed description of is on the website. A reference library provides public access, but appointments are required. The Historian's *Handbook for Putnam County History and Genealogy* is updated annually and available for purchase.

Putnam County – All Municipal Historians
While not authorized to answer genealogical inquiries, town and village historians can provide valuable historical information and research advice; some maintain collections and webpages which may include transcribed records, local histories, and other genealogical

material. See contact information at *www.putnamcountyny.com/countyhistorian/town-village-links* or at the website of the Association of Public Historians of New York State at *www.aphnys.org*.

Putnam County History Museum, Putnam County Historical Society and the Foundry School Museum
63 Chestnut Street • Cold Spring, NY 10516 • (845) 265-4010
Email: office@pchs-fsm.org or library@pchs-fsm.org • *www.pchs-fsm.org*

The Society operates a museum in a historic foundry. Collections include business records, photographs, and papers of the Ludington and Kemble families, manuscripts, maps, newspapers, periodicals, and genealogy files on local families.

Putnam County Public Libraries
Putnam is part of the Mid-Hudson Library System; see *www.midhudson.org* to access each library. Many hold genealogy and local history collections such as local newspapers; some are online and accessed from their websites. For example, Brewster Public Library has digitized the *Brewster Standard*, 1870–1982 and Mahopac Public Library has digitized the *Putnam County Courier*, 1849–1930. Also see listing below for Alice Curtis Desmond & Hamilton Fish Library and its online archive.

REGIONAL REPOSITORIES & RESOURCES
See listings in the Dutchess County Guide

LOCAL REPOSITORIES & RESOURCES
Alphabetized by location

Landmark Preservation Society of Southeast
Old Southeast Church and Walter Brewster House
43 Oak Street • Brewster, NY 10509 • (845) 279-7429
Email: walterbrewsterhouse@yahoo.com • *www.landmarksse.org*

Headquarters of the Enoch Crosby Chapter of the DAR, which has transcribed vast numbers of records in Putnam County. Holdings include photographs and contents of Old Southeast Church.

Southeast Museum
67 Main Street • Brewster, NY 10509 • (845) 279-7500
Email: info@southeastmuseum.org • *www.southeastmuseum.org*

Documents history of Harlem Line Railroad, Tilly Foster Mine, Croton Reservoir System, and Early American Circus. Archives include the 1825 New York state census for Town of Patterson, business ledgers, deeds, letters, and handwritten rolls of residents

Alice Curtis Desmond & Hamilton Fish Library: Livingston-Svirsky Archives
472 Route 203 • PO Box 265 • Garrison, NY 10524 • (845) 424-3020
dflstaff@highlands.com • *www.desmondfishlibrary.org*

The website gives access to the Livingston-Svirsky Archive, a digitized local history collection of books, articles, maps, and photographs, many with countywide relevance. Library collections include more than 26,000 family histories and local histories, microfilmed census and other records, and other material.

Kent Historical Society
PO Box 123 • Kent, NY 10512 • (845) 225-4882
Email: kenthistoricalsociety@gmail.com • Facebook page

Documents history of the one room schoolhouse 1900–1944, and of Farmers Mills, a large five mill town. Holdings include photographs, slide collection, and oral history of area residents.

Town of Carmel Historical Society and Museum
40 McAlpin Avenue • PO Box 456 • Mahopac, NY 10541-2301
(845) 628-0500 • Email: carmelhistory@aol.com
www.carmelhistory.blogspot.com

Books, albums and journals, business ledgers, maps, newspapers, phone books, yearbooks, photographs, personal papers, poorkeeper records 1768–1812, town and county minutes documenting history of Carmel, Mahopac, and Mahopac Falls. Working to transcribe and digitize records, newspapers, and maps.

Patterson Historical Society
Patterson Court House • 1167 Route 311
Patterson, NY 12563-0416 • Email: info@pattersonhistoricalsociety.org
www.pattersonhistoricalsociety.org

Holdings include school-related memorabilia, photographs, materials related to Town of Patterson.

Putnam Valley Historical Society and Schoolhouse Museum
301 Peekskill Hollow Road • PO Box 297 • Putnam Valley, NY 10579
(845) 528-1024 • Email: pvhistoricalsociety@verizon.net
Facebook page

Holdings include photographs, genealogical material, and 19th-century manuscripts. Will provide research assistance.

SELECTED PRINT AND ONLINE RESOURCES

Below is a selection of resources relevant for research in this borough. The list is representative, not exhaustive. Additional titles—particularly of abstracts, indexes, transcriptions, and local histories—are available; consult the introduction to Part Two for further information. For guidance on how to identify and locate community directories and local newspapers, see chapter 11, City Directories, and chapter 12, Newspapers, in Part One of this book.

Abstracts, Indexes & Transcriptions

See also the Dutchess County Guide for abstracts and transcriptions of early records that pre-date Putnam County's formation in 1812.

Bailey, Carol, and Catherine Wargas, comps. *Putnam County Men in the Civil War.* Brewster, NY: Putnam County Historian, 2008. Book includes names and service records.

Buys, Barbara Smith. *Old Gravestones of Putnam County, New York, Together with Information from Ten Adjacent Dutchess County Burying Grounds: Eleven Thousand Eight Hundred Inscriptions of Persons Born up to and Including 1850.* Baltimore: Gateway Press, 1975. Index available from Berkshire Family History Association.

Calkins, H., Jr. "The Records of Philippi [Congregational Church], now Southeast, Putnam Co., N.Y." *NYG&B Record,* vol. 32 (1901) no. 2: 100–104, no. 3: 169–172. [NYG&B eLibrary]

Daughters of the American Revolution, comps. *New York DAR Genealogical Records Committee Report.* Since 1913 DAR volunteers have transcribed many thousands of unpublished cemetery, church, and town records throughout New York. The reports are at the DAR Library; copies are at the NYSL and the NYPL. The DAR has a searchable name index to all the GRC reports at *http://services.dar.org/Public/DAR_Research/search/?Tab_ID=6.* See Jean Worden's index below for a listing by county of the New York record sets that were transcribed by the DAR before 1998.

Daughters of the American Revolution. Enoch Crosby Chapter, Helen G. Daniels, Florence D. Hopkins, and Harriet Akin Ferris. "Historical Records of Enoch Crosby Chapter; Putnam, Dutchess and Westchester Counties, New York." 3 vols. Typescript, 1944–1959. DAR Library, Washington, DC. Includes indexes. [Microfilm at FHL]

Daughters of the American Revolution, Enoch Crosby Chapter, Libby Baker, Carol Bailey, and Jeanne Marie Perry. *Gravestones of Revolutionary War Patriots in Putnam County, NY.* Carmel, NY: NSDAR, 2011.

Dutchess County Historical Society. "Town of Southeast, Tax List, 1779." *The Dutchess,* vol. 15, no. 3 (1988): 97–99.

Dykeman, W. Jerome. "Tombstone Inscriptions in the Old Cemetery at Tilly Foster, Putnam Co., New York." *NYG&B Record,* vol. 45, no. 2 (1914): 116. [NYG&B eLibrary]

———. "Tombstone Inscriptions from the Old Fowler Family Cemetery, Tilly Foster, Putnam Co., New York." *NYG&B Record,* vol. 45, no. 4 (1914): 307. [NYG&B eLibrary]

Eaderley, William Applebie. "Putnam County, New York, Cemeteries, 1794–1914." Typescript, 1917. NYPL, New York.

Fisher, Floyd. *They All Rest Together: Burial Sites of Early Settlers—Southern Dutchess and Putnam Counties.* Holmes, NY: The Author, 1972.

Foster, Emma J., and Julia R. Livingston. "Inscriptions from the Old Baptist Burying Ground, Carmel, N.Y." *NYG&B Record,* vol. 35, no. 1 (1904): 56–60. [NYG&B eLibrary]

———. "Inscriptions in Milltown Cemetery, Southeast, N.Y." *NYG&B Record,* vol. 38 (1907) no. 4: 273–277; vol. 39 (1908) no. 1: 42–46. [NYG&B eLibrary]

Frost, Josephine C. "Cemetery Inscriptions, Haviland Hollow and Quaker Hill, NY." Typescript, 1936. NYPL, New York. [NYG&B eLibrary]

———. "Inscriptions from Ten Cemeteries in Putnam County, New York." Typescript, 1911. NYPL, New York.

———. "Inscriptions from 13 Old Cemeteries in Putnam County, New York." Typescript, 1912. Library of Congress, Washington, DC. [*Archive.org*]

———. "Putnam County Cemetery Inscriptions, New York." Typescript, 1910. NYPL, New York.

Haacker, Frederick C. "Early Settlers of Putnam County, New York." Typescript, 1946. Library of Congress, Washington, DC. [*Archive.org*]

———. "Records of Early Settlers of Putnam County and Cortlandt Manor." Typescript, 1954. NYPL, New York. On microfilm at various libraries.

Horton, William P. "Gravestone Inscriptions from the Churchyard, St. Philip's Protestant Episcopal Church, Garrisons, N.Y." *NYG&B Record,* vol. 55 (1924) no. 1: 78–84, no. 2: 168–170. [NYG&B eLibrary]

———. "Graveyard Inscriptions, Methodist Churchyard, South Highlands, Putnam Co., N.Y." *NYG&B Record,* vol. 55, no. 2 (1924): 185–190. [NYG&B eLibrary]

———. "Graveyard Inscriptions, North Highlands, Putnam Co., N.Y." *NYG&B Record,* vol. 55 (1924) no. 2: 190–192, no. 3: 236–240. Cemetery "on the State Road back of Cold Springs." [NYG&B eLibrary]

———."Graveyard Inscriptions, Putnam County, N.Y." *NYG&B Record*, vol. 49 (1918) no. 1: 76–82, no. 2: 177–181, no. 3: 288–294, no. 4: 308–317. Includes Peekskill Hollow, Adams Corners, and Lafayette Avenue cemeteries, and others. [NYG&B eLibrary]

———."Graveyard Inscriptions, Putnam County, N.Y." *NYG&B Record*, vol. 56 (1925) no. 1: 68–73, no. 3: 288–294, no. 4: 308–317. Includes Lake Mahopac Methodist Churchyard, Farmers Mills Baptist Church, Barrett Cemetery, Halstead Cemetery, and others. [NYG&B eLibrary]

———."Putnam and Westchester Counties Cemetery Inscriptions and Marriage Dates." Typescript, 1928. NYPL, New York. [FHL microfilm]

MacCormick, Elizabeth J. "Abstracts of Wills of Putnam County, N.Y." Typescript, 1942. NYPL, New York. Covers Libers A–D.

Nicholson, William A. "Inscriptions from Clift or Drew Cemetery, about Two Miles South of Brewsters in the Town of South East, Putnam County, N.Y." *NYG&B Record*, vol. 49, no. 4 (1918): 326–329. [NYG&B eLibrary]

Old Southeast Cemetery: A History and Handbook. Brewster, NY: Landmarks Preservation Committee, 1976.

Southeast Museum. *1898 and 1902 Enumeration of the Inhabitants, Brewster, Putnam County, New York*. Brewster, NY. Handwritten lists in the Southeast Museum.

Ruddock, William T. *Confiscated Properties of Philipse Highland Patent Putnam County New York 1780–1785*. Westminster, MD: Heritage Books, 2012.

Wheeler, Glendon E. *Burials and Gravestones: Families Associated with Putnam County, New York*. Rhinebeck, NY: Kinship, 1998. Separate index by the author.

———, comp. *Index of Gravestones for the People of Putnam County, New York*. Rhinebeck, NY: Kinship, 1997.

———. *Town Records: Frederickstown to Kent, 1788–1841, Dutchess/Putnam Counties, New York*. Rhinebeck, NY: Kinship, 2002.

Wheeler, Glendon E., and Betty M. L. Behr. *State Census, Town of Kent, Putnam County, N.Y., 1845*. Rhinebeck, NY: Kinship, 2005.

Worden, Jean D. "Book 1, Subject Index." In *Revised Master Index to the New York State Daughters of the American Revolution Genealogical Records Volumes*. Zephyrhills, FL: J. D. Worden, 1998. The Subject Index includes a listing by county of the cemeteries, churches, towns, and other sources of records transcribed by the DAR.

Other Resources

Blake, William J. *The History of Putnam County, New York; with an Enumeration of Its Towns, Villages, Rivers, Creeks, Lakes, Ponds, Mountains, Hills, and Geological Features; Local Traditions; and Short Biographical Sketches of Early Settlers, etc.* Middletown, NY: T. Emmett Henderson, 1849.

Boyer, Donna, ed. *An Introduction to the Availability of the Historical and Genealogical Primary Sources in Eastern Putnam County*. Carmel, NY: Kent Library, 1986.

Commemorative Biographical Record of the Counties of Dutchess and Putnam, New York: Containing Biographical Sketches of Prominent and Representative Citizens and of Many of the Early Settled Families. Chicago: J. H. Beers, 1897.

Conklin, Henry S. "Maps of Lots Sold by the New York Commissioners of Forfeitures, 1779–1786." Drafted by Henry Conklin, 1885, held by the Putnam County Historian, Brewster, NY.

Historical and Genealogical Record, Dutchess and Putnam Counties, New York. Poughkeepsie, NY: Oxford Publishing, 1912.

Historical Records: Putnam, Dutchess, and Westchester Counties of New York State. Carmel, NY: DAR, Enoch Crosby Chapter.

Lustenberger, Anita. "When Connecticut Became New York: Researching in the Oblong before 1800." *Connecticut Ancestry*, vol. 47, no. 2 (2004): 169–178.

New York Genealogical and Biographical Society. *Putnam County Church Surveys*. Digitally published by New York Genealogical and Biographical Society, 2012. Identifies records held by St. Philips in the Highlands, St. James' Chapel, and Gilead Presbyterian Church, ca. 1900. [NYG&B eLibrary]

New York Historical Resources Center. *Guide to Historical Resources in Putnam County, New York, Repositories*. Ithaca, NY: Cornell University, 1989. [books.FamilySearch.org]

Pelletreau, William Smith. *History of Putnam County, New York: With Biographical Sketches of Its Prominent Men*. Philadelphia: W. W. Preston, 1886.

Putnam County Historian. *A Handbook for Putnam County History and Genealogy*. Brewster, NY: Office of the County Historian, 2012.

Town of Patterson, Christina Mucciolo, Ezra Ayres, James H. Cornwall, Samuel Cornwall, Benjamin Cowl, James C. Hayt, John Hayt, and Cyrus B. Laurence. *Patterson (N.Y.) Town Clerk Records, 1795–1863*. Rhinebeck, NY: Kinship, 2007.

Town of Putnam Valley, Christina Mucciolo, and Christine O'Connor. *Town of Putnam Valley Town Records, 1839–1916*. Rhinebeck, NY: Kinship, 2008.

U.S. Census Office. *Special Schedules of the 11th Census (1890) Enumerating Union Veterans and Widows of Union Veterans of the Civil War New York, Bundle 109 (Columbia, Dutchess, Putnam, and Westchester Counties)*. Washington: National Archives, 1948.

Zimm, Louise Hasbrouck. *Southeastern New York: History of the Counties of Ulster, Dutchess, Orange, Rockland, and Putnam*. 3 vols. New York: Lewis Historical Publishing, 1946. Index available from Berkshire Family History Association.

Additional Online Resources

Ancestry.com

There are vast numbers of records on *Ancestry.com* that pertain to people who have lived in New York State. See chapter 16 for a description of *Ancestry.com*'s resources and its partnership with the New York State Archives. A search of the online card catalog by county may reveal lesser known resources that pertain to a locality, such as town records, abstracts, transcriptions, city directories, and local histories.

FamilySearch.org

FamilySearch has extensive collections of New York records, including religious records, which are searchable by name and location, but not by county. The following collections include record images (browsable, but not searchable) that are organized by county:

- "New York, Land Records, 1630–1975." Includes land and property records. *familysearch.org/search/collection/2078654*

- "New York, Probate Records, 1629–1971." Includes wills, letters of administration, and guardianship papers. *familysearch.org/search/collection/1920234*

For both collections, choose the browse option and then select Putnam to view the available records sets. Select Dutchess County to view early records that pre-date Putnam County's formation in 1812. A detailed description of *FamilySearch.org* resources is found in chapter 16.

Historic Patterson
www.historicpatterson.org
> Articles, photographs, information on local churches, industry, American Indians, agriculture, education, place names, etc.

Hudson River Valley Heritage (HRVH)
www.hrvh.org/cdm
> The HRVH website provides free access to digital collections of historical material from more than 40 organizations in Columbia, Greene, Dutchess, Ulster, Sullivan, Rockland, Orange, Putnam, and Westchester counties.

New York Heritage Digital Collections: New York State Newspaper Project
www.nyheritage.org/newspapers
> The website provides links to digital newspapers collections in 26 counties (currently) made accessible through New York Heritage, New York State Historic Newspapers, HRVH Historical Newspapers, and other providers.

NYGenWeb Project: Putman County
www.rootsweb.ancestry.com /~nyputnam
> Part of the national, USGenWeb volunteer initiative, the website provides information and resources for county research.

Old Fulton New York Postcards
www.FultonHistory.com
> The website provides free access to a vast collection of digitized New York newspapers, including three titles for Putnam County.

Preserve Putnam County
www.preserveputnam.org/thennow.html
> Online articles and images that trace Putnam County's development and give background on historical places.

Rensselaer County

Formed February 7, 1791

Parent County   Albany
Daughter Counties None
County Seat   City of Troy

Major Land Transactions
See chapter 7, Land Records
Rensselaerwyck 1629
Saratoga Patent 1684

Town Boundary Map
★ - County seat

Towns (and Cities)	Villages and other Settlements		Notes
Berlin 1806 Formed from towns of Peterburgh, Schodack, and Stephentown 1812 Daughter town Sand Lake formed	Berlin Berlin Center Bucks Corner Center Berlin	Cherry Plain South Berlin West Berlin	
Brunswick 1807 Formed from City of Troy 1814 Ceded land to City of Troy 1839 Annexed land from Town of Lansingburgh	Brunswick Brunswick Center Clum(s) Corner(s) Cropseyville Eagle Mills	East Brunswick Hayner(s)ville Millville Tamarac(k)	• Brunswick Center also Centre Brunswick • East Brunswick also Rock Hollow • Hayner(s)ville also Cooksborough; formerly in Town of Pittstown • Tamarac(k) also Platestown, formerly Plattstown
Clinton Name for Town of East Greenbush 1855–1858			
East Greenbush 1855 Formed as Clinton from Town of Greenbush 1858 Name changed to East Greenbush 1902 Ceded land to City of Rensselaer	Best Clinton Heights Couse East Greenbush Greenbush Hampton Manor	Hampton Park Luther Prospect Heights Sherwood Park Woodland Park	• Couse also Couse Corners
Grafton 1807 Formed from Town of Petersburgh and City of Troy	Babcock Lake East Grafton	Grafton Quackenkill	• Grafton also Grafton Center, formerly Patroon Mills
Greenbush 1792–1897 (see East Greenbush, North Greenbush and City of Rensselaer) 1792 Formed from district of Rensselaerwyck (see Albany County) 1795 Second act of incorporation 1812 Daughter town Sand Lake formed 1843 Annexed land from Town of Sand Lake 1855 Daughter towns Clinton (now East Greenbush) and North Greenbush formed leaving the Village of Greenbush coterminous with the town 1897 Incorporated as a city and name changed to Rensselaer	East Albany Greenbush (v)		• East Albany was the northern section of Village of Greenbush • Village of Greenbush inc. 1815; from 1855 the village and the town boundaries were coterminous; became City of Rensselaer in 1897
Hoosick 1688 Hoosick Patent granted 1772 Formed as a district 1788 Recognized as a town in Albany County 1791 Transferred to new county of Rensselaer	Buskirk Eagle Bridge East Buskirk East Hoosick Hoosick Hoosick Corner(s) Hoosick Falls (v) Hoosick Junction Junction Mapletown North Hoosick	Petersburg Junction Potter Hill Potterville San Coick Southwest Hoosick Tiashoke Trumanville Walloomsac(k) West Hoosick White Creek Station	• Buskirk also Buskirk(s) Bridge • Village of Hoosick Falls inc. 1827 • Junction was on Schaghticoke town line • North Hoosick also McNamarasville, McNarasville, and St. Croix • Petersburg Junction on Petersburgh town line

Towns (and Cities)	Villages and other Settlements	Notes
Lansingburgh 1807–1900 1807 Formed from towns of Petersburgh and City of Troy 1819 Annexed land from Town of Schaghticoke 1836 Ceded land to City of Troy 1839 Ceded land to Town of Brunswick 1900 Town ceded to City of Troy	Lansingburgh (v) Spiegeltown	• Village of Lansingburgh founded 1770 (formerly New City); incorporated 1790 in Rensselaerwyck; 1791 located in new Town of Troy when it was also known as North Troy; 1807 ceded to new Town of Lansingburgh; became part of City of Troy 1900 • Spiegeltown in Town of Schaghticoke before 1819
Nassau 1806 Formed as Philipstown from towns of Petersburgh, Schodack, and Stephentown 1808 Name changed to Nassau	Alps Jacks Corners Brainard(s) Lyons Lake Brainard Station Miller(s) Corners Central Nassau Nassau (v) Denault Corners Nassau Mills Dunham Hollow North Nassau East Nassau Ontikehomawck Hoag(s) Corner(s) West Nassau	• Brainards formerly Brainards Bridge • Village of Nassau inc. 1819; shared with Town of Schodack • Ontikehomawck formerly a Stockbridge Indian village • West Nassau formerly Schermerhorns Village, Schermerhorns, and Union Village
North Greenbush 1855 Formed from Town of Greenbush 1902 Ceded Village of Bath to City of Rensselaer	Bath (v) Defreestville North Greenbush Snyder(s) Corners Snyders Lake Wynantskill	• Village of Bath inc. 1874; also Bath-on-the-Hudson, ceded to City of Rensselaer 1902 • Defreestville also Defriestville; formerly Blooming Grove, name changed due to confusion with Blooming Grove, Orange County • Snyder(s) Corner on Poestenkill town line
Petersburgh 1791 Formed from Town of Stephentown 1806 Daughter towns of Berlin and Philipstown (now Nassau) formed 1807 Daughter towns Grafton and Lansingburgh formed	North Petersburgh Petersburg(h) Petersburgh Four Corners Petersburgh Junction Stillham	• Hamlet of Petersburg(h) formerly Rensselaer Mills and South Petersburgh • Petersburgh Junction on Hoosick town line • Stillham also Stillman
Philipstown Name for Town of Nassau 1806–1808		
Pittstown 1650 Settlement commenced 1761 Became a township by patent in Albany County (part of Schaghticoke District) 1788 Recognized as town by State of New York 1791 Transferred to new county of Rensselaer	Boynton North Pittstown Boyntonville Pittstown East Pittstown Prospect Hill Factory Hollow Raymertown Hayner(s)ville Shermans Mills Johnsonville Tomhannock Little Red Schoolhouse Valley Falls (v) Millertown	• Hayner(s)ville also Cooksborough; now in Town of Brunswick • Johnsonville also Akins Junction, Hooses Mills, and The Lick • Pittstown also Pittstown Corners • Village of Valley Falls inc. 1902; also Pittstown Station; shared with Town of Schaghticoke
Poestenkill 1848 Formed from Town of Sand Lake	Barberville Poestenkill East Poestenkil Snyder(s) Corners Ives Corners	• East Poestenkill also Columbia • Snyder(s) Corner on North Greenbush town line

Towns (and Cities)	Villages and other Settlements		Notes
Rensselaer (city) 1897 Town and Village of Greenbush incorporated as City of Rensselaer * 1902 Annexed Village of Bath, Town of North Greenbush, and western part of Town of East Greenbush	Bath (on-Hudson) De Laets Burg East Albany		* Town of Greenbush coterminous with Village of Greenbush • East Albany formerly part of Village of Greenbush
Sand Lake 1812 Formed from towns of Berlin and Greenbush 1843 Ceded land to Town of Greenbush 1848 Daughter town Poestenkill formed	Aiken Averill Park Glass House Glass Lake McLarens Mill Rensselaer	Sand Lake Sliter(s) Sliters Corners South Sand Lake Taborton West Sand Lake	• Glass House formerly Rensselaer Village • West Sand Lake formerly Ulinesville
Schaghticoke 1772 Formed as a district in Albany County 1788 Recognized as a town by State of New York 1791 Transferred to new county of Rensselaer 1819 Ceded land to Town of Lansingburgh	East Schaghticoke Grant(s) Hollow Hemstreet Park Junction Melrose Old Schaghticoke Pleasantdale	Reynolds Schaghticoke (v) Schaghticoke Hill Speigeltown The Borough Valley Falls (v) West Valley Falls	• Junction on Hoosick town line • Village of Schaghticoke inc. as Harts Falls 1867; name changed to Schaghticoke in 1881; formerly Schaghticoke Point • Spiegeltown in Town of Lansingburgh after 1819 • Village of Valley Falls inc. 1902; also Pittstown Station; shared with Town of Pittstown
Schodack 1795 Formed from Rensselaerwyck (see Albany County) 1806 Daughter towns Berlin and Philipstown (now Nassau) formed	Braeside Brookview Bunker Hill Castleton-on-Hudson (v) East Schodack Mastens Corners Morey Park Muitzes Kill Nassau (v) North Schodack	Post Road Crossing Rice Corners Rosecrans Park Schodack Schodack Center Schodack Landing Shivers Corners South Schodack Stony Point Van Hoesen Station	• Brookview also Schodack Depot • Village of Castleton-on-Hudson inc. 1827; also Castleton, formerly Morriches Hastie • East Schodack also Scotts Corners • Muitzes Kill also Muitzeskill • Village of Nassau inc. 1819; shared with Town of Nassau
Stephentown 1784 Formed from Rensselaerwyck (see Albany County) 1788 Recognized as a town by State of New York 1791 Transferred to new county of Rensselaer; daughter town Petersburgh formed 1806 Daughter towns Berlin and Philipstown (now Nassau) formed	Garfield North Stephentown South Stephentown Stephentown Stephentown Center Stephentown Flats Stephentown Station West Stephentown Wyomanock		• Stephentown Center formerly Mechanicsville

Towns (and Cities)	Villages and other Settlements	Notes
Troy (city) ∗ Settled pre-Revolution by Dutch; settlement known as Ashleys Ferry and Vanderheydens Ferry 1789 Name Troy adopted in Albany County 1791 Transferred to new county of Rensselaer; formed as a town from Rensselaerwyck, Albany County 1807 Daughter towns Brunswick, Grafton, and Lansingburgh formed 1814 Annexed land from Town of Brunswick 1816 City charter 1836 Ceded land to Town of Greenbush; annexed land from Town of Lansingburgh 1900 Annexed Town of Lansingburgh	Albia Downtown East Side Frear Park Lansingburg(h) North Central South Central South Troy Sycaway The Hill Troy (v)	∗ County seat at Troy from 1791 when county was formed • Lansingburgh also North Troy, formerly in Town of Lansingburgh • Village of Troy inc. 1801, reinc. 1806; dissolved and became part of City of Troy 1816

NEW YORK STATE CENSUS RECORDS
See also chapter 3, Census Records

County originals at Rensselaer County Clerk's Office
1855, 1865*, 1875, 1905, 1915, 1925 (1825, 1835, 1845, and 1892 are lost)

State originals at the NYSA: 1915, 1925

Microfilm at the FHL, NYPL, and NYSL; many years are online at *FamilySearch.org* and *Ancestry.com*.

*1865 City of Troy index online at *www.connorsgenealogy.com/troy*

NATIONAL/STATEWIDE REPOSITORIES & RESOURCES
See chapter 16

COUNTYWIDE REPOSITORIES & RESOURCES

Rensselaer County Clerk
105 Third Street • Troy, NY 12180 • (518) 270-4080
www.rensco.com/departments_countyclerk.asp

Land records, court records, naturalization records 1824–1908, and original copies of the New York state census for Rensselaer County 1855, 1865, 1875, 1905, 1915, and 1925.

Rensselaer County – City, Town, and Village Clerks
Birth, marriage, and death records are maintained by the clerk of the municipality in which the event occurred; see Introduction to County Guides for details of other records which may also be held by municipal clerks. For contact information, see *www.rensselaercounty. org/Index.htm*.

Rensselaer County Surrogate's Court
Rensselaer County Courthouse • 1504 Fifth Avenue
Troy, NY 12180 • (518) 285-6100

Holds microfilm probate records from 1794 to the present. See also chapter 6, Probate Records.

Rensselaer County Public Libraries
Rensselaer County is part of the Upper Hudson Library System; see *www.uhls.org* to access each library. Information about special collections relating to local history, genealogy, and archival materials can be found at *www.uhls.org/NICHE/Libraries.htm*. Troy Public Library and Valley Falls Free Library have particularly strong collections and are listed below.

Troy Public Library: Troy Room Collection of Genealogy and Local History
100 Second Street • Troy, NY 12180 • (518) 274-7071
Email: troyref@thetroylibrary.org • *www.thetroylibrary.org*
Research Guide: *www.thetroylibrary.org/pdf/FindAncestors.pdf*

Books and periodicals, biographies, census microfilm, church and cemetery records, city directories, immigration books and naturalization record microfilms, military records, newspapers and newsletters, school records, scrapbooks, newspaper vital record indexes, wills, and Local History and Portrait Index. A 21-page research guide provides details of special collections at the library.

Rensselaer County Historical Society and Historian
57 Second Street • Troy, NY 12180 • (518) 272-7232
Email: research@rchsonline.org • *www.rchsonline.org*

Holds origina probate records from 1794 to early–1900s, business records, diaries, letters, maps and atlases (early 1800s–1990), photographs, scrapbooks, ephemera, city directories, county and family histories, social and labor histories, and town and village histories. Special Collections include papers of local institutions, businesses, and families. Offers research services for a fee. Publishes *Current History*, quarterly.

Rensselaer County – All Municipal Historians
While not authorized to answer genealogical inquiries, town and village historians can provide valuable historical information and research advice; some maintain collections and webpages which may include transcribed records, local histories, and other genealogical material. See contact information at *www.rootsweb.ancestry.com/~nyrensse/history.htm* or at the website of the Association of Public Historians of New York State at *www.aphnys.org*.

REGIONAL REPOSITORIES & RESOURCES

University at Albany, SUNY: M. E. Grenander Department of Special Collections and Archives
See listing in Albany County Guide

Bard College Archives and Special Collections
See listing in Dutchess County Guide

Capital District Genealogical Society
See listing in Albany County Guide

Fulton-Montgomery Community College: Evans Library: The Kenneth R. Dorn Regional History Study Center
See listing in Fulton County Guide

LOCAL REPOSITORIES & RESOURCES
Alphabetized by location

Brunswick Historical Society
The Garfield School: 605 Brunswick Road • Eagle Mills, NY 12180
(518) 279-4024 • *Society*: PO Box 1776 • Cropseyville, NY 12052
Email: president@bhs-ny.org • *www.bhs-ny.org*

Genealogies, surname files, books, church and cemetery records, census microfilm, newspaper files (1960–present), photographs, and ephemera. Offers research services for a fee.

Grafton Historical Society
Grafton Town Hall • 2379 Route 2 • PO Box 244 • Grafton, NY 12082
(518) 641-9660 • Email: historicgrafton@aol.com
www.graftonny.org/wordpress/historical

Genealogies (list of surnames on website), Hydorn Collection, newspapers (*Defender*, 1942–1955), obituary database, photographs, school records, and scrapbooks.

Hoosick Township Historical Society and Museum
166 Main Street • Hoosick Falls, NY 12090 • (518) 686-4682
Email: Staff@HoosickHistory.com • *www.hoosickhistory.com*

Holdings include cemetery information and name index for local families; website includes online articles, biographies, local history timeline, and photographs.

City of Rensselaer Historian and Rensselaer City History Research Center
Rensselaer City Hall, Second Floor • 62 Washington Street
Rensselaer, NY 12144 • (518) 694-3126
www.rensselaerny.gov/departments/Historian.aspx

Histories and genealogies, family papers, directories, maps, newspapers, photographs, and yearbooks documenting history of City of Rensselaer and villages of Bath-on-the-Hudson, Greenbush, East Albany, and Rensselaerwyck.

The Knickerbocker Historical Society and Knickerbocker Mansion

132 Knickerbocker Road • PO Box 29 • Schaghticoke, NY 12154
(518) 664-1700 • Email: knickinfo@aol.com • www.knickmansion.com

Documents Knickerbocker genealogy and Old Schaghticoke history. Publishes the *Knickerbocker* semiannually.

Stephentown Historical Society and Museum & Library

5 Staples Road • PO Box 11 • Stephentown, NY 12168
(518) 733-6070 • Email: shs@fairpoint.net
www.stephentown-historical.org

Cemetery records, newspapers, and town records. Website includes local cemetery list (locations and lists of burials), and name index to cemetery records.

Lansingburgh Historical Society and Herman Melville House

Two 114th Street • PO Box 219 • Lansingburgh Station
Troy, NY 12182-0219 • (518) 235-7647
Email: lhssecretary@gmail.com • www.lansingburghhistoricalsociety.org

Most of Society's collection of diaries, business records, maps, photographs, town and village records, and other documents are held at Rensselaer County Historical Society Library (see above). Society maintains collection of documents relating to history of Town of Lansingburgh.

Pittstown Historical Society

PO Box 252 • Valley Falls, NY 12185 • (518) 686-7514
Email: pittstownhs@gmail.com
http://pittstown.us/historical_society/pittstown_historical_society.htm

Family histories, local history books, transcriptions of early Baptist records, diaries, and photographs. Some digitized records on website.

Troy Irish Genealogy Society

Email address on website • Facebook page
www.rootsweb.ancestry.com/~nytigs

Society transcription projects are ongoing. The website includes: online indexed death and marriage announcements from local newspapers 1812–1885 transcribed by the DAR with support from the WPA, an index of 240 Rensselaer County newspapers, a wide range of transcribed local records and indexes, meeting minutes, surname list, research tips, and list of resources and links.

SELECTED PRINT & ONLINE RESOURCES

Below is a selection of resources relevant for research in this county. The list is representative, not exhaustive. Additional titles—particularly of abstracts, indexes, transcriptions, and local histories—are available; consult the introduction to Part Two for further information. For guidance on how to identify and locate community directories and local newspapers, see chapter 11, City Directories, and chapter 12, Newspapers, in Part One of this book.

Abstracts, Indexes & Transcriptions

Broderick, Frances D. *Lansingburgh Village Cemeteries, Rensselaer County, NY, 1786–1951*. Rhinebeck, NY: Kinship, 2002. Originally published as *Burial Grounds of Lansingburgh*. Rensselaer County, New York, 1965.

Cook, William B., Jr. "Schaghticoke Dutch Reformed Church Records, Schaghticoke, Rensselaer County, New York." *NYG&B Record*, vol. 63 (1932) no. 1: 52–59, no. 2: 191–198, no. 3: 291–298, no. 4: 366–373; vol. 64 (1933) no. 1: 73–82, no. 2: 191–196, no. 3: 280–287, no. 4: 388–395; vol. 65 (1934) no. 1: 74–82, no. 2: 174–182, no. 3: 266–275. [NYG&B eLibrary]

Coons, W. S. "Inscriptions from the Second Cemetery of Zion's Lutheran Church, West Sandlake, Rensselaer Co., NY." Typescript, n.d. NYPL, New York. [NYG&B eLibrary]

County of Rensselaer Abstracts. Syracuse: Central New York Genealogical Society, 2000. Abstracts for a range of genealogical records originally published in the quarterly *Tree Talks*.

Daughters of the American Revolution, comps. *New York DAR Genealogical Records Committee Report*. Since 1913 DAR volunteers have transcribed many thousands of unpublished cemetery, church, and town records throughout New York. The reports are at the DAR Library; copies are at the NYSL and the NYPL. The DAR has a searchable name index to all the GRC reports at http://services.dar.org/Public/DAR_Research/search/?Tab_ID=6. See Jean Worden's index below for a listing by county of the New York record sets that were transcribed by the DAR before 1998.

Kelly, Arthur C. M. *Index to Tree Talks County Packet: Rensselaer County*. Rhinebeck, NY: Kinship, 2002.

Nial, Loretta M. *Tombstone Inscriptions in Cemeteries in Troy, Rensselaer County, N.Y., Indicating a Foreign Place of Origin*. Troy, NY: The Author, 1976.

Phillips, Ralph D. "Inscriptions from Rensselaer County, N.Y., Gravestones." Typescript, 1939. NYPL, New York.

————. "Wills of Rensselaer County, New York: Abstracts of All Wills, 1794–1850." Typescript, 1937. Index available from Berkshire Family History Association. [Ancestry.com]

Shepard, Charles, and Milton Thomas. *Some Rensselaer County Gravestone Inscriptions*. Washington, DC: Charles Shepard, 1923. Book includes Groesbeck, Reed, Barberville, Peek, Slouter, Barringer, Sharp, Myers, and East Poestenkill Cemeteries.

Stearns, J. W., comp. *Membes: Sabbatarian Brethren at Little Hoosack of the Seventh Day Baptist Church (Petersburgh, Stephentown, Berlin, in Rensselaer Co., N.Y.)*. 1946. Reprint, Pittsfield, MA: Berkshire Family History Association, 1990.

Tax Records of Stephentown, New York, for 1789, 1790, and 1791. Pittsfield, MA: Berkshire Family History Association, 1992. Index available from Berkshire Family History Association.

Thomas, Milton. "Records of the Park Presbyterian Church of Troy, NY." Typescript, n.d. NYPL, New York. [NYG&B eLibrary]

Vosburgh, Royden Woodward, ed. "Records of the First Presbyterian Church of Lansingburgh in the Town of Lansingburgh, Rensselaer County, N.Y., Vol. 2." Typescript, 1915. NYPL, New York. [NYG&B eLibrary]

————, ed. "Records of the Reformed Protestant Dutch Church in the Town of Nassau, Rensselaer County, NY." Typescript, 1919. NYPL, New York. [NYG&B eLibrary]

————, ed. "Records of the Second Street Presbyterian Church in the City of Troy, Rensselaer County, N.Y." Typescript, 1915. NYPL, New York. [NYG&B eLibrary]

Worden, Jean D. "Book I, Subject Index." In *Revised Master Index to the New York State Daughters of the American Revolution Genealogical Records Volumes*. Zephyrhills, FL: J. D. Worden, 1998. The Subject Index includes a listing by county of the cemeteries, churches, towns, and other sources of records transcribed by the DAR.

Other Resources

Anderson, George B. *Landmarks of Rensselaer County, New York*. Syracuse, 1897. Book includes biographies and family sketches. Index available from Berkshire Family History Association.

Beers, F. W. *County Atlas of Rensselaer, New York: From Recent and Actual Surveys and Records*. New York, 1876.

Capital District Genealogical Society Newsletter. Albany: Capital District Genealogical Society, 1982–present. [capitaldistrictgenealogicalsociety.org]

Child, Hamilton. *Gazetteer and Business Directory of Rensselaer County, N.Y., for 1870–71*. Syracuse, 1870.

County Atlas of Rensselaer, New York: From Recent and Actual Surveys and Records. New York, 1876.

Clark, Donna K. *Rensselaer County, New York, Directory of Genealogical Records by TAD*. Arvada, CO: Ancestor Publishers, 1986.

Craib, Stephanie H., and Roderick H. Craib. *Our Yesterdays: a History of Rensselaer County*. Troy, NY: n.p., 1948.

Foley, Janet W. *Early Settlers of New York State: Their Ancestors and Descendants*. 9 vols. Akron, NY: 1934–1942. Reprint, 2 vols. Baltimore, Genealogical Publishing Co., 1993.

Hayner, Rutherford. *Troy and Rensselaer County, New York: A History*. 3 vols. New York: Lewis Historical Publishing Company, 1925. Index available from Berkshire Family History Association. [OneBigFamilyTree.com (vol. 3)]

Hudson River Valley Review: A Journal of Regional Studies. Poughkeepsie, NY: Hudson River Valley Institute at Marist College, 2002–present. [hudsonrivervalley.org]

Kelly, Arthur C. M. *The Capital*. Rhinebeck, NY: Kinship, quarterly 1986–1998, annually 1999–2001.

———. *Valley Quarterlies*. Directory of articles (vols. 1–15) and every-name index to the *Capital*, the *Columbia*, the *Mohawk*, and the *Saratoga*. Rhinebeck, NY: Kinship, CD-ROM, 2000.

Lisk, Edward H. *Representative Young Irish-Americans of Troy, N. Y.* Troy, NY, 1889.

Miller, Richard Joseph. "Patroons of Modernization: The Economic Elite of Rensselaer County, New York, 1800–1860." Thesis (B.A.), Williams College, Department of American Studies, 1986.

New York Historical Resources Center. *Guide to Historical Resources in Rensselaer County, New York, Repositories*. Ithaca, NY: New York Historical Resources Center, Olin Library, Cornell University, 1983.

Rittner, Don. *Legendary Locals of Troy, New York*. Charleston, SC: Arcadia Press, 2011.

———. *Troy*. Charleston, SC: Arcadia Press, 2007.

Sylvester, Nathaniel B. *History of Rensselaer Co., New York: With Illustrations and Biographical Sketches of its Prominent Men and Pioneers*. Philadelphia, 1880. Index available from Berkshire Family History Association.

Walkowitz, Daniel J. *Worker City, Company Town: Iron and Cotton-Worker Protest in Troy and Cohoes, New York, 1855–84*. Urbana: University of Illinois Press, 1978.

Weise, Arthur James. *History of the Seventeen Towns of Rensselaer County: From the Colonization of the Manor of Rensselaerwyck to the Present Time*. Troy, NY, 1880.

Weise, Arthur James. *Troy's One Hundred Years 1789–1889*. Troy, NY: William H. Young, 1891

———. *Troy's One Hundred Years: 1789–1889*. Troy, NY, 1891.

Additional Online Resources

Ancestry.com
> There are vast numbers of records on *Ancestry.com* that pertain to people who have lived in New York State. See chapter 16 for a description of *Ancestry.com*'s resources and its partnership with the New York State Archives. A search of the online card catalog by county may reveal lesser known resources that pertain to a locality, such as town records, abstracts, transcriptions, city directories, and local histories.

Connors Genealogy: City of Troy, Rensselaer County
www.connorsgenealogy.com/troy
> Website includes indexes for naturalization 1844–1884 (mainly Irish), censuses both New York State (1855, 1865, 1875) and federal (1880, 1900), Civil War deaths, cemetery inscriptions (mainly Irish), records of baptisms at St. Joseph's R.C. church 1820–1893, name index Court of Common Pleas 1855–1857, and local directories. The website also has an online surname registry (list of surnames being researched with contact information on researchers) and lookups (list of repositories that local researchers will search for records).

FamilySearch.org
> FamilySearch has extensive collections of New York records, including religious records, which are searchable by name and location, but not by county. The following collections include record images (browsable, but not searchable) that are organized by county:
>
> * "New York, Land Records, 1630–1975." Includes land and property records. *familysearch.org/search/collection/2078654*
> * "New York, Probate Records, 1629–1971." Includes wills, letters of administration, and guardianship papers. *familysearch.org/search/collection/1920234*
>
> For both collections, choose the browse option and then select Rensselaer to view the available records sets.
>
> A detailed description of *FamilySearch.org* resources is found in chapter 16.

NYGenWeb Project: Rensselaer County
www.rootsweb.ancestry.com/~nyrensse
> Part of the national, USGenWeb volunteer initiative, the website provides information and resources for county research.

Old Fulton New York Postcards
www.FultonHistory.com
> The website provides free access to a vast collection of digitized New York newspapers, including six titles for Rensselaer County.

Rockland County

Formed February 23, 1798

Parent County	Orange
Daughter Counties	None
County Seat	New City, Town of Clarkstown

Major Land Transactions
See table in chapter 7, Land Records
Kakiat(e) Patent 1696
Chesecock Patent 1707

Putnam County

Orange County

Stony Point

Hudson River

Haverstraw

★

Ramapo

Clarkstown

Westchester County

NEW JERSEY

Orangetown

Town Boundary Map
★ - County seat

Towns (and Cities)	Villages and other Settlements	Notes
Clarkstown Settled pre-revolution by Dutch 1791 Formed in Orange County from Town of Haverstraw 1798 Transferred to new county of Rockland	Bardonia Bardons Station Brownsell Corner Cedar Grove Corners Centenary Central Nyack Clarksville Congers Dutch Factory Germond Nanuet New City Nyack (v) Oakbrook Old Rockland Rockland Lake Snedekers Landing South Nyack Spring Valley (v) Strawtown Upper Nyack (v) Valley Cottage Waldberg Green West Nyack	• Cedar Grove Corners also Waldberg • Clarksville also Mount Moor and Nyack Turnpike • Nanuet also Clarkstown • New City county seat from 1798 when county was formed • Village of Nyack inc. 1883; shared with Town of Orangetown; most of village located in Orangetown • Rockland Lake also Slaughters Landing • Snedekers Landing also Waldberg Landing • Village of Spring Valley inc. 1902; also Pascack and Pot Cheese; shared with Town of Ramapo • Village of Upper Nyack inc. 1872; also Sarvents Landing
Hampstead Name of Town of Ramapo 1797–1828		
Haverstraw Part of Chesecock, Kakiat(e), and several smaller patents 1616 On Dutch maps as Haverstroo 1719 Separated from Orangetown as Precinct of Haverstraw 1788 Recognized as a town in Orange County by State of New York 1791 Daughter towns Clarkstown and New Hampstead (now Ramapo) formed 1798 Transferred to new county of Rockland 1865 Daughter town Stony Point formed	Felters Corners Garnerville Grassy Point Haverstraw (v) Johnsontown Jones Point Ladentown Mount Ivy Mo(u)ntville North Haverstraw Pomona (v) Rosa Villa Samsondale St. John St. Johns in the Wilderness St. Johnland Thiells Tomkins Cove West Haverstraw (v) Willow Grove	• Grassy Point in Town of Stony Point from 1865 • Village of Haverstraw (also Averstroo and Haverstroo) inc. 1854 as Warren; name changed to Haverstraw in 1874 • Jones Point formerly Caldwells Landing and Gibraltar; in Town of Stony Point from 1865 • Mount Ivy also Gurnees Corners • Mountville in Town of Stony Point from 1865 • North Haverstraw in Town of Stony Point from 1865, see hamlet of Stony Point • Village of Pomona inc. 1967; shared with Town of Ramapo • Thiells also Theilis Corners • Tom(p)kins Cove also Lime Kilns and Thompsons Cove; in Town of Stony Point from 1865 • Village of West Haverstraw inc. 1883 • Willow Grove on Stony Point town line
New Hampstead Name of Town of Ramapo 1791–1797		

Towns (and Cities)	Villages and other Settlements	Notes
Orangetown	Blauvelt	• Blauvelt also Blauveltville
1680 Settled by Dutch	Camp Shanks	• Camp Shanks was the largest WWII
1686 Orangetown patent, also called	Grand-View-on-	army embarkation camp in the USA;
Tappan Patent, in Orange County	Hudson (v)	1945 became a prisoner of war camp;
1702 First courts were held in	Mansfield Station	after the war until 1954 it was veterans
Tappantown, county seat for	Nauraushaun	housing called Shanks Village
Orange County	Nyack (v)	• Village of Grand-View-on-Hudson inc.
1719 Precinct of Haverstraw formed	Orangeburg(h)	1910 as Grand View, reinc. 1918 as
from Precinct of Orangetown	Orange Mills	Grand-View-on-Hudson excluding Upper
1788 Recognized as a town in Orange	Orangeville	Grandview
County by State of New York	Orangeville Station	• Village of Nyack inc. 1883; shared with
1798 Transferred to new county of	Palisades	Town of Clarkstown; most of village
Rockland	Pearl River	located in Orangetown
	Piermont (v)	• Pearl River also Middletown and Muddy
	Rockland	Creek
	Sickletown	• Village of Piermont inc. 1850
	South Nyack (v)	• Rockland also Snedens Landing
	Sparkill	• Village of South Nyack inc. 1878
	Tappan	• Tappantown was a county seat for
	Tappantown	Orange County 1702–1773
	Upper Grandview	
Ramapo	Airmont (v)	* Some sources give the spelling New
1791 Formed in Orange County as	Antrim	Hampstead and Hampstead
New Hempstead from Town of	Blauvelts Foundry	• Village of Airmont inc. 1991
Haverstraw *	Camp Hill	• Village of Chestnut Ridge inc. 1986
1797 Name changed to Hempstead *	Chestnut Ridge (v)	• Forshays (Corners) also Ackermans and
1798 Transferred to new county of	Forshays (Corners)	Cassadys
Rockland	Furmanville	• Village of Hilburn inc 1893; formerly
1828 Name changed to Ramapo	Hempstead	Woodburn
	Hillburn (v)	• Village of Kaser inc. 1990
	Hillcrest	• Monsey formerly Kakiat and Monsey
	Kaser (v)	Depot
	Ladentown	• Village of Montebello inc. 1986
	Mill of Abbot Cooper	• Village of New Hempstead inc. 1983;
	Monsey	also known as Kakiat
	Montebello (v)	• Village of New Square inc. 1961
	New Hempstead (v)	• Village of Pomona inc. 1967; shared with
	New Square (v)	Town of Haverstraw
	Pomona (v)	• Ramapo also Ramapo Works
	Pomona Heights	• Sandyfield submerged in 1928 to create
	Ramapo	Lake Welch
	Sandyfield	• Village of Sloatsburg(h) inc. 1929; also
	Scotland	Pothat and Pothod
	Sherwoodville	• Village of Spring Valley inc. 1902; also
	Sloatsburg(h) (v)	Pascack and Pot Cheese; shared with
	South Monsey	Town of Clarkstown
	Spring Valley (v)	• Sterlington formerly a railroad junction
	Sterlington	called The Y, also Piersons Depot and
	Suffern	Sterling Junction
	Suffern Park	• Suffern also New Antrim and Point of
	Summit Park	the Mountains
	Tallman(s)	• Viola formerly known as Mechanicstown
	Talma	and Mechanicsville
	Viola	• Village of Wesley Hills inc. 1982
	Wesley Hills (v)	

Towns (and Cities)	Villages and other Settlements		Notes
Stony Point * 1865 Formed from Town of Haverstraw	Bear Mountain Benson Corners Bulsontown Caldwell Camp Deer Trail Park Cedar Flats Cricketown Doodletown Fort Clinton Grassy Point	Iona Island Jones Point Kidds Dam Mo(u)ntville Pingyp Hill Sinnipink Stony Point Tomkins Cove Willow Grove	* Former names for Stony Point include Antioch and Knights Corners • Grassy Point in Town of Haverstraw before 1865 • Iona Island formerly known as Waggons • Jones Point formerly Caldwells Landing and Gibraltar; in Town of Haverstraw before 1865 • Mo(u)ntville in Town of Haverstraw before 1865 • Stony Point formerly North Haverstraw and Florus Falls; in Town of Haverstraw before 1865 • Tom(p)kins Cove also Lime Kilns and Thompsons Cove; in Town of Haverstraw before 1865 • Willow Grove on Stony Point town line

NEW YORK STATE CENSUS RECORDS

See also chapter 3, Census Records

County originals at Rockland County Clerk's Office: 1855, 1865, 1875, 1892, 1905, 1915, 1925 (1825, 1835, and 1845 are lost)

State originals at the NYSA: 1915, 1925

Microfilm at the FHL, NYPL, and NYSL; many years are online at *FamilySearch.org* and *Ancestry.com*.

NATIONAL/STATEWIDE REPOSITORIES & RESOURCES

See chapter 16

COUNTYWIDE REPOSITORIES & RESOURCES

Rockland County Clerk

Rockland County Courthouse • One South Main Street, Suite 100
New City, NY 10956-5070 • (845) 638-5070
Email: rocklandcountyclerk@co.rockland.ny.us
www.rocklandcountyclerk.com

Court records; land records 1884–1929; naturalization records 1907–1960; declarations of intent 1884–1929; and the New York state censuses for Rockland County 1855, 1865, 1875, 1892, 1905, 1915, and 1925. The clerk has an index to naturalization records; actual records are kept by the County Archives (see below). Selection of records on website.

Rockland County – Town and Village Clerks

Birth, marriage, and death records are maintained by the clerk of the municipality in which the event occurred; see Introduction to County Guides for details of other records which may also be held by municipal clerks. See municipal websites for contact information.

Rockland County Surrogate's Court

One South Main Street • New City, NY 10956 • (845) 483-8300

Holds probate records from 1900 to the present. Also see chapter 6, Probate Records.

Rockland County Archives

Pomona Health Complex, Building S • Sanatorium Road
Pomona, NY 10970 • (845) 364-3675
www.rocklandcountyclerk.com/archives.html

Census records 1855–1925; court records 1798–2001; marriage records 1908–1935; naturalization records 1812–1991; Orange County deeds and mortgages 1703–1800; Rockland County deeds 1798–1921; Rockland County mortgages 1798–1931; wills 1798–1965; and maps and atlases. Guide to holdings on website.

Rockland County Public Libraries

Rockland is part of the Ramapo Catskill Library System; see *www.rcls.org* to access each library. Many libraries hold local history and genealogy collections. For example, Blauvelt Free Library holds information on the Blauvelt family. Also see listings below for New City Library, Nyack Library, Palisades Free Library, Pearl River Public Library, and Suffern Free Library. Rockland also maintains the Library Association of Rockland County; see *www.larclib.org* for more information or to access the Hudson River Valley Heritage Images Project.

Rockland County Historian

12 Ashwood Lane • Garnerville, NY 10923 • (845) 357-6383

Rockland County – All Municipal Historians

While not authorized to answer genealogical inquiries, town and village historians can provide valuable historical information and research advice; some maintain collections and webpages which may include transcribed records, local histories, and other genealogical material. For contact information, see municipal websites or the website of the Association of Public Historians of New York State at *www.aphnys.org*.

African American Historical Society of Rockland County

See listing under African American in chapter 16, Peoples of New York

The Genealogical Society of Rockland County

PO Box 444 • New City, NY 10956 • *www.rocklandgenealogy.org*

Maintains reference collections at the New City Library and the Records Management and Archives Department in Pomona. Holdings include cemetery records and genealogies. Offers research services. Website includes guide to genealogical resources in Rockland County.

The Historical Society of Rockland County

20 Zukor Road • New City, NY 10956 • (845) 634-9629
Email: info@rocklandhistory.org • *www.rocklandhistory.org*

Family Bibles, deeds, diaries, lantern slides, ledgers, letters, drawings, maps and atlases, and photographs; manuscripts and ephemera documenting the Dutch-American Blauvelt family. Website includes list of local historians and article "A Brief History of Rockland County." Publishes a journal on Rockland County history called *South of the Mountains*.

REGIONAL REPOSITORIES & RESOURCES

Bard College Archives and Special Collections

See listing in Dutchess County Guide

LOCAL REPOSITORIES & RESOURCES

Alphabetized by location

New City Library: Rockland Room

220 North Main Street • New City, NY 10956
(845) 634-4997, ext. 139 • *www.newcitylibrary.org/taxonomy/term/20*

Local histories and genealogies, census materials, maps, newspapers on microfilm 1847–present, telephone books 1883–present, print materials, vertical files, and *Rockland County Messenger*, 1847–1898. Documents relating to the history of the Town of Clarkstown, 1752–1789, are online.

Historical Society of the Nyacks at the DePew House

50 Piermont Avenue, Suite L-2 • PO Box 850 • Nyack, NY 10960
(845) 418-4430 • Email: info@nyackhistory.org • *www.nyackhistory.org*

Holdings include historical papers on history of the Nyacks.

The Nyack Library: Local History Collection

59 South Broadway • Nyack, NY 10960 • (845) 358-3370 ext. 223
Email: history@nyacklibrary.org • *www.nyacklibrary.org/local-history.html*

Books and pamphlets, genealogies, maps, photographs, and yearbooks. Nyack Library Local History Image Collection and *Rockland County Journal*, online. Website includes finding aids and guides to Library's resources.

Orangetown Historical Museum & Archives at the DePew House

196 Blaisdell Road • Orangeburg, NY 10962 • (845) 398-1302 • Email: otownmuseum@optonline.net • *www.orangetownmuseum.com*

Eclectic document library and archives, open to researchers.

Palisades Free Library: Local History Collection
19 Closter Road • Palisades, NY 10964 • (845) 359-0136
Email: pal@rcls.org • *www.palisadeslibrary.org/palisades/localhistory.asp*

Maps, photographs, Gesner Diary (1829–1850), and Palisades local newsletter, *10964* (1977–present). Website includes local history articles.

Pearl River Public Library: Local History and Archives
80 Franklin Avenue • Pearl River, NY 10965 • (845) 735-4084
www.pearlriverlibrary.org/pearlriver/localhistory.asp

Ephemera and photographs (1872–present) documenting history of local schools, government, and institutions; information on local cemeteries.

Piermont Historical Society
50 Ash Street • PO Box 362 • Piermont, NY 10968
www.piermonthistorysociety.org

Website includes gallery of local photographs.

Sloatsburg Historical Society
Orange Turnpike • Sloatsburg, NY 10974 • (845) 753-2030
Email: info@sloatsburgny.com • *www.sloatsburgny.com/History.htm*

Website includes history of local structures and cemeteries and selected family histories. Society accepts research requests.

Suffern Free Library: Ramapo Room
210 Lafayette Avenue • Suffern, NY 10901 • (845) 357-1237
www.suffernfreelibrary.org/local_history_and_photos.aspx

Holdings include books, census materials, city directories, newspapers, and photographs.

Tappantown Historical Society
PO Box 71 • Tappan, NY 10983 • *www.tappantown.org*

Website includes maps and photographs.

SELECTED PRINT & ONLINE RESOURCES

Below is a selection of resources relevant for research in this county. The list is representative, not exhaustive. Additional titles—particularly of abstracts, indexes, transcriptions, and local histories—are available; consult the introduction to Part Two for further information. For guidance on how to identify and locate community directories and local newspapers, see chapter 11, City Directories, and chapter 12, Newspapers, in Part One of this book.

Abstracts, Indexes & Transcriptions

Ackerman, Herbert S., and Arthur J. Goff, comps. *New York and New Jersey Cemeteries*. Ridgewood, NJ: The Compilers, 1947. Includes cemeteries in Bardonia, Kakeath (West New Hempstead), Monsey, Nanuet, Pearl River, and Orangeburg.

Barber, Gertrude Audrey. "Abstracts of Wills of Rockland County, New York: Copied from the Original Records at the Surrogate's Office, New City, Rockland County, NY." 4 vols. Typescript, 1950–1953. [*Ancestry.com*]

———. "Graveyard Inscriptions of Rockland County, NY." Typescript, 1931. NYPL, New York.

"Betrothals and Marriages of the Dutch Reformed Church of Tappan, Rockland County, New York." *NYG&B Record*, vol. 84 (1953) no. 3: 162–169, no. 4: 235–238; vol. 85 (1954) no. 2: 98–106, no. 3: 168–171, no. 4: 239–245; vol. 86 (1955) no. 2: 111–119, no. 3: 169–176, no. 4: 169–176. [NYG&B eLibrary]

Budke, George H. *Abstracts of Early Deeds, Patents, Mortgages, and Other Instruments Affecting the Land Titles of Rockland County, NY*. New York: Library Association of Rockland County, 1975.

———. *Patents Granted for Lands in the Present County of Rockland, New York, with Biographical Notices of the Patentees*. New York: Library Association of Rockland County, 1975.

Cohen, Minnie. "Abstracts of Wills of Rockland County, New York, 1786–1845." 3 vols. Typescript, 1937–1939. NYPL, New York. [*Ancestry.com*]

Cole, David, and Walter Kenneth Griffin. "Records of the Reformed Dutch Church of Kakiat." Typescript, n.d. NYPL, New York. From church records and private registers, 1774–1864. [NYG&B eLibrary]

Daughters of the American Revolution, comps. *New York DAR Genealogical Records Committee Report*. Since 1913 DAR volunteers have transcribed many thousands of unpublished cemetery, church, and town records throughout New York. The reports are at the DAR Library; copies are at the NYSL and the NYPL. The DAR has a searchable name index to all the GRC reports at *http://services.dar.org/Public/DAR_Research/search/?Tab_ID=6*. See Jean Worden's index below for a listing by county of the New York record sets that were transcribed by the DAR before 1998.

Noel, John V., and Pierre, Charles G. *Rockland County Red Book and Classified Directory*. Valley Cottage, NY: Noel Press, 1926.

Rockland County, NYG&B Church Surveys Collection. NYG&B, New York. [NYG&B eLibrary]

Worden, Jean D. "Book 1, Subject Index." In *Revised Master Index to the New York State Daughters of the American Revolution Genealogical Records Volumes*. Zephyrhills, FL: J. D. Worden, 1998. The Subject Index includes a listing by county of the cemeteries, churches, towns, and other sources of records transcribed by the DAR.

Other Resources

Baker, Norman R. *The Way It Was in North Rockland*. Orangeburg, NY: Historical Society of Rockland County, 1973.

Bedell, Cornelia F. *Now and Then and Long Ago in Rockland County, New York*. Suffern, NY: Ramapo Valley Independent, 1941.

Beers, F. W. *County Atlas of Rockland, New York: From Recent and Actual Surveys and Records*. New York, 1875.

Chapman Publishing Company. *Portrait and Biographical Record of Rockland and Orange Counties, New York: Containing Portraits and Biographical Sketches of Prominent and Representative Citizens of the Counties. Together with Biographies and Portraits of All the Presidents of the United States*. 2 vols. New York, 1895.

Cohen, David S. *The Ramapo Mountain People*. New Brunswick, NJ: Rutgers University Press, 1974. Results of a genealogical inquiry into the origins of the Ramapo Mountain People of Rockland County and New Jersey.

Cole, David. *History of Rockland County, New York, with Biographical Sketches of Its Prominent Men*. New York, 1884.

French, F. F. *Map of Orange and Rockland Counties, New York: From Actual Surveys*. Philadelphia, 1859. Wall map.

Greater Hudson Heritage Network. *History Keepers' Companion: Guide to Sites & Sources of the Lower Hudson Valley and Western*

Connecticut. Fleischmanns, N.Y: Purple Mountain Press, 1998. The Greater Hudson Heritage Network is in the process of updating and creating an online version of this publication; information is at *www.greaterhudson.org/history-keepers-companion.html.*

Green, Frank B. *The History of Rockland County.* New York: Historical Society of Rockland County, 1989. First published 1886.

Haley, Jacquetta M. *Rockland County, New York in the 1790s.* New York: Historical Society of Rockland County, 1997.

Hudson River Valley Review: A Journal of Regional Studies. Poughkeepsie, NY: Hudson River Valley Institute at Marist College, 2002–present. [*hudsonrivervalley.org*]

New York Historical Resources Center. *Guide to Historical Resources in Rockland County, New York, Repositories.* Ithaca, NY: Cornell University, 1990. [*books.FamilySearch.org*]

Nordstrom, Carl. *A Finding List of Bibliographical Materials Relating to Rockland County, New York.* Orangeburg, NY: Tappan Zee Historical Society, 1959.

Penfold, Saxby V. *Suffern's Contribution to the Founding of Rockland County: Written in Commemoration of the Rockland County Sesquicentennial, 1798–1948.* Suffern, NY: Suffern Historical Society, 1948.

Rockland County Almanac and Year Book, 1934: Most Complete Fact Book Ever Compiled About Rockland County, New York. Rockland County, NY: 1934.

Rockland County Planning Board. *Rockland County Data Book.* New York: The Board, 1970.

Tholl, C. K. *Landmarks of Rockland County : with old roads and early buildings / The Historical Society of Rockland County.* [New City, NY]: The Society, 1975. Map.

Tompkins, Arthur S. *Historical Record to the Close of the Nineteenth Century of Rockland County, New York.* Nyack, NY: Van Deusen & Joyce, 1902.

Zimm, Louise H. *Southeastern New York: History of the Counties of Ulster, Dutchess, Orange, Rockland, and Putnam.* 3 vols. New York: Lewis Historical Publishing Co., 1946. Index available from Berkshire Family History Association.

Zimmerman, Linda. *Rockland County Century of History.* New York: Historical Society of Rockland County, 2002.

Additonal Online Resources

Ancestry.com
There are vast numbers of records on *Ancestry.com* that pertain to people who have lived in New York State. See chapter 16 for a description of *Ancestry.com*'s resources and its partnership with the New York State Archives. A search of the online card catalog by county may reveal lesser known resources that pertain to a locality, such as town records, abstracts, transcriptions, city directories, and local histories.

Dutch Door Genealogy
www.dutchdoorgenealogy.com
The website provides free access to a selection of transcribed census and religious records and historical information for Orange and Rockland counties.

FamilySearch.org
FamilySearch has extensive collections of New York records, including religious records, which are searchable by name and location, but not by county. The following collections include record images (browsable, but not searchable) that are organized by county:
- "New York, Land Records, 1630–1975." Includes land and property records. *familysearch.org/search/collection/2078654*
- "New York, Probate Records, 1629–1971." Includes wills, letters of administration, and guardianship papers. *familysearch.org/ search/collection/1920234*

For both collections, choose the browse option and then select Rockland to view the available records sets.

A detailed description of *FamilySearch.org* resources is found in chapter 16.

Hudson River Valley Heritage (HRVH)
www.hrvh.org/cdm
The HRVH website provides free access to digital collections of historical material from more than 40 organizations in Columbia, Greene, Dutchess, Ulster, Sullivan, Rockland, Orange, Putnam, and Westchester counties.

New York Heritage Digital Collections: New York State Newspaper Project
www.nyheritage.org/newspapers
The website provides links to digital newspapers collections in 26 counties (currently) made accessible through New York Heritage, New York State Historic Newspapers, HRVH Historical Newspapers, and other providers.

NYGenWeb Project: Rockland County
www.rootsweb.ancestry.com/~nyrockla
Part of the national, USGenWeb volunteer initiative, the website provides information and resources for county research.

Rockland County Archivist Naturalization Database
www.rootsweb.ancestry.com/~nyrockla/rcnaturalizations.htm
Searchable index of Declarations of Intention 1812–1991 and Naturalization Oaths 1836–1896 for Rockland County; listing gives name, date, and place of origin. Index can be browsed by surname at *www.usgwarchives.net/ny/rockland/court/courttoc.htm.*

Saratoga County

Formed February 7, 1791

Parent County   Albany
Daughter Counties   None
County Seat   Village of Ballston Spa, Towns of Ballston and Milton

Major Land Transactions
See table in chapter 7, Land Records
Saratoga Patent 1684
Kayaderosseras Patent 1708

Town Boundary Map
★ - County seat

Towns (and Cities)	Villages and other Settlements		Notes
Ballston 1763 First settled 1775 Formed as a district of Albany County 1788 Recognized as a town by State of New York 1791 Transferred to new county of Saratoga 1792 Daughter towns Charlton, Galway, and Milton formed 1795 Boundary with Charlton changed	Academy Hill Ballston Ballston Center Ballston Lake Ballston Manor Ballston Spa (v) Burnt Hills East Line Garrison Manor		• Ballston also Long Lake • Ballston Center also Balltown • Ballston Lake formerly South Ballston; on Clifton Park town line • Village of Ballston Spa inc. 1807; also Ballston Springs; shared with Town of Milton; county seat from 1791 when county was formed • East Line on Malta town line
Charlton 1774 Settled 1792 Formed from Town of Ballston	Blue Corners Charlton Harmony Corners Holbrook Corners Komar Park	Little Troy Scotch Church Tucker Heights West Charlton	• Little Troy also Slab Troy
Clifton Name for Town of Clifton Park 1828–1829			
Clifton Park Settled before 1700 1708 Patent granted 1828 Formed as Clifton from Town of Halfmoon 1829 Name changed to Clifton Park	Ballston Lake Clifton Park Clifton Park Center Country Knolls Dry Dock Elnora Flagler Corners	Forts Ferry Groom(s) Corners Jonesville Rexford Ushers Vischer Ferry	• Ballston Lake on Ballston town line • Country Knolls on Malta town line • Dry Dock also Clutis Dry Dock • Groom(s) Corners also Grooms • Rexford formerly Rexford Flats • Ushers on Halfmoon town line • Vischer(s) Ferry also Amity and Vis(s)-cher(s) Ferry
Concord Name for Town of Day 1819–1827			
Corinth 1790 Settled 1818 Formed from Town of Hadley 1848 Annexed land from Town of Moreau	Clothier Hollow Corinth (v) East Corinth Glade Jessup(s) Landing Mooleyville	Mount McGregor Palmer Palmer Falls Randall Corner South Corinth Spier Falls	• Clothier Hollow also Clothier Holley • Village of Corinth inc. 1886 • Mount McGregor shared with towns of Moreau and Wilton; now a Correctional Facility
Day 1819 Formed as Concord from towns of Edinburgh and Hadley 1827 Name changed to Day	Allentown Conklingville Crowerville Day Center Day Corners West Day		• Original hamlets of Conklingville, Day Center, and West Day flooded for construction of Sacandaga Reservoir in 1930; current names refer to areas along banks of Sacandaga Lake near original locations • Conklingville, also West Hadley, on Hadley town line • Day Center formerly Day • West Day also Huntsville and Westday

Towns (and Cities)	Villages and other Settlements		Notes
Edinburg(h) 1790 Settled 1801 Formed as Northfield from Town of Providence 1808 Name changed to Edinburgh 1819 Daughter town Concord (now Day) formed	Batchel(l)erville Clarkville Edinburg(h) Fox Hill(s) Tenantville		• Edinburg(h) also Beechers Hollow
Galway 1774 Settled by Scots from Galway 1792 Formed from Town of Ballston 1796 Daughter town Providence formed	Birchton Bunn Corners East Galway Edgecombs Corners Fairweather Corners Galway (v) Green Corners Hagedorn(s) Mills Holsapple Corners Mosherville	North Galway O'Brien Corners Parkis Mills Ruback Camp Shuttleworth Corners South Galway South Galway Corner Stimpsons Corners West Galway Whiteside Corners	• East Galway also Yorks Corners • Village of Galway inc. 1838; also New Galloway • Green Corners on Providence town line • Hagedorn(s) Mills on Providence town line
Greenfield 1784 Settled 1793 Formed from towns of Milton and Saratoga 1801 Daughter town Hadley formed	Chatfield Corner Frink Corner Greenfield Greenfield Center Kings King(s) Station Lake Desolation	Middle Grove Mount Pleasant North Greenfield Pages Corner(s) Porter(s) Corners South Greenfield West Greenfield	• King(s) Station on Wilton town line • Middle Grove also Jamesville
Hadley 1788 Settled 1801 Formed from towns of Greenfield and Northumberland 1808 Boundaries amended 1818 Daughter town Corinth formed 1819 Daughter town Concord (now Day) formed	Conklingville Hadley Lynnwood Quarry		• Conklingville also West Hadley; most of original hamlet is underwater due to construction of Sacandaga Reservoir in 1930; on Day town line • Lynnwood also Linwood
Halfmoon 1772 Formed as a district in Albany County * 1788 Recognized as a town by State of New York 1791 Transferred to new county of Saratoga 1816 Name changed to Orange, daughter town Waterford formed 1820 Name changed back to Halfmoon 1828 Daughter town Clifton (now Clifton Park) formed	Brookwood Clifton Park Coons Crescent Dunsbach Ferry Gray(s) Corners Halfmoon Halfmoon Beach Mechanic(s)ville (v) Newtown Smithtown Ushers		* 1709 Albany County tax list includes people with Dutch names living in "Halvemaen" • Hamlet of Halfmoon also Middletown • Village of Mechanic(s)ville was shared with Town of Stillwater; inc. 1859, reinc. 1870; became a city in 1915 • Ushers on Clifton Park town line
Malta Settled before the Revolution 1802 Formed from towns of Saratoga and Stillwater	Country Knolls Deming Street Dunning Street East Line Francis Corners Halls Corners Luther Forest	Malta Malta Ridge Maltaville Mannings Cove Riley Cove Round Lake (v)	• Country Knolls on Clifton Park town line • East Line on Ballston town line • Riley Cove also China Town due to use of Chinese lanterns at local camps • Village of Round Lake inc. 1969

Towns (and Cities)	Villages and other Settlements		Notes
Mechanicville (city) 1915 Incorporated as a city from the Village of Mechanic(s)ville that was shared between the towns of Halfmoon and Stillwater	Mechanicville		
Milton Settled before the Revolution 1792 Formed from Town of Ballston 1793 Daughter town Greenfield formed	Ballston Spa (v) Bloodville Cranesville Factory Village Milton	Milton Center North Milton Rock City Falls West Milton	• Village of Ballston Spa inc. 1807; also Ballston Springs; shared with Town of Milton; county seat from 1791 • Cranesville formerly Crane(s) Village • Rock City Falls also Rock City Mills • West Milton formerly Clutes Corners and Spiers Corners
Moreau Settled before the Revolution 1805 Formed from Town of Northumberland 1848 Ceded land from Town of Corinth	Clark(s) Corners Feeder Dam Fenimore Fernwood Fortsville	Moreau Station Mount McGregor Reynolds Corners South Glens Falls (v) Spier Pines	• Mount McGregor shared with towns of Corinth and Wilton; now a Correctional Facility • Village of South Glens Falls inc. 1877
Northfield Name for Town of Edinburg(h) 1801–1808			
Northumberland 1755 Fort Miller built 1798 Formed from Town of Saratoga 1801 Daughter town Hadley formed 1805 Daughter town Moreau formed 1818 Daughter town Wilton formed	Ashfords Way Bacon Hill Callahans Corners Gansevoort Jewell Corner Northumberland Starks Knob		• Bacon Hill formerly Fiddletown and Popes Corners
Orange Name for Town of Halfmoon 1816–1820			
Providence Settled before the Revolution then abandoned 1796 Formed from Town of Galway 1801 Daughter town Northfield (now Edinburgh) formed	Barker(s)ville Fayville Glenwild Green Corners Hagedorn(s) Mills Long Corners	Providence Shaw Corners Skinner Corners West Providence Wiley Corners	• Green Corners on Galway town line • Hagedorn(s) Mills formerly Hagadorns Hollow; on Galway town line
Saratoga Settled in the early 1700s 1772 Formed as district in Albany County 1788 Recognized as a town by State of New York 1789 Daughter town Easton formed * 1791 Transferred to new county of Saratoga 1793 Daughter town Greenfield formed 1798 Daughter town Northumberland formed 1802 Daughter town Malta formed 1819 Daughter town Saratoga Springs formed	Burgoyne Cedar Bluff(s) Coveville Dean(s) Corners Gates Grangerville Maple Shade Meyer Corners Quaker Springs Schuylerville (v) Smithville Victory (v) Victory Mills		* Town of Easton in Washington County from 1791 • Village of Schuylerville inc. 1831 • Village of Victory inc. 1849

Towns (and Cities)	Villages and other Settlements		Notes
Saratoga Springs (city) 1915 Incorporated as a city from Town of Saratoga	Travers Manor		
Saratoga Springs (town) 1819–1915 1819 Formed from Town of Saratoga 1915 Became City of Saratoga Springs	Saratoga Springs (v)		• Village of Saratoga Springs inc. 1826; now City of Saratoga Springs
Stillwater 1750 Settled 1772 Part of Halfmoon District in Albany County 1788 Recognized as a town by State of New York 1789 Daughter town Easton formed * 1791 Transferred to new county of Saratoga 1802 Daughter town Malta formed	Bemis Heights East Saratoga Junction Jobville Ketchum(s) Corners Mechanic(s)ville (v) Riverside	Snake Hill Stillwater (v) Stillwater Center Stillwater Junction Wayville Willow Glen	* Town of Easton in Washington County from 1791 • Village of Mechanic(s)ville was shared with Town of Halfmoon; inc. 1859, reinc. 1870; became a city in 1915 • Village of Stillwater inc. 1816; reinc. 1950
Waterford Settled by the Dutch 1816 Formed from Town of Halfmoon	Northside Prospect Hill	Waterford (v) West Waterford	• Village of Waterford inc. 1794, also Half Moon Point
Wilton 1774–75 Settled 1818 Formed from Town of Northumberland	Ballard Corners Barnes Corners Dimmick Corners Emerson(s) Corners Gurn Spring(s) King(s) Station	Mount McGregor South Wilton Summit Station Travers Corners Wilton	• King(s) Station on Greenfield town line • Mount McGregor shared with towns of Corinth and Moreau; now a Correctional Facility

NEW YORK STATE CENSUS RECORDS
See also chapter 3, Census Records

County originals at Saratoga County Clerk's Office: 1845*, 1855, 1865, 1875, 1892, 1905, 1915, 1925 (1825 and 1835 are lost)

State originals at the NYSA: 1915, 1925

Microfilm at the FHL, NYPL, and NYSL; many years are online at *FamilySearch.org* and *Ancestry.com*.

*1845—only the original statistics pages survive. The county historian's office has an undated typescript for the Town of Hadley which lists the names of head of household and the number in people in each family.

NATIONAL/STATEWIDE REPOSITORIES & RESOURCES
See chapter 16

New York State Military Museum and Veterans Research Center
See chapter 16

COUNTYWIDE REPOSITORIES & RESOURCES

Saratoga County Clerk
40 McMaster Street • Ballston Spa, NY 12020
(518) 885-2213 ext. 4420 • *www.saratogacountyny.gov*

Land records, court records, naturalization records 1800–1950s, and original copies of the New York state censuses for Saratoga County 1855–1925. Website includes select land records and, after applying for access, naturalization records.

Saratoga County – City, Town, and Village Clerks
Birth, marriage, and death records are maintained by the clerk of the municipality in which the event occurred; see Introduction to County Guides for details of other records which may also be held by municipal clerks. For contact information, see *www.saratogacountyarchiveind ex.com/ari/contact.*

Saratoga County Surrogate's Court
Municipal Center • 30 McMaster Street
Ballston Spa, NY 12020 • (518) 451-8830

Holds probate records from 1791 to the present. See also chapter 6, Probate Records.

Saratoga County Public Libraries
Saratoga is part of the Southern Adirondack Library System; see *http://directory.sals.edu* to access each library. Many hold genealogy and local history collections. Also see listings below for Ballston Spa Public Library, Clifton Park-Halfmoon Public Library, and Saratoga Springs Public Library.

Saratoga County Historical Society and Brookside Museum
6 Charlton Street • Ballston Spa, NY 12020 • (518) 885-4000
Email: info@brooksidemuseum.org • *www.brooksidemuseum.org*

Society's collections, archives, and research library are searchable through the online catalog. Website includes list of surnames documented in genealogy collection. Offers research services for a fee.

Saratoga County Historian
Municipal Center • 40 McMaster Street • Ballston Spa, NY 12020
(518) 884-4749 • Email: historian@saratogacountyny.gov
www.saratogacountyny.gov

Town files, church, cemetery, and historic place records; surname files; subject files; federal census on microfilm 1800–1840, 1860–1870, and 1890–1930; New York state census on microfilm 1855–1925; map

collection; assessment records and early town records on microfilm; military history; family papers; field books; voter lists; warrant records; tax lists; photographs; and information on veterans. Holds an undated typescript of 1845 census for Hadley.

Saratoga County – All Municipal Historians
While not authorized to answer genealogical inquiries, city, town, and village historians can provide valuable historical information and research advice; some maintain collections and webpages which may include transcribed records, local histories, and other genealogical material. See contact information at *www.brooksidemuseum.org* or at the website of the Association of Public Historians of New York State at *www.aphnys.org*.

Heritage Hunters of Saratoga County
PO Box 270 • Saratoga Springs, NY 12866-0270 • (518) 587-5852
www.saratoganygenweb.com/gwsarhh.html

Meetings at Saratoga Town Hall. Collection of books, periodicals, local histories, and documents at the Brookside Museum in Ballston Spa. Publishes a newsletter which includes genealogical articles (online index at *http://saratoganygenweb.com/HHNLalph.htm*).

Skidmore College: Lucy Scriber Library Special Collections: Anita Pohndorff Yates Collection of Saratogiana
815 North Broadway • Saratoga Springs, NY 12866
(518) 580-5509 • *www.lib.skidmore.edu*

The Yates Collection, which documents the local history of Saratoga Springs and surrounding areas, consists of five series: Documents and Ephemera; Newspapers, Magazines and Maps; Photographs and Scrapbooks; Prints and Artwork; and Objects. Website includes finding aid.

REGIONAL REPOSITORIES & RESOURCES

Adirondack Museum Library
See listing in Hamilton County Guide

Capital District Genealogical Society
See listing in Albany County Guide

Fulton-Montgomery Community College: Evans Library: The Kenneth R. Dorn Regional History Study Center
See listing in Fulton County Guide

Gerald B. H. Solomon Saratoga National Cemetery
200 Duell Road • Schuylerville, NY 12871-1721
(518) 581-9128 • *www.cem.va.gov/cems/listcem.asp*

A national veterans' cemetery.

LOCAL REPOSITORIES & RESOURCES
Alphabetized by location

Ballston Spa Public Library: Local History Collection
21 Milton Avenue • Ballston Spa, NY 12020 • (518) 885-5022
http://bspl.sals.edu/index.php/special-collections

Books, pamphlets, and clippings; name card file; city directories 1893–present including Ballston Spa and other towns; *Ballston Journal,* in print and microfilm April 1847–present, with indexes for marriages and deaths 1847–1900 and by subject 1847–1865; Saratoga County Epitaphs compiled in the 1870s; family histories (website includes list of surnames); maps and atlases; and church records.

Charlton Historical Society and Museum

2009 Maple Avenue • Charlton, NY 12019 • (518) 399-3797

www.charltonnyhs.org

Website includes antique postcards, maps, and photographs.

Clifton Park-Halfmoon Public Library

475 Moe Road • Clifton Park, NY 12065 • (518) 371-8622

www.cphlibrary.org

Records of local organizations, New York state census microfilm for Saratoga County, school records, photographs, letters, and diaries. Finding aids on website.

Corinth Town Museum

609 Palmer Avenue • Corinth, NY 12822

Email: info@townofcorinthny.com

www.townofcorinthny.org/townmuseum.aspx

Photographs, advertisements from local businesses, school records, house histories, cemetery records, 1906 village census, Corinth Baptist Church records, and published genealogies.

Edinburg Historical Society and Museum

PO Box 801 • Edinburg, NY 12134 • (518) 863-2034

www.edinburg-hist-soc.org

Offers assistance with genealogy research.

Halfmoon Historical Society

2 Halfmoon Town Plaza • Halfmoon, NY 12065

www.townofhalfmoon.org/historicalsociety

Holdings include photographs and interview transcripts.

Saratoga Springs History Museum

One East Congress Street • PO Box 216 • Saratoga Springs, NY 12866

(518) 584-6920 • Email: info@saratogahistory.org

www.saratogahistory.org

Holdings include George S. Bolster Collection, including photographic negatives of Saratoga Springs, 1855–1980, and Beatrice Sweeney Archive of documents and business records.

Saratoga Springs Public Library: Saratoga Room

49 Henry Street • Saratoga Springs, NY 12866-3271

(518) 584-1957 ext. 255 • *www.sspl.org/research/local_history*

Books and pamphlets, local histories, city directories, newspapers on microfilm 1840–present, oral histories maps, photographs, prints, clippings, and scrapbooks documenting history of Saratoga Springs and surrounding area. Collection searchable through online catalog.

Waterford Historical Museum and Cultural Center

2 Museum Lane • Waterford, NY 12188 • (518) 238-0809

Email: info@waterfordmuseum.com • *www.waterfordmuseum.com*

Houses George and Annabel O'Connor Library for Local History, which includes genealogical materials.

SELECTED PRINT & ONLINE RESOURCES

Below is a selection of resources relevant for research in this county. The list is representative, not exhaustive. Additional titles—particularly of abstracts, indexes, transcriptions, and local histories—are available; consult the introduction to Part Two for further information. For guidance on how to identify and locate community directories and local newspapers, see chapter 11, City Directories, and chapter 12, Newspapers, in Part One of this book.

Abstracts, Indexes & Transcriptions

Becker, Edith V., Melvin W. Lethbridge, and Leslie A. Frye. *Cemetery Records of Saratoga, Herkimer, and Hamilton Counties.* New York: Montgomery County (NY) Department of History and Archives, 1939. Includes index.

Calkins, H., Jr. "An Exact Copy of the Records of the Congregational Church of Greenfield, Saratoga Co., N.Y." *NYG&B Record,* vol. 34 (1903) no. 2: 141–143, no. 3: 212–216, no. 4: 284–288; vol. 35 (1904) no. 1: 29–33. [NYG&B eLibrary]

Cormack, Marie N., and Katherine A. Furman. "New York State Cemetery Inscriptions: Albany County, Herkimer County, Montgomery County, Saratoga County, Schenectady County." Typescript, 1940. [microfilm at FHL, NYSL]

County of Saratoga Abstracts. Syracuse: Central New York Genealogical Society, 2000. Abstracts for a range of genealogical records originally published in the quarterly *Tree Talks.*

Daughters of the American Revolution, comps. *New York DAR Genealogical Records Committee Report.* Since 1913 DAR volunteers have transcribed many thousands of unpublished cemetery, church, and town records throughout New York. The reports are at the DAR Library; copies are at the NYSL and the NYPL. The DAR has a searchable name index to all the GRC reports at *http://services.dar.org/Public/DAR_Research/search/?Tab_ID=6.* See Jean Worden's index below for a listing by county of the New York record sets that were transcribed by the DAR before 1998.

Dunn, Violet B., Robert S. Hayden, and Clayton H. Brown. *Saratoga County Heritage.* N.p., 1974.

Durkee, Cornelius E. "Index to Marriage and Death Notices in the Saratoga Sentinel: 1819–1837." Typescript, 1919. New York State Library, Albany.

———. "Saratoga County, N.Y. Epitaphs." *NYG&B Record,* vol. 44 (1913) no. 2: 177–184, no. 3: 177–184, no. 4: 389–396; vol. 45 (1914) no. 1: 81–89, no. 2: 126; vol. 47 (1916) no. 3: 233–240, no.4: 403–409; vol. 48 (1917) no. 1: 15–19, no. 2: 185–190, no. 3: 245–250. [NYG&B eLibrary]

Ellsberry, Elizabeth P. "Cemetery Records of Saratoga County, New York, Vol. I." Typescript, n.d. New York State Historical Association Library, Cooperstown, NY. A database of the records is at *Ancestry.com.*

———. *Will Records of Saratoga County, New York, 1796–1805.* Typescript, 1965. New York State Historical Association Library, Cooperstown, NY.

Federal Writers' Project, Works Progress Administration, State of New York "Sweetman and West Charlton Cemeteries: Saratoga County, New York." Typescript, 1938. NYPL, New York. [NYG&B eLibrary]

Harris, Edward D. "Grantors in the Registry of Deeds of Saratoga Co., NY: As Contained in Libers A–S, 1792–1831." Typescript, 1903. NYPL, New York.

Keefer, Donald A. "Cemetery Records of the Town of Charlton, Saratoga County, NY." Typescript, 1971. NYPL, New York.

Kelly, Arthur C. M. *Index to Tree Talks County Packet: Saratoga County.* Rhinebeck, NY: Kinship, 2002.

Post, Paul. *Soldiers of Saratoga County: From Concord to Kabul.* Charleston, SC: History Press, 2010. Book includes cemetery records, military lists, award recipients, genealogies of military families, casualties of war, etc.

Register of Revolutionary War Soldiers in Saratoga County, New York. 3 vols. N.p.: Sons of the American Revolution, n.d. Book includes birth/ death dates, burial place, tombstone inscriptions, service records, family descriptions.

Ritchie, Henry C. "Saratoga County, NY, Miscellaneous Cemetery Inscriptions." Typescript, 1943. NYPL, New York.

Samuelsen, W. David. Saratoga County, New York, 1799–1921: Index to Will Books. Salt Lake City: Sampubco., 1992.

Saratoga County, NYG&B Church Surveys Collection. NYG&B, New York. [NYG&B eLibrary]

University of the State of New York. Division of Archives and History. The Records of Ballston Spa, Saratoga County. Albany: University of the State of New York, 1921.

Vosburgh, Royden Woodward, ed. "Records of the United Presbyterian Church at West Charlton, in the Town of Charlton, Saratoga County, NY." Typescript, 1921. NYPL, New York. [NYG&B eLibrary]

Worden, Jean D. "Book 1, Subject Index." In Revised Master Index to the New York State Daughters of the American Revolution Genealogical Records Volumes. Zephyrhills, FL: J. D. Worden, 1998. The Subject Index includes a listing by county of the cemeteries, churches, towns, and other sources of records transcribed by the DAR.

Other Resources

Anderson, George B. Our County and Its People: A Descriptive and Biographical Record of Saratoga County, New York. Boston, 1899.

Beers, S. N. New Topographical Atlas of Saratoga County, New York: From Actual Surveys. Philadelphia, 1866. [NYPL Digital Gallery]

Brandow, John H. The Story of Old Saratoga: The Burgoyne Campaign, to Which is Added New York's Share in the Revolution. Albany: Fort Orange Press: The Brandow Print Co., 1919.

Capital District Genealogical Society Newsletter. Albany: Capital District Genealogical Society, 1982–present. [capitaldistrictgenealogicalsociety.org]

Child, Hamilton. Gazetteer and Business Directory of Saratoga County, New York, and Queensbury, Warren County, for 1871. Syracuse, 1870.

Foley, Janet W. Early Settlers of New York State: Their Ancestors and Descendants. 9 vols. Akron, NY: 1934–1942. Reprint, 2 vols. Baltimore: Genealogical Publishing Co., 1993.

Guide to Local Historical Materials: A Union List of Holdings of Public Libraries in Saratoga, Warren, Washington, and Hamilton Counties. Saratoga Springs, NY: Southern Adirondack Library System, 1977.

Hay, William. History of Temperance in Saratoga County, NY: Containing Biographical Sketches of Billy J. Clark, Rev. Lebbeus Armstrong, Mr. James Mott, Gardner Stow, Esq., and Hon. Esek Cowen; The First Four Having Survived the Last, and All Other Original Members of the Union Temperate Society of Moreau and Northumberland, Which Association Was Organized in April A.D. 1808. Saratoga Springs, NY, 1854.

Horne, Philip F. Genealogical Guide to Saratoga County, New York. Ballston Spa, NY: Saratoga County Historical Society, 1980.

Kelly, Arthur C. M. The Saratoga. Rhinebeck, NY: Kinship, quarterly 1986–1998, annually 1999–2001.

———. Valley Quarterlies. Directory of articles (vols. 1–15) and every-name index to the Capital, the Columbia, the Mohawk, and the Saratoga. Rhinebeck, NY: Kinship, CD-ROM, 2000.

New York Historical Resources Center. Guide to Historical Resources in Saratoga County, New York, Repositories. Ithaca, NY: Cornell University, 1983. [books.FamilySearch.org]

Stone, William L. Reminiscences of Saratoga and Ballston. New York: Worthington Co., 1988. First published 1875.

Sylvester, Nathaniel B. History of Saratoga County, New York: With Historical Notes on Its Various Towns. Chicago, 1893.

———. History of Saratoga County, New York: With Illustrations And Biographical Sketches Of Some of Its Prominent Men And Pioneers. Philadelphia, 1877. Index available from Berkshire Family History Association.

The Patents: The Northeastern New York Genealogical Society Newsletter. Queensbury, NY: Northeastern New York Genealogical Society, 1981–present. [www.rootsweb.ancestry.com/~nywarren/community/nnygs.htm]

Additional Online Resources

Ancestry.com

There are vast numbers of records on Ancestry.com that pertain to people who have lived in New York State. See chapter 16 for a description of Ancestry.com's resources and its partnership with the New York State Archives. A search of the online card catalog by county may reveal lesser known resources that pertain to a locality, such as town records, abstracts, transcriptions, city directories, and local histories.

FamilySearch.org

FamilySearch has extensive collections of New York records, including religious records, which are searchable by name and location, but not by county. The following collections include record images (browsable, but not searchable) that are organized by county:

- "New York, Land Records, 1630–1975." Includes land and property records. familysearch.org/search/collection/2078654
- "New York, Probate Records, 1629–1971." Includes wills, letters of administration, and guardianship papers. familysearch.org/search/collection/1920234

For both collections, choose the browse option and then select Saratoga to view the available records sets.

A detailed description of FamilySearch.org resources is found in chapter 16.

NYGenWeb Project: Saratoga County

saratoganygenweb.com

Part of the national, USGenWeb volunteer initiative, the website provides information and resources for county research.

Old Fulton New York Postcards

www.FultonHistory.com

The website provides free access to a vast collection of digitized New York newspapers, including eight titles for Saratoga County.

Saratoga County Archival Records Interactive Index

www.saratogacountyarchiveindex.com

Searchable database of historical repositories in Saratoga County with information about their holdings, created by the Saratoga County Clerk and New York State Archives.

Schenectady County

Formed March 7, 1809

Parent County   Albany
Daughter Counties   None
County Seat   City of Schenectady

Major Land Transactions
See table in chapter 7, Land Records
Kayaderosseras Patent 1708

Town Boundary Map
★ - County seat

Towns (and Cities)	Villages and other Settlements		Notes
Duanesburg(h) 1765 Settlement began and formed as a district in Albany County 1788 Recognized as a town by State of New York 1809 Transferred to new county of Schenectady	Braman(s) Corners Delanson (v) Duane Duane Lake Duanesburg Churches Duanesburg(h) Eaton(s) Corners	Esperance Station Kelleys Station Mariaville Mariaville Lake Millers Corners Quaker Street Scotch Church	• Village of Delanson inc. 1921; formerly Toad Hollow and Quaker Street Station • Duanesburg(h) formerly Duanes Bush
Glenville 1665 Settlement 1820 Formed from fourth ward of City of Schenectady	Alpau Craig East Glenville Glenville (Station) Glenville Center Green(s) Corners High Falls High Mills	Hoffman(s) Mohawk Station Reeseville Scotia (v) Stoodley Corners Thomas Corners West Glenville	• Alpaus also Aalplaats, Aelplatts and Alplatts • Hoffmans formerly Hoffmans Ferry • Village of Scotia inc. 1904 • Stoodley Corners also Town Center
Niskayuna 1640 Settled 1809 Formed from Town of Watervliet, Albany County 1853 Annexed land from City of Schenectady	Aqueduct Avon Crest Avon Crest North Catherines Woods Estates Edison Woods Forest Oaks Grand Blvd Estates Hawthorne Hill Hexam Gardens	Karen Crest Locust Grove Niskayuna Niskayuna Center Orchard Park Rosendale Estates Stanford Heights Watervliet Center Windsor Estates	• Stanford Heights shared with Town of Colonie, Albany County
Princetown 1798 Formed in Albany County from City of Schenectady 1809 Transferred to new county of Schenectady	Corrysbush Gifford(s) Pattersonville Princetown Ryners Corners		• Normansville formerly Upper Hollow • North Albany in Town of Watervliet before 1870 • Westerlo Island in Town of Bethlehem before 1926
Rotterdam 1661 Settled 1820 Formed from third ward of City of Schenectady 1853 Annexed land from the City of Schenectady 1903 Ceded land (Bellvue and Mont Pleasant) to City of Schenectady	Antonia Hills Athens Junction Bellevue Carman Cold Brook Colonial Manor Eldorado Acres Factoryville Lower Rotterdam Junction Mohawkville	Mont Pleasant Pattersonville Rotterdam Rotterdam Junction Rotterdam Station Rynex Corners Schonowe South Schenectady Van Vechten West Rotterdam Woodlawn	• Bellvue and Mont Pleasant in City of Schenectady after 1903
Schenectady (city) * 1798 Incorporated as a city from the Town of Schenectady in Albany County 1809 Transferred to new county of Schenectady 1820 Daughter towns Glenville and Rotterdam formed 1853 Land ceded to towns of Niskayuna and Rotterdam 1903 Annexed land from Town of Rotterdam (Bellevue and Mont Pleasant)	Bellevue Frog Alley Hamilton Hill Mont Pleasant Stockade The Plot Woodlawn		* City of Schenectady county seat from 1809 when county was formed • Bellevue and Mont Pleasant in Town of Rotterdam before 1903 • The Plot, also General Electric Realty Plot, dates from the late 1800s, one of the first planned residential neighborhoods in the United States

Towns (and Cities)	Villages and other Settlements	Notes
Schenectady (town) * **c. 1661** Settled **1684** Patented in Albany County **1765** Chartered as a borough **1772** Incorporated as a district **1788** Recognized as a town by the State of New York **1798** Incorporated as a city in Albany County		* Site of 1690 massacre, and numerous forts including: Dongan 1661; Queens 1705; Fort Crosby 1735

NEW YORK STATE CENSUS RECORDS

See also chapter 3, Census Records

County originals at Schenectady County Clerk's Office: 1835, 1855, 1865, 1875, 1892, 1905, 1915, 1925 (1825 is lost)

County original at Schenectady County Historical Society: 1845* (Town of Rotterdam only)

State originals at the NYSA: 1915, 1925

Microfilm at the FHL, NYPL, and NYSL; many years are online at *FamilySearch.org* and *Ancestry.com*.

*For 1845 transcription, see Keefer in Abstracts, Indexes & Transcriptions below.

NATIONAL/STATEWIDE REPOSITORIES & RESOURCES

See chapter 16

COUNTYWIDE REPOSITORIES & RESOURCES

Schenectady County Clerk
620 State Street • Schenectady, NY 12305 • (518) 388-4220
www.schenectadycounty.com

Historic land and railroad maps, court records, land records, naturalization records early-1800s–present, and Schenectady County originals of the New York state censuses for 1835, 1855, 1865, 1875, 1892, 1905, 1915, and 1925.

Schenectady County – City, Town, and Village Clerks
Birth, marriage, and death records are maintained by the clerk of the municipality in which the event occurred; see Introduction to County Guides for details of other records which may also be held by municipal clerks. For contact information, see *www.schenectadyhistory. org/contacts.html*.

Schenectady County Surrogate's Court
612 State Street • Schenectady, NY 12305 • (518) 285-8455

Holds probate records from 1809 to the present. See also chapter 6, Probate Records.

Schenectady County Public Libraries
99 Clinton Street • Schenectady, NY 12305 • (518) 388-4500
Email: scplresearch@mvls.info • *www.scpl.org*

Atlases, census microfilms and materials 1790–1920, church histories, city directories and phone books, newspapers 1822–present, and yearbooks. Schenectady County Public Library and its branches are part of the Mohawk Valley Library system. Information on special collections can be found on a separate webpage at *www.mvls.info/lhg*.

Schenectady County Historical Society, Museum, and Grems-Dolittle Library and Archives
32 Washington Avenue • Schenectady, NY 12305 • (518) 374-0263
Email: librarian@schist.org • *www.schist.org*

Documents history of the Schenectady City and County. Holdings include books, manuscripts, local histories, family Bibles, genealogies and family files, almshouse records, broadsides, city directories, deeds, newspapers (1790–1943) and newspaper vital records indexes, oral histories, periodicals, photographs, postcards, scrapbooks, and yearbooks. Selection of indexes is available on website, along with research guides and bibliographies. Has published SCHS Newsletter bimonthly since 1971.

Schenectady County Historian
835 Central Parkway • Schenectady, NY 12309
Email: historian@nycap.rr.com • *www.schenectadyhistory.org*

Schenectady County – All Municipal Historians
While not authorized to answer genealogical inquiries, city, town, and village historians can provide valuable historical information and research advice; some maintain collections and webpages which may include transcribed records, local histories, and other genealogical material. See contact information at *www.schenectadyhistory.org/ contacts.html* or at the website of the Association of Public Historians of New York State at *www.aphnys.org*.

Schenectady County Community College Library: Local History Resources
Begley Library • 78 Washington Ave • Schenectady, NY 12305
(518) 381-1239 • *www.sunysccc.edu/library*

Website includes Local History Research Guide to local history books, local repositories, and online resources.

REGIONAL REPOSITORIES & RESOURCES

Capital District Genealogical Society
See listing in Albany County Guide

Fulton-Montgomery Community College: Evans Library: The Kenneth R. Dorn Regional History Study Center
See listing in Fulton County Guide

University at Albany, SUNY: M. E. Grenander Department of Special Collections and Archives
See listing in Albany County Guide

LOCAL REPOSITORIES & RESOURCES

Alphabetized by location

Duanesburg Historical Society Local History Collection
PO Box 421 • Duanesburg, NY 12056 • (518) 895-2632
www.duanesburghistorical.com • Email access on website

Newspapers, photographs, pamphlets, and old textbooks. Website includes list of the Society's publications.

Town of Glenville History Center
24 Glenridge Road • Glenville, NY 12302 • (518) 982-0643
Email: glenvillehistorian@gmail.com
www.townofglenville.org/Public_Documents/GlenvilleNY_Historian

Cemetery records, census materials, city directories, maps, newspapers, town and school records, obituaries 1812–present, will abstracts, yearbooks, and information on local buildings and archaeology. Located behind the Glenville Branch Library.

City of Schenectady: Efner History Center, Research Library, and City Archives
Schenectady City Hall • 105 Jay Street • Schenectady, New York 12305
(315) 382-5199 • *www.cityofschenectady.com/efner_city_archives.html*

Municipal records and city directories; collections of local labor unions, civic organizations, public schools, and businesses; postcards and photographs; maps and atlases; military records; posters and pamphlets; and manuscripts by local historians.

Union College: Schaffer Library: Schenectady Collection
807 Union St • Schenectady, NY 12308 • (518) 388-6277
www.union.edu/library

Holdings include books, atlases, and government publications.

SELECTED PRINT & ONLINE RESOURCES

Below is a selection of resources relevant for research in this county. The list is representative, not exhaustive. Additional titles—particularly of abstracts, indexes, transcriptions, and local histories—are available; consult the introduction to Part Two for further information. For guidance on how to identify and locate community directories and local newspapers, see chapter 11, City Directories, and chapter 12, Newspapers, in Part One of this book.

Abstracts, Indexes & Transcriptions

Barber, Gertrude Audrey. "Abstracts of Wills of Schenectady County, NY." Typescript, 1941. Index available from Berkshire Family History Association. [*Ancestry.com*]

Brinkman, William A. "Records from Family Cemeteries Near Schenectady." Typescript, 1914. Schenectady County Historical Society, Schenectady, NY.

Cormack, Marie N., and Katherine A. Furman. "*New York State Cemetery Inscriptions: Albany County, Herkimer County, Montgomery County, Saratoga County, Schenectady County.*" Typescript, 1940. [microfilm at FHL, NYSL]

County of Schenectady Abstracts. Syracuse: Central New York Genealogical Society, 2000. Abstracts for a range of genealogical records originally published in the quarterly *Tree Talks.*

Daughters of the American Revolution, comps. *New York DAR Genealogical Records Committee Report.* Since 1913 DAR volunteers have transcribed many thousands of unpublished cemetery, church, and town records throughout New York. The reports are at the DAR Library; copies are at the NYSL and the NYPL. The DAR has a searchable name index to all the GRC reports at *http://services.dar.org/Public/DAR_Research/search/?Tab_ID=6*. See Jean Worden's index below for a listing by county of the New York record sets that were transcribed by the DAR before 1998.

Davenport, David P. *The 1855 Census of Schenectady County, New York: An Index.* Rhinebeck, NY: Kinship Books, 1989.

"First Dutch Reformed Church of Schenectady, N.Y." *NYG&B Record*, vol. 73 (1942) no. 1: 36–63, no. 2: 106–108. [NYG&B eLibrary]

Foote, Clarence. *The Cemeteries of Duanesburg and Princetown.* Schenectady, NY: Schenectady County Historical Society, 2002.

Keefer, Donald, comp. "1845 State Census—Town of Rotterdam, Schenectady Co." *The Mohawk*, vol. 8 (1991) no. 3: 105-108, no. 4: 127-130; vol. 9 (1992) no. 1: 35.

Kelly, Arthur C. M. *Index to Tree Talks County Packet: Schenectady County.* Rhinebeck, NY: Kinship, 2002.

"A List of the Freeholders of Schenectady, Before the Grant of Gov. Dongan." *NYG&B Record*, vol. 3, no. 2 (1872): 71. [NYG&B eLibrary]

Luckhurst, Charlotte T. "Copies of Schenectady County Family Bible Records." Typescript, 1930. Library of Congress, Washington, DC. [*HathiTrust.org*]

— — —. "Early Schenectady Cemetery Records: First Reformed Church of Schenectady." Typescript, 1914. NYPL, New York.

— — —. "Schenectady Dutch Church Members, 1694–1839." Typescript, 1914. NYPL, New York.

— — —. "Scotia-Glenville, Cemetery Records." Typescript, 1924 NYPL, New York.

— — —. "Vale Cemetery Records, Schenectady, NY." Typescript, 1926. NYPL, New York. Index available from Berkshire Family History Association.

Reynolds, Neil B. "Schenectady County Genealogy from Surrogate's Records: Genealogical Data from Wills, Probate Proceedings, Guardianship Petitions, etc., Filed in The Office of the Surrogate of Schenectady County." Typescript, 1949. NYPL, New York.

Schenectady County, NYG&B Church Surveys Collection. NYG&B, New York. [NYG&B eLibrary]

Worden, Jean D. "Book 1, Subject Index." In *Revised Master Index to the New York State Daughters of the American Revolution Genealogical Records Volumes.* Zephyrhills, FL: J. D. Worden, 1998. The Subject Index includes a listing by county of the cemeteries, churches, towns, and other sources of records transcribed by the DAR.

Other Resources

Beers, S. N. *New Topographical Atlas of the Counties of Albany and Schenectady, New York: From Actual Surveys.* Philadelphia, 1866. [NYPL Digital Gallery]

Burke, Thomas E. *Mohawk Frontier: The Dutch Community of Schenectady, New York, 1661–1710.* Ithaca, NY: Cornell University Press, 1991.

Capital District Genealogical Society Newsletter. Albany: Capital District Genealogical Society, 1982–present. [*capitaldistrict genealogicalsociety.org*]

Child, Hamilton. *Gazetteer and Business Directory of Albany and Schenectady Co., NY, for 1870–1.* Syracuse, 1870.

Clark, Donna K. *Schenectady County, NY, List of Depositories.* Arvada, CO: Ancestor Publishers, 1986.

Foley, Janet W. *Early Settlers of New York State: Their Ancestors and Descendants.* 9 vols. Akron, NY: 1934–1942. Reprint, 2 vols. Baltimore: Genealogical Publishing Co., 1993.

Greene, Nelson. *History of the Mohawk Valley, Gateway to the West, 1614–1925; Covering the Six Counties of Schenectady, Schoharie, Montgomery, Fulton, Herkimer, and Oneida.* Chicago: S. J. Clarke, 1925.

Hanson, Willis T. *A History of Schenectady during the Revolution: To Which is Appended a Contribution to the Individual Records of the Inhabitants of Schenectady District during That Period.* Interlaken, NY: Heart of the Lakes Publishing, 1988. First published 1916.

Howell, George R., and John H. Munsell. *History of the County of Schenectady, NY, from 1662 to 1886.* New York, 1885.

Kelly, Arthur C. M. *The Mohawk.* Rhinebeck, NY: Kinship, quarterly 1986–1998, annually 1999–2001.

— — —. *Valley Quarterlies.* Directory of articles (vols. 1–15) and every-name index to the *Capital*, the *Columbia*, the *Mohawk*, and the *Saratoga.* Rhinebeck, NY: Kinship, CD-ROM, 2000.

Monroe, Joel H. *Schenectady, Ancient and Modern: A Complete and Connected History of Schenectady from the Granting of the First Patent In 1661 to 1914, Presenting Many Historic Pictures and*

Portraits of Those Who Have Been Conspicuous Figures in Its History. Geneva, NY: Press of W. F. Humphrey, 1914.

New York Historical Resources Center. *Guide to Historical Resources in Schenectady County, New York, Repositories*. Ithaca, NY: Cornell University, 1983.

Pascucci, Robert R. "Electric City Immigrants: Italians and Poles of Schenectady, N.Y., 1880–1930." PhD diss., State University of New York at Albany, Department of History, 1984.

Pearson, Jonathan. *Contributions for the Genealogies of the Descendants of the First Settlers of the Patent and City of Schenectady, from 1662 to 1800*. Baltimore: Genealogical Publishing Co., 1982. First published 1873.

Rittner, Don. *Schenectady: Frontier Village to Colonial City*. Charleston, SC: The History Press, 2011.

— — —. *Schenectady: Then & Now*. Charleston, SC: Arcadia Publishing, 2007.

Rosenthal, Susan C. *Schenectady*. Charleston, SC: Arcadia Publishing, 2000.

Staffa, Susan J. *Schenectady Genesis: How a Dutch Colonial Village Became an American City, 1661–1800*. Fleischmanns, NY: Purple Mountain Press, 2004.

Toll, Daniel J. *A Narrative, Embracing the History of Two or Three of the First Settlers and Their Families, of Schenectady*. Schenectady, NY, 1847.

Van Santvoord, C. *A History of the County of Schenectady*. Schenectady, 1887.

Yates, Austin A. *Schenectady County, New York: Its History to the Close of the Nineteenth Century*. New York: New York History Co., 1902. Index available from the Berkshire Family History Association.

Additional Online Resources

Ancestry.com

There are vast numbers of records on *Ancestry.com* that pertain to people who have lived in New York State. See chapter 16 for a description of *Ancestry.com*'s resources and its partnership with the New York State Archives. A search of the online card catalog by county may reveal lesser known resources that pertain to a locality, such as town records, abstracts, transcriptions, city directories, and local histories.

FamilySearch.org

FamilySearch has extensive collections of New York records, including religious records, which are searchable by name and location, but not by county. The following collections include record images (browsable, but not searchable) that are organized by county:

- "New York, Land Records, 1630–1975." Includes land and property records. *familysearch.org/search/collection/2078654*

- "New York, Probate Records, 1629–1971." Includes wills, letters of administration, and guardianship papers. *familysearch.org/search/collection/1920234*

For both collections, choose the browse option and then select Schenectady to view the available records sets.

A detailed description of *FamilySearch.org* resources is found in chapter 16.

Old Fulton New York Postcards
www.FultonHistory.com

The website provides free access to a vast collection of digitized New York newspapers, including six titles for Schenectady County.

Schenectady Digital History Archive:
Schenectady County History and Genealogy
www.schenectadyhistory.org

A service of the Schenectady County Public Library, the website is also the home of the county's NYGenWeb page. The extensive resources for Schenectady County history and genealogy research include genealogies, biographies, an obituary index with more than 100,000 citations (with some records for Albany, Fulton, Hamilton, Montgomery, Rensselaer, Saratoga, Schoharie, Warren, and Washington counties), and links to articles and resources. A comprehensive bibliography and links to numerous digitized books is at *www.schenectadyhistory.org/resources/index.html*.

Schoharie County

Formed April 6, 1795

Parent Counties   Albany • Otsego
Daughter Counties   None
County Seat   Village of Schoharie

Montgomery County

Schenectady County

Sharon

Carlisle

Esperance

Seward

Cobleskill

Schoharie ★

Wright

Otsego County

Richmondville

Middleburgh

Albany County

Summit

Fulton

Broome

Jefferson

Blenheim

Gilboa

Conesville

Delaware County

Greene County

Town Boundary Map
 - County seat

Towns (and Cities)	Villages and other Settlements		Notes
Blenheim Settled by German Palatines and Dutch before 1761 **1797** Formed from Town of Schoharie **1803** Daughter town Jefferson formed **1848** Daughter town Gilboa formed	Blenheim Blenheim Hill Burnt Hill Cole Hollow	Eminence Minekill Falls North Blenheim Ruth	• Eminence formerly Dutch Hill; on Summit town line • North Blenheim also Patchin Hollow
Bristol Name for Town of Broome 1797–1808			
Broome **1797** Formed as Town of Bristol from Town of Schoharie **1808** Name changed to Broome **1836** Daughter town Conesville formed **1848** Daughter town Gilboa formed **1849** Annexed land from Town of Middleburgh	Bates Franklinton Gilboa Livingstonville Smithto(w)n		• Franklinton also The Vly • Gilboa in Town of Gilboa from 1848
Carlisle **c.1760** Settled **1807** Formed from towns of Cobleskill and Sharon	Argusville Becker Corners Carlisle	Carlisle Center Grovenor(s) Corners Little York	• Argusville formerly Molicks Mills; on Sharon town line • Carlisle Center formerly Bradts Corners
Cobleskill **1750** Settled **1797** Formed from Town of Schoharie **1807** Daughter town Carlisle formed **1819** Daughter town Summit formed **1849** Daughter town Richmondville formed	Barnerville Bramanville Cobleskill (v) Cobleskill Center East Cobleskill Greenbush Howe(s) Cave	Lawyersville Mineral Springs Punchkill Richmondville Sagendorf Corners Shutts Corners	• Barnerville also Bernerville • Bramanville also Braymanville • Village of Cobleskill inc. 1868 • Lawyersville, also New Boston; on Seward town line • Punchkill formerly Schoharie Mountain • Richmondville in Town of Richmondville from 1849
Conesville **1764** Settled **1836** Formed from towns of Durham (Greene County) and Broome	Conesville Manorkill West Conesville		• Conesville also Stone Bridge • Manorkill also Manor Kill • West Conesville also Strykersville
Esperance **c.1711** First settled by Palatines **1846** Formed from Town of Schoharie **1850** Ceded land to Town of Schoharie	Burtonsville Central Bridge Dwelly Corners Esperance (v)	Kneiskerns Dorf Schoharie Junction Sloansville	• Central Bridge formerly Smithville • Village of Esperance inc. 1818 • Kneiskerns Dorf one of the earliest settlements
Fulton **c.1711** First settlements by Dutch and Palatines **1828** Formed from Town of Middleburgh	Br(e)akabeen Fairland Fultonham Greenbush Housons Corners Patria	Petersburgh Pleasant Valley Vintonto(w)n Vromansland Watsonville West Fulton	• West Fulton formerly Byrneville and Sapbush Hollow
Gilboa **1764** Settled **1848** Formed from towns of Blenheim and Broome	Broome Center Five Corners Flat Creek Gilboa Mackey Mine Kil Falls	Owlsville South Gilboa South Gilboa Station Welch Corners West Gilboa	• Broome Center also Mackies (Mackeys) Corners, formerly Tibbetts • Gilboa in Town of Broome before 1848 • Mine Kil Falls also Minekill Falls

Towns (and Cities)	Villages and other Settlements		Notes
Jefferson c. 1794 Settlers from New England 1803 Formed from Town of Blenheim 1819 Daughter town Summit formed	Arabia Baird Corners East Jefferson Jefferson Jerome	Morseville South Jefferson Stewart West Jefferson Westkill	
Middleburgh c. 1711 Settled by Palatines 1797 Formed as Town of Middletown from Town of Schoharie 1798 Ceded land to Town of Schoharie 1801 Name changed to Middleburgh 1828 Daughter town Fulton formed 1849 Ceded land to Town of Broome	East Cobleskill Huntersland Middleburgh (v) Mill Valley West Middleburgh		• Huntersland also Hunters Land, formerly Huntersville • Village of Middleburgh inc. 1881; formerly Weisers Dorp, also Middletown • West Middleburgh also Polly Hollow
Middletown Name for Town of Middleburgh 1797–1801			
Richmondville 1764 Settled near Warnerville 1849 Formed from Town of Cobleskill 1851 Annexed land from Town of Seward	Beards Hollow Richmondville (v) Warnerville West Richmondville		• Beards Hollow on Summit town line • Village of Richmondville inc. 1881; in Town of Cobleskill before 1849 • Warnerville formerly Manns Valley • West Richmondville formerly Caryleville
Schoharie c. 1711 Settled by Palatines 1772 Formed as Schoharie District 1788 Formed as town in Albany County 1795 Transferred to new county of Schoharie 1797 Daughter towns Blenheim, Bristol (now Broome), Cobleskill, and Middletown (now Middleburgh) formed 1798 Annexed land from Town of Middletown (now Middleburgh) 1846 Daughter towns Esperance and Wright formed 1850 Annexed land from Town of Esperance	Barton Hill Central Bridge East Cobleskill Esperance Gallopsville Garlocks Dorf Hartmans Dorf Howes Cave Old Central Bridge Schoharie (v) Sidney Corners Sloansville Vroman Corners		• Village of Schoharie inc. 1867; formerly Brunnendorf, Brunnen Dorp, Fountain Town, and Sommersville; county seat 1795–present
Seward 1754 Settled by Germans as New Dorlach 1840 Formed from Town of Sharon 1851 Ceded land to Town of Richmondville	Clove Dorloo Gardner(s)ville Hyndsville Janesville	Lawyersville Seward Seward Station Weber(s) Corners Zeh Corners	• Clove formerly Clauver Kloof (Clover Valley) • Dorloo formerly New Dorlach • Lawyersville, also New Boston; on Cobleskill town line • Seward also Neeleys Hollow and Seward Valley

Towns (and Cities)	Villages and other Settlements	Notes
Sharon **c. 1781** Settlers from New England **1792** Formed in Otsego County as Dorlach from Town of Cherry Valley * **1795** Transferred to new county of Schoharie: name changed to Sharon **1797** Sharon was officially incorporated **1807** Daughter town Carlisle formed **1840** Daughter town Seward formed	Argusville Beekman(s) Corners Engleville Gilbert(s) Corners Leesville Rockville Sharon Sharon Center Sharon Hill Sharon Springs (v) Staleyville	* Dorlach referred to as New Dorlach in some county supervisor's minutes • Argusville also Molicks Mills; on Carlisle town line • Engleville also Engellville and Engles Mills • Sharon also Moaks Hollow • Village of Sharon Springs inc. 1871
Summit **1794** Settlers from Dutchess County **1819** Formed from towns of Cobleskill and Jefferson	Beards Hollow Charlotteville Eminence Lutheranville Summit	• Beards Hollow on Richmondville town line • Eminence formerly Dutch Hill; on Blenheim town line • Lutheranville also Tar Hollow • Summit formerly Four Corners
Wright Settled before Revolution **1846** Formed from Town of Schoharie	Gallupville Shutter(s) Corners Waldenville	

NEW YORK STATE CENSUS RECORDS

See also chapter 3, Census Records

County originals at Schoharie County Clerk's Office (affected by 2011 floods): 1825*, 1835, 1855, 1865, 1875, 1892, 1905, 1915, 1925 (1845 is lost)

State originals at the NYSA: 1915, 1925

Microfilm at the FHL, NYPL, and NYSL; many years are online at *FamilySearch.org* and *Ancestry.com*.

*1825 census transcription and index available from the Central New York Genealogical Society

NATIONAL/STATEWIDE REPOSITORIES & RESOURCES

See chapter 16

COUNTYWIDE REPOSITORIES & RESOURCES

Schoharie County Clerk
284 Main Street • PO Box 549 • Schoharie, NY 12157
(518) 295-8316

Holdings include Schoharie County originals of New York state censuses for 1825, 1835, 1855, 1865, 1875, 1892, 1905, 1915, and 1925; land records 1797–present; and naturalization records 1810–1955. Many records damaged by Hurricane Irene are undergoing conservation.

Schoharie County – Town and Village Clerks
Birth, marriage, and death records are maintained by the clerk of the municipality in which the event occurred; see Introduction to County Guides for details of other records which may be held by municipal clerks. For contact information, see *www.schohariechamber.com/pdf/2011CountyDirectory.pdf*.

Schoharie County Surrogate's Court and Family Court
Schoharie County Courthouse • 290 Main Street • PO Box 669
Schoharie, NY 12147 • (518) 453-6999 ext. 3

Probate records begin in 1795. However, all records from the years 1795–1987 were badly damaged in Hurricane Irene; recovered records have been digitized (*www.schoharie-ny.gov/remote/OpeningScreen?menuItem=43*), and new website is expected in 2015. See also records on FHL microfilm. All probate records after 1987 are on the Surrogate's Court's computers. Also see chapter 6, Probate Records.

Schoharie County Public Libraries
Schoharie is part of the Mohawk Valley Library System; see *www.mvls.info* to access each library. Many libraries maintain special collections relating to local history and genealogy, and more information can be found on a separate webpage at *www.mvls.info/lhg*. Also see listing below for Middleburgh Free Library.

Schoharie County Historical Society, Old Stone Fort Museum, and Old Stone Fort Library
145 Fort Road • Schoharie, NY 12157 • (518) 295-7192
Email: Office@SchoharieHistory.net • *http://theoldstonefort.org*

Manuscripts, periodicals, atlases, cemetery records, church records, census records, directories, maps, military information, newspapers, vertical files, family papers, Bible records, genealogical charts, published genealogies, vital records, and wills and abstracts. Publishes *Schoharie County Historical Review*, semi-annually.

Schoharie County Historian
4994 State Route 145 • Cobleskill, NY 12043 • 518-234-7241

Schoharie County – All Municipal Historians
While not authorized to answer genealogical inquiries, town and village historians can provide valuable historical information and research advice; some maintain collections and webpages which may include transcribed records, local histories, and other genealogical material. See contact information at *www.theoldstonefort.org/Library/historians.html* or at the website of the Association of Public Historians of New York State at *www.aphnys.org*.

Iroquois Indian Museum
See listing in chapter 14, Peoples of New York, American Indian

REGIONAL REPOSITORIES & RESOURCES

Capital District Genealogical Society
See listing in Albany County Guide

Fulton-Montgomery Community College: Evans Library: The Kenneth R. Dorn Regional History Study Center
See listing in Fulton County Guide

LOCAL REPOSITORIES & RESOURCES

Alphabetized by location

Cobleskill Historical Society
PO Box 423 • Cobleskill, NY 12043
Email: CHS@SchoharieHistory.net
www.schohariehistory.net/CHS/CHShome.htm

Website includes history of Cobleskill, photographs, and postcards.

SUNY College of Agriculture and Technology at Cobleskill: Van Wagenen Library
142 Schenectady Avenue • Cobleskill, NY 12043-1702
(518) 255-5841 • Email: library@cobleskill.edu
www.cobleskill.edu/library

Holdings include materials relating to Cobleskill and Schoharie County history and genealogy.

Middleburgh Free Library: History and Genealogy Room
323 Main Street • Middleburgh, NY 12122 • (518) 827-5142
www.middleburghlibrary.info

Books and genealogies, church and cemetery records, master name file, 1855 Middleburgh census index, military information, family Bibles, and town records.

Richmondville Historical Society
The Bunn Mill, High Street • PO Box 316 • Richmondville, NY 12149
www.richmondvillehistoricalsociety.com

Website includes biographies of Richmondville residents, historical photographs, and other information on the history of Richmondville.

SELECTED PRINT & ONLINE RESOURCES

Below is a selection of resources relevant for research in this county. The list is representative, not exhaustive. Additional titles—particularly of abstracts, indexes, transcriptions, and local histories—are available; consult the introduction to Part Two for further information. For guidance on how to identify and locate community directories and local newspapers, see chapter 11, City Directories, and chapter 12, Newspapers, in Part One of this book.

Abstracts, Indexes & Transcriptions

Barber, Gertrude Audrey. "Abstracts of Wills, Letters of Administration and Guardianship of Schoharie County, New York." Typescript, 1938. NYPL, New York.

— — —. "Cemetery Records, Schoharie County, New York." Typescript, 1932. NYPL, New York.

Barnello, Kathleen, Joan Green, Harriet M. B. Hall, and Joyce Mason. *Abstract of the 1825 New York State Census of Schoharie County, New York.* Syracuse: Central New York Genealogical Society, 1994. Originally published in *Tree Talks*, vol. 34, no. 4 (1994): 1–47. Index: 49–66, introduction: i–vii.

Cady, Henry. "Schoharie County Genealogical Records." 10 vols. Manuscript, n.d. NYPL, New York. Manuscript ledger books containing transcriptions of birth, marriage, death, census, and cemetery records of Schoharie County.

Cady, Henry, and Charlotte T. Luckhurst. *Deaths and Burials in Schoharie County, NY.* Salem, MA: Higginson Book Co., 2007.

Cohen, Minnie. *Vital Records of the Gilboa Reformed Church, Gilboa, Schoharie County, NY: Baptisms 1801–1882, Marriages 1803–1884; and the Blenheim Reformed Church, Blenheim, Schoharie County, NY, Baptisms 1797–1839.* Indexed by Lawrence V. Rickard in 1999. Rhinebeck, NY: Kinship, 1999.

County of Schoharie Abstracts. Syracuse: Central New York Genealogical Society, 2000. Abstracts for a range of genealogical records originally published in the quarterly *Tree Talks.*

Daughters of the American Revolution, comps. *New York DAR Genealogical Records Committee Report.* Since 1913 DAR volunteers have transcribed many thousands of unpublished cemetery, church, and town records throughout New York. The reports are at the DAR Library; copies are at the NYSL and the NYPL. The DAR has a searchable name index to all the GRC reports at *http://services.dar.org/Public/DAR_Research/search/?Tab_ID=6.* See Jean Worden's index below for a listing by county of the New York record sets that were transcribed by the DAR before 1998.

Davenport, David. *The 1855 Census of Schoharie County, New York: An Index.* Rhinebeck, NY: Kinship, 1988.

Index to Deeds, Schoharie County, 1795–1940. Microfilm. Salt Lake City: Reproduction Systems for the Genealogical Society of Utah, 1971. Includes land and property records and grantor/grantee index; microfilm of original records in the Schoharie County Courthouse.

Kelly, Arthur C. M. *Index to Tree Talks County Packet: Schoharie County.* Rhinebeck, NY: Kinship, 2002.

— — —. *Schoharie County, New York, Early Records: Family Lists, Marriages, Deaths, 1730–1904.* Rhinebeck, NY: Kinship, 2001. Book includes records of the Schoharie Lutheran Church, Cobleskill Lutheran Church, and the Schoharie Reformed Church.

Lamb, Jr., VanBuren. "Small Cemeteries of Schoharie Co., NY." Typescript, 1957. NYPL, New York. [NYG&B eLibrary]

Rickard, Lawrence V. *Records of the Rev. John Daniel Shafer, Schoharie County, New York: Baptisms 1819–1838, Marriages 1830–1838.* Rhinebeck, NY: Kinship, 2000.

Schoharie County, NYG&B Church Surveys Collection. NYG&B, New York. [NYG&B eLibrary]

Spencer, Frances B. "Cemetery Inscriptions in Schoharie County, New York." Typescript, 1959. NYSHA, Cooperstown, NY.

Vosburgh, Royden Woodward, ed. "Records of St. Paul's Evangelical Lutheran Church in the Town of Schoharie, Schoharie County, NY." Typescript, 1914–1915. NYPL, New York.

— — —, ed. "Records of the Reformed Church in the Village of Gilboa, Schoharie County, NY, Formerly the Reformed Dutch Church in Dyse's Manor, in the Town of Broome; and Records of the Reformed Dutch Church in Blenheim, in the Old Village of Blenheim, Schoharie County, NY." Typescript, 1918. NYPL, New York. [NYG&B eLibrary]

— — —. "Vital Records of the Lawyersville Reformed Church: Lawyersville, Schoharie County, NY." Typescript, 1915. NYSHA, Cooperstown, NY.

Worden, Jean D. "Book 1, Subject Index." In *Revised Master Index to the New York State Daughters of the American Revolution Genealogical Records Volumes.* Zephyrhills, FL: J. D. Worden, 1998. The Subject Index includes a listing by county of the cemeteries, churches, towns, and other sources of records transcribed by the DAR.

Other Resources

Adams, Arthur G., ed. *The Catskills: An Illustrated Historical Guide with Gazetteer.* New York: Fordham University Press, 1990. First published 1975.

Beers, S. N. *New Topographical Atlas of Schoharie Co., New York.* Philadelphia, 1866. [NYPL Digital Gallery]

Brown, John M. *A Brief Sketch of the First Settlement of the County of Schoharie.* Schoharie, NY, 1823.

Cady, Henry. *Genealogical Notes of Schoharie County, NY, Families.* Retyped and indexed by Frances B. Spencer. Middleburgh, NY: 1959–1960.

Capital District Genealogical Society Newsletter. Albany: Capital District Genealogical Society, 1982–present. [*capitaldistrict genealogicalsociety.org*]

Child, Hamilton. *Gazetteer and Business Directory of Schoharie County, NY, for 1872–3.* Syracuse, 1871.

Cornell, Fanchon D., and Alicia T. Cornell. *Blenheim History, 1710–1991, Schoharie County, New York: With a Brief 1994 Update.* Albany: Fort Orange Press, 1994.

Greene, Nelson. *History of the Mohawk Valley, Gateway to the West, 1614–1925; Covering the Six Counties of Schenectady, Schoharie, Montgomery, Fulton, Herkimer, and Oneida.* Chicago: S. J. Clarke, 1925.

Kelly, Arthur C. M. *The Mohawk.* Rhinebeck, NY: Kinship, quarterly 1986–1998, annually 1999–2001.

— — —. *Valley Quarterlies.* Directory of articles (vols. 1–15) and every-name index to the *Capital,* the *Columbia,* the *Mohawk,* and the *Saratoga.* Rhinebeck, NY: Kinship, CD-ROM, 2000.

Luckhurst, Charlotte T. "Schoharie County, NY, Families." Typescript, 1922. NYPL, New York.

New York Historical Resources Center. *Guide to Historical Resources in Schoharie County, New York, Repositories.* Ithaca, NY: Cornell University, c. 1983.

Noyes, Marion F. *A History of Schoharie County.* Richmondville, NY: Richmondville Phoenix, 1954.

Rockwell, Charles. *The Catskill Mountains and the Region Around* . . . . New York, 1869.

Roscoe, William E. *History of Schoharie County, New York: With illustrations and Biographical Sketches of Some of Its Prominent Men and Pioneers.* Bowie, MD: Heritage Books, 1994. First published 1882.

Sias, Solomon. *A Summary of Schoharie County, Giving the Organization, Geography, Geology, History. Prepared at the Request of the County Teachers' Association.* Middleburgh, NY: P. W. Danforth Press, 1904.

Simms, Jeptha R. *History of Schoharie County: And Border Wars of New York, Containing Also a Sketch of the Causes Which Led to the American Revolution and Interesting Memoranda of the Mohawk Valley* . . . . Albany, 1845.

Sloughter's Instant History of Schoharie County, 1700–1900: With a Few Folk Tales, Maps, and Illustrations Thrown in for Good Measure and Good Reading. Schoharie, NY: Schoharie County Historical Society, 1988. Compiled from Brown, Simms, Roscoe, Warner, and Hagan, the Schoharie County Historical Review, and other published works.

Van Schaick, John, Jr. *The Little Hill Farm; Or, Cruisings in Old Schoharie.* Boston: Universalist Pub. House, 1930.

Additional Online Resources

Ancestry.com

There are vast numbers of records on *Ancestry.com* that pertain to people who have lived in New York State. See chapter 16 for a description of *Ancestry.com*'s resources and its partnership with the New York State Archives. A search of the online card catalog by county may reveal lesser known resources that pertain to a locality, such as town records, abstracts, transcriptions, city directories, and local histories.

FamilySearch.org

FamilySearch has extensive collections of New York records, including religious records, which are searchable by name and location, but not by county. The following collections include record images (browsable, but not searchable) that are organized by county:

- "New York, Land Records, 1630–1975." Includes land and property records. *familysearch.org/search/collection/2078654*

- "New York, Probate Records, 1629–1971." Includes wills, letters of administration, and guardianship papers. *familysearch.org/search/collection/1920234*

For both collections, choose the browse option and then select Schoharie to view the available records sets.

A detailed description of *FamilySearch.org* resources is found in chapter 16

Gilboa Historical Society

www.gilboahome.com

Society's website includes oral histories, newsletter archives (2006–2012), maps, photographs, and articles documenting the history and pre-history of Gilboa.

NYGenWeb Project: Schoharie County

www.rootsweb.ancestry.com/~nyschoha

Part of the national, USGenWeb volunteer initiative, the website provides information and resources for county research.

Schuyler County

Formed April 17, 1854

Parent Counties   Chemung • Steuben • Tompkins
Daughter Counties   None
County Seat   Village of Watkins Glen, Towns of Dix and Reading

Major Land Transactions
See chapter 7, Land Records
New Military Tract 1782–1791
Phelps and Gorham Purchase 1788
Watkins and Flint Purchase 1794

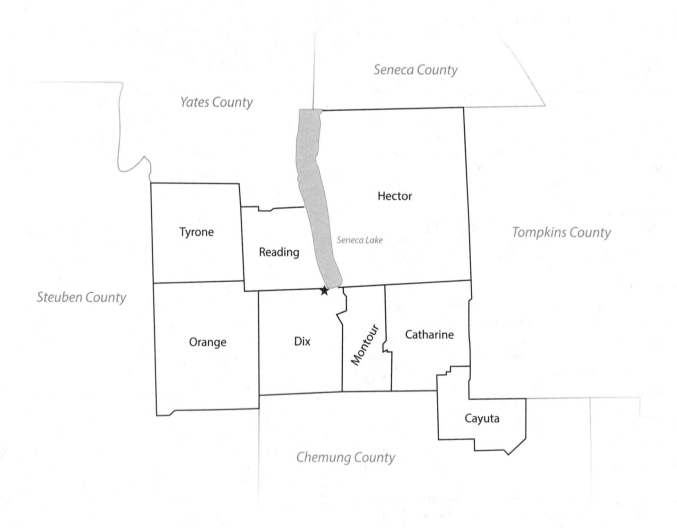

Town Boundary Map
 - County seat

Towns (and Cities)	Villages and other Settlements	Notes
Catharine 1798 Formed in Tioga County from Town of Newtown (now Elmira) * 1823 Daughter towns Catlin and Veteran formed (now Chemung County) 1836 Transferred to new county of Chemung 1854 Transferred to new county of Schuyler; ceded land to Town of Cayuta 1860 Daughter town Montour formed	Alpine Catharine(s) Cayutaville Havana (v) Lawrence Malarys Settlement Odessa (v)	* Town of Newton (now Elmira) in Chemung County from 1836 • Alpine on Cayuta town line • Catherine(s) also Johnsons Settlement • Cayutaville on Hector town line • Havana formerly Catherines Town and Mills Landing, named Havana in 1829; inc. 1836 in Chemung County; 1854 transferred to new Schuyler County and served as county seat 1854–1867; transferred to new Town of Montour in 1860; renamed Village of Montour Falls 1895 • Village of Odessa inc. 1903; shared with Town of Montour
Cayuta 1801 Settled 1824 Formed in Tioga County from Town of Spencer 1854 Transferred to new county of Schuyler; annexed land from Town of Catharine; daughter town Van Etten formed in Chemung County	Alpine Alpine Junction Cayuta	• Alpine on Catherine town line • Cayuta also West Cayuta
Dix 1800 Settled 1835 Formed in Tioga County from Town of Catlin 1836 Transferred to new county of Chemung 1854 Transferred to new county of Schuyler 1869 Annexed land from Town of Hector	Beaver Dams Montour Falls (v) Moreland Moreland Station Townsend Watkins Glen (v) Wedgewood Wedg(e)wood Station	• Village of Montour Falls inc. 1836 as Havana; name changed to Montour Falls in 1895; shared with Town of Catherine before 1860 and then with Town of Montour; see Town of Montour for county seat information • Moreland also Crawford Settlement • Village of Watkins Glen formerly Salubria and Savoy, inc. 1842 as Jefferson, renamed Watkins in 1852, and Watkins Glen in 1926; village shared with Town of Reading; Village of Watkins Glen (Watkins) county seat 1867–present; 1854–1867 county seat at Village of Montour Falls (Havana) with second courthouse in Watkins 1854–1857; county seat contested until 1877
Hector * 1791 Settled 1802 Formed in Cayuga County from Town of Ovid * 1804 Transferred to new county of Seneca 1817 Transferred to new county of Tompkins 1854 Transferred to new county of Schuyler 1869 Ceded land to towns of Dix and Reading	Bennetsburgh Peach Orchard Burdett (v) Peach Orchard Point Cayutaville Perry City East Steamburg Polkville Hector Reynoldsville Hector Station Searsburg(h) Logan Seneca McIntyre Settlement Smith Valley Mecklenburgh Spaulding Corner North Hector Steamburgh North Hector Station Valois	* Hector was the name of one of the 28 Military Tract townships * Ovid in Seneca County from 1804 • Village of Burdett inc. 1898 • Cayutaville on Catherine town line

Towns (and Cities)	Villages and other Settlements		Notes
Jersey Name for Town of Orange 1813–1836			
Montour 1794 Settled near current Village of Montour Falls 1860 Formed from Town of Catharine	Deckertown Montour Falls (v) Odessa (v)		• Village of Montour Falls inc. 1836 as Havana in Town of Catherine; transferred to Town of Montour 1860; name changed to Montour Falls March 20, 1895; shared with Town of Dix • Village of Montour Falls (Havana) was county seat 1854–1857 with second courthouse at Watkins; sole county seat 1857–1867; 1867 county seat moved to Watkins—contested until 1877 • Village of Odessa inc. 1903; shared with Town of Catherine
Orange 1799 Settlers from Monterey 1813 Formed in Steuben County as Town of Jersey from Town of Wayne 1836 Name changed to Orange; daughter town Bradford formed 1854 Transferred to new county of Schuyler	East Orange Monterey Orange Orangetown Pine Creek Sugar Hill		
Reading 1806 Formed in Steuben County from Town of Frederickstown (now Wayne) 1824 Daughter town Starkey formed in Yates County 1854 Reading transferred to new county of Schuyler 1869 Annexed land from Town of Hector	Chapmans Corners Coal Point Coles Corners Gabriels Junction Halls Corners Ireland Mills	Irelandville North Reading Reading Reading Center Watkins Glen (v) Watkins Glen Station	• Halls Corners on Tyrone town line • Village of Watkins Glen inc. 1842; shared with Town of Dix; see Town of Dix for county seat and name change information
Tyrone 1800 Settled 1822 Formed in Steuben County from Town of Wayne 1854 Transferred to new county of Schuyler	Altay Gingerbread Corners Halls Corners Pine Grove	Shorewood Tyrone Wayne Weston	• Halls Corners on Reading town line

NEW YORK STATE CENSUS RECORDS

See also chapter 3, Census Records

County originals at Schuyler County Clerk's Office: 1855, 1865, 1875, 1915, 1925 (1892 and 1905 are lost)

State originals at the NYSA: 1915, 1925

Microfilm at the FHL, NYPL, and NYSL; many years are online at *FamilySearch.org* and *Ancestry.com*.

NATIONAL/STATEWIDE REPOSITORIES & RESOURCES

See chapter 16

COUNTYWIDE REPOSITORIES & RESOURCES

Schuyler County Clerk

105 Ninth Street, Unit 8 • Watkins Glen, NY 14891
(607) 535-8133 • *www.schuylercounty.us*

Holdings include a name index to deeds, leases, mortgages, judgments, federal tax liens, court proceedings, business names, and corporations; federal censuses 1860, 1870, 1880, and the New York state census 1855, 1865, 1875, for Schuyler County; some marriage records 1908–1935; and naturalization records 1864–1954. Holdings also include deeds from 1796 (transcribed from Chemung County, towns of Catherine, Cayuta, Dix, and Montour), from 1798 (transcribed from Steuben County, towns of Orange, Reading, and Tyrone), and from 1817 (transcribed from Tompkins County, Town of Hector).

Schuyler County – Town and Village Clerks

Birth, marriage, and death records are maintained by the clerk of the municipality in which the event occurred; see Introduction to County Guides for details of other records which may also be held by municipal clerks. A PDF with contact information can be downloaded at *www.schuylercounty.us/DocumentCenter*

Schuyler County Surrogate's Court

Schuyler County Courthouse • 105 Ninth Street, Unit 35
Watkins Glen, NY 14891 • (607) 535-7144

Holds probate records from 1850 to the present. See also chapter 6, Probate Records.

Schuyler County Public Libraries

Schuyler is part of the Southern Tier Library System; see *www.stls.org/libraries* to access each library. Many hold genealogy and local history collections. Also see listing below for Montour Falls Memorial Library.

Schuyler County Historical Society

108 North Catharine Street (Route 14) • PO Box 651
Montour Falls, NY 14865 • (607) 535-9741
Email: info@schuylerhistory.org • *www.schuylerhistory.org*

Histories, genealogies, cemetery records, maps, newspapers, military records, business records, school records, town records, vital record listings, and records of local institutions, clubs, and societies. Website includes surname list.

Schuyler County Historian

2470 County Route 16 • Watkins Glen, NY 14891
(607) 535-4730 • *www.schuylercounty.us/historian.htm*

Schuyler County – All Municipal Historians

While not authorized to answer genealogical inquiries, town and village historians can provide valuable historical information and research advice; some maintain collections and webpages which may

include transcribed records, local histories, and other genealogical material. A PDF with contact information can be downloaded at *www.schuylercounty.us/DocumentCenter* or see the website of the Association of Public Historians of New York State at *www.aphnys.org*.

LOCAL REPOSITORIES & RESOURCES

Alphabetized by location

Montour Falls Memorial Library: Historic Resource Room

406 West Main Street • PO Box 486 • Montour Falls, NY 14865-0486
(607) 535-7489 (front desk) • 594-2062 (Historic Resource Room)
www.montourfallslibrary.org

Local histories and genealogies, cemetery listings, information on local businesses, newspapers, atlases and maps, scrapbooks, school records, town records, and photographs. Offers research services for a fee.

SELECTED PRINT & ONLINE RESOURCES

Below is a selection of resources relevant for research in this county. The list is representative, not exhaustive. Additional titles—particularly of abstracts, indexes, transcriptions, and local histories—are available; consult the introduction to Part Two for further information. For guidance on how to identify and locate community directories and local newspapers, see chapter 11, City Directories, and chapter 12, Newspapers, in Part One of this book.

Abstracts, Indexes & Transcriptions

Anhalt, Edith Pratz, and the Daughters of the American Colonists, Ga–Ha–Da Chapter. "Cemetery Records, Bible Records of Seneca County and Schuyler County, New York." Bound typescript, 1961. NYPL, New York.

County of Schuyler Abstracts. Syracuse, NY: Central New York Genealogical Society, 2000. Abstracts for a range of genealogical records originally published in the quarterly *Tree Talks*.

Daughters of the American Revolution, comps. *New York DAR Genealogical Records Committee Report.* Since 1913 DAR volunteers have transcribed many thousands of unpublished cemetery, church, and town records throughout New York. The reports are at the DAR Library; copies are at the NYSL and the NYPL. The DAR has a searchable name index to all the GRC reports at *http://services.dar.org/Public/DAR_Research/search/?Tab_ID=6*. See Jean Worden's index below for a listing by county of the New York record sets that were transcribed by the DAR before 1998.

Jackson, Mary Smith. *Marriage and Death Notices from Schuyler County, New York, Newspapers.* Westminster, MD: Heritage Books, 2006.

Kelly, Arthur C. M. *Index to Tree Talks County Packet: Schuyler County.* Rhinebeck, NY: Kinship, 2002.

Sheldon, Nellie M. *Name Index, History of Tioga, Chemung, Tompkins and Schuyler Counties, New York: Compiled by H. B. Peirce and D. Hamilton Hurd, Published by Everts and Ensign, 1879.* N.p: The Author, 1965.

Worden, Jean D. "Book 1, Subject Index." In *Revised Master Index to the New York State Daughters of the American Revolution Genealogical Records Volumes.* Zephyrhills, FL: J. D. Worden, 1998. The Subject Index includes a listing by county of the cemeteries, churches, towns, and other sources of records transcribed by the DAR.

Other Resources

A Biographical Record of Schuyler County, New York. New York: The S. J. Clarke Publishing Co., 1903.

Child, Hamilton. *Gazetteer and Business Directory of Chemung and Schuyler Counties, N.Y., for 1868–9.* Syracuse, 1868.

Cleaver, Mary Louise Catlin. *The History of the Town of Catharine, Schuyler County, NY.* Rutland, VT: Tuttle, 1945.

Fay, Loren V. *Schuyler County, New York Genealogical Research Secrets.* Albany: L.V. Fay, 1982.

Foley, Janet W. *Early Settlers of New York State: Their Ancestors and Descendants.* 9 vols. Akron, NY: 1934–1942. Reprint, 2 vols. Baltimore: Genealogical Publishing Co., 1993.

Hoiland, Doris Reynolds. *Pioneers of the Southern Tier: Schuyler and Tioga Counties.* Elmira, NY: Commercial Service Bureau, 1977. Originally published as *The History of Seven Countries,* 1885.

Journal of the Schuyler County Historical Society. Watkins Glen, NY: The Society, 1965–present. Periodical.

New York Historical Resources Center. *Guide to Historical Resources in Schuyler County, New York, Repositories.* Ithaca, NY: Cornell University, 1981.

Nichols, Beach. *Atlas of Schuyler County, New York.* Philadelphia, 1874. [NYPL Digital Gallery]

Peirce, Henry B. *History of Schuyler County, New York: With Illustrations and Biographical Sketches of Some of Its Prominent Men and Pioneers.* Ovid, NY: W. E. Morrison & Co., 1975. First published 1879.

Peirce, Henry B., and D. Hamilton Hurd. *History of Tioga, Chemung, Tompkins and Schuyler Counties, New York: With Illustrations and Biographical Sketches of Some of Its Prominent Men and Pioneers.* Philadelphia, 1879. See above for a name index by Nellie Sheldon.

Portrait and Biographical Record of Seneca and Schuyler Counties, New York: Containing Portraits and Biographical Sketches of Prominent and Representative Citizens of the Counties. Together with Biographies and Portraits of All the Presidents of the United States. New York, 1895.

Records of the Ithaca College Study Center for Early Religious Life in Western New York, 1978–1981. Division of Rare and Manuscript Collections, Cornell University Library. A description of the holdings for each county is at *http://rmc.library.cornell.edu/eguides/lists/churchlist1.htm.*

Schuyler County Historical Society. *Schuyler County, New York: History and Families.* Paducah, KY: Turner Publishing Co., 2005.

Sexton, John L. *An Outline History of Tioga and Bradford Counties in Pennsylvania, Chemung, Steuben, Tioga, Tompkins, and Schuyler in New York: By Townships, Villages, Boro's and Cities.* Elmira, NY, 1885.

Stillman, Louise V. *Schuyler Around and About.* Montour Fall, NY: W. E. Morrison, 1994.

Additional Online Resources

Ancestry.com

There are vast numbers of records on *Ancestry.com* that pertain to people who have lived in New York State. See chapter 16 for a description of *Ancestry.com*'s resources and its partnership with the New York State Archives. A search of the online card catalog by county may reveal lesser known resources that pertain to a locality, such as town records, abstracts, transcriptions, city directories, and local histories.

FamilySearch.org

FamilySearch has extensive collections of New York records, including religious records, which are searchable by name and location, but not by county. The following collections include record images (browsable, but not searchable) that are organized by county:

- "New York, Land Records, 1630–1975." Includes land and property records. *familysearch.org/search/collection/2078654*
- "New York, Probate Records, 1629–1971." Includes wills, letters of administration, and guardianship papers. *familysearch.org/search/collection/1920234*

For both collections, choose the browse option and then select Schuyler to view the available records sets.

A detailed description of *FamilySearch.org* resources, which include the catalog of the Family History Library, is found in chapter 16.

NYGenWeb Project: Schuyler County
www.rootsweb.ancestry.com/~nyschuyl

Part of the national, USGenWeb volunteer initiative, the website provides information and resources for county research.

Old Fulton New York Postcards
www.FultonHistory.com

The website provides free access to a vast collection of digitized New York newspapers, including seven titles for Schuyler County.

Seneca County

Formed March 24, 1804

Parent County   Cayuga
Daughter Counties Tompkins 1817 • Wayne 1823
County Seat   Village of Waterloo, Towns of Fayette and Waterloo

Major Land Transactions
See chapter 7, Land Records
New Military Tract 1782–1791

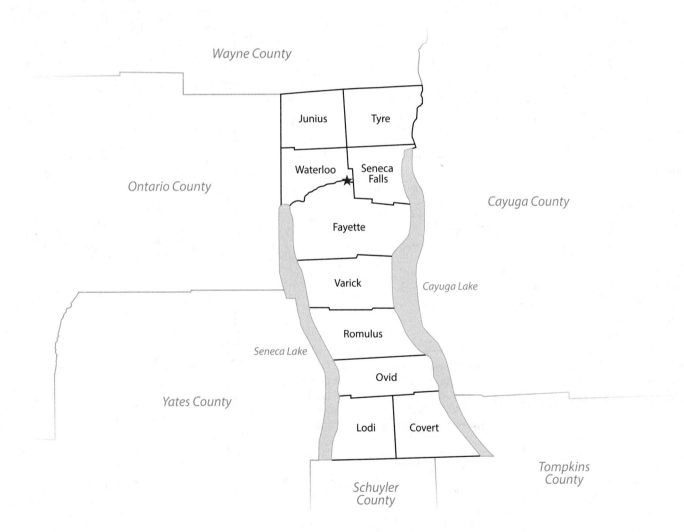

Town Boundary Map
★ - County seat

Towns (and Cities)	Villages and other Settlements		Notes
Covert c.1793 Settled at Goodwins Point 1817 Formed in new Tompkins County from Town of Ovid 1819 Transferred back to Seneca County * 1826 Daughter town Lodi formed	Bergen Beach Cold Springs Covert Dawson Corners Hall(s) Corners Holton Beach Interlaken (v)	Interlaken Beach Kelly Corners Osgood Landing Port Deposit Six Corners Trumansburg Landing	* Tompkins County formed from Seneca and Cayuga counties 1817 • Hamlet of Covert also Pratts Corners • Village of Interlaken inc. 1904; formerly Farmerville (before 1865), Farmer Village (1865–1892), Farmer (1892–1904); became Interlaken in 1904
Fayette 1789 Settlers from Pennsylvania 1800 Formed in Cayuga County as Town of Washington from Town of Romulus 1803 Daughter town Junius formed 1804 Transferred to new county of Seneca 1808 Name changed to Fayette	Canoga Canoga Springs Fayette Kuneytown MacDougall Pastime Park Rose Hill South Waterloo Teall Beach Waterloo (v) West Fayette Yale Yost Corners		• Hamlet of Fayette also Bearytown; on Varick town line • MacDougall on Varick town line • South Waterloo part of incorporated Village of Waterloo, south of Seneca River • Village of Waterloo, inc. 1824; called New Hudson in 1807 when land was purchased; name changed to Waterloo in 1816; former names include Scauyes, Scauyz, Scawas, Scawyace, and Schoyes; shared with Town of Junius until 1829, then with Town of Waterloo; see Town of Waterloo for county seat dates • Yale also Yale Station; on Varick town line
Galen * In Seneca County 1812–1823			* See Wayne County
Hector * In Seneca County 1804–1817			* See Schuyler County
Junius * 1795 Settled 1803 Formed in Cayuga County from Town of Washington (now Fayette) 1804 Transferred to new county of Seneca 1807 Daughter town Wolcott formed 1812 Daughter town Galen formed 1829 Daughter towns Seneca Falls, Tyre, and Waterloo formed	Dublin Junius Corners Malcon Stone Church Corner Thompson Thorntons Corners Waterloo (v)		* Junius was the name of one of the 28 Military Tract townships • Dublin also Junius • Thompson also Thompson Station • Village of Waterloo inc. 1824 ceded to Town of Waterloo 1829
Lodi 1789 Settlers from Pennsylvania 1826 Formed from Town of Covert	Butcher Hill Cat Elbow Corner Caywood Kelly Corners Lamoreaux Landing	Lodi (v) Lodi Center Lodi Landing Lodi Station Townsendville	• Village of Lodi inc. 1926
Ovid * 1789 Settlers from New Jersey and Pennsylvania 1794 Formed as a town in Onondaga County 1799 Transferred to new county of Cayuga 1802 Daughter town Hector formed	Coan Corners Gilbert Kidders Ovid (v) Ovid Center Scott(s) Corners		* Ovid was the name of one of the 28 Military Tract townships • Kidders formerly Kidders Ferry • Village of Ovid inc. 1816, dissolved 1849, reinc. 1852; also Verona; shared with Town of Romulus; county seat 1804–1817, in 1822 served again as county seat with Village of Waterloo; Ovid rarely used as county seat after 1921 *(Ovid continued on next page)*

Towns (and Cities)	Villages and other Settlements		Notes
Ovid (continued) 1804 Transferred to new county of Seneca 1817 Daughter town Covert formed in new Tompkins County *	Sheldrake Sheldrake Springs Starrett Corners Willard		* Daughter town Covert transferred back to Seneca County 1819 • Sheldrake also Sheldrake Point • Willard formerly Ovid Landing: on Romulus town line; location of Willard Psychiatric Center 1869–1995
Romulus * 1789 Settled 1794 Formed as a town in Onondaga County 1799 Transferred to new county of Cayuga 1800 Daughter town Washington (now Fayette) formed 1804 Transferred to new county of Seneca 1830 Daughter town Varick formed	Cooleys Elm Beach Freleighs Points Hayt(s) Corners Jacacks Landing Kendaia Marsh Corner Ovid (v) Pontius Landing	Poplar Beach Romulus Romulus Center Sacketts Landing Sampson Tannery Corners Whitneys Landing Willard	* Romulus was the name of one of the 28 Military Tract townships • Hayt(s) Corners formerly Hyatts Corners • Village of Ovid inc. 1816, dissolved 1849, reinc. 1852; also Verona; shared with Town of Romulus; county seat 1804–1817, in 1822 served again as county seat with Village of Waterloo; Ovid rarely used as county seat after 1921 • Poplar Beach also Poplar Shore • Willard formerly Ovid Landing; on Ovid town line
Seneca Falls 1787 Settlers from Ulster County 1829 Formed from Town of Junius	Bridgeport Halsey Corners Kingdom Lehigh Valley Junction	Nichols Corners Seneca Falls (v) Seneca Junction West Cayuga	• Village of Seneca Falls inc. 1831 and dissolved 12/31/2011
Tyre 1794 Settlers from New Jersey 1829 Formed from Town of Junius	Cruso Evans Corner Magee	Mays Point Munsons Corner Tyre	• Magee also Magees Corners • Tyre also Tyre City
Varick 1789 Settled 1830 Formed from Town of Romulus	Deys Landing East Varick Fayette Fayette Siding MacDougall	McDuffee Town Romulus Romulus Town Varick Yale	• Fayette also Bearytown; on Fayette town line • MacDougall on Fayette town line • McDuffee Town also McDuffietown • Yale also Yale Station; on Fayette town line
Washington Name for Town of Fayette 1800–1808			
Waterloo 1759 Settlers from Rhode Island 1829 Formed from Town of Junius	Border City Dobbins Corner East Geneva Packwood Corners Parr Harbour Waterloo (v)		• Village of Waterloo inc. 1824, called New Hudson in 1807 when land was purchased; name changed to Waterloo in 1816; former names include Scauyes, Scauyz, Scawas, Scawyace, and Schoyes; ceded from Town of Junius to Town of Waterloo 1829; shared with Town of Fayette. Village of Waterloo sole county seat 1817–1822, county seat shared with Village of Ovid from 1822 though Ovid rarely used after 1921
Wolcott * In Seneca County 1807–1823			* See Wayne County

NEW YORK STATE CENSUS RECORDS
See also chapter 3, Census Records

County originals at Seneca County Clerk's Office: 1905, 1915, 1925 (1825, 1835, 1845, 1855, 1865, 1875, and 1892 are lost)

State originals at the NYSA: 1915, 1925

Microfilm at the FHL, NYPL, and NYSL; many years are online at *FamilySearch.org* and *Ancestry.com*.

NATIONAL/STATEWIDE REPOSITORIES & RESOURCES
See chapter 16

COUNTYWIDE REPOSITORIES & RESOURCES

Seneca County Clerk
Seneca County Office Building • One Di Pronio Drive
Waterloo, NY 13165 • (315) 539-1771
www.co.seneca.ny.us/dpt-clerkserv-clerk.php

Land records 1804–present, court records, naturalization records 1830–1948, and the New York state census for Seneca County 1905, 1915, 1925. Also see county historian located in same building.

Seneca County – Town and Village Clerks
Birth, marriage, and death records are maintained by the clerk of the municipality in which the event occurred; see Introduction to County Guides for details of other records which may be held by municipal clerks. For contact information, see *www.rootsweb.ancestry. com/~nyseneca/hstrns.htm*.

Seneca County Surrogate's Court
48 West Williams Street • Waterloo, NY 13165 • (315) 539-7531

Holds probate records from 1804 to the present. See also chapter 6, Probate Records.

Seneca County Public Libraries
Seneca is part of the Finger Lakes Library System; see *www.flls.org* to access each library. Many hold genealogy and local history collections such as local newspapers. Seneca Falls Library hosts a Genealogy Club. See also listing below for Waterloo Library and Historical Society.

Seneca County Historian
Seneca County Office Building • One DiPronio Drive
Waterloo, NY 13165 • (315) 539-1785
www.co.seneca.ny.us/dpt-genserv-historian.php

Genealogies and histories, extensive family files, naturalization records (mid-1800s–1920s), cemetery records, census records (hard copies of federal 1880, 1920 and New York State 1905, 1915, 1925; more on microfilm), local histories, information compiled from marriage and death records, and land records. The historian conducted original research on the history of the Underground Railroad and abolitionism in the area; the material and the final report are in the historian's office. Website includes list of local historians and historical societies, historic photographs, maps, and articles on the history of Seneca County covering American Indian history, geography, county boundaries, place names, the women's rights movement and other reform movements, abolitionism, agriculture and industry, legend and folklore, churches, and many other topics.

Seneca County – All Municipal Historians
While not authorized to answer genealogical inquiries, town and village historians can provide valuable historical information and research advice; some maintain collections and webpages which may include transcribed records, local histories, and other genealogical material. See contact information at *www.rootsweb.ancestry.com/~nyseneca/hstrns.htm* or see the website of the Association of Public Historians of New York State at *www.aphnys.org*.

REGIONAL REPOSITORIES & RESOURCES

SUNY at Oswego: Local History Collection
See listing in Oswego County Guide

LOCAL REPOSITORIES & RESOURCES
Alphabetized by location

Interlaken Historical Society
Interlaken Public Library • 8389 and 8395 Main Street
PO Box 270 • Interlaken, NY 14847 • (607) 532-8899
Email: museum@interlakenhistory.org • *www.interlakenhistory.org*

Cemetery records, church records, histories and genealogies, local newspapers, maps and atlases, photographs, and gazetteers. A selection of documents is on the Society's website. Quarterly newsletter, *Between the Lakes*.

Lodi Historical Society
8297 North Lower Lake Road • PO Box 279 • Lodi, NY 14860
(607) 582-6077 • Email: info@lodihistoricalsociety.com
www.lodihistoricalsociety.com

Holdings include census materials. Website includes historic photos.

Waterloo Library and Historical Society
Library: 31 East Williams Street • Waterloo, NY 13165 • (315) 359-0533
National Memorial Day Museum: 35 East Main Street
Waterloo, NY 13165 • (315) 539-9611 • *www.wlhs-ny.org*

Library holdings include histories, death and marriage notices 1807–1908, and local newspapers. A significant amount of the Library's genealogy holdings is located in the National Memorial Day Museum, a Civil War Museum that is also maintained by the Waterloo Library and Historical Society.

SELECTED PRINT & ONLINE RESOURCES

Below is a selection of resources relevant for research in this county. The list is representative, not exhaustive. Additional titles—particularly of abstracts, indexes, transcriptions, and local histories—are available; consult the introduction to Part Two for further information. For guidance on how to identify and locate community directories and local newspapers, see chapter 11, City Directories, and chapter 12, Newspapers, in Part One of this book.

Abstracts, Indexes & Transcriptions
Anhalt, Edith Pratz. "Birth Records of Fayette (1882–1884) and Burial Records of Waterloo, Seneca County, New York." Bound typescript, 1959–1960. NYPL, New York.

Anhalt, Edith Pratz, and the Daughters of the American Colonists, Ga–Ha–Da Chapter. "Cemetery Records, Bible Records of Seneca County and Schuyler County, New York." Bound typescript, 1961. NYPL, New York

County of Seneca Abstracts. Syracuse: Central New York Genealogical Society, 2000. Abstracts for a range of genealogical records originally published in the quarterly *Tree Talks*.

Daughters of the American Revolution, comps. *New York DAR Genealogical Records Committee Report*. Since 1913 DAR volunteers have transcribed many thousands of unpublished cemetery, church, and town records throughout New York. The reports are at the DAR Library; copies are at the NYSL and the NYPL. The DAR has a searchable name index to all the GRC reports at *http://services.dar.org/Public/DAR_Research/search/?Tab_ID=6*. See Jean Worden's index below for a listing by county of the New York record sets that were transcribed by the DAR before 1998.

Delafield, John. *A General View and Agricultural Survey of the County of Seneca: Taken under the Direction of the New-York State Agricultural Society*. Albany, 1851.

Finch, Jesse H. *Vital Records from the Ovid Bee: Published at Ovid Village, Seneca Co., NY, 1822–1869*. New York: The J. Finch Committee, 1971.

Fischer, Carl W. "Index of the 1850 Census of Some Towns of Tompkins and Seneca Counties." Typescript, 1966. NYPL, New York.

Kelly, Arthur C. M. *Index to Tree Talks County Packet: Seneca County*. Rhinebeck, NY: Kinship, 2002.

MacRae, Cameron F. "Inscriptions from the McNeil Cemetery, Ovid, Seneca County, New York." *NYG&B Record*, vol. 101 (1970) no. 4: 230–234; vol. 102 (1971) no. 2: 118–121, no. 3: 175–178, no. 4: 228–230. [NYG&B eLibrary]

Seneca County, NYG&B Church Surveys Collection. NYG&B, New York. [NYG&B eLibrary]

Worden, Jean D. "Book 1, Subject Index." In *Revised Master Index to the New York State Daughters of the American Revolution Genealogical Records Volumes*. Zephyrhills, FL: J. D. Worden, 1998. The Subject Index includes a listing by county of the cemeteries, churches, towns, and other sources of records transcribed by the DAR.

Other Resources

Becker, John D. *A History of the Village of Waterloo, New York: And Thesaurus of Related Facts*. Waterloo, NY: Waterloo Library and Historical Society, 1949.

Brigham, A. Delancey. *Brigham's Geneva, Seneca Falls, and Waterloo Directory and Business Advertiser for 1862 and 1863: Including the Towns of Phelps, Flint Creek, Seneca Castle and Stanley Corners, with Histories of the Towns from Their Earliest Settlement*. Geneva, NY, 1862.

Child, Hamilton. *Gazetteer and Business Directory of Seneca County, NY, for 1867–8*. Syracuse, 1867.

———. *Reference and Business Directory of Seneca County, NY, 1894–5*. New York, 1894.

Foley, Janet W. *Early Settlers of New York State: Their Ancestors and Descendants*. 9 vols. Akron, NY: 1934–1942. Reprint, 2 vols. Baltimore, Genealogical Publishing Co., 1993.

History of Seneca County, New York: With Illustrations Descriptive of Its Scenery, Palatial Residences, Public Buildings, Fine Blocks, and Important Manufactories. Ovid, NY: W. E. Morrison, 1976. Reprint of the 1876 edition.

New York Historical Resources Center. *Guide to Historical Resources in Seneca County, New York, Repositories*. Ithaca, NY: Cornell University, 1980. [*books.FamilySearch.org*]

Nichols, Beach. *Atlas of Seneca County, New York: From Actual Surveys by and under the Direction of Beach Nichols*. Philadelphia, 1874.

Portrait and Biographical Record of Seneca and Schuyler Counties, New York: Containing Portraits and Biographical Sketches of Prominent and Representative Citizens of the Counties. Together with Biographies and Portraits of all the Presidents of the United States. New York, 1895.

Records of the Ithaca College Study Center for Early Religious Life in Western New York, 1978–1981. Division of Rare and Manuscript Collections, Cornell University Library. A description of the holdings for each county is at *http://rmc.library.cornell.edu/eguides/lists/churchlist1.htm*.

Spafford, Horatio G. *The History of Seneca County, New York, 1786–1876, with Illustrations*. Ovid, NY: W. E. Morrison, 1976.

Waltrous, Hilda R. *The County Between the Lakes: A Public History of Seneca County, New York, 1876–1982*. Waterloo, NY: Seneca County Board of Supervisors, 1982.

Willers, Diedrich. *Centennial Historical Sketch of the Town of Fayette, Seneca County, New-York, 1800–1900*. Ovid, NY: W. E. Morrison, 1982. First published 1900 by W. F. Humphrey.

Additional Online Resources

Ancestry.com
There are vast numbers of records on *Ancestry.com* that pertain to people who have lived in New York State. See chapter 16 for a description of *Ancestry.com*'s resources and its partnership with the New York State Archives. A search of the online card catalog by county may reveal lesser known resources that pertain to a locality, such as town records, abstracts, transcriptions, city directories, and local histories.

FamilySearch.org
FamilySearch has extensive collections of New York records, including religious records, which are searchable by name and location, but not by county. The following collections include record images (browsable, but not searchable) that are organized by county:

- "New York, Land Records, 1630–1975." Includes land and property records. *familysearch.org/search/collection/2078654*
- "New York, Probate Records, 1629–1971." Includes wills, letters of administration, and guardianship papers. *familysearch.org/search/collection/1920234*

For both collections, choose the browse option and then select Seneca to view the available records sets.

A detailed description of *FamilySearch.org* resources, which include the catalog of the Family History Library, is found in chapter 16.

NYGenWeb Project: Seneca County
www.rootsweb.ancestry.com/~nyseneca
Part of the national, USGenWeb volunteer initiative, the website provides information and resources for county research.

Steuben County

Formed March 18, 1796

Parent County   Ontario
Daughter County   Schuyler 1854
County Seat   Village of Bath

Major Land Transactions
See chapter 7, Land Records
Phelps and Gorham Purchase 1788

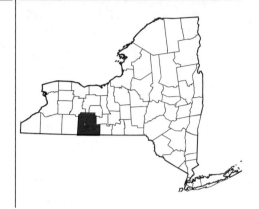

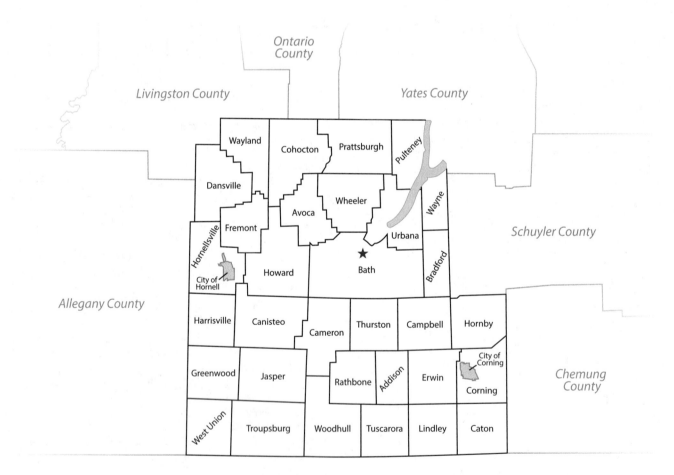

Town Boundary Map
★ - County seat

Towns (and Cities)	Villages and other Settlements		Notes
Addison 1791 Settled 1796 Formed as Town of Middletown in new county of Steuben 1808 Name changed to Addison; daughter town Troupsburg(h) formed 1822 Daughter town Cameron formed 1828 Daughter town Woodhull formed 1856 Daughter town Rathbone formed 1859 Daughter town Tuscarora formed	Addison (v) Addison Hill Goodhue Lake Jones Corners Rathbunville South Addison West Addison		• Village of Addison inc. 1854, reinc. 1873 • Addison Hill and South Addison in Town of Tuscarora from 1859 • Rathbunville and West Addison in Town of Rathbone from 1856
Avoca c. 1790 Settled 1843 Formed from towns of Bath, Cohocton, Howard, and Wheeler	Avoca (v) Bloomerville Greenville	Neils Creek Wallace	• Village of Avoca inc. 1883; called Eight Mile Tree before it was an incorporated village; in Town of Bath before 1843
Barrington * In Steuben County 1822–1826			* See Yates County
Bath 1793 Settled by 15 families, mostly German and Scottish 1796 Formed as town in new county of Steuben 1808 Daughter town Pulteney formed 1812 Daughter towns Cohocton and Howard formed 1820 Daughter town Wheeler formed 1822 Daughter town Urbana formed 1839 Annexed land from Town of Urbana 1843 Daughter town Avoca formed	Avoca Bath (v) Buck Settlement Campbells Creek Coss Corners Dudley Settlement East Union Haverling Heights	Kanona Knight Settlement Mud Creek Pineville Savona (v) Sonora Thomas Corners Unionville	• Avoca in Town of Avoca from 1843 • County seat at Bath from 1796 when county was formed; Village of Bath inc. 1816 • Kanona formerly Canona and Kennedyville • Village of Savona inc. 1883
Bradford 1793 Settlers from New Jersey 1836 Formed from Town of Jersey (now Orange)	Bradford Jersey South Bradford		
Cameron 1800 Settled 1822 Formed from Town of Addison 1844 Daughter town Thurston formed 1856 Daughter town Rathbone formed	Bonny Hill Boyds Corners Cameron Cameron Mills	North Cameron South Cameron West Cameron	
Campbell 1800 Settled 1831 Formed from Town of Hornby	Campbell Campbelltown Curtis	East Campbell Hammonds Mills Meads Creek	

Towns (and Cities)	Villages and other Settlements	Notes
Canisteo 1789 Settlers from Pennsylvania 1796 Formed as a town in new county of Steuben 1808 Daughter town Troupsburg(h) formed 1818 Ceded land to Town of Troupsburg(h) 1820 Daughter town Hornellsville formed 1827 Daughter towns Greenwood and Jasper formed	Adrian Allens Station Bennetts Bennett(s) Creek Browns Crossing Canisteo (v) Canisteo Center Crosbyville East Canisteo South Canisteo Swale	• Village of Canisteo inc. 1873 • Canisteo Center also Center Canisteo
Caton 1819 Settlers from Connecticut 1839 Formed as Town of Wormly from Town of Painted Post (now Corning) 1840 Name changed to Caton	Brown(s)town Caton Hittown West Caton	• Hamlet of Caton also Caton Center
Cohocton 1796 Settled at Bivens Corners 1812 Formed from towns of Bath and Dansville 1843 Daughter town Avoca formed 1848 Daughter town Wayland formed	Atlanta Bowles Corners Cohocton (v) Kirkwood Liberty North Cohocton Patchins Mills	• Atlanta formerly Bloods, Bloods Corners, and Bloods Depot • Village of Cohocton inc. 1891 • North Cohocton formerly Bivens Corners • Patchins Mills see Patchinville in Town of Wayland from 1848
Corning (city) 1890 Formed as a city from Village of Corning, Town of Corning		
Corning (town) 1788 Settled 1796 Formed as Town of Painted Post in new county of Steuben 1826 Daughter towns Erwin and Hornby formed 1839 Daughter town Wormly (now Caton) formed 1852 Name changed to Corning 1856 Ceded land to Town of Erwin 1890 Daughter city Corning formed from Village of Corning	Browns Crossing Centerville Corning (v) Corning Manor Denmark East Corning East Painted Post Frenchs Mill Gibson Knoxville Riverside (v) South Corning (v)	• Village of Corning inc. 1848, became City of Corning 1890 • Knoxville also Port Barton; became part of the 5th ward of the City of Corning c. 1890 • Village of Riverside inc. 1922 • Village of South Corning inc. 1920
Dansville 1795 Settled 1796 Formed in new county of Steuben 1812 Daughter towns Cohocton and Howard formed 1822 Ceded land, including Dansville village, to Town of Sparta, Livingston County 1848 Daughter town Wayland formed 1854 Daughter town Fremont formed	Beachville Bluff Point Burns Cream Hill Dansville Dotys Corners Forest Lawn North Oak Hill Oak Hill Rogersville South Dansville	• Hamlet of Dansville was first settlement in the town; now an incorporated village in Town of North Dansville, Livingston County

Towns (and Cities)	Villages and other Settlements		Notes
Erwin 1787 Settled 1826 Formed from Town of Painted Post (now Corning) 1837 Daughter town Lindley formed 1856 Annexed land from Town of Corning	Cooper(s) Plains Erwin(s) Gang Mills Painted Post (v)		• Village of Painted Post inc. 1860, reinc. 1893
Frederickstown Name for Town of Wayne 1796–1808			
Fremont 1812 Settled 1854 Formed from towns of Dansville, Hornellsville, Howard, and Wayland	Big Creek Fremont Haskinville	Jobs Corner Seely Creek Stephens Mills	• Hamlet of Fremont formerly Fremont Center • Stephens Mills also Stevens Mills
Greenwood 1820 Settled 1827 Formed from towns of Canisteo and Troupsburg(h) 1845 Daughter town West Union formed 1848 Annexed land from Town of Jasper	Bennetts Greenwood Krusens Corners Norton Norton Hollow Rough and Ready West Greenwood		
Hartsville 1809 Settled 1844 Formed from Town of Hornellsville	Hartsville Hartsville Center	Purdy Creek Webb Hollow	
Hornby 1814 Settlers from Otsego County 1826 Formed from Town of Painted Post (now Corning) 1831 Daughter town Campbell formed	Dyke Ferenbaugh Hornby	Nash Settlement Palmer Settlement Shady Grove	• Hamlet of Hornby also Hornby Forks
Hornell (city) 1790 Settled at Upper Canisteo 1852 Village of Hornellsville established in Town of Hornellsville 1888 Formed as City of Hornellsville from Village of Hornellsville 1906 Name changed to Hornell			
Hornellsville 1790 Settled at Upper Canisteo 1820 Formed from Town of Canisteo 1844 Daughter town Hartsville formed 1854 Daughter town Fremont formed 1888 Daughter city Hornellsville (now Hornell) formed from Village of Hornellsville	Almond (v) Arkport (v) Hornellsville (v) North Hornell (v) South Hornell Upper Canisteo Webbs Crossing		• Village of Almond inc. 1921; shared with Town of Almond, Allegany County • Village of Arkport inc. 1913 • Village of Hornellsville inc. 1852, became City of Hornellsville 1888 • Village of North Hornell inc. 1924
Howard 1806 Settled 1812 Formed from towns of Bath and Dansville	Buena Vista Butcher Corners Fowlersville Goffs Mills	Howard South Howard Towlesville	

(Howard continued on next page)

Towns (and Cities)	Villages and other Settlements		Notes
Howard (continued) 1843 Daughter town Avoca formed 1854 Daughter town Fremont formed			
Jasper 1807 Settled 1827 Formed from towns of Canisteo and Troupsburg(h) 1848 Ceded land to Town of Greenwood	Adamsport Craigs Corners Dennis Corners Hampshire Jasper Jasper Five Corners	Jasper Four Corners Marlatts Corners North Jasper South Hill West Jasper	
Lindley 1790 Settlers from New Jersey 1837 Formed from Town of Erwin	East Lindley Lawrenceville	Lindley Presho	• Hamlet of Lindley formerly Lindleytown • Presho formerly Erwin Center
Middletown Name for Town of Addison 1796–1808			
Orange * In Steuben County 1813–1854			* See Schuyler County
Painted Post Name for Town of Corning 1796–1852			
Prattsburgh 1801 Settled 1813 Formed from Town of Pulteney 1820 Daughter town Wheeler formed	Beans Beans Station Daball Corners Ingleside	Lynn Prattsburgh (v) Rikers Hollow	• Village of Prattsburgh inc. 1848 and dissolved 9/22/1972
Pulteney 1802 Settled 1808 Formed from Town of Bath 1813 Daughter town Prattsburgh formed 1848 Ceded land to Town of Urbana	Brown Corners Catawba Elmbois Gibson Landing Gloade(s) Corners Gulicksville Harmonyville	Peltonville Pine Grove Pulteney Roffs Landing South Pulteney Stewart Corners	• Elmbois formerly Scuttsville • Gulicksville also Boyds Landing, Briggs Point, and Wagners Landing • Harmonyville formerly Sodum • Roffs Landing formerly Millers Point • South Pulteney formerly Bluffport
Rathbone 1793 Settled 1856 Formed from towns of Addison, Cameron, and Woodhull	Cameron Mills Derby Switch Rathbone	Rathboneville West Addison	• Cameron Mills formerly Hubbard(s)ville • Rathboneville (also Rathbunville) and West Addison; in Town of Addison before 1856
Reading * In Steuben County 1806–1854			* See Schuyler County
Thurston 1813 Settled at Bonny Hill 1844 Formed from Town of Cameron	Bonny Hill North Thurston Risingville	South Thurston Thurston	• Hamlet of Thurston formerly Merchantville
Troupsburg(h) 1805 Settlers from Connecticut 1808 Formed from Town of Middletown (now Addison) and Canisteo 1818 Annexed land from Town of Canisteo 1827 Daughter towns Greenwood and Jasper formed 1828 Daughter town Woodhull formed	Alice East Troupsburgh Highup Lila South Troupsburg(h)	Troupsburg(h) Troupsburgh Center West Troupsburgh Young Hickory	

Towns (and Cities)	Villages and other Settlements		Notes
Tuscarora 1792–93 Settled 1859 Formed from Town of Addison	Addison Hill Freeman Nichols South Addison	Tuscarora Center Van Vleet Woods Corner(s)	• Addison Hill and South Addison in Town of Addison before 1859 • Freeman formerly Steamtown
Tyrone * In Steuben County 1822–1854			* See Schuyler County
Urbana 1793 Settlers from Pennsylvania at Pleasant Valley 1822 Formed from Town of Bath 1839 Ceded land to Town of Bath, annexed land from Town of Wheeler 1848 Annexed land from Town of Pulteney	Cold Spring(s) Glen Brook Glen Grove Hammondsport (v) Hermitage Mitchellsville	Mount Washington North Urbana Pleasant Valley Rheims Taggart Urbana	• Village of Hammondsport inc. 1856
Wayland 1806 Settled 1848 Formed from towns of Cohocton and Dansville 1854 Daughter town Fremont formed	Loon Lake Patchinville Perkinsville Wayland (v) Wayland Depot		• Patchinville formerly Patchins Mills; in Town of Cohocton before 1848 • Village of Wayland inc. 1877
Wayne 1791 Settled 1796 Formed as Town of Fredericksto(w)n in new county of Steuben 1806 Daughter town Reading formed 1808 Name changed to Wayne 1813 Daughter town Jersey (now Orange) formed 1814 Ceded land to towns of Jerusalem and Middlesex in Ontario County * 1822 Daughter towns Barrington and Tyrone formed	Grove Springs Keuka North Urbana Sylvan Beach Wayne Wayne Four Corners		* Towns of Jerusalem and Middlesex in Yates County from 1823 • Hamlet of Wayne also Wayne Hotel
West Union 1822 Settled at Rexville 1845 Formed from Town of Greenwood	Barney Mills McGraw(s) Rexville Saunders	Venus West Union Wiley(s)ville	
Wheeler 1799 Settlers from Albany County 1820 Formed from towns of Bath and Prattsburgh 1839 Ceded land to Town of Urbana 1843 Daughter town Avoca formed	Dinehart(s) Jordans Marshalls Mitchellsville	Renchans Stickneys Wheeler Wheeler Center	
Woodhull 1805 Settled 1828 Formed from towns of Addison and Troupsburg(h) 1856 Daughter town Rathbone formed	Borden East Woodhull Hedgesville Newville	Tubbsville Woodhull (v) Wylies Corners	• Village of Woodhull (also Newville) inc. 1899 and dissolved 1/13/1986

NEW YORK STATE CENSUS RECORDS
See also chapter 3, Census Records

County originals at Steuben County Clerk's Office:* 1825, 1835, 1845, 1855, 1865, 1875, 1892, 1905, 1915, 1925

State originals at the NYSA: 1915, 1925

Microfilm at the FHL, NYPL, and NYSL; many years are online at *FamilySearch.org* and *Ancestry.com*.

* The Steuben County Census Index is kept by the Steuben County Historian.

NATIONAL/STATEWIDE REPOSITORIES & RESOURCES
See chapter 16

COUNTYWIDE REPOSITORIES & RESOURCES

Steuben County Clerk
3 East Pulteney Square • Bath, NY 14810
(607) 664-2563 • *www.steubencony.org*

Court records, land records, naturalization records index 1820–1909 and 1930; death and marriage records 1885–1940s; and Steuben County New York state censuses 1825, 1835, 1845, 1855, 1865, 1875, 1892, 1905, 1915, and 1925.

Steuben County – City, Town, and Village Clerks
Birth, marriage, and death records are maintained by the clerk of the municipality in which the event occurred; see Introduction to County Guides for details of other records which may also be held by municipal clerks. For contact information, see *www.steubencony.org*.

Steuben County Surrogate's Court
County Court Building • 13 Pulteney Square E • Bath, NY 14810
(607) 622-8221

Holds probate records from 1796 to the present. Also see chapter 6, Probate Records.

Steuben County Public Libraries
Steuben is part of the Southern Tier Library System; see *www.stls. org/libraries* to access each library. Many libraries hold local history collections and genealogical materials. For example, Prattsburg Free Library has a collection of yearbooks and information on local cemeteries; Wayland Free Library has local newspapers dating back to 1893; also see listings below for the Avoca Free, Howard Public, and Southeast Steuben County Libraries.

Steuben County Historical Society
One Cohocton Street • PO Box 349 • Bath, NY 14810
(607) 776-9930 • Email: steuben349@yahoo.com
www.steubenhistoricalsociety.org

The society, archives, and learning center are located in the Magee House. Holdings include genealogies, censuses with Steuben County Census Index, cemetery records, church records, maps and atlases, probate records, and military history. The office of the county historian is also located in Magee House. Quarterly journal, *Steuben Echoes*, 1974–present.

Steuben County Historian
Mailing address: 3 East Pulteney Square • Bath, NY 14810
(607) 776-2199 • Email access on website • *www.steubencony.org*

The office of the county historian is in Magee House, Steuben County Historical Society. Collections include: Steuben County burial records (printouts on request), many Steuben County newspapers from 1831–1960 on microfilm, indexed abstracts of Steuben County surrogate records of probate 1790–1900, genealogical records, and Steuben County census index. Website includes online cemetery and obituary listings, list of local historians, and useful links.

Steuben County – All Municipal Historians
While not authorized to answer genealogical inquiries, city, town, and village historians can provide valuable historical information and research advice; some maintain collections and webpages which may include transcribed records, local histories, and other genealogical material. See contact information on county historian's page at *www.steubencony.org* or at the website of the Association of Public Historians of New York State at *www.aphnys.org*.

REGIONAL REPOSITORIES & RESOURCES

Bath National Cemetery
Veterans Affairs Medical Center • San Juan Avenue • Bath, NY 14810
(607) 664-4853 • *www.cem.va.gov/cems/nchp/bath.asp*

Established in 1877 and became part of the National Cemetery System in 1973.

Milne Library at SUNY Geneseo: Special Collections: Genesee Valley Historical Collection
See listing in Livingston County Guide

Painted Hills Genealogy Society
See listing in Allegany County Guide

LOCAL REPOSITORIES & RESOURCES
Alphabetized by location

Avoca Free Library
18 North Main Street • Avoca, NY 14809
(607) 566-9279 • *www.stls.org/avoca*

Family files, genealogies of local families, and books on the history of Avoca and Steuben County.

Corning Painted Post Historical Society
Benjamin Patterson Inn • 59 West Pulteney Street
Corning, NY 14830 • (607) 937-5281 •
Email: pattersoninnmuseum@stny.rr.com • *www.pattersoninnmuseum.org*

Holdings include local histories, archives, and city directories 1930s–1980s.

Hornby Historical Society Museum
185 South Place • Corning, NY 14830 • (607) 962-4471

Holdings include census records, obituaries, and books. Museum is open select days in July and August and by appointment.

Southeast Steuben County Library
300 Nasser Civic Center Plaza • Corning, NY 14830
(607) 936-3713 • *www.ssclibrary.org*

Collection includes newspapers. Offers local history and genealogy research requests for a fee.

Howard Public Library: Genealogy Research
3607 County Route 70A • Hornell, NY 14843
(607) 566-2412 • Facebook page

Holdings include local and family histories, obituaries and cemetery index, and early tax rolls.

SELECTED PRINT & ONLINE RESOURCES

Below is a selection of resources relevant for research in this county. The list is representative, not exhaustive. Additional titles—particularly of abstracts, indexes, transcriptions, and local histories—are available; consult the introduction to Part Two for further information. For guidance on how to identify and locate community directories and local newspapers, see chapter 11, City Directories, and chapter 12, Newspapers, in Part One of this book.

Abstracts, Indexes & Transcriptions

Bostwick, Retta. "Inscriptions from the Lindsley-Mulford Cemetery, Township of Lindsley, Steuben County, New York." *NYG&B Record*, vol. 85, no. 4 (1954): 223–227. [NYG&B eLibrary]

County of Steuben Abstracts. Syracuse: Central New York Genealogical Society, 2000. Abstracts for a range of genealogical records originally published in the quarterly *Tree Talks*.

Daughters of the American Revolution, comps. *New York DAR Genealogical Records Committee Report.* Since 1913 DAR volunteers have transcribed many thousands of unpublished cemetery, church, and town records throughout New York. The reports are at the DAR Library; copies are at the NYSL and the NYPL. The DAR has a searchable name index to all the GRC reports at *http://services.dar.org/Public/DAR_Research/search/?Tab_ID=6.* See Jean Worden's index below for a listing by county of the New York record sets that were transcribed by the DAR before 1998.

Dennis, Faye, comp. "Addison Rural Cemetery Transcriptions of Steuben County, New York." Typescript, 1981. NYPL, New York.

"Federal Census, 1800, Steuben County, New York." *NYG&B Record*, vol. 60, no. 2 (1929): 118–119. [NYG&B eLibrary]

Jackson, Edward F., and Mary S. Jackson. *1850 Census for the Town of Howard, Steuben County, New York, and Genealogical Data on the Families Who Lived There.* Bowie, MD: Willow Bend Books, 2004.

———. *Death Notices from Steuben County, New York, Newspapers, 1797–1884.* Bowie, MD: Heritage Books, 1998.

———. *Marriage Notices from Steuben County, New York, Newspapers, 1797–1884.* Bowie, MD: Heritage Books, 1998. Includes almost 8,000 notices.

Kelly, Arthur C. M. *Index to Tree Talks County Packet: Steuben County.* Rhinebeck, NY: Kinship, 2002.

Martin, Yvonne E. *Marriages and Deaths from Steuben County, New York, Newspapers, 1797–1868.* Bowie, MD: Heritage Books, 1988.

Worden, Jean D. "Book 1, Subject Index." In *Revised Master Index to the New York State Daughters of the American Revolution Genealogical Records Volumes.* Zephyrhills, FL: J. D. Worden, 1998. The Subject Index includes a listing by county of the cemeteries, churches, towns, and other sources of records transcribed by the DAR.

Other Resources

Babbitt, John S., and Sue Babbit. *Steuben County.* Charleston, SC: Arcadia, 2010.

Beers, G. W. *Atlas of Steuben County, New York: From Actual Surveys and Official Records.* Philadelphia, 1873. [NYPL Digital Gallery]

Child, Hamilton. *Gazetteer and Business Directory of Steuben County, NY, for 1868-9.* Syracuse, 1868.

Clayton, W. W. *A History of Steuben County, New York: With Illustrations and Biographical Sketches of Some of Its Prominent Men and Pioneers.* Philadelphia, 1879. Book includes a list of Civil War soldiers organized by town.

Folts, James D. *Indian Paths of Steuben County.* Bath, NY: Steuben County Historical Society, 1974.

Hakes, Harlo. *Landmarks of Steuben County, New York.* Mt. Vernon, IN: Windmill Publications, 1992. First published 1896 by D. Mason.

Hoiland, Doris R. *Pioneers of the Southern Tier; Steuben County.* New York: The Author, 1974.

McMaster, Guy H. *History of the Settlement of Steuben County, NY: Including Notices of the Pioneer Settlers and Their Adventures.* Bath, NY, 1853.

Mulford, Uri. *Pioneer Days and Later Times in Corning and Vicinity, 1789–1920.* Corning, NY: The Author, 1922.

Near, Irvin W. *A History of Steuben County, New York, and Its People.* Chicago: Lewis Publishing Co., 1911.

New York Historical Resources Center. *Guide to Historical Resources in Steuben County, New York, Repositories.* Ithaca, NY: Cornell University, 1981. [books.FamilySearch.org]

Records of the Ithaca College Study Center for Early Religious Life in Western New York, 1978–1981. Division of Rare and Manuscript Collections, Cornell University Library. A description of the holdings for each county is at *http://rmc.library.cornell.edu/eguides/lists/churchlist1.htm.*

Roberts, Millard F. *Historical Gazetteer of Steuben County, New York: With Memoirs and Illustrations.* Syracuse, 1891.

Sexton, John L., Jr. *An Outline History of Tioga and Bradford Counties in Pennsylvania; Chemung, Steuben, Tioga, Tompkins, and Schuyler in New York.* Elmira, NY, 1885.

Sherer, Richard. *Steuben County: The First 200 Years, a Pictorial History.* Virginia Beach, VA: The Donning Company, 1996.

Stuart, William M. *Who's Who in Steuben: A Biographical Record of Many of the Prominent Residents of Steuben County, New York.* Dansville, NY: F. A. Owen Publishing Co., 1935.

Thrall, W. B. *Pioneer History and Atlas of Steuben County, NY: Compiled from Historical, Statistical, and Official Records.* Perry, NY: Thrall, 1942.

Turner, Orsamus. *Pioneer History of Phelps & Gorham's Purchase, and Morris' Reserve: Embracing the Counties of Monroe, Ontario, Livingston, Yates, Steuben, Most of Wayne and Allegany, and Parts of Orleans, Genesee, and Wyoming.* Rochester, 1852.

Wilson, Hugh M. *Early Southern Steuben County and Some of Its People from Pioneer Days to World War I.* Bath, NY: Lois J. Wilson, 1975.

Additional Online Resources

Ancestry.com

There are vast numbers of records on *Ancestry.com* that pertain to people who have lived in New York State. See chapter 16 for a description of *Ancestry.com*'s resources and its partnership with the New York State Archives. A search of the online card catalog by county may reveal lesser known resources that pertain to a locality, such as town records, abstracts, transcriptions, city directories, and local histories.

FamilySearch.org

FamilySearch has extensive collections of New York records, including religious records, which are searchable by name and location, but not by county. The following collections include record images (browsable, but not searchable) that are organized by county:

- "New York, Land Records, 1630–1975." Includes land and property records. *familysearch.org/search/collection/2078654*

- "New York, Probate Records, 1629–1971." Includes wills, letters of administration, and guardianship papers. *familysearch.org/ search/collection/1920234*

For both collections, choose the browse option and then select Steuben to view the available records sets.

A detailed description of *FamilySearch.org* resources, which include the catalog of the Family History Library, is found in chapter 16.

NYGenWeb Project: Steuben County
www.rootsweb.ancestry.com/~nysteube

Part of the national, USGenWeb volunteer initiative, the website provides information and resources for county research.

Painted Hills Genealogy Society, Steuben County, New York Index Page
www.paintedhills.org/steuben.html

The county webpage of this regional society has direct links to numerous records transcriptions of cemeteries for the county, as well as census information, family histories, biographies, maps, and other historical resources.

St. Lawrence County

Formed March 3, 1802

Parent County   Clinton
Daughter Counties   None
County Seat   Village of Canton

Major Land Transactions
See table in chapter 7, Land Records
St. Lawrence Ten Towns 1787
Macomb Purchase 1792

Town Boundary Map
★ - County seat

Towns (and Cities)	Villages and other Settlements	Notes
Brasher 1817 Settled 1825 Formed from Town of Massena 1828 Daughter town Lawrence formed	Brasher Center Brasher Falls Brasher Iron Works Helena Ironton	
Canton * 1800 Settled 1805 Formed from Town of Lisbon	Brick Chapel Langdon Corners Bullis Island Little River Butterfield Mills Morley Canton (v) Pyrites Champlin Island Rensselaer Falls (v) Cousintown South Canton Crary Mills Woodbridge Corners Eddy Woods High Falls York Jerusalem	* Canton was the name for town 6 of the Ten Towns tract surveyed 1787 • Village of Canton inc. 1845; county seat from 1828; 1802–1828 county seat at Village of Ogdensburg, Town of Oswegatchie • Crary Mills on Pierrepont and Potsdam town lines • Morley formerly Long Rapids • Village of Rensselaer Falls inc. 1912; formerly Canton Falls and Tateville
Clare 1880 Formed from Town of Pierrepont	Brouses Corners Clarksboro Canton Farm Gleasons Mill Clare Newbridge	
Clifton 1868 Formed from Town of Pierrepont	Benson(s) Mines Cook Corners Catamount Island Cranberry Lake Chair Rock Island Freds Islands Chaumont Newton Falls	
Colton 1824 Settled at Colton Village 1843 Formed from Town of Parishville 1851 Annexed land from Town of Parishville	Brandy Brook Sevey Corners Colton South Colton Granshue Club Stark Irish Settlement Wildwood Corner Sevey	
De Kalb * 1803 Settlers from Otsego County 1806 Formed from Town of Oswegatchie 1825 Daughter town De Peyster formed 1830 Daughter town Depau (now Hermon) formed	Bigelow Kendrew Corners Blink Bonny Kendrews Cooper(s) Falls Richville (v) DeKalb Richville Station DeKalb Junction Stella Mines East DeKalb Stellaville Farrs Crossing	* De Kalb was the name for town 7 of the Ten Towns tract surveyed 1787 • Hamlet of DeKalb formerly Coopers Village and Williamstown • Village of Richville inc. 1880
Depau Name for Town of Hermon 1830–1834		
De Peyster 1802 Settlers from Vermont 1825 Formed from towns of De Kalb and Oswegatchie	De Peyster De Peyster Corners Edenton Kokomo Corners	• Kokomo Corners formerly Kings Corners
Edwards 1812 Settled along St. Lawrence Turnpike 1827 Formed from Town of Fowler 1830 Daughter town Depau (now Hermon) formed 1850 Annexed land from Town of Hermon	Earl Island Edwards (v) Edwardsville Freemansburg Pond Settlement South Edwards Talcville	• Village of Edwards inc. 1893, dissolved 12/31/2012 • South Edwards formerly Shawville • Talcville formerly Freemansville

Towns (and Cities)	Villages and other Settlements		Notes
Fine c. 1825 Settled 1844 Formed from towns of Pierrepont and Russell	Aldrich Bloomfield Briggs Coffin Mills Collins Emilyville Fine Hardscrabble Inlet Jayville	Lower Oswegatchie Oswegatchie Sarahsburgh Scriba Star Lake Star Lake Inn Stemberg The Plains Wanakena	• Hamlet of Fine also Andersonville and Smithville • Oswegatchie formerly The Crossing • Sarahsburgh was on Russell town line
Fowler 1807 Settled at Hailesboro(ugh) 1816 Formed from towns of Rossie and Russell 1827 Daughter town Edwards formed 1836 Daughter town Pitcairn formed	Balmat Emeryville Fowler Fuller(s)ville Fullerville Iron Works Hailesboro(ugh)	Homers Factory Kellogg Corners Osborneville Shingle Creek West Fowler	• Hamlet of Fowler also Little York
Gouverneur * 1805 Settled 1810 Formed from Town of Oswegatchie 1841 Daughter town Macomb formed	Caledonia Elmdale Gouverneur (v) Halls Corners Hermon Crossroad Holcomb Mills Homestead	Little Bow Little Bow Corners Natural Dam North Gouverneur Olds Mills Staplin Corners	* Gouverneur formerly Cambray—the name for town 10 of the Ten Towns tract surveyed 1787 • Village of Gouverneur inc. 1847, reinc. 1850; formerly Morrisville • Olds Mills formerly Smiths Mills
Hammond Sparsely settled from 1812; settled by Scots west of Hammond village 1818–1821 1827 Formed from towns of Morristown and Rossie 1842 Ceded land to Town of Macomb 1844 Ceded land to Town of Rossie	Bilberry Island Brush Island Bullhead Island Calaboga Chippewa Chippewa Bay Chokeberry Island Crossover Island Crows Nest Garden Island	Grants Island Hammond (v) Indian Chief Islands Jug Island North Hammond Oak Island Oak Point Oakvale Schermerhorn Landing South Hammond	• Village of Hammond inc. 1901 • Oakvale also Oakvale Station
Hermon c. 1812 Settled 1830 Formed as Depau from towns of De Kalb and Edwards 1834 Name changed to Hermon 1850 Ceded land to Town of Edwards	Bell Isle Crofton Graham Island Hermon (v)	Kents Corners Marshville Podunk Simpson	• Graham Island formerly Jordan Island and J. S. Brown Island • Village of Hermon inc. 1877
Hopkinton 1802 Settled 1805 Formed from Town of Massena 1807 Daughter town Russell formed 1818 Daughter town Parishville formed 1828 Daughter town Lawrence formed 1900 Daughter town Piercefield formed	Catherineville Childwold Days Mill Fernwood Hall Fort Jackson Hopkinton	Kildare Nichol(s)ville Otter Sylvan Falls Youngs Camp	• Childwold formerly Atherton and Mortlake; on Piercefield town line • Fort Jackson also Port Jackson • Nichol(s)ville formerly Sodom, mostly in Town of Lawrence
Lawrence 1806 Settled 1828 Formed from towns of Brasher and Hopkinton	Coteys Corner Fort Jackson Laverys Corner Lawrenceville McEwens Corner	Nichol(s)ville North Lawrence Taylors Corner Wagstaff Corner	• Nichol(s)ville formerly Sodom, small part in Town of Hopkinton

Towns (and Cities)	Villages and other Settlements		Notes
Lisbon * 1799 Settled 1801 Formed as a town in Clinton County 1802 Transferred to new county of St. Lawrence; daughter towns Madrid and Oswegatchie formed 1805 Daughter town Canton formed	Baycroft Island Benedict Island Boice Camp Island Chimney Island Flackville Galop Island Gregory Corners Hague Crossing	Lisbon Lisbon Center Lisbon Station Lotus Island North Corners Pine Grove Red Mills Tilden	* Lisbon was the name for town 5 of the Ten Towns tract surveyed 1787; in 1801 the new Town of Lisbon included all land in the Ten Towns tract • Chimney Island formerly Oraquointon, later Fort Levis
Louisville * 1800 Settled 1810 Formed from Town of Massena 1823 Daughter town Norfolk formed 1844 Annexed land from Town of Norfolk	Aults Island Bradford Island Chats Island Chase(s) Mills Croil Island Dishaw	Gooseneck Island Louisville Louisville Corner Louisville Landing Massena (v) Tucker Terrace	* Louisville was the name for town 1 of the Ten Towns tract surveyed 1787 • Aults Island formerly Loux Island • Chase(s) Mills on Waddington town line • Croil Island formerly Baxter, Gods Acre, Ille au Chamailles, Stacy Island, and Tsiiowenkwakarate • Dishaw on Norfolk town line • Louisville also Millersville • Village of Massena inc. 1886; shared with Town of Massena
Macomb 1805–06 Settled on Old State Road 1841 Formed from towns of Gouverneur and Morristown 1842 Annexed land from Town of Hammond	Apple Island Brasie Corners Hickory Macomb	Pierces Corners Pope(s) Mills Ruby Corner Washburnville	
Madrid * 1798 Settled 1802 Formed from Town of Lisbon 1806 Daughter town Potsdam formed 1859 Daughter town Waddington formed	Allen Corners Chase(s) Mills Cogswell Corners Columbia Village Dixon Corners Isle au Rapid Plat	Madrid Madrid Springs Ruthersville Turnbull Corner Waddington (v)	* Madrid was the name for town 4 of the Ten Towns tract surveyed 1787 • Chase(s) Mills in Town of Waddington after 1859 • Hamlet of Madrid also Columbia Village; formerly Grass River Falls and Roberts Mills; named Madrid in 1826 • Village of Waddington inc. 1839; formerly Hamilton; in Town of Waddington after 1859
Massena 1798 Settled on Revolutionary grants 1802 Formed as a town 1805 Daughter town Hopkinton formed 1806 Daughter town Stockholm formed 1810 Daughter town Louisville formed 1825 Daughter town Brasher formed	Barnhart Island Barnharts Bridges Place Crocker Delaney Island Hatfield Long Sault Island Massena (v)	Massena Center Massena Point Massena Springs Massena Springs Station Minklers Corners Raquette River Rooseveltown	• Village of Massena inc. 1886; shared with Town of Louisville • Raquette River also Racket River • Rooseveltown also Nyando
Morristown * 1799 Settled 1821 Formed from Town of Oswegatchie 1827 Daughter town Hammond formed 1841 Daughter town Macomb formed	Black Lake Bogardus Island Bowman Island Brier Hill Brier Hill Station Cedars Edgewater Park	Edward(s)ville English Settlement Longs Corners Morristown (v) Morristown Center Terrace Park	* Morristown formerly Hague—the name for town 9 of the Ten Towns tract surveyed 1787 • Black Lake formerly in Town of Oswegatchie • Edwardsville formerly Marysborough, Marysburgh, and The Narrows • Village of Morristown inc. 1884

Towns (and Cities)	Villages and other Settlements		Notes
Norfolk 1809 Settled at Raymondsville 1823 Formed from towns of Louisville and Stockholm 1844 Ceded land to Town of Louisville	Attwaters Falls Dishaw East Norfolk Grantville Houghville Norfolk	Norwood (v) Plumbrook Raymondville Tiernan Ridge Yaleville	• Dishaw on Louisville town line • Village of Norwood inc. 1871; shared with Town of Potsdam; Norwood also North Potsdam and Potsdam Station; formerly Potsdam Junction, Racketville, and Raquetteville • Raymondville formerly Racketon • Yaleville on Potsdam town line
Ogdensburg (city) 1817 Village of Oswegatchie incorporated 1868 Formed as a city from Village of Ogdensburg in Town of Oswegatchie	Heuvelton		
Oswegatchie * Abandoned by British; resettled in 1796 1802 Formed from Town of Lisbon 1806 Daughter town De Kalb formed 1810 Daughter town Gouverneur formed 1821 Daughter town Morristown formed 1825 Daughter town De Peyster formed 1868 Village of Ogdensburgh became the City of Ogdensburg	Black Lake Galilee Heuvelton (v) Lost Village Northrup Corners Ogdensburg (v)		* Oswegatchie was the name for town 8 of the Ten Towns tract surveyed 1787 • Black Lake in Town of Morristown after 1821 • Village of Heuvelton inc. 1912; formerly Heuvel • Village of Ogdensburg inc. 1817, became City of Ogdensburg 1868; county seat 1802–1828
Parishville 1810 Settled 1818 Formed from Town of Hopkinton 1843 Daughter town Colton formed 1851 Ceded land to Town of Colton	Abbot Hill Allen Falls Blake Cookham High Flats Joe Indian Long Bow Parishville	Parishville Center Picket(t)ville Reuben Hill Sinclair Corner Stafford Corners West Parishville Wick	• Joe Indian called Sterlingwick until 1920
Piercefield 1900 Formed from Town of Hopkinton 1913 Ceded land to Town of Altamont (now Tupper Lake) Franklin County	Childwold Childwold Park Conifer Ferrys Gale Horseshoe Massawepie	Mount Arab Mount Arab Station Piercefield Pleasant Lake Sabattis Veterans Mountain Camp	• Childwold formerly Atherton and Mortlake; on Hopkinton town line
Pierrepont 1806–07 Settled 1818 Formed from Town of Russell 1844 Daughter town Fine formed 1868 Daughter town Clifton formed 1880 Daughter town Clare formed	Austins Corners Claflins Corners Crary Mills Deans Corners Hamiltons Corners Hannawa Falls Pierrepont	Sellecks Corners Vebber Corners Washburn Corners West Pierrepont Willisville Wilson Corners	• Crary Mills on Canton and Potsdam town lines • Hannawa Falls formerly Coxs Mill, East Pierrepont, and Ellsworth • Vebber Corners also Cook(s) Corners
Pitcairn 1824 Settlers from Potsdam 1836 Formed from Town of Fowler	Backus Bacon Bacons Crossing Bacon Station Collins	East Bacon East Pitcairn Geers Corners Kalurah Pitcairn	

Towns (and Cities)	Villages and other Settlements		Notes
Potsdam * 1803 Settled 1806 Formed from Town of Madrid	Bucks Bridge Casey Corners Crary Mills Eben Grays Mills Hewittville Norwood (v) Potsdam (v)	Russell Turnpike Sisson Sissonville Slab City Unionville West Potsdam Yaleville	* Potsdam was the name for town 3 of the Ten Towns tract surveyed 1787 • Crary Mills on Canton and Pierrepont town lines • Hewittville also Glenwood • Village of Norwood inc. 1871; shared with Town of Norfolk; Norwood also North Potsdam and Potsdam Station; formerly Potsdam Junction, Racketville, and Raquetteville • Village of Potsdam inc. 1831 • West Potsdam formerly Smiths Corners • Yaleville on Norfolk town line
Rossie 1807 Settled 1810 Scottish immigrants arrived 1813 Formed from Town of Russell 1816 Daughter town Fowler formed 1827 Daughter town Hammond formed 1844 Annexed land from Town of Hammond	Keenes Keenes Station Lead Mines Nelson Corner Pikes Corner Rossie Shingle Creek Somerville Spragueville Wegatchie		• Spragueville formerly Keenesville and Spragues Corners • Wegatchie also Church(s) Mills, formerly Caledonia and Howards Mills
Russell 1804 Settled 1807 Formed from Town of Hopkinton 1813 Daughter town Rossie formed 1816 Daughter town Fowler formed 1818 Daughter town Pierrepont formed 1844 Daughter town Fine formed	Clarks Corners Coopers Corners Danes Corners Degrasse Derbys Corners Devils Elbow Downerville Fairbanks Corners Fordhams Corners Frier Settlement Grant Knox Settlement North Russell	Owens Corners Palmer(s)ville Putnams Corners Reynolds Corners Russell Sarahsburgh Scotts Corners Silver Hill South Russell Stalbird Stammerville Van House Corners	• Degrasse formerly Monterey • Hamlet of Russell formerly Ballybeen; site of Russell Arsenal in 1809 • Sarahsburgh was on Fine town line
Stockholm * 1802 Settled 1806 Formed from Town of Massena 1823 Daughter town Norfolk formed	Armstrong Corners Beechertown Bicknellville Brasher Station Brookdale Buckton Converse East Part East Stockholm Holmes Hill Jenkins Corners	Kellogg Knapps Knapp(s) Station North Brookdale North Stockholm Sanfordville Skinnerville Southville Stockholm Center West Stockholm Winthrop	* Stockholm was the name for town 2 of the Ten Towns tract surveyed 1787 • Brookdale formerly Scotland • Buckton also Bucks Corners • Southville formerly South Stockholm • West Stockholm formerly Bickneyville • Winthrop formerly Stockholm and Stockholm Depot
Waddington 1798 Settled 1859 Formed from Town of Madrid	Chamberlain(s) Corners Chase(s) Mills Chipman Corrigans Island Dalton Crossing Drews Corner	Halfway House Corners Henrys Corners Irish Settlement Rutherford Waddington (v) Wagners Corners	• Chase(s) Mills formerly in Town of Madrid; on Louisville town line • Village of Waddington inc. 1839; formerly Hamilton; in Town of Madrid before 1859

Note on St. Lawrence County

Though St. Lawrence was formed from Clinton County March 7, 1802, the land had not been part of Clinton County for very long. On April 3, 1801 and March 3, 1802 Clinton gained land from Herkimer and Montgomery counties and it was this recently acquired land that became St. Lawrence County.

NEW YORK STATE CENSUS

County originals at St. Lawrence County Clerk's Office: 1845*, 1865**, 1905, 1915, 1925 (1825, 1855, 1875, and 1892*** are lost)

County original at NYSL: 1835 (Town of Gouverneur only)

State originals at the NYSA: 1915, 1925

Microfilm at the FHL, NYPL, and NYSL; some years are online at *FamilySearch.org* and *Ancestry.com*.

*1845: Transcriptions for the towns of Brasher, Hopkinton, and Warwick at St. Lawrence County Historical Association; for the towns of Brasher and Lawrence, see Nyando Roots Genealogical Club in Abstracts, Indexes & Transcriptions

**1865: Transcriptions for the towns of Madrid, Massina, Morristown, Norfolk, Oswegatchie, and Parishville at St. Lawrence County Historical Association

***1892: For the Town of Parishville, see Young in Abstracts, Indexes & Transcriptions

NATIONAL/STATEWIDE REPOSITORIES & RESOURCES

See chapter 16

COUNTYWIDE REPOSITORIES & RESOURCES

St. Lawrence County Clerk
Building #2 • 48 Court Street • Canton, NY 13617 • (315) 379-2237
www.co.st-lawrence.ny.us/Departments/CountyClerk

Business certificates, court records, land records 1802–present, naturalization records 1802–1906, marriages 1908–1936, survey maps, and St. Lawrence county original of the New York state census for 1905. Website has a list of local clerks' offices.

St. Lawrence County – City, Town, and Village Clerks
Birth, marriage, and death records are maintained by the clerk of the municipality in which the event occurred; see Introduction to County Guides for details of other records which may also be held by municipal clerks. For contact information, see *www.co.st-lawrence. ny.us/Departments/CountyClerk/Certificates.*

St. Lawrence County Surrogate's Court
St. Lawrence County Courthouse • 48 Court Street
Canton, NY 13617 • (315) 379-2217

Holds probate records from the early 1800s to the present. See also chapter 6, Probate Records.

St. Lawrence County Public Libraries
St. Lawrence is part of the North Country Library System; see *http:// ncls.northcountrylibraries.org* to access each library. Many hold genealogy and local history collections. For example, Canton Free and Rensselaer Falls Libraries hold local ephemera, including scrapbooks accessible online. Also see listings below for Hepburn Library of Lisbon, Ogdensburg Public Library, and Russell Public Library.

St. Lawrence County Historical Association, County Historian, and Silas Wright Museum
3 East Main Street • PO Box 8 • Canton, NY 13617 • (315) 386-8133
Email: slcha@northnet.org • *www.slcha.org*

Holdings include cemetery records and census transcriptions, including 1845 and 1865 for some towns. Also books, manuscripts, maps, photographs, and letters relating to the Civil War (serving soldiers and military units), the Woman's Christian Temperance Union, region-wide industrial history, and many genealogies. Special collections include the Macomb Purchase Papers (late 18th-century records of the purchase of the future St. Lawrence County), the Silas Wright Collection (letters and books of U.S. Senator and NYS Governor Silas Wright 1795–1847) and the Isaac Johnson papers (freed slave builder and architect). The society publishes the *Quarterly*.

St. Lawrence County –All Municipal Historians
While not authorized to answer genealogical inquiries, city, town, and village historians can provide valuable historical information and research advice; some maintain collections and webpages which may include transcribed records, local histories, and other genealogical material. See contact information at *www.slcha.org/information/ historians.php* or at the website of the Association of Public Historians of New York State at *www.aphnys.org.*

St. Lawrence Valley Genealogical Society
PO Box 205 • Canton, NY 13617-0205
www.rootsweb.ancestry.com/~nystlawr/html/slvgs.html

Society's research library is located in the Potsdam Public Museum (see below).

REGIONAL REPOSITORIES & RESOURCES

Adirondack Genealogical-Historical Society
See listing in Franklin County Guide

Adirondack Museum Library
See listing in Hamilton County Guide

Saranac Lake Free Library: The William Chapman White Memorial Room: Adirondack Research Center
See listing in Franklin County Guide

St. Lawrence University:
Special Collections and Vance University Archives
Owen D. Young Library • Park Street • Canton, NY 13617 • (315) 229-5476 or 229-5956 • *www.stlawu.edu/library/special-collections*

Holdings may be searched through the library's online catalog and include books and manuscripts, diaries and correspondence, journals, maps and atlases, newspapers, photographs, and other materials relating to St. Lawrence University history and the history of northern New York.

State University of New York at Oswego:
Local History Collection
See listing in Oswego County Guide

LOCAL REPOSITORIES & RESOURCES

Alphabetized by location

Pierrepont Museum

872 State Highway 68 • Canton, NY 13617 • (315) 379-0804

Holdings include histories, genealogies, and cemetery records.

Colton Historical Society and Museum

89 Main Street • PO Box 223 • Colton, NY 13625 • (315) 262-2524
Email: collib@nnyln.net • www.coltonmuseum.org/more

Holdings include ledgers, papers, photographs, and scrapbooks.

Town of De Kalb Historical Association, Museum, and Historian's Office

Old Methodist Meetinghouse Museum, 2nd Floor
696 East De Kalb Road • PO Box 111 • De Kalb Junction, NY 13630
(315) 347-1900 • Email: deputyhist@tds.net • www.dekalbnyhistorian.org

Cemetery records, church records, land records, ledgers, maps, scrapbooks, and photographs dating from 1806–present. Website includes virtual archives, list of local historical societies, searchable indexes, and articles on local history. Publishes the *Williamstown Gazette*.

Edwards Historical Association, Historian, and History & Genealogy Center

Edwards Town Hall • 161 Main Street • Edwards, NY 13635
(315) 562-3500 • Email: historian@edwardshistory.org
www.edwardshistory.org

Books, church records, family histories, military records, newspapers, obituaries, scrapbooks, and vital statistics.

Gouverneur Historical Association and Museum

30 Church Street • Gouverneur, NY 13642 • (315) 287-0570
Email: gouverneurmuseum@centralny.twcbc.com
www.gouverneurmuseum.org

Holdings include local histories, directories, documents, photographs, and newspapers.

R.T. Elethorp Historical Society and Hammond Historical Museum

Route 37 • PO Box 107 • Hammond, NY 13646 • (315) 324-5517
www.blacklakeny.com/hammondmuseum

Holdings include family histories, scrapbooks, maps, photographs, and artifacts.

Hermon Heritage Hall

117 Main Street • Hermon, NY 13652 • (315) 347-2373 or 347-3311
Email: hermonheritagehall@yahoo.com

Holdings include biographies and genealogies, newspapers 1874–1906, and artifacts.

Hepburn Library of Lisbon

6899 Country Route 10 • Lisbon, NY 13658 • (315) 393-0111
Email: lislib@ncls.org • www.hepburnlibraryoflisbon.com

Holdings include books, photographs, scrapbooks, and tombstone transcriptions.

Massena Town Museum and Historical Association

200 East Orvis Street • Massena, NY 13662 • (315) 769-8571
Email: historian@massenaworks.com

Holdings include genealogies, photographs, and scrapbooks.

Norfolk Town Historical Museum

42 ½ West Main Street • PO Box 643 • Norfolk, NY 13667
(315) 384-3136 or 384-4575 • Email: norfolk@centralny.twcbc.com
www.norfolknymuseum.com

Holdings include documents, family files, and photographs.

Norwood Historical Association & Susan C. Lyman Historical Museum

39 North Main Street • PO Box 163 • Norwood, NY 13668
(315) 353-2751 (museum) • (315) 384-3273 (historian)

Holdings include family archives, photographs, and artifacts.

Ogdensburg Public Library: Local History Room and Archives

312 Washington Street • Ogdensburg, NY 13669 • (315) 393-4325
www.ogdensburgpubliclibrary.org

Cemetery records, census microfilms, church records, city directories, maps, newspapers, scrapbooks, and yearbooks (Ogdensburg Free Academy, various years, some online). See website for a full list of special collections.

Parishville Historical Association and Museum

1785 East Main Street • PO Box 534 • Parishville, NY 13672
(315) 265-7619 • http://www.parishvilleny.us/history.html

Holdings include information on over 400 Parishville families.

Potsdam Public Museum

Civic Center • 2 Park Street • PO Box 5168
Potsdam, NY 13676-5168 • (315) 265-6910
Email: museum@vi.potsdam.ny.us • www.potsdampublicmuseum.org

Archives include books and journals, cemetery records, family files, letters, town and village records, photographs, and yearbooks. Collections include photographs and documents. Website includes an archive subject index and list of family surnames. Local newspapers 1861–1989 are online.

Richville Historical Association

24 Depot Street • PO Box 207 • Richville, NY 13681 • (315) 287-0182
www.richvillenyhistory.blogspot.com

Holdings include genealogies, World War II memorabilia, and photographs. Information on Wayside and Maple Grove cemeteries available online.

Russell Public Library and Museum

24 Pestle Street • PO Box 510 • Russell, NY 13684
(315) 347-2115 • Email: ruslib@ncls.org • www.russellny.org/library.html

Books, cemetery records, information on the Russell Arsenal (War of 1812), and the *St. Lawrence County Historical Association Quarterly*, 1950s–present.

Moore Museum and Waddington Historian

79 West St. Lawrence Avenue • PO Box 277
Waddington, NY 13694 • (315) 388-5967
Email: wadhist@northnet.org

Family histories, cemetery records, census materials, military information, photographs, and biographies of prominent residents documenting the history of St. Lawrence County and nearby areas of Canada.

Stockholm Historical Organization

607 State Highway 11C • PO Box 206 • Winthrop, NY 13697
(315) 389-5062 or 384-4764 • Email: stckhmhistorg@slic.com

Cemetery records, church records, maps, scrapbooks, and information relating to local veterans of the Civil War, World War I, and World War II.

SELECTED PRINT & ONLINE RESOURCES

Below is a selection of resources relevant for research in this county. The list is representative, not exhaustive. Additional titles—particularly of abstracts, indexes, transcriptions, and local histories—are available; consult the introduction to Part Two for further information. For guidance on how to identify and locate community directories and local newspapers, see chapter 11, City Directories, and chapter 12, Newspapers, in Part One of this book.

Abstracts, Indexes & Transcriptions

County of St. Lawrence Abstracts. Syracuse: Central New York Genealogical Society, 2000. Abstracts for a range of genealogical records originally published in the quarterly *Tree Talks.* A name index is on the CNYGS website.

Daughters of the American Revolution, comps. *New York DAR Genealogical Records Committee Report.* Since 1913 DAR volunteers have transcribed many thousands of unpublished cemetery, church, and town records throughout New York. The reports are at the DAR Library; copies are at the NYSL and the NYPL. The DAR has a searchable name index to all the GRC reports at *http://services.dar.org/Public/DAR_Research/search/?Tab_ID=6.* See Jean Worden's index below for a listing by county of the New York record sets that were transcribed by the DAR before 1998.

Fuller, Joyce Rockwood. "St. Lawrence County, New York, Death Records." Manuscript, 2001. New York State Library, Albany.

Jackson, Ronald Vern, W. David Samuelson, and Scott Rosenkilde. *New York 1815 Census Index.* Bountiful, UT: Accelerated Indexing Systems, 1984. Names compiled from tax assessment rolls. Also see FHL microfilm titled: *Transcript of Information from Tax Assessment Roll and Other Sources for Potsdam, New York.* Salt Lake City: Genealogical Society of Utah, 1968.

Kelly, Arthur C. M. *Index to Tree Talks County Packet: St. Lawrence County.* Rhinebeck, NY: Kinship, 2002.

Lacy, Cindy Clowe. *Some Cemeteries of St. Lawrence Co., NY.* Painted Post, NY: C. C. Lacy, 1994.

Nyando Roots Genealogical Club. "1845 New York State Census for Towns of Brasher and Lawrence, St. Lawrence County." *Nyando Roots,* vol. 16, no. 4 (1999): 2–16 [towns of Brasher and Lawrence]; vol. 17, no. 1 (2000): 8–16 [Lawrence continued]; vol. 17, no. 2 (2000): 12–18 [Lawrence continued].

Worden, Jean D. "Book 1, Subject Index." In *Revised Master Index to the New York State Daughters of the American Revolution Genealogical Records Volumes.* Zephyrhills, FL: J. D. Worden, 1998. The Subject Index includes a listing by county of the cemeteries, churches, towns, and other sources of records transcribed by the DAR.

Young, Norman, comp. "Parishville Census, Enumerator's Blotter 3rd Election District, 1892 New York State Census." *SLVGS News,* vol. 12, no. 1 (1995): 11–12; vol. 12, no. 2 (1995): 10–11.

Other Resources

Beers, S. N. *New Topographical Atlas of St. Lawrence Co., New York: From Actual Surveys.* Philadelphia, 1865. [NYPL Digital Gallery]

Carson, Patricia Harrington. *St. Lawrence County Portraits.* Charleston, SC: Arcadia, 2005.

Child, Hamilton. *Gazetteer and Business Directory of St. Lawrence County, N.Y., for 1873–4.* Syracuse: Printed at the Journal Office, 1873.

Curtis, Gates. *Our County and Its People: A Memorial Record of St. Lawrence County, New York.* Syracuse, 1894.

Durant, Samuel W. *History of St. Lawrence Co., New York, with Illustrations and Biographical Sketches of Some of Its Prominent Men and Pioneers.* Interlaken, NY: Heart of the Lakes Publishing, 1982.

Fay, Loren V. *St. Lawrence County, New York, Genealogical Research Secrets.* Albany: L. V. Fay, 1981.

Harder, Kelsie B., and Mary H. Smallman. *Claims to Name: Toponyms of St. Lawrence County.* Utica, NY: North Country Books, 1992.

Hough, Franklin Benjamin. *A History of St. Lawrence and Franklin Counties, New York, From the Earliest Period to the Present Time.* Baltimore, MD: Regional Publishing Co., 1970. First published 1853.

James, Patricia R. *Upstate New York Researcher: Principally for Research in Jefferson, Oneida, and St. Lawrence Counties.* Boise, ID: Family Tree, 1991.

New York Historical Resources Center. *Guide to Historical Resources in St. Lawrence County, New York Repositories.* Ithaca, NY: Cornell University, 1987. [books.FamilySearch.org]

Northern New York Library Network. *Directory of Archival and Historical Document Collections.* 2011–2013 edition; published digitally at *http://nny.nnyln.org/archives/ArchivalDirectory.pdf.* Online indexes at *http://nny.nnyln.org/archives/page01.html.* Describes collections held by organizations in Clinton, Essex, Franklin, Jefferson, Lewis, Oswego, and St. Lawrence counties.

Saint Lawrence County Historical Association. *The Quarterly.* Canton, NY: St. Lawrence County Historical Association, 1956—present. An index is online at *www.slcha.org/quarterly/quarterlyindex.php.*

St. Lawrence County History ... A View from the People: A Photographic Portrait by Those Who Live Here. Canton, NY: St. Lawrence County Historical Association, 1975.

Additional Online Resources

Ancestry.com

There are vast numbers of records on *Ancestry.com* that pertain to people who have lived in New York State. See chapter 16 for a description of *Ancestry.com*'s resources and its partnership with the New York State Archives. A search of the online card catalog by county will reveal lesser known resources that pertain to a locality, such as town records, abstracts, transcriptions, city directories, and local histories. In addition, the Drouin Collection: Early U.S. French Catholic Church Records 1695–1954 contains some records pertaining to Clinton, Franklin, St. Lawrence, and Essex counties.

FamilySearch.org

FamilySearch has extensive collections of New York records, including religious records, which are searchable by name and location, but not by county. The following collections include record images (browsable, but not searchable) that are organized by county:

- "New York, Land Records, 1630–1975." Includes land and property records. *familysearch.org/search/collection/2078654*
- "New York, Probate Records, 1629–1971." Includes wills, letters of administration, and guardianship papers. *familysearch.org/search/collection/1920234*

For both collections, choose the browse option and then select St. Lawrence to view the available records sets.

A detailed description of *FamilySearch.org* resources is found in chapter 16.

New York Heritage Digital Collections: New York State Newspaper Project

www.nyheritage.org/newspapers

> The website provides links to digital newspapers collections in 26 counties (currently) made accessible through New York Heritage, New York State Historic Newspapers, HRVH Historical Newspapers, and other providers.

NYGenWeb Project: St. Lawrence County

www.rootsweb.ancestry.com/~nystlawr

> Part of the national, USGenWeb volunteer initiative, the website provides information and resources for county research.

St. Lawrence County Cemeteries

www.stlawrencecountycemeteries.org

> Gravestone transcriptions, photographs of, and articles relating to selected cemeteries in St. Lawrence County.

Suffolk County

Parent County	Original County
Daughter Counties	None
County Seat	Hamlet of Riverhead

Major Land Transactions
See table in chapter 7, Land Records

Gardiner's Island Manor 1665, Shelter Island Manor 1666, Fishers Island Manor 1668, Plum Island Manor 1675, Queens Village Manor 1685, Eaton Manor 1686, St. George Manor 1693

Indian Territories
See chapter 14, Peoples of New York, American Indian

Unkechaug Nation: Poospatuck Reservation (1859–present)
Shinnecock Indian Nation: Shinnecock Reservation (1859–present)

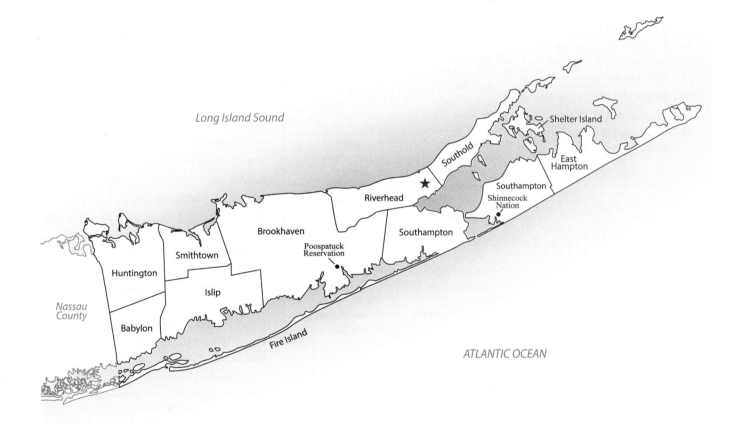

Town Boundary Map
★ - County seat

Towns (and Cities)	Villages and other Settlements		Notes
Babylon 1872 Formed from Town of Huntington, formerly called Huntington South	American Venice Amity Harbor Amityville (v) Amityville Heights Argyle Park Babylon (v) Broad Hollow Captree Island Colonial Springs Copiague Copiague Harbor Deer Park East Babylon East Farmingdale Farmingdale Fire Island Frontier Park	Gilgo(e) Beach Lindenhurst (v) Lower Melville Maywood Muncie Island North Amityville North Babylon North Lindenhurst Oak Beach Oak Island Pinelawn Sampawam Point Venetian Shores West Babylon West Gilgo Beach Wheatley Heights Wyandanch	• Village of Amityville inc. 1894; formerly West Neck; in Town of Huntington before 1872 • Village of Babylon inc. 1893; formerly New Babylon; in Town of Huntington before 1872 • Captree Island on Islip town line • Colonial Springs formerly Colonial Manor • Copiague also East Amityville, formerly Copiag Neck; in Town of Huntington before 1872 • Deer Park in Town of Huntington before 1872 • Fire Island shared with towns of Brookhaven and Islip • Village of Lindenhurst inc. 1923; formerly Breslau; in Town of Huntington before 1872 • Lower Melville on Huntington town line • North Amityville formerly Brush Plains; in Town of Huntington before 1872; on Oyster Bay town line • North Babylon in Town of Huntington before 1872 • West Gilgo Beach also Gilgo and Sand Point • Wyandanch formerly Half Way, Hollow Hills, West Deer Park, and Wyandance
Brookhaven 1655 Settlers purchased land from Setauket Indians, founded Cromwell Bay, now Setauket 1661 Became part of colony of Connecticut 1664 Became part of colony of New York 1666 Incorporated by patent 1788 Recognized as a town by the State of New York	Atlantic Beach, Fire Is. Artist Lake Bayberry Dunes Bay View Park Belle Croft Belle Terre (v) Bellport (v) Bellview Beach Blue Point Brookhaven Canaan Carman Mills Cedar Beach Center Moriches Centereach Cherry Grove, Fire Is. Coram Crane(s) Neck Crystal Brook Cumsewogue Davis Park, Fire Is. East Manor East Moriches East Patchogue Eastport East Setauket East Shoreham Edenvale Farmingville Fire Island Fire Island Pines Foxwood Village Germantown Crossing Gordon Heights Greenwood Village	Hagerman Hallock Landing Holbrook Holtsville Lake Grove (v) Lakeland Lake Ronkonoma Lakeview Park Manorville Mastic Mastic Beach (v) Masury Point Medford Middle Island Middletown Miller(s) Place Mittyville Moriches Mount Sinai Mount Vernon Nassakeag North Bellport North Manor North Patchogue North Shore Beach Oakleyville Ocean Bay Park, Fire Is. Old Field (v) Old Mastic Patchogue (v) Patchogue Highlands Point O'Woods, Fire Is. Poquott (v) Port Jefferson (v) Port Jefferson Station Ridge	• Village of Belle Terre inc. 1931 • Village of Bellport inc. 1908 • Hamlet of Brookhaven called Fire Place until circa 1871 • Centereach formerly New Village • Coram also Corum • Crane(s) Neck in Old Field Village • Eastport formerly Seacotauk and Seatuck; on Southampton town line • Fire Island shared with towns of Babylon and Islip • Gordon Heights also Coram Hill and Jordan Heights • Holbrook on Islip town line • Holtsville formerly Waverly; small part in Town of Islip • Village of Lake Grove inc. 1968 • Lakeland on Islip town line • Manorville formerly St. Georges Manor (granted 1693) • Mastic formerly Forge • Village of Mastic Beach inc. 2010 • Mount Sinai also Mount Vernon, Old Mans Harbor, Old Mans, and Ould Mans • Ocean Bay Park on Islip town line • Village of Old Field inc. 1927, included Conscience Bay, Oldfield, and West Meadow, later included Cranes Neck • Village of Patchogue inc. 1893; also Milltown • Village of Poquott inc. 1931 • Village of Port Jefferson inc. 1963; formerly Drowned Meadowland • Port Jefferson Station also Echo • Ridge also Randalville and Ridgeville

(Brookhaven continued on next page)

Towns (and Cities)	Villages and other Settlements		Notes
Brookhaven (continued)	Rocky Point Rocky Point Landing Ronkonkoma Seatuck Grove Seaview, Fire Is. Selden Setauket Shirley Shoreham (v) Sigfield Park Smiths Point Sound Beach Sound View South Haven South Manor South Medford South Setauket South Yaphank	Squassux Landing Stony Brook Strongs Neck Swezys Landing Swezeytown Tangier Terryville Upton Wampmissic Water Island, Fire Is. West Manor West Meadow Beach West Moriches West Yaphank Woodhull Landing Yaphank	• Ronkonkoma on Islip town line • Seatuck Grove on Southampton town line • Seaview on Islip town line • Selden formerly Westfield • Setauket originally Cromwell Bay, also formerly Ashford • Village of Shoreham inc. 1913; formerly Woodville • Sigfield Park also Siegfield Park • Upton also Camp Upton • Yaphank formerly Brookfield and Millville
East Hampton * 1639 Gardiners Island granted to Lion Gardiner 1648 Western part of town purchased from Montauk Indians by Governors of Connecticut and New Haven, and conveyed to settlers from Southampton, LI 1657 Became part of colony of Connecticut 1664 Became part of colony of New York 1666 Incorporated by patent 1788 Recognized as a town by the State of New York	Acabonack Amaganset(t) Apaquoga Barnes Hole Bartlett Beach Hampton Devon Ditch Plains Divinity Hill East Hampton (v) Eastside Fire Place Freetown Gardiners Island Georgica Gerard Park Grace Estate Grassy Hollow Hard Scrabble Hither Plains Jericho Kingsto(w)n	Lazy Point Maidstone Landing Maidstone Park Midhampton Montauk Montauk Beach Montauk Point Montauk Station Napeague Northwest Harbor Pantigo Powder Hill Promised Land Sag Harbor (v) Shepherd Neck Springs Star Island The Creek Beach Three Mile Harbor Wainscott West Amagansett	* First called Maidstone after English home of some of the settlers; name changed to Easthampton and in 1885 to East Hampton • Amaganset(t) also Amergansett and Amerbnasett • Village of East Hampton inc. 1920 • Gardiners Island also Gardeners Island; (Gardiner's Island Manor granted 1665) • Montauk also Montank • Northwest Harbor also Northwest and Northwest Woods • Village of Sag Harbor inc. 1846; incorporated as a fire district in 1803, law passed 1819 allowed the election of trustees who could make by-laws and levy fines; also Sagaponack Harbor; shared with Town of Southampton • Wainscott also Wainscut and Wenscoat
Huntington 1653 Purchased from Matinecock Indians and settled by English from New England and other parts of LI 1660 Became part of colony of Connecticut 1664 Became part of colony of New York 1666 Incorporated by patent 1788 Recognized as a town by the State of New York 1872 Daughter town Babylon formed 1886 Annexed Lloyds Neck from Town of Oyster Bay, Queens County (now Nassau County)	Amityville (v) Asharoken (v) Babylon Bay Crest Bell Crest Breslau Brush Plains Cedarcroft Centerport Cold Spring Harbor Commack Copiag Neck		• Village of Amityville, formerly West Neck, inc. 1894; in Town of Babylon after 1872 • Village of Asharoken inc. 1925 • Babylon formerly New Babylon; in Town of Babylon after 1872 • Breslau, now Lindenhurst, in Town of Babylon after 1872 • Brush Plains now North Amityville; in Town of Babylon after 1872; on Oyster Bay town line • Centerport formerly Centreport and Little Cow Harbor • Cold Spring Harbor also Cold Spring; partly in Town of Oyster Bay, Nassau County • Commack also Winne-Comack and Wanecommack; on Smithtown town line • Copiag Neck also East Amityville, now Copiague; in Town of Babylon after 1872

(Huntington continued on next page)

Towns (and Cities)	Villages and other Settlements		Notes
Huntington (continued)	Crab Meadow	Lefferts Mill	• Deer Park in Town of Babylon after 1872
	Deer Park	Little Neck	• East Northport also Larkfield and Clay Pits
	Dix Hills	Little Plains	• Eaton(s) Neck part of Eaton Manor (granted 1686)
	East Northport	Lloyd Harbor (v)	• Fort Salonga on Smithtown town line
	Eaton(s)Neck	Lloyd(s) Neck	• Greenlawn formerly Old Fields
	Elwood	Long Swamp	• Half Hollow also Half Hollow Hills and Half Way Hollow Hills
	Fort Hill	Lower Melville	
	Fort Salonga	Melville	• Village of Huntington Bay inc. 1924; formerly East Neck, includes Wincoma
	Great Neck	Middleville	
	Greenlawn	North Babylon	• Huntington Station formerly Fairgrounds
	Halesite	Northport (v)	• Village of Lloyd Harbor inc. 1926
	Half Hollow	Pidgeon Hill	• Lloyd(s) Neck peninsula formerly Caumsett, Horse Neck, Manor of Queen's Village (manor granted 1685); annexed from Town of Oyster Bay, Queens County, in 1886; now part of Village of Lloyd Harbor
	Huntington	South Huntington	
	Huntington Bay (v)	Vernon Valley	
	Huntington Beach	West Hills	
	Huntington Harbor	West Neck	
	Huntington Manor	Wincoma	• Lower Melville on Babylon town line
	Huntington Station		• Melville formerly Sweet Hollow
			• Middleville on Smithtown town line
			• North Babylon in Town of Babylon after 1872
			• Village of Northport inc. 1894; formerly Cow Harbor and Great Cow Harbor
			• Vernon Valley formerly Red Hook
			• West Hills includes Mount Misery
			• West Neck now part of Village of Lloyd Harbor
			• Wincoma part of Village of Huntington Bay
Islip * Originally inhabited by Patchogue and Secatogue Indians **1683** First land purchase from Indians, first of several patents granted **1683–1710** Settled by patentees and others from Suffolk, Queens, and NYC **1710** Recognized as a precinct by colonial government **1788** Recognized as a town by the State of New York	Atlantique, Fire Is.	Kismet	* Islip first called Secatague
	Bayport	Lakeland	• Bayport also Middle Road and Midroadville
	Bay Shore	Lonelyville	• Bay Shore formerly Mechanicville and Penataquit
	Bayberry Point	Middle Village	• Brentwood formerly Modern Times
	Baywood	North Bay Shore	• Village of Brightwater(s) inc. 1916
	Bedford Park	North Great River	• Captree Island on Babylon town line
	Bohemia	North Islip	• Fire Island shared with towns of Babylon and Brookhaven
	Brentwood	Oakdale	
	Brightwater(s) (v)	Ocean Beach, Fire Is. (v)	• Happauge formerly Wheeler Settlement; on Smithtown town line
	Captree Island	O-Co-Nee	
	Carlton Park	Pine Aire	• Holbrook on Brookhaven town line
	Central Islip	Robbins Rest	• Holtsville formerly Waverly; mostly in Town of Brookhaven
	Club House	Ronkonkoma	
	Connetquot Park	Saltaire, Fire Is. (v)	• Village of Islandia inc. 1985
	Deer Run	Sayville	• Lakeland on Brookhaven town line
	East Brentwood	Sayville Heights	• Middle Village part of Bayport
	East Islip	Sea Breeze	• Oakdale also Oakdale Station
	Edgewood	Seaview, Fire Is.	• Village of Ocean Beach inc. 1921
	Fair Harbor, Fire Is.	Slater Park	• Ronkonkoma on Brookhaven town line
	Ferndale	South Great River	• Village of Saltaire inc. 1917
	Fire Island	The Moorings	• Seaview on Brookhaven town line
	Great River	Thompsons Station	
	Hauppauge	Timber Point	
	Holbrook	West Bay Shore	
	Holtsville	West Islip	
	Idle Hour	West Sayville	
	Islandia (v)	Youngport	
	Islip		
	Islip Terrace		

Towns (and Cities)	Villages and other Settlements		Notes
Riverhead * **c. 1659** Settled as part of Southold **1728** Riverhead hamlet becomes county seat **1792** Formed from Town of Southold	Aquebogue Baiting Hollow Calverton Centerville Fresh Pond Landing Friar Head Landing Glenwood Village Herod Point Hulse Landing Jamesport Lakewood Park Laurel Luce Landing Northville (v)	Polishtown Reeves Park Riverhead Roanoke Roanoke Landing Second Avenue South Jamesport Sweyze Upper Aquebogue Upper Mills Wading River Wildwood Woodcliff Park	* County Seat: hamlet of Riverhead 1728–present; earlier courts met in Southold, Southampton, and Brookhaven, the clerk's home was his office; some present-day county offices are in Riverside, Town of Southampton • Calverton also Baiting Hollow Station and Hulses Turnout • Jamesport formerly Lower Aquebogue and Old Aquebogue • Laurel formerly Franklinville; on Southold town line • Northville inc. 1921 as Village of Sound Avenue, formerly Success, named Northville 1927; dissolved 5/16/1930 • Hamlet of Riverhead—small part in Town of Southampton
Shelter Island Originally inhabited by Manhasset Indians **1652** Settled **1666** Incorporated by patent (Shelter Island Manor), but government shared with Southold until 1730 **1788** Recognized as a town by the State of New York	Coeckles Harbor Dering Harbor (v) Menantic Montclair Colony Ram Island Sachems Neck Shelter Island	Shelter Island Heights Silver Beach South Ferry Stearns Point West Neck Westmoreland	• Village of Dering Harbor inc. 1916
Smithtown * **1659** Wyandance, Sachem of the Montauks conveyed land to Lion Gardiner as a free gift **1663** Richard Smith purchases site of Smithtown from Gardiner **1664** Became part of colony of New York **1665** Patented by Governor **1788** Recognized as a town by the State of New York	Bread and Cheese Hollow Commack Darlington East Hauppauge Flowerfield Fort Salonga Fresh Pond Hallock Acres Hauppauge Head of the Harbor (v) Indian Head Kings Park Meadow Glen Middleville Mills Pond	Nesconset Nissequogue (v) North Smithtown San Remo Smithtown Smithtown Landing St. James St. Johnland Sunken Meadow The Branch The Landing Village of the Branch (v) Village of the Landing (v) West Hauppauge	* Smithtown first called Smithfield and Nesaquake • Commack also Comac, Winne-Comack; on Huntington town line • Fort Salonga on Huntington town line • Happauge also Hoppouge formerly Wheeler Settlement; on Islip town line • Village of Head of the Harbor inc. 1928 • Middleville on Huntington town line • Village of Nissequogue inc. 1926; formerly Nesaquake, Nissaquag, and Nissequague • Smithtown also Head of the Landing • St. James also St. Jamesville • Sunken Meadow also Sunk Meadow • Village of the Branch inc. 1927, formerly Smithtown Branch • Village of the Landing inc. 1927, dissolved 5/25/1939, now The Landing

Towns (and Cities)	Villages and other Settlements		Notes
Southampton	Art Village	Red Creek	• Bridgehampton formerly Bullhead
1640 Settlers from Lynn, MA purchased land from patentee Earl of Stirling	Bay Point	Redwood	• Eastport formerly Seacotauk and Seatuck; on Brookhaven town line
	Bridgehampton	Remsenburg	
	Canoe Place	Riverhead	• East Quogue formerly Atlanticville
1644 Became part of colony of Connecticut	Cedar Crest	Riverside	• Ketchabonec also Kitcaboneck
	Cobb	Rose Grove	• Village of North Haven inc. 1931
1664 Became part of colony of New York	Deerfield	Sagaponack (v)	• Village of Pine Valley inc. 3/15/1988 and dissolved 4/4/1990
	Eastport	Sag(g)	
1676 Incorporated by patent	East Quogue	Sagg Scuttle Hole	• Quioque also Quiogue
	Flanders	Sag Harbor (v)	• Village of Quogue inc. 1928
1788 Recognized as a town by the State of New York	Fly(ing) Point	Scuttle Hole	• Riverside was sometimes known as Brooklyn in the 19th century because it was across the water from Riverhead—as the City of Brooklyn was in relation to New York City; some county offices in Riverside
	Hampton Bays	Sebonac	
	Hampton Park	Seven Ponds	
	Hayground	Shinnecock	
	Hog Neck	Shinnecock Hills	
	Jessup Neck	Southampton (v)	
	Ketchabonec	Southport	• Village of Sagaponack inc. 2005
	Littleworth	Speonk	• Village of Sag Harbor inc. 1846, also Sagaponack Harbor; shared with Town of East Hampton
	Mecox	Springville	
	Newtown	Squiretown	
	Northampton	Suffolk Downs	• Sebonac also Sebonack and Sebonnecke
	North Haven (v)	Suffolk Pines	• Village of Southampton inc. 1894, also Sud Hampton
	North Sea	Tiana	
	Noyac(k)	Tuckahoe	• Water Mill formerly Mill Neck
	Oakville	Union Place	• Village of Westhampton Beach inc. 1928
	Old Town	Water Mill(s)	• Village of West Hampton Dunes inc. 1993
	Pine Neck	Westhampton	
	Pine Valley (v)	Westhampton Beach (v)	
	Ponquoque	West Hampton Dunes (v)	
	Potunk	West Mecox Village	
	Poxabogue	West Tiana	
	Quantuck Bay	Wickapogue	
	Quioque		
	Quogue (v)		
	Rampasture		
Southold *	Arshamonaque	Mattituck	* Southold's Indian name was Yennicott
1640 Settlers from New Haven Colony purchased land from Corchaug Indians; became part of New Haven Colony	Bay Haven	Mattituck Light	• Cutchogue formerly Cuchoge and Corchaug
	Bay View	Nassau Farms	• East Marion also Rocky Point, formerly Upper Neck
	Beixedon	Nassau Point	
	Cedar Beach Point	New Suffolk	
1662 Became part of colony of Connecticut	Cutchogue	Orient	• Fishers Island formerly Vischers Island; (Fishers Island Manor granted 1668)
	Cutchogue Station	Orient Point	
1664 Became part of colony of New York	Duck Pond Point	Paradise Point	• Village of Greenport inc. 1838; formerly Green Hill, Sterling, Stirling, and Winter Harbor
	East Cutchogue	Peconic	
1676 Incorporated by patent	East Marion	Plum Island	
	Eastwind Shores	Reydon Shores	• Gull Island also Great Gull Island
1788 Recognized as a town by the State of New York	Fishers Island	Robins Island	• Laurel formerly Franklinville; on Riverhead town line
	Fleets Neck	Shore Acres	
1792 Daughter town Riverhead formed	Fort Terry	Southold	• Orient formerly Lower Neck, also Oyster Ponds
	Founders Landing	Stirling	
	Greenport (v)	Terry Waters	• Peconic formerly Hermitage
	Greenport West	The Cove	• Plum Island Manor (granted 1675)
	Gull Island	Waterville	
	Horton Point	West Southold	
	Laughing Waters	Yennicott	
	Laurel		

Note on Suffolk County

1640–1664 People from New England founded the initial settlements, most of which affiliated with colonies of Connecticut or New Haven

1664–1683 All eastern Long Island became East Riding of Yorkshire in Colony of New York

1673–1674 Briefly occupied by the Dutch

1683 East Riding became Suffolk County

NEW YORK STATE CENSUS RECORDS

See also chapter 3, Census Records

County original at East Hampton Public Library: 1865 (1825*, 1835, 1845*, 1855, 1875, 1892*, 1905, 1915, and 1925 are lost)
State originals at the NYSA: 1915, 1925

Microfilm at the FHL, NYPL, and NYSL; many years are online at *FamilySearch.org* and *Ancestry.com*.

* In Abstracts, Indexes & Transcriptions below, see Horton for 1825 for Baiting Hollow (Riverhead), see Blydenburgh, et al., for 1845 for Smithtown, and see "St. James, Suffolk County, New York Census of 1892," for 1892.

Federal Census

The 1890 federal census for Suffolk County is lost with the exception of part of the Town of Brookhaven.

Note on early censuses

For a census of 1698 for Southampton and Southold, see O'Callaghan in Abstracts, Indexes & Transcriptions.

For censuses of 1771 and 1776 for Shelter Island, see Mallman in Abstracts, Indexes & Transcriptions.

For a census of 1776 for all towns except Huntington, see *Calendar of Historical Manuscripts Relating …* , in Abstracts, Indexes & Transcriptions.

For a census of 1790 for Huntington (not the same as 1790 federal census), see Street in Town Records section below.

NATIONAL/STATEWIDE REPOSITORIES & RESOURCES

See chapter 16

COUNTYWIDE REPOSITORIES & RESOURCES

Suffolk County Clerk

310 Center Drive • Riverhead, NY 11901-3392 • (631) 852-2000
Email: countyclerk@suffolkcountyny.gov
www.suffolkcountyny.gov/Departments/countyclerk.aspx

Land and court records, some online. Naturalization records from 1853 to 1990. Clerk's office maintains Historic Documents Library (see below) (1600s–present) of land records, maps, and atlases. Website includes directory of repositories and list of local historical societies.

Suffolk County – Town and Village Clerks

Birth, marriage, and death records are maintained by the clerk of the municipality in which the event occurred; see Introduction to County Guides for details of other records which may also be held by municipal clerks. For contact information, see *www.suffolkcountyny. gov/Community/TownsandVillage.aspx*.

Suffolk County Surrogate's Court

320 Center Drive • Riverhead, NY 11901 • (631) 852-1746

Holds probate records from the late 1600s to the present. The NYSA holds most probate records prior to 1787. Pre-1787 probate records are on *FamilySearch.org* under New York County where most Suffolk estates were processed; estates processed locally were transcribed by Pelletreau and Cooper, see below. Probate records 1787–present are available only at the Surrogate's Court in Riverhead.

Suffolk County Archivist

310 Center Drive • Riverhead, NY 11901-3392
(631) 852-2000 ext. 700

Suffolk County Historical Documents Library

Holding include deeds, recorded mortgages (from 1755), naturalization records 1853–1990, court actions 1758–1900, coroners inquests, oaths of office (as early as 1700s), almshouse records, orphanage records, county jail records 1932–1975, marriage certificates 1926–1936 and registers 1909–1929, clerk's minutes as early as 1724, lis pendens, atlases and Sanborn maps, and vessel liens 1875–1968.

Suffolk County Public Libraries

For the Suffolk Cooperative Library System see *www.suffolklibrary system.org*. Most libraries have local history and genealogy collections including newspapers, maps, local histories, photographs, yearbooks, scrapbooks, pamphlets, diaries, town records, and oral histories and some hold archival materials. See also libraries listed below.

Suffolk County Historical Society, Museum, and Library & Archives

300 West Main Street • Riverhead, NY 11901 • (631) 727-2881
Email: schsociety@optonline.net • *www.suffolkcountyhistoricalsociety.org*

Account books, deeds, wills, federal and New York state census on microfilm, letters, diaries and journals, maps and atlases, photographs and scrapbooks, and vertical files. Library & Archives serve as the repository for the collection of the now defunct National Society of the Daughters of the Revolution of 1776 ("D of R"; a distinct society from the DAR), including genealogies, biographies, periodicals, town records, ledgers, diaries, photographs, postcards, maps and atlases, cemetery transcriptions, ancestor charts, scrapbooks, family Bible records, and newspapers. The Society accepts research requests for a fee.

Suffolk County Historian

See Suffolk County Historical Society

Suffolk County – All Municipal Historians

While not authorized to answer genealogical inquiries, town and village historians can provide valuable historical information and research advice; some maintain collections and webpages which may include transcribed records, local histories, and other genealogical material. For contact information, see *www.suffolkcountyny.gov/Community/ TownsandVillage.aspx* or the website of the Association of Public Historians of New York State at *www.aphnys.org*.

REGIONAL REPOSITORIES & RESOURCES

Glen Cove Public Library:
The Robert R. Coles Long Island History Collection
See listing in Nassau County Guide

Hofstra University Library Special Collections Department:
Long Island Studies Institute
See listing in Nassau County Guide

Patchogue-Medford Library:
Celia M. Hastings Local History Room
54-60 Main Street • Patchogue, NY 11772 • (631) 654-4700 ext. 240
www.pmlib.org/genealogy

One of ten locations in NYS holding the New York state vital records indexes. Strong genealogical collection includes books, maps, atlases, newspapers, journals, photographs, postcards, oral histories, genealogies and archives documenting Patchogue-Medford Area, Long Island and NY state history. Website has genealogy section, online resources on New York State, Long Island, Suffolk County, Brookhaven Town, and the Patchogue-Medford Area, with links to digital editions of local history books and record transcriptions (usually full-text, searchable, and downloadable), online research guides and handouts— including bibliography of genealogy resources at the library; additional offline electronic resources and in house publications accessible at the library. Comprehensive guide to collections on website.

Stony Brook University: Center for Global and Local History
Stony Brook University Department of History
Stony Brook, NY 11794-4348 • (631) 632-7488
www.stonybrook.edu/globalhistory

Stony Brook University: Special Collections & Archives
Frank Melville Jr. Memorial Library, Room E-2320
Stony Brook, NY 11794-3323 • (631) 632-7119
www.stonybrook.edu/libspecial

Library contains extensive collection of local history materials. Website contains Digital Long Island Collections. Includes a manuscript regarding St. George Manor in the collection of "Harpur, Robert, 1731–1825" (SC 42); Microfilm Collection of the Institute for Colonial Studies, reel HK, contains papers regarding the Manor of St. George.

LOCAL REPOSITORIES & RESOURCES
Alphabetized by location

Amagansett Historical Association
129 Main Street • PO Box 7077 • Amagansett, NY 11930-7077
(631) 267-3020 • Email access on website • *www.amagansethistory.org*

Association maintains Carleton Kelsey Archive of historical photographs at the Phebe Edwards Mulford House.

Amityville Historical Society & Lauder Museum
170 Broadway • PO Box 764 • Amityville, NY 11701 • (631) 598-1486
Email: amhist@hotmail.com • Facebook page

Historical Research Library includes local historical publications, newspapers, family records, cemetery records, and records of the German Genealogical Society.

Bay Shore Historical Society, Gibson-Mack-Holt House, and Historical Reference Library
22 Maple Avenue • Bay Shore, NY 11706 • (631) 665-1707
Email: contactus@BayShoreHistoricalSociety.org
www.bayshorehistoricalsociety.org

Historical Reference Library includes local history books, maps, photographs, and ephemera. Selection of photographs on website.

Bellport-Brookhaven Historical Society and Museum
31 Bellport Lane • Bellport, NY 11713 • (631) 776-7640
Email: president@bbhsmuseum.org • *www.bbhsmuseum.org*

Research facility includes manuscripts, documents, and photographs.

Brentwood Public Library: Local History Room
34 Second Avenue • Brentwood, NY 11717• (631) 273-7883
Email: history@suffolk.lib.ny.us • *www.brenhis.blogspot.com*

Books and pamphlets, newspapers, scrapbooks, photographs, maps, yearbooks, and oral histories relating to the history of Brentwood and Long Island. Website has digitized documents and links to resources for Suffolk County research.

Bridgehampton Historical Society
2539-A Montauk Highway • PO Box 977 • Bridgehampton, NY 11932
(631) 613-6730 • Email: bhhs@optonline.net
www.bridgehamptonhistoricalsociety.org

Books, family Bibles, letters, photographs, ephemera, and artifacts from Bridgehampton and Long Island.

Cutchogue-New Suffolk Historical Council
Route 25 at Case's Lane • PO Box 714 • Cutchogue, NY 11935-0714
Email: info@cutchoguenewsuffolkhistory.org
www.cutchoguenewsuffolkhistory.org

Maintains Old Burying Ground (est. 1717) and Cutchogue-New Suffolk Free Library, which is home to its Local History Center.

East Hampton Public Library: Long Island Collection
159 Main Street • East Hampton, NY 11937 • (631) 324-0222 ext. 4
www.easthamptonlibrary.org/history

Holds an extensive collection of books, atlases, deeds (over 800 online), family records, histories and genealogies, letters, maps, manuscripts, newspapers, whaling logs, and wills. Census holdings include original copies of 1865 New York state census for Suffolk County and transcript of 1845 New York state census for the Town of Smithtown, Suffolk County. Transcriptions of past history lectures online. Many items digitized at *www.easthamptonlibrary.org/history/digitalli.html*.

Greenlawn-Centerport Historical Association
Russel B. Brush Research Center: Harborfields Public Library
31 Broadway • Greenlawn, NY 11740
Association: PO Box 354 • Greenlawn, NY 11740 • (631) 754-1180
Email: GCHA-info@usa.net • *www.gcha.info*

Association's Research Center is located in the Harborfields Public Library; list of family names documented is on Association's website.

Hampton Bays Historical Society
140 West Montauk Highway • Hampton Bays, NY 11946-0588
(631) 728-0887 • *www.hamptonbayshistoricalsociety.org*

Holdings include books, periodicals, maps, photographs and postcards.

Huntington Historical Society: Resource Center & Archives, Museum, and Genealogy Workshop
209 Main Street • Huntington, NY 11743 • (631) 427-7045
www.huntingtonhistoricalsociety.org

Genealogies, books, atlases and maps, church records, cemetery records, manuscripts, military records, land records, newspapers, oral histories, photographs, and vertical files. Website includes detailed information on holdings, including list of family names documented in Special Collections.

Lake Ronkonkoma Historical Society and Museum
326 Hawkins Avenue • PO Box 2716 • Lake Ronkonkoma, NY 11779
(631) 467-3152 • Email: info@lakerhs.org • *www.lakerhs.org*

Holdings include photographs, artifacts, and archives.

Mattituck-Laurel Historical Society and Museums
Main Road (Route 25) at Cardinal Drive • PO Box 766
Mattituck, NY 11952 • (631) 298-5248
Email: webmaster@mlhistoricalsociety.org
www.mlhistoricalsociety.org

Maintains local history archive.

Moriches Bay Historical Society
15 Montauk Highway • Center Moriches, NY 11934 • (631) 878-1776
www.mbhs.info

Maintains local history collections.

Oysterponds Historical Society
Village Lane • PO Box 70 • Orient, NY 11957 • (631) 323-2480
www.oysterpondshistoricalsociety.org

Donald H. Boerum Research Library houses books, articles, photographs, and other materials documenting history of Orient and East Marion. Website includes archive location aid.

Greater Patchogue Historical Society
PO Box 102 • Patchogue, NY 11772 • (631) 475-7871
Email: gphsociety@yahoo.com
www.greaterpatchoguehistoricalsociety.com

Website includes information on and photographs of Swan River School House; lists and information on local men who served in Civil War; historic local postcards; and indexed photographs of local historic hotels.

The Historical Society of Greater Port Jefferson and Mather House Museum
115 Prospect Street • PO Box 586 • Port Jefferson, NY 11777
(631) 473-2665 • Email: info@portjeffhistorical.org
www.portjeffhistorical.org

Holdings include books, photographs, and artifacts.

Port Jefferson Village Digital Archive
101A East Broadway • Port Jefferson, NY 11777 • (631) 802-2165
Email: historian@portjeff.com • *www.portjeff.com/village-history*

Website includes historic photographs of local people, businesses, events, and buildings; list and information on local Civil War soldiers; and maps.

Quogue Historical Society
114 Jessup Avenue • PO Box 1207 • Quogue, NY 11959-1207
(631) 996-2404 • *www.quoguelibrary.org/history.htm*

Holds census materials, family Bible records, diaries, familiy trees and genealogies, letters, maps, and memorabilia.

Rocky Point Historical Society
PO Box 1720 • Rocky Point, NY 11778 • Email address on website
www.rockypointhistoricalsociety.org

Society published and sells the *Noah Hallock Cemetery of Rocky Point*, which includes complete transcriptions, cemetery maps, and genealogies of those interred.

John Jermain Memorial Library
34 West Water Street • Sag Harbor, NY 11963 • (631) 725-0049
www.johnjermain.org

Genealogies, maps, newspapers (1822–present), photographs, town records, information on local American Indian groups, and Sag Harbor births, deaths, and marriages.

Sag Harbor Historical Society
174 Main St. • PO Box 1709 • Sag Harbor, NY 11963-1709
(631) 725-5092 • Email: sagharborhist@gmail.com
www.sagharborhistoricalsociety.org

Books and documents, ledgers, letters and diaries, photographs, and postcards documenting history of Sag Harbor.

Three Village Historical Society
93 North Country Road • Setauket, NY 11733 • (631) 751-3730
Email: info@tvhs.org • *www.threevillagehistoricalsociety.org*

Society documents history of Villages of Old Field, Poquott, the eight Setaukets, and Stony Brook. Holdings include genealogical collection, deed history, and Captain R. Rhodes Memorial Collection of Local History. Society currently building genealogical database of over 60,000 individuals, based on primary source material.

Shelter Island Historical Society and Old Havens House
16 South Ferry Road • PO Box 847 • Shelter Island, NY 11964-0847
(631) 749-0025 • Email: sihissoc@optonline.net
www.ShelterIslandHistorical.org

Maps, correspondence, land surveys, publications, police records, legal records, photos, and town records beginning in the 1600s.

Smithtown Historical Society
239 Middle County Road • Smithtown, NY 11787 • (631) 265-6703

Holdings include account books, deeds, family Bibles, ledgers, cemetery records (private and public), diaries, recipe books, photographs, and personal papers from the Smith and other early families.

Smithtown Main Library:
Richard H. Handley Collection of Long Island Americana
One North Country Road • Smithtown, NY 11787
(631) 265-2072 ext. 189 • *www.smithlib.org/long-island-room*

Books, pamphlets, maps, archival boxes, historical account books, photographs, scrapbooks, and newspapers. Offers access to *Long Island Historical Journal: Digital Edition*.

Southampton Historical Museums and Research Center
17 Meeting House Lane • PO Box 303 • Southampton, NY 11969
(631) 283-2494 • Email: info@southamptonhistoricalmuseum.org

Family histories and genealogies, cemetery records, whaling logs, deeds, minutes of societies, account books, photographs and postcards, scrapbooks, family memorabilia, and maps.

Rogers Memorial Library: Long Island Collection
91 Coopers Farm Road • Southampton, NY 11968 • (631) 283-0774
Email: info@myrml.org • *www.myrml.org*

Books and periodicals, records, photographs and postcards, scrapbooks, vertical files, videos, and more documenting history and genealogy of Southampton, Shinnecock Indians, and the library. Website includes digital documents and photographs.

Southold Historical Society
54325 Main Road • PO Box 1 • Southold, NY 11971 • (631) 765-5500
Email: sohissoc@optonline.net • *www.southoldhistoricalsociety.org*

Holdings include collections of local photographers (1890s–1910s), family papers, information on African American and Polish/Lithuanian families (partial list of family names on website), and information on Camp Pinecrest Dunes (1931–1970).

SELECTED PRINT & ONLINE RESOURCES

Below is a selection of resources relevant for research in this county. The list is representative, not exhaustive. Additional titles—particularly of abstracts, indexes, transcriptions, and local histories—are available; consult the introduction to Part Two for further information. For guidance on how to identify and locate community directories and local newspapers, see chapter 11, City Directories, and chapter 12, Newspapers, in Part One of this book.

See also Selected Print and Online Resources—Long Island.

Abstracts, Indexes & Transcriptions

Bailey, Rosalie Fellows. "The Account Books of Henry Lloyd of the Manor of Queens Village." *Journal of Long Island History*, vol. 2, no. 1 (1962): 26–49.

Baldwin, Evelyn Briggs. "Marriages and Baptisms Performed by the Rev. Joshua Hartt [Smithtown, New York. First Presbyterian Church Records 1751–1867]." *NYG&B Record*, vol. 42 (1911) no. 2: 128–143, no. 3: 277–293. [NYG&B eLibrary] See also Robbins, William A., below.

Barber, Gertrude Audrey. "Deaths Taken from *The Republican Watchman*: A Newspaper Published Every Saturday Morning at Greenport, Suffolk County, NY, Covering Death Records for The Whole County." 5 vols. Typescript, 1949. NYPL, New York. Covers 1859–1900; vols. 4–5 also include deaths taken from the *South Side Signal*, Babylon, L.I., 1885–1900.

———. "Marriages of Suffolk County, NY: Taken from *The Republican Watchman*, A Newspaper Published at Greenport, NY." Typescript, 1950. *http://longislandgenealogy.com/MarriagesofSuffolk.pdf*

Barck, Dorothy C., ed. *Papers of the Lloyd Family of the Manor of Queens Village, Lloyd's Neck, Long Island, New York, 1654–1826.* Vols. 59–60 of *Collections of The New-York Historical Society*, New York: The Society, 1926–1927.

Blydenburgh, Jonas B., Albert G. Mulford, and J. Wickham Case, Marshall. "Smithtown Census, 1845." Typescript, 1941. East Hampton Library, East Hampton, NY.

Brown, Russell K. "Records of the Congregational Church, Orient, Long Island." *NYG&B Record*, vol. 136 (2005) no. 3: 173–182, no. 4: 285–295. [NYG&B eLibrary]

Calendar of Historical Manuscripts Relating to the War of the Revolution . . . . 2 vols. Albany: Weed, Parsons, 1868. 1776 census of Suffolk County, vol. 1: 378–417.

Cooper, Thomas W. *The Records of the Court of Sessions of Suffolk County in the Province of New York, 1670–1688.* Bowie, MD: Heritage Book, 1993.

Craven, Charles E. *A History of Mattituck, Long Island, NY.* Mattituck, NY: The Author, 1906. Includes Presbyterian church records of Mattituck and Aquebogue, 1751–1809.

Daughters of the American Revolution, comps. *New York DAR Genealogical Records Committee Report.* Since 1913 DAR volunteers have transcribed many thousands of unpublished cemetery, church, and town records throughout New York. The reports are at the DAR Library; copies are at the NYSL and the NYPL. The DAR has a searchable name index to all the GRC reports at *http://services.dar.org/Public/DAR_Research/search/?Tab_ID=6.* See Jean Worden's index below for a listing by county of the New York record sets that were transcribed by the DAR before 1998.

Dyson, Verne. *Deerpark—Wyandanch History.* Brentwood, NY: Brentwood Village Press, 1957. *http://cdm16373.contentdm.oclc.org/cdm/ref/collection/p15281coll20/id/445*

Eaton, James Waterbury. *History and Records of the First Presbyterian Church of Babylon, New York (1783–1857).* Babylon: The Church, 1912.

Harris, Edward Doubleday. *Ancient Long Island Epitaphs from the Towns of Southold, Shelter Island, and Easthampton, New York.* Baltimore: Genealogical Publishing Co., 2000. First published 1903 by David Clapp. From Harris's original records in NYG&B Collection, NYPL, which also include inscriptions from towns of Babylon, Brookhaven, Huntington, Riverhead, and Southampton.

Hazelton, Henry Isham. *The Boroughs of Brooklyn and Queens, Counties of Nassau and Suffolk, Long Island, New York, 1609–1924.* 6 vols. New York: Lewis Historical Publishing, 1925.

Healy, Clement. *South Fork Cemeteries.* Charleston, SC: Arcadia, 2006.

Hoff, Henry B. "[Episcopal] Baptisms at Islip, Long Island, 1782–1789." *NYG&B Record*, vol. 121, no. 3 (1990): 135–138. [NYG&B eLibrary]

———. "Families and Sources in the Suffolk County Historical Society Register." *NYG&B Newsletter* (now *New York Researcher*), Fall 2000. Updated May 2011 and published as a Research Aid on *NewYorkFamilyHistory.org.*

Horton, Jonathan. "Baiting Hollow Census, 1825. With Notes, by James F. Young." N.p., 1906. See also *Suffolk County Historical Register*, vol. 7, no. 4 (Mar 1982).

Howell, George Rogers. *The Early History of Southampton, L.I., New York, with Genealogies.* 2nd edition. Albany: Weed, Parsons, 1887.

Huntting, Rev. Nathaniel. "Records of Marriages, Baptisms, and Deaths in East Hampton, L.I., from 1696 to 1746 [Records of the First Church [Presbyterian] of East Hampton, New York]." *NYG&B Record*, vol. 24 (1893) no. 4: 183–194; vol. 25 (1894) no. 1: 35–40, no. 3: 139–142, no. 4: 196–197; vol. 26 (1895) no. 1: 38–44; vol. 28 (1897) no. 2: 109–110; vol. 29 (1898) no. 1: 18–21, no. 3: 166–170; vol. 30 (1899) no. 1: 40–42; vol. 33 (1902) no. 2: 81–86, no. 3: 150–156, no. 4: 223–227; vol. 34 (1903) no. 1: 7–11, no. 2: 112–117, no. 3: 166–171, no. 4: 251–258. [NYG&B eLibrary]

Jefferson, Wayland. *Cutchogue, Southold's First Colony.* New York: The Author, 1940. Includes Presbyterian church records of Cutchogue: 142–166.

Jefferson, Wayland, and DeWitt Van Buren. "Records of the First Church [Presbyterian] of Southold, Long Island." *NYG&B Record*, vol. 64 (1933) no. 3: 217–227, no. 4: 322–330; vol. 65 (1934) no. 1: 47–55, no. 2: 152–158, no. 3: 261–266, no. 4: 339–344; vol. 66 (1935) no. 1: 51–58, no. 3: 257–269. Baptismal records 1763–1832, marriages 1769–1891. [NYG&B eLibrary]

Jones, John H. "Inscriptions on Gravestones: Inscriptions Taken from the Old Cemetery at Huntington, Suffolk Co., L.I., 1701–1850." *NYG&B Record*, vol. 31 (1900) no. 2: 111–115, no. 3: 142–144, no. 4: 247–250; vol. 32 (1901) no. 1: 47–52, no. 2: 89–96, no. 3: 176–179, no. 4: 228–230; vol. 33 (1902) no. 2: 97–100. [NYG&B eLibrary]

Kearney, Michael. "A List of Persons in Suffolk County, Long Island, Who Took the Oath of Allegiance and Peaceable Behavior before Governor Tryon, 1778." *NYG&B Record*, vol. 142 (2011): no. 2: 98–106, no. 3: 226–236, no. 4: 260–264; vol. 143 (2012) no. 1: 65–74. [NYG&B eLibrary]

Kelby, William. "Brookhaven (Long Island) Epitaphs." *NYG&B Record*, vol. 16 (1885) no. 3: 131–133; vol. 17 (1886) no. 4: 259–260; vol. 21 (1890) no. 2: 73–81. [NYG&B eLibrary]

King, Rufus. "Long Island (NY) Marriages and Deaths from the *Suffolk Gazette*." *NYG&B Record*, vol. 24 (1893) no. 2: 86–88, no. 4: 159–161; vol. 25 (1894) no. 1: 6–8, no. 2: 89–92, no. 3: 137–139, no. 4: 161–164. [NYG&B eLibrary]

"List of Freeholders, Smithtown, Long Island, NY [1810–1820]." *NYG&B Record*, vol. 56, no. 2 (1925): 102–103. [NYG&B eLibrary]

Lloyd, J. *Tombstone Names in Suffolk County, New York*. Long Beach, CA: M. S. Lloyd, 1986.

MacCormick, Elizabeth Janet, comp. "Inscriptions from Six Cemeteries of Suffolk County, Long Island, New York." Typescript, 1938. NYPL, New York. [NYG&B elibrary]

Macoskey, Arthur R. *Long Island Gazetteer: A Guide to Historic Places*. Brooklyn: Eagle Library, 1939.

Mallman, Jacob. *Historical Papers on Shelter Island and Its Presbyterian Church* . . . . New York, 1899. Census of Shelter Island for 1771: 62 and 1776: 63.

Marriages and Deaths from the Account Book of Darling Whitney and Daniel Darling Whitney of Woodbury, Long Island, New York 1808–1848: Towns of Huntington and Oyster Bay. Huntington, NY: Huntington American Revolution Bicentennial Committee, 1977.

Meigs, Alice. *Suffolk County Cemeteries [Inscriptions]*. 7 vols. Typescript. Queens Library Archives, Queens, New York, 1935. [FHL] For the 125 cemeteries covered, see *www.queenslibrary.org/item/suffolk-county-cemeteries*.

New York Genealogical and Biographical Record. New York, NY: The Society, 1870–present. Numerous Suffolk Bible records have been transcribed in the *Record* [NYG&B eLibrary]; multiple indexes to the *Record* are freely available on *NewYorkFamilyHistory.org*.

O'Callaghan, Edmund B. *Documentary History of the State of New York*. 4 vols. Albany, 1849–1851. vol. 1, census 1698, vol. 2 town rate lists 1675, 1683; vol. 4, list of freeholders 1737.

Pelletreau, William S. "A Complete List of all the Brownstone and Slate Tombstone Inscriptions in the North End Burying Ground, Southampton, Long Island." *NYG&B Record*, vol. 46, no. 1 (1915): 19–26. [NYG&B eLibrary]

———. *Early Long Island Wills of Suffolk County, 1691–1703: An Unabridged Copy of the Manuscript Volume Known as "The Lester Will Book," Being the Record of the Prerogative Court of the County of Suffolk, New York: With Genealogical and Historical Notes*. New York, 1897.

Rattray, Jeannette Edwards. *East Hampton History Including Genealogies of Early Families*. East Hampton, NY: The Author, 1953.

The Revised Statutes of the State of New-York, Passed During the Years One Thousand Eight Hundred and Twenty-Seven, and One Thousand Eight Hundred and Twenty-Eight: To Which Are Added, Certain Former Acts Which Have Not Been Revised. 3 vols. Albany, 1829.

Robbins, William A. "The Records of the Presbyterian Church of Smithtown, Suffolk Co." *NYG&B Record*, vol. 44 (1913) no. 3: 279–285, no. 4: 384–389; vol. 45 (1914) no. 1: 8–16. See also Baldwin, above. [NYG&B e-library]

———. "The Salmon Records [Vital Records, Southold, New York]." *NYG&B Record*, vol. 47 (1916) no. 4: 344–360; vol. 48 (1917) no. 1: 20–32, no. 2: 134–179; no. 3: 275–290; no. 4: 341–351; vol. 49 (1918) no. 1: 64–75, no. 2: 154–165, no. 3: 265–279. [NYG&B eLibrary]

Roberts, David. *Deaths Reported by the* Long Islander *1878–1890*. Bowie, MD: Heritage Books, 1998. Roberts also produced a similar index to marriages, published on *longislandgenealogy.com*, which includes his "Long Island Gazetteer" identifying places named in the death notices, with useful notes.

Scott, Kenneth. "Absentee Patriots from British-Occupied Suffolk County, L.I., 1778," *NYG&B Record*, vol. 107, no. 2 (1978): 73–78. [NYG&B eLibrary]

———. "Middle Island Court Records, 1774–1776." *Journal of Long Island History*, vol. 4, no. 1 (1964).

———. "Suffolk County Inhabitants in 1778." *NYG&B Record*, vol. 104, no. 4 (1973): 225–230. [NYG&B eLibrary]. A different version in Scott, Kenneth. "Suffolk County, New York, 1778 Census." *National Genealogical Society Quarterly*, vol. 63, no. 4 (1975): 276–283.

Scudder, Moses L. *Records of the First Church [Presbyterian] in Huntington, Long Island, 1723–1779, Being the Record Kept by the Rev. Ebenezer Prime* . . . . Huntington, NY, 1899. Original records including later years are on microfilm NYPL.

Smith, Edward H. L. III. "1798 Property Valuations for Western Suffolk County." *NYG&B Record*, vol. 127, no. 1 (1996): 12–16. [NYG&B eLibrary]

Smith, Leroy. "Marriages, Cutchogue, New York, 1787–1797." *The American Genealogist*, vol. 18, no. 2 (1941): 118.

———. "Middle Island Presbyterian Church, Marriages 1818–1862." *The American Genealogist*, vol. 19, no. 2 (1942): 110.

"St. James, Suffolk County, New York Census of 1892." Manuscript. NYPL: Milstein Division, New York Genealogical and Biographical Society Collection: Locale Files: NYGB Loc 2008-001.

Stryker-Rodda, Harriet Mott. "Land Records of Huntting, Mulford & Allied Families of East Hampton, Suffolk Co., NY, 1705–80." Manuscript, 1975. Manuscript & Archives Division, New York Genealogical and Biographical Society Localities Files. NYPL, New York.

Suffolk County Church Surveys. Digitally published by New York Genealogical & Biographical Society, 2012. [NYG&B elibrary]

Van Buren, Elizabeth R. "Abstracts of Wills of Suffolk County, New York, 1787–1847." 3 vols. Typescript, n.d. NYPL, New York.

———. "Intestate Records of Suffolk County Recorded at Riverhead, New York." Typescript, n.d. NYPL, New York. Contains transcription of libers A–F, 1787–1840.

Worden, Jean D. "Book 1, Subject Index." In *Revised Master Index to the New York State Daughters of the American Revolution Genealogical Records Volumes*. Zephyrhills, FL: J. D. Worden, 1998. The Subject Index includes a listing by county of the cemeteries, churches, towns, and other sources of records transcribed by the DAR.

Town Records

Alphabetized by town; for Babylon, see Huntington

Weeks, William J., Osborn Shaw, et al., eds. *Records of the Town of Brookhaven Book A 1657–1679 and 1790–1798; Book B 1679–1756; Book C 1687–1879*. New York: Derrydale Press, 1930–1932.

Records of the Town of East-Hampton, Long Island, Suffolk Co., NY: With Other Ancient Documents of Historic Value. 9 vols. Sag Harbor, NY: J. Hunt, 1887–1957.

Langhans, Rufus B., ed. Huntington/Babylon Land Deeds 1663–1797. 6 vols. Huntington and Babylon, NY: The Towns of Huntington and Babylon, 1985.

———, ed. Huntington Ear Marks and Stray Sheep 1745–1831. Huntington, NY: Town of Huntington, 1989.

———. Index Huntington Land Grant Surveys 1697–1787, and Land Grants 1688–1802. Huntington, NY: Office of the Town Historian, 1980.

———. Personal Name Index to Huntington Town Records Including Babylon ... 1653–1873, Volumes I, II, III. Huntington, NY: Office of Historian, 1978. Index to Street, see below.

———. School Trustee Annual Census Reports, 1827–1863. Huntington, NY: Town of Huntington, 1982. The censuses show parent's name and number of his or her children in school that year.

———, ed. Town of Huntington, Records of the Overseers of the Poor: Addendum, 1729–1843. Huntington, NY: Town of Huntington, 1992.

Langhans, Rufus B., and Dorothy Flowers Koopman, eds. Huntington Court Records 1657–1700 and Duke's Law[s], 1664. Huntington, NY: Town Board, 1994.

Langhans, Rufus B., ed. Manumission Book of the Towns of Huntington & Babylon ... 1800–1824. Huntington, NY: Office of the Town Historian, 1980.

———, eds, Vital Statistics, Marriage, Deaths, & Births, Town of Huntington ... 1847–1849. Huntington, NY: Office of the Town Historian, 1980.

O'Neil, John J., Rufus B. Langhans, and Town of Huntington NY, eds. Town of Huntington Records of the Overseers of the Poor: Part 1, 1752–1804, [bonds for births out of wedlock] and Part 2, 1805–1861 [Accounts for care of the poor]. Huntington, NY: Town of Huntington, 1986.

Street, Charles R., ed. Huntington Town Records, Including Babylon, Long Island, NY, 1776–1873, with Introduction, Notes and Index. 3 vols. Huntington and Babylon, 1887–1889. Vol. 1, 1653–1688, vol. 2, 1688–1775, vol. 3 1776–1873. Census of Huntington, 1790, vol. 3: 147–158

Starace, Carl A., ed. Book One of the Minutes of Town Meetings and Register of Animal Ear Marks of the Town of Islip 1720–1851. Islip: The Town, 1982.

Riverhead Town Records 1792–1886. Huntington, NY: Long Islander for the Town, 1967.

Pelletreau, William S., ed. Town Records of Smithtown, Long Island, NY, with Other Documents of Historical Value. Huntington, NY, 1898.

Records of the Town of Southampton 1639–1927. 8 vols. Southampton: By the Town, 1874–1930.

Case, J. Wickham, ed. Southold Town Records. 2 vols. New York, 1882–1884. Libers A–C, including history of Plum Island Manor. See also Southold Town Records, below.

Southold Town Records, Vol. 3 (Liber D, 1683–1856). Southold: Academy Printing, 1983. See also Case, above.

Other Resources

Atlas of a Part of Suffolk County, Long Island, New York. South Side—Ocean Shore. Complete in Two Volumes. Based upon Actual Measurements by Our Own Corps of Engineers, Maps on File at County Offices, Also Maps from Actual Surveys Furnished by Individual Owners. New York: E. Belcher Hyde, 1915–1916.

Barstow, Belle. Setauket, Alias Brookhaven: The Birth of a Long Island Town: With the Chronological Records, 1655–1679. Bloomington, IN: Author House, 2004.

Bayles, Richard M. Historical and Descriptive Sketches of Suffolk County and Its Towns, Villages, Hamlets, Scenery, Institutions, and Important Enterprises: With a Historical Outline of Long Island, from Its First Settlement by Europeans. Port Jefferson, NY, 1874.

Bayles, Thomas R. The Ten Towns of Suffolk County, Long Island, New York. Middle Island, NY: T. R. Bayles, 1964.

Bi-Centennial History of Suffolk County: Comprising the Addresses Delivered at the Celebration of the Bi-Centennial of Suffolk County, NY, in Riverhead, November 15, 1883. Babylon, NY, 1885.

Duffield, Rev. Howard, D. The Tangier Smith Manor of St. George: Address ... Order of the Colonial Lords of the Manor .... Baltimore: n.p., 1921. Publication No. 8. [persi.heritagequestonline.com]

Eberlein, Harold Donaldson. Manor Houses and Historic Homes of Long Island and Staten Island. New York: J. B. Lippincott, 1928.

Ferguson, Henry L. Fishers Island, NY, 1614–1925. New York: n.p., 1925.

Gardiner, David. Chronicles of the Town of Easthampton, County of Suffolk, New York. New York, 1871. Book includes transcript of original grant for Gardiner's Island.

Halsey, Abigail. Two Hundred and Seventy-Five Years of East Hampton, Long Island, New York: A Historical Sketch, by Samuel Seabury, Together with the Book of the Pageant Celebrating the Two Hundred and Seventy-Fifth Anniversary of the Founding of the Town. East Hampton, NY: Published for the Community, 1926.

Havemeyer, Harry W. Along the Great South Bay: From Oakdale to Babylon, the Story of a Summer Spa 1840–1940. Mattituck, NY: Amereon House, 1996.

———. East on the Great South Bay: Sayville and Bayport 1860–1960. Mattituck, NY: Amereon House, 2001.

Hedges, Henry P. A History of East Hampton: Including an Address Delivered at the Celebration of the Bi-Centennial Anniversary of Its Settlement in 1849, Introductions to the Four Printed Volumes of Its Records, and Other Historical Material, and Appendix and Genealogical Notes. Sag-Harbor, NY, 1897. Index available; supplements publishers' index with index of genealogy section.

History of Suffolk County, New York: With Illustrations, Portraits, and Sketches of Prominent Families and Individuals. New York, 1882.

Home Town Long Island: The History of Every Community on Long Island in Stories and Photographs. Melville, NY: Newsday, 1999.

Horsford, Cornelia. The Manor of Shelter Island; An Address Read before the Annual Meeting of the Order of Colonial Lords and Manors in America on April 23, 1931. New York: The Society, 1934. [Ancestry.com]

Howell, Nathaniel R. Know Suffolk, the Sunrise County, Then and Now. Islip, NY: Buys Bros, 1952.

Jacobson, Judy. *Southold Connections: Historical and Biographical Sketches of Northeastern Long Island*. Baltimore: Genealogical Publishing Co., 1991.

Jefferson, Wayland, and S. Wentworth Horton. *Southold Town, Suffolk County, New York With Genealogies of the Founding Families*. Mattituck, NY: Mattituck Press, 1938.

Lightfoot, Frederick S., Linda B. Martin, and Bette S. Weidman. *Suffolk County, Long Island, In Early Photographs, 1867–1951*. New York: Dover, 1984.

McDermott, Charles J. *Suffolk County*. New York: J. H. Heineman, 1965.

Moore, Charles B. *Town of Southold, Long Island: Personal Index Prior to 1698 and Index of 1698*. New York: J. Medole, 1868.

Nicoll, Henry. *Early History of Suffolk County, L.I.* Brooklyn, 1866.

Onderdonk, Henry. *Revolutionary Incidents of Suffolk and Kings Counties; with an Account of the Battle of Long Island and the British Prisons and Prison-Ships at New York*. Port Washington, NY: Kennikat Press, 1970. First published 1849.

Petty, Joseph H. "Collections, Historical & Genealogical, of Suffolk County, New York." Manuscript. 1878. NYPL, New York.

Portrait and Biographical Record of Suffolk County (Long Island) New York: Containing Portraits and Biographical Sketches of Prominent and Representative Citizens of the County. . . . New York and Chicago, 1896.

Scott, Kenneth, and Susan E. Klaffky. *A History of the Joseph Lloyd Manor House*. Setauket, NY: Society for the Preservation of Long Island Antiquities, 1976.

The Setaukets, Old Field, and Poquott. Charleston, SC: Arcadia, 2005.

Simpson, Robert L. *An Index to the* Long Islander *1865–1881 Marriages-Deaths*. Huntington, NY: Huntington American Revolution Bicentennial Committee, 1976. See also Stevens, below.

Spinzia, Raymond E., and Judith A. Spinzia. *Long Island's Prominent Families in the Town of Southampton, Their Estates and Their Country Homes*. College Station, TX: VirtualBookworm. 2010.

———. *Long Island's Prominent South Shore Families: Their Estates and Their Country Homes in the Towns of Babylon and Islip*. College Station, TX: VirtualBookworm, 2007. With maiden names, occupations, architects, etc.

Stevens, Marian F. *An Index to the* Long Islander *1839–1864 Marriages–Deaths*. Huntington, NY: Huntington Historical Society and Huntington American Revolution Bicentennial Committee, 1974. See Simpson, above, for later years,

Stone, Gaynell. *The History and Archaeology of the Montauk*. Stony Brook, NY: Suffolk County Archaeological Association: Nassau County Archaeological Committee, 1993.

Suffolk County Historical Society Register. Riverhead, NY: Suffolk County Historical Society, 1975–present.

Titus, Stephen A. *History of Suffolk County*. Babylon, NY, 1885.

Tyler, Sarah Gardiner. *The Gardiner Manor*. Baltimore: n.p., 1916.

Voyse, Mary, and Sydney Bevin. *History of Eaton's Neck, Long Island, Together with Its Geological Background*. N.p., 1955.

Windesheim, Susan, and Peter Windesheim, eds., *Index to the Huntington Rural Cemetery 1853–1990*. Huntington, NY: Huntington Historical Society Genealogy Workshop, 1998.

Wood, Silas. *A Sketch of the First Settlement of the Several Towns on Long Island: With Their Political Condition, to the End of the American Revolution*. Brooklyn, NY, 1828.

Wood, Simeon. *A History of Hauppauge, Long Island: With Genealogies of the Wheeler, Smith, "Bull" Smith, Blydenburgh, Wood, Rolph, Hubbs, Price, McCrone, and Germond Families*. Hauppauge, NY: J. Marr Publishing, 1981. Originally published 1920.

Woolsey, Rev. Lloyd M. *The Winthrop Manor of Fishers Island*. Baltimore: n.p., 1927.

Additional Online Resources

Ancestry.com

> There are vast numbers of records on *Ancestry.com* that pertain to people who have lived in New York State. See chapter 16 for a description of *Ancestry.com*'s resources and its partnership with the New York State Archives. A search of the online card catalog by county may reveal lesser known resources that pertain to a locality, such as town records, abstracts, transcriptions, city directories, and local histories.

Brookhaven/South Haven Hamlets and Their People

www.brookhavensouthhaven.org/hamletpeople/tng/index.php

> Histories and Genealogies of the Families of Brookhaven and South Haven Hamlets, Suffolk County, NY.

Brooklyn Genealogy Information

http://bklyn-genealogy-info.stevemorse.org

> Contains information relating to New York City and Long Island, including links and tips for general genealogical research. Particular records relating to Suffolk County include: directories (1868–1869 and 1909–1913), history of local post offices, Pelletreau's *Early Long Island Wills* (1691–1703), historic maps, military information, *Long Island Star* extracts, and house of worship directories.

FamilySearch

> FamilySearch has extensive collections of New York records, including religious records, which are searchable by name and location, but not by county. The following collection includes record images (browsable, but not searchable) that are organized by county:

> • "New York, Land Records, 1630–1975." Includes land and property records. *familysearch.org/search/collection/2078654*

> Choose the browse option and then select Suffolk to view the available records sets.

> A detailed description of *FamilySearch.org* resources, which include the catalog of the Family History Library, is found in chapter 16.

German Genealogy Group and Italian Genealogy Group:
The Suffolk County Naturalization Project/Index

www.germangenealogygroup.com or *www.italiangen.org/suffolk.stm*

> Searchable index of Suffolk County Petitions for Naturalization and Declarations of Intention, 1853–1990.

> German Genealogy Group databases include Index to the Orville B. Ackerly Collection at the Suffolk County Historical Society, a huge collection of transcriptions of early unrecorded Suffolk deeds and other documents, and an index to notices of births, marriages, deaths, etc., in the newspaper the *Amityville Record*, 1904–1944.

Live-Library.com

suffolktopicguides.org

This webpage is offered by the Public Libraries of Suffolk County. The webpage has a list of research topics, including genealogy. The genealogy page is divided into subjects ranging from census records to New York State records. Each subject page has a YouTube video on the basics of research that topic, and has links to online, Long Island, New York State, and general genealogical resources.

New York Heritage Digital Collections:
New York State Newspaper Project

www.nyheritage.org/newspapers

The website provides links to digital newspapers collections in 26 counties (currently) made accessible through New York Heritage, New York State Historic Newspapers, HRVH Historical Newspapers, and other providers.

NYGenWeb Project: Suffolk County

www.rootsweb.ancestry.com/~nysuffol

Part of the national, USGenWeb volunteer initiative, the website provides information and resources for county research.

Suffolk County Historical Newspaper Archive

www.live-brary.com/historic-newspapers

This database includes local newspaper titles including the *Corrector* (Sag Harbor, 1822–1911); the *Long Island Traveler* (Cutchogue, 1872–1898); the *Long Islander* (Huntington, 1839–1974); the *Mid–Island Mail* (Medford Station, 1935–1941); the *Patchogue Advance* (1926–1948); the *Port Jefferson Echo* (1892–1931); *Sag Harbor Express* (1885–1898); *South Side Signal* (Babylon, 1869–1879): *Suffolk County News* (Saville, 1888–1953; 1996–2007).

Sullivan County

Formed March 27, 1809

Parent County   Ulster
Daughter Counties   None
County Seat   Village of Monticello, Town of Thompson

Major Land Transactions
See table in chapter 7, Land Records
Minisink Patent 1704
Hardenbergh Patent 1708

Town Boundary Map
★ - County seat

Towns (and Cities)	Villages and other Settlements		Notes
Bethel c. 1798 Settled 1809 Formed from Town of Lumberland 1828 Daughter town Cochecton formed	Bethel Black Lake Briscoe Bushville Forestine Fulton Settlement	Hurd Kauneonga Lake Mongaup Valley Smallwood White Lake	• Bethel (Yasgur's Farm) was the location of the Woodstock music festival in 1969 • Bushville on Thompson town line • Fulton (Fuller) Settlement settled c.1806 • Hurd also Hurd Settlement • Kauneonga Lake formerly North White Lake • Mongaup Valley formerly Mongaup Mill • Smallwood formerly Mountain Lakes
Callicoon 1814 Settled 1842 Formed from Town of Liberty 1851 Daughter town Fremont formed	Buck Brook Callicoon Callicoon Center Jeffersonville (v)	North Branch Shandelee Wood Settlement Youngsville	• Buck Brook on Fremont town line • Callicoon also Callicoon Depot and Collikoon; on Delaware town line • Callicoon Center formerly Thu(r)mansville • Village of Jeffersonville inc. 1924; also Village of Winkelried
Cochecton Settled pre-Revolution, then abandoned 1828 Formed from Town of Bethel 1869 Daughter town Delaware formed	Beech Wood Callicoon Depot Cochecton Cochecton Center East Cochecton Fosterdale	Lake Huntington Nobody Station Pike Pond Skinners Falls Tylertown	• Beech Wood in Town of Delaware after 1869 • Callicoon Depot in Town of Delaware after 1869 • Hamlet of Cochecton formerly Cushetunk, also Cashington • Cochecton Center formerly Stephensburgh • Pike Pond now Kenoza Lake in Town of Delaware
Delaware 1768 Settlers from New Jersey, abandoned during the Revolutionary War 1869 Formed from Town of Cohecton	Beech Wood Callicoon Falls Mills Hortonville Kenoza Lake	Kohlertown Lower Beechwood Nobodys Rock Run Upper Beechwood	• Beech Wood in Town of Cochecton before 1869 • Callicoon formerly Callicoon Depot; on Callicoon town line • Kenoza Lake formerly Pike Pond in Town of Cochecton
Fallsburg(h) Settled by Germans pre-Revolution, then abandoned 1826 Formed from towns of Neversink and Thompson	Bradley Dennistons Ford Divine(s) Corners Fallsburg(h) Gardnerville Glen Wild Glenwood Hasbrouck Hurleyville	Hurleyville Station Loch Sheldrake Luzon Station Mountain Dale Prince's Hollow South Fallsburg(h) Woodbourne Woodridge (v)	• Bradley on Neversink town line • Hamlet of Fallsburg(h) formerly Falls of the Neversink, Lockwoods Mills, Neversink Falls, and Old Falls • Glen Wild formerly Miller Settlement; on Thompson town line • Loch Sheldrake also Schoonmaker Settlement • Mountain Dale also Sandburg(h) • South Fallsburg(h) formerly Fallsburgh Station and Mitchell Station • Village of Woodridge inc. 1911; formerly Centreville and Centerville Station; incorporated as Woodridge

Towns (and Cities)	Villages and other Settlements		Notes
Forestburgh Settled pre-Revolution; settled again in 1795 1837 Formed from towns of Mamakating and Thompson	Barnums Station Barryville Draketown Forestburg(h) Forestburgh Corners Forest Glen Fowler(s)ville Gillmans Station Handy Town	Hartwood Hartwood Club Merriewold Park Newfoundland Oakland Valley Perkinsville Philwold Saint Josephs Squirrels Corner	
Fremont 1851 Formed from Town of Callicoon	Acidalia Basket Buck Brook Fernwood Fremont Center Hankins Hankins Station	Lakewood Long Eddy Mileses Obernburg(h) Pleasant Valley Tennanah Lake	• Buck Brook on Callicoon town line • Hankins Station renamed Fremont Station 1851, but soon reverted to Hankins Station • Long Eddy also Basket Switch, Basket Station, and Douglass Village • Mileses formerly Milesville • Obernburg(h) also Fremont • Tennanah Lake formerly Long Pond
Highland Settled at Narrow Falls late 1700s 1853 Formed from Town of Lumberland	Barryville Eldred Highland Lake	Minisink Ford Narrow Falls Yulan	• Eldred formerly Half-Way Brook and Lumberland; see Town of Lumberland before 1853
Liberty 1793–94 Settlers from Connecticut near Liberty village 1807 Formed in Ulster County from Town of Lumberland 1809 Transferred to new county of Sullivan 1842 Daughter town Callicoon formed, ceded land to Town of Thompson	Blue Mountain Settlement Cooley Dahlia Egypt Ferndale Glen Cove Liberty (v) Liberty Falls	Liberty Village Loomis Marcy Heights Parksville Red Brick Strongtown Swan Lake White Sulphur Springs	• Ferndale formerly Liberty; on Thompson town line • Glen Cove formerly Dowtonville • Village of Liberty inc. 1870 • Swan Lake formerly Stevensville • White Sulphur Springs formerly Robertsonville or Robinsonville
Lumberland Settled before Revolution 1798 Formed in Ulster County from Town of Mamakating 1807 Daughter town Liberty formed 1809 Transferred to new county of Sullivan; daughter town Bethel formed 1853 Daughter towns Highland and Tusten formed	Carpenters Basin Deckers Dock Glen Spey Hillside Kings Eddy Lebanon Lumberland Mohican Lake	Mongaup Narrowsburg(h) Parkers Glen Pond Eddy Rosas South Lebanon Upper Mongaup	• Lumberland, see Eldred in Town of Highland after 1853 • Mohican Lake also Long Pond • Narrowsburg(h) also Big Eddy and Homans Eddy; in Town of Tusten after 1853 • Pond Eddy also Kilgour
Mamakating c. 1700 Settled 1743 Mamakating precinct formed in Ulster County; area previously called Wagackkemeck and embraced all of future Sullivan County and part of Orange County * 1788 Recognized as a town by State of New York	Bloomingburg(h) (v) Burlingham Culvertown Haven High View		* Mamakating also Mama-Kating and Mame-Kating; Wagackkemeck also Warensackemack • Village of Bloomingburg(h) inc. 1833; county seat in 1809 when county was formed; in 1810 county seat moved to Monticello • Burlingham also Searsville • Haven also Brownville • High View also Highview Station

(Mamakating continued on next page)

Towns (and Cities)	Villages and other Settlements		Notes
Mamakating (continued) 1798 Daughter towns formed: Deerpark in Orange County and Lumberland in Ulster County 1803 Daughter town Thompson formed 1809 Transferred to new county of Sullivan 1837 Daughter town Forestburgh formed	Homowack Mamakating Park Mount Prosper New Vernon Phillipsport Pleasant Valley Red Hill	Roosa Gap Spring Glen Summitville West Brookville Winterton Wurtsboro (v) Yankee Lake	• Homowack shared with Town of Wawarsing, Ulster County • Phillipsport also Lockport • West Brookville formerly Bashshusville or Bashasville • Village of Wurstboro inc. 1866; formerly Rome; also Mamakating Hollow, Wirtzboro, and Wurtsborough, and Wurtzboro
Neversink 1743 Settled; abandoned during Revolution 1798 Formed in Ulster County from Town of Rochester 1809 Transferred to new county of Sullivan; daughter town Rockland formed 1826 Daughter town Fallsburg(h) formed	Aden Bittersweet Bradley Cat's Paw Claryville Curry(s) Dewittsville Eureka	Grahamsville Hall(s) Mills Hog Rock Le Roy Corners Lowes Corners Neversink Unionville Willowemoc	• Bittersweet destroyed by Neversink Reservoir • Bradley on Fallsburg(h) town line • Eureka flooded for Roundout Reservoir • Neversink formerly Neversink Flats; original settlement flooded for Neversink Reservoir; current settlement was built nearby • Willowemoc formerly Willowcanoe; on Rockland town line
Rockland 1789 Settlers from Middletown, CT 1809 Formed from Town of Neversink	Anderson Beaverkill Craigie Clair Debruce Deckertown Grooville Hazel Joscelyn	Lew Beach Livingston Manor Morsston Parkston Rockland Roscoe Willowemoc	• Craigie Clair also Craigeclare • Grooville formerly Emmonsville • Lew Beach also Lewbeach, formerly Shin Creek • Livingston Manor not part of Livingston Manor patent; called Purvis before 1882 • Hamlet of Rockland also Westfield Flats • Roscoe formerly Westfield Flats • Willowemoc formerly Willowcanoe; on Neversink town line
Thompson Settled at Thompsonville 1803 Formed in Ulster County from Town of Mamakating 1809 Transferred to new county of Sullivan 1826 Daughter town Fallsburg(h) formed 1837 Daughter town Forestburgh formed 1842 Annexed land from Town of Liberty	Bridgeville Bushville Coopers Corners Emerald Green Ferndale Gales Glen Wild Harris Kiamesha Lake Maplewood Melody Lake	Monticello (v) Rock Hill Sackett Lake South Woods Starlight Strong Settlement Tannersdale Thompsons Station Thompsonville Washington Heights	• Bushville on Bethel town line • Ferndale on Liberty town line • Glen Wild formerly Miller Settlement; on Fallsburg(h) town line • Kiamesha Lake called Kiamesha before 1938 • Village of Monticello inc. 1830; county seat from 1810; county seat formerly at Bloomingburg, Town of Mamakating • Thompsonville formerly Albion
Tusten 1853 Formed from Town of Lumberland	Beaver Brook (Corners) Delaware Bridge Dutch Settlement Hunts Corners Irish Settlement	Lava Narrowsburg(h) Neweiden Smith Switch Ten Mile River (Village) Tusten	• Narrowsburg(h) also Big Eddy and Homans Eddy; in Town of Lumberland before 1853 • Neweiden also Swamp Mills • Tusten formerly Tusten Settlement

NEW YORK STATE CENSUS RECORDS

See also chapter 3, Census Records

County originals at Sullivan County Historical Society: 1855, 1865, 1875, 1892, 1915, 1925 (1825, 1835, 1845, and 1905 are lost)

State originals at the NYSA: 1915, 1925

Microfilm at the FHL, NYPL, and NYSL; many years are online at *FamilySearch.org* and *Ancestry.com*.

NATIONAL/STATEWIDE REPOSITORIES & RESOURCES

See chapter 16

COUNTYWIDE REPOSITORIES & RESOURCES

Sullivan County Clerk
Sullivan County Government Center • 100 North Street
PO Box 5012 • Monticello, NY 12701-5012 • (845) 807-0411
www.co.sullivan.ny.us

Holdings include land records, naturalization records (1903–1950s), and court records.

Sullivan County – Town, and Village Clerks
Birth, marriage, and death records are maintained by the clerk of the municipality in which the event occurred; see Introduction to County Guides for details of other records which may also be held by municipal clerks. For contact information, see the Sullivan County Directory at *www.co.sullivan.ny.us*.

Sullivan County Surrogate's Court
Sullivan County Government Center • 100 North Street
Monticello, NY 12701 • (845) 807-0690

Holds probate records from 1800 to the present. Also see chapter 6, Probate Records.

Sullivan County Public Libraries
Sullivan is part of the Ramapo Catskill Library System; see *www.rcls. org* to access each library. Many hold local history collections. For example, Liberty Public Library's collection includes local yearbooks dating from 1919.

Sullivan County Historical Society and Museum
265 Main Street • PO Box 247 • Hurleyville, NY 12747
(845) 434-8044 • Email: SCHS@SullivanCountyHistory.org
www.sullivancountyhistory.org

Holdings include original Sullivan County censuses 1855, 1865, 1875, 1892, 1915, and 1925, and *Liberty Register* and *Liberty Gazette* on microfilm. Website includes cemetery information, local history articles for Sullivan County towns, and historical photographs. Offers genealogical research services for a fee. Has published the *Observer*, bimonthly since 1963.

Sullivan County Historian
PO Box 185 • Barryville, NY 12719

Sullivan County – All Municipal Historians
While not authorized to answer genealogical inquiries, city, town and village historians can provide valuable historical information and research advice to family historians; some maintain collections with genealogical material. Some historians also have webpages with local histories, transcribed records, links to useful resources and other genealogical information. For contact information, see County Directory at *www.co.sullivan.ny.us*.

REGIONAL REPOSITORIES & RESOURCES

Bard College Archives and Special Collections
See listing in Dutchess County Guide

LOCAL REPOSITORIES & RESOURCES

Alphabetized by location

Fort Delaware Museum
6615 Route 97 • Narrowsburg, NY 12764
(845) 807-0261 (September-April) • (845) 252-6660 (May-August)
www.co.sullivan.ny.us/?TabId=3192

A living history museum, documenting the lives of 18th-century Delaware Company pioneers. Offers genealogical research services.

Tusten Historical Society
Western Sullivan Public Library • 198 Bridge Street • PO Box 18
Narrowsburg, NY 12764 • (845) 252-3360
Email: tustenroots@lycos.com • *www.tusten.org/historya.htm*

Local histories and genealogies, federal census microfilm for Sullivan County 1820–1920, early church record microfilms, ledgers, newspapers on microfilm, tax rolls 1859–1956, photographs, and scrapbooks. Website includes some digitized images. Genealogical research services offered for a fee.

Mamakating Historical Society
Summitville Road • PO Box 163 • Summitville, NY 12781
(845) 866-1607 • *www.nyow.org/mhs.html*

Deeds, photographs, and town histories; family files for Mamakating and other nearby towns. Currently working to transcribe vital and cemetery records.

SELECTED PRINT & ONLINE RESOURCES

Below is a selection of resources relevant for research in this county. The list is representative, not exhaustive. Additional titles—particularly of abstracts, indexes, transcriptions, and local histories—are available; consult the introduction to Part Two for further information. For guidance on how to identify and locate community directories and local newspapers, see chapter 11, City Directories, and chapter 12, Newspapers, in Part One of this book.

Abstracts, Indexes & Transcriptions
Barber, Gertrude Audrey. "The Church Record of the Kenoza Lake Charge of the Methodist Episcopal Church: Heard Settlement - Foster - Dale - Jeffersonville - Youngsville - Pike Pond, Now Known as Kenoza Lake; All in Sullivan County, N.Y." Typescript, 1929. NYPL, New York.

— — —. "Gravestone Inscriptions of Sullivan County, NY." 10 vols. Typescript, 1929–1934. NYPL, New York. [*Ancestry.com*]

———. "Graveyard Inscriptions of Bloomingburgh Cemetery, Bloomingburgh, Sullivan County, New York." Typescript, 1930. NYPL, New York. [*Ancestry.com*]

———. "Index of Wills, Sullivan County, New York, 1876–1909." Typescript, 1929. NYPL, New York. [*Ancestry.com*]

———. "Index to Proceedings in Administration of Intestates Estates: At the Surrogate's office, Monticello, Sullivan County, NY." Typescript, 1949. NYPL, New York.

———."Records of the First Congregational Church in the Town of Lumberland, Sullivan County, New York: Formerly Known as the First Presbyterian Congregational Church of Narrow Falls and Also as the Narrow Falls and Middlebrook Church." Typescript, 1929. NYPL, New York.

———."Sullivan County Church Records." 20 parts in 3 vols. Typescripts, 1929–1931. NYPL, New York. [*Ancestry.com*]

Calkin, Lydia. "Sullivan County, NY, Cemetery Gravestone Inscriptions and Chart of Grave Locations, Old Bethel, NY, Cemetery: A 1957 Resurvey of and Additions to Records Made in 1936 by Gertrude Audrey Barber." Typescript, 1957. NYPL, New York.

Daughters of the American Revolution, comps. *New York DAR Genealogical Records Committee Report*. Since 1913 DAR volunteers have transcribed many thousands of unpublished cemetery, church, and town records throughout New York. The reports are at the DAR Library; copies are at the NYSL and the NYPL. The DAR has a searchable name index to all the GRC reports at *http://services.dar.org/Public/DAR_Research/search/?Tab_ID=6*. See Jean Worden's index below for a listing by county of the New York record sets that were transcribed by the DAR before 1998.

Worden, Jean D. "Book 1, Subject Index." In *Revised Master Index to the New York State Daughters of the American Revolution Genealogical Records Volumes*. Zephyrhills, FL: J. D. Worden, 1998. The Subject Index includes a listing by county of the cemeteries, churches, towns, and other sources of records transcribed by the DAR.

Other Resources

Adams, Arthur G., ed. *The Catskills: An Illustrated Historical Guide with Gazetteer*. New York: Fordham University Press, 1990. First published 1975.

Beers, F. W. *County Atlas of Sullivan, New York: From Recent Surveys and Records, under the Superintendence of F. W. Beers*. New York, 1874.

Brass Buttons and Leather Boots: Sullivan County and the Civil War. South Fallsburg, NY: Printed by Steingart Associates, 1963.

Child, Hamilton. *Gazetteer and Business Directory of Sullivan County, NY, for 1872–3*. Syracuse, 1871.

Conway, John. *Remembering the Sullivan County Catskills*. Charleston, SC: The History Press, 2008.

———. *Retrospect: An Anecdotal History of Sullivan County, New York*. Fleischmanns, NY: Purple Mountain Press Ltd., 1996.

———. *Sullivan County: A Bicentennial History in Images*. Charleston, SC: The History Press, 2009.

Curley, Edward F. *Old Monticello*. Monticello, NY: Printed by the Republican Watchman, 1930.

Evers, Alf. *The Catskills; From Wilderness to Woodstock*. Garden City, NY: Doubleday, 1972.

Gold, David M. *The River and the Mountains: Readings in Sullivan County History*. South Fallsburg, NY: Marielle Press, 1994.

New York Historical Resources Center. *Guide to Historical Resources in Sullivan County, New York, Repositories*. Ithaca, NY: Cornell University, 1988. [*books.FamilySearch.org*]

Quinlan, James E. *History of Sullivan County: Embracing an Account of Its Geology, Climate, Aborigines, Early Settlement, Organization . . . with Biographical Sketches . . . .* Liberty, NY, 1872.

Rockwell, Charles. *The Catskill Mountains and the Region Around . . . .* New York, 1869.

Additional Online Resources

Ancestry.com

There are vast numbers of records on *Ancestry.com* that pertain to people who have lived in New York State. See chapter 16 for a description of *Ancestry.com*'s resources and its partnership with the New York State Archives. A search of the online card catalog by county may reveal lesser known resources that pertain to a locality, such as town records, abstracts, transcriptions, city directories, and local histories.

FamilySearch.org

FamilySearch has extensive collections of New York records, including religious records, which are searchable by name and location, but not by county. The following collection includes record images (browsable, but not searchable) that are organized by county:

- "New York, Land Records, 1630–1975." Includes land and property records. *familysearch.org/search/collection/2078654*

Choose the browse option and then select Sullivan to view the available records sets.

A detailed description of *FamilySearch.org* resources is found in chapter 16.

Hudson River Valley Heritage (HRVH)
www.hrvh.org/cdm

The HRVH website provides free access to digital collections of historical material from more than 40 organizations in Columbia, Greene, Dutchess, Ulster, Sullivan, Rockland, Orange, Putnam, and Westchester counties.

NYGenWeb Project: Sullivan County
www.rootsweb.ancestry.com/~nysulliv

Part of the national, USGenWeb volunteer initiative, the website provides information and resources for county research.

Tioga County

Formed • February 16, 1791

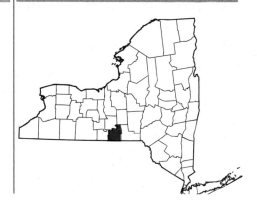

Parent County   Montgomery

Daughter Counties   Onondaga 1794 • Chenango 1798
                          Broome 1806 • Chemung 1836

County Seat   Village of Owego

Major Land Transactions
See table in chapter 7, Land Records
Boston Ten Towns 1787
Watkins and Flint Purchase 1794

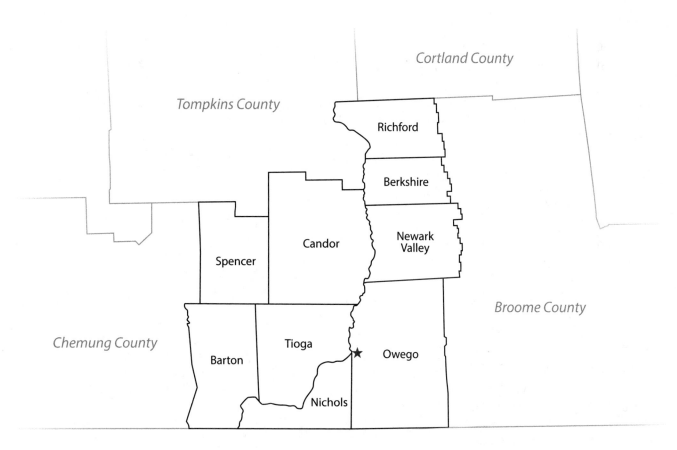

Town Boundary Map
★ - County seat

Towns (and Cities)	Villages and other Settlements		Notes
Barton 1791 Settled 1824 Formed from Town of Tioga	Barton Barton Center East Waverly Ellistown Glencairn Halsey Valley	Lockwood North Barton North Waverly Reniff Waverly (v)	• Hamlet of Barton also Barton City • East Waverly formerly part of Factoryville • Halsey Valley called Girls Flats c. 1836; on Tioga town line • Lockwood formerly Binghams Mills • Village of Waverly inc. 1854; formerly part of Factoryville ; reincorporation of 1876 added more land from Factoryville
Berkshire 1791 Settlers at Browns Settlement 1808 Formed in Broome County from Town of Tioga (now Town of Owego) * 1822 Town transferred to Tioga County 1823 Daughter Town of Westville (now Newark Valley) formed 1831 Daughter town Arlington (now Richford) formed	Berkshire East Berkshire Wilson Creek		* Town of Tioga renamed Owego in 1813 and now in Tioga County • Berkshire also Browns Settlement
Big Flats * In Tioga County 1822–1836			* See Chemung County
Candor 1793 Settlers from Connecticut 1811 Formed from Town of Spencer	Candor (v) Catatonk East Candor Fairfield Gridleyville Hubbardtown Perryville	Strait(s) Corners Upper Fairfield Weltonville West Candor Willseyville Wright	• Village of Candor inc. 1900; created from both Candor Center and Candor Corners • Catatonk also Catatunk • East Candor settled 1795 • Fairfield settled 1809 • Gridleyville also Boothtown, settled c. 1805 • Hubbardtown also Hubbardville and South Candor • Perryville settled 1816 • Strait(s) Corners formerly Straights Corners, included Rhoadville; settled 1825; on Tioga town line • Upper Fairfield also Blinns Settlement, East Candor, and Honeypot • Weltonville settled 1795 • West Candor includes Snyder settled 1796 • Willseyville formerly Big Flatt settled 1792
Caroline * In Tioga County 1811–1822			* See Tompkins County
Catharine * In Tioga County 1798–1836			* See Schuyler County
Catlin * In Tioga County 1823–1836			* See Chemung County

Cities and Towns	Villages, Settlements, Neighborhoods	Notes
Cayuta * In Tioga County 1811–1822		* See Town of Newfield, Tompkins County
Cayuta * In Tioga County 1824–1854		* See Schuyler County
Chemung * In Tioga County 1791–1836		* See Chemung County
Chenango * In Tioga County 1791–1806		* See Broome County
Danby * In Tioga County 1811–1822		* See Tompkins County
Elmira * In Tioga County 1792–1836		* See Chemung County
Erin * In Tioga County 1822–1836		* See Chemung County
Jericho * In Tioga County 1791–1798		* See Town of Bainbridge, Chenango County
Lisle * In Tioga County 1801–1806		* See Broome County
Newark Name for Town of Newark Valley 1824–1862		
Newark Valley 1791 Settlers from Berkshire County, MA 1823 Formed as Town of Westville from Town of Berkshire 1824 Name changed to Newark 1862 Name changed to Newark Valley	East Newark Jenksville Ketchumville New Connecticut Newark Valley (v) West Newark	• New Connecticut formerly the New Connecticut District • Village of Newark Valley inc. 1894; also Westville • West Newark also Cross Road
Nichols 1787 Settled 1824 Formed from Town of Tioga	Briggs Hollow Nichols (v) East Nichols Osborn Hooper(s) Valley Waits Litchfield Wappasening Lounsberry	• Lounsberry formerly Canfield Corners • Village of Nichols inc. 1903; formerly Hooper(s) Valley, also Rushville • Osborn also Litchfield Station
Norwich (town) * In Tioga County 1793–1798		* See Chenango County
Owego * Name for Town of Tioga before 1813		* Towns of Owego and Tioga switched names in 1813

Towns (and Cities)	Villages and other Settlements		Notes
Owego 1786 Settled at Owego village 1800 Formed as Town of Tioga from Town of Union in Tioga County 1806 Transferred to new county of Broome; daughter town Spencer formed 1808 Daughter Town of Berkshire formed 1813 Name changed to Owego (towns of Tioga and Owego switched names) 1822 Transferred back to Tioga County	Apalachin Apalachin Corners Bornt Hill Campville Caskills Corners Cornell Hollow Danby Deans Tannery Fleming(s)ville Foster Gaskill	Gibson Corners Hiawatha Hull(s)ville Oakley Corners Owego (v) Riverside South Apalachin South Owego Waits Whittemore Willsboro	• Campville formerly East Owego • Danby formerly Beers • Fleming(s)ville settled 1808 • Foster also Foster Hollow • Gaskill also Gaskill Corners • Village of Owego established by charter 1827; county seat from 1836; 1822–1836 shared county seat with Village of Elmira (now City of Elmira in Chemung County); 1811–1822 county seat at Spencer; 1791–1811 county seat at Newtown Point (now Elmira) and Chenango, Town of Union • Waits formerly Waite Settlement • Whittemore also Whittemore Hill
Richford 1831 Formed as Town of Arlington from Town of Berkshire 1832 Name changed to Richford	De Maraudeville Hollow Dunhamville East Richford	Padlock Richford West Richford	
Southport * In Tioga County 1822–1836			* See Chemung County
Spencer c. 1794 Settled 1806 Formed from Town of Tioga (now Owego) 1811 Daughter towns Candor, Caroline, Cayuta (now Newfield), and Danby formed * 1824 Daughter town Cayuta formed *	Cowells Corners Crum Town East Spencer Florence North Spencer Spencer (v) Spencer Springs Swamp Siding West Candor		* Town of Cayuta, renamed Newfield, transferred to Tompkins County in 1822 * Town of Cayuta transferred to Schuyler County 1854 • Florence in new Town of Cayuta after 1811; see Newfield in Tompkins County after 1822 • North Spencer formerly Huggtown, also Spencer Summit • Village of Spencer inc. 1886; comprises former Bradleytown and Drakes Settlement; county seat 1812–1822
Tioga * Name for Town of Owego before 1813			* Towns of Owego and Tioga switched names in 1813
Tioga 1785 Settlers from Wyoming, PA 1791 Formed as Town of Owego when Tioga County was formed 1813 Name changed to Tioga (towns of Tioga and Owego switched names) 1824 Daughter towns Barton and Nichols formed	Catlin Hill Germany Hill Goodrich Halsey Valley Horton Crossing	Jenksville Smithboro Strait(s) Corners Tioga Tioga Center	• Germany Hill formerly German Settlement • Goodrich also Goodrich Settlement • Halsey Valley called Girls Flats c. 1836; on Barton town line • Smithboro also Smithsborough • Strait(s) Corners formerly Straights Corners; on Candor town line
Union * In Tioga County 1791–1806			* See Broome County
Veteran * In Tioga County 1823–1836			* See Chemung County

NEW YORK STATE CENSUS RECORDS
See also chapter 3, Census Records

County originals at Tioga County Clerk's Office: 1825*, 1835, 1855, 1865, 1875, 1892, 1905, 1915, 1925 (1845** is lost)

State originals at the NYSA: 1915, 1925

Microfilm at the FHL, NYPL, and NYSL; many years are online at *FamilySearch.org* and *Ancestry.com*.

* For 1825 census abstract and index, see Barnello, et al., in Abstracts, Indexes & Transcriptions, below.

** For 1845 census transcription of Factoryville, see Miles in Abstracts, Indexes & Transcriptions, below and Anderson in Other Resources.

NATIONAL/STATEWIDE REPOSITORIES & RESOURCES
See chapter 16

COUNTYWIDE REPOSITORIES & RESOURCES

Tioga County Clerk
16 Court Street • PO Box 307 • Owego, NY 13827
(607) 687-8660 • *www.tiogacountyny.com/departments/county-clerk.html*

Land records, court records, naturalization records 1854–1955, and the New York state census for Tioga County 1825, 1835, 1855, 1865, 1875, 1892. County deeds 1790–1835 held by Chemung County Clerk.

Tioga County – Town and Village Clerks
Birth, marriage, and death records are maintained by the clerk of the municipality in which the event occurred; see Introduction to County Guides for details of other records which may also be held by municipal clerks. For contact information, see *www.tiogacountyny.com/towns-villages.html*.

Tioga County Surrogate's Court
20 Court Street • PO Box 10 • Owego, NY 13827 • (607) 689-6099
www.tiogacountyny.com/courts/surrogates-court-owego.html

Holds probate records from the early 1800s to the present. See also chapter 6, Probate Records.

Tioga County Public Libraries
Tioga is part of the Finger Lakes Library System; see *www.flls.org* to access each library. Many libraries hold local history books or genealogical materials. See listings below for Berkshire Free Library, Candor Public Library, and Coburn Free Library.

Tioga County Historical Society Museum
110-112 Front Street • Owego, NY 13827 • (607) 687-2460
Email: museum@tiogahistory.org • *www.tiogahistory.org*

Holds local and family histories, microfilm, and a 300,000 surname index compiled from censuses, newspapers, family Bibles, and family folders.

Tioga County Historian
56 Main Street • Owego, NY 13827 • (607) 687-8646
www.tiogacountyny.com/departments/historian.html

Tioga County – All Municipal Historians
While not authorized to answer genealogical inquiries, town and village historians can provide valuable historical information and research advice; some maintain collections and webpages which may include transcribed records, local histories, and other genealogical material. See contact information at *www.tiogacountyny.com/towns-villages.html* or at the website of the Association of Public Historians of New York State at *www.aphnys.org*.

REGIONAL REPOSITORIES & RESOURCES

Afton Historical Society and Museum
See listing in Chenango County Guide

Central New York Genealogical Society
See listing in Onondaga County Guide

LOCAL REPOSITORIES & RESOURCES
Alphabetized by location

Berkshire Free Library and Berkshire History Museum
12519-1 State Route 38 • PO Box 151 • Berkshire, NY 13736
(607) 657-4418 • Email: bfl@htva.net
www.berkshireny.com/museum.htm

Holds local and family history books. Library houses and operates the museum, which includes photographs and ephemera.

Candor Public Library
2 Bank Street • PO Box 104 • Candor, NY 13743
(607) 659-7258 • Email: candorli@twcny.rr.com
www.flls.org/memberpages/candor.htm • *www.candorlibrary.blogspot.com*

Family histories, *Candor Chronicle* 1800s–1950s, New York State Civil War records, and local history books.

Coburn Free Library
275 Main Street • Oswego, NY 13827 • (607) 687-3520
Email: coburnlibrary@clarityconnect.com • *www.coburnfreelibrary.org*

Family and local histories, including materials relating to the Daughters of the American Revolution and Mayflower descendants.

Spencer Historical Society
22 Spencer Street • PO Box 71 • Spencer, NY 14883 • (607) 589-6134

Local collection of census records 1825, 1835, 1855; birth and death records 1880s–1915; newspapers 1888–present; and family files. Quarterly newsletter.

SELECTED PRINT & ONLINE RESOURCES
Below is a selection of resources relevant for research in this county. The list is representative, not exhaustive. Additional titles—particularly of abstracts, indexes, transcriptions, and local histories—are available; consult the introduction to Part Two for further information. For guidance on how to identify and locate community directories and local newspapers, see chapter 11, City Directories, and chapter 12, Newspapers, in Part One of this book.

Abstracts, Indexes & Transcriptions
Barnello, Kathleen, Harriet Hall, Joan Green, Joyce Mason, and Harold Witter. *Abstract of the 1825 New York State Census of Tioga County, New York*. Syracuse: Central New York Genealogical Society, 1996. Originally published in *Tree Talks*, vol. 37, no. 4 (1996): 1–57. Index: 58–78, introduction: iii, maps iv–v.

Canfield, Amos. "Abstracts of Wills Taken from the Probate Records of Tioga County, New York." *NYG&B Record*, vol. 57 (1926) no. 4: 381–386; vol. 58 (1927) no. 1: 67–76, no. 3: 277–287. [NYG&B eLibrary]

"Cemetery Records of Tioga County, New York." Manuscript, 1966. Filmed by the Genealogical Society of Utah, 1971.

County of Tioga Abstracts. Syracuse: Central New York Genealogical Society, 2000. Abstracts for a range of genealogical records originally published in the quarterly *Tree Talks.*

Daughters of the American Revolution, comps. *New York DAR Genealogical Records Committee Report.* Since 1913 DAR volunteers have transcribed many thousands of unpublished cemetery, church, and town records throughout New York. The reports are at the DAR Library; copies are at the NYSL and the NYPL. The DAR has a searchable name index to all the GRC reports at *http://services.dar.org/Public/DAR_Research/search/?Tab_ID=6.* See Jean Worden's index below for a listing by county of the New York record sets that were transcribed by the DAR before 1998.

Kelly, Arthur C. M. *Index to Tree Talks County Packet: Tioga County.* Rhinebeck, NY: Kinship, 2002.

Miles, Ernie. "1845 Census of Factoryville, N.Y." NYGenWeb Project. *www.tioga.nygenweb.net/factory.htm.* Information abstracted from the *History of Waverly, N.Y. and Vicinity* by Albertson, below.

Sheldon, Nellie M. *Name Index, History of Tioga, Chemung, Tompkins and Schuyler Counties, New York: Compiled by H. B. Peirce and D. Hamilton Hurd, Published by Everts and Ensign, 1879.* N.p: The Author, 1965.

Tioga County, NYG&B Church Surveys Collection. NYG&B, New York. [NYG&B eLibrary]

Worden, Jean D. "Book 1, Subject Index." In *Revised Master Index to the New York State Daughters of the American Revolution Genealogical Records Volumes.* Zephyrhills, FL: J. D. Worden, 1998. The Subject Index includes a listing by county of the cemeteries, churches, towns, and other sources of records transcribed by the DAR.

Other Resources

Albertson, Charles L. *History of Waverly, N.Y. and Vicinity.* Waverly, NY: Waverly Sun, 1943. [*Ancestry.com*]

Beers, F. W. *Atlas of Tioga Co., New York: From Actual Surveys by and under the Direction of F. W. Beers, Assisted by Geo. P. Sanford and Others.* New York, 1869.

Child, Hamilton. *Gazetteer and Business Directory of Broome and Tioga Counties, New York, for 1872–3.* Syracuse, 1872.

Gay, W. B. *Historical Gazetteer of Tioga County, New York, 1785–1888.* Bowie, MD: Heritage Books, 1991. Index available from Berkshire Family History Association.

Hoiland, Doris R. *Pioneers of the Southern Tier: Schuyler and Tioga Counties.* Elmira, NY: The Author, 1977.

Hunt, Joan, Ray Hunt, and Linda Williams. *History of Tioga Schools.* Tioga, NY: Tioga County Historical Society, 2010.

Kingman, LeRoy W. *Our County and Its People: A Memorial History of Tioga County, New York.* Elmira, NY, 1897.

———. *Owego: Some Account of the Early Settlement of the Village in Tioga County, NY, Called Ah-wa-ga by the Indians, Which Name was Corrupted by Gradual Evolution into Owago, Owego, Owegy, and Finally Owego.* Owego, NY: Owego Gazette, 1907.

McEnteer, Thomas C. *Seasons of Change: An Updated History of Tioga County, New York.* Owego, NY: Tioga County Legislature, 1990.

New York Historical Resources Center. *Guide to Historical Resources in Tioga County, New York, Repositories.* Ithaca, NY: Cornell University, 1981. [*books.FamilySearch.org*]

Peirce, Henry B., and D. Hamilton Hurd. *History of Tioga, Chemung, Tompkins and Schuyler Counties, New York: With Illustrations and Biographical Sketches of Some of Its Prominent Men and Pioneers.* Philadelphia, 1879. See above for a name index by Nellie Sheldon.

Quest, Richard. *Tioga County, New York.* Charleston, SC: Arcadia, 1999.

Sexton, John L. *An Outline History of Tioga and Bradford Counties in Pennsylvania; Chemung, Steuben, Tioga, Tompkins and Schuyler in New York: By Townships, Villages, Boro's and Cities.* Elmira, NY, 1885.

Watrous, Hilda R. *Owego Reflections, 1887–1987.* New York: Tioga County Historical Society, 1994.

Additional Online Resources

Ancestry.com

There are vast numbers of records on Ancestry.com that pertain to people who have lived in New York State. See chapter 16 for a description of *Ancestry.com*'s resources and its partnership with the New York State Archives. A search of the online card catalog by county may reveal lesser known resources that pertain to a locality, such as town records, abstracts, transcriptions, city directories, and local histories.

FamilySearch.org

FamilySearch has extensive collections of New York records, including religious records, which are searchable by name and location, but not by county. The following collections include record images (browsable, but not searchable) that are organized by county:

- "New York, Land Records, 1630–1975." Includes land and property records. *familysearch.org/search/collection/2078654*
- "New York, Probate Records, 1629–1971." Includes wills, letters of administration, and guardianship papers. *familysearch.org/search/collection/1920234*

For both collections, choose the browse option and then select Tioga to view the available records sets.

A detailed description of *FamilySearch.org* resources is found in chapter 16.

NYGenWeb Project: Tioga County

tioga.nygenweb.net

Part of the national, USGenWeb volunteer initiative, the website provides information and resources for county research.

Tompkins County

Formed April 17, 1817

Parent Counties   Cayuga • Seneca
Daughter County   Schuyler 1854
County Seat   City of Ithaca

Major Land Transactions
See chapter 7, Land Records
New Military Tract 1782–1791
Boston Ten Towns 1787
Watkins and Flint Purchase 1794

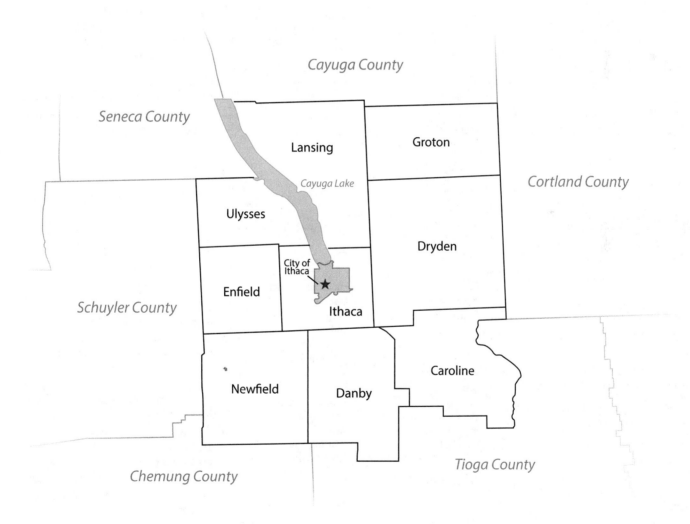

Cayuga County

Seneca County

Lansing

Groton

Cayuga Lake

Cortland County

Ulysses

Dryden

City of Ithaca

★

Enfield

Schuyler County

Ithaca

Caroline

Newfield

Danby

Chemung County

Tioga County

Town Boundary Map
 - County seat

Towns (and Cities)	Villages and other Settlements		Notes
Caroline 1795–96 Settlers from Vermont and New Jersey 1811 Formed in Tioga County from Town of Spencer 1822 Transferred to Tompkins County 1839 Ceded land to Town of Danby	Bald Hill Besemer Boiceville Brearley Brooktondale Buffalo Road Canaan Cantines Great Caroline Caroline Center Caroline Depot	Guide Board Corners Honeypot Pugsleys Depot Ransom Hollow Rawson Hollow Slaterville Springs Speedsville Taft Hill Terryville West Slaterville White Church	• Besemer on Dryden town line • Brooktondale also Brookton (1883–1926), Cantinesburgh, Cantines Little Location, Cantines Mill, Cantinesville, Motts Corners, Motts Hollow, Motts Mill, and Mottsville • Canaan formerly Union Valley in Town of Dryden; transferred to Town of Caroline and renamed in 1885 • Cantines Great also Cantines Little and Cantines Mill • Hamlet of Caroline formerly Tobeytown and Yankee Settlement • Caroline Center formerly Centreville • Slaterville Springs formerly Dutch Settlement and Slaterville • Speedsville formerly Jenksville (1800–1830s) and The Corners • Taft Hill formerly Hardscrabble Hill
Covert * In Tompkins County 1817–1819			* See Seneca County
Danby 1797 Settled 1811 Formed in Tioga County from Town of Spencer 1822 Transferred to Tompkins County 1839 Annexed land from Town of Caroline 1856 Ceded land to Town of Dryden	Danby Michigan Hollow South Danby Summit The Pinnacles West Danby		• South Danby formerly Beers Settlement • The Pinnacles formerly Thatchers Pinnacles
Division Name for Town of Groton 1817–1818			
Dryden * 1797 Settled 1803 Formed in Cayuga County from Town of Ulysses 1817 Transferred to new county of Tompkins 1856 Annexed land from Town of Danby	Barney Besemer Bethel Grove California Canaan Dryden (v) Dusenbury Hollow Ellis Etna Fall Creek Parke Freeville (v) Gee Hill Genung Corners Gilesville	Hibbards Corner Irish Settlement Lac(e)y Corners Ludwig Malloryville McLean Red Mills Ryngewood Snyder Union Valley Varna Wernnickville West Dryden Willow Glen	* Dryden was the name of one of the 28 Military Tract townships • Besemer on Caroline town line • Canaan also Land of Canaan, formerly Canaan Valley and The Happy Land of Canaan • Village of Dryden inc. 1857; called Dryden Corners until 1811, also Dryden Four Corners • Etna formerly Millers Settlement (1800–1815), Columbia (1815–1823), and Millers Corners • Village of Freeville inc. 1887; formerly Whites Corner, Whites Mill, and Whitesville • Gee Hill also Gee Town • Irish Settlement formerly South Hill (Dryden continued on next page)

Towns (and Cities)	Villages and other Settlements		Notes
Dryden (continued)			• McLean was Moscow until 1824; on Groton town line • Union Valley transferred to Town of Caroline and renamed Canaan in 1885 • Willow Glen formerly Stickles Corners
Enfield 1821 Formed from Town of Ulysses	Applegate(s) Corner(s) Black Oak Corners Bostwick Corners Christian Hill Enfield	Enfield Falls Honeypot Kennedy(s) Corner(s) Millers Corners West Enfield	• Hamlet of Enfield also Enfield Center and The Center • Honeypot formerly Meadowbrook • Millers Corners also Sandy Creek, The Corners, and The Store
Groton Settlers from Massachusetts and Connecticut in late 1700s 1817 Formed as Division from Town of Locke, Cayuga County 1818 Name changed to Groton	Benson(s) Corners Bensonville Fall Creek Fitts Corners Franklinville Groton (v) Groton City Grotto	Jones Corners Lafayette Corners McLean Nubia Peruton Peruville Pleasant Valley West Groton	• Village of Groton inc. 1860; was Groton Hollow before 1860, also Drouton Hollow • Groton City formerly Slab City and Fall Creek Post Office (1824–1841) • McLean was Moscow until 1824; on Dryden town line • Nubia formerly Footville and Gooseville; name changed to Nubia in 1893 • Peruville also Peruton, formerly Peru
Hector * In Tompkins County 1817–1854			* See Schuyler County
Ithaca (city) * 1888 Formed as a city from Village of Ithaca in Town of Ithaca	Brandon Place Bryant Park Collegetown Dunmore Place Fall Creek Goose Pasture Hog(s) Hole Klondike	Northside Rhine South Hill Southside The Commons The Nook Wheat Street	* County seat at Ithaca (hamlet, village, and city) from 1817 • Brandon Place and Dunmore Place formerly Irish Nob • Bryant Park also Bryant Tract • Klondike on Ithaca town line • South Hill formerly Brewery Hill, Michigan Hill, and Prospect Hill
Ithaca (town) Settlers from New York, Pennsylvania and New Jersey at The Flats * 1821 Formed from Town of Ulysses 1888 Village of Ithaca became City of Ithaca	Auburn Junction Booltown Cayuga Heights (v) Conover Coreorgonel Eastern Heights East Ithaca Forest Home Glenside	Ithaca (v) Klondike Pewtown Remingtown Point Renwick Renwick Heights South Hill Vetsburg	* Ithaca formerly called The Flats • Village of Cayuga Heights inc. 1915 • Coreorgonel was a pre-Revolution Tutelo Indian village, now Tutelo Park • Forest Home formerly Flea Hollow, Free Hollow, and Sydneys Mill • Village of Ithaca inc. 1821, became City of Ithaca 1888; county seat from 1817 • Klondike on Ithaca town line • Remington Point also Elm Tree Point
Lansing 1792 Settlers from New Jersey 1817 Formed from Town of Genoa, Cayuga County	Asbury Dublin East Lansing Esty(s) Fiddlers Green Forest City Hill Crest Ladoga Lake Ridge	Lansing (v) Lansing Station Lansingville Libertyville Ludlowville McKinneys Midway Mill Point Myers	• Esty formerly Forest City • Fiddlers Green formerly Genoa • Hill Crest formerly Bean Hill, name changed 1954 • Lake Ridge also Lake Ridge Point, formerly Heddens and Himrods Point • Village of Lansing inc. 1974

(Lansing continued on next page)

Towns (and Cities)	Villages and other Settlements		Notes
Lansing (continued)	North Lansing Nortons Landing Portland Portland Point Sage South Lansing Taughannock		• Lansing Station formerly Lehigh Valley • Lansingville formerly Teetertown, name changed 1828 • Ludlowville formerly Ludlows Mill(s), Ludlowtown, Ludlow Village, and Ludlowville Falls • Myers formerly (The) Ploughs (1880–1882) • North Lansing formerly Beardsleys Corners • Nortons Landing also Norton, formerly Kimples Landing • Portland Point formerly Collins Point, Koplins Point, and Shergours; named Portland Point in 1900 • Sage formerly Jacktown and Midway • South Lansing formerly Libertyville, Rogues Harbor, and The Harbor
Newfield 1811 Formed in Tioga County as Cayuta from Town of Spencer 1822 Transferred to Tompkins County; name changed to Newfield	Jackson Jackson Hollow Newfield (v) Nina Picnic Corners Pon(e)y Hollow	Sebring Settlement South Newfield Stratton Trumbull(s) Corners Windfall Settlement	• Village of Newfield inc. 1895 and dissolved 12/2/1926; formerly Cayuta and Florence • Nina formerly East Newfield • Trumbull(s) Corners also North Newfield and Rumsey Corners
Ulysses * 1792 Settled at Trumansburgh 1799 Formed as a town in Cayuga County 1803 Daughter town Dryden formed 1817 Transferred to new county of Tompkins 1821 Daughter towns Enfield and Ithaca formed	Crowbar Point Glenwood Halseyville Jacksonville Krum Corner Mack Settlement Middleburgh Podunk Presbyterian Row	Quaker Settlement Taughannock Falls Taughannock Point Trumansburg (v) Updike Settlement Waterburg Willow Creek	* Ulysses was the name of one of the 28 Military Tract townships • Glenwood formerly Glenwood Falls • Jacksonville called Harlows Corners until 1815, also Van Cortland • Mack Settlement also Macktown • Taughannock Point formerly Weyburns Point • Village of Trumansburg inc. 1872; formerly McLallens Tavern, Shin Hollow, Tremain Village, Tremansburg, Tremans Mill, and Tremansville

Note about Tompkins County

Tompkins is one of four "County Registration Districts" which have consolidated the administration of birth and death records. These civil records are kept at the Tompkins County Health Department, Vital Records office; see details below. Civil birth and death records earlier than 1880 may still be found with city, town, or village clerks.

NEW YORK STATE CENSUS RECORDS

See also chapter 3, Census Records

County originals at Tompkins County Clerk's Office: 1825, 1835, 1865, 1875, 1892, 1905, 1925 (1845, 1855 and 1915 are lost)

State originals at the NYSA: 1915, 1925

Microfilm at the FHL, NYPL, and NYSL; many years are online at *FamilySearch.org* and *Ancestry.com*.

For 1825 transcription, see Tompkins County Genealogical Society in Abstracts, Indexes & Transcriptions.

NATIONAL/STATEWIDE REPOSITORIES & RESOURCES

See chapter 16

Cornell University Library: Genealogical Research at Cornell
See listing in chapter 16

COUNTYWIDE REPOSITORIES & RESOURCES

Tompkins County Clerk
320 North Tioga Street • Ithaca, NY 14850 • (607) 274-5431
Email: countyclerkmail@tompkins-co.org
www.tompkinscountyny.gov/cclerk

Census records 1825–1925, incomplete, court records, land records 1817–present, marriage records 1908–1935, naturalization records 1817–present, and survey maps. Vital records in Tompkins County are kept by the Tompkins County Health Department (see below).

Tompkins County – City, Town, and Village Clerks
Birth, marriage, and death records are maintained by the clerk of the municipality in which the event occurred; see Introduction to County Guides for details of other records which may also be held by municipal clerks. For contact information, see *www.tompkins-co.org/cclerk/links.htm*.

Tompkins County Surrogate's Court
Tompkins County Courthouse • 320 North Tioga Street
PO Box 70 • Ithaca, NY 14850 • (607) 277-0622

Holds probate records from 1817 to the present. See also chapter 6, Probate Records.

Tompkins County Health Department: Vital Records
55 Brown Road • Ithaca, NY 14850 • (607) 274-6642
www.tompkins-co.org/health/vitals/index.htm

Village of Dryden births and deaths 1887–present, Village of Freeville births and deaths 1894–present, Town of Ithaca births 1886–present, Town of Ithaca deaths 1893–present, Town of Ulysses births and deaths 1922–present, Town of Trumansburg births and deaths 1914–present, birth and death records from all other areas of Tompkins County 1880–present.

Tompkins County Public Libraries

Tompkins is part of the Finger Lakes Library System; see *www.flls.org* to access each library. Many hold genealogy and local history collections. For example, the collection of the Newfield Historical Society is held at the Newfield Public Library. Also see listings below for Southworth Library Association and Tompkins County Public Library.

Tompkins County Public Library: Local History
101 East Green Street • Ithaca, NY 14850 • (607) 272-4557
www.tcpl.org/local-history.php

Biographies and histories, atlases and maps, church records, gravestone inscriptions, local gazetteers and directories including *Ithaca Directory*, 1868–2000, materials from local organizations, American Indian history, newspapers (*Ithaca Journal*, 1849–present and *Ithaca Times*, 1974–2005), *Ithaca Journal* Obituary Index (1860–1876, 1900–1914, 1980–1999), Index to Trumansburgh Newspapers 1827–1940, school histories including *Cornell University Guide*, 1875, and voter lists 1912, 1913. A wide selection of the library's local history collection is available on the website.

The History Center in Tompkins County Local History
401 East State/MLK Jr. Street • Ithaca, NY 14850 • (607) 273-8284
www.thehistorycenter.net

Manuscripts, books, census materials (1790 summary, 1825 abstract), city directories, family files, cemetery and obituary listings, death and marriage notices, ledgers, scrapbooks, maps, and photographs. The Center offers research services for a fee. It was formerly known as the Dewitt Historical Society of Tompkins County and the Tompkins County Museum.

Tompkins County Historian
125 East Court Street • Ithaca, NY 14850
www.tompkinscountyny.gov/historian

Website includes county and town histories, information on town place names, and contact information for local historians.

Tompkins County – All Municipal Historians
While not authorized to answer genealogical inquiries, city, town, and village historians can provide valuable historical information and research advice; some maintain collections and webpages which may include transcribed records, local histories, and other genealogical material. For contact information, see *www.tompkinscountyny.gov/historian* or the website of the Association of Public Historians of New York State at *www.aphnys.org*.

REGIONAL REPOSITORIES & RESOURCES

Central New York Genealogical Society
See listing in Onondaga County Guide

LOCAL REPOSITORIES & RESOURCES

Alphabetized by location

Dryden Town Historical Society
36 West Main Street • PO Box 69 • Dryden, NY 13053
(607) 844-9209 • Email: historyhouse@odyssey.net
www.drydennyhistory.org

Holdings include genealogies, cemetery records, maps, newspaper clipping scrapbooks, and photographs. Society offers genealogical research services. Quarterly newsletter.

Southworth Library Association: Local History Resources
24 West Main Street • PO Box 45 • Dryden, NY 13053
(607) 844-4782 • Email: southworth@twcny.rr.com
www.southworthlibrary.org

Books, census materials (microfilm, abstract of 1825 and transcriptions), local history, military records, newspapers (1856–present), photographs, scrapbooks, and records of local organizations.

Willow Glen Cemetery Association
PO Box 397 • Dryden, NY 13053
www.nytompki.org/cemeteries/willow_glen_cem_assn_a.htm

Website includes gravestone transcriptions and cemetery map. Cemetery is located on Route 13, west of Dryden Village.

Groton Historical Society
168 Main Street (NYS Route 38) • PO Box 142 • Groton, NY 13073
(607) 898-5787 or 898-5725 • *www.historicgroton.com/page2a.html*

Holdings include genealogy files and records of the Town of Groton.

Historic Ithaca
212 Center Street • Ithaca, NY 14850 • (607) 273-6633
www.historicithaca.org

Books, city directories, magazines, maps, scrapbooks, resource surveys, and ephemera documenting local history and architecture.

Lansing Historical Association
PO Box 100 • Lansing, NY 14882 • (607) 533-4514
www.lansinghistory.com

Holdings include early school records and photographs, some of which are featured on the Association's website. Website features list of local schools and churches and other historical information.

Newfield Historical Society
262 Van Kirk Road • Newfield, NY 14876 • (607) 564-7778
Email: newfieldarchives@gmail.com • *www.newfieldhistoricalsociety.org*

The Society's archives are held on the second floor of the Newfield Public Library and include church and telephone directories, genealogies and histories, ledgers, maps, newspapers (*Newfield News*, 1973–1979, 1980–2008; *Newfield Tribune*, 1888–1890), photographs and postcards, school documents, town records, and yearbooks (1939–1992).

Town of Caroline Historical Room
Caroline Town Hall • 2670 Slaterville Road • PO Box 136
Slaterville Springs, NY 14881 • (607) 539-6400
Email: Carolinehistorian@yahoo.com • *www.carolinehistorian.org*

The Historical Room is maintained by the Caroline town historian. Holdings include books, church records, diaries and journals, genealogies and family files, government records, magazines, newspapers, photographs, scrapbooks, and town records.

The Ulysses Historical Society Museum
39 South Street • PO Box 445 • Trumansburg, NY (607) 387-6666
Email: uhs@fltg.net • *http://nytompki.org/ulysses/ulysses_hs.htm*

Census material, cemetery records, genealogies and histories, local newspapers (*Free Press*, 1885–present), maps, and Revolutionary War soldiers' grants.

SELECTED PRINT & ONLINE RESOURCES

Below is a selection of resources relevant for research in this county. The list is representative, not exhaustive. Additional titles—particularly of abstracts, indexes, transcriptions, and local histories—are available; consult the introduction to Part Two for further information. For guidance on how to identify and locate community directories and local newspapers, see chapter 11, City Directories, and chapter 12, Newspapers, in Part One of this book.

Abstracts, Indexes & Transcriptions

Barber, Gertrude Audrey. "Abstracts of Wills of Tompkins County, New York, 1803–1838." Typescript, 1941. New York State Library, Albany.

County of Tompkins Abstracts. Syracuse: Central New York Genealogical Society, 2000. Abstracts for a range of genealogical records originally published in the quarterly *Tree Talks*.

Daughters of the American Revolution, comps. *New York DAR Genealogical Records Committee Report*. Since 1913 DAR volunteers have transcribed many thousands of unpublished cemetery, church, and town records throughout New York. The reports are at the DAR Library; copies are at the NYSL and the NYPL. The DAR has a searchable name index to all the GRC reports at *http://services.dar.org/Public/DAR_Research/search/?Tab_ID=6*. See Jean Worden's index below for a listing by county of the New York record sets that were transcribed by the DAR before 1998.

Greene-Young, Nancy E. *Death and Marriage Notices, Tompkins County, New York, 1870–1890*. Bowie, MD: Heritage Books, 1996.

Haynes, Myrte R., Marjorie S. Dows, and Virginia Moscrip. "Abstracts of Intestate Estates, Tompkins County, New York, 1850–1875." Typescript, 1966. NYPL, New York.

Ireland, Harriet D. "Honor Roll of Tompkins County, New York: Being a List of Names of the Soldiers of the Revolution of Tompkins County." Typescript, 1910. NYPL, New York.

Jackson, Mary S., and Edward F. *Marriage and Death Notices from Tompkins County, New York, Newspapers*. Macedon, NY: The Authors, 1993.

Kelly, Arthur C. M. *Index to Tree Talks County Packet: Tompkins County*. Rhinebeck, NY: Kinship, 2002.

Martin, Catherine M. *Records of Tompkins County, New York: Wills, Intestates, Bible, Church, and Family Records: Wills, 1817 mid-1839, Liber A through C, with Added Wills and Notes Concerning Tompkins County, New York, Early Families, as Taken from LDS Roll 085,070*. Durand, MI: The Author, 1995.

Sandwick, Charles M. *The Old Cemetery of Dryden, Tompkins County, New York: Records of Inscriptions and Genealogical Notes*. Ithaca, NY: Dewitt Historical Society, 1970.

Sheldon, Nellie M. *Name Index, History of Tioga, Chemung, Tompkins and Schuyler Counties, New York: Compiled by H. B. Peirce and D. Hamilton Hurd, Published by Everts and Ensign, 1879*. N.p: The Author, 1965.

Tompkins County Genealogical Society. *The New York State Census 1825 for Tompkins County*. Ithaca, NY: The Society, 1991.

Worden, Dora P. "Tompkins County Gravestone Inscriptions." *NYG&B Record*, vol. 52 (1921), no. 2: 130–150, no. 3: 268–285, no. 4: 350–372; vol. 53 (1922) no. 1: 75–88, no. 2: 181–195, no. 3: 288–300, no. 4: 393–401; vol. 54 (1923) no. 1: 73–85, no. 2: 167–176, no. 3: 285–291, no. 4: 358–392; vol. 55 (1924) no. 1: 15–16. [NYG&B eLibrary]

Worden, Jean D. "Book 1, Subject Index." In *Revised Master Index to the New York State Daughters of the American Revolution Genealogical Records Volumes*. Zephyrhills, FL: J. D. Worden, 1998. The Subject Index includes a listing by county of the cemeteries, churches, towns, and other sources of records transcribed by the DAR.

———. *Tompkins County, New York, Church Records.* Franklin, OH: The Author, 1985.

Other Resources

Abt, Henry E. *Ithaca.* Ithaca, NY: Ross W. Kellogg, 1926.

Bishop, Morris. *A History of Cornell.* Ithaca, NY: Cornell University Press, 1962.

Burns, Thomas W. *Initial Ithacans: Comprising Sketches and Portraits of the Forty-Four Presidents of the Village of Ithaca (1821 to 1888) and the First Eight Mayors of the City of Ithaca (1888 to 1903).* Ithaca, NY: Ithaca Journal, 1904.

Child, Hamilton. *Gazetteer and Business Directory of Tompkins County, NY, for 1868.* Syracuse, 1868.

Cutter, William R. *Genealogical and Family History of Central New York: A Record of the Achievements of Her People in the Making of a Commonwealth and the Building of a Nation.* New York: Lewis Historical Publishing Co., 1912.

Dieckmann, Jane M. *A Short History of Tompkins County.* Ithaca, NY: DeWitt Historical Society of Tompkins County, 1986.

———. *The Towns of Tompkins County: From Podunk to the Magnetic Springs.* Ithaca, NY: DeWitt Historical Society of Tompkins County, 1998.

Fay, Loren V. *Tompkins County, New York, Genealogical Research Secrets.* Albany: The Author, 1982.

Hesch, Merrill, and Richard Pieper. *Ithaca Then & Now.* Ithaca, NY: McBooks Press, 1983.

Kammen, Carol, ed. *The Peopling of Tompkins County: A Social History.* Interlaken, NY: Heart of the Lakes Pub., 1985. May be downloaded at *www.tompkins-co.org/historian/PlaceNames/index.html.*

———. *Place Names of Tompkins County.* Ithaca, NY: Office of the Tompkins County Historian, 2004.

Kurtz, D. Morris. *Ithaca and Its Resources: Being an Historical and Descriptive Sketch of the "Forest City" and Its Magnificent Scenery, Glens, Falls, Ravines, Cornell University, and the Principal Manufacturing and Commercial Interests.* Ithaca, NY, 1883.

Lewis, Helen F. *New York's Finger Lakes Pioneer Families Especially Tompkins County: A Genealogical Notebook.* Rhinebeck, NY: Kinship, 1991.

New York Historical Resources Center. *Guide to Historical Resources in Tompkins County, New York, Repositories.* Ithaca, NY: Cornell University, 1981.

Peirce, Henry B., and D. Hamilton Hurd. *History of Tioga, Chemung, Tompkins and Schuyler Counties, New York: With Illustrations and Biographical Sketches of Some of Its Prominent Men and Pioneers.* Philadelphia, 1879. See above for a name index by Nellie Sheldon.

Records of the Ithaca College Study Center for Early Religious Life in Western New York, 1978–1981. Division of Rare and Manuscript Collections, Cornell University Library. A description of the holdings for each county is at *http://rmc.library.cornell.edu/eguides/lists/churchlist1.htm.*

Sears, Lydia. *A History of Trumansburg, New York, 1792–1967.* Ithaca, NY: Art Craft of Ithaca, 1968.

Selkreg, John H., and Waterman T. Hewett. *Landmarks of Tompkins County, New York: Including a History of Cornell University by Prof. W. T. Hewitt.* Syracuse, 1894.

Stone & Stewart. *New Topographical Atlas of Tompkins County, New York: From Actual Surveys Especially for This Atlas.* Philadelphia, 1866. [NYPL Digital Gallery]

The Towns of Tompkins County: From Podunk to the Magnetic Springs. Ithaca, NY: DeWitt Historical Society of Tompkins County, 1998.

Additional Online Resources

Ancestry.com

There are vast numbers of records on *Ancestry.com* that pertain to people who have lived in New York State. See chapter 16 for a description of *Ancestry.com*'s resources and its partnership with the New York State Archives. A search of the online card catalog by county may reveal lesser known resources that pertain to a locality, such as town records, abstracts, transcriptions, city directories, and local histories.

The Cornell Daily Sun

http://cdsun.library.cornell.edu

Digitizing this college newspaper is an ongoing project of the Cornell University Library. Issues for September of 1880 through May of 1979 with some omissions are online and searchable. The years 1974–1989 are not yet fully digitized.

FamilySearch.org

FamilySearch has extensive collections of New York records, including religious records, which are searchable by name and location, but not by county. The following collections include record images (browsable, but not searchable) that are organized by county:

- "New York, Land Records, 1630–1975." Includes land and property records. *familysearch.org/search/collection/2078654*
- "New York, Probate Records, 1629–1971." Includes wills, letters of administration, and guardianship papers. *familysearch.org/search/collection/1920234*

For both collections, choose the browse option and then select Tompkins to view the available records sets.

A detailed description of *FamilySearch.org* resources, which include the catalog of the Family History Library, is found in chapter 16.

NYGenWeb Project: Tompkins County

www.nytompki.org

Part of the national, USGenWeb volunteer initiative, the website provides information and resources for county research.

Old Fulton New York Postcards

www.FultonHistory.com

The website provides free access to a vast collection of digitized New York newspapers, including eight titles for Tompkins County.

Ulster County

Formed November 1, 1683

Parent County	Original county
Daughter Counties	Delaware 1797 • Greene 1800 • Sullivan 1809
County Seat	City of Kingston

Major Land Transactions
See table in chapter 7, Land Records
Fox Hall Manor 1672
Hardenburgh Patent 1708

Town Boundary Map
★ - County seat

Towns (and Cities)	Villages and other Settlements		Notes
Catskill * In Ulster County 1798–1800			* See Greene County
Colchester * In Ulster County 1792–1797			* See Delaware County
Denning **1849** Formed from Town of Shandaken **1859** Daughter town Hardenburgh formed	Branch Bull Run Denning Dewitt(s)ville Frost Valley	Greenville Ladleton Peekamoose Red Hill Sundown	
Esopus **1650s** Settled **1811** Formed from Town of Kingston **1818** Annexed land from Town of Hurley; ceded land to Town of Kingston **1842** Annexed land from Town of New Paltz	Arnoldton Atkarton Connelly Dashville Ellmores Cove Esopus Heightsburgh New Salem	Pelham Farms Port Ewen Rifton (v) Sleightsburg St. Remy Ulster Park Union Center West Park	• Arnoldton also Rifton Glen • Atkarton also Arkarkaten • Connelly formerly South Rou(n)dout • Dashville in Town of New Paltz before 1842; part of Village of Rifton 1901–1919 • Hamlet of Esopus formerly Ellmores Corners • New Salem formerly Freerville • Village of Rifton inc. 1901, dissolved 1919; village included Perrines Bridge, Rifton Glen, Saltpeterville, and Swartekill • Ulster Park formerly Amesville and Norris Corners • Union Center formerly Kallicoon Hook
Gardiner Settled by French Huguenots **1853** Formed from towns of New Paltz, Rochester, and Shawangunk	Benton Corners Bruynswick Church Corners Forest Glen Gardiner(s) Guilford Ireland Corner(s) Jenkinstown	Kettleborough Lake Minnewaska Libertyville Rutsonville Tuthill Tuthilltown Wallkill Camp	• Lake Minnewaska on Rochester town line • Libertyville in Town of New Paltz before 1853 • Rutsonville on Shawangunk town line • Tuthilltown formerly called Tuthill, before Tuthill was separate hamlet; also Ganaghote
Hardenburgh **1859** Formed from towns of Denning and Shandaken	Beaver Kill Belle Ayr Dry Brook Grants Mills Hardenburg(h) Mapledale	Millbrook Seager Shin Creek Turnwood Yorktown	• Belle Ayr also Belleayre • Dry Brook formerly West Shokan
Hurley **1662** Settled by Dutch as Nieuw Dorp * **1669** Renamed Horley by English governor **1708** Hurley Patent granted **1787** Daughter town Woodstock formed **1788** Recognized as Town of Hurley by State of New York **1789** Annexed part of Hardenburgh Patent **1809** Ceded land to Town of New Paltz	Ashton Bristol Hill Eagles Nest Glenford Hurley Jockey Hill Morgan Hill Riverside Park Rolling Meadows Ston(e)y Hollow West Hurley		* Nieuw Dorp is Dutch for new village • Hamlet of Hurley formerly Old Hurley • Jockey Hill in Town of Kingston before 1879 • Ston(e)y Hollow in Town of Kingston before 1879

(Hurley continued on next page)

Towns (and Cities)	Villages and other Settlements	Notes
Hurley (continued) 1818 Ceded land to Town of Esopus 1823 Daughter town Olive formed 1844 Daughter town Rosendale formed 1853 Ceded land to Town of Woodstock 1879 Annexed land from Town of Kingston		
Kingston (city) * 1872 Formed as a city from Villages of Rondout and Kingston, Town of Kingston	Rondout	* County seat at Kingston (hamlet, village, and city); Kingston was also the county seat for Dutchess County 1683–1713
Kingston (town) 1614 Settled by Dutch, later abandoned 1652 Settled again and abandoned 1661 Chartered as Wiltwijck * 1667 Incorporated by patent as Kingston 1702 Recognized as a town by colony of New York 1787 Annexed Fox Hall Patent * 1788 Recognized as a town by State of New York 1811 Daughter towns Esopus and Saugerties formed 1818 Annexed land from Town of Esopus 1832 Land ceded to Town of Saugerties 1872 Villages of Kingston and Rondout become City of Kingston 1879 Daughter town Ulster formed; ceded land to towns of Hurley and Woodstock	Dutch Settlement East Kingston Eddyville Flatbush Fly Mountain Fox Hall Halihan Hill Jockey Hill Kingston (v) Rondout (v) Sawkill South Rondout Ston(e)y Hollow Sweet Meadows Wilbur	* Wiltwijck also Wiltwyck and Wiltwick * Fox Hall Patent was Fox Hall Manor (granted 1672) * Dutch Settlement, East Kingston, Eddyville, Flatbush, and Fly Mountain formed part of new Town of Ulster 1879 • Fox Hall name still in use in 1860s for the district that had been Fox Hall Manor • Jockey Hill in Town of Hurley after 1879 • Village of Kingston inc. 1805, became part of new City of Kingston 1872; county seat from 1701 • Village of Rondout inc. 1849; formerly Bolton and The Strand; became part of new City of Kingston 1872 • Ston(e)y Hollow in Town of Hurley from 1879 • Wilbur also Twalfskill
Liberty * In Ulster County 1807–1809		* See Sullivan County
Lloyd Original settlement was named Paltz 1845 Formed from Town of New Paltz	Blue Point Lloyd Centerville Nippityville Clintondale Oakes Clintondale Station Pancake Hollow Etling Corners Perkinsville Highland Plutarch Highland Landing Riverside Lewisburg	• Clintondale formerly Quaker Street; on Plattekill town line • Highland also Eltings Landing and Philips Folly • Highland Landing formerly New Paltz Landing; see Town of New Paltz before 1845 • Plutarch formerly Cold Spring Corners; on New Paltz town line
Lumberland * In Ulster County 1798–1809		* See Sullivan County
Mamakating * In Ulster County 1743–1809		* See Sullivan County

Towns (and Cities)	Villages and other Settlements		Notes
Marbletown 1669 Settled 1703 Marbletown Patent granted 1788 Recognized as a town by State of New York 1823 Daughter town Olive formed 1844 Daughter town Rosendale formed	Atwood Bruceville Davis Corners High Falls Kripplebush Lomontville	Lyonsville Marbletown Mohonk Lake Pacama Stone Ridge The Vly	• Bruceville and High Falls on Rosendale town line • Davis Corners on Olive town line • Kripplebush also Kripple Bush • Lomontville also Lamontville
Marlborough c. 1725 Settled 1772 Formed as New Marlborough Precinct from Newburgh Precinct 1788 Recognized as Town of New Marlborough by State of New York 1800 Daughter town Plattekill formed; name changed to Marlborough	Baileys Gap Lattinto(w)n Marlborough (v) Milton Tuckers Corners		• Village of Marlborough mapped in 1764, inc. 1906, dissolved 4/20/1928; now Marlboro • Tuckers Corners, formerly New Hurley; shared with Town of Plattekill
Middletown * In Ulster County 1789–1797			* See Delaware County
Montgomery * In Ulster County 1772–1798			* See Orange County
Neversink * In Ulster County 1798–1809			* See Sullivan County
Newburgh * In Ulster County 1762–1798			* See Orange County
New Paltz Settled by French Huguenots 1677 New Paltz Patent granted by English governor 1775 Bounds enlarged 1785 Formed as Town of New Paltz 1788 Recognized as a town by State of New York 1809 Annexed land from Town of Hurley 1842 Ceded land to Town of Esopus 1844 Daughter town Rosendale formed 1845 Daughter town Lloyd formed 1853 Daughter town Gardiner formed	Butterville Dashville Libertyville New Paltz (v) New Paltz Landing Ohioville Plutarch Put(t) Corners Springtown		• Butterville also Butlerville • Dashville in Town of Esopus after 1842 • Libertyville in Town of Gardiner after 1853 • Village of New Paltz inc. 1887 • New Paltz Landing see Highland Landing in Town of Lloyd after 1845 • Plutarch formerly Cold Spring Corners; on Lloyd town line
New Windsor * In Ulster County 1762–1798			* See Orange County

Towns (and Cities)	Villages and other Settlements		Notes
Olive **c.1740** Settled in the Esopus Valley 1823 Formed from towns of Hurley, Marbletown, and Shandaken 1853 Ceded and annexed land with Town of Woodstock	Ashokan Beechford Bishop Falls Boiceville Brodhead Brodheads Bridge Brown Station Bush Kill Caseville Cold Brook Davis Corners	Krumville Olive Olivebridge Olive City Samsonville Shokan Traver Hollow Watson Hollow West Shokan Winchell	• Beechford on Shandaken town line • Brodheads Bridge, Brown Station (called Brooks Crossing until 1880), and Olive City were submerged by the Ashokan reservoir in 1913 • Davis Corners on Marbletown town line • Olivebridge also Olive Bridge, formerly Tongore, moved location after original site was flooded by Ashokan reservoir in 1913
Plattekill **c.1700** Settled 1800 Formed from Town of Marlborough	Ardonia Clintondale Modena Modena Gardens New Hurley Plattekill Sylva The Flint Tuckers Corners		• Ardonia formerly Brookside and Palmers Corners • Clintondale shared with Town of Lloyd; formerly Quaker Street • Modena formerly Clarks Corners • New Hurley on Shawangunk town line • Plattekill formerly Pleasant Valley • Sylva formerly Unionville • Tuckers Corners, formerly New Hurley; shared with Town of Marlborough
Rochester **c.1680** Settled by Dutch, area called Mombaccus * 1703 Rochester Patent granted 1788 Recognized as a town by State of New York 1789 Daughter towns Middletown formed 1798 Daughter town Neversink formed 1806 Daughter town Wawarsing formed 1823 Annexed land from Town of Wawarsing 1853 Daughter town Gardiner formed	Accord Alligerville Cherrytown Fantinekill Granite Kerhonkson Kyserike Lake Minniwaska Leibhart Mettacahonts Mill Hook Mombaccus	Palentown Pataukunk Pine Bush Potterville Rock Hill Saint Josen Tabasco The Clove Vantine Hill Vernoy Falls Whitfield Yagerville	* Mombaccus also Mombackus • Accord formerly Port Jackson and Rochester Center • Kerhonkson on Wawarsing town line • Lake Minnewaska also Minnewaska; on Gardiner town line • Mombaccus formerly Cherrytown and Newton • Rock Hill formerly Pleasant Ridge • The Clove also Clove Valley • Whitfield formerly Newtown; on Wawarsing town line • Yagerville on Wawarsing town line
Rosendale **c.1680** Settled by Dutch 1844 Formed from towns of Hurley, Marbletown, and New Paltz	Binnewater Bloomington Bruceville Cottekill Creeklocks Hickory Bush High Falls	Kallops Corners Lawrenceville Lefevre Falls Maple Hill Rosendale (v) Tillson Whiteport	• Bruceville and High Falls on Marbletown town line • Creeklocks also Creek Locks, formerly Hurley Common and Wagondale • Village of Rosendale inc. 1890; dissolved 1979 • Tillson also Rosendale Plains

Towns (and Cities)	Villages and other Settlements		Notes
Saugerties c.1663 Settled by Dutch 1710 German Palatinates settled at West Camp 1811 Formed from Town of Kingston 1832 Annexed land from Town of Kingston	As(h)bury Barclay Heights Bethel Blue Mountain Browersville Canoe Hill Cedar Grove Centerville E(a)vesport Fish Creek Flatbush Glasco Glenerie High Woods Katsbaan	Malden-on-Hudson Manorville Mount Marion Mount Marion Park Petersons Corner Pine Grove Quarryville Saugerties (v) Saxton Shultis Corners Trumpbourville Vanaken Mills Veteran West Camp West Saugerties	• Flatbush, also Foxhall, in Town of Kingston before 1879; on Ulster town line • Glenerie formerly Gleanearie • Katsbaan also Caatsban • Malden-on-Hudson formerly Malden • Village of Saugerties was incorporated as the Village of Ulster in 1831, name was officially changed to Saugerties in 1855 • Vanaken Mills also Van Akens Mills • Veteran formerly Toodlum and Unionville
Shandaken 1770s Settled 1804 Formed from Town of Woodstock 1823 Daughter town Olive formed 1849 Daughter town Denning formed 1859 Daughter town Hardenburgh formed	Allaben Beechford Big Indian Bushnellsville Chichester Claryville Highmount Ladleton	Mount Pleasant Mount Summit Mount Tremper Oliverea Phoenicia Pine Hill (v) Shandaken Woodland	• Allaben formerly Fox Hollow • Beechford on Olive town line • Chichester also Chichester Village • Highmount formerly Summit, also Grand Hotel Station • Ladleton also Ladelton • Mount Pleasant formerly Longyear and Riseleys • Mount Tremper formerly Ladew Corners and The Corner • Village of Pine Hill inc. 1895; dissolved 1985/6 • Shandaken also Shandaken Center
Shawangunk Settled by Dutch along valley of Shawangunk River 1680–1700 c.1709 Formed as Shawangunk Precinct attached to New Paltz 1743 Shawangunk Precinct reestablished 1788 Recognized as a town by State of New York 1853 Daughter town Gardiner formed	Awosting Bruynswick Crawford Dwaarkill Galeville Jamesburgh New Fort New Hurley	New Prospect Red Mills Rutsonville St. Elmo Ulsterville Walker Valley Wallkill Watchtower	• Dwaarkill also Dwaar(s) Kill • Galeville also Galeville Mills • New Hurley on Plattekill town line • Rutsonville on Gardiner town line • Wallkill formerly Shawangunk
Stamford * In Ulster County 1792–1797			* See Delaware County
Thompson * In Ulster County 1803–1809			* See Sullivan County
Ulster 1879 Formed from Town of Kingston	East Kingston Eddyville Flatbush Fly Mountain Goldricks Landing	Lake Katrine Lincoln Park Ruby Ulster Landing	• East Kingston, Eddyville and Fly Mountain in Town of Kingston before 1879 • Flatbush also Foxhall in Town of Kingston before 1879; on Saugerties town line • Lake Katrine formerly Auntrens Pond • Ruby formerly Dutch Settlement in Town of Kingston before 1879

Towns (and Cities)	Villages and other Settlements		Notes
Wallkill * In Ulster County 1743–1798			* See Orange County
Wawarsing **c.1708** Settled by Dutch **1806** Formed from Town of Rochester **1823** Ceded land to Town of Rochester	Briggs Brown(s)ville Cragsmoor Dairyland Ellenville (v) Evensville Greenfield Park Homowack Honk Hill Kerhonkson Lackawack Leurenkill	Napanock/h Oak Ridge Port Ben Port Hixon Sams Point Spring Glen The Cape Ulster Heights Wawarsing Whitfield Yagerville	• Village of Ellenville inc. 1856; also Fairchild City • Greenfield Park formerly Greenfield • Homowack formerly Newspring Glen; shared with Town of Mamakating, Sullivan County • Kerhonkson on Rochester town line • Port Ben formerly Port Benjamin • Port Hixon also Port Nixon • Ulster Heights formerly Drowned Land, Sholam, and Soccannissins • Whitfield formerly Newtown; on Rochester town line • Yagerville on Rochester town line
Windham * In Ulster County 1798–1800			* See Greene County
Woodstock **c.1762** Settled by Palatine Germans **1787** Formed from Town of Hurley **1789** Daughter town Middletown formed **1798** Daughter town Windham formed **1804** Daughter town Shandaken formed **1853** Annexed land from Town of Hurley; annexed and ceded land with Town of Olive	Bearsville Bristol Bristol Center Lake Hill Mink Hollow Montoma Shady Willow Wittenberg Woodstock Yankeetown Zena		

NEW YORK STATE CENSUS RECORDS
See also chapter 3, Census Records

County originals at Ulster County Clerk's Office: 1855, 1865, 1875, 1905, 1915, 1925 (1825, 1835, 1845, and 1892 are lost)

State originals at the NYSA: 1915, 1925

Microfilm at the FHL, NYPL, and NYSL; many years are online at *FamilySearch.org* and *Ancestry.com*.

NATIONAL/STATEWIDE REPOSITORIES & RESOURCES
See chapter 16

COUNTYWIDE REPOSITORIES & RESOURCES

Ulster County Clerk
Ulster County Office Building • 244 Fair Street • Kingston, NY 12401
(845) 340-3288 • Email: countyclerk@co.ulster.ny.us
www.co.ulster.ny.us/countyclerk

Civil and criminal records from Ulster County Supreme and County Courts, civil action cases, divorce files, land records 1685–present, naturalization records 1800–1903, marriages 1903–1935, and the New York state census for Ulster County 1855, 1865, 1875, 1905, 1915, 1925. The Ulster County Records Management & Archives (see below) also holds town clerk returns of vital records for select years (usually kept by the town clerks in NYS).

Ulster County – City, Town, and Village Clerks
Birth, marriage, and death records are maintained by the clerk of the municipality in which the event occurred; see Introduction to County Guides for details of other records which may also be held by municipal clerks. For contact information, see *www.co.ulster.ny.us/countyclerk/townClerks.html*.

Ulster County Surrogate's Court
240 Fair Street • Kingston, NY 12401 • (845) 340-3348

Holds probate records 1787 to the present. The NYSA holds most probate records prior to 1787. See also chapter 6, Probate Records.

Ulster County Records Management & Archives
Ulster County Record Center • 300 Foxhall Avenue
Kingston, NY 12401 • (845) 340-3415
www.co.ulster.ny.us/countyclerk/recordsmgment.html (Records Management) • *www.co.ulster.ny.us/archives/index.html* (Archives)

Administered by the county clerk. Holdings 1600s–present and include census and indexes; city directories; Dutch Colonial records; historic maps and atlases; marriage records 1908–1935; naturalizations 1800–1992; poorhouse records; and town clerk returns of births, deaths, and marriages 1847–1850, 1873–1884. Many records are searchable and/or viewable through the Archives website.

Ulster County Public Libraries
Ulster is part of the Mid-Hudson Library System; see *midhudson.org* to access each library. Many libraries hold local history and genealogy collections. For example, Saugerties Public Library has a collection of local newspapers on microfilm. Also see listings below for Elting Memorial Library, Kingston Library, Marlboro Free Library, and Rosendale Library. Ulster is also part of the Ramapo Catskill Library System; see *www.rcls.org* to access each library. Ellenville Public Library houses local newspapers 1849–present, obituaries, and a museum.

Ulster County Historian
38 Roundout Harbor • Port Ewen, NY 12466 • (845) 331-7380
Email: ulsterhistorian@aol.com

Ulster County– All Town Historians
While not authorized to answer genealogical inquiries, city, town, and village historians can provide valuable historical information and research advice; some maintain collections and webpages which may include transcribed records, local histories, and other genealogical material. For contact information, see *www.ulstercountyny.gov/historian* or the website of the Association of Public Historians of New York State at *www.aphnys.org*.

Ulster County Genealogical Society
17 Main Street • PO Box 536 • Hurley, NY 12443
Email: librarian@ucgsny.org (Librarian) • *www.ucgsny.org*

Society's research library includes Bible records, cemetery records, church records, directories and gazetteers, genealogies, maps, naturalizations, newspapers and newsletters, obituaries, surname files, tax lists, undertaker records, vital records, and wills. A selection of records is on the website, along with lists of museums, societies, historic places, libraries, archives, etc. Publishes the *Ulster County Gazette*, 1963–present, and a newsletter.

Ulster County Historical Society and Bevier House Museum
Museum: 2682 Route 209 • Marbletown, NY 12401
Society: PO Box 279 • Stone Ridge, NY 12484-027 • (845) 338-5614
Email: museum@bevierhousemuseum.org • *www.ulstercountyhs.org*

Society's Library and Archives are open only by appointment. Collections include diaries, letters, land records, maps, and town histories.

REGIONAL REPOSITORIES & RESOURCES

Bard College Archives and Special Collections
See listing in Dutchess County Guide

Elting Memorial Library: Historical and Genealogical Department and Haviland-Heidgerd Historical Collection
93 Main Street • New Paltz, NY 12561 • (845) 255-5030
Email: havilandheidgerd@yahoo.com
www.eltinglibrary.org/historical-collection

Holdings document the history and genealogy of Ulster County and the Hudson Valley and include genealogical and biographical information; church, cemetery, and Bible records; maps; directories; obituaries, birth, and marriage announcements (1860–present); census microfilm (federal and NYS); genealogies, vertical files, and special subject files; house and building books; newspapers (1860–present); periodicals, magazines, newsletters, and yearbooks; photographs, slides, and postcards; and special collections. Holdings are searchable through the Mid-Hudson online catalog (*www.midhudson.org*).

LOCAL REPOSITORIES & RESOURCES
Alphabetized by location

Friends of Historic Rochester, Museum and Genealogical Research Library
12 Main Street • PO Box 22 • Accord, NY 12404 • (845) 626-7104
Email: FriendsHistRoch@aol.com • *www.historicrochester.eyeswrite.com*

Library contains the Eleanor Rosakranse Genealogical Research Collection, consisting of hundreds of books and documents. Additionally, the museum and library house local history books, cemetery records, notebooks, and photographs.

Kingston Library: Marilyn Beichert Powers Local History Room
55 Franklin Street • Kingston, NY 12401 • (845) 331-0988
Email: localhistory@kingstonlibrary.org
www.kingstonlibrary.org/historyroom.php

Local directories, local newspapers on microfilm, maps, vertical files, architectural surveys, Kingston Historic Preservation League collection, and yearbooks.

Old Dutch Reformed Church
272 Wall Street • Kingston, NY 12401 • (845) 338-6759
Email: info@olddutchchurch.org • *www.olddutchchurch.org*

The church's records, available on microfilm, are one of the most complete collections of church records in the country and begin in 1660. Dutch records have been translated into English.

Marlboro Free Library
1251 Route 9W • PO Box 780 • Marlboro, NY 12542
(852) 236-7272 • Email: eamodeo@marlborolibrary.org
www.marlborolibrary.org

Cemetery records, census materials, church records, Bible records, directories, marriage records, obituaries, postcards, photographs, and yearbooks.

Historic Huguenot Street
(formerly Huguenot Historical Society)
88 Huguenot Street • New Paltz, NY 12561 • (845) 255-1660
Email: info@huguenotstreet.org • *www.huguenotstreet.org*

Society's Schoonmaker Library documents the Huguenot and Dutch settlers of New Paltz, allied families, and their descendants and includes local history and genealogies, Bible records, cemetery records, census materials, church records, wills and deeds; has an online catalog. Special Collections (1582–1989) include personal and family papers and records, Bibles, rare books, genealogy collections (including 1,000 family files), maps, newspapers, photographs, reference works, and more. Historic Huguenot Street Corporate Records (1894–present) contains material related to Historic Huguenot Street/the Huguenot Historical Society and similar organizations. Website contains a list of surnames that are represented in the organization's genealogy files, family crests, and other genealogical information.

Town of Shandaken Historical Museum
26 Academy Street • PO Box 627 • Pine Hill, NY 12465 • (845) 688-3116
www.shandaken.us/services/town-of-shandaken-historical-museum
www.catskillpark.com/museum.html

Holdings include genealogy files and local histories documenting the 12 hamlets of the town of Shandaken.

Rosendale Library
264 Main Street • PO 482 • Rosendale, NY 12472 • (845) 658-9013
Email: rosendalelibrary@hvi.net • *www.rosendalelibrary.org*

Church records, directories, maps, obituaries, voter lists, and history books.

Historical Society of Shawangunk and Gardiner
PO Box 570 • Wallkill, NY 12589 • (845) 895-3321
www.wallkillhistory.com

Website includes history of Wallkill Prison; 1800 and partial 1860 federal census of Shawangunk (images and transcriptions); a history of Shawangunk written in 1959; information on and photographs of local buildings, schools and railroads; historic maps of Shawangunk; historic postcards; select family histories; and history of Walker Valley United Methodist Church. The society will research historical residents of the area upon request.

Historical Society of Woodstock and Eames House
20 Comeau Drive • PO Box 841 • Woodstock, NY 12498
(845) 679-2256 • Email: historical.society.woodstock@gmail.com
www.historicalsocietyofwoodstock.org

Society's Archives contain books and manuscripts, documents, and correspondence.

SELECTED PRINT & ONLINE RESOURCES

Below is a selection of resources relevant for research in this county. The list is representative, not exhaustive. Additional titles—particularly of abstracts, indexes, transcriptions, and local histories—are available; consult the introduction to Part Two for further information. For guidance on how to identify and locate community directories and local newspapers, see chapter 11, City Directories, and chapter 12, Newspapers, in Part One of this book.

Abstracts, Indexes & Transcriptions

Anjou, Gustave. *Ulster County, NY, Probate Records in the Office of the Surrogate, at Kingston, NY, at the Surrogate's Office, New York, and in the Library of the Long Island Historical Society: . . Wills, Letters of Administration . . . Inventories . . . Historical Notes*. New York: Gustave Anjou, 1906.

Baptismal and Marriage Registers of the Old Dutch Church of Kingston, Ulster County, New York. New York, 1891.

"Baptisms of the Katsbaan Dutch Church in Saugerties, Ulster County, New York." *NYG&B Record*, vol. 76 (1945) no. 4: 146–157; vol. 78 (1947) no. 2: 58–69; vol. 79 (1948) no. 1: 29–35, no. 2: 93–97, no. 4: 204–208. [NYG&B eLibrary]

Behr, Betty M. Light. *Index to Old Gravestones of Ulster County, NY, Poucher & Terwilliger, 1931*. Carmel, NY: The Author, 1979.

Daughters of the American Revolution, comps. *New York DAR Genealogical Records Committee Report*. Since 1913 DAR volunteers have transcribed many thousands of unpublished cemetery, church, and town records throughout New York. The reports are at the DAR Library; copies are at the NYSL and the NYPL. The DAR has a searchable name index to all the GRC reports at *http://services.dar.org/Public/DAR_Research/search/?Tab_ID=6*. See Jean Worden's index below for a listing by county of the New York record sets that were transcribed by the DAR before 1998.

Hasbrouck, Kenneth E. "Marriages of the Dutch Reformed Church of Shawangunk, Ulster County, New York." *NYG&B Record*, vol. 87 (1956) no. 1: 31–36, no. 2: 96–101, no. 3: 137–148. [NYG&B eLibrary]

Heidgerd, Ruth P. *New Paltz Rural Cemetery Records, 1860–1962*. New Paltz, NY: n.p, 1991. [*books.FamilySearch.org*]

Historical Records Survey. *WPA Transcriptions of Early County Records of New York State: Records of the Road Commissioners of Ulster County, 1722–1769*. Albany, NY: Historical Records Survey, 1940.

Hoes, Roswell R., and Jean D. Worden. *Baptismal and Marriage Registers of the Old Dutch Church of Kingston, Ulster County, New York, 1660–1809*. Franklin, OH: The Authors, 1981.

Klinkenberg, Audrey M. *The Annotated Records of the Saugerties United Methodist Church, Saugerties, Ulster County, New York, up to 1899*. Saugerties, NY: The Church, 1996.

"Marriages of the Katsbaan Dutch Church in Saugerties, Ulster County, New York." *NYG&B Record*, vol. 83 (1952) no. 1: 19–23; vol. 91 (1960) no. 1: 17–28, no. 2: 80–89, no. 4: 242–245; vol. 92 (1961) no. 1: 35–49. [NYG&B eLibrary]

Mearns, Shirley A., comp. *Melancholy—Awful and Etc.: (Deaths, Marriages, and Other Genealogical Bits) from "The Ulster Republican" (sic) Published at Kingston, New York, 1837–1845.* Kingston, NY: The Author, 1983.

Poucher, J. Wilson, and Byron J. Terwilliger, eds. *Old Gravestones of Ulster County, New York: Twenty-Two Thousand Inscriptions.* Hurley, New York: Ulster County Genealogical Sociey, 1931. [Ancestry.com]

Roney, Lila J., comp. "Gravestone Inscriptions of Old Hurley, Ulster County, NY." Typescript, 1927. NYPL, New York. [NYG&B eLibrary]

———, comp. and ed. "Gravestone Inscriptions of Ulster County, NY." 4 vols. Typescript, 1924–1928. NYPL, New York. [NYG&B eLibrary]

Totten, John R., ed. "Ulster County, New York, Tax Lists, 1709, 1709–10, 1711–12, 1718–19 and 1720–21." *NYG&B Record*, vol. 62, no. 2 (1931): 146–150. [NYG&B eLibrary].

Ulster County, NYG&B Church Surveys Collection. NYG&B, New York. [NYG&B eLibrary]

Worden, Jean D. "Book 1, Subject Index." In *Revised Master Index to the New York State Daughters of the American Revolution Genealogical Records Volumes.* Zephyrhills, FL: J. D. Worden, 1998. The Subject Index includes a listing by county of the cemeteries, churches, towns, and other sources of records transcribed by the DAR.

———. *Katsbaan and Saugerties Reformed Church, Ulster County, New York.* Franklin, OH: Jean D. Worden, 1982. Includes baptismal records, marriages, and an index.

———. *Marbletown Reformed Dutch Church, Ulster County, New York, 1737–1944; Baptisms 1746–1944; Marriages 1796–1930; Stone Ridge Methodist Church, Ulster County, New York; Marriages 1848–1875; Baptisms 1875–1884.* Franklin, OH: Jean D. Worden, 1987.

———. *New Paltz Reformed Dutch Church, New Paltz, New York, 1817–1882; New Paltz and Plattekill Methodist Episcopal Circuit, 1842–1867; Shokan Reformed Dutch Church, Olive, Ulster County, New York, 1799–1892; Death Notices from Kingston, New Paltz, and Poughkeepsie Newspapers, 1865–1895; Quaker Records from Plains Monthly Meeting, Ulster County, New York, 1787–1864.* Franklin, OH: Jean D. Worden, 1987.

———. *Wawarsing Reformed Church, Ulster County, New York, 1745–1883; New Prospect Reformed Dutch Church, Ulster County, New York, 1816–1886; Bloomington Dutch Reformed Church, Ulster County, New York, 1796–1859; Newburgh Circuit, Methodist Episcopal Church, 1789–1834.* Franklin, OH: Jean D. Worden, 1987.

Zimm, Louise H. "Earliest English Deeds of Ulster County, New York." 2 vols. Typescript, 1936. NYPL, New York.

Other Resources

Adams, Arthur G., ed. *The Catskills: An Illustrated Historical Guide with Gazetteer.* New York: Fordham University Press, 1990.

Anson, Shirley V. *Quaker History and Genealogy of the Marlborough Meeting, Ulster County, NY, 1804–1900.* Clintondale, NY: Gateway Press, 1980.

Beers, F. W. *County Atlas of Ulster, New York: From Recent and Actual Surveys and Records.* New York, 1874.

Brink, Benjamin Myer. *Olde Ulster: An Historical and Genealogical Magazine.* 10 vols. Kingston, NY: Benjamin Myer Brink. 1905–1914.

Child, Hamilton. *Gazetteer and Business Directory of Ulster County, NY, for 1871–2.* Syracuse, 1870.

Clearwater, Alphonso T. *The History of Ulster County, New York.* Kingston, NY: W. J. Van Deusen, 1907.

Cochrane, Charles H. *The History of the Town of Marlborough, Ulster County, New York: From the First Settlement in 1712, by Capt. Wm. Bond, to 1887.* Poughkeepsie, 1886.

DeWitt, William C. *People's History of Kingston, Rondout, and Vicinity: The First Capital of New York State (1820–1943).* New Haven, CT: Tuttle, Morehouse & Taylor, 1944.

Donahue, Donald C., Jack K Middaugh, and Audrey M Klinkenberg. *The Ulster County Genealogical Society's Families of Ulster County.* Hurley, NY: The Society, 1995.

"The Erection of Foxhall Manor," *Olde Ulster*, vol. 2 (1906): 97–104.

"Executive Minutes of the New York Colonial Council from 1668–1783." In *Documents of the Senate of the State of New York, Volume 8.* Albany: The Argus Company, 1903.

Fay, Loren V. *Ulster County, New York, Genealogical Research Secrets.* Albany: Loren V. Fay, 1983.

Fried, Marc B. *The Early History of Kingston and Ulster County, New York.* Marbletown, NY: Ulster County Historical Society, 1975.

Gentile, Nancy, and Eric J. Roth. *Historic Huguenot Street and Its Founding Families.* New Paltz, New York: Huguenot Historical Society, 2004.

Greater Hudson Heritage Network. *History Keepers' Companion: Guide to Sites & Sources of the Lower Hudson Valley and Western Connecticut.* Fleischmanns, N.Y: Purple Mountain Press, 1998. The Greater Hudson Heritage Network is in the process of updating and creating an online version of this publication; information is at *www.greaterhudson.org/history-keepers-companion.html.*

Griffiths, George R. *Dutch Families of Old Kingston (Ulster County, New York).* Chandler, AZ: George R. Griffiths, 1995.

Hasbrouck, Kenneth E. *Births, Marriages, Deaths, New Paltz, Ulster County, New York: 1847–1850: Taken from an Early Town Clerk's Record.* N.p., 1990. [DunhamWilcox.net]

Heidgerd, Ruth P. *Ulster County in the Revolution: A Guide to Those Who Served.* A project of the Ulster County Bicentennial Commission. New Paltz, NY: The Commission, 1977.

Heidgerd, William. *Black History of New Paltz.* New Paltz, NY: Haviland-Heidgerd Historical Collection, Elting Memorial Library, 1986.

Historical Records Survey, New York State. *Inventory of the County Archives of New York State (Exclusive of the Five Counties of New York City) No. 51. Ulster County.* Albany: Work Projects Administration, Historical Records Survey, 1940.

History of Delaware County, NY: With Illustrations, Biographical Sketches, and Portraits of Some Pioneers and Prominent Residents. New York, 1880.

The History of Ulster County, with Emphasis upon the Last 100 Years, 1883–1983. Kingston, NY: Ulster County Historians, 1984.

Hudson River Valley Review: A Journal of Regional Studies. Poughkeepsie, NY: Hudson River Valley Institute at Marist College, 2002–present. [hudsonrivervalley.org]

LeFevre, Ralph. *History of New Paltz, New York, and Its Old Families (from 1678 to 1820): Including The Huguenot Pioneers and Others Who Settled in New Paltz Previous to The Revolution; with an Appendix Bringing Down the History of Certain Families and Some Other Matter to 1850.* Albany: Fort Orange Press, 1903.

New York Historical Resources Center. *Guide to Historical Resources in Ulster County, New York, Repositories.* Ithaca, NY: Cornell University, 1988. [books.FamilySearch.org]

Plank, Will. *Banners and Bugles: A Record of Ulster County, New York, and the Mid-Hudson Region in the Civil War.* Marlborough, NY: Centennial Press, 1963.

Prehn, Florence. *Early Ulster County Genealogies.* Saugerties, NY: KTB Associates, 1978.

Quinlan, James Eldridge. *History of Sullivan County: Embracing an Account of Its Geology, Climate, Aborigines, Early Settlement, Organization; the formation of Its Towns with Biographical Sketches of Prominent Residents.* Liberty, NY, 1873.

Rockwell, Charles. *The Catskill Mountains and the Region Around . . . .* New York, 1867.

Ruttenber, E. M. *History of the Town of Newburgh.* Newburgh, NY, 1859.

Schoonmaker, Marius. *The History of Kingston, New York: From Its Early Settlement to the Year 1820.* Kingston, NY, 1888.

Sylvester, Nathaniel B. *History of Ulster County, New York: With Illustrations and Biographical Sketches of Its Prominent Men and Pioneers.* Philadelphia: Everts & Peck, 1880. Book includes general history, history of towns, lists of Ulster County men who served in the Civil War. Index available from Berkshire Family History Association.

University of the State of New York. Division of Archives and History. *Historical account and inventory of records of the city of Kingston.* Albany, University of the State of New York, 1918.

Van Buren, Augustus H. *A History of Ulster County under the Dominion of the Dutch.* Kingston, NY: n.p., 1923.

— — —. *Index to Old Ulster.* Kingston, NY: Senate House Museum, 1963.

Woolsey, C. M. *History of the Town of Marlborough, Ulster County, New York: From Its Earliest Discovery.* Albany: J. B. Lyon Company, 1908.

Zimm, Louise H. *Southeastern New York: History of the Counties of Ulster, Dutchess, Orange, Rockland, and Putnam.* 3 vols. New York: Lewis Historical Publishing Co., 1946. Index available from Berkshire Family History Association.

Additional Online Resources

Ancestry.com

There are vast numbers of records on *Ancestry.com* that pertain to people who have lived in New York State. See chapter 16 for a description of *Ancestry.com*'s resources and its partnership with the New York State Archives. A search of the online card catalog by county may reveal lesser known resources that pertain to a locality, such as town records, abstracts, transcriptions, city directories, and local histories.

FamilySearch.org

FamilySearch has extensive collections of New York records, including religious records, which are searchable by name and location, but not by county. The following collections include record images (browsable, but not searchable) that are organized by county:

- "New York, Land Records, 1630–1975." Includes land and property records. *familysearch.org/search/collection/2078654*
- "New York, Probate Records, 1629–1971." Includes wills, letters of administration, and guardianship papers. *familysearch.org/search/collection/1920234*

For both collections, choose the browse option and then select Ulster to view the available records sets.

A detailed description of *FamilySearch.org* resources is found in chapter 16.

Hudson River Valley Heritage (HRVH)
www.hrvh.org/cdm

The HRVH website provides free access to digital collections of historical material from more than 40 organizations in Columbia, Greene, Dutchess, Ulster, Sullivan, Rockland, Orange, Putnam, and Westchester counties.

New York Heritage Digital Collections: New York State Newspaper Project
www.nyheritage.org/newspapers

The website provides links to digital newspapers collections in 26 counties (currently) made accessible through New York Heritage, New York State Historic Newspapers, HRVH Historical Newspapers, and other providers.

NYGenWeb Project: Ulster County
www.hopefarm.com/geneatop.htm

Part of the national, USGenWeb volunteer initiative, the website provides information and resources for county research.

Warren County

Formed March 12, 1813

Parent County   Washington
Daughter Counties   None
County Seat   Town of Queensbury

Major Land Transactions
See table in chapter 7, Land Records
Totten and Crossfield Purchase 1771–1787

Town Boundary Map
★ - County seat

Towns (and Cities)	Villages and other Settlements		Notes
Athol Name for Town of Thurman 1792–1852			

Bolton
1792   Settlers from New England
1799   Formed in Washington County
      from Town of Athol (now
      Thurman)
1807   Daughter town Rochester (now
      Hague) formed
1810   Daughter town Caldwell (now
      Lake George) formed
1813   Transferred to new county of
      Warren
1838   Daughter town Horicon formed
	Bolton
	Bolton Landing
	North Bolton
	Riverbank
	Sagamore		

Caldwell Name for Town of Lake George 1810–1962			

Chester
Settled in late 1700s
1799   Formed in Washington County
      from Town of Athol (now
      Thurman)
1813   Transferred to new county of
      Warren
	Chestertown
	Darrowsville
	Hyde
	Igerna
	Landon Hill
		Pottersville
		Riparius
		Starbuckville
		The Glen
			• Riparius, also Riverside, on Johnsburg
			  town line
			• Starbuckville on Horicon town line

Glens Falls (city)
1908   Incorporated as a city from the
      Village of Glens Falls in the Town
      of Queensbury			

Hague
1796   Settled
1807   Formed in Washington County
      as Town of Rochester from
      Town of Bolton
1808   Name changed to Hague
1813   Transferred to new county of
      Warren
1838   Daughter town Horicon formed
	Brant Lake
	Graphite
	Hague
	Indian Kettles
	Sabbath Day Point
	Silver Bay
	Wardboro
			• Brant Lake in Town of Horicon after 1838
			• Wardboro also Wards

Horicon
c.1810   Settled
1838   Formed from towns of Bolton
      and Hague
	Adirondack
	Brant Lake
	Haysburgh
	Horicon Center
		Pottersville
		South Horicon
		Starbuckville
			• Adirondack formerly The Elbow and
			  Mill Brook
			• Brant Lake in Town of Hague before 1838;
			  variant names Bartonville and Horicon
			• Starbuckville on Chester town line

Johnsburg(h)
Settled soon after Revolutionary War
1805   Formed in Washington County
      from Town of Athol (now
      Thurman)
1813   Transferred to new county of
      Warren
	Baker(s) Mills
	Garnet Lake
	Holcombville
	Johnsburg(h)
	North Creek
		North River
		Riparius
		Sodom
		The Glen
		Wevertown
			• Riparius also Riverside, on Chester
			  town line
			• Sodom also Sodom Corners
			• The Glen on Thurman town line
			• Wevertown also Nobles Corners and
			  Weavertown

Towns (and Cities)	Villages and other Settlements	Notes
Lake George Settled before Revolution 1810 Formed in Washington County as Town of Caldwell from towns of Athol (now Thurman), Bolton, and Queensbury 1813 Transferred to new county of Warren 1962 Name changed to Lake George	Big Hollow Crosbyside Diamond Point Lake George (v)	• Crosbyside site of Wiawaka vacation house established 1903 for female factory workers • Diamond Point also High View and Hillview • Village of Lake George inc. 1903; called Caldwell before 1903; county seat 1813–1963; 1963–present courthouses in Queensbury and mailing address Lake George
Lake Luzerne 1770 Settled 1792 Formed in Washington County as Town of Fairfield from Town of Queensbury 1808 Name changed to Luzerne 1813 Transferred to new county of Warren 1963 Name changed to Lake Luzerne	Beartown Danielstown Fourth Lake Hartman Lake Luzerne Lake Vanare Luzerne	
Luzerne Name for Lake Luzerne 1808–1963		
Queensbury * c. 1760 Settled 1762 Incorporated by patent as a township in Washington County 1786 Erected as Town of Queensbury by New York State * 1792 Daughter towns Athol (now Thurman) and Fairfield (now Lake Luzerne) formed 1810 Daughter town Caldwell (now Lake George) formed 1813 Transferred to new county of Warren 1908 Village of Glens Falls incorporated as City of Glen Falls	Assembly Point Brayton Cleverdale French Mountain Glens Falls (v) Harrisena Oneida Corners Paradise Beach Queensbury Rockhurst West Glens Falls	* County courthouses in Queensbury from 1963 * In 1786 Town of Queensbury coterminous with future Warren County • Village of Glens Falls inc. 1839; became City of Glen Falls 1908; formerly Glenville, Pearl Village, The Corners, Wings Corners, and Wings Falls • Oneida Corners also Oneida
Stony Creek 1795 Settled 1852 Formed from Town of Thurman	Bakertown Knowelhurst Creek Center Stony Creek Harrisburg	• Harrisburg also West Stony Creek
Thurman Settled in late 1700s 1792 Formed in Washington County as Town of Athol from the Town of Queensbury 1799 Daughter towns Bolton and Chester formed 1805 Daughter town Johnsburg(h) formed 1810 Daughter town Caldwell (now Lake George) formed	Athol Fullers High Street The Glen Thurman	• The Glen on Johnsburg(h) town line • Thurman also Kenyontown

(Thurman continud on next page)

Towns (and Cities)	Villages and other Settlements	Notes
Thurman (continued) 1813 Transferred to new county of Warren; daughter town Warrensburgh formed 1852 Athol renamed Thurman; daughter town Stony Creek formed		
Warrensburg(h) Settled shortly after Revolution 1813 Formed from Town of Athol (now Thurman)	Riverbank Warrensburg(h)	

NEW YORK STATE CENSUS RECORDS

See also chapter 3, Census Records

County originals at Warren County Records Center & Archives: 1855, 1865, 1875, 1892, 1905, 1915, 1925 (1825, 1835, and 1845 are lost)

State originals at the NYSA: 1915, 1925

Microfilm at the FHL, NYPL, and NYSL; many years are online at *FamilySearch.org* and *Ancestry.com*.

NATIONAL/STATEWIDE REPOSITORIES & RESOURCES

See chapter 16

COUNTYWIDE REPOSITORIES & RESOURCES

Warren County Clerk, Records Center & Archives
Warren County Municipal Center • 1340 State Route 9
Lake George, NY 12845 • (518) 761-6455
www.warrencountyny.gov/clerk

Holdings include land records 1813–present, court records, naturalization records 1813–1955, almshouse records 1855–1979, bastardy papers 1813–1913, book of dower 1821–1858, book of wills 1813–1974, census records 1830–1925, business records, Civil War town clerks' registers 1865, executions 1834–1974, jail record book 1868–1883, jury lists 1813–1985, maps 1786–present, marriage records and index 1908–1935, military discharge records 1887–1914, mortgage records 1813–present, Revolutionary War Service Affidavits 1818–1845, school district records 1831–1960, and miscellaneous town records 1795–1968. A full list of collections is available on the clerk's website. Select collections are online.

Warren County –Town and Village Clerks
Birth, marriage, and death records are maintained by the clerk of the municipality in which the event occurred; see Introduction to County Guides for details of other records which may also be held by municipal clerks. For contact information, see *www.warrencountyny. gov/gov/phone.php*.

Warren County Surrogate's Court
Warren County Municipal Center • 1340 State Route 9
Lake George, NY 12845 • (518) 761-6514

Holds probate records from 1813 to the present. See also chapter 6, Probate Records.

Warren County Public Libraries
Warren is part of the Southern Adirondack Library System; see *http:// directory.sals.edu* to access each library. Many hold genealogy and local history collections.

Crandall Public Library: Folklife Center
251 Glen Street • Glens Falls, NY 12801 • (518) 792-6508 ext. 239
www.crandalllibrary.org/folklife

Holds a copy of the New York State Vital Records Indexes. The Center maintains the library's Special Collections and Archives, consisting of books and periodicals, cemetery transcriptions (Warren, Washington, and Saratoga counties), church record transcriptions, city directories, family papers, maps (including Sanborn Maps), manuscripts, 61,000 photographs, scrapbooks, vertical files, and yearbooks.

Warren County Historian
Warren County Municipal Center
Room 7-122, Warren County Clerk's Wing • 1340 State Route 9
Lake George, NY 12845 • (518) 761-6544
www.warrencountyny.gov/historian

Family papers and genealogies, census records and indexes, cemetery records, church records, directories, histories, maps, military records (French & Indian War, Revolutionary War, Civil War, World War I), letters, divorce actions 1860–1897, jury lists, Surrogate's Court Dower Book 1821–1830, naturalizations 1789 and 1813–1940, assessment rolls, abstracts of wills 1813–1850, abstracts of deeds 1813–1825, guardianship records, homestead exemptions 1851–1940, and town records. Website includes complete list of holdings and select records.

Warren County – All Municipal Historians
While not authorized to answer genealogical inquiries, town and village historians can provide valuable historical information and research advice; some maintain collections and webpages which may include transcribed records, local histories, and other genealogical material. See contact information at *www.warrencountyny.gov/ historian/historians.php* or at the website of the Association of Public Historians of New York State at *www.aphnys.org*.

Warren County Historical Society
195 Sunnyside Road • Queensbury, NY 12804
(518) 743-0734 • Email: mail@warrencountyhistoricalsociety.org
www.warrencountyhistoricalsociety.org

Society's Research Library includes local histories, family histories and surname files. Its collection consists of archaeological and early American Indian artifacts, historic postcards, and records. Publishes *Pastimes*, quarterly.

REGIONAL REPOSITORIES & RESOURCES

Adirondack Museum Library
See listing in Hamilton County Guide

Fulton-Montgomery Community College: Evans Library: The Kenneth R. Dorn Regional History Study Center
See listing in Fulton County Guide

Northeastern New York Genealogical Society
See Warren County Historical Society for contact information
www.rootsweb.ancestry.com/~nywarren/community/nnygs.htm

In mid-2014, the Northeastern Historical Society began working closely with the Warren County Historical Society and the organizations may merge in the future. *Patents: The Northeastern New York Genealogical Society Bulletin*, published bi-monthly since 1962, covers Warren, Washington, Saratoga and Essex counties.

SUNY Adirondack: Hill Collection of Local History
Scoville Learning Center • 640 Bay Road • Queensbury, NY 12804
(518) 743-2260 • Email: librarian@sunyacc.edu
http://libguides.sunyacc.edu/hillcollection

Books, manuscripts, pamphlets, county and town histories, scrapbooks, and clippings documenting the history of the Glen Falls area from the 1700s to the present.

LOCAL REPOSITORIES & RESOURCES
Alphabetized by location

Historical Society of the Town of Bolton and Bolton Historical Museum
4924 Main Street • Bolton Landing, NY 12814 • (518) 644-9960
Email: info@boltonhistorical.org • www.boltonhistorical.org

Census materials, land, military, political, and vital records. Website includes collection of transcribed records, cemetery histories, census transcriptions and indexes, and sketches from History of Warren County (1963).

Chapman Historical Museum
348 Glen Street • Glens Falls, NY 12801 • (518) 793-2826
Email: ContactUs@ChapmanMuseum.org
www.chapmanmuseum.org

Museum documents the history of Glens Falls, Queensbury, and the Southern Adirondacks through programs and events, exhibits, and archives. Research services are offered for a fee.

Hague Historical Society and Hague Historical Museum
Museum: 9793 Graphite Mountain Road
Hague, NY 12836 • (518) 543-6161
www.townofhague.org/townofhague/Museum/MuseumHome.htm
Society: PO Box 794 • Hague, NY 12836-0794
Email: haguehistoricalsociety@yahoo.com • Facebook page

Books, genealogies, church records, cemetery records, military records, vital records, and local memorial markers. Museum includes historical information and photographs.

Warrensburg Historical Society
Museum: 3754 Main Street (VFW Building)
Society: PO Box 441 • Warrensburg NY 12885
Email: whs7396@yahoo.com • www.whs12885.org

Published bicentennial book with biographies and historical notes, indexed. Quarterly newsletter.

SELECTED PRINT & ONLINE RESOURCES
Below is a selection of resources relevant for research in this county. The list is representative, not exhaustive. Additional titles—particularly of abstracts, indexes, transcriptions, and local histories—are available; consult the introduction to Part Two for further information. For guidance on how to identify and locate community directories and local newspapers, see chapter 11, City Directories, and chapter 12, Newspapers, in Part One of this book.

Abstracts, Indexes & Transcriptions
Barber, Gertrude Audrey. "Abstracts of Wills of Warren County, N.Y., from 1813–1850: Copied from the Original Records at the Surrogate's Office, Glens Falls, N.Y." Typescript, 1937. NYPL, New York.

County of Warren Abstracts. Syracuse: Central New York Genealogical Society, 2000. Abstracts for a range of genealogical records originally published in the quarterly *Tree Talks.*

Daughters of the American Revolution, comps. *New York DAR Genealogical Records Committee Report.* Since 1913 DAR volunteers have transcribed many thousands of unpublished cemetery, church, and town records throughout New York. The reports are at the DAR Library; copies are at the NYSL and the NYPL. The DAR has a searchable name index to all the GRC reports at *http://services.dar.org/Public/DAR_Research/search/?Tab_ID=6.* See Jean Worden's index below for a listing by county of the New York record sets that were transcribed by the DAR before 1998.

Harris, Edward D. "Inscriptions in the Luzerne Cemetery, Warren County, New York, as Found in 1912." Manuscript, 1912. NYPL, New York.

Haviland, Mrs. Frank. "Essex and Warren County Cemetery Records." Typescript, 1925. NYPL, New York.

Kelly, Arthur C. M. *Index to Tree Talks County Packet: Warren County.* Rhinebeck, NY: Kinship, 2002.

Warren County, NYG&B Church Surveys Collection. NYG&B, New York. [NYG&B eLibrary]

Worden, Jean D. "Book 1, Subject Index." In *Revised Master Index to the New York State Daughters of the American Revolution Genealogical Records Volumes.* Zephyrhills, FL: J. D. Worden, 1998. The Subject Index includes a listing by county of the cemeteries, churches, towns, and other sources of records transcribed by the DAR.

Other Resources
Beers, F. W. *County Atlas of Warren, New York.* New York, 1876.

Brown, William H. *History of Warren County, New York.* Queensbury, NY: Board of Supervisors of Warren County, 1963.

Child, Hamilton. *Gazetteer and Business Directory of Saratoga County, N.Y., and Queensbury, Warren County, for 1871.* Syracuse, 1871.

Fay, Loren V. *Warren County, New York, Genealogical Research Secrets.* Albany: L.V. Fay 1983.

Guide to Local Historical Materials: A Union List of the Holdings of Public Libraries in Saratoga, Warren, Washington and Hamilton Counties. Saratoga Springs, NY: Southern Adirondack Library System, 1977.

Holden, A. W. *A History of the Town of Queensbury, in the State of New York: With Biographical Sketches of Many of Its Distinguished Men and Pioneers, and Some Account of the Aborigines of Northern New York.* Albany, 1874.

Hyde, Louis F. *History of Glens Falls, New York, and its Settlement.* Glens Falls, NY: n.p., 1936.

Metcalfe, Ann B. *The Schroon River: A History of an Adirondack Valley and Its People.* Lake George, NY: Warren County Historical Society, 2000.

New York Historical Resources Center. *Guide to the Historical Resources in Warren County, New York Repositories.* Cornell University, 1982. [*books.FamilySearch.org*]

The Patents: The Northeastern New York Genealogical Society Newsletter. Queensbury, NY: Northeastern New York Genealogical Society, 1982–present. *www.rootsweb.ancestry.com/~nywarren/community/nnygs.htm*

Smith, H. P. *History of Warren County With Illustrations and Bibliographical Sketches of Some of Its Prominent Men and Pioneers.* Syracuse, 1885. Reprint, Interlaken, NY: Heart of the Lakes Publishing, 1981.

Warren County Historical Society (NY). *Warren County: (New York): Its People & Their History Over Time.* Virginia Beach, VA: Donning Co., 2009.

Writers' Program of the Works Project Administration in the State of New York. *Warren County: A History and Guide.* New York: The Warren County Board of Supervisors, 1942.

Additional Online Resources

Ancestry.com

There are vast numbers of records on *Ancestry.com* that pertain to people who have lived in New York State. See chapter 16 for a description of *Ancestry.com*'s resources and its partnership with the New York State Archives. A search of the online card catalog by county may reveal lesser known resources that pertain to a locality, such as town records, abstracts, transcriptions, city directories, and local histories.

FamilySearch.org

FamilySearch has extensive collections of New York records, including religious records, which are searchable by name and location, but not by county. The following collections include record images (browsable, but not searchable) that are organized by county:

- "New York, Land Records, 1630–1975." Includes land and property records. *familysearch.org/search/collection/2078654*
- "New York, Probate Records, 1629–1971." Includes wills, letters of administration, and guardianship papers. *familysearch.org/search/collection/1920234*

For both collections, choose the browse option and then select Warren to view the available records sets.

A detailed description of *FamilySearch.org* resources is found in chapter 16.

NYGenWeb Project: Warren County

www.rootsweb.ancestry.com/~nywarren

Part of the national, USGenWeb volunteer initiative, the website provides information and resources for county research.

Washington County

Formed March 12, 1772

County Name	Originally named Charlotte County Name changed to Washington April 2, 1784
Parent County	Albany
Daughter Counties	Clinton 1788 • Warren 1813
County Seat	Village of Fort Edward

Major Land Transactions
See table in chapter 7, Land Records
Saratoga Patent 1684

Town Boundary Map
★ - County seat

Towns (and Cities)	Villages and other Settlements		Notes
Argyle 1764 Arglye patent granted in Albany County 1765 Settled 1772 Lands become part of newly formed Charlotte County * 1786 Erected as Town of Argyle by New York State 1803 Daughter town Greenwich formed 1818 Daughter town Fort Edward formed	Argyle (v) Evansville Goose Island Lick Springs North Amboy North Argyle South Argyle (The) Hook		* Charlotte County renamed Washington County 1784 • Village of Argyle inc. 1838 • North Argyle also Stevensons Corner
Athol * In Washington County 1792–1813			* See Town of Thurman in Warren County
Bolton * In Washington County 1799–1813			* See Warren County
Caldwell * In Washington County 1810–1813			* See Town of Lake George, Warren County
Cambridge 1761 Cambridge patent granted in Albany County 1761–63 Settled 1772 Formed as a district of Albany County 1788 Recognized as a town in Albany County by New York State 1791 Town transferred to Washington County 1815 Daughter towns Jackson and White Creek formed	Buskirk(s) Bridge Cambridge (v) Center Cambridge Coila Fly Summit Lee North Cambridge Oak Hill South Cambridge Summit Station West Cambridge		• Village of Cambridge inc. 1866; shared with Town of White Creek; also Dorrs Corners, and North White Creek • Coila also Green Settlement and Stevensons Corner; on Jackson town line • Fly Summit also Vly Summit; on Easton town line
Chester * In Washington County 1799–1813			* See Warren County
Crown Point * In Washington County 1786–1788			* See Essex County
Dresden 1784 Settled 1822 Formed as Town of South Bay from Town of Putnam; name changed to Dresden one month later	Clemons Dresden Dresden Center	Huletts Landing Snody Dock South Bay	
Easton Settled late 1600s 1789 Formed in Albany County from towns of Saratoga and Stillwater 1791 Town transferred to Washington County	Archdale Bangall Barkers Grove Beadleys Corners Crandalls Corners Easton	Fly Summit Greenwich (v) Middle Falls North Easton South Easton	• Fly Summit also Vly Summit; on Cambridge town line • Village of Greenwich inc. 1809; shared with Town of Greenwich; formerly Whipple City 1804–1809; Union Village 1809–1867 • Middle Falls was Arkansaw and Galesville before 1875; on Greenwich town line • North Easton also Easton Corners

Towns (and Cities)	Villages and other Settlements		Notes
Fort Ann 1757 Queens Fort renamed Fort Ann for daughter of King George 1786 Erected as Town of Westfield by New York State 1793 Daughter town Hartford formed 1806 Daughter town Putnam formed 1808 Name changed to Fort Ann	Canes Falls Comstock Dewey Bridge Fort Ann (v) Furnace Hollow Head of South Bay Hogtown Johnnycake Corners	Katskill Bay Pattens Mills Pilot Knob Shelving Rock South Bay Tripoli West Fort Ann	• Comstock formerly Comstock(s) Landing • Village of Fort Ann inc. 1820 • Tripoli formerly Griswolds Mills
Fort Edward 1709 Site of Fort Nicholson 1818 Formed from Town of Argyle	Durkeetown Fort Edward (v) Fort Edward Center Fort Miller Moses Kill		• Village of Fort Edward county seat 1994–present; 1773–1779 courts held in homes and hotels in Fort Edward and New Perth (Salem); 1779 county seat est. New Perth; 1792–1796 Fort Edward shares county seat; 1796–1994 Village of Salem shares county seat with Village of Sandy Hill (now Hudson Falls), Town of Kingsbury • Moses Kill also Mock
Granville 1764 First patents awarded to those who fought in the French and Indian war c.1770 Settlers from New England 1786 Erected as Town of Granville by New York State	Bakers Corners Granville (v) Hillsdale Jamesville Middle Granville North Granville Raceville	Slyboro South Granville Truthville West Granville West Granville Corners	• Village of Granville inc. 1849; formerly Bishops Corners
Greenwich Settled by Dutch mid-1700s 1803 Formed from Town of Argyle	Bald Mountain Battenville Center Falls Clarks Mills Cossayuna East Greenwich Fort Miller Greenwich (v) Middle Falls Mountain North Greenwich Spraguetown Thomson Trionds		• Battenville also Battenkill • Center Falls formerly Franklin and Hardscrabble • Cossayuna formerly Hog Hollow, Lake, and Lakeville • East Greenwich formerly Slab City • Village of Greenwich inc. 1809; shared with Town of Easton; formerly Whipple City 1804–1809 and Union Village 1809–1867 • Middle Falls was Arkansaw and Galesville before 1875; on Easton town line • North Greenwich formerly Antioch and Reids Corners
Hague * In Washington County 1807–1813			* See Warren County
Hampton Settled before the Revolution 1786 Erected as Town of Hampton by New York State	Hampton Hampton Corners	Hampton Flats Low Hampton	
Hartford 1764 Provincial Patent granted to 26 commissioned officers of New York Infantry 1793 Formed from Town of Westfield (now Fort Ann)	Adamsville East Hartford Hartford Log Village South Hartford		• Hamlet of Hartford also North Hartford

Towns (and Cities)	Villages and other Settlements		Notes
Hebron Known as District of Black Creek before 1774 **1769–70** Settled **1774** Patents granted to soldiers, especially Scottish Highlanders who had served in the French and Indian war **1786** Erected as Town of Hebron by New York State	Belcher Clarks Mills East Hebron North Hebron Porter Slateville Tiplady West Hebron West Pawlett		• East Hebron also Hebron • North Hebron also Munros Meadows • West Hebron formerly Chamberlain Mills
Jackson **1761–65** Settled **1762** Part of Anaquassacook Patent **1815** Formed from Town of Cambridge	Anaquass(a)cook Coila Eagleville	Jackson Center Shushan The Plains	• Coila also Green Settlement and Stevensons Corners; on Cambridge town line • Eagleville also East Salem; on Salem town line • Shushan on Salem town line
Johnsburg(h) * In Washington County 1805–1813			* See Warren County
Kingsbury **1762** Kingsbury Patent granted; first settlers from New York City **1786** Erected as Town of Kingsbury by New York State	Adamsville Baldwin Corner Dunham(s) Basin Hudson Falls (v) Kingsbury	Langdon(s) Corners Moss Street Pattens Mills Smith(s) Basin Vaughns Corners	• Village of Hudson Falls inc. 1810 as Village of Sandy Hill, name changed 1910; shared county seat with Village of Salem 1796–1994
Luzerne (named Fairfield 1792–1808) * In Washington County 1792–1813			* See Town of Lake Luzerne, Warren County
Plattsburgh * In Washington County 1785–1788			* See Clinton County
Putnam Settled before Revolution **1806** Formed from Town of Westfield (now Fort Ann) **1822** Daughter town South Bay (now Dresden) formed	Glenburnie (on Lake George) Gull Bay Putnam Putnam Station Wright		• Putnam also Putnam Center and Putnam Corners
Queensbury * In Washington County 1762–1813 *			* See Warren County * Washington County called Charlotte County until 1784
Salem **1761** Settled **1764** Patent granted and soon divided * **1774** Land tracts combined under township of New Perth **1786** Erected as Town of Salem by New York State	Baxter Mills Clapps Mills Eagleville Fitch(es) Point Greenwich Junction Rexleigh Salem (v) Shushan		* Some deeds refer to land as New Perth and others as White Creek • Eagleville also East Salem; on Jackson town line • Village of Salem county seat 1779–1994—shared with Fort Edwards 1792–1796, shared with Village of Sandy Hill (now Hudson Falls) 1796–1994; courts held here 1773–1779 • Shushan on Jackson town line
Skenesborough Name for Town of Whitehall 1765–1786			

Towns (and Cities)	Villages and other Settlements		Notes
Westfield Name for Town of Fort Ann 1788–1808			
White Creek Part of Walloomsac Patent, settled by Dutch 1815 Formed from Town of Cambridge	Ash Grove Briggs Corners Brighton Corners Cambridge (v) Center White Creek Dorrs Corners Eagle Bridge	Martindale Corners North White Creek Post(s) Corners Pumpkin Hook White Creek White Martindale Corners	• Irish Methodists settled 1770 near Ash Grove • Village of Cambridge inc. 1866; shared with Town of Cambridge; also Dorrs Corners and North White Creek
Whitehall 1761 Settled 1765 Incorporated by patent as Skenesborough 1786 Erected as Town of Whitehall by New York State	Chubbs Dock East Whitehall Grays Corner Whitehall (v)		• Village of Whitehall inc. 1806 as Whitehall Landing; reinc. 1820 as Whitehall, and chartered 1850

NEW YORK STATE CENSUS RECORDS
See also chapter 3, Census Records

County originals at Washington County Clerk's Office: 1825*, 1835, 1855, 1865, 1875, 1892, 1905, 1915, 1925 (1845 is lost)

State originals at the NYSA: 1915, 1925

Microfilm at the FHL, NYPL, and NYSL; many years are online at *FamilySearch.org* and *Ancestry.com*.

*For 1825 census abstract and index, see Barnello, et al., in Abstracts, Indexes & Transcriptions.

NATIONAL/STATEWIDE REPOSITORIES & RESOURCES
See chapter 16

COUNTYWIDE REPOSITORIES & RESOURCES

Washington County Clerk
Municipal Center, Building A • 383 Broadway
Fort Edward, NY 12828(518) 746-2170 •
www.co.washington.ny.us/Departments/cclerk/clk1.htm

The New York state censuses for Washington County 1825, 1835, 1855, 1865, 1875, 1892, 1905, 1915, and 1925; deeds 1794–present, unrecorded conveyances 1742–1870; naturalization records 1794–1952, Dec 1977–Oct 1991 (restricted); births, deaths, and marriages 1848–1849; marriage licenses 1908–1935; probate records 1786–1900; books of record and disposition of real property 1900–present; land records; and court records.

Washington County –Town and Village Clerks
Birth, marriage, and death records are maintained by the clerk of the municipality in which the event occurred; see Introduction to County Guides for details of other records which may also be held by municipal clerks. For contact information, see the County-Town-Village Directory at *www.co.washington.ny.us*.

Washington County Surrogate's Court
383 Broadway • Fort Edward, NY 12828 • (518) 746-2545

Holds probate records from 1787 to the present. Also see chapter 6, Probate Records.

Washington County Archives
Municipal Center, Building A, Basement • 383 Broadway
Fort Edward, NY 12828 • (518) 746-2136
www.co.washington.ny.us/departments/cclerk/clk1.htm • *www.wchs-ny.org*

Maintained by the county clerk. Holdings include birth and death records 1847–1849; marriage records 1847–1849 and 1905–1935; assessment records and tax rolls 1850–present; census records; coroners' inquests 1787–1932; civil and criminal court records 1773–present; deeds and mortgages 1773–present; indictments 1782–1910; insolvency papers 1795–1912; naturalization records 1794–1955; Revolutionary War pension applications 1820–1831; surrogate's court records 1783–1915.

Washington County Public Libraries
Washington is part of the Southern Adirondack Library System; see *http://directory.sals.edu* to access each library. Many libraries hold genealogy and local history collections, including maps and newspapers. For example, Bancroft Public Library has digitized transcriptions of cemetery records, Easton Library's holdings include records of the Quakers, and Cambridge Public Library holds the *Washington County Post*, 1849–present. Also see listings below for Pember Library and Greenwich Library.

Washington County Historical Society
167 Broadway • Fort Edward, NY 12828 • (518) 747-9108
Email: wchs@wchs-ny.org • *www.wchs-ny.org*

Society's Historical Research Library contains books, biographies, local histories and genealogies, deeds, diaries and letters, maps and atlases, periodicals, and photographs. Website contains lists of historical resources in Washington County.

Washington County Historian
Municipal Center, Building A, Records Room • 383 Broadway
Fort Edward, NY 12828 • (518) 746-2178
Email: wchist@co.washington.ny.us
www.co.washington.ny.us/Departments/His/His1.htm

Local histories and genealogies, cemetery records, church records, family Bibles, ledgers, letters and correspondence, military/pension records, newspapers on microfilm, poorhouse records, school records, vital records 1847–1849, Asa Fitch Papers on Washington County genealogy and history, the Goodspeed Collection of fifty boxes of genealogical research contributed by Aaron Godspeed (1862–1932), and other special collections. Many records online.

Washington County – All Municipal Historians
While not authorized to answer genealogical inquiries, city, town and village historians can provide valuable historical information and research advice; some maintain collections and webpages which may include transcribed records, local histories, and other genealogical material. For contact information, see *www.wchs-ny.org/archives.html* or the website of the Association of Public Historians of New York State at *www.aphnys.org*.

REGIONAL REPOSITORIES & RESOURCES

Adirondack Museum Library
See listing in Hamilton County Guide

Capital District Genealogical Society
See listing in Albany County Guide

Fulton-Montgomery Community College: Evans Library: The Kenneth R. Dorn Regional History Study Center
See listing in Fulton County Guide

Northeastern New York Genealogical Society
See listing in Warren County Guide

LOCAL REPOSITORIES & RESOURCES
Alphabetized by location

Dr. Asa Fitch Historical Society
RD 1 Box 336A • Cambridge, NY 12816 • (518) 854-3888
www.salem-ny.com/asafitchpage.html

Society publishes local history books. Website includes the Cruikshank Civil War Letters.

Fort Edward Historical Association and Old Fort House Museum
22 & 29 Lower Broadway • PO Box 106 • Fort Edward, NY 12828
(518) 747-9600 • Email: old-fort-house-museum@juno.com
www.oldforthousemuseum.com

Documents local history and genealogy of Fort Edward and Hudson Falls.

Rogers Island Visitors Center

11 Rogers Island Drive (off Route 197) • PO Box 208
Fort Edward, NY 12828 • (518) 747-3693
Email: rogersisland@gmail.com • www.rogersisland.org

Documents history of Rogers Island and the Revolutionary War.

Pember Library: Local History Collection

33 West Main Street • Granville, NY 12832 • (518) 642-2525
http://gralib.sals.edu/index.php/local-history-collection

Books, pamphlets, brochures, directories and gazetteers, genealogy files, maps and atlases, newspapers, obituary index, periodicals, and photographs.

Greenwich Library: I. V. H. Gill Room

148 Main Street • Greenwich, NY 12834 • (518) 692-7157
Email: pember.library@gmail.com
www.greenwichfreelibrary.com/index.php/local-history/gill-room

Books, documents, census microfilms, genealogies, newspaper microfilms, and Asa Fitch manuscripts.

Hartford Museum and Howard Hanna Memorial Civil War Enlistment Center

44 County Route 23 • Hartford, NY 12838 • (518) 632-5993
www.hartfordny.com/history/museum-civil-war-enlistment-center

Museum documents the history of the Civil War and the Town of Hartford; collections include artifacts, photographs, and books.

The Archives of the Village and Town of Salem, NY

Town Archives: Historic Salem Courthouse • 58 East Broadway
Salem, NY 12865 • Email: HSCPA@salemcourthouse.org
Village Archives: Bancroft Public Library • 181 South Main Street
Salem, NY 12865 • (518) 854-3510
www.salem-ny.com/historicarchives.html

The archives of the Town of Salem include court records, genealogical files, ledgers, maps, taxation and assessment, town clerk's files, town records, and more. Archives of the village include journals, newspapers, town records, and vital records.

Skenesborough Museum

Skenesborough Drive • PO Box 238
Whitehall, NY 12887 • (518) 499-1155

Holdings include artifacts, maps, and photographs documenting the history of Whitehall, the Revolutionary War, the War of 1812, and transportation.

SELECTED PRINT & ONLINE RESOURCES

Below is a selection of resources relevant for research in this county. The list is representative, not exhaustive. Additional titles—particularly of abstracts, indexes, transcriptions, and local histories—are available; consult the introduction to Part Two for further information. For guidance on how to identify and locate community directories and local newspapers, see chapter 11, City Directories, and chapter 12, Newspapers, in Part One of this book.

Abstracts, Indexes & Transcriptions

Barber, Gertrude Audrey. "Abstracts of Wills of Washington County, New York, 1788–1825." Typescript, 1937. New York State Library, Albany. [Ancestry.com]

———. "Cemetery Located at Putnam, Washington County, NY." Typescript, 1931. NYPL, New York. [NYG&B eLibrary]

———. "Meadow Knoll Cemetery Located at Putnam, Washington County, NY." Typescript, 1932. NYPL, New York.

Barnello, Kathleen, Joan Green, Joyce Mason, and Harold Witter. "Abstract of the 1825 New York State Census of Washington County, New York." Syracuse: Central New York Genealogical Society, 1998. Originally published in Tree Talks, vol. 38, no. 4 (1998): 1–92. Index: 94–144, introduction: iii–xi.

Bates, Loretta. Those Called Paupers. Queensbury, NY: The Author, 2013. Includes a listing of 600 children in poorhouse records 1829–1853 with name, birth date, and to whom indentured.

County of Washington Abstracts. Syracuse: Central New York Genealogical Society, 2000. Abstracts for a range of genealogical records originally published in the quarterly Tree Talks.

Daughters of the American Revolution, comps. New York DAR Genealogical Records Committee Report. Since 1913 DAR volunteers have transcribed many thousands of unpublished cemetery, church, and town records throughout New York. The reports are at the DAR Library; copies are at the NYSL and the NYPL. The DAR has a searchable name index to all the GRC reports at http://services.dar.org/Public/DAR_Research/search/?Tab_ID=6. See Jean Worden's index below for a listing by county of the New York record sets that were transcribed by the DAR before 1998.

Fitch, Asa, comp. The Asa Fitch Papers. Fort Campbell, KY: Sleeper Co., 1997.

Hill, Mrs. H. C. "Graveyard Inscriptions from the Towns of Easton and Greenwich, Washington County, NY." Typescript, 1916. NYPL, New York. [NYG&B eLibrary]

Hulslander, Laura P. Abstracts of Deeds of Washington County, New York. Colorado Springs, CO: The Sleeper Co., 1991.

———. Washington County, New York, Vital Records, 1847–1849. New York: The Author, 1993.

Jackson, Mary S., and Edward F. Death Notices from Washington County, New York, Newspapers, 1799–1880. Bowie, MD: Heritage Books, 1995.

———. Marriage Notices from Washington County, New York, Newspapers, 1799–1880. Bowie, MD: Heritage Books, Inc., 1995.

Moore, Charles B. Cemetery Records of the Township of [Argyle, Cambridge, Dresden, Easton, Fort Ann, Granville, Hampton, Hartford, Hebron, Kingsbury, Putnam, Salem, Whitehall] Washington County, New York. 12 vols. Glens Falls, NY: Historical Data Services, 1993–2009. Index available from Berkshire Family History Association.

Vosburgh, Royden Woodward, ed. "Records of the Protestant Presbyterian Congregation of Cambridge in the Village of Cambridge, Washington County, NY." Typescript, 1916. NYPL, New York. [NYG&B eLibrary]

Washington County, NYG&B Church Surveys Collection. NYG&B, New York. [NYG&B eLibrary]

Other Resources

Capital District Genealogical Society Newsletter. Albany: Capital District Genealogical Society, 1982–present. [capitaldistrictgenealogicalsociety.org]

Child, Hamilton. Gazetteer and Business Directory of Washington County, NY, for 1871. Syracuse, 1871.

Corey, Allen. Gazetteer of the County of Washington, NY: Comprising a Correct Statistical and Miscellaneous History of the County and Several Towns. Schuylerville, NY, 1849. [Ancestry.com]

Fitch, Asa. *Early History of the Town of Salem: From Its First Settlement in 1761 to the Close of the Revolutionary War, Together with Incidents of Pioneer Days in Other Towns of Washington County, NY.* Salem, NY: Salem Press, 1927.

———. "History of Washington County, NY." Manuscript, n.d. NYPL, New York. Also see Index by Kenneth Perry.

Foley, Janet W. *Early Settlers of New York State: Their Ancestors and Descendants.* 9 vols. Akron, NY: 1934–1942. Reprint, 2 vols. Baltimore: Genealogical Publishing Co., 1993.

Gibson, James, and William H. Hill. *History of Washington County, New York: The Gibson Papers; The History of Washington Academy; The Bench and Bar of Washington County for a Century.* Fort Edward, NY: Honeywood Press, 1932. Index available from Berkshire Family History Association.

Guide to Local Historical Materials: A Union List of Holdings of Public Libraries in Saratoga, Warren, Washington and Hamilton Counties. Saratoga Springs, NY: Southern Adirondack Library System, 1977.

Hill, William H. *Old Fort Edward Before 1800: An Account of The Historic Ground Now Occupied by the Village of Fort Edward, New York.* Fort Edward, NY: n.p, 1929.

History and Biography of Washington County and the Town of Queensbury, New York. New York, 1894.

Johnson, Crisfield. *History of Washington County, New York with Illustrations and Biographical Sketches of Some of Its Prominent Men and Pioneers.* Philadelphia, 1878.

McLean, J. P. *An Historical Account of the Settlements of Scotch Highlanders in America.* Cleveland, OH: Helman-Taylor, 1900.

New York Historical Resources Center. *Guide to Historical Resources in Washington County, New York, Repositories.* Ithaca, NY: Cornell University, 1983. [*books.FamilySearch.org*]

Perry, Kenneth A. *The Fitch Gazetteer: An Annotated Index to Dr. Asa Fitch's Manuscript History of Washington County, NY.* Bowie, MD: Heritage Books, 1999.

The Patents: The Northeastern New York Genealogical Society Newsletter. Queensbury, NY: Northeastern New York Genealogical Society, 1981–present. [*www.rootsweb.ancestry.com/~nywarren/community/nnygs.htm*]

Salem Historical Committee. *The Salem Book: Records of the Past and Glimpses of the Present.* Salem, NY: Salem Review Press, 1896.

Stone, William L. *Washington County, New York: Its History to the Close of the Nineteenth Century.* New York: New York History Co., 1901. Index available from Berkshire Family History Association.

Stone & Stewart. *New Topographical Atlas of Washington County, New York: From Actual Surveys Especially For This Atlas.* Philadelphia, 1866.

Additional Online Resource

Ancestry.com

There are vast numbers of records on *Ancestry.com* that pertain to people who have lived in New York State. See chapter 16 for a description of *Ancestry.com*'s resources and its partnership with the New York State Archives. A search of the online card catalog by county may reveal lesser known resources that pertain to a locality, such as town records, abstracts, transcriptions, city directories, and local histories.

FamilySearch.org

FamilySearch has extensive collections of New York records, including religious records, which are searchable by name and location, but not by county. The following collections include record images (browsable, but not searchable) that are organized by county:

• "New York, Land Records, 1630–1975." Includes land and property records. *familysearch.org/search/collection/2078654*

• "New York, Probate Records, 1629–1971." Includes wills, letters of administration, and guardianship papers. *familysearch.org/search/collection/1920234*

For both collections, choose the browse option and then select Washington to view the available records sets.

A detailed description of *FamilySearch.org* resources is found in chapter 16.

NYGenWeb Project: Washington County

washington.nygenweb.net

Part of the national, USGenWeb volunteer initiative, the website provides information and resources for county research.

Old Fulton New York Postcards

www.FultonHistory.com

The website provides free access to a vast collection of digitized New York newspapers, including six titles for Washington County.

Wayne County

Formed April 11, 1823

Parent Counties   Ontario • Seneca
Daughter Counties   None
County Seat   Village of Lyons

Major Land Transactions
See chapter 7, Land Records
New Military Tract 1782–1791
Phelps and Gorham Purchase 1788

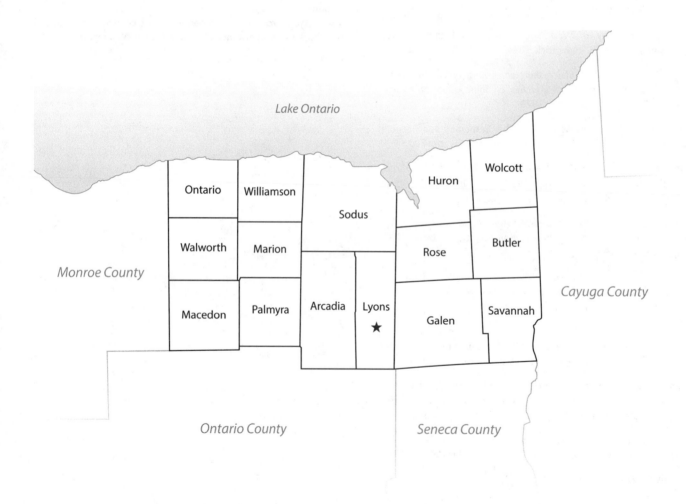

Lake Ontario

Ontario

Williamson

Sodus

Huron

Wolcott

Monroe County

Walworth

Marion

Rose

Butler

Cayuga County

Macedon

Palmyra

Arcadia

Lyons
★

Galen

Savannah

Ontario County

Seneca County

Town Boundary Map
 - County seat

Towns (and Cities)	Villages and other Settlements		Notes
Arcadia 1791 Settled 1825 Formed from Town of Lyons	Arcadia (v) Fairville Fairville Station Hyde(s)ville Jessups Corners	Marbletown Minsteed Newark (v) Stebbins Corner Zurich	• Village of Arcadia inc. 1839, dissolved and became part of Village of Newark in 1853; formerly Lockville • Village of Newark inc. 1853; includes Village of Arcadia; formerly Millers Basin, also East Newark and Newark-Arcadia
Butler 1802–03 Settled 1826 Formed from Town of Wolcott	Butler Center Butler Settlement South Butler	West Butler Westbury Wolcott (v)	• South Butler formerly Harringtons Corner • Westbury shared with Town of Victory, Cayuga County • Village of Wolcott inc. 1852, reinc. 1873; largely located in Town of Wolcott
Galen * 1800 Settled 1812 Formed in Seneca County from Town of Junius 1823 Transferred to new county of Wayne 1824 Daughter town Savannah formed	Angel(ls) Corners Clyde (v) Fergusons Corner Hunt Corner(s) Lock Berlin Lockpit Marengo	Meadville Noble Corner Pangburn Corners Shepards Corner White Schoolhouse Corners	* Galen was the name of one of the 28 Military Tract townships • Village of Clyde inc. 1835; formerly Block House then Lauraville, name changed to Clyde in 1818
Huron 1796 Settled 1826 Formed as Town of Port Bay from Town of Wolcott 1834 Name changed to Huron	Bonni Castle East Bay Park Furnace Village Huron Lake Bluff Lummisville	North Huron Resort Rice Mill Sunset View York	• East Bay Park also East Bay • Furnace Village on Wolcott town line • Huron also South Huron • Resort formerly Port Glasgow • York also York Settlement
Lyons 1789 Settled 1811 Formed in Ontario County from Town of Sodus 1823 Transferred to new county of Wayne; land annexed from Town of Phelps, Ontario County 1825 Daughter town Arcadia formed	Alloway Lyons (v) Pilgrimport Thompson Station Zurich		• Village of Lyons inc. 1831, reinc. 1854; county seat from 1823 as hamlet and village; also called The Forks
Macedon 1789 Settled 1823 Formed from Town of Palmyra	Cator Corners Gananda Huddle Macedon (v) Macedon Center	North Macedon Walworth Station Wayneport Yellow Mills	• Gananda originally conceived as a city; community formed 1973; on Walworth town line • Village of Macedon inc. 1856 • Wayneport formerly West Macedon
Marion 1795–06 Settled 1825 Formed as Town of Winchester from Town of Williamson 1826 Name changed to Marion	Lower Corners Marion Owls Nest Upper Corners		
Ontario 1806 Settlers from Rhode Island * 1807 Formed in Ontario County as Town of Freetown from Town of Williamson 1808 Name changed to Ontario 1823 Transferred to new county of Wayne 1829 Daughter Walworth formed	Bear Creek Fruitland Furnaceville Lakeside Lakeside Station New Boston	Ontario Ontario Center Ontario-on-the-Lake Union Hill Union Hill Station West Ontario	* Some sources say first settler, Freeman Hopkins, was from Massachusetts • Furnaceville formerly Furnace Village

Towns (and Cities)	Villages and other Settlements		Notes
Palmyra **1789** Created as district of Tolland in Ontario County * **1796** Named Town of Palmyra **1823** Transferred to new county of Wayne; daughter town Macedon formed	Cooney Crossing East Palmyra Palmyra (v)		* District of Tolland also known as Swift or Swifts Landing • Village of Palmyra inc. 1819
Port Bay Name for Town of Huron 1826–1834			
Rose **1805** Settled **1826** Formed from Town of Wolcott	Glenmark Lockwood Corners Maunders Corners North Rose	Rose Stewart Corners Wayne Center	• Glenmark formerly Glenmark Falls • North Rose formerly Lambs Corners • Hamlet of Rose formerly Valentine, Albion, and Rose Valley
Savannah **1812** Settled **1824** Formed from Town of Galen	Crusoe Evans Corner Fort Hill Mays Point Noble Corner	Pangburn Corners Savannah (v) Savannah Depot Seneca River Station	• Village of Savannah inc. 1867 and dissolved 4/25/1979
Sodus **1789** Formed in Ontario County **1802** Daughter town Williamson formed **1811** Daughter town Lyons formed **1823** Transferred to new county of Wayne	Alton Joy Salmon Creek Sodus (v) Sodus Center	Sodus Point (v) South Sodus Thorntons Corner Wallington	• Village of Sodus inc. 1917 • Village of Sodus Point inc. 1957 • Wallington also Calciana
Walworth **1800** Settled **1829** Formed from Town of Ontario	Gananda Huddle Lincoln Walworth West Walworth		• Gananda on Macedon town line • Lincoln also Lincklaen • Hamlet of Walworth formerly Douglass Corners
Williamson **1802** Formed in Ontario County from Town of Sodus **1807** Daughter town Freetown (now Ontario) formed **1823** Transferred to new county of Wayne **1825** Daughter town Winchester (now Marion) was formed	East Williamson Pultneyville Williamson		
Wolcott **1805** Settled **1807** Formed in Seneca County from the Town of Junius **1823** Transferred to new county of Wayne **1826** Daughter towns Butler, Port Bay (now Huron), and Rose formed	Desbrough Park Duncans Corners Furnace Furnace Village	North Wolcott Red Creek (v) Wolcott (v) Yellow Red Corners	• Furnace Village on Huron town line • Village of Red Creek inc. 1852; also Jacksonville • Village of Wolcott inc. 1852, reinc. 1873; small part of village in Town of Butler

NEW YORK STATE CENSUS RECORDS

See also chapter 3, Census Records

County originals at Wayne County Historian's Office: 1865, 1875, 1892, 1905, 1915, 1925 (1825, 1835, 1845, and 1855* are lost)

State originals at the NYSA: 1915, 1925

Microfilm at the FHL, NYPL, and NYSL; many years are online at *FamilySearch.org* and *Ancestry.com*.

*Typescript at Wayne County Historian's Office: 1855

NATIONAL/STATEWIDE REPOSITORIES & RESOURCES

See chapter 16

COUNTYWIDE REPOSITORIES & RESOURCES

Wayne County Clerk and Records Center

9 Pearl Street • PO Box 608 • Lyons, NY 14489 • (315) 946-7470
www.co.wayne.ny.us/departments/ctyclerk/ctyclerk.htm

Grantor/grantee indexes 1794–1823, land records 1823–present, the New York state census for Wayne County 1865, 1875, 1892, 1905, 1915, 1925, maps, marriage records 1907–1934, naturalization records 1836–1957, oaths of office, and veterans discharges. The clerk offers a genealogical research service for a fee.

Wayne County – Town and Village Clerks

Birth, marriage, and death records are maintained by the clerk of the municipality in which the event occurred; see Introduction to County Guides for details of other records which may also be held by municipal clerks. For contact information, see *www.co.wayne.ny.us/departments/addressbook.htm*.

Wayne County Surrogate's Court

Wayne County Hall of Justice • 54 Broad Street
Lyons, NY 14489 • (315) 946-5430

Holds probate records 1820s to the present. See also chapter 6, Probate Records.

Wayne County Public Libraries

Wayne is part of the Pioneer Library System; see *www.pls-net.org* or *www.owwl.org* to access each library. Many hold genealogy and local history collections, including books and newspapers. For example, Clyde-Savannah Public Library has a digital archive of ten local newspapers, 1844–2003, and family files (names index on website, *sites.google.com/site/clydesavannahpubliclibrary/Home*).

Wayne County Historian

9 Pearl Street, Suite 3 • PO Box 608 • Lyons, NY 14489
(315) 946-5470 • Email: historian@co.wayne.ny.us
www.co.wayne.ny.us/departments/historian/historian.htm

Cemetery inscriptions from all Wayne County cemeteries (indexed), census microfilm (federal 1790–1880, 1900, 1910, 1920; typescript of NYS 1855 (except Rose, Savannah, Sodus, Walworth, Williamson, and Wolcott), 1865, 1875, 1892, 1905, 1915, 1925), newspapers 1817–1970s, wills and estate records 1823–present, vital statistics 1847, 1848, 1849 all towns; 1850 Rose only. Historian offers genealogy search requests for a fee. Website includes list of public record types and where to find them in Wayne County, 1850 census index, list of local historical societies and historians, and searchable online surname database.

Wayne County – All Municipal Historians

While not authorized to answer genealogical inquiries, town and village historians can provide valuable historical information and research advice; some maintain collections and webpages which may include transcribed records, local histories, and other genealogical material. See contact information at *www.co.wayne.ny.us/departments/historian/LocalHistorians.htm* or at the website of the Association of Public Historians of New York State at *www.aphnys.org*.

Wayne County Historical Society and Museum of Wayne County History

21 Butternut Street • Lyons, NY 14489 • (315) 946-4943
Email: info@waynehistory.org • *www.waynehistory.org*

The museum is housed in the former Wayne County Jail and Sheriff's residence 1856–1960. Archival collections include photographs and military history.

Wayne County Genealogical Society

PO Box 502 • Newark, NY 14513-0502 • (315) 221-8682
Email: info@wcnygs.com • *www.wcnygs.com*

Formed in October 2012; see website for current information.

REGIONAL REPOSITORIES & RESOURCES

SUNY at Oswego: Local History Collection

See listing in Oswego County Guide

LOCAL REPOSITORIES & RESOURCES

Alphabetized by location

Galen Historical Society

PO Box 43 • Clyde, NY 14433 • (315) 573-6643
Email: Galenhistoricals@aol.com • *www.galenhistoricalsociety.org*

Holdings include a genealogy collection and records documenting local businesses, churches, civic organizations, military, and transportation. Society accepts research requests.

Newark-Arcadia Historical Society and Museum

120 High Street • Newark, NY 14513 • (315) 331-6409
Email: arcadiahistory@gmail.com • *http://newarkarcadiamuseum.org*

The society's research room includes census and other genealogical material.

Rose Historical Society

10798 Wolcott Road • North Rose, NY 14516-9622 • (315) 587-4532

Holdings include genealogies, cemetery records, military records, photographs, and artifacts.

Historic Palmyra, Inc. at Palmyra Historical Museum

132 Market Street • Palmyra, NY 14522 • (315) 597-6981
www.historicpalmyrany.com

Museum houses a research facility of archives 1781–2000, which includes information on local history (religious, business, agricultural, industrial and military); as well as the suffrage movement, abolition, and the Underground Railroad. Palmyra was once known as the "Queen of Erie Canal towns" and the collections include information on the Erie Canal and transportation.

Williamson-Pultneyville Historical Society

4130 Mill Street • PO Box 92 • Pultneyville, NY 14538
Email: info@w-phs.org • www.w-phs.org

Holdings include an archival collection. Website contains local history information, photographs, and a guide to historic landmarks.

Sodus Bay Historical Society

7606 North Ontario Street • PO Box 94 • Sodus Point, NY 14555
(315) 483-4936 • Email: sbhslighthouse@gmail.com
www.soduspointlighthouse.org

The Society maintains the D. Russell Chamberlain Maritime Library, which contains books and periodicals, charts, manuscripts and essays, and audio and videotapes documenting the history of the Sodus Bay area. Exhibits contain information on local history including early pioneers, Shakers, transportation, etc.

Walworth Historical Society and Museum

2257 Academy Street • PO Box 142 • Walworth, NY 14568
(315) 524-9205 • www.walworthhistoricalsociety.org

Currently involved in a project to map historic places in Walworth. Website includes historic photographs.

Wolcott Historical Society

PO Box 51 • Wolcott, NY 14590 • (315) 594-9494
Email: admin@wolcottnyhistory.com • www.wolcottnyhistory.com

Website includes gallery of historic maps, postcards, and photographs.

SELECTED PRINT & ONLINE RESOURCES

Below is a selection of resources relevant for research in this county. The list is representative, not exhaustive. Additional titles—particularly of abstracts, indexes, transcriptions, and local histories—are available; consult the introduction to Part Two for further information. For guidance on how to identify and locate community directories and local newspapers, see chapter 11, City Directories, and chapter 12, Newspapers, in Part One of this book.

Abstracts, Indexes & Transcriptions

County of Wayne Abstracts. Syracuse: Central New York Genealogical Society, 2000. Abstracts for a range of genealogical records originally published in the quarterly *Tree Talks.*

Daughters of the American Revolution, comps. *New York DAR Genealogical Records Committee Report.* Since 1913 DAR volunteers have transcribed many thousands of unpublished cemetery, church, and town records throughout New York. The reports are at the DAR Library; copies are at the NYSL and the NYPL. The DAR has a searchable name index to all the GRC reports at *http://services.dar.org/Public/DAR_Research/search/?Tab_ID=6.* See Jean Worden's index below for a listing by county of the New York record sets that were transcribed by the DAR before 1998.

Kelly, Arthur C. M. *Index to Tree Talks County Packet: Wayne County.* Rhinebeck, NY: Kinship, 2002.

Meyer, Mary K., S. D. Van Alstine, and Harriet M. Wiles. *Genealogical Abstracts from Palmyra, Wayne County, New York Newspapers, 1810–1854.* Mount Airy, MD: Pipe Creek Publications, 1996.

Wiles, Harriett M. "Cemetery Inscriptions from Palmyra Cemetery, Palmyra, Wayne County, N.Y." 4 vols. Typescript, 1934–1938. NYPL, New York.

———. "Church Record of the Presbyterian Church of East Palmyra, Wayne County, New York." Typescript, 1933. NYPL, New York.

———. "Church Records of the Western Presbyterian Church of Palmyra, Wayne County, New York." Typescript, 1933. NYPL, New York. [NYG&B eLibrary]

———. "Marriages and Deaths of Wayne County, New York: Copied from the *Newark Weekly Courier,* Published at Newark, New York." Manuscript, 1941. NYPL, New York.

———. "Records of the Presbyterian Church of Lyons, Wayne County, Nw (sic) York". Typescript, 1952. NYPL, New York.

Worden, Jean D. "Book 1, Subject Index." In *Revised Master Index to the New York State Daughters of the American Revolution Genealogical Records Volumes.* Zephyrhills, FL: J. D. Worden, 1998. The Subject Index includes a listing by county of the cemeteries, churches, towns, and other sources of records transcribed by the DAR.

Other Resources

Barthel, Otto. *New Century Atlas of Wayne County, New York, with Farm Records.* Philadelphia: Century Map Co., 1904.

Beers, D. G. & Co. *Atlas of Wayne Co., New York, from Actual Surveys and Official Records.* Philadelphia, 1874. [NYPL Digital Gallery]

Cowles, George W. *Historical and Biographical Record of Wayne County, New York.* Salem, MA: Higginson Book Co., 1997.

———. *Landmarks of Wayne County, New York.* Syracuse: D. Mason, 1895. Book includes biographies and family sketches. Index available from Berkshire Family History Association.

Curtis, Vera. *History of the Town of Marion, Wayne County, State of New York 1795–1937.* Marion, NY: n.p., 1937.

Espenschied, Lloyd. *Early Wayne County Settlers and Their Rhineland Origins.* Westminster, MD: Heritage Books, 2011. Originally published in the Lyons Republican and Clyde Times in 1958.

Fay, Loren V. *Wayne County, New York, Genealogical Research Secrets.* Albany: L. V. Fay, 1982.

Foley, Janet W. *Early Settlers of New York State: Their Ancestors and Descendants.* 9 vols. Akron, NY: 1934–1942. Reprint, 2 vols. Baltimore: Genealogical Publishing Co., 1993.

Jacobs, Stephen W. *Wayne County: The Aesthetic Heritage of a Rural Area: A Catalog for the Environment.* Lyons, NY: Wayne County Historical Society, 1979.

McIntosh, W. H. *History of Wayne County, New York: With Illustrations Descriptive of Its Scenery, Palatial Residences, Public Buildings, Fine Blocks, and Important Manufactories.* Philadelphia, 1877.

New York Historical Resources Center. *Guide to Historical Resources in Wayne County, New York, Repositories.* Ithaca, NY: Cornell University, 1981. [books.FamilySearch.org]

Rochester Regional Library Council. *Guide to Local History and Archives Collections in the Genesee Valley.* Digitally published June 2006. The guide provides collection descriptions for 150 organizations in the region. *http://rrlc.org/wp-content/uploads/uploads/2013/02/dhp_Local-History-Guide-June-2006.pdf*

Additional Online Resources

Ancestry.com
There are vast numbers of records on *Ancestry.com* that pertain to people who have lived in New York State. See chapter 16 for a description of *Ancestry.com*'s resources and its partnership with the New York State Archives. A search of the online card catalog

by county may reveal lesser known resources that pertain to a locality, such as town records, abstracts, transcriptions, city directories, and local histories.

FamilySearch.org

FamilySearch has extensive collections of New York records, including religious records, which are searchable by name and location, but not by county. The following collections include record images (browsable, but not searchable) that are organized by county:

- "New York, Land Records, 1630–1975." Includes land and property records. *familysearch.org/search/collection/2078654*
- "New York, Probate Records, 1629–1971." Includes wills, letters of administration, and guardianship papers. *familysearch.org/search/collection/1920234*

For both collections, choose the browse option and then select Wayne to view the available records sets.

A detailed description of *FamilySearch.org* resources, which include the catalog of the Family History Library, is found in chapter 16.

New York Heritage Digital Collections:
New York State Newspaper Project
www.nyheritage.org/newspapers

The website provides links to digital newspapers collections in 26 counties (currently) made accessible through New York Heritage, New York State Historic Newspapers, HRVH Historical Newspapers, and other providers.

NYGenWeb Project: Wayne County
http://wayne.nygenweb.net

Part of the national, USGenWeb volunteer initiative, the website provides information and resources for county research, including an extensive selection of cemetery transcriptions, indexes, and census abstracts that can be accessed from the Historical Articles section of the website.

Old Fulton New York Postcards
www.FultonHistory.com

The website provides free access to a vast collection of digitized New York newspapers, including 27 titles for Wayne County.

Westchester County

Formed November 1, 1683

Parent County   Original County

Daughter Counties None (land ceded to New York County 1874 and 1895, which became Bronx County in 1914)

County Seat   City of White Plains

Major Land Transactions

See chapter 7, Land Records

Fordham Manor 1671; Pelham Manor 1687; Philipsburg(h) Manor 1693; Cortlandt Manor 1697; Morrisania Manor 1697; Scarsdale Manor 1701; Oblong (tract) 1731

Town Boundary Map

★ - County seat

Towns (and Cities)	Villages and other Settlements	Notes
Bedford **1680** Settlers from Stamford, CT **1682** Established as Bedford "Plantation" by Hartford, CT court of election **1697** Town formed by patent in Colony of Connecticut; subsequently contested between Connecticut and New York **1704** Became part of Westchester County, New York Colony **1788** Recognized as a town by State of New York **1977** Daughter town Mount Kisco formed	Bedford Bedford Center Bedford Four Corners Bedford Hills Cantitoe Corners Haines Corners Katonah Katonah Ridge Kirbyville Lake Katonah Mount Kisco (v) Succabone Corners Sutton Corners Valley Pond Estates Whitlockville	• Bedford shared the county seat with White Plains 1787–1868; also Bedford Village • Bedford Hills formerly Bedford Station • Cantitoe Corners also Cantatoe Corners • Katonah was Mechanicsville before 1852 and Whitlockville 1830–1852; moved to current location in 1897 after Cross River Reservoir flooded original location • Kirbyville in Town of Mount Kisco after 1977 • Lake Katonah on Lewisboro town line • Village of Mount Kisco inc. 1875; shared with Town of New Castle until 1977; coterminous with Town of Mount Kisco 1977
Cortlandt Manor * **1683** Stephanus Van Cortlandt begins buying land in northern Westchester **1697** Van Cortlandt land patented as a Manor **1788** Manor divided by State of New York into five towns, Cortlandt, Salem (now Lewisboro), North Salem, Stephentown (now Somers), and Yorktown, as well as a small part of the Town of Pound Ridge.		* Cortlandt Manor also called Van Cortlandt Manor
Cortlandt Part of Cortlandt Manor (see above) **1788** Recognized as a town by State of New York **1940** Village of Peekskill became City of Peekskill	Annsville Bakers Landing Blue Mountain Boscobel Buchanan (v) Camp Smith Centerville Chimney Corners Cornwall Dam Cortlandt Manor Cortlandtown Crompond Croton Landing Station Croton-on-Hudson (v) Croton Point Crugers Dixie Furnace Woods Gallows Hill Harmon Harmon-on-Hudson Mohegan Colony Mohegan Lake Montrose Montroses Point Mount Airy New Haverstraw Station Oregon Oscawana	• Bakers Landing also Peekskill Landing • Village of Buchanan inc. 1928 • Camp Smith military training site established 1882 as Camp Townsend, name changed 1919 • Centerville formerly Buchanan and Verplanck • Cornwall Dam also Cornell Dam, Croton Dam, and New Croton Dam • Crompond on Yorktown town line • Village of Croton-on-Hudson inc. 1898; known as Col(l)abaugh Landing, Cortlandt Town, Croton, and Croton Landing before incorporation • Croton Point formerly Enoch Point, Navish Point, Sarahs Point, Senasqua Neck, Slaupers Haven, Tellers Point, and Verdrida Hooke • Dixie affected by flooding for Lake Croton 1892, also in Town of Yorktown before 1892 • Mohegan Lake on Yorktown town line • Montrose formerly Centreville, East Haverstraw, and Lyell • Oscawana formerly Cortlandt-on-Hudson

(Cortlandt continued on next page)

Towns (and Cities)	Villages and other Settlements		Notes
Cortlandt (continued)	Oscawana-on-Hudson Peekskill (v) Pleasantside Quaker Bridge Riveredge Trailer Park Roe Park Rycks Patent Sunset	Teatown Hill Toddville Valeria Home Van Cortlandville Varian Mills Verplanck Verplancks Point Woodybrook	• Village of Peekskill inc. 1816; became City of Peekskill 1940 • Rycks Patent also Camp Smith • Van Cortlandtville formerly Bakers Landing, Cortlandtville, Sutton Mills, and Van-Cortlandt Manor
Eastchester * *Southern part of Eastchester now part of the Bronx, see Bronx County Guide* **c. 1642** Settled by Anne Hutchinson and children; destroyed in 1643 massacre **1654** Land acquired from American Indians **1664** Settled by ten families from Connecticut and known as Ten Farms **1667** Established by patent as a part of Town of Westchester; residents believed the patent established Eastchester as its own town; colonial government treated Eastchester as a separate town with its own officials **1672** Eastchester and Westchester agreed on a boundary demarcating the two towns **1788** Recognized as a town by State of New York **1892** Village of Mount Vernon became City of Mount Vernon; Eastchester was divided north and south of the city **1895** Land south of the Mount Vernon border ceded to New York County; becomes part of the 24th ward of New York City; now in Bronx County	Baychester Bronxville (v) Bronxville Manor Burpos Corners California Ridge Central Mount Vernon Chester Hill Chester Heights Crestwood Eastchester East Mount Vernon Fleetwood Jacksonville Lakeville Lawrence Park Long Reach Patent Mount Vernon (v) Sebastopol South Washingtonville Ten Farms Tuckahoe (v) Union Corners Upper Tuckahoe Wakefield (v) Washingtonville Waverly West Mount Vernon (v)		• Eastchester also East Chester, formerly known as Hutchinsons (after Anne Hutchinson 1591–1643), and later Ten Farms • Baychester ceded to New York County in 1895; now in Bronx County • Village of Bronxville inc. 1898; formerly Underhills Crossing; was part of Long Reach Patent • Central Mount Vernon see note for Village of West Mount Vernon • Chester Heights crosses borders of Town of Pelham and cities of Mount Vernon and New Rochelle • Chester Hill in City of Mount Vernon after 1892 as Chester Hill Park • Crestwood neighborhood on both sides of Tuckahoe-Yonkers border • Hamlet of Eastchester ceded to New York County in 1895, now in Bronx County; on Mount Vernon city line • East Mount Vernon see note for Village of Mount Vernon • Fleetwood (Fleetward) neighborhood in City of Mount Vernon after 1892 • Lawrence Park in Village of Bronxville; formerly called Sunset Hill • Village of Mount Vernon inc. 1853; reinc. 1874 including East Mount Vernon; reinc. 1878 including former Village of West Mount Vernon; 1892 became City of Mount Vernon • South Washingtonville ceded to New York County in 1895; now in Bronx County • Ten Farms shared with City of Mount Vernon 1892–1895; divided between City of Mount Vernon and New York County 1895–1914; shared between City of Mount Vernon and Bronx County 1914–present • Village of Tuckahoe inc. 1902; part of Long Reach Patent; railroad station est. 1844 and PO in 1847 • Village of Wakefield inc. 1889 as Village of South Mount Vernon; encompassed Jacksonville and Washingtonville; name changed to Wakefield 1894; ceded to New York County in 1895; now in Bronx County • Village of West Mount Vernon inc. 1869 including village of Central Mount Vernon; see Village of Mount Vernon 1878–1892; now in City of Mount Vernon

Towns (and Cities)	Villages and other Settlements		Notes
Greenburgh Part of Philipsburg(h) Manor (see below) **1788** After division of former manor, Greenburgh recognized as a town by State of New York	Abbotsville Ardsley (v) Ardsley-on-Hudson Briggsville Chauncey Dobbs Ferry (v) East Irvington Eastview Elmsford (v) Fairview Glenville Greenville Hartsdale Hastings-on-Hudson (v) Irving Irvington (v) Knollwood Manor	Lower Cross Road Manhattan Park Middletown Mount Hope Nob Hill North Elmsford Orchard Hill Parkway Gardens Parkway Homes Poets Corner South Ardsley Tarrytown (v) Uniontown Valhalla Wickers Creek Woodlands Worthington	• Village of Ardsley inc. 1896; formerly Ashford • Ardsley-on-Hudson formerly also Abbotsford, Irvington, and West Ardsley • Village of Dobbs Ferry, formerly New Wales, founded 1698 as Dobbs Ferry, but incorporated as Village of Greenburgh 1873; name changed back to Dobbs Ferry in 1882 • East Irvington formerly also Dublin • Eastview on Mount Pleasant town line • Village of Elmsford inc. 1910; formerly Saw Mill River Hamlet 1834–1883, Greenburg, Halls Corners, and Storms Bridge; annexed Nob Hill in 1990s • Greenville also Edgemont • Hartsdale formerly Barnes Corners, Harts Corners, and Moringville • Village of Hastings-on-Hudson inc. 1879; Hastings-upon-Hudson 1849–1935, formerly Hastings • Village of Irvington inc. 1872; called Dearman 1817–1853, formerly Dearmans Landing and Irvington-on-Hudson • Village of Tarrytown inc. 1870; also Alipkonk, Tarry Town, and Tarwe Dorp • Uniontown within Hastings-on-Hudson • Valhalla mostly in Mount Pleasant, partly in North Castle, zip code includes part of Greenburgh
Harrison **1695** John Harrison acquired land from American Indians, attracted Quaker settlers from Long Island; administered as part of Rye **1774** Became a separate precinct **1788** Recognized as a town by State of New York **1975** Village of Harrison incorporated; coterminous with town	Blackberry Row Blind Brook Brentwood Plaza East White Plains Fenmore Park Harrison (v) Hortons Hill Merritts Hill Purchase Sunset Ridge		• Blackberry Row was an African-American settlement • East White Plains formerly Silver Lake and West Harrison • Village of Harrison inc. 1975 • Hortons Hill also Stony Hill • Purchase formerly Harrisons Purchase, The Purchase, and Thomasville
Kingsbridge 1872–1874 *Town of Kingsbridge now part of the Bronx, see Bronx County Guide* **1872** Formed as a town from southern part of Town of Yonkers **1874** Ceded to New York County; becomes part of 24th ward of New York City; now part of Bronx County	Fort Independence Kingsbridge Kingsbridge Heights Kingsbridge Village Little Yonkers Lower Yonkers Mosholu (Village) Mount St. Vincent	Orloff Park Paparinemo Island Riverdale (Park) Spuyten Duyvil Van Cortlandt (Park) Warnerville Woodlawn Heights	• Paparinemo Island also Hummock Island, Island Farm, Kingsbridge Village, and Paparinemin

Towns (and Cities)	Villages and other Settlements		Notes

Lewisboro
Part of Cortlandt Manor and Oblong known as Lower Salem (see Salem) *
 	
1788 Lower Salem recognized as Town of Salem by the State of New York
 	
1806 Name changed to South Salem
 	
1840 Name changed to Lewisborough
 	
1890s Name changed to Lewisboro
	Averys Corners
	Colony
	Cross Pond
	Cross River
	Dibbles Long Cabin
	    Corners
	East ward of
	    Cortlandt Manor
	Goldens Bridge
		Kitchawan
		Lake Katonah
		Lewisboro
		Mill River
		South Salem
		Truesdale Lake
		Vista
		Waccabuc
			* Researchers may need to consult records of the pre-1731 Connecticut towns of Norwalk, Ridgefield, or Stamford
			
			• Cross Pond also Lake Kitchawan
			
			• Goldens Bridge formerly Goldings Bridge
			
			• Lake Katonah on Bedford town line
			
			• Hamlet of Lewisboro formerly Lewisborough
			
			• Mill River now submerged by Mill River Reservoir
			
			• Waccabuc also Lake Waccabuc

Mamaroneck 1660 Purchased from Indians; first English settlers arrive 1701 Part purchased by Caleb Heathcote and included in his Scarsdale Manor patent 1788 Recognized as town by State of New York	Chatsworth Harbor Heights Harbor Island Park Heathcote Hill Kelloggsville Larchmont (v)	Larchmont Gardens Mamaroneck (v) Orienta Shore Acres Washingtonville	• Village of Larchmont inc. 1891; formerly Munros Neck • Larchmont Gardens was Hickory Grove until 1912 • Village of Mamaroneck inc. 1895; shared with Town of Rye
Morrisania 1788–1791 (first) 1676 First land patent to Lewis Morris 1697 Manor of Morrisania established by patent 1788 Recognized as town by State of New York 1791 Became part of Town of Westchester	Broncksland Shingle Plain Stony Island Turners Patent		
Morrisania 1855–1874 (second) *Town of Morrisania now part of the Bronx, see Bronx County Guide* Note: the boundaries of the first and second Morrisanias were not identical; the second included Hunts Point 1855 Formed from Town of West Farms 1874 Ceded to New York County; becomes the 23rd ward of New York City; now part of Bronx County	Bensonia Claremo(u)nt Devoes Neck East Melrose East Morrisania Eltona Forest Grove Grove Hill Highbridgeville Melrose	Morrisania (v) Morris Dock Mott Haven North New York Old Morrisania Port Morris South Melrose West Morrisania Wilton Woodstock	• Claremo(u)nt on West Farms town line • Highbridgeville also High Bridgeville; now Highbridge in Bronx County • Village of Morrisania inc. 1864 and dissolved 1874; in Town of West Farms before 1855 • Old Morrisania formerly Central Morrisania
Mount Kisco Settled before Revolutionary War 1875 Incorporated as a village in towns of Bedford and New Castle 1977 Formed as a town from towns of Bedford and New Castle; coterminous with Village of Mount Kisco *	Kirbyville Mount Kisco (v) New Castle Corner		* Act passed December 1977, effective Jan 1, 1978 • Kirbyville in Town of Bedford before 1977 • Village of Mount Kisco incorporated in the towns of Bedford and New Castle in 1875; village became coterminous with new Town of Mount Kisco in 1977 • New Castle Corner in Town of New Castle before 1977

Towns (and Cities)	Villages and other Settlements		Notes
Mount Pleasant Part of Philipsburg(h) Manor (*see below*) 1788 After division of former manor, Mount Pleasant recognized as a town by State of New York 1845 Daughter town Ossining formed	Archville Beekman Briarcliff Manor (v) Buckhout Corners Eastview Graham Hawthorne Lower Cross Roads Mount Pleasant Philipse Manor Pinckney Heights Pleasantville (v) Pocantico Hills Reynolds District Sherman Park Sing Sing (v) Sleepy Hollow (v) Sleepy Hollow Sleepy Hollow Manor Sparta Thornwood Upper Cross Roads Usonia Valhalla Whitson		• Village of Briarcliff Manor inc. 1902; shared with Town of Ossining; formerly Briarcliff Farm • Eastview formerly East Tarrytown and Knapps Corners; on Greenburgh town line • Hawthorne formerly Hammonds Mills, Neperan, and Unionville • Village of Pleasantville inc. 1897; formerly Clarks Corners (1797–1828) and Mechanicsville • Pocantico Hills formerly Tarrytown Heights • Village of Sing Sing: inc. 1813; in Town of Ossining from 1845; renamed Village of Ossining 1901 • Village of Sleepy Hollow formerly Upper Mills (of Philipsburg(h) Manor), Beekmantown (1835–1874); inc. 1874 as North Tarrytown; name changed to Sleepy Hollow in 1996 • Sleepy Hollow was a small hamlet in the 1800s, north of the hamlet of Beekmantown (Beekmantown renamed Sleepy Hollow in 1996) • Sparta see Town of Ossining from 1845 • Thornwood formerly Hillside, Nanahagen, and Sherman Park • Valhalla formerly Davis Brook; mostly in Mount Pleasant, partly in North Castle, zip code includes part of Greenburgh; site of Kensico Cemetery • Whitson was shared with Town of Ossining
Mount Vernon (city) 1878 Incorporated as Village of Mount Vernon in the Town of Eastchester 1892 Village incorporated as City of Mount Vernon	Chester Heights Chester Hill Park East Mount Vernon Elmsmere Fleetwood Hunts Bridge	Hunts Woods North Side Park Side South Side Sunny Brae Vernon Park	• Chester Heights crosses borders of towns of Eastchester and Pelham and City of New Rochelle • Chester Hill Park in town of Eastchester as Chester Hill before 1892 • East Mount Vernon and Fleetwood formerly settlements in the Town of Eastchester
New Castle 1791 Formed from West Patent of Town of North Castle 1977 Daughter town Mount Kisco created from Village of Mount Kisco	Chappaqua Chappaqua Springs Millwood Mount Kisco (v)	New Castle New Castle Corner Stanwood Tompkins Corners	• Millwood formerly Merritts Corners, Sarlesville, and Sarles Corners • Village of Mount Kisco inc. 1875; shared with Town of Bedford until 1977; coterminous with Town of Mount Kisco 1977 • New Castle Corner in Town of Mount Kisco after 1977

Towns (and Cities)	Villages and other Settlements		Notes
New Rochelle (city) Part of Pelham Manor 1688 Settled by French Huguenots 1689 Purchased for settlement of Huguenot refugees from France 1699 Organized as a colonial town by this date 1788 Recognized as Town of New Rochelle by the State of New York 1899 Town incorporated as City of New Rochelle	Bayberry Park Beaufort Point Beechmont Beechmont Woods Bonnie Crest Chester Heights Clifford Island Coopers Corner Daisy Farms Davenport Neck Davids Island DeVeau Town Forest Heights Forest Knolls French Ridge Glen Island Glenwood Lake Halcyon Park Hazlehurst Park Highland Park Homestead Park Hudson Park Huguenot Park Isle of San(s) Souci Maplewood Middleto(w)n Neptune Park	New Jerusalem New Rochelle (v) Petersville Pine Brook Pinebrook Heights Premium Point Pugsleys Hollow Quaker Ridge Residence Park Rochelle Heights Rochelle Park Scarsdale Downs Sun Haven Sutton Manor Sycamore Park Upper New Rochelle Victory Park Ward Acres West Neck West New Rochelle White Birches Wilmot Woods Winyah Park Woodside Wykagyl Wykagyl Park	• Chester Heights crosses borders of towns of Eastchester and Pelham and City of Mount Vernon • Davenport Neck also Laglers, LeCounts, Leislers, Myers, Pells Little, and Rodmans Neck • Davids Island also Allens, Boutelliers, Hewletts, Morses, Myers, and Rodmans Island • Glen Island also Davenport, Locust, Starins Glen Island, and Wooleys • Neptune Park also Residence Park 1886–1903 • Village of New Rochelle inc. 1857; dissolved 1899 when town became a city • Petersville also New Jerusalem • Pugsleys Hollow was a free black community • Scarsdale Downs on Scarsdale town line
North Castle 1640–1705 Many sales by Indians; largest purchase 1696 1702 Patented in three parts, the East, Middle, and West Patents 1718–20 Settlement begins, particularly by Long Island Quakers 1721 Town of North Castle receives patent of incorporation 1788 Recognized as a town by State of New York 1791 Daughter town New Castle formed from West Patent	Anns Bridge Patent Armonk Banksville California Patent Castle Heights Kensico Middle Patent North Castle	North White Plains Paynes Corners Quarry Heights Quarter Station Tuckertown Valhalla West Middle Patent	• Armonk also Mile Square and Mill Square • Castle Heights also Heights of North Castle • Kensico also Fishers Mills, Robins Mills, and Wrights Mills; flooded by Kensico Dam, 1917; Kensico Cemetery is in Valhalla, Mount Pleasant • North White Plains formerly North Castle; on White Plains city line • Paynes Corners formerly Downes Corners • Valhalla formerly Davis Brook; mostly in Mount Pleasant, partly in North Castle, zip code includes part of Greenburgh; site of Kensico Cemetery
North Salem Part of Cortlandt Manor and Oblong, and known as Upper Salem (see Salem) 1788 Upper Salem recognized as Town of North Salem by State of New York	Butlerville Cat Ridge Cotswold Croton Falls Dingle Grant Corner Lake Purdy Lobdell Corners	North Salem Peach Lake Purdys Purdys Station Salem Center Twin Lakes Village Yerkes Corners	• Croton Falls was Owensville before 1843; on Somersa town line • Purdys Station, settled 1700 under authority of Connecticut

Towns (and Cities)	Villages and other Settlements		Notes
Ossining Part of Philipsburg Manor (see below) **1845** Formed from Town of Mount Pleasant	Briarcliff Manor (v) Chilmark Crotonville Fernbrook Park Mariandale Mouth of Croton	Ossining (v) Prospect Hill Scarborough Sparta Spring Valley Whitson	• Village of Briarcliff Manor inc. 1902; shared with Town of Mount Pleasant • Named Ossining 1901; village inc. 1813 as Sing Sing in Town of Mount Pleasant; formerly Mount Pleasant and Hunters Landing • Scarborough formerly Scarboro (1864–1928) and Wescora • Sparta see Town of Mount Pleasant before 1845 • Whitson was shared with Town of Mount Pleasant
Peekskill (city) **1816** Incorporated as Village of Peekskill in Town of Cortlandt **1940** Village incorporated as City of Peekskill			
Pelham *Southern part of Pelham now part of the Bronx, see Bronx County Guide* **1642** Settled, but later abandoned **1654** Thomas Pell purchases land from American Indians **1666** Pell's land established as a manor—unnamed **1687** Second patent established name of Pelham Manor **1788** Recognized as a town by State of New York **1895** Southern portion of town ceded to New York County including Bartow, City Island, Hart Island, Rodmans Neck, and Pells Point; becomes part of the 24th ward of New York City; now part of Bronx County	Barton-on-Sound Bartow Chester Heights City Island Hart Island Hunter(s) Island North Pelham (v) Pelham (v)	Pelham Heights Pelham Manor (v) Pelham Neck Pelham Priory Pelhamwood Pells Point Prospect Hill Rodmans Neck	• Bartow ceded to New York County in 1895, now part of Bronx County • Chester Heights crosses borders of Town of Eastchester and cities of Mount Vernon and New Rochelle • City Island also Minnewits Island, Minnifers, Minnifords, and Mulberry; now part of Bronx County • Hart Island also Little Minneford Island and Spectacle Island; now part of Bronx County • Hunter(s) Island now part of Bronx County • Village of North Pelham inc. 1896; became part of Village of Pelham in 1975; formerly Pelhamville • Village of Pelham inc. 1896, reinc. 1975 when it merged with Village of North Pelham • Village of Pelham Manor inc. 1891 • Pelhamwood also Clifford and Colonel Lathers Farm • Pelham Neck, Pells Point, and Rodmans Neck ceded to New York County in 1895
Philipsburg Manor **1672–84** Frederick Philipse purchased lands along the Hudson, attracted Dutch settlers **1693** Patented as Manor of Philipsburg(h) **1779** Manor confiscated by State of New York after attainder of Philipse heirs for opposing Revolution; sequestered land sold off to many individuals **1788** Former manor divided into towns of Greenburgh, Mount Pleasant, and Yonkers			

Towns (and Cities)	Villages and other Settlements		Notes
Pound Ridge * 1685 Part of future town included in patent for Town of Stamford, CT 1731 Connecticut–New York boundary settlement cedes area to New York 1744 Settlers from Stamford, Connecticut 1788 Recognized as a town by State of New York	Boutonville Dantown East Woods Horseshoe Hill Long Ridge Pound Ridge Sarles Corners Scotts Corners		* Pound Ridge also Poundridge • Boutonville also Boutontown and Boretontown • Sarles Corners formerly Taylors Corner
Rye (city) 1904 Incorporated as Village of Rye in Town of Rye 1942 Village incorporated as City of Rye	Greenhaven Manursing Island Milton	Peningo(e) (Neck) Rye Beach West Rye	• See notes under Town of Rye
Rye (town) * 1660 Settled at Hastings (Manursing Island) in Town of Rye 1665 Act passed by CT court forming "plantation" of Rye * 1683 Ceded to New York Colony 1685 Received a Connecticut patent; confirmed in 1697 1700 Connecticut court upheld New York colony possession 1774 Harrison became a separate precinct 1788 Rye recognized as a town by State of New York 1942 Village of Rye became City of Rye; Town of Rye was divided in two parts— north and south of the city	Apawamis Blind Brook Glenville Greenhaven Kingstreet Mamaroneck (v) Manursing Island Milton Point Parsons Wood Peningo(e) (Neck) Port Chester (v) Purdys Grove Rye (v) Ryebeach Rye Brook (v) Rye Neck Ryeport Tamarack Garden		* 1665 act merged the villages of Hastings and Rye • Blind Brook also Hog Pen Ridge • Greenhaven in City of Rye from 1942 • Village of Mamaroneck inc. 1895; shared with Town of Mamaroneck • Manursing Island also Manussing Island; formerly site of Hastings village; in City of Rye from 1942 • Milton (Point) in City of Rye from 1942 • Parsons Wood now in the Rye Nature Center • Peningo(e) (Neck) in City of Rye from 1942 • Village of Port Chester inc. 1868; formerly Sawpits 1732–1837 and Saw Log Swamp • Village of Rye inc. 1904, became City of Rye 1942 • Ryebeach (Rye Beach) in City of Rye from 1942 • Village of Rye Brook inc. 1982 • Rye Neck—name for the part of Village of Mamaroneck in Town of Rye
Salem Name applied to easternmost part of Cortlandt Manor (see above) 1731 Oblong tract along eastern border ceded by Connecticut to New York, added to Salem * 1751 First mention of Salem as a town 1760 First mention of Upper and Lower Districts 1783/84 Upper and Lower Districts officially recognized as Upper Salem and Lower Salem 1788 New York State recognized Upper Salem as Town of North Salem and Lower Salem as Town of Salem (now Lewisboro)			* As the South Salem/Lewisboro strip was part of Connecticut before 1731, researchers may need to consult records of the pre-1731 towns of Norwalk, Ridgefield, and Stamford, CT

Towns (and Cities)	Villages and other Settlements		Notes
Salem Name for Town of Lewisboro 1788–1806			
Scarsdale 1660 Purchased from Indians, patented by Dutch 1662, patented by English 1668 1701 Purchased by Caleb Heathcote, patented as Manor of Scarsdale; settled at Heathcote 1788 Recognized as a town by State of New York 1915 Village of Scarsdale incorporated; coterminous with town	Arthur Manor Berkley in Scarsdale Bramlee Heights Colonial Acres Drake Edgewood East Heathcote Fox Meadow Greenacres Green Farms Heathcote Heath Ridge Murdock Woods Murray Hill	Overhill Quaker Ridge Scarsdale (v) Scarsdale Downs Scarsdale Manor Scarsdale Meadows Scarsdale Park Scarsdale Station Secor Farms Secor Gardens Sherbrooke Farms West Quaker Ridge	• Green Farms formerly The Dickel Farm • Murray Hill formerly Middle Heathcote • Village of Scarsdale inc. 1915 • Scarsdale Downs on New Rochelle city line • Scarsdale Park formerly Edgewood
Somers Part of Cortlandt Manor (see above) 1701 Settled at Amawalk 1788 Recognized as Town of Stephentown by the State of New York 1808 Name changed from Stephentown to Somers	Amawalk Baldwin Place Croton Falls Grasslands Granite Springs Greenbriar Hanover Heritage Hills Horton Estates	Lake Lincolndale Lincolndale North Shenorock Owenville Shenorock Somers Westchester Whitehall Corners Woodsbridge	• Amawalk on Yorktown town line • Croton Falls was Owensville before 1843; on North Salem town line • Granite Springs formerly Lents Corners and West Somers • Lincolndale formerly Somers Center and Teeds Corner • Shenorock also Lake Shenorock • Somers formerly Somerstown Plains • Hamlet of Westchester formerly Putnam 1932–1966
South Salem Name for Town of Lewisboro 1806–1840			
Stephentown Name for Town of Somers 1788–1808			
Westchester 1664–1895 * *Town of Westchester now part of the Bronx, see Bronx County Guide* 1639 Dutch West India Company and Jonas Bronck purchased land from Indians 1642 English settlement at Throggs Neck, called Vreedlandt by Dutch 1654–55 English settlement at village called Oostdrop or Easttown by Dutch, later called Westchester Village 1664 English rule begins; recognized as Town of Westchester 1664–83 Part of colonial jurisdiction North Riding of Yorkshire with own court 1683 Shire-town (county seat) of new Westchester County 1686 Patent granted by Governor Dongan	Bedford Park Bronxdale Bronxwood Park Castle Hill (Neck) Centerville Clason Point Cherry Tree Point Connersville Cornells Neck Edenwald Ferry Point Fordham Fort Schuyler Hunts Point Integrity Jerome (Park)	Laconia Middletown Morris Park Morrisania Olinville Oostdorp Pennyfield Schuylerville Stinardtown Throg(g)s Neck Van Nest Unionport Vreedlandt Westchester (Village) West Farms (Village) Williamsbridge (v)	* Westchester also West Chester; county seat 1683–1759 • Castle Hill (Neck) also Cromwells Neck and Wilkins Neck; now Castle Hill in Bronx County • Clason Point also Classons Point • Cornells Neck now Harding Park in Bronx County • Fordham, Hunts Point, and Jerome in Town of West Farms after 1846 • Morrisania in Town of West Farms Village—see Town of West Farms 1846–1855 and Town of Morrisania after 1855 • West Farms (Village) in Town of West Farms after 1846 • Village of Williamsbridge (Williams Bridge) inc. 1888, dissolved 1895; mostly in Town of West Farms after 1846, expanded in Westchester after 1874; when Williamsbridge reservoir opened in 1890 the neighborhood name was used more widely; now part of Norwood in the Bronx (Westchester continued on next page)

Towns (and Cities)	Villages and other Settlements		Notes
Westchester 1664–1895 (continued)	Wrights Island		• Wrights Island now Locust Point in Bronx County
1696 Made a Borough Town, with a Mayor			
1788 Recognized as Town by the State of New York			
1791 Annexed the first Town of Morrisania			
1846 Daughter town West Farms formed (included land from former Town of Morrisania)			
1895 Became part of the 24th ward of New York City and County; now part of Bronx County			
West Farms 1846–1874 *Town of West Farms now part of the Bronx, see Bronx County Guide*	Belmont Central Morrisania Claremo(u)nt East Morrisania East Tremont Eltona Fairmount Fordham (v) Fordham Heights Forest Grove Grove Hill Highbridgeville Hunts Point Jerome (Park) Melrose Monterey Morrisania	Morris Dock Mott Haven Mount Eden Mount Hope North Melrose Port Morris Rose Hill South Belmont South Fordham Springhurst Tremont Upper Morrisania Wardsville West Farms (Village) West Tremont Williamsbridge Woodstock	• Central Morrisania became Old Morrisania in Town of Morrisania after 1855 • Claremo(u)nt on Morrisania town line • East Morrisania and Eltona in Town of Morrisania after 1855 • Village of Fordham inc. 1846, dissolved 1874; see Town of Westchester before 1846 • Forest Grove and Grove Hill in Town of Morrisania after 1855 • Highbridgeville also High Bridgeville; in Town of Morrisania after 1855; now Highbridge in Bronx County • Melrose, Morrisania, Morris Dock, and Mott Haven in Town of Morrisania after 1855 • Mount Hope formerly Adamsville • Port Morris in Town of Morrisania after 1855 • Tremont formerly South Fordham and Upper Morrisania • West Farms in Town of Westchester 1791–1846; formerly known as Bycancks Mills, DeLanceys Mills, Hive Town, Richardsons Mills, and Twelve Farms • Williamsbridge (Williams Bridge) mostly in Town of West Farms after 1846, expanded in Westchester after 1874 to become an incorporated village in 1888 • Woodstock in Town of Morrisania after 1855
1664 Settled by twelve families from village of Westchester			
1671 Manor of Fordham patented, owned by Dutch Church 1693–1753, part of Westchester from 1753			
1697 Manor of Morrisania patented (see first Town of Morrisania), part of Westchester from 1791			
1846 Town of West Farms formed from Town of Westchester west of Bronx River, including former manors			
1855 Daughter town Morrisania formed			
1874 Ceded to New York County; becomes part of 24th ward of New York City; now part of Bronx County			
White Plains (city) ∗	Battle Hill Carhart Chatterton Hill Colonial Corners Eastview Ferris Avenue Fisher Hill Fulton Street Gedney Farms Gedney Way	Greenburgh Avenue Greenridge Park Havilands Manor Highlands Hillair Circle Holbrooke Idle Forest Mount Misery North Broadway North White Plains	∗ White Plains county seat 1759–present (shared with Bedford 1787–1868); county seat in Town of Westchester 1683–1759 • Battle Hill was part of Chatterton Hill from 1731–1905 • Fisher Hill existed in 18th and 19th centuries, possibly at different locations • North White Plains on North Castle town line
1683 Purchased from American Indians and settled by English from Rye; title disputed for many years			
1721/22 Charter granted			
1759 County seat moves to White Plains from Westchester			

(White Plains continued on next page)

Towns (and Cities)	Villages and other Settlements		Notes
White Plains (city) (continued) 1788 Recognized as Town of White Plains by the State of New York 1916 Town incorporated as City of White Plains	Oak Ridge Prospect Park Purdy Hill Reynal Park Ridgeway Rosedale Saxon Woods	Soundview The Crags Vivian Heights Wanawaking Park Washington Heights Westminster Ridge White Plains (Village)	• Reynal Park also Rocky Dell • Vivian Heights now part of Battle Hill • Washington Heights now part of Battle Hill
Yonkers (city) 1646 Part of the Dutch grant to patroon Jonkheer Adriaen van der Donck; called Colendonck or Jonkheer's land, hence the name Yonkers 1655 Van der Donck dies, settlement laid waste by Indians 1672 Frederick Philipse begins to acquire land 1693 Manor of Philipsburg created (see Philipsburg) 1788 After division of former manor, Town of Yonkers recognized by State of New York 1872 Town incorporated as City of Yonkers; daughter town Kingsbridge formed	Armour Villa Armour Villa Hill Park Beech Hill Beverly Crest Bronxville Heights Bryn Mawr Heights Bryn Mawr Park Caryl Cecil Park Cedar Knolls Chicken Island Colen Donck Colonial Heights Crestwood Crestwood Gardens Dunwoodie Dunwoodie Heights Gedney Way Getty Square Glendale Glen Washington Grey Oaks Greystone Guions Mills Gunther Park Homefield Homewood Kingsbridge Kinross Heights Lincoln Heights Lincoln Park	Locust Hill Lower Mills Lowerre Ludlow McLean Heights Mile Square Mohegan Heights Moorelands Mosquette Park Nepera Park Nepperhan Nepperhan Heights Nodine Hill Oak Hill Park Hill Prospect Hill Riverdale Runyon Heights Sherwood Park South Yonkers Spring Hill Grove Spuyten Duyvil Strathmore Teatown The Hollow Tuckahoe Valentine Hill Wakefield Park Woodstock Park Yonkers (v) Yonkers Park	• Colen Donck also Colendonck • Colonial Heights also Tuckahoe Hills • Crestwood on Eastchester town line • Kingsbridge, Riverdale, South Yonkers, and Spuyten Duyvil see Town of Kingsbridge 1872–1874; now in Bronx County • Ludlow formerly Ludlows Landing • Oak Hill also Hog Hill • Nodine Hill also Naudin Hill and Dundee Heights • Park Hill formerly Yonkers Ridge • Village of Yonkers inc. 1855; dissolved 1872 when town became a city
Yorktown Part of Cortlandt Manor 1788 Recognized as a town by State of New York	Amawalk Crompond Croton Dam Croton Heights Croton Lake Dixie Fieldhome Florenceville Groveville Hallocks Mills Hanover Heights of North Castle Huntersville Jefferson Valley Jefferson Village	Kitchawan Lake Mohegan Manhattan Park Mohansic Lake Mohegan Mohegan Heights Mohegan Lake Old Croton Dam Osceola Osceola Heights Osceola Lake Pine(s) Bridge Shrub Oak Yorktown Yorktown Heights	• Amawalk on Somers town line • Crompond on Cortlandt town line • Croton Dam flooded by Croton Lake in 1892 • Dixie on Cortlandt town line; affected by flooding for Lake Croton 1892; see Town of Cortlandt from 1892 • Kitchawan formerly known as Cornell • Mohegan Lake on Cortlandt town line • Old Croton Dam was flooded by Croton Reservoir c. 1837 • Hamlet of Yorktown formerly Crompond, before Crompond was separate hamlet • Yorktown Heights formerly Underhill

Notes on Westchester County

The name Westchester is not exclusive to the county; the Town of Westchester and the village of Westchester separated from Westchester County in 1895 and became part of New York County and later Bronx County.

The Municipal Archives of New York City (MUNI) holds city, town, and village records, ca. 1663–1898, for places in the Bronx that were annexed from Westchester County, including Eastchester, Kingsbridge, Morrisiania, South Mount Vernon, Wakefield, Westchester, and Williamsbridge. See the MUNI entry in see Citywide Resources.

For archival material pertaining to Philipsburg Manor and Cortlandt (Van Cortlandt) Manor, see the Historic Hudson Valley entry and the Philipse-Gouverneur Family Papers, ca. 1653–1874, at Columbia University's Butler Library. Van Cortlandt-Van Wyck Family Papers 1667–1912 are at the NYPL and have been microfilmed. See Gordon Remington's "Robert[2] Huestis of Westchester County" for information on Pelham Manor papers, which are in private hands. Selected print resources on colonial manors are listed in the bibliography. See Sung Kim's *Landlord and Tenant in Colonial New York* for extensive references to both archival and printed materials.

NEW YORK STATE CENSUS RECORDS

See also chapter 3, Census Records

County original at the Scarsdale Public Library: 1845*

County originals at the Westchester County Archives: 1905, 1915, 1925 (1825, 1835, 1855, 1865, 1875, and 1892 are lost)

State originals at the NYSA: 1915, 1925

Microfilm at the FHL, NYPL, and NYSL; many years are online at *FamilySearch.org* and *Ancestry.com*.

* Most of the 1845 New York state census for Westchester County is lost; see Walker for Scarsdale and Smith for Mamaroneck in Abstracts, Indexes & Transcriptions.

Note on Early Censuses

For published censuses in Abstracts, Indexes & Transcriptions, see Miller for 1698 Eastchester, Fordham, and (town of) Westchester; Randolph for 1698 Mamaroneck and New Rochelle; Horne for 1710 Bedford; and Smith for 1771 New Rochelle.

NATIONAL/STATEWIDE REPOSITORIES & RESOURCES

See chapter 16

COUNTYWIDE REPOSITORIES & RESOURCES

See also the Bronx Borough Guide for information relevant to communities that were once part of Westchester County.

Westchester County Clerk

110 Dr. Martin Luther King Jr. Blvd. • White Plains, NY 10601
(914) 995-3080 • *www.westchesterclerk.com*

Deeds, land records, maps, and property surveys; legal records; judgments and liens; divorce records; and trades licenses. A searchable database of land and legal records is on the website. Naturalization records held at the County Archives; a collections description and an online index are at *http://archives.westchestergov.com*.

Westchester County – City, Town, and Village Clerks

Birth, marriage, and death records are maintained by the clerk of the municipality in which the event occurred. Westchester is the only county in New York State where warrant tax rolls are retained by towns and not by the county. Unlike most city clerks, the Yonkers city clerk holds some vital records not available at the New York State Department of Health; see full listing below. See *www.westchester clerk.com* for a list of city, town, and village clerks in Westchester County.

Westchester County Surrogate's Court

111 Dr. Martin Luther King Jr. Blvd., 19th Floor
White Plains, NY 10601 • (914) 824-5656

Wills 1942–present, and estate files 1922–present. Earlier records 1788–1921, are held at the Westchester County Archives. The NYSA holds most probate records prior to 1787.

Westchester County Archives (WCA)

2199 Saw Mill River Road • Elmsford, NY 10523 • (914) 231-1500
Email: archivesreferencedesk@westchestergov.com
http://archives.westchestergov.com

Almshouse records 1854–1917; atlases 1867–1930, with gaps; bastardy proceedings 1788–1846; court records 1768–1911, with gaps; deeds 1684–1898; estate records 1775, 1783–1921; farm names register 1912–1949; guardianship records 1802–1931; marriage records 1908–1935; naturalization records 1808–1960; New York State census originals 1905, 1915, 1925; school reports 1828–1968, gaps; wills 1788–1941; returns of births, marriages, and deaths 1842, 1847–1848. Online list of holdings along with indexes and guides to research. Online records include naturalizations indexed by name: 1808–1928 A-Z and 1928–1955 A-L; 1928–1955 M-Z is in progress. Website also includes maps, photographs and searchable indexes. Some records are on FHL film or online at *FamilySearch.org*. The WCA and the WCHS (below) are located in the same facility.

Westchester County Historian
Westchester County Historical Society (WCHS)

2199 Saw Mill River Road • Elmsford, NY 10523 • (914) 592-4323
Email: info@westchesterhistory.com • *www.westchesterhistory.com*

The Society fulfills the role of county historian and shares a building with the WCA. Holdings include books, manuscripts, and pamphlets; Genealogy Collection with cemetery records, censuses, church records, family histories, marriages and deaths from local newspapers, genealogy files of over 2,800 families; maps and atlases (1700s–present); gazetteers, directories, and phone books; orphanage and almshouse records; newspapers, periodicals, scrapbooks, and pictures. Publishes the *Westchester Historian* (formerly the *Westchester County Historical Bulletin*) 1925–present. Online indexes to cemetery, church, and other collections, recent acquisitions, a list of libraries with local history collections, a list of local historians, and virtual archives.

Westchester County – All Municipal Historians

While not authorized to answer genealogical inquiries, town and village historians can provide valuable historical information and research advice; some maintain collections and webpages which may include transcribed records, local histories, and other genealogical material. See contact information at *www.westchesterhistory.com/index.php/historians/municipal* or at the website of the Association of Public Historians of New York State at *www.aphnys.org*.

Westchester County – Public Libraries

For the Westchester Library System (WLS) see *www.westchester libraries.org*. Most town and village libraries have special collections and archival materials relating to local history and genealogy including newspapers, maps, local histories, photographs, yearbooks, scrapbooks, pamphlets, and city directories. An overview of holdings can be found on each library's website. Libraries with additional collections are listed below under Local Repositories & Resources. For a list of WLS member libraries see *www.westchesterlibraries.org./ about-wls/member-libraries/list-of-member-libraries*.

Westchester County Genealogical Society

PO Box 518 • White Plains, NY 10603-0518
www.rootsweb.ancestry.com/~nywcgs

Meetings held at Aldersgate United Methodist Church, 600 Broadway, Dobbs Ferry, NY. Offers research services for a fee. Website includes research guide for Westchester County with list of resources. Holdings, including books and genealogies, are held at the Yorktown Family History Center at 801 Kitchawan Road, Ossining, NY.

Historic Hudson Valley (HHV)

639 Bedford Road • Pocantico Hills, NY 10591 • (914) 631-8200
www.hudsonvalley.org

Historic Hudson Valley preserves and interprets the history and material culture of the Hudson Valley. It maintains five historic sites in Westchester County—in Tarrytown, Sleepy Hollow, and Croton-on-Hudson—and one in Red Hook, Dutchess County. Its decorative art collections comprise 16,000 objects from the 17th through 19th centuries; the website has links to online exhibitions. Its library collections include more than 4,000 rare books and 3,000 manuscripts, as well as maps, pamphlets, prints, and microfilm. The HHV is custodian to Van Cortlandt Manor and Philipsburg Manor and holds archival material pertaining to both properties. A project is under way to create an all-name index for every document in the collection.

REGIONAL REPOSITORIES & RESOURCES

Bard College Archives and Special Collections

See listing in Dutchess County Guide

Hudson River Valley Heritage

www.hrvh.org
See listing in Ulster County Guide

Hudson River Valley Institute

www.hudsonrivervalley.org
See listing in Dutchess County Guide

LOCAL REPOSITORIES & RESOURCES

Alphabetized by location; village resources appear under the heading of the associated town.

Town of Bedford

Bedford Historical Society and Museum

612 Old Post Road • PO Box 491 • Bedford, NY 10506
(914) 234-9751 • Email: info@bedfordhistoricalsociety.org
www.bedfordhistoricalsociety.org

Books, atlases, cemetery records, genealogy files, town records and minutes, land records, and military information.

Friends of Bedford Burying Grounds

PO Box 152 • Bedford, NY 10506
Email: friendsofbedfordburyinggrounds@gmail.com
http://friendsofbedfordburyinggrounds.org

Conducts historical and genealogical research and also conducts conservation work on historic burying grounds. Holdings include thousands of gravestone transcriptions, genealogical data, photographs, and cemetery maps.

Katonah Village Library and Katonah Historical Museum

26 Bedford Road • Katonah, NY 10536 • (914) 232-1233
Email: katref@wlsmail.org • *www.katonahlibrary.org*

Holdings include books, pamphlets, cemetery records, maps, newspapers, oral history, and photographs.

Town of Cortlandt

Van Cortlandtville Historical Society

297 Locust Avenue • Cortlandt Manor, NY 10567 • (914) 736-7868
Email: society@vancort.net • *www.vancort.net*

Holdings include books and memorabilia.

Croton Historical Society

One Van Wyck Street • Croton-on-Hudson, NY 10520
(914) 271-4574 • *www.crotononhudson-ny.gov*

Local histories, genealogies, books and documents, maps, oral histories, periodicals, photographs, and information on history of Croton Dam and railroad.

Town of Eastchester

Bronxville Historical Conservancy

PO Box 989 • Bronxville, NY 10708
bronxvillehistoricalconservancy.org

Preserves and interprets the cultural heritage of the village; publishes a semiannual newsletter and the Bronxville Journal; art collection displayed in Village Hall.

Bronxville Public Library, Local History Room

201 Pondfield Road • Bronxville, New York 10708 • (914) 337-7680
bronxvillelibrary.org/us/history

Archives include documents, photographs, local newspapers and periodicals; accessible by appointment; managed by the Village Historian.

Eastchester 350th Anniversary Inc.

www.eastchester350.org

A nonprofit formed to celebrate the town's 350th anniversary in 2014; website includes online archive of founding documents and other records, photographs, oral histories, and lesson plans.

Eastchester Historical Society and Marble School House

388 California Road • PO Box 37 • Eastchester, NY 10709
(914) 793-1900 • Email: marbleschoolhouse@yahoo.com
www.eastchesterhistoricalsociety.org

Books, records of Town of Eastchester (1664–present), genealogical records, maps 1845–1920s, and burial records of St. Paul's Church (historic Eastchester, now City of Mount Vernon).

Town of Greenburgh

Ardsley Historical Society at Ardsley Public Library

Ardsley Public Library, 2nd Floor • 9 American Legion Drive
PO Box 523 • Ardsley, NY 10502 • (914) 693-6027
www.ardsleyvillage.com/historical.html • *www.ardsleylibrary.org*

Selection of documents and photographs online. Library's collection includes histories, documents, photographs, special collections, and artifacts.

Dobbs Ferry Historical Society
The Mead House • 12 Elm Street • Dobbs Ferry, NY 10522
(914) 674-1007 • Email: DFHistory@optimum.net
www.dobbsferryhistory.org

Books, oral histories, programs and pamphlets, photographs and postcards, local school district archives, and local newspapers on microfilm 1884–present. Website includes video interviews with local historians on the topic "The American Revolution in the Hudson River Valley" conducted by Dobbs Ferry village historian in 2009.

Hastings Historical Society
407 Broadway • Hastings-on-Hudson, NY 10706 • (914) 478-2249
Email: hhscottage@hastingshistorical.org • *www.hastingshistorical.org*

Books, documents, dissertations, family papers, maps, pamphlets, photographs and postcards, oral histories, videotapes, yearbooks, artifacts, and fine art. Selection of documents online.

Irvington Historical Society and History Center
131 Main Street • PO Box 23 • Irvington, NY 10533
(914) 591-1020 • Email: curator@irvingtonhistoricalsociety.org
www.irvingtonhistoricalsociety.org

Publishes a newsletter; produces exhibitions from its collections; presents lectures; accepts research requests. Website has a list of historic sites in Irvington.

Historical Society, Inc. of Tarrytown and Sleepy Hollow
One Grove Street • Tarrytown, NY 10591 • (914) 631-8374
Email: historyatgrove@aol.com • *www.thehistoricalsociety.net*

Books, local directories, local newspapers (1875–present), subject files, photographs and postcards, maps and atlases, and manuscripts.

Town of Harrison

Harrison Historical Society and Charles Dawson History Center
Two East Madison Street • West Harrison, NY 10604
Mailing address: PO Box 1696 • Harrison, NY 10528 • (914) 948-2550
Email: harrisonhistoricalsociety@gmail.com
www.town.harrison.ny.us/historian

Official Town Archives holds original 1696 patent; town records 1774–present, genealogies and family files, church histories, immigration history, maps, diaries, postcards and photographs, records of Visiting Nurse Association of Harrison 1913–present, and school records.

Town of Lewisboro

A history of the town is at *www.lewisborogov.com/Community/history/index.html*. Contact information for the town historian at *www.westchesterhistory.com/index.php/historians/municipal*.

Town of Mamaroneck

Larchmont Historical Society and Archives
Mamaroneck Town Center • 740 West Boston Post Road
PO Box 742 • Mamaroneck, NY 10543 • (914) 381-2239
Email: archives@larchmonthistory.org • *www.larchmonthistory.org*

Books, documents, family papers, maps and atlases, newspapers (1912–present), plans, artifacts, and photographs. Online special collections include Cemeteries in Larchmont and Mamaroneck, Engine One, Historical Photography Collection, Larchmont War Memorials, NY Soldiers of the Great War, and Slavery in Mamaroneck Township.

Mamaroneck Historical Society at the Mamaroneck Public Library, Historical Research Room
Library: 136 Prospect Avenue • Mamaroneck, NY 10543 • (914) 698-1250
Society mailing address: PO Box 776 • Mamaroneck, NY 10543
www.mamaroncklibrary.org/historical_society.html

The Society's collection is located in Mamaroneck Public Library Historical Research Room. Holdings include archives, books, maps, oral history, and artifacts.

Town of Mount Kisco

Mount Kisco Historical Society
PO Box 263 • Mount Kisco, NY 10549 • Email access on website
http://mountkiscohistoricalsociety.org

Holdings include newspapers and photographs.

Mount Kisco Public Library
100 East Main Street • Mount Kisco, NY 10549 • (914) 666-8041
www.mountkiscolibrary.org

Books, cemetery guides, census and indexes, church histories, local directories, genealogies, maps and atlases, and newspapers.

Town of Mount Pleasant

Briarcliff Manor-Scarborough Historical Society
162 Macy Road • PO Box 11 • Briarcliff Manor, NY 10510
(914) 941-7016 • Email: mail@briarcliffhistory.org
http://briarcliffhistory.org

School, organization, and institution records; artifacts, photographs, and scrapbooks.

Mount Pleasant Public Library: Local History Center
350 Bedford Road • Pleasantville, NY 10570 • (914) 769-0548
Email: loc.hist@mountpleasantlibrary.org
www.mountpleasantlibrary.org/blog/local-history.html

Histories and genealogies, newspapers, periodicals, obituary indexes, photographs, subject files, yearbooks, and maps.

Friends of the Old Dutch Church & Burying Ground, Sleepy Hollow, NY
PO Box 832 • Sleepy Hollow, NY 10591 • (914) 631-4497
Email: info@odcfriends.org • *www.odcfriends.org*

Burying Ground contains 1,700 burials (1700s–late 1800s). Friends' website includes inscriptions recorded in 1926 and 1953.

Sleepy Hollow Cemetery: Information for Genealogists
540 North Broadway • Sleepy Hollow, NY 10591 • (914) 631-0081
Email: info@sleepyhollowcemetery.org • *www.sleepyhollowcemetery.org*

Cemetery contains 45,000 documented burials from 1849 to the present. Website includes cemetery maps.

Mount Pleasant Historical Society
One Town Hall • Valhalla, NY 10595 • (914) 769-4734

Holdings include manuscripts, books, original records, photographs, ephemera, and drawings.

City of Mount Vernon

Mount Vernon Public Library:
Virginia McCullen Moskowitz Local History Room
28 First Avenue • Mount Vernon, NY 10550 • (914) 668-1840, ext. 227
mtvref@wlsmail.org • *www.mountvernonpubliclibrary.org/local-history*

The Local History Room is currently closed to the public, and its resources are accessible by appointment only; a written request should be sent by email. Holdings include books and genealogies, family files, maps and atlases, newspapers (1800s–present), ethnic collections (Italian, Jewish, and African American), city directories (1885–present), telephone books (1933–present), yearbooks, artifacts, and city government reports. The *Mount Vernon Daily Argus*, the city's oldest newspaper, is on microfilm in the library's periodical collection.

St. Paul's Church National Historic Site

897 South Columbus Avenue • Mount Vernon, NY 10550
(914) 667-4116 • www.nps.gov/sapa

Founded in 1665 as the Church of Eastchester, it was used as a field hospital by British and Hessian soldiers during the American Revolution, and both Loyalists and Patriots are buried in its cemetery, as are Hessians. A selection of St. Paul's archives, including the church record book and registers of interments for the St. Paul's Churchyard and the Mount Vernon City cemetery can be viewed online at www.mhsarchive.org.

Town of New Castle

New Castle Historical Society

The Horace Greeley House • 100 King Street • PO Box 55
Chappaqua, NY 10514 • (914) 238-4666
Email: director@newcastlehs.org • www.newcastlehs.org

Holdings include books, family files, maps, local newspapers, oral histories, photographs and postcards 1700s–1900s, letters, and diaries.

City of New Rochelle

Huguenot & New Rochelle Historical Association and Thomas Paine Cottage

20 Sicard Avenue • New Rochelle, NY 10804-4131 • (914) 633-1776
Email: PaineCottage@optonline.net • www.thomaspainecottage.org

Operates a historic house museum that was Thomas Paine's last home in North America; it includes a permanent exhibit on the Huguenot settlement of New Rochelle. Education programs on topics relevant to local history, such as African American, Civil War, American Indian, women's, and general colonial history.

Iona College Ryan Library:
Thomas Paine National Historical Association Collection

715 North Avenue • New Rochelle, NY 10801 • (914) 633-2343
www.iona.edu

Iona College is custodian of a collection that includes the only surviving personal effects of Thomas Paine, as well as documents, manuscripts, letters, and ephemera. Online exhibits from the collection are at www.iona.edu/Academics/Libraries/About/TPNHA-Collection.aspx. The College has also established an Institute for Thomas Paine Studies.

New Rochelle Public Library: Local History Collection and the E. L. Doctorow Local History Room

One Library Plaza • New Rochelle, NY 10801 • (914) 632-7878
Email: refdesk@nrpl.org • www.nrpl.org/localhistorycollection

The primary repository of archival materials and other resources relating to New Rochelle's history. Online Local History Index at www.nrpl.org/pages/NRPLLclHstryCndnsdIndx.pdf. Holdings include books and pamphlets, maps and atlases, photographs, postcards, newspapers and clippings, scrapbooks, and federal census for selected counties. Digital collections include post cards; photographs; Coutant Cemetery Centennial; manuscripts; WWII newspaper clippings; and the Davids Island/Fort Slocum Cultural Resources Digital Repository. A portion of its Oral History Collection has been digitized at www.hrvh.org.

Town of North Castle

North Castle Historical Society

440 Bedford Road • Armonk, NY 10504 • (914) 273-4510

Holdings include books, photographs, and maps.

Town of North Salem

North Salem Historical Society

81 Keeler Lane • North Salem, NY • (914) 274-7206
Email: northsalemhistoricalsociety@gmail.com • www.nshs.info

Holdings include manuscripts, maps 1700s–present, periodicals, books, and photographs.

Town of Ossining

Ossining Historical Society Museum

196 Croton Avenue • Ossining, NY 10562 • (914) 941-0001
Email: info@ossininghistorical.org • www.ossininghistorical.org

Genealogy files, maps, newspapers 1818–present, photographs, oral histories, historical materials of Sing Sing Prison, military material, slides and films, a military exhibit, and a library of over 1,000 volumes. Society maintains Historic Sparta Cemetery, which contains burials dating to colonial times.

City of Peekskill

Field Library: Colin T. Naylor Jr. Archives

4 Nelson Avenue • Peekskill, NY 10566 • (914) 737-1212
www.peekskill.org/local-history

Subjects include history of Peekskill, Westchester County, New York State, and the American Revolution. Holdings include cemetery records, maps 1700s–present, newspapers 1800s–present, photographs and prints, obituary index, telephone directories 1860–present, subject files, and Couch genealogical files. Research requests are accepted.

Peekskill Museum

The Herrick House • 124 Union Avenue • PO Box 84
Peekskill, NY 10566 • (914) 736-0473
Email: info@peekskillmuseum.org • www.peekskillmuseum.org

Holdings include books, genealogies and histories, maps, newspapers (*Peekskill Evening Star*, 1937–1985), and village directories 1889–1940.

Town of Pelham

Pelham Preservation & Garden Society

PO Box 8129 • Pelham, NY 10803
info@pelhampreservationsociety.com • pelhampreservationsociety.com

Promotes appreciation of the town's architecture and natural environment; the website includes a history of the town. It assists members to obtain copies of historical residential photographs and documents.

Historic Pelham

Email: historian@townofpelham.com • http://historicpelham.blogspot.com

The blog of the Pelham town historian features posts about local history and genealogy and has a link to the archive of the Historic Pelham website, which provides online access to numerous resources for Pelham research.

Town of Pound Ridge

Hiram Halle Memorial Library (Pound Ridge Library)

271 Westchester Avenue • Pound Ridge, NY 10576 • (914) 764-5085
www.poundridgelibrary.org

Holdings include local histories, genealogies, cemetery records, and church records.

Pound Ridge Historical Society and Museum & Library

255 Westchester Avenue • PO Box 51 • Pound Ridge, NY 10576
(914) 764-4333 • www.prhsmuseum.org

Church records, vital records, marriage records, oral histories, photographs, and histories.

City of Rye

Rye Historical Society, Square House Museum & Knapp House Archives
Society Offices and Museum: One Purchase Street • Rye, NY 10580
(914) 967-7588 • Email: ryehistory@verizon.net • *www.ryehistory.org*
Library and Archives: 265 Rye Beach Avenue • Rye, NY 10580
(914) 967-8657

Holdings include Bible records, census materials, cemetery records, church records, genealogies, manuscripts and pamphlets, maps, newspapers, photographs, artifacts, and Parsons Family Papers.

Town of Rye

Port Chester Public Library
One Haseco Avenue • Port Chester, NY 10573 • (914) 939-6710
www.portchester-ryebrooklibrary.org

Local directories 1890–present, maps and atlases, newspapers, genealogies, obituary indexes (*Port Chester Journal* 1868–1911, *Daily Item,* 1918–1942), and school yearbooks 1914–present.

Rye Historical Society
See the listing above under the City of Rye.

Town of Scarsdale

Scarsdale Historical Society
Cudner-Hyatt House • 937 White Plains Post Road • PO Box 431
Scarsdale, NY 10583 • (914) 723-1744 • Email: history@cloud9.net
www. scarsdalehistoricalsociety.org

Holdings include genealogies, histories, maps, oral histories, personal papers, historical photographs, pamphlets, Quaker material, and family Bibles. The website offers a selection of digitized articles (including one on Scarsdale streets and place names), books, and photographs; links to other valuable resources; and a blog. The society has partnered with the Scarsdale Public Library and other organizations on digitization projects.

Scarsdale Public Library
54 Olmsted Road • Scarsdale, NY 10583 • (914) 722-1300
http://scarsdalelibrary.org

The library's special collections include historical photographs, indexed clipping and pamphlet files, maps, and documents, such as the original 1845 New York state census for Scarsdale. Digitized resources accessible from the website include *Scarsdale Town Minutes: 1787-1864, Scarsdale Inquirer* (1901–1935), and a collection of local history photographs.

Town of Somers

Somers Historical Society and Museum
Somers Town Hall • 335 U.S. Route 202 • Somers, NY 10589
(914) 277-4977 • *www.somershistoricalsoc.org*

The Society is located in the historic Elephant Hotel where it maintains the Alice Minnerly Runyon Reference Library, with collections on the early 19th-century American circus, genealogy, local history, and theater; exhibition galleries; and its archives. Some of its collections have been digitized at *www.hrvh.org.*

City of White Plains

City of White Plains: City Archives
255 Main Street • White Plains, NY 10601-2409 • (914) 422-1450
Email: webpo@ci.white-plains.ny.us • *www.cityofwhiteplains.com*

Assessment rolls, census materials, maps, manuscripts, military rolls, minutes, photographs, scrapbooks, school census, town records, yearbooks, artifacts, and archives of White Plains government.

White Plains Historical Society
Jacob Purdy House • 60 Park Avenue • White Plains, NY 10603
(914) 328-1776 • Email: info@whiteplainshistory.org
www.whiteplainshistory.org

The Society holds meetings and events at the Jacob Purdy House, a former headquarters of General George Washington on the National Register of Historic Places. It publishes a newsletter and has a website with online exhibits from its collections and a list of links to historic sites in the City of White Plains.

White Plains Public Library: Local History Collection
100 Martine Avenue • White Plains, NY 10601 • (914) 422-1480 –
http://whiteplainslibrary.org/local-history

Holdings include books and pamphlets, census materials, city directories, genealogies, newspapers (including obituary index), maps and atlases, photographs and postcards, vertical files, and yearbooks. A complete description of holdings on the website; local history inquiries may be submitted to the Reference Desk via a form online.

City of Yonkers

Yonkers City Clerk
City Hall, Room 107 • 40 South Broadway • Yonkers, NY 10701
(914) 377-6020 • Email: wp@mail.cloud9.net or webpo@ci.white-plains.ny.us • *www.cityofyonkers.com*

Birth, marriage, and death records 1875–present. Records from 1875–1913 are only available at this repository. Birth and death records from 1914–present, and marriage records 1908–present are also available at the New York State Department of Health in Albany.

Yonkers Historical Society
Society: PO Box 190 • Yonkers, NY 10710 • *www.yonkershistory.org*
Collections: Grinton I. Will Library • 1500 Central Park Avenue
Yonkers, NY 10710 • (914) 961-8940

Collections include postcards, photographs, maps, and manuscripts. Digitized articles from *Yonkers History: The Journal of the Yonkers Historical Society* on the website; publications and CDs of Yonkers genealogy and history are available for purchase.

Yonkers Public Library
Riverfront Library • One Larkin Center • Yonkers, New York 10701
Reference desk: (914) 375-7966
Local History Librarian: (914) 337-1500, ext. 486 • *www.ypl.org*

The Library's Local History Room is accessible by appointment. The website provides access to selected online genealogy and local history resources.

Hudson River Museum (HRM)
511 Warburton Avenue • Yonkers, NY 10701 • 914-963-4550
www. hrm.org

The HRM produces exhibitions and education programs that explore the cultural and environmental history of the Hudson River Valley region. The HRM is custodian of the historic 1877 Glenview Mansion. Collections include art and archival materials relevant to Yonkers and the regional history the Hudson River Valley. A portion of its Oral History Collection has been digitized at *www.hrvh.org.*

Town of Yorktown

John C. Hart Memorial Library
1130 Main Street • Shrub Oak, NY 10588 • *www.yorktownlibrary.org*

Holdings include books, diaries, scrapbooks, ledgers, and newspapers.

Yorktown Historical Society

Yorktown Town Hall • PO Box 355 • Yorktown Heights, NY 10598
(914) 962-5722 ext. 440 • www.yorktownhistory.org

Website includes census records, letters, cemetery records, oral histories, church records, journals and publications, and local histories.

Yorktown Museum and Doris & Cortland Auser Research Room

Yorktown Community and Cultural Center, Top Floor
1974 Commerce Street • Yorktown Heights, NY 10598 • (914) 962-2970
Email: museum@yorktownny.org • www.yorktownmuseum.org

Research Room includes local history and genealogical materials, maps, and documents. Subjects represented in exhibits include history of Mohegan Indians, agricultural history, railroad history, and domestic life (1750–1850).

SELECTED PRINT & ONLINE RESOURCES

Below is a selection of resources relevant for research in this county. The list is representative, not exhaustive. Additional titles—particularly of abstracts, indexes, transcriptions, and local histories—are available; consult the introduction to Part Two for further information. For guidance on how to identify and locate community directories and local newspapers, see chapter 11, City Directories, and chapter 12, Newspapers, in Part One of this book.

Abstracts, Indexes & Transcriptions

Bacon, Edgar M. *First English Record Book of the Dutch Reformed Church in Sleepy Hollow, Formerly the Manor of Philipsburgh, Now the First Reformed Church of Tarrytown.* Tarrytown, NY: Tarrytown Historical Society, 1931. The records cover 1791–1836.

Baird, Rev. Charles W. "Marriage Records of the Society of Friends in the Town of Harrison, N.Y. [Purchase Monthly Meeting, 1742–1785]." *NYG&B Record*, vol. 3, no. 1 (1872): 45–51. [NYG&B eLibrary] From the original records now on microfilm at the FHL.

Becker, E. Marie. "The 801 Westchester County Freeholders of 1763 and the Cortlandt Manor Land-Case which Occasioned Their Listing." *New-York Historical Society Quarterly*, vol. 35 (July 1951): 312.

Bristol, Theresa Hall. "Abstracts of Wills Recorded at White Plains, Westchester County, N.Y., Subsequent to May 1, 1787." *NYG&B Record*, vol. 55 (1924) no. 2: 143–154, no. 3: 262–269, no. 4: 330–338; vol. 56 (1925) no. 2: 118–126; vol. 57 (1926) no. 1: 5–10, no. 2: 102–107, no. 3: 248–253, no. 4: 320–325; vol. 58 (1927) no. 1: 40–44, no. 2: 143–149, no. 3: 202–208, no. 4: 381–388; vol. 59 (1928) no. 1: 26–32; vol. 60 (1929) no. 2: 149–155. Covers libers A–G, 1787–1812. [NYG&B eLibrary]

———. "Westchester County, N.Y., Miscellanea." *NYG&B Record*, vol. 50 (1919) no. 3: 240–242; vol. 51 (1920) no. 1: 39–46, no. 3: 252–258; vol. 52 (1921) no. 1: 71–78, no. 2: 170–174, no. 3: 224–229, no. 4: 319–325; vol. 53 (1922) no. 1: 20–26, no. 3: 220–224, no. 4: 325–329; vol. 54 (1923) no. 1: 44–48, no. 2: 132–137, no. 3: 278–285, no. 4: 392–400; vol. 55 (1924) no. 1: 27–36, no. 2: 177–185, no. 3: 202–211, no. 4: 384–393; vol. 56 (1925) no. 2: 137–142, no. 3: 281–287, no. 4: 317–322. Abstracts of County Deed libers A–M, 1683–1801, and Mortgage libers A–E, 1755–1796. [NYG&B eLibrary] The original records are on microfilm at the FHL and the NYPL; the deeds are online at *FamilySearch.org*.

———. "Westchester County, N.Y., Miscellanea." *NYG&B Record*, vol. 57 (1926) no. 3: 240–248, no. 4: 315–319; vol. 58 (1927) no. 1: 34–39, no. 2: 102–110, no. 3: 242–245, no. 4: 348–351. Abstracts of deeds from three volumes of Rye land records. Covers Rye libers B, C, D (Liber A being lost), ca. 1670–1772. Includes Harri-

son to 1772. [NYG&B eLibrary] The complete original Rye town records 1660–1992 and village records of Port Chester are on microfilm at the NYSL.

Burhans, Samuel, Jr. "Records of Baptisms of the Reformed Dutch Church of Cortlandtown, Westchester County, New York [1741–1748 and 1781–1830]." *NYG&B Record*, vol. 73 (1942) no. 2: 136–143, no. 3: 190–199, no. 4: 281–286. [NYG&B eLibrary]

Canfield, Amos. "Westchester County, N.Y., Miscellanea: Abstracts from the Records of the Town of Westchester, New York . . . ." *NYG&B Record*, vol. 60 (1929) no. 2: 105–114, no. 3: 256–264, no. 4: 303–312. Covers Books 1–5, 1655–1725. [NYG&B eLibrary] Original records at MUNI; FHL film.

Cole, Rev. David. *First Record Book of the "Old Dutch Church of Sleepy Hollow" Organized in 1697 and Now the First Reformed Church, Tarrytown, N.Y.* Yonkers Historical and Library Association, 1901. Reprint, Rhinebeck, NY: Palatine Transcripts, 1986. The church was originally called the Church of the Manor of Philipsburgh. Records cover 1697–1791.

Cox, John. "Quaker Records: Chappaqua Monthly Meeting: Westchester County, New York: To Which is Appended Chappaqua Burial Ground, Armonk Burial Ground." Typescript, 1900. NYPL, New York. [*Ancestry.com*]

Daughters of the American Revolution, comps. *New York DAR Genealogical Records Committee Report.* Since 1913 DAR volunteers have transcribed many thousands of unpublished cemetery, church, and town records throughout New York. The reports are at the DAR Library; copies are at the NYSL and the NYPL. The DAR has a searchable name index to all the GRC reports at *http://services.dar.org/Public/DAR_Research/search/?Tab_ID=6*. See Jean Worden's index below for a listing by county of the New York record sets that were transcribed by the DAR before 1998.

———. *Historical Records: Putnam, Dutchess, and Westchester Counties of New York State.* 3 vols. Carmel, NY: Enoch Crosby Chapter, n.d.

Eardeley, William B., and Robert B. Miller. "St. Mark's Episcopal Cemetery, Mount Kisco, NY." Typescript, 1939. Transcriptions made 1909–1914 and copied 1939. [*Ancestry.com*]

Eastchester Historical Society. *Burial Records of St. Paul's Church, Eastchester: 897 S. Columbus Avenue, Mt. Vernon, New York.* Eastchester, NY: The Society, 1973.

Farrell, Charles, "Marriages by a Justice of the Peace in Morrisania." *NYG&B Record*, vol. 129, no. 3 (1998): 189–90. [NYG&B eLibrary]

Fox, Dixon Ryan, and G. B. Harrington. *The Minutes of the Court Sessions 1657–1696, Westchester County, New York.* White Plains, NY: Westchester County Historical Society, 1924.

Frost, Josephine C., and Robert B. Miller. "Cemetery Inscriptions from Westchester County, NY." Typescript, 1915. NYPL, New York. Also titled "Eleven Westchester County Cemeteries." Includes (sic): St. Mark Episcopal at Mt. Kisco; Travis, between Mt. Kisco and Bedford; Reformed Dutch, Elmsford; Zarr at Bedford; Bethel at Croton Village; on road from Poundridge to Bedford; Poundridge, Hobby, at Poundridge; Hoyt, on road from Poundridge to New Canaan; Cooke, Hastings on Hudson; Murphy's Corners at Poundridge. [NYG&B eLibrary]

———. *Cemetery Inscriptions from Westchester County, NY.* N.d. Includes (sic): Tarrytown, Dutch Church Cemetery; Tarrytown, Old Dutch Church Cemetery; Sleepy Hollow Cemetery; Scarborough, Sparta Presbyterian Church Yard; Amawalk, Quaker Cemetery; Purchase Quaker Burial Ground; Chappaqua, Quaker Burial Ground; Croton Village, Bethel Cemetery; Mt. Kisco, St. Mark's Episcopal and Methodist Church Yards. Microfilm, FHL.

Grundset, Eric G. "Some Suppliers to the Continental Army in Westchester County, 1780–1782." *NYG&B Record*, vol. 142, no. 1 (2011): 65–72. [NYG&B eLibrary]

Haacker, Frederick C. *Westchester County, New York, and the French and Indian Wars, 1755–1762: Muster Rolls.* New York: F. C. Haacker, 1952. [*Ancestry.com*]

Harris, William A. "Records Related to Slave Manumissions: Pelham, New York." *NYG&B Record*, vol. 123, no. 3 (1992): 145–147. [NYG&B eLibrary]

Horne, Field, "Customers and Others in the Ledger of Caleb Fowler of New Castle 1754–1760." *NYG&B Record*, vol. 132, no. 3 (2001): 171–176. [NYG&B eLibrary]

———. "New Rochelle Inhabitants, 1767 and 1771." *NYG&B Record*, vol. 107, no. 4. (1976): 194–198 [NYG&B eLibrary]

Horton, William P. "Burials in Hillside Cemetery, Peekskill, Westchester Co., New York. Vol. 1, inscriptions prior to 1888; vol. 2, 1888–1921. Typescript, 1928. NYPL, New York. [Vol. 1 only, NYG&B eLibrary]

———. "Cemetery Inscriptions of Westchester County, New York." 2 vols. Typescript, 1928. NYPL, New York. Vol. 1 includes Amawalk, Bedford Center, Elmsford, Groveville, North Castle, Ossining, Pleasantside, Shrub Oaks, Somers, Sunset, Tarrytown, Vancortlandtville, and Yorktown; vol. 2 includes in Peekskill. [*Ancestry.com*]

———. "Graveyard Inscriptions, Westchester County." Typescript, 1925. Including Selleck Yard (Croft's Corners, north of Peekskill), Tompkins Cemetery and Tompkins Plot (near Ossining), and Lafayette Avenue (North Pleasantside). [NYG&B eLibrary]

Kelly, Arthur C. M. *Vital Records of the Cortlandtown Reformed Church, Montrose, N.Y., 1741–1894.* Rhinebeck, NY: Kelly, 1980. See also Burhans "Records of Baptisms of the Reformed Dutch Church of Cortlandtown."

Leach, Josiah G. *The Journal of the Rev. Silas Constant, Pastor of the Presbyterian Church at Yorktown, N.Y.* Philadelphia, 1903. Includes marriages 1784–1825.

Lustenberger, Anita A. "Cortlandt Manor Leases for Three-Lives." *NYG&B Record*, vol. 133, no. 1 (2002): 19–22. [NYG&B eLibrary]

———. "North Salem, Westchester County, Presbyterian Church Members, 1856." *NYG&B Record*, vol. 137, no. 3 (2006): 178. [NYG&B eLibrary]

———. "Tenants of the Commissioners of Sequestration in Westchester Co. 1778–1783." *NYG&B Record*, vol. 123 (1992) no. 4: 203–206; vol. 124 (1993) no. 1: 30–33. [NYG&B eLibrary]

———. "Unrecorded Deeds, Westchester County [1722–1813]." *NYG&B Record*, vol. 139, no. 4 (2008): 283–284. [NYG&B eLibrary]

Mackenzie, Grenville. "Families of the Colonial Manor of Philipsburgh." Typescript, n.d. Westchester County Historical Society, Elmsford, NY. A name index to the typescript, which contains genealogical data on more than 200 tenant families prior to the Revolution, is accessible on the website; copies may be requested.

Manville, Margaret R. *Revolutionary War Soldiers Buried in Cemeteries in Westchester County, New York.* White Plains, NY: The Author, 1966.

Miller, Robert B. "New York Colonial Manuscripts." *NYG&B Record*, vol. 38 (1907) no. 2: 129–135, 1698 census for Eastchester, Fordham, and Town of Westchester; no. 3: 218–222, 1710 census of Bedford. [NYG&B eLibrary]

New York Genealogical and Biographical Society. "Freeholders to be Jurors, New Rochelle, Westchester County, 1811." *NYG&B Record*, vol. 140, no. 4 (2009): 287–288. [NYG&B eLibrary]

———. "Road List, New Rochelle, Westchester County, 1798." *NYG&B Record*, vol. 140, no. 3 (2009): 207. [NYG&B eLibrary]

———. "The Town Book of the Manor of Philipsburgh." *NYG&B Record*, vol. 59, no. 3 (1928): 203–213. Record of "town" meetings 1742–1779. [NYG&B eLibrary]

Randolph, Howard S. F. "The Census of 1698 for Mamaroneck, Morrisania, and New Rochelle, Westchester County, New York." *NYG&B Record*, vol. 59, no. 2 (1928): 103–107. [NYG&B eLibrary]

"Records of the Church of Christ in Salem, Westchester County, New York [1752–1823]." *NYG&B Record*, vol. 31 (1900) nos. 2–4; vol. 32 (1901) nos. 1–4 ; vol. 33 (1902) nos. 1–4; vol. 34 (1903) nos. 1–4; vol. 35 nos. (1904) 1–2 . [NYG&B eLibrary] For page numbers, see the "Index to Articles in the *Record* by Title and by Author" on *NewYorkFamilyHistory.org*.

"Records of the French Church at New Rochelle, N.Y." *New-York Historical Society Quarterly*, vol. 1 (1917): 77–81, covers 1703–1712.

"Records of the French Church at New Rochelle, New York, Subsequently Known as Trinity Church." Typescript and manuscript, 1930–1950. NYPL, New York. Covers 1726–1727 and 1753–1765.

Sherman, Thomas T. "Vital Records of Christ's Church at Rye, Westchester County, New York [1790–1879]." *NYG&B Record*, vol. 37 (1906) nos. 1, 2, 4; vol. 38 (1907) nos. 1–4; vol. 46 (1915) nos. 3–4; vol. 47 (1916) nos. 1–4; vol. 48 (1917) nos. 1–4. [NYG&B eLibrary] For page numbers, see the "Index to Articles in the *Record* by Title and by Author" on *NewYorkFamilyHistory.org*.

Smith, Mable W. "Unpublished 1845 Census of Mamaroneck, Westchester County, New York; 1850 Census of Mamaroneck, Westchester County, New York; Military Enlistments—Civil War, 1862." Typescript, 1955–1956. DAR Library, Washington. [FHL microfilm]

Spies, Francis Ferdinand. "Rye, Westchester Co., N.Y., Inscriptions from the Graveyards." Mt. Vernon, NY: The Author, 1932.

———. "Inscriptions from Quaker Burying Grounds with Notes: Purchase, West Chester Co; Chappaqua, West Chester Co.; Pawling, Dutchess Co. (Quaker Hill); Bethel, Dutchess Co., Index." Typescript, 1923. [*Ancestry.com*]

Spies, Francis Ferdinand, and Mildred Struble. "Inscriptions from the Cemetery Yard of the Old Methodist Church in Pleasantville, NY." Typescript, 1951. [NYG&B eLibrary]

St. John's Episcopal Church, Tuckahoe, NY, 1853–1939. Typescript, 1948. NYPL, New York. Selected records and registers of the church, which is located in the Colonial Heights neighborhood of Yonkers, NY. [NYG&B eLibrary]

Struble, Mildred, Mable Jordan, and Natalie Seth. "Deaths and Cemetery Inscriptions, Poundridge, Westchester County, NY—Accounts of an Unnamed Undertaker, 1860–1871; Tombstone Records of Eighteen Cemeteries." Typescript, 1941. NYPL, New York. [NYG&B eLibrary]

Vosburgh, Royden Woodward. *Records of the Reformed Church of Fordham in the Borough of the Bronx, City of New York, Formerly the Reformed Protestant Dutch Church of Fordham in the Town of West Farms, Westchester County, N.Y.* New York: New York Genealogical and Biographical Society, 1921. Covers 1793–1888.

Walker, Eldon L. "1845 New York State Census, Scarsdale, Westchester County, NY." *Westchester County Historical Bulletin,* vol. 54, no. 3 (1978): 64–68.

Webb, Morrison DeSoto, "Baptisms, Marriages, and Burials, Christ's Church, Rye, Westchester County, 1880–1898." *NYG&B Record,* vol. 141 (2010) no. 1: 43–52, no. 2: 142–146, no. 3: 230–234. [NYG&B eLibrary]

"Westchester County Administrations 1707." *NYG&B Record,* vol. 124, no. 2 (1993): 90–91. [NYG&B eLibrary]

Westchester County Almshouse. *Records 1854–1908.* Archival collection. NYSA, Albany, NY. NYSL microfilm.

Westchester County Church Surveys. Includes information about the archives of six churches in Westchester ca. 1900. Digitally published by New York Genealogical and Biographical Society, 2012. [NYG&B eLibrary]

Worden, Jean D. "Book 1, Subject Index." In *Revised Master Index to the New York State Daughters of the American Revolution Genealogical Records Volumes.* Zephyrhills, FL: J. D. Worden, 1998. The Subject Index includes a listing by county of the cemeteries, churches, towns, and other sources of records transcribed by the DAR.

Town Records

Town of Bedford. *Bedford Historical Records.* 9 vols. Bedford, NY: The Town, 1966–present. Includes land records, 1680–1800; cemetery records, 1681–1975; soldiers of the revolution; meeting minutes; genealogies.

Town of Eastchester. *Records of the Town of Eastchester.* 9 vols. Eastchester Historical Society, 1964–1966.

Town of Greenburgh. "Town and Village Records, 1845–1993." NYSL microfilm.

Town of Harrison, and David N. Haviland, "Town/Village of Harrison Records, 1696–1966." NYSL microfilm.

Town of Mamaroneck, and Mary O. C. English. *Early Town Records of Mamaroneck, 1697–1881.* Larchmont: Larchmont Public Library, 1979. The complete town records of Mamaroneck plus the village records of Mamaroneck and Larchmont to 1993 are on microfilm at the NYSL.

Town of New Rochelle, and Jeanne A. Forbes. *Records of the Town of New Rochelle 1699–1828.* New Rochelle, NY: Paragraph Press, 1916.

Town of North Castle, Richard N. Lander, and Barbara S. Massi. *North Castle Historical Records: Minutes of Town Meetings, 1791–1848, Maps, Census of 1800, Census of 1850, Illustrations, Articles of Historical Interest.* Armonk, NY: The Town, 1986.

Town of Westchester. *Records of the Town of Westchester, New York, 1665–1827.* N.p., 1900. FHL microfilm.

Other Resources

Akerly, Lucy D. *The Morris Manor.* Publication No. 4. New York: The Order of Colonial Lords of Manors in America, 1916.

Baird, Charles W. *Chronicle of a Border Town, History of Rye, Westchester County, New York, 1660–1870, Including Harrison.* New York, 1871.

Beers, J. B., & Co. *County Atlas of Westchester, New York.* New York, 1872. [NYPL Digital Gallery]

Bien, Joseph R. *Atlas of Westchester County.* New York: Julius Bien & Company, 1893. [NYPL Digital Gallery]

Bolton, Robert, Jr. *A History of the County of Westchester, from Its First Settlement to the Present Time.* 2 vols. New York, 1848.

———. *A History of Several Towns, Manors, and Patents of the County of Westchester from Its First Settlement to the Present Time.* 2 vols. New York, 1881. Includes genealogies of county families.

Bristol, Theresa Hall. "Genealogical Gleanings from Land and Probate Records at White Plains and Rye, New York." *NYG&B Record,* vol. 49 (1918) no. 2: 170–176, no. 3: 292–303, no. 4: 381–389. Early families of White Plains, with map showing their landholdings. [NYG&B eLibrary]

Caro, Edythe Quinn. *"The Hills" in the Mid-Nineteenth Century: The History of a Rural Afro-American Community in Westchester County, New York.* Valhalla, NY: Westchester County Historical Society, 1988.

Cushman, Elisabeth. *Historic Westchester, 1683–1933: Glimpses of County History.* Tarrytown, NY: Westchester County Publishers, Inc., 1933.

Davis, Norman. *Westchester Patriarchs: A Genealogical Dictionary of Westchester County, New York, Families Prior to 1755.* Bowie, MD: Heritage Books, 1988.

Dawson, Henry B. *Westchester County, New York, during the American Revolution.* New York, 1886.

De Lancey, Edward F., *The Origin and History of Manors in New York and in the County of Westchester.* New York, 1886. Also published as a chapter in Scharf's *History of Westchester County* below.

———. "Original Family Records, Morris of Morrisania, Westchester Co., New York," *NYG&B Record,* vol. 7, no. 1 (1876): 16–18.

Dunkak, Harry M. *Freedom, Culture, Labor: The Irish of Early Westchester County, New York.* New Rochelle, NY: Iona College Press, 1994.

Forliano, Richard, and Eloise L. Morgan, eds. *Out of the Wilderness: The Emergence of Eastchester, Tuckahoe, and Bronxville, 1664–2014.* Eastchester, NY: Eastchester 350th Celebration Committee, 2014.

French, Alvah P. *History of Westchester County, New York.* 5 vols. New York: Lewis Historical Publishing Co., 1925–1927. [vols. 1–4, *books. FamilySearch.org*]

Fuller, Elizabeth Green. *Indexes to Westchester County Names in the Federal Censuses, 1790–1840.* Elmsford, NY: Westchester County Historical Society, 1994.

———. *Index to the Westchester Historian, vols. 1–65, 1925–1989.* Elmsford, Westchester Historical Society.

Fuller, Elizabeth Green, and Diana D. Deichert. *Index to the Westchester Historian, vols. 66–86, 1990–2012.* Elmsford, Westchester Historical Society.

Graziano, Jackie. "Westchester County Archives." *New York Researcher*, Spring 2014; also a Research Aid on *NewYorkFamilyHistory.org.*

Griffin, Ernest F., ed. *Westchester County and Its People, A Record.* 3 vols. New York: Lewis Historical Publishing. Co., 1946 [*HathiTrust.org*]

Hall, Edward Hagaman. *Philipse Manor Hall at Yonkers, NY: The Site, the Building, and Its Occupants.* New York: American Scenic and Historic Preservation Society, 1912.

Hoff, Henry B. "Hudson Valley Research: The East Side." This extensive bibliography of resources in Westchester and other Hudson Valley counties was originally prepared for the NEHGS-NYG&B Joint Conference, Tarrytown, NY, July 25–26, 1997; digitally published as a Research Aid at *NewYorkFamilyHistory.org.*

———. "MacKenzie's Families of Philipsburgh." *NYG&B Newsletter* (now *New York Researcher*), Fall 1994. Published as a Research Aid on *NewYorkFamilyHistory.org.*

Horne, Field. "A Guide to the Churches and Their Records in Westchester County, New York, 1674–1880." Typescript, 1977. NYPL, New York.

———. "The Philipsburg Manor Rent Roll of 1760," *NYG&B Record*, vol. 110, no. 2 (1979): 102–104.

Hufeland, Otto. *A Check List of Books, Maps, Pictures, and Other Printed Matter Relating to the Counties of Westchester and Bronx.* White Plains, NY: Westchester County Historical Society, 1929. [*Ancestry.com*]

———. *Westchester County during the American Revolution.* White Plains, NY: Westchester County Historical Society, 1926. [*Ancestry.com*]

Jacob Judd, ed. *Van Cortlandt Family Papers* [1748–1848]. 4 vols. Tarrytown, NY: Sleepy Hollow Restorations, 1976–1981.

Jordan, Alvin, and Maureen L. Koehl, eds. *A History of the Town of Lewisboro, Westchester County, New York.* South Salem, NY: Lewisboro History Book Committee, 1981. Reprinted, South Salem, NY: South Salem Library Association, 1994.

Kim, Sung B. *Landlord and Tenant in Colonial New York: Manorial Society, 1664-1775.* Chapel Hill: Published for the Institute of Early American History and Culture, Williamsburg, Va., by the University of North Carolina Press, 1978. See "A Note on Sources," pp. 425–431, for detailed information about archival and printed material related to Westchester County's historic Manors.

———. "The Manor of Cortlandt and Its Tenants, 1697–1783," PhD diss., Michigan State University, 1966.

Leggett, Theodore A., and Abraham Hatfield, eds. "Early Settlers of West Farms, Westchester County, N.Y." *NYG&B Record*, vol. 44 (1913) nos. 3–4; vol. 45 (1914) nos. 1–4; vol. 46 (1915) nos. 1–4; vol. 47 (1916) nos. 1–2. [*NYG&B eLibrary*] For page numbers, see the "Index to Articles in the *Record* by Title and by Author" on *NewYorkFamilyHistory.org.*

Lewis Publishing. *Biographical History of Westchester County, New York.* 2 vols. Chicago, 1899.

Macy, Harry, Jr. "Westchester County Resources in the *NYG&B Record.*" *NYG&B Newsletter* (now *New York Researcher*), Spring 1998. Updated June 2011 and published as a Research Aid on *NewYorkFamilyHistory.org.*

McKernan, Maureen. "Old Families of Westchester." Typescript, 1951. NYPL, New York. Clippings of a series of 22 articles.

Mellick, Harry C. W. *The Manor of Fordham and Its Founder.* New York: Fordham University Press, 1950

Morris, Fordham. *The Borough Town of Westchester, An Address Delivered by Fordham Morris, October 28, 1896.* White Plains, NY, 1896.

New York Historical Resources Center. *Guide to Historical Resources in Westchester County, New York Repositories.* Ithaca, NY: Cornell University Library, 1991. [*books.FamilySearch.org*]

Pallen, Condé B., ed. *New Rochelle, Her Part in the Great War: Historical and Biographical Sketches of Individuals and Organizations Who Rendered Valuable Service to Their Country During the Great World War.* New Rochelle, NY: W. C. Tindall, 1920.

Pell, Captain Howland. *The Pell Manor.* Publication No. 5. New York: The Order of Colonial Lords of Manors in America, 1917.

Pelliana: Pell of Pelham. Vol. 1, nos. 1–6, 1934–1941; new series vol. 1, nos. 1 and 2, 1962–1965. A series of pamphlets published privately by the Pell Family are at the NYPL; microfilm is at the FHL.

Raftery, Patrick J. *The Cemeteries of Westchester County.* 3 vols. Elmsford, NY: Westchester County Historical Society, 2011. This comprehensive reference is nearly 800 pages and includes more than 1,200 illustrations.

———. "The Westchester County Historical Society." *New York Researcher*, Winter 2013/2014; also a Research Aid on *NewYorkFamilyHistory.org.*

Remington, Gordon L., "Robert[2] Huestis of Westchester County: His Ancestry and Descendants," *NYG&B Record*, vol. 129 (1998) no. 1: 1–12, no. 2: 97–108, no. 3: 191–206, (A/C) 260–261, no. 4: 276–284; vol. 130 (1999) no. 1: 54–60. See vol. 129, no. 4: 277–279 for information relevant to Pelham Manor and Philipsburgh Manor. [*NYG&B eLibrary*]

Renino, Marjorie Chamberlain Herrmann, comp. *The Guide to Genealogical Research for Westchester County, New York.* Elmsford, NY: Westchester County Historical Society, 2003. This is an authoritative, and virtually exhaustive, guide.

Scharf, J. Thomas. *History of Westchester County, New York, Including Morrisania, Kings Bridge, and West Farms, Which Have Been Annexed to New York City.* 2 vols. Philadelphia, 1886. Indexed by Elizabeth G. Fuller in 1988.

Seacord, Morgan H. *Biographical Sketches and Index of the Huguenot Settlers of New Rochelle, 1687–1776.* New Rochelle, NY: Huguenot and Historical Association of New Rochelle, 1941.

Shargel, Baila. *The Jews of Westchester: A Social History.* Fleischmanns, NY: Purple Mountain Press, 1994.

Shonnard, Frederic. *History of Westchester County, New York, from Its Earliest Settlement to the Year 1900.* Harrison, NY: Harbor Hill Books, 1974. [*books.FamilySearch.org*]

Smith, Henry T. *Manual of Westchester County, Past and Present.* White Plains, NY, 1898.

Swanson, Susan C., and E. G. Fuller. *Westchester County, a Pictorial History*. Norfolk, VA: Donning Co., 1982

Weigold, Marilyn E. *Westchester County: The Past Hundred Years, 1883–1983*. Harrison, NY: Harbor Hill Books for Westchester County Historical Society, Valhalla, 1984.

Wheeler, Charles B. *The Heathcote Manor of Scarsdale*. Publication No. 11. New York: The Order of Colonial Lords of Manors in America, 1923.

Additional Online Resources

Ancestry.com

There are vast numbers of records on *Ancestry.com* that pertain to people who have lived in New York State. See chapter 16, National and Statewide Repositories & Resources, for a description of *Ancestry.com*'s resources and its partnership with the New York State Archives. A search of the online card catalog by county may reveal lesser known resources that pertain to a locality, such as town records, abstracts, transcriptions, city directories, and local histories.

FamilySearch.org

FamilySearch has extensive collections of New York records, including religious records, which are searchable by name and location, but not by county. The following collections include record images (browsable, but not searchable) that are organized by county:

- "New York, Land Records, 1630–1975." Includes land and property records. *familysearch.org/search/collection/2078654*

- "New York, Probate Records, 1629–1971." Includes wills, letters of administration, and guardianship papers. *familysearch.org/search/collection/1920234*

For both collections, choose the browse option and then select Westchester to view the available records sets.

A detailed description of *FamilySearch.org* resources, which include the catalog of the Family History Library, is found in chapter 16, National and Statewide Repositories & Resources.

NYGenWeb Project: Westchester County
www.rootsweb.ancestry.com/~nywestch

Part of the national, USGenWeb volunteer initiative, the website provides information and resources for county research.

Old Fulton New York Postcards
www.FultonHistory.com

The website provides free access to a vast collection of digitized New York newspapers, including 18 titles for Westchester County.

Wyoming County

Formed May 19, 1841

Parent County   Genesee
Daughter Counties   None
County Seat   Village of Warsaw

Major Land Transactions
See chapter 7, Land Records
Morris Reserve 1791
Holland Land Company Purchase 1792–1796

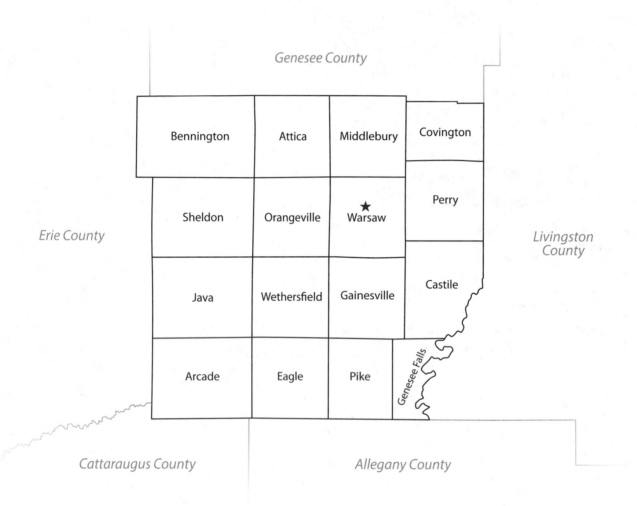

Town Boundary Map
★ - County seat

Towns (and Cities)	Villages and other Settlements		Notes
Arcade 1807 Settlers from New England 1818 Formed in Genesee County as Town of China from Town of Sheldon 1832 Daughter town Java formed 1841 Transferred to new county of Wyoming 1866 Name changed from China to Arcade; ceded land to Town of Eagle	Arcade (v) Arcade Center East Arcade East China Punkshire Corners West Eagle		• Village of Arcade inc. 1871
Attica 1802 Settled 1811 Formed in Genesee County from Town of Sheldon 1816 Daughter town Orangeville formed 1841 Transferred to new county of Wyoming	Attica (v) Attica Center Sierks South Attica Vernal Corners		• Village of Attica inc. 1837; small part of village in Town of Alexander, Genesee County • Vernal Corners formerly Vernal, on Middlebury town line
Bennington 1802 Settlers from Vermont 1818 Formed in Genesee County from Town of Sheldon 1841 Transferred to new county of Wyoming	Bennington Bennington Center Bennington Corner Cowlesville Danley Corner(s)	Earls Corner East Bennington Folsomdale Poland Hill	
Castile c. 1780 Settlers at Gardeau Flats, near St. Helena 1821 Formed in Genesee County from Town of Perry 1841 Transferred to new county of Wyoming	Bishop Corners Castile (v) Castile Center Chase Fairview Five Corners Oak Hill	Perry (v) Silver Lake Silver Lake Junction Sowerby Corners St. Helena Walkers Whaley	• Village of Castile inc. 1877 • Chase also Chase Station • Village of Perry inc. 1830; shared with Town of Perry
China Name for Town of Arcade 1818–1866			
Covington 1807 Settled 1817 Formed in Genesee County from towns of LeRoy and Perry 1841 Daughter town Pavilion formed in Genesee County; Covington transferred to new county of Wyoming	Boyds Corners Covington LaGrange Orrs Corners Pearl Creek Peoria Quinlan(s) Corners		• Covington also Covington Center
Eagle 1808 Settlers from Cayuga County 1823 Formed in Allegany County from Town of Pike 1846 Transferred to Wyoming County 1866 Annexed land from Town of Arcade	Bliss Eagle Eagle Center Eagle Village Hillside(s) Howes Wing		

Towns (and Cities)	Villages and other Settlements		Notes
Gainesville 1805 Settlers from Columbia County and Vermont 1814 Formed in Genesee County as Town of Hebe from Town of Warsaw 1816 Name changed to Gainesville 1841 Transferred to new county of Wyoming	East Gainesville Gainesville (v) Gainesville Center Gainesville Creek Hardy(s)	Newburg North Gainesville Rock Glen Silver Springs (v)	• Village of Gainesville inc. 1902 • Rock Glen formerly called Newburg • Village of Silver Springs inc. 1895
Genesee Falls 1804 Settled 1846 Formed from towns of Portage (Livingston County) and Pike	Bigelow Corners Bishop Corners Letchworth Park Portageville		
Hebe Name for Town of Gainesville 1814–1816			
Java 1810 Settlers from Lowell, MA 1832 Formed in Genesee County from Town of China (now Arcade) 1841 Transferred to new county of Wyoming	Curriers Currier(s) Corners East Java Java Java Center Java Village	North Java Strykersville Union Corners Waldos Corners Williamsville	• Strykersville mostly in Town of Sheldon • Union Corners on Wethersfield town line
Middlebury 1802 Settlers from Rutland County, VT, near Wrights Corners 1812 Formed in Genesee County from Town of Warsaw 1841 Transferred to new county of Wyoming	Belknap Crossing Dale Ewells Corner(s) Lambs Corner(s) Middlebury Millers Corner(s) Millers Crossing	Saltvale Thompsons Crossing Vernal Corners West Middlebury Wrights Corner(s) Wyoming (v)	• Vernal Corners on Attica town line • Village of Wyoming inc. 1916
Orangeville 1816 Formed in Genesee County from Town of Attica 1823 Daughter town Wethersfield formed 1841 Transferred to new county of Wyoming	Dutch Flats East Orangeville Halls Corner(s) Johnsonburg Orangeville Orangeville Center Quakertown		• East Orangeville county seat 1841–1842 • Johnsonburg on Sheldon town line
Perry 1806 Settlers from Vermont 1814 Formed in Genesee County from Town of Leicester * 1817 Daughter town Covington formed 1821 Daughter town Castile formed 1841 Transferred to new county of Wyoming	Buffalo Corners Burk Hill Perry (v) Perry Center Simmons Corners Sucker Brook West Perry West Perry Center		* Town of Leicester now in Livingston County • Village of Perry inc. 1830; formerly Beechville, Columbia, Ninevah, Shacksberg, and Slabtown; shared with Town of Castile

Towns (and Cities)	Villages and other Settlements		Notes
Pike 1806 Settlers from Whitehall, NY 1818 Formed in Allegany County from Town of Nunda * 1819 Daughter town Centerville formed in Allegany County 1822 Daughter town Hume formed in Allegany County 1823 Daughter town Eagle formed 1846 Transferred to Wyoming County 1846 Daughter town Genesee Falls formed	East Koy East Pike Griffith(s) Corners Lamont Pike (v) Pike Five Corners		* Town of Nunda now in Livingston County • East Koy formerly East Coy • Village of Pike inc. 1848, dissolved 12/31/2009
Sheldon 1804 Settled 1808 Formed in Genesee County from Town of Batavia 1811 Daughter town Attica formed 1818 Daughter towns China (now Arcade) and Bennington formed 1841 Transferred to new county of Wyoming	Cobble Hill Dutch Hollow Frinks Corner(s) Harris Corners Humphrey Hollow Johnsonburg North Sheldon Persons Corners	Plants Corner Sheldon Sheldon Center Straubs Corners Strykersville Toziers Corner Varysburg	• Johnsonburg on Orangeville town line • Strykersville on Java town line
Warsaw 1803 Settled at Warsaw Village 1808 Formed in Genesee County from Town of Batavia 1812 Daughter town Middlebury formed 1814 Daughter town Hebe (now Gainesville) formed 1841 Transferred to new county of Wyoming	East Warsaw Erie Martinsville Newburg Oatka	Pierce Corners South Warsaw Thompsons Crossing Warsaw (v)	• County seat at Warsaw from 1842, courts held at East Orangeville, Town of Orangeville 1841–1842; Village of Warsaw inc. 1843
Wethersfield 1810 Settlers from Jefferson County 1823 Formed in Genesee County from Town of Orangeville 1841 Transferred to new county of Wyoming	Eastman Corners Hermitage North Wethersfield Ontario	Poplar Tree Corners Smiths Corner(s) Union Corners Wethersfield Springs	• Smiths Corner(s) also Wethersfield • Union Corners on Java town line

NEW YORK STATE CENSUS RECORDS

See also chapter 3, Census Records

County originals at Wyoming County Clerk's Office: 1875, 1915, 1925 (1845, 1855, 1865, 1892* and 1905 are lost)

State originals at the NYSA: 1915, 1925

Microfilm at the FHL, NYPL, and NYSL; many years are online at *FamilySearch.org* and *Ancestry.com*.

*1892 New York State census is lost with the exception of the schedules for the Town of Orangeville. For a partial transcription of surviving census records, see Wilson and Ripstein in Abstracts, Indexes & Transcriptions.

NATIONAL/STATEWIDE REPOSITORIES & RESOURCES

See chapter 16

COUNTYWIDE REPOSITORIES & RESOURCES

Wyoming County Clerk

143 North Main Street, Suite 104 • Warsaw, NY 14569
(585) 786-8810 • Email: county.clerk@wyomingco.net
www.wyomingco.net/cclerk/main.html

Land and court records; military discharge documents; naturalization records 1851–1929, and petitions of intention 1841–present; birth, marriage, and death records; and the New York state censuses for Wyoming County 1875, 1915, and 1925.

Wyoming County – Town and Village Clerks

Birth, marriage, and death records are maintained by the clerk of the municipality in which the event occurred; see Introduction to County Guides for details of other records which may also be held by municipal clerks. For contact information, see *www.wyomingco.net/ Board/rosters/Roster_Book.pdf*.

Wyoming County Surrogate's Court

Wyoming County Courthouse • 147 North Main Street
Warsaw, NY 14569 • (585) 786-3148

Holds probate records from 1848 to the present. See also chapter 6, Probate Records.

Wyoming County Public Libraries

Wyoming is part of the Pioneer Library System; see *www.pls-net.org* or *www.owwl.org* to access each library. Many hold genealogy and local history collections, including books, newspapers, and gazetteers. See also listing below for Warsaw Public Library.

Wyoming County Historian

26 Linwood Avenue • Warsaw, NY 14569 • (585) 786-8818
www.gahwny.org/p/wyoming.html

Website includes list of local historians, museums, and historical societies with contact information. Since 1947, the county historian has edited the quarterly journal *Historical Wyoming*, which includes local histories, biographies, genealogical queries, and record transcriptions. *Historical Wyoming* is widely available from public libraries, and issues 1947–1987 are on *http://FultonHistory.com*.

Wyoming County – All Municipal Historians

While not authorized to answer genealogical inquiries, town and village historians can provide valuable historical information and research advice; some maintain collections and webpages which may include transcribed records, local histories, and other genealogical material.

See contact information at the Government Appointed Historians of Western New York at *www.gahwny.org/p/wyoming.html* or at the website of the Association of Public Historians of New York State at *www.aphnys.org*.

REGIONAL REPOSITORIES & RESOURCES

Milne Library at SUNY Geneseo: Special Collections: Genesee Valley Historical Collection
See listing in Livingston County Guide

SUNY Fredonia: Daniel A. Reed Library: Archives & Special Collections
See listing in Chautauqua County Guide

University of Rochester: Rare Books, Special Collections, and Preservation: Manuscript and Special Collections: Rochester, Western New York, and New York State
See listing in Monroe County Guide

Western New York Genealogical Society
See listing in Erie County Guide

Western New York Heritage Press
See listing in Erie County Guide

LOCAL REPOSITORIES & RESOURCES
Alphabetized by location

Arcade Historical Society and Gibby House

331 West Main Street • Arcade, NY 14009 • (585) 492-4466
Email: office@arcadehistoricalsociety.org
www.arcadehistoricalsociety.org

Documents, newspapers, obituaries, scrapbooks, and photographs documenting local history 1865–present.

Attica Historical Society and Museum

130 Main Street • Attica, NY 14011 • (585) 591-2161
www.townofattica.net/history.htm

Holdings include local histories and genealogies.

Castile Historical Society and Museum

17 East Park Road • Castile, NY 14427 • (585) 493-5370
Email: castilehistory@peoplepc.com

Genealogical records, cemetery records, census materials, newspapers, photographs, scrapbooks, and artifacts.

Bennington Historical Society

211 Clinton Street • Cowlesville, NY 14037 • (585) 591-2601
www.benningtonny.com/history.htm

Website includes local history and photographs.

Sheldon Historical Society and Museum

3859 Main Street • PO Box 122
Strykersville, NY 14145 • (585) 457-7033
Email: Sheldonhistoricalsociety@hotmail.com • Facebook page

Holdings include family files, cemetery lists and information, obituaries, historical maps, histories, and gazetteers. The Society publishes a quarterly newsletter and accepts genealogical and local history inquiries. The museum is a restored 1890 schoolhouse.

Warsaw Historical Society, Gates House Museum, and Research Library
15 Perry Avenue • Warsaw, NY 14569 • (585) 786-5240
Email: gateshouse@basicisp.net • *www.warsawhistory.org*

Books, documents, maps, newspapers, and photographs chronicling the history of Warsaw, with focus on the history of the Underground Railroad, Suffrage Movement, and local agricultural and industrial history.

Warsaw Public Library: Local History and Genealogy Resources
130 North Main Street • Warsaw, NY 14569
(585) 786-5650 • Email: warsawlibrarydirector@owwl.org
www.warsawpubliclibraryhome.blogspot.com

Holdings include local histories, gazetteers, directories, and newspapers 1836–present.

Middlebury Historical Society and Middlebury Academy Museum
22 South Academy Street • PO Box 198
Wyoming, NY 14591 • Facebook page

Small collection of local history and genealogy.

SELECTED PRINT & ONLINE RESOURCES

Below is a selection of resources relevant for research in this county. The list is representative, not exhaustive. Additional titles—particularly of abstracts, indexes, transcriptions, and local histories—are available; consult the introduction to Part Two for further information. For guidance on how to identify and locate community directories and local newspapers, see chapter 11, City Directories, and chapter 12, Newspapers, in Part One of this book.

Abstracts, Indexes & Transcriptions

Bannister, Doris A. *Wyoming County Vital Records, Deaths, 1847–1851 & Warsaw Deaths, 1863.* Wyoming, NY: Doris A. Bannister, 2008.

Barber, Gertrude Audrey. "Cemetery Inscriptions, Wyoming County, N.Y." Typescript, 1931. NYPL, New York. Includes Curriers Corners and Old Strikersville cemeteries. [NYG&B eLibrary].

———. "Gravestone Inscriptions of Wyoming County, N.Y.: Including Cemeteries in Sheldon and Bennington, N.Y." Typescript, 1933. NYPL, New York. [NYG&B eLibrary].

———. "Gravestone Inscriptions of Wyoming County, N.Y.: Including Cemeteries in Silver Springs, Hermitage, and Genesee Falls." Typescript, 1932. NYPL, New York.

———. "Gravestone Inscriptions, Sundry Cemeteries in Cattaraugus, Erie and Wyoming Counties, NY." Typescript. NYPL, New York. [NYG&B eLibrary]

———. "Wyoming County, N.Y., Cemetery Inscriptions." Typescript, 1930–1932. NYPL, New York. Includes cemeteries in Pike, Java, and Weathersfield. [NYG&B eLibrary].

———. "Wyoming County, N.Y., Cemetery Inscriptions." Typescript, 1931. NYPL, New York. Includes cemeteries in Orangeville and Strikersville. [NYG&B eLibrary].

County of Wyoming Abstracts. Syracuse: Central New York Genealogical Society, 2000. Abstracts for a range of genealogical records originally published in the quarterly *Tree Talks*. A name index is on the CNYGS website.

Daughters of the American Revolution, comps. *New York DAR Genealogical Records Committee Report.* Since 1913 DAR volunteers have transcribed many thousands of unpublished cemetery, church, and town records throughout New York. The reports are at the DAR Library; copies are at the NYSL and the NYPL. The DAR has a searchable name index to all the GRC reports at *http://services.dar.org/Public/DAR_Research/search/?Tab_ID=6*. See Jean Worden's index below for a listing by county of the New York record sets that were transcribed by the DAR before 1998.

Kelly, Arthur C. M. *Index to Tree Talks County Packet: Wyoming County.* Rhinebeck, NY: Kinship, 2002.

Samuelsen, W. David. *Wyoming County, New York, Probate Records, 1841–1900.* Salt Lake City: Kokaubeam Company, 1988.

Wilson, John G., and Anita Ripstein, eds. "Town of Orangeville—1892 Census." *Historical Wyoming,* vol. 31 (April 1985) no. 4: 109–111; vol. 32 (January 1986) no. 3: 84. This is a partial transcription of the schedule of the Orangeville 1892 New York state census.

Worden, Jean D. "Book 1, Subject Index." In *Revised Master Index to the New York State Daughters of the American Revolution Genealogical Records Volumes.* Zephyrhills, FL: J. D. Worden, 1998. The Subject Index includes a listing by county of the cemeteries, churches, towns, and other sources of records transcribed by the DAR.

Wyoming County (NY) Board of Supervisors. *List of Names of the Soldiers, Sailors, and Marines of Wyoming County, NY in the World War of 1917–1918.* Attica, NY: Attica News, 1919.

Wyoming County, NYG&B Church Surveys Collection. NYG&B, New York. [NYG&B eLibrary]

Other Resources

Beers, S. N., and D. G. Beers. *New Topographical Atlas of Genesee and Wyoming Counties, New York.* Philadelphia, 1866.

Biographical Review: This Volume Contains Biographical Sketches of the Leading Citizens of Livingston and Wyoming Counties, New York. Boston, 1895.

Child, Hamilton. *Gazetteer and Business Directory of Wyoming County, NY, for 1870–1.* Syracuse, 1870.

Douglass, Harry S. *Famous Sons and Daughters of Wyoming County, New York.* Warsaw, NY: Wyoming County Newspapers, 1935.

Foley, Janet W. *Early Settlers of New York State: Their Ancestors and Descendants.* 9 vols. Akron, NY: 1934–1942. Reprint, 2 vols. Baltimore, Genealogical Publishing Co., 1993.

Historical Wyoming. Warsaw, NY: Wyoming County Historian, 1947–present, quarterly. Indexes to articles 1947–2008 at *http://wyoming.bettysgenealogy.org/hw.htm*. Many issues online at *www.fultonhistory.com*. Published census transcriptions include 1810, 1820, and 1830 for various towns and a partial transcription of the 1892 census for the Town of Orangeville, see Wilson and Ripstein above.

History of Wyoming County, NY: With Illustrations, Biographical Sketches, and Portraits of Some Pioneers and Prominent Residents. New York, 1880.

New Century Atlas of Wyoming County, New York, with Farm Records. Philadelphia: Century Map Co., 1902.

New York Historical Resources Center. *Guide to Historical Resources in Wyoming County, New York, Repositories.* Ithaca, NY: Cornell University, 1983.

Pierce, Preston E. *Western New York Oral History Collections in Livingston County, Monroe County, Ontario County, Wayne County, Wyoming County.* Fairport, NY: Rochester Regional Library

Council, 2009. *http://rrlc.org/wp-content/uploads/2013/02/dhp_Oral-History-Inventory.pdf*

Records of the Ithaca College Study Center for Early Religious Life in Western New York, 1978–1981. Division of Rare and Manuscript Collections, Cornell University Library. A description of the holdings for each county is at *http://rmc.library.cornell.edu/eguides/lists/churchlist1.htm*.

Western New York Genealogical Society Journal. Hamburg, NY: Western New York Genealogical Society, 1974–present. [wnygs.org]

Wyckoff, William. *The Developer's Frontier: The Making of the Western New York Landscape.* New Haven: Yale University Press, 1988.

Young, Andrew W. *History of the Town of Warsaw, New York, from Its First Settlement to the Present Time: With Numerous Family Sketches and Biographical Notes.* New York, 1869.

Additional Online Resources

Ancestry.com

There are vast numbers of records on *Ancestry.com* that pertain to people who have lived in New York State. See chapter 16 for a description of *Ancestry.com*'s resources and its partnership with the New York State Archives. A search of the online card catalog by county may reveal lesser known resources that pertain to a locality, such as town records, abstracts, transcriptions, city directories, and local histories.

FamilySearch.org

FamilySearch has extensive collections of New York records, including religious records, which are searchable by name and location, but not by county. The following collections include record images (browsable, but not searchable) that are organized by county:

- "New York, Land Records, 1630–1975." Includes land and property records. *familysearch.org/search/collection/2078654*

- "New York, Probate Records, 1629–1971." Includes wills, letters of administration, and guardianship papers. *familysearch.org/search/collection/1920234*

For both collections, choose the browse option and then select Wyoming to view the available records sets.

A detailed description of *FamilySearch.org* resources, which include the catalog of the Family History Library, is found in chapter 16.

NYGenWeb Project: Wyoming County
www.wyoming.bettysgenealogy.org

Part of the national, USGenWeb volunteer initiative, the website provides information and resources for county research.

Old Fulton New York Postcards
www.FultonHistory.com

The website provides free access to a vast collection of digitized New York newspapers, including 14 titles for Wyoming County.

Yates County

Formed February 5, 1823

Parent County   Ontario
Daughter Counties   None
County Seat   Village of Penn Yan, Towns of Benton, Jerusalem, and Milo

Major Land Transactions
See chapter 7, Land Records
Phelps and Gorham Purchase 1788

Ontario County

Canandaigua Lake

Middlesex

Potter

Benton

Seneca County

Italy

Keuka Lake

Jerusalem

Torrey

Milo

Seneca Lake

Barrington

Starkey

Steuben County

Schuyler County

Town Boundary Map
★ - County seat

Towns (and Cities)	Villages and other Settlements	Notes
Augusta Name for Town of Middlesex 1789–1808		
Barrington 1800 Settled 1822 Formed in Steuben County from Town of Wayne 1826 Transferred to Yates County *	Barrington Crosby Crystal Spring(s) East Barrington Porter(s) Corner	* Act of April 1824, "that from and after January 1, 1826, Barrington … . should be annexed to Yates County" • Hamlet of Barrington also Warsaw
Benton 1789 Settlers from Catskill, Greene County 1803 Formed in Ontario County as Town of Vernon from Town of Jerusalem 1808 Name changed to Snell 1810 Name changed to Benton 1818 Daughter town Milo formed 1823 Transferred to new county of Yates 1851 Daughter town Torrey formed	Angus Bellona Bellona Station Benton Benton Center Cashong Dresden Earl Ferguson(s) Corners Gage Havens Corners Penn Yan (v)	• Bellona also Pinkneyville, Slab Hollow, and Woods Hollow • Benton also Benton Station • Village of Penn Yan inc. 1833; shared with Town of Jerusalem and Town of Milo; county seat from 1823 when county was formed
Italy 1793 Settled at West Hollow 1815 Formed in Ontario County from Town of Naples 1823 Transferred to new county of Yates	Barker Church West Italy Italy West River Italy Hill Woodville Italy Hollow	• Barker Church also Italy-Naples • Italy also Italy Valley • Italy Hill on Jerusalem town line
Jerusalem 1789 Formed in Ontario County; settled same year 1803 Daughter town Vernon (now Benton) formed 1814 Annexed land from Town of Wayne, Steuben County 1823 Transferred to new county of Yates	Agayago Italy Hill Bluff Point Jerusalem Branchport (v) Keuka Park Cinconia Kinneys Corners Darby Corners Penn Yan (v) Dunnings Shermans Hollow Friend Yatesville Guyanoga	• Village of Branchport formerly Esperanza; incorporated as a village 1867 and dissolved 1876 • Italy Hill mostly in Town of Italy • Kinneys Corners formerly Fox's Corners • Village of Penn Yan inc. 1833; shared with Town of Benton and Town of Milo; county seat from 1823 when county was formed • Yatesville mostly in Town of Potter
Middlesex * 1789 Settled 1797 Formed as Town of Augusta in Ontario County 1808 Name changed to Middlesex 1814 Annexed land from Town of Wayne, Steuben County 1823 Transferred to new county of Yates 1832 Daughter town Potter formed 1856 Ceded land to Town of Potter	Middlesex Middlesex Center North Middlesex Overackers Corners Pine Corners Valley View Vine Valley Williams Corner	* Middlesex also colloquially known as Potterstown and Suckerstown

Towns (and Cities)	Villages and other Settlements		Notes
Milo **1788–89** Settlers from Rhode Island **1818** Formed in Ontario County from Town of Benton **1823** Transferred to new county of Yates **1851** Daughter town Torrey formed	Cascade Mills Himrod Keuka Mills Mays Mill(s) Milo Center Milo Mills Milo Station	Penn Yan (v) Randall Crossing Second Milo Seneca Mills Thayer Corners Townsend Corners Willow Grove	• Himrod formerly Himrods Corners and Milo • Mays Mill(s) on Torrey town line • Milo Center formerly Nichols Corners • Village of Penn Yan inc. 1833; shared with Town of Benton and Town of Jerusalem; county seat from 1823 when county was formed
Potter **1788** Settled **1832** Formed from Town of Middlesex **1856** Annexed land from Town of Middlesex	Cole Corners East Potter Potter	Rushville (v) Voak Yatesville	• Potter also Potter Center • Village of Rushville inc. 1866, reinc. 1876; shared with Town of Gorham, Ontario County • Yatesville on Jerusalem town line
Snell Name for Town of Benton 1808–1810			
Starkey **1800** Settled **1824** Formed from Town of Reading, Steuben County *	Barnes Station Big Stream Dundee (v) Glenora Lakemont Rock Stream Shannon(s) Corners Starkey Starkey Corners		* Town of Reading now in Schuyler County • Village of Dundee inc. 1848; also Harpendings Corners • Glenora also Glenara, formerly Big Stream Point • Lakemont formerly Eddytown • Mays Mill(s) on Milo town line • Rock Stream also Hathaways Corners and Hurds Corners
Torrey **1788** Settlers from New England **1851** Formed from towns of Benton and Milo	Cascade Mills Dresden (v) Long Point	Mays Mill(s) Ryal(s) Corners Townsend Corners	• Village of Dresden inc. 1867; formerly West Dresden
Vernon Name for Town of Benton 1803–1808			

NEW YORK STATE CENSUS RECORDS

See also chapter 3, Census Records

County originals at Yates County Clerk's Office: 1825, 1835, 1845*, 1855, 1865, 1875, 1892, 1905, 1915, 1925

State originals at the NYSA: 1915, 1925

Microfilm at the FHL, NYPL, and NYSL; many years are online at *FamilySearch.org* and *Ancestry.com.*

*1845 census records only survive for three towns—Barrington, Italy, and Potter. Indexes for all years of the NYS census are online at the website of the county historian.

NATIONAL/STATEWIDE REPOSITORIES & RESOURCES

See chapter 16

COUNTYWIDE REPOSITORIES & RESOURCES

Yates County Clerk

Yates County Office Building • 417 Liberty Street, Suite 1107
Penn Yan, NY 14527 • (315) 536-5120
Email: countyclerk@yatescounty.org • *www.yatescounty.org*

Land records, court records, census records, survey maps, naturalization records 1823–1965, and the New York state censuses for Yates County 1825–1925.

Yates County – Town and Village Clerks

Birth, marriage, and death records are maintained by the clerk of the municipality in which the event occurred; see Introduction to County Guides for details of other records which may also be held by municipal clerks. For contact information, see *www.newyorkroots.org/yates/yatesresources.htm.*

Yates County Surrogate's Court

Yates County Court Building • 415 Liberty Street
Penn Yan, NY 14527 • (315) 536-5130

Holds probate records 1823 to the present. See also chapter 6, Probate Records.

Yates County Public Libraries

Yates is part of the Southern Tier Library System; see *www.stls.org/libraries* to access each library. Many hold genealogy and local history collections. See listings below for Dundee Library and Penn Yan Public Library.

Yates County Office of Public History/Historian's Office

Yates County Office Building • 417 Liberty Street
Penn Yan, NY 14527 • (315) 536-5147 • Email: history@yatescounty.org
www.yatescounty.org/upload/12/historian/index.html

Indexed copies of all extant federal (through 1910) and state (through 1925) censuses for Yates County, online indexes for federal censuses, 1790–1870, and NY state censuses, 1825–1925 (*www.yatescounty.org/upload/12/historian/census.html*); land records 1788–present; cemetery records in book format and available on onsite computer database; tax rolls 1790s–present; military records (Revolutionary War, War of 1812, Civil War, World War I); newspapers 1823–present; probate record index 1823–1903; court records; town and village records; index to vital records 1881–1913; some church record; and reference books. Website has extensive online resources including information on records

for all towns and villages (what survives and where they can be viewed); select records (census, court, estate, immigration, land, and military); maps; and articles about people, places, and topics that have been important to the county's history.

Yates County – All Municipal Historians

While not authorized to answer genealogical inquiries, town and village historians can provide valuable historical information and research advice; some maintain collections and webpages which may include transcribed records, local histories, and other genealogical material. See contact information at *www.yatescounty.org/upload/12/historian/others.html* or at the website of the Association of Public Historians of New York State at *www.aphnys.org.*

Yates County Genealogical & Historical Society, Inc.

107 Chapel Street • Penn Yan, NY 14527 • (315) 536-7318
Email: ycghs@yatespast.org • *www.yatespast.com*

County maps 1790–1969, marriage and death records 1820s–1990s, census indexes 1790–1865, county and Penn Yan directories 1879–1990, family files, history files, local history publications, cemetery records, school records, land records 1792–1949, newspapers, diaries, almanacs, photographs, scrapbooks, and personal correspondence. Monthly newsletter *Yates Past,* 2004–present, some articles online.

LOCAL REPOSITORIES & RESOURCES

Alphabetized by location

Dundee Area Historical Society

26 Seneca Street • Dundee, NY 14873 • (607) 243-7047
Email: dundeehistory@live.com • Facebook page

Obituaries, cemetery records, family files, and historical records for the south end of the county.

Dundee Library

32 Water Street • Dundee, NY 1483
(607) 243-5938 • *www.dundeelib.org*

Holdings include census indexes, *Dundee Observer* (1879–present), and published histories.

Middlesex Heritage Group

Middlesex Town Hall • Route 364
Middlesex, NY 14507 • Facebook page

Cemetery records, family files, and information on the history of local churches, schools, American Indians, and the Lehigh Valley Railroad.

Penn Yan Public Library

214 Main Street • Penn Yan, NY 14527
(315) 536-6114 • *www.pypl.org*

Holdings include local histories, census indexes, and a comprehensive collection of newspapers. Staff will assist with genealogy research.

SELECTED PRINT & ONLINE RESOURCES

Below is a selection of resources relevant for research in this county. The list is representative, not exhaustive. Additional titles—particularly of abstracts, indexes, transcriptions, and local histories—are available; consult the introduction to Part Two for further information. For guidance on how to identify and locate community directories and local newspapers, see chapter 11, City Directories, and chapter 12, Newspapers, in Part One of this book.

Abstracts, Indexes & Transcriptions

Abstract of the 1825 New York State Census of Yates County. Syracuse: Central New York Genealogical Society, 1988.

Cleveland, Stafford C., and Thelma E. Burton Bootes. "Inscriptions From Three Abandoned Cemeteries in Yates County, New York: Friends Burying Ground, Stoddard Family Cemetery, Thomas Family Cemetery. With Index and Family History. Copied from History of Yates County, by S. C. Cleveland, 1873, by Thelma Burton Bootes (Mrs. Fenton E. Bootes)." Typescript, n.d. NYPL, New York.

County of Yates Abstracts. Syracuse: Central New York Genealogical Society, 2000. Abstracts for a range of genealogical records originally published in the quarterly *Tree Talks.*

Daughters of the American Revolution, comps. *New York DAR Genealogical Records Committee Report.* Since 1913 DAR volunteers have transcribed many thousands of unpublished cemetery, church, and town records throughout New York. The reports are at the DAR Library; copies are at the NYSL and the NYPL. The DAR has a searchable name index to all the GRC reports at *http://services.dar.org/Public/DAR_Research/search/?Tab_ID=6.* See Jean Worden's index below for a listing by county of the New York record sets that were transcribed by the DAR before 1998.

Dumas, Frances. *Yates County Cemeteries and Cemetery Burials.* Penn Yan, NY: F. Dumas, 1997.

Kelly, Arthur C. M. *Index to Tree Talks County Packet: Yates County.* Rhinebeck, NY: Kinship, 2002.

Stark, Helen. "Graveyard Inscriptions from Some Yates Co., N.Y., Cemeteries." Manuscript, 1915. NYPL, New York.

Stenzel, Dianne. *Genealogical Gleanings Abstracted from the Early Newspapers of Penn Yan, Yates County, New York, 1823–1833 and 1841–1855.* Bowie, MD: Heritage Books, 1991.

———. *Genealogical Gleanings Abstracted from the Yates County Chronicle, Penn Yan, New York, May 1856 to October 1867.* Bowie, MD: Heritage Books, 1992.

Worden, Jean D. "Book 1, Subject Index." In *Revised Master Index to the New York State Daughters of the American Revolution Genealogical Records Volumes.* Zephyrhills, FL: J. D. Worden, 1998. The Subject Index includes a listing by county of the cemeteries, churches, towns, and other sources of records transcribed by the DAR.

Other Resources

Aldrich, Louis C. *History of Yates County, New York: With Illustrations and Biographical Sketches of Some of the Prominent Men and Pioneers.* Syracuse, 1891.

Cleveland, Stafford C. *History and Directory of Yates County.* 2 vols. Penn Yan, NY, 1873. Reprint, Penn Yan, NY: Carlton L. Wheeler, 1951. Index available from Berkshire Family History Association.

Everts, Ensign & Everts. *Combination Atlas Map of Yates County, NY.* Philadelphia, 1875.

Foley, Janet W. *Early Settlers of New York State: Their Ancestors and Descendants.* 9 vols. Akron, NY: 1934–1942. Reprint, 2 vols. Baltimore, Genealogical Publishing Co., 1993.

New York Historical Resources Center. *Guide to Historical Resources in Yates County, New York, Repositories.* Ithaca, NY: New York Historical Resources Center, Olin Library, Cornell University, 1984.

Records of the Ithaca College Study Center for Early Religious Life in Western New York, 1978–1981. Division of Rare and Manuscript Collections, Cornell University Library. A description of the holdings for each county is at *http://rmc.library.cornell.edu/eguides/lists/churchlist1.htm.*

Slater-Putt, Dawne. "John and Elizabeth (Halbert) Blair of Ontario and Yates Counties, New York." *NYG&B Record,* vol. 142 (2011) no. 3: 179–194, no. 4: 265–276. [NYG&B eLibrary]

Turner, Orsamus. *Pioneer History of Phelps & Gorham's Purchase, and Morris' Reserve: Embracing the Counties of Monroe, Ontario, Livingston, Yates, Steuben, Most of Wayne and Allegany, and Parts of Orleans, Genesee, and Wyoming.* Geneseo, NY: James Brunner, 1976.

Wolcott, Walter. *The Military History of Yates County, N.Y.: Comprising a Record of the Services Rendered by Citizens of This County in the Army and Navy, from the Foundation of Government to the Present Time.* Penn Yan, NY, 1895.

Additional Online Resources

Ancestry.com

There are vast numbers of records on *Ancestry.com* that pertain to people who have lived in New York State. See chapter 16 for a description of *Ancestry.com*'s resources and its partnership with the New York State Archives. A search of the online card catalog by county may reveal lesser known resources that pertain to a locality, such as town records, abstracts, transcriptions, city directories, and local histories.

FamilySearch.org

FamilySearch has extensive collections of New York records, including religious records, which are searchable by name and location, but not by county. The following collections include record images (browsable, but not searchable) that are organized by county:

- "New York, Land Records, 1630–1975." Includes land and property records. *familysearch.org/search/collection/2078654*
- "New York, Probate Records, 1629–1971." Includes wills, letters of administration, and guardianship papers. *familysearch.org/search/collection/1920234*

For both collections, choose the browse option and then select Yates to view the available records sets.

A detailed description of *FamilySearch.org* resources, which include the catalog of the Family History Library, is found in chapter 16.

NYGenWeb Project: Yates County
www.yatescounty.org/upload/12/historian/genweb.html

Part of the national, USGenWeb volunteer initiative, the website provides information and resources for county research.

New York City

Formed January 1, 1898

Boroughs:
 Bronx (Bronx County)
 Brooklyn (Kings County)
 Manhattan (New York County)
 Queens (Queens County)
 Staten Island (Richmond County)

Timeline: New York City

1609	Henry Hudson, representing the Dutch East India Company, explored the area around the future New York Harbor
1614	The colony of New Netherland established in the area between the Delaware and Connecticut rivers
1621	Dutch West India Company (WIC) chartered, its jurisdiction to include New Netherland
1624	WIC sent out first European settlers, mostly French-speaking Walloons, on ship *Eendracht*; eight men began a settlement on *Nooten Eylandt* (present-day Governors Island)
1625	• WIC chose Manhattan Island for first permanent settlement and seat of New Netherland government, later called New Amsterdam • Construction of Fort Amsterdam and settler housing on Manhattan Island began
1626	• Manhattan Island acquired from the American Indians • Settlers at Fort Orange and other outposts in the colony relocated to Manhattan, joined by Dutch, French, and other Europeans, and first enslaved Africans
1636	First European settlement on Long Island, in future Kings County
1638	First attempt to settle on Staten Island did not succeed
1639	First European settlement in future Bronx County
1642	First European settlement in future Queens County
1653	New Amsterdam chartered as a city
1661	First permanent settlement on Staten Island
1664	• New Amsterdam surrendered to the English, who changed its name to New York and made it the capital of the new colony of New York • English colonial jurisdictions known as the Yorkshire Ridings established; West Riding included future Kings and Richmond counties and North Riding included future Queens and Bronx counties; Manhattan Island and Fordham area were in the Town of New York judicial district
1665	City of New York created by charter with jurisdiction over all of Manhattan Island, New Harlem receiving its own subordinate patent
1673–1674	New York City renamed New Orange during brief recapture by the Dutch
1683	Colony of New York divided into 12 counties, including Kings, New York, Queens, and Richmond counties; Westchester County included present-day Bronx County
1776–1783	New York, Kings, Queens, Richmond, and southern Westchester counties occupied by British troops
1783	New York's capital, temporarily located at Kingston and Poughkeepsie during the Revolution, reestablished in New York City after British evacuation
1785	New York City served as capital of the United States under the Articles of Confederation 1785–1788 and first capital of the United States under the Constitution 1789–1790
1798	New York state capital moved from New York City to Albany

1874	New York County (then coterminous with New York City) annexed part of Westchester County (now the western Bronx)
1895	New York County annexed more land from Westchester County (now the eastern Bronx)
1895	Voters in New York, Kings, Queens, and Richmond counties approve the creation of a unified city consisting of five boroughs; 57% were in favor, 43% opposed
1898	The consolidated City of New York established, comprising five boroughs created from four counties: Kings County (Borough of Brooklyn), Richmond County (Borough of Richmond), western Queens County (Borough of Queens), New York County (Borough of Manhattan and Borough of the Bronx)
1899	Towns of Hempstead, North Hempstead, and Oyster Bay separated from Queens County to become Nassau County
1914	Borough of the Bronx separated from New York County, becoming New York's most recently created county—Bronx County
1975	• Borough of Richmond renamed the Borough of Staten Island, but Richmond County's name was not changed • Community Districts established by New York City for the five boroughs

Notes on the City of New York

New York City was consolidated in its current form—comprising the five boroughs of the Bronx, Brooklyn, Manhattan, Queens, and Staten Island (known officially as Richmond until 1975)—in 1898. Until the late-19th century, when it annexed parts of Westchester County, New York City consisted only of Manhattan Island and a few adjacent islands. Harry Macy Jr. provides an authoritative account of the city's evolution in "Before the Five-Borough City: The Old Cities, Towns and Villages That Came Together to Form 'Greater New York'."

Each borough today is a self-contained county. With the exception of Bronx County (established in 1914), the county names have existed for more than 300 years. However, their modern boundaries may differ from historical ones.

- Borough of the Bronx /Bronx County
- Borough of Brooklyn /Kings County
- Borough of Manhattan / New York County
- Borough of Queens/Queens County
- Borough of Staten Island /Richmond County

Knowing the borough or county name is essential for identifying genealogical records in New York City. Correspondence can provide clues to location, but researchers should note that mailing addresses are specific to each borough and somewhat idiosyncratic. Mail to Manhattan has always been addressed to "New York, NY." Mail to Queens has traditionally been addressed to the neighborhood name, e.g. "Forest Hills, NY;" this has occasionally been the case for neighborhoods in other boroughs, such as Riverdale (the Bronx) and Brooklyn Heights. And prior to consolidation, mail would have been addressed to the old town or old village name.

Vital record keeping in New York City takes place at the city level, but is organized by borough. Other records may be kept by either city, county, or borough offices. The section below describes repositories and resources that are pertinent to all five boroughs. A separate guide to each borough follows, which identifies resources for genealogical research specific to each borough/county.

CITYWIDE REPOSITORIES AND RESOURCES

Government Repositories

New York City Department of Records and Information Services (DORIS)

www.nyc.gov/html/records/html/home/home.shtml

New York City government records are preserved and managed by DORIS, which oversees the Municipal Archives (see below), the City Hall Library, and the Visitor Center. The website provides access to the online catalog of the City Hall Library; a digital collection of nearly one million historical photographs of New York City; and a Family History Research page that describes collections and procedures.

Municipal Archives of New York City (MUNI)

31 Chambers Street, Room 103 • New York, NY 10007
(212) 639-9675 (outside NYC)   311 (inside NYC)
www.nyc.gov/html/records/html/archives/archives.shtml

MUNI preserves New York City vital records, including birth, death, and marriage records; see table 1 for a list of vital records held at MUNI for each borough and chapter 2, Vital Records, for detailed information. Online indexes to MUNI's vital records may be accessed for free at *germangenealogygroup.com, italiangen.org*, and *Ancestry.com*. The birth and death records may be viewed on microfilm at MUNI, as can New York City Department of Health marriage certificates through 1937 and City Clerk marriage licenses 1908–1929 (with an index through 1951); certified copies may be requested remotely. Many vital records held at MUNI, and corresponding indexes, are on microfilm at the Family History Library (FHL) and can be identified by the online catalog at *FamilySearch.org*.

MUNI's Old Town Records collection, ca. 1663–1898, comprises bound volumes of records of the historic towns, cities, and villages that were consolidated to form New York City in 1898, including places that originally were annexed from Westchester County. Other MUNI holdings include city directories, court records, coroner's records, Bodies in Transit records, almshouse records, legislative and

Table 1: Summary of Vital Records Held at MUNI by Borough
(For more recent records, see the listings below for the City Clerk and the Department of Health)

Borough	Birth	Marriage	Death	Notes on Early Records
The Bronx	1898–1909	1898–1937	1898–1948	For places annexed from Westchester County in 1874 and 1875, see Westchester County for records made before annexation. For these places from annexation to 1898, see Manhattan.
Brooklyn	1866–1909	1866–1937	1847–1853 1857–1948	Includes what records exist for the City of Brooklyn since its founding; extant vital records from the municipalities annexed by the City of Brooklyn to 1896 are at MUNI. The earliest are from 1847.
Manhattan	1847–1848 1853–1909	1847–1848 1853–1937	1795 1802–1804 1808 1812–1948	Except for deaths, the earliest records are sparse. See also notes on early records of the Bronx in this table, above.
Queens	1898–1909	1898–1937	1898–1948	Also includes records from towns and villages of Queens created 1847–1849 and 1881–1897, and from Long Island City 1871–1897.
Richmond/Staten Island	1898–1909	1898–1937	1898–1948	Includes records created before 1898 by towns and villages on Staten Island dating from 1847–1859 and 1881–1897.

mayoral administration records, and photographs. Two collections of tax photographs document every building in New York City from 1939 to 1941 and from 1983 to 1988; the latter collection may be viewed online for free. MUNI has launched an initiative to present historical records of New York City government and early settlements online at *www.archives.nyc*, beginning with the digital collection Records of New Amsterdam, Ordinances 1647–1661.

Office of the City Clerk, Marriage Bureau
Executive Office • 141 Worth Street • New York, NY 10013
(212) 639-9675 (outside NYC)   311 (inside NYC)
www.cityclerk.nyc.gov/html/marriage/records.shtml

Holds marriage records 1930–present from all boroughs. Access to records is unrestricted after 50 years. See website for information about obtaining copies of more recent records. See also chapter 2, Vital Records.

New York City Department of Health and Mental Hygiene (NYCDH)
125 Worth Street, CN-4, Room 133 • New York, NY 10013
(212) 639-9675 (outside NYC)   311 (inside NYC)
Email: nycdohvr@health.nyc.gov
www.nyc.gov/html/doh/html/services/vr.shtml

The NYCDH holds records of births (1910–present) and deaths (1949–present) for all boroughs. Instructions for ordering certificate copies are on the website. For further information, see chapter 2, Vital Records.

New York City Office of the City Register
www1.nyc.gov/nyc-resources/service/2266/property-record-information

Holds land and property records for four boroughs—the Bronx, Brooklyn, Manhattan, and Queens. Staten Island records are held by the Richmond County Clerk. Records 1966–present may be accessed online through the Automated City Register Information System (ACRIS). Earlier records must be requested in person at the borough office. See the individual Borough Guides for contact information and other details.

New York County Clerk, State Supreme Court, Division of Old Records
31 Chambers Street, Room 703 • New York, NY 10007 • (646) 386-5395
www.nycourts.gov/courts/1jd/supctmanh/county_clerk_operations.shtml

Holdings include colony-wide Supreme Court records and Chancery Court records for southern counties of New York. See chapter 5, Court Records, for details.

National Archives at New York City (NARA-NYC)
Alexander Hamilton U.S. Customs House
One Bowling Green, 3rd Floor • New York, NY 10004
(866) 840-1752 • Email: newyork.archives@nara.gov
www.archives.gov/nyc

Holds immigration, naturalization, federal agency, military service, and court records for New York City dating from the colonial period. See chapter 16, National and Statewide Repositories & Resources, for a detailed description.

Other Repositories and Societies

The following repositories and societies have collections and resources of relevance to all five boroughs of New York City. Repositories and societies with borough-specific collections will be found in the individual Borough Guides.

Museum of the City of New York (MCNY)
1220 Fifth Avenue • New York, NY 10029 • (212) 534-1672
Email: research@mcny.org • *mcny.org*

Founded in 1923, the MCNY preserves and interprets the history and culture of New York City through its exhibitions, publications, and collections. Archival holdings include papers of prominent New York families; material related to events and cultural activities in New York City, including a large theater collection; postcards, early maps, and photographs; and the Collection on Real Estate of New York City and Surrounding Areas, 1646–1941. More than 150,000 digitized images from the museum's collections may be viewed on the website and browsed by theme or by borough.

New-York Historical Society (N-YHS)
170 Central Park West • New York, NY 10024 • (212) 873-3400
Email: info@nyhistory.org (general information) or reference@nyhistory.org (research inquiries) • *nyhistory.org*

The N-YHS was founded in 1804 and is New York City's oldest museum, as well as a major research library. Its collections and archival holdings are national in scope, with strong components that pertain to all five boroughs of New York City and New York State. The library's collection is described at *www.nyhistory.org/library/collections*. Holdings include business records, New York City directories, genealogies, local histories, maps, New York military records, newspapers, photographs, probate abstracts, records of religious institutions and charitable organizations, and records of slavery in New York City. Online catalogs to the library collection and the museum collection are accessible on the website. For more details, see chapter 16, National and Statewide Repositories & Resources.

New York Public Library (NYPL)
www.nypl.org

The vast collections of the NYPL's research libraries are described in detail in chapter 16, National and Statewide Repositories & Resources. The NYPL also operates branch libraries in Manhattan, Staten Island, and the Bronx, some of which maintain local history collections. The public libraries of Queens and Brooklyn are independently operated. See the individual Borough Guides for information about public library resources for each borough.

New York City New York Family History Center
125 Columbus Avenue • New York, New York 10023-6514
(212) 799-2414 • *nynyfhc.blogspot.com*

Microfilms from the Family History Library (FHL) may be ordered online at *www.familysearch.org* and viewed at the Center, which also has more than 3,000 on-site microfilms and access to nine family history subscription websites. Consult the website for hours. The Center for Jewish History also serves as a Family History Center; see chapter 16 for details.

New York Genealogical and Biographical Society (NYG&B)
36 West 44th Street, 7th Floor • New York, NY 10036-8105
(212) 755-8532 • Email: education@nygbs.org
www.NewYorkFamilyHistory.org

The NYG&B, founded in 1869, is the oldest and largest genealogical society in New York, and the only one that is statewide. Its two quarterly publications, the *New York Genealogical and Biographical Record* (1870–present) and the *New York Researcher* (1990–present), and a long series of books have significantly contributed to the genealogical scholarship on New York City families and New York City history. The NYG&B's website provides access to numerous tools for New York City research, some free to the public and others restricted to members. The NYG&B's research collections are now at the NYPL. See chapter 16, National and Statewide Repositories & Resources, for a more detailed description.

Ethnic Genealogical Societies

The following societies serve the New York City area; for descriptions, see chapter 14, Peoples of New York.

Afro-American Historical and Genealogical Society, Jean Sampson Scott Greater New York Chapter	*aahgs-newyork.org*
German Genealogy Group	*germangenealogygroup.com*
Hispanic Genealogical Society of New York	*hispanicgenealogy.com*
Irish Family History Forum	*ifhf.org*
Italian Genealogical Group	*italiangen.org*
Jewish Genealogical Society, Inc.	*jgsny.org*
New York Irish History Roundtable	*irishnyhistory.org*

University and College Libraries

The libraries of Columbia University and New York University hold collections of interest for New York State—as well as New York City—research and are described in detail in chapter 16, National and Statewide Repositories & Resources. See the individual Borough Guides for university and college libraries with local history collections of particular interest.

City University of New York (CUNY)

cuny.edu

The CUNY network of colleges extends over 20 campuses across the five boroughs and includes more than 21 libraries. Collections of particular genealogical interest are noted in the relevant subject and Borough Guide bibliographies. Below are two CUNY resources of broad interest for New York City Research.

Gotham Center for New York City History

The Graduate Center, CUNY, Room 6103 • 365 Fifth Avenue New York, NY 10016-4309 • (212) 817-8460
Email: gotham@gc.cuny.edu • www.gothamcenter.org

The Gotham Center was founded in 2000 by historian Mike Wallace, coauthor of the outstanding reference book, *Gotham: A History of New York City to 1898.* Its website identifies a robust selection of online resources for New York City research and gathers nonfiction essays about New York City history in its "Gotham History Blotter."

John Jay College of Criminal Justice

524 West 59th Street • New York, NY 10019
guides.lib.jjay.cuny.edu/SpecialCollections

The special collections of the college's Sealy Library include published and unpublished material about crime in New York City. Digitized collections include the "Crime in New York Archive 1850–1950," which documents nearly a century of New York City's criminal history.

Historic House Trust of New York City

historichousetrust.org

The Trust is custodian to 23 historic sites across all five boroughs, spanning 350 years of New York City. The website provides information about each site that can provide historical context for genealogical research. Locations with research collections are identified in the relevant Borough Guides.

SELECTED PRINT & ONLINE RESOURCES

Below is a selection of key resources for New York City research. Resources specific to each of the five boroughs are listed in the individual Borough Guides. This list is representative, not exhaustive. Additional resources are in the subject-based bibliographies in each chapter throughout Part One of this book.

Bailey, Rosalie Fellows. *Guide to Genealogical and Biographical Sources for New York City (Manhattan), 1783–1898.* New York: The Author, 1954. [*books.FamilySearch.org*] Reprinted with a new introduction by Harry Macy Jr. Baltimore: Clearfield Co., 1998. Provides detailed advice for using sources, including many obscure titles. After 60 years still an essential tool for the researcher.

Burrows, Edwin G., and Mike Wallace. *Gotham: A History of New York City to 1898.* New York: Oxford University Press, 1999.

Corn, Leslie. "New York City Research Guide, Part One: Vital Records, Property Records, and Estate Records." "New York City Research Guide, Part Two: Naturalization and Immigration Records, Court Records, and City Directories;" "New York City Research Guide, Part Three: Censuses, Cemetery Records, Military Records, Newspapers, and Libraries." New England Historic Genealogical Society. *www.americanancestors.org/articles*

Daughters of the American Revolution, comps. New York DAR Genealogical Records Committee Report. Since 1913 DAR volunteers have transcribed many thousands of unpublished cemetery, church, and town records throughout New York. The reports are at the DAR Library; copies are at the NYSL and the NYPL. The DAR has a searchable name index to all the GRC reports at *http://services.dar.org/Public/DAR_Research/search/?Tab_ID=6.* See Jean Worden's index below for a listing by county of the New York record sets that were transcribed by the DAR before 1998.

DeGrazia, Laura Murphy. *Research in New York City, Long Island, and Westchester County.* Arlington, VA: National Genealogical Society, 2013.

Family History Library. *Register of New York City Birth Records.* Salt Lake City: Church of Jesus Christ of Latter-day Saints, 2006. [*FamilySearch.org*]

———. *Register of New York City Marriage Records.* Salt Lake City: Church of Jesus Christ of Latter-day Saints, 2006. [*FamilySearch.org*]

Goodfriend, Joyce D. *Before the Melting Pot: Society and Culture in Colonial New York City, 1664-1730.* Princeton, NJ: Princeton University Press, 1992.

Grundset, Eric. *New York in the American Revolution: A Source Guide for Genealogists and Historians.* Washington: National Society Daughters of the American Revolution, 2012.

Guzik, Estelle M., ed. *Genealogical Resources in New York.* New York: Jewish Genealogical Society, 2003.

Homberger, Eric. *The Historical Atlas of New York City: A Visual Celebration of Nearly 400 Years of New York City's History.* New York: Henry Holt, 2005 (revised and updated edition; originally published 1998).

Jackson, Kenneth T., ed. *The Encyclopedia of New York City.* 2nd edition. New Haven, CT: Yale University Press, 2010.

Jensen, Howard M. *Aid to Finding Addresses in the 1890 New York City Police Census.* Bowie, MD: Willow Bend Books, 2003.

Macy, Harry, Jr., "Before the Five-Borough City: The Old Cities, Towns and Villages That Came Together to Form 'Greater New York'." *NYG&B Newsletter* (now *New York Researcher*), Winter 1998. Updated June 2011 and published as a Research Aid on *NewYorkFamilyHistory.org*.

Risse, Louis A. *General Map of the City of New York, Consisting of Boroughs of Manhattan, Brooklyn, Bronx, Queens and Richmond . . . .* New York: Board of Public Improvements, Topographical Bureau, 1900. [NYPL Digital Gallery]

Seitz, Sharon, and Stuart Miller. *The Other Islands of New York City: A History and Guide.* Woodstock, VT: Countryman Press, 2001.

Weeks, Lyman Horace. *Prominent Families of New York: Being an Account in Biographical Form of Individuals and Families Distinguished as Representatives of the Social, Professional, and Civic Life of New York City.* New York, 1898.

Worden, Jean D. "Book 1, Subject Index." In Revised Master Index to the New York State Daughters of the American Revolution Genealogical Records Volumes. Zephyrhills, FL: J. D. Worden, 1998. The Subject Index includes a listing by county of the cemeteries, churches, towns, and other sources of records transcribed by the DAR.

Additional Online Resources

Ancestry.com

There are vast numbers of records on *Ancestry.com* that pertain to people who have lived in New York State in general, and New York City in particular. See chapter 16 for a description of *Ancestry.com's* resources and its partnership with the New York State Archives (NYSA). A search of the online card catalog by county may reveal lesser-known resources that pertain to a locality, such as town records, abstracts, transcriptions, city directories, and local histories. Chapter 2, Vital Records, provides detailed information on New York City birth, marriage, and death records accessible on *Ancestry.com*.

FamilySearch.org

FamilySearch has extensive collections of New York City records and reference material that can be identified through a search for New York state collections, then, as is the case for Land and Probate collections, by county name. A detailed description of *FamilySearch.org* resources, which include the catalog of the Family History Library (FHL), is found in chapter 16, National and Statewide Repositories & Resources.

Forgotten New York

www.forgotten-ny.com

The website/blog posts articles and images about New York City history that illuminate vestiges of a forgotten past, as well as streets, buildings, and other places that no longer exist.

German Genealogy Group and Italian Genealogical Group

www.GermanGenealogyGroup.com or *www.ItalianGen.org*

Free, online indexes to New York City vital records and naturalization records for all boroughs except Brooklyn.

New York City Department of City Planning, Community Portal

www.nyc.gov/html/dcp/html/neigh_info/nhmap.shtml#

The Community Portal tool allows users to select from a list of neighborhood names within a borough to view a map with present-day boundaries and adjacent neighborhoods. Other resources include maps of 2010 census neighborhood tabulation areas for each borough and maps that identify the geographic distribution of several ethnic groups throughout the five boroughs based on the 1920 federal census.

Old Fulton New York Postcards

www.FultonHistory.com

The website provides free access to a vast collection of digitized New York newspapers, including 60 titles for New York City, such as the *New York Sun* (1843–1945), the *New York Times* (1852–1921), and the *New York Tribune* (1841–1922). Chapter 12, Newspapers and Periodicials, provides more detail on this resource and other newspaper sources for New York City.

One-Step Webpages

www.SteveMorse.org

This website provides optimal searching across a wide range of records from many different online sources. One-Step resources for New York City research include vital records search tools and an Assembly District and Election District finder for the 1890–1925 New York state censuses.

Borough of the Bronx/Bronx County

County formed	1914
Borough formed	1898
Parent County	New York County (Bronx created from land that came from Westchester County)
Daughter Counties	None

Major Land Transactions
See chapter 7, Land Records

Fordham Manor 1671; Pelham Manor 1687; Morrisania Manor 1697

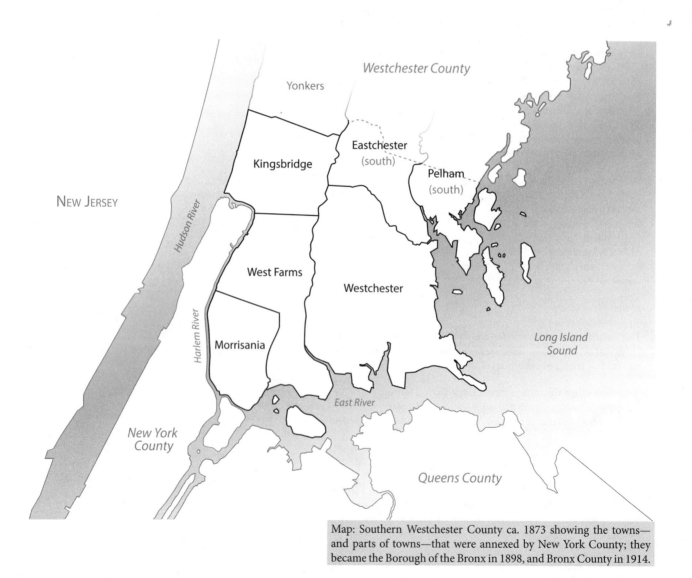

Map: Southern Westchester County ca. 1873 showing the towns—and parts of towns—that were annexed by New York County; they became the Borough of the Bronx in 1898, and Bronx County in 1914.

1639	Dutch West India Company (WIC) and Jonas Bronck acquired land from American Indians; settlement began along the Harlem River
1642	English settled at Throggs Neck, called Vreedlandt by the Dutch
1654–1655	English settlement at future village of Westchester, called Oostdorp or Easttown by Dutch
1664	• British captured colony of New Netherland renaming it New York; territory north of Manhattan Island was named Westchester • English colonial jurisdictional divisions known as the Yorkshire Ridings established, lasting until 1683; the Bronx was part of the North Riding, with the exception of Fordham which was part of the judicial district called the Town of New York; North Riding court was at Jamaica (in present-day Queens County)
1683	English colony of New York divided into 12 counties; today's Bronx was part of Westchester County, whose first county seat was the Village of Westchester
1759	White Plains became the seat of Westchester County
1787–1868	Bedford shared the Westchester county seat with White Plains
1788	Towns of Eastchester, Morrisania, Pelham, Westchester, and Yonkers recognized by New York State
1791	Town of Westchester annexed the Town of Morrisania
1846	Town of West Farms formed from Town of Westchester (including land from former Town of Morrisania)
1855	A new Town of Morrisania formed from Town of West Farms (the boundaries of the first and second Morrisanias were not identical; the second included Hunts Point)
1868	Westchester county seat located solely in Town of White Plains
1872	Town of Kingsbridge formed from southern part of Town of Yonkers
1874	Westchester County towns of Kingsbridge, Morrisania, and West Farms ceded to New York County (New York City); Morrisania became the 23rd ward, and Kingsbridge and West Farms became the 24th ward; the annexed lands were known collectively as the Annexed District; at this time, the old records of Morrisania, West Farms, and Kingsbridge were transferred to New York City authorities
1895	Areas east of the Bronx River, including the Town of Westchester and the southern parts of the towns of Eastchester and Pelham, were ceded to New York County (New York City) and became part of the 24th ward; the records of the former towns were transferred to New York City authorities
1898	The consolidated City of New York created with five boroughs; the 23rd and 24th wards of New York County became the Borough of the Bronx, and the Borough of the Bronx remained within New York County
1914	Borough of the Bronx separated from New York County; Bronx County formed—coterminous with the existing Borough of the Bronx

Towns (and Cities)	Villages and other Settlements	Notes
Eastchester (south of Mount Vernon) *Also see Town of Eastchester in Westchester County Guide* 1895 Town of Eastchester south of Mount Vernon city border ceded to New York County; becomes part of 24th ward of New York City 1898 Forms part of the Borough of the Bronx—one of five boroughs in a new consolidated New York City; remains in New York County 1914 Borough of the Bronx ceded from New York County, becomes Bronx County	Baychester Eastchester Jacksonville South Washingtonville Ten Farms Wakefield (v) Washingtonville	• Jacksonville was part of the Village of Wakefield after 1889 • Ten Farms shared with City of Mount Vernon, Westchester County 1892–1895; divided between City of Mount Vernon and New York County 1895–1914; shared between City of Mount Vernon and Bronx County 1914–present • Village of Wakefield, originally incorporated as the Village of South Mount Vernon 1889, name changed to Wakefield in 1894, dissolved 1895 • Washingtonville was part of the Village of Wakefield after 1889
Kingsbridge *Also see towns of Kingsbridge and Yonkers in Westchester County Guide* 1872 Formed from southern part of Town of Yonkers (now City of Yonkers) in Westchester County 1874 Ceded to New York County; becomes part of 24th ward of New York City 1898 Forms part of the Borough of the Bronx—one of five boroughs in a new consolidated New York City; remains in New York County 1914 Borough of the Bronx ceded from New York County, becomes Bronx County	Fort Independence Kingsbridge Kingsbridge Heights Kingsbridge Village Little Yonkers Lower Yonkers Mosholu (Village) Mount St. Vincent Orloff Park Paparinemo Island Riverdale South Yonkers Spuyten Duyvil Van Cortlandt (Park) Warnerville Woodlawn Heights	
Morrisania *Also see both towns of Morrisania in Westchester County Guide* 1855 Formed from Town of West Farms 1874 Ceded to New York County; becomes 23rd ward of New York City 1898 Forms part of the Borough of the Bronx—one of five boroughs in a new consolidated New York City; remains in New York County 1914 Borough of the Bronx ceded from New York County, becomes Bronx County	Bensonia Claremo(u)nt Devoes Neck East Melrose East Morrisania Eltona Forest Grove Grove Hill Highbridge Melrose Morrisania (v) Morris Dock Mott Haven North New York Old Morrisania Port Morris South Melrose West Morrisania Wilton Woodstock	• Claremo(u)nt on West Farms town line • Village of Morrisania inc. 1864 and dissolved 1874 • Old Morrisania formerly Central Morrisania in Town of West Farms

Towns (and Cities)	Villages and other Settlements		Notes
Pelham (south) *Also see Town of Pelham in Westchester County Guide* **1895** Southern part of Pelham ceded to New York County; becomes part of 24th ward of New York City **1898** Forms part of the Borough of the Bronx—one of five boroughs in a new consolidated New York City; remains in New York County **1914** Borough of the Bronx ceded from New York County, becomes Bronx County	Bartow City Island Hart Island Hunter(s) Island Pelham Neck Pells Point Rodmans Neck		• Hart Island also Heart Island
Westchester *Also see Town of Westchester in Westchester County Guide* **1791** Annexed the Town of Morrisania **1846** Daughter town West Farms created (included land from former Town of Morrisania) **1895** Town of Westchester ceded to New York County; becomes part of 24th ward of New York City **1898** Forms part of the Borough of the Bronx—one of five boroughs in a new consolidated New York City; remains in New York County **1914** Borough of the Bronx ceded from New York County, becomes Bronx County	Bedford Park Bronxdale Bronxwood Park Castle Hill (Neck) Centerville Cherry Tree Point Clason Point Connersville Cornells Neck Edenwald Ferry Point Fordham Fort Schuyler Hunts Point Integrity Jerome (Park) Laconia Middletown	Morrisania Morris Park Olinville Oostdorp Pennyfield Schuylerville Stinardtown Throg(g)s Neck Unionport Van Nest Vreedlandt Westchester (Village) West Farms (Village) Williamsbridge (v) Wrights Island	• Cornells Neck now Harding Park in Bronx County • Fordham, Hunts Point, and Jerome, in Town of West Farms after 1846 • Morrisania in Town of West Farms after 1846 and Town of Morrisania after 1855 • West Farms (Village) in Town of West Farms after 1846 • Village of Williamsbridge (Williams Bridge) inc. 1888, dissolved 1895; mostly in Town of West Farms after 1846, expanded in Westchester after 1874; when Williamsbridge reservoir opened in 1890 the neighborhood name was used more widely; this area also called Norwood • Wrights Island now Locust Point in Bronx County
West Farms *Also see Town of West Farms in Westchester County Guide* **1846** Formed from Town of Westchester **1855** Daughter town Morrisania formed **1874** Ceded to New York County; becomes part of 24th ward of New York City **1898** Forms part of the Borough of the Bronx—one of five boroughs in a new consolidated New York City; remains in New York County **1914** Borough of the Bronx ceded from New York County, becomes Bronx County	Belmont Central Morrisania Claremo(u)nt East Morrisania East Tremont Eltona Fairmount Fordham (v) Fordham Heights Forest Grove Grove Hill Highbridge(ville) Hunts Point Jerome (Park) Melrose Monterey Morrisania Morris Dock	Mott Haven Mount Eden Mount Hope North Melrose Port Morris Rose Hill South Belmont South Fordham Springhurst Tremont Upper Morrisania Wardsville West Farms (Village)(v) West Tremont Williamsbridge Woodstock	• Central Morrisania becomes Old Morrisania in Town of Morrisania after 1855 • Claremo(u)nt on Morrisania town line • East Morrisania and Eltona in Town of Morrisania after 1855 • Village of Fordham inc. 1846 and dissolved 1874; in Town of Westchester before 1846 • Forest Grove and Grove Hill in Town of Morrisania after 1855 • Highbridgeville in Town of Morrisania after 1855; now Highbridge in Bronx County • Melrose, Morrisania, Morris Dock, Mott Haven, and Port Morris in Town of Morrisania after 1855 • Village of West Farms inc. 1846, dissolved 1874; in Town of Westchester 1791–1846 • Williamsbridge (Williams Bridge) mostly in Town of West Farms 1846–1874; expanded in Town of Westchester after 1874 to become an incorporated village in 1888 • Woodstock in Town of Morrisania after 1855

Many of the names of early cities, towns, villages, and settlements listed in the preceding gazetteer, have survived as neighborhood names—although their boundaries may have changed. Sources consulted to compile this list of neighborhoods and communities are identified in the introduction to Part Two; they include the Community Portal of the New York City Department of City Planning, the Geographic Names Information System (GNIS), and the New York State Department of Health Gazetteer, 2007.

Allerton	Fordham	Pelham Bay
Bathgate	Fordham Heights	Pelham Gardens
Baychester	Harding Park	Pelham Parkway
Bedford Park	Hart Island *	Port Morris
Belmont	Highbridge	Rikers Island *
Bronx River	Hunts Point	Riverdale
Bronx Park South	Indian Village	Schuylerville
Bronxdale	Jerome Park	Silver Beach
Castle Hill	Kingsbridge	Soundview
Charlotte Gardens	Kingsbridge Heights	Spencer Estates
City Island	Laconia	Spuyten Duyvil
Claremont	Locust Point	Throggs Neck
Clason Point	Longwood	Tremont
Concourse	Marble Hill *	Unionport
Concourse Village	Melrose	University Heights
Co-op City	Middletown	Van Cortlandt
Country Club	Morris Heights	Van Nest
Crotona Park East	Morris Park	Violet Park
Dodgewood	Morrisania	Wakefield
Eastchester	Mott Haven	West Concourse
East Concourse	Mount Eden	West Farms
East Tremont	Mount Hope	Westchester
Edenwald	North Riverdale	Westchester Heights
Edgewater Park	Norwood	Williamsbridge
Fieldston	Olinville	Woodlawn
Fish Bay	Parkchester	Woodstock

* Hart Island—situated off the eastern coast of the Bronx, see chapter 9, Cemetery Records, for more information on the New York City potter's field located there

* Marble Hill—used to be part of Manhattan island and, though it is now north of the Spuyten Duyvil Creek (Harlem River), it is still part of the Borough of Manhattan/New York County; however, it is included in Bronx community district 8

* Rikers Island—see Queens County before 1884; jail located here since 1832

Notes on the Borough of the Bronx / Bronx County

The Municipal Archives of New York City (MUNI) holds city, town, and village records, ca. 1663–1898, for places in the Bronx that were annexed from Westchester County, including Eastchester, Kingsbridge, Morrisania, South Mount Vernon, Wakefield, Westchester, and Williamsbridge. See the MUNI entry in Citywide Resources.

See the Westchester County Guide for additional resources that pertain to Bronx locations that were annexed from Westchester.

The New York County Clerk holds county records for the Bronx from 1874 to 1914. The Bronx County Clerk holds county records for the Bronx from 1914 to the present.

NEW YORK STATE CENSUS RECORDS
See also chapter 3, Census Records

County originals at the Bronx County Historical Society: 1915, 1925

State originals at the NYSA: 1915, 1925

For census records for the Bronx before 1915, see New York and Westchester counties.

Microfilm at the FHL, NYPL, and NYSL; both years are online at *FamilySearch.org* and *Ancestry.com*.

NATIONAL/STATEWIDE REPOSITORIES & RESOURCES
See chapter 16

CITYWIDE REPOSITORIES AND RESOURCES

Vital records for the Bronx are held at the Municipal Archives of New York City (MUNI). For a description of MUNI and other resources that pertain to all five boroughs, see Citywide Repositories & Resources in the Introduction to the Borough Guides.

COUNTYWIDE REPOSITORIES & RESOURCES

Bronx County Clerk
851 Grand Concourse, Room 118 • Bronx, NY 10451
(866) 797-7214 • *bronxcountyclerksoffice.com/en/home*

Court records, business records, naturalization records 1914–1952 (a searchable index is at *www.germangenealogygroup.com* and *www.italiangen.org*).

Bronx County Surrogate's Court
851 Grand Concourse • Bronx, NY 10451 • (718) 618-2300

Holds probate records from the early-20th century to the present. See also chapter 6, Probate Records.

Office of the City Register: Borough of the Bronx
Bronx Business Center • 1932 Arthur Avenue, Third Floor
Bronx, NY 10457 • (718) 579-6820
www.nyc.gov/html/dof/html/contact/contact_visit_bronx.shtml

Holdings include land records, deeds, and mortgages. *FamilySearch.org* "New York Land Records" has a selection of records.

Board of Elections, Bronx Borough Office
1780 Grand Concourse • Bronx, NY 10457 • (212) 299-9017

Bronx voter registration records 1897–present. Record copies are made by staff and should be requested in advance.

Bronx County Archives (BCA)
3313 Bainbridge Avenue • Bronx, NY 10467
Email: librarian@bronxhistoricalsociety.org

The Archives has been managed by the Bronx County Historical Society since 1974 (see below) and is housed in an adjacent building. Research is by appointment only. See the bibliography for a 2014 collections guide by Kathleen McAuley and Elizabeth Nico, as well as a comprehensive inventory conducted by the Historical Records Survey of the Work Projects Administration.

Bronx County Historical Society (BCHS)

Administration Office and Research Library
3309 Bainbridge Avenue • Bronx, NY 10467 • (718) 881-8900
Email: administration@bronxhistoricalsociety.org
www.bronxhistoricalsociety.org/library

The Society's holdings include books, manuscripts, city directories, documents, maps, and newspapers that document the history of the Bronx, New York City, and Westchester County. Research is by appointment only, and research inquiries are accepted. The BCHS published the *Bronx County Historical Journal* (1964–present) and the *Bronx Historian* newsletter, which is accessible on the website. Links to digital resources for the BCHS's Bronx Latino History Project and Fordham's Bronx African American History Project can be accessed from the website. The Society is custodian of the Valentine-Varian House/Museum of Bronx History (Bainbridge Avenue) and the Edgar Allan Poe Cottage (Grand Concourse at East Kingsbridge Road).

Bronx Borough Historian

Bronx County Historical Society • 3309 Bainbridge Avenue
Bronx, NY 10467 • (718) 881-8901

While not authorized to answer genealogical inquiries the borough historian can provide historical information and research advice. For personal contact information see the website of the Association of Public Historians of New York State at *www.aphnys.org*.

New York Public Library—The Bronx

Bronx Library Center • 310 East Kingsbridge Road (at Briggs Ave)
Bronx, NY 10458 • (718) 579-4257

The Bronx is served by the New York Public Library (NYPL) system. A detailed description of NYPL resources is in chapter 16, National and Statewide Repositories & Resources. A list of NYPL branch libraries in the Bronx is at *www.nypl.org/locations*. Some branches have local history, heritage, or other special collections. For example, the Bronx Library Center holds the NYPL's Latino and Puerto Rican Heritage Collection; the Belmont Library and Enrico Fermi Cultural Center has an Italian heritage collection.

Cemeteries

See table 1 in chapter 9, Cemetery Records, for a selected list of Bronx cemeteries with their website addresses.

Other Repositories and Societies

Fordham University Library: Archives and Special Collections

Walsh Library at Rose Hill • Bronx, NY 10458 • (718) 817-3560
www.library.fordham.edu/archives/archive.html

Fordham University was founded in 1841 by Bishop John Hughes to serve New York's Catholic immigrant community and is today one of the nation's most prominent Jesuit educational institutions. A descriptive list of archival collections is on the website. Digitized collections accessible from the website include Maps of New Netherland, New Amsterdam, and New England; a selection of resources on the Hudson River; and historical photographs. Fordham's Bronx African American History Project seeks to identify, preserve, and catalog collections that document the African American experience in the Bronx and make them accessible to the public. A description of the project and links to digital collections

and archival collections is at *www.fordham.edu/academics/programs_at_fordham_/bronx_african_americ*.

Lehman College: Leonard Lief Library: Special Collections

250 Bedford Park Boulevard West • Bronx, NY 10468 • (718) 960-8603
Email: libref@lehman.cuny.edu
www.lehman.edu/library/special-collections.php

The Bronx Institute Archives include local history books, documents, maps and atlases, newspapers, photographs and postcards, and oral history. Holdings include the Fordham Manor Reformed Church Collection and the Bronx Chamber of Commerce Collection, both of which have been microfilmed, and the Riverdale Neighborhood House Collection. The digital exhibitions "Bronx Business for Everybody" and "Childhood in the Bronx" are accessible on the website.

City Island Historical Society
City Island Nautical Museum & Library

190 Fordham Street • PO Box 82 • City Island, NY 10464
(718) 885-0008 • Email: CIHS@cityislandmuseum.org
www.cityislandmuseum.org

The museum chronicles City Island's history as a center of yacht-building and shipbuilding, as well as its role during the American Revolution. The website includes historic photographs of local people, schools, and businesses.

East Side Settlement House Archives

Columbia University • Rare Book and Manuscript Library
Butler Library, 6th Floor East • 535 West 114th Street
New York, NY 10027 • (212) 854-5153
Email: rbml@libraries.cul.columbia.edu
http://library.columbia.edu/locations/rbml.html

Holdings (18 linear feet) date from 1851 to 1991 and document the history of the East Side House Settlement, established in 1891 on the Upper East Side of Manhattan to serve the community's growing immigrant population, and relocated to the Bronx in 1963. The website has a detailed finding aid.

Huntington Free Library

9 Westchester Square • Bronx, NY 10461-3583 • (718) 829-7770
www.bronxnyc.com/Huntington_Free_Library_MIE.html

The library has served the Westchester Square community since 1893 and is not affiliated with the NYPL. Collections include historical photographs, books, and ephemera on the Bronx. The Huntington Free Library Native American Collection was transferred to Cornell University in 2004; a collection description and finding aids are at http://ebooks.library.cornell.edu/h/hunt.

Kingsbridge Historical Society (KHS)

www.kingsbridgehistoricalsociety.org

Established in 1949 as the Bronx's first historical society, the KHS serves the greater Kingsbridge area of the northwest Bronx, including the present-day neighborhoods of Riverdale, Kingsbridge, Spuyten Duyvil, Marble Hill, Inwood, Van Cortlandt, and Fieldston. Its website provides access to digital books, articles, and photographs about the community's history.

Morris High School Museum

Morris High School Campus • 1100 Boston Road • Bronx, NY 10456
(718) 542-3700

The museum documents the history of New York City's first coeducational high school, established in 1897, and of the surrounding community. Holdings include diplomas, letters, literary journals, personal papers, photographs, and yearbooks and range from 1900 to the present.

SELECTED PRINT AND ONLINE RESOURCES

Below is a selection of resources relevant for research in this borough. The list is representative, not exhaustive. Additional titles—particularly of abstracts, indexes, transcriptions, and local histories—are available; consult the introduction to Part Two for further information. For guidance on how to identify and locate community directories and local newspapers, see chapter 11, City Directories, and chapter 12, Newspapers, in Part One of this book.

Abstracts, Indexes & Transcriptions

See the Westchester County Guide for abstracts and transcriptions pertaining to the Bronx.

Other Resources

Beers, J. B., & Co. *County Atlas of Westchester, New York*. New York, 1872. Includes maps of Fordham, Morrisania, Riverdale, Tremont, West Farms, Woodlawn, and the Town of Westchester that were then part of Westchester County. [NYPL Digital Gallery]

Bronx County Historical Society Journal. Bronx County Historical Society, 1964–present. www.bronxhistoricalsociety.org

Bronx County Historical Society Journal 25 Year Index, 1964–"1988. New York: Bronx County Historical Society, 1991.

Comfort, Randall. *History of Bronx Borough, City of New York*. New York: North Side News Press, 1906. Book includes information on indigenous people and their place names, first white settlers, development of the Bronx and Westchester, Revolutionary War, transportation, geographical features, architecture, churches, institutions, clubs, parks, industry, law, education, and biographical sketches of prominent people.

Cook, Harry Tecumseh. *The Borough of the Bronx, 1639–1913: Its Marvelous Development and Historical Surroundings*. New York: The Author, 1913. Book includes information on early settlement, Revolutionary War, industries, transportation, parks, geographical features, prominent people (including the Van Cortlandts), churches, clubs, education, and local legends.

Edsall, Thomas H. *History of the Town of Kings Bridge, Now Part of the 24th Ward of New York City*. New York, 1887.

Fluhr, George J. A. *The Bronx Through the Years: A Geography and History*. New York: Aidan Press, 1964.

Gonzalez, Evelyn Diaz. *The Bronx*. New York: Columbia University Press, 2004.

Hibbitts, Megan. 2007. "Treasures of The Bronx: The Bronx County Historical Society's Archives." *Metropolitan Archivist*, vol. 12, no. 2 (2007): 15–16, 22.

Historical Records Survey. *Inventory of the Borough Archives of the City of New York, No. 1, Bronx County*. New York: Work Projects Administration, 1942. [NYG&B eLibrary]

———. *Inventory of the County Archives of the City of New York, No. 1, Bronx County*. New York: Work Projects Administration, 1940. [NYG&B eLibrary]

Hufeland, Otto. *A Check List of Books, Maps, Pictures, and Other Printed Matter Relating to the Counties of Westchester and Bronx*. White Plains, NY: Westchester County Historical Society, 1929.

Jenkins, Stephen. *The Story of the Bronx: From the Purchase Made by the Dutch from the Indians in 1639 to the Present Day*. New York: G. P. Putnam's Sons, 1912. Includes information on transportation, communication, churches, cemeteries, colonial and Revolutionary history, and locations.

McAuley, Kathleen A. *The Bronx*. Charleston, SC: Arcadia Pub., 2010. Book is primarily pictorial, part of the *Then & Now* series.

McNamara, John. *History in Asphalt: The Origin of Bronx Street and Place Names, the Bronx, New York City*. New York: Bronx County Historical Society, 1996.

Mellick, Harry C.W. *The Manor of Fordham*. New York: Fordham University Press, 1950.

Munch, Janet Butler. *Bibliography of the Bronx*. New York: Bronx County Historical Society, 1974.

New York Historical Resources Center. *Guide to Historical Resources in Bronx County, New York, Repositories*. Ithaca, NY: Cornell University, 1988.

Nico, Elizabeth, Gary Hermalyn, and Laura Tosi. *Ethnic Groups in the Bronx: Selected Bibliographies from the Collections of the Bronx County Historical Society*. New York: Bronx County Historical Society, 2013.

Rand-McNally. *New Standard Map of the Borough of Bronx*. 1903. [NYPL Digital Gallery]

Sartain, Dorthea, and Peter Derrick. *Guide to the Collections of the Bronx County Archives*. New York: Bronx County Historical Society, May 2007.

Scharf, J. Thomas. *History of Westchester County, New York, including Morrisania, Kings Bridge, and West Farms, Which Have Been Annexed to New York City*. 2 vols. Philadelphia: L. E. Preston & Co, 1886.

Sgambettera, Mark. *Newspaper Titles of the Bronx*. New York: Bronx County Historical Society, 2007.

Tieck, William. *Riverdale, Kingsbridge, Spuyten Duyvil, New York City: A Historical Epitome of the Northwest Bronx*. Old Tappan, NY: Fleming H. Revell, 1968.

Tosi, Laura. *Media Collection: The Audio & Visual Collections of the Bronx County Historical Society Research Library*. Edited by Gary Hermalyn. New York: Bronx County Historical Society, 2007.

———. *Microfilm and Microfiche Collection of the Bronx County Historical Society Research Library*. Edited by Gary Hermalyn. The Bronx County Historical Society, 2005.

Tosi, Laura, and Frank Wilmot. *The Bronx In Print: An Annotated Catalogue of Books, Dissertations, Pamphlets, Scripts and Manuscripts About the Bronx*. Edited by Gary Hermalyn and Kathleen A. McAuley. 5th edition. New York: Bronx County Historical Society and New York Public Library, 2006.

Tosi, Laura, and Gary Hermalyn. *Article Titles and Contributing Authors of The Bronx County Historical Society Journal, 1964–2006*. New York: Bronx County Historical Society, 2007.

Tosi, Laura, Janet Butler Munch, and Gary Hermalyn. *Genealogy in the Bronx: An Annotated Guide to Sources of Information*. New York: Bronx County Historical Society, 1986.

Ultan, Lloyd. *The Beautiful Bronx, 1920–1950*. New Rochelle, NY: Arlington Press, 1979.

———. *The Birth of the Bronx, 1609–1900*. New York: Bronx County Historical Society, 2000. Book draws from diaries, letters, and other records.

———. *Blacks in the Colonial Bronx: A Documentary History*. New York: Bronx County Historical Society, 2012.

———. *The Bronx in the American Revolution*. New York: Bronx County Historical Society, 1975.

———. *The Bronx in the Frontier Era: From the Beginning to 1696*. Dubuque, IA: Kendall Hunt, 1993.

———. *The Bronx: It was Only Yesterday, 1935–1965*. New York: Bronx County Historical Society, 1992.

———. *The Northern Borough: A History of the Bronx*. New York: Bronx County Historical Society, 2009.

Wells, James, et al. *The Bronx and Its People: A History, 1609–1927*. New York: Lewis Historical Publishing Co., 1927.

Wuttge, Frank. Portal of History: Connotations of Name Origins of Bronx Streets and Avenues." Typescript, 1964. NYPL, New York.

Additional Online Resources

Ancestry.com

There are vast numbers of records on *Ancestry.com* that pertain to people who have lived in New York State. See chapter 16 for a description of *Ancestry.com*'s resources and its partnership with the New York State Archives. A search of the online card catalog by county may reveal lesser known resources that pertain to a locality, such as town records, abstracts, transcriptions, city directories, and local histories. Chapter 2, Vital Records, provides detailed information on Bronx birth, marriage, and death records accessible on *Ancestry.com*.

FamilySearch.org

FamilySearch has extensive collections of New York records, including religious records, which are searchable by name and location, but not by county. The collection "New York, Land Records, 1630–1975" has record images (browsable, but not searchable) that are organized by county, and includes records for the Bronx, 1874–1888. It is accessible at *familysearch.org/search/collection/2078654* by choosing the browse option and then selecting Bronx to view the available records sets. As of this printing, the collection "New York, Probate Records, 1629–1971," which is also browsable by county, did not include any Bronx records. However, the collection Bronx Probate Estate Files 1914–1931 is in the process of being posted; Administration Files 1914–1916 are now accessible. A detailed description of *FamilySearch.org* resources, which include the catalog of the Family History Library, is found in chapter 16.

German Genealogy Group and Italian Genealogical Group

www.GermanGenealogyGroup.com or *www.ItalianGen.org*

Free, online indexes to New York City vital records and Bronx County naturalization records 1914–1952.

NYGenWeb Project: Bronx County

http://www.rootsweb.ancestry.com/~nybronx

Part of the national, USGenWeb volunteer initiative, the website provides information and resources for county research.

Borough of Brooklyn/Kings County

County formed	1683
Borough formed	1898
Parent County	Original county
Daughter Counties	None

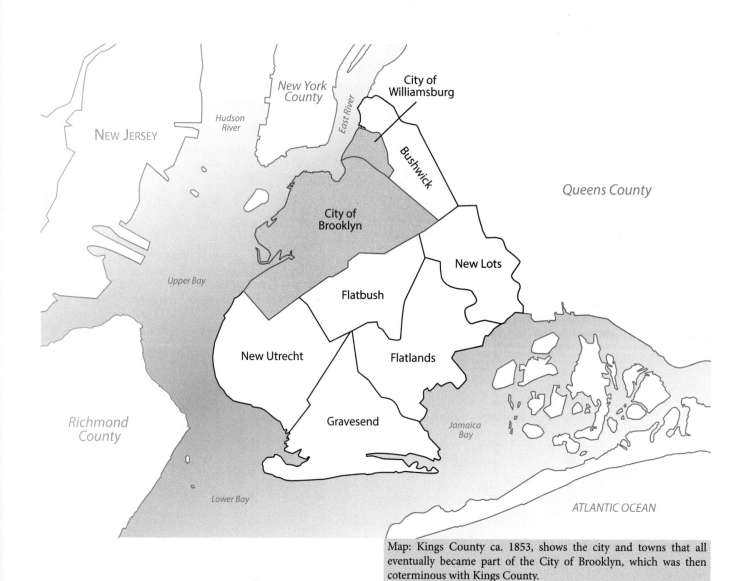

Map: Kings County ca. 1853, shows the city and towns that all eventually became part of the City of Brooklyn, which was then coterminous with Kings County.

1636–1637	First land acquired from American Indians at Keskachauge in future towns of Flatlands and Flatbush, and in Gowanus and Wallabout in future Town of Brooklyn; settlement followed by French and Walloon, Dutch, Scandinavian, Italian, German, and other nationalities
1638	Dutch West India Company (WIC) acquired land in future Town of Bushwick from American Indians; settlement began by 1650
1639	New Netherland Director General Willem Kieft granted tract on future New Utrecht-Gravesend border to Moroccan-Dutch settler Anthony Jansen (thought to be first Muslim settler); patented 1643 and known as Turk's Plantation
1645	New Netherland government granted English religious dissenters, led by Lady Deborah Moody, a patent to settlement at Gravesend
1646	New Netherland government granted dorp (village) of Breuckelen (including Gowanus and Wallabout) its own court
1647	Name of Nieuw Amersfoort (Flatlands) first appears on record
1652	New Netherland government granted dorp of Midwout/Vlackebos (Flatbush) a patent and its own court
1652	New Netherland government granted patent for Nyack (later Nieuw Utrecht)
1661	New Netherland government granted dorps of Nieuw Amersfoort (Flatlands) and Boswijck (Bushwick) their own courts
1662	New Netherland government granted dorp of (Nieuw) Utrecht its own court
1664–1683	• English colonial jurisdictional divisions known as the Yorkshire Ridings established 1664–1665; Kings County in West Riding; West Riding court sat at Flatbush 1665–1668 and Gravesend 1668–1683 • New English government recognized the towns of Boswick (Bushwick), Breuckelen, Gravesend, Midwout (Flatbush), Nieuw Amersfoort (Flatlands), and Nieuw Utrecht (New Utrecht), granting patents to each 1667–1668
1670	Flatbush settlers laid out "the new lots" in their town's east end, and began settlement
1677	Flatbush received separate patent for New Lots section
1683	English province of New York divided into 12 counties; Kings County established with its county seat at Gravesend
1685	Kings county seat moved from Gravesend to Flatbush
1776–1783	Kings County occupied by British troops
1788	New York State recognized towns of Brooklyn, Bushwick, Flatbush, Flatlands, Gravesend, and New Utrecht
1832	County seat moved from Flatbush to Brooklyn
1834	Town and Village of Brooklyn incorporated as City of Brooklyn
1840	Town of Williamsburgh created from Village of Williamsburgh, which was previously part of Town of Bushwick
1851	Town of Williamsburgh became a city
1852	Town of New Lots formed from Town of Flatbush
1854	City of Brooklyn annexed City of Williamsburgh and Town of Bushwick, afterwards known as the Eastern District (E.D.); rest of Brooklyn briefly called Western District (W.D.)
1886	City of Brooklyn annexed Town of New Lots
1894	City of Brooklyn annexed towns of Flatbush, Gravesend, and New Utrecht
1896	City of Brooklyn annexed Town of Flatlands, with the result that the City of Brooklyn became coterminous with Kings County
1898	The consolidated City of New York created with five boroughs; City of Brooklyn dissolved, becoming the Borough of Brooklyn, still coterminous with Kings County

Towns (and Cities)	Villages and other Settlements		Notes

Brooklyn (city) 1834–1898 *

1834	Town and village of Brooklyn incorporated as a city
1854	Annexed City of Williamsburg and Town of Bushwick which were afterwards known as the Eastern District (E.D.), rest of Brooklyn briefly called Western District (W.D.)
1886	Annexed Town of New Lots
1894	Annexed towns of Flatbush, Gravesend, and New Utrecht
1896	Annexed Town of Flatlands; City of Brooklyn then constituted all of Kings County (city and county were coterminous)
1898	City dissolved, becomes Borough of Brooklyn—one of the five boroughs of New York City

Villages and other Settlements:

Bedford
Bergen (Heights)
Brooklyn
Brooklyn Heights
Bushwick
Bushwick Cross Roads
Bushwick Green
Carrville
Cobble Hill
Eastern District
Fort Greene
Fulton Ferry
Gowanus
Greenpoint
New Brooklyn
Park Slope
Prospect Heights
Prospect Park
Red Hook
Ridgewood
South Brooklyn
Stuyvesant Heights
Vinegar Hill
Wallabout
Weeksville
Western District
Williamsburg(h)
Windsor Terrace

Notes:

* County seat in Brooklyn from 1832 (county and borough offices now in Downtown Brooklyn); also see Gravesend and Flatbush
• Bushwick Cross Roads and Bushwick Green in Town of Bushwick before 1854
• Eastern District see 1854 in column 1
• Fulton Ferry formerly The Ferry
• Greenpoint also Green-Point and Green Point; see Bushwick before 1854
• Prospect Park on Flatbush town line
• Ridgewood extends into Queens County; towns of Newtown an Bushwick both laid claim to the area
• Wallabout also East Brooklyn
• Western District see 1854 in column 1
• Williamsburg(h) was city of Williamsburg until 1854

Brooklyn (town) 1636–1834 *

1636–37	First land purchases from American Indians, at Gowanus and Wallabout, followed by French and Walloon, Dutch, Scandinavian, Italian, German, and other settlers
1646	New Netherland government gives dorp (village) of Breuckelen (including Gowanus and Wallabout) its own court
1664	Town recognized by new English government; part of English colonial jurisdiction of the West Riding of Yorkshire
1788	Recognized as a town by State of New York
1834	Town and village of Brooklyn incorporated as City of Brooklyn

Villages and other Settlements:

Bay Ridge
Bedford
Bergen
Brooklyn (v)
Brooklyn Heights
Fort Greene
Fort Lawrence
Fort Swift
Gowanus
Red Hook
The Ferry
Wallabout

Notes:

* Brooklyn also Breuckelen (Dutch) and Brookland (English)
• Bay Ridge formerly Yellow Hook; on New Utrecht town line
• Village of Brooklyn incorporated as fire district 1801, as village 1816, dissolved 1834
• Fort Greene formerly Fort Putnam
• Gowanus had many early variants including Guanos
• The Ferry also Dutch 't Veer
• Wallabout also Wallaboght, also 't Wale-quartier (the Walloon quarter) and Wale-bocht or Wallaboght

Bushwick 1650–1854 *

1638	Dutch West India Company purchased area from American Indians
1650	European settlers arrived by this date, Dutch, Scandinavians, later French and Walloons
1661	New Netherland government recognized village (dorp) of Boswijck with its own court
1664	Town recognized by new English government; part of English colonial jurisdiction of the West Riding of Yorkshire; town patented 1667

Villages and other Settlements:

Bushwick (Village)
Bushwick Cross Roads
Bushwick Green
Green Point
Het Strand
Williamsburgh (v)

Notes:

* Bushwick called Boswijck ("wooded district") by the Dutch, also spelled Boswyck
• Bushwick (Village) also Het Dorp
• Bushwick Cross Roads also The Crossroads, formerly Het Kivis Padt (?Kruis Padt)
• Green Point formerly Cherry Point, later Green-Point and Greenpoint; see City of Brooklyn after 1854
• Het Strand meaning "the beach," later site of Williamsburgh and Greenpoint

(Bushwick continued on next page)

Towns (and Cities)	Villages and other Settlements	Notes
Bushwick 1650–1854 (continued) 1788 Recognized as a town by State of New York 1840 Daughter town Williamsburgh created from Village of Williamsburgh 1854 Town dissolved, becomes wards 17 and 18 of the City of Brooklyn, part of the Eastern District (E.D.) of the city		• Williamsburgh before 1827 was Cripplebush; Village of Williamsburgh inc. 1827, annexed land from the town in 1835 and was divided into districts: South Side, North Side, and a third district which had several different names including Dutchtown; Williamsburgh becomes a town in 1840
Flatbush 1651–1894 * 1651 Settled by this date by Dutch and others 1652 New Netherland government gave (dorp) village a patent and its own court 1664 Town recognized by new English government; part of English colonial jurisdiction of the West Riding of Yorkshire; town patented 1667 1677 Received separate patent for New Lots section 1788 Recognized as a town by State of New York 1852 Daughter town New Lots formed 1894 Town dissolved, becomes ward 29 of the City of Brooklyn	East New York Flatbush (Village) Kensington New Lots Parkville Prospect Hill Prospect Park Rugby Rustenberg	* Called by the Dutch Midwout (Midwood) and Vlackebos (Flatbush) * County seat at Flatbush 1683–1832 • East New York part of Town of New Lots in 1852 • New Lots also Oostwood or East Woods; became Town of New Lots in 1852 • Parkville formerly Greenfield; borders towns of Gravesend and New Utrecht • Prospect Park on Brooklyn town line
Flatlands 1636–1896 * 1636 Dutch purchased land from American Indians and began settlement 1647 Settlements combined to form dorp (village) of Nieuw Amersfoort 1661 New Netherland government granted Nieuw Amersfoort its own court 1664 Town recognized by new English government; part of English colonial jurisdiction of the West Riding of Yorkshire; town patented 1667 as "Amersfoort alias Flatlands" 1788 Recognized as Town of Flatlands by State of New York 1896 Town dissolved, becomes ward 32 of the City of Brooklyn	Barren Island Bergen Beach Canarsie Flatlands	* Also called Nieuw Amersfoort, Achtervelt, Keskachague (many spellings), and The Bay

Towns (and Cities)	Villages and other Settlements		Notes
Gravesend 1645–1894 *	Brighton Beach	Sea Gate	* Called 's-Gravensande (sic) by Dutch, Gravesend by English
1645 English settlers from New England, led by Lady Deborah Moody, granted patent by New Netherland Director-General Kieft *	Coney Island	Sheepshead Bay	
	Gravesend	The Cove	* County seat at Gravesend 1683–1685
	Manhattan Beach	Unionville	
	Schryers Hook		* Lady Deborah Moody also see Baptist section, chapter 15, Religious Records
1664 Town recognized by new English government			
1788 Recognized as a town by State of New York			
1894 Town dissolved, becomes ward 31 of the City of Brooklyn			
New Lots 1852–1886	Brownsville		
1670 Flatbush settlers laid out "the new lots" in their town's east end, and begin settlement	Cypress Hills		
	East New York		
1677 Flatbush received separate patent for New Lots section			
1852 Formed from Town of Flatbush			
1886 Town dissolved, becomes ward 26 of the City of Brooklyn			
New Utrecht 1639–1894 *	Bath		* New Utrecht also alled Nieuw Utrecht, or just Utrecht by the Dutch
1639 Director-General Kieft granted tract on future New Utrecht-Gravesend border patented 1643, known as Turk's Plantation	Bay Ridge		
	Bensonhurst		• Bath also Bath Beach
	Blythebourne		• Bay Ridge formerly Yellow Hook; on Brooklyn town line
	Fort Fayette		
	Fort Hamilton		• Fort Fayette formerly Fort Diamond
1652 Nyack patent granted	Fort Lewis		
1657 Settlement of Utrecht established	New Utrecht (Village)		• Fort Hamilton formerly Nyack
1662 New Netherland government gave dorp (village) of (Nieuw) Utrecht its own court			
1664 Recognized as Town of New Utrecht by new English government			
1788 Recognized as a town by State of New York			
1894 Town dissolved, becomes ward 30 of the City of Brooklyn			
Williamsburg (town/city) 1840–1854			
1840 Village of Williamsburgh in Town of Bushwick becomes Town of Williamsburgh			
1851 Town of Williamsburgh becomes the City of Williamsburgh			
1852 City removes the "h" from Williamsburgh			
1854 City dissolved; the three wards of Williamsburg become wards 13, 14, 15, 16, and part of 19 of the City of Brooklyn; constituted part of the Eastern District (E.D.) of the City of Brooklyn			

Many of the names of early cities, towns, villages, and settlements listed in the preceding gazetteer, have survived as neighborhood names—although their boundaries may have changed. Sources consulted to compile this list of neighborhoods and communities are identified in the introduction to Part Two; they include the Community Portal of the New York City Department of City Planning, the Geographic Names Information System (GNIS), and the New York State Department of Health Gazetteer, 2007.

Adelphi	East Williamsburg	Northside
Barren Island	Eastern Parkway	Ocean Parkway
Bath Beach	Farragut	Paerdegat (Basin)
Bay Ridge	Flatbush	Park Slope
Bedford	Flatlands	Parkville
Bedford-Stuyvesant	Fort Greene	Plumb Beach
Bensonhurst	Fort Hamilton	Pratt
Bergen Beach	Fulton Ferry	Prospect Heights
Boerum Hill	Georgetown	Prospect Lefferts
Borough Park	Gerritsen	Prospect Lefferts
Brevoort	Gerritsen Beach	Gardens
Brighton Beach	Gowanus	Prospect Park South
Broadway Junction	Gravesend	Red Hook
Brooklyn Heights	Gravesend Beach	Remsen Village
Brooklyn Navy Yard	Greenpoint	Rugby
Brownsville	Highland Park	Ryder
Bushwick	Homecrest	Sea Gate
Canarsie	Industry City	Sheepshead Bay
Carroll Gardens	Kensington	South Brooklyn
City Line	Kings Highway	Southside
Clinton Hill	Kouwenhoven	Spring Creek
Cobble Hill	Lefferts Manor	Starrett City
Coney Island	Manhattan Beach	Stuyvesant Heights
Crown Heights	Manhattan Terrace	Sunset Park
Crown Heights	Mapleton	Times Plaza
South	Marine Park	Tompkins Park North
Cypress Hills	Metropolitan	Vinegar Hill
Ditmas Park	Midwood	Weeksville
Downtown	Mill Basin	West Brighton
Brooklyn	Mill Island	Williamsburg
DUMBO	New Lots	Windsor Terrace
Dyker Heights	New Utrecht	Wingate
East Flatbush	Northeast	Wyckoff Heights
East New York	Flatbush	

Repositories and Resources

Notes on Early Town and City Records

Kings County has extensive town and city records, but only small fragments of them have been published or made available online. The original records are preserved and available on microfilm at the Municipal Archives of the City of New York (MUNI). The microfilmed records cover Bushwick, Flatbush, Flatlands, Gravesend, New Lots, New Utrecht, and Williamsburg, as well as the City of Brooklyn. See detailed lists in Estelle Guzik's *Genealogical Resources in New York* and B-Ann Moorhouse's "Kings County Records from the St. Francis Collection."

Notes on Early Censuses

The 1698 and 1731 censuses for the entire county are in Edmund O'Callaghan's *Documentary History of the State of New-York*. See also Harry Macy Jr. and Henry Hoff's "'1738 Census' of Kings County Was Actually Taken in 1731." Citations for both titles are in Selected Print and Online Resources below.

NEW YORK STATE CENSUS RECORDS
See also chapter 3, Census Records

County originals at the Kings County Clerk: 1855, 1865, 1875, 1892, 1905, 1915, and 1925; 1825, 1835, and 1845—except Flatbush—are lost; microfilm at MUNI, which also has original 1845 census for Flatbush

State originals at the NYSA: 1915, 1925

Microfilm at the FHL, NYPL, and NYSL; many years are online at *FamilySearch.org* and *Ancestry.com*.

NATIONAL/STATEWIDE REPOSITORIES & RESOURCES
See chapter 16

CITYWIDE REPOSITORIES & RESOURCES

Vital records for Brooklyn are held at the Municipal Archives of New York City (MUNI). For a description of MUNI and other resources that pertain to all five boroughs, see Citywide Repositories & Resources in the introduction to the Borough Guides.

COUNTYWIDE REPOSITORIES & RESOURCES

Kings County Clerk
Supreme Court Building • 360 Adams Street, Room 189
Brooklyn, NY 11201 • (347) 404-9772
www.nycourts.gov/courts/2jd/kingsclerk/index.shtml

Holdings include court records, naturalization records 1856–1924 (a searchable index for 1907–1924 is at *jgsnydb.org*), and the New York state census for Kings County 1855, 1865, 1875, 1892, 1905, 1915, and 1925.

Kings County Surrogate's Court
Two Johnson Street • Brooklyn, NY 11201 • (347) 404-9700

Holds probate records from 1787 to the present. *FamilySearch.org* "New York Probate Records" include wills 1787–1915, letters of administration 1787–1866, indexes to both 1787–1923; also some nineteenth-century proceedings, inventories, final accountings, administration records, and general card index 1787–1941. Also *FamilySearch.org* "Kings County Estate Files" 1866–1923. NYPL has microfilm of wills 1787–1881, letters of administration 1787–1866, indexes 1787–1923. The NYSA holds most probate records prior to 1787. See also chapter 6, Probate Records.

Office of the City Register, Borough of Brooklyn

Brooklyn Business Center • Brooklyn Municipal Building
210 Joralemon Street, Room 2 • Brooklyn, NY 11201 • (718) 802-3590
http://nyc.gov/html/dof/html/contact/contact_visit_brooklyn.shtml

Holdings include deeds and mortgages 1679 to date. *FamilySearch. org* "New York Land Records" has deeds 1679–1886, indexes 1679–1949, mortgages 1927–1945. NYPL has microfilm of deeds 1679–1850, indexes 1679–1950. The Queens office of the City Register holds Brooklyn Real Property books; microfilm/microfiche available at the Brooklyn office.

Board of Elections, Kings County

345 Adams Street, 4th Floor • Brooklyn, New York 11201 • (718) 797-8800

Brooklyn voter registration records 1890–present. Record copies are made by staff and should be requested in advance.

Brooklyn Borough Historian

Office of the Brooklyn Borough President • Brooklyn Borough Hall
210 Joralemon Street • Brooklyn, NY 11201 • (718) 802-3700

While not authorized to answer genealogical inquiries the borough historian can provide historical information and research advice. For personal contact information see the website of the Association of Public Historians of New York State at *www.aphnys.org*.

Brooklyn Historical Society (BHS)

128 Pierrepont Street at Clinton Street • Brooklyn, NY 11201
(718) 222-4111 • Email: library@brooklynhistory.org
brooklynhistory.org

The Brooklyn Historical Society was founded in 1863 as the Long Island Historical Society and renamed in 1985. The holdings of its Othmer Library cover the full geographic extent of Long Island—Kings, Queens, Nassau, and Suffolk counties—and include census material; Brooklyn and Manhattan city directories; family histories; maps and atlases; newspapers (*Long Island Star* 1809–1863; excerpts from the *Brooklyn Evening Star* 1809–1845); scrapbooks; vital statistics; will abstracts; and special collections, such as the Eardeley Genealogy Collection, which contains will abstracts 1787–1835 and research notes compiled by the prodigious genealogist William Applebie Daniel Eardeley. The website offers an online catalog, research subject guides, online exhibits, and a Brooklyn history timeline. See also Rawls' *Century Book of the Long Island Historical Society*, Rodda's *Long Island Genealogical Source Material*, and Moorhouse, "Eardeley Collection" and "Wardwell Collection."

Brooklyn Public Library (BPL)

Grand Army Plaza • Central Library • Brooklyn, NY 11238
(718) 230-2762 • bklynpubliclibrary.org

The Brooklyn Public Library is entirely separate from the New York Public Library. Its principal resources for family history research are gathered in the Brooklyn Collection, which is located in the local history division at the Central Library. It includes city directories; manuscripts and archives; maps; newspapers (1835–1999); photographs; prints; and yearbooks. Digital collections accessible on the website include City Directories 1856–1908, the *Brooklyn Daily Eagle* 1841–1955 (with excellent search and copy functionality), Brooklyn in the Civil War, and historical photographs. The website also gives access to an online catalog, finding aids to the collections, and a guide to genealogical resources in New York City.

Cemeteries

See chapter 9, Cemetery Records, for a selected list of Brooklyn cemeteries with their website addresses.

Other Repositories and Societies

Brooklyn College Library: Brooklyniana Collection

2900 Bedford Avenue • Brooklyn, NY 11210-2889 • (718) 951-5346
http://library.brooklyn.cuny.edu/resources

Local histories, genealogies, maps, and professional papers; the Brooklyn Historical Photographic Collection; and the St. Francis College Local History Research Files.

Brooklyn Museum: Libraries and Archives

200 Eastern Parkway • Brooklyn, NY 11238-6052 • (718) 638-5000
Email: information@brooklynmuseum.org
www.brooklynmuseum.org/opencollection/archives

Digital collections accessible on the website include "The Brooklyn Bridge and the Brooklyn Museum: Spanning Art and History" and historical photographs of Brooklyn. Its Library and Archives hold materials that document the Museum's history which dates to 1823, as well as material relevant to the history the City of Brooklyn and the role the Museum played in its development.

Erasmus Hall Academy Archives

Erasmus Hall Academy was founded in 1786 in Flatbush and is the oldest secondary school in New York State. Its original building survives and sits in the center of a contemporary public high school complex. The New-York Historical Society (see Citywide Resources) holds some records for the years 1775–1975; the Brooklyn Historical Society (see above) holds some records for the years 1787–1896, including an account book listing all students and tuition payments 1787–1792. A history is at *www.nyc.gov/html/lpc/downloads/pdf/reports/ehall.pdf*. The NYG&B holds some papers relating to the establishment of the school in its Lefferts Papers collection.

Friends of Historic New Utrecht

1831 84th Street • Brooklyn, NY 11214 • (718) 256-7173
Email: mail@historicnewutrecht.org • *historicnewutrecht.org*

Holdings include archives and genealogical records of the historic town of New Utrecht.

Weeksville Society and Heritage Center

1698 Bergen Street • PO Box 130120 • Brooklyn, NY 11213
(718) 756-5250 • Email: info@weeksvillesociety.org
weeksvillesociety.org

The Society documents the history of Weeksville, a 19th-century free black community.

The Wyckoff House and Association

5816 Clarendon Road • Brooklyn, NY 11203 • (718) 629-5400
Email: info@wyckoffassociation.org • *wyckoffmuseum.org*

The Association documents the history of the Wyckoff family and maintains a 17th-century farmhouse as a museum. Genealogical services are available to members.

SELECTED PRINT AND ONLINE RESOURCES

Below is a selection of resources relevant for research in this county. The list is representative, not exhaustive. Additional titles—particularly of abstracts, indexes, transcriptions, and local histories—are available; consult the introduction to Part Two for further information. For guidance on how to identify and locate community directories and local newspapers, see chapter 11, City Directories, and chapter 12, Newspapers, in Part One of this book. Other valuable sources for Brooklyn research will be found in the listings of Citywide Repositories and Resources, Long Island Print and Online Resource, and in the subject-based bibliographies throughout Part One.

Abstracts, Indexes & Transcriptions

Barber, Gertrude Audrey. "Deaths Taken from the Brooklyn Eagle, 1841–1880." 19 vols. Typescript, 1963–1966. NYPL, New York.

———. *Index of Wills Probated in Kings County, New York: From January 1, 1850 to December 31, 1890.* Salem, MA: Higginson Book Co., 1997. For later years, see Thomas below.

———. "Marriages Taken from the Brooklyn Eagle, 1841–1880." Typescript, 1962–1966. NYPL, New York. [*Ancestry.com*]

———. "Miscellaneous Vital Statistics Other Than Death and Marriage Notices Taken from the *Brooklyn Eagle*." Typescript, 1963. NYPL, New York.

Biebel, Frank A. *Methodist Protestants and the Union Cemeteries of Brooklyn, 1844–1894.* New York: New York Genealogical and Biographical Society, 2007. [NYG&B eLibrary]

Cohen, Minnie. "Greenwood Cemetery Inscriptions." 3 vols. Typescript, 1932. Brooklyn Historical Society, New York. The inscriptions on some of the monuments differ from the cemetery's burial records.

Cropsey, Frances Bergen, and Harriet M. Stryker-Rodda. "Records of the Reformed Dutch Church of New Utrecht." *NYG&B Record*, vol. 112 (1981) no. 3: 130–134, no. 4: 205–211; vol. 113 (1982) no.1: 10–14, no. 2: 74–80, no. 3: 169–173, no. 4: 220–222; vol. 114 (1983) no. 1: 36–39, no. 2: 86–92, no. 3: 131–136, no. 4: 220–224; vol. 115 (1984) no. 1: 19–22, no. 2: 88–90. Includes transcriptions of baptism records, 1718–1741, 1786–1879; marriages 1835–1880. [NYG&B eLibrary]

Eardeley, William Applebie. *Cemeteries in Kings and Queens Counties, Long Island, New York: 1753–1913.* Brooklyn: n.p., 1916. Covers three Brooklyn cemeteries—Humboldt Street; Canarsie; Bay Ridge.

Frost, Josephine C. "Genealogical Gleanings from Book No. 2 of Conveyances, Brooklyn, Kings Co., N.Y." *NYG&B Record*, vol. 54 (1923) no. 2: 105–111, no. 3: 241–251, no. 4: 303–319. [NYG&B eLibrary]

Gohari, Carol Elaine. "Historical Forfeitures of Land in Kings County, NY." *Brooklyn Record*, April 9–15, 2002. A photocopy of the article is at the NYPL.

Hagemeyer, Frank E. "Seat Owners, Brooklyn Dutch Reformed Church, 1769/1778." *NYG&B Record*, vol. 141, no. 2 (2010): 129–132. [NYG&B eLibrary]

Hoff, Henry B. "1761 Assessment List of Flatbush, Kings County." *NYG&B Record*, vol. 137, no. 3 (2006): 188–190. [NYG&B eLibrary]

———. "The 1781 Tax List of Flatbush, Kings County." *NYG&B Record*, vol. 137, no. 4 (2006): 291–293. [NYG&B eLibrary]

———. "Some Kings County Marriages 1694–95." *NYG&B Record*, vol. 132, no. 1 (2001): 27. [NYG&B eLibrary]

McQueen, David. "Kings County, N.Y., Wills." *NYG&B Record*, vol. 47 (1916) no. 2: 161–170, no. 3: 227–232. Wills, 1650–1707, Deeds, Book No. 1 of the Conveyances, Brooklyn, Kings Co., N.Y. [NYG&B eLibrary]

———. "Kings County, New York, Deeds." *NYG&B Record*, vol. 48 (1917) no. 2: 110–118, no. 3: 291–298, no. 4: 355—361. [NYG&B eLibrary]

Moorhouse, B-Ann, and Joseph M. Silinonte. *Kings County, New York, Administration Proceedings, 1817–1856.* New York: New York Genealogical and Biographical Society, 2006. [NYG&B eLibrary]

Nash, Edward W. *Kings County Genealogical Club Collections.* Vol. 1, nos. 1–6. Brooklyn, 1882–1894. Includes gravestone inscriptions from Reformed Dutch Church cemeteries in New Utrecht, Flatlands, Gravesend, and Bushwick.

Nichols, Joan M. "Oaths of Intention to Become Citizens, Kings Co. Court of Common Pleas 1821–49." *NYG&B Record*, vol. 123 (1992) no. 2: 75–78, no. 3: 148–152. [NYG&B eLibrary]

O'Callaghan, Edmund B. *Documentary History of the State of New-York.* 4 vols. Albany: State of New York, 1849–51. See vol. 3, pp. 133–138, for the 1698 and 1731 censuses for the entire county.

Scott, Kenneth. "Manumissions in Kings County, NY, 1797–1825." *National Genealogical Society Quarterly*, vol. 65, no. 3 (1977): 177–180.

———. "Slave Births in Kings County, after 1800." *National Genealogical Society Quarterly*, vol. 66, no. 2 (1978): 97–103.

Silinonte, Joseph M. *Bishop Laughlin's Dispensations, Diocese of Brooklyn, Genealogical Information from the Marriage Dispensation Records of the Roman Catholic Diocese of Brooklyn: Kings, Queens and Suffolk Counties, New York, Volume 1 1859–1866.* Brooklyn: The Author, 1996.

———. *Tombstones of the Irish-Born: Cemetery of the Holy Cross, Flatbush, Brooklyn.* Concord, ON: Becker Associates, 1992.

Sisser, Fred, III. "Brooklyn Residents of May 1713." *NYG&B Record*, vol. 117, no. 4 (1986): 225–226. [NYG&B eLibrary]

———. "Flatlands Church Bell Subscription List of 1686." *NYG&B Record*, vol. 120, no. 3 (1989): 148–149. [NYG&B eLibrary]

Stiles, Henry R. *Brooklyn in 1796, or the First Directory of the Village.* New York: By Subscription.

Stillwell, William H. *History of the Reformed Protestant Dutch Church of Gravesend, Kings County, NY.* Brooklyn, 1892.

Stryker-Rodda, Harriet M., "Gravesend 1762–1763 Baptisms." *NYG&B Record*, vol. 119, no. 1 (1988): 5. [NYG&B eLibrary]

Stryker-Rodda, Harriet M., and Kenn Stryker-Rodda. "Records of the Reformed Dutch Church of Flatlands 1737–1914." 3 vols. Typescript, n.d. NYPL, New York.

Stryker-Rodda, Kenn. "Extracts from Acmon P. Van Gieson's Journal [1856–57]." *NYG&B Record*, vol. 114, no. 1 (1983): 29–35. [NYG&B eLibrary]

———. "Marriages by a Brooklyn Baptist Minister, 1866–1887." *NYG&B Record*, vol. 116 (1985) no. 2: 94–99, no. 3: 132–140, no. 4: 220–228. [NYG&B eLibrary]

Thomas, Milton Halsey. *Index to the Wills, Administrations, and Guardianships of Kings County, New York, 1650–1850.* Washington: C. Shepard, 1926. For later years see Barber above.

Van Buren, DeWitt. *Abstracts of Wills of Kings County, Recorded at Brooklyn.* 1934. Reprint, Dublin, PA: Bergen Historic Books, 2005. Covers the years 1787–1843.

Van Cleef, Frank L., "Records of the Reformed Protestant Dutch Church of Flatbush." Typed by Josephine C. Frost. 5 vols. Typescript, 1915. NYPL, New York. Including baptisms 1722, 1725, 1750–1754; marriages 1742–1757; and marriage and burial fees collected by the deacons, churchmasters, ministers and trustees 1663–1741; scattered entries 1763–1786. [Microfilm at the FHL] See also Voorhees, below.

Van der Linde, A. P. G. Jos. *Old First Dutch Reformed Church of Brooklyn, New York: First Book of Records, 1660–1752.* Baltimore: Genealogical Publishing. Co., 1983. (The version of these records in 1897 *Year Book of the Holland Society of New York* is available online but is very unreliable.)

Voorhees, David W. *Records of the Reformed Protestant Dutch Church of Flatbush, Kings County, New York.* 2 vols. New York: Holland Society of New York, 1998–2009. Vol. 1, 1677–1720, contains baptisms, marriages, and membership for the *vier dopen*, the four villages of Flatbush, Brooklyn, Flatlands, and New Utrecht. (The version of these records in the 1897 *Year Book of the Holland Society of New York* is available online, but is very unreliable.) Vol. 2 contains Midwood Deacons Accounts 1654–1709. Holland Society has photocopies of the original records and Van Cleef's transcripts/translations for later years; see also Van Cleef, above.

Other Resources

Abelow, Samuel Philip. *History of Brooklyn Jewry.* Brooklyn: Scheba Publishing Company, 1937.

Abromovitich, Ilana, et al. *Jews of Brooklyn.* Hanover, NH: University Press of New England for Brandeis University Press, 2002.

Armbruster, Eugene L. *The Eastern District of Brooklyn.* New York: n.p., 1912.

Bergen, Teunis G. *Register in Alphabetical Order of the Early Settlers of Kings County, Long Island, New York: From Its First Settlement by Europeans to 1700.* Baltimore: Clearfield, 1997.

Bishop, William G. *Map of the Consolidated City of Brooklyn, for Bishop's Manual of the Corporation.* 1859. [NYPL Digital Gallery]

Bromley, G. W., & Co. *Atlas of the Borough of Brooklyn, City of New York (Volume One).* 1907. [NYPL Digital Gallery]

Brooklyn Daily Eagle Almanac. Published annually 1886–1929. Contains a wide variety of information on Brooklyn, the other boroughs, and Nassau and Suffolk counties. Many issues are accessible for free at *HathiTrust.org.* For a sampling of its contents see below for Harry Macy Jr., "The *Brooklyn Eagle Almanac.*"

Brooklyn, the Home Borough of New York City: Its Family Life, Educational Advantages, Civic Virtues, Physical Attractions, and Varied Industries. Brooklyn: Municipal Club of Brooklyn, 1912.

Citizens Committee for New York City. *The Neighborhoods of Brooklyn.* New Haven, CT: Yale University Press, 1998.

Dikeman, John. *The Brooklyn Compendium.* Brooklyn, 1869. Book includes Common Council manual, election returns for 1869, election districts, local judiciary, constables, commissioners of deeds, fire dept., buildings department, park commissioners, police department, city court, water department, City Court, almshouse, valuation of property and rates of taxation, county government, etc.

Ditmas, Charles Andrew. *Historic Homesteads of Kings County.* Brooklyn: The Author, 1909. Includes biographical information on original/early residents.

Historical Records Survey. Inventory of the County Archives of the City of New York, No. 2, Kings County. New York: Work Projects Administration, 1942. [NYG&B eLibrary]

Landesman, Alter F. *A History of New Lots, Brooklyn to 1887, Including the Villages of East New York, Cypress Hills, and Brownsville.* Port Washington, NY: Kennikat Press, 1977.

Macy, Harry, Jr. "Before the Five-Borough City: The Old Cities, Towns and Villages That Came Together to Form Greater New York." *NYG&B Newsletter* (now *New York Researcher*), Winter 1998. Updated June 2011 and published as a Research Aid on *NewYorkFamilyHistory.org.*

———. "The *Brooklyn Eagle Almanac.*" *New York Researcher,* Winter 2005. Published 2011 as a Research Aid on *NewYorkFamilyHistory.org.*

———. "Brooklyn/Kings County Church Records Since 1783." *NYG&B Newsletter* (now *New York Researcher*), Summer 2000. Updated June 2011 and published as a Research Aid on *NewYorkFamilyHistory.org.*

———. "Kings County's Colonial Church Records." *NYG&B Newsletter* (now *New York Researcher*), Winter 1997. Updated June 2011 and published as a Research Aid on *NewYorkFamilyHistory.org.*

———. "Provost's Early Settlers of Bushwick." *New York Researcher,* Winter 2006. Updated June 2011 and published as a Research Aid on *NewYorkFamilyHistory.org.*

Macy, Harry, Jr., and Henry B. Hoff. " '1738 Census' of Kings County Was Actually Taken in 1731." *NYG&B Record,* vol. 123, no. 2 (1992): 85–86. [NYG&B eLibrary]

Ment, David. *The Shaping of a City: A Brief History of Brooklyn.* Brooklyn: Brooklyn Educational and Cultural Alliance, 1979.

Mills, Thomas. *Rediscovering Brooklyn History: A Guide to Research Collections.* Brooklyn: Brooklyn Educational and Cultural Alliance, 1978.

Moorhouse, B-Ann. "The Eardeley Collection at the Brooklyn Historical Society." *NYG&B Newsletter* (now *New York Researcher*), Fall 1995. Published 2011 as a Research Aid on *NewYorkFamilyHistory.org.*

———. "Kings County Records from the St. Francis College Collection now at the Municipal Archives of the City of New York." *NYG&B Newsletter* (now *New York Researcher*), Spring 1994. Published 2011 as a Research Aid on *NewYorkFamilyHistory.org.*

———. "The Wardwell Collection of Genealogical Notes on Local Families at the Brooklyn Historical Society." *NYG&B Newsletter* (now *New York Researcher*), Summer 1995. Published 2011 as a Research Aid on *NewYorkFamilyHistory.org.*

Neighborhood History Guides. Published by the Brooklyn Historical Society: *Red Hook Gowanus,* 2000; *Williamsburg,* 2005; *DUMBO Fulton Ferry, Vinegar Hill,* 2001; *Greenpoint,* 2001; *Bay Ridge Fort Hamilton,* 2003. Flatbush, 2008, and Park Slope, 2008 (Fort Greene/Clinton Hill audio tour online).

New York Historical Resources Center. *Guide to Historical Resources in Kings County (Brooklyn), New York, Repositories.* Ithaca, NY: Cornell University, 1987. [books.FamilySearch.org]

Onderdonk, Henry, Jr. *Revolutionary Incidents of Suffolk and Kings Counties; with an Account of the Battle of Long Island and the British Prisons and Prison-Ships at New York.* Port Washington, NY: Kennikat Press, 1970.

Ostrander, Stephen M. *A History of the City of Brooklyn and Kings County*. 2 vols. Brooklyn, 1893.

Provost, Andrew J. *Early Settlers of Bushwick, Long Island, New York, and Their Descendants*. Darien, CT: The Author, 1949. For contents see above for Harry Macy Jr., "Provost's Early Settlers of Bushwick."

Rawls, Walton H., ed., *The Century Book of the Long Island Historical Society*. Brooklyn: The Society, 1964.

Roman Catholic Diocese of Brooklyn. "Chronological List of Brooklyn Parishes, 1822–2008." Available for download at *dioceseofbrooklyn.org*.

Scott, Kenneth, and Stryker-Rodda, Kenn. *Long Island Genealogical Source Material*. Arlington, VA: National Genealogical Society, 1962.

Stiles, Henry R. *The Civil, Political, Professional, and Ecclesiastical History, and Commercial and Industrial Record of the County of Kings and the City of Brooklyn, NY, from 1683 to 1884*. New York, 1883.

———. *A History of the City of Brooklyn: Including the Old Town and Village of Brooklyn, the Town of Bushwick, and the Village and City of Williamsburgh*. Brooklyn: 1869.

Vanderbilt, Gertrude Lefferts. *The Social History of Flatbush, and Manners and Customs of the Dutch Settlers in Kings County*. New York, 1899.

Van Wyck, Frederick. *Keskachauge, or the First White Settlement on Long Island*. New York: G. P. Putnam and Sons, 1924. Covers the area of Brooklyn that became known as Flatlands.

Walsh, Kevin. *Forgotten New York: Views of a Lost Metropolis*. New York: Collins, 2006.

Walter, John F. *The Confederate Dead in Brooklyn: Biographical Sketches of 513 Confederate POWs*. Bowie, MD: Heritage Books, 2003. Book includes information on Confederate soldiers who died while being held as prisoners of war in the New York area and were buried in Cypress Hills National Cemetery in Brooklyn: summaries of military careers, corrections of names/units incorrectly given in cemetery records, causes of death, dates of death, etc. Book also includes appendices, bibliography, and full name index of individuals for whom biographies do not exist.

Wexelstein, Leon. *Building Up Greater Brooklyn: With Sketches of Men Instrumental in Brooklyn's Amazing Development*. Brooklyn: Brooklyn Biographical Society, 1925.

Additional Online Resources

Ancestry.com

There are vast numbers of records on *Ancestry.com* that pertain to people who have lived in New York State. See chapter 16 for a description of *Ancestry.com*'s resources and its partnership with the New York State Archives. A search of the online card catalog by county may reveal lesser known resources that pertain to a locality, such as town records, abstracts, transcriptions, city directories, and local histories. Chapter 2, Vital Records, provides detailed information on Brooklyn birth, marriage, and death records accessible on *Ancestry.com*.

Brooklyn Genealogy Information Page
http://bklyn-genealogy-info.stevemorse.org

The website has assembled a large number of digital resources for Brooklyn research, including links to city directories; birth, marriage, and death indexes and extracts; cemetery information;

residency lists from the early 1700s; jail, asylum, school, and convent census abstracts; history of local post offices; information on fire companies and the police force; military information; orphanage information; teacher appointments, school graduate lists, and information on schools; society and club member lists; historic maps; and ward boundary maps.

Brooklyn Revealed
brooklynrevealed.com

The website provides online histories of the original six towns of Brooklyn and street name origins (written by Joseph Ditta, Reference Librarian, New-York Historical Society), an interactive map, and historic photographs.

FamilySearch.org

FamilySearch has extensive collections of New York records, see the Surrogate's Court and City Register enteries in this section for a description fo prbate and land records.

A detailed description of *FamilySearch.org* resources, which include the catalog of the Family History Library, is found in chapter 16.

Forgotten New York
www.forgotten-ny.com

The website/blog posts articles and images about New York City history that illuminate vestiges of a forgotten past, as well as streets, buildings, and other places that no longer exist; it includes a street necrology for some Brooklyn neighborhoods.

German Genealogy Group and Italian Genealogical Group
GermanGenealogyGroup.com or *ItalianGen.org*

Free, online indexes to New York City vital records.

Jewish Genealogy Society
jgsnydb.org

The website has a searchable index for 1907–1924 Brooklyn naturalization records.

NYGenWeb Project: Kings County
www.rootsweb.ancestry.com/~nykings

Part of the national, USGenWeb volunteer initiative, the website provides information and resources for county research.

Old Fulton New York Postcards
www.FultonHistory.com

The website provides free access to a vast collection of digitized New York newspapers, including seven titles for Kings County.

Borough of Manhattan/New York County

County formed	1683
Borough formed	1898
Parent County	Original county
Daughter County	Bronx 1914

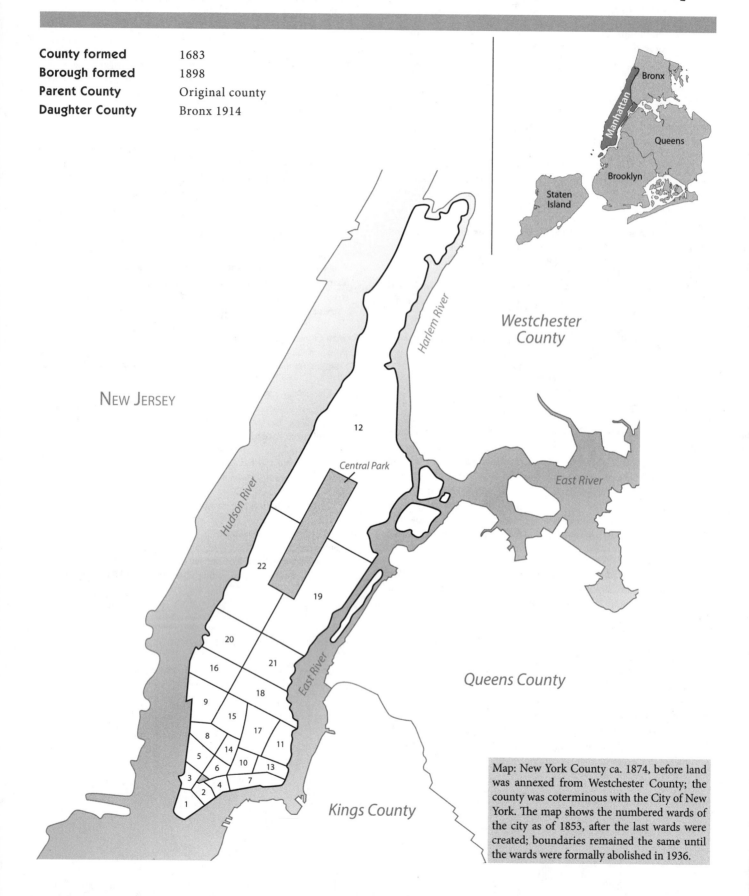

New Jersey

Westchester County

Harlem River

Central Park

Hudson River

East River

12

22

19

20

21

16

18

9

15

17

8

14

11

5

6

10

13

3

2

4

7

1

East River

Queens County

Kings County

Map: New York County ca. 1874, before land was annexed from Westchester County; the county was coterminous with the City of New York. The map shows the numbered wards of the city as of 1853, after the last wards were created; boundaries remained the same until the wards were formally abolished in 1936.

Bronx

Manhattan

Queens

Brooklyn

Staten Island

1624	First European settlers, mostly Walloons, arrived on ship *Eendracht*, leaving eight men on Nooten Eylandt (present-day Governors Island)
1625	• Dutch West India Company (WIC) selected southern tip of Manhattan Island as site of first permanent settlement and seat of New Netherland government • Construction of Fort Amsterdam and settler housing began
1626	• Manhattan Island acquired from American Indians • Settlers at Fort Orange and other outposts in the colony relocated to Manhattan, joined by Dutch, French, and other Europeans, and first enslaved Africans • Manhattan settlement later known as New Amsterdam
1653	New Amsterdam chartered as a city
1658	Dorp (village) of *Nieuw Haarlem* (New Harlem) laid out; Nieuw Haarlem village and Dutch Reformed Church of Harlem chartered 1660
1664	• New Amsterdam surrendered to the English, who changed its name to New York and made it the capital of the new colony of New York • English colonial jurisdictional divisions established; in addition to Manhattan, the Town of New York had jurisdiction over Fordham area on the mainland (now in Bronx County)
1665	City of New York created by charter with jurisdiction over all of Manhattan Island, New Harlem receiving its own subordinate patent
1683	• New York divided into 12 counties, Manhattan Island becoming New York County • New York City divided into five wards called the North, South, East, West, and Dock wards; all of Manhattan Island north of the Wall (an early fortification at present-day Wall Street) was the Out Ward, consisting of the Harlem and Bowery Divisions
1776–1783	Manhattan occupied by British troops
1791	Wards reconfigured and names replaced with numbers
1811	City commissioners laid out the "grid" of numbered streets and avenues from Houston Street (former North Street) to the north end of the Island
1874	New York City and County annexed Westchester County towns of Kingsbridge, West Farms, and Morrisania; they became wards 23 and 24 of New York County and were known as the Annexed District or North Side
1881	New York City and County annexed North Brother Island from Long Island City, Queens County, to house hospital for infectious diseases
1884	New York City and County annexed Rikers Island from Town of Newtown, Queens County, for a prison farm
1895	City and County annexed Westchester County town of Westchester and southern part of Eastchester and Pelham which became part of the 24th ward of New York County; these additions also referred to as part of the Annexed District
1898	• The consolidated City of New York created with five boroughs • New York County divided into two boroughs—the Borough of Manhattan (the Island of Manhattan and present-day Marble Hill) and the Borough of the Bronx (the 23rd and 24th wards of New York County plus North Brother and Rikers islands)
1914	New York County divided into two counties: New York County became coterminous with the existing Borough of Manhattan, and the new Bronx County was formed, which then became coterminous with the existing Borough of the Bronx

EARLY NEW YORK CITY WARDS

In October 1683 the City of New York, then entirely south of the Wall (now Wall Street), was divided into five wards, or political units, called the North, South, East, West, and Dock wards. All of Manhattan Island north of the Wall was the Out Ward, consisting of the Harlem and Bowery Divisions. Over the next 100 years the city grew north to about Chambers Street, extending the North, West and East wards and in 1730 adding a seventh ward on the east side, called Montgomerie's Ward after John Montgomerie, governor of New York and New Jersey (1728–1731).

In 1791 the seven old wards were dissolved and seven new wards created, with different boundaries and designated by numbers. Between 1791 and 1853 the number of wards was increased to 22. When the future Bronx was annexed it was divided into wards 23 and 24.

In the 19th century New York City politics was based on the wards, and most city dwellers were very conscious of the ward in which they resided, especially if they lived below 14th Street where 16 of the 22 wards were located. The wards became increasingly associated with fraud and were stripped of political significance by the end of the 19th century. They were abolished in 1936.

Table 1: Wards of the Old City of New York, now Borough of Manhattan			
Ward	**When Created (and Divided)**	**Boundaries**	**Neighborhoods Old and Current**
1	1791	South of Liberty St. and Maiden Lane	*New Amsterdam*, Financial District, Battery
2	1791	East side, Liberty St. and Maiden Lane north to Spruce St., Ferry St., and Peck Slip, from Broadway and Park Row to East River	South Street Seaport, *The Swamp*, Financial District
3	1791	West side, Liberty St. north to Reade St., from Broadway to Hudson River	*Lower West Side*, Financial District (World Trade Center), Tribeca
4	1791	East side, Spruce St., Ferry St., and Peck Slip northeast to Catharine St., from Park Row, Chatham Sq. and East Broadway to East River	Parts of Chinatown, Lower East Side, South Street Seaport
5	1791	West side, Reade St. north to Canal St., from Broadway to Hudson River	*Lower West Side*, *St. John's Park* (Hudson Square), Tribeca
6	1791	A middle ward, (future) City Hall Park north to Walker and Canal Sts., from Broadway east to Park Row, Chatham Sq., and Bowery	*Commons* (City Hall Park), Civic Center, *Five Points*, original Chinatown
7	1791 (1803 see 8, 9, 1808 see 10)	1791 all Manhattan north of wards 1–6 (and 8–9 as of 1803). Reduced 1808 to south of Division and Grand Sts. east of Catharine St., along East River	(1808–present) Lower East Side, Corlears Hook, part of Chinatown
8	1803, from 7 (1827 see 14)	West side, Canal St. north to Houston (North St.), from Bowery to Hudson River. 1827 east boundary changed from Bowery to Broadway.	(1827–present) *Lower West Side*, South Village/ Hudson Square, SoHo, *part Little Italy*
9	1803, from 7 (1832 see 15)	West side, Houston St. north to (future) 14th St., from Fourth Ave./Bowery to Hudson River. 1832 east boundary changed from Fourth Ave./Bowery to Sixth Ave.	(1832–present) Greenwich Village (West Village), Meatpacking District, *part Little Italy*. Mid-19th century wards 9 and 15 had highest percentage of native-born residents so were called the "American wards."
10	1808, from 7 (1825 see 11, 12, 1827 see 13)	1808 all Manhattan north of wards 1–9. 1825 reduced to East side, Division and Grand Sts. north to Rivington St., from Bowery to East River. 1827 east boundary changed from East River to Norfolk St.	(1827–present) Lower East Side, part of Chinatown

Table 1: Wards of the Old City of New York, now Borough of Manhattan			
Ward	**When Created (and Divided)**	**Boundaries**	**Neighborhoods Old and Current**
11	1825, from 10 (1837 see 17)	East side, Rivington St. north to 14th St., from Fourth Ave./Bowery to East River. 1837 west boundary changed from Fourth Ave./Bowery to Avenue B.	(1837–present) parts of Lower East Side, *Little Germany*, East Village
12	1825, from 10 (1835 see 16, 1850 see 19)	All Manhattan north of 14th St. 1835 all Manhattan north of 40th St. 1850 all Manhattan north of 86th St.	(1850–present) parts of Upper East Side (Yorkville), Upper West Side (*Bloomingdale*), and *Seneca Village*. East Harlem, (Central) Harlem, West Harlem, Morningside Heights, Washington Heights, Inwood, Marble Hill
13	1827, from 10	East side, Division and Grand Sts. north to Rivington St., from Norfolk St. to East River	Lower East Side
14	1827, from 8	A middle ward, Walker and Canal Sts. to Houston St., from Broadway to Bowery	Little Italy, parts of Chinatown, SoHo
15	1832, from 9	A middle ward, Houston St. north to 14th St., between Sixth Ave. and Fourth Ave./Bowery	Greenwich Village, Washington Sq., parts of NoHo, Astor Place, Union Sq., *Little Italy*. See ward 9.
16	1835, from 12 (1846 see 18, 1851 see 20)	1835 all Manhattan between 14th and 40th Sts. 1846 divided, now west of Sixth Ave. to Hudson River. 1851 divided again, north boundary 26th St.	(1851–present) Chelsea; parts of Meatpacking and *Tenderloin*
17	1837, from 11	East Side, Rivington St. north to 14th St., Fourth Ave./Bowery east to Avenue B	*Little Germany*, East Village, Lower East Side, parts of Astor Place and NoHo
18	1846, from 16 (1853 see 21)	East Side, 14th to 40th Sts. from Sixth Ave. to East River. 1853 divided, north boundary 26th St.	(1853–present) Union Sq., Madison Sq., Stuyvesant Sq., Gramercy Park, Flatiron, Ladies Mile, Bellevue, *Gashouse District*, part of *Tenderloin*
19	1850, from 12 (1853 see 22)	1850 all Manhattan between 40th and 86th Sts. 1853 divided, now Sixth Ave. and Central Park to East River.	(1853–present) Turtle Bay, Sutton Place, most of Upper East Side; parts of *Tenderloin*, Midtown, Yorkville
20	1851, from 16	West Side, 26th to 40th Sts. from Sixth Ave. to Hudson River	Parts of Chelsea, Hell's Kitchen, Garment District, *Tenderloin*, Midtown
21	1853, from 18	East Side, 26th to 40th Sts. from Sixth Ave. to East River	Murray Hill, Kips Bay, Rose Hill, parts of *Tenderloin*, Midtown, Bellevue
22	1853, from 19	West Side, 40th to 86th Sts. from Sixth Ave. and Central Park to Hudson	Parts of Hell's Kitchen, *Tenderloin*, Midtown, Upper West Side (*Bloomingdale*), *Seneca Village*
Table created by Harry Macy Jr., 2014			

MANHATTAN NEIGHBORHOODS
PAST AND PRESENT

Unlike all other counties in New York State, present-day New York County, coterminous with the modern-day Borough of Manhattan, was never divided into villages, towns, or cities. But it did not lack for place names. As John Homer French wrote in his 1860 gazetteer, the city "… has localities known by distinct names as villages or neighborhoods." His belief that "… most of them will soon be known only to the student of history" certainly proved false, because a large number of old Manhattan neighborhood names have survived, while new ones have been adopted. Since the disappearance of the wards, it is safe to say that Manhattan residents identify with their neighborhoods (or addresses) as much as with the borough or city.

Table 2 outlines the best known and historically most significant place names, from the Dutch colonial period to the present; disused names are in italics. The list is not exhaustive. And it does not contain places in the Bronx that were part of New York County from 1874 to 1914; for these place names, see the Bronx Borough/County Guide. The names on the list were identified from 19th-century New York State gazetteers, neighborhood histories, atlases and maps, historical and contemporary guides to New York City, and other sources.

Table 2: Neighborhoods of the Borough of Manhattan / New York County	
Name	**Notes (most boundaries are approximate)**
The Battery (Ward 1)	Park at southern tip of Manhattan and adjacent area, almost entirely landfill. See Castle Clinton/Castle Garden, below. Just north of park at foot of Broadway is Bowling Green, the oldest city park (1733).
Battery Park City	New neighborhood created beginning in 1974 on landfill along the Hudson south and west of the Financial District.
Bedloe's Island (now Liberty Island)	In NY Harbor between Manhattan and Staten islands, site of Statue of Liberty erected 1886, renamed Liberty Island 1956. Now under National Park Service. Expanded by landfill which is part of New Jersey.
Bellevue (Wards 18, 21)	25th to 30th Sts., First Ave. to East River, site of city hospital since 1794, was Bellevue estate of Dutch Keteltas family. Name sometimes applied to neighboring blocks.
Blackwell's Island (now Roosevelt Island)	In East River opposite 51st to 86th Sts. Called after owners Manning's Island 1668–early 1700s, then Blackwell's. Acquired by City 1828 for prison, almshouse, workhouse, hospitals. Renamed Welfare Island 1921. Since 1971 Roosevelt Island, converted to residential area.
Bloomingdale (Wards 22, 12)	Name (from Dutch Bloemendael) for much of the Upper West Side from 1700s until mid- to late 1800s. Included Harsenville, 68th to 81st Sts., and Stryker's Bay, 81st to 99th Sts., first settled by 18th-century Dutch farmers. See Upper West Side.
Bowery (Wards 10, 14, 15, 17)	Original division of Out Ward between 18th-century city and Harlem, name later restricted to area around street of same name on Lower East Side from Canal St. to Cooper Square (4th St.). Name derives from Dutch bouwerie, referring to the farm of New Netherland Director-General Stuyvesant to which the street led.
Castle Clinton/Castle Garden (Ward 1)	Built 1808–1811 at southern tip of Manhattan on small island created by landfill, now part of Battery Park. First a fort called Southwest Battery, renamed Castle Clinton 1817, converted to Castle Garden entertainment center 1823–1854, Emigrant Landing Depot 1855–1890, City Aquarium 1896–1941, now restored as Castle Clinton.
Central Park	Manhattan's largest park, constructed beginning in 1857 from 59th to 110th Sts. between Fifth and Eighth Aves. Area previously included Seneca Village (see below).
Chelsea (Ward 16, 20)	From Hudson River to Sixth Ave., 14th to 30th Sts., settled early by Dutch and English farmers, part purchased 1750 by Thomas Clarke and named Chelsea after the London borough.
Chinatown (Ward 6)	Began in mid-1800s as small Chinese neighborhood between Pell and Doyer Sts., before WW II sometimes called the "Bachelor Society" as few Chinese women and children entered United States due to restrictive immigration laws. Since 1965 increased immigration has expanded Chinatown east into the Lower East Side and north into Little Italy and the Bowery.
Civic Center (Ward 6)	20th-century name for area including City Hall and city, state, and federal courts and offices. Between Chinatown and Tribeca, north of Financial District and south of SoHo and Little Italy. Earlier names The Commons, The Fields, The Park. Includes the African Burial Ground, cemetery of the city's early black population both slave and free, some of whom also lived in the area. See also Five Points.

Table 2: Neighborhoods of the Borough of Manhattan / New York County

Name	Notes (most boundaries are approximate)
East Harlem (Ward 12)	That part of Harlem from Park Ave. to the East River, between 96th and 142nd Sts. Site of original Harlem Dutch settlement. Area on East River at 116th St. once called *Benson's Point*. Development began by 1860s, attracting many immigrants, Irish followed by Jewish and Italian, the latter forming a *Little Italy*. In 20th century became first center of city's Puerto Rican population, known as El Barrio or Spanish Harlem.
East Village (Wards 11, 17)	20th-century name for Houston to 14th St., Bowery and Fourth Ave. to East River, including part of Astor Place; northern end of the Lower East Side. Most of area formerly part of *Little Germany* (see below).
Ellis Island	In NY Harbor between Manhattan and Staten islands, formerly *Oyster*, *Bucking*, and *Gibbet Island*, purchased by Samuel Ellis 1785, acquired by U.S. Government 1808 for a fort. Site of federal immigration center 1892–1924, museum since 1990. Island greatly expanded by landfill which is part of New Jersey.
Financial District (Wards 1, 2, 3)	20th–century name for area south of City Hall housing much of the financial industry, centering on Wall Street but including the World Trade Center and World Financial Center. Site of original city of *New Amsterdam*. Stock Exchange dates from 1792. For many years a commercial area, the district now has a growing residential population.
Five Points (Ward 6)	Former intersection of five streets centering on present-day Columbus Park between Chinatown and Civic Center. Notorious slum from about 1820 until acquired by City 1887–1894. "All that is loathsome, drooping, and decayed is here" (Charles Dickens, *American Notes*, 1842).
Flatiron District (Ward 18)	Between Chelsea and Gramercy, 14th to 23rd Sts. from Sixth Ave. to Park Ave. South. Name derived from the 1902 Flatiron building on block formed by Fifth Ave., Broadway, 22nd and 23rd Sts. Includes *Ladies' Mile* historical shopping districts.
Gashouse District (Ward 18)	From Fourth Ave. (now Park Ave. South) to East River, 14th to 27th Sts., named for gas storage tanks along the river, replaced 1947–1948 by Stuyvesant Town and Peter Cooper Village apartment complexes.
Governors Island	In NY Harbor between Manhattan and Brooklyn, formerly *Nooten Eylandt* (*Nut Island*), site of first European settlement 1624, residence of colonial governors beginning 1698, U.S. military base 1800–1996, now a public park owned by City.
Gramercy Park (Ward 18)	18th to 23rd Sts. between Third Ave. and Fourth Ave. (Park Ave. South), surrounding the 1831 private park. Name evolved from Dutch *Krom Moerasje* (little crooked swamp).
Greenwich Village (Wards 9, 15)	Also "The Village," between the Bowery/Fourth Ave. and Hudson River, from Houston to 14th St. Early names *Noortwyck* and *Bossen Bouwerie* (farm in the woods). Includes Washington Square (see below) and a large historic district. Area west of Sixth Ave. is West Village. See also Meatpacking District.
Hamilton Heights (Ward 12)	Part of West Harlem, between 135th and 155th Sts. from Hudson River to Edgecombe Ave. and Colonial Park, named for Alexander Hamilton's country home "The Grange" (1804). Earlier part of *Harlem Heights*. Includes Sugar Hill Historic District and campuses of City College of New York.
Harlem (Ward 12)	Central Harlem extends north from 110th St. (Central Park North) to the Harlem River, between Fifth Ave. on east and Morningside Heights and St. Nicholas Ave. on west. Originally a Dutch farming village laid out in 1658 in what is now East Harlem, and named *Nieuw Haarlem* after the city in Holland. In 1665 English granted patent as a town within the limits of the City of New York, and attempted unsuccessfully to rename it *Lancaster*. Harlem continued to have its own court for many years, but was also one of the two divisions of the City's Out Ward, covering all of northern Manhattan. 19th century brought development and European immigrants, gradually replaced in 20th century as Central Harlem became capital of black America. See also East Harlem and West Harlem.

Table 2: Neighborhoods of the Borough of Manhattan / New York County

Name	Notes (most boundaries are approximate)
Hell's Kitchen (Wards 20, 22)	Between 30th and 59th Sts. from Eighth Ave. to the Hudson River, north of Chelsea and south of Upper West Side. Developed in 19th century as an immigrant neighborhood, largely Irish, called Hell's Kitchen from about 1870 because of poor living conditions. Renamed Clinton in 1959 and also called Midtown West or West Midtown, but the old name persists even though it is becoming an expensive residential area.
Inwood (Ward 12)	Northernmost tip of Manhattan, above Fairview Ave. and Fort George Ave. Includes the Dyckman House, the borough's only surviving colonial farm house. Inwood is supposed to be where Peter Minuit purchased Manhattan from the Indians in 1626.
Kips Bay (Ward 21)	About East 27th to 34th Sts., and Third Ave. to the East River, south of Murray Hill. Named for Dutch Kip family's 17th–18th century farm, at a bay from the river, now filled in. Some place southern boundary at 23rd, western boundary anywhere from 2nd Ave. to Lexington.
Little Germany (Wards 11, 17)	*Kleindeutschland*, also *Deutschlandle* and *Dutchtown*, from Division and Grand Sts. on Lower East Side north to East 16th St., between Fourth Ave./the Bowery and East River. Starting in 1830s the city's largest German immigrant neighborhood. Avenue B was "German Broadway." After 1900 German community left, many going to Yorkville. Included Tompkins Square. Now East Village. Blocks adjoining Avenues A, B, C, D later acquired nickname Alphabetville or Alphabet City; early Irish settlement near Avenue A south of 14th St. called *Mackerelville*, name disappeared in 1880s. In 20th century Puerto Ricans settled in area.
Little Italy (Wards 14, 15, 8, 9)	First developed in late 19th century in 14th Ward, east of present-day SoHo between Houston and Canal Sts. and Mulberry St. and Broadway. As Italian immigration increased Little Italy spread especially into the Village. Recent years has seen it diminish to Mulberry between Canal and Spring Sts. For another *Little Italy* see East Harlem.
Lower East Side (Wards 7, 10, 13, parts of 11, 17)	Area east of the Bowery and south of Houston St., to the East River. After the Revolution large Dutch and English landholdings were sold and developed, attracting a mostly native-born middle and working-class population. The northernmost developed area of the city, it was often called just the *East Side*, but as city grew steadily northward, the name Lower East Side was coined to distinguish it from affluent areas further north. By mid-19th century the earlier population was replaced by German, Irish, and other European immigrants. At beginning of 20th century, population became largely Jewish, its crowded tenements making it the city's most densely settled section. Later the area attracted large numbers of Puerto Ricans, who called it "Loisaida." End of 20th century saw expansion of Chinatown into western blocks, and beginning of gentrification. Many of the worst slums had already been replaced by new housing built by the City and unions. At the southeast corner of the Lower East Side is Corlears Hook, on the East River south of Grand St., named for its early Dutch owner, the name preserved in a local park and housing. The Lower East Side is also described more broadly to cover 14th St. south as far as Fulton St., and Broadway to the East River, to include the East Village, *Little Germany*, Little Italy, and Chinatown; see separate entries for those neighborhoods.
Lower West Side (Wards 3, 5, 8)	Former name for area south of Houston St. and west of Broadway, now in South Village, Tribeca and Financial District. It included *Dominies Hook*, along the Hudson from Duane to Canal Sts.; *Kings Garden*, west of Broadway from Fulton to Reade Sts.; *Lispenards Swamp*, Duane to Spring Sts., and Wooster to Greenwich Sts., drained in 1730s and renamed *Lispenards Meadows*; *St. John's Park* (now Hudson Square), North Moore to Laight Sts. west of Varick St., settled after the Revolution; and *Washington Market*, large wholesale food market built 1812 on Washington St. between Fulton and Vesey Sts., continued in various forms until 1956, now Washington Market Park in Tribeca. Wards 5 and 8 were home to many of city's free African Americans in early 19th century. Much of this area was owned by Trinity Church.
Madison Square (Wards 18, 21)	Area around Madison Square Park, 23rd to 26th Sts., Madison to Fifth Aves., above the Flatiron District. In early 1800s a potter's field, arsenal and barracks, became a park in 1847, soon surrounded by a wealthy residential neighborhood.

Table 2: Neighborhoods of the Borough of Manhattan / New York County	
Name	**Notes (most boundaries are approximate)**
Manhattanville (Ward 12)	A 19th-century village on Broadway vicinity of 125th St., now part of West Harlem, north of Morningside Heights, south of Hamilton Heights.
Marble Hill (Ward 12)	Former northernmost tip of Manhattan, separated from the island when Harlem Ship Channel was created in 1895 to improve ship access from Harlem River to the Hudson. When former route of Harlem River around north side of Marble Hill was filled in, it became attached to the Bronx, but it remains part of Manhattan Borough and New York County.
Meatpacking District (Wards 9, 16)	Also *Gansevoort Market*, former center of city's meatpacking industry, is at the northwest corner of Greenwich Village, Hudson River to Greenwich Ave. and Bethune to 16th St. Historic district.
Midtown (Wards 19–22)	Manhattan's largest business district since the 1920s, roughly from 30th to 59th Sts., Eighth to Third Aves. Includes most of Garment District, 34th to 42nd Sts., Ninth to Fifth Aves.; Herald and Greeley Squares at intersection of Sixth Ave., Broadway, and 34th St., and Times Square (formerly *Long Acre Square*) at intersection of Seventh Ave. and Broadway above 42nd St. Earlier these were residential blocks and also part of the *Tenderloin*.
Morningside Heights (Ward 12)	North of Upper West Side and south of West Harlem, between 110th and 123rd Sts., Morningside Park to the Hudson, home of Columbia University and other institutions; formerly *Vandewater Heights*, *Harlem Heights*, *Cathedral Heights*, and *Columbia Heights*. Earlier settlement *Carmansville*, on Tenth Ave. above 115th St., built after 1835 downtown fire on land of Richard Carman.
Murray Hill (Ward 21)	East Side residential area, 34th to 40th Sts., Madison to Third Aves., extended to East River after Third Ave. "El" torn down 1956. Named for Murray family whose estate *Inclenberg* was part of area.
New Amsterdam	Original Dutch settlement 1626–1664, incorporated as city 1653. Part of present-day Financial District south of *the Wall* (Wall Street), except for blocks west of Broadway and east of Pearl St., created by 18th-century landfill, and Battery Park, 19th-century landfill. First called *Fort Amsterdam* from fort on site of U.S. Customs House; name *New Amsterdam* in use by 1640s.
NoHo (formerly Wards 15, 17)	20th-century acronym for North of Houston, between Greenwich Village and East Village—Houston to 9th St., Mercer St. to Third Ave. and Bowery, including Astor Place. Site of 18th century *Vauxhall Gardens* on Bond St.
Randalls Island	Formerly *Barent Eylandt*, *Little Barn Island*, *Belleisle*, and *Montresors Island*, named Randall's 1784 after then-owner. Sold to city 1830 and used for potter's field and institutions for the poor, sick, and "undesirable." Now a city park, connected to Wards Island.
Rose Hill (Ward 21)	27th to 29th Sts. east of Fourth Ave. (Park Ave. South), name of 1787 estate of John Watts.
Seneca Village (Wards 12, 22)	Largely African American village between what would have been 82nd and 89th Sts. and Seventh and Eighth Aves., now in Central Park. Settled 1825, razed 1857 for construction of park.
SoHo (Wards 8, part 14)	20th-century acronym for South of Houston. Canal to Houston Sts. from Crosby St. to West Broadway, though name also applied to area further west (South Village). Settled early by Dutch and free black farmers, developed in mid-19th century as major commercial area, subsequently deserted as business moved uptown. Saved from destruction with creation of historic district in 1973 to preserve its cast iron architecture.
South Street Seaport (Wards 2, 4)	Includes designated historic district along East River below Brooklyn Bridge, comprising several blocks of 19th-century buildings including Schermerhorn Row, and piers and historic ships. Center of the much larger port and shipbuilding industry approximately 1815–1860. Immigrants landed here before Castle Garden opened in 1855. West of the district, in blocks bordered by Gold, Frankfort, Pearl, and Ferry Sts., was *Beekman's Swamp* (*The Swamp*), once center of tanning and related leather industries.
South Village (Ward 8)	Canal St. north to Houston, from West Broadway (formerly *Laurens St.*) to the Hudson, overlapping with SoHo. Includes Hudson Square and a historic district.
Sutton Place (Ward 19)	East 53rd to 59th Sts., First Ave. to East River, developed by Effingham B. Sutton beginning 1875, gentrified beginning 1920 and main street (Avenue A) renamed Sutton Place.

Table 2: Neighborhoods of the Borough of Manhattan / New York County

Name	Notes (most boundaries are approximate)
Tenderloin (Wards 16, 18–22)	West 24th to 42nd Sts., Fifth to Seventh Aves. In the 1870s and 1880s famous for its "saloons, brothels, gambling parlors, and dance halls." Now part of Midtown.
Tribeca	20th-century acronym for Triangle Below Canal, part of *Lower West Side* from Canal St. south to World Trade Center, from Broadway west to the Hudson.
Turtle Bay (Ward 19)	East Side 43rd to 52nd Sts., Lexington Ave. to East River, neighborhood since 1600s, name evolved from Dutch *Deutal* Bay. Includes Beekman Place, 49th to 51st Sts., First Ave. to East River (south of Sutton Place), site of 1765 Beekman mansion. To south is Tudor City apartment complex, opposite the United Nations. All of this area sometimes called Midtown East.
Union Square (Junction of Wards 18, 15, 17)	Neighborhood surrounding Union Square Park at intersection of Broadway and Fourth Ave./Park Ave. South between 14th and 17th Sts. First called *Union Place*. Before 1815 a potter's field, a park since 1839.
Upper East Side (Wards 19, 12)	The area between Central Park and the East River, from about 59th to 96th Sts., including Fifth Ave. Sparsely populated before 1840s, blocks west of Third Ave. developed into Manhattan's richest section while blocks east of the Third Ave. "El" were filled with tenements housing poor European immigrants. Demolition of the "El" in 1956 opened the blocks east of Third Ave. to redevelopment.
	Included *Hamilton Square*, 65th to 69th Sts., Fifth to Third Aves., set aside as a park in 1811 grid plan but eliminated 1865–1868. Includes Lenox Hill, 60th to 77th Sts., Fifth to Lexington Aves., once Robert Lenox's farm, where townhouses were built from the 1880s. See Yorkville (below) for northern neighborhoods.
Upper West Side (Wards 22, 12)	West 59th to 110th Sts. from Central Park to the Hudson River (some define the north boundary as 125th, see Morningside Heights). Formerly rural area known as *Bloomingdale* (see above). Main development began about 1878 and area was called *The End* and *West End* before settling on Upper West Side.
	Includes Lincoln Square around intersection of Broadway and Columbus Ave. between 65th and 66th Sts., former site of *San Juan Hill* possibly named for a post-1898 settlement of black Spanish-American War veterans. Now site of Lincoln Center cultural complex. Section from 100th to 110th Sts., Central Park West to Columbus Ave., is called Manhattan Valley, earlier *Clendening Valley*.
Wall Street	Original site of wall marking north boundary of *New Amsterdam*. Later developed into financial center of the nation. Now part of Financial District which is often referred to as Wall Street.
Wards Island	Formerly *Great Barcutor* and *Great Barn Island*, called Wards after the Revolution. Acquired by City 1955, site of various institutions but now mostly a park. Joined to Randalls Island.
Washington Heights (Ward 12)	West 155th St. north to Inwood, between the Harlem and Hudson rivers. Sometimes called *Harlem Heights* in 19th century. Current name in use by 1870s, recalling Fort Washington on the Hudson near 162nd St. and Eleventh Ave. Much of area remained rural as late as 1900, developed after arrival of rapid transit. Now home to Manhattan's largest Dominican community, succeeding, Irish, German-Jewish, and other groups.
Washington Square (Ward 15)	Neighborhood around Washington Square Park in Greenwich Village, formerly a potter's field (1797–1825) and military parade ground (1826–ca. 1871). Developed as fashionable residential area from 1830s. Site of main campus of New York University.
West Harlem (Ward 12)	West Side between Morningside Heights and Washington Heights, from 123rd to 155th Sts., from St. Nicholas Park, Edgecomb Ave. and Colonial Park to the Hudson. See Hamilton Heights and Manhattanville.
Yorkville (Wards 19, 12)	Part of Upper East Side, originally a village centered at 86th St. and Third Ave. Name now applied to broader area from 72nd to 96th Sts., East River to Central Park, excluding 20th-century neighborhoods Gracie Square between 79th and 92nd Sts., York Ave. to East River, and Carnegie Hill and part sometimes called West SoHo between 86th and 98th Sts., Fifth to Lexington Aves. Yorkville succeeded *Little Germany* as Manhattan's main German neighborhood, and was also called *Germantown*. There were also many Czechs and Hungarians in the area, but these separate ethnic enclaves have now largely disappeared from this affluent section.

Table created by Harry Macy Jr., 2014

Notes on the Borough of Manhattan

Until 1874 the City of New York consisted of Manhattan Island and several small adjacent islands. Except for the early Dutch period the name Manhattan was not officially used until the borough's creation in 1898. The island itself even appears on many 18th and 19th century maps as New York Island.

Today's Borough of Manhattan comprises Manhattan Island, as well as several adjacent islands and Marble Hill, which is now on the mainland, but was physically part of Manhattan Island until 1895.

Notes on Early Censuses of New York City

For the 1703 New York City Census, see Edmund O'Callaghan in Abstracts, Indexes & Transcriptions below. See chapter 3, Census Records, for information about the New York City Jury Censuses of 1817 and 1819, and the 1821 New York City Electoral Census.

NEW YORK STATE CENSUS RECORDS
See also chapter 3, Census Records

County originals at New York County Clerk's Office: 1855,* 1905, 1915, 1925 (1825, 1835, 1845, 1865, 1875, and 1892 are lost)

* Ward 17 of the 1855 New York state census was not microfilmed. A digitized version is available only in the NYG&B's eLibrary.

State originals at the NYSA: 1915, 1925

Microfilm at the FHL, NYPL, and NYSL; many years are online at *FamilySearch.org* and *Ancestry.com.*

NATIONAL/STATEWIDE REPOSITORIES & RESOURCES
See chapter 16

CITYWIDE REPOSITORIES AND RESOURCES

Vital records for Manhattan are held at the Municipal Archives of New York City (MUNI). For a description of MUNI and other resources that pertain to all five boroughs, see Citywide Repositories & Resources in the introduction to the Borough Guides.

COUNTYWIDE REPOSITORIES & RESOURCES

New York County Clerk
New York County Courthouse • 60 Center Street, Room 161
New York, NY 10007 • (646) 386-5955
www.nycourts.gov/courts/1jd/supctmanh/county_clerk_operations.shtml
Division of Old Records • 31 Chambers Street, Room 703
New York, NY 10007 • (646) 386-5395

Business records, court records (dating from the late-17th century), naturalization records (1824–1959), divorce records, name changes, and various records from the New York state census for New York County. Detailed description of holdings, the rules for access, and the files requiring advance ordering from offsite storage is on the website. The Division of Old Records also holds colony-wide Supreme Court records.

New York County Surrogate's Court
31 Chambers Street • New York, NY 10007 • (646) 386-5000
Email: probate_general@courts.state.ny.us (Probate Department)
www.nycourts.gov/courts/1jd/surrogates

Probate records beginning 1665, many records online at *FamilySearch. org* and on microfilm at NYPL. For most original pre-1787 records, originals are at NYSA, and Surrogate has copies made in 19th and 20th centuries.

New York City Clerk: Manhattan Office
141 Worth Street • New York, NY 10013
311 (in New York City) • (212) 639-9675 (outside New York City)
www.cityclerk.nyc.gov/html/home/home.shtml

Marriage records for all five boroughs, 1930–present. Index up to 1951 is at MUNI, which also holds earlier marriage records.

New York City Register: Borough of Manhattan
Manhattan Business Center • 66 John Street, 13th Floor
New York, NY 10038

Holds land records, including deeds since 1654 and mortgages since 1754. Deeds also online at *www.FamilySearch.org*; NYPL has microfilm of deeds 1654–1850, deeds index 1654–1890, mortgages 1754–1800.

Board of Elections, New York County
200 Varick Street, 10th Floor • New York, NY 10014 • (212) 886-2100

Manhattan voter registrations, 1916–1920 (with gaps) and 1923–present. Record copies are made by staff and should be requested in advance.

Manhattan Borough Historian and Community Historians
Municipal Building • One Centre Street, 19th Floor
New York, NY 10007 • (212) 669-8089

While not authorized to answer genealogical inquiries, borough and community historians can provide historical information and research advice. See contact information at the website of the Association of Public Historians of New York State at *www.aphnys.org.*

New York Public Library (NYPL)
www.nypl.org

The vast collections of the NYPL's research libraries that are pertinent for genealogical research are described in detail in chapter 16, National and Statewide Repositories & Resources. Some library branches in Manhattan offer instructional workshops on genealogy, and some hold ethnic heritage collections.

Cemeteries
See chapter 9, Cemetery Records, for information about the practice of disinterment, which was common in Manhattan as the city grew, as well as a selected list of New York City cemeteries with their website addresses. See also, Rosalie Fellows Bailey's guide, pp. 44–45, which lists the oldest cemeteries with disinterment dates when applicable.

History Museums and Repositories in the Borough of Manhattan
There are many museums with historical collections in the Borough. The larger institutions are in the citywide resources section and in chapter 16, National and Statewide Repositories & Resources. See especially the entries for the New-York Historical Society and the Museum of the City of New York. Other museums and cultural institutions are listed in sections of chapter 14, Peoples of New York.

African Burial Ground National Monument
290 Broadway, 1st Floor • New York, NY 10007
(212) 637-2019 • *www.nps.gov/afbg*
A National Monument on the burial site of approximately 15,000 slaves and free blacks who died during the late-17th through the late-18th centuries.

Dyckman Farmhouse Museum

4881 Broadway at 204th Street • New York, NY 10034 • (212) 304-9422
Email: info@dyckmanfarmhouse.org • www.dyckmanfarmhouse.org

The only surviving Dutch-Colonial farmhouse in Manhattan was built in 1784 by William Dyckman. Website includes Dyckman informational handouts, Dyckman family tree and timeline, floorplans, historic images and documents, and information on genealogy research.

Fraunces Tavern Museum

54 Pearl Street • New York, NY 10004 • (212) 509-3467
Email: curator@frauncestavernmuseum.org
www.frauncestavernmuseum.org

Operated by the Sons of the Revolution in the State of New York, the museum is housed in a colonial tavern that was witness to significant events during the Revolutionary War. Holdings include artifacts, drawings and documents, and paintings.

Lower East Side Tenement Museum

97 Orchard Street • New York, NY • (212) 982-8420
Email: lestm@tenement.org • www.tenement.org

The rooms of this 1863 tenement building have been restored to various points in time, representing different families who lived there and reflecting immigration history from the late-19th to the early-20th century. Archives include documents, artifacts, photographs, and oral history. A searchable photo archive is accessible on the website.

National Park Service (NPS), Manhattan Historic Sites Archive

www.mhsarchive.org

The NPS operates five historic sites in Manhattan: Federal Hall, the Ulysses S. Grant Memorial, Hamilton Grange (which was home to Alexander Hamilton), the Theodore Roosevelt Birthplace, and Castle Clinton. This website provides access to digital collections pertaining to each of these sites, as well as St. Paul's Church in Mount Vernon.

Rose Museum at Carnegie Hall

154 West 57th Street • New York, NY 10019 • (212) 903-9600
www.carnegiehall.org/Information/Rose-Museum

A significant archive of interest to researchers studying musicians and people prominent in the performing arts. The museum has a plan to digitize its extensive records.

South Street Seaport Museum

12 Fulton Street • New York, NY 10038 • (212) 748-8600
www.southstreetseaportmuseum.org

The Museum is custodian of a historic district of 19th-century commercial buildings and holds art and archival collections that document the history of the Port of New York and its crucial role in the development of New York City, as well as a fleet of historic ships. It produces exhibitions and education programs and formerly published *Seaport* magazine. Some digital collections are accessible on the website.

SELECTED PRINT AND ONLINE RESOURCES

Below is a selection of resources relevant for research in Manhattan. The list is representative, not exhaustive. Additional titles—particularly of abstracts, indexes, transcriptions, and local histories—are available and can be found in the bibliographies in chapter 15, Religious Records of New York; consult the Introduction to Part Two for further information. For guidance on how to identify and locate community directories and local newspapers, see chapter 11, City Directories, and chapter 12, Newspapers, in Part One of this book. Other valuable sources for Manhattan research will be found in Citywide Repositories, and in the subject-based bibliographies throughout Part One.

Abstracts, Indexes & Transcriptions

Barber, Gertrude A. "Index of the Letters of Administration Filed in New York County, New York from 1743–1875." Typescript, 1950–1951. NYPL, New York.

Barck, Dorothy C. *List of 500 Inhabitants of New York City in 1775 with Their Occupations and Addresses*. New York: New-York Historical Society, 1939.

Beach, Moses Yale. *The Wealth and Biography of the Wealthy Citizens of New York City ... Persons Estimated to be Worth $100,000 and upwards ....* New York: The Sun Office, 1844.

Bloch, Dr. Julius M., Leo Hershkowitz, and Kenneth Scott. "New York City Assessment Rolls, February 1730." *NYG&B Record*, vol. 95 (1964) no. 1: 27–32; no. 3: 166–84; no. 4: 197–202. [NYG&B eLibrary] See also Research Aid "New York City Assessment Rolls 1699–1734," originally published in the *NYG&B Newsletter* (now *New York Researcher*), Fall 1996. Updated June 2011 and published on *NewYorkFamilyHistory.org*.

The Burghers of New Amsterdam and the Freemen of New York, 1675–1866. Collections of The New-York Historical Society, vol. 18, 1885. Includes pre-1675 lists of New Amsterdam burghers, followed by roll of freemen with occupations and dates registered. In English colonial period only a Freeman could conduct a business or practice a trade; it also qualified them to vote.

Darling, William A. *List of Persons, Co-partnerships and Corporations Who Were Taxed on Seventeen Thousand Five Hundred Dollars and Upwards in the City of New York: In the Year 1850*. New York, 1851. [Ancestry.com]

Farrell, Charles. "Index to Matrimonial Actions [Divorces, Annulments, Legal Separations] 1784–1840, at the New York County Clerk's Office." *NYG&B Record*, vol. 129, no. 2 (1998): 81–88. [NYG&B eLibrary]

Fernow, Berthold, trans. and ed. *The Records of New Amsterdam from 1653 to 1674*. 7 vols. New York, 1897. Reprint, Baltimore: Genealogical Publishing Co., 1976.

Grim, Charles F. *An Essay towards an Improved Register of Deeds, City and County of New-York to Dec. 31, 1799, Inclusive*. New York: Gould, Banks, and Co, 1832. Index to New York County deeds recorded in Manhattan and Albany. References some deeds not in official *Index of Conveyances*, below.

New York County (NY). *Index of Conveyances Recorded in the Office of the Register of the City and County of New York*. 51 vols. Vol. 21, New York, 1857–1864: deeds and other land records indexed by grantors and grantees, and one volume of corporate grantors including masters in chancery and sheriffs.

New York (NY) Board of Assessors. "Tax Lists of the City of New York, December, 1695–July 15th, 1699." *Collections of the New-York Historical Society*, vol. 43 (1910): 1–208; vol. 44 (1911): 209–315. See also Bloch, above.

O'Callaghan, Edmund B. *Documentary History of the State of New York*. Vol. 1. Albany: Weed, Parsons, 1849. See pp. 611–624 for the transcript of the 1703 census.

Pelletreau, William S. *Abstracts of Wills on File in the Surrogate's Office, City of New York [1665–1800]*. 17 vols. Collections of The New-York Historical Society, vols. 25–41, 1892–1908. Abstracts wills and administrations filed at the New York County Surrogate's Court. Vols. 16–17 contain corrections. [books.FamilySearch.org]

Pool, David de Sola. *Portraits Etched in Stone: Early Jewish Settlers 1682–1831*. New York: Columbia University Press, 1952. Gravestone inscriptions from Manhattan's three oldest Jewish cemeteries.

Riker, James Jr. "The James Riker Papers." Collection W94-a231. NYPL Manuscripts and Archives Division, New York. Finding aid available online. Includes original records of the Town of Harlem 1662–after 1800.

Sawyer, Ray C. "Gravestone Inscriptions of Trinity Cemetery, New York City, New York." Typescript, 1931. NYPL, New York. [*Ancestry.com*] Trinity Cemetery at Broadway and 155th Street, successor to Trinity's cemeteries downtown.

———. "Index of Wills for New York County (New York City) from 1662–[1875]." Typescript, 1930, 1950–1951. NYPL, New York.

Sawyer, Ray C., and Gertrude A. Barber. "Abstracts of Wills for New York County, New York [1801–1856]." 20 vols. Typescript, 1934–1960. NYPL, New York.

Other Resources

Bailey, Rosalie Fellows. *Guide to Genealogical and Biographical Sources for New York City (Manhattan), 1783–1898*. New York: The Author, 1954. [*books.FamilySearch.org*] Reprinted with a new introduction by Harry Macy Jr. Baltimore: Clearfield Co., 1998. Provides detailed advice for using sources, including many obscure titles. After 60 years still an essential tool for the researcher.

Beck, Louis J. *New York's Chinatown: An Historical Presentation of Its People and Places*. New York: Bohemia Publishing, 1898.

Brown, Anne Wright. *New York Marble Cemetery Interments, 1830–1937: With Additional Biographical Information Gathered from Descendants, Family Genealogies, Newspapers, and City Directories*. Rhinebeck, NY: Kinship, 1999.

Cohen, Paul E., and Robert T. Augustyn. *Manhattan in Maps 1527–1995*. New York: Rizzoli, 2006. Reproductions of historic and contemporary maps with commentary document Manhattan's development.

Dallett, Nancy, and Jannelle Warren-Findley. *Governor's Island National Monument Historic Resources Study*. New York: National Park Service, 2007. www.nps.gov/history/history/online_books/gois/gois_hrs.pdf

Diner, Hasia R., et al. *Remembering the Lower East Side: American Jewish Reflections*. Bloomington: Indiana University Press, 2000.

Dolan, Jay P. *The Immigrant Church: New York's Irish and German Catholics, 1815–1865*. Baltimore: Johns Hopkins University Press, 1975.

Dolkart, Andrew J. *Morningside Heights, A History of Its Architecture and Development*. New York: Columbia University Press, 1998.

Franks, David. *The New York Directory for 1786: Illustrated with a Plan of the City, Also Changes in the Names of Streets*. New York: H. J. Sachs & Co., 1905. [*Ancestry.com*]

Freeman, Rhoda Golden. *The Free Negro in New York City in the Era Before the Civil War*. New York: Garland Publishing, 1994. Based on a study conducted from 1927–1986.

Gill, Jonathan. *Harlem: The Four Hundred Year History from Dutch Village to Capital of Black America*. New York: Grove Press, 2011.

Goodfriend, Joyce D. *Before the Melting Pot, Society and Culture in Colonial New York City, 1664–1730*. Princeton, NJ: Princeton University Press, 1992. History as experienced by the major ethnic groups of the period.

Gurock, Jeffrey S. *When Harlem Was Jewish, 1870–1930*. New York: Columbia University Press, 1979.

Guzik, Estelle M., ed. *Genealogical Resources in New York*. New York: Jewish Genealogical Society, 2003. Detailed descriptions of 29 Manhattan repositories.

Harris, Leslie M. *In the Shadow of Slavery: African Americans in New York City, 1626–1863*. Chicago: University of Chicago Press, 2003.

Hindus, Milton, ed. *The Old East Side: An Anthology*. Philadelphia: Jewish Publication Society of America, 1969.

Historical Records Survey. *Guide to Vital Statistics in the City of New York, Borough of Manhattan: Churches*. New York: Work Projects Administration, 1942.

Hobart, George H. *The Negro Churches of Manhattan: A Study Made in 1930*. New York: The Greater New York Federation of Churches, 1930.

Hoff, Henry B. New York County section of "Pre-1750 New York Lists: Censuses, Assessment Rolls, Oaths of Allegiance, and Other Lists." *NYG&B Newsletter* (now *New York Researcher*), Fall 1992. Published as a Research Aid on *NewYorkFamilyHistory.org*. Identifies the lists and where they were published.

———. "Using the Publications of the New-York Historical Society." *NYG&B Newsletter* (now *New York Researcher*), Winter 1992. Published as a Research Aid on *NewYorkFamilyHistory.org*. List of books and articles relating to New York history and genealogy.

Jensen, Howard M. *Aid to Finding Addresses in the 1890 New York City Police Census*. Bowie, MD: Willow Bend Books, 2003.

Kouwenhoven, John A. *The Columbia Historical Portrait of New York, an Essay in Graphic History in Honor of the Tricentennial of New York City and the Bicentennial of Columbia University*. Garden City, NY: Doubleday, 1953. Prints, maps, and photographs illustrating the history of Manhattan 1614–1953.

Longworth's American Almanac, New York Register, and City Directory. David Longworth published 1796–1817; Thomas Longworth continued into the 1840s.

Lowenstein, Steven M. *Frankfurt on the Hudson: The German-Jewish Community of Washington Heights, 1933–1983, Its Structure and Culture*. Detroit: Wayne State University Press, 1989.

Macy, Harry, Jr. "James Riker's Publications and Papers." *NYG&B Newsletter* (now *New York Researcher*), vol. 13, nos. 2–3, Spring–Summer 2002. Riker's papers at NYPL include Harlem town records and church records. See Riker, above.

———. *Protestant Church Records of New York City (Manhattan)*. Series in *The NYG&B Newsletter* (now *New York Researcher*), Fall 1992–Spring 1996. Updated May 2011 as six Research Aids and published on *NewYorkFamilyHistory.org*. Finding aids for published and unpublished records of Dutch Reformed, Episcopal, Lutheran, Methodist, Presbyterian, and other Protestant denominations.

———. "The Records of St. Peter's, New York City's Oldest Catholic Parish." *NYG&B Newsletter* (now *New York Researcher*), Winter 2002. Updated May 2011 and published as a Research Aid on *NewYorkFamilyHistory.org*.

Markel, Howard. *Quarantine! East European Jewish Immigrants in New York City and the Epidemics of 1892*. Baltimore: Johns Hopkins University Press, 1999.

Mott, Hopper S. *The New York of Yesterday: A Descriptive Narrative of Old Bloomingdale*. New York and London: G. P. Putnam's Sons, 1908.

Nadel, Stanley. "Kleindeutschland: New York City's Germans, 1845–1880." Thesis (PhD), Columbia University, 1981.

———. *Little Germany: Ethnicity, Religion, and Class in New York City, 1845–80*. Urbana: University of Illinois Press, 1990.

New York (NY). *Minutes of the Common Council of the City of New York [1675–1776]*. 8 vols. New York: Dodd, Mead, 1905. [vols. 1–7, *HathiTrust.org*; vol. 8, *books.google.com*]

New York (NY), and Arthur E. Peterson. *Minutes of the Common Council of the City of New York [1784–1831]*. 19 vols. New York: City of New York, 1917.

Osofsky, Gilbert. *Harlem, the Making of a Ghetto: Negro New York, 1890–1930*. Chicago: Ivan R. Dee, 1996.

Purple, Edwin R. *Contributions to the History of Ancient Families of New Amsterdam and New York*. New York, 1881.

Riker, James Jr., and Henry P. Toler, *Revised History of Harlem*. New York: New Harlem Publishing Co., 1904.

Rischin, Moses. *The Promised City, New York's Jews 1870–1914*. New York: Harper & Row, 1962. Focuses on the Lower East Side.

Roskolenko, Harry. *The Time That Was Then: The Lower East Side, 1900–1914: An Intimate Chronicle*. New York: Dial Press, 1971.

Schoener, Allon. *Harlem on My Mind: Cultural Capital of Black America, 1900–1968*. New York: New Press, 1995.

———. *Portal to America: The Lower East Side, 1870–1925*. New York: Holt, Rinehart, and Winston, 1967.

Singleton, Esther. *Social New York under the Georges, 1714–1776: Houses, Streets, and Country Homes, with Chapters on Fashions, Furniture, China, Plate and Manners*. New York: Appleton, 1902.

Stokes, Isaac Newton Phelps, comp. *The Iconography of Manhattan Island, 1498–1909*. 6 vols. New York, 1915–1928. Includes detailed chronology; title histories of New Amsterdam lots and early Manhattan farms; inventories of New York City and County records; maps; and prints. A goldmine of information.

Toler, Henry P. *The New Harlem Register: A Genealogy of the Descendants of the Twenty-Three Patentees of the Town of New Harlem, Containing Proofs of Births, Baptisms, and Marriages from the Year 1630 to Date*. New York: New Harlem Publishing Co., 1903. See also Henry B. Hoff, "Principal Families in the *New Harlem Register*," *NYG&B Newsletter* (now *New York Researcher*), Summer 1998. Published as a Research Aid on *NewYorkFamilyHistory.org*.

Walker, George E. *The Afro-American in New York City, 1827–1860*. New York: Garland Publishing, 1993.

Weeks, Lyman Horace. *Prominent Families of New York: Being an Account in Biographical Form of Individuals and Families Distinguished as Representatives of the Social, Professional, and Civic Life of New York City*. New York, 1898.

White, Mrs. William R. "Records of the Reformed Dutch Church of Harlem." *NYG&B Record*, vol. 117 (1986) no. 4: 228–233; vol. 118 (1987): no. 1: 31–38; no. 2: 95; no. 3: 161–164; no. 4: 217–222; vol. 119 (1988): no. 1: 16–17. [NYG&B eLibrary]

Wilson, James Grant. *The Memorial History of the City of New-York*. 4 vols. New York, 1892.

Wilson, Sherrill D. *New York City's African Slaveowners: A Social and Material Culture History*. New York: Garland Publishing, 1994.

Additional Online Resources

Ancestry.com
There are vast numbers of records on *Ancestry.com* that pertain to people who have lived in New York State. See chapter 16 for a description of *Ancestry.com*'s resources and its partnership with the New York State Archives. A search of the online card catalog by county may reveal lesser known resources that pertain to a locality, such as town records, abstracts, transcriptions, city directories, and local histories. Chapter 2, Vital Records, provides detailed information on Manhattan birth, marriage, and death records accessible on *Ancestry.com*.

Brooklyn Genealogy Information Page
http://bklyn-genealogy-info.stevemorse.org
The website also contains information relating to other parts of New York City and Long Island, including general links and tips for genealogy research. Particular records relating to Manhattan include: medical, city, business, and house of worship directories; 1703 census; historic maps (1600s–1900s); ward boundary maps; marriage indexes; military information; and information on schools.

FamilySearch.org
FamilySearch has extensive collections of New York records, including land and probate records described in the entries for the Surrogate's Court and City Register of this section.

A detailed description of *FamilySearch.org* resources, which include the catalog of the Family History Library, is found in chapter 16.

Forgotten New York
www.forgotten-ny.com
The website/blog posts articles and images about New York City history that illuminate vestiges of a forgotten past, as well as streets, buildings, and other places that no longer exist; it includes a street necrology for some Manhattan neighborhoods.

German Genealogy Group and Italian Genealogical Group
www.GermanGenealogyGroup.com or *www.ItalianGen.org*
Free, online indexes to New York City vital records and Manhattan naturalization records 1906–1959 from the Southern District Court.

NYGenWeb Project: New York County
www.rootsweb.ancestry.com/~nymanhat
Part of the national, USGenWeb volunteer initiative, the website provides information and resources for county research.

Borough of Queens/Queens County

County formed	1683
Borough formed	1898
Parent County	Original county
Daughter County	Nassau 1899

Major Land Transactions
See table in chapter 7, Land Records
Queens Village Manor 1685

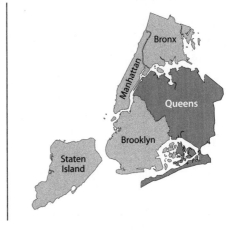

Map: Queens County ca. 1870, before it was divided into two counties. The western part later formed the Borough of Queens, and the eastern towns of Hempstead (except the Rockaway peninsula), North Hempstead, and Oyster Bay became Nassau County.

1639	Dutch West India Company (WIC) claimed Hempstead area by deed from American Indians
1642	New Netherland government granted a patent for English settlement at Mespat (Newtown), joining Dutch and English farmers already in the area
1644	Hempstead (as *Heemstede*) granted by patent to English settlers by Dutch governor Willem Kieft
1645	Flushing (as *Vlissengen*) granted by patent to English settlers by Governor Kieft
1652	Newtown (as *Middelburg*) granted to English settlers by patent by Dutch governor Pieter Stuyvesant
1653	Oyster Bay acquired from American Indians by English settlers, not affiliated with any colony
1656	Jamaica (as *Rustdorp*) granted to English settlers by patent by Governor Stuyvesant
1657	The Flushing Remonstrance forced the Dutch government to end persecution of Quakers, who found many converts in all the towns of future Queens County
1662	Middelburg (Newtown) renamed Hastings after changing allegiance from New Netherland to Connecticut
1664	• British captured colony of New Netherland renaming it New York; existing English towns on Long Island added to the new colony • English colonial jurisdictional divisions known as the Yorkshire Ridings were established, lasting until 1683; most of Queens County was in the North Riding (Flushing, Hempstead, Jamaica, Oyster Bay); Newtown was in the West Riding; North Riding court sat at Jamaica
1665	Hastings and adjacent settlements combined to form Town of Newtown, part of English colonial West Riding of Yorkshire
1667	Towns of Newtown and Oyster Bay received patents from English governor Richard Nicolls
1683	English colony of New York divided into 12 counties, including Queens County; county seat at Jamaica until 1787
1776–1783	Queens County occupied by British troops
1784	• Town of North Hempstead formed from Town of Hempstead • Town of Hempstead changed name to South Hempstead
1787	Courthouse in North Hempstead west of present-day Mineola 1787–1877; offices of County Clerk and Surrogate remained at Jamaica
1788	Towns of Flushing, Jamaica, Newtown, North Hempstead, Oyster Bay, and South Hempstead recognized by New York State
1796	Town of South Hempstead changed name back to Hempstead
1870	Long Island City created from Town of Newtown
1877–1898	Queens County courthouse moved to Long Island City
1886	Lloyd's Neck (former Queens Village Manor) ceded from Town of Oyster Bay to Town of Huntington, Suffolk County
1898	• The consolidated City of New York created with five boroughs • Queens County divided into two parts: the towns of Flushing, Jamaica, and Newtown, and the Rockaway peninsula of Hempstead were dissolved and combined to form the Borough of Queens; the eastern part became Nassau County (see below)
1899	Nassau County created from the eastern Queens County towns of North Hempstead, Oyster Bay, and Hempstead
1940	Borough Hall moved from Long Island City neighborhood to Kew Gardens; County Clerk, Supreme Court, Civil Court, Surrogate's Court, and City Register remain in Jamaica

Towns (and Cities)	Villages and other Settlements	Notes
Flushing * **1645** Land patent granted to English settlers by government of New Netherland **1664** Part of English colonial jurisdiction of the North Riding of Yorkshire **1683** Formed part of original Queens County; a few Dutch and French settlers began to arrive **1788** Recognized as a town by State of New York **1898** Town dissolved; became ward 3, Borough of Queens, New York City	Alley Bayside Black Stump College Point (v) Douglaston Flammersburg Floral Park Flushing (v) Fresh Meadows Head of Vleigh Ireland Little Neck Marathon Rock(y) Hill Spring Hill Springville Strattonport Union Place Whitestone (v) Wilkins Point Willets Point	* Called Vlissingen after town in the Netherlands, which the English called Flushing • Village of College Point inc. 1867, dissolved 1898; formerly Lawrence(s) Neck and Tews Neck • Flammersburg included in Village of College Point 1870 • Floral Park formerly Hinsdale, on Hempstead and North Hempstead town lines • Head of Vleigh later Queens Valley and then Kew Gardens Hills • Village of Flushing inc. 1813, dissolved 1898 • Springville also Spring Vale • Strattonport included in Village of College Point 1870 • Village of Whitestone inc. 1869, dissolved 1898; formerly Clintonville and Cookie Hill • Wilkins Point formerly Thornes Neck, also called Willets Point but not same as current Willets Point; purchased by U.S. Govt. 1857, renamed Fort Totten 1898
Hempstead * (See Nassau County from 1899) **1639** Dutch claim area by deed from American Indians **1643** Indians deed land to English settlers from Connecticut **1644** New Netherland Governor Kieft grants patent to the settlement **1664** Part of English colonial jurisdiction of the North Riding of Yorkshire **1666** Town patent confirmed by English Governor Nicolls **1683** Formed part of original Queens County; about this time Dutch begin to settle in parts of town **1784** Daughter town of North Hempstead formed **1784** Name changed to South Hempstead **1788** Recognized as a town by State of New York **1796** Name changed back to Hempstead **1898** Rockaway peninsula becomes ward 5 of the Borough of Queens **1899** Transferred to new county of Nassau with the exception of the Rockaway peninsula	Arverne (v) Atlantic Baldwin(s) Bellmore Cedarhurst East Hempstead East Meadow East Rockaway Far Rockaway (v) Floral Park Fosters Meadows Franklin Square Freeport (v) Garden City Greenwich Point Hempstead (v) Hempstead Plains Hewlett Inwood Island Trees Jerusalem Lawrence (v)	* Called Heemstede by the Dutch, Hempstead by the English • Arverne inc. 1895 as Village of Arverne-on-Sea, dissolved 1899; part of Rockaway peninsula which remains in Queens County • Baldwin(s) formerly Baldwin(s)ville, Foxborough, Hicks Neck, and Millburn Corners • Bellmore included former Bridge Haven and New Bridge • East Rockaway formerly Near Rockaway • Village of Far Rockaway inc. 1888, dissolved 1899; part of Rockaway peninsula which remains in Queens County • Floral Park formerly Hinsdale, on North Hempstead and Flushing town lines • Fosters Meadows—also see Springfield in Town of Jamaica • Village of Freeport inc. 1853; formerly Hempstead South, Raynortown, Raynorville, and Rum Point • Greenwich Point also Greenwich and Greenville Point • Village of Hempstead inc. 1853 • Hempstead Plains, former large tract of grassland on north side of Town of Hempstead and south side of Town of North Hempstead, also Salisbury Plains • Hewlett also Fenhurst and Hewletts; formerly Cedar Grove • Inwood formerly Westville or North West Point • Village of Lawrence inc. 1897

(Hempstead continued on next page)

Towns (and Cities)	Villages and other Settlements	Notes
Hempstead (continued)	Long Beach Lynbrook Merrick Mil(l)burn Munson New Bridge New Hyde Park Norwood Ocean Point Oceanside Rockaway Beach (v) Rockville Centre (v) Seaford Smithville South Uniondale Valley Stream Wantagh Washington Square Woodmere Woodsburgh	• Long Beach now a city • Lynbrook formerly Pearsalls or Pearsalls Corner(s) • Merrick also Merie, Merilohe, and Moroke • New Bridge formerly Little Neck, later part of Bellmore • New Hyde Park, formerly Hyde Park; on North Hempstead town line • Norwood also Woodfield, now Malverne in Nassau County • Oceanside formerly South Bay, Christian Hook, Oceanville, also Ocean Side • Village of Rockaway Beach inc. 1897, dissolved 1899; inlcuded Hammels and Holland(s); part of Rockaway peninsula which remains in Queens County • Village of Rockville Centre inc. 1893 • Seaford was Jerusalem South until 1866, also Atlanticville, Verity Town, and Seamans Neck • Smithville South formerly Smithville • Uniondale formerly Turtle Hook • Valley Stream included former Brookfield • Wantagh formerly Jerusalem and Ridgewood
Jamaica * 1656 Land patent granted to English settlers by government of New Netherland 1664 Part of English colonial jurisdiction of the North Riding of Yorkshire 1683 Formed part of original Queens County; major migration of Dutch families from Kings County began at about this time 1788 Recognized as a town by State of New York 1898 Town dissolved; became ward 4, Borough of Queens, New York City	Centerville Clarenceville Dunton East Jamaica Hollis Hopedale Jamaica (v) Jamaica Heights Little Plains Morris Park Ozone Park Queens Richmond Hill (v) South Woodhaven Springfield Unionville The Raunt Willow Tree Woodhaven	* Called Rustdorp by Dutch, and Crawford and Jamaica by English • Clarenceville included in Village of Richmond Hill 1894 • Dunton also West Jamaica • East Jamaica also Hillside • Hopedale on Newtown town line; now part of Kew Gardens • Jamaica was Queens County seat 1683–1787 (also see Queens County Timeline); Village of Jamaica inc. 1814, dissolved 1898 • Morris Park included in Village of Richmond Hill 1894 • Queens, formerly Brushville, now Queens Village • Village of Richmond Hill inc. 1894, dissolved 1898; on Newtown town line • South Woodhaven now Aqueduct • Springfield now Springfield Gardens; eastern section formerly part of Fosters Meadows, Town of Hempstead • Woodhaven formerly Woodville
Long Island City * 1870 Formed as a city from Town of Newtown 1898 City dissolved; became ward 1, Borough of Queens, New York City	Astoria (v) Blissville Dutch Kills Hunters Point Long Island City Middleto(w)n North Brother Island Ravenswood South Brother Island Steinway Sunnyside The Bowery	* Long Island City was Queens County seat 1877–1898 (also see Queens County Timeline) • Village of Astoria inc. 1839 and dissolved 1870 when it became part of Long Island City • North Brother Island now in Bronx County, transferred to New York County 1881 • South Brother Island now in Bronx County, transferred 1964 • The Bowery also Bowery Bay

Towns (and Cities)	Villages and other Settlements	Notes
Newtown **1642** New Netherland granted patent for English settlement at Mespat, joining Dutch and English farmers already in area **1652** Patent rights extended to new English settlement at Middelburg **1662** Middelburg renamed Hastings after changing allegiance from New Netherland to Connecticut **1664** Hastings and adjacent settlements combined to form Town of Newtown, part of English colonial jurisdiction of the West Riding of Yorkshire **1667** Received patent from Governor Nicolls **1683** Formed part of original Queens County **1788** Recognized as a town by State of New York **1870** Daughter city Long Island City created; included Village of Astoria and hamlets of Blissville, Bowery Bay, Dutch Kills, Hunters Point, Middleto(w)n, Ravenswood, Steinway, and Sunnyside **1898** Town dissolved; became ward 2, Borough of Queens, New York City	2 Brothers Islands Astoria (v) Berlin Blissville Bowery Bay Charlotteville Columbusville Corona Cypress Avenue Dutch Kills East Williamsburgh Fort Stevens Fresh Pond Glendale Hopedale Hunters Point Jackson Heights Laurel Hill Lawrenceville Linden Hill(s) Locust Grove Maspeth Melvina Middleto(w)n Middle Village New Astoria Newtown Newtown Landing Penny Bridge Ravenswood Richmond Hill (v) Ridgewood Rikers Island South Williamsburgh Steinway St. Ronans Well Sunnyside Whitepot Winantsville Winfield (Junction) Woodside	• 2 Brothers Islands also North Brother Island and South Brother Island became part of Long Island City 1870 • Village of Astoria inc. 1839, dissolved 1870; formerly Hallets Cove; became part of Long Island City in 1870 • Blissville and Dutch Kills become part of Long Island City in 1870 • Bowery Bay also The Bowery, formerly the Armen Bouwery, Dutch Reformed Church farm for support of the poor; became part of Long Island City 1870 • Charlotteville or North Woodside former names for part of Woodside • Columbusville former name of part of Maspeth • Corona also West Flushing • Cypress Avenue named for railroad station • East Williamsburgh former name for part of Ridgewood • Hopedale on Jamaica town line; now part of Forest Hills • Hunters Point formerly Dominies Hook, became part of Long Island City 1870 • Jackson Heights formerly Trains Meadow • Linden Hills—the cemetery still exists; there is now a different Linden Hills in Flushing • Maspeth also Mashpeag, Mespat, Mispat, and English Kills • Middleto(w)n, Ravenswood, Steinway, and Sunnyside became part of Long Island City in 1870 • Middle Village includes former Juniper Swamp • Newtown renamed Elmhurst 1896 • Village of Richmond Hill inc. 1894, dissolved 1898; on Jamaica town line • Ridgewood extends into Kings County; towns of Newtown and Bushwick both laid claim to area, in 1708 colonial governor declared neither owned the land; also Evergreen and Old Germania Heights • Rikers Island formerly Hewletts Island; transferred to New York County 1884, and to Bronx County 1914; jail located here since 1832 • Whitepot now Forest Hills and Rego Park • Winfield (Junction) former name for part of Woodside

Towns (and Cities)	Villages and other Settlements	Notes
North Hempstead * (See Nassau County from 1899) 1784 Formed in Queens County from Town of Hempstead 1788 Recognized as a town by State of New York 1899 Transferred to new county of Nassau	Albertson Bar Beach Brookdale Carl(e) Place Clowesville East Williston Farmers Village Floral Park Flower Hill Glenwood Landing Great Neck Hempstead Plains Herricks Lakeville Manhasset Mineola New Cassel New Hyde Park North Roslyn Old Westbury Plattsdale Port Washington Red Ground Roslyn Sands Point Searingtown Thomaston Westbury	* County seat in North Hempstead west of present-day Mineola 1787–1877 (also see Queens County Timeline) • Carle Place also Frog Hollow • Clowesville also North Hempstead or Queens Court House, site of county courthouse 1787–1877 (also see Queens County Timeline); now Garden City Park in Nassau County • East Williston formerly North Side and Williston • Floral Park formerly Hinsdale, on Flushing and Hempstead town lines • Glenwood Landing formerly Duck Cove, Motts Cove, and Glenwood; on Oyster Bay town line • Great Neck also Madnans Neck • Hempstead Plains, former large tract of grassland south side of Town of North Hempstead and on north side of Town of Hempstead, also Salisbury Plains • Lakeville formerly Success • Manhasset formerly Tan Yard and Cow Neck • Mineola formerly Hempstead Branch; named Mineola in 1858 • New Hyde Park, formerly Hyde Park; on Hempstead town line • North Roslyn also Bulls Head • Port Washington formerly Cow Bay, on Cow Neck penisula • Roslyn formerly Hempstead Harbor, part formerly Montrose • Westbury formerly Woodedge
Oyster Bay (See Nassau County from 1899) 1653 Purchased from American Indians by English settlers, not affiliated with any colony 1664 Part of English colonial jurisdiction of the North Riding of Yorkshire 1667 Town patent granted by Governor Nicolls 1683 Formed part of original Queens County 1788 Recognized as a town by State of New York 1886 Lloyds Neck ceded to Town of Huntington, Suffolk County 1899 Transferred to new county of Nassau	Bayville Bedelltown Bethpage Brookville Brushy Plains Centre Island Cold Spring Harbor Cove Neck Dosoris East Norwich Farmingdale Glen Cove Glen Head	• Bayville formerly Oak Neck and Pine Island • Bethpage originally a large area including Farmingdale and Plainedge; in early 1850s renamed Jerusalem Station, and in 1867 Central Park • Brookville formerly Wolver Hollow • Brush Plains also Brushy Plains, shared with Town of Babylon, Suffolk County • Centre Island formerly Hog Island, Hog Neck Island, and Barnums Island • Cold Spring Harbor also Cold Spring; mostly in Town of Huntington, Suffolk County • Dosoris in City of Glen Cove after 1917 • East Norwich formerly Norwich • Farmingdale formerly Hardscrabble; originally part of Bethpage • Glen Cove formerly Musquito Cove, Moscheto Cove, Musketa Cove, also sometimes Pembroke and The Place, renamed Glen Cove in 1834; see City of Glen Cove in Nassau County • Glen Head formerly part of Cedar Swamp and Greenvale; sometimes Glenhead

(Oyster Bay continued on next page)

Towns (and Cities)	Villages and other Settlements	Notes
Oyster Bay (continued)	Glenwood Landing Greenvale Hicksville Jericho Killingworth Lattingtown Laurelton Lloyd(s) Neck Locust Valley Massapequa Matinecock Mill Neck Oyster Bay Pine Hollow Piping Rock Plainedge Plainview Sea Cliff (v) Syosset The Cove Wheatley Woodbury	• Glenwood Landing formerly Duck Cove, Motts Cove, Glenwood; on North Hempstead town line • Greenvale formerly Little Plains, Cedar Swamp • Jericho also Lusum, Springfield, and The Farms; part formerly Tappentown • Killingworth, also Cillingworth and Kenilworth, early names for Underhill and adjacent properties in old Matinecock • Lloyd(s) Neck formerly Caumsett, Horse Neck, and Manor of Queens Village (manor granted to James Lloyd 1685/6); ceded to Town of Huntington, Suffolk County, in 1886 • Locust Valley formerly Buckram • Massapequa, also South Oyster Bay, Fort Neck • Matinecock formerly the north shore of Oyster Bay west of Mill Neck, not same as the present incorporated village • Oyster Bay formerly also Town Spot • Plainedge originally part of Bethpage, includes former Williamsville • Plainview formerly Mannetto Hill, renamed 1885 • Village of Sea Cliff inc. 1883, formerly Littleworth • Syosset formerly Little East Woods • Woodbury formerly East Woods
South Hempstead Name for Town of Hempstead 1784–1796		

Place names 1898–present

Many of the names of early cities, towns, villages, and settlements listed in the preceding gazetteer, have survived as neighborhood names—although their boundaries may have changed. Sources consulted to compile this list of neighborhoods and communities are identified in the introduction to Part Two; they include the Community Portal of the New York City Department of City Planning, the Geographic Names Information System (GNIS), and the New York State Department of Health Gazetteer, 2007.

Arverne	Fresh Meadows	New Hyde Park
Astoria	Fresh Pond	North Corona
Astoria Heights	Glen Oaks	North Springfield
Auburndale	Glendale	Gardens
Bay Terrace	Hamilton Beach	Oakland Gardens
Bayside	Hammels	Old Howard Beach
Bayswater	Hillcrest	Ozone Park
Beechhurst	Hillside	Pomonok
Bellaire	Hollands	Queens Village
Belle Harbor	Hollis	Queensboro Hill
Bellerose	Hollis Hills	Ravenswood
Bellerose Manor	Holliswood	Rego Park
Blissville	Howard Beach	Richmond Hill
Breezy Point	Hunters Point	Ridgewood
Briarwood	Jackson Heights	Rochdale
Broad Channel	Jamaica	Rockaway Park
Brooklyn Manor	Jamaica Center	Rockaway Point
Brookville	Jamaica Estates	Rosedale
Bushwick Junction	Jamaica Hills	Roxbury
Cambria Heights	Kew Gardens	Saint Albans
Clearview	Kew Gardens Hills	Seaside
College Point	Kissena Park	Somerville
Corona	Laurel Hill	South Corona
Corona Heights	Laurelton	South Jamaica
Douglaston	Lefrak City	South Ozone Park
Downtown Flushing	Linden Hill	Springfield Gardens
Dutch Kills	Lindenwood	Steinway
East Elmhurst	Little Neck	Sunnyside
Edgemere	Locust Manor	Sunnyside Gardens
Elmhurst	Long Island City	The Rockaways
Far Rockaway	Malba	Utopia
Floral Park	Maspeth	Waldheim
Flushing	Middle Village	Whitestone
Forest Hills	Mott Creek	Willets Point
Forest Hills Gardens	Murray Hill	Woodhaven
Forest Park	Neponsit	Woodside

Repositories and Resources

Note on Queens County

Queens County has extensive town records; selected ones are listed under town records, below. The original records are preserved and available on microfilm at the Municipal Archives of the City of New York (MUNI). The microfilmed records cover Flushing, Jamaica, and Newtown. See detailed lists in Estelle Guzik's *Genealogical Resources in New York*.

NEW YORK STATE CENSUS RECORDS

See also chapter 3, Census Records

County originals at Queens County Supreme Court, Jamaica: 1892, 1915 and 1925 (1825, 1835, 1845, 1855, 1865, 1875, and 1905 are lost)

State originals at the NYSA: 1915, 1925

Microfilm at the FHL, NYPL, and NYSL; many years are online at *FamilySearch.org* and *Ancestry.com*.

Early Censuses

For 1698, 1771 and 1781 published census lists, see Blank, Gardner, Harris, Macy, and O'Callaghan in Abstracts, Indexes & Transcriptions, below.

NATIONAL/STATEWIDE REPOSITORIES & RESOURCES

See chapter 16

CITYWIDE REPOSITORIES AND RESOURCES

Vital records for Queens are generally held at the Municipal Archives of New York City (MUNI). For a description of MUNI and other resources that pertain to all five boroughs, see Citywide Repositories & Resources in the introduction to the Borough Guides. See chapter 2, Vital Records for details on early town vital records.

COUNTYWIDE REPOSITORIES & RESOURCES

Queens County Clerk
88-11 Sutphin Blvd. • Jamaica, NY 11435 • (718) 298-0609
www.nycourts.gov/courts/11jd/queensclerk/index.shtml
(see the German Genealogy and Italian Genealogical indexes)

Court records; naturalization records 1906–1941; New York state census 1892, 1915 and 1925; no land records. *FamilySearch.org* "New York County Naturalization Records" includes Queens County declarations of intention 1824–1926, petitions for naturalization 1794–1906, indexes 1794–1941. For some court records see Onderdonk's "Notes," in Abstracts, Indexes & Transcriptions, below.

Queens County Surrogate's Court
88-11 Sutphin Blvd. • Jamaica, NY 11435 • (718) 298-0400 or 298-0500
Email: qnssurr-info@courts.state.ny.us

Holds probate records from 1787 to the present. The NYSA holds most probate records prior to 1787. *FamilySearch.org* "New York Probate Records" includes an index 1787–1987, wills and letters of administration 1787–1916, proceedings 1830–1865, accounts 1800–1888; "Queens County Probate Files" contains similar record categories with some different date ranges, and mixed proceedings 1899–1932. See also NYPL microfilm: indexes 1787–1923, wills 1787–1881 (including personal wills 1835–1898), letters of administration 1787–1916, probate proceedings 1830–1865, accounts 1800–1880. See also chapter 6, Probate Records.

Office of the City Register: Borough of Queens

Queens Business Center • 144-06 94th Avenue • Jamaica, NY 11435

Holdings include land records, deeds 1683–present, mortgages 1754–present. Available microfilm: FHL deeds to 1886 and indexes to 1951; NYPL deeds to 1850, indexes to 1950; Queens Library Archives deeds to 1806, mortgages 1754–1815. Microfilm of pre-1899 records at the Nassau County Clerk's office and Hofstra University Long Island Room Studies Institute. No records online. Hold Brooklyn Real Property books; microfilm/microfiche available at the Brooklyn office.

Board of Elections, Queens County

126-06 Queens Boulevard • Kew Gardens, NY 11415
(718) 730-6730 • (718) 797-8800

Queens voter registration records 1957–present. Records 1949–1956 are missing. Earlier records at MUNI.

Public Libraries in Queens County

Queens Library, formerly the Queens Borough Public Library, is an independent library and not part of the New York Public Library. It has 62 libraries, plus seven adult learning centers. Genealogical holdings are kept at the Central Library; see The Archives at Queens Library. Online catalog, including the manuscripts catalog at *www.queenslibrary.org.*

The Archives at Queens Library

Central Library • 89-11 Merrick Boulevard • Jamaica, NY 11432
(718) 990-0770 • *www.queenslibrary.org/research/archives*

Extensive holdings of the Archives (formerly the Long Island Collection or Division) include books and manuscripts, city directories (various locations and years, 1796–1934), court records on microfilm, genealogies, local histories, maps, military materials (manuscript and other), serial publications, newspapers (various 1835–present), photographs, broadsides, wills and probate on microfilm, town records on microfilm, and vertical files documenting the history of all of Long Island (Kings, Queens, Nassau, and Suffolk counties) from the 17th century to the present. See also Moorhouse in Other Resources in the Long Island Print and Online Resources for finding aids of items. See Herbert F. Seversmith and Kenn Styker-Rodda's *Long Island Genealogical Source Material (A Bibliography)*. Examples of the extensive manuscript collection: Abstracts of deeds—4 libers 1683–1785; WPA guide for Surrogates Court 1787–1835; WPA guide to Queens County wills; an index of Queens County wills; Brooklyn: Registry, 5th election district, 18th ward for 1877; Suffolk County Cemetery listings, 7 vols.

Queens Borough Historian

While not authorized to answer genealogical inquiries; the borough historian can provide historical information and research advice. Contact the Queens borough president's office or see contact information on the website of the Association of Public Historians of New York State at *www.aphnys.org.*

Queens Historical Society

Weeping Beech Park • 143-135 37th Avenue • Flushing, NY 11354
(718) 939-0647 • Email: queenshistoricalsociety@verizon.net
www.queenshistoricalsociety.org

Holdings include manuscripts 1700s–present, maps 1820–present, and photographs 1850–present. Certain collections are available online.

Queens Museum

New York City Building • Flushing Meadows Corona Park
Queens, NY 11368 • (718) 592-9700
Email: info@queensmuseum.org • *queensmuseum.org*

The Panorama of the City of New York, originally created for the 1964–1965 World's Fair and last updated in 1992, shows 895,000 buildings, streets, parks, bridges, and encompasses the 320 square miles of New York City.

La Guardia Community College/CUNY: La Guardia and Wagner Archives: Queens Local History Collection

31-10 Thomson Ave., Room E-238 • Long Island City, NY 11101
(718) 482-5065 • *www.laguardiawagnerarchive.lagcc.cuny.edu*

Selected documents are available online. The entire collection is searchable online.

Cemeteries

Queens County has numerous cemeteries, some established to in order to relocate then-New York City (Manhattan) cemeteries. See chapter 9, Cemetery Records, table 1, for a selected list of Queens cemeteries with their website addresses.

LOCAL REPOSITORIES & RESOURCES
Alphabetized by location

Bayside Historical Society

208 Totten Avenue • Fort Totten • Bayside, NY 11359 • (718) 352-1548
Email: info@baysidehistorical.org • *www.baysidehistorical.org*

The Society is headquartered in the Fort Totten of the Civil War. Holdings include genealogies, business records, directories, diaries and correspondence, ephemera, films and sound recordings, maps, personal papers, scrapbooks, and yearbooks.

Douglaston/Little Neck Historical Society

328 Manor Road • Douglaston, NY 11363 • (718) 225-4403
www.dlnhs.org

Holdings include drawings, maps and blueprints, photographs, and artifacts.

Barnes Historical Society

JFK Station • PO Box 300049 • Jamaica, NY 11430-0049
(718) 658-2515

The Society is conducting an oral history project documenting the lives of local African Americans.

King Manor Museum

Mailing address: 90-04 161st Street, Suite 704 • Jamaica, NY 11432
(718) 206-0545 • contact@kingmanor.org • *kingmanor.org*
Museum: King Park, 150-03 Jamaica Avenue • Jamaica, NY

The museum is the former home of the King family. Archival materials include books and pamphlets, diaries and journals, drawings and prints, ledgers, letters, photographs and postcards, scrapbooks, and ephemera relating to the history of Jamaica and the King family from the 18th to 20th centuries.

Greater Astoria Historical Society

Quinn Building • 35-20 Broadway, 4th Floor
Long Island City, NY 11106 • (718) 278-0700
Email: info@astorialic.org • *www.astorialic.org*

Website contains digitized photographs, maps, and other images.

Richmond Hill Historical Society and Archival Museum

85-03 114 Street • Richmond Hill, NY 11418 • (718) 704-9317
Email: richmond.hill.historical@gmail.com • *www.richmondhillhistory.org*

Website includes church histories, list of former street names, maps, videos, photographs, and general local history.

Greater Ridgewood Historical Society, Vander Ende-Onderdonk House, and Queens Genealogy Workshop
1820 Flushing Avenue • Ridgewood, NY 11385 • (718) 456-1776
Email: info@onderdonkhouse.org • onderdonkhouse.org

Archives include genealogies, books, photographs, surname files, and other materials relating to the history of Long Island.

Newtown Historical Society
1883 Stockholm Street • Ridgewood, NY 11385 • (718) 366-3715
Email: newtownhistory@gmail.com • www.newtownhistorical.org

The Society does not provide genealogical research services. Website includes photographs and maps, publications, and the *Annals of Newtown*, from 1852.

SELECTED PRINT AND ONLINE RESOURCES

Below is a selection of resources relevant for research in this county. The list is representative, not exhaustive. Additional titles—particularly of abstracts, indexes, transcriptions, and local histories—are available; consult the introduction to Part Two for further information. For guidance on how to identify and locate community directories and local newspapers, see chapter 11, City Directories, and chapter 12, Newspapers, in Part One of this book.

Many additional Queens resources are identified in Scott and Stryker-Rodda, *Long Island Genealogical Source Material*. See also Citywide Repositories and Resources and Long Island Print and Online Resources in this book. See the Nassau County Guide for resources pertaining specifically to that county.

Abstracts, Indexes & Transcriptions

Betts, The Rev. Beverley R., et al., eds. "The Register Book for the Parish of Jamaica Kept by the Rev. Thomas Poyer, Rector from 1710 to 1732," *NYG&B Record*, vol. 19 (1888) no. 1: 5–12, no. 2: 53–59. [NYG&B eLibrary]

Blank, John A., comp. "Census of 1781 [Part of Oyster Bay]," *Nassau County Historical Journal*, vol. 13, no. 1 (1951): 1–9; vol. 13, no. 2 (1952): 39–52.

Canfield, Amos. "Abstracts of Early Wills of Queens County, New York, Recorded in Libers A and C of Deeds, Now in the Register's Office at Jamaica, New York." *NYG&B Record*, vol. 65 (1934) no. 2: 114–120, no. 3: 245–251, no. 4: 319–328. [NYG&B eLibrary] Continued in Eardeley, below.

Case, Dudley. "Personal Wills 1835–1875." Typescript, 1940. Queens Library, New York. See also abstracts by MacCormick and Sawyer, below.

Case, Dudley, and Walter Beck. "Wills of Real Estate, Queens County, New York." 6 vols. Typescript, 1937–1939. Queens Library, New York. Microfilm at NYPL. Covers 1787–1852. See also abstracts by MacCormick and Sawyer, below.

Daughters of the American Revolution, comps. *New York DAR Genealogical Records Committee Report*. Since 1913 DAR volunteers have transcribed many thousands of unpublished cemetery, church, and town records throughout New York. The reports are at the DAR Library; copies are at the NYSL and the NYPL. The DAR has a searchable name index to all the GRC reports at *http://services.dar.org/Public/DAR_Research/search/?Tab_ID=6*. See Jean Worden's index below for a listing by county of the New York record sets that were transcribed by the DAR before 1998.

Eardeley, William A. D. "Records in the Office of the County Clerk at Jamaica, Long Island, 1680–1781. Wills and Administrations, Guardians and Inventories." 2 vols. Typescript, 1918. NYPL, New

York. A planned vol. 3 was never completed. These records are from the deed books, now in the City Register's office.

Frost, Josephine C. "Baptismal Record of the Reformed Dutch Church at Newtown, Long Island, New York, 1736 to 1846 [and marriages 1835–1846]." Typescript, 1913. NYPL, New York. Copied from manuscript transcriptions by Henry Onderdonk, Jr.

Gardner, Charles Carroll, comp. "Census, 1698, Newtown, Long Island," *The American Genealogist*, vol. 24. no. 3 (1948): 133–137.

Gritman, Charles T. "An Index to Land Records of Queens County, Long Island, New York [Deed libers A–H only]." Typescript, 1920. NYPL, New York.

Harris, Edward Doubleday. "The Hempstead Census of 1698," *NYG&B Record*, vol. 45, no. 1 (1914): 54–68. [NYG&B eLibrary]

Hinshaw, William W., and John Cox, Jr., *Encyclopedia of American Quaker Genealogy*. Vol. 3. New York: Edwards Bros., 1940. Includes New York and Flushing Monthly Meetings. Microfilm of original records available at FHL, NYPL.

Hoff, Henry B. "A New Look at the Newtown (L.I.) Presbyterian Church Records." *New York Researcher*, Winter 2010. Published as a Research Aid on *NewYorkFamilyHistory.org*.

Huntington, Edna, Harriet Stryker-Rodda, and Kenn Stryker-Rodda. "Vital Records from the Long Island Farmer and Queens County Advertiser." 3 vols. Typescript, 1946–1955. Brooklyn Historical Society, New York. Covers 1821–1841.

Kelly, Arthur C. M. *St. James Episcopal Church, Newtown, Queens County, NY, 1803–1888*. Rhinebeck, NY: Kinship Books, 2001.

Ladd, Horatio O. *The Origin and History of Grace Church [Episcopal], Jamaica, New York*. New York: Shakespeare Press, 1914. Includes baptismal records and marriages 1710–1732, 1769–1866, some deaths or burials. Records for 1710–1732 also transcribed in Betts, above.

Lobel, Alexander. "Abstracts of Deeds, Queens County, New York, Libers A to D (1683–1785)." 5 vols. Typescript, 1938–1940. Queens Library, New York. Liber A, 1683–1702/3; Liber B1, 1684–1701; Liber B2, 1703–1714; Liber C, 1714–1724, 1755–1785; Liber D, 1721–1765.

MacCormick, Elizabeth Janet. "Abstracts of Wills, Queens County, NY, 1848–1856." Typescript, n.d. NYPL, New York. Includes index.

MacCormick, Elizabeth Janet, and Marian Otis Reeves. "Burials in Springfield Cemetery, Springfield, L.I., N.Y." Typescript, 1946. NYPL, New York. Arranged alphabetically. [NYG&B eLibrary]

Macy, Harry, Jr. "Newtown Census of 1771." *NYG&B Record*, vol. 117, no. 1 (1986): 7–9. [NYG&B eLibrary]

O'Callaghan, Edmund B. *Documentary History of the State of New-York*. 4 vols. Albany: State of New York, 1849–1851. See vol. 1: 433–437 for the 1698 census for Flushing.

Onderdonk, Henry, Jr. *Documents and Letters Intended to Illustrate the Revolutionary Incidents of Queens County, with Connecting Narratives, Explanatory Notes, and Additions*. New York, 1845. Supplement (called second edition), 1884. Reprinted, New Orleans: Polyanthos, 1976.

———. "Notes on the History of Queens County." *Journal of Long Island History*, vol. 7, nos. 1–2, 1967. Includes "Extracts from Minutes of the Court of Assizes of Queens County 1722 to 1787" from Minutes of General Sessions of the Peace at County Clerk's Office.

———. *Queens County in Olden Times: Being a Supplement to the Several Histories There of.* Jamaica, NY, 1864.

Powell, Charles Underhill, and Alice H. Meigs. *Description of Private and Family Cemeteries in the Borough of Queens.* Jamaica, NY: Long Island Collection, Queens Borough Public Library, 1932.

"Presbyterian Marriages at Jamaica, Queens County, 1775–1848." *NYG&B Record*, vol. 129 (1998) no. 1: 36–42, no. 2: 121–124, no. 3: 170–173; vol. 130 (1999) no. 1: 60–63, no. 2: 89–90, no. 3: 217, no. 4: 301–302; vol. 131 (2000): no. 1: 62–63, no. 2: 146. [NYG&B eLibrary]

Sammis, A. Higbee. "Records of the First Methodist Episcopal Church of Flushing." *NYG&B Record*, vol. 125 (1994) no. 1: 24–29, no 2: 93–95, no. 3: 167–169. Includes marriages 1835–1878. Additional records of this church at NYPL. [NYG&B eLibrary]

Sawyer, Ray C. "Abstracts of Wills, Queens County, subsequent to 1787 [to 1848]." 4 vols. Typescript, 1934–1938. NYPL, New York.

Scott, Kenneth. "Records of St. George's (Episcopal) Church, Flushing, Long Island." *NYG&B Record*, vol. 110 (1979) no. 1: 1–6, no. 2: 67–74, no. 3: 154–163, no. 4: 223–226; vol. 111 (1980) no. 1: 39–50, no. 2: 105–110, no. 3: 164–170; vol. 112 (1981) no. 1: 41–45, no. 2: 106–109, no. 3: 140–144, no. 4: 234–238; vol. 113 (1982) no. 1: 16–20, no. 2: 85–92. Includes marriages 1782–1885, burials 1803–1896, baptismal records 1788–1880. [NYG&B eLibrary]

Stryker-Rodda, Kenn. "Records of the First Reformed Dutch Church of Jamaica, Long Island." Baptismal records 1702–1851, 1871–1876; Marriages 1803–1851, 1871–1876; Members 1786–1887; Deaths 1835–1898. *NYG&B Record*, vol. 105 (1974) no. 1– 4; vol. 106 (1975) no. 1–4; vol. 107 (1976) no. 1–4; vol. 108 (1977) no. 1–4; vol. 109 (1978) no. 1–4; vol. 110 (1979) no. 1–4; vol. 111 (1980) no. 1–4; vol. 112 (1981) no. 1–4. [NYG&B eLibrary] For page numbers, see the Index to Articles in the *Record* by Title and by Author on *NewYorkFamilyHistory.org*.

White, Arthur. "Records of the Presbyterian Church, Newtown (now Elmhurst), Queens County, Long Island, NY. [1709–1882]." *Collections of the New York Genealogical and Biographical Society*, vol. 8, 1928. Previously published in *NYG&B Record*, vols. 55–56 (1924–1925). See also Hoff, "A New Look" [NYG&B eLibrary]

Wilson, John Ewell. "Index of Administrations of Queens County, New York, 1707–1908." Typescript, 1938. Queens Library, New York.

———. "Index to the Wills of Queens County, New York, 1787–1906." Typescript, 1937. Queens Library, New York.

Worden, Jean D. "Book 1, Subject Index." In *Revised Master Index to the New York State Daughters of the American Revolution Genealogical Records Volumes.* Zephyrhills, FL: J. D. Worden, 1998. The Subject Index includes a listing by county of the cemeteries, churches, towns, and other sources of records transcribed by the DAR.

Town Records
Alphabetized by Town

See also Note on Queens County.

Gibbs, Alicia. "Records of the Town of Flushing." 3 vols. Typescript, 1939. Queens Library, New York. Covers 1790–1885. Original records 1790–1896 may be found at MUNI. Earlier records destroyed in 1790 fire.

Henry Onderdonk papers: 1729–1895, Series 1: Historical Manuscripts and Notes. Brooklyn Historical Society, New York. Box 4: Lists from Long Island Towns—Tax Lists, Names from Town Records, Student

Names, Supervisor's Book Extracts, Patentees, 1653–1844. Tax lists include 1784 and 1788 for Flushing, Hempstead, Jamaica, and Oyster Bay; Newtown 1786, Hempstead 1792, 1797. Finding aid available at *http://dlib.nyu.edu/findingaids/html/bhs/arc_045_henry_onderdonk/index.html*.

Fielder, Leland. "Records of the Town of Jamaica." 4 vols. Typescript, 1939. Queens Library, New York. Covers 1749–1897. Original records, 1660–1897 at MUNI.

Frost, Josephine C., ed. *Jamaica, Long Island, Town Records 1656–1751.* 3 vols. Brooklyn: Long Island Historical Society, 1914. Original records 1660–1897 at MUNI.

Historical Records Survey. *Minutes of the Town Courts of Newtown, Long Island, 1656–1690.* Work Projects Administration, 1940–1941. [Ancestry.com] Original records 1692–1897 (with gaps) available at MUNI.

Historical Records Survey. *Town Minutes of Newtown 1653–1734.* Work Projects Administration, 1940.

Other Resources

Beers, F. W. *Atlas of Long Island, New York, from Recent and Actual Surveys and Records.* New York, 1873.

Copquin, Claudia Gryvatz. *The Neighborhoods of Queens.* New York: Citizens Committee for New York City, 2007.

Erhardt, Davis, et al. *A Short Guide to Genealogical Sources in the Official Government Records in the Borough of Queens.* New York: n.p., 1971.

Guzik, Estelle, ed. *Genealogical Resources in New York.* New York: Jewish Genealogical Society, 2003. Pages 250–265 have detailed descriptions of holdings of major Queens County repositories.

History of Queens County, New York, with Illustrations, Portraits, and Sketches of Prominent Families and Individuals. New York, 1882.

Hobart, George H. *The Negro Churches of the Borough of Queens, New York City: A Study Made in 1931.* New York: Greater New York Federation of Churches, 1931.

Kross, Jessica. *The Evolution of an American Town: Newtown, New York 1642–1775.* Philadelphia: Temple University Press, 1983.

Liberman, Janet E. *City Limits: A Social History of Queens.* Dubuque, IA: Kendall Hunt Publishing, 1983.

MacMaster, Frank J. *Queens in the Civil War.* Queens, NY: F. J. MacMaster, 1960.

Macy, Harry, Jr. "Religious Records of Queens and Nassau Counties," *NYG&B Newsletter* (now *New York Researcher*), Spring 2003. Updated June 2011 and published a Research Aid on *NewYorkFamilyHistory.org*. Identifies religious records not listed under Abstracts, Indexes & Transcriptions, above.

New York Historical Resources Center. *Guide to Historical Resources in Queens County, New York, Repositories.* Ithaca, NY: Cornell University, 1988.

Onderdonk, Henry, Jr. *History of the Reformed Dutch Church of Jamaica, Long Island.* Jamaica, NY, 1884.

Peyer, Jean B. *Jamaica, Long Island, 1656–1776, A Study of the Roots of American Urbanism.* PhD diss., City University of New York, 1974.

Portrait and Biographical Record of Queens County (Long Island). New York, 1896.

Riker, James. *The Annals of Newtown in Queens County, New-York: Containing Its History from Its First Settlement, Together with Many Interesting Facts Concerning the Adjacent Towns: Also, a Particular Account of Numerous Long Island Families Now Spread Over This and Various Other States of the Union.* New York, 1852.

Scott, Kenneth, and Kenn Stryker-Rodda. *Long Island Genealogical Source Material.* Arlington, VA: National Genealogical Society, 1962. Identifies numerous sources not listed here.

Seyfried, Vincent F. *300 Years of Long Island City, 1630–1930.* Garden City, NY: V. F. Seyfried, 1984.

Seyfried, Vincent F., and Jon A. Peterson. *A Research Guide to the History of the Borough of Queens, New York City: Historical Sketches, Population Data, Chronologies, Bibliography, and Other Aids.* Flushing, NY: Department of History, Queens College, City University of New York, 1987.

Sherman, Franklin J. *Building Up Greater Queens Borough: An Estimate of Its Development and the Outlook.* New York: The Brooklyn Biographical Society, 1929.

Ullitz, Hugo. *Atlas of the Borough of Queens, City of New York.* New York: E. Belcher Hyde, 1907.

Von Skal, Georg. *Illustrated History of the Borough of Queens, New York City.* Flushing, NY: Flushing Journal, 1908.

Waller, Henry D. *History of the Town of Flushing.* Flushing, NY, 1899.

Warren, Wini, and James Driscoll. *Angels of Deliverance: The Underground Railroad in Queens, Long Island, and Beyond.* Flushing, NY: Queens Historical Society, 1999.

Additional Online Resources

Ancestry.com

There are vast numbers of records on *Ancestry.com* that pertain to people who have lived in New York State. See chapter 16 for a description of *Ancestry.com*'s resources and its partnership with the New York State Archives. A search of the online card catalog by county may reveal lesser known resources that pertain to a locality, such as town records, abstracts, transcriptions, city directories, and local histories. Chapter 2, Vital Records, provides detailed information on Queens birth, marriage, and death records accessible on *Ancestry.com*.

Brooklyn Genealogy Information Page

http://bklyn-genealogy-info.stevemorse.org—see also Long Island Print and Online Resources

Particular records relating to Queens County include Long Island City birth and death extracts, history of local post offices, medical directories, ward boundary maps, historic maps, *Daily Star* and *Long Island Star* extracts, information on schools, and house of worship directories.

FamilySearch.org

FamilySearch has extensive collections of New York records, as described in the County Clerk and Surrogate Court entries, above, as well as religious records.

A detailed description of *FamilySearch.org* resources, which include the catalog of the Family History Library, is found in chapter 16.

German Genealogy Group and Italian Genealogical Group

www.germangenealogygroup.org or *www.italiangen.org*

Fre online indexes to NYC vital records, plus Queens County naturalizations in federal Eastern District and county courts. Projects are ongoing. See also the listing in chapter 16. and chapter 2, Vital Records.

NYGenWeb Project: Queens County

www.rootsweb.ancestry.com/~nyqueens

Part of the national, USGenWeb volunteer initiative, the website provides information and resources for county research.

Old Fulton New York Postcards

www.FultonHistory.com

The website provides free access to a vast collection of digitized New York newspapers, including ten titles for current-day Queens County and seven for Nassau.

Queens Genealogical Resources

www.pefagan.com/gen/queens/qnsres1.htm

Guide to Queens related sources with some useful information on repositories and libraries, FHL film numbers, city directories, and other resources.

Borough of Staten Island/Richmond County

County formed	1683
Borough formed	1898
Parent County	Original county
Daughter Counties	None

Major Land Transactions
See chapter 7, Land Records
Bentley Manor 1687; Cassiltown(e) Manor 1687

Map: Staten Island ca. 1860, shows the towns that existed before Richmond County became a New York City borough in 1898.

1609	Island visited by Henry Hudson
1630	The island was acquired from American Indians by Michael Pauw, and became part of land tract known as *Pavonia*; venture failed and land ceded to Dutch West India Company (WIC) in 1636
1636	David deVries obtained possession of Staten Island from Governor van Twiller; settlement began in 1638, but attempt to create a permanent colony was unsuccessful
1640	Cornelis Melijn granted all of Staten Island by Governor General Willem Kieft except a farm reserved for David deVries; Melijn and successors Van Reede and Van der Capellen created settlement at modern Tompkinsville with mostly Dutch colonists; settlement destroyed in 1655 by American Indians
1661	First permanent settlement made by Walloons, French (Huguenots), and Dutch at the Oude Dorp (Old Village)
1664	British captured colony of New Netherland renaming it New York; English colonial jurisdictional divisions known as the Yorkshire Ridings established, lasting until 1683; Staten Island part of West Riding; West Riding court sat at Flatbush 1665–1668 and Gravesend 1668–1683; separate Staten Island "town" court began 1678
1683	• English colony of New York divided into 12 counties • Richmond County established and divided into four judicial precincts: North, South, West, and the (Castleton) Manor; courts held where convenient, but by the early 1700s they were regularly held at Stony Brook
1729	County seat established at Richmond (Richmondtown) in the Town of Southfield
1776–1783	Richmond County occupied by British troops
1788	Towns of Northfield, Southfield, Westfield, and Castleton established by State of New York—the boundaries similar to those of the four precincts
1860	Town of Middletown formed from towns of Northfield and Southfield
1898	The consolidated City of New York created with five boroughs; the towns of Richmond County were dissolved forming the Borough of Richmond, coterminous with Richmond County
1906	On completion of the new Borough Hall, the administration moved from Richmondtown to St. George; the new courthouse in St. George opened in 1919
1975	Name changed from Borough of Richmond to Borough of Staten Island; name of Richmond County remained unchanged

Towns (and Cities)	Villages and other Settlements	Notes
Castleton * 1664 Part of English colonial jurisdiction of the West Riding of Yorkshire 1683 Formed as judicial precinct "The Manor" in Richmond County * 1788 Recognized as a town by State of New York, boundaries similar to 1683 precinct 1860 Daughter town Middletown created 1898 Town dissolved, becomes ward 1, Borough of Richmond, New York City	Butcherville Castleton Corners Centreville Clove Hills Livingston Morganville New Brighton (v) North Shore Sailors Snug Harbor St. George Tompkinsville West New Brighton	* Castleton also The Manor and Castletown * Cassiltown(e) Manor granted 1687 encompassed both the Manor precinct and much of the North precinct • Castleton Corners also Four Corners, formerly Centerville • Centreville see Town of Middletown after 1860 • Livingston also Elliotsville • Village of New Brighton inc. 1866, reinc. 1872 when it was greatly enlarged, dissolved 1898; New Brighton included Elliotsville and Factoryville • St. George originally name of ferry terminal c. 1882, part of New Brighton; became neighborhood name as borough and county municipal buildings relocated here; Staten Island Borough Hall opened 1906 • Tompkinsville on Middletown town line, shared between New Brighton and Edgewater villages • West New Brighton formerly Factoryville; included Cork Town and Silent Village; site of the Cassiltown manor house
Middletown 1860 Formed from towns of Castleton and Southfield 1898 Town dissolved, becomes ward 2, Borough of Richmond, New York City	Centreville Clifton Edgewater (v) Egbert(s)ville New Dorp Stapleton Todt Hill Tompkinsville	• Centreville see Town of Castleton before 1860 • Village of Edgewater inc. 1866 included Clifton, Stapleton, and part of Tompkinsville; reinc. 1870; on Southfield town line; dissolved 1895; Village of Edgewater vital records survive in addition to town records • Egbert(s)ville on Northfield town line; see Southfield before 1860 • New Dorp on Southfield town line • Stapleton in Town of Southfield before 1860 • Tompkinsville on Castleton town line, shared between villages of Edgewater and New Brighton
Northfield * 1664 Part of English colonial jurisdiction of the West Riding of Yorkshire 1683 Formed as judicial precinct "The North Precinct" in Richmond County 1788 Recognized as a town by State of New York, boundaries similar to 1683 precinct 1898 Town dissolved, becomes ward 3, Borough of Richmond, New York City	Bulls Head Chelsea Egbertsville Fresh Kills Graniteville Howland(s) Hook Long Neck Mariners Harbor New Springville Old Place Port Richmond(v)	* Northfield also known as North Quarter • Bulls Head formerly Phoenixville and London Bridge • Egbertsville also Tipperary Corners, New Dublin and Young Ireland; on Southfield town line before 1860, and Middletown town line after 1860 • Graniteville also Granite Village • Howland(s) Hook also Hollins Hook, Hollands Hook, and Jacksonville • New Springville also Springville, formerly Karles or Charles Neck • Old Place formerly Tunissens Creek; used to include Summerville which was formerly called Skunks Town • Village of Port Richmond inc. 1866, dissolved 1898; formerly Bristol and New Bristol; vital records survive in addition to town records (Northfield continued on next page)

Towns (and Cities)	Villages and other Settlements	Notes
Northfield (continued)	Richmondtown Travis The Kills	• Richmondtown also Richmond and Richmond Village; formerly Cucklestowne also Cuckold-stown; on Southfield town line; county seat 1729–1906 • Travis also Decker Town and Travisville; formerly Linoleumville
Southfield * 1661 Permanent Dutch and French settlement of Oude Dorp established 1664 Part of English colonial jurisdiction of the West Riding of Yorkshire 1683 Formed as judicial precinct "The South Precinct" in Richmond County 1788 Recognized as a town by State of New York, boundaries similar to 1683 precinct 1860 Daughter town Middletown created 1898 Town dissolved, becomes ward 4, Borough of Richmond, New York City	Bayview Cedar Grove Clifton Concord Dongan Hill(s) Dover Edgewater (v) Egbertsville Fort Hudson Fort Tompkins Giffords Grant City Linden Park New Dorp Oakwood Oceanville Old Town Oude Dorp Richmondtown Signal Hill South Beach South Side Stapleton Stony Brook	* Southfield also known as South Quarter • Concord formerly Dutch Farms • Dover included Oude Dorp • Village of Edgewater inc. 1866, reinc. 1870, dissolved 1898; on Middletown town line; Village of Edgewater vital records survive in addition to town records • Dongan Hill(s) also Garretsons • Egbert(s)ville on Northfield town line; see Middletown after 1860 • Giffords formerly Newton • Grant City also New Paris and French Town • New Dorp on Middletown town line • Oakwood formerly Court House • Oceanville also Oceana • Old Town located near former Oude Dorp • Oude Dorp (earliest settlement) was located near present day South Beach • Richmondtown also Richmond and Richmond Village; formerly Cucklestowne also Cuckold-stown; on Northfield town line; county seat 1729–1898 • Stapleton in Town of Middletown after 1860 • Stony Brook was the location for courts in early 1700s
Westfield * 1664 Part of English colonial jurisdiction of the West Riding of Yorkshire 1683 Formed as judicial precinct "The West Precinct" in Richmond County 1788 Recognized as a town by State of New York, boundaries similar to 1683 precinct 1898 Town dissolved, becomes ward 5, Borough of Richmond, New York City	Annadale Bentley Bloomfield Greenridge Huguenot Kreischerville Lemon Creek Pleasant Plains Princes Bay Richmond Valley Rossville Sandy Ground Seaside Southside Tottenville (v) Unionville Woodrow	* Westfield also known as West Quarter • Bentley named for Bentley Manor (granted 1687) which was 1163 acres including present-day Tottenville • Bloomfield formerly Merriltown, also Watchogue • Greenridge also Green Ridge; was Marshland formerly Marshall Land, and Kleine Kill • Huguenot formerly Blooming View • Kreischerville also Androvetteville and Charles-town • Lemon Creek also Pleasant Plains • Sandy Ground also Little Africa and Harrisville • Seaside formerly South Side and South Shore, later Eltingville • Village of Tottenville's legal papers for 1869 incorporation reportedly improperly drawn—reincorporated in 1894, dissolved 1898; Village of Tottenville vital records survive in addition to town records; Tottenville also Arentsville

Place names 1898–present

Many of the names of early cities, towns, villages, and settlements listed in the preceding gazetteer, have survived as neighborhood names—although their boundaries may have changed. Sources consulted to compile this list of neighborhoods and communities are identified in the introduction to Part Two; they include the Community Portal of the New York City Department of City Planning, the Geographic Names Information System (GNIS), and the New York State Department of Health Gazetteer, 2007.

Annadale	Fort Wadsworth	Livingston
Arden Heights	Fox Hills	Manor Heights
Arlington	Fresh Kills	Mariner's Harbor
Arrochar	Giffords	Midland Beach
Bay Terrace	Graniteville	Mount Loretta
Bloomfield	Grant (City)	New Brighton
Bulls Head	Grasmere	New Dorp
Butler Manor	Great Kills	New Dorp Beach
Castleton Corners	Greenridge	New Springville
Charleston	Grymes Hill	Oakwood
Chelsea	Gulfport	Oakwood Beach
Clifton	Hamilton Park	Old Place
Concord	Heartland Village	Old Town
Crookers Point	Howland Hook	Park Hill
Dongan Hills	Huguenot (Park)	Pleasant Plains
Egbertville	Kreischerville	Port Ivory
Elm Park	La Tourette	Port Richmond
Eltingville	LightHouse Hill	Prince's Bay
Emerson Hill	Linden Park	Randall Manor
Fairview Heights	Linoleumville	Richmond (Town)

Repositories and Resources

Notes on the Borough of Staten Island/Richmond County

The Borough of Staten Island was named the Borough of Richmond from 1898 to 1975.

Notes on Early Census Records

A census was taken about 1707. See Stillwell and Hatcher in Abstracts, Indexes & Transcriptions below.

NEW YORK STATE CENSUS RECORDS

See also chapter 3, Census Records

County originals at Staten Island Historical Society Library: 1835

County originals at New York City Municipal Archives: 1855, 1865, 1875, 1915, 1925 (1825, 1845, 1892, and 1905 are lost).

State originals at the NYSA: 1915, 1925

Microfilm at the FHL, NYPL, and NYSL; many years are online at *FamilySearch.org* and *Ancestry.com*.

NATIONAL/STATEWIDE REPOSITORIES & RESOURCES

See chapter 16

CITYWIDE REPOSITORIES & RESOURCES

Vital records for Staten Island are held at the Municipal Archives of New York City (MUNI). For a description of MUNI and other resources that pertain to all five boroughs, see Citywide Repositories & Resources in the Introduction to the Borough Guides.

COUNTYWIDE REPOSITORIES & RESOURCES

Richmond County Clerk
130 Stuyvesant Place, 2nd Floor • Staten Island, NY 10301
(718) 675-7700 • *www.richmondcountyclerk.com*

Holdings include court records, land records 1638–present (searchable online), maps, naturalization records 1820–1962 (free online index at *GermanGenealogyGroup.com*, *ItalianGen.org*), and veterans' discharges. *FamilySearch.org* has deeds 1683–1901, mortgages 1756–1851, and indexes to later dates (with gaps); NYPL has copies of FHL films of deeds 1683–1851, mortgages 1754–1800, and indexes to later dates (with gaps).

Richmond County Surrogate's Court
18 Richmond Terrace • Staten Island, NY 10301 • (718) 675-8500
www.nycourts.gov/courts/13jd/surrogates/index.shtml

Holds probate records from 1787 to the present. The NYSA holds most probate records prior to 1787. See also chapter 6, Probate Records. *FamilySearch.org* has wills 1787–1967, Letters of Administration and Guardianship 1787–1866, and index to wills 1787–1931; NYPL has copy of FHL film of wills 1787–1829.

Municipal Archives of the City of New York (MUNI)—Special Staten Island Collections
31 Chambers Street (Manhattan) • New York, NY 10007
(212) 788-8604 • Email: archives@records.nyc.gov
www.nyc.gov/html/records

In addition to vital records and other records noted on MUNI's website, MUNI holds Old Town Records for Castletown, Middletown, Edgewater, Southfield, New Brighton, Northfield, Port Richmond, and Westfield; Staten Island court records 1839–1942; divorce judgments 1861–1920; deeds and mortgages; naturalization records 1820–1940; and miscellaneous records of other kinds. These have been inventoried, but not cataloged, indexed, or filmed. The inventory is in—or shortly will be added to—the NYG&B eLibrary. The College of Staten Island describes the collection at *www.library.csi.cuny.edu/ archives/GuideSIResearch.htm*.

Staten Island Historian
460 Brielle Avenue • Staten Island, NY 10314
Email: sihistorian@aol.com • *www.statenislandhistorian.com*

Website features publications, pictures, maps, and histories of Staten Island American Indians, women, Italians, and place names. It also provides links to resources for genealogical research.

Staten Island Historical Society
Historic Richmond Town
441 Clarke Avenue • Staten Island, NY 10306 • (718) 351-1611
Email: sihs-library@si.rr.com • *www.historicrichmondtown.org*

The Society operates Historic Richmond Town, a living history museum which includes numerous original historic structures, as well as a working farm. Collections include local history and genealogy books, archives of local organizations, land records, licenses, newspapers on microfilm, vital records, the 1835 New York state census for Richmond County, and WPA documentation of Staten Island families (1940s). A collections database is online at *http://statenisland.pastperfect-online.com*.

New York Public Library—Staten Island
St. George Library Center • 5 Central Avenue
Staten Island, NY 10301 • (718) 442-8560

Staten Island is served by the New York Public Library (NYPL) system. A detailed description of NYPL resources is in chapter 16, National and Statewide Repositories & Resources. A list of NYPL branch libraries is at *www.nypl.org/locations*. Some branches have local history, heritage, or other special collections. For example, St. George Library Center has the *Staten Island Advance* on microfilm 1921–present and the *Staten Island Historian*.

Cemeteries
See chapter 9, Cemetery Records, table 1, for a selected list of Staten Island cemeteries with their website addresses.

Other Repositories and Societies

Alice Austen House
Two Hylan Boulevard • Staten Island, NY 10305 • (718) 816-4506
www.aliceausten.org

This historic house museum is the former home of pioneering photographer Alice Austen (1866–1952). The collections include early photographs of Staten Island and New York City. A searchable, online catalog is at *http://aliceausten.org/collection*.

College of Staten Island: Archives and Special Collections
Library, 1L-216 • 2800 Victory Boulevard • Staten Island, NY 10314
(718) 982-4128 • Email: archives@csi.cuny.edu
www.library.csi.cuny.edu/archives/index.htm

Printed materials in all formats (directories, pamphlets, broadsides, maps, and photographs) relevant to understanding the history of Richmond County are collected. The Archives & Special Collections also spearheaded an effort to collect and document the community response to the events of September 11, 2001. This collection includes speeches, photographs, ephemera, and newspaper clippings. The college's guide to Staten Island Research Materials at Other Institutions is at *www.library.csi.cuny.edu/archives/GuideSIResearch.htm*

Friends of Abandoned Cemeteries of Staten Island
158 Myrtle Avenue • Staten Island, NY 10310 • (917) 545-3309
Email: SICemetery@aol.com
www.rootsweb.ancestry.com/~nyrichmo/facsi/index.html
Website includes select cemetery records.

Sailors' Snug Harbor
1000 Richmond Terrace • Staten Island, NY 10301 • (718) 448-2500
snug-harbor.org
Archives: SUNY Maritime College • 6 Pennyfield Avenue
Throggs Neck, NY 10465 • (718) 409-7200 • *www.sunymaritime.edu*

Established in its Staten Island location in 1833, the Sailors' Snug Harbor provided a home and social services to sailors in need for over 140 years. Today its campus of historic buildings, architectural landmarks of national distinction, is operated as a cultural center. Its archives are housed at SUNY Maritime College at Fort Schuyler in the Bronx. A description of the collections is at *http://sunymaritime.edu/ stephenblucelibrary/sailorssnugharbor*.

Sandy Ground Historical Society, Museum & Library
1538 Woodrow Road • Staten Island, NY 10309 • (718) 317-5796
http://sandygroundmuseum.org

Society documents the history of Sandy Ground, a community established by former New York slaves in the early–19th century. Holdings include books, artifacts, film, and photographs.

Staten Island Museum, History Archives & Library
(also known as the Staten Island Institute of Arts and Sciences)
1000 Richmond Terrace • Snug Harbor Campus, Building H
Staten Island, NY 10301 • (718) 727-1135
Email: info@statenislandmuseum.org • *www.statenislandmuseum.org*

Archives include books and periodicals, business records, documents, genealogies, family Bibles, maps, photographs, and postcards from throughout Staten Island's history, as well as the Anthon family interviews of local residents (1840–1865). Collections are searchable online.

Tottenville Historical Society, Research Library & Archives
Library: 19 Winant Place • Staten Island, NY 10309
Society: PO Box 70185 • Staten Island, NY 10307-0185 • (646) 291-7005
Email: info@tottenvillehistory.com • *www.tottenvillehistory.com*

Books, prints, family histories, maps, microfilm, photographs, postcards, ephemera, telephone books, and school yearbooks.

Wagner College
One Campus Road • Staten Island, NY 10301 • (718) 390-3100
www.wagner.edu

The Horrmann Library's holdings include papers of the poet Edwin Markham, who lived on Staten Island; the Sutter Archive, including the archives of the Metropolitan New York Synod of the Evangelical Lutheran Church (see the section on Lutherans in chapter 15); and the college's own archives.

SELECTED PRINT AND ONLINE RESOURCES
Below is a selection of resources relevant for research in this borough. The list is representative, not exhaustive. Additional titles—particularly of abstracts, indexes, transcriptions, and local histories—are available; consult the introduction to Part Two for further information. For guidance on how to identify and locate community directories and local newspapers, see chapter 11, City Directories, and chapter 12, Newspapers, in Part One of this book. Other valuable sources for Staten Island research will be found in the listings of Citywide Repositories and Resources and in the subject-based bibliographies throughout Part One of this book.

Abstracts, Indexes & Transcriptions

Daughters of the American Colonists, Brooklyn Chapter, comp. "Chiefly Bible Records Copied from Those of the Staten Island Hist. Society at Port Richmond, Staten Island, NY." Typescript, 1956. NYPL, New York.

Eichholz, Alice, and James Rose. "Slave Births in Castleton, Richmond County, New York." *NYG&B Record*, vol. 110, no. 4 (1979): 196–197. [NYG&B eLibrary]

Fast, Frances S. "Richmond Co., N.Y.: [Abstracts of] Wills 1787–1863, Letters of Administration and Guardianship 1787–1866," and "Index of Wills and Administrations." Typescripts, n.d. NYPL, New York.

"Federal Census, 1800, Richmond County, New York." *NYG&B Record*, vol. 60, no.4 (1929): 313–325. [NYG&B eLibrary]

Frost, Josephine C. *Cemetery Inscriptions from Richmond, Staten Island, NY.* Typescript, n.d. NYPL, New York.

Hatcher, Patricia Law. "The Staten Island Census, A List Analysis." *NYG&B Record*, vol. 140, no. 4 (2009): 261–271. [NYG&B eLibrary]

Hix, Charlotte Megill. *Staten Island Wills and Letters of Administration: Richmond County, New York, 1670–1800.* Bowie, MD: Heritage Books, 1993. Copies of Richmond County will and administration abstracts are from the New-York Historical Society series *Abstracts of Wills*, by William S. Pelletreau (see chapter 6, Probate Records).

McMillen, Loring. *Transcriptions of the Earliest Court Records of Staten Island, 1668–1688.* Staten Island, NY: Borough Historian, 1989.

New York Genealogical and Biographical Society. *Richmond County Church Surveys.* Digitally published by NYG&B, 2012 [NYG&B eLibrary]. This survey was made in the early-20th century and inventories records held by Italian Calvary Church, All Saints Church, and Church of the Ascension.

New York Historical Resources Center. *Guide to Historical Resources in Richmond County (Staten Island), New York, Repositories.* Ithaca, NY: Cornell University, 1980.

Ojelade, Julie Moody, and Richard L. Dickenson. *Afro-American Vital Records and 20th-Century Abstracts: Richmond County/Staten Island 1915 and 1925.* New York: Sandy Ground Historical Society, 1985.

Salmon, Patricia M. *Realms of History: The Cemeteries of Staten Island.* New York: Staten Island Museum, 2006.

Steinmeyer, Elinor. *Chiefly Bible Records Copied from Those of the Staten Island Hist. Society at Port Richmond, Staten Island, NY.* Brooklyn: New York State Society, Daughters of the American Colonists, Brooklyn Chapter, 1956.

Stillwell, John E., comp. *Historical and Genealogical Miscellany,* Vol. 1. New York, n.p., 1903. Includes Liber A, Richmond Co. Records (1680–1735, see also Hatcher, below); Baptismal Register of the Dutch Church of Staten Island (1696–1745 and 1786–1790, for those years this is a superior version to that in Wright, below); and Census of Staten Island in the Year 1706 (see also Hatcher, above, for dating census 1707.)

Tooker, Holly. "Index to Staten Island Marriages and Deaths in the *New York Herald.*" Typescript, 2000. NYPL, New York.

Vosburgh, Royden Woodward. "Marriage Records of the Reformed Dutch Church on Staten Island [1790–1825]." *NYG&B Record*, vol. 124 (1993) no. 1: 9–12, no. 2: 8–90, no. 3: 157–160, no. 4: 230–232. Copied from Vosburgh's Staten Island Church Records, below. [NYG&B eLibrary]

———. *Staten Island Church Records.* 8 vols. Staten Island Institute of Arts and Sciences, 1922–1925. Records of eight Episcopal, Methodist, and Reformed churches, see list in Harry Macy Jr., "The Vosburgh Collection of New York State Church Records," *NYG&B Newsletter* (now *New York Reasearcher*), Fall 1998. Updated August 2011 and published as a Research Aid on *NewYorkFamilyHistory.org.*

———. *Staten Island Gravestone Inscriptions: Copied in 1923–1924.* New York: Staten Island Institute of Arts and Sciences, 1925.

Worden, Jean D. "Book 1, Subject Index." In *Revised Master Index to the New York State Daughters of the American Revolution Genealogical Records Volumes.* Zephyrhills, FL: J. D. Worden, 1998. The Subject Index includes a listing by county of the cemeteries, churches, towns, and other sources of records transcribed by the DAR.

Wright, Tobias Alexander, ed. *Staten Island Church Records.* Vol. 4 of Collections of the NYG&B Society, 1909. Includes records of the Staten Island Reformed Dutch Church, United Brethren or Moravian Church, and St. Andrew's Episcopal Church. See Vosburgh for later records of the Reformed church and St. Andrew's. See also Stillwell, above. [NYG&B eLibrary, *Ancestry.com*]

Other Resources

Anderson, Albert J. *Indians of Staten Island: Sections of Archaeology and Natural History.* New York: Staten Island Museum, 2000.

Bayles, Richard Mather. *History of Richmond County (Staten Island), New York: From Its Discovery to the Present Time.* New York, 1887. Reprinted, Salem, MA: Higginson Book Company, 1999.

Beers, F. W. *Atlas of Staten Island, Richmond County, New York: From Official Records and Surveys Compiled and Drawn by F. W. Beers.* New York, 1873.

Brooks, Erastus. *Historical Records of Staten Island: Centennial and Bicentennial, for Two Hundred Years and More.* New York, 1883.

Charitis, Christine Victoria. *Staten Island's Greek Community.* Charleston, SC: Arcadia Publishing, 2005.

Clute, J. J. *Annals of Staten Island: From Its Discovery to the Present Time.* New York, 1876. (Extracts of the genealogies comprise Clute's *Old Families of Staten Island.* Baltimore: Genealogical Publishing Co., 2003.)

Dickenson, Richard B. *Census Occupations of Afro-American Families on Staten Island, 1840–1875.* New York: Staten Island Institute of Arts and Sciences, 1981.

———. *Holden's Staten Island: The History of Richmond County: Revised Resource Manual Sketches for the Year 2002.* New York: Center for Migration Studies, 2003.

Du Bois, Theodora. *Staten Island Patroons.* New York: Staten Island Historical Society, 1961.

Eberlein, Harold D. *Manor Houses and Historic Homes of Long Island and Staten Island.* Philadelphia & London: J. B. Lippincott Co., 1928.

Hampton, Vernon B. *Staten Island in Transition: A Timely Capsule of Historical Highlights, Problems and Prospects of New York's "Cinderella" Borough.* New York: Richmondtown Social Studies Project, 1970.

———. *Staten Island's First Permanent Settlement.* New York: Staten Island Historical Society, 1960.

Hatcher, Patricia Law. "Richmond County Deeds, 'Liber A'—A Mystery Solved." *NYG&B Newsletter* (now *New York Researcher*), Winter 1999: 7–8. [NYG&B eLibrary]

Historic Records Survey. *The Earliest Volume of Staten Island Records, 1678–1813.* New York: Work Projects Administration, 1942. Sometimes erroneously called Liber A, see Hatcher, above. [*Ancestry.com*]

Illustrated Sketch Book of Staten Island, New York, Its Industries and Commerce. New York, 1886.

Jackson, Ronald David. *African American History in Staten Island: Slave-holding Families and Their Slaves.* New York: Staten Island Historical Society, 1995.

Kolff, Cornelius G. *A Short History of Staten Island.* Rosebank, NY: The Author, 1926.

Leng, Charles W., and William T. Davis. *Staten Island and Its People, a History, 1609–1933.* New York: Lewis Historical Publishing, 1930. [*Ancestry.com*]

Lundrigan, Margaret. *Irish Staten Island.* Charleston, SC: Arcadia Publishing, 2009.

Matteo, Thomas W. *Staten Island.* Charleston, SC: Arcadia Publishing, 2006.

McMillen, Harlow. *A History of Staten Island, New York, during the American Revolution.* New York: Staten Island Historical Society, 1976.

McMillen, Loring. *Staten Island: The Cosmopolitan Era, from 1898.* New York: Staten Island Historical Society, 1952.

Morris, Ira K. *Morris's Memorial History of Staten Island, New York.* New York: Memorial Publishing, 1900.

Papas, Phillip. *That Ever Loyal Island: Staten Island and the American Revolution.* New York: New York University Press, 2007.

Prominent Men of Staten Island, 1893. New York, 1893.

Robinson, E. *Atlas of the Borough of Richmond, City of New York: From Official Records, Private Plans, and Actual Surveys Compiled by and under the Supervision of E. Robinson.* New York, 1898.

Rosenfeld, Michael, and Charles LaCerra. *Community, Continuity, and Change: New Perspectives on Staten Island History.* New York: Pace University Press, 1999.

Salmon, Patricia M. *Realms of History: The Cemeteries of Staten Island.* New York: Staten Island Museum, 2006.

Steinmeyer, Henry G. *Staten Island, 1524–1898.* New York: Staten Island Historical Society, 1987.

Tango, Jenny. *The Jewish Community of Staten Island.* Charleston, SC: Arcadia Publishing, 2004.

Weintrob, Lori, and Philip Papas. *When New York State Spoke French: The Huguenots and Walloons of Staten Island: A Research Guide.* This publication, sponsored by the NYG&B, is nearing completion and will be added to the NYG&B eLibrary when finished.

Youssef, Nadia Hagg. *Changing Population Dynamics on Staten Island: The Transition from Homogeneity to Racial and Ethnic Diversity.* New York: Center for Migration Studies, 1991.

Additional Online Resources

Ancestry.com

There are vast numbers of records on *Ancestry.com* that pertain to people who have lived in New York State. See chapter 16 for a description of *Ancestry.com*'s resources and its partnership with the New York State Archives. A search of the online card catalog by county may reveal lesser known resources that pertain to a locality, such as town records, abstracts, transcriptions, city directories, and local histories. Chapter 2, Vital Records, provides detailed information on Staten Island birth, marriage, and death records accessible on *Ancestry.com*.

FamilySearch.org

FamilySearch has extensive collections of New York records, including religious records, which are searchable by name and location, but not by county. The following collections include record images (browsable, but not searchable) that are organized by county:

- "New York, Land Records, 1630–1975." Includes land and property records. *familysearch.org/search/collection/2078654*
- "New York, Probate Records, 1629–1971." Includes wills, letters of administration, and guardianship papers. *familysearch.org/search/collection/1920234*

For both collections, choose the browse option and then select Richmond to view the available records sets as described in the County Clerk and Surrogate Court entries, above. A detailed description of *FamilySearch.org* resources, which include the catalog of the Family History Library, is found in chapter 16.

German Genealogy Group and Italian Genealogical Group
GermanGenealogyGroup.com or *ItalianGen.org*

Free, online indexes to New York City vital records and Richmond County Naturalizations.

NYGenWeb Project: Richmond County
www.rootsweb.ancestry.com/~nyrichmo

Part of the national, USGenWeb volunteer initiative, the website provides information and resources for county research.

Old Staten Island: Staten Island History
www.statenislandhistory.com

The website of John Louis Sublett, who has authored six books on Staten Island, has historical photographs, timelines, and a wide variety of information on people and places in the borough's history.

Long Island

Counties:
Kings County
Queens County
Nassau County
Suffolk County

The name "Long Island" derives from "Lange Eylandt" which dates from no later than the mid-17th century. Surrounded by water, it is the largest island in the continental United States. Until 1883 when the Brooklyn Bridge was built, the only way to get to Long Island was by boat. Today, Long Island is comprised of Kings, Queens, Nassau and Suffolk counties.

Long Island was first settled in the 17th century. By the 1650 Treaty of Hartford, a line was drawn just west of Oyster Bay, between Dutch New Netherland to the west and English settlements mostly tied to Connecticut. Lion Gardiner acquired the adjacent Gardiners Island in 1637, and English settlers founded towns in present-day Suffolk County as well as Oyster Bay. In the New Netherland portion of the island there were both Dutch and English settlements.

When the British took over New Netherland in 1664, all of Long Island became part of the newly-created Yorkshire. In 1683 Yorkshire was abolished and Long Island was divided into Kings, Queens, and Suffolk counties. The English designated the islands in Long Island Sound as part of New York, which explains why Fishers Island is part of New York rather than Connecticut.

Largely rural until the early-19th century, when western Long Island began to develop rapidly and identify economically with New York City, the whole of Long Island as a place had a singular identity. For decades, it was mainly agricultural, incorporating some industry, for example shipbuilding and whaling. As the population grew, the western portion became densely urban and industrialized, and outlying areas became more suburban.

"Long Island" has never existed as a political entity. In 1898 when the modern, five-borough City of New York was formed, Kings County became the Borough of Brooklyn, the western portion of Queens County became the Borough of Queens, and the eastern portion became the newly created Nassau County in 1899. Today, people referring to Long Island generally mean Nassau and Suffolk counties.

Due to the nearly 400 years of overlapping municipal jurisdictions, genealogists will find that Long Island history, peoples, organizations, publications, and records do not fall neatly into the modern political boundaries. Hence the need for this section.

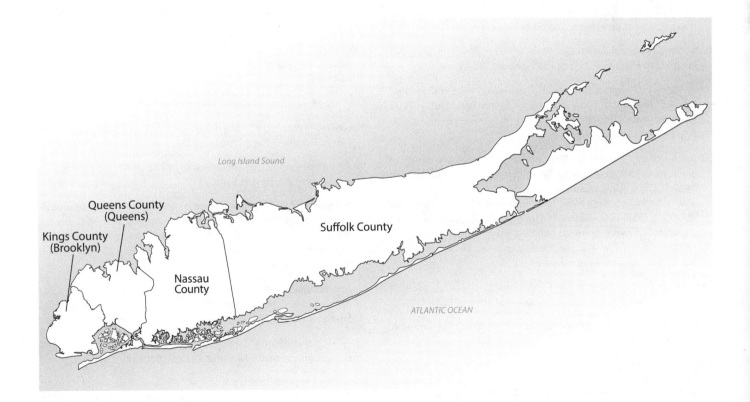

SELECTED PRINT AND ONLINE RESOURCES — LONG ISLAND

In a work of this size it is not possible to include every relevant work, therefore, the following is a sampling of the types of transcriptions, research guides, and published works that are available. See also the respective County Guides for more resources.

Abstracts, Indexes & Transcriptions

Eardeley, William Applebie. *Cemeteries in Kings and Queens Counties, Long Island, New York, 1753–1913*. Brooklyn: n.p., 1916.

Frost, Josephine C. "Long Island Cemetery Inscriptions." 13 vols. Typescript, 1913. NYPL, New York. A list of the more than 100 cemeteries in this series will be found in Seversmith and Stryker-Rodda's *Long Island Genealogical Source Material* (see below), pp. 26–27. [NYG&B eLibrary]

———, comp. "Marriages on Long Island, New York, 1802–1855." Typescript, 1914. NYPL, New York.

Gritman, Charles T. "Genealogical Data of Many Families: Gathered from Numerous Sources, Land Records, Wills & etc. Supplement by Charles T. Gritman, Jr." 3 vols. Typescript, n.d. NYPL, New York.

Harris, Edward D. "Long Island Epitaphs: Kings County, Flatbush, New-Utrecht, Astoria." Manuscript, 1885–1877. NYPL, New York. Autograph manuscript in red and black ink. Transcriptions made between 1877 and 1885. Epitaphs in the ground prior to 1840 only, includes index.

Hoff, Henry B. "Marriage and Death Notices in Long Island Newspapers." *NYG&B Newsletter* (now *New York Researcher*), Summer 1991. Updated December 2000 and published as a Research Aid on *NewYorkFamilyHistory.org*.

LongIslandGenealogy.com—see the listing below for links to transcription of cemeteries and other records.

Long Island Historical Society Quarterly, Brooklyn, New York. Brooklyn: Long Island Historical Society, 1939–present. [FHL]

Macy, Harry Jr. "Religious Records of Queens and Nassau Counties," *NYG&B Newsletter* (now *New York Researcher*), Spring 2003. Updated June 2011 and published as a Research Aid on *NewYorkFamilyHistory.org*.

Silinonte, Joseph M. *Bishop Loughlin's Dispensations, Diocese of Brooklyn: Genealogical Information from the Marriage Dispensation Records of the Roman Catholic Diocese of Brooklyn, Kings, Queens, and Suffolk Counties, New York*. Brooklyn: The Author, 1996. Volume 1, 1859–1866. Abstracts data on 5,200 marriages for which dispensations were granted, including many where one of the parties was not Catholic. The diocese included all of Long Island. No further volumes were published.

Sniffin, Irene G. *The Index to the Long Islander . . . [1832–1862]*. 4 vols. Huntington, NY: Huntington Historical Society, 1977–1992.

Van Wyck, Frederick. *Long Island Colonial Patents*. Boston: A. A. Beauchamp, 1935.

Other Resources

Bailey, Paul. *Long Island: A History of Two Great Counties, Nassau and Suffolk*. 3 vols. New York: Lewis Historical Publishing Co., 1949.

Beers, F. W. *Atlas of Long Island New York: From Recent and Actual Surveys and Records*. New York, 1873. One of several atlases that are useful because they show names of landowners.

Bookbinder, Bernie. *Long Island: People and Places, Past and Present*. New York: Abrams, 1998.

Bunker, Mary Powell. *Long Island Genealogies: Families of Albertson, Andrews, Bedell, Birdsall . . . Willets, Williams, Willis, Wright, and Other Families. Being Kindred Descendants of Thomas Powell, of Bethpage, L.I., 1668*. Baltimore: Genealogical Publishing Co., 1976. Reprint of 1895 edition.

Cocks, George William. "Long Island Families and Families of Long Island Origin." Manuscript, n.d. Manuscripts & Archives Division, New York Genealogical and Biographical Society Family Files 1644–2002. NYPL, New York. Microfilm of manuscripts, New York, 1975

Eberlein, Harold Donaldson. *Manor Houses and Historic Homes of Long Island and Staten Island*. New York: J. B. Lippincott, 1928.

Hazelton, Henry Isham. *The Boroughs of Brooklyn and Queens, Counties of Nassau and Suffolk, Long Island, New York, 1609–1924*. 5 vols. New York; Chicago: Lewis Historical Publishing Co., 1925.

Hoff, Henry B. *Genealogies of Long Island Families: From the New York Genealogical and Biographical Record*. Baltimore: Genealogical Publishing Co., 1987.

———. *Long Island Source Records: From the New York Genealogical and Biographical Record*. Baltimore: Genealogical Publishing Co., 1987.

Inventory of the Church Archives of New York City: Protestant Episcopal Church, Diocese of Long Island. New York: New York City Historical Records Survey, 1940.

Journal of Long Island History. Brooklyn: [Brooklyn] Long Island Historical Society, 1961–1979. 18 vols.

King, Rufus. "Genealogical Items from the *Long Island Star* [1809–1811]." *NYG&B Record*, vol. 48, no. 4 (1917): 411–413. [NYG&B eLibrary]

Long Island, Our Story. Melville, NY: Newsday, 1998.

Macoskey, Arthur R., ed. *Long Island Gazetteer: A Guide to Historic Places*. Brooklyn: Eagle Library, 1939.

Mather, Frederic G. *The Refugees of 1776 from Long Island to Connecticut*. Albany: J. B. Lyon, 1913.

Moorhouse, B-Ann. "The Long Island Division of the Queens Borough Public Library." *NYG&B Newsletter* (now *New York Researcher*), Winter 1994. Published as a Research Aid on *NewYorkFamilyHistory.org*. The library is now called the Queens Library and the division is called the Archives.

Naylor, Natalie A. *Bibliography of Dissertations and Theses on Long Island Studies*. Hempstead, NY: Hofstra University Long Island Studies Institute, 1999.

———, ed. *Exploring African-American History: Long Island and Beyond*. Hempstead, NY: Hofstra University, 1995.

Proehl, Karl H., and Barabara A. Shupe. *Long Island Gazetteer: A Guide to Current and Historical Place Names*. Bayside, NY: LDA Publishers, 1984.

Pullen, Sharon. "Archives and Manuscript Repositories in Nassau and Suffolk Counties." Office of the Suffolk County Clerk, Historical Documents Library, 2000. *www.suffolkcountyny.gov/Departments/ CountyClerk/HistoricDocumentsLibrary/RepositoryDirectory.aspx*

Ross, Peter, and William S. Pelletreau. *A History of Long Island: From its Earliest Settlement to the Present Time.* 3 vols. New York: Lewis Publishing Company, 1902–1905. Vol. 1 by Ross and vols. 2–3 by Pelletreau.

Sealock, Richard B., and Seely, Pauline A. *Long Island Bibliography.* Ann Arbor, MI: Edwards Brothers, 1940.

Seversmith, Herbert F. *Colonial Families of Long Island, New York, and Connecticut . . . .* 5 vols. Washington: privately printed, 1939–1958. [*Hathitrust.org*]

Seversmith, Herbert F., and Kenn Stryker-Rodda. *Long Island Genealogical Source Material: A Bibliography.* Arlington, VA: National Genealogical Society, 1987.

Siminoff, Farnen R. *Crossing the Sound: The Rise of the Atlantic American Communities in the Seventeenth-Century Eastern Long Island.* New York: New York University Press, 2004.

Spinzia, Raymond E., and Judith A. Spinzia. *Long Island's Prominent North Shore Families: Their Estates and Their Country Homes.* College Station, TX: VirtualBookworm.com Publishing, 2006.

Thompson, Benjamin Franklin. *History of Long Island from Its Discovery and Settlement to the Present Time: With Many Important and Interesting Matters; including Notices of Numerous Individuals and Families; also a Particular Account of the Different Churches and Ministers.* New York: E. French, 1839.

Vahey, Mary Feeney. *A Hidden History: Slavery, Abolition, and the Underground Railroad in Cow Neck and on Long Island.* Port Washington, NY: Cow Neck Peninsula Historical Society, 1998. Contains sections on: Slavery on Long Island; Long Island Quakers help fugitive slaves; Genealogy; Will of Thomas Pearsall (of Long Island).

Weigold, Marilyn E. *The Long Island Sound: A History of Its People, Places, and Environment.* New York: New York University Press, 2004.

Werner, Charles J. comp. *Genealogies of Long Island Families: . . . Dickerson, Mitchill, Wickham, Carman, Raynor, Rushmore, Satterly, Hawkins, Arthur Smith, Mills, Howard, Lush, Greene.* New York: The Complier, 1919. Complied mainly from records left by the late Benjamin F. Thompson.

Wilson, Rufus Rockwell. *Historic Long Island.* New York: Berkeley Press, 1902.

Wood, Silas. *A Sketch of the First Settlement of the Several Towns on Long Island.* Brooklyn: A. Spooner, 1824.

Selected Repositories

Brooklyn Historical Society (BHS)
See full listing in Kings County (Borough of Brooklyn)
Founded as the Long Island Historical Society, its collections cover all of Long Island. See Seversmith and Stryker-Rodda above.

Patchogue Medford Library
See full listing in Suffolk County

This public library has a particularly large genealogical collection, NYS Vital Records Indexes, and an active educational program featuring speakers of national reputation. It is a Family History Center Affiliate Library through which FHL microfilm may be borrowed. The library offers a catalog search function tailored to genealogical sources.

State University of New York at Stony Brook
Frank Melville, Jr. Memorial Library • Stony Brook, NY 11794
(631) 632-7119 • *stonybrook.edu/libspecial*

Special Collections and University Archives contains material concerning Long Island history, including maps, atlases, land records and deeds (some dating from the late eighteenth century), personal papers, and many links to familiar and unfamiliar sources of information about Long Island history and culture.

Queens Library: The Archives
See full listing in Queens County

The Archives at Queens Library hold materials regards the four counties on Long Island: Kings (Brooklyn), Queens, Nassau, and Suffolk. Some 17th century material is included, and there is extensive material from the 18th century to the present. See Seversmith and Stryker-Rodda above.

Additional Online Resources
Brooklyn Genealogy Information Page
http://bklyn-genealogy-info.stevemorse.org
> Contains information relating to New York City and Long Island, including general links and tips for genealogy research. See listing in the County and Borough Guides.

Computer Genealogy Society of Long Island
http://freepages.genealogy.rootsweb.ancestry.com/~cgsli
> Society dedicated to computer-based genealogy; contact information and newsletter archive accessible on website.

GenealogyWise
www.genealogywise.com/group/longislandgenealogy
> Long Island Genealogy is a social media group for researchers of Long Island genealogy.

German Genealogy Group (GGG) and Italian Genealogy Group (IGG)
germangenealogygroup.com and *italiangen.org.*
> In addition to German- and Italian-related genealogy, the GGG & IGG have extensive indexes online, as well as monthly presentations. The indexes cover vital records of New York City, church records, cemetery records, naturalization records, veterans, and yearbooks. Projects are ongoing so researchers will want to check these site regularly.

Long Island Genealogy
longislandgenealogy.com
> While not a resource for original records, the site includes biographies, photographs, postcards, maps, newspaper clippings, local histories, military histories, information on old homes, information on maritime activities, video footage from the 1930s, links to general resources, and information on local genealogical societies. It maintains the Long Island Surname Index listing more than 400,000 names and family trees of Long Island families at *longislandsurnames.com.* The site can be challenging in finding items, e.g., *longislandgenealogy.com/Cem* is the present-day link to find the cemetery transcriptions. Researchers should use the search function to unearth the extensive information on the site

Long Island, New York (Kings, Queens, Nassau & Suffolk counties) – Index
http://dunhamwilcox.net/ny/li_index.htm
> Long Island Index is a selection of re-transcribed church record and gravestones transcriptions covering Kings, Queens, Nassau, and Suffolk counties; dates range from late 1700s to early 1900s. Researchers should use this site only as a finding aid to locating original sources.

Index to Place Names in the Gazetteers

This index catalogs more than 11,000 place names that are listed in the gazetteer sections of the County Guides in Part Two of this book. It does not include place names that are mentioned elsewhere in the County Guides or in Part One. See the annotated Table of Contents for subjects covered in Part One.

Corrections, Additions, and Omissions

The Introduction to Part Two of this book includes a bibliography of New York State gazetteers, the first of which was published in 1813. It was compiled by Horatio Gates Spafford, who painstakingly collected data over three years, corresponding with and interviewing experts in communities across the state. Nevertheless, Mr. Spafford noted in the introduction to his gazetteer that ". . . although I have made my best efforts, under such circumstances, to render it worthy its high public patronage, I am still constrained to apologize for its many defects, and to solicit the indulgence of the public." So, too, this publication undoubtedly contains omissions and errors. Corrections, omissions, and additions with citations may be sent to NYGuide@nygbs.org, with the sincere thanks of the editors.

Bellvale, 548
Bellview Beach, 650
Bellville, 295
Bellwood, 461
Belmont, 293, 409, 724, 759, 760
Belmont Centre, 409
Belvidere, 293
Belvidere Station, 293
Bemis Heights, 603
Bemus, 327
Bemus Point, 326
Bend (The), 422
Benders Corners, 560
Benedict, 416
Benedict Beach, 482
Benedict Island, 642
Benedicts Corners, 416
Bennets Corners, 417
Bennetsburgh, 621
Bennett, 538
Bennett Bridges, 561
Bennett Hollow, 371
Bennetts, 296, 632, 633
Bennetts Corners, 424, 474, 475, 525, 555
Bennett(s) Creek, 632
Bennetts Settlement, 423
Bennettsville, 340
Bennington, 737
Bennington Center, 737, 737
Benson, 437
Benson Centre/Center, 437
Benson(s) Corners, 595, 677
Benson(s) Mines, 640
Benson's Point, 779
Bensonhurst, 768, 769
Bensonia, 718, 758
Bensonville, 677
Bent Settlement, 461
Bentley, 802
Bentley Manor, 799, 802
Bentleys Corners, 451
Benton, 744
Benton Center, 744
Benton Corners, 318, 683
Benton Station, 744
Berbank, 381
Berea, 546
Bergen, 422, 766
Bergen Beach, 626, 767, 769
Bergen Corners, 422
Bergen (Heights), 766
Berghol(t)z, 509
Berkley in Scarsdale, 723
Berkshire, 417, 670
Berkshire Terrace, 577
Berlin, 585, 791
Berlin Center, 585
Bern(e), 282
Bernerville, 614
Berneville, 282
Bernhards Bay, 560
Berry Brook, 370
Berryville, 491
Berwyn, 527
Besemer, 676
Bessboro, 404
Best, 585
Bethany, 423
Bethany Center, 423
Bethel, 318, 382, 444, 536, 664, 687
Bethel Corners, 318
Bethel Grove, 676
Bethford, 394
Bethlehem, 282, 285, 484, 544
Bethlehem Center, 282
Bethlehem Heights, 282
Bethpage, 499, 500, 792
Bethunville, 438
Betts Corners, 526
Bettsburg, 340
Beulah, 484, 536

Beverly Crest, 725
Beverly Inn Corners, 568
Beverwyck, 282
Beyers Corners, 418
Bicknellville, 644
Bickneyville, 644
Big Bend, 526
Big Brook, 515, 519
Big Creek, 633
Big Eddy, 665, 666
Big Elm, 578
Big Flats, 334, 343
Big Flatt, 670
Big Hollow, 432, 695
Big Indian, 687
Big Island, 545, 548
Big Moose, 446
Big Stream, 745
Big Stream Point, 745
Big Tree, 394, 467, 468
Big Tree Corners, 394
Big Tupper, 411
Big Wolfe Lake, 411
Bigelow, 640
Bigelow Corners, 738
Bilberry Island, 641
Billings, 381
Billings Gap, 381
Billington Heights, 394
Billsboro, 536
Billsboro Corners, 536
Billyville, 424
Biltmore Shores, 499
Bingham(s) Mills, 357, 670
Binghampton, 301
Binghamton, 301
Bingley, 473, 474
Bingley Mills, 473, 474
Bingley Station, 474
Bingotown, 411
Binnewater, 686
Birchton, 601
Bird, 310
Bird Grove, 498
Birdsall, 294
Birdsall Center, 294
Birmingham Corners, 446
Birmingham Falls, 348, 402
Bisby Lodge, 446
Bishas Mill, 461
Bishop Corners, 737, 738
Bishop Falls, 686
Bishop Street, 452
Bishops Corners, 451, 702
Bishopville, 293
Bittersweet, 666
Bivens Corners, 632
Black Bridge, 438
Black Brook, 348
Black Corners, 325
Black Creek (district), 295, 445, 703
Black Falls, 343
Black Grocery, 356
Black Hills, 393
Black Lake, 642, 643, 664
Black Oak Corners, 677
Black River, 453, 454
Black Rock, 318, 355, 392, 393
Black Stump, 789
Blackberry Row, 717
Blackmans Corners, 518
Blacksmith Corners, 536
Blackwell's Island, 778
Blaine, 490
Blairville, 508
Blake, 643
Blakeley, 392
Blakeslee, 474, 475, 476
Blakeslee Station, 476
Blanchard(s) Corners, 452, 461
Blanchards Settlement, 461
Blasdell, 394

Blatchley, 303
Blauvelt, 594
Blauvelts Foundry, 594
Blauveltville, 594
Bleecker, 416
Bleecker Center, 416
Blenheim, 614
Blenheim Hill, 614
Blennes Corner, 514
Blind Brook, 717, ,
Blind Brook, 722
Blink Bonny, 640
Blinns Settlement, 670
Bliss, 737
Bliss Corner, 418
Bliss Corners, 475
Blissville, 790, 791, 794
Blivinville, 430
Block House, 709
Blockville, 327
Blodgett Landing, 461
Blodgett Mills, 364
Bloods, 632
Bloods Corners, 632
Bloods Depot, 632
Bloodville, 602
Bloomerville, 631
Bloomfield, 535, 641, 802, 803
Blooming Grove, 544, 586
Blooming Grove Station, 544
Blooming View, 802
Bloomingburg(h), 665
Bloomingdale, 404, 410, 777, 778
Bloomington, 686
Blooms Corners, 548
Bloomvale, 383
Bloomville, 372
Blossom, 394, 396
Blossoms Mills, 394
Blossvale, 514
Blue Corners, 600
Blue Mountain, 687, 715
Blue Mountain Lake, 437
Blue Mountain Settlement, 665
Blue Point, 650, 684
Blue Ridge, 404
Blue Store, 357
Bluff Beach, 482
Bluff Point, 350, 632, 744
Bluffport, 634
Blythebourne, 768
Boardmanville, 311
Boerum Hill, 769
Bog Lake, 438
Bogardus Island, 642
Boght, 286
Boght Corners, 283, 286
Bogusville, 343
Bohemia, 652
Boice, 642
Boiceville, 676, 686
Bolivar, 294, 476
Bolton, 545, 684, 694
Bolton Landing, 694
Bolts Corners, 319
Bombay Corners, 409
Bombay (Village), 409
Bonaparte, 461
Bonila, 326
Bonita, 326
Bonney, 343
Bonni Castle, 709
Bonnie Crest, 720
Bonny Hill, 631, 634
Booltown, 677
Boomertown, 325
Boonville, 514
Booth, 445
Boothtown, 670
Boquet, 402
Borden, 635
Border City, 536, 627
Boreas River, 403

Boretontown, 722
Bornt Hill, 672
Borodino, 528
Borodino Landing, 528
Borough (The), 587
Borough Park, 769
Boscobel, 715
Bosley Corner, 468
Bossen Bouwerie, 779
Boston, 392
Boston Center, 392
Boston Corner(s), 382, 355, 392
Boston Ten Towns, 300, 363, 669, 675
Bostwick Corners, 677
Boswell Corners, 355, 539
Boswijck, 766
Boswyck, 766
Botsford Corners, 319
Bouckville, 475
Boughton Hill, 539
Boulton Beach, 452
Bourne, 570
Boutelliers, 720
Boutontown, 722
Boutonville, 722
Bouwerie (The), 778, 779
Bovina, 370
Bovina Center, 370
Bovina Valley, 370
Bowen, 312
Bowen Corners, 563
Bowens Corners, 560
Bowens Settlement, 342
Bowers Corners, 302, 318
Bower(s)to(w)n, 569
Bowersville, 467
Bowery (The), 587, 778
Bowery Bay, 790, 791
Bowler, 295
Bowlers Corners, 416
Bowles Corners, 632
Bowling Green, 497, 778
Bowman Island, 642
Bowmans Creek, 490
Bowmansville, 395
Bows Corners, 469
Boyd, 462
Boyds Corners, 577, 631, 737
Boyds Landing, 634
Boydsville, 577
Boyes Corners, 341
Boyle, 539
Boylston, 560
Boylston Center, 560
Boylston Corner, 560
Boynton, 586
Boyntonville, 586
Brackel, 342
Brackle, 340
Braddock Heights, 482
Bradford, 631
Bradford Hills, 528
Bradford Island, 642
Bradford Junction, 309
Bradley, 664, 666
Bradley Corners, 409
Bradley Point Kiln, 349
Bradleytown, 672
Bradts Corners, 614
Bradtville, 416
Braeside, 587
Brag Village, 535
Braggs Corners, 555
Brainard Corners, 568
Brainard(s), 586
Brainard Station, 586
Brainards Bridge, 586
Brainards Forge, 404
Brainardsville, 409
Brakel Township, 340, 342
Braman(s) Corners, 608
Bramans Corners, 286

Bramanville, 614
Bramlee Heights, 723
Bran(d)t, 392
Branch (The), 653, 683
Branchport, 744
Brandon, 409
Brandon (Center), 409, 411
Brandon Place, 677
Brandreth, 446
Brandreth Lake, 438
Brandy Brook, 349, 640
Brandys Corners, 492
Brant Lake, 694
Brantingham, 461
Brasher, 640
Brasher Center, 640
Brasher Falls, 640
Brasher Iron Works, 640
Brasher Station, 644
Brasie Corners, 642
Braymanville, 614
Brayton, 695
Brayton Hollow, 409
Brayton(s) Corners, 444
Bread and Cheese Hollow, 653
Br(e)akabeen, 614
Breakneck, 578
Brearley, 676
Breckville, 334
Breed, 402
Breed(s) Hill, 402
Breesport, 335
Breeze Hill, 549
Breezy Point, 794
Brentwood, 652
Brentwood Plaza, 717
Breslau, 650, 651
Breucklelen, 766
Brevoort, 769
Brewer Corners, 295, 310, 518
Brewerton, 525, 560
Brewery Hill, 677
Brewster, 578
Brewster Heights, 578
Brewster Hill, 578
Brewsters Corner, 383
Brewsters Station, 578
Brewsterville, 561
Briar Park, 497
Briarcliff Farm, 719
Briarcliff Manor, 719, 721
Briarwood, 525, 794
Brice, 555
Brice Station, 555
Brick Chapel, 640
Brick Church, 317
Brick House Corners, 424
Brick Tavern, 355
Bridge Haven, 789
Bridgehampton, 654
Bridgeport, 476, 525, 627
Bridges Corners, 475
Bridges Place, 642
Bridgeville, 666
Bridgewater, 514
Bridgewater Center, 514
Brier Hill, 642
Brier Hill Station, 642
Brier Street, 372
Briggs, 641, 688
Briggs Corners, 570, 704
Briggs Hollow, 671
Briggs Point, 634
Briggs Station, 381
Briggsville, 717
Brigham, 328
Brightman Neighborhood, 473
Brighton, 396, 409, 481, 571
Brighton Beach, 768, 769
Brighton Corners, 571, 704
Brightside, 438
Brightwater(s), 652
Brinckherhoff, 380

Crosbyside, 695
Crosbyville, 632
Cross, 403
Cross Pond, 718
Cross River, 718
Cross Road(s) (The), 328, 671, 766
Cross Roads Station, 320
Crossing (The), 641
Crossman Corners, 526
Crossover Island, 641
Croton, 371, 715
Croton Dam, 715, 725
Croton Falls, 720, 723
Croton Heights, 725
Croton Lake, 725
Croton Landing, 715
Croton Landing Station, 715
Croton Point, 715
Croton Station, 445
Crotona Park East, 760
Croton-on-Hudson, 715
Crotonville, 721
Crouse(s) Store, 384
Crow Hill, 383
Crowbar Point, 678
Crowerville, 600
Crowley Corners, 348
Crown(e) Point, 402
Crown(e) Point Center, 402
Crown Heights, 383, 769
Crown Heights South, 769
Crown Village, 499
Crowningshield, 403
Crows Hollow, 529
Crows Nest, 641
Crugers, 715
Crum(b) Hill, 473
Crum Creek, 417
Crum Elbow, 380, 381, 383
Crum Elbow Precinct, 379, 380, 381, 382, 384
Crum Town, 672
Cruso, 627
Crusoe, 710
Crystal Beach, 536
Crystal Brook, 650
Crystal Dale, 463
Crystal Lake, 285, 309
Crystal Run, 548
Crystalrun, 548
Crystal Spring(s), 744
Cuba, 294
Cuba Lake, 310
Cuba Summit, 294
Cuchoge, 654
Cucklestowne, 802
Cuckoldstown, 802
Cuddeback, 538
Cuddebackville, 545
Cuif Summit, 302
Cullen, 445
Culver Meadows, 482
Culvers Point, 319
Culvertown, 665
Cumberland, 276
Cumberland Head, 350
Cummings Bridge, 561
Cummings Crossing, 365
Cummings Mills, 561
Cummingsville, 468
Cumminsville, 468
Cumsewogue, 650
Curriers, 738
Currier(s) Corners, 738
Curry(s), 666
Currytown, 492
Curtis, 445, 631
Curtis Corner
Curtis Corner(s), 445, 538, 555
Cushetunk, 664
Cutchogue, 654
Cutchogue Station, 654

Cutting, 326
Cuyler, 364, 365
Cuyler Hill, 364
Cuylerville, 468
Cypress Avenue, 791
Cypress Hills, 768, 769

D

Daball Corners, 634
Daboll Corners, 529
Dadville, 462
Daggettsville, 475
Dahlia, 665
Dairyland, 688
Daisy Farms, 720
Dakins Corners, 516
Dale, 738
Dalrymples Mill, 475
Dalton, 468
Dalton Crossing, 644
Damascus, 303
Dams Corner, 518
Danby, 672, 676
Danes Corners, 644
Danforth, 528
Danielstown, 695
Danley Corner(s), 737
Dann Corner, 482
Dannattsburg, 461
Dannemora, 349, 350
Dannemora Crossing, 348, 349
Dans Kamer (The), 547
Dansville, 404, 468, 469, 632
Dansville Station, 468
Dantown, 722
Danube, 442
Danville, 302
Darby Corners, 744
Darby Flats, 311
Darien, 423
Darien Center, 423
Darien City, 423
Darlington, 653
Darrow, 357
Darrowsville, 694
Darts Corner(s), 474
Dashville, 683, 685
Davenport, 370, 720
Davenport Center, 370
Davenport Corners, 578
Davenport Neck, 720
Davids Island, 720
Davis Brook, 719, 720
Davis Corners, 473, 490, 685, 686
Davis Crossing, 341
Davis Hollow, 370
Davis Park, 650
Davistown, 548
Davys Corners, 442
Daws, 422, 423
Daws Corners, 422, 423
Dawson Corners, 626
Day, 600
Day Center, 600
Dayansville, 463
Day(s) Corners, 443, 600
Days Mill, 641
Days Rock, 443
Daysville, 562
Daysville Corner, 562
Dayton, 308
Daytonville, 516
De La Farge Corners, 453
De Laets Burg, 587
De Launeys Mill, 454
De Maraudeville Hollow, 672
De Peyster, 640
De Peyster Corners, 640
Dead Water Iron Works, 404
Deadwater, 404
Dean, 325

Dean Chase Settlement, 348
Dean(s) Corners, 372, 578, 602, 643
Deans Mill, 432
Deans Tannery, 672
Deansboro, 516
Deansville, 516
Dearman, 717
Dearmans Landing, 717
Debruce, 666
DeCantillon Landing, 381
Decatur, 568
Deck, 444, 445
Decker Town, 802
Deckers, 545
Deckers Dock, 665
Deckertown, 622, 666
Deer Creek, 295
Deer Park, 650, 652
Deer River, 461
Deer River Falls, 410
Deer River Station, 461
Deer Run, 652
Deerfield, 514, 654
Deerfield Corners, 514
Deerfield Heights, 394, 514
Deerhead, 403
Deerland, 438
Deerpark, 545
Deferiet, 455
Deforest Corners, 578
Deforno, 452
Defreestville, 586
Defriestville, 586
Degrasse, 644
Degroff, 319
DeKalb, 640
DeKalb Junction, 640
DeLanc(e)y, 371, 473
DeLancey Corners, 473
DeLanceys Mills, 724
Delaney Island, 642
Delanson, 608
Delanti, 328
Delaware, 282, 369–373, 664
Delaware Bridge, 666
Delevan, 312, 392
Delhi, 370
Dellwood, 392, 395
Delmar, 282
Delphi, 527
Delphi Falls, 527
Delphi Falls Park, 527
Delphi Station, 473
Delta, 515, 519
Deming Street, 601
Dempster Corners, 416
Demster, 561
Demster Beach, 561
Demster Grove, 561
Denault Corners, 586
Denison(s) Corner(s), 538
Denley Station, 462
Denmark, 461, 632
Dennies Crossing, 417
Dennies Hollow, 417
Denning, 578, 683
Dennis Corners, 634
Dennison, 442, 443
Dennison Corners, 327, 442, 443
Denniston, 547
Dennistons Ford, 664
Dennytown, 578
Denton, 328, 549
Dentons Corners, 328, 562
Denver, 372
Depau, 641
Depauville, 452
Depew, 393, 395
Deposit, 302, 370, 373
Derby, 394
Derby Switch, 634
Derbys Corners, 644

Dering Harbor, 653
Derrick, 411
DeRuyter, 473
Desbrough Park, 710
Despatch, 481
Deutal Bay, 782
Deutschlandle, 780
DeVeau Town, 720
Develville, 578
Devereaux, 309, 445
Devereaux Station, 309
Devils Elbow, 644
Devils Halfacre, 371, 373
Devils Hole, 507
Devins Corners, 348
Devoes Neck, 718, 758
DeVoice Corners, 455
Devon, 651
Dewells Corners, 394
Dewey Bridge, 702
Dewey Corners, 514
Deweys Corners, 561
Deweyville, 463
DeWitt, 525, 528
Dewitt Mills, 379
DeWitts Valley, 294
DeWittsburgh, 294, 431
DeWittsville, 294, 666
Dewitt(s)ville, 683
Dewittville, 325
Dexter, 451
Dexter Corners, 308
Dexter Junction, 451
Dexterville, 326, 560
Deys Landing, 627
Diamond, 455
Diamond Hill, 445
Diamond Point, 695
Diana, 461
Diana Center, 461
Diana Station, 461
Dibble Corner, 343
Dibbles Long Cabin Corners, 718
Dibbletown, 518
Dickel Farm (The), 723
Dickerson City, 370
Dickersonville, 507
Dickinson, 302, 410
Dickinson Center, 410
Dickinsons Station, 373
Dicktown, 577
Didell, 380, 384
Dillen, 454
Dillenbeck Corners, 442
Dimmick Corners, 603
Dimmick Hollow, 569
Dinehart(s), 635
Dingle, 720
Dingle Hill, 370
Disco, 348
Dishaw, 642, 643
Ditch Plains, 651
Ditmas Park, 769
Divine(s) Corners, 664
Divinity Hill, 651
Division, 677
Dix, 519, 621
Dix Hills, 652
Dixie, 715, 725
Dixon Corners, 642
Doanesburg(h), 578, 578
Doansburg
Dobbins Corner(s), 538, 627
Dobbs Ferry, 717
Dodge, 325
Dodges Creek, 295
Dodgewood, 760
Dogtail Corners, 380
Dolgeville, 417, 444
Dominies Hook, 780
Donattsburg, 461
Dongan Hill(s), 802, 803
Donnellys Corners, 411

Doodletown, 595
Doolins Crossing, 453
Doonan Corners, 372
Dora, 301
Doraville, 301
Doris Park, 560
Dorlach, 616
Dorloo, 615
Dormansville, 286
Dorrs Corners, 701, 704
Dorwood Park, 509
Dosoris, 497, 499, 792
Dotys Corners, 632
Douglass, 371
Douglass Corners, 710
Douglass Crossing, 454
Douglass Village, 665
Douglaston, 789, 794
Douwsburgh, 284
Dover, 380, 802
Dover Furnace, 380
Dover Plains, 380
Downersport, 473
Downerville, 644
Downes Corners, 720
Downing, 492
Downing Station, 492
Downsville, 370
Downtown, 588
Downtown Brooklyn, 769
Downtown Flushing, 794
Downtown Syracuse, 528
Dowtonville, 665
Doxtater Corner, 417
Doyle, 393
Drake Edgewood, 723
Drakes Corner, 563
Drakes Settlement, 672
Draketown, 665
Dresden, 701, 744, 745
Dresden Center, 701
Dresserville, 319
Drews Corner, 644
Drewville Heights, 578
Driftwood, 326
Drouton Hollow, 677
Drowned Land(s), 546, 548, 688
Drowned Meadowland, 650
Dry Brook, 327, 683
Dry Brook Settlement, 372
Dry Dock, 600
Dry Hill, 454
Dryden, 676
Dryden Corners, 676
Dryden Four Corners, 676
Duane, 410, 608
Duane Center, 410
Duane Lake, 608
Duanes Bush, 608
Duanesburg Churches, 608
Duanesburg(h), 608
Dublin, 626, 677, 717
DuBois Mills, 547
Ducharm, 349
Duck Cove, 792, 793
Duck Pond Point, 654
Dudley Settlement, 631
Duells Corner, 395
Dugway, 560
Dukes, 276
Dumbarton, 518
DUMBO, 769
Dunbar, 303
Dunbars Mills, 474
Dunbarton, 518
Duncans Corners, 710
Dundee, 745
Dundee Heights, 725
Dunes, 282
Dunham Hollow, 586
Dunham(s) Basin, 703
Dunhams Grove, 424
Dunhamville, 672

Elgin, 310
Elizabeth Town, 442
Elizabethtown, 402
Elizaville, 356, 357
Elk Brook, 371
Elk Creek, 569, 571
Elka Park, 431
Elkcreek, 569, 571
Elkdale, 310
Elko, 309
Ellenburg, 349
Ellenburg Center, 349
Ellenburg Corners, 349
Ellenburg(h) Depot, 348, 349
Ellenville, 688
Ellenwood Hollow, 475
Ellerslie, 356, 357, 383
Ellery, 326
Ellery Center, 326
Ellicott, 326, 395
Ellicott Mills, 422, 425
Ellicottville, 309
Ellington, 326
Elliotsville, 801
Ellis, 676
Ellis Island, 749, 779
Ellis Village, 452
Ellisburg(h), 452
Ellisons Point, 497
Ellistown, 670
Ellmores Corners, 683
Ellmores Cove, 683
Ellsworth, 318, 643
Elm(s) (The), 308, 563
Elm Beach, 627
Elm Creek, 308
Elm Flat, 328
Elm Grove, 569
Elm Park, 803
Elm Point, 498
Elm Tree, 327, 578
Elm Tree Point, 677
Elm Valley, 293, 296
Elma, 394
Elma Center, 394
Elmbois, 634
Elmcrest, 525, 528
Elmdale, 641
Elmendorph Corner, 383
Elmer Hill, 515
Elmgrove, 481, 482
Elmhurst, 317, 326, 791, 794
Elmira, 334, 335
Elmira Heights, 334, 335
Elmont, 497
Elmsford, 717
Elmsmere, 719
Elmwood, 296, 319, 528
Elmwood Village, 392
Elnora, 600
Elpis, 518
Elsinor(e), 350
Elsinore, 350
Elsmere, 282
Eltings Landing, 684
Eltingville, 802, 803
Elton, 309
Elton Station, 309
Eltona, 718, 724, 758, 759
Elwood, 652
Emburys Corners, 475
Emerald Green, 666
Emerick, 283
Emerson, 317
Emerson Hill, 803
Emerson(s) Corners, 603
Emeryville, 641
Emilyville, 641
Eminence, 614, 616
Emmons, 570
Emmons Siding, 560
Emmons Station, 569
Emmonsburg(h), 445, 418

Emmonsville, 666
Empeyville, 515
Enchanted Lake, 311
End (The), 782
Endicott, 303
Endorlin, 544
Endwell, 303
Enfield, 677
Enfield Center, 677
Enfield Falls, 677
Engellville, 616
Engles Mills, 616
Engleville, 616
English Kills, 791
English Settlement, 642
Ennerdale, 536
Ennerdale Station, 536
Ennis, 411
Eno Point, 526
Enoch Point, 715
Enos, 515
Ensenore, 319
Ensenore Point, 319
Enterprise, 381
Ephratah, 416
Eppie Corners, 417
Erie, 391–396, 739
Erie Village, 526
Erietown, 475
Erieville, 475
Erin, 335
Ervine Mills, 308
Erwin Center, 634
Erwin(s), 633
Escarpment, 507
Esopus, 683
Esperance, 614, 615
Esperance Station, 608
Esperanza, 744
Esperanzay, 430
Esquire Coons Corners, 473
Essex, 401–404
Esty(s), 677
Etling Corners, 684
Etna, 676
Euba Mills, 402
Euclid, 525
Eureka, 519, 666
Evans, 394
Evans Beach Park, 394
Evans Center, 394
Evans Center Station, 394
Evans Corner, 627, 710
Evans Mills, 453
Evans Patent, 544, 546, 547
Evans Station, 453
Evansville, 453, 701
Evensville, 688
Evergreen, 791
Everton, 411
Ewells Corner(s), 474, 738
Excelsior Springs, 467
Exeter, 568
Exeter Center, 568
Exeter Corner, 568
Ezraville, 411

F

Fabius, 526
Fabius Center, 526
Factory Hill, 355
Factory Hollow, 539, 586
Factory Village, 602
Factoryville, 402, 608, 801
Fahnestock Corners, 578
Fair Harbor, 652
Fair Haven, 320, 365, 555
Fair Oaks, 548
Fair Point, 325
Fairbanks, 326, 328
Fairbanks Corners, 644

Fairchild City, 688
Fairchilds Corners, 417
Fairdale, 560
Fairfield, 442, 670, 695
Fairgrounds, 652
Fairland, 614
Fairmount, 525, 724, 759
Fairport, 335, 483
Fairview, 294, 296, 309, 383, 717, 737
Fairview Corners, 445
Fairview Heights, 803
Fairville, 709
Fairville Station, 709
Fairway West, 525
Fairweather Corners, 601
Falcon Manor, 507
Falconer, 326, 327
Falconer Junction, 326
Falkirk, 395
Fall Bridge, 570
Fall Clove, 370
Fall Creek, 677
Fall Creek Parke, 676
Fall Creek Post Office, 677
Falls Mills, 664
Falls of the Neversink, 664
Fallsburg(h), 664
Fallsburgh Station, 664
Fancher, 556
Fancy Tract, 309, 310
Fanlon Corners, 350
Fantinekill, 686
Far Rockaway, 789, 794
Fargo, 423, 455
Farley Corners, 562, 563
Farley(s), 320
Farm (The), 793
Farmbrook, 536
Farmer, 626
Farmer Village, 626
Farmers Corners, 562
Farmers Hill, 382
Farmers Mills, 515, 577
Farmers Village, 792
Farmersville, 309
Farmersville Center, 309
Farmersville Station, 309
Farmerville, 626
Farmingdale, 499, 544, 650, 792
Farmington, 536, 555
Farmington Station, 536
Farmingville, 650
Farmton, 536
Farnham, 392
Farragut, 769
Farrel Corner, 444
Farrs Crossing, 640
Farwells Mills, 555
Fauconnier Patent, 381
Faust, 411
Fay, 411
Fayette, 327, 341, 626, 627
Fayette Siding, 627
Fayetteville, 526
Fayville, 437, 602
Fecoe Corners, 416
Federal Store(s), 382, 355
Feeder Dam, 602
Fellows Corners, 320
Felters Corners, 593
Felts Mills, 454
Fenhurst, 789
Fenimore, 602
Fenmore Park, 717
Fenner, 474
Fenner Corners, 474
Fenner Grove Station, 444
Fenton, 302
Fentonville, 325
Ferenbaugh, 633
Ferguson(s) Corner(s), 709, 744
Fergusonville, 370

Fernbrook Park, 721
Ferndale, 652, 665, 666
Fernwood, 562, 602, 665
Fernwood Hall, 641
Fero, 334
Ferris Avenue, 724
Ferrona, 348
Ferry(s) (The), 643, 766
Ferry Point, 723, 759
Ferry Village, 394
Feura Bush, 282, 285
Fey Mill, 462
Fical(s) Corner(s), 341, 416
Fickles Corner, 340
Fiddlers Green, 677
Fiddletown, 602
Field Crossing, 569
Fieldhome, 725
Fields (The), 778
Fields Corners, 578
Fields Settlement, 452, 454
Fieldston, 760
Filer Corners, 569
Filkinville, 384
Fillmore, 295
Fillmore Chapel, 508
Fillmore Corner, 526
Financial District, 776, 779
Finch Hollow, 303
Finchville, 547
Findley, 327
Findley(s) Lake, 327
Fine, 641
Fineview, 453
Fink Hollow, 517
Finks Basin, 442
Finksville, 570
Finnegans Corner, 545
Fintches Corners, 320
Fire Island, 650, 652
Fire Island Pines, 650
Fire Place, 650, 651
Firthcliffe, 544, 547
Firthcliffe Heights, 544, 547
Fish Bay, 760
Fish Creek, 462, 463, 518, 687
Fish Creek Landing, 517, 518
Fish Creek Ponds, 411
Fish Creek Station, 518
Fish House, 416, 417
Fish Island, 301, 451
Fish Lake, 309
Fisher Hill, 724
Fishers, 539
Fishers Corners, 327
Fishers Eddy, 371
Fishers Island, 654
Fishers Island Manor, 649, 654
Fishers Landing, 453
Fishers Mills, 720
Fishers Station, 539
Fisherville, 334
Fisherville Station, 539
Fishkill, 380
Fishkill Furnace, 380
Fishkill Furnace Hook, 380
Fishkill Furnace Plains, 380
Fishkill Hook, 380
Fishkill Landing, 379, 380
Fishkill Plains, 380
Fishkill Precinct, 380
Fishkill-on-Hudson, 380
Fish(s) Eddy, 371
Fitch, 309, 310
Fitch Bridge, 334
Fitch Hill, 570
Fitch(es) Point, 703
Fitchs (Corners), 319, 562
Fitts Corners, 677
Fitzgerald, 461
Five Chimneys Corner, 475

Five Corners, 293, 318, 341, 422, 423, 424, 453, 473, 474, 475, 514, 517, 527, 555, 614, 737
Five Mile, 310
Five Mile Point, 302, 528
Five Mile Run, 308
Five Points, 310, 483, 484, 538, 776, 779
Five Waters Corners, 538
Flackville, 642
Flagg, 403
Flagler Corners, 600
Flammersburg, 789
Flanders, 654
Flat Creek, 492, 614
Flat Iron, 343
Flat Rock, 451
Flatbrook, 355
Flatbush, 684, 687, 767, 769
Flatbush Village, 767
Flatiron, 777
Flatiron District, 779
Flatlands, 767, 769
Flats (The), 342, 430, 432, 677
Flea Hollow, 677
Fleets Neck, 654
Fleetwood, 716, 719
Fleischmanns, 372
Fleming, 318
Fleming(s)ville, 672
Fletchers Corners, 535
Flint (The), 538, 686
Flint Creek, 538
Flint Town, 514
Flints Corners, 562
Floodport, 473
Floodwood, 411
Floral Park, 497, 498, 789, 792, 794
Floral Park Center, 497, 498
Floral Park Crest, 497
Florence, 515, 672
Florence Hill, 515
Florenceville, 725
Florida, 490, 545, 548
Floridaville, 318
Florus Falls, 595
Flower Hill, 498, 792
Flowerfield, 653
Flowers, 303
Floyd, 515
Floyd Corners, 515
Flushing, 789, 794
Fluvanna, 326
Fly Creek, 570
Fly Mountain, 684, 687
Fly Summit, 701
Flycreek, 570
Fly(ing) Point, 654
Foggingto(w)n, 578
Folsomdale, 737
Folts Corners, 319
Fonda, 491
Fondas Bush, 416
Font Grove, 282
Footes, 393
Foots Corner(s), 467
Footville, 677
Ford Brook, 293
Ford Clearing, 461
Ford Corner, 482
Fordham, 723, 724, 759, 760
Fordham Heights, 724, 759, 760
Fordham Manor, 714, 724, 756
Fordhams Corners, 644
Fordsborough, 491
Fordsbush, 491
Forest, 348
Forest Beach, 525
Forest City, 461, 677
Forest Glen, 665, 683
Forest Grove, 718, 724, 758, 759
Forest Heights, 720

Jordan, 461
Jordan, 526
Jordan Falls, 461
Jordan Heights, 650
Jordan Island, 641
Jordans, 635
Jordanville, 445
Joscelyn, 666
Joshua, 527
Joslins Corners, 476
Joy, 710
Judd Corners, 308
Juddville, 473
Jug City, 424
Jug Island, 641
Juhelville, 453
Jump Corners, 318
Junction (The), 349, 424, 526, 585, 587
Juniper Swamp, 791
Junius, 538, 626
Junius Corners, 626

K

Kaaterskill, 431
Kaaterskill Falls, 431
Kaaterskill Junction, 431
Kaaterskill Station, 431
Kabob, 328
Kahes Bridge, 393
Kaisertown, 392, 546
Kakiat, 594
Kakiat(e) Patent, 592, 593
Kallicoon Hook, 683
Kallops Corners, 686
Kalurah, 643
Kanadesaga, 538
Kanona, 631
Kansas, 380
Karen Crest, 608
Karles Neck, 801
Karlsfeld, 282, 283
Karner, 283
Karr Valley, 293
Karrdale, 293
Karter, 455
Karter Crossing, 455
Kaser, 594
Kasoag, 563
Kast Bridge, 443
Kast Bridge Station, 443
Katonah, 715
Katonah Ridge, 715
Katsbaan, 687
Katskill Bay, 702
Kattelville, 301
Kauneonga Lake, 664
Kavanaugh Corners, 409
Kayaderosseras Patent, 415, 489, 599, 607
K Cat Corner(s), 320
Keaches Corners, 327
Keck(s) Center, 417
Keefer(s) Corners, 283
Keene, 403
Keene Center, 403
Keene Flat, 403
Keene Valley, 403
Keenes, 451
Keenes Mills, 451
Keenes Station, 644
Keenesville, 644
Keeney, 364
Keeney(s) Settlement, 364, 365, 526
Kecpawa, 438, 446
Keese Corners, 348
Keese Mills, 409
Keeseville, 348, 402
Keisertown, 546
Kelleys Station, 608

Kellogg, 644
Kellogg Corners, 641
Kelloggs Mills, 528
Kelloggsville, 319, 718
Kellogville, 296
Kelly(s) Corners, 328, 372, 626, 527
Kelpytown, 462
Kelsey, 373
Kelseys Landing, 484
Kelseys Mills, 462
Kempton, 410
Kempville, 508
Kempwick, 560
Kendaia, 627
Kendall, 334, 555
Kendall Corners, 310
Kendall Mills, 555
Kendall(s) Mills, 482
Kendrew Corners, 640
Kendrews, 640
Kenilworth, 396, 793
Kenmore, 396
Kennedy, 327
Kennedy(s) Corner(s), 677
Kennedys Mills, 326, 327
Kennedyville, 327, 631
Kenoza Lake, 664
Kensico, 720
Kensington, 327, 392, 498, 767, 769
Kent, 555, 577
Kent Cliffs, 577
Kent Corners, 577
Kent Hills, 577
Kents Corners, 641
Kentwood Estates, 577
Kenwell, 437
Kenwells, 437
Kenwood, 282, 283, 475
Kenwood Station, 475
Kenyon Corners, 474
Kenyontown, 695
Kenyonville, 555
Kerhonkson, 686, 688
Kerleys Corners, 383
Kerrs Corners, 395
Kerry Siding, 371
Kerryville, 371, 373
Keskachague, 767
Ketchabonec, 654
Ketchamtown, 544
Ketchum, 570
Ketchum(s) Corners, 603
Ketchums Corners, 302
Ketchumville, 671
Kettleborough, 683
Kettleville, 301
Keuka, 635
Keuka Mills, 745
Keuka Park, 744
Kew Gardens, 790, 794
Kew Gardens Hills, 789, 794
Keys Mill, 411
Kiamesha, 666
Kiamesha Lake, 666
Kiantone, 327
Kidders, 626
Kidders Ferry, 626
Kidds Dam, 595
Kiffville, 372
Kildare, 411, 641
Kildare Station, 411
Kiley Bridge, 473
Kilgore Spur, 371
Kilgour, 665
Kills (The), 802
Kill Buck, 309, 312
Killawog, 302
Killingworth, 793
Kilmartin Corners, 492
Kimball Mill, 461
Kimball Stand, 326

Kimmeys Corners, 283
Kimples Landing, 678
Kinderhook, 357
Kinderhook Station, 357
King Ferry Station, 318
King(s) Ferry, 318
King(s) Settlement, 341, 342
King(s) Station, 601, 603
Kingdom (The),402, 442, 445, 627
Kings, 601, 749, 764–769, 807
Kings Corners, 319, 325, 423, 640
Kings District, 355
Kings Eddy, 665
Kings Falls, 461
Kings Garden, 451, 780
Kings Highway, 769
Kings Park, 653
Kings Point, 498
Kings School Corner, 325, 326
Kingsboro, 416
Kingsboro Settlement, 416
Kingsboro Station, 417
Kingsborough, 416
Kingsborough Patent, 415
Kingsbridge, 717, 725, 758, 760
Kingsbridge Heights, 717, 758, 760
Kingsbridge Village, 717, 758
Kingsbury, 703
Kingsland District, 443
Kingston, 684
Kingsto(w)n, 651
Kingstreet, 722
Kinne(y) Corners, 442, 443
Kinneys Corners, 744
Kinney(s) (Four) Corners, 560
Kinross Heights, 725
Kipps, 545
Kips Bay, 777, 780
Kipsbergen, 383
Kipsburgh Manor-Rhinebeck Patent, 378
Kipville, 328
Kirbytown, 549
Kirbyville, 715, 718
Kirchehock, 383
Kirk, 343
Kirkland, 515
Kirks Crossing, 482
Kirkville, 526
Kirkwood, 301, 302, 632
Kirkwood Center, 302
Kirschnerville, 463
Kiryas Joel, 546
Kiskatom, 430
Kismet, 652
Kissena Park, 794
Kitcaboneck, 654
Kitchawan, 718, 725
Kleindeutschland, 780
Kleine Kill, 802
Kline, 490
Klocks Corners, 563
Klocks Field, 492
Klondike, 455, 677
Knapp Creek, 308
Knapps, 644
Knappsburg, 341
Knapps Corners, 719
Knapps Creek, 308
Knapp(s) Station, 644
Knappville, 418
Kneiskerns Dorf, 614
Knickerbocker Corner, 538
Knight(s) Creek, 296
Knight Settlement, 631
Knights, 416
Knights Corners, 595
Knob Street, 381
Knollwood Manor, 717
Knowelhurst, 695
Knowersville, 284
Knowlesville, 453, 469, 556

Knowlesville Station, 556
Knox, 284
Knox Corners, 514
Knox Settlement, 644
Knoxboro, 514
Knoxville, 475, 632
Koenigs Point, 319
Kohlertown, 664
Kokomo Corners, 640
Komar Park, 600
Koplins Point, 678
Kortright, 372
Kortright Center, 372
Kossuth, 294
Kosterville, 462
Kouwenhoven, 769
Kraus Landing, 525
Kreischerville, 802, 803
Kringsbush, 417
Kripple Bush, 685
Kripplebush, 685
Krum Corner, 678
Krumville, 686
Krusens Corners, 633
Kuckville, 555
Kuneytown, 626
Kushagua, 410
Kyserike, 686
Kysorville, 469

L

La Fargeville, 453
La Fayetteville, 381
La Grange, 327
La Salle, 508
La Tourette, 803
Lac(e)y Corners, 676
Lacey Field, 547
Lackawack, 688
Lackawanna, 395
Lacona, 563
Laconia, 723, 759, 760
Ladelton, 687
Ladentown, 593, 594
Lader(s) Point, 528
Ladew Corner, 687
Ladies Mile, 777, 779
Ladleton, 683, 687
Ladoga, 677
LaFayette, 526
Lafayette Corners, 677
Laglers, 720
LaGrange, 381, 545, 548, 737
LaGrangeville, 381
Laidlaw, 309
Laird Corners, 526
Lairdsville, 519
Lake, 548, 702
Lake Arbutus, 403
Lake Beach, 482
Lake Bluff, 709
Lake Bonaparte, 461
Lake Bonaparte Station, 461
Lake Carmel, 577
Lake Clear, 411
Lake Clear Junction, 411
Lake Colby, 411
Lake Delaware, 370
Lake Delta, 515, 519
Lake Desolation, 601
Lake Erie Beach, 394
Lake George, 695
Lake Grove, 650
Lake Hill, 370, 688
Lake Huntington, 664
Lake Katonah, 715, 718
Lake Katrine, 687
Lake Kitchawan, 718
Lake Kushagua, 410
Lake Lila, 438
Lake Lincolndale, 723

Lake Luzerne, 695
Lake Minnewaska, 683
Lake Minniwaska, 686
Lake Mohegan, 725
Lake Osiris Colony, 546
Lake Peekskill, 578
Lake Placid, 403
Lake Pleasant, 437
Lake Purdy, 720
Lake Ridge, 677
Lake Ridge Point, 677
Lake Road, 509
Lake Ronkonoma, 650
Lake Sapphire, 546
Lake Shenorock, 723
Lake Shore Road, 394
Lake Station, 548
Lake Success, 498
Lake Vanare, 695
Lake View, 394
Lake View Terrace, 312
Lake Waccabuc, 718
Lakeland, 526, 650, 652
Lakemont, 745
Lakeport, 476
Lakeside, 526, 555, 709
Lakeside Park, 325, 555
Lakeside Station, 709
Lakeview, 343, 365, 497, 563
Lakeview Park, 650
Lakeville, 343, 468, 498, 548, 702, 716, 792
Lakewood, 325, 665
Lakewood Park, 653
Lamberton, 328
Lambs Corner(s), 286, 302, 340, 561, 710, 738
Lamont, 739
Lamontville, 685
Lamoreaux Landing, 626
Lamoree, 384
Lamson, 526
Lancaster, 341, 395, 779
Lancktons Corner, 423
Land of Canaan, 676
Landing (The), 430, 497, 544, 653
Landon Hill, 694
Lanesburg, 462
Lanesville, 431
Langdon, 302
Langdon(s) Corners, 640, 703
Langford, 395
Langton(s) Corners, 423
Lansing, 371, 563, 677
Lansing Station, 677
Lansingburg(h), 586, 588
Lansingville, 371, 677
Laona, 328
Lapeer, 364
Lapham(s), 349, 358
Lapham(s) Mills, 349
LaPlant Corners, 560
Larchmont, 718
Larchmont Gardens, 718
Larkfield, 652
Lassellsville, 416
Latham, 283
Lathams Corners, 341
Lattinto(w)n, 499, 685, 793
Laughing Waters, 654
Lauraville, 709
Laurel, 653, 654
Laurel Hill, 791, 794
Laurel Hollow, 499
Laurel House, 431
Laurel House Station, 431
Laurel Ridge, 548
Laurelton, 482, 500, 793, 794
Laurens, 569
Laurensville, 569
Lava, 666
Laverys Corner, 641
Lawless Corners, 348, 350

Uniontown, 717
Unionville, 283, 285, 454, 483, 538, 546, 631, 644, 666, 686, 687, 719, 768, 790, 802
Unitaria, 301
University Gardens, 499
University Heights, 760
Updike Settlement, 678
Upper Aquebogue, 653
Upper Barbourville, 370
Upper Beaver Meadow, 342
Upper Beechwood, 664
Upper Benson, 437
Upper Brookville, 500
Upper Canisteo, 633
Upper Chateaugay Lake, 349
Upper Corners, 381, 709
Upper Cross Roads, 719
Upper East Side, 777, 782
Upper Ebenezer, 394, 396
Upper Fairfield, 670
Upper Falls, 404
Upper Genegantslet Corner, 341
Upper Grandview, 594
Upper Green River, 355
Upper Hollow, 282, 283, 608
Upper Hollowville, 355
Upper Iron Works, 403
Upper Jay, 403
Upper Kilns, 348, 409
Upper Landing, 430
Upper Lisle, 302
Upper Mills, 653
Upper Mills (of Philipsburg(h) Manor), 719
Upper Mongaup, 665
Upper Morrisania, 724, 759
Upper Neck, 654
Upper New Rochelle, 720
Upper Nyack, 593
Upper Red Hook, 383
Upper Red Hook Landing, 383
Upper Salem, 720
Upper Saranac, 411
Upper St. Johnsville, 492
Upper St. Regis, 411
Upper Town Landing, 453
Upper Tuckahoe, 716
Upper Village, 327, 546
Upper West Side, 777, 782
Upperville, 343
Upson Corners, 562
Upton, 422, 651
Upton Lake, 384
Urbana, 635
Urlton, 430
Ushers, 600, 601
Usonia, 719
Utica, 518, 519
Utopia, 296, 794
Utrecht, 768

V

Vails Gate, 547
Vails Gate Junction, 547
Vail(s) Mills, 417
Valatie, 357
Valatie Colony, 357
Valcour, 349
Valcour Island(s), 349
Valentine, 312, 710
Valentine Hill, 725
Valentines Beach, 525
Valentines Corners, 319
Valeria Home, 716
Valhalla, 717, 719, 720
Valley (The), 402, 528
Valley Brook, 491
Valley Cottage, 593
Valley Falls, 586, 587
Valley Mills, 475

Valley Pond Estates, 715
Valley Stream, 498, 790
Valley View, 744
Valleyville, 578
Vallonia Springs, 301, 302
Valois, 621
Van Akens Mills, 687
Van Buren, 529
Van Buren Bay, 328
Van Buren Center, 529
Van Buren Harbor, 328
Van Buren Point, 328
Van Burens Corners, 341
Van Burenville, 548
Van Cortland, 678
Van Cortlandt, 760
Van Cortlandt (Park), 717, 758
Van Cortlandt Manor, 715, 716
Van Cortlandville, 716
Van Deusenville, 490
Van Duyn, 528
Van Epps Swamp, 491
Van Etten, 335
Van Etten Junction, 335
Van Ettenville, 335
Van Hoesen Station, 587
Van Hornesville, 445
Van House Corners, 644
Van Keuren(s), 383, 544
Van Leuvens Corners, 286
Van Nest, 723, 759, 760
Van Nostrand Crossing, 295
Van Schaick Island, 283
Van Tines Corners, 393
Van Vechten, 608
Van Vleet, 635
Van Vranken, 416
Van Vranken Corners, 416
Van Wagner, 383
Van Wies Point, 283
Vanaken Mills, 687
Vanburen, 563
Vandalia, 308
Vandemark, 293
Vandermark Creek, 296
Vandewater Heights, 781
Vansville, 319
Vantine Hill, 686
Vanvranken Corners, 416
Varian Mills, 716
Varick, 627
Varna, 676
Varysburg, 739
Vaughns Corners, 703
Vauxhall Garden, 781
Vebber Corners, 643
Vedersburgh, 490
Vega, 372
Venetian Shores, 650
Venice, 320
Venice Center, 320
Venus, 635
Vera Cruz, 561
Verbank, 384
Verbank Station, 384
Verbank Village, 384
Verdoy, 284
Verdrida Hooke, 715
Verity Town, 790
Vermillion, 561, 562
Vermont, 326
Vermont Sufferers Tract, 339
Vermontville, 410
Vernal, 737
Vernal Corners, 737, 738
Vernon, 518, 744
Vernon Center, 518
Vernon Park, 719
Vernon Valley, 652
Vernoy Falls, 686
Verona, 348, 518, 626, 627
Verona Beach, 518
Verona Depot, 518

Verona Mills, 518
Verona Springs, 518
Verona Station, 518
Verplanck, 715, 716
Verplancks Point, 716
Versailles, 311, 393
Vesper, 529
Vestal, 303
Vestal Center, 303
Vestal Corner, 303
Vestal Hills, 303
Veteran, 335, 687
Veterans Mountain Camp, 643
Vetsburg, 677
Vickerys Settlement, 526
Victor, 539
Victor Station, 539
Victoria, 327
Victory, 320, 602
Victory Lake, 381
Victory Mills, 602
Victory Park, 720
Vienna, 518, 538
Viewmonte, 355, 356, 357
Village (The), 779
Village Green, 529
Village of Sound Avenue, 653
Village of the Branch, 653
Village of the Landing, 653
Villenova, 328
Vincent, 535
Vincent Corners, 526
Vine Valley, 744
Vinegar Hill, 766, 769
Vineyard, 328
Vintonto(w)n, 614
Viola, 594
Violet Park, 760
Virgil, 365
Vischers Island, 654
Vis(s)cher(s) Ferry, 600
Vis-Kill, 380
Vista, 718
Vivian Heights, 725
Vlackebos, 767
Vlissingen, 789
Vly (The), 614, 685
Vly Summit, 701
Voak, 745
Volney, 560, 563
Volney Center, 563
Volney Corners, 563
Volusia, 328
Voorheesville, 285, 491
Vorca, 561
Vorhees, 562
Vosburg, 293, 294
Vreedlandt, 723, 759
Vroman Corners, 615
Vromansland, 614
Vukote, 325

W

Waccabuc, 718
Waddington, 642, 644
Wadham Mills Station, 404
Wadhams, 404
Wadham(s) Mills, 404
Wading River, 653
Wadsworth, 469
Wadsworth Cove, 467
Wagackkemeck, 665
Waggons, 595
Wagners Corners, 644
Wagners Landing, 634
Wagondale, 686
Wagstaff Corner, 641
Wahmeda, 325
Wainscott, 651
Wainscut, 651
Waite Settlement, 672

Waits, 671, 672
Wait(s) (Corners), 328
Wake, 303
Wakefield, 716, 758, 760
Wakefield Park, 725
Walbridge Flats, 568
Waldberg, 593
Waldberg Green, 593
Waldberg Landing, 593
Walden, 393, 546
Walden Cliffs, 394
Waldenville, 616
Waldheim, 794
Waldos Corners, 738
Waldron Corners, 342
Wales, 396
Wales Center, 396
Wales Hollow, 396
Walesville, 519
Walker(s), 411, 482, 563, 737
Walker(s) Corners, 342, 469, 475, 514
Walker(s) Mills, 357
Walker Valley, 687
Walkleys Landing, 467
Wall Street, 779, 782
Wallabout, 766
Wallace Hills, 350
Wallington, 710
Wallins Corners, 490
Wallkill, 548, 687
Wallkill Camp, 683
Walloomsac(k), 585
Walloomsac Patent, 704
Walmore, 509
Walnut Creek, 327
Walnut Falls, 327
Walrath Hollow, 442
Walton, 373
Walton Park, 544, 546
Walton Tract, 528
Walworth, 710
Walworth Station, 709
Wampmissic, 651
Wampsville, 475
Wanakah, 394
Wanakena, 641
Wanawaking Park, 725
Wanecommack, 651
Wango, 328
Wantagh, 498, 790
Wappasening, 671
Wappinger, 384
Wappingers Falls, 381, 383, 384
Wappingers Landing, 383
Ward, 296
Ward Acres, 720
Wardboro, 694
Wardner, 409
Wards, 694
Wards Corner(s), 319
Wards Island, 782
Wards Mill, 383
Ward(s)ville, 422, 563, 724, 759
Wardwell, 452
Warensackemack, 665
Warner Corners, 538
Warners, 525, 529
Warners Lake, 282
Warnerville, 615, 717, 758
Warren, 445, 451, 693–696
Warren Settlement, 451
Warrens Corners, 507, 508
Warrensburg(h), 696
Warsaw, 739, 744
Warwick, 548
Washburn Corners, 643
Washburnville, 642
Washiack, 379
Washington, 286, 384, 544, 626, 700–704

Washington Four Corners, 384
Washington Heights, 548, 666, 725, 777, 782
Washington Hollow, 383, 384
Washington Hunt, 469
Washington Lake, 547
Washington Market, 780
Washington Mills, 516
Washington Park, 282, 453
Washington Square, 547, 777, 782, 790
Washingtonville, 544, 563, 716, 718, 758
Wassaic, 379
Watchogue, 802
Watchtower, 687
Water Island, 651
Water Mill(s), 654
Water Valley, 394
Waterboro, 326, 327
Waterburg, 678
Waterbury Hill, 379, 381, 384
Waterford, 603
Waterloo, 626, 627
Waterloo Mills, 546
Waterman Corners, 326
Waterman District, 473
Waterport, 555
Waterport Station, 555
Watertown, 454
Watertown Center, 454
Watertown Junction, 454
Watervale, 527
Waterville, 373, 453, 490, 516, 517, 654
Waterville Corners, 393
Watervliet, 286
Watervliet Center, 286, 608
Watkins, 621
Watkins and Flint Purchase, 333, 620, 669, 675
Watkins Glen, 621, 622
Watkins Glen Station, 622
Watkinstown, 537
Watson, 463
Watson Hollow, 686
Watsonville, 614
Wattles Ferry, 372
Wattlesburg, 328
Watts Flats, 327
Waverly, 311, 650, 652, 670, 716
Wawarsing, 688
Wawayanda, 549
Wawayanda Patent, 543, 545, 546, 548
Wawayanda Station, 549
Wawbeek, 411
Wawbeek Center Station, 411
Wayland, 635
Wayland Depot, 635
Wayne, 622, 635, 708–710
Wayne Center, 710
Wayne Four Corners, 635
Wayne Hotel, 635
Wayneport, 709
Wayville, 603
Weatheridge, 525
Weaver Corner, 476
Weaver Hollow, 356
Weavertown, 694
Webatuck, 380
Webb, 446
Webb Corners, 342
Webb Hollow, 526, 633
Webbs Crossing, 633
Webb(s) Mills, 335
Weber(s) Corners, 615
Webster Corners, 395, 571
Webster Mills, 555
Webster Pond, 528
Webster(s) Crossing, 469
Webster Settlement, 327
Websters Landing, 528